Women's Health Psychology

Edited by

MARY V. SPIERS
PAMELA A. GELLER
JACQUELINE D. KLOSS

WILEY

John Wiley & Sons, Inc.

Library of Congress Cataloging-in-Publication Data:

Women's health psychology / edited by Mary V. Spiers, Pamela A. Geller, and Jacqueline D. Kloss.
      pages ; cm
  Includes bibliographical references and index.
  ISBN 978-0-470-89066-0 (paper); ISBN 978-1-118-41819-2 (ebk); ISBN 978-1-118-41551-1 (ebk); ISBN 978-1-118-43351-5 (ebk)
  1. Women–Health and hygiene–Psychological aspects.   I. Spiers, Mary, editor of compilation.   II. Geller, Pamela A., editor of compilation.   III. Kloss, Jacqueline D., 1970- editor of compilation.
  RA564.85.W6833 2013
  613'.04244—dc23

                                                                                                2012032035

Printed in the United States of America

10 9 8 7 6 5 4 3 2 1

Contents

Foreword   ix

Preface   xi

Acknowledgments   xiii

List of Contributors   xv

SECTION I: Women's Health in Context

Chapter 1 Historical Roots of Women's Healthcare   3

Heather Munro Prescott and Wendy Kline

Chapter 2 Retheorizing Women's Health Through Intersectionality's Prism   25

Lisa Bowleg

Chapter 3 Employment and Women's Health   46

Nancy L. Marshall

Chapter 4 Effects of Intimate Partner Violence Against Women   64

Kathy McCloskey and Deidre Hussey

SECTION II: Well-Being and Health Challenges

Chapter 5 Alcohol Use in Women   91

Nancy Vogeltanz-Holm, Kaitlin Lilienthal, Allison Kulig, and Sharon C. Wilsnack

Chapter 6 Women and Smoking   123

Bradley N. Collins and Uma S. Nair

Chapter 7 Obesity in Women   149

Michael R. Lowe, Meghan L. Butryn, and Alice V. Ely

Chapter 8   Eating and Weight-Related Disorders   173

Matthew Fuller-Tyszkiewicz, Ross Krawczyk, Lina Ricciardelli, and J. Kevin Thompson

Chapter 9   Cosmetic Medical Procedures and Body Adornment   199

Canice E. Crerand, Leanne Magee, Jacqueline Spitzer, and David B. Sarwer

Chapter 10   Women's Sleep Throughout the Lifespan   223

Jacqueline D. Kloss and Christina O. Nash

Chapter 11   Promotion of Physical Activity for Women's Health   255

Dori Pekmezi, Sarah Linke, Sheri Hartman, and Bess H. Marcus

Section III: Reproductive Health

Chapter 12   Women's Sexual Health   281

Patricia J. Morokoff and Maggie L. Gorraiz

Chapter 13   Premenstrual Dysphoric Disorder   305

Simone N. Vigod and Meir Steiner

Chapter 14   The Stress of Infertility   328

Lauren B. Prince and Alice D. Domar

Chapter 15   The Psychology of Agency in Childbearing   355

Pamela A. Geller, Alexandra R. Nelson, and Efrat Eichenbaum

Chapter 16   Psychiatric Symptoms and Pregnancy   389

Danielle M. Novick and Heather A. Flynn

Chapter 17   Breastfeeding and Maternal Mental and Physical Health   414

Jennifer Hahn-Holbrook, Chris Dunkel Schetter, and Martie Haselton

Chapter 18   Rethinking Menopause   440

Paula S. Derry and Heather E. Dillaway

Section IV: Disability and Chronic Conditions

Chapter 19   Women's Responses to Disability   467

Rhoda Olkin

Chapter 20   The Experience of Cancer in Women   491

Annette L. Stanton and Betina Yanez

Chapter 21   The Psychology of Irritable Bowel Syndrome   514

Sarah K. Ballou and Laurie Keefer

**Chapter 22   Stress and Resilience in Women
With Rheumatic Disease**   539

Sharon Danoff-Burg

Chapter 23   Neurological Disorders in Women   556

M. Meredith Gillis, Kara R. Douglas-Newman, and Mary V. Spiers

**Chapter 24   Converging Issues in Heart Disease, Stroke,
and Alzheimer's Disease in Women**   581

Mary V. Spiers

Author Index   605
Subject Index   637

Foreword

NANCY E. ADLER, PhD

omen's Health Psychology provides an important overview and analysis of key issues affecting women's health and well-being. In 2010 I had the privilege of chairing an Institute of Medicine (IOM) committee charged with evaluating progress in women's health research. The committee was composed of eminent researchers and clinicians representing a wide range of aspects of women's health. The committee considered whether the right questions had been asked about women's health, whether the right methods had been used to answer those questions, and whether the findings had been communicated effectively and had resulted in better health outcomes for women. In reading the contributions to *Women's Health Psychology*, I was struck by the resonance between the lessons the committee learned from our review and this volume.

The first thing that struck me was the broad perspective that the editors of this volume took in defining women's health. Women's health has sometimes been defined narrowly, referring only to health associated with women's reproductive organs and hormones, but this view has evolved. Just as the IOM committee embraced a wider definition that included diseases that are more prevalent among women than among men, present differently (e.g., differences in age of onset or in typical presenting symptoms), respond differently to treatment, or represent a major burden of

illness for women, this book covers an impressive array of health issues that affect women and/or differ in their impact for women than for men. Although one section of the book deals specifically with reproductive health, spanning menstruation and sexual health, infertility and pregnancy, breastfeeding, and menopause, the remaining sections cover a wide swath of health problems. The authors of the various chapters highlight both commonalities and differences in the etiology and treatment of these conditions.

In addition to considering a wide range of health conditions, the editors have also included chapters that deal both with sex differences (those caused by biological differences between the sexes) and gender differences (those caused by socially determined factors to which men and women are differentially exposed). The IOM committee observed that the social determinants of women's health had received relatively less attention than the biological underpinnings. Social determinants are important in understanding how gender effects impact on health, as well as in understanding, within groups of women, why there are marked disparities in health status between those who are socially disadvantaged versus those who live in more favorable social conditions. *Women's Health Psychology* highlights the critical role of these factors in the initial section that discusses the intersectionality among different bases of social disadvantage. The stage is set by considering the historical context and then discusses two domains in which women encounter social threats to their health: employment and intimate partner violence.

Finally, almost every chapter in this volume touches on the importance of quality of life, not just longevity. Women live longer lives than do men, but they suffer more years of disability. The burden of diseases such as Alzheimer's, which occur primarily late in life, fall disproportionately upon women. Even earlier in life, women are more prone to diseases that are not fatal but that interfere with well-being and full functioning. These include autoimmune diseases, depression and other mood disorders, and unintended pregnancy. The IOM committee observed that relatively less attention had been paid to nonfatal diseases and that less progress had occurred for many of these disorders. This volume underlines the importance of well-being and the burden to women of health challenges such as irritable bowel syndrome, rheumatic disease, multiple sclerosis, and Alzheimer's. Importantly, it also includes chapters that analyze the role of risk factors such as alcohol and tobacco use, weight and eating disorders, sleep and sedentary behaviors that may contribute to a range of diseases and that may impair quality of life.

In sum, this volume covers a wide array of conditions, causes, and approaches to understanding and improving health among women. It will serve as a valuable reference for health and mental health providers, researchers, and those in training for professional or research careers.

Preface

In the 1990s, when specific courses and texts in women's health psychology emerged, Annette Stanton and Sheryle Gallant (Stanton & Gallant, 1995) commented on questions they faced relating to the advisability of presenting such specialized content. Both the empirical foundations and the reasons for separating women's health psychology from "general" health psychology were questioned. At that time, the study of women's health psychology was just beginning to blossom. For the first time, the United States was seeing the development of organizations such as the Office of Research on Women's Health in 1990, national initiatives to include women in clinical health trials (the Women's Health Equity Act, 1990), federal research requirements to include women and individuals from diverse ethnic-racial groups (the NIH Revitalization Act of 1993), physician (the Council on Graduate Medical Education, 1995) and clinical psychology (the American Psychological Association) training in women's health. In the years following, several U.S.-based programs and organizations became cornerstones in the field of women's health, including the American Medical Women's Association, Division 35 of the American Psychological Association (i.e., Society for the Psychology of Women), the Office of Research on Women's Health, the Society for Women's Health Research, and the Women's Health Initiative (WHI).

From that foundation, the interest and impact of women's health and women's health psychology continues to be evidenced by the increase in women's health programs instituted by hospitals and universities and the number of professional organizations that have identified women's health as a focus area. General booksellers now have entire sections devoted to narratives and educational information on women's health for consumers. One of the questions facing us at the inception of this book was whether the research work in women's health psychology has kept pace with the interest it has garnered.

In this second decade of the 21st century, the empirical foundation of women's health psychology has become both broader and deeper. It has grown into a specialty area that in some instances converges with research and theories of general health psychology in common with men while in other instances reflects unique or different needs of women. Perhaps one of the major advancements is that today, more than ever, the field of women's health psychology recognizes that women are a diverse group. There is also more attention to the idea that women's health can be impacted by a variety of factors related to economic and social backgrounds and practices, as well as cultural, political, and relational contexts, and that women will face a variety of issues during different life stages related to reproduction, family, and work.

With these issues in mind, *Women's Health Psychology* was designed to focus on important health psychology issues of women spanning from young adulthood to post-menopause. It is intended to describe how behaviors, attitudes, and lifestyle choices influence women's health, to examine interactions between psychological and physical health, and to present these findings within a developmental and diverse socio-cultural context.

Our goal is to present current research in women's health psychology that incorporates the broad and diverse context of women's lives. The book is divided into four sections. The first section of the book considers several important general issues of historical and current context for women's health that help to expand thinking related to intersections of women's health with wider social issues, employment, and relationships. The section "Well-Being and Health Challenges" includes chapters related to a number of behaviors and conditions known to enhance and/or compromise healthy lifestyles among women. The manifestation of addictive behaviors (namely smoking and alcohol use) among women and strategies tailored *to women* and *for women* are presented. The importance of physical activity and sleep throughout women's lives, coupled with the impairments related to sleep disturbance and sedentary lifestyle, are highlighted. The growing epidemic of obesity, along with eating disorders and body image, are addressed within a socio-cultural context. Likewise, the increasing popularity of cosmetic treatments and their hypothesized underlying motives are discussed. The next section presents a range of reproductive health topics that women encounter during their lifespan including sexual health issues, decision-making surrounding childbearing, breastfeeding, and menopause, as well as topics that may be experienced by a subset of women, including premenstrual dysphoric disorder, infertility, and psychiatric symptoms during the perinatal period. The final section, "Disability and Chronic Conditions," opens with a chapter on women's responses to disability followed by chapters dealing with some of the more important health threats and chronic conditions experienced by women. These include the experience of cancer in women, the psychology of irritable bowel syndrome, neurological disorders in women, and converging issues in heart disease, stroke, and Alzheimer's disease in women.

Authors were invited to provide a critical review of an area, focusing on one to two key issues and to address, where possible, how the health behavior, reproductive issue, or disorder might interact with developmental milestones or cultural, socioeconomic, or social identity (e.g., gender orientation or disability). We anticipate that this book will be useful to a broad range of practitioners, including psychologists, mental health counselors, physicians, nurses, allied health professionals, and medical social workers as well as students, educators, and researchers in the medical and social sciences who are interested in the evidence-based foundation for offering effective services to women.

REFERENCE

Stanton, A. L., & Gallant, S. J. (Eds). (1995). *The psychology of women's health: Progress and challenges in research and application*. Washington, DC: American Psychological Association.

Acknowledgments

We are grateful to the many people who gave of their time and expertise in support of this book's completion. First, the development of this book would not have been possible without the efforts of our contributing authors. Our selection of authors was designed to reflect the current state of the field of women's health psychology. Authors represent both well established and "up and coming" researchers and clinicians. We wish to thank our graduate students Alexa Bonacquisti, Casey Burkard, Efrat Eichenbaum, Meredith Gillis, Sara Levine Kornfield, Mitra Khaksari, Alexandra R. Nelson, Emily Reid O'Connor, and Victoria Wright for their assistance in proposal and chapter development research and initial conceptualization of the book sections. We thank them, as well as Katherine Alvarez, Jessica Bartholow, Lindey Bartolucci, Elizabeth Culnan, Kara Douglas, Aimee Hildenbrand, Sarah Horsey, Christina Nash, Colleen Walsh, and Maisa Ziadni, for their assistance with editing, referencing, and many administrative tasks.

To our wonderful editorial assistants, Alexa Bonacquisti and Emily Reid O'Connor (1981–2011), we want to express our heartfelt gratitude. Emily's dedication and passion for women's health psychology was infectious. Although her passing left us with deep sadness, she also engendered in us a resolve to live life fully and always ask the important questions, as she did. Alexa's amazing organizational abilities, initiative, and positive attitude contributed immensely to the management of this project. Alexa was truly "the hub" and often anticipated our needs before we could voice them. We are grateful that our editorial assistants were willing to abide by our editors' edict to "nourish our spirits by holding all meetings *away* from our offices" and repeatedly accompanied us to coffee shops and restaurants as we hashed out the details of the book. Also, to our editor, Patricia Rossi, and the staff at John Wiley & Sons, our many thanks for your advice and input in guiding the development and publication of the manuscript.

We are grateful to our families and friends who have provided unwavering support and enthusiasm throughout this process, particularly our spouses (Sean Duffy, Steve Nocella, and Brian Kloss) who have supported us, not only with this professional endeavor, but who also, on a daily basis, enable us to achieve a healthy work-life balance. And to the Kloss girls—the assistants, Ella and Abby—and the Geller Nocella boys—Ean and Maxwell—for their smiles, giggles, boundless energy, and curiosity that give inspiration every day. It is our children who remind us to plant seeds to grow future generations of health and happiness.

Finally, with this book, we pay homage to the generations of women who came before us and those who will come after, united in our engagement in multiple roles that influence women's physical, psychological, and spiritual health and well-being (including roles as mothers, sisters, daughters, wives and partners, primary caretakers, workers, and friends).

List of Contributors

Sarah K. Ballou, BA
Northwestern University, Feinberg
School of Medicine, Chicago, IL

Lisa Bowleg, PhD
Drexel University, School of Public Health,
Philadelphia, PA

Meghan L. Butryn, PhD
Drexel University, Philadelphia, PA

Canice E. Crerand, PhD
University of Pennsylvania,
School of Medicine, Philadelphia

Bradley N. Collins, PhD
Temple University, Philadelphia, PA

Sharon Danoff-Burg, PhD
San Diego State University & UCSD
Moores Cancer Center, CA

Paula S. Derry, PhD
Paula Derry Enterprises in Health
Psychology, Baltimore, MD

Heather E. Dillaway, PhD
Wayne State University, Detroit, MI

Alice D. Domar, PhD
Domar Center for Mind/Body Health,
Waltham, MA

Kara R. Douglas-Newman, MS
Drexel University, Philadelphia, PA

Alice V. Ely, MS
Drexel University, Philadelphia, PA

Efrat Eichenbaum, MS
Drexel University, Philadelphia, PA

Heather A. Flynn, PhD
Florida State University, Tallahassee

Matthew Fuller-Tyszkiewicz, PhD
Deakin University, Victoria, Australia

Pamela A. Geller, PhD
Drexel University, Philadelphia, PA

M. Meredith Gillis, PhD
Emory University, Atlanta, GA

Maggie L. Gorraiz, MA
University of Rhode Island, Kingston

Jennifer Hahn-Holbrook, PhD
University of California, Los Angeles

Sheri Hartman, PhD
UCSD Moores Cancer Center,
San Diego, CA

Martie Haselton, PhD
University of California, Los Angeles

Deidre Hussey
University of Hartford, CT

Laurie Keefer, PhD
Northwestern University, Feinberg
School of Medicine, Chicago, IL

Wendy Kline, PhD
University of Cincinnati, OH

Jacqueline D. Kloss, PhD
Drexel University, Philadelphia, PA

Ross Krawczyk, MA
University of South Florida, Tampa

Allison Kulig, MA
University of North Dakota, Grand Forks

Kaitlin Raines Lilienthal, MS
University of North Dakota, Grand Forks

Sarah Linke, PhD, MPH
University of California, San Diego

Michael R. Lowe, PhD
Drexel University, Philadelphia, PA

Leanne Magee, PhD
University of Pennsylvania School of
Medicine, Philadelphia

Bess H. Marcus, PhD
University of California, San Diego

Nancy L. Marshall, EdD
Wellesley College, Wellesley, MA

Kathy McCloskey, PhD, PsyD, ABPP
University of Hartford, CT

Patricia J. Morokoff, PhD
University of Rhode Island, Kingston

Dori Pekmezi, PhD
University of Alabama at Birmingham

Heather Munro Prescott, PhD
Central Connecticut State University,
New Britain

Uma S. Nair, PhD
Temple University, Philadelphia, PA

Christina O. Nash, M.S.
Drexel University, Philadelphia, PA

Alexandra R. Nelson, PhD
Drexel University, Philadelphia, PA

Danielle L. Novick, PhD
University of Michigan Medical School,
Ann Arbor

Rhoda Olkin, PhD
California School of Professional
Psychology, Los Angeles

Lauren B. Prince, BA
Wake Forest University, Winston-Salem, NC

Lina Ricciardelli, PhD
Deakin University, Victoria, Australia

David B. Sarwer, PhD
University of Pennsylvania School of
Medicine, Philadelphia

Chris Dunkel Schetter, PhD
University of California, Los Angeles

Mary V. Spiers, PhD
Drexel University, Philadelphia, PA

Jacqueline Spitzer, MSEd
University of Pennsylvania School of
Medicine, Philadelphia

Annette L. Stanton, PhD
University of California, Los Angeles

Meir Steiner, MD, PhD, FRCPC
McMaster University and St. Joseph's
Healthcare, Ontario, Canada

J. Kevin Thompson, PhD
University of South Florida, Tampa

Simone N. Vigod, MD, MSc, FRCPC
Women's College Hospital, University of
Toronto, Canada

Nancy Vogeltanz-Holm, PhD
University of North Dakota School of
Medicine and Health Sciences, Grand Forks

Sharon C. Wilsnack, PhD
University of North Dakota School of
Medicine and Health Sciences, Grand Forks

Betina Yanez, PhD
Northwestern University Feinberg School
of Medicine, Chicago, IL

WOMEN'S HEALTH IN CONTEXT

Historical Roots of Women's Healthcare

HEATHER MUNRO PRESCOTT AND WENDY KLINE

INTRODUCTION

From childhood to old age, what it means to be female in American society has changed over time. There is a large body of literature on the history of women's health in the United States, and this subject continues to draw major interest from scholars and lay readers alike. As 21st-century politics reminds us, the role of reproduction and female sexuality in contemporary society are regularly up for debate. What distinguishes women from men—the capacity to conceive—is both a physiological and a historical phenomenon. As this chapter illustrates, the relationship among women, their bodies, and what is considered "healthy" is grounded in particular assumptions and contexts. As a result, medical theories and diagnoses sometimes radically reverse course when social conventions change.

This chapter approaches the history of women's health from a thematic perspective, offering readers a sense of the myriad issues that have confronted women over the past century. Topics include child and adolescent health, sexuality and sex education, birth control, pregnancy and childbirth, reproductive rights, the women's health movement, abortion, sterilization abuse, sexual assault, and gender equality in medical research. It is by no means comprehensive, but taken together, the issues fleshed out here illustrate the contested terrain that women still encounter when negotiating their healthcare. Understanding the origins of contemporary women's health issues is a crucial step toward improving the psychology of women's health today.

CHILD AND ADOLESCENT HEALTH

During the early 20th century, pediatricians and other medical experts argued that high rates of infant and child mortality were caused by mothers' lack of accurate scientific knowledge about how to prevent and manage childhood diseases. The solution to this problem was to make motherhood more "scientific" by instructing women to rely on pediatricians and other scientific experts for advice on the proper ways to raise healthy children. These principles of "scientific motherhood" were promoted in high school and college courses in home economics, advice manuals, government pamphlets issued by the U.S. Children's Bureau, and popular advice columns in women's magazines. By the 1920s, women had become accustomed to seeking childcare advice from medical and scientific experts rather than from neighbors, friends, and relatives (Apple, 2006).

Women reformers of the early 20th century were also instrumental in gaining congressional support for the Sheppard-Towner Maternity and Infancy Act (1921). This law appropriated federal funds for maternal and child healthcare for low-income families free of charge. Unfortunately, conservative male politicians in Congress opposed this program and refused to reauthorize the program in 1927 (Muncy, 1991).

School boards attempted to control the spread of disease by requiring schoolchildren and adolescents to be vaccinated against smallpox, diphtheria, and other diseases before attending school. Then as now, some parents objected strongly to compulsory vaccination. Some believed that vaccination was dangerous, whereas others resented the intrusion of state officials into private family matters. In order to prevent the spread of disease and protect the health of students, schools began in the 1890s to hire physicians as medical inspectors. These physicians identified a set of diseases that seemed to be caused and/or exacerbated by the environment of 19th-century schools, many of which lacked adequate light, ventilation, heat, or sanitary facilities. Medical experts noted that American schoolrooms, especially those in urban areas, were breeding grounds for the spread of disease, and they called for reforms that would eliminate hazards to student health. At the same time, child welfare reformers successfully lobbied for legislation that outlawed child labor and mandated school attendance through the age of 16 in most states (Meckel, 2002).

During the late 1910s and 1920s, the educational psychologist Lewis Terman argued that public schools should do more than detect and prevent illness: They should treat physical illnesses and defects that could affect students' academic success. Terman

proposed that schools hire nurses, who would not only examine students at school but also follow up on cases by visiting the students' homes to ensure that medical treatment was being followed. Terman also realized that many families, especially immigrant, urban, and rural poor families, could not afford medical care on their own. Therefore, he argued that the second essential step in promoting the health of students was to create medical clinics in the nation's schools. Terman's suggestions met with fierce opposition from the American Medical Association (AMA) and other medical organizations, who saw this as the first step toward "socialized medicine." Terman replied that free medical and dental clinics for the nation's children and youth were no different from universal public school education supported by taxpayer dollars. Opposition from the AMA led public schools to abandon school medical clinics as a healthcare strategy and limit their role to ensuring that students were properly vaccinated and in sufficiently good health to attend school (Sedlak & Schlossman, 1985).

ADOLESCENT GROWTH AND DEVELOPMENT

Surveys of schoolchildren and child laborers conducted by public health officials during the late 19th and early 20th centuries illustrated the negative effects of modern industrial life on young bodies. Physicians found that native-born, White, middle-class children who did not work for wages were on average larger and heavier than immigrant, working-class children of the same age. They also found that children who endured too much pressure in school had smaller and weaker bodies than those whose education was more suited to their age. At the same time, surveys indicated a steadily declining age of menarche and sexual maturity among children of the white, native-born middle classes (Tanner, 1981). Today, pediatricians attribute this decline in the average age of puberty to improvements in nutrition and child health, but in the late 19th and early 20th centuries, this change was alarming, especially for adolescent girls who were menstruating earlier but marrying later. Some parents and doctors tried to slow girls' physical maturation by eliminating foods that were considered "stimulating," such as cloves, pickles, and meat (Brumberg, 1997).

By the 1930s, a substantial amount of data had been accumulated on the average heights and weights of the nation's children and youth and incorporated into standardized height and weight charts. One of the main tasks of pediatricians in the post–World War II era was to measure their patients' growth and development against standardized tables of height and weight. Initially, deviation from the standardized norm was taken as a sign of disease or malnutrition, but soon "abnormal" height itself became a disease in need of treatment. This medical demarcation between "normal" and "abnormal" was reinforced by gender expectations for girls and boys. Experts warned that "tallness can be a real handicap for a girl," especially in the postwar era when women were expected to marry and have children. Girls could be "saved from spinsterhood" by receiving a new "wonder" drug—the synthetic estrogen diethylstilbestrol (DES), which when administered during early puberty would keep their adult height within socially accepted norms.

Children who were considered below average in height received the height-enhancing human growth hormone (hGH). This drug was initially developed to treat pituitary dwarfism, but soon anxious parents were bringing short children, boys especially, to pediatric endocrinologists in the hopes their children could attain a "socially acceptable height." These "wonder drugs" did not always live up to their promise, as tall girls continued to grow and short children did not reach their predicted height. Moreover, these treatments often caused severe medical problems. Tall girls who received synthetic estrogen experienced weight gain, nausea, vomiting, and extremely heavy and painful menstrual periods. Later in life, these women were more likely to develop fertility problems and cancer of the breast and reproductive organs.

During the 1980s, women who had received DES as teenagers organized Tall Girls Inc. Like other women's health organizations that emerged out of the second wave of feminism, this group criticized the medical profession's unethical treatment of girls and women as research subjects. Tall Girls, Inc. also helped promote pride among and social acceptance of tall women. Although growth attenuation still continues today, being a tall woman is no longer a "pitiable fate" but a ticket to a career on the runway or basketball court (Cohen & Cosgrove, 2009).

At the same time, the average age at which children first exhibit development of secondary sexual characteristics has steadily declined over the past 50 years: It is not unusual for breast development to occur in girls as early as age 7, and for testicular enlargement to occur in boys as young as age 8. Some experts blame the declining age of puberty on a host of modern societal ills, including pesticides and other environmental toxins, hormones in meat and milk, the epidemic of obesity in American society, and the ubiquity of sexualized messages in the mass media that some believe may trigger changes in the brain that in turn promote sexual development. At the same time, the average heights of adolescents have increased, which means that heights that were considered average in the mid-20th century (5 feet 2 inches for women, 5 feet 6 inches for men) are now below average. As tall stature in women has become not only acceptable but desirable, many parents show a preference for tallness in both girls and boys. Some pediatric endocrinologists recommend giving the hormone lupron to early-developing girls not only to slow their sexual maturation but also to ensure that they reach their full adult height (Cohen & Cosgrove, 2009).

SEXUALITY AND SEX EDUCATION

During World War I, the incidence of sexually transmitted diseases among American young people increased dramatically. Although sexually transmitted infections (STIs) had vexed medical experts for centuries, infection rates as high as 25% in some regions gave new urgency to campaigns to eliminate these deadly scourges. At the same time, it was becoming clear that young people's sexual practices were changing radically. Dr. Max J. Exner, Public Health Officer for the Young Men's Christian Association (YMCA), reported that more than half of his sample of 948 college men had engaged in sexual practices of some kind. More than 60% had practiced "self-abuse" (masturbation), 17% of these had also engaged in intercourse, and 2% described engaging in "various perverted practices,"

which Exner did not specify. Studies of the sexual behavior of female college graduates conducted by Clelia Duel Mosher at Stanford, and by New York City Corrections Commissioner Katherine Bement Davis in the 1910s and 1920s, indicated that similar changes were occurring on a smaller scale among female undergraduates. Reformers had long been concerned about "declining morals" among working-class, immigrant youth. The fact that "respectable" college and university students were also engaging in such "radical" sexual practices was disturbing to many parents, health professionals, and educators in public schools (Munro Prescott, 2007).

To address these concerns, public health experts created new initiatives in what they called "social hygiene," a term that represented both a euphemism for the control of "venereal diseases," as well as a new approach to prevention of these afflictions. Social hygiene differed from earlier "purity crusades," which shielded young people from moral and physical dangers via a "conspiracy of silence" about sexual matters. Social hygienists attacked the sexual double standard, supporting total abstinence before marriage for both men and women. Yet, social hygienists believed education rather than scare tactics was the best way to protect the health of the nation's youth. Social hygienists believed sex education was especially important for female students, because so many young women became teachers and mothers. Yet they were also concerned about preserving sexual propriety; therefore, they developed separate curricula for each gender and insisted that girls should receive instruction in sex education separately from boys. Even then, sex education programs advocated total abstinence before marriage. Nevertheless, sex education programs were as controversial then as they are now, and supporters of these programs tended to camouflage their efforts by using titles such as "family and marriage education" to describe their courses (Moran, 2000).

The social hygiene movement eventually paved the way for significant changes in theories about adolescent female psychology. Before the 1920s, most writers on adolescent female psychology argued that healthy female development involved protecting the young girl from premature awakening of sexual instincts and longings. Rather than label these girls as delinquents, experts in adolescent mental hygiene revised their views of female adolescent psychology and made sexual curiosity and a certain degree of sexual experimentation a normal part of healthy female development. In fact, mental hygiene experts worried more about girls who did *not* adopt an avid interest in the opposite sex by the middle years of adolescence. Mental hygienists argued that such girls might become lesbians or otherwise fail to attain a normal adult feminine role (Lunbeck, 1994).

Efforts to control the spread of sexually transmitted diseases led some gynecologists to recommend routine pelvic examinations for young women who were about to be married. The cytological cancer-screening vaginal smear, developed by George Papanicolaou in the 1920s, became a fundamental part of the move toward routine annual gynecological checkups following World War II (Casper & Clarke, 1998). Yet, routine pelvic examinations for young teenage patients were controversial. Most gynecologists recommended that this procedure be avoided except in cases of gross physical disease, and even then should only be performed under anesthesia (Munro Prescott, 1998). By adopting such a course, noted one

gynecology textbook from the 1930s, "there will be less danger of inducing morbid introspection and of engendering psychosis that cannot fail to have an unfavorable effect on the patient" (Sturgis, 1962).

Nevertheless, during the 1940s and 1950s, a few gynecologists began to suggest that regular gynecological exams and Pap smears should be made part of standard medical care for adolescent girls (Allen, 1958; Schauffler, 1964). These gynecologists argued that routine care during adolescence was crucial because of two major demographic trends at this time: First, the percentage of married teenaged girls increased markedly. By 1959, 47% of all brides had married before the age of 19, and the percentage of girls married between 14 and 17 had grown by one-third since 1940 (Bailey, 1988). Second, Alfred Kinsey's study entitled *Sexual Behavior in the Human Female* disclosed that more than 50% of the women in his sample had engaged in premarital sex (Kinsey, 1953). In a paper presented at the 91st Annual Meeting of the American Public Health Association in Kansas City in 1963, Helen Manley, Executive Director of the Social Health Association of Greater Saint Louis, commented on the problems that resulted from the rise in early marriage and motherhood. Manley observed that between 1940 and 1958, the overall marriage rate had increased by 231%, but the number of teen marriages had grown by 500%. Half of all teen brides were pregnant at the time of marriage (Manley, 1964). Like now, health experts like Manley were concerned about growing rates of teenage pregnancy, but these experts were concerned not only with unwed mothers but also with the problems of *married* teenage mothers. Manley was part of a larger cohort of women reformers in the city of Saint Louis who, beginning in the 1920s, attempted to stamp out prostitution and venereal disease through aggressive public health campaigns and sex education programs in youth groups and public schools (Wagman, 2009).

As a result of these reform efforts, sex education programs were gradually incorporated first into colleges and universities and later into public high schools during the 1940s and 1950s. During that time, support for sex education emerged amidst intense concern about the consequences of adolescent sexual behavior, especially increasing rates of "illegitimate" pregnancies and a growing incidence of sexually transmitted diseases. Although many of these anxieties targeted young people of color and low-income whites, the "declining morals" of white, middle-class, suburban teenagers were also cause for concern. Unlike our own day, creation of sex education programs following World War II inspired very little popular opposition at the time, partly because these programs emphasized that sexual intercourse should be reserved for marriage (Freeman, 2008).

At the same time, experts warned of the social and medical dangers of early marriage. Manley observed that the rate of divorce for teenage marriages was three times higher than that for older couples, with three out of every four teenage marriages breaking up. Young people who were wed before age 20 not only shortened their own schooling but also affected the health of the next generation. Teenaged parents had a higher percentage of premature babies, leading to higher rates of illness and death resulting from lack of prenatal care (Manley, 1964).

These anxieties about the dangers of teen marriage for girls also appeared in epidemiological studies of cervical cancer. Several epidemiological studies published in the 1950s and early 1960s indicated that women who married before age 20 appeared to be at higher risk for this disease. Some speculated that women who had multiple "broken marriages" were especially susceptible. Isadore D. Rotkin of the Cancer Research Project at the Kaiser Foundation in California elaborated on this research, and found that age at first coitus was the most significant variable distinguishing cervical cancer patients from controls. In a study of more than 400 patients, 85% of whom were Caucasian, twice as many cancer patients as controls began coitus at ages 15 to 17, comparatively few began after age 21, and almost none started as late as age 27. Rotkin hypothesized that some kind of infectious agent transmitted by male partners was a contributing factor, and that the adolescent cervix was especially vulnerable to "epithelial transformation" by exposure to such an agent. Although Rotkin acknowledged that measures aimed at improving male sexual hygiene could reduce the incidence of the disease, he argued that postponement of marriage for young women—and limitation of sexual intercourse to marriage—was the most effective means of prevention (Rotkin, 1967).

These findings lent further weight to the argument that regular gynecological exams and Pap smears should be made part of standard medical care for adolescent girls. Edward Allen, Professor of Obstetrics and Gynecology at University of Illinois, observed that: "Further advances in the detection of early pelvic cancer will probably not occur until we educate our young women as to the ease and necessity of routine pelvic examination before the sex inhibitions become so fixed" (Allen, 1954). Allen's allusion to "sex inhibitions" indicates that more was at stake than accurate diagnosis of gynecological disease: He and other gynecologists were worried that many of the adolescent girls they saw in their practices had an "unhealthy" attitude toward their genitals, expressed in excessive modesty or anxiety in regards to this area of their bodies. Physicians claimed that the pelvic exam helped foster normal sexual adjustment within marriage frigidity, dyspareunia (painful intercourse), sterility, and hostility toward her spouse (Schauffler, 1964).

Sex education programs came under increasing attack not during the conservative 1950s, but during the late 1960s, led by anticommunist organizations and the early beginnings of an organized religious right. By the end of the 20th century, opposition to increasingly controversial topics, such as condoms, HIV/AIDs, and gay, lesbian, bisexual, and transgendered sexual identities, led to the creation of the abstinence-only programs we are familiar with today (Freeman, 2008). Many parents object to mandatory vaccines that prevent the human papilloma virus (HPV), which has been linked to cervical cancer. These parents claim that mandatory vaccination violates parental rights and "promotes promiscuity" by protecting girls from the consequences of their sexual behavior (Charo, 2007).

THE BIRTH CONTROL MOVEMENT

In the 21st century, women face numerous options for controlling their fertility, from barrier methods to hormonal contraceptives. Yet despite an increase of choices, birth control remains controversial and fraught with complications. More and more women have come to rely on hormonal methods, which are highly effective in terms of preventing

pregnancy, but also introduce new health risks and side effects into otherwise healthy patient populations. In addition, the question of choice has become more complex, as individuals and groups debate the safety and legitimacy of certain types of hormonal contraceptives, as well as their use on minority populations and the disabled.

The term "birth control" was coined by Margaret Sanger, the leading activist for contraceptive prevention in the 20th-century United States. Specializing in obstetrics, she witnessed women struggling to deliver and raise baby after baby in crowded urban conditions with little money or power. She recalls the many women who begged her to tell them the "secret" to preventing conception. All she could recommend, however, were condoms or withdrawal, both of which required the cooperation of the male partner. She vowed to make this her lifelong crusade—making birth control accessible to all women. She began publishing *The Woman Rebel* in 1914, a magazine intended for working women to educate them about sexuality and contraception. She also used this publication to challenge the Comstock Law, in effect since 1873, which prohibited the importation and mailing of contraceptive information and devices in the United States. She used the term "birth control" in her magazine to replace more awkward phrases such as "family limitation" or "voluntary motherhood" (Chesler, 1992). After seven issues of the magazine, the paper was shut down, deemed "unmailable" by the U.S. Post Office (under the Comstock Obscenity Laws). In 1916, Sanger opened the first birth control clinic in Brownsville, New York. Although the clinic did not stay open for long, the experience made her realize the importance of obtaining medical support for birth control.

Although birth control was not openly discussed in public in the early 20th century, there was plenty of evidence it was already in use, at least within certain socioeconomic groups. College-educated, middle-class white women demonstrated, by a dramatic drop in fertility, that they were practicing some form of birth control in the 1920s. Katharine Bement Davis's massive 10-year study (published in 1929), entitled *Factors in the Sex Lives of Twenty-two Hundred Women*, revealed the extent to which certain women were familiar with forms of birth control. Seventy-four percent of 1,000 college-educated women who were queried admitted to using some form of contraception, although information on birth control had "virtually been driven underground." Many middle-class social reformers couched their concern in eugenic terms, fearing that the Anglo-Saxon population would soon be overcome by immigrants and African Americans. Over the course of the 20th century, the White middle-class birthrate had dropped by nearly half, from seven to just over three children per woman. Although Teddy Roosevelt and others had sparked a widespread concern about "race suicide" at the turn of the century, the white middle-class birthrate dropped even lower in the 1920s. The rate of childlessness reached a record high in the 1920s and 1930s, and the birthrate would not actually begin to increase until the postwar era (May, 1995).

Though the declining birthrate demonstrated that many women (predominantly in the middle and upper classes) still managed to gain access to birth control, it was not widely talked about in public. Most professionals, including physicians and even feminists, avoided such a controversial topic, which they believed might undermine their credibility. Physicians, as James Reed points

out, had "no strong motive for a positive attitude toward birth control," often because they, too, were concerned about the declining birthrate and the change in sexual mores. As a result, physicians "betrayed a startling reticence and lack of information on the subject." They often perceived contraceptives as both morally and physically dangerous. Since its antiabortion campaign in the 1870s, the profession regarded itself as "the gatekeepers of women's virtue" (Chesler, 1992; Reed, 1978).

Given the reluctance of medical professionals (and even many feminists) to support her cause, Sanger took another approach. Rather than directly challenging the Comstock Law, she sought to reform it. She toned down her argument that women had a right to control their own bodies, instead marketing her crusade as a public health campaign. She began pushing for a "doctors only" bill that would exempt doctors from criminal prosecution. Eventually, this strategy would prove effective. With massive financial backing from her wealthy second husband, Noah Slee, Sanger helped establish the first birth control firm that would sell birth control devices directly to doctors, the Holland-Rantos company (Tone, 2001). This approach encouraged more doctors to support the medicalization of birth control, providing a financial incentive. For example, they could purchase diaphragms directly from Holland-Rantos, then prescribe them to their patients at a profit. In the 1930s, for example, doctors marked up the price of individual diaphragms anywhere from 75 cents to more than $3, depending on the design (Tone, 2001).

Two events in the 1930s further legitimized the use of physician-controlled contraceptive use. First, in a landmark decision,

U.S. v. One Package of Japanese Pessaries (1936), the U.S. Supreme Court permitted the modification of the Comstock Law to allow physicians (only) to order contraceptives through the mail. Second, the American Medical Association voted in the following year to endorse physician-prescribed contraceptives. As a result, birth control gained legitimacy in the eyes of many people. In the process, however, birth control fell under the direction of doctors rather than women—a far cry from what many envisioned. Some historians have viewed Sanger's collaboration with the medical professionals as a betrayal of Sanger's earlier commitment to grass-roots feminist birth control activism. They have also rightly criticized Sanger for tacitly endorsing the population movement's tendency to focus their population control efforts on poor people of color in the United States and developing countries (Gordon, 1990).

The *One Package* decision only affected federal laws regarding contraception, but individual states could and did impose additional restrictions on the sale and distribution of contraceptive advice and devices. The state of Connecticut had one of the most restrictive laws in the nation: Even physicians were prohibited from giving contraceptives to their patients, and the law did not make any exceptions for women whose health or lives would be endangered by pregnancy (Garrow, 1998). Connecticut did, like many states, have a compulsory sterilization law for women who were deemed "unfit" to reproduce by the state, but it imposed severe restrictions on voluntary sterilization for women who requested this method of fertility control. Women had to be married, and the number of children they had plus their age had to equal 30 or more (Kluchin, 2009). Consequently,

sterilization was the only legal means of contraception in Connecticut (Garrow, 1998).

In 1958, Dr. C. Lee Buxton, chair of Yale Medical School's department of Obstetrics and Gynecology, and three of his patients filed a lawsuit claiming that Connecticut's laws prohibiting the sale, distribution, and use of contraceptive drugs and devices were unconstitutional. The suit reached the U.S. Supreme Court in June 1961, but the court dismissed the case because no state laws had been violated. Yet, the court opinion that accompanied the decision also declared that Connecticut's laws were "dead words and harmless, empty shadows." On November 1st of that year, the Planned Parenthood League of Connecticut, led by Buxton and Planned Parenthood's Executive Director Estelle Griswold, decided to test the validity of the court's opinion, and opened a birth control clinic in New Haven. Nine days later, Buxton and Griswold were arrested for violating state laws outlawing contraception. The defendants appealed their case all the way to the U.S. Supreme Court, culminating in the court's decision in *Griswold v. Connecticut* (1965) declaring that Connecticut's birth control law unconstitutionally intruded upon the right of marital privacy (Johnson, 2005).

The *Griswold* decision only applied to married individuals. Although Connecticut removed restrictions on contraception for the unmarried as well, most states were silent on the issue of whether the unwed had the same privacy rights. Massachusetts and Wisconsin explicitly outlawed prescribing or distributing contraceptives to unmarried individuals (Pilpel & Wechsler, 1969). In 1967, the Boston vice squad arrested contraceptive salesman Bill Baird for "crimes against chastity" when he gave a can of Emko contraceptive foam to an unmarried teenaged girl following a lecture at Boston University. Two years later, Baird was again arrested after a demonstration at Northland College in Ashland, Wisconsin. In 1972, the U.S. Supreme Court heard the criminal case against Baird, and declared in its decision *Eisenstadt v. Baird*: "If the right of privacy means anything, it is the right of the individual, married or single, to be free from unwarranted governmental intrusion into matters so fundamentally affecting a person as the decision whether to bear or beget a child" (Munro Prescott, 2007).

The introduction of hormonal contraceptives guaranteed that birth control would remain steadfastly under the control of doctors. When the U.S. Food and Drug Administration (FDA) approved the first birth control pill in 1960, debates about contraceptive use took on a whole new turn. Emerging at the dawn of the sexual revolution, the pill raised expectations that women were sexually available. By 1965, more than 6 million women had taken oral contraceptives. Planned Parenthood noted that 70% of all women using its services for birth control chose to get a prescription for the pill. By 1990, more than 80% of American women born in the postwar era had tried it (Watkins, 1998). The pill offered many advantages over barrier methods of birth control: It was highly effective, convenient, and entirely separated from the act of intercourse. It also did not require the consent or even awareness of a male sexual partner. Both doctors and female patients initially expressed enthusiasm for this new form of birth control. Yet, by the end of the 1960s, many had lost confidence in this new form of birth control.

The first pill, Enovid, contained approximately 10 times the amount of progesterone and 4 times the amount of estrogen used in later doses. Many women suffered from severe side effects, including blood clots and heart attacks. In 1969, the U.S. Senate conducted hearings on the safety of the pill, resulting in the requirement that makers of the product include a patient package insert warning of potential side effects of the pill. As a result, pill use dropped by 20%, but it remained the most popular contraceptive.

Other controversies continued to complicate the debate surrounding hormonal contraceptives. Growing cynicism and a rising women's health movement (see later section) raised new questions regarding the validity of prescribing hormonal contraceptives to millions of healthy women. Many people accused scientists and doctors of using women as guinea pigs whose health was expendable in the name of scientific research. One of the most controversial forms of hormonal birth control was Depo-Provera, which was injected intramuscularly every 90 days to prevent ovulation. Although highly effective in preventing pregnancy, Depo-Provera's availability to and higher use among poor and minority patient populations before it received FDA approval in 1992 generated concern among activists that the drug was a dangerous tool for population control advocates. Journalists reported that women were lining up by the thousands for contraceptive injections in developing countries, funded by international family planning organizations. One Namibian physician noted that injections were "simply banged into black and colored women, without discussion, explanation or even permission" in the 1980s (Lindsay, 1991). These reports generated concern about racist population control policies, and also drew attention to poor scientific research methods.

Clinical trials conducted in these countries failed to follow up with patients who discontinued use of the drug and did not adequately document the risks and side effects, from weight gain to heavy bleeding to cancer. As a result, the FDA repeatedly turned down Upjohn's attempts to market Depo as a contraceptive in the United States in the 1970s and 1980s. Not until 1992, after a long-term World Health Organization Study suggested the overall risk of cancer to be minimal, would the FDA approve Depo-Provera for contraceptive marketing. Nonetheless, thousands of American women received Depo injections to prevent pregnancy during these decades, either through clinical trials or through off-label use, as Depo was approved by the FDA for the treatment of endometrial cancer.

Depo-Provera finally received FDA approval in 1992, but the story did not end there. The FDA announced a label change for Depo as a result of data on the drug submitted by now-owner Pfizer. It included a black box warning linking prolonged use of the drug with loss of bone density (and thus the potential to develop osteoporosis), and a warning that Depo should not be used for more than 2 years "unless other birth control methods are inadequate" (Food and Drug Administration [FDA], 2004). New evidence continues to raise questions about cancer risks, and the side effects remain a problem for many users. Depo-Provera illustrates the complex nature of birth control in American society. In addition to potential health risks from certain types of birth control, the question of how to balance accessibility with protection from abuse of certain patient populations continues to divide the feminist community.

THE WOMEN'S HEALTH MOVEMENT

Although women have always had an important relationship with healthcare issues, the interest in tracking the history of women's health is a more recent phenomenon, coming directly out of the social movements of the 1960s and 1970s. For the first time, many women began to see their individual struggles as women—whether psychological, economic, or sexual—as forms of societal oppression. In activist groups, college campuses, and literary circles, some women employed the terms *misogyny*, *sexism*, and *medicalization* to describe how their bodies were being used against them. Before looking at the specific issues that the women's health movement addressed, it is important to look at the historical context that allowed this movement to surface.

Women's health emerged as a major social and political issue in a turbulent decade. A new generation of Americans expressed dismay that the wealthiest, most powerful nation in the world could not adequately provide for nor protect those at home, and they sought alternative solutions. Students for a Democratic Society (SDS) issued their manifesto of New Left Activism, the Port Huron Statement, in 1962 (Patterson, 1996). The following summer, more than 250,000 civil rights protesters marched on Washington, DC, for freedom and jobs in the largest political demonstration in U.S. history. In 1968, radical feminists staged a series of dramatic protests, such as crowning a sheep at the Miss America pageant to protest the sexual objectification of women. The final year of the decade brought about 5 days of rioting in Greenwich Village, in New York City, fueling the gay liberation movement. In this unsettled period, no issue was left unexplored, no political structure unchallenged. By its end, a postwar climate of confidence had been replaced by cynicism and doubt, which included disillusionment with the medical profession.

Science and medicine had enjoyed unprecedented authority and power in post-WWII America, when medical care became one of the nation's largest industries. But by 1970, medicine, along with other social institutions, had suffered a "stunning loss of confidence" (Starr, 1982). Beginning in the mid-1960s, according to David Rothman, the practice of medicine became thoroughly transformed, a process completed within just a decade. An intrusion of outsiders, including academic scholars, government officials, lawyers, and judges, completely altered the doctor–patient relationship and brought "new rules to medicine." Exposés on patient experimentation and unethical treatment challenged the notion that the doctor had the patient's best interest in mind (Rothman, 1991). In this social climate, only outsiders, who were presumed to be objective, could effectively regulate and monitor a doctor's decisions. As they brought these concerns to light, popular agitation ensured that patients' rights would join the broader spectrum of civil rights. Patients, like African Americans, gays and lesbians, and women, were easily exploited as human subjects and therefore required a language of rights.

Several new health programs emerged in the 1960s to address what many were pronouncing a national healthcare crisis. Congress approved Medicare and Medicaid programs in 1965, and President Lyndon Johnson's Office of Economic Opportunity legislation included funding for neighborhood health centers by the following year

(Starr, 1982). These centers were designed to improve access to healthcare, particularly for the poor. Johnson became the first president to establish federal funding of family planning (excluding abortion) and maternal health programs (Nelson, 2003). In addition, hundreds of free clinics opened in the late 1960s, providing treatment that was less expensive or less hierarchical than traditional services (Ruzek, 1978). For some women, however, these measures did not begin to scrape the surface of what they believed to be an even more fundamental problem in American society: sexism.

Of all social movements, the women's health movement had its most direct roots in women's liberation. By the late 1960s, women who were inspired by the civil rights movement and the demand for equal citizenship created a new wave of feminist activism (Evans, 2003). Although it was a fragmented movement (historians refer to several branches of feminism, including liberal, socialist, radical, cultural, and multiracial), the unifying characteristic was the claim that the personal is political (Thompson, 2002). By challenging the divide between the two, feminists asserted that the most private aspects of their identity—relationships, sexuality, health, and family life— were indeed political issues. Ideas and personal stories, rather than goals or strategies, united a broad range of women who came to identify themselves as feminists. Women's liberation, according to Sara Evans, depended "on the ability of women to tell each other their own stories, to claim them as the basis of political action." For many women, these stories and their political implications emerged through "consciousness raising," a process in which the sharing of personal stories led to a "click"—a sudden recognition and clarity that sexism lay at the root of their struggles. Coined by early members of the New York Radical Women, *consciousness-raising* became "an intense form of collective self-education" (Evans, 2003).

Thus, at a time when medical authority was already undermined, when activists sought protection for human rights, and when feminists argued that deeply personal issues had political consequences, renewed activism in women's health appears almost inevitable. Female bodies, argued health feminists, had been subjected to male medical authority; women could not achieve full equality without the right to reclaim their bodies. Doctors were overwhelmingly male (in 1970, 7.6% of physicians and 7.2% of obstetrician-gynecologists were female), and according to critics, they were paternalistic, condescending, and judgmental (Weisman, 1998). In addition, they had medicalized reproductive issues and turned women into human guinea pigs, argued activists at hearings on abortion, Depo-Provera, and childbirth.

Women's health activists used a wide range of strategies to increase women's control over their own bodies, including advocacy, education, and the creation of alternative healthcare organizations (Weisman, 1998). By 1974, more than 1,200 women's groups were providing health services in the United States, according to a nationwide survey, although many of these groups were short-lived experiments. Other groups worked through legislative channels to ensure protection and services, from abortion to FDA regulation of contraception (Ruzek, 1978). As more women became active consumers in the healthcare industry, they sought out accurate, easy-to-understand information on women's health.

Such information became available from women's health literature. The first and most comprehensive book to provide information about women's health and sexuality was *Our Bodies, Ourselves*. Beginning as a 130-page newsprint manual in 1971, this comprehensive book on women's health was by 2005 an 832-page treatise (complete with a companion website) that had sold 4 million copies and had been translated and/or culturally adapted into 18 different languages. The topics that the authors chose to cover in multiple editions of *Our Bodies, Ourselves* attest to some of the important themes in women's health that were emerging in the mid-to-late 20th century: pregnancy and childbirth, sterilization abuse, and reproductive rights.

PREGNANCY AND CHILDBIRTH

In the first edition of *Our Bodies, Ourselves*, the Boston Women's Health Book Collective authors noted that American women had been "kept in the dark" about what to expect physically and emotionally in pregnancy and birth. This was more than a decade before the pregnancy guide *What to Expect When You're Expecting* was published—a book that went on to regularly top the *New York Times* Best Seller list in the advice books category. In the 1970s, most births took place in the hospital and were attended by an obstetrician, a trend that began at the turn of the 20th century. Before this trend, childbirth was an all-female event that took place in the home under the direction of a female midwife. As birth moved to the hospital, expectant mothers lost their ability to play an active role in the delivery process. Birth became an entirely medical event, dictated by doctors who sought to standardize and regulate delivery.

Some women welcomed these changes, in particular the use of obstetrical anesthesia, to ease the pain of childbirth (Wolf, 2009). In the early 20th century, American women discovered a miraculous new practice that was being used on their German sisters: *Dammerschlaf*, or Twilight Sleep. Two female journalists writing for *McClure's* magazine in 1914 embarked on a mission to report the effects of Twilight Sleep by traveling to Germany (one delivered her baby while there under Twilight Sleep and described her experience in the article). Their enthusiastic report generated a massive reader response (the largest *McClure's* had ever seen) from American women who were interested in the latest benefits of modern medicine to relieve the pain and suffering of childbirth. Although American doctors were reluctant to mess with the delicate balance of morphine and scopolamine, which could be very dangerous, they eventually conceded to try it—after all, it was an additional guarantor of obstetric patients as more women chose the hospital as the ideal setting in which to give birth. Despite the death of one of the most active supporters of Twilight Sleep, the practice persisted well into the mid-20th century. Supporters, publishing in popular magazines, "described childbirth as 'torture' and suggested that the prospect of pain deterred many women from becoming pregnant, particularly upper-class and better-educated women, who, they said, should be the ones to have the largest families" (Caton, 1999).

But by mid-century, some people began to challenge the belief that the best childbirth was one forgotten. Opposition to medicated childbirth originated not with feminists, but with a controversial, flamboyant British obstetrician who believed that women should give birth "as God intended"—with as little medical intervention as possible (Caton, 1999). Grantley

Dick-Read believed that childbirth was a spiritual experience, guided by "mother love" as a powerful force. A woman's "true emancipation," he argued, "lies in freedom to fulfill her biological purpose" (Caton, 1999). *Childbirth Without Fear*, which was first published in the United States at the start of the postwar baby boom (1945), celebrated traditional womanhood. This pro-natalist purpose problematized "natural childbirth" for later feminists, who disagreed with the meaning behind the message. They perceived "natural childbirth" as emancipation from the medical profession, not as a return to traditional motherhood.

A second challenge came from Soviet doctors, who introduced the "psychoprophylactic method" of relaxation and breathing patterns to lessen the pain associated with childbirth. This method was then promoted by French obstetrician Ferdinand Lamaze and popularized in the United States by the 1959 publication of Marjorie Karmel's *Thank You, Dr. Lamaze: A Mother's Experience in Painless Childbirth*. Karmel then founded the American Society for Prophylaxis in Obstetrics (ASPO) in 1960 to provide labor coaches, and by 1986, there were 10,000 Lamaze instructors in the United States, a testament to its growing popularity and acceptance (the organization is now called Lamaze International).

Another challenge to medicalized childbirth came from the media. In 1958, the *Ladies' Home Journal*—more known for affirming traditional roles for women than for challenging them—published a series of articles based on hundreds of letters written by women who had recently given birth in American hospitals. "JOURNAL READERS REPORT SADISTIC PRACTICES: CRUELTY IN MATERNITY WARDS" exclaimed the *LHJ* editors in bold print on the cover of the May 1958 issue. Juxtaposed with recipes for coconut cream pie and tips for organizing a successful dinner party lay horror stories of helpless women strapped down for hours, slapped by nurses who held their legs together to keep the baby from coming out while the doctor finished his golf game. "My first was born in a Chicago suburban hospital," wrote one woman. "I wonder if the people who ran that place were actually human. My lips were parched and cracked, but the nurses refused to even moisten them with a damp cloth. I was left alone all night in a labor room." Mrs. WSB was more direct: "I believe that there exists among nurses a definite hostility toward women in childbirth," she wrote. "There seems to be a feeling that a woman in childbirth has brought her troubles on herself and so deserves no kindness."

The introduction of new childbirth methods and techniques, along with media exposés such as the *Ladies' Home Journal* article, galvanized some people to demand changes to hospital practice. Childbirth educators, along with expectant parents, challenged hospital protocol for the treatment of women in labor and delivery. Until the 1970s, most hospitals did not allow husbands in labor or delivery rooms; they utilized routine interventions during labor; and they separated the baby from the mother immediately after birth. Fathers, along with mothers, demanded changes to these hospital routines, resulting in more freedoms for mother, father, and baby (Leavitt, 2009).

Yet for some consumers, these changes did not go far enough. In 1977, Suzanne Arms published *Immaculate Deception: A New Look at Women and Childbirth in America*, an instant bestseller that questioned the medical management of birth. Arms challenged even the use of the term "natural childbirth," which had come to mean anything short of a Cesarean section. She argued that the only way "normal" childbirth could be reclaimed by women would be to grant the midwife "her rightful place in the American way of birth" (Arms, 1977). *Immaculate Deception* documented the work of new midwives who were beginning to appear on the American landscape. This, in turn, led to greater consumer interest in alternative birthing practices and out-of-hospital births. Small organizations began to form, such as the National Association of Parents and Professionals for Safe Alternatives in Childbirth (NAPSAC) and Home Oriented Maternity Experience (HOME). Ironically, at the same time that the alternative birth movement was increasing, the rates of Cesarean section increased dramatically. Between 1965 and 1987, C-section rates rose 455%, from 4.5% to 25% of births. By 2006, it was up to 31% (Wolf, 2009).

In the 21st century, childbirth remains primarily a medical event, with more than 99% of all American births taking place in hospitals. Although midwifery has become a more accepted and growing profession, midwives continue to struggle to increase their influence on hospital births. Meanwhile, the rate of Cesarean section continues to rise, along with infant and maternal mortality rates.

ABORTION, STERILIZATION ABUSE, AND REPRODUCTIVE RIGHTS

For many activists, legalizing abortion was a key component of their agenda. It is difficult to track the varieties of abortion activism in the period shortly before and after *Roe v.*

Wade. States varied in their responses and implementation of the 1973 decision that upheld a woman's right to an abortion during the first trimester of pregnancy. While more women came together to protest restrictive abortion laws and later attempts to dismantle *Roe*, they were not the first group to demand reform. In response to greater suppression of abortion practices in the 1950s, doctors and public health workers who witnessed the physical damages and deaths from illegal abortions sought legal changes. This increasingly repressive climate triggered a widespread reaction from those who witnessed the repercussions on women's health. According to historian Leslie Reagan, abortion rights activism "arose out of the deteriorating conditions of abortion and the frustrations of both women and physicians." Though most states had outlawed abortion by the late 19th century, it was generally accepted as an "open secret" well into the 20th century. "The social movement to decriminalize abortion," continues Reagan, "drew upon and brought into the open a longstanding acceptance of abortion" (Reagan, 1997).

Abortion reform changed in the hands of feminists, who began in the late 1960s to perceive it as more than a medical or public health issue, but as a "collective problem for all women" (Reagan, 1997). Abortion, according to activist Laura Kaplan, was a touchstone. If women could not make decisions regarding their own bodies, then other gains were "meaningless" (Kaplan, 1995). Feminists introduced new tactics, including abortion speak-outs, in which women shared stories of illegal abortions and anger over their lack of rights to control their bodies. *Village Voice* reporter and future feminist Susan Brownmiller remembered her introduction to the women's movement

when she first encountered a women's group talking about abortions in 1968:

> Saying "I've had three illegal abortions" aloud was my feminist baptism, my swift immersion in the power of sisterhood. A medical procedure I'd been forced to secure alone, shrouded in silence, was not "a personal problem" any more than the matter of my gender in the newsroom was "a personal problem."
>
> (Brownmiller, 2000)

Many socialist feminists emphasized how racism affected reproductive rights. Black women were twice as likely as White women to be sterilized in 1970, for example, sometimes having to choose between having their tubes tied and receiving a welfare check. For these women, access to reproductive health services had to be matched with protective regulations (such as waiting periods for sterilization) that would protect vulnerable women from abuse. These different priorities made compromise and coalition building across race and class boundaries all the more challenging (Kluchin, 2009). In certain contexts, feminists found themselves on opposing sides of policy decisions. For example, historian Rebecca Kluchin describes the "direct and irreconcilable conflict" between different reproductive rights groups in the mid-1970s over proposed new sterilization guidelines that were designed to protect women from abuse. Specifically, the National Organization for Women (NOW) and the National Abortion Rights Action League (NARAL) objected to a mandatory waiting period and age minimums for sterilization, reflecting their privileging of abortion rights over other reproductive rights issues and their concern that if the government could prevent women from receiving sterilization on demand, it could use this precedent to prohibit women from accessing abortion on demand.

(Kluchin, 2009)

At the same time, women of color pushed for a wider vision of reproductive rights that included a critique of the coercive politics of the mainstream population movement. Women of color resisted externally imposed policies to limit their fertility while asserting their rights to bodily self-determination. For women of color, reproductive freedom meant not only the legal right to abortion and contraception, but also the freedom to have children if they so desired (Silliman, Gerber Fried, Ross, & Gutierrez, 2004).

SEXUAL ASSAULT AND THE ANTIRAPE MOVEMENT

Before the mid-1960s, physicians tended to ignore the problem of sexual abuse of children and adolescents. Pediatricians who treated sexually transmitted diseases in their young patients insisted that these infections were acquired from innocent sources such as toilet seats that had been contaminated with infectious material. Physicians were especially likely to use these modes of transmission to explain cases in which the family was White, well-to-do, and socially prominent. Even when the family was from a lower socioeconomic group, child and adolescent cases of venereal disease were usually attributed to the filth and squalor of most lower-

class homes, rather than to sexual abuse by family members. Pediatricians and gynecologists seldom learned how to perform pelvic exams on girls and young women: In fact, the practice was actively discouraged by most pediatric and gynecological textbooks. Physicians were therefore ill equipped to recognize the signs of sexual abuse in girls and young women (Evans, 2005).

The criminal justice system was even less helpful to women and girls who were victims of sexual assault. During the first half of the 20th century, legal discussions of rape tended to focus on the psychopathology of the perpetrator rather than on the mental health needs of the victim. Mental health professionals argued that rapists suffered from a character disorder and that these individuals needed medical treatment, not punishment. At the same time, psychologists and sexologists argued that female sexual pleasure was both normal and desirable. This had the unintended consequence of reframing rape as a crime in which women played a role in their own victimization by tempting men who were unable to control their sexual impulses. In other words, many believed that women who were raped had provoked their attackers by behaving in a sexually provocative manner. Rape laws allowed the victim's prior sexual history to be admitted as evidence during criminal proceedings, effectively putting women on trial along with their abusers (Donat & D'Emilio, 1992).

During the mid-1960s, rape victims and their supporters began to challenge these views. In 1965, a woman who had been raped in the District of Columbia complained bitterly to the local and national press about the inhumane treatment she received from law enforcement and emergency medical personnel. The victim reported that police treated her more like a "cold statistic than a human being," holding her for 3 hours of questioning before taking her to the hospital. She then waited nearly 2 hours in the emergency room before being examined by a physician, who did not offer her any methods to prevent pregnancy. Eventually the fed-up patient went to a private physician, who treated her for more than 7 hours following the initial assault. This scandal prompted the District's public health department to improve treatment for sexually assaulted females. They were especially intent on helping children and adolescents from lower socioeconomic levels who did not have access to a family physician (Hayman, Lewis, Stewart, & Grant, 1967).

In 1966, John McLean Morris and Gertrude van Wagenen of Yale University School of Medicine announced that they had used a new "morning-after pill" to treat rape victims at Yale-New Haven Hospital. In an interview with the *New York Times*, Morris underscored the significance of the morning-after pill for the young rape victims he saw at Yale-New Haven Hospital: "It means that the girl who has been raped and has a good chance of becoming pregnant doesn't have to worry," he said, because she will "know that there is available retroactive contraception" (Brody, 1966).

By the 1970s, feminist activists argued that rape was not only a private tragedy but, as New York Radical Feminists put it, "a political crime against women." The first rape crisis centers were started by radical feminists in the Washington, DC area, who saw the antirape movement as an integral part of their larger struggle for women's liberation. The activism of radical feminists eventually compelled the liberal feminist organization the National Organization for Women to enter the arena of antirape activism, leading to the creation of the NOW Rape Task Force in 1973 (Brownmiller, 2000).

Although the antirape movement, like the women's movement more generally, initially consisted almost entirely of White, middle-class women, it was not long before this branch of feminist action sought ways to bring minority and working-class women into their organizations. According to Washington, DC antirape activist Loretta Ross, she and other women of color were active in the movement almost from the beginning. Ross was drawn to the antirape movement because she had been kidnapped and raped when she was 11 years old, and she became pregnant at age 14 in 1968 as a result of incest committed by an older cousin. Legal abortion in the United States was not an option, and her family decided against taking her to Mexico for an abortion because they considered it too dangerous. After delivering her son in a home for unwed mothers, Ross decided to keep the child and give up a scholarship to Radcliffe College. Two years later, Ross became pregnant from a gang rape during her first year at Howard University, but she was able to obtain a legal abortion in Washington, DC. Ross and other women of color were instrumental in convincing white antirape activists that racism, poverty, and imperialism were just as important as male supremacy in the struggle to combat violence against women (Nelson, 2010). By the early 1990s, rape had become a "bridge issue" that brought together women from a variety of political and racial backgrounds (Bevacqua, 2008).

GENDER EQUALITY AND MEDICAL RESEARCH

One of the consequences of the modern women's health movement was growing awareness of gender disparities in medical research. As Eileen Nechas and Denise Foley show in their book *Unequal Treatment*,

> Decisions on what aspect of health to study, on what research protocol to fund" are based "not only on scientific merit . . . but on a judgment of social worth. What is valuable to medicine is who is valuable to society, and that is white men.
>
> (Nechas & Foley, 1994)

Activists and government officials began to address these concerns during the 1980s. In 1983, James O. Mason, Assistant Secretary for Health, created a Public Health Service Task Force on Women's Health Issues to study disease risks that were unique to women, with special attention to assessing women's health across the life stages. After 2 years of investigation, the Task Force issued a report on its findings and recommendations. The Task Force was careful to acknowledge that "not all women are alike," and environmental, social, and demographic characteristics influence women's health risks. The report observed: "If a woman is a member of an ethnic or cultural minority, if she is physically or mentally disabled, or if, for any reasons, she is outside the normal range of what society expects, her health is at greater risk." Nevertheless, the Task Force found that there were several common areas where "the circumstances for women are unique, the noted condition is more prevalent, the interventions are different for women than for men, or the health risks are greater for women than for men." The report recommended that the Public Health Service needed to take the lead in ensuring

that the unique health needs of women were adequately addressed by healthcare services and regulatory agencies, and that biomedical and behavioral research made the conditions and diseases that were unique to or more prevalent in women in all age groups a priority (Women's Health, 1985). In response to these recommendations, Mason established the Public Health Service Coordinating Committee on Women's Health Issues. This Committee implemented some Task Force recommendations and increased public and congressional awareness of, and interest in, women's health issues (Office on Women's Health, 2001).

During the late 1980s and early 1990s, Congresswomen Patricia Schroeder (D–CO) and Olympia Snowe (R–ME) co-chaired the Congressional Caucus for Women's Issues. One of the main goals of the Caucus was to put pressure on the National Institutes of Health (NIH) to increase resources for women's health research. At the same time, Dr. Florence Haseltine, an obstetrician-gynecologist at NIH, organized fellow members of the American Congress of Obstetricians and Gynecologists (ACOG) and other experts in women's health to demand that more attention be given at NIH to gynecological research and women's health needs more generally. In 1990, Haseltine and her colleagues founded the Society for the Advancement of Women's Health Research (SAWR) to provide leadership on the issue of healthcare equity.

That same year, SAWR and the Congressional Caucus requested that the General Accounting Office (GAO) conduct an audit of NIH procedures regarding women and clinical research. The GAO reported that NIH had made little progress in this area. The resulting outcry on Capitol Hill and the national media led to important changes at

NIH, including the creation of the Office of Research on Women's Health and the appointment of Dr. Bernadine Healy as director of NIH, the first woman to ever hold that post. Members of the Congressional Caucus introduced the Women's Health Equity Act, which included support not only for new research but also improved access to healthcare and treatment for women (Bass & Howes, 1992). This activism led to the creation in 1991 of the Office on Women's Health (OWH) within the Department of Health and Human Services. The mission of OWH is

> to improve the health of American women by advancing and coordinating a comprehensive women's health agenda throughout HHS to address health care prevention and service delivery, research, public and health care professional education, and career advancement for women in the health professions and in scientific careers.
> (Office on Women's Health, 2001)

The rise of gender-based medicine has challenged not only traditional medical research practices by demanding that women be included in biomedical and behavioral studies but also interpretations of results that tend to view the male body as normal and the female body as deviant or pathological. For example, symptoms of heart attack in women are described as atypical in comparison to the typical symptoms seen in men. Yet some feminist scholars warn that too heavy an emphasis on gender distinctions might reinforce rather than challenge biologically deterministic views about women's health (Fausto-Sterling, 2005).

REFERENCES

Allen, E. D. (1954). Pelvic examination of the pre-adolescent and adolescent girl. *Transactions of the American Gynecological Society*, 77, 109–110.

Allen, E. D. (1958, February). Examination of the genital organs in the prepubescent and in the adolescent girl. *Pediatric Clinics of North America*, 19–34.

Apple, R. (2006). *Perfect motherhood: Science and child-rearing in America*. New Brunswick, NJ: Rutgers University Press.

Arms, S. (1977). *Immaculate deception: A new look at women and childbirth in America*. New York, NY: Bantam Books. doi:10.1111/j.1552-6909.1976.tb01278.x

Bailey, B. (1988). *From front porch to back seat: Courtship in twentieth-century America*. Baltimore, MD: Johns Hopkins University Press.

Bass, M., & Howes, J. (1992). Women's health: The making of a powerful new public issue. *Women's Health Issues*, 2, 3–5. doi:10. 1016/S1049-3867 (05)80130-6.

Bevacqua, M. (2008). Reconsidering violence against women: Coalition politics in the antirape movement. In S. Gilmore (Ed.), *Feminist coalitions: Historical perspectives on second-wave feminism in the United States*. Chicago and Urbana: University of Illinois Press.

Brody, J. E. (1966). Human tests considered. *New York Times*, May 1, p. 1.

Brownmiller, S. (2000). *In our time: Memoir of a revolution*. New York, NY: The Dial Press.

Brumberg, J. J. (1997). *The body project: An intimate history of American girls*. New York, NY: Vintage Books.

Casper, M. J., & Clarke, A. E. (1998). Making the pap smear into the "right tool" for the job: Cervical cancer screening in the USA, circa 1940–95. *Social Studies of Science*, 28, 255–290. doi:10. 1177/030631298028002003.

Caton, D. (1999). *What a blessing she had chloroform: The medical and social response to pain in childbirth from 1800 to the present*. New Haven, CT: Yale University Press.

Charo, R. A. (2007). Politics, parents, and prophylaxis—Mandating HPV vaccination in the United States. *New England Journal of Medicine*, 356, 1905–1908.

Chesler, E. (1992). *Woman of valor: Margaret Sanger and the birth control movement in America*. New York, NY: Doubleday.

Cohen, S., & Cosgrove, C. (2009). *Normal at any cost: Tall girls, short boys, and the medical industry's quest to manipulate height*. New York, NY: Jeremy P. Tarcher/Penguin.

Donat, P. L. N, & D'Emilio, J. (1992). A feminist redefinition of rape and sexual assault: Historical foundations and change. *Journal of Social Issues, 48*, 11–13.

Evans, H. H. (2005). Physician denial and child sexual abuse in America, 1870–2000. In C. K. Walsh & V. Strong-Boag (Eds.), *Children's health issues in historical perspective* (pp. 327–353). Waterloo, Ontario: Wilfrid Laurier Press.

Evans, S. M. (2003). *Tidal wave: How women changed America at century's end*. New York, NY: Free Press.

Fausto-Sterling, A. (2005). The bare bones of sex: Part 1—Sex and gender. *Signs, 30*(2), 1491–1527. doi:10. 1086/424932.

Food and Drug Administration (2004). Recalls and Safety Alerts November 2004. http://www.fda.gov/ForConsumers/ByAudience/ForWomen/ucm118632.htm

Freeman, S. K. (2008). *Sex goes to school: Girls and sex education before the 1960s*. Urbana and Chicago: University of Illinois Press.

Garrow, D. J. (1998). *Liberty and sexuality: The right to privacy and the making of* Roe v. Wade. Berkeley: University of California Press.

Gordon, L. (1990). *Woman's body, woman's right: Birth control in America*. New York, NY: Penguin.

Hayman, C. R., Lewis, F. R., Stewart, W. F., & Grant, M. (1967). A public health program for sexually assaulted females. *Public Health Reports, 82*(6), 497–504.

Johnson, J. W. (2005). Griswold v. Connecticut:*Birth control and the constitutional right of privacy*. Lawrence: University of Kansas Press.

Kaplan, L. (1995). *The story of Jane: The legendary feminist abortion service*. Chicago, IL: University of Chicago Press.

Kinsey, A. C. (1953). *Sexual behavior in the human female*. Philadelphia, PA: W. B. Saunders.

Kluchin, R. (2009). *Fit to be tied: Sterilization and reproductive rights in America, 1950–1980*. New Brunswick, NJ: Rutgers University Press.

Leavitt, J. W. (2009). *Make room for Daddy: The journey from waiting room to birthing room*. Chapel Hill: University of North Carolina Press.

Lindsay, J. (1991). The politics of population control in Namibia. In M. Turshen (Ed.), *Women and health in Africa*. Trenton, NJ: Africa World Press.

Lunbeck, E. (1994). *The psychiatric persuasion: Knowledge, gender, and power in modern America*. Princeton, NJ: Princeton University Press.

May, E. (1995). *Barren in the promised land: Childless Americans and the pursuit of happiness*. New York, NY: Basic Books.

Manley, H. (1964). Wed before twenty, trouble aplenty. *Public Health Reports, 79*(3), 247.

Meckel, R. A. (2002). Going to school, getting sick: The social and medical construction of school diseases in the late nineteenth century. In A. Minna Stern & H. Markel (Eds.), *Formative years: Child health in the United States, 1880–2000* (pp. 185–207). Ann Arbor: University of Michigan Press.

Moran, J. (2000). *Teaching sex: The shaping of adolescence in the 20th century*. Cambridge, MA: Harvard University Press.

Muncy, R. (1991). *Creating a female dominion in American reform, 1890–1935*. New York, NY: Oxford University Press.

Munro Prescott, H. (1998). *A doctor of their own: The history of adolescent medicine*. Cambridge, MA: Harvard University Press.

Munro Prescott, H. (2007). *Student bodies: The impact of student health on American society and medicine*. Ann Arbor: University of Michigan Press.

Nechas, E., & Foley, D. (1994). *Unequal treatment: What you don't know about how women are mistreated by the medical community*. New York, NY: Simon & Schuster.

Nelson, J. (2003). *Women of color and the reproductive rights movement*. New York: New York University Press.

Nelson, J. (2010). "All this that has happened to me shouldn't happen to nobody else": Loretta Ross and the Women of Color Reproductive Freedom Movement of the 1980s. *Journal of Women's History, 22*, 136–160.

Office on Women's Health. (2001). *A century of women's health 1900–2000*. Washington, DC: U.S. Department of Health and Human Services.

Patterson, J. T. (1996). *Grand expectations: The United States, 1945–1974.* New York, NY: Oxford University Press.

Pilpel, H. F., & Wechsler, N. F. (1969). Birth control, teenagers, and the law. *Family Planning Perspectives, 1*(1), 29–35.

Reagan, L. J. (1997). *When abortion was a crime: Women, medicine, and law in the United States, 1867–1973.* Berkeley: University of California Press.

Reed, J. (1978). *From private vice to public virtue: The birth control movement and American society since 1830.* New York, NY: Basic Books.

Rotkin, I. D. (1967). Adolescent coitus and cervical cancer: Associations of related events with increased risk. *Cancer Research, 27*(4), 603–617.

Rothman, D. (1991). *Strangers at the bedside: A history of how law and bioethics transformed medical decision making.* New York, NY: Basic Books.

Ruzek, S. (1978). *The women's health movement: Feminist alternatives to medical control.* New York, NY: Praeger.

Schauffler, G. (1964). *Guiding your daughter to confident womanhood.* Englewood Cliffs, NJ: Prentice-Hall.

Sedlak, M. W., & Schlossman, S. (1985). The public school and social services: Reassessing the progressive legacy. *Educational Theory, 35,* 371–383. doi:10.1111/j.1741-5446.1985.00371.x

Silliman, J., Gerber Fried, M., Ross, L., & Gutierrez, E. R. (2004). *Undivided rights: Women of color organize for reproductive justice.* Boston, MA: South End Press.

Starr, P. (1982). *The social transformation of American medicine.* New York, NY: Basic Books.

Sturgis, S. H. (1962). *The gynecologic patient: A psychoendocrine study.* New York, NY: Grune & Stratton.

Tanner, J. M. (1981). Menarcheal age. *Science, 214* (4521), 604, 606.

Thompson, B. (2002). Multiracial feminism: Recasting the chronology of second wave feminism. *Feminist Studies, 28,* 337–360.

Tone, A. (2001). *Devices and desires: A history of contraceptives in America.* New York, NY: Hill & Wang.

Wagman, J. S. (2009). Women reformers respond during the Depression: Battling St. Louis's disease and immorality. *Journal of Urban History, 35*(5), 698–717. doi:10. 1177/0096144209335858.

Watkins, E. (1998). *On the pill: A social history of oral contraceptives, 1950–1970.* Baltimore, MD: Johns Hopkins University Press.

Weisman, C. S. (1998). *Women's health care: Activist traditions and institutional change.* Baltimore, MD: Johns Hopkins University Press.

Wolf, J. (2009). *Deliver me from pain: Anesthesia and childbirth in America.* Baltimore, MD: Johns Hopkins University Press.

Women's Health: Report of the Public Health Service Task Force on Women's Health Issues. (1985). *Public Health Reports, 100*(1), 73–105.

2 Retheorizing Women's Health Through Intersectionality's Prism

LISA BOWLEG

"Get a body that's slim, strong, sexy: Drop pounds. Blast more fat with this fast shape-up plan."

(*Fitness* magazine, June 2011)

"1-2-3 Abs! Easy Steps to a Lean Sexy Belly!"

(*Women's Health*, June 2011)

"Lose Belly Fat – Easy Summer Eating Plan"

(*Ladies Home Journal*, July 2011)

"Win at Weight Loss. Exactly What to Do to Reveal Toned Abs, Legs, and Arms."

(*Self*, June 2011)

Curious about which topics about women's health I might find in women's magazines as I prepared to write this chapter, I ventured over to my local magazine stand. The aforementioned headlines jumped off the covers in large, eye-catching, brightly colored fonts. If you knew no better, you would naturally think that women's health was synonymous with weight loss. With striking unanimity, the covers extolled the virtue of the thin, toned body. Nor was the main heading the only one on the subject. Often, as was the case with the *Women's Health*

cover, subheadings were just as emphatic: "Eat More, Weigh Less! No Cravings, No Crankiness. Just Results." Although the *Women's Health* cover also advertised content relevant to other health issues, such as the need for sunscreen ("Is Any Amount of Sun Healthy? The Final Answer") and the importance of stress reduction ("Boost Your Bliss. New Ways to Escape Stress"), headlines and straplines (yes, that is what they call the subheadlines in the magazine business) about weight loss and toning dominated the covers by far.

The covers unanimously shared another visual: the image of a White, thin, often bikini-clad, smiling, able-bodied, presumably middle-class woman (in the case of the *Women's Home Journal*, the cover model was Jenny Craig weight-loss program spokesperson, the newly thin actress Valerie Bertinelli). While it might be easy to dismiss the health information on the cover of women's magazines as folly, the fact is, health information in magazines matters. In 2003, a majority of respondents in the Health Information National Trends Survey (HINTS) reported paying "a lot" (25%) or "some" (30%) attention to health or medical topics in magazines (National Cancer Institute, 2003). The Internet trailed behind magazines, with only 13% and 16% of people responding that they paid "a lot" or "some" attention, respectively, to health or medical topics on the Internet. The booming growth of the Internet and digital magazine content has presumably presaged the decline of magazines that you can pick up and flip through since 2003. Nonetheless, women's magazine covers are instructive. They are normative in the sense that they define and establish norms about women's health. They are informative in the sense that they indicate the topics that are most likely to attract women buyers and readers. And they are prescriptive in the sense that they signal to women what our health priorities ought to be.

National health statistics provide a considerably different image of women's health than that of the glossy words and photographs that grace the covers of women's magazines. These data document that heart disease, cancer, and stroke are the top three leading causes of death for women in the United States (U.S. Department of Health and Human Services, Health Resources and Services Administration, & Maternal and Child Health Bureau, 2007). Heart disease is the leading cause of death for Black, White, and Latina women. For Asian and Pacific Islander women and American Indian and Alaskan Native women, cancer is the leading cause of death, followed by heart disease. Because most of the leading causes of morbidity and mortality in the United States are avoidable, prevention is obviously a top national public health priority. Accordingly, public health officials routinely issue health tips such as "eat smart, exercise regularly, and get routine health screenings" (U.S. Department of Health and Human Services, n.d.) or "eat healthy, be active, protect yourself, manage stress, and get check-ups" (Centers for Disease Control and Prevention, 2011b).

The most recent and noteworthy recognition of the value of prevention of disease and illness is the nation's new *National Prevention Strategy: America's Plan for Better Health and Wellness* (U.S. Department of Health and Human Services, 2011). Released on June 16, 2011, the plan— pursuant to a mandate in the federal Affordable Care Act—relies on evidence-based science to address seven priority areas: tobacco-free living, prevention of drug abuse and excessive alcohol use, healthy eating, active living, injury and violence-free living, reproductive and sexual health, and mental and emotional well-being. In a refreshing departure from the individualistic bent of most health behavior advocacy, the new plan recognizes that health promotion transcends the mere provision of health information. Although it acknowledges the importance of health information, the plan also asserts that "communities must reinforce and support health, for example, by making healthy choices easy and affordable" (p. 6).

Psychosocial theories of health behavior, such as the Health Belief Model, the Theory of Reasoned Action/Planned Behavior, Social Cognitive Theory, and the Transtheoretical Model or Stages of Change, have made critically important contributions to understanding how attitudes, beliefs, and cognitions promote and hinder a variety of health behaviors, such as condom use, tobacco control, weight loss, and exercise. Yet, a major limitation of these theories is that they tend to adhere to the same individualistic script as do the women's health magazines and public health messages (at least public health messages that predate the new National Prevention Strategy). The implicit message is that health is an exclusively individual act; all women need to do to be healthy is eat well, stay physically active, lose weight, protect themselves, and get checkups.

The reality of women's health, however, is far more complex. Numerous factors beyond the level of the individual woman, including but not limited to the neighborhood in which she lives, her income and/or that of her household, the color of her skin, the person with whom she forms intimate relationships and/or has sex, and whether she has health insurance, will all influence the extent to which she can actually be healthy. If she is a woman of color, particularly a low-income woman of color, the intersections of her race, sex, and socioeconomic status will interlock with systems of oppression such as racism, sexism, and classism (to name just a few) to ensure that she (and other women like her) experiences adverse health outcomes more disproportionately than her White and middle-class counterparts. Thus, approaching women's health from the standpoint of low-income women of color offers greater promise of improving the health of all women, rather than focusing on the health of women with more resources and opportunities for health—traditionally White, middle-class, heterosexual, able-bodied women.

In light of this approach, this chapter aims to retheorize women's health through the prism of intersectionality. Rooted in Black feminist scholarship, intersectionality is a theoretical perspective that examines how multiple social identities, such as race, ethnicity, sex, gender, sexual orientation, and socioeconomic status (SES), in individual lives (i.e., the micro level) intersect with interlocking systems of oppression, such as racism, sexism, heterosexism, and classism (i.e., the macro level), to produce a variety of disparate health, social, and economic

outcomes (Collins, 1995; Crenshaw, 1991, 1995; Davis, 2008). I have organized the chapter into four sections. In the first section, I provide a historical overview of intersectionality. Next, I briefly review five of the most popular psychosocial health behavior theories: the Health Belief Model, the Theory of Reasoned Action, the Theory of Planned Behavior, Social Cognitive Theory, and the Transtheoretical Model of Change. Thereafter, I critique these theories in terms of their neglect of the macro-level realities of the lives of low-income women of color.

Throughout the chapter, I will infuse theory and research on women and HIV/AIDS to exemplify my central thesis that women's health is best understood from an intersectionality perspective that accounts for the intersection of multiple social identities (e.g., race, sex, gender, sexual orientation, socioeconomic status) at the micro level with interlocking systems of oppression (e.g., racism, sexism, heterosexism, and classism) at the macro level. Finally, I will conclude with some recommendations, framed from an intersectionality perspective, for how students of psychology and psychologists can enhance and advance women's health theory, research, and advocacy.

INTERSECTIONALITY: A BRIEF HISTORY OF AN INTENSELY USEFUL BUT UNDERUTILIZED THEORY IN PSYCHOLOGY

Although intersectionality is in relative infancy within psychology, the concept is hardly new. Freed slave Sojourner Truth's (1851) interrogation of the intersections of race and sex in her famous "Ain't I a Woman?" speech at the 1851 Women's

Convention in Akron, Ohio is one of the earliest recorded accounts of intersectionality. In the speech, Truth challenged the notion that being a woman (i.e., sex) and Black (i.e., race) are wholly separate constructs:

> That man over there says that women need to be helped into carriages, and lifted over ditches, and to have the best place everywhere. Nobody ever helps me into carriages, or over mud-puddles, or gives me any best place! And ain't I a woman?

In 1977, the Combahee River Collective, a collective of Black feminist activists, issued a statement in which they introduced the intersectionality concept in their opening paragraph:

> The most general statement of our politics at the present time would be that we are actively committed to struggling against racial, sexual, heterosexual, and class oppression, and see as our particular task the development of integrated analysis and practice based upon the fact that the major systems of oppression are interlocking. The synthesis of these oppressions creates the conditions of our lives. (p. 272)

Kimberle Crenshaw (1991) coined the term *intersectionality* to describe the exclusion of Black women from White feminist discourse (which equated women with White) and antiracist discourse (which equated men with Black). Intersectionality has thrived in feminist and women's studies circles, prompting McCall (2005) to extol intersectionality as "the most important contribution that women's studies has made so far" (p. 1771). Intersectionality is also frequently the topic of interdisciplinary scholarship. Intersectionality and women's health is the subject of the interdisciplinary book *Gender, Race, Class and Health: Intersectional Approaches* published in 2006 (Schulz & Mullings, 2006). Two years later, the interdisciplinary journal *Sex Roles* published a special issue focused on gender and intersectionality (Shields, 2008). Another special issue of the journal focusing on intersectionality among gay, lesbian, and bisexual people of color is forthcoming.

By contrast, intersectionality theory has been relatively invisible in the discipline of psychology. Notable exceptions are the contributions of many psychologists to the gender and intersectionality *Sex Roles* special issue and a 2009 *American Psychologist* article on "Intersectionality and Research in Psychology" that attributed psychologists' slow adoption of intersectionality to an absence of guidelines for how to incorporate intersectionality within research (Cole, 2009). This is possibly true, but I believe that a more likely explanation is that with few exceptions (community psychology and multicultural psychology come to mind), psychologists are not typically trained to consider how factors beyond the level of the individual shape health and other behaviors. A unifying factor of the five psychological health behavior theories reviewed in the following section is that they stem from the field of social psychology, where individual attitudes, beliefs, and cognitions are core components (Noar, 2005).

THE INDIVIDUAL AS QUEEN: A REVIEW OF FIVE PSYCHOLOGICAL THEORIES OF HEALTH BEHAVIOR

Five theories dominate much of the psychological literature on health behavior: The Health Belief Model (Janz & Becker, 1984; Rosenstock, 1974), the Theory of Reasoned Action/Planned Behavior (Ajzen & Fishbein, 1980; Fishbein & Ajzen, 1975), Social Cognitive Theory (Bandura, 1977), and the Transtheoretical Model or Stages of Change (Prochaska & DiClemente, 1983; Prochaska, Velicer, et al., 1994). A comprehensive review, comparison, and analysis of the literature applying these theories to a variety of health behaviors is beyond the scope of this article, but can be found in Noar (2005). As any PubMed or PsycInfo search will quickly attest, the health behavior and health psychology literature is replete with empirical studies demonstrating the successful application of these theories to a variety of health behaviors, including, but not limited to, eating fruits and vegetables (Laforge, Greene, & Prochaska, 1994), sexual risk and condom use (Albarracin, Johnson, Fishbein, & Muellerleile, 2001; Bandura, 1990; Downing-Matibag & Geisinger, 2009; Fishbein, 2000; Norris & Ford, 1995; Prochaska, Redding, Harlow, Rossi, & Velicer, 1994; Rosenstock, Strecher, & Becker, 1994), exercise (Laforge, Rossi, Prochaska, Velicer, & Levesque, 1999), and smoking (Prochaska & DiClemente, 1983).

The Health Belief Model

The Health Belief Model (HBM) proposes that when an individual perceives a threat of disease or other adverse health outcome, she or he is motivated to avoid that threat. The *perceived threat* concept includes two components: *perceived susceptibility*, the perception that one is at risk for the disease or outcome; and *severity*, how serious the person perceives the risk to be. The HBM asserts than when both aspects of perceived threat are high, the person will be motivated to take action. The model also includes *perceived benefits* and *barriers*. If a person perceives that the benefits of engaging in a certain behavior outweigh the barriers of doing so, she or he will be more likely to act. The model also includes demographic factors (e.g., age, sex, race) that influence perceived benefits and threats, and cues to action (e.g., a media story, the illness of a friend or family member, advice), stimuli that can affect perceived threat and prompt action. Later versions of the HBM include *self-efficacy*, the conviction that one can successfully engage in a certain behavior (Rosenstock, Strecher, & Becker, 1988).

The Theory of Reasoned Action (TRA) and the Theory of Planned Behavior (TPB)

The TRA and TPB theorize that a person's *behavioral intentions* to perform a specific behavior (e.g., workout three times a week vs. lose weight) are the best predictor of that behavior (Ajzen & Fishbein, 1980; Fishbein & Ajzen, 1975). *Behavioral intentions* include two components: *attitudes* and *subjective norms*. Attitudes include *behavioral beliefs*, beliefs that engaging in a certain behavior will produce positive outcomes; and the *evaluation* of how valuable these outcomes are. Subjective norms include *normative beliefs*, a person's beliefs about whether other people that the person values approve or disapprove of the behavior; and the *motivation to comply* with the beliefs of these valued others. The TRA asserts that the more positive a person's attitudes and subjective norms are, the higher the likelihood that a person will develop the intention to engage in a certain behavior, and will actually engage in the behavior. So, if a woman who has a positive attitude about exercising to lose weight perceives that people she values will favorably view her intention to lose weight, and she feels motivated to comply with those subjective beliefs, then she is likely to develop a specific intention (i.e., biking three times per week to lose weight) and follow through on it.

The TPB shares the aforementioned components of the TRA, but adds perceived behavioral control as a third major variable to account for behaviors that are not completely under a person's control. *Perceived behavioral control* includes two components: *control beliefs*, the individual's perception that some factors and resources may either help or hinder the health behavior, and *perceived power*, the perceived impact of these factors and resources. Take condom use, for example. Women do not wear (male) condoms; they must rely on men to wear condoms or negotiate condom use with male sex partners. Thus, under the TPB a woman who intends to use condoms will do so to the extent that she believes that it will be easy to negotiate condom use with her partner and that she has the power to successfully negotiate condom use.

Social Cognitive Theory (SCT)

SCT (Bandura, 1977, 1998) posits that a dynamic interaction exists between the environment, personal cognitive factors (e.g., attitudes, perceptions, cognitions), and behavior. Self-efficacy, one's certainty that one can successfully engage in a behavior to gain a desired outcome, is central to and one of the best-known aspects of SCT. The higher a person's self-efficacy, the more likely it is that she will engage in a behavior. For example, the higher a person's self-efficacy that she can eat healthy foods, the more likely she is to eat healthily.

Transtheoretical Model (TTM) and Stages of Change

Frequently called the Stages of Change model, the TTM posits that people progress through one of five stages on their way to changing a behavior (Prochaska & DiClemente, 1983; Prochaska, Velicer, et al., 1994). *Precontemplation*, the first stage, describes a stage in which a person has no intention of changing a behavior (e.g., a person who has no intention of quitting smoking). *Contemplation*, the next stage, describes a person's intention to change a behavior in the future (e.g., a person who is considering stopping smoking in the next 6 months). *Preparation* describes the stage in which a person is planning a change in the near future (e.g., a person who enrolls in a smoking cessation program starting next week). *Action* describes the stage in which a person has changed in the past 6 months (e.g., the person has stopped smoking). *Maintenance* refers to the stage in which a person has changed and maintained behavior change for 6 months and is en route to changing the behavior permanently (e.g., the person who has quit smoking for 6 months and plans to never smoke again).

FLIPPING THE INDIVIDUALISTIC SCRIPT: CRITIQUES OF PSYCHOSOCIAL HEALTH BEHAVIOR THEORIES

The Health Belief Model, the Theory of Reasoned Action/Planned Behavior, Social

Cognitive Theory, and the Transtheoretical Model or Stages of Change are all well respected and empirically validated theories of health behavior. Each has made invaluable contributions to enhancing understanding about how people's attitudes, beliefs, and thoughts influence their health behaviors. Yet, because the individual is their primary unit of analysis, these theories typically ignore factors beyond the level of the individual, such as neighborhoods, intimate partners, social networks, structural context (e.g., SES), and social discrimination (e.g., racism, sexism, heterosexism, ableism), that constrain the ability of the individual to engage in health-promoting behaviors. Although virtually any disease or condition that has a disparate impact on low-income women of color would suffice (and there are many), the HIV/AIDS epidemic among women aptly illuminates many of the limitations of exclusively individualistic approaches to women's health.

Critics of these approaches—intersectionality theorists, feminist psychologists, health psychologists, social epidemiologists, and public health researchers among them—consistently advocate for theory and research in women's health to consider the structural contexts and realities of women's lives (Amaro, 1995; Amaro & Raj, 2000; Amaro, Raj, & Reed, 2001; Bowleg, 2008a; Cochran & Mays, 1993; Dworkin & Ehrhardt, 2007; Krieger, 1996; Krieger, Chen, Waterman, Rehkopf, & Subramanian, 2003; Krieger, Rowley, Herman, Avery, & Phillips, 1993; Mays & Cochran, 1988; Teti et al., 2010; Weber, 1998, 2006; Weber & Fore, 2007; Weber & Parra-Medina, 2003; Wingood & DiClemente, 2000; Zierler & Krieger, 1997, 1998). In this section, I outline some of the general critiques of traditional psychosocial/biobehavioral/

biomedical approaches to women's health. Thereafter, using the HIV/AIDS epidemic among women as an example, I demonstrate how traditional individualistic approaches ignore the contexts and realities of women's lives to ill effect.

Although they differ substantially in content and aim, the women's magazine covers, the national health statistics, and the psychosocial health behavior theories are united in their adherence to the biomedical paradigm. The traditional biomedical paradigm typically involves the use of multidimensional models to identify environmental, social, psychological, behavioral, and biological "risk factors" for health (Weber & Fore, 2007; Weber & Parra-Medina, 2003). In an excellent chapter on intersectionality and women's health, Weber and Parra-Medina summarize key differences between the psychosocial/biobehavioral/biomedical models and intersectionality approaches to women's health (see Weber & Parra-Medina, 2003).

In the section that follows, I interweave three of these themes—individual vs. social structural factors, dominant vs. oppressed group centered, and independent single inequalities vs. intersecting multiple inequalities—to assert that envisioning women's health in general, and HIV/AIDS in particular, through the prism of intersectionality provides a more insightful and comprehensive view of women's health than that provided by traditional psychosocial/biobehavioral/biomedical models of health.

HIV/AIDS: THE OTHER WEIGHTY ISSUE

The women's health magazines are to some extent rightly obsessed with the subject of women's weight. National statistics attest that obesity is a growing public health crisis in the United States, with estimates that 33% of U.S. adults are overweight (i.e., have a Body Mass Index [BMI] between 25 and 29.9) and 34% are obese (i.e., a BMI greater than 30) (Khan et al., 2009). National health statistics also demonstrate the increasing prevalence of obesity among women. Between 2007 and 2008, for example, the prevalence of obesity among women was 35.5%, compared with 32.2% among men (Flegal, Carroll, Ogden, & Curtin, 2010). Women of color are also disproportionately more obese than White women. Age-adjusted obesity trends demonstrate that Black women account for 49.6% of obese women, compared with 45.1% for Mexican American women and 33% for White women between 2007 and 2008. But whereas the women's health magazines highlight only the vanity-related benefits of women's weight loss (i.e., "lean sexy bellies," "toned abs, legs, and arms," and the like), the health benefits of weight loss have more dire implications for morbidity and mortality. Being overweight/obese is associated with increased risk for several of the leading causes of death among women: diabetes, hypertension, high cholesterol, stroke, heart disease, certain cancers, and arthritis (Malnick & Knobler, 2006).

By contrast, the topic of sexually transmitted infections (STIs), especially HIV/AIDS, was notably absent from the covers of the women's magazines that I observed. When White women are the reference group, as they typically are in psychosocial/biobehavioral/biomedical models of women's health as well as the women's health magazines, diseases such as HIV/AIDS are virtually invisible. And rightly so. HIV/AIDS appears once in the top leading causes of death for all White women when the top 10 major causes of death are stratified by age. HIV disease was the ninth leading cause of death for White women between the ages of 35 and 44 in 2006 (Centers for Disease Control and Prevention, Office of Women's Health, 2010b). When Black women are the reference group, however, an entirely different image of HIV/AIDS morbidity and mortality emerges. For instance, HIV/AIDS is the leading cause of death for all Black women between the ages of 20 and 64. For Black women in the 20–24 age group, HIV/AIDS is the 6th leading cause of death; for those in the 25–34 age group it is the 4th leading cause of death; for those aged 35–44 it is the 3rd leading cause of death; for those in the 45–54 age category it is the 4th leading cause of death; and for those aged 55–64, it is the 10th leading cause of death (Centers for Disease Control and Prevention, Office of Women's Health, 2010a).

Indeed, the HIV/AIDS epidemic has had an especially devastating impact on women of color in the United States, particularly Black women. Black women represent just 14% of the female population in the United States, but they accounted for 66% of HIV cases among women in 2009 (Centers for Disease Control and Prevention, 2011a). Figure 2.1 shows the disproportionate impact of the HIV/AIDS epidemic on women of color in the United States. Thus, centering in on the experiences of low-income Black women as a starting point for analysis provides an apt illustration of intersectionality; that is, how multiple social identities at the micro level (i.e., race, sex, and SES) intersect with macro-level structural factors (i.e., poverty, racism, and sexism) when we examine HIV risk from their vantage point.

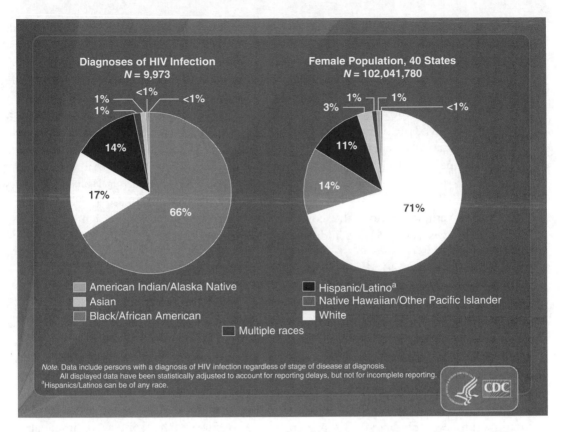

Figure 2.1 Diagnoses of HIV Infection and Population Among Adult and Adolescent Females in 40 States, by Race/Ethnicity, 2009 (CDC, 2011)

Contextualizing HIV/AIDS Among Women

The feminist psychology and public health literature is replete with insightful critiques of the individualistic bent of most of the psychosocial behavioral health theories applied to women's HIV risk (Amaro, 1995; Bowleg, 2008a; Bowleg, Lucas, & Tschann, 2004; Cochran & Mays, 1993; Dworkin & Ehrhardt, 2007; Mays & Cochran, 1988; Wingood & DiClemente, 2000). In 1988, just 7 years after the discovery of HIV and during an era in which the media, public health officials, and the public still perceived HIV/AIDS as a predominantly gay men's disease, Mays and Cochran, in an *American Psychologist* article, issued one of the earliest and most provocative critiques of how individualistic and context-neutral psychosocial approaches neglected the realities of low-income women of color who were at increased risk for HIV.

Take the notion of risk perception, for example. Risk perception is a core component of the Health Belief Model, the notion that perception of a severe-enough threat might motivate action to reduce the threat. Using risk perception as their focus, Mays and Cochran adroitly illustrate how the realities of low-income women of color might trump concern about their HIV risks: "The key to poor ethnic women's responses to AIDS is their perception of its danger relative to the hierarchy of other risks present in their lives and the existence of resources available to act differently" (p. 951). As for those who perceived the severity of the HIV threat, Mays and Cochran noted that women who perceived HIV to be a severe threat might not have the resources to protect themselves from HIV infection. Thus, they exemplified how the context of women's lives can override individual perception of risk.

Another problem with the psychosocial health behavior theories is their presumption of rationality and the primacy of cognition. Implicit in most of these theories is a clear presumption that social cognitive processes (e.g., perceiving risk, forming an intention, contemplating an action) should translate into HIV risk protection. Oh, how lovely it would be to live in a world where social cognitive processes predicted HIV prevention behaviors. Alas, as almost anyone who has ever been in love or deep-seated lust can readily attest, irrationality is often a hallmark of sexual and emotional relationships, especially in their early stages. Moreover, rationality exists in the eye of the beholder. Some poor ethnic minority women may deem it irrational to forgo condom use when exchanging sex for money or drugs (Cochran & Mays, 1993).

Five years after their *American Psychologist* article, Cochran and Mays (1993) honed their critiques on several of the psychosocial health behavior theories that I reviewed previously. In so doing, they pondered whether the tendency for these theories to omit the structural context of Black people's lives (e.g., racism, poverty, imbalanced sex ratios) limited their ability to "capture the relevant determinants of [Black people's] risk behaviors" (p. 142). Since then, feminist psychologists have been especially critical of theoretical approaches that neglect the structural and gendered contexts of women's lives (e.g., Amaro, 1995; Amaro & Raj, 2000; Pulerwitz, Amaro, DeJong, Gortmaker, & Rudd, 2002; Wingood & DiClemente, 2000). In her seminal article, *Love, Sex and Power: Considering Women's Realities in HIV Prevention,* Amaro (1995) criticized traditional approaches that ignored the historical context of unequal sexual and relationship power between women and men and advocated for theories and interventions to "consider women's realities" (p. 437). Amaro asserted that condom use, a core HIV prevention strategy, was not only a different behavior for men and women, but a behavior that intrinsically reflected issues of gender and power:

> [Hetero]sexual behavior [often] occurs in the context of unequal power and in a context that socializes women to be passive sexually and in other ways. . . . For men, the behavior is wearing the condom; for women, the behavior is persuading the male partner to wear a condom, or in some cases, deciding not to have sex when the male partner refuses to wear a condom. (p. 440)

The notion that sexual and relationship power in heterosexual relationships are key determinants of women's HIV risk is bolstered by an abundant empirical literature that documents the role of actual or threatened violence in response to a woman's request for condom use with a male partner (e.g., Beadnell, Baker, Morrison, &

Knox, 2000; Brown-Peterside, Ren, Chiasson, & Koblin, 2002; Campbell, Sefl, & Ahrens, 2004; Dunkle et al., 2004; Frye et al., 2011; Gruskin et al., 2002; Hamburger et al., 2004; Lichtenstein, 2005; Raj, Reed, Welles, Santana, & Silverman, 2008; Teitelman, Ratcliffe, Morales-Aleman, & Sullivan, 2008). In sum: The gendered and relational context of a woman's life (e.g., a violent partner, a partner who refuses to use condoms) can readily override her social cognitive resources.

A macro perspective of the HIV/AIDS epidemic in the United States demonstrates that protecting oneself from the virus, particularly if you are a poor Black woman, is not simply a matter of individualized metrics such as health beliefs, self-efficacy, or stage of readiness. Rather, individual risk and protection from risk are embedded within a larger context of health risk. Just as women's social cognitive resources can be overridden by relational context, this macro-level context is one where individual risk or protection from risk can be readily trumped by larger structural forces, such as the concentration of HIV within the neighborhood and social networks in which one lives and socializes. Indeed, findings from a nationally representative study found that Black young adults were at increased risk for STIs even when their sexual and drug use behaviors were fairly normative (Hallfors, Iritani, Miller, & Bauer, 2007). By contrast, Whites were only at increased STI risk when their behaviors were very risky. The authors attributed these disparities in risk to be reflective of "environmental, institutional, and contextual differences between Blacks and Whites" (p. 6), such as race-segregated sexual mating patterns in which Blacks were more likely than Whites to encounter high-risk and low-risk sexual partners when choosing their sexual partners. Relevant to the limitations of individualistic approaches to HIV risk, Hallfors et al. asserted that HIV prevention approaches that focus on "risk behaviors at the individual level" (p. 6) may be more appropriate for Whites than for Blacks. In short, for Black young adults, the environmental contexts of their lives accounted for a larger proportion of their actual STI risk than their individual risk behaviors.

Socioeconomic Status: The Dollars and Cents of Women's HIV Risk

Paradoxically, the best predictor of a woman's—indeed of anyone's—health status is the one that is the least mentioned, theorized, and researched in psychology and public health: SES (Krieger, Williams, & Moss, 1997). Across centuries, SES has emerged as the most robust and consistent predictor of health (Adler, Boyce, Chesney, Folkman, & Syme, 1993; Adler & Newman, 2002; Adler & Ostrove, 1999; Krieger et al., 1993). Simply put, the more money and social and economic resources you have, the better your health will be. This, though, as intersectionality scholars indicate, is not always the case. There exists an intersectionality paradox whereby Black middle-class women and men with more education and higher incomes do not accrue the same health or wealth benefits as do Whites (Jackson & Williams, 2006). This paradox notwithstanding, nor does stronger SES just confer better health advantages at the top and fewer health advantages at the lower rungs. A socioeconomic gradient exists whereby people at the highest SES level enjoy better health than those in the middle, who in turn have better health than those at the bottom (Adler et al., 1994).

The HIV/AIDS epidemic provides an apt example of the social gradient of HIV risk. In Philadelphia, for example, the incidence of AIDS increased 14%, 88%, and 113% in high-, middle-, and low-income tracts respectively between 1988 and 1990 (Fife & Mode, 1992).

Despite overwhelming evidence about the relationship between SES and health, the United States pales in comparison to other countries in terms of conducting national research on SES and health (Krieger et al., 1997). This is presumably because of the pervasive cultural myth about the role of meritocracy in the United States and/or the notion that because most researchers are middle class, they cognitively distance themselves from people who are poor and issues that are most relevant to low-income people (Lott, 2002). The lack of national data on SES and health shapes how the nation responds to health disparities. That is, instead of developing structural approaches, such as job training, employment, and economic opportunities for low-income women, policy makers seem more content to focus attention and resources on individualistic interventions that are doomed to fail. This was the conclusion that my colleagues and I reached after examining the impact of the Protect and Respect intervention for women living with HIV/AIDS (Teti et al., 2010). Although the goal of the intervention was to increase the women's use of condoms with male partners, findings from the intervention groups highlighted several factors, such as poverty, substance abuse, and violent partners, that posed barriers to condom use. This prompted us to conclude:

> Women bring their painful histories, lack of formal education opportunities, isolation, abusive partnerships, and myriad other life challenges that affect sexual decision making to interventions. They need a space to discuss their lives before they can successfully implement the skills that they have learned in the intervention. (p. 576)

An abundant literature documents the relationship between low SES and increased risk, particularly for low-income Black and Latina women (Zierler & Krieger, 1997), but you would be hard pressed to find any SES data in the Centers for Disease Control and Prevention's surveillance reports. The reports collect and present HIV/AIDS prevalence and incidence data by sex, race, ethnicity, age, geographic region, and exposure category (e.g., injection drug use, high-risk heterosexual contact) but not by SES (Sutton et al., 2009). Yet, by the agency's own admission, the majority of the nation's HIV/AIDS cases are concentrated among Black and Latino populations who live in impoverished urban areas (Centers for Disease Control and Prevention, 2010a, 2010b). Indeed, evidence exists of a generalized HIV epidemic in the United States for impoverished urban areas (Denning & DiNenno, 2010). The United Nations for AIDS (UNAIDS) declares an epidemic to be generalized when its prevalence within a population exceeds 1% (UNAIDS, 2010). In some U.S. cities, the 2.1% prevalence of HIV/AIDS is on par with or higher than the epidemic found in poor countries such as Burundi, Ethiopia, Angola, and Haiti.

The intersectionality perspective also highlights how SES factors into health messages, which are typically framed from the vantage point of middle-class people. Implicit in HIV prevention messages that direct women to "negotiate" condom use with partners or talk to sexual partners about HIV risk and condom use is a middle-class bias about what intimate relationships are or should be (Mays & Cochran, 1988). This "rather middle class notion" (Mays & Cochran, 1988, p. 954) may be unrealistic and inapplicable to the lives of poor women who "may not bother to ask men about previous sexual or drug use behaviors because they know the men will lie or discount the risk" (p. 954). Mays and Cochran advise developers of HIV prevention messages for low-income women of color to remember that "poor people do not always have the luxury of honesty, which is much easier when there is sufficient money and resources to guide one's choices" (p. 954). Nor is the middle-class presumption unique to HIV/AIDS prevention. People who are middle and upper middle class, not those who are poor or low income, are often the prime beneficiaries of the results of psychological and public health research, because they have the resources to effect health-promotion behaviors, such as buying condoms or enrolling in smoking cessation programs (Adler & Newman, 2002).

Social Inequality, Women, and HIV Risk

One of intersectionality's signature tenets is the notion that social inequalities are multiple, intersecting, and simultaneously constructed at both the micro level of individual lives as well as the macro level of social inequalities (Weber & Parra-Medina, 2003). This view contrasts substantially with the traditional biomedical/psychosocial/biobehavioral paradigm that conceptualizes social inequality as independent and discrete and often involving just two dimensions (e.g., race and sex). By contrast, empirical research on the intersectionality of multiple social

inequalities (e.g., racism, sexism, social class) is woefully scarce, presumably because of the methodological challenges involved in conducting intersectionality research (Bowleg, 2008b; Cole, 2009). Krieger et al. (1993) go a step farther by indicating not only the "narrow vision" of epidemiological research in the United States for failing to conduct intersectionality research, but also questioning whether researchers are reluctant to investigate topics such as intersectional oppression "whose remedies lie outside the bounds of traditional public health interventions" (p. 99). Applied to psychology, individual problems have individual solutions. Like the epidemiologists Krieger and colleagues criticize, many psychologists too may be reluctant to investigate complex topics, such as women's experiences of multiple and interlocking systems of social inequalities, whose solutions lie well beyond psychology's purview.

This dearth of research on intersectionality and women's health in general also serves as a beacon for research on the topic of intersectionality (namely, intersections of racism, sexism, classism) and women's HIV risk. In light of the disproportionate impact of HIV on women of color in the United States, research examining the intersectional impact of racism, sexism, and classism relevant to women of color and HIV risk is curiously absent. In fact, compared to the abundant research on racism and diminished physical and mental health (Williams, 2008; Williams, Neighbors, & Jackson, 2003, 2008; Williams, Yan, Jackson, & Anderson, 1997), research on social inequality and HIV risk, even on single types of social inequality like racism, is scarce. The exception to this rule is an HIV prevention study with Latino gay and bisexual men that documented a relationship between the men's reports of more financial hardship, racism, and hetero-sexism and more reports of HIV-risk behaviors (Diaz, Ayala, & Bein, 2004; Diaz, Ayala, Bein, Henne, & Marin, 2001).

Research on the relationship among gender, sexism, and health is also relatively rare (Krieger et al., 1993). Not surprisingly, this dearth of research on sexism and women's health in general also extends to the women and HIV/AIDS epidemic. Only a handful of studies exist on the topic of sexism and women's HIV risk. Among them is a study with women attending family planning clinics in the San Francisco Bay Area that found that the vast majority of women (83%) reported having sexist experiences, and having more sexist experiences predicted risky sexual behaviors with casual partners, but not main sex partners (Bowleg, Neilands, & Choi, 2008). A major limitation of the research was that 60% of the sample was White, limiting opportunities to investigate how multiple forms of social discrimination (e.g., the intersectionality of racism and sexism) might predict increased HIV risk for women of color. To state the obvious, there is a dire need for more theory and research on how the interlocking experiences of racism, sexism, and classism shape HIV risk at the micro and macro levels.

OPTIMISM RISING AND FALLING: TOWARD AN INTERSECTIONALITY-INFORMED UNDERSTANDING OF WOMEN'S HEALTH

Intersectionality theorists and many public health scholars are realistically pessimistic about the prospect of reducing, much less eliminating, health disparities in the United States. This is because the majority of health disparities are not rooted solely in individualistic determinants of behavior, but in larger macro and interlocking structural processes such as racism, sexism, and poverty (Krieger et al., 1993; Link & Phelan, 1995, 1996, 2000; Ruzek, Olesen, & Clarke, 1997; Weber & Fore, 2007; Weber & Parra-Medina, 2003).

Steeped so long in our individualistic stew, many psychologists might find it difficult to envision how variables beyond the level of the individual could improve women's health. The irony here is that ample evidence shows that structural interventions for health issues, such as physical activity, nutrition, and smoking cessation, have been strikingly successful (Katz, 2009). For example, increased excise taxes on cigarettes have prompted many people to quit smoking; bans on the use of trans fats in restaurants have improved healthy eating. Even so, attempts to integrate intersectionality's focus on micro- and macro-level factors that shape women's health are likely to be fraught with frustration. Incorporating a macro-level focus would violate one of psychology's most sacrosanct tenets: the perception that individuals are, or ought to be, solely responsible for their health outcomes (Katz, 2009; Sumartojo, 2000).

Nor is intersectionality the panacea for all that ails the individualistic approach to women's health. Intersectionality is not a testable theory in the way that the psychosocial health behavioral theories are. Moreover, the methodological challenges of conducting intersectionality research, particularly using quantitative methods, is daunting at best (Bowleg, 2008b; Cole, 2009). Nonetheless, psychologists need not be deterred by the lack of guidelines for conducting research on intersectionality nor the methodological challenges of intersectionality. Here, I recommend five ways that psychologists can play a larger role in theorizing, researching, and practicing intersectionality in service of advancing women's health:

1. *Read the original and contemporary literature on intersectionality.* The women's studies, feminist, and interdisciplinary literature is chock full of engaging and insightful articles on intersectionality (see this chapter's reference list for a start).

2. *Consider intersectionality as an interpretative and analytical tool.* Regardless of sample size or whether research participants explicitly articulate intersectionality, researchers can highlight the relationship between social structures (i.e., macro-level factors such as racism, poverty, sexism) and individual accounts (Cuadraz & Uttal, 1999).

3. *Use the term* intersectionality *in relevant work.* Scholars from multiple disciplines, psychology included, routinely conduct studies that are relevant to intersectionality either in content, participants, results, or interpretation of findings. Puzzlingly, the word *intersectionality* is often nowhere to be found in these studies (see e.g., Schulman et al., 1999; Van Ryn & Burke, 2000) or even articles that fervently advocate for evaluations of the conjoined impact of race/ethnicity, class, and sex on social inequalities in health (see e.g., Krieger et al., 1993, 1997). In order to advance and refine theory, research, and analysis about intersectionality and its application to the health of women and other populations, we need a common language. Where applicable, theorists and researchers should use and cite references on intersectionality and use *intersectionality* as a keyword in manuscript submissions.

4. *Practice "asking the other question."* Matsuda (1991) provides an extremely useful metric for understanding the interlocking nature of social inequalities that she calls "ask the other question":

   When I see something that looks racist, I ask, "Where is the patriarchy in this?" When I see something that looks sexist, I ask, "Where is the heterosexism in this?" When I see something that looks homophobic, I ask, "Where are the class interests in this?" (p. 1189)

5. *Traverse disciplinary boundaries.* It is easy to get stuck in disciplinary myopia—the inability to see beyond the disciplines in which we are trained. The interdisciplinary nature of intersectionality is one of its many strengths. An interdisciplinary approach that incorporates different disciplines (e.g., anthropology, demography, political science, women's studies, sociology) as well as diverse philosophical paradigms (e.g., social constructionist, interpretive, feminist, critical race theory) promises new and enriching ways of addressing women's health disparities.

THE REVERBERATIONS OF "AIN'T I A WOMAN?": CONCLUDING THOUGHTS

There is a reason that 160 years after Sojourner Truth's "Ain't I a woman?" query, the scholarly appeal of intersectionality persists. In this way, intersectionality bears all of the hallmarks of a successful social theory in terms of addressing fundamental concerns about social differences and inequalities; providing a novel way of looking at old issues; appealing to both generalists and specialists; and providing, through its ambiguity and incompleteness, seemingly endless opportunities for debate, theorizing, and research (Davis, 2008).

Although these factors may explain intersectionality's success as a theory, I believe that intersectionality's longevity is better traced to practical realities. Recognizing the seeming intractability of health disparities, despite decades of excellent research focused on the individual, many scholars of women's health and health disparities now recognize the limitations of an exclusively individualistic approach to reducing or eliminating disparities in women's health and the public's health in general. Indeed, this is why I find the nation's new *National Prevention Plan* (U.S. Department of Health and Human Services, 2011), with its recognition that communities need to create the conditions to foster health and well-being, to be heartening. It accords with intersectionality's notion that "health is located in families and communities, not simply in individual bodies" (Weber & Parra-Medina, 2003, p. 222). But try as they might, individuals alone do not strengthen communities. Individuals and macro- and structural-level interventions gird communities to facilitate and support healthy behaviors

(e.g., local and state tax policies that fund neighborhoods and schools, regulations that zone out businesses that discourage health and encourage businesses that do, and federal bans on smoking in restaurants, urban design to improve places to exercise) (Katz, 2009).

Mt. Airy, the vibrant and progressive middle-class community in which I live in Philadelphia, provides ample and easy access to a variety of stores that sell healthy foods. This is not the case in the poorer and more racially segregated neighborhoods of Philadelphia that are relative "food deserts" with no or limited access to healthy food, but ample access to stores that sell liquor and fatty and other junk foods (Chilton & Booth, 2007). Thus, the elimination of health disparities will require a concerted change in social structures and intersectional social inequalities, the "fundamental causes" that create the disparities in the first place (Link & Phelan, 1995, 1996, 2000). Only then will we be able to envision a society in which eating well, staying active, losing weight, protecting ourselves, and getting checkups are enough for women to be healthy.

REFERENCES

Adler, N. E., Boyce, T., Chesney, M. A., Cohen, S., Folkman, S., Kahn, R. L., & Syme, S. L. (1994). Socioeconomic status and health: The challenge of the gradient. *American Psychologist, 49*(1), 15–24.

Adler, N. E., Boyce, W. T., Chesney, M. A., Folkman, S., & Syme, S. L. (1993). Socioeconomic inequalities in health: No easy solution. *JAMA, 269*(24), 3140–3145.

Adler, N. E., & Newman, K. (2002). Socioeconomic disparities in health: Pathways and policies. Inequality in education, income, and occupation exacerbates the gaps between the health "haves" and "have-nots." *Health Affiliates, 21*(2), 60–76.

Adler, N. E., & Ostrove, J. M. (1999). Socioeconomic status and health: What we know and what we don't. *Annals of the New York Academy of Sciences*, *896*, 3–15.

Ajzen, I., & Fishbein, M. (1980). *Understanding attitudes and predicting social behavior*. Englewood Cliffs, NJ: Prentice-Hall.

Albarracin, D., Johnson, B. T., Fishbein, M., & Muellerleile, P. A. (2001). Theories of reasoned action and planned behavior as models of condom use: A meta-analysis. *Psychological Bulletin*, *127*(1), 142–161.

Amaro, H. (1995). Love, sex, and power: Considering women's realities in HIV prevention. *American Psychologist*, *50*, 437–447.

Amaro, H., & Raj, A. (2000). On the margin: Power and women's HIV risk reduction strategies. *Sex Roles*, *42*(7–8), 723–749.

Amaro, H., Raj, A., & Reed, E. (2001). Women's sexual health: The need for feminist analyses in public health in the Decade of Behavior. *Psychology of Women Quarterly*, *25*(4), 324–334.

Bandura, A. (1977). Self-efficacy: Toward a unifying theory of behavioral change. *Psychological Review*, *84*(2), 191–215.

Bandura, A. (1990). Perceived self-efficacy in the exercise of control over AIDS infection. *Evaluation and Program Planning*, *13*(1), 9–17.

Bandura, A. (1998). Health promotion from the perspective of Social Cognitive Theory. *Psychology and Health*, *13*, 623–649.

Beadnell, B., Baker, S. A., Morrison, D. M., & Knox, K. (2000). HIV/STD risk factors for women with violent male partners. *Sex Roles*, *42*(7–8), 661–689.

Bowleg, L. (2008a). The health risks of being Black, Latina, woman, and/or poor: Redefining women's health within the context of social inequality. In J. C. Chrisler, C. Golden, & P. D. Rozee (Eds.), *Lectures on the psychology of women* (4th ed., pp. 205–219). New York, NY: McGraw-Hill.

Bowleg, L. (2008b). When Black + lesbian + woman ≠ Black lesbian woman: The methodological challenges of qualitative and quantitative intersectionality research. *Sex Roles*, *59*, 312–325.

Bowleg, L., Lucas, K. J., & Tschann, J. M. (2004). "The ball was always in his court": An exploratory analysis of relationship scripts, sexual scripts, and condom use among African American women. *Psychology of Women Quarterly*, *28*, 70–82.

Bowleg, L., Neilands, T. B., & Choi, K. H. (2008). Evaluating the validity and reliability of a modified Schedule of Sexist Events: Implications for public health research on women's HIV risk behaviors. *Women & Health*, *47*(2), 19–40.

Brown-Peterside, P., Ren, L., Chiasson, M. A., & Koblin, B. A. (2002). Double trouble: Violent and nonviolent traumas among women at sexual risk of HIV infection. *Women and Health*, *36*(3), 51–64.

Campbell, R., Sefl, T., & Ahrens, C. E. (2004). The impact of rape on women's sexual health risk behaviors. *Health Psychology*, *23*(1), 67–74.

Centers for Disease Control and Prevention. (2010a, September 9). HIV/AIDS among African Americans. Retrieved from http://www.cdc.gov/hiv/topics/aa/pdf/aa.pdf

Centers for Disease Control and Prevention. (2010b, December 1). HIV/AIDS among Hispanics/Latinos. Retrieved from http://www.cdc.gov/hiv/hispanics/index.htm

Centers for Disease Control and Prevention. (2011a, May 20). Diagnoses of HIV infection and population among adult and adolescent females, by race/ethnicity, 2009—40 states. *HIV Surveillance in Women*. Retrieved from http://www.cdc.gov/hiv/topics/surveillance/resources/slides/women/slides/Women4.pdf

Centers for Disease Control and Prevention. (2011b, March 15, 2011). Tips for a safe and healthy life. Retrieved from http://www.cdc.gov/family/tips/index.htm

Centers for Disease Control and Prevention, Office of Women's Health. (2010a, February 19). Leading causes of death by age group, Black females—United States, 2006. *Leading causes of death in females, United States 2006*. Retrieved from http://www.cdc.gov/women/lcod/06_black_females.pdf

Centers for Disease Control and Prevention, Office of Women's Health. (2010b, February 19). Leading causes of death by age group, White females—United States, 2006. *Leading causes of death in females, United States 2006*. Retrieved from http://www.cdc.gov/women/lcod/06_white_females.pdf

Chilton, M., & Booth, S. (2007). Hunger of the body and hunger of the mind: African American women's perceptions of food insecurity, health and violence. *Journal of Nutrition Education and Behavior*, *39*(3), 116–125.

Cochran, S. D., & Mays, V. M. (1993). Applying social psychological models to predicting HIV-related sexual risk behaviors among African-Americans. *Journal of Black Psychology, 19*, 142–154.

Cole, E. R. (2009). Intersectionality and research in psychology. *American Psychologist, 64*(3), 170–180.

Collins, P. H. (1995). Symposium: On West and Fenstermaker's "Doing difference." *Gender & Society, 9*(4), 491–513.

Combahee River Collective. (1977). The Combahee River Collective Statement. In B. Smith (Ed.), *Home girls: A black feminist anthology* (pp. 272–282). New York, NY: Kitchen Table, Women of Color Press.

Crenshaw, K. W. (1991). Mapping the margins: Intersectionality, identity politics, and violence against women of color. *Stanford Law Review, 43*, 1241–1299.

Crenshaw, K. W. (1995). The intersection of race and gender. In K. W. Crenshaw, N. Gotanda, G. Peller, & K. Thomas (Eds.), *Critical race theory: The key writings that formed the movement* (pp. 357–383). New York, NY: The New Press.

Cuadraz, G. H., & Uttal, L. (1999). Intersectionality and in-depth interviews: Methodological strategies for analyzing race, class, and gender. *Race, Gender & Class, 6*, 156–186.

Davis, K. (2008). Intersectionality as buzzword: A sociology of science perspective on what makes a feminist theory successful. *Feminist Theory, 9*(1), 67–85. doi: 10.1177/1464700108086364

Denning, P., & DiNenno, E. (2010). Communities in crisis: Is there a generalized HIV epidemic in impoverished urban areas of the United States? Retrieved from http://www.cdc.gov/hiv/topics/surveillance/resources/other/poverty.htm

Diaz, R. M., Ayala, G., & Bein, E. (2004). Sexual risk as an outcome of social oppression: Data from a probability sample of Latino gay men in three U.S. cities. *Cultural Diversity & Ethnic Minority Psychology, 10*(3), 255–267.

Diaz, R. M., Ayala, G., Bein, E., Henne, J., & Marin, B. V. (2001). The impact of homophobia, poverty, and racism on the mental health of gay and bisexual Latino men: Findings from 3 US cities. *American Journal of Public Health, 91*(6), 927–932.

Downing-Matibag, T. M., & Geisinger, B. (2009). Hooking up and sexual risk taking among college students: A Health Belief Model perspective. *Qualitative Health Research, 19*(9), 1196–1209. doi: 10.1177/1049732309344206.

Dunkle, K. L., Jewkes, R. K., Brown, H. C., Gray, G. E., McIntryre, J. A., & Harlow, S. D. (2004). Gender-based violence, relationship power, and risk of HIV infection in women attending antenatal clinics in South Africa. *Lancet 363*(9419), 1415–1421.

Dworkin, S. L., & Ehrhardt, A. A. (2007). Going beyond "ABC" to include "GEM": Critical reflections on progress in the HIV/AIDS epidemic. *American Journal of Public Health 97*(1), 13–18.

Fife, D., & Mode, C. (1992). AIDS prevalence by income group in Philadelphia. *Journal of Acquired Immune Deficiency Syndrome, 5*(11), 1111–1115.

Fishbein, M. (2000). The role of theory in HIV prevention. *AIDS Care, 12*(3), 273–278. doi: 10.1080/09540120050042918.

Fishbein, M., & Ajzen, I. (1975). *Belief, attitude, intention and behavior: An introduction to theory and research.* Reading, MA: Addison-Wesley.

Flegal, K. M., Carroll, M. D., Ogden, C. L., & Curtin, L. R. (2010). Prevalence and trends in obesity among US adults, 1999–2008. *JAMA, 303*(3), 235–241. doi: 10.1001/jama.2009.2014.

Frye, V., Ompad, D., Chan, C., Koblin, B. A., Galea, S., & Vlahov, D. (2011). Intimate partner violence perpetration and condom use-related factors: Associations with heterosexual men's consistent condom use. *AIDS and Behavior, 15*(1), 153–162.

Gruskin, L., Gange, S. J., Celentano, D., Schuman, P., Moore, J. S., Zierler, S., & Vlahov, D. (2002). Incidence of violence against HIV-infected and uninfected women: Findings from the HIV Epidemiology Research (HER) study. *Journal of Urban Health, 79*(4), 512–524.

Hallfors, D. D., Iritani, B. J., Miller, W. C., & Bauer, D. J. (2007). Sexual and drug behavior patterns and HIV and STD racial disparities: The need for new directions. *American Journal of Public Health, 97*(1), 125–132. doi: 10.2105/AJPH.2005.075747.

Hamburger, M. E., Moore, J., Koenig, L. J., Vlahov, D., Schoenbaum, E. E., Schuman, P., & Mayer, K. (2004). Persistence of inconsistent condom use: Relation to abuse history and HIV serostatus. *AIDS & Behavior, 8*(3), 333–344.

Jackson, P. B., & Williams, D. R. (2006). The intersection of race, gender and SES: Health paradoxes. In A. J. Schulz & L. Mullings (Eds.), *Gender, race, class, & health: Intersectional approaches* (pp. 131–162). San Francisco, CA: Jossey-Bass.

Janz, N. K., & Becker, M. H. (1984). The Health Belief Model: A decade later. *Health Education Quarterly, 11*(1), 1–47.

Katz, M. H. (2009). Structural interventions for addressing chronic health problems. *JAMA, 302*(6), 683–685. doi: 10.1001/jama.2009.1147.

Khan, L. K., Sobush, K., Keener, D., Goodman, K., Lowry, A., Kakietek, J., & Zaro, S. (2009). Recommended community strategies and measurements to prevent obesity in the United States. *Morbidity and Mortality Weekly Report, 58*(RR07) 1–26.

Krieger, N. (1996). Inequality, diversity, and health: Thoughts on "race/ethnicity" and "gender." *Journal of the American Medical Women's Association, 51*(4), 133–136.

Krieger, N., Chen, J. T., Waterman, P. D., Rehkopf, D. H., & Subramanian, S. V. (2003). Race/ethnicity, gender, and monitoring socioeconomic gradients in health: A comparison of area-based socioeconomic measures—The Public Health Disparities Geocoding Project. *American Journal of Public Health, 93*(10), 1655–1671.

Krieger, N., Rowley, D. L., Herman, A. A., Avery, B., & Phillips, M. T. (1993). Racism, sexism, and social class: Implications for studies of health, disease, and well-being. *American Journal of Preventive Medicine, 9*(6), 82–122.

Krieger, N., Williams, D. R., & Moss, N. E. (1997). Measuring social class in U.S. public health research: Concepts, methodologies, and guidelines. *Annual Review of Public Health, 18*, 341–378.

Laforge, R. G., Greene, G. W., & Prochaska, J. O. (1994). Psychosocial factors influencing low fruit and vegetable consumption. *Journal of Behavioral Medicine, 17*(4), 361–374.

Laforge, R. G., Rossi, J. S., Prochaska, J. O., Velicer, W. F., & Levesque, D. A. (1999). Stage of regular exercise and health-related quality of life. *Preventive Medicine, 28*, 349–360.

Lichtenstein, B. (2005). Domestic violence, sexual ownership, and HIV risk in women in the American deep south. *Social Science & Medicine, 60*(4), 701–714.

Link, B. G., & Phelan, J. (1995). Social conditions as fundamental causes of disease. *Journal of Health and Social Behavior, Spec No*, 80–94.

Link, B. G., & Phelan, J. C. (1996). Understanding sociodemographic differences in health: The role of fundamental social causes. *American Journal of Public Health, 86*(4), 471–473.

Link, B. G., & Phelan, J. C. (2000). Evaluating the fundamental cause explanation for social disparities in health. In C. Bird, P. Conrad, & A. M. Fremont (Eds.), *Handbook of medical sociology* (5th ed., pp. 33–46). Upper Saddle River, NJ: Prentice Hall.

Lott, B. (2002). Cognitive and behavioral distancing from the poor. *American Psychologist, 57*(2), 100–110.

Malnick, S. D., & Knobler, H. (2006). The medical complications of obesity. *Quarterly Journal of Medicine, 99*(9), 565–579. doi: 10.1093/qjmed/hcl085.

Matsuda, D. J. (1991). Beside my sister: Facing the enemy: Legal theory out of coalition. *Stanford Law Review, 43*(6), 1183–1192.

Mays, V. M., & Cochran, S. D. (1988). Issues in the perception of AIDS risk and risk reduction activities by Black and Hispanic/Latina women. *American Psychologist, 43*(11), 949–957.

McCall, L. (2005). The complexity of intersectionality. *Signs, 30*(3), 1771–1800.

National Cancer Institute. (2003). How much attention do you pay to information about health or medical topics in magazines? *Health Information National Trends Survey.* Retrieved from http://hints.cancer.gov/hints/questions/question-details.jsp?qid=684&dataset=2003

Noar, S. M. (2005). A health educator's guide to theories of health behavior. *International Quarterly of Community Health Education, 24*(1), 75–92.

Norris, A. E., & Ford, K. (1995). Condom use by low-income African-American and Hispanic Youth with a well-known partner: Integrating the Health Belief Model, Theory of Reasoned Action, and the Construct Accessibility Model. *Journal of Applied Social Psychology, 25*(20), 1801–1830.

Prochaska, J. O., & DiClemente, C. C. (1983). Stages and processes of self-change of smoking: Toward an integrating model of change. *Journal of Consulting and Clinical Psychology, 51*(3), 390–395.

Prochaska, J. O., Redding, C. A., Harlow, L. L., Rossi, J. S., & Velicer, W. F. (1994). The transtheoretical model of change and HIV prevention: A review. *Health Education Quarterly, 21*(4), 471–486.

Prochaska, J. O., Velicer, W. F., Rossi, J. S., Goldstein, M. G., Marcus, B. H., Rakowski, W., . . .

& Rossi, S. R. (1994). Stages of change and decisional balance for 12 problem behaviors. *Health Psychology*, *13*(1), 39–46.

Pulerwitz, J., Amaro, H., DeJong, W., Gortmaker, S. L., & Rudd, R. (2002). Relationship power, condom use and HIV risk among women in the USA. *AIDS Care*, *14*(6), 789–800.

Raj, A., Reed, E., Welles, S. L., Santana, M. C., & Silverman, J. G. (2008). Intimate partner violence perpetration, risky sexual behavior, and STI/HIV diagnosis among heterosexual African American men. *American Journal of Mens Health*, *2*(3), 291–295. doi: 10.1177/1557988308320269.

Rosenstock, I. M. (1974). The Health Belief Model and preventive health behavior. *Health Education Monographs*, *2*(4), 354–386.

Rosenstock, I. M., Strecher, V. J., & Becker, M. H. (1988). Social learning theory and the Health Belief Model. *Health Education Quarterly*, *15*(2), 175–183.

Rosenstock, I. M., Strecher, V. J., & Becker, M. H. (1994). The health belief model and HIV risk behavior change. In R. J. DiClemente & J. L. Peterson (Eds.), *Preventing AIDS: Theories and methods of behavioral interventions* (pp. 5–24). New York, NY: Plenum Press.

Ruzek, S., Olesen, V., & Clarke, A. (Eds.). (1997). *Women's health: Complexiities and differences*. Columbus: Ohio State University Press.

Schulman, K. A., Berlin, J. A., Harless, W., Kerner, J. F., Sistrunk, S., Gersh, B. J., . . . Escarce, J. J. (1999). The effect of race and sex on physicians' recommendations for cardiac catheterization. *New England Journal of Medicine*, *340*(8), 618–626.

Schulz, A. J., & Mullings, L. (2006). *Gender, race, class and health: Intersectional approaches*. San Francisco, CA: Jossey-Bass.

Shields, S. A. (2008). Gender: An intersectionality perspective. *Sex Roles*, *59*, 301–311.

Sumartojo, E. (2000). Structural factors in HIV prevention: Concepts, examples, and implications for research. *AIDS*, *14S*(1) S3–S10.

Sutton, M. Y., Jones, R. L., Wolitski, R. J., Cleveland, J. C., Dean, H. D., & Fenton, K. A. (2009). A review of the Centers for Disease Control and Prevention's response to the HIV/AIDS crisis among blacks in the United States, 1981–2009. *American Journal of Public Health*, *99*, S351–S359.

Teitelman, A. M., Ratcliffe, S. J., Morales-Aleman, M. M., & Sullivan, C. M. (2008). Sexual relationship power, intimate partner violence, and condom use among minority urban girls. *Journal of Interpersonal Violence*, *23*(12), 1694–1712. doi: 10.1177/0886260508314331.

Teti, M., Bowleg, L., Cole, R., Lloyd, L., Rubinstein, S., Spencer, S., . . . Gold, M. (2010). A mixed methods evaluation of the effect of the Protect and Respect intervention on the condom use and disclosure practices of women living with HIV/AIDS. *AIDS & Behavior*, *14*(3), 567–579.

Truth, S. (1851). Ain't I a woman? Retrieved from http://afroamhistory.about.com/od/sojournertruth/a/aintiawoman.htm

U.S. Department of Health and Human Services. (2011, June 16). National prevention strategy: America's plan for better health and wellness. Retrieved from http://www.healthcare.gov/center/councils/nphpphc/strategy/report.pdf

U.S. Department of Health and Human Services. (n.d.). Prevention. Retrieved from http://www.hhs.gov/safety/index.html

U.S. Department of Health and Human Services, Health Resources and Services Administration, & Maternal and Child Health Bureau. (2007). Ten leading causes of death among women aged 18 and older, by race/ethnicity, 2007. *Women's Health USA 2010*. Retrieved from http://mchb.hrsa.gov/whusa10/hstat/hi/pages/208lcd.html

UNAIDS. (2010). UNAIDS report on the global AIDS epidemic. Retrieved from http://www.unaids.org/documents/20101123_GlobalReport_em.pdf

Van Ryn, M., & Burke, J. (2000). The effect of patient race and socio-economic status on physicians' perceptions of patients. *Social Science & Medicine*, *50*(6), 813–828. doi: 10.1016/s0277-9536(99)00338-x.

Weber, L. (1998). A conceptual framework for understanding race, class, gender, and sexuality. *Psychology of Women Quarterly*, *22*(1), 13–32.

Weber, L. (2006). *Reconstructing the landscape of health disparities research: Promoting dialogue and collaboration between feminist intersectional and biomedical paradigms*. San Francisco, CA: Jossey-Bass.

Weber, L., & Fore, M. E. (2007). Race, ethnicity, and health: An intersectional approach. In H. Vera & J. R. Feagin (Eds.), *Handbook of the sociology of racial and ethnic relations* (pp. 191–218). New York, NY: Springer.

Weber, L., & Parra-Medina, D. (2003). Intersectionality and women's health: Charting a path to eliminating health disparities. *Advances in Gender Research*, 7, 181–230.

Williams, D. R. (2008). Racial/ethnic variations in women's health: The social embeddedness of health. *American Journal of Public Health*, *98*(Supplement 1) S38–S47.

Williams, D. R., Neighbors, H. W., & Jackson, J. S. (2003). Racial/ethnic discrimination and health: Findings from community studies. *American Journal of Public Health*, *93*(2), 200–208.

Williams, D. R., Neighbors, H. W., & Jackson, J. S. (2008). Racial/ethnic discrimination and health: Findings from community studies. *American Journal of Public Health*, *98*(S1) S29–S37.

Williams, D. R., Yan, Y., Jackson, J. S., & Anderson, N. B. (1997). Racial differences in physical and mental health. *Journal of Health Psychology*, *2*(3), 335–351. doi: 10.1177/135910539700200305.

Wingood, G. M., & DiClemente, R. J. (2000). Application of the theory of gender and power to examine HIV-related exposures, risk factors, and effective interventions for women. *Health Education & Behavior*, *27*(5), 539–565.

Zierler, S., & Krieger, N. (1997). Reframing women's risk: Social inequalities and HIV infection. *Annual Review of Public Health*, *18*, 401–436.

Zierler, S., & Krieger, N. (1998). HIV infection in women: Social inequalities as determinants of risk. *Critical Public Health*, *8*(1), 13–32.

CHAPTER 3

Employment and Women's Health

Nancy L. Marshall

Employment is a significant context for women's health. Historically, pundits have argued that higher education would damage women's health (Morantz & Zschoche, 1980), and that employment would interfere with women's roles as mothers and wives (Coontz, 1992), or lead to rising health risks as women become "like men" and therefore at risk for cardiovascular disease and other "men's diseases" (Haynes & Feinleib, 1980). While each of these perspectives had some support in its day, in the 21st century, the context of employment for women's health has changed dramatically. Women are now almost as likely to be employed as men are, and, as such, are equally vulnerable to the effects of poor working conditions. However, women's position in the economy is often different from that of men from similar backgrounds. In addition, women continue to have greater responsibility for caring for children and extended family, which creates additional demands on women. This chapter reviews the latest research on employment and women's health, in the context of the changing economy and changing family lives of the 21st century.

Women's participation in the labor force has changed dramatically in the past 60 years, rising from 34% of women in the labor force in 1950 to almost 60% in 2009 (Smith & Bachu, 1999). The largest gain in

the labor force participation rate was by women with children under age 6, from a participation rate of 39% in 1975 to 64% in 2009. In 2009, more than 65 million women in the United States were in the workforce. Of these, more than 48 million, or 74%, were employed full time (BLS, 2010a).[1] By 2050, it is projected that women's labor force participation rate will almost equal that of men (Toossi, 2002).

The rising rate of women's employment in the second half of the 20th century led to a debate about the effects of employment on women's health. Some argued that women's employment would conflict with their family responsibilities, and that full-time employment would create role overload, which would negatively affect their health and well-being; this perspective was referred to as the *scarcity hypothesis* (Goode, 1960). Others argued that employment would provide women with an additional arena in which to develop competencies, self-esteem, and social connections, and that the combination of roles would actually enhance women's health (Marks, 1977; Sieber, 1974). In an extensive review of the research conducted between 1950 and 2000 on the relation between employment status—whether or not a woman is employed—and health,

---

[1]Compared to 72% of men who were in the labor force; 87% of employed men were employed full time.

Klumb and Lampert (2004) found that employment either had no effect on women's health or had positive effects.

While the rise of women's employment has not meant a decline in women's health, it has meant the need to incorporate women into research on the effects of working conditions on health, and has led to new research on the effects of combining work and family responsibilities on the lives of women and men. Working women face health risks at work that are similar to those faced by men, such as stress from the organization of work (e.g., job demands, little control over work, work schedule). Trends in the new economy, including downsizing and outsourcing of core functions, increasing use of contingent labor, flatter management structures, and lean production technologies, have contributed to reduced job stability and increased workload (Hertz & Marshall, 2001; Sauter et al., 2002). A significant proportion (25% to 30%) of workers report high levels of emotional exhaustion at the end of the workday (Sauter et al., 2002). Workers in their prime family-formation years are working longer hours at a time when their workload demands at home are also higher (Gerson & Jacobs, 2001). While men also experience stressful employment conditions, rates of stress–related illness, including depression, are nearly twice as high for women as for men (NIOSH, 2001; NORA, 2003). Work and family balance issues are an additional health risk factor for women with children (Sauter et al., 2002).

WORKING CONDITIONS AND HEALTH

Existing research has identified several characteristics of work organization that are associated with poorer health, including greater demands, reduced worker control, lower levels of substantive complexity, and reduced work-related social support (Caplan, Cobb, French, Van Harrison, & Pinneau, 1975; House & Wells, 1978; Kohn & Schooler, 1983). One of the leading theoretical models in the field of occupational health is the demand-control model, developed by Karasek and colleagues (Karasek & Theorell, 1990). The demand-control model posits that the combination of heavy demands and limited control or decision latitude to moderate those demands results in job strain, which in turn, leads to negative health consequences. Several studies have supported this model. The demand-control model has been confirmed in random samples of male workers in the United States and Sweden (Karasek, 1979), and for men and women using the U.S. Quality of Employment Surveys data in 1972 and 1977 (Karasek & Theorell, 1990), as well as in studies of specific occupations, including clerical workers in the finance industry, employees in manufacturing, and German metalworkers (Dwyer & Ganster, 1991; Karasek & Theorell, 1990). Reviews of the research have found the strongest support for the job strain (high demands combined with low control) model for psychological distress or well-being outcomes (de Lange, Taris, Kompier, Houtman, & Bongers, 2003) and cardiovascular disease risk (Belkic, Landsbergis, Schnall, & Baker, 2004).

The demand-control model receives greatest support in studies conducted before the recent rise in the service industries, or on samples drawn from the manufacturing industry. Muntaner and colleagues have posited that Karasek's job characteristics scales are limited to domains that are more characteristic of traditional industrial jobs

(Muntaner, Eaton, & Garrison, 1993). In response to these limitations, research on the service industries has examined additional characteristics of work demands and rewards. For example, Soderfeldt and colleagues (Soderfeldt et al., 1996, 1997) examined the role of emotional demands.

Marshall and colleagues examined emotional demands and the intrinsic rewards from service to others in their studies of licensed practical nurses and social workers, and of two-earner couples (Marshall, Barnett, Baruch, & Pleck, 1991; Marshall, Barnett, & Sayer, 1997). Giardini and Frese (2006) examined emotion work—which they defined as the required effort to express employer-desired emotions—as a source of work stress for workers in the service industries.

The demand-control model has also been expanded to include the importance of social support to workers' psychological health (Johnson & Hall 1988; Johnson, Hall, & Theorell, 1989). Early research on occupational health identified the importance of social support, particularly work-related social support, to men's health (cf. House & Wells, 1978). In the 1990s, research on women and health established the importance of social support for women workers as well (Loscocco & Spitze, 1990; Marshall & Barnett, 1992; Vermeulen & Mustard, 2000). In a review of the research on the demand-control-social support model conducted between 1998–2007, Hausser and colleagues (Hausser, Mojzisch, Niesel, & Schulz-Hardt, 2010) found that workers with stronger social support reported greater psychological well-being in 60% of studies that examined simultaneously the main effects of all three dimensions (demand, control, support).

Some have argued that any observed links between employment and health are spurious; workers in poor health are likely to leave the workforce, or to have never entered it, and associations between employment and health are artifacts of this—a result of the selection of healthy workers into the workforce. Waldron and colleagues (Waldron, Herold, Dunn, & Staum, 1982) argued that most of the cross-sectional association between health and employment for women is a result of such self-selection, particularly for women who were married, white-collar, or White.

To address this critique, Ross and Mirowsky (1995) used two waves of data from a national probability sample, collected in 1979–1980, to estimate both the effects of health on employment and the effects of employment on health, for separate samples of women and men ages 20–64. They found that full-time employment predicted a slower decline in health over time for both genders and for Whites and non-Whites, married and nonmarried; part-time employment was unrelated to health. At the same time, physical functioning increased the odds of getting or keeping a full-time job for both women and men. While acknowledging the role of selection, Ross and Mirowsky argue that their analyses support the conclusion that "full-time employment keeps healthy workers healthy" (p. 241).

Occupational Segregation and Women's Health

Although women's labor force participation rates are approaching men's rates, women and men often have very different experiences at work, as a function of the types of occupations they hold. In 2009, 44.6% of women were concentrated in just 20 occupations, and most of these occupations were heavily female, including secretaries and administrative assistants; registered nurses; elementary and middle school teachers; cashiers; nursing, psychiatric, and home health aides; restaurant servers; maids and housekeeping cleaners; customer service representatives; childcare workers; book-keeping, accounting, and auditing clerks; and receptionists and information clerks.[2] By comparison, only 34.1% of men are concentrated in their top 20 occupations, most of which are heavily male, including drivers/sales workers and truck drivers, janitors and building cleaners, laborers and material movers, construction laborers, carpenters, chief executives, grounds main-tenance workers, construction managers, wholesale and manufacturing sales represen-tatives, stock clerks and order fillers, auto-motive service technicians and mechanics, and computer software engineers. This occupational segregation means that women and men are differentially exposed to partic-ular occupational health hazards.[3]

More than one-third (36%) of all women workers are employed in education and health services industries (BLS, 2010a). Across all industries in the United States, there are 3.9 reported cases of nonfatal occupational inju-ries and illnesses per 100 full-time workers; in the education and health services industries there are 5.0 reported cases per 100 full-time workers. According to the Bureau of Labor Statistics, there were 100,000 or more cases of

nonfatal occupational injuries and illnesses in general medical and surgical hospitals (7.3 cases per 100 full-time workers), nursing care facilities (8.9 cases per 100 full-time workers), and elementary and secondary schools (5.0 cases per 100 full-time workers) (BLS, 2010b). Occupational health risks include low-back pain (nurses, childcare workers; McGrath, 2007; Tan, 1991), asthma (health-related industries and teaching; McHugh, Symanski, Pompeii, & Delclos, 2010), noise exposures that can contribute to reduction in hearing sensitivity and increased stress (teaching; Grebennikov & Wiggins, 2006; Seetha et al., 2008), and exposure to infectious, biological, or chemi-cal hazards (nurses, childcare workers; McGrath, 2007; Tan, 1991).

Sexual Harassment and Women's Health

The U.S. Equal Employment Opportunity Commission (Facts About Sexual Harass-ment, 2002) defines *sexual harassment* as:

> Unwelcome sexual advances, requests for sexual favors, and other verbal or physical conduct of a sexual nature constitutes sexual harassment when submission to or rejection of this conduct explicitly or implicitly affects an individual's employment [*quid pro quo* harass-ment], unreasonably interferes with an individual's work perform-ance or creates an intimidating, hostile or offensive work environ-ment [hostile environment].

In the psychological literature, *sexual harassment* is defined more broadly, to include unwanted sex-related experiences

---

[2]Calculated from Table 11 of *Women in the Labor Force: A Databook* (Department of Labor, 2010a).

[3]I am not arguing that men are not exposed to occupational health hazards, only that women and men are exposed to different health hazards in the different occupations that they hold, and that an understanding of women's health requires an under-standing of the health hazards of women's occupa-tions, such as registered nurses and elementary school teachers.

and the individual's perception of having been sexually harassed, whether or not the behavior meets the legal test. Reported rates of sexual harassment of women vary with the questions asked and the research methods used; Ilies and colleagues (Ilies, Hauserman, Schwochaum, & Stibal, 2003) conducted a meta-analysis of 55 studies with probability samples, and found that, on average, 24% of women have experienced sexual harassment at work, while 58% of women have experienced potentially harassing behaviors.

Sexual harassment is more common in organizations that have a higher tolerance for sexual harassment, that is, a climate in which employees believe that reports of sexual harassment will not be taken seriously, will not have consequences for the harasser, or where reporting sexual harassment may have negative consequences for the reporter (Fitzgerald, Drasgow, Hulin, Gelfand, & Magley, 1997; Willness, Steel, & Lee, 2007). A series of studies have examined the profiles of men who are likely to harass and have found that men who believe that social dominance is linked to sexuality, view themselves as more masculine and less feminine, and have more hostile attitudes toward women are more likely to become sexual harassers (O'Leary-Kelly, Bowes-Sperry, Bates, & Lean, 2009). Men with this profile are more likely to act on their inclinations in organizations that are more tolerant of sexual harassment (Pryor, LaVite, & Stoller, 1993).

Other organizational factors are also important. Women are more likely to experience sexual harassment when they work in a setting with fewer women and more men, or in an occupation that is traditionally male (Berdahl, 2007; Willness et al., 2007). O'Leary-Kelly and colleagues (2009) reviewed recent research on sexual harassment and found that women with less power within organizations—in lower-status occupations, or from race/ethnic minorities—were more likely to experience sexual harassment.

Sexual harassment has direct effects on the well-being of women (and men) who have been sexually harassed. Two recent meta-analyses were conducted, one by Willness and colleagues (2007) of 41 studies, and one by Chan and colleagues (Chan, Lam, Chow, & Cheung, 2008) of 49 studies. While the meta-analyses differed in the ways they coded physical health and mental health outcomes, and in some of the details of their analyses, their findings are consistent. Experiencing sexual harassment was associated with negative job outcomes, including decreased job satisfaction, lower organizational commitment, greater work withdrawal (missing work, neglecting work tasks), and reduced productivity (Chan et al., 2008; Willness et al., 2007). Sexual harassment also directly affects health and well-being. Chan and colleagues (2008) argued that sexual harassment is a stressful condition, and that individuals often report what Selye (1993) calls "diseases of adaptation," such as headaches, gastrointestinal disorders, and sleep disturbances. Sexual harassment was significantly associated with lower physical health satisfaction and greater physical symptomatology (Chan et al., 2008; Willness et al., 2007). In addition, sexual harassment was significantly associated with reduced psychological well-being (self-esteem and life satisfaction) and increased psychological distress (depression, anxiety, PTSD symptoms) (Chan et al., 2008; Willness et al., 2007). Sexual harassment also affects co-workers' job behavior and psychological health, particularly when the harassment is part of a hostile work environment (O'Leary-Kelly et al., 2009).

WORK-FAMILY BALANCE AND HEALTH

We know that employment has many benefits for women, as for men, including more positive perceptions of health and improved physical functioning (Ross & Mirowsky, 1995). However, combining work and family can lead to experiences of work-family conflict and other stressors that may negatively affect health (Byron, 2005). The apparent paradox inherent in these two research findings—that employment status has health benefits, but combining work and family may have negative health consequences—has led to a body of research on women's employment and health. While men may also experience work-family conflict, women continue to spend more time in family labor than do men. For example, Bianchi, Robinson, and Milkie (2006) found that married mothers spent an average of 41 hours per week on domestic tasks, compared to 21 hours per week for married fathers. While men spend more hours, on average, in paid labor than women do, women's second shift can lead to work-family conflict. In the following section, we discuss the different models of work-family balance and the links between work-family conflict and women's health.

Models of Work-Family Balance and Health

There is growing recognition of the importance of multilevel analysis in health research (Bachrach & Abeles, 2004). Sauter and colleagues (2002) outline a multilevel concept of work organization that "illustrates the continuity between (1) broad economic and public policy and other forces at the national and international level, (2)

organization-level structures and processes, and (3) job demands and conditions in the workplace." In their introduction to the special issue of the *Journal of Occupational Health Psychology* on work-family research, Westman and Piotrkowski (1999) called for the use of systems theory as a starting point in theorizing work-family research in occupational health, because "it allows for a broad, unifying theoretical perspective in which both workplaces and families are considered semiopen systems with permeable boundaries." Ecological systems theory combines systems theory with a multilevel model, placing the microsystems of workplaces and families within the exosystem of economic and public-sector institutions and policies, which are embedded in a macrosystem of societal and cultural beliefs and practices (Bronfenbrenner, 1989). Since Westman and Piotrkowski's call, several important articles have appeared that use ecological systems theory in occupational health and/or work-family research (Ettner & Grzywacz, 2001; Grzywacz & Marks, 2000; Voydanoff, 2002).

Research over the past three decades has explored a range of individual responses to variations in the work-family system, including *work-family strain*, *work-family conflict*, and *work-family balance*. Although these terms are often used interchangeably, they arise from different theoretical perspectives. Multiple roles research examines the additive or cumulative impact of participation in both the work and family systems. The scarcity hypothesis posits that *work-family strain* occurs when the combined demands of the work and family systems are too great for available resources (cf. Goode, 1960; Slater, 1963). Role enhancement theory suggests that occupying multiple roles enhances the performance in individual roles and leads to *work-family gains*, such as greater self-esteem, social recognition, and social involvement (cf. Marks, 1977; Sieber, 1974).

Another perspective focuses on the *interface* between the two systems; work–family conflict occurs when the tasks or responsibilities of one system interfere with those of the other system (Burke, 1988; Frone, Russell, & Cooper, 1991; Marshall & Barnett, 1993a). For example, when the schedules of paid work and family demands are incompatible, mothers of young children may choose nonday work schedules to facilitate combining work and family—working evenings or nights, while the father works days. However, Voydanoff (1989) found that women working nonday shifts experienced higher levels of work–family conflict, possibly because their lives were out of sync with the lives of their societal supports, including family and friends, as well as with formal childcare. Hattery (2001) found that, while couples liked working opposite shifts because it allowed them to save on childcare costs and to be with their children, it also led to a lack of marital couple time.

Workplaces also vary in their norms and expectations of workers' behavior in negotiating the borders between work and family. Some workplaces view borders as rigid—family needs should not interfere with work responsibilities. Other workplaces view borders as temporally or spatially flexible—workers may select semipermanent employment schedules that fit their family needs, or may use flexplace options (working from home). Still other workplaces view borders as permeable, allowing workers considerable day-to-day flexibility in managing the needs of family and work. Shockley and Allen (2007) found that flexible work arrangements were particularly important to

women with greater family responsibility, and that flextime was more strongly linked to reducing work interference with family life than was flexplace. In general, while workplace flextime policies do not in and of themselves make a consistent difference (Christensen & Staines, 1990), workplace cultures that supported worker-controlled flexibility were associated with improved work-family balance (Galinsky & Johnson, 1998; Glass & Camarigg, 1992; Hill, Hawkins, Ferris, & Weitzmann, 2001).

Drawing on all of these perspectives as well as on exchange theory, Pittman (1994) suggests that individuals are engaged in a "multidimensional exchange between a family and work organization." A core tenet of exchange theory is that individual actors seek to maximize their benefits through their exchanges with other individuals or with aggregate groups, such as the workplace (Turner, 1987). From this perspective, work-family balance refers to the individual's cognitive assessment of the extent to which his or her exchanges between the family system and the paid work system are in equilibrium, so that the benefits of combining work and family are maximized and the conflicts are minimized.

The linkages between the work-family system and work-family conflict have often been studied from the perspective of stress theory, which examines the relations among events or conditions (stressors), individual reactions to stressors (stress), and individual or family outcomes, such as depression, parenting behaviors, or child well-being. Stress theory places individuals' experiences of stress and strain within specific structural contexts (Pearlin, 1989), such as the family system or paid work system. In an extensive review of the research on stress and health, Thoits (2010) found that, when stressors are measured comprehensively, including considering chronicity, the research clearly shows an impact on physical and mental health. Chronic stress leads to wear and tear or allostatic load, which can suppress immune function and increase susceptibility to disease (McEwen & Seeman, 1999).

Voydanoff (2002) proposed specific characteristics of the microsystem of paid work that are related to work-family conflict and individual well-being, including structure, social organization, norms and expectations, support, orientation, and quality. Individual work systems may vary in structure—organization size, pay and benefits, work schedules—and in norms and expectations, as expressed in official policies or in workplace culture. Individual work systems also vary in the support available from co-workers and supervisors, the quality of the work performed—job performance and productivity—and in the individual's orientation to work—level of involvement or commitment as evidenced in the number of hours spent at work and in the sense of community or connection to paid work. Finally, work systems vary in the social organization of the work itself—the level of demand or burden, the autonomy or skill discretion of workers, and the challenge or complexity of the work.

A large body of research has found that the social organization of work—reflected in such working conditions as job demands and autonomy—is a significant contributor to work-family conflict, such that more stressful jobs are associated with greater conflict between the demands of work and family. Similarly, work structure (the amount of time that women with children spend at work) is an important aspect of the context in which employment is experienced.

Women with young children may be employed part-time or full-time, and full-time employment can range from 35 to 80 hours per week or more. Working long hours has been linked to greater work-family conflict (Burke, 1988; Judge, Boudreau, & Bretz, 1994). Haines, Marchand, and Rousseau (2008) found that shift work was associated with greater work-family conflict for both women and men. Work-family conflict is also more common among working mothers than among employed fathers (Marshall & Barnett, 1993b), reflecting, in part, the fact that mothers continue to bear greater responsibility for day-to-day parenting despite fathers' increased involvement with their children (Bianchi, Milkie, Sayer, & Robinson, 2000).

Work-family conflict, in turn, is associated with emotional or psychological distress (Haines et al., 2008). In a survey of a representative national sample of 2,700 U.S. adults who were either married or the parent of a child under 19, Frone (2000) found that women (and men) who reported higher levels of work-family conflict were more likely to have clinically significant diagnoses of mood, anxiety, and substance dependence disorders. Work-family conflict is also associated with overall physical health (Frone et al., 1991; Frone, Russell, & Barnes, 1996; Grandey & Cropanzano, 1999; Grywacz, 2000), physical health symptoms (Burke & Greenglass, 2001; Thomas & Ganster, 1995), hypertension, and high blood pressure (Frone et al., 1991; Thomas & Ganster, 1995).

Life Stage Variations

A lifespan perspective that recognizes changes in the individual organism from the prenatal period through death is broadly used, particularly in research on children, but increasingly in research on adults. Such a perspective is important in understanding both specific stages of adulthood and trajectories of adult development (Moen, Robison, & Dempster-McClain, 1995). Over the life course, individuals move in and out of roles and relationships, becoming parents, partnering or marrying, spending time single, and living with extended family or friends. At the same time, individuals follow employment trajectories or careers, finding employment as young adults or after leaving school, changing jobs and even occupations, accumulating experience, and sometimes advancing to better paid positions, eventually entering a period of peri-retirement—perhaps returning to work after official retirement, perhaps leaving the labor force completely.

These two trajectories—relationships/families and employment/careers—are intertwined. Although there are a variety of paths, most women spend some time working before having children. After having a child, more than half of women return to work within a few months, while others stay out of the labor force for a longer period. Some women (with or without children) stay in the labor force continuously until retirement; others move in and out, or shift from full-time to part-time work as needed or required. These interlocking trajectories create recognizable stages, but not all individuals move through all of the stages, nor do they move through them at the same pace or in the same sequence. Nevertheless, considering the characteristics of these stages for working women provides new insights into the role of employment in women's health. We examine three major stages: women with young children, women with school-age children, and women over 50, with young adult or adult children.

Women With Young Children Employment rates among mothers with a child under the age of 3 years rose from 34% in 1975 to 61% by 2009 (BLS, 2010a). The lifespan perspective is important to an interpretation of the finding from the multiple roles tradition that, while combining employment and family is positive for many women, women with young children are likely to report greater work-family strains (cf. Barnett & Gareis, 2000; Killien, Habermann, & Jarrett, 2001; Marshall & Barnett, 1993a; Tausig & Fenwick, 2001). A recent study of trends over time concluded that, on balance, women's employment has positive health effects; however, these benefits are reduced for working mothers of young children (Schnittker, 2007). The reduced health benefits for working mothers of young children parallel research that shows that these mothers report greater conflicts between work and family responsibilities than do mothers of older children (Higgins, Duxbury, & Lee, 1995).

Employment rates among mothers of infants had risen to 55% by 2007 (U.S. DOL, 2008), and most new mothers return to work by the time their baby is 3 months old (U.S. DOL, 2004). While the Family and Medical Leave Act provides unpaid leave for eligible employees for up to 12 weeks, more than 90% of parents who take leave to care for a newborn or adopted child return to paid work at the end of the 12-week period (Cantor et al., 2001). Research on postpartum health has identified challenges faced by women, including physical recovery from childbirth, postpartum blues or depression, stresses in the marital relationship, and health problems of the newborn, which are specific to the postpartum period (cf. Ellis & Hewitt 1985). Emergent research in occupational health in the postpartum period has focused on maternity leave and found that longer time off from work has a positive relation to maternal health and quality of life (Chatterji & Markowitz, 2005; Gjerdingen & Chaloner, 1994; Hyde, Klein, Essex, & Clark, 1995; McGovern et al., 1997). In a study of more than 700 working mothers of infants, Marshall and Tracy (2009) found that, while employment provided these working mothers and their families with important income and other benefits, women in jobs with poor working conditions, or who experienced greater work-family conflict because they were single mothers or caring for infants who were sick more often than other infants, reported poorer emotional health.

Women With School-Age Children
Labor force participation rates among women with school-age children (between the ages of 6 and 17, with no children under 6) rose from 55% in 1975 to 78% in 2009. Women at this life stage have the highest labor force participation rates across all of the life stages. At this point in life, women either have reentered the labor force after having children or have several years of work experience; some women have advanced in their careers to positions that, while potentially more demanding, may also offer better pay and benefits. The parenting needs of school-age children are different from those of young children under three. Infants and preschoolers require constant supervision and regular physical caretaking, as well as nurturing. School-age children are increasingly able to meet their own physical caretaking needs, and, even when still requiring supervision, this often takes the form of distal supervision—contact with children by telephone or through responsible others. As every parent of a school-age child knows,

homework and children's activities benefit from parental presence, but the repertoire of parenting behaviors expands. These characteristics of this life stage contribute to the findings that women with school-age children report lower levels of work-family conflict than do women with preschool-age children, although they report higher work-family conflict compared to workers without children (Grzywacz, 2000; Marshall & Barnett, 1993a; Martinengo, Jacob, & Hill, 2010; Roehling, Moen, & Batt, 2003).

Employed Women Over 50
Almost 60% of women between the ages of 55 and 64 were in the labor force in 2009, compared to 70% of men ages 55–64 (BLS, 2010a). The number and proportion of older workers in the workforce is growing as the "baby-boom" generation ages and there are fewer younger workers from the "baby-bust" generation (1964–1980s) (Farr, Tesluk, & Klein, 1998; Salthouse & Maurer, 1996). Many of today's aging baby boomers will remain in the labor force longer than members of recent cohorts because of a variety of individual and societal factors: increased longevity, financial concerns, societal concerns about the economic costs of early retirement, a shortage of younger workers, and the beginning of disincentives toward early retirement in public and private retirement plans (Schooler, Caplan, & Oates, 1998). Even when workers retire, retirement does not always signal the end of employment. Various studies suggest that approximately one-third of older workers become reemployed postretirement; this is especially likely among workers with a college degree and among women who have been intermittently employed before retirement (Beck, 1986; Han & Moen, 1999). The research to date suggests that most older

adults are physically and mentally able to continue employment in later years (Sterns & Sterns, 1995).

These factors combine to create labor force participation rates among older workers that are dramatically different from those of 30 years ago, particularly among women (Federal Interagency Forum on Aging Related Statistics, 2000). At the same time, the longer lifespan of Americans has raised concerns about the caregiving needs of the growing numbers of the elderly. Although Americans live longer and are healthier than in the past, 15% of people 65 and older need assistance with one or more activities of daily living (ADLs) (Treas, 1995) and many more need assistance with chores, errands, or transportation. Most of this assistance is provided by family members; one study of women and men ages 53 to 63 found that 26% of women and 15% of men reported spending at least 100 hours per year caring for or helping their older parents (Johnson & Lo Sasso, 2000). Another study of caregivers of the elderly found that 75% of caregivers were women, and that most of the caregivers were between the ages of 50 and 64 (Barrah, Shultz, Baltes, & Stoltz, 2004).

Parenting responsibilities also extend into late midlife. While most children of older parents (over 50) are themselves adults (over the age of 18), parental care of offspring in the form of financial support, and sometimes co-residence or other assistance, often continues until children are in their mid-twenties (Boaz, Hu, & Ye, 1999). For a significant portion of older Americans, caregiving demands are potentially in direct conflict with their involvement in the labor force. As the National Academies of Science notes in *Health and Safety Needs of Older Workers* (NRC, 2004, p. 93): "The health and safety needs of older workers arise not only from their paid employment, but also from their unpaid work roles, including . . . caregiving responsibilities and other household responsibilities." This is particularly likely to be true among older female workers.

Research on employed caregivers has provided important information about the extent of caregiving among older workers and the health of older workers who are also caregivers. A national survey, conducted for the National Alliance for Caregiving and AARP (NAC/AARP, 2004), found that 59% of current caregivers were also employed, and most were employed full time. The majority of employed caregivers reported that caregiving responsibilities affected their work; the most frequent impact, reported by 57% of employed caregivers, was going in late, leaving early, or taking time off. Scharlach and colleagues (Scharlach, 1994; Scharlach & Boyd, 1989; Scharlach, Sobel, & Roberts, 1991) have found that, while caregivers report that their caregiving sometimes interferes with their employment, this is outweighed by the positive returns to caregiving, including a sense of accomplishment and enhanced interpersonal relationships. Similarly, studies by Spitze and colleagues (Spitze, Logan, Joseph, & Lee, 1994) and Stoller and Pugliesi (1989) found that the negative health effects of caregiving were reduced by employment. Stephens, Franks, and Atienza (1997) found that caregivers with rewarding full-time jobs experienced less caregiving stress than did caregivers with less-rewarding jobs or who were employed part time. Using three waves of the *American Changing Lives Study*, Rozario, Morrow-Howell, and Hinterlong (2004) found that older caregivers who also worked and/or volunteered reported better health.

IMPLICATIONS

Employment has become a normative experience for women as well as for men, and employment, per se, does not lead to poor health for women. It is clear that women are not leaving the workplace, and their continuing presence calls attention to the importance of addressing environmental stressors in the lives of women and men. Women are as at risk for the negative health consequences of poor working conditions as are men. Women's (and men's) health can be protected in the workplace by reengineering jobs to reduce demands, increasing worker control over the pace, timing, and performance of tasks, and increasing support at work from co-workers and supervisors. Because women are concentrated in occupations with higher emotional demands, rather than physical demands, it is crucial that research continues to examine emotional work and that employers identify ways to reduce the wear and tear of emotionally demanding jobs. Healthcare providers can assist women in identifying stressful working conditions as a potential risk factor, and can support women's exploration of ways to reduce the stressors and provide balance through increasing control, support, and other rewards, or expanding their ability to cope with the stress associated with poor working conditions. Women are also at greater risk for sexual harassment, particularly in certain workplaces and occupations; employers can reduce the negative consequences of sexual harassment by implementing policies that create a climate that does not tolerate sexual harassment, including policies that specify consequences for harassers and supports for employees who report sexual harassment. Healthcare providers can assist women

who report sexual harassment by screening for possible emotional health effects, including symptoms of posttraumatic stress disorder, and for possible links between the harassment and physical symptoms.

Work-family conflict, particularly for mothers of young children, creates an additional health risk for women. Policies, such as paid parental leave, can reduce the work-family conflict of mothers with infants. Other policies, such as generous sick leave benefits that can be used to care for sick children and older relatives, or financial support for childcare and elder-care costs, can reduce the conflicts between employment and caregiving. However, to the extent that these policies are utilized only by women, they will perpetuate the second shift for women and open the door for employers who view women employees as "too expensive." To address the effects of work-family conflict, it is important that men are as involved in the day-to-day parenting responsibilities as women. This would reduce the number of hours women spend in the second shift and increase the incentive for employers to support both women and men in balancing work and family.

Although work-family conflict is a health risk for some women, many women, particularly women with older children and women without children at home, do not report such conflict, or report that combining work and family is rewarding. It is important that this be understood so that we do not create well-intentioned policies that actually perpetuate women's second shift. In addition, when girls and young women consider their career options, it is important that they understand this, so that they do not limit their choices to those occupations that are considered female-friendly, such as teaching or nursing. In fact, employers that have workforces that are not either predominantly female or predominantly male are more likely to offer work-family benefits such as extended sick leave, and these benefits are most likely to be offered to workers who are highly educated or trained, or in unions that have bargained for these benefits. Small business employers may also offer less formal flexible work arrangements (Hertz & Marshall, 2001).

Addressing the challenges of employment for women requires an understanding of both the ways in which women and men are similar in their experiences of, and reactions to, poor working conditions, as well as the differences in women's experiences in the workplace, and, especially for mothers of young children, with the second shift. Responses must be as varied as women's labor force experiences, including reengineering jobs, expanding work-family benefits, and addressing the role of men in the family.

REFERENCES

Bachrach, C. A., & Abeles, R. P. (2004). Social science and health research: Growth at the National Institutes of Health. *American Journal of Public Health, 94,* 22–28.

Barnett, R. C., & Gareis, K. C. (2000). "Reduced-hours job-role quality and life satisfaction among married women physicians with children." *Psychology of Women Quarterly, 24,* 358–364.

Barrah, J. L., Shultz, K. S., Baltes, B., & Stolz, H. E. (2004). Men's and women's elder care based work family conflict: Antecedents and work related outcomes. *Fathering, 2,* 305–330.

Beck, S. H. (1986). Mobility from preretirement to postretirement job. *The Sociological Quarterly, 27,* 515–531.

Belkic, K. L., Landsbergis, P. A., Schnall, P. L., & Baker, D. (2004). Is job strain a major source of cardiovascular disease risk? *Scandinavian Journal of Work & Environmental Health, 30,* 85–128.

Berdahl, J. L. (2007). The sexual harassment of uppity women. *Journal of Applied Psychology, 92,* 425–437.

Bianchi, S. M., Milkie, M. A., Sayer, L. C., & Robinson, J. P. (2000). Is anyone doing the housework? Trends in the gender division of household labor. *Social Forces, 79,* 191–228.

Bianchi, S. M., Robinson, J. P., & Milkie, M. A. (2006). *Changing rhythms of American family life.* New York, NY: Russell Sage.

Boaz, R. F., Hu, J., & Ye, Y. J. (1999). The transfer of resources from middle-aged children to functionally limited elderly parents: Providing time, giving money, sharing space. *Gerontologist, 39,* 648–657.

Bronfenbrenner, U. (1989). Ecological systems theory. *Annals of Child Development, 6,* 187–249.

Bureau of Labor Statistics (BLS). (2010a). *Workplace injuries and illnesses—2009.* News Release. USDL-10-1451.

Bureau of Labor Statistics (BLS). (2010b). *Women in the labor force: A databook.* Report 1026. U.S. Department of Labor.

Burke, R. J. (1988). Some antecedents and consequences of work-family conflict. In E.B. Goldsmith (Ed.), *Work and family: Theory, research and applications* (pp. 287–302). Newbury Park, CA: Sage.

Burke, R. J., & Greenglass, E. R. (2001). Hospital restructuring, work-family conflict and psychological burnout among nursing staff. *Psychological Health, 58,* 95–114.

Byron, K. (2005). A meta-analytic review of work–family conflict and its antecedents. *Journal of Vocational Behavior, 67,* 169–198.

Cantor, D., Waldfogel, J., Kerwin J., McKinley Wright, M., Levin, K., Rauch, J., . . . Kudela, M. S. (2001). *Balancing the needs of families and employers: Family and medical leave surveys, 2000 Update.* Rockville, MD: Westat.

Caplan, R. D., Cobb, S., French, J. R. P., Van Harrison, R. V., & Pinneau, S. R. (1975). *Job demands and worker health: Main effects and occupational differences.* Washington, DC: U.S. Government Printing Office.

Chan, D. K.-S., Lam, C. B., Chow, S. Y., & Cheung, S. F. (2008). Examining the job-related, psychological, and physical outcomes of workplace sexual harassment: A meta-analytic review. *Psychology of Women Quarterly*, *32*, 362–376.

Chatterji, P., & Markowitz, S. (2005). Does the length of maternity leave affect maternal health? *Southern Economic Journal*, *72*, 16–41.

Christensen, K. E., & Staines, G. L. (1990). Flextime: A viable solution to work/family conflict? *Journal of Family Issues*, *11*, 455–476.

Coontz, S. (1992). *The way we never were: American families and the nostalgia trap*. New York, NY: Basic Books.

de Lange, A. H., Taris, T. W., Kompier, M. A. J., Houtman, I. L. D., & Bongers, P. M. (2003). "The *very* best of the millennium": Longitudinal research and the demand-control-(support) model. *Journal of Occupational Health Psychology*, *8*, 282–305.

Dwyer, D. J., & Ganster, D. C. (1991). The role of negative affectivity in work-related stress. *Journal of Social Behavior and Personality*, *6*, 319–330.

Ellis, D., & Hewitt, R. (1985). Mother's postpartum perceptions of spousal relationships. *Journal of Gynecological and Neonatal Nursing*, *14*, 140.

Ettner, S. L., & Grzywacz, J. G. (2001). Workers' perceptions of how jobs affect health: A social ecological perspective. *Journal of Occupational Health Psychology*, *6*, 101–113.

Facts About Sexual Harassment. (2002, June 27). *The U.S. Equal Employment Opportunity Commission*. Retrieved from www.eeoc.gov/facts/fs-sex.html

Farr, J. L., Tesluk, P. E., & Klein, S. R. (1998). Organizational structure of the workplace and the older worker. In K. W. Schaie & C. Schooler (Eds.), *Impact of work on older workers* (pp. 143–185). New York, NY: Springer.

Federal Interagency Forum on Aging Related Statistics. (2000). *Older Americans 2000: Key Indicators of Well-being*. Available at www.agingstats.gov

Fitzgerald, L. F., Drasgow, F., Hulin, C. L., Gelfand, M. J., & Magley, V. J. (1997). Antecedents and consequences of sexual harassment in organizations: A test of an integrated model. *Journal of Applied Psychology*, *82*, 578–589.

Frone, M. R. (2000). Work-family conflict and employee psychiatric disorders: The national comorbidity survey. *Journal of Applied Psychology*, *85*, 888–895.

Frone, M. R., Russell, M., & Barnes, G. M. (1996). Work-family conflict, gender, and health-related outcomes: A study of employed parents in two community samples. *Journal of Occupational Health Psychology*, *1*, 57–69.

Frone, M. R., Russell, M., & Cooper, M. L. (1991). Relationship of work and family stressors to psychological distress: The independent moderating influence of social support, mastery, active coping, and self-focused attention. *Journal of Social Behavior and Personality*, *6*, 227–250.

Galinsky, E., & Johnson, A. A. (1998). *Reframing the business case for work-life initiatives*. New York, NY: Families and Work Institute.

Gerson, K., & Jacobs, J. A. (2001). Changing the structure and culture of work: Work and family conflict, work flexibility, and gender equity in the modern workplace. In R. Hertz & N. L. Marshall (Eds.), *Working families: The transformation of the American home* (pp. 207–226). Berkeley: University of California Press.

Giardini, A., & Frese, M. (2006). Reducing the negative effects of emotion work in service occupations: Emotional competence as a psychological resource. *Journal of Occupational Health Psychology*, *11*, 63–75.

Gjerdingen, D. K., & Chaloner, K. M. (1994). The relationship of women's postpartum mental health to employment, childbirth and social support. *Journal of Family Practice*, *38*, 465–472.

Glass, J., & Camarigg, V. (1992). Gender, parenthood, and job-family compatibility. *American Journal of Sociology*, *98*, 131–151.

Goode, W. J. (1960). A theory of role strain. *American Sociological Review*, *25*, 483–496.

Grandey, A. A., & Cropanzano, R. (1999). The conservation of resources model applied to work-family conflict and strain. *Journal of Vocational Behavior*, *54*, 350–370.

Grebennikov, I., & Wiggins, M. (2006). Psychological effects of classroom noise on early childhood teachers. *Australian Educational Researcher*, *33*, 35–53.

Grzywacz, J. G. (2000). Work-family spillover and health during midlife: Is managing conflict everything? *American Journal of Health Promotion*, *14*, 236–243.

Grzywacz, J. G., & Marks, N. F. (2000). Reconceptualizing the work-family interface: An ecological perspective on the correlates of positive and negative spillover between work and family. *Journal of Occupational Health Psychology*, *5*, 111–126.

Haines, V. Y., Marchand, A., & Rousseau, V. (2008). The mediating role of work-to-family conflict in the relationship between shiftwork and depression. *Work and Stress*, *22*, 341–356.

Han, S., & Moen, P. (1999). Clocking out: Multiplex time in retirement. *The American Journal of Sociology*, *105*, 191–236.

Hattery, A. J. (2001). Tag-team parenting: Costs and benefits of utilizing nonoverlapping shift work in families with young children. *Families in Society*, *82*, 419–427.

Hauser, J. A., Mojzisch, A., Niesel, M., & Schulz-Hardt, S. (2010). Ten years on: A review of recent research on the Job Demand-Control (-Support) model and psychological well-being. *Work & Stress*, *24*, 1–35.

Haynes, S. G., & Feinleib, M. (1980). Women, work and coronary heart disease: Prospective findings from the Framingham heart study. *American Journal of Public Health*, *70*, 133–141.

Hertz, R., & Marshall, N. L. (2001). *Working families: The transformation of the American home*. Berkeley: University of California Press.

Higgins, C., Duxbury, L., & Lee, C. (1995). Impact of life-cycle stage and gender on the ability to balance work and family responsibilities. In G. L. Bowen & J. F. Pittman (Eds.), *The work and family interface* (pp. 313–324). Minneapolis, MN: National Council on Family Relations.

Hill, E. J., Hawkins, A. J., Ferris, M., & Weitzman, M. (2001). Finding an extra day a week: The positive influence of perceived job flexibility on work and family life balance. *Family Relations*, *50*, 49–58.

House, J. S., & Wells, J. A. (1978). Occupational stress, social support, and health. In A. McLean, G. Black, & M. Colligan (Eds.), *Reducing occupational stress: Proceedings of a conference* (Publication No. 78-140; pp. 8–29). Cincinnati, OH: Department of Health, Education and Welfare (National Institute of Occupational Safety and Health).

Hyde, J. S., Klein, M. H., Essex, M. J., & Clark, R. (1995). Maternity leave and women's mental health. *Psychology of Women Quarterly*, *19*, 257–285.

Ilies, R., Hauserman, N., Schwochau, S., & Stibal, J. (2003). Reported incidence rates of work-related sexual harassment in the United States: Using meta-analysis to explain reported rate disparities. *Personnel Psychology*, *56*, 607–631.

Johnson, J. V., & Hall, E. M. (1988). Job strain, work place social support, and cardiovascular disease: A cross-sectional study of a random sample of Swedish working populations. *American Journal of Public Health*, *78*, 1336–1342.

Johnson, J. V., Hall, E. M., & Theorell, T. (1989). Combined effects of job strain and social isolation on cardiovascular disease morbidity and mortality in a random sample of Swedish male working population. *Scandinavian Journal of Work, Environment and Health*, *15*, 271–279.

Johnson, R. W., & Lo Sasso, A. T. (2000). *The trade-off between hours of paid employment and time assistance to elderly parents at midlife*. Washington, DC. The Urban Institute.

Judge, T., Boudreau, J., & Bretz, R. (1994). Job and life attitudes of male executives. *Journal of Applied Psychology*, *79*, 767–782.

Karasek, R. A. (1979). Job demands, job decision latitude and mental strain: Implications for job redesign. *Administrative Science Quarterly*, *24*, 285–308.

Karasek, R. A., & Theorell, T. (1990). *Healthy work*. New York, NY: Basic Books.

Killien, M. G., Habermann, B., & Jarrett, M. (2001). Influence of employment characteristics on postpartum mothers' health. *Women and Health*, *33*, 63–83.

Klumb, P. L., & Lampert, T. (2004). Women, work, and well-being 1950–2000: A review and methodological critique. *Social Science & Medicine*, *58*, 1007–1024.

Kohn, M., & Schooler, C. (1983). *Work and personality: An inquiry into the impact of social stratification*. New York, NY: Ablex.

Loscocco, K. A., & Spitze, G. (1990). Working conditions, social support, and the well-being of female and male factory workers. *Journal of Health and Social Behavior*, *31*, 313–327.

Marks, S. (1977). Multiple roles and role strain: Some notes on human energy, time, and commitment. *American Sociological Review*, *42*, 921–936.

Marshall, N. L., & Barnett, R. C. (1992). Work-related support among women in caregiving occupations. *Journal of Community Psychology*, *20*, 36–42.

Marshall, N. L., & Barnett, R. C. (1993a). Variations in job strain across nursing and social work specialties. *Journal of Community and Applied Social Psychology*, *3*, 261–271.

Marshall, N. L., & Barnett, R. C. (1993b). Work-family strains and gains among two-earner couples. *Journal of Community Psychology*, *21*, 64–78.

Marshall, N. L., Barnett, R. C., & Sayer, A. (1997). The changing workforce, job stress and psychological distress. *Journal of Occupational Health Psychology, 2,* 99–107.

Marshall, N. L., Barnett, R. C., Baruch, G. K., & Pleck, J. (1991). More than a job: Women and stress in caregiving occupations. In H. Z. Lopata & J. A. Levy (Eds.), *Current research on occupations and professions* (Vol. VI, pp. 61–81). Greenwich, CT: JAI Press.

Marshall, N.L. & Tracy, A.J. (2009). After the baby: Work-family conflict and working mothers' psychological health. *Family Relations, 58,* 380–391.

Martinengo, G., Jacob, J. I., & Hill, E. J. (2010). Gender and the work-family interface: Exploring differences across the family life course. *Journal of Family Issues, 31,* 1363–1390.

McEwen, B. S., & Seeman, T. (1999). Protective and damaging effects of mediators of stress: Elaborating and testing the concepts of allostasis and allostatic load. *Annals of the New York Academy of Sciences, 896,* 30–47.

McGovern, P., Dowd, B., Gjerdingen, D., Muscovice, I., Kochevar, L., & Lohman, W. (1997). Time off work and the postpartum health of employed women. *Medical Care, 35,* 507–21.

McGrath, B. J. (2007). Identifying health and safety risks for childcare workers. *American Association of Occupational Health Nurses Journal, 55,* 321–325.

McHugh, M., Symanski, E., Delclos, G. L., & Pompeii, L. A. (2010). Prevalence of asthma by industry and occupation in the U.S. working population. *American Journal of Industrial Medicine, 53,* 463–475. PMID: 20187006.

Moen, P., Robison, J., & Dempster-McClain, D. (1995). Caregiving and women's well-being: A life course approach. *Journal of Health and Social Behavior, 36,* 259–273.

Morantz, R. M., & Zschoche, S. (1980). Professionalism, feminism, and gender roles: A comparative study of nineteenth-century medical therapeutics. *The Journal of American History, 67,* 568–588.

Muntaner, C., Eaton, W. W., & Garrison, R. (1993). Dimensions of the psychosocial work environment in a sample of the US metropolitan population. *Work and Stress, 7,* 351–363.

National Alliance for Caregiving and American Association of Retired Persons (NAC/AARP). (2004). *Caregiving in the U.S.* Bethesda, MD: Author.

National Institute for Occupational Safety and Health (NIOSH). (2001). *Women's safety and health issues at work.* DHHS (NIOSH) Publication Number 2001-123.

National Occupational Research Agenda (NORA). *Update* 2003. Department of Health and Human Services, Centers for Disease Control and Prevention, National Institute for Occupational Safety and Health. DHHS (NIOSH) Publication Number 2003-148.

National Research Council and the Institute of Medicine (NRC). (2004). *Health and safety needs of older workers.* Committee on the Health and Safety Needs of Older Workers. D. H. Wegman & J. P. McGee (Eds.), Division of Behavioral and Social Sciences and Education. Washington, DC: The National Academies Press.

O'Leary-Kelly, A. M., Bowes-Sperry, L., Bates, C. A., & Lean, E. R. (2009). Sexual harassment at work: A decade (plus) of progress. *Journal of Management, 35,* 503–536.

Pearlin, L. I. (1989). The sociological study of stress. *Journal of Health and Social Behavior, 30,* 241–256.

Pittman, J. F. (1994). Work/family fit as a mediator of work factors on marital tension: Evidence from the interface of greedy institutions. *Human Relations, 47,* 183–209.

Pryor, J. B., LaVite, C. M., & Stoller, L. M. (1993). A social psychological analysis of sexual harassment: The person/situation interaction. *Journal of Vocational Behavior, 42,* 68–83.

Roehling, P. V., Moen, P., & Batt, R. (2003). When work spills over into the home and home spills over into work. In P. Moen (Ed.), *It's about time: Couples and careers.* Ithaca, NY: Cornell University Press.

Ross, C. E., & Mirowsky, J. (1995). Does employment affect health? *Journal of Health and Social Behavior, 36,* 230–243.

Rozario, P. A., Morrow-Howell, N., & Hinterlong, J. E. (2004). Role enhancement or role strain: Assessing the impact of multiple productive roles on older caregiver well-being. *Research on Aging, 26,* 413–428.

Salthouse, T. A., & Maurer, T. J. (1996). Aging, job performance, and career development. In J. E. Birren & K. W. Schaie (Eds.), *Handbook of the psychology of aging* (pp. 353–364). San Diego, CA: Academic Press.

Sauter, S. L., Brightwell, W. S., Colligan, M. J., Hurrell, Jr., J. J., Katz, T. M., LeGrande,

D. E., . . . Tetrick, L. E. (2002). *The changing organization of work and the safety and health of working people: Knowledge gaps and research directions*. DHHS (NIOSH) Publication Number 2002-116.

Scharlach, A. E. (1994). Caregiving and employment: Competing or complementary roles? *Gerontologist, 34*, 378–385.

Scharlach, A. E., & Boyd, S. L. (1989). Caregiving and employment: Results of an employee survey. *Gerontologist, 29*, 382–387.

Scharlach, A. E., Sobel, E. L., & Roberts, R. E. (1991). Employment and caregiver strain: An integrative model. *Gerontologist, 31*, 778–787.

Schnittker, J. (2007). Working more and feeling better: Women's health, employment and family life, 1974–2004. *American Sociological Review, 72*, 221–238.

Schooler, C., Caplan, L., & Oates, G. (1998). Aging and work: An overview. In K. W. Schaie & C. Schooler (Eds.), *Impact of work on older adults* (pp. 1–19). New York, NY: Springer.

Seetha, P., Karmegam, K., Ismail, M. Y., Sapuan, S. M., Ismail, N., & Moli, L. T. (2008). Effects to teaching environment of noise level in school classrooms. *Journal of Scientific & Industrial Research, 67*, 659–664.

Selye, H. (1993). History of the stress concept. In L. Goldberger & S. Breznitz (Eds.), *Handbook of stress: Theoretical and clinical aspects* (2nd ed.; pp. 7–17). New York, NY: Free Press.

Shockley, K. M., & Allen, T.D. (2007). When flexibility helps: Another look at the availability of flexible work arrangements and work-family conflict. *Journal of Vocational Behavior, 71*, 479–493.

Sieber, S. D. (1974). Toward a theory of role accumulation. *American Sociological Review, 39*, 567–578.

Slater, P. (1963). On social regression. *American Sociological Review, 28*, 339–364.

Smith, K. E., & Bachu, A. (1999). *Women's labor force attachment patterns and maternity leave: A review of the literature*. Population Division Working Paper No. 32. Washington, DC: U.S. Bureau of the Census.

Söderfeldt, B., Söderfeldt, M., Jones, K., O'Campo, P., Muntaner, C., Ohlson, C. G., & Warg, L. E. (1997). Does organization matter? A multilevel analysis of the demand-control model applied to human services. *Social Science & Medicine, 44*, 527–534.

Soderfeldt, B., Soderfeldt, M., Muntaner, C., O'Campo, P., Warg, L., & Ohlson, C. (1996). Psychosocial work environment in human service organisations: A conceptual analysis and development of the demand-control model. *Social Science & Medicine, 42*, 1217–1226.

Spitze, G., Logan, J. R., Joseph, G., & Lee, E. J. (1994). Middle generation roles and the well-being of men and women. *Journals of Gerontology, 49*, S107–S116.

Stephens, M. A. P., Franks, M. M., & Atienza, A. A. (1997). Where two roles intersect: Spillover between parent care and employment. *Psychology and Aging, 12*, 30–37.

Sterns, H. L., & Sterns, A. A. (1995). Health and the employment capability of older Americans. In S. A. Bass (Ed.), *Older and active: How Americans over 55 are contributing to society* (pp. 10–34). New Haven, CT: Yale University Press.

Stoller, E. P., & Pugliesi, K. L. (1989). The transition to the caregiving role: A panel study of helpers of elderly people. *Research on Aging, 11*, 312–330.

Tan, C. C. (1991). Occupational health problems among nurses. *Scandinavian Journal of Work and Environmental Health, 17*, 221–230.

Tausig, M., & Fenwick, R. (2001). Unbinding time: Alternate work schedules and work-life balance. *Journal of Family and Economic Issues, 22*, 101–119.

Thoits, P. A. (2010). Stress and health: Major findings and policy implications. *Journal of Health and Social Behavior, 51*, S41–S53.

Thomas, L. T., & Ganster, D. C. (1995). Impact of family-supportive work variables on work-family conflict and strain: A control perspective. *Journal of Applied Psychology, 80*, 6–15.

Toossi, M. (2002). A century of change: The U.S. labor force, 1950–2050. *Monthly Labor Review, 125*, 15–28.

Treas, J. (1995). Older Americans in the 1990s and beyond. *Population Bulletin, 50*, 2–46.

Turner, J. 1987. Social exchange theory: Future directions. In K. S. Cook (Ed.), *Social exchange theory* (pp. 223–238). Newbury Park, CA: Sage.

U.S. Department of Labor, Bureau of Labor Statistics (DOL). (2004). *Employment characteristics of families*. Press Release April 20 2004. USDL 04-719. Retrieved from http://stats.bls.gov/news.release/pdf/famee.pdf

U.S. Department of Labor, Bureau of Labor Statistics (DOL). (2008, May 30). *Employment characteristics of families in 2007.* Press Release. USDL 08-0731. Retrieved from http://stats.bls.gov/news.release/pdf/famee.pdf

Vermeulen, M., & Mustard, C. (2000). Gender differences in job strain, social support at work, and psychological distress. *Journal of Occupational Health Psychology, 5,* 428–440.

Voydanoff, P. (1989). Work and family: A review and expanded conceptualization. In E. B. Goldsmith (Ed.), *Work and family: Theory, research and applications* (pp. 1–22). Newbury Park, CA: Sage.

Voydanoff, P. (2002). Linkages between the work-family interface and work, family, and individual outcomes. *Journal of Family Issues, 23,* 138–164.

Waldron, I., Herold, J., Dunn, D., & Staum, R. (1982). Reciprocal effects of health and labor force participation among women: Evidence from two longitudinal studies. *Journal of Occupational Medicine, 24,* 126–132.

Westman, M., & Piotrkowski, C. S. (1999). Work-family research in occupational health psychology. *Journal of Occupational Health Psychology, 4,* 301–306.

Willness, C. R., Steel, P., & Lee, K. (2007). A meta-analysis of the antecedents and consequences of workplace sexual harassment. *Personnel Psychology, 60,* 127–162.

4

Effects of Intimate Partner Violence Against Women

Kathy McCloskey and Deidre Hussey

DEFINITION OF INTIMATE PARTNER VIOLENCE (IPV)

The frequency and severity of violence against women worldwide within the context of intimate relationships is devastating, yet so common in both developed and poverty-stricken countries that it has become commonplace and, in many cases, simply invisible (Watts & Zimmerman, 2002). Due to this situation, in order to truly grasp the extent of the problem, it is necessary to concisely define what is meant when using the phrase *intimate partner violence* (IPV).

At first glance, defining IPV should be simple and straightforward. We often assume we can easily identify IPV when it happens because it seems so obvious. However, a perusal of the literature clearly demonstrates this is not the case (e.g., Malloy, McCloskey, Grigsby, & Gardner, 2003). Does calling your intimate partner a derogatory name constitute IPV? Is a shove in frustration also considered IPV? Must a mark, bruise, or broken bones or teeth be a result in order to classify as "true" IPV?

We can loosely describe this meaning-making problem by highlighting the

tensions between two categories: (1) injury and other physical damage–related definitions of IPV (mostly reflected within legal statutes and often used in medical settings), and (2) emotional-injury definitions of IPV (Nicolaidis & Paranjape, 2009). Commonly, legal definitions are predicated on physical assault upon a person or property. For example, legal statutes across the United States rarely if ever include emotional abuse over time within their definitions of prosecutable IPV offenses, with the notable exception of relatively new stalking laws (Norris, Huss, & Palarea, 2011; Rajan & McCloskey, 2009). Instead, there must be evidence of physical pain and/or damage inflicted upon a person or property in order to meet statutory requirements for criminal justice system intervention (note that sexual assault would also fall under this general construct).

Additionally, two interesting assumptions are embedded within this definitional approach: (1) because physical pain/injury or property damage are centralized within this definition, the discrete assaultive event becomes of paramount importance, and any other related types of events are thereby obscured; and (2) because physical pain/

Acknowledgments: We would like to thank Dr. Shari Miles-Cohen and Ms. Tanya Burrell of the American Psychological Association (APA) Women's Program Office for their assistance in identifying key references for this effort.

injury or property damage must be present for IPV to "legally" occur, negative emotional sequelae are assumed to arise primarily from physical damage, and therefore any negative emotional impact is unfortunately viewed as secondary or of lesser importance (Blasco-Ros, Sanchez-Lorente, & Martinez, 2010; Rajan & McCloskey, 2009; Saltzman & Houry, 2009).

In contrast, emotional-injury definitions of IPV include patterned abusive behavior over time and do not assume that physical pain/injury or property damage must be present in order to inflict severe damage upon a victim (Blasco-Ros et al., 2010). However, an emotional-injury definitional approach requires a thorough understanding of abusive patterns within intimate relationships *across time*, as well as the common terrorist-like tactics abusers effectively use against their partners (e.g., Basile & Hall, 2011). Therefore, law enforcement, as well as healthcare providers in general, are often unable to accurately identify the presence of IPV, especially if the infliction of obvious physical pain/injury is absent [see Saltzman (2000a, 2000b) and Saltzman, Fanslow, McMahon, & Shelley (2002) for detailed discussions of these definitional issues].

In addition, if professionals cannot come to agreement on an acceptable IPV definition, then we certainly cannot expect individuals within the general population to provide accurate reports about the incidence or prevalence of their own IPV experiences. More often than not, individuals do not readily self-define themselves as abusers or victims of IPV, even in the presence of physical pain/assault. For example, while a slap or shove both meet the criteria of a legal assault, individuals typically do not classify these actions as IPV unless contextually prompted with concrete definitions (DeKeseredy, 2000). It also appears that psychological and emotional abuse alone will not prompt individuals to classify such behavior as IPV, even though the long-term effects can be devastating (e.g., Blasco-Ros et al., 2010).

Obviously, these types of definitional issues directly lead to population measurement problems and impact the quality of information available to us concerning IPV incidence and prevalence. For the purposes of this effort, we will use the IPV definition provided by the United States Centers for Disease Control and Prevention (CDC). This definition is the result of years of work and consensus building, which culminated in the publication of two special editions of the *Violence Against Women* journal (Saltzman, 2000a, 2000b), as well as other relevant publications since that time. As can be seen in Table 4.1, the two general IPV constructs outlined previously (physical and emotional) have each been broken down into two categories: (1) physical injury has been separated into physical and sexual, and (2) emotional injury has been separated into threats and psychological/emotional abuse. It is important to note that within this definition, property damage has been moved from the physical category into the emotional category, stalking has been included in the emotional category, and threats against or actual violence toward loved ones (e.g., children, extended family members, friends, co-workers, pets) as a controlling tactic, are altogether missing.

Given the definition of IPV in Table 4.1, there appears to be a disconnect between the legal definitions reviewed earlier and those used for UnitedStates public health surveillance by the CDC. This causes further inaccuracies to arise when collecting incidence and prevalence data regarding IPV. As shown later, accurate "base rates" (and

Table 4.1   Definition of IPV

Type of IPV	Definition
Physical Injury Physical Violence	The intentional use of physical force with the potential for causing death, disability, injury, or harm; includes but is not limited to scratching; pushing; shoving; throwing; grabbing; biting; choking; shaking; slapping; punching; burning; use of a weapon; and use of restraints or one's body, size, or strength against another person.
Sexual Violence	Is divided into three categories: 1. Use of physical force to compel a person to engage in a sexual act against his or her will, whether or not the act is completed 2. Attempted or completed sex act involving a person who is unable to understand the nature or condition of the act, to decline participation, or to communicate unwillingness to engage in the sexual act (e.g., because of illness, disability, or the influence of alcohol or other drugs, or because of intimidation or pressure) 3. Abusive sexual contact

Emotional Injury
  Threats of Physical/
  Sexual Violence
	The use of words, gestures, or weapons to communicate the intent to cause death, disability, injury, or physical harm.

Psychological/Emotional Violence	Involves trauma to the victim caused by violent physical/sexual acts, threats of violent acts, or coercive tactics and can include but is not limited to humiliating the victim, controlling what the victim can and cannot do, withholding information from the victim, deliberately doing something to make the victim feel diminished or embarrassed, isolating the victim from friends and family, and denying the victim access to money or other basic resources (it is also considered psychological/emotional violence when there has been prior physical/sexual violence or prior threat of such). *Stalking* generally refers to repeated harassing or threatening behavior, such as following a person, appearing at a person's home or place of business, making harassing phone calls, leaving written messages or objects, or vandalizing a person's property, etc.

Adapted from Saltzman (2000a, 2000b); Saltzman, Fanslow, McMahon, and Shelley (2002); and Tjaden and Thoennes (2000a).

by implication, risk factors) within the population are difficult to come by for use in clinical work, because determining rates and risk factors depend on a variety of measurement issues. Nevertheless, known risk factors are reviewed in the following section.

RISK FACTORS FOR IPV IN THE UNITED STATES

Homicides

Gender Homicides are the easiest form of IPV phenomena to track because they are the most discrete and verifiable of violent acts (note that correct classification of an IPV-related homicide continues to be somewhat problematic because it requires a thorough

and accurate investigation by law enforcement (e.g., O'Dell, 2009; Saltzman et al., 2002). Since data on IPV-related murders have been tracked within the United States, large-scale public health surveillance programs have shown a sharp decrease in the number of males killed by females, whereas the number of females killed by males has not displayed the same decline. For instance, Paulozzi, Saltzman, Thompson, and Holmgren (2001) found that homicides between 1981 and 1998 had declined overall by about 47%; however, this decline was the result of a 68% reduction in male homicide victims, whereas the proportion of female victims remained roughly the same. Similarly, Fox and Zawitz (2003) found that the overall downward trend in the number of homicides had continued since 1998, but that this reduction was mainly the result of a decreased number of males being killed by their partners, whereas women were killed by their partners at the same rate as seen approximately 30 to 40 years ago. Fox and Zawitz (2003) also found that the number of IPV-related homicides dramatically declined for all racial groups, with the exception of White women being killed at the hands of their male partners. Thus, the perpetration of IPV-related homicides is an overwhelmingly *male* phenomenon, while the victims are predominantly *female*.

Age   In terms of age, women of all ethnicities aged 35 to 49 are victims of IPV homicide at greater rates than any other age group, according to the National Crime Victimization Survey; in contrast, those aged 12 to 15 and 50 or older (youngest and oldest) have the lowest rates of IPV homicide victimization (Rennison, 2001, 2002; Rennison & Rand, 2003). This pattern can be explained as reflecting standard relationship patterns within the United States; that is, women aged 35 to 49 are the most likely to have been married and then separated and/or divorced; thus, separation and/or divorce increases the risk of IPV homicide victimization quite dramatically.

Race/Ethnicity   Because Whites presently constitute the single largest demographic group in the United States, perhaps it is not surprising that they also constitute the largest number of those killed in IPV-related homicides. On the other hand, when we examine the *proportion* of those killed in IPV-related homicides by demographic group, another picture emerges. Per capita, women of color (African American, Hispanic, Native American, Pacific Islander, etc.) are

proportionately more likely than Whites to be killed by their partners (e.g., Azziz-Baumgartner, McKeown, Melvin, Dang, & Reed, 2011). However, race/ethnicity seems to be a poor stand-alone risk factor, because when these data are adjusted for socioeconomic status (SES), these findings no longer hold (e.g., Fox & Zawitz, 2003; Rennison, 2001, 2002). That is, once adjusted for SES, women of color are no more likely than White women to be killed by an intimate partner; instead, *women of color are more likely to be located in lower SES strata and thus overall more likely than White women to be homicide victims of IPV*.

Nonlethal Physical and Sexual Assault

Gender   It has been known for some time that girls and boys suffer from simple and aggravated assaults at approximately the same rates across multiple environments (home, community, school, etc.); however, as girls approach the age of 18, the risk of both sexual and physical assault combined, increases until it dramatically passes that of boys (Finkelhor & Asdigian, 1996; Finkelhor, Ormrod, Turner, & Hamby, 2005). This is due to the greater risk of sexual assault victimization for females of all ages. Females are almost always the victims of sexual assault, whereas males are almost always the perpetrators, regardless of the victim's age (McCloskey & Raphael, 2005; Snyder, 2000; Snyder & Sickmund, 1999; U.S. Department of Justice, 2000). Furthermore, as noted by McCloskey (2009):

> Similar to rape statistics . . . regardless of whether the victim was a female or male, perpetrators of non-lethal physical violence are overwhelmingly male. . . . Furthermore, compared to men, women are

overwhelmingly victimized within the home. (p. 13)

In large population samples, the prevalence rates for female IPV physical and sexual victimization at the hands of males range from about 1.3% to 12%, while estimates derived from clinical populations range from a whopping 36% to 58% [see Jose & O'Leary (2009) for a review of these data]. Thus, depending on the methods used to collect information about IPV, general population rates look much different than the higher clinical rates. This is especially important for clinicians to understand, as noted in more detail as follows.

Age   Age is also a large covariate. According to the National Crime Victimization Survey, younger women of all ethnicities tend to have higher population rates of nonlethal IPV in comparison to older women, with the highest rates occurring for those aged 16 to 24 (Rennison, 2001). Rennison (2001) also noted that "women experienced [IPV] at rates that were about equal among different ethnic or racial groups. . . . Only among women age 20–24 did blacks experience more [IPV] than whites" (p. 1).

In a study of high school students within the United States who answered the single question, "Did your boyfriend or girlfriend ever hit, slap, or physically hurt you on purpose?," Black, Noonan, Legg, Eaton, and Breiding (2003) found that:

8.9% of students (8.9% of males and 8.8% of females) reported [IPV] victimization during the preceding 12 months and that students reporting victimization were more likely to engage in four out of five risky behaviors (i.e., sexual intercourse,

attempted suicide, episodic heavy drinking, and physical fighting). (p. 532)

Thus, it seems as if teen dating violence does *not* show the same gender pattern as IPV in adults, and instead appears to be roughly equal in both perpetration and victimization rates.

However, when sexual assault is added to the equation, this pattern changes quite dramatically. Females in this age group are once again the most likely victims of both physical and sexual assault within intimate relationships. As Raghavan, Bogart, Elliot, Vestal, and Schuster (2004) demonstrated, adolescent females are sexually assaulted in very high numbers during their high school dating years, and this pattern continues into college-age years. Fisher, Cullen, and Turner (2000) have also found that young adult women on college campuses are actually at higher risk for rape victimization than are women in the general population. Therefore, the single largest risk factor for teen/early-adult IPV victimization is being female, while other bidirectional factors include substance abuse, early sexual activity, and a greater number of sexual partners (Black et al., 2003; Fisher et al., 2000; Raghavan et al., 2004).

As noted earlier, women of all ethnicities between the ages of 16 and 49 are at highest risk for IPV assaults and homicide (Rennison, 2001, 2002, 2003). However, victimization rates for those 50 and older have held steady over the years, despite declines seen among other age groups, which continues to pose a serious health problem for women as they age. As shown later, women 50 and older must also contend with increased risk for other types of domestic abuse, most notably abuse by nonintimate relatives.

According to Klein, Tobin, Salomon, and Dubois (2008), while women 50 to 59 years old are at risk of being physically and sexually abused by a current or former intimate partner, they were also at risk of being abused by relatives. For women aged 60 years or older, their risk for overall abuse was even higher. While the risk of IPV remained virtually the same as for those in the 50- to 59-year-old range, the risk of being abused by a nonintimate relative sky rocketed for those aged 60 or older, accounting for the overall increase in risk. Nevertheless, the risk of IPV victimization for women remained high regardless of age. This has implications for health providers in that screening for IPV (as well as violence perpetrated from relatives) should be routine practice regardless of age; service providers may need to overcome the conventional wisdom that victimization decreases with age in order to conduct adequate screenings.

Race/Ethnicity   In regards to IPV and ethnicity, results depend on the data collection method used. Similar to homicide rates, many authors have found that nonlethal IPV for people of color (African American, Hispanic, Native American, Pacific Islander, etc.) is more common than for Whites (e.g., Ho, 2000; Thompson et al., 2006; Tjaden & Thoennes, 2000a, 2000b). However, once again, methodological issues often determine whether such patterns are found. For example, McCloskey, Sitaker, Grigsby, and Malloy (2006) examined the differences in the racial composition of groups that accessed various IPV-related community resources and found that African Americans were overrepresented in police calls but underrepresented in both court-ordered referrals to a batterers' treatment program

and self-referred visits to a victims' advocacy center. Thus, it is difficult to determine the actual rates of IPV among different racial or ethnic groups. With the exception of gender and age, all other demographic categories are suspect in terms of IPV rates because they co-vary so strongly with poverty (see later section). As noted by Saltzman and Houry (2009): "The true incidence and prevalence rates of IPV are still not clear" (p. 27). However, vulnerable populations in general are more likely to suffer from overall intimate, domestic, and community violence in all their forms.

Other Vulnerable Populations

People Living in Poverty   Poverty as a strong risk factor for IPV has a long and storied history, often fraught with controversy (e.g., Humphreys, 2007). However, it has become clear over time that the same structural and political inequalities found in poverty-stricken areas intersect with ethnic risk factors for victimization of all kinds. For example, when SES is controlled, high rates of IPV victimization among women with ethnic minority status tend to disappear (Humphreys, 2007). Nevertheless, the intersectionality of oppressive forces based on gender, ethnicity, and poverty can lock many women into situations where escape routes from violent situations are cut off, social safety nets are either nonexistent or spotty at best, and access to healthcare is negligible (Brush, 2001; Cole, 2001; Davis, 2009; Hirsch, 2001; Humphreys, 2007). Women's low wage status, primary responsibility for childcare and safety, lack of healthcare, and high rates of IPV victimization in all its forms can interact to create a hopeless situation; furthermore, recent reductions in welfare rolls, Aid to Dependent Children, and other TANF-based social safety nets within the United States have left many battered women with few resources to secure the assistance they need (Cole, 2001; Davis, 2009; Hirsch, 2001).

In addition to the challenges that IPV imposes, healthcare providers should also understand the many other structural and political barriers to safety and healing that poverty-stricken women face every day; such barriers include lack of insurance, inability to pay for medical visits and/or medications, lack of access to affordable/reliable transportation, lack of appropriate nutritional foodstuffs, homelessness, racial/ethnic biases, and a multitude of other hurdles within the environment (Brush, 2001).

Lesbian and Transgender Women
Women who identify as lesbian or transgender are especially vulnerable as a result of social stigma, structural barriers in the environment, and discriminatory practices by others. Women who are attracted to or in relationships with other women also violate social norms of compulsory heterosexuality. As Fontes and McCloskey (2011) state:

> Because lesbian girls and women are subjected to the double whammy of being both female and nonconforming in their sexual orientation, they are discriminated against severely, including being subject to peer and family rejection, harassment, job and housing discrimination, and physical assault, rape, and murder. It shouldn't be surprising, given the amount of societal discrimination and violence against lesbians, that many lesbians internalize the message that they are not normal and do not deserve basic human rights, or that they turn on each other in relationships. Intimate partner violence does occur in lesbian relationships . . . and similar to heterosexual battering, it cuts across class, race, and ethnic lines. (p. 160)

The exact risk for IPV within lesbian relationships is currently unknown. Ristock and Timbang (2005) state that while many researchers believe that IPV victimization among lesbian and transgender women are at rates similar to or higher than those who identify as heterosexual, they note the jury is still out. The lack of data is because there are virtually no nationally representative surveys available to determine actual prevalence/incidence rates within this population, with only one exception—the National Violence Against Women Survey (NVAWS; Tjaden & Thoennes, 2000a, 2000b). Results from the NVAWS showed that women living with women reported less IPV than those living with men. About 25% of women living with men reported being physically assaulted and/or raped by their male partners, while only 11% of women living with women reported such assaults; conversely, about 15% of males living with men reported being physically and/or sexually assaulted compared to 8% of males living with women (Tjaden & Thoennes, 2000a). Based on these findings, living with a male, regardless of sexual orientation, presented the highest risk for IPV victimization.

Furthermore, even less is known about the rates of violence among transgender women. Using data obtained from 14 regions throughout the United States, the National Coalition of Anti-Violence Programs (NCAVP, 2008) reported that transgender women constituted 3% of all sexual/gender minority IPV victimization contacts made to antiviolence programs nationwide. However, data from the NCAVP does not represent a national survey, and clearly fails to compare rates with those found for heterosexual individuals. Nevertheless, healthcare providers should learn to routinely screen for IPV when working with lesbians and transgender women and overcome biases and stereotypes about this vulnerable population.

People With Disabilities   Other vulnerable individuals are those who are perceived to be less physically or cognitively able to protect themselves from others, including those with disabilities (Cramer & Plummer, 2009). For example, Mitra, Mouradian, and Diamond (2011) found that individuals with a disability were at higher risk for all types of sexual victimization. Lifetime prevalence for sexual victimization was approximately 30% for women with disabilities versus 14% for those without, while prevalence for men with disabilities was about 17% versus 4.5% for those without, respectively. Similarly, Rand and Harrell (2009) found that females were more likely than males to be both physically and sexually abused by an intimate partner, regardless of disability status. Overall, the presence of a disability further increased the risk of IPV victimization for both women and men, although once again, women were at a higher risk than men regardless of their disability status. Clearly, healthcare providers must learn to routinely screen for IPV when working with this vulnerable population and overcome stereotypes and biases about relationships and sexuality when dealing with those who have disabilities.

Pregnant Women   Pregnancy can create an especially vulnerable situation for many women. Because women are most likely to

be victims of IPV, and only women can become pregnant, it should come as no surprise that: "[IPV] is as prevalent during pregnancy as other commonly screened-for complications such as gestational diabetes and preeclampsia . . . [and] femicide is a leading cause of maternal death" (Goodman, 2009, p. 253). Indeed, it is strongly suggested that all pregnant women should be routinely screened for IPV, because the negative pre- and postpartum outcomes for both mother and fetus can be extremely severe (Campbell, Woods, Chouaf, & Parker, 2000; Chambliss, 2008; Chu, Goodwin, & D'Angelo, 2010; Goodman, 2009; Huth-Bocks, Levendosky, & Bogat, 2002). Negative outcomes for pregnant women related to IPV victimization include a higher likelihood of the following: (a) premature labor, (b) miscarriage, (c) later identification of pregnancy and entrance into prenatal care, (d) maternal substance abuse, (e) undiagnosed/untreated sexually transmitted diseases (STDs), (f) postpartum depression, (g) increased physical trauma (the abdomen is especially targeted), (h) increased sexual trauma, and (i) femicide (Chambliss, 2008; Chu et al., 2010; Huth-Bocks et al., 2002).

During delivery, Goodman (2009) also notes that IPV victimization for pregnant women is related to a higher than normal risk for "premature rupture of membranes, placental abruption [and] acute maternal distress" (p. 255). Furthermore, IPV victimization also negatively affects fetal health. For example, Huth-Bocks et al. (2002) and Goodman (2009) found that maternal IPV victimization was associated with intrauterine growth retardation, lower infant birth weight, premature birth, and substance use withdrawal syndromes in fetuses and newborns. Clearly, without routine IPV screening and appropriate interventions during pregnancy, the risk of negative outcomes for both mother and child can only increase.

Summary

From this short review, it seems clear that IPV victimization poses a serious health risk to women throughout the United States. Because of this, healthcare providers should be aware of the ubiquitous presence of negative physical and mental health sequelae related to IPV in women's lives. To this end, the next section reviews the known health-related outcomes of IPV victimization.

THE NEGATIVE HEALTH EFFECTS OF IPV VICTIMIZATION

Physical Effects

Direct Outcomes It has been known for some time that female victims of IPV suffer from multiple acute health problems as a direct result of physical/sexual assaults (Campbell, 2002; Campbell et al., 2000; Coker, Smith, Bethea, King, & McKeown, 2000; Coulthard & Warburton, 2007; Dutton et al., 2005, 2006; Gallant, Keita, & Royak-Shaler, 1997; Plichta, 2004; Sheridan & Nash, 2007; WHO, 2002, 2005). Table 4.2 summarizes both the acute and long-term direct effects.

According to Sheridan and Nash (2007), the most common form of physical injury resulting from IPV victimization is blunt force trauma to the head or neck after being struck by a hand or fist, followed by being kicked and/or hit with an inanimate object. Strangulation (compression of the neck structures by hand) was the second most common form of assault, resulting in anoxia, petechiae in the

eyes and face, and internal injury to the throat. Sheridan and Nash (2007) note, however, that signs of strangulation are rarely assessed within medical settings.

Besides injury to the face and neck, other common patterns include bruising and lacerations to the upper arms (holding, squeezing) and lower arms (defensive/blocking injuries). More severe forms of injury can also result from blunt force trauma to the abdomen, back, and head (e.g., concussion), as well as the use of weapons (knives, guns, etc.), which can result in internal organ compromise and threat of death (Campbell, 2002; Sheridan & Nash, 2007). However, such severe types of injury are more commonly seen in emergency room venues in comparison to regularly scheduled healthcare appointments with general practitioners, specialists, and/or dentists.

Indirect Outcomes Besides the direct acute and long-term effects of IPV injury, there are also indirect effects on physical health (Campbell, 2002; Campbell et al., 2000; Coker et al., 2000; Plitchta, 2004). As Campbell (2002) stated:

> Women who are abused are frequently treated within health-care systems, however, they generally do not present with obvious trauma, even in accident and emergency departments. . . . [IPV] has long-term negative health consequences for survivors, even after the abuse has ended. These effects can manifest as poor health status, poor quality of life, and high use of health services. Battering is a significant direct and indirect risk factor for various physical health problems. (p. 1331)

Table 4.2   Acute and Long-Term Direct Effects of IPV Physical/Sexual Assault

Acute Effects	Long-Term Effects

Life-threatening injury
    Disfigurement
    Permanent disability
    Dismemberment
    Death
	Cognitive compromise
	    Traumatic brain injury
	    Strangulation

Lacerations and bruises throughout the body
    Skin/nail trauma (blunt force, squeezing,
    burning, biting, hair pulling)
	Functional damage to internal organs
	    Cardiovascular
	    Gastrointestinal
	    Neurological
	    Gynecological (including infertility)

Internal injury to soft tissues
    Traumatic brain injury
    Eye/throat injuries
    Soft abdominal organ trauma
    Genital trauma
	Chronic pain
	    Headaches
	    Back/neck pain
	    Joint pain
	    Abdominal pain

Internal injury to bones (fracture/dislocation)
    Skull
    Facial/jaw/teeth
    Neck/shoulder
    Arms/hands
    Spinal injury/pelvis
    Hips/legs/feet
	Overall suppression of immune/hormonal system due to chronic stress, leading to multiple disease processes:
	    Hypertension
	    Heart disease
	    Diabetes
	    Other systemic diagnoses

Complications to or loss of pregnancy as a result of trauma
    Miscarriage or induced abortion
    Fetal insult/damage
	Sexually transmitted diseases
	    HIV/AIDs
	    Gonorrhea/syphilis
	    Chlamydia, genital warts, etc.

Adapted from Campbell (2002), Campbell et al. (2000), Coker et al. (2000), Coulthard and Warburton (2007), Plichta (2004), Sheridan and Nash (2007), WHO (2002, 2005).

As shown in Table 4.3, the indirect effects of IPV victimization negatively impact women's health in a wide range of areas; such outcomes range from higher rates of cardiovascular disease to higher rates of immune system disorders. Many people believe that these negative effects are a result of both repeated physical and sexual injury and ongoing psychological and emotional distress, leading to an overall loss of bodily integrity and health over time (Campbell, 2002; Coker et al., 2000).

Psychological Effects

Direct Outcomes   It has also been known for some time that female victims of IPV suffer from multiple acute mental health problems as a direct result of physical and sexual assaults (Campbell, 2002; Dutton et al., 2005, 2006; Pico-Alfonso et al., 2006; WHO, 2002, 2005; see Table 4.4). However, even the threat of physical or sexual violence, as well as the presence of psychological and emotional abuse, can have devastating and immediate

Table 4.3   Chronic Health Issues Indirectly Associated With IPV Victimization

Higher Use of Healthcare Services	Higher Rates of Disability
Outpatient services	Partial disability
Inpatient/hospital services	Full disability
Emergency services	Permanent disfigurement
Diagnostic testing services	
Prescription use	
Higher Rates of Cardiovascular Disease	Higher Rates of Gastrointestinal Problems
Hypertension	Constipation/diarrhea
Heart disease/angina	Spastic colon/gastric reflux
Stroke	Nausea/loss of appetite
Arteriosclerosis/atherosclerosis	Binging/purging
Diabetes	Abdominal/stomach pain
	Ulcers
Higher Rates of Urogenital Problems	Higher Rates of Central Nervous System Disorders
Bladder/kidney infection	Cognitive compromise and memory loss
Problems with urination	Seizures and convulsions
Vaginal infection, itching, bleeding	Fainting/loss of consciousness
Sexually transmitted disease	Dizziness
Pelvic/genital pain	Vision/hearing loss
Painful intercourse/sexual dysfunction	Paralysis
Fibroids/hysterectomy	Left/right side weakness
Pregnancy complications/infertility	
Higher Rates of Immune System Disorders	Higher Rates of Chronic Pain Syndromes
Arthritis	Headaches (including migraines)
Influenza or colds	Temporomandibular joint disorder (TMJ)
Other systemic disorders	Fibromyalgia
	Neck/back pain
	Joint pain

Adapted from Campbell (2002), Campbell et al. (2000), Coker et al. (2000), and Plichta (2004).

mental health consequences (Pico-Alfonso, 2005). In addition, considerable evidence suggests that mental health problems increase with the amount (frequency, intensity, and duration) of physical, sexual, and psychological victimization; that is, there appears to be a "dose effect" for IPV and the severity of mental health outcomes (Campbell, 2002; Graham-Bermann, Sularz, & Howell, 2010; Pico-Alfonso et al., 2006; WHO, 2005).

For example, the World Health Organization (WHO, 2005), in a report of the results from a multicountry study that examined the effects of IPV on women, found that the risk of suicidal ideation, attempts, and completed suicides rose steadily as women reported greater severity of IPV victimization, especially emotional and sexual abuse. Similarly, Martinez-Torteya et al. (2009) reported that the severity of depressive and posttraumatic stress disorder (PTSD) symptoms were associated with women's increased stressfulness appraisals resulting from IPV victimization, and women who reported extremely high levels of IPV were more likely to have comorbid depression and PTSD symptoms.

Indirect Outcomes   It should not be surprising that the direct negative effects on mental health (shown in Table 4.4) can often result in certain mental health syndromes if IPV victimization, especially emotional

Table 4.4   Direct Mental Health Effects of IPV Physical/Sexual Assault

Fear
   Scanning of the environment for threats
   (hypervigilance)
   Paranoia
   Heightened startle response
   Sense of a foreshortened future
	Dissociation
	   Derealization
	   Depersonalization
	   Emotional numbing and/or constriction
	   Traumatic amnesia

Anxiety
   Restlessness/psychomotor agitation
   Apprehensive expectations
   Worry and negative predictions about the future
   Obsessive thought patterns
   Isolation and avoidance
	Depression
	   Helplessness/hopelessness/low self-efficacy
	   Worthlessness/guilt/shame
	   Feeling sad, empty, depressed, cries easily
	   Weight increase/decrease
	   Recurrent thoughts of death and/or suicide

Cognitive Deficits
   Cognitive slowing
   Memory loss/deficits
   Problems with concentration and attention
   Mind going "blank"
   Characterological changes
	Fatigue
	   Exhaustion
	   Diminished interest and/or pleasure in significant activities (work,
	   play, sex, etc.)
	   Lowered quality of life caused by lack of energy

Intrusive Thoughts
   Recurrent distressing recollections
   Reexperiencing of the trauma (flashbacks and
   hallucinations)
	Rage
	   Heightened anger and/or outbursts
	   Heightened physiological response to threats
	   Irritability

Sleep Disturbances
   Nightmares/disturbing dreams
   Trouble falling and/or staying asleep
   Insomnia or hypersomnia
	Substance Use
	   Self-medication as coping mechanism
	   Increased alcohol use
	   Increased prescription/illegal drug use

Adapted from Blasco-Ros et al. (2010), Campbell (2002), Dutton et al. (2005, 2006), Kamo (2009), Karam, Salamoun, and El-Sabbagh (2009), Martinez-Torteya et al. (2009), Pico-Alfonso et al. (2006), WHO (2002, 2005).

and/or sexual abuse, continues over time. In other words, the indirect mental health outcome for many victimized women is the development of full-blown chronic mental health diagnoses caused by ongoing IPV. The most common categories used to diagnose victimized women are (a) PTSD (including acute stress disorder and adjustment disorders), (b) depression/mood disorders (including bipolar disorder), (c) anxiety disorders (including agoraphobia and panic attacks), (d) personality disorders (including borderline, avoidant, histrionic, paranoid, dependent, and obsessive-compulsive disorders), (e) somatoform disorders, (f) substance use disorders, (g) dissociative and psychotic disorders, (h) sleep disorders, and (i) sexual dysfunction disorders. It should be noted, however, that for many abused women, negative mental health effects can and do abate over time once IPV victimization has ended (e.g., WHO, 2002, 2005).

Summary

Given the direct and indirect negative effects of IPV victimization on both the physical and mental health of women, it seems crucial that healthcare providers of all types should know how to assess every client for the presence of victimization. The context of IPV may be missed without routine screening and assessment within every healthcare milieu, possibly leading to misdiagnosis at best and harmful interventions at worst.

THE NEED FOR ROUTINE HEALTHCARE SCREENING

Some of the most commonly stated reasons for not conducting routine IPV screenings within the healthcare professions include (a) the belief that IPV is very rare in clinical settings, (b) the belief that even if IPV is present, it does not greatly impact treatment or outcomes, (c) a lack of knowledge about how to conduct screenings, and (d) a lack of confidence in handling IPV issues once they are identified, including possible mandatory reporting issues (Chang et al., 2011; Gutmanis, Beynon, Tutty, Wathen, & MacMillan, 2007; Roark, 2010; Spangaro, Poulos, & Zwi, 2011; Spangaro, Zwi, Poulos, & Man, 2010; Waalen, Goodwin, Spitz, Peterson, & Saltzman, 2000). As explained earlier, IPV victimization is extremely common for women presenting for medical and/or mental health services, and IPV clearly impacts physical and mental health in a negatively profound way. Nevertheless, all healthcare providers still need to be educated about this state of affairs in order to change prevailing belief structures (e.g., McCloskey & Grigsby, 2005).

Once attitudes and beliefs are brought in line with what we know scientifically, further attitude change is needed; that is, providers need to believe that screening is helpful, that it adds value to the clinical milieu, and that there are resources available to help those who are suffering from IPV victimization. The following sections review the available literature regarding these topics.

Resistance to IPV Screening

There is some debate about whether routine IPV screening should be completed by healthcare providers to either increase correct differential diagnosis (taking the context of IPV etiology into consideration) or to decrease IPV victimization itself (e.g., Koziol-McLain et al., 2010). This debate can also add to provider confusion as to the overall point of the screening. It appears that the answer is both: that is, screening should be done to aid in correct diagnosis *and* to decrease the negative impact of IPV, not one or the other.

However, there is also some concern that IPV screening and subsequent disclosure to a healthcare professional can be "associated with short-term harm . . . including reprisal violence [by the abuser], psychological distress, family disruption, and risk of a child being removed from a mother's care following child protective services involvement [due to IPV in the home]" (MacMillan et al., 2009, p. 499). Disclosure of IPV to a healthcare professional prompts the need to assess for safety issues and also raises the concern of possible mandatory reporting requirements. Well-controlled studies that have examined negative outcomes for women as a result of IPV screening have shown no harm to date (e.g., MacMillan et al., 2009). Nevertheless, the United States Preventative Services Task Force (2004) has cautioned that there is insufficient evidence to recommend for or against routine screening, even though many professional medical societies have provided guidelines for such screening (American Medical Association, American Nursing Association, The American College of Obstetricians and Gynecologists, etc.). It appears that studies examining the outcomes of routine IPV screening, while showing no harm to women as a result, also fail to show reductions in IPV victimization.

This should come as no surprise. At the very least, knowing that IPV victimization is occurring in a woman's life can only help in fine-tuning medical etiology, diagnosis, intervention, and prognosis; at best, it also gives an opportunity for providers to educate their clientele on community resources and perhaps referrals to IPV specialists that can help reduce the violence in their lives, but it does not *require* victimized women to access such resources.

For medical professionals, one of the first things any provider must do is determine what IPV assistance can be given within practice and time constraints once its presence is known. First, standard IPV safety assessments (including lethality evaluations) should be obtained and used subsequent to a positive IPV screen, and relevant local and/or state mandatory reporting requirements must be followed (and limits of confidentiality conveyed to all women during IPV screening). Second, the immediate availability of IPV-targeted referrals varies widely, from in-house counseling and case-management services to outside referral agencies; therefore, the parameters of these extra-medical services must be understood thoroughly by medical providers prior to implementing screening practices (see following discussion).

Once all of these pieces are in place, IPV screening can be as simple as initiating discussions about the topic within routine practice arenas [although see Rabin, Jennings, Campbell, & Bair-Merritt (2009) and/or Basile, Hertz, & Back (2007) for a review of validated IPV screening tools]. Gutmanis et al. (2007) surveyed physicians and nurses in Canada and found that about 32% of

nurses and 42% of physicians reported routinely initiating discussions of IPV in their practices. They also found that those physicians most likely to initiate IPV discussions were either working in emergency departments or were relatively new to the profession. This suggests that physicians in an emergency room (ER) may see more IPV-related injury and thus be sensitized to the topic, and that those who are newly trained may have had more access to IPV screening and intervention education during their training histories.

A nursing training program was instituted at a hospital in the rural American South in order to educate nurses about IPV seriousness and prevalence within their caseloads (Roark, 2010). Nurses also participated in training that taught them to include a one-sentence IPV screening question in the admissions intake folder, and then how to make appropriate community referrals when needed. While including a one-sentence IPV screening question during intake did not increase the number of patient disclosures at pre- versus post-training, the quality of appropriate IPV outside referrals (as well as follow-through) did increase for nurses receiving this training.

Another effort to train nurses appeared to be more problematic. Nursing staff in the public health department of a large university located in the American Midwest were provided training programs on two different days (Davila, 2006). For those nurses who reported their own history of IPV victimization, 8 of the 11 (73%) failed to show for the second training program. Davila (2006) suggested that the high no-show rate for the second program was a major reason that there were no differences between IPV knowledge and screening ability pre- and post-tests. She highlighted the fact that any

IPV training program must take into account each provider's own IPV history in order to be effective, especially since nurses as a group are overwhelmingly female and therefore at higher risk for their own IPV victimization.

In Australia, a screening policy was instituted statewide in antenatal, mental health, and substance abuse services; however, even after the policy was instituted, actual screening rates among healthcare providers was only in the range of 62% to 75% (Spangaro et al., 2011). Nevertheless, providers reported that familiarity with the procedure and women's favorable reactions helped reinforce the practice. Furthermore, cards were printed that were given to all women during the screening that included contact numbers for IPV service providers and other IPV-related referrals. The actual Australian screening, modeled on the Abuse Assessment Screen form, was very straightforward (Spangaro et al., 2011, p. 131):

EXPLAIN:

- In this health service, we ask all women the same questions about violence in the home.
- This is because violence in the home is very common and can be serious, and we want to improve our response to women experiencing domestic violence.
- You don't have to answer the questions if you don't want to.
- What you say will remain confidential to the health service except when you give us information that indicates there are serious safety concerns for you or your children.

ASK:

- Within the last year, have you been hit, slapped, or hurt in other ways by your partner or ex-partner? ___Yes ___No
- Are you frightened of your partner or ex-partner? ___Yes ___No

If the woman answers "NO" to both questions, give the information card to her and say, "Here is information that we give to all women about domestic violence."

If the woman answers "YES" to either or both questions, continue.

- Are you safe to go home when you leave here? ___Yes ___No
- Would you like some assistance with this? ___Yes ___No

In addition to physicians and nurses, dental care providers should also know how to screen for IPV victimization. As noted earlier, women's faces are common targets for blunt force trauma during IPV assaults. Such assaults can result in broken or dislocated teeth, injury to the hard palate, jaw, or other facial bones, and injury to the soft tissues of the mouth and throat (Coulthard & Warburton, 2007). Thus, it is vital for dental care providers to universally screen for IPV victimization, understanding that "the purpose of identification of domestic violence is referral on to the appropriate agency and so this process must be considered prior to starting screening" (Coulthard & Warburton, 2007, p. 637).

Clearly, dentists, nurses, primary care physicians, physician specialists (especially obstetric/gynecology), and other medically related personnel should know (a) how to screen for the presence of IPV victimization within women's lives, (b) mandatory reporting requirements and limits of confidentiality, (c) how to conduct safety evaluations, and (d) how to appropriately refer to local resources. However, healthcare providers (including mental health specialists) must first overcome preconceived notions that may block their adoption of routine screening practices.

Overcoming Attitudinal Barriers to IPV Screening

Spangaro et al. (2011) and Gutmanis et al. (2007) identified common attitudinal barriers reported by healthcare providers that included (a) unpreparedness and lack of confidence about IPV issues, (b) fear of offending patients and other negative consequences for women (e.g., breaking of confidentiality, mandatory reporting), (c) lack of practitioner comfort following disclosure and lack of knowledge about what to do, and (d) lack of ability to make IPV stop (patients remained in abusive relationships). Besides attitudinal barriers, providers also reported concrete environmental barriers within the healthcare milieu that included (a) presence of the abuser (e.g., accompanying victim to medical appointments), (b) lack of time and other practice pressures to adequately complete an IPV screen, (c) lack of appropriate IPV training resources (e.g., safety/planning and lethality evaluations), and (d) lack of contact with or knowledge about appropriate IPV referral resources within the community.

On the other hand, Spangaro et al. (2011) and Gutmanis et al. (2007) also identified factors that increased the propensity to conduct universal and routine IPV screenings: (a) preparedness and appropriate training, (b) availability of straightforward scripted screening language, (c) availability

of referral materials/contact information, and (d) experience with the screening process. According to Spangaro et al. (2011), this latter factor seemed especially important; healthcare providers reported that they crossed from "prying to inquiring" (p. 135) without being judgmental of those women who stayed within IPV relationships, were able to simply "open the door" (p. 134) to the topic by using scripted screening questions that did not take up large amounts of time, found that "all I had to do was ask" (p. 135) in order to gain access to and build relationships with outside referral resources, and that with continued use of the screening tools and referral materials, providers became more comfortable with the process and received positive feedback from the women they served. Spangaro et al. (2011) also found that:

> A related experience for health workers was the phenomenon of disclosures that surprised them from *the well-groomed professional mother(s)*. [Italics original.] This was a tangible lesson for health workers about the extent of IPV and the risk of making assumptions about which women experience abuse. Disclosures at a subsequent visit following initial denial were also common. (p. 136)

Thus, while there are certainly attitudinal and practice barriers to overcome in order to institute routine universal IPV screening, healthcare providers and patients alike would nevertheless reap the benefits of such screening when implemented.

Psychologists, counselors, social workers, family therapists, case managers, and other mental health workers may face a unique situation when screening for IPV. Similar to other healthcare providers, there is some confusion about whether routine IPV screening should be specifically targeted by mental health providers to either increase correct differential diagnosis (taking the context of IPV into consideration) or decrease IPV victimization. However, a crucial difference between medical and mental health providers is that medical providers are trained to treat only the physical sequelae resulting from IPV victimization, and decreasing IPV victimization is therefore outside of their competency area (with the notable exception of psychiatrists). Conversely, mental health providers by definition are trained to treat psychological, emotional, and behavioral problems, whether or not they are exacerbated by or result from trauma.

Similar to medical professionals, however, competency levels in dealing with the sequelae of IPV, including screening, safety planning, or attempts at reducing IPV victimization, vary widely throughout the mental health arena (see later discussion). This is unfortunate, because IPV victimization is also highly prevalent within mental health populations; similar to medical providers, mental health specialists can only benefit from knowing whether IPV victimization is occurring in a woman's life. Such knowledge is beneficial because mental health etiology, diagnosis, intervention, and prognosis are also directly and indirectly affected by trauma. Furthermore, mental health providers may have more time to help educate their clientele about the presence of other community resources, most notably advocacy centers, housing, legal aid, and other justice system resources.

Although many mental health professional organizations require some level of competency with IPV issues (e.g., American Psychological Association, American Counseling Association, etc.), not all mental health providers have received training or have experience with IPV screening. For example, Chang et al. (2011) found that many clients (63% of women and 32% of men) within a sample obtained from emergency, inpatient, and outpatient psychiatric settings reported IPV victimization, whereas only 44% reported that mental health providers had asked them about IPV.

Dudley, McCloskey, and Kustron (2008) also found that, overall, therapists are not effective in identifying critical IPV issues within clinical presentations. A vignette was given to respondents where a heterosexual couple had come for therapy because of violent behavior and drinking on the husband's part, and suspicions by the husband that the wife was having an affair. The wife was also considering leaving the relationship. Although 78% of the entire sample of psychologists, social workers, marriage and family therapists, and other mental health workers identified violent conflict as the primary presenting problem, 43% said the source of the conflict was couple dynamics, and only one respondent was concerned about lethality issues. None predicted lethal violence, and only one predicted an increase in violence as possible outcomes. When comparing these results to a similar study completed decades earlier, Dudley et al. (2008) noted an increase in the ability of mental health providers to identify violence within relationships, but also noted poor improvement in their ability to assess lethality, as well as to identify risk-reducing interventions.

As McCloskey and Grigsby (2005) have noted, mental health providers can only benefit from receiving educational materials about the effects of IPV on mental health, as well as obtaining suggested screening approaches and initial safety planning techniques. For example, these authors provide a very clear, step-by-step procedure to screen individuals and couples who present for therapy. They also provide procedures relevant to history taking, primary batterer and victim assessment, and lethality evaluations for use after determining that IPV is present, as well as templates for safety planning. Even though such information is available, many mental health providers are not trained in utilizing such materials.

Whether seeing individuals, couples, or families (McCloskey & Grigsby, 2005; Stith & McCollumn, 2009; Stith, McCollum, & Rosen, 2011), or providing case management services within inpatient or outpatient mental health settings (e.g., Renner, 2011), mental health professionals need to know how to conduct appropriate IPV screenings with every client, as well as the necessary steps to take if the screening is positive (Conner, Nouer, Mackey, Tipton, & Lloyd, 2011).

FUTURE DIRECTIONS

It seems clear that given the information presented above, simply asking about IPV in women's lives is itself an intervention. Asking about IPV conveys that the topic is important, that the healthcare provider is aware that IPV can have negative health outcomes, and that the woman has a safe place where disclosure may take place (e.g., McCloskey & Fraser, 1998). If this is so, then IPV screenings should include certain domains that healthcare providers should cover. Conner et al. (2011) developed the Physician Readiness to Manage Intimate Partner Violence Survey (PREMIS) based on such domains, including (a) legal

requirements/processes (e.g., mandatory reporting), (b) preparation and IPV-related skills, (c) willingness to universally screen, (d) provider self-efficacy relative to IPV screening processes, (e) belief in and support for victim autonomy, and (f) understanding the victim's worldview (e.g., understanding all the reasons why a victim may not leave an abusive relationship or does not follow through with other staff recommendations; see especially Rhatigan, Shorey, & Nathanson [2011] for factors that influence leaving an abusive relationship). If these competency domains are embraced by providers, then the treatment of immediate physical injury and ensuring safety during a crisis situation may become more effective.

Currently, healthcare providers should know about the plethora of services available for women dealing with IPV victimization, from medical and mental health treatment for immediate IPV sequelae to the availability of community resources that include IPV hotlines (24-hour telephone crisis intervention), local advocacy centers (social services redress including aid and housing), emergency shelters, specialized IPV legal resources (protection orders, police, arrest, prosecution), and other multidisciplinary approaches that may include coordinated community responses to IPV perpetrators designed to hold batterers accountable for their abuse (Heyman, Slep, & Nelson, 2011; McCloskey & Grigsby, 2005; Tiefenthaler, Farmer, & Sambria, 2005; Vaddiparti & Varma, 2009).

In addition, healthcare providers should also understand that the field of IPV as both a science and practice competency is constantly evolving, and continuing IPV education should be part of every provider's professional development. For example, the overall field of gender-sensitive healthcare for women continues to expand (e.g., Rondon, 2009), and the knowledge base concerning the unique effects of IPV victimization on minority populations, such as African American women (Lilly & Graham-Bermann, 2009; Rose, House, & Stepleman, 2010; Wright, Perez, & Johnson, 2010), recent immigrant populations such as Mexican Americans (Galvez, Mankowski, McGlade, Ruiz, & Glass, 2011), Chinese Americans (Wong, Tiwari, Fong, Humphreys, & Bullock, 2011), sexual minorities (Klosterman, Kelley, Milletich, & Mignone, 2011), and other vulnerable populations such as those on welfare (Tolman & Rosen, 2001) also continues to expand. Clearly, effective healthcare provision is now understood to be predicated on gender and multicultural competency (e.g., Bernal, 2006).

Fortunately, prevention efforts also continue to expand, and community-based interventions that reflect primary prevention have proliferated (Cismaru, Jensen, & Lavack, 2010; Foshe, Reyes, & Wycokk, 2009; Stith, 2006). Although the success of programs that target victims has been known for some time, programs that target perpetrators have had less success, and the need to validate programs that effectively prevent IPV is ongoing (Feder et al., 2011; Murphy, Meis, & Eckhardt, 2009; Stith, 2006). Clearly, healthcare providers will continue to routinely treat women who are suffering from IPV victimization in large numbers until our primary prevention efforts become much more effective. In the meantime, IPV will loom large within the healthcare practice arena.

REFERENCES

Azziz-Baumgartner, E., McKeown, L., Melvin, P., Dang, Q., & Reed, J. (2011). Rates of femicide in women of different races, ethnicities, and places of birth: Massachusetts, 1993–2007. *Journal of Interpersonal Violence, 26*(5), 1077–1090.

Basile, K. C., & Hall, J. E. (2011). Intimate partner violence perpetration by court-ordered men: Distinctions and intersections among physical violence, sexual violence, psychological abuse, and stalking. *Journal of Interpersonal Violence, 26*(2), 230–253.

Basile, K. C., Hertz, M. F., & Back, S. E. (2007) *Intimate partner violence and sexual violence victimization assessment instruments for use in healthcare settings.* Atlanta, GA: Centers for Disease Control and Prevention, National Center for Injury Prevention and Control. Retrieved from http://www.cdc.gov/NCIPC/pub-res/ipv_and_sv_screening.htm

Bernal, G. (2006). Intervention development and cultural adaption research with diverse families. *Family Process, 45*(2), 143–151.

Black, M. C., Noonan, R., Legg, M., Eaton, D., & Breiding, M. J. (2003). Physical dating violence among high school students—United States, 2003. *Mortality and Morbidity Weekly Report, 55*(19), 532–535.

Blasco-Ros, C., Sanchez-Lorente, S., & Martinez, M. (2010). Recovery from depressive symptoms, state anxiety and post-traumatic stress disorder in women exposed to physical and psychological, but not to psychological intimate partner violence alone: A longitudinal study. *BioMed Central Psychiatry, 10*(98). Retrieved from http://www.biomedcentral.com/1471-244X/10/98

Brush, L. D. (2001). Poverty, battering, race, and welfare reform: Black-White differences in women's welfare-to-work transitions. *Journal of Poverty, 5*(1), 67–90.

Campbell, J. (2002). Health consequences of intimate partner violence. *The Lancet, 359*, 1331–1336.

Campbell, J. C., Woods, A. B., Chouaf, K. L., & Parker, B. (2000). Reproductive health consequences of intimate partner violence: A nursing research review. *Clinical Nursing Research, 9*(3), 217–237. Available at: http://cnr.sagepub.com/cgi/content/abstract/9/3/217

Chambliss, L. R. (2008). Intimate partner violence and its implication for pregnancy. *Clinical Obstetrics & Gynecology, 51*(2), 385–397.

Chang, J., Cluss, P., Burke, J., Hawker, L., Dado, D., Goldstrohm, S., & Scholle, S. (2011). Partner violence screening in mental health. *General Hospital Psychiatry, 33*(1), 58–65.

Chu, S. Y., Goodwin, M. M., & D'Angelo, D. V. (2010). Physical violence against U.S. women around the time of pregnancy, 2004–2007. *American Journal of Preventative Medicine, 38*(3), 317–322.

Cismaru, M., Jensen, G., & Lavack, A. (2010). If the noise coming from next door were loud music, you'd do something about it: Using mass media campaigns encouraging bystander intervention to stop partner violence. *Journal of Advertising, 39*(4), 69–82.

Coker, A. L., Smith, P. H., Bethea, L., King, M. R., & McKeown, R. E. (2000). Physical health consequences of physical and psychological intimate partner violence. *Archives of Family Medicine, 9,* 451–457.

Cole, P. (2001). Impoverished women in violent partnerships: Designing services to fit their reality. *Violence Against Women, 7*(2), 222–233.

Conner, P. D., Nouer, S. S., Mackey, S. N., Tipton, N. G., & Lloyd, A. K. (2011). Psychometric properties of an intimate partner violence tool for health care students. *Journal of Interpersonal Violence, 26*(5), 1012–1035.

Coulthard, P., & Warburton, A. L. (2007). The role of the dental team in responding to domestic violence. *British Dental Journal, 203,* 645–648.

Cramer, E., & Plummer, S. (2009). People of color with disabilities: Intersectionality as a framework for analyzing intimate partner violence in social, historical, and political contexts. *Journal of Aggression, Maltreatment & Trauma, 18*(2), 162–181.

Davila, Y. (2006). Increasing nurses' knowledge and skills for enhanced response to intimate partner violence. *Journal of Continuing Education in Nursing, 37*(4), 171–177.

Davis, D.A. (2009). Non-violent survival strategies in the face of IPV and economic discrimination. In K. McCloskey & M. Sitaker (Eds.), *Backs against the wall: Battered women's resistance strategies* (pp. 113–142). New York, NY: Routledge.

DeKeseredy, W. (2000). Current controversies on defining nonlethal violence against women in intimate heterosexual relationships: Empirical implications. *Violence Against Women, 6,* 728–746.

Dudley, D. R., McCloskey, K., & Kustron, D. A. (2008). Therapist perceptions of intimate partner violence: A replication of Harway and Hansen's study after more than a decade. *Journal of Aggression, Maltreatment, & Trauma, 17*(1), 80–102.

Dutton, M. A., Green, B. L., Kaltman, S. I., Roesch, D. M., Zeffiro, T. A., & Krause, E. D. (2006). Intimate partner violence, PTSD, and adverse health outcomes. *Journal of Interpersonal Violence, 21*(7), 955–968.

Dutton, M. A., Kaltman, S., Goodman, L. A., Weinfurt, K., & Vankos, N. (2005). Patterns of intimate partner violence: Correlates and outcomes. *Violence & Victims, 20*(5), 483–497.

Feder, L., Niolon, P., Campbell, J., Wallinder, J., Nelson, R., & Larrouy, H. (2011). The need for experimental methodology in intimate partner violence: Finding programs that effectively prevent IPV. *Violence Against Women, 17*(3), 340–358.

Finkelhor, D., & Asdigian, N. L. (1996). Risk factors for youth victimization: Beyond a lifestyles/routine activities approach. *Violence & Victims, 11*(1), 3–19.

Finkelhor, D., Ormrod, R., Turner, H., & Hamby, S. L. (2005). The victimization of children and youth: A comprehensive national survey. *Child Maltreatment, 10*(1), 5–25.

Fisher, B. S., Cullen, F. T., & Turner, M. G. (2000). *The sexual victimization of college women* [NCJ-182369]. Washington, DC: U.S. Department of Justice, National Institute of Justice. Retrieved from https://www.ncjrs.gov/pdffiles1/nij/182369.pdf

Fontes, L., & McCloskey, K. (2011). A cultural perspective on violence against women. In C. Renzetti, J. L. Edelson, & R. K. Bergen (Eds.), *Sourcebook on violence against women* (2nd ed pp. 151–169). Thousand Oaks, CA: Sage.

Foshe, V. A., Reyes, H. L. M., & Wycokk, S. C. (2009). Approaches to preventing psychological, physical, and sexual partner abuse. In K. D. O'Leary & E. M. Woodin (Eds.), *Psychological and physical aggression in couples* (pp. 165–189). Washington, DC: American Psychological Association.

Fox, J. A., & Zawitz, M. W. (2003). *Homicide trends in the United States: 2000 update.* Washington, DC: U.S. Department of Justice, Bureau of Justice Statistics Crime Data Brief [NCJ-197471].

Gallant, S. J., Keita, G. P., & Royak-Shaler, R. (1997). *Health care for women: Psychological, social, and behavioral influences.* Washington, DC: American Psychological Association.

Galvez, G., Mankowski, E. S., McGlade, M. S., Ruiz, M. E., & Glass, N. (2011). Work-related intimate partner violence among employed immigrants from Mexico. *Psychology of Men & Masculinity*, *12*(3), 230–246.

Goodman, P. E. (2009). Intimate partner violence and pregnancy. In C. Mitchell & D. Anglin (Eds.), *Intimate partner violence: A health perspective* (pp. 253–263). New York, NY: Oxford University Press.

Graham-Bermann, S., Sularz, A., & Howell, K. (2010). Additional adverse events among women exposed to intimate partner violence: Frequency and impact. *Psychology of Violence*, *1*(2), 136–149.

Gutmanis, I., Beynon, C., Tutty, L., Wathen, C. N., & MacMillan, H. L. (2007). Factors influencing identification of and response to intimate partner violence: A survey of physicians and nurses. *BioMed Central Public Health*, *7*(12). doi:10. 1186/1471-2458-7-12.

Heyman, R. E., Slep, A. M. S., & Nelson, J. P. (2011). Empirically guided community interventions for partner abuse, child maltreatment, suicidality, and substance misuse. In S. M. Wadsworth & D. Riggs (Eds.), *Risk and resilience in U.S. military families* (pp. 85–107). New York, NY: Springer.

Hirsch, A. E. (2001). "The world was never a safe place for them": Abuse, welfare reform, and women with drug convictions. *Violence Against Women*, *7*(2), 159–175.

Ho, T. (2000). Domestic violence in a southern city: The effects of a mandatory arrest policy on male-versus-female aggravated assault incidents. *American Journal of Criminal Justice*, *25*, 107–118.

Humphreys, C. (2007) A health inequalities perspective on violence against women. *Health & Social Care in the Community*, *15*(2), 120–127.

Huth-Bocks, A. C., Levendosky, A. A., & Bogat, G. A. (2002). The effects of domestic violence during pregnancy on maternal and infant health. *Violence and Victims*, *17*(2), 169–185.

Jose, A., & O'Leary, K. D. (2009). Prevalence of partner aggression in representative and clinical samples. In K. D. O'Leary & E. M. Woodin (Eds.), *Psychological and physical aggression in couples: Causes and interventions* (pp. 15–35). Washington, DC: American Psychological Association.

Kamo, T. (2009). The adverse impact of psychological aggression, coercion, and violence in the intimate partner relationship on women's mental health. In P. S. Chandra et al. (Eds.), *Contemporary topics in women's mental health* (pp. 550–558). Hoboken, NJ: Wiley.

Karam, E. G., Salamoun, M. M., & El-Sabbagh, S. (2009). Psychiatric consequences of trauma in women. In P. S. Chandra et al. (Eds.), *Contemporary topics in women's mental health* (pp. 149–168). Hoboken, NJ: Wiley.

Klein, A., Tobin, T., Salomon, A., & Dubois, J. (2008). A statewide profile of abuse of older women and the criminal justice response [NCJ 222459]. Washington, DC: U.S. Department of Justice. Retrieved from https://www.ncjrs.gov/pdffiles1/nij/grants/222459.pdf

Klostermann, K., Kelley, M., Milletich, R., & Mignone, T. (2011). Alcoholism and partner aggression among gay and lesbian couples. *Aggression and Violent Behavior*, *16*(2), 115–119.

Koziol-McLain, J., Garrett, N., Fanslow, J., Hassall, I., Dobbs, T., Henare-Toka, T., & Lovell, V. (2010). A randomized controlled trial of a brief emergency department intimate partner violence screening intervention. *Annals of Emergency Medicine*, *56*(4), 413–423.

Lilly, M., & Graham-Bermann, S. (2009). Ethnicity and risk for symptoms of posttraumatic stress following intimate partner violence: Prevalence and predictors in European American and African American women. *Journal of Interpersonal Violence*, *24*(1), 3–19.

MacMillan, H. L., Wathen, C. N., Jamieson, E., Boyle, M. H., Shannon, H. S., Ford-Gilbe, M., . . . McMaster Violence Against Women Research Group. (2009). Screening for intimate partner violence in health care settings: A randomized trial. *JAMA*, *302*(5), 493–501.

Malloy, K., McCloskey, K., Grigsby, N., & Gardner, D. (2003). Women's use of violence within intimate relationships. *Journal of Aggression, Maltreatment, & Trauma*, *6*, 37–59.

Martinez-Torteya, C., Bogat, G.A., von Eye, A., Levendosky, A. A., & Davidson, W. S. (2009). Women's appraisals of intimate partner violence stressfulness and their relationship to depressive and PTSD symptoms. *Violence & Victims*, *24*(6), 707–722.

McCloskey, K. (2009). Are half of all IPV perpetrators women? Putting context back into the intimate partner violence research field. In K. McCloskey & M. Sitaker (Eds.), *Backs against the wall: Battered* women's resistance strategies (pp. 7–23). New York, NY: Routledge.

McCloskey, K. A., & Fraser, J. S. (1998). Using feminist MRI brief therapy during initial contact with victims of domestic violence. *Psychotherapy: Theory, Research, Practice, Training, 34*(4), 433–446.

McCloskey, K., & Grigsby, N. (2005). The ubiquitous clinical problem of intimate partner violence: The need for routine assessment. *Professional Psychology: Research and Practice, 36*(6), 264–275.

McCloskey, K., & Raphael, D. (2005). Adult perpetrator gender asymmetries in child sexual assault victim selection: Results from the 2000 National Incident-Reporting System. *Journal of Child Sexual Abuse, 14*(4), 1–24.

McCloskey, K., Sitaker, M., Grigsby, N., & Malloy, K. (2006). Over-representation of people of color as intimate partner violence perpetrators: The case for examining multiple points of contact. *Journal of Aggression, Maltreatment, & Trauma, 13*(1), 21–42.

Mitra, M., Mouradian, V. E., & Diamond, M. (2011). Sexual violence victimization against men with disabilities. *American Journal of Preventative Medicine, 41*(5), 494–497.

Murphy, C., Meis, L., Eckhardt, C. (2009). Individualized services and individual therapy for partner abuse perpetrators. In K. O'Leary, K. Daniel, & E. M. Woodin (Eds.), *Psychological and physical aggression in couples: Causes and interventions* (pp. 211–231). Washington, DC: American Psychological Association.

National Coalition of Anti-Violence Programs (NCAVP). (2008). *Lesbian, gay, bisexual, and transgender domestic violence in the United States, 2007.* New York, NY: Author.

Nicolaidis, C., & Paranjape, A. (2009). Defining intimate partner violence: Controversies and implications. In C. Mitchell & D. Anglin (Eds.), *Intimate partner violence: A health-based perspective* (pp. 19–29). New York, NY: Oxford University Press.

Norris, S. M., Huss, M. T., & Palarea, R. E. (2011). A pattern of violence: Analyzing the relationship between intimate partner violence and stalking. *Violence & Victims, 26*(1), 103–115.

O'Dell, A. (2009). Why do police arrest victims of domestic violence? The need for comprehensive training and investigative protocols. In K. McCloskey & M. Sitaker (Eds.), *Backs against the wall: Battered women's resistance strategies* (pp. 49–68). New York, NY: Routledge.

Paulozzi, L. J., Saltzman, L. E., Thompson, M. P., & Holmgren, P. (2001). Surveillance for homicide among intimate partners: United States 1981–1998. *Morbidity and Mortality Weekly Report, 50* (SS03) 1–16.

Pico-Alfonso, M. A. (2005). Psychological intimate partner violence: The major predictor of posttraumatic stress disorder in abused women. *Neuroscience & Biobehavioral Review, 29*(1), 181–193.

Pico-Alfonso, M. A., Garcia-Linares, M. I., Celda-Navarro, N., Blasco-Ros, C., Echeburúa, E., & Martinez, M. (2006). The impact of physical, psychological, and sexual intimate male partner violence on women's mental health: Depressive symptoms, posttraumatic stress disorder, state anxiety, and suicide. *Journal of Women's Health, 15*(5), 599–611.

Plichta, S. (2004). Intimate partner violence and physical health consequences: Policy and practice implications. *Journal of Interpersonal Violence, 19*(11), 1296–1323. Available at: http://jiv.sagepub.com/cgi/content/abstract/19/11/1296

Rabin, R. F., Jennings, J., M., Campbell, J. C., & Bair-Merritt, M. H. (2009). Intimate partner violence screening tools. *American Journal of Preventative Medicine, 36*(5), 439–445.

Raghavan, R., Bogart, L. M., Elliot, M. N., Vestal, K. D., & Schuster, M. A. (2004). Sexual victimization among a national probability sample of adolescent women. *Perspectives on Sexual and Reproductive Health, 36*(6), 225–232.

Rajan, M., & McCloskey, K. (2009). Victims of IPV: Arrest rates across recent studies. In K. McCloskey & M. Sitaker (Eds.), *Backs against the wall: Battered women's resistance strategies* (pp. 24–48). New York, NY: Routledge.

Rand, M. R., & Harrell, E. (2009). *Crime against people with disabilities, 2007* [NCJ 227814] Washington, DC: Bureau of Justice Statistics, U.S. Department of Justice.

Renner, L. (2011). "I'm wondering if I am completely missing that": Foster care case managers and supervisors report on their IPV training. *Children and Youth Services Review, 33*(2), 386–394.

Rennison, C. M. (2001). *Intimate partner violence and age of victim, 1993–1999.* Washington, DC: U.S. Department of Justice.

Rennison, C. M. (2002). *Rape and sexual assault: Reporting to police and medical attention, 1992–2000.* Washington, DC: U.S. Department of Justice, Bureau of Justice Statistics. Selected Findings [NCJ-194530].

Rennison, C. M. (2003). *Intimate partner violence, 1993–2001.* Washington, DC: U.S. Department of Justice, Bureau of Justice Statistics. Crime Data Brief [NCJ-197838].

Rennison, C. M., & Rand, M. R. (2003). *Criminal victimization, 2002.* Washington, DC: U.S. Department of Justice, Office of Justice Programs [NCJ-199994].

Rhatigan, D., Shorey, R., & Nathanson, A. (2011). The impact of posttraumatic symptoms on women's commitment to a hypothetical violent relationship: A path analytic test of post-traumatic stress, depression, shame, and self-efficacy on investment model factors. *Psychological Trauma: Theory, Research, Practice, & Policy, 3*(2), 181–191.

Ristock, J., & Timbang, N. (2005). *Relationship violence in lesbian/gay/bisexual/transgender/queer (LGBTQ) communities: Moving beyond a gender-based framework.* St. Paul: Minnesota Center Against Violence and Abuse. Retrieved from http://www.mincava.umn.edu/documents/lgbtqviolence/lgbtqviolence.html

Roark, S. (2010). Intimate partner violence: Screening and intervention in the health care setting. *The Journal of Continuing Education in Nursing, 41*(11), 490–495.

Rondon, M. B. (2009). Gender sensitive care for adult women. In P. S. Chandra et al. (Eds.), *Contemporary topics in women's mental health* (pp. 323–336). Hoboken, NJ: Wiley.

Rose, R., House, A., & Stepleman, L. (2010). Intimate partner violence and its effects on the health of African American HIV-positive women. *Psychological Trauma: Theory, Research, Practice, and Policy, 2*(4), 311–317.

Saltzman, L. E. (2000a). Building data systems for monitoring and responding to violence against women, part I. *Violence Against Women, 6*(7).

Saltzman, L. E. (2000b). Building data systems for monitoring and responding to violence against women, part II. *Violence Against Women, 6*(8).

Saltzman, L. E., Fanslow, J. L., McMahon, P. M., & Shelley, G.A. (2002). *Intimate partner violence surveillance: Uniform definitions and recommended data elements, Version 2.0.* Atlanta, GA: Centers for Disease Prevention and Control.

Saltzman, L. E., & Houry, D. (2009). Prevalence of nonfatal and fatal intimate partner violence in the United States. In C. Mitchell & D. Anglin (Eds.), *Intimate partner violence: A health-based perspective* (pp. 31–38). New York, NY: Oxford University Press.

Sheridan, D. J., & Nash, K. R. (2007). Acute injury patterns of domestic violence victims. *Trauma, Violence, & Abuse, 8*(3), 281–289.

Snyder, H. N. (2000). *Sexual assault of young children as reported to law enforcement: Victim, offender, and incident characteristics* (NCJ 182990) Washington, DC: U.S. Department of Justice, Bureau of Justice Statistics (www.ncjrs.org).

Snyder, H. N., & Sickmund, M. (1999). *Juvenile offenders and victims: 1999 National Report* (NCJ 178257) Washington, DC: U.S. Department of Justice, Office of Juvenile Justice and Delinquency Prevention (www.ncjrs.org).

Spangaro, J., Poulos, R. G., & Zwi, A. B. (2011). Pandora doesn't live here anymore: Normalization of screening for intimate partner violence in Australian antenatal, mental health, and substance abuse services. *Violence & Victims, 26*(1), 130–144.

Spangaro, J., Zwi, A., Poulos, R., & Man, W. (2010). Who tells and what happens: Disclosure and health service responses to screening for intimate partner violence. *Health & Social Care in the Community, 18*(6), 671–680.

Stith, S. (2006). Future directions in intimate partner violence prevention research. *Journal of Aggression, Maltreatment, & Trauma, 13*(3–4), 229–244.

Stith, S. M., & McCollum, E. E. (2009). Couples treatment for psychological and physical aggression. In K. D. O'Leary & E. M. Woodin (Eds), *Psychological and physical aggression in couples* (pp. 233–250). Washington, DC: American Psychological Association.

Stith, S., McCollum, E., & Rosen, K. (Eds.) (2011). *Couples therapy for domestic violence: Finding safe solutions.* Washington, DC: American Psychological Association.

Thompson, R., Bonomi, A., Anderson, M., Reid, R., Dimer, J., Carrell, D., & Rivara, F. (2006). Intimate partner violence: Prevalence, types, and chronicity in adult women. *American Journal of Preventive Medicine, 30*(6), 447–457.

Tiefenthaler, J., Farmer, A., & Sambira, A. (2005). Services and intimate partner violence in the United States: A county-level analysis. *Journal of Marriage and Family, 67*(3), 565–578.

Tjaden, P., & Thoennes, N. (2000a). *Extent, nature, and consequences of intimate partner violence: Findings from the National Violence Against Women Survey* (NCJ-181867) Washington, DC: U.S. Department of Justice.

Tjaden, P., & Thoennes, N. (2000b). Prevalence and consequences of male-to-female and female-to-male intimate partner violence as measure by the National Violence Against Women Survey. *Violence Against Women, 6*, 142–161.

Tolman, R., M., & Rosen, D. (2001). Domestic violence in the lives of women receiving welfare: Mental health, substance dependence, and economic well-being. *Violence Against Women, 7*(2), 141–158.

U.S. Department of Justice. (2000). Children as victims: 1999 National Report Series Juvenile Justice Bulletin (NCJ-180753). Rockville, MD: Juvenile Justice Clearing House. Retrieved from http://www.ncjrs.org

U.S. Preventive Services Task Force. (2004). Screening for family and intimate partner violence. *Annals of Internal Medicine, 140*(5), 382–386.

Vaddiparti, K., & Varma, D. (2009). Intimate partner violence interventions. In P. S. Chandra et al. (Eds.), *Contemporary topics in women's mental health: Global perspectives in a changing society* (pp. 387–403). Hoboken, NJ: Wiley.

Waalen, J., Goodwin, M. M., Spitz, A. M., Peterson, R., & Saltzman, L. E. (2000). Screening for intimate partner violence by health care providers: Barriers and interventions. *American Journal of Preventive Medicine, 19*(4), 230–237.

Watts, C., & Zimmerman, C. (2002). Violence against women: Global scope and magnitude. *Lancet, 259*(9313), 1232–1237.

Wong, J., Tiwari, A., Fong, D., Humphreys, J., & Bullock, L. (2011). Depression among women experiencing intimate partner violence in a Chinese community. *Nursing Research, 60*(1), 58–65.

World Health Organization (WHO). (2002). *First world report on violence and health*. Geneva, Switzerland: Author.

World Health Organization (WHO). (2005). *WHO multi-country study on women's health and domestic violence against women*. Geneva, Switzerland: Author.

Wright, C., Perez, S., & Johnson, D. (2010). The mediating role of empowerment for African American women experiencing intimate partner violence. *Psychological Trauma: Theory, Research, Practice, and Policy, 2*(4), 266–272.

WELL-BEING AND HEALTH CHALLENGES

5 Alcohol Use in Women

NANCY VOGELTANZ-HOLM, KAITLIN LILIENTHAL, ALLISON KULIG, AND
SHARON C. WILSNACK

INTRODUCTION

In the past decade, understanding the epidemiology of U.S. women's alcohol use and
related problems has been greatly enhanced
by the collection of data from several large
nationally representative general population
samples. Some of these surveys include very
large numbers of women of different ages
and ethnicities, and a few are longitudinal,
allowing analyses that have the potential to
map how women's drinking and its consequences are influenced by a myriad of factors
across the lifespan. However, there is still a
great need for researchers to examine epidemiological data disaggregated by gender,
age, and race/ethnicity—variables that are
often controlled in analyses, but not fully
explored, thus masking potentially important subgroup differences.

Fortunately, the largest general population study of alcohol use to date—Wave 1 of
the National Epidemiologic Survey of Alcohol and Related Conditions (NESARC)—
was completed in 2002 and is providing
unparalleled opportunities for enhanced
understanding of the patterns, antecedents,
and consequences of adult women's alcohol
use across the lifespan. (Wave 2 NESARC
data were collected in 2004–2005. At the
time of writing this chapter, papers had
reported cross-sectional findings in the

Wave 2 data, but merged public-use data
files had not yet become available that would
support longitudinal analyses of Wave 1 and
Wave 2 data.) The data from NESARC and
several other national surveys, together with
in-depth clinical and community studies,
have the potential to suggest new and effective alcohol-related health messages for
women and girls, and to inform the design
of more effective prevention and intervention strategies.

The first section of this chapter reviews
the most recent epidemiological findings on
women's alcohol use, the health and social
consequences of women's drinking, and
antecedents/risk factors associated with
women's problem drinking. These findings
may be summarized as follows:

1. The majority of U.S. women drink
   alcohol, but do so at low levels.
2. Women's drinking levels generally
   peak before age 25, drop off, then
   steadily decline across the lifespan.
3. Women drink less and have significantly fewer alcohol problems than
   men, but gender gaps in younger
   cohorts of drinkers have narrowed
   from previous decades.
4. Women who are heavier drinkers
   have more serious health and social
   complications of their drinking

compared to men who are heavier drinkers.

5. Women likely derive some cardio-vascular and potentially osteo-porotic benefit from light drinking, but concurrently increase their risk of breast and other cancers.

6. Women's problem drinking is associated with younger age, White or American Indian race/ethnicity, family history of alcohol problems, their partners' heavy drinking, child and adult victimization, and certain comorbid disorders.

The second part of the chapter reviews the most effective strategies for assessing, treating, and preventing women's alcohol problems. Rates of screening for risky drinking and delivering brief interventions in medical settings—a setting in which women often feel more comfortable discussing their alcohol use—remain very low despite national recommendations for routinely providing these services and evidence for their effectiveness in reducing drinking. These services seem particularly important for preventing women's development of alcohol use disorders, which have risen in the past decade (Grant et al., 2004).

The majority of women and men who meet criteria for an alcohol use disorder do not perceive a need for treatment, which remains a primary reason for very low utilization of alcohol intervention programs. However, unlike in previous decades, women are now as likely as men to enter treatment when there is perceived need, and their treatment completion and success rates equal or exceed men's rates. New intervention studies, in particular the large Combined Pharmacotherapies and Behavioral Interventions for Alcohol Dependence

(COMBINE) study completed in 2004, have provided new evidence for effective treatment approaches that may be especially appropriate for women's treatment needs and conducive to women's recovery.

Finally, we review strategies for the prevention of drinking and high-risk drinking in girls and young women—recent research emerging from national initiatives to prevent and reduce underage drinking. Recommendations include raising the price of alcohol, reducing the density of alcohol outlets, enforcing restrictions on youth access, restricting advertising and promotions that target youth, and increasing screening and brief interventions in health settings for persons of all ages. We begin with an overview of recent data on patterns and prevalence of alcohol use and related problems among U.S. women.

PATTERNS OF ALCOHOL USE AND ALCOHOL PROBLEMS IN WOMEN

Determining the prevalence and patterns of women's alcohol use and alcohol-related problems across the lifespan has important implications for understanding the risks and benefits of drinking, and for identifying needs for prevention and treatment. The national survey data included in this section, unless otherwise noted, refer to past-12-month drinking and are reported as percentages or rates of the total U.S. general population or as percentages/rates among current drinkers (any drinking in the past year). As defined by the National Institute on Alcohol Abuse and Alcoholism (NIAAA), a component of the National Institutes of Health, a "drink" refers to about 14 grams of pure alcohol (ethanol) in a 12-ounce (355 ml) regular beer, a 5-ounce (148 ml) serving of wine, or 1.5 ounces (44 ml) of 80-proof distilled spirits (NIAAA, 2010).

The most commonly reported alcohol consumption measures include (a) drinking status (abstainers vs. drinkers); (b) average drinking levels (light, moderate, and heavier; see definitions in Table 5.1); and (c) the frequency of heavy or "risky" drinking, defined as four or more drinks per day/occasion for women and five or more for men (Chen et al., 2006; NIAAA, 2010) (or in some surveys, five or more drinks per day for both women and men [NIAAA, 2009]). This review covers the range of women's problem drinking, from drinking patterns that put women at risk for problems to the development of diagnosed alcohol use disorders (AUDs).

Prevalence of Women's Drinking and Average Drinking Levels

The largest U.S. national survey to date designed specifically to measure adult alcohol use and related problems is the National Epidemiologic Survey on Alcohol and Related Conditions (NESARC), administered by the NIAAA. Wave I of the NESARC was conducted in 2001–2002 with 43,093 adults surveyed. It is the first U.S. national survey to permit analyses of 10-year changes in AUDs using current (*DSM-IV*) psychiatric diagnostic criteria, through comparisons with data from the NIAAA's 1992 National Longitudinal Alcohol Epidemiologic Survey (NLAES; Grant et al., 2004). The National Health Interview Survey (NHIS) from the Centers for Disease Control and Prevention (CDC) has been ongoing since 1957. The NHIS interviews up to 100,000 persons from more than 40,000 households on a range of health and disability topics, including questions on alcohol use patterns and related problems. Both the NESARC and the NHIS are representative of the year 2000 U.S. civilian, noninstitutionalized population of approximately 100 million men and 108 million women aged 18 years and older (Chen et al., 2006; NIAAA, 2009). A final national survey, of women only, is the National Study of Health and Life Experiences of Women (NSHLEW), which interviewed nationally representative samples of U.S. women aged 21 and older in 1981, 1991, and 2001 and new samples of women aged 21 to 30 in 1991 and 2001 (Wilsnack, Kristjanson, Wilsnack, & Crosby, 2006). Smaller than the NESARC and NHIS, and with a slightly

Table 5.1 Past-12-Month Average Drinking Levels in U.S. Women and Men, 2008 National Health Interview Survey (NHIS)

Drinking Level	Women	Men	Total
Abstainer (%)	41.7	28.9	35.5
Light Drinker (%)	45.1	42.2	43.7
Moderate Drinker (%)	8.3	22.6	15.1
Heavier Drinker (%)	5.0	6.4	5.6

Abstainer = No drinking in the past 12 months including lifetime abstainers.
Light drinker ≤ 3 drinks/week. Moderate drinker = 4–7 drinks/week for women; 4–14 drinks/week for men. Heavier drinker = > 1 drink/day for women; > 2 drinks/day for men.

From NIAAA *Database Resources and Statistical Tables, National Health Interview Survey, 2008*, Centers for Disease Control & Prevention. Retrieved from http://www.niaaa.nih.gov/Resources/DatabaseResources/QuickFacts/AlcoholConsumption

different age range (21 and older), the NSHLEW provides complementary information about time trends in women's drinking and related problems over a 20-year period.

As shown in Table 5.1, the 2008 NHIS indicates that almost 60% of U.S. adult women aged 18 and older reported drinking during the past 12 months, compared with about 71% of men (NIAAA, 2009). Results from the earlier 2001–2002 NESARC found nearly identical rates (Chen et al., 2006). The 2001 NSHLEW found that 65.8% of women reported consuming at least some alcohol in the past 12 months (Wilsnack et al., 2006); the higher rate of drinkers likely reflects the NSHLEW's slightly older sample (age 21 and older). Table 5.1 also shows that the distributions of abstention rates and drinking levels differ considerably between women and men. Women were much more likely to be abstainers than men, and were much less likely to report drinking at moderate or heavy levels. Table 5.1 highlights the importance of examining drinking rates by gender, as national totals are substantially influenced by men's drinking levels.

Table 5.2 highlights the equally important need to examine women's drinking levels across the lifespan. Average overall drinking levels in women 55 and older are considerably lower than in younger women. Women's heavier drinking appears to peak by around age 24 and then drop considerably, followed by declines after ages 45 to 54. Abstention rates increase to over 62% in women 65 and older. In a large 1996 Australian sample of healthy older persons living in the community, about 30% of women ages 70 to 75 reported weekly drinking, compared to 66% of men 65 to 79 (McCaul et al., 2010).

These drinking rates, applied to the U.S. population of adult women, indicate that about 5.4 million women drink more than the U.S.-government-recommended one drink per day, and 18.5 million report heavy drinking (four or more drinks per day) in the past year (Chen et al., 2006; NIAAA, 2009). These drinking levels significantly increase women's risks of experiencing multiple adverse consequences.

Finally, although we do not include here a review of the epidemiology of drinking in youth, it is important to keep in mind that prevention of women's problem

Table 5.2 Past-12-Month Average Drinking Levels in U.S. Women, by Age, 2008 National Health Interview Survey (NHIS)

Drinking Level	Years of Age						
	Total	18–24	25–34	35–44	45–54	55–64	65+
Abstainer (%)	41.7	41.7	32.0	35.6	35.3	43.3	62.4
Light Drinker (%)	45.1	42.1	55.0	52.2	49.7	43.0	27.2
Moderate Drinker (%)	8.3	8.1	8.5	7.3	9.4	9.3	7.2
Heavier Drinker (%)	5.0	8.1	4.4	4.9	5.6	4.4	3.2

Abstainer = No drinking in the past 12 months including lifetime abstainers.
Light drinker ≤ 3 drinks/week. Moderate drinker = 4–7 drinks/week for women; 4–14 drinks/week for men. Heavier drinker = > 1 drink/day for women; > 2 drinks/day for men.

From NIAAA *Database Resources and Statistical Tables, National Health Interview Survey, 2008*, Centers for Disease Control & Prevention. Retrieved from http://www.niaaa.nih.gov/Resources/DatabaseResources/QuickFacts/AlcoholConsumption

drinking will be improved by reducing risky drinking in girls. Findings from the 2004 national report on reducing underage drinking (National Research Council [NRC] and Institute of Medicine [IOM], 2004) indicate that, although drinking rates in youth have remained relatively stable since 1993 (about 50% of high school seniors drink), rates of heavy drinking (five or more drinks per day) have increased, especially in full-time college students (also see Chen, Dufour, & Yi, 2004). Gender and race/ethnicity differences in youth drinking generally reflect trends in adults: The gender gap for recent use is relatively small but becomes larger for heavy drinking, with rates generally highest in White and American Indian youth. For example, a recent national survey showed that White males aged 18 to 20 have heavy drinking (five or more drinks per day) rates that are 13% higher than those of White females, but men are only 6% higher for any recent use (NRC & IOM, 2004).

Prevalence of Women's Alcohol Problems and Disorders

Current concepts and definitions of women's problem drinking range from risky drinking patterns to drinking that results in actual adverse physiological, psychological, and/or social consequences, including the more serious and extreme problem of alcohol use disorders (AUDs). AUDs are the relatively reliable psychiatric diagnostic conditions of alcohol abuse and alcohol dependence—with dependence often referred to as *alcoholism.*

Risky drinking (sometimes termed *heavy drinking* or *heavy episodic drinking*) is defined in the NESARC survey as drinking four or more drinks per day for women and five or more drinks for men, and as five or more drinks per day/occasion for both women and men in the NHIS. Using the five or more drinks definition, women's overall rate of 14.2% is substantially lower than men's rate of 31.9% (NIAAA, 2008). Table 5.3 shows the 2008 NHIS population frequency of women reporting any days of consuming five or more drinks in the past year, disaggregated by age. Almost 30% of the women aged 18 to 24 years reported at least one episode of heavy drinking (five or more drinks), compared to only about 2% of the oldest women.

Table 5.4 reports data from the 2001–2002 NESARC on the percentage of current drinkers who reported drinking to

Table 5.3 Past-12-Month Average Number of Heavy Drinking Days (5+ Drinks/Day) in U.S. Women, by Age, 2008 National Health Interview Survey (NHIS)

Frequency of 5 or more drinks/day	Years of Age						
	Total	18–24	25–34	35–44	45–54	55–64	65+
Abstainer (%)	41.9	42.4	32.2	35.8	35.5	43.4	62.6
None (%)	43.8	29.2	43.5	47.8	52.2	51.2	35.2
1–11 days (%)	9.6	17.0	16.6	12.0	8.6	3.6	1.7
12 or more days (%)	4.6	11.4	7.6	4.3	3.7	1.8	0.5*

Abstainer = fewer than 12 drinks in lifetime or no drinks in past year.
* = fewer than 30 respondents in the category.

From NIAAA *Database Resources and Statistical Tables, National Health Interview Survey, 2008,* Centers for Disease Control & Prevention. Retrieved from http://www.niaaa.nih.gov/Resources/DatabaseResources/QuickFacts/AlcoholConsumption

Table 5.4 Past 12-Month Risky Drinking Behaviors in U.S. Current Drinkers, 2001–2002 National Epidemiologic Survey on Alcohol and Related Conditions (NESARC)

Drinking Behavior/Family History	Women %	Men %	Total %
Drank enough to feel drunk			
1–11 times	24.7	27.1	25.9
12+ times	7.0	13.6	10.5
Driving after 3+ drinks	8.9	22.2	15.9
Getting into potentially harmful			
situations after drinking	1.4	4.1	2.8
Started drinking before age 18	27.3	37.8	32.8
Started drinking before age 15	5.6	8.6	7.2

Current drinkers = any drinking the past 12 months.

From NIAAA, *2001–2002 National Epidemiologic Survey on Alcohol and Related Conditions*, Chen et al., 2006. Retrieved from http://pubs.niaaa.nih.gov/publications/manual.htm

drunkenness, driving and engaging in other risky behaviors after drinking, and who began drinking at an early age. Men were higher than women on all measures, with the greatest gender gap observed for engaging in risky behaviors after drinking. Women and men were relatively similar in rates of feeling drunk 1 to 11 times in the past year, but rates were again much higher in men for the more extreme behavior of feeling drunk 12 or more times in the past year.

Data from a 20-year national longitudinal study of women's drinking found that self-reported intoxication increased significantly between 1981 and 2001, particularly among women under age 50 (Wilsnack et al., 2006). As shown in Table 5.5, in nationally representative samples of U.S. women aged 21 and older, rates of drinking (nonabstention) did not change significantly between 1981 and 1991 but increased between 1991 and 2001. Although rates of heavy episodic drinking (defined as six or more drinks in a drinking day) among drinkers declined between 1981 and 2001, rates of intoxication increased significantly in women aged 21 to 50. The increase in

reports of intoxication may reflect in part women's greater awareness of, and willingness to report, intoxicating effects of alcohol, due perhaps to alcohol education campaigns and media warnings. In addition, it is possible that some women, younger women in particular, have become increasingly motivated toward and skilled at drinking intentionally to become intoxicated. Guidelines for low-risk drinking (e.g., eating while drinking or drinking beverages with lower ethanol content) can be reversed to produce heightened intoxication (e.g., drinking high-ethanol-content beverages after fasting). Such intentional or "efficient" drinking to attain intoxication, also seen in the common phenomenon of predrinking or pregaming among young adults (Borsari et al., 2007; Wells et al., 2009), deserves further research attention and may help explain the apparent paradox of increased intoxication without increased overall consumption among younger U.S. women.

When alcohol problems become recurrent and cause significant distress and/or functional impairment, a drinker may then be diagnosed with an AUD. The current psychiatric diagnostic definition (American

Table 5.5   Percentage of U.S. Women Reporting Drinking; and Among Past 12-Month Drinkers, Percentage Reporting Past 12-Month Heavy Episodic Drinking and Intoxication, By Age, 1981, 1991, and 2001, National Study of Health and Life Experiences of Women (NSHLEW)

Age	Percentage of Women Reporting Drinking		
	1981 % (weighted *n*)	1991 % (weighted *n*)	2001 % (weighted *n*)
21–30	75.5 (169)	73.7 (174)	79.7 (167)
31–40	72.1 (145)	69.3 (163)	78.8 (196)
41–50	66.3 (92)	66.2 (141)	72.9 (160)
51–60	55.9 (83)	51.3 (72)	61.3 (118)
61 70	38.8 (47)	40.6 (59)	46.0 (48)
≥71	33.0 (25)[a]	24.2 (30)[a]	33.5 (50)[a]
Total sample	61.7 (562)	58.4 (639)	65.8 (740)[b]

[a]Age trend, p<.001; [b]difference, 1991–2001, p<.001.

Age	Percentage of Women Drinkers Reporting Heavy Episodic Drinking		
	1981 % (weighted *n*)	1991 % (weighted *n*)	2001 % (weighted *n*)
21–30	51.3 (108)	37.2 (78)	29.2 (56)[a]
31–40	30.5 (53)	24.9 (49)	25.1 (57)
41–50	30.2 (34)	13.9 (23)	24.3 (45)
51–60	16.6 (17)	21.1 (18)	12.9 (18)
61-70	22.6 (12)	14.5 (10)	14.3 (8)
≥71	2.8 (1)[b]	8.6 (3)[b]	1.5 (50)[b]
Total sample	32.9 (224)	23.7 (182)	21.6 (185)[a]

[a]Historical trend, p<.001; [b]age trend, p<.001.

Age	Percentage of Women Drinkers Reporting Intoxication		
	1981 % (weighted *n*)	1991 % (weighted *n*)	2001 % (weighted *n*)
21–30	47.6 (100)	55.2 (115)	62.7 (121)[a]
31–40	24.4 (42)	50.5 (100)	52.6 (119)[a]
41–50	21.5 (24)	19.4 (33)	46.3 (86)[a]
51–60	14.2 (15)	25.2 (22)	24.4 (33)
61–70	8.9 (5)	9.1 (6)	8.8 (53)
≥71	2.8 (1)[b]	4.7 (2)[b]	3.9 (2)[b]
Total sample	27.4 (187)	36.2 (278)	42.9 (365)[a]

Data from R. Wilsnack, Kristjanson, S. Wilsnack, & Crosby, 2006.
Age group *n*'s may not sum to total sample *N* because of rounding.
[a]Historical trend, p<.001; [b]age trend, p<.001.

Psychiatric Association [APA], 1994) for abuse is the continued use of alcohol despite distress or impairment in one or more of several areas, including role impairment, legal problems, hazardous use, or social and interpersonal problems. A diagnosis of alcohol dependence requires that three of seven criteria be met, among which are

physiological tolerance, withdrawal symptoms, and a desire or unsuccessful efforts to
cut down on use (APA, 1994). Current
efforts are underway in the development
of the new *DSM-5* to combine alcohol
abuse and dependence into a single disorder
(*addiction*), in which two or more problem
areas lead to the diagnosis, with specifications for severity and the presence or absence
of physiological dependence (see http://
www.dsm5.org for updates on this issue).

In the most comprehensive epidemiological report to date, Grant et al. (2004)
provided gender-, age-, and race/ethnicity-
specific current, and 10-year changes in,
U.S. rates of AUDs. Overall, 4.9% of
women and 12.4% of men aged 18 and
older met diagnostic criteria for an AUD,
resulting in a male-to-female ratio of about
2.5:1—a smaller gender difference than the
3:1 ratio found in 1991–1992 (Grant et al.,
2004; Vogeltanz & Wilsnack, 1997). White
women and men aged 30 to 44 showed the

greatest gender convergence in rates of
dependence from 1991 to 2001.

Another recent analysis of the 2001–
2002 NESARC found that women and
men born between 1913 and 1932 had a
gender gap of about 4.7:1 in lifetime dependence rates compared to a 1.8:1 ratio for
cohorts born between 1968 and 1984 (Keyes,
Grant, & Hasin, 2008). Keyes et al. concluded
that the narrowing of the gender gap is most
likely a result of the greater social acceptability
of women's drinking, which led to increased
drinking and related problems, as well as
women's greater willingness to accurately
report their use. This conclusion is supported
by findings that at similar levels of drinking,
women are more likely than men to perceive
their drinking in negative terms (see Nolen-
Hoeksema, 2004; Vogeltanz-Holm et al.,
2004).

Table 5.6 shows AUD rates for women
by age groups and race/ethnicity (Grant
et al., 2004). Similar to the pattern of age-

**Table 5.6 Percentage of Past 12-Month Alcohol Use Disorders (AUDs) in U.S. Women, by Age and Race/
Ethnicity, 2001–2002 National Epidemiologic Survey on Alcohol and Related Conditions (NESARC)**

AUDs	Years of Age				
	Total %	18–29 %	30–44 %	45–64 %	65+ %
Abuse (Total)	2.55	4.57	3.31	1.70	0.38
American Indian/Alaska Native	4.18	6.68	6.52	0.00	4.12
White	2.92	5.56	4.13	2.02	0.36
Black	1.41	2.10	1.51	1.25	0.12
Latina	1.65	3.04	1.46	0.63	0.00
Asian	1.13	3.89	0.23	0.20	0.00
Dependence (Total)	2.32	5.52	2.61	1.15	0.13
American Indian/Alaska Native	4.49	8.73	5.77	2.53	0.00
White	2.37	6.38	2.84	1.15	0.08
Black	2.39	3.79	2.53	1.74	0.71
Latina	1.94	3.85	1.65	0.46	0.00
Asian	1.34	4.27	0.59	0.15	0.00

Data are from Grant et al., 2004.

related decreases in drinking (Tables 5.3 and 5.5), slightly more than 10% of the youngest women met criteria for an AUD, whereas less than 1% of the oldest women met criteria, although the degree of decline in AUDs across the lifespan varied by race/ethnicity. American Indian/Alaska Native and White women had the highest rates of AUDs (abuse and dependence combined). Ten-year trend analyses of NLAES and NESARC data from Caetano, Baruah, Ramisetty-Mikler, and Ebama (2010) indicate that Black, Latina, and White women's monthly drinking remained stable from 1991 to 2001; and, consistent with Grant et al. (2004) findings, White women were significantly more likely to drink to intoxication compared to Black and Latina women.

HEALTH AND SOCIAL CONSEQUENCES OF WOMEN'S DRINKING

Gender Differences in Alcohol-Related Morbidity and Mortality

As in earlier reviews (e.g., Greenfield, 2002; Vogeltanz & Wilsnack, 1997), the research summarized as follows continues to confirm that regular heavy drinking substantially increases drinkers' risks of developing cirrhosis of the liver and cardiovascular disease (CVD), and that even light drinking increases risks for certain cancers. Women have equal or higher risks than men for these problems at the same or lower levels of drinking, and they often develop cirrhosis more quickly. Less consistent evidence indicates that women are more vulnerable than men to alcohol-related cardiomyopathy, epilepsy, short- and long-term cognitive impairment, nerve damage, and type 2 diabetes mellitus.

Conversely, consistent evidence across multiple studies shows that light-to-moderate drinking in both older women and older men is correlated with reduced risk of coronary heart disease (CHD), and more recently some studies show associations with increased bone density, especially with beer and wine consumption (Allen et al., 2009; Bagnardi, Blangiardo, La Vecchia, & Corrao, 2001; Breslow & Graubard, 2008; NIAAA, 1999, 2004; Rehm, Gmel, Sempos, & Trevisan, 2002; Seitz et al., 1993; Tucker et al., 2009; Turner & Sibonga, 2001).

Why women have greater risks than men for most alcohol-related health problems is not fully understood, but is likely related to at least two factors. First, women have generally lower levels of body water in which alcohol may be distributed and therefore achieve higher blood alcohol levels (BALs) per equivalent alcohol dose than men, even when body weight is controlled (Lieber, 1997; York & Welte, 1994). This same process likely contributes to greater health risks in older compared to younger persons. Also implicated is women's relatively faster rate of eliminating (metabolizing) alcohol from the liver, per volume of blood (Kwo et al., 1998), thus elevating their levels of toxic acetaldehyde in the body (NIAAA, 2007). At least two reports (Mumenthaler, Taylor, O'Hara, & Yeasavage, 1999; Ramchandani, Bosron, & Li, 2001) have shown that gender differences in "first-pass" metabolism of alcohol in the stomach are small and less important in explaining women's increased risk for alcohol-related morbidity than previously believed (Lieber, 1997).

Cancer Morbidity and Mortality A recent large population study of risk for alcohol-related cancers in women involved

more than 1.3 million middle-aged women (mean age 55 years) from the United Kingdom (Allen et al., 2009). Analyses adjusted for region of residence, age, socioeconomic status, smoking, physical activity, and use of oral contraceptives or hormone replacement therapy. Relative to drinking an average of two or fewer drinks per week (abstainers were excluded from analyses), each additional one drink per day increased women's relative risk for breast cancer by 12%, by 24% for liver cancer, and by 10% for rectal cancer. Among smokers, the additional one drink per day increased the risk for cancers of the oral cavity, pharynx, esophagus, and larynx by 44% for drinkers of wine only, and by 67% for drinkers of other alcoholic beverages. The authors estimate that in developed countries in women age 75 and younger, every additional drink per day increases the incidence of breast cancer by 11 cases per 1,000 women, from a baseline of 95 breast cancer cases per 1,000. This study confirms findings from a previous meta-analysis that found significant and dose-dependent relationships between drinking (versus abstaining) and cancers of the upper aerodigestive tract (in smokers), rectum, liver, and in women, the breast. At the same level of consumption, women's risks exceeded men's for esophageal and liver cancer (Bagnardi et al., 2001).

Until recently, studies found no consistent link between pancreatic cancer and drinking (American Institute for Cancer Research, 2007; Bagnardi et al., 2001). However, a recent pooled analysis of 14 large population studies found a small but statistically significant relationship in women, but not in men, when drinking two or more drinks per day compared to no drinking (Genkinger et al., 2009).

Individual risk for alcohol-related cancer is moderated by various genetic, lifestyle, and drinking patterns factors, but in general, findings suggest there is no safe level of regular (frequent) drinking for women who wish to reduce their overall risk of certain cancers. For women who smoke, the evidence is strong that regular drinking at even light levels substantially increases the risks for upper aerodigestive tract cancers.

Cardiovascular Disease Morbidity and Mortality

There is consistent evidence that regular light-to-moderate alcohol use—relative to no drinking or heavier/riskier drinking—reduces the risk for coronary heart disease (CHD), and less consistently, ischemic stroke, in both women and men after controlling for important sociodemographic confounders and beverage type (Elkind et al., 2006; McCaul et al., 2010; Mukamal & Rimm, 2001; Rehm et al., 2002). Moderate drinking's protective effects on CHD and stroke appear similar in women and men and related to reduction of arterial plaque and/or blood clot formation (reviewed in Mukamal & Rimm, 2001).

In summary, middle-aged and older women's potential for alcohol-related harm will be related to their drinking levels and drinking patterns, and to their individual and family risks for diseases that are causally influenced by alcohol use. Methodological research currently underway, focusing in particular on misclassification of "abstainers" (vs. former drinkers) and on uncontrolled confounding, may eventually produce more precise estimates of risks and benefits of alcohol consumption within various population subgroups (see Chikritzhs, Fillmore, & Stockwell, 2009; Fillmore, Kerr, Stockwell, Chikritzhs, & Bostrom, 2006).

Women's Reproductive Health

Animal studies have shown that moderate alcohol consumption disrupts mammalian female puberty, and one human study found that adolescent girls' estrogen levels were depressed for up to 2 weeks following moderate drinking, suggesting the potential for disruptions in pubertal maturation and bone health in girls. Moderate alcohol consumption has also been associated with disruptions in normal menstrual cycling in both animals and humans, and with increases in estradiol in postmenopausal women (reviewed by Emanuele, Wezeman, & Emanuele, 2002). Moderate and, more certainly, heavier drinking increases women's risks of infertility and spontaneous abortion in the first trimester of pregnancy (Eggert, Theobald, & Engfeldt, 2004; Grodstein, Goldman, & Cramer, 1994; Henriksen et al., 2004; Kesmodel, Wisborg, Olsen, Henriksen, & Secher, 2002). Evidence is unequivocal that prolonged heavier drinking and/or multiple heavy drinking episodes in pregnancy lead to severe fetal harm, including fetal alcohol syndrome (FAS), and are the leading cause of preventable mental retardation (Institute of Medicine, 1996; Jacobson & Jacobson, 1994). Fetal alcohol spectrum disorder (FASD) is a term used for a broad and diverse range of less severe adverse physical and behavioral outcomes related to prenatal alcohol exposure (Riley, Clarren, Weinberg, & Jonsson, 2010).

Studies show inconsistent relationships between women's light-to-moderate drinking during pregnancy and fetal harm. Several studies have found increased fetal abnormalities and infant/child behavioral decrements at light-to-moderate levels of drinking (e.g., Jacobson & Jacobson, 1994), but the clearest evidence is that even at low overall levels, episodes of heavy drinking, especially in the first few weeks of pregnancy, are the most harmful (Barr & Streissguth, 2001; Jacobson & Jacobson, 1994; Maier & West, 2001).

A recent large longitudinal study in the United Kingdom (Kelly et al., 2012) found that 5-year-old children of mothers who reported drinking one to two drinks per week or per episode during pregnancy did not have higher risks of cognitive and behavioral problems than children whose mothers did not drink, after adjusting for several confounders. The study also confirmed the consistent finding that children are at high risk for experiencing cognitive and behavioral problems when their mothers report heavy drinking (seven or more drinks per week or six or more drinks per occasion). Because there is no clear consensus about how much alcohol can be safely consumed during pregnancy, U.S. health policy continues to advise that abstinence is the only safe choice (Office of the U.S. Surgeon General, 2005).

Nonetheless, significant numbers of women drink during pregnancy. Findings from the large 2001–2002 NESARC survey (Caetano, Ramisetty-Mikler, Floyd, McGrath, 2006) showed that 38.8% of women who reported being pregnant during the past year also drank during the past year but without any occurrence of heavy drinking (four or more drinks per day). Another 16.7% of past-year pregnant women reported drinking with at least one occurrence of heavy drinking (four or more drinks per day), and 3.6% met criteria for an AUD. In comparison, 41.9%, 19.3%, and 8.3% of women who were not pregnant in the past year reported drinking without heavy episodes, drinking with heavy episodes, and meeting criteria for an AUD, respectively. Caetano and colleagues estimated that at least 50% of pregnant women drank at some level, and up to

20% of pregnant drinkers reported a heavy drinking episode.

Given that drinking and heavy drinking in pregnant and nonpregnant women of child-bearing age were not largely different, it seems that the abstinence-during-pregnancy public health message is not working well, especially among women who are under age 30, single, White, and have higher incomes (Caetano et al., 2006). These data indicate that more effective (evidence-based) strategies are needed for preventing, detecting, and minimizing harm from alcohol use in women who are pregnant or may become pregnant. The recent consensus guidelines from the Society of Obstetricians and Gynaecologists of Canada (Carson et al., 2010) exemplify this position.

Adverse Psychological and Social Consequences of Women's Problem Drinking

Although the majority of women who drink do so in moderation and without serious adverse consequences, there remain significant numbers of U.S. women who experience a range of psychological and social problems as a consequence of their drinking. For example, women who engage in heavy episodic drinking, especially college students, are at increased risk for sexual assault (Hingson, Heeren, Zakocs, Kopstein, & Wechsler, 2002; Mohler-Kuo, Dowdall, Koss, & Wechsler, 2004). Intimate partner violence (IPV) is a highly prevalent form of alcohol-related violence, with estimates that up to 40% of men and 34% of women were drinking at the time they were violent toward their partners (Caetano, Schafer, & Cunradi, 2001). The association between alcohol use and IPV is not limited to the United States and has been reported in numerous other countries worldwide

(Graham, Bernards, Munné, & Wilsnack, 2008; Graham, Bernards, Wilsnack, & Gmel, 2010). And although U.S. adult women are less likely than men to report driving after drinking or to die in an alcohol-related fatal crash, at equivalent blood alcohol concentrations (BACs), fatal crashes are just as likely in women as in men; such crashes increased significantly between 1995 and 2007 in women aged 19 to 24 (Chou et al., 2006; Tsai, Anderson, & Vaca, 2010; Zador, Krawchuk, & Voas, 2000).

Women meeting criteria for an AUD are, by definition, experiencing considerable impairment in health and/or social functioning, with the most serious impairment occurring in women with alcohol dependence (APA, 1994). NESARC data from 2001–2002 show strong relationships, in both women and men, between alcohol dependence and other substance use disorders, and significant but somewhat weaker relationships with mood, anxiety, and personality disorders (Hasin, Stinson, Ogburn, & Grant, 2007). As discussed later, AUDs appear to be both antecedents and outcomes of other psychological disorders and adverse life experiences. In addition to antecedent psychological disorders, the following section discusses several other personal and environmental factors that increase women's risks of problem drinking.

RISK FACTORS FOR WOMEN'S PROBLEM DRINKING

Understanding Gender Differences in Alcohol use and Related Problems

It seems obvious that women have fewer alcohol-related problems than men because women drink considerably less than men, and in particular engage in less heavy and risky drinking. But one may ask, *why* do women drink less than men?—a nearly universal finding (Gefou-Madianou, 1992; McDonald, 1994; Wilsnack et al., 2009). As with most complex phenomena, the answer involves the interaction of biology, learning, and sociocultural context. As discussed by Wilsnack, Vogeltanz, and Wilsnack (2000), women are more sensitive to the physiological effects of alcohol—an evolutionary advantage—and this biological sex difference is magnified within cultures as a way of controlling women's drinking, both for protective purposes (e.g., of offspring) and for differentiation of gender roles (e.g., to reinforce male privilege and social dominance). In support of this theory, epidemiological data show that women's drinking is most similar to men's in countries where women have more control over their reproduction (Social Issues Research Centre, 1998) and where there are smaller differences in gender roles (Wilsnack, Wilsnack, & Obot, 2005).

Genetic and Familial Risks

Twin studies in recent decades have consistently confirmed a genetic contribution to the development of severe AUDs in men, accounting for as much as 60% of the risk. Although some studies have suggested that the genetic contribution to AUD risk may be smaller for women than men, Prescott and colleagues (Prescott, Aggen, & Kendler, 1999), using data from the Virginia Adult Twin Study (Kendler, Heath, Neale, Kessler, & Eaves 1992), found equally large (50% to 60% of variance) genetic contributions for alcohol dependence in women and men. Men's and women's genetic risk for—or protection from—severe AUDs is also likely influenced by sex-specific genetic factors (e.g., greater impulsivity in men and greater sensitivity to alcohol in women), which in turn interact with environmental influences on AUD development (see Prescott, 2002).

Drinking before age 13 is also strongly associated with increased AUD risk in both men and women, with evidence suggesting that the causal mechanism is an interaction between genetic and various social, psychological, and cultural influences on drinking (Agrawal et al., 2009). For example, Grucza and Colleagues (Grucza, Norberg, Bucholz, & Bierut, 2008) used longitudinal data from the NLAES and NESARC surveys to show that increases in women's AUD rates in recent decades are substantially accounted for by their earlier age at onset of drinking relative to previous cohorts of women. The social, psychological, and cultural factors that influence girls' and women's drinking—including age at onset of drinking—are of even greater importance when considering strategies for reducing women's risks for AUDs and for less severe, but more prevalent, alcohol-related problems.

Demographic Correlates and Psychosocial Risk Factors

Age, Ethnicity, Income, Marital, and Employment Status Demographic predictors of women's problem drinking mirror the subgroup prevalence data presented earlier (e.g., younger women and women of White or American Indian race/ethnicity generally have higher rates of problem drinking). The etiology of age differences in drinking levels between younger and older women likely parallels the etiology of gender differences (i.e., biological sensitivity interacting with social and cultural norms). Public health and prevention messages should (and often do) take into account the enormous effect of age on women's risk for drinking problems across the lifespan.

We have shown how women's problem drinking rates vary considerably between racial/ethnic groups, with White and

American Indian women reporting the highest rates. Racial/ethnic differences are also likely influenced by biological sensitivity. For example, Asian women appear to be most sensitive to alcohol's effects and also have the lowest rates of alcohol-related problems (Collins & McNair, 2002). But ethnic differences may be even more strongly associated with economic, psychological, and sociocultural differences that affect women's opportunities for drinking and others' responses to their drinking. Of the major U.S. racial/ethnic groups, White women have the highest rates of heavier and problem drinking (Caetano et al., 2010; Grant et al., 2004). Several studies have described aspects of African American and Latina culture that protect and/or restrict women's heavier drinking, including religiosity and gender-role norms, and how adoption of majority culture values—acculturation—increases Latina women's risks for alcohol problems (Collins & McNair, 2002).

The effects of employment and marital status on women's risk for problem drinking are complex, but data from the NESARC provide some updated information. Women who are unemployed or unmarried, compared with employed and/or married women, have higher rates of alcohol problems (Caetano et al., 2010). Among employed women, higher rates of AUDs occurred in women reporting their occupations as farming, forestry, or fishing (14.1%), followed by women employed in a private household as maids, housekeepers, or childcare workers (12.2%) (Chen et al., 2006). Studies in the United States have found consistently that heavier drinking and adverse drinking consequences are more common among cohabiting women than among married women, controlling for age, with similar patterns observed for

men (Caetano et al., 2006; Duncan, Wilkerson, & England, 2006; Marcussen, 2005).

Recent analyses of survey data from 19 countries were generally consistent with U.S. findings: Cohabitation (vs. marriage) was associated with increased risk of heavy episodic drinking (six or more drinks per day) among both women and men drinkers, with the association stronger among women than men (Li, Wilsnack, Wilsnack, & Kristjanson, 2010). Sexual-minority women, in particular bisexual women, have substantially higher rates of problem drinking than heterosexual women. These differences may reflect sexual minority women's higher levels of other risk factors for alcohol problems in women— childhood sexual abuse, early onset of drinking, and mood disorders—as well as effects of discrimination and other stressors related to minority status (Drabble, Midanik, & Trocki, 2005; Wilsnack et al., 2008).

In general, and as found with other psychological and substance use disorders, there is a consistent relationship between lower socioeconomic status (SES) and severe alcohol problems/dependence (Curran et al., 1999). However, as Keyes and Hasin (2008) found in the NESARC data, less severe alcohol problems, including abuse, are associated with higher SES. In dissecting this relationship, the authors showed that most of the relationship was related to the presence of a specific type of alcohol problem—hazardous use involving drinking and driving—which typically implies sufficient income for car ownership. Similarly, Caetano et al. (2010) found strong associations between lower education and income and drinking to intoxication at least once a month in the past year, but for any intoxication in the past year, higher income (more than $75,000 per year) and education (college graduate) were significantly more predictive. Gender differences were not examined in the NESARC analyses of SES, but international and older studies suggest that SES is a more important predictor of men's excessive alcohol problems than women's (Curran et al., 1999; Van Oers, Bongers, Van de Goor, & Garretsen, 1999).

Partner's Drinking Married women and other women in relationships are at higher risk for problem drinking when their partners are problem drinkers, and partners also have similarities in AUD presence/absence (Grant et al., 2007; Leonard & Homish, 2008). These patterns most likely reflect interactions among assortative mating, social learning, and marital and relationship stress (Jacob & Bremer, 1986; Merline, Schulenberg, O'Malley, Bachman, & Johnston, 2008; Yamaguchi & Kandel, 1997).

Social Stressors Economic disadvantage and a range of other life stressors likely exert their influence on the development of drinking problems through relatively well-understood learning mechanisms that interact with women's unique vulnerabilities and lifestyles. Alcohol's pharmacologic effects, and the social milieu in which drinking typically occurs, may both reduce feelings of stress, thus drinking becomes a negatively reinforced behavior that may become habitual, which in turn increases the potential for problem drinking. NESARC data showed that for each additional health, social, legal, or job-related stressor reported in the previous year, women's frequency of heavy drinking (four or more drinks per day) increased by 13% and daily drinking increased by 8%. Relationships were strongest for legal and job-related stress, with low income increasing risks from job-related stress (Dawson, Grant, & Ruan, 2005).

Childhood Victimization Numerous studies, including clinical (e.g., Miller, Downs, & Testa, 1993), U.S. general population (Wilsnack, Vogeltanz, Klassen, & Harris, 1997), and national population twin studies (Sartor et al., 2007), have found an association between increased risks for problem drinking in women and a history of childhood sexual abuse (CSA), after controlling for potential confounds in several of the studies. In a comprehensive review of studies that tested causal relationships, Vogeltanz-Holm (2002) concluded that CSA in women was causally but modestly related to several forms of adult psychopathology, after controlling for familial and environmental risks, and that the risk for alcohol dependence was most consistently supported. Possible causal paths include the use of alcohol to cope with sexual dysfunction and/or negative affectivity resulting from sexual abuse in childhood, or as part of a maladaptive lifestyle that includes drinking at an early age—the latter finding receiving support from an analysis of the developmental course from CSA to women's AUDs in a large twin study (Sartor et al., 2007; Vogeltanz & Wilsnack, 1997).

A recent comprehensive analysis of associations between seven types of childhood and adult victimization experiences and past-year substance use disorders (SUDs) used Wave 2 (2004–2005) NESARC data from nearly 35,000 respondents, including 577 (2%) sexual-minority women and men (Hughes, McCabe, Wilsnack, West, & Boyd, 2010). The study found strong associations between victimization and past-year SUDs, with the strongest associations between childhood victimization experiences (CSA, childhood physical abuse, and especially childhood neglect) and SUDs. Sexual-minority women and men reported

more lifetime victimization than did heter-
osexuals, and the odds of SUDs were highest
among both women and men, regardless of
sexual identity, who reported multiple (two
or more) victimization experiences.

Adult Violent Victimization   As discussed
earlier, heavy drinking is an antecedent factor in 30% to 40% of violent assaults in
couples, but violent assaults may also
increase women's risks for problem drinking
(Abbey, Zawacki, Buck, Clinton, & McAuslan, 2001; Kilpatrick, Acierno, Resnick,
Saunders, & Best, 2000). Etiological mechanisms in the development of traumatic
stress syndromes and disorder (PTSD) and
AUDs in women have been described in
detail elsewhere (Epstein, Saunders, Kilpatrick, & Resnick, 1998; Stewart, 1996), but
in brief, they involve similar social learning
mechanisms as occur with less traumatic
stressors. The most recent national study
examining SUDs and women's adult experiences of violent victimization found an
increased risk for SUDs in women with
histories of sexual assault, partner violence,
and nonpartner violence, with risks 2 to 4
times greater in women who experienced
multiple episodes of violent victimization
(Hughes et al., 2010).

Sexual Dysfunction   Sexual dysfunction is
often reported by women who have experienced sexual assault, as well as by women with
AUDs, again implicating comorbid etiological
pathways (Sanjuan, Langenbucher, & Labouvie, 2009). Research in this area by Becker and
colleagues (Becker, Skinner, Abel, & Cichon,
1986), S. Wilsnack and colleagues (Wilsnack,
Plaud, Wilsnack, & Klassen, 1997), and others
supports a central mediating role for women's
sexual dysfunction in the development and
maintenance of AUDs. Heavy drinking may

cause sexual dysfunction via impairments
in physiology as discussed previously, and
may be used to cope with impaired sexual
functioning.

Depression and Anxiety   Wave 1
NESARC data confirmed previous findings
that, with the exception of other substance
abuse disorders, the most common comorbid
disorders occurring in women with AUDs
are depression and anxiety disorders (Hasin
et al., 2007). AUDs are considered a potential
risk factor for the development of mood
disorders, especially depression. However,
depression and anxiety disorders, including
PTSD, also contribute to the development of
AUDs. As reviewed by Anthenelli (2010),
compared to men, women are more likely to
report AUDs emerging after the onset of a
stress-related mood or anxiety disorder, and
to report more symptoms and worse health
outcomes from depression. Women continue
to have higher rates of PTSD than men, and,
self-medicative alcohol use plays an important role in the development of problem
drinking patterns among persons with
PTSD—potentially a greater antecedent
contribution to women's compared to
men's AUDs (Sonne, Back, Zuniga, Randall,
& Brady, 2003). Women's comorbid depression and anxiety disorders are important
AUD treatment considerations.

ASSESSMENT, INTERVENTION, AND PREVENTION OF ALCOHOL PROBLEMS IN WOMEN

Screening and Assessment for Women's Problem Drinking

Identification of women's problem drinking
may occur by self-assessment, by significant

others, at the workplace, through the legal system, or by healthcare professionals. Unfortunately, even when women's drinking meets criteria for an AUD, their perceived need for intervention/treatment is low. In the 2001–2002 NESARC survey, only 11% of persons diagnosed with an AUD either believed they needed treatment or were currently receiving treatment, and women were no more likely than men to perceive a need for treatment after controlling for diagnostic symptoms (Edlund, Booth & Feldman, 2009).

The NESARC data also showed that women and men had similar rates of seeking treatment—over 60%—when they perceived a need for it (Edlund et al., 2009). However, perceived need was most strongly associated with more severe symptoms, the strongest association being with recurrent alcohol-related legal problems. Women's lower likelihood of experiencing these types of problems (e.g., only about 14% of DUI offenders are women; Schwartz, 2008) may suggest that women will continue to be underrepresented in treatment settings (Green, 2006; Weisner, Greenfield, & Room, 1995). Earlier research suggests that women may be especially likely to perceive a need for treatment if their alcohol dependence is related to comorbid prescription drug dependence (Wu & Ringwalt, 2004).

In a review of gender differences in use of alcohol treatment services, Green (2006) concluded that women's alcohol problems are generally less likely than men's to be detected and referred or mandated for treatment by employers, through the criminal justice system, or by their families—the one exception being that women are more likely to be referred for treatment by social/family services agencies. Clearly, women experience unique barriers to entering treatment. These include greater stigma (perhaps especially

toward women with children), lack of support from family members, and economic barriers such as costs of transportation and childcare services (Wu & Ringwalt, 2004). And even though women's problem drinking is less detected than men's in healthcare settings, general health settings continue to be the most broadly effective locations for the detection and assessment of women's alcohol problems (Brienza & Stein, 2002; Johnson, Jackson, Guillaume, Meier, & Goyder, 2010).

Screening in Healthcare Settings In 1990, the Institute of Medicine recommended that patients in all medical settings be screened for alcohol use and related problems as a way to broaden the scope of prevention and detection of substance use problems (IOM, 1990). In 2004, the U.S. Preventive Services Task Force (USPSTF; Whitlock, Polen, Green, Orleans & Klein, 2004) found good evidence that screening for alcohol problems in primary healthcare settings could accurately identify drinkers who may be at risk for health problems but who do not meet criteria for an AUD (Whitlock et al., 2004).

Unfortunately, routine screenings for risky drinking rarely occur, despite USPSTF recommendations and the fact that patients expect and accept questions about alcohol from their healthcare providers (Denny, Serdula, Holtzman, & Nelson, 2003; Johnson et al., 2010). An earlier study found that, among providers who asked new patients about their alcohol use, only about one-half asked about maximum use, and only 13% used recommended screening instruments (Friedmann, McCullough, Chin, & Saitz, 2000). Barriers to healthcare providers' screening for alcohol problems include lack of financial and staff resources and lack of knowledge and training to perform screenings (Johnson et al., 2010).

Screening may be especially important for preventing and detecting women's problem drinking, because their drinking levels are often below criteria for an AUD but nonetheless increase their risks for health problems. A brief intervention that follows screening results is an effective and economical intervention for reducing risky drinking.

Recommended Screening Instruments for Women

Because providers vary in their time and resources for alcohol screening, the NIAAA recommends screening strategies along a continuum, based on available time and resources (Fleming, 2004; NIAAA, 2005b). Level 1 screening is a single question: "How many times in the past year have you had five or more drinks (four or more drinks for women) in a day?" For patients who report one or more times, Level 2 screening is more detailed and asks patients about their average frequency of drinking (how many days per week), the average quantity (how many drinks on a typical drinking day), as well as the maximum number of drinks on an occasion in the past month. Women reporting risky drinking patterns (more than seven drinks per week or four or more drinks per occasion) should be offered a brief intervention for their drinking. When time and resources permit, and/or if the clinician feels the woman may be minimizing her drinking, administering a validated screening questionnaire (Level 3 screening) is advised.

The most widely validated screening instruments for use with women are the 10-item Alcohol Use Disorders Identification Test (AUDIT) (Babor, Biddle-Higgins, Saunders, & Monteiro, 2001), which includes questions about drinking patterns and related problems, and the 5-item TWEAK—an acronym that stands for Tolerance, Worried, Eye-opener, Amnesia, and Kut-down (Bradley, Boyd-Wickizer, Powell, & Burman, 1998; Fleming, 2004) (see Figures 5.1 and 5.2). The TWEAK and the AUDIT-C—a 3-item version of the AUDIT that includes only the consumption questions—have also been shown to be effective alcohol use screeners for pregnant women who drink. Such screeners should be routinely used by healthcare providers despite findings of providers' reluctance to assess and treat pregnant women for their drinking problems (Burns, Gray, & Smith, 2010).

In addition to screening tools, the NIAAA has recommended several diagnostic tools for clinicians to use in determining the extent and type of alcohol use problems (NIAAA, 2005a). As discussed by Hester and Miller (2006), many of these diagnostic instruments can be self-administered and are available online, thus providing patients with options for increased satisfaction and confidentiality with the diagnostic process, which in turn often leads to greater disclosure and diagnostic accuracy.

Gender Differences in Outcome of Treatment for Alcohol Dependence

When women's problem drinking reaches the level of alcohol dependence, intensive and/or specialized treatment may be required, often, though not always, with a goal of abstinence from drinking. Before reviewing major treatment approaches, this section summarizes current knowledge about gender differences in alcohol dependence treatment outcomes. Research from previous decades reported that women were less likely to seek specialized treatment for AUDs, were less likely to complete

Questions	0	1	2	3	4	Score
1. How often do you have a drink containing alcohol?	Never	Monthly or less	2 to 4 times a month	2 to 3 times a week	4 or more times a week	
2. How many drinks containing alcohol do you have on a typical day when you are drinking?	1 or 2	3 or 4	5 or 6	7 to 9	10 or more	
3. How often do you have more than five or more drinks on one occasion?	Never	Less than monthly	Monthly	Weekly	Daily or almost daily	
4. How often during the last year have you found that you were not able to stop drinking once you had started?	Never	Less than monthly	Monthly	Weekly	Daily or almost daily	
5. How often during the last year have you failed to do what was normally expected of you because of drinking?	Never	Less than monthly	Monthly	Weekly	Daily or almost daily	
6. How often during the last year have you needed a first drink in the morning to get yourself going after a heavy drinking session?	Never	Less than monthly	Monthly	Weekly	Daily or almost daily	
7. How often during the last year have you had a feeling of guilt or remorse after drinking?	Never	Less than monthly	Monthly	Weekly	Daily or almost daily	
8. How often during the last year have you been unable to remember what happened the night before because of your drinking?	Never	Less than monthly	Monthly	Weekly	Daily or almost daily	
9. Have you or someone else been injured because of your drinking?	No		Yes, but not in the last year		Yes, during the last year	
10. Has a relative, friend, doctor or other health care worker been concerned about your drinking or suggested you cut down?	No		Yes, but not in the last year		Yes, during the last year	

Scoring: NIAAA (2005, p. 10) recommends a score of 8 or more for men ages 18–60 and a score of 4 or more for all women and for men ages 61 and older as an indication of hazardous drinking.

Figure 5.1   The Alcohol Use Disorders Identification Test (AUDIT)

Tolerance: How many drinks can you hold? ("hold" version; >6 drinks indicates tolerance), or How many drinks does it take before you begin to feel the first effects of the alcohol? ("high" version; >3 drinks indicates tolerance)

Worried: Have close friends or relatives worried or complained about your drinking in the past year?

Eye opener: Do you sometimes take a drink in the morning when you first get up?

Amnesia: Has a friend or family member ever told you about things you said or did while you were drinking that you could not remember?

Kut down: Do you sometimes feel the need to cut down on your drinking?

Scoring: 2 points each for positive responses to Tolerance and **W**orried questions; 1 point each for positive responses to **E**ye opener, **A**mnesia and **K**ut down (Total of 0 to 7 points). A score of 2 or more is an indication of women's harmful drinking.

From Russell (1994).

Figure 5.2   The TWEAK Questionnaire

treatment, and typically experienced poorer treatment outcomes, relative to men. Although women continue to face unique barriers to treatment, current evidence shows that women are as likely to seek treatment as men when they perceive the need (although both genders have low perceived need), but are more likely than men to seek treatment from their primary care providers than at specialized alcohol treatment centers. Regardless of treatment setting or approach, women are just as likely as men to complete treatment for their alcohol dependence, and with equally good or better outcomes, including lower relapse rates and more abstinent recovery (Dawson, Grant, Stinson, et al., 2005; Green, 2006; Greenfield, Pettinati, O'Malley, Randall, & Randall, 2010; Project Match Research Group, 1997). Nonetheless, women may prefer treatment settings specialized for women, although these programs are relatively few. Green (2006) suggests that pregnant, perinatal, and lesbian women may be better served by specialized or gender-specific treatment programs than by mixed-gender programs.

Evidence-Based Interventions for Women's Problem Drinking

There are numerous treatment approaches for women's problem drinking. Drinking goals range from reducing risky drinking to abstinence; other goals include improving interpersonal, occupational, and health functioning. The most effective and widely used interventions include brief interventions, cognitive-behavioral approaches, 12-step/self-help approaches, and pharmacotherapies.

Brief Interventions   When women report drinking at risky levels but have not yet developed an AUD, their healthcare professional should provide a brief intervention (BI). BIs are generally of relatively short duration (typically one to five sessions), usually delivered in health settings (but could also be delivered in criminal justice or child services settings), and are designed to reduce alcohol consumption and related problems, especially risky/heavy drinking patterns. Although not typically recommended for individuals with AUDs, BIs can be used in a stepped approach to assist dependent drinkers to seek more intensive treatment (Moyer & Finney, 2004; Vasilaki, Hosier, & Cox, 2006). Similar to the levels approach used for screening, Fleming (2004) described Level 1 BIs as simple provider feedback and advice about their patients' drinking (e.g., expressing concern that drinking is above safe levels and may lead to certain problems) and providing a recommendation that the patient reduce or stop drinking. Level 2 BIs consist of at least two sessions, about one month apart, with follow-up phone calls after each session. These sessions typically also include goal setting and clear advice on how to change drinking behaviors. Level 3 BIs generally are used with persons who have more serious problem drinking. They involve longer session times (around 20 minutes), often add the use of motivational strategies, and are often used to facilitate a referral for more specialized treatment.

A USPSTF review of 12 controlled trials of BIs confirmed that the most efficacious BIs involved multiple contacts (at least two) and included providing feedback and advice, assisting with goal setting, and providing assistance with referrals/ additional contacts. These BIs resulted in 6- to 12-month reductions in drinking that were 13% to 34% greater than for patients who did not receive BIs. BIs were found to be equally effective in women and men, and in older and younger adults (Whitlock et al., 2004). Fleming and colleagues (2002) found that Level 2 BIs delivered to risky drinkers in primary care settings reduced alcohol use, hospitalizations, and emergency room use up to 4 years after the BI, compared to control group patients. However, most studies to date have not included very heavy or dependent drinkers, leading Saitz (2010) to caution that current evidence does not yet support the use of BIs with alcohol-dependent persons.

Motivational Interviewing Brief interventions frequently adopt a motivational approach to the treatment of problem drinking, based on findings that level of patient motivation for changing drinking behavior is a consistent predictor of positive treatment outcomes (see Miller & Rollnick, 2002). Designed as an alternative to the direct confrontation traditionally used in alcohol treatment, Miller and Rollnick describe motivational interviewing (MI) as client-centered but directive, with an emphasis on targeting problem drinkers' ambivalence about changing their drinking behavior. Five key provider techniques are used: (1) expressing empathy, (2) facilitating clients' awareness of discrepancy (between their positive/ideal life goals and their problem-causing drinking behavior), (3) avoiding argumentation, (4) rolling with resistance, and (5) supporting the client's self-efficacy.

In a 2006 meta-analysis of studies examining the efficacy of MI as a brief intervention for reducing risky drinking (Vasilaki, Hosier, & Cox, 2006), the authors found that slightly more than 1 hour of MI was better than no treatment in reducing drinking among nondependent drinkers, but the effects were consistently better only in the short-term (3 months or less). Although an hour of MI was more effective than a group of alternative treatments, the authors could not determine if MI was better than any single alternative treatment. Although it is not clear which components of MI are most effective, one recent study examined findings from the 1997 Project MATCH (described following) and found that clients engaging in "change talk"— sincere expressions of their reasons and desires for making changes—was the most important predictor of positive outcomes (Moyers, Martin, Houck, Christopher, & Tonigan, 2009).

Cognitive-Behavioral Interventions
Cognitive-behavioral treatment (CBT) models for AUDs are based on the theory that problem drinking is a learned behavior that can be modified through the development of more adaptive thought processes and behaviors that promote awareness of triggers (e.g., depression and anger) that precede problem drinking episodes, and through the development of behavioral skills for coping, refusing alcohol, and preventing relapse (see, e.g., Marlatt & Gordon, 1985; Miller & Hester, 2003; Monti, Abrams, Kadden, & Cooney, 1989). CBT for AUDs can be delivered via group or individual therapies, and in both inpatient and outpatient settings as well as in brief interventions. CBT is often combined with pharmacotherapy and/or couples therapy. As a group of therapies, CBT is the most widely evaluated alcohol treatment method to date, with findings generally supporting its efficacy relative to no treatment (Magill & Ray, 2009; Miller et al., 1995; Morgenstern & Longabaugh, 2000).

The most recent and comprehensive meta-analysis of controlled trials of CBT for adults with AUDs (and other drugs) found a small but significant advantage for CBT compared to other alcohol treatments, but with diminishing effects across 12 months of follow-up. CBT's effectiveness for AUDs was less than its effectiveness in treating other SUDs. Overall effects (across all alcohol and drug studies) were larger for CBT combined with an additional psychosocial treatment, compared to CBT with pharmacotherapy or to CBT alone. CBT was equally effective in group or individual formats. Overall, the effects were larger for women and for briefer interventions (Magill & Ray, 2009).

Alcoholics Anonymous   Alcoholics Anonymous (AA), although not a formal alcohol treatment, is a free, mutual-support recovery program that is used more often than any other specific program or treatment approach for alcohol problems in the United States. Based on a 12-step approach to sobriety, AA is commonly recommended as an adjunct to traditional specialized alcohol treatments (Groh, Jason, & Keys, 2008; Weisner et al., 1995). Research on the effectiveness of AA is limited, but available data generally support modest improvements in both drinking outcomes and psychosocial functioning when participants regularly attend meetings, as well as improved abstinence rates when AA is combined with other effective treatments (Connors, Tonigan, & Miller, 2001; Groh et al., 2008; Moos & Moos, 2006).

Specific active components of AA are not known, but research suggests that faith development, social networking, improving coping skills, and helping others with their alcohol problems are important components predicting positive outcomes. Pagano, Friend, Tonigan, and Stout's (2004) analyses of data from Project MATCH found that AA members who helped others were almost twice as likely to remain abstinent at 1-year follow-up compared to AA participants who did not help others (40% vs. 22%), regardless of the number of meetings attended. However, 76% of the sample studied were men, and gender effects were not reported. To our knowledge, there are no empirical studies indicating differential effectiveness of AA for men compared to women.

Other Mutual-Support Groups for Women   Women for Sobriety (WFS), a recovery program specifically for women, shares AA's emphasis on abstinence as the only acceptable recovery goal. However, unlike AA's focus on God or another higher power, WFS's 13-step program encourages positive self-affirmations, spiritual growth, and daily meditation (Center for Substance Abuse Treatment, 2008). At least one study reported that alcohol-dependent women attending a WFS mutual-help group chose not to attend AA because they felt that AA was too negative, focused on the past, and was geared toward men's needs (Kaskutas, 1994). The SMART (Self-Management and Recovery Training) program is another mutual-help group that is growing in popularity. It differs from 12-step programs such as AA in that it emphasizes a cognitive-behavioral approach that includes principles of motivation to abstain, coping with urges, and learning to manage negative cognitions and behaviors. SMART recovery also has online meetings and discussion boards (Center for Substance Abuse Treatment, 2008).

The COMBINE Study The largest clinical trial to date, the 3-year, 11-site Combined Pharmacotherapies and Behavioral Interventions for Alcohol Dependence (COMBINE) study evaluated the effects of pharmacotherapy and a combined behavioral intervention on 1,383 patients treated for alcohol dependence. All eight treatment groups received medical management (MM), with four groups receiving (a) 100 mg per day of the drug naltrexone (which blocks opioid receptors involved in craving), (b) 3 g per day of the drug acamprosate (which reduces symptoms of protracted abstinence), (c) both drugs, or (d) placebo pills; and the other four groups receiving, in addition, up to 20 sessions of a combined behavioral intervention (CBI). The CBI consisted of cognitive-behavioral skills training, motivational enhancement therapy, and encouragement to participate in a self-help/AA group.

Overall results were that patients who received naltrexone, CBI sessions (with placebo pill), or both had the best drinking outcomes after 16 weeks of outpatient treatment, which also included nine brief sessions of MM provided by a healthcare professional. Importantly, patients receiving both naltrexone and CBI sessions did not have better outcomes than patients who received either of these treatments alone (Anton et al., 2006). Greenfield and colleagues (2010) analyzed the data separately for men and women and found the same results as in the overall study, with no gender differences in treatment outcomes. A lack of gender differences in treatment outcomes was also observed in the earlier Project MATCH study (Matching Alcoholism Treatments to Client Heterogeneity), which tested numerous matching hypotheses for client characteristics, including gender, across three treatment modalities (i.e., CBT, 12-step facilitation, and motivational enhancement). Although only one client characteristic—degree of psychopathology—interacted with treatment modality to predict outcome, both women and men in all three treatment modalities showed significant improvement at 1-year follow-up (Project MATCH Research Group, 1997, 1998).

Taken together, findings from the COMBINE study and Project MATCH are encouraging for women with alcohol dependence, given women's greater likelihood of seeking treatment in primary care or general mental health settings in which any of the treatment approaches in the two studies could be widely implemented—

and for providing women with several equally effective treatment options.

Prevention of Risky Drinking in Women and Girls

This review has outlined the continuum of women's alcohol use, its associated antecedents and consequences, and approaches for assisting women who develop problem drinking patterns. Although most women, especially middle-aged and older women, drink at low-risk levels, a substantial number, especially younger adult and underage women drinkers, engage in high-risk drinking (Office of Applied Studies, SAMHSA, 2002). As a result, national initiatives have been developed in the past decade for preventing underage drinking and risky drinking in college students and young adults. These initiatives, along with emerging research on the prevention of high-risk drinking in youth, have identified several important areas that must be addressed (National Research Council & Institute of Medicine, 2004; Office of Juvenile Justice and Delinquency Prevention, 2005; Office of the Surgeon General, 2007; Task Force of the National Advisory Council on Alcohol Abuse and Alcoholism, 2002). Proposed strategies include the following:

1. Alcohol prices should be increased, which will lower youth consumption. Due to a lack of excise tax increases over the years, real costs of alcohol have been dropping, with costs of cheap beer now on par with costs of nonalcoholic soft drinks.

2. The number of new alcohol outlets should be restricted, as this too decreases youth drinking. Alcohol outlet density is high, especially in low-income communities, where alcohol is often more available than basic supplies.

3. Restricting youth access to alcohol, in both public and private settings, is an effective preventive strategy, but enforcement and laws should be strengthened.

4. Effectively reducing and controlling alcohol advertising and promotions should provide at least a modest reduction in youth uptake of alcohol.

5. Importantly for both youth and adults, providers in general medical and public health settings should increase screening and brief interventions that include behavioral and motivational components, which have been shown to be modestly effective in reducing risky drinking. Motivational strategies used in women-only college student groups have also been effective (LaBrie et al., 2009).

CONCLUSIONS AND FUTURE DIRECTIONS

This review of alcohol use in women has highlighted important new scientific knowledge that can inform prevention, assessment, and intervention strategies for risky drinking and related consequences. On the positive side, the large majority of adult women in the United States—approximately 87% in 2008—report either no drinking or light/low-risk drinking. Women 25 and older continue to report much lower rates of heavy drinking and drinking-related problems than men, most likely because of their greater biological sensitivity to alcohol and to several other psychological, social, and cultural influences that reduce women's risks for problem drinking. New evidence indicates that women are as likely as men to enter treatment for drinking problems when they perceive a need, and that their treatment outcomes are equally or more favorable than men's. Encouragingly, new and effective pharmacological and behavioral treatments for AUDs can be provided on an outpatient basis, thus reducing barriers to accessing treatment that existed for women in previous decades. Our public health institutions have recently dedicated considerable resources toward reducing underage and college student drinking, and women now have more information than ever before about the risks associated with heavier drinking, the potential benefits of light drinking, and circumstances and conditions under which any drinking poses risks. We know to a large degree which subgroups of women are at higher risk for drinking-related problems, thus allowing more effective identification and assistance to women in a wide range of community, workplace, educational, and healthcare settings.

Our review also highlights several areas of concern related to women's alcohol use. Similar to findings in the previous decade, women under 25 continue to rival men in high-risk drinking and consequently experience considerable adverse consequences of their drinking. More than 18 million women in the United States reported some level of past-year risky drinking, and almost 5%—approximately 5.3 million women—reported an AUD in 2001–2002 (Grant et al., 2004). The majority of these women did not perceive a need for alcohol treatment services, but this may be in part because healthcare providers do not routinely assess, advise, and assist women with their risky drinking. New evidence indicates that women are more likely to drink to

intoxication than in the previous decade, are just as genetically vulnerable to alcohol dependence as men, and are particularly vulnerable to developing AUDs after traumatic life experiences. Although women may derive some heart and bone health benefits from light drinking, the evidence is now clear that even light drinking increases women's risks for breast cancer. Data show that many women continue to drink during pregnancy, including evidence of substantial numbers of women who report heavy drinking occasions, which clearly increase risks to fetal health.

Fortunately, there are solutions to these problems. Reducing risky drinking in young persons can be achieved, and recent findings show a clear path to progress in this area. As more effective public health strategies emerge for nudging both young and older adults toward lower-risk drinking, accepted cultural norms for heavy/binge drinking should gradually change to norms of greater moderation. Essential to these efforts is comprehensive training of health, education, and social services professionals in evidence-based assessment and brief interventions for risky drinking—training goals that health psychologists are uniquely qualified to assist. Already in place are excellent national surveillance systems of women's drinking and related consequences. These surveys, coupled with research ranging from basic science to controlled intervention trials, will continue to be the foundation for improving women's health and well-being as it relates to their use of alcohol.

REFERENCES

Abbey, A., Zawacki, T., Buck, P. O., Clinton, A. M., & McAuslan, P. (2001). Alcohol and sexual assault. *Alcohol Research & Health*, *25*, 43–51.

Agrawal, A., Sartor, C. E., Lynskey, M. T., Grant, J. D., Pergadia, M. L., Grucza, R., . . . Heath, A. C. (2009). Evidence for an interaction between age at first drink and genetic influences on DSM-IV alcohol dependence symptoms. *Alcoholism: Clinical and Experimental Research, 33,* 2047–2056.

Allen, N. E., Beral, V., Casabonne, D., Kan, S. W., Reeves, G. K., Brown, A., . . . Million Women Study Collaborators. (2009). Moderate alcohol intake and cancer incidence in women. *Journal of the National Cancer Institute, 101,* 296–305.

American Institute for Cancer Research and World Cancer Research Fund. (2007). *Food, nutrition, physical activity and the prevention of cancer: A global perspective.* Retrieved from www.dietandcancerreport.org

American Psychiatric Association (APA). (1994). *Diagnostic and statistical manual of mental disorders* (4th ed.). Washington, DC: Author.

Anthenelli, R. M. (2010). Focus on: Comorbid mental health disorders. *Alcohol Research & Health, 33,* 109–117.

Anton, R. F., O'Malley, S. S., Ciraulo, D. A., Cisler, R. A., Couper, D., Donovan, D. M., . . . Zweben, A. (2006). Combined pharmacotherapies and behavioral interventions for alcohol dependence. *JAMA, 295,* 2003–2017.

Babor, T. F., Biddle-Higgins, J. C., Saunders, J. B., & Monteiro, M. G. (2001). *AUDIT: The Alcohol Use Disorders Identification Test: Guidelines for use in primary health care.* Geneva, Switzerland: World Health Organization.

Bagnardi, V., Blangiardo, M., La Vecchia, C., & Corrao, G. (2001). Alcohol consumption and the risk of cancer. *Alcohol Research & Health, 4,* 263–270.

Barr, H. M., & Streissguth, A. P. (2001). Identifying maternal self-reported alcohol use associated with fetal alcohol spectrum disorders. *Alcoholism: Clinical and Experimental Research, 25,* 283–287.

Becker, J., Skinner, L., Abel, G., & Cichon, J. (1986). Levels of post assault sexual functioning in rape and incest victims. *Archives of Sexual Behavior, 15,* 37–49.

Borsari, B., Boyle, K. E., Hustad, J. T., Barnett, N. P., O'Leary Tevyaw, T., & Kahler, C. W. (2007). Drinking before drinking: Pregaming and drinking games in mandated students. *Addictive Behaviors, 32,* 2694–2705.

Bradley, K. A., Boyd-Wickizer, J., Powell, S. H., & Burman, M. L. (1998). Alcohol screening questionnaires in women: A critical review. *JAMA, 280,* 166–171.

Breslow, R. A., & Graubard, B. I. (2008). Prospective study of alcohol consumption in the United States: Quantity, frequency, and cause-specific mortality. *Alcoholism: Clinical and Experimental Research, 32,* 513–521.

Brienza, R. S., & Stein, M. D. (2002). Alcohol use disorders in primary care. *Journal of General Internal Medicine, 17,* 387–397.

Burns, E., Gray, R., & Smith, L. A. (2010). Brief screening questionnaires to identify problem drinking during pregnancy: A systematic review. *Addiction, 105,* 601–614.

Caetano, R., Baruah, J., Ramisetty-Mikler, S., & Ebama, M. S. (2010). Sociodemographic predictors of pattern and volume of alcohol consumption across Hispanics, Blacks, and Whites: 10-year trend (1992–2002). *Alcoholism: Clinical and Experimental Research, 34,* 1782–1792.

Caetano, R., Ramisetty-Mikler, S., Floyd, R., & McGrath, C. (2006). The epidemiology of drinking among women of childbearing age. *Alcoholism: Clinical and Experimental Research, 30,* 1023–1030.

Caetano, R., Schafer, J., & Cunradi, C. B. (2001). Alcohol-related intimate partner violence among White, Black, and Hispanic couples in the United States. *Alcohol Research & Health, 25,* 58.

Carson G., Cox, L. V., Crane, J., Croteau, P., Graves, L., Kluka, S., Koren, G., . . . Wood, R. (2010). Alcohol use and pregnancy consensus clinical guidelines. *Journal of Obstetrics and Gynaecology Canada, 32,* S1–S32.

Center for Substance Abuse Treatment, Substance Abuse and Mental Health Services Administration (SAMHSA). (2008). An introduction to mutual support groups for alcohol and drug abuse. *Substance Abuse in Brief Fact Sheet, 5.* Rockville, MD: SAMHSA.

Chen, C. M., Dufour, M. C., & Yi, H. (2004/2005). Alcohol consumption among young adults ages 18–24 in the United States: Results from 2001–2002 NESARC survey. *Alcohol Research & Health, 28,* 269–280.

Chen, C. M., Yi, H., Falk, D. E., Stinson, F. S., Dawson, D. A., & Grant, B. F. (2006). *Alcohol use and alcohol use disorders in the United States: Main findings from the*

2001–2003 *National Epidemiologic Survey on Alcohol and Related Conditions (NESARC)*. (NIH Publication No. 05-5737). Bethesda, MD: National Institutes of Health, National Institute on Alcohol Abuse and Alcoholism.

Chikritzhs, T., Fillmore, K., & Stockwell, T. (2009). A healthy dose of skepticism: Four good reasons to think again about protective effects of alcohol on coronary heart disease. *Drug and Alcohol Review, 28*, 441–444.

Chou, S. P., Grant, B. F., Dawson, D. A., Stinson, F. S., Saha, T., & Pickering, R. P. (2006). Twelve-month prevalence and changes in driving after drinking: United States, 1991–1992 and 2001–2002. *Alcohol Research & Health, 29*, 143.

Collins, R. L., & McNair, L. D. (2002). Minority women and alcohol use. *Alcohol Research & Health, 26*, 251–256.

Connors, G. J., Tonigan, J. S., & Miller, W. R. (2001). A longitudinal model of intake symptomatology, AA participation and outcome: Retrospective study of the project MATCH outpatient and aftercare samples. *Journal of Studies on Alcohol, 62*, 817–825.

Curran, G. M., Stoltenberg, S. F., Hill, E. M., Mudd, S. A., Blow, F. C., & Zucker, R. A. (1999). Gender differences in the relationships among SES, family history of alcohol disorders and alcohol dependence. *Journal of Studies on Alcohol, 60*, 825.

Dawson, D. A., Grant, B. F., & Ruan, W. J. (2005). The association between stress and drinking: Modifying effects of gender vulnerability. *Alcohol and Alcoholism, 40*, 453–460.

Dawson, D. A., Grant, B. F., Stinson, F. S., Chou, P. S., Huang, B., & Ruan, W. J. (2005). Recovery from DSM-IV alcohol dependence: United States, 2001–2002. *Addiction, 100*, 281–292.

Denny, C. H., Serdula, M. K., Holtzman, D., & Nelson, D. E. (2003). Physician advice about smoking and drinking: Are U.S. adults being informed? *American Journal of Preventive Medicine, 24*, 71–74.

Drabble, L., Midanik, L. T., & Trocki, K. (2005). Reports of alcohol consumption and alcohol-related problems among homosexual, bisexual, and heterosexual respondents: Results from the 2000 National Alcohol Survey. *Journal of Studies on Alcohol, 66*, 111–120.

Duncan, G. J., Wilkerson, B., & England, P. (2006). Cleaning up their act: The effects of marriage and cohabitation on licit and illicit drug use. *Demography, 43*, 691–710.

Edlund, M. J., Booth, B. M., & Feldman, Z. L. (2009). Perceived need for treatment for alcohol use disorders: Results from two national surveys. *Psychiatric Services, 60*, 1618–1628.

Eggert, J., Theobald, H., & Engfeldt, P. (2004). Effects of alcohol consumption on female fertility during an 18-year period. *Fertility and Sterility, 81*, 379–383.

Elkind, M. S. V., Sciacca, R., Boden-Albala, B., Rundek, T., Paik, M. C., & Sacco, R. L. (2006). Moderate alcohol consumption reduces risk of ischemic stroke: The Northern Manhattan Study. *Stroke, 37*, 13–19.

Emanuele, M. A., Wezeman, F., & Emanuele, N. V. (2002). Alcohol's effects on female reproductive function. *Alcohol Research & Health, 26*, 274.

Epstein, J. N., Saunders, B. F., Kilpatrick, D. G., & Resnick, H. S. (1998). PTSD as a mediator between childhood rape and alcohol use in adult women. *Child Abuse and Neglect, 22*, 223–234.

Fillmore, K. M., Kerr, W. C., Stockwell, T., Chikritzhs, T., & Bostrom, A. (2006). Moderate alcohol use and reduced mortality risk: Systematic error in prospective studies. *Addiction Research and Theory, 14*, 101–132.

Fleming, M. F., Mundt, M. P., French, M. T., Manwell, L. B., Stauffacher, E. A., & Barry, K. L. (2002). Brief physician advice for problem drinkers: Long-term efficacy and benefit-cost analysis. *Alcoholism: Clinical and Experimental Research, 26*, 36–43.

Fleming, M. F. (2004). Screening and brief intervention in primary care settings. *Alcohol Research & Health, 28*, 57–62.

Friedmann, P. D., McCullough, D., Chin, M. H., & Saitz, R. (2000). Screening and intervention for alcohol problems. *Journal of General Internal Medicine, 15*, 84–91.

Gefou-Madianou, D. (Ed.). (1992). *Alcohol, gender and culture*. London, UK: Routledge.

Genkinger, J. M., Spiegelman, D., Anderson, K. E., Bergkvist, L., Bernstein, L., van den Brandt, P. A., . . . Smith-Warner, S. A. (2009). Alcohol intake and pancreatic cancer risk: A pooled analysis of fourteen cohort studies. *Cancer Epidemiology, Biomarkers & Prevention 18*, 765–776.

Graham, K., Bernards, S., Munné, M., & Wilsnack, S. C. (Eds.). (2008). *Unhappy hours: Alcohol and partner aggression in the Americas*. Washington, DC: Pan American Health Organization.

Graham, K., Bernards, S., Wilsnack, S. C., & Gmel, G. (2011). Alcohol may not cause partner violence but it seems to make it worse: A cross national comparison of the relationship between alcohol and severity of partner violence. *Journal of Interpersonal Violence*, *26*(8), 1503–1523.

Grant, B. F., Dawson, D. A., Stinson, F. S., Chou, S. P., Dufour, M. C., & Pickering, R. P. (2004). The 12-month prevalence and trends in DSM-IV alcohol abuse and dependence: United States, 1991–1992 and 2001–2002. *Drug and Alcohol Dependence*, *74*, 223–234.

Grant, J. D., Heath, A. C., Bucholz, K. K., Madden, P. A. F., Agrawal, A., Statham, D. J., & Martin, N. G. (2007). Spousal concordance for alcohol dependence: Evidence for assortative mating or spousal interaction effects? *Alcoholism: Clinical and Experimental Research*, *31*, 717–728.

Green, C. A. (2006). Gender and use of substance abuse treatment services. *Alcohol Research & Health*, *29*, 55–62.

Greenfield, S. F. (2002). Women and alcohol use disorders. *Harvard Review of Psychiatry*, *10*, 76–85.

Greenfield, S. F., Pettinati, H. M., O'Malley, S., Randall, P. K., & Randall, C. L. (2010). Gender differences in alcohol treatment: An analysis of outcome from the COMBINE study. *Alcoholism: Clinical and Experimental Research*, *34*, 1803–1812.

Grodstein, F., Goldman, M. B., & Cramer, D. W. (1994). Infertility in women and moderate alcohol use. *American Journal of Public Health*, *84*, 1429–1432.

Grucza, R. A., Norberg, K., Bucholz, K., & Bierut, L. J. (2008). Dependence and age of drinking onset among women in the United States. *Alcoholism: Clinical and Experimental Research*, *32*, 1493–1501.

Groh, D. R., Jason, L. A., & Keys, C. B. (2008). Social network variables in Alcoholics Anonymous: A literature review. *Clinical Psychology Review*, *28*, 430–450.

Hasin, D. S., Stinson, F. S., Ogburn, E., & Grant, B. F. (2007). Prevalence, correlates, disability, and comorbidity of DSM-IV alcohol abuse and dependence in the United States: Results from the National Epidemiologic Survey on Alcohol and Related Conditions. *Archives of General Psychiatry*, *64*, 830–842.

Henriksen, T. B., Hjollund, N. H., Jensen, T. K., Bonde, J. P., Andersson, A.-M., Kolstad, H., . . . Olsen, J. (2004). Alcohol consumption at the time of conception and spontaneous abortion. *American Journal of Epidemiology*, *160*, 661–667.

Hester, R. K., & Miller, J. H. (2006). Computer-based tools for diagnosis and treatment of alcohol problems. *Alcohol Research & Health*, *29*, 36–40.

Hingson, R. W., Heeren, T., Zakocs, R. C., Kopstein A., & Wechsler, H. (2002). Magnitude of alcohol-related mortality and morbidity among U.S. college students ages 18–24. *Journal of Studies on Alcohol*, *63*, 136–144.

Hughes, T., McCabe, S. E., Wilsnack, S. C., West, B. T., & Boyd, C. J. (2010). Victimization and substance use disorders in a national sample of heterosexual and sexual minority women and men. *Addiction*, *105*, 2130–2140.

Institute of Medicine. (1990). *Broadening the base of treatment for alcohol problems*. Washington, DC: National Academy Press.

Institute of Medicine. (1996). *Fetal alcohol syndrome: Diagnosis, epidemiology, prevention and treatment*. Washington, DC: National Academy Press.

Jacobson, J. L., & Jacobson, S. W. (1994). Prenatal alcohol exposure and neurobehavioral development: Where is the threshold? *Alcohol Health & Research World*, *18*, 30–36.

Jacob, T., & Bremer, D. A. (1986). Assortative mating among men and women alcoholics. *Journal of Studies on Alcohol*, *47*, 219–222.

Johnson, M., Jackson, R., Guillaume, L., Meier, P., & Goyder, E. (2010). Barriers and facilitators to implementing screening and brief intervention for alcohol misuse: A systematic review of qualitative evidence. *Journal of Public Health*, *33*(3), 412–421. doi: 10.1093/pubmed/fdq095

Kaskutas, L. A. (1994). What do women get out of self-help? Their reasons for attending Women for Sobriety and Alcoholics Anonymous. *Journal of Substance Abuse Treatment*, *11*, 185–195.

Kelly, Y. J., Sacker, A., Gray, R., Kelly, J., Wolke, D., Head, J., & Quigley, M. (2012). Light drinking during pregnancy: Still no increased risk for socioemotional difficulties or cognitive deficits at 5 years of age? *Journal of Epidemiology and Community Health*, *66*(1), 41–48. doi: 10.1136/jech.2009.103002.

Kendler, K. S., Heath, A. C., Neale, M. C., Kessler, R. C., & Eaves, L. J. (1992). A population-based twin study of alcoholism in women. *JAMA, 268*, 1877–1882.

Kesmodel, U., Wisborg, K., Olsen, S., Henriksen T., & Secher, N. (2002). Moderate alcochol intake in pregnancy and the risk of spontaneous abortion. *Alcohol & Alcoholism, 37*, 87–92.

Keyes, K. M., Grant, B. F., & Hasin, D. S. (2008). Evidence for a closing gender gap in alcohol use, abuse, and dependence in the United States population. *Drug and Alcohol Dependence, 93*, 21–29.

Keyes, K. M., & Hasin, D. S. (2008). Socio-economic status and problem alcohol use: The positive relationship between income and the DSM-IV alcohol abuse diagnosis. *Addiction, 103*, 1120–1130.

Kilpatrick, D. G., Acierno, R. E., Resnick, H. S., Saunders, B. E., & Best, C. L. (2000). Risk factors for adolescent substance abuse and dependence: Data from a national sample. *Journal of Consulting and Clinical Psychology, 68*, 19–30.

Kwo, P. Y., Ramchandani, V. A., O'Connor, S., Amann, D., Carr, L. G., Sandrasegaran, K., . . . Li, T. K. (1998). Gender differences in alcohol metabolism: Relationship to liver volume and effect of adjusting for body mass. *Gastroenterology, 115*, 1552–1557.

LaBrie, J. W., Hutching, K. K., Lac, A., Tawalbeh, S., Thompson, A. D., & Larimer, M. E. (2009). Preventing risky drinking in first-year college women: Further validation of a female specific motivational-enhancement group intervention. *Journal of Studies on Alcohol and Drugs*, S1677–85.

Leonard, K. E., & Homish, G. G. (2008). Predictors of heavy drinking and drinking problems over the first four years of marriage. *Psychology of Addictive Behaviors, 22*, 25–35.

Li, Q., Wilsnack, R. W., Wilsnack, S. C., & Kristjanson, A. F. (2010). Cohabitation, gender, and alcohol consumption in 19 countries: A multilevel analysis. *Substance Use & Misuse, 45*, 2481–2502.

Lieber, C. S. (1997). Gender differences in alcohol metabolism and susceptibility. In R. W. Wilsnack & S. C. Wilsnack (Eds.), *Gender and alcohol: Individual and social perspectives* (pp. 77–89). New Brunswick, NJ: Rutgers Center of Alcohol Studies.

Magill, M., & Ray, L. A. (2009). Cognitive-behavioral treatment with adult alcohol and illicit drug users:

A meta-analysis of randomized controlled trials. *Journal of Studies on Alcohol and Drugs, 70*, 516–527.

Maier, S. E., & West, J. R. (2001). Drinking pattern and alcohol-related birth defects. *Alcohol Research and Health, 25*, 168.

Marcussen, K. (2005). Explaining differences in mental health between married and cohabiting individuals. *Social Psychology Quarterly, 68*, 239–257.

Marlatt, G. A., & Gordon, J. R. (Eds.). (1985). *Relapse prevention: Maintenance strategies in the treatment of addictive behaviors.* New York, NY: Guilford Press.

McCaul, K. A., Almeida, O. P., Hankey, G. J., Jamrozik, K., Byles, J. E., & Flicker, L. (2010). Alcohol use and mortality in older men and women. *Addiction, 105*, 1391–1400.

McDonald, M. (Ed.). (1994). *Gender, drink and drugs.* Oxford, UK: Berg.

Merline, A. C., Schulenberg, J. E., O'Malley, P. M., Bachman, J. G., & Johnston, L. D. (2008). Substance use in marital dyads: Premarital assortment and change over time. *Journal of Studies on Alcohol and Drugs, 69*, 352–361.

Miller, W. R., Brown, J. M., Simpson, T. L., Handmaker, N. S., Bien, T. H., Luckie, L. F., . . . Tonigan, J. S. (1995). What works? A methodological analysis of the alcohol treatment outcome literature. In R. K. Hester & W. R. Miller (Eds.), *Handbook of alcoholism treatment approaches: Effective alternatives* (2nd ed., pp. 12–44). Boston, MA: Allyn & Bacon.

Miller, B. A., Downs, W. R., & Testa, M. (1993). Interrelationships between victimization experiences and women's alcohol use. *Journal of Studies on Alcohol*, S11109–117.

Miller, W. R., & Hester, R. K. (2003). Alcoholism treatment: Towards an informed eclecticism. In R. K. Hester & W. R. Miller (Eds.), *Handbook of alcoholism treatment approaches: Effective alternatives* (3rd ed.). Boston, MA: Allyn & Bacon.

Miller, W. R., & Rollnick, S. (2002). *Motivational interviewing: Preparing people for change.* New York, NY: Guilford Press.

Mohler-Kuo, M., Dowdall, G. W., Koss, M., & Wechsler, H. (2004). Correlates of rape while intoxicated in a national sample of college women. *Journal of Studies on Alcohol, 65*, 37–45.

Monti, P. M., Abrams, D. B., Kadden, R. M., & Cooney, N. L. (1989). *Treating alcohol dependence:*

A coping skills training guide. New York, NY: Guilford Press.

Moos, R. H., & Moos, B. S. (2006). Participation in treatment and Alcoholics Anonymous: A 16-year follow-up of initially untreated individuals. *Journal of Clinical Psychology, 62,* 735–750.

Morgenstern, J., & Longabaugh, R. (2000). Cognitive-behavioral treatment for alcohol dependence: A review of evidence for its hypothesized mechanisms of action. *Addiction, 95,* 1475–1490.

Moyer, A., & Finney, J. W. (2004). Brief interventions for alcohol problems. *Alcohol Research & Health, 28,* 44–50.

Moyers, T. B., Martin, T., Houck, J. M., Christopher, P. J., & Tonigan, J. S. (2009). From in-session behaviors to drinking outcomes: A causal chain for motivational interviewing. *Journal of Consulting and Clinical Psychology, 77,* 1113–1124.

Mukamal, K., J., & Rimm, E. B. (2001). Alcohol's effects on the risk for coronary heart disease. *Alcohol Research & Health, 25,* 255.

Mumenthaler, M. S., Taylor, J. L., O'Hara, R., & Yesavage, J. A. (1999). Gender differences in moderate drinking effects. *Alcohol Research and Health, 23,* 55–61.

National Institute on Alcohol Abuse and Alcoholism. (1999). Are women more vulnerable to alcohol's effects? *Alcohol Alert, 46.* Retrieved at http://www.niaaa.nih.gov/Publications/AlcoholAlerts/Pages/AlcoholAlertsArchives.aspx

National Institute on Alcohol Abuse and Alcoholism. (2004). Alcohol's damaging effects on the brain. *Alcohol Alert, 63,* 1–7.

National Institute on Alcohol Abuse and Alcoholism. (2005a). *Helping patients who drink too much: A clinician's guide.* Retrieved from http://pubs.niaaa.nih.gov/publications/practitioner/cliniciansguide2005/guide.pdf

National Institute on Alcohol Abuse and Alcoholism. (2005b). Screening for alcohol use and alcohol-related problems. *Alcohol Alert, 65,* 1–7.

National Institute on Alcohol Abuse and Alcoholism. (2007). Alcohol metabolism: An update. *Alcohol Alert, 72,* 1–5.

National Institute on Alcohol Abuse and Alcoholism. (2009). *Database Resources and Statistical Tables, National Health Interview Survey, 2008,* Centers for Disease Control and Prevention. Retrieved from http://www.niaaa.nih.gov/Resources/Database Resources/QuickFacts/AlcoholConsumption/Pages/dkpat25.aspx

National Institute on Alcohol Abuse and Alcoholism. (2010). *Rethinking drinking.* Retrieved from http://pubs.niaaa.nig.gov/publications/RethinkingDrinking/Rethinking_Drinking.pdf

National Research Council & Institute of Medicine. (2004). In R. J. Bonnie & M. E.O'Connell (Eds.), *Reducing underage drinking: A collective responsibility.* Washington, DC: National Academies Press.

Nolen-Hoeksema, S. (2004). Gender differences in risk factors and consequences for alcohol use and problems. *Clinical Psychology Review, 24,* 981–1010.

Office of Applied Studies, Substance Abuse and Mental Health Services Administration. (2002). *National survey on drug use and health.* Rockville, MD: Author. Retrieved at http://www.oas.samhsa.gov/nhsda/2k2nsduh/Results/2k2Results.htm

Office of Juvenile Justice and Delinquency Prevention. (2005). *Drinking in America: Myths, realities, and prevention policy.* U.S. Department of Justice, Office of Justice Programs, Office of Juvenile Justice and Delinquency Prevention. Retrieved from www.udetc.org/documents/Drinking_in_America.pdf

Office of the Surgeon General. (2005). Press release: *U.S. Surgeon General releases advisory on alcohol use in pregnancy.* Retrieved from www.hhs.gov/surgeongeneral/pressreleases/sg02222005.html

Office of the Surgeon General. (2007). *The Surgeon General's call to action to prevent and reduce underage drinking.* Retrieved from www.surgeongeneral.gov/topics/underagedrinking

Pagano, M. E., Friend, K. B., Tonigan, J. S., & Stout, R. L. (2004). Helping other alcoholics in Alcoholics Anonymous and drinking outcomes: Findings from Project MATCH. *Journal of Studies on Alcohol, 65,* 766–773.

Prescott, C. A., Aggen, S. H., & Kendler, K. S. (1999). Sex differences in the sources of genetic liability to alcohol abuse and dependence in a population-based sample of U.S. twins. *Alcoholism: Clinical and Experimental Research, 23,* 1136–1144.

Prescott, C. A. (2002). Sex differences in the genetic risk for alcoholism. *Alcohol Research & Health, 26,* 264.

Project MATCH Research Group. (1997). Matching alcoholism treatment to client heterogeneity: Project MATCH posttreatment drinking outcomes. *Journal of Studies on Alcohol, 58,* 7–29.

Project MATCH Research Group. (1998). Matching alcoholism treatment to client heterogeneity: Treatment main effects and matching effects on drinking during treatment. *Journal of Studies on Alcohol, 59*, 631–639.

Ramchandani, V. A., Bosron, W. F., & Li, T. K. (2001). Research advances in ethanol metabolism. *Pathologie Biologie, 49*, 676–682.

Rehm, J., Gmel, G., Sempos, C. T., & Trevisan, M. (2002). Alcohol-related morbidity and mortality. *Alcohol Research & Health, 27*, 39–51.

Riley, E. P., Clarren, S., Weinberg, J., & Jonsson, E. (2010). *Fetal Alcohol Spectrum Disorder: Management and policy perspectives of FASD*. Hoboken, NJ: Wiley.

Russell, M. (1994). New assessment tools for drinking in pregnancy: T-ACE, TWEAK, and others. *Alcohol Health & Research World, 18*, 55–61.

Saitz, R. (2010). Alcohol screening and brief intervention in primary care: Absence of evidence for efficacy in people with dependence or very heavy drinking. *Drug and Alcohol Review, 29*, 623–640.

Sanjuan, P. M., Langenbucher, J. W., & Labouvie, E. (2009). The role of sexual assault and sexual dysfunction in alcohol/other drug use disorders. *Alcoholism Treatment Quarterly, 27*, 150–163.

Sartor, C. E., Lynskey, M. T., Bucholz, K. K., McCutcheon, V. V., Nelson, E. C., Waldron, M., & Heath, A. C. (2007). Childhood sexual abuse and the course of alcohol dependence development: Findings from a female twin sample. *Drug and Alcohol Dependence, 89*, 139–144.

Schwartz, J. (2008). Gender differences in drunk driving prevalence rates and trends: A 20-year assessment using multiple sources of evidence. *Addictive Behaviors, 33*, 1217–1222.

Seitz, H. K., Egerer, G., Simanowski, U. A., Waldherr, R., Eckey, R., Agarwal, D. P., . . . von Wartburg, J. P. (1993). Human gastric alcohol dehydrogenase activity: Effect of age, sex and alcoholism. *Gut, 34*, 1433–1437.

Social Issues Research Centre. (1998). *Social and cultural aspects of drinking: A report to Amsterdam Group*. Retrieved from http://www.sirc.org/publik/social_drinking.pdf

Sonne, S. C., Back, S. E., Zuniga, C. D., Randall, C. L., & Brady, K. T. (2003). Gender differences in individuals with comorbid alcohol dependence and post-traumatic stress disorder. *American Journal on Addictions, 12*, 412–423.

Stewart, S. H. (1996). Alcohol abuse in individuals exposed to trauma: A critical review. *Psychological Bulletin, 120*, 83–112.

Task Force of the National Advisory Council on Alcohol Abuse and Alcoholism. (2002). *A call to action: Changing the culture of drinking at U.S. colleges*. Retrieved from http://www.collegedrinkingprevention.gov/NIAAACollegeMaterials/TaskForce/TaskForce_TOC.aspx

Tsai, V. W., Anderson, C. L., & Vaca, F. E. (2010). Alcohol involvement among young female drivers in US fatal crashes: Unfavourable trends. *Injury Prevention, 16*, 17–20.

Tucker, K. L., Jugdaohsingh, R., Powell, J. J., Qiao, N., Hannan, M. T., Sripanyakorn, S., . . . Kiel, D. P. (2009). Effects of beer, wine, and liquor intakes on bone mineral density in older men and women. *The American Journal of Clinical Nutrition, 89*, 1188–1196.

Turner, R. T., & Sibonga, J. D. (2001). Effects of alcohol use and estrogen on bone. *Alcohol Research & Health, 25*, 276–281.

Van Oers, J. A. M., Bongers, I. M. B., Van de Goor, L. A. M., & Garretsen, H. F. L. (1999). Alcohol consumption, alcohol-related problems, problem drinking, and socioeconomic status. *Alcohol & Alcoholism, 34*, 78.

Vasilaki, E. I., Hosier, S. G., & Cox, W. M. (2006). The efficacy of motivational interviewing as a brief intervention for excessive drinking: A meta-analytic review. *Alcohol & Alcoholism, 41*, 328–335.

Vogeltanz, N. D., & Wilsnack, S. C. (1997). Alcohol problems in women: Risk factors, consequences and treatment strategies. In S. Gallant, G. P. Keita, & R. Royal-Schaler (Eds.), *Health care for women: Psychological, social, and behaviorial influences* (pp. 75–95). Washington, DC: American Psychological Association.

Vogeltanz-Holm, N. D. (2002). Childhood sexual abuse and risk for adult psychopathology. In N. J. Smelser & P. B. Baltes (Eds.), *International encyclopedia of the social and behavioral sciences* (Vol. 3, pp. 1712–1716). Amsterdam-New York: Elsevier.

Vogeltanz-Holm, N. D., Neve, R. J. M., Greenfield, T. K., Wilsnack, R. W., Kubicka, L., Wilsnack, S. C., . . . Spak, F. (2004). A cross-cultural analysis of women's drinking and drinking-related problems in five countries: Findings from the

International Research Group on Gender and Alcohol. *Addiction Research and Theory, 12*, 31–40.

Weisner, C., Greenfield, T., & Room, R. (1995). Trends in the treatment of alcohol problems in the US general population, 1979–1990. *American Journal of Public Health, 85*, 55–60.

Wells, S., Graham, K., & Purcell, J. (2009). Policy implications of the widespread practice of "pre-drinking" or "pre-gaming" before going to public drinking establishments: Are current prevention strategies backfiring? *Addiction, 104*, 4–9.

Whitlock, E. P., Polen, M. R., Green, C. A., Orleans, T., & Klein, J. (2004). Behavioral counseling interventions in primary care to reduce risky/harmful alcohol use by adults: A summary of evidence for the U.S. Preventive Services Task Force. *Annals of Internal Medicine, 140*, 557–568.

Wilsnack, R. W., Kristjanson, A. F., Wilsnack, S. C., & Crosby, R. D. (2006). Are U.S. women drinking less (or more)?: Aging and historical trends, 1981–2001. *Journal of Studies on Alcohol, 67*, 341–348.

Wilsnack, R. W., Vogeltanz, N. D., & Wilsnack, S. C. (2000). Gender differences in alcohol consumption and adverse drinking consequences: Cross-cultural patterns. *Addiction, 95*, 251–265.

Wilsnack, R. W., Wilsnack, S. C., Kristjanson, A. F., Vogeltanz-Holm, N. D., & Gmel, G. (2009). Gender and alcohol consumption: Patterns from the multinational GENACIS project. *Addiction, 104*, 1487–1500.

Wilsnack, R. W., Wilsnack, S. C., & Obot, I. S. (2005). Why study gender, alcohol, and culture? In I. S. Obot & R. Room (Eds.), *Alcohol, gender and drinking problems: Perspectives from low and middle income countries* (pp. 1–23). Geneva, Switzerland: World Health Organization.

Wilsnack, S. C., Hughes, T. L., Johnson, T. P., Bostwick, W. B., Szalacha, L. A., Benson, P., . . . Kinnison, K. E. (2008). Drinking and drinking-related problems among heterosexual and sexual minority women. *Journal of Studies on Alcohol and Drugs, 69*, 129–139.

Wilsnack, S. C., Plaud, J. J., Wilsnack, R. W., & Klassen, A. D. (1997). Sexuality, gender, and alcohol use. In R. W. Wilsnack & S. C. Wilsnack (Eds.), *Gender and alcohol: Individual and social perspectives* (pp. 250–288). New Brunswick, NJ: Rutgers Center of Alcohol Studies.

Wilsnack, S. C., Vogeltanz, N. D., Klassen, A. D., & Harris, T. R. (1997). Childhood sexual abuse and women's substance abuse: National findings. *Journal of Studies on Alcohol, 58*, 264–271.

Wu, L., & Ringwalt, C. L. (2004). Alcohol dependence and use of treatment services among women in the community. *The American Journal of Psychiatry, 161*, 1790–1797.

Yamaguchi, K., & Kandel, D. B. (1997). The influence of spouses' behavior and marital dissolution on marijuana use: Causation or selection? *Journal of Marriage and the Family, 59*, 22–36.

York, J. L., & Welte, J. W. (1994). Gender comparisons of alcohol consumption in alcoholic and nonalcoholic populations. *Journal of Studies on Alcohol, 55*, 743–750.

Zador, P. L., Krawchuk, S. A., & Voas, R. B. (2000). Alcohol-related relative risk of driver fatalities and driver involvement in fatal crashes in relation to driver age and gender: An update using 1996 data. *Journal of Studies on Alcohol, 61*, 387.

CHAPTER 6

Women and Smoking

BRADLEY N. COLLINS AND UMA S. NAIR

INTRODUCTION

Tobacco use among women has increased recently both in the United States and globally. Due to enormous tobacco-related morbidity and mortality (MM) burdens, the World Health Organization (WHO) and U.S. federal agencies have declared tobacco control among women a public health priority, particularly for those in low-to-middle-income (LTMI) and medically underserved communities. Priorities include efforts aiming to (1) stem tobacco use initiation among girls; (2) reduce smoking and secondhand smoke exposure (SHSe) among pregnant women; (3) reduce children's SHSe; (4) combat tobacco industry advertising targeting females; and (5) improve cessation rates among women across the lifespan.

This chapter begins by presenting the global significance of tobacco use among women. Understanding the scope of current trends underscores concerns about tobacco-related MM highlighted in the section that follows. In the next sections, we focus predominantly on cigarette smoking because it is the most commonly used form of tobacco globally. We also provide an overview of factors related to smoking initiation and dependence and describe current smoking cessation intervention approaches, unique barriers to cessation among women, and

important strategies to facilitate smoking behavior change. We also draw attention to issues related to special subgroups of women, disparities, and high-risk groups across chapter sections. The chapter closes with a brief look at future directions related to tobacco control targeting women.

SIGNIFICANCE AND CURRENT TRENDS

Despite well-publicized evidence of the detrimental effects of tobacco use and widely implemented tobacco control policies and interventions, approximately 1.3 billion adults use tobacco, with numbers increasing globally (Shafey, Eriksen, Ross, & Mackay, 2009). Worldwide, about 80% of smokers reside in LTMI countries. Although smoking prevalence has always been lower among women than men globally (Kelly, Blair, & Pechacek, 2001; Samet & Yoon, 2010), the gender gap narrowed considerably in industrialized nations from the mid-1960s through the 1980s. With the number of women in the world expected to increase dramatically during the 21st century, even if prevalence levels remain steady, the actual number of women who smoke will continue to increase. This trend, coupled with increased prevalence rates among women in many subpopulations (Shafey et al., 2009), justifies the urgency of tobacco control efforts targeting women.

In the Americas and Europe, approximately 17% to 22% of women smoke, rates that are similar to males. Approximately 4% to 5% of Asian-Pacific women smoke, compared to 37% to 57% of their male counterparts (Samet & Yoon, 2010). However, underreporting in countries where cultural norms discourage women from using tobacco exaggerates this gender gap, and recent trends suggest that this gap will continue to narrow as it did in the 20th century in the United States and Europe. In emerging countries, smoking rates among women are highest in well-educated, affluent, urban populations and are spreading to broader segments of the population as women's spending power expands. The rise in smoking prevalence among females can be attributed to the positive effects of globalization, such as women's increased freedom and earning power, and declining sociocultural constraints. However, such sociocultural shifts are also associated with increasingly aggressive tobacco industry marketing efforts aimed at normalizing tobacco use among girls and women (Ho, Shi, Ma, & Novotny, 2007). Rates of tobacco use also differ across the tobacco use continuum (initiation through cessation), and these differences emerge across socioeconomic groups, races, and ethnicities (Centers for Disease Control and Prevention [CDC], 2007; Fagan, Moolchan, Lawrence, Fernander, & Ponder, 2007). In many high-income countries, the increasing concentration of smoking in low-income and racial minority populations of women is an important contributor to tobacco-related health disparities (Amos, Greaves, Nichter, & Bloch, 2011).

The use of specific types of tobacco products varies across cultures and customs.

In Asia, a ballooning population of women use chewing tobacco and snuff, whereas a relatively low proportion (less than 10%) smoke commercial cigarettes. Still, very high rates of smoking are found in specific pockets of Asia, such as Papua New Guinea, Nepal, and Beijing, where up to 80% of women smoke. In India, 50% to 60% of women use smokeless tobacco (Samet & Yoon, 2010). Those who smoke typically use *bidis*, small cigar-like products manufactured by cottage industries throughout India, or *chutta*, hand-rolled, heavy-bodied cigars. About 65% of female smokers "reverse smoke" by inhaling after the burning end of the cigar is placed inside the mouth. This process dramatically increases the risk of oral cancers (Gupta, Mehta, & Pindborg, 1984).

Stemming tobacco use initiation is a primary focus of tobacco control. Globally, use of tobacco among girls is increasing (Samet & Yoon, 2010). Every year in the United States, more than 350,000 children under the age of 18 become regular, daily smokers (CDC, 2010). Disparities in tobacco initiation trends among female youth have also emerged across racial, ethnic, and socioeconomic groups. For example, smoking among Caucasian girls declined from the mid-1970s to the early 1980s but then increased dramatically in the early 1990s. Among Black girls, close to two decades of declining smoking rates have been followed by increasing since the mid-1990s (Kelly et al., 2001).

Maternal smoking is another specific tobacco control priority because of numerous tobacco-related health consequences to mothers and their children who are exposed to SHS. In high-income countries, about 22% of women smoke cigarettes during pregnancy and postpartum, with rates varying by age, relationship status, education, income, race/ethnicity, level of nicotine addiction, presence of comorbid mental health and substance abuse problems, and social network influences (e.g., Holtrop et al., 2009; Mousa et al., 2009). One of the many major consequences of maternal smoking is that SHS-exposed children are 2 to 3 times more likely than nonexposed children to become smokers themselves.

The world's first international public health treaty, WHO's Framework Convention on Tobacco Control (FCTC), has influenced tobacco control and prevention efforts around the world. It urges countries to "address gender-specific risks when developing tobacco-control strategies" (Samet & Yoon, 2010). To date, most LTMI countries have endorsed the FCTC, requiring that they implement evidence-based tobacco control policy, prevention, and smoking cessation interventions. This treaty stresses the urgent need to better understand the unique risks and the multifactorial influences on women's tobacco use across the lifespan to ensure that effective policies and interventions are implemented. With this challenge in mind, the following sections highlight the current state of knowledge about the most relevant topics that can facilitate improved understanding of the complex, multidetermined public health problem of tobacco use in women.

TOBACCO-RELATED MORBIDITY AND MORTALITY

Compared to men, women suffer increased tobacco-related morbidity and mortality (MM). Tobacco smoke contains more than 60 carcinogens and numerous toxicants (Rodgman & Perfetti, 2009). Tobacco use is causally linked to numerous diseases

including cancers in at least 18 different organ sites (ACS, 2009; CDC, 2008; IARC, 2008). Smoking and child SHSe are leading preventable causes of illness and premature death, including cardiovascular and respiratory diseases (CDC, 2008). In countries with the longest history of smoking among women (e.g., U.S., UK, Japan), lung cancer has overtaken breast cancer as the leading cause of female cancer deaths (Jemal et al., 2004), and tobacco-related cardiovascular diseases are a major cause of female deaths. The following section highlights unique risks and concerns related to women. Encouragingly, the risk of tobacco-related disease dramatically decreases after one quits smoking.

Cancer

Compared to nonsmoking females, women who smoke have increased risk of multiple cancers. Women have greater risk than men for certain tobacco-related cancers, such as lung cancer (Gasperino & Rom, 2004; Zang & Wynder, 1996), potentially because of gender differences in the biotransformation of carcinogens, hormonal factors, and nicotine metabolism rate (e.g., Meireles et al., 2010). For example, cytochrome P450 enzymes (e.g., *CYP2A6*), which mediates the first phase of metabolism of nicotine and other toxic chemicals in tobacco smoke, are expressed more in females than males (e.g., Yamanaka et al., 2005). Thus, women metabolize nicotine at a faster rate than men, which could lead to more frequent nicotine dosing and higher levels of bioactivated chemicals in the blood, thereby increasing exposure to toxicants in tobacco smoke. Unique tobacco-related cancers also exist among women. Smoking relates to increased risk for cervical cancer (CDC, 2001), potentially creating synergistic risk with the human papillomavirus infection. Smoking and SHSe are also linked to breast cancer risk. Although antiestrogenergic effects of smoking could actually reduce breast cancer risk among smokers, this protective effect is most likely outweighed by the negative effects of tobacco toxicants and carcinogens (e.g., *N*-nitrosamines, aromatic amines) that are related to breast cancer risk (Ambrosone & Shields, 2001; Vainio, Weiderpass, & Kleihues, 2001). Tobacco carcinogens are easily stored in breast tissue and get activated or metabolized by mammary epithelial cells (Terry & Rohan, 2002), further increasing breast cancer risk. Risk appears to be higher among premenopausal versus postmenopausal smokers, with higher incidence in both age groups among smokers who started younger and who had longer smoking histories (Xue et al., 2011).

Respiratory and Cardiovascular Diseases

Causal relationships exist between smoking and risk of both respiratory disease and cardiovascular disease (CVD). Moreover, women who smoke may be more susceptible than men to the development of chronic obstructive pulmonary disease (COPD) (Dransfield, Davis, Gerald, & Bailey, 2006), with risk increasing with amount and duration of lifetime cigarette use. While it remains unclear whether females experience greater declines in overall lung function than males as a result of smoking (Rahmanian, Diaz, & Wewers, 2011), key indices of lung function deteriorate more dramatically in current female smokers than men (Gan, Man, Postma, Camp, & Sin, 2006). Female smokers may also have greater risk of myocardial infarction (MI) than males (Downs et al., 2005; Prescott, Hippe, Schnohr, Hein, &

Vestbo, 1998). Women who smoke, compared to nonsmokers, have greater risk of ischaemic heart disease, peripheral vascular atherosclerosis, ischemic stroke, and subarachnoid hemorrhage. Even light smokers (those smoking one to four cigarettes per day) suffer from adverse consequences of smoking and an increased risk of developing and dying from CVD and pulmonary disease (Bjartveit & Tverdal, 2005).

Reproductive Health

Smoking affects women's reproductive health across the lifespan. It is linked to irregular menstrual cycles, painful cramps, infertility, greater menstrual bleeding, and variability in menstrual cycle regularity and length (e.g., Mishra, Dobson, & Schofield, 2000). It may also influence levels of steroid hormones (oestradiol and progesterone) and gonadotropins (follicle-stimulating hormone and luteinising hormone) (e.g., Tanko & Christiansen, 2004). Female smokers are more likely to enter menopause at an earlier age than nonsmokers (Kato et al., 1999), thus placing them at greater risk for osteoporosis. Additional consequences include delayed conception (e.g., Olsen, 1991), increased risk of miscarriage (Mishra et al., 2000), and ectopic pregnancies (Stroud et al., 2009). Greater difficulty with conception is linked to tobacco's effects on ovulatory function, depletion of oocytes, tubal dysfunction, and impaired implantation (USDHHS, 2001). Particular concerns exist among smokers who use oral contraception, leading health professionals to advise women to avoid smoking if they use contraceptives (Schiff et al., 1999). Smoking and oral contraceptive use independently increase CVD risk, but their synergistic effects dramatically increase CVD risk. This risk contributes to smokers' discontinuing oral contraceptives, increasing their chance of unplanned pregnancy (Westhoff et al., 2009). Moreover, smoking increases estrogen catabolism, leading to an increased likelihood of adverse effects on menstrual cycle control among oral contraceptive users, such as increased frequency of bleeding (Rosenberg, Waugh, & Stevens, 2006).

Maternal Smoking and Child SHSe

Apart from the effects on maternal health, smoking during pregnancy affects child health. It is causally linked to premature rupture of membranes, placenta previa, placental abruption, preterm delivery, low birth weight, and sudden infant death syndrome (SIDS). Smoking during pregnancy and postpartum is also associated with pediatric health consequences, such as otitis, asthma, respiratory infection, cancers, CVD risk, and behavior problems (CDC, 2001; USDHHS, 2006). Child SHSe is a significant public health problem globally. Maternal smoking is a primary source of SHSe, with younger, medically underserved, and minority children bearing excess SHSe-related MM burden. SHSe is a particular concern for babies because of their dependence on others to avoid exposure. SHS contains numerous toxins and carcinogens. Because there is no safe level of SHSe (USDHHS, 2006), the only way to protect children from SHSe is to completely eliminate tobacco smoke in indoor spaces. Postpartum smoking also affects child health indirectly by affecting breastfeeding (Collins, DiSantis, & Nair, 2011; DiSantis, Collins, & McCoy, 2010). Not only do smokers have less intention to breastfeed (Goldade et al., 2008), but smoking also inhibits breastfeeding initiation and influences earlier-than-intended weaning (e.g., Horta, Victora, Menezes, & Barros,

1997). Smoking may interfere with two hormones closely connected to milk ejection, prolactin and oxytocin, which could lead to early weaning and to milk that has lower fat content among smokers compared to nonsmokers (Horta et al., 1997).

SHSe and Nonsmoking Women's Health

SHSe is causally linked to lung cancer and CVD risk among women who have never smoked, and research shows an increased risk of breast cancer in SHS-exposed women (USDHHS, 2006). However, research in this area is not entirely conclusive (IARC, 2008). There are at least 20 known or suspected human carcinogens present in SHS (Phillips, Martin, & Grover, 2001). These comparative results, together with an analysis of 30 recent articles on the subject, could be considered sufficient confirmation of the link between SHSe and breast cancer risk (see Johnson, 2005). Even nonsmoking women experiencing SHSe incur risks to their fetus. For example, compared to unexposed mothers, SHS-exposed pregnant women have an increased risk of babies who present intrauterine growth retardation, and they experience elevated odds for still birth, preterm birth, and low-birth-weight babies (Peppone et al., 2009; USDHHS, 2006). Female offspring exposed to SHS in utero also demonstrate reduced fecundity later in life compared to nonexposed females (Jensen et al., 2006).

Health Disparities and High-Risk Groups

Greater tobacco-related MM has long been observed in underserved, minority populations (e.g., Ahluwalia, Dang, Choi, & Harris,

2002; Fagan et al., 2007). African Americans bear a greater risk of lung and other tobacco-related cancers (Mazas & Wetter, 2003). They also experience nearly twice the risk for cerebrovascular disease, partly because of their greater sensitivity to tobacco smoke and higher levels of nicotine dependence (Ahluwalia et al., 2002; Perez-Stable, Herrera, Jacob, & Benowitz, 1998) compared to Caucasian smokers. Differential sensitivity and dependence is attributed to the slower metabolism of cotinine (a metabolite of nicotine), as well as to increased volume of nicotine intake among African Americans as compared to Caucasians. Greater nicotine intake may result from use of mentholated cigarettes, which are far more popular among African American smokers (Giovino et al., 2004). Menthol's local anesthetic effects facilitate deeper inhalation and increased exposure to tobacco smoke toxins. Potential gender differences in MM among menthol users have not been clearly established.

PSYCHOSOCIAL CORRELATES OF SMOKING INITIATION

Most smokers begin tobacco use during adolescence. Voorhees and colleagues (2011) suggested that an amalgamation of peer influence, tobacco advertising exposure, and SHSe predict greater risk of initiation. Specifically for girls, depressive symptoms, weight concerns, exposure to targeted tobacco advertisements, and lower tobacco use risk perceptions are also important factors. Describing how these factors interrelate to increase the probability of smoking is beyond the scope of this chapter. However, the following individual, inter-personal, and environmental factors strongly influence the initiation of smoking among females.

Media Influence

Globally, a major factor influencing tobacco use initiation is the aggressive efforts of the tobacco industry to exploit females' attitudes and insecurities through their marketing campaigns (CDC, 2001; Pierce & Gilpin, 1995). Industry market researchers identify the psychosocial needs of different groups of women at different life stages; then specific advertising campaigns portray how cigarettes can satisfy these needs. For example, brands for younger women stress female camaraderie, self-confidence, and independence, whereas brands for older women address needs for pleasure, relaxation, and social acceptability (Boyd, Boyd, & Greenlee, 2003), while avoiding or downplaying imagery reflecting the dangers of smoking (Toll & Ling, 2005). Often, advertising exploits the perceived "value" of thinness and the widespread belief that smoking facilitates weight loss. Zucker et al. (2001) found that female smokers who were exposed to media depicting thinness were more likely to believe that cigarettes control weight and were less skeptical about tobacco advertising.

Parents and Peers

Parental influence is a more important predictor of smoking initiation among females, consistent with findings that girls might be more susceptible to social influences in general compared to boys (e.g., Flay et al., 1994). Positive parental influence *reduces* risk, whereas parental smoking increases the risk of smoking initiation during adolescence (e.g., Otten, Engels, van de Ven, &

Bricker, 2007). Although parent support and active engagement with teens are known to increase resilience to peer pressure to smoke, social network influences remain a primary predictor of smoking initiation (USDHHS, 2001). Peer smoking significantly increases the likelihood of experimental and regular use (e.g., Alexander, Piazza, Mekos, & Valente, 2001). Girls are more likely to report pro-smoking social norms and peer pressure as reasons to initiate smoking (Hu, Flay, Hedeker, Siddiqui, & Day, 1995; Waldron, Lye, & Brandon, 1991). Although parental smoking is persuasive among early adopters, peer smoking plays a greater role in smoking initiation later as girls develop and place increasing influence on friends' behavior.

Predictors of smoking initiation vary little across race/ethnicity (Nichols, Birnbaum, Birnel, & Botvin, 2006). A study by Nichols, Graber, Brooks-Gunn, and Botvin (2004) with urban adolescent girls showed that normative expectations of adult smoking were related to lifetime smoking rates regardless of ethnicity. However, a couple of studies suggest that Caucasian girls may be more influenced by perceived norms and peers than are racial minorities (Mermelstein, 1999). This influence may account for racial/ethnic differences in girls' smoking rates: Caucasians and Native Americans show the highest rates, Latinas have intermediate rates, and African Americans and Asian Americans have the lowest rates (USDHHS, 2001).

Psychological Factors

Weight Concerns and Depressive Symptoms
Females tend to experience greater weight and body concerns than males. The belief that smoking controls body weight can be a strong motivator to initiate smoking (e.g., Tomeo, Field, Berkey, Colditz, & Frazier, 1999), especially among those with increased weight concerns, high body mass index, or who describe themselves as overweight (e.g., Cawley, Markowitz, & Tauras, 2004). Negative body image and weight concerns overlap with other psychosocial factors linked to smoking initiation, such as lower self-esteem and negative affect (NA) states. The constellation of moods defined within the construct of NA includes subsyndromal depressive and anxiety symptoms, boredom, anger, and disgust, among others. Although many of these moods are tied to the maintenance of smoking, depressive symptoms are a key determinant of smoking initiation, particularly among females. Depressed versus nondepressed youth are more likely to initiate smoking (Munafo, Hitsman, Rende, Metcalfe, & Niaura, 2008); however, there is still controversy about the direction of causality in this relationship (e.g., Boden, Fergusson, & Horwood, 2010). Evidence appears to favor depressive symptoms as an important risk factor for smoking initiation rather than vice versa. Higher levels of depression are associated with higher self-reported daily smoking rates among high school and college students (Vogel, Hurford, Smith, & Cole, 2003), and college students are 5 to 7 times more likely to use tobacco within the past month if they have a lifetime diagnosis of depression (McChargue, Spring, Cook, & Neumann, 2004).

Psychiatric Comorbidity and the Gateway Hypothesis
Many psychiatric disorders and psychosocial problems relate with smoking initiation, including major depression, drug and alcohol abuse, anxiety, and behavior disorders (e.g., conduct disorder,

attention-deficit/hyperactivity disorder). Both early-onset cigarette smoking (before 13 years old) and conduct problems are robust markers of comorbid psycho-pathology. Patton and colleagues (1998) revealed that depression and anxiety pre-dicted tobacco initiation and transition to daily smoking. This finding was more robust among females reporting that most of their friends smoked. Sonntag and colleagues (2000) found social phobia associated with higher rates of tobacco initiation, consistent with other studies (e.g., Wittchen, Stein, & Kessler, 1999). Nicotine abuse/dependence and other psychiatric disorder comorbidities, along with nicotine abuse and other substance abuse comorbidities, lend some support to viewing tobacco use as a gateway drug among high-risk youth.

FACTORS ASSOCIATED WITH NICOTINE DEPENDENCE

Most factors that relate to experimentation and initiation of smoking also relate to con-tinued use and nicotine dependence among females. For men and women, higher smok-ing rates occur among psychiatric popula-tions compared to the general population, with especially high rates of smoking among patients with mood, anxiety, and psychotic disorders (e.g., de Leon, Diaz, Rogers, Browne, & Dinsmore, 2002; Lasser et al., 2000). Other key factors for nicotine depen-dence include NA and weight concerns.

Negative Affect

Associations between negative affect (NA) and nicotine dependence in females are well established. Adolescents who smoke to manage NA are more likely to continue to use tobacco (Stevens, Colwell, Smith, Robinson, & McMillan, 2005). In a recent behavioral laboratory study, Collins, Nair, and Komaroff (2011) demonstrated that women experiencing greater non-with-drawal-related NA during repeated, unrein-forced exposures to cigarette smoking cues (conditioned stimuli) were more likely to report maintained urges to smoke over time compared to women experiencing less NA. This observation supports previous evi-dence that NA is closely tied to motivation to smoke. There is also a robust association between depressive symptoms and nicotine dependence. Women are about 2 times more likely than men to experience lifetime depres-sion, and depression in women is more com-monly comorbid with nicotine dependence (Husky, Mazure, Paliwal, & McKee, 2008; McChargue, Cohen, & Cook, 2004).

Weight Concerns

Several cross-sectional studies have demon-strated evidence of weight concerns and smoking association in females (e.g., Collins, Nair, Hovell, & Audrain-McGovern, 2009; Voorhees, Schreiber, Schumann, Biro, & Crawford, 2002). Due to greater concerns about their body shape and weight (Clark et al., 2005), women are more likely to use cigarettes to manage weight-related anxiety and concerns (Camp, Klesges, & Relyea, 1993; Copeland & Carney, 2003; Pinto et al., 1999). The belief that quitting smoking is followed by weight gain is not unfounded: smokers weigh less than nonsmokers because of reduced calorie intake and increased meta-bolic rate (Pomerleau, Pomerleau, Namenek, & Mehringer, 2000; Wack & Rodin, 1982); and smokers gain weight during abstinence periods because of withdrawal processes that contribute to temporarily increased appetite and reduced metabolism (Blitzer, Rimm, & Giefer, 1977; Klesges et al., 1997; Swan & Carmelli, 1995). Because smoking becomes an effective, albeit maladaptive weight control tool, weight-concerned women maintain smoking to manage fear of postcessation weight gain (Perkins, Levine, Marcus, & Shiffman, 1997; Pomerleau, Zucker, & Stewart, 2001; Weekley, Klesges, & Reylea, 1992). In treatment, they are also less likely to be abstinent (Meyers et al., 1997) and more likely to drop out (Copeland, Martin, Geiselman, Rash, & Kendzor, 2006; Mizes et al., 1998).

Race and Socioeconomic Factors

Racial and economic factors influence differential risk for nicotine dependence in the general population. Caucasian females, compared to African American females tend to start smoking at later ages, smoke fewer cigarettes per day, and prefer mentholated cigarette brands (e.g., Moon-Howard, 2003). Although smoking prevalence among African American women exceeds the U.S. national average and that of Caucasian women (Delva et al., 2005; Manfredi, Lacey, Warnecke, & Buis, 1992), the heterogeneity among African Americans may obscure some differences in smoking behavior patterns between African Americans and Caucasian women. For example, low-income, urban African American women begin smoking earlier in adolescence than other African American women and smoke at higher rates than Caucasian women (e.g., Manfredi et al., 1992). Psychological stress, resulting from environmental demands of poverty, which is higher among low-income urban African Americans (Ewart & Suchday, 2002), may contribute to their smoking behavior. Low-income African

American women are known to have greater exposure to multiple sources of daily stress, including poor access to healthcare, substandard housing, and lower wages than other female subgroups.

Webb et al. (2008) found increased odds of smoking for older women who had less education, lower income, greater perceived stress, and increased alcohol use. Droomers, Schrijvers, and Mackenbach (2002) concluded that smoking maintenance in less-educated individuals was explained by poor perceived general health, financial problems, fewer coping resources, low perceived control, and higher neuroticism. Many of these factors also influence postpartum smoking and child SHSe, especially in low-income underserved communities (Secker-Walker, Solomon, Flynn, Skelly, & Mead, 1998; Stotts, DiClemente, Carbonari, & Mullen, 2000) and play a pivotal role in influencing relapse rates among postpartum African American mothers (Kahn, Certain, & Whitaker, 2002; Secker-Walker et al., 1998).

Molecular Genetics

Several genetic polymorphisms have been identified that contribute to variability in nicotine dependence and smoking behaviors. Increased knowledge of genetic influences on smoking behavior may improve our understanding of gender differences in tobacco use. For example, genetic variants in the nicotine-metabolizing enzymes have been implicated in prediction of nicotine dependence and cessation. Genetic variations in *CYP2A6* have been associated with smoking behavior (e.g., Malaiyandi et al., 2006). Women from predominately Caucasian populations appear to have (a) higher nicotine elimination rates, (b) lower steady-state plasma levels of nicotine per cigarette, and (c) higher *CYP2A6* activity (Benowitz & Wilson, 2000; Mweni-fumbo, Sellers, & Tyndale, 2007; Zeman, Hiraki, & Sellers, 2002). These observations suggest faster clearance of nicotine, thereby contributing to more frequent nicotine dosing among females.

SMOKING CESSATION AND RELAPSE: INTERVENTION ISSUES UNIQUE TO WOMEN

Nicotine Replacement Therapy

Nicotine replacement therapy (NRT) was introduced a few decades ago and has become the most commonly used treatment for smoking cessation (Burton, Gitchell, & Shiffman, 2000). Available as gum, transdermal patches, lozenges, and inhalers, NRT delivers nicotine via routes of administration with slower and/or steadier absorption rates than smoking. This process allows smokers to reduce and taper nicotine levels, thereby alleviating the severity of withdrawal symptoms. Although NRT is superior to placebo in promoting cessation (Fiore et al., 2000), men respond better to NRT compared to women (e.g., Fiore et al., 2000; Perkins & Scott, 2008). In a meta-analysis of NRT effectiveness studies, Cepeda-Benito, Reynoso, and Erath (2004) found that while men and women benefitted from NRT in the short-term (3 months), NRT efficacy was greater in men compared to women at long-term follow-ups (6 to 12 months). This gender difference may be explained by lower reinforcement value of nicotine among women (e.g., Perkins et al., 2001), greater expectancies of nicotine to manage affect and prevent weight gain (e.g., Cepeda-Benito & Reig Ferrer, 2000), and differential reactivity to smoking-related cues

between genders (Collins, Nair, & Komaroff, 2011). Thus, many women are likely to benefit from smoking interventions that combine NRT with other treatment components, such as behavioral counseling and medication.

Nicotine Withdrawal Medications

In addition to NRT, pharmaceutical companies have tested off-label medications and developed new medications to alleviate withdrawal and facilitate smoking cessation. The most frequently prescribed medications for smoking cessation are Bupropion (an antidepressant) and Varenicline (a nicotine receptor agonist).

Antidepressants affect neural pathways and receptors that are also involved in the maintenance of nicotine addiction (Benowitz & Wilson, 2000; Kotlyar, Golding, Hatsukami, & Jamerson, 2001). Typically, they are used for smoking cessation to treat withdrawal-induced depressive symptoms in nondepressed smokers and to prevent major depressive episodes among smokers with comorbid mood disorders. A meta-analysis showed that Bupropion, a widely prescribed smoking cessation medication, was equally effective for men and women (Scharf & Shiffman, 2004). However, results from other studies suggest that certain subgroups of women may benefit more than others. In a trial with counseling plus Bupropion versus placebo (Collins et al., 2004), it was demonstrated that among women on Bupropion, lighter smokers had about twice the abstinence rates as those on placebo, but heavier smokers experienced little benefit from Bupropion compared to those on counseling plus placebo. Because lighter smokers tend to experience less intense nicotine withdrawal than heavier smokers, perhaps Bupropion's negative affect-attenuating effects were more salient among lighter than heavier smokers. In another study with smokers presenting COPD, women demonstrated a larger treatment effect on Bupropion than men (ORs = 2.7 versus 1.7), although the difference was not statistically significant (Tashkin et al., 2001). Thus, Bupropion plus counseling may be superior to placebo and counseling for specific subgroups of women.

Another effective smoking cessation medication is Varenicline (e.g., Cahill et al., 2009). A selective a4b2 neuronal nicotinic acetylcholine receptor (nAChR) partial agonist, Varenicline attenuates nicotine's effect on dopamine release. Its agonist function minimizes craving and withdrawal, while its antagonist properties attenuate the reinforcing effects of nicotine, thereby reducing satisfaction from smoking and decreasing relapse likelihood (Foulds, 2006). A recent meta-analysis concluded that Varenicline's effectiveness is generally greater than that of NRT or Bupropion, although further studies are needed to substantiate this conclusion (Wu, Wilson, Dimoulas, & Mills, 2006). There currently exists a dearth of studies that explore gender differences in response to Varenicline. Among studies that have examined gender and drug effects, abstinence rates appear to be equivalent between genders.

Behavioral Interventions

Behavioral counseling strategies are effective in promoting tobacco cessation, and they represent important treatment components that address many of the unique cessation barriers many women experience. However, compared to pharmacotherapy development, dramatically fewer research and development resources have been dedicated to the improvement of evidence-based behavioral interventions, even though counseling is essential to successful cessation programs. All provider guidelines and public health recommendations for evidence-based treatment emphasize the importance of using a combination of behavioral and pharmaceutical intervention. While NRT and withdrawal medications assist smokers in the initial phases of a quit attempt, counseling helps smokers develop skills that minimize the risk of smoking relapse in the long run.

Fundamental components of behavioral interventions enhance motivation for cessation; promote urge, stress, and mood management skills; enable the development of adaptive problem solving; facilitate support for cessation and general social support; expand the range of reinforcing activities to replace smoking; and generalize smoking behavior change across contexts. For women, behavioral interventions are effective in addressing unique challenges to cessation by enhancing social support and providing skills training to assist with weight concerns and mood management.

Behavioral Shaping, Harm Reduction, and Stepped Care Approaches

Behavioral shaping is a long-established process by which reinforcers are provided for approximations toward end-goal behavior. This approach increases the probability that target behaviors become reflexive and generalizable across contexts. A relevant example would be rewarding creation of smoke-free rooms as parents work toward a long-term goal of a smoke-free home. Reinforcement that is contingent upon these harm-reduction steps increases the probability that short-term efforts lead to the ultimate goal(s). Shiffman, Mason, and Henningfield (1998) specify principles that guide the harm-reduction philosophy in tobacco control. As Niaura and Abrams (2002) describe, the approach is based on data suggesting a strong dose-dependent relationship between exposure to tobacco toxins and subsequent MM (Burns, 1997) and evidence that there are public health benefits to reducing harm associated with tobacco use (e.g., reducing child SHSe). In a recent behavioral intervention trial (Collins et al., in submission), initial behavioral goals focused on child SHSe reduction to encourage participation of high-risk smokers who typically do not enroll in formal smoking cessation interventions. Shaping facilitated progress through sequentially more difficult smoking behavior change efforts leading to a quit attempt.

Unique Challenges and Barriers to Smoking Cessation for Women

Menstrual Cycle and Hormones Fluctuations in estrogen and progesterone during the menstrual cycle (MC) influence women's smoking behavior. For example, compared to women in the follicular phase (and to men), women during the luteal (premenstrual) phase smoke more cigarettes (Snively, Ahijevych, Bernhard, & Wewers, 2000), experience increased NA and nicotine withdrawal (Allen, Allen, & Pomerleau, 2009; Pomerleau, Garcia, Pomerleau, & Cameron, 1992), and report greater cue-induced craving when exposed to smoking-related stimuli (Franklin et al., 2004). Research attempting to understand the influence of the MC on smoking intervention outcomes has yielded mixed results. One intervention study using the nicotine patch plus counseling showed that women quitting during the follicular phase had higher quit rates compared to women quitting during the luteal phase (Carpenter, Saladin, Leinbach, Larowe, & Upadhyaya, 2008; Franklin et al., 2008).

In contrast, Mazure, Toll, McKee, Wu, and O'Malley (2011) found that women receiving Bupropion without NRT were more likely to be abstinent after 6 weeks of intervention if they quit during the luteal phase, perhaps because Bupropion attenuates NA and withdrawal symptoms (e.g., Lerman et al., 2002), phenomena that are generally greater during the luteal versus follicular phase. A third trial randomized women to quit during either the follicular or luteal phases and used only behavioral counseling without pharmacotherapy (Allen, Bade, Center, Finstad, & Hatsukami, 2008). In this trial, women who quit during the luteal phase versus the follicular phase had lower relapse rates or longer periods of abstinence after quitting. Similarly, Allen and colleagues (Allen, Allen, Lunos, & Hatsukami, 2009) found that women who self-selected a luteal phase quit date had significantly longer abstinence than women who chose a follicular phase quit date. The results of these last two studies were attributed to the higher levels of estrogen that occur during the follicular phase and that may influence nicotine metabolism and reinforcement in ways that undermine quit success (see Allen et al., 2008). Thus, while there is evidence of the influence of sex hormones on smoking quit attempts, additional research is needed to disentangle the current mixed evidence.

Negative Affect and Depression Negative affect (NA) is strongly associated with smoking and relapse in women compared to men (e.g., Husky et al., 2008; Piasecki, Kenford, Smith, Fiore, & Baker, 1997). A meta-analysis examining depression history and smoking treatment outcome associations found no relationship in the context of clinic-based treatment (Hitsman, Borrelli, McChargue, Spring, & Niaura, 2003; Niaura & Abrams, 2002). However, this meta-analysis did not distinguish among studies with smokers in enhanced treatment versus placebo or standard treatment, potentially masking the effect of depression reduction on the ability to stop smoking (Covey, 2004). Moreover, increased levels of depressive symptoms are related to greater attrition rate from treatment programs, poorer cessation outcomes post-treatment, and increased relapse rates, suggesting that concurrent depressive symptoms, even if subsyndromal, are more predictive of cessation treatment outcomes than is a history of depression (Levine, Marcus, & Perkins, 2003). Depression may hinder cessation success and increase relapse risk through a meditational process: Depressed smokers are vulnerable to psychosocial stressors that can undermine cessation attempts. Turner et al. (2008) found that, among lower-educated women smokers, depressed women who had high levels of social support were as likely to quit as women who did not have a recent history of depression, potentially indicating the mediating effect of social support.

Weight Concerns Concern about weight gain and actual weight gain are potential reasons for poor cessation outcomes among women (Levine, Perkins, & Marcus, 2001; Meyers et al., 1997; Mizes et al., 1998). Hence, some smoking interventions are beginning to include weight concerns/control components to improve women's cessation outcomes. These interventions integrate standard cognitive behavioral therapy (CBT) for smoking cessation with physical activity and diet, to address weight

concerns. Several clinical trials have demonstrated a positive impact of physical activity on abstinence and reductions in weight gain (e.g., Jonsdottir & Jonsdottir, 2001). Engaging in physical activity is effective in reducing withdrawal symptoms, cravings, and NA among sedentary women who smoke (Bock, Marcus, King, Borrelli, & Roberts, 1999; Nair, Collins, & Napolitano, under review). Marcus et al. (2000) found that weight-concerned women who engaged in vigorous-intensity physical activity achieved higher levels of continuous abstinence and gained less weight at the end of treatment and 1 year post-treatment than did other women. Subsequent studies have been unable to reveal consistent evidence of mechanisms underlying the association between physical activity and smoking treatment outcomes due in part to methodological variations in length, type, and timing of physical activity sessions and to differential adherence rates to protocols across studies.

Results from intervention studies using diet/weight control strategies to prevent post-cessation weight gain have been inconclusive. In a study demonstrating the potential efficacy of combining physical activity and diet/weight control strategies, smokers who quit did not experience significant changes in weight (Talcott et al., 1995).

Poor body image may contribute to preoccupation with weight among female smokers (Cavallo, Duhig, McKee, & Krishnan-Sarin, 2006). Negative body image is associated with greater difficulty quitting (King et al., 2006) and maintaining abstinence (Clark et al., 2005; Pomerleau et al., 2001). CBT may be an important approach to attenuate smoking-related weight concerns. Perkins et al. (2001) found that women who received CBT focusing on weight concerns not only had higher abstinence rates but also gained less weight after quitting than those who received weight control training (e.g., reducing snacking). Thus, weight concerns, rather than actual post–cessation weight gain, may be the crucial behavior influencing smoking abstinence among these women (Perkins, 2001), and CBT that includes skills training to manage weight concerns may be an effective intervention in smoking cessation programs.

Pregnancy and Smoking Cessation

Despite being aware of the negative consequences of smoking, most pregnant women who smoked before conceiving continue to smoke at some point during pregnancy. The U.S. Public Health Service Clinical Practice Guidelines recommends that pregnant smokers be offered augmented psychosocial smoking interventions (e.g., CBT), combined with self-help materials, as the first-line approach to smoking cessation (Nielsen & Fiore, 2000). Although they are safer than smoking, the use of pharmacological interventions during pregnancy is recommended only when first line interventions fail because of health concerns to the fetus (Rigotti, Park, Chang, & Regan, 2008). Moreover, conventional doses of NRT may be insufficient for helping pregnant women quit smoking, because the metabolic clearances of nicotine and cotinine (the principal metabolite of nicotine) are increased by 60% and 140%, respectively (Dempsey, Jacob, & Benowitz, 2002). Thus, CBT interventions are the most widely used strategy for smoking cessation.

Currently, most smoking behavior counseling tends to be provided by prenatal clinic staff, but few actually provide cessation-related advice. In a population–based survey of 4,473 postpartum smokers, only 57%

reported that a provider counseled them to quit smoking. Moreover, while brief behavioral counseling at a prenatal visit is the standard practice, it produces only modest smoking cessation (Berg, Park, Chang, & Rigotti, 2008). It is important to understand potential barriers that the clinic staff face to deliver required advice, because the prenatal visit is a good opportunity to assess smoking status and provide credible advice, referral, and encouragement to quit smoking. Interventions that target barriers to cessation during pregnancy are needed (e.g., Berg et al., 2008; Linares Scott, Heil, Higgins, Badger, & Bernstein, 2009). Moreover, counseling in the context of pregnancy often does not generalize to the postpartum period. In a recent study examining the efficacy of counseling intervention among pregnant women, Hannover et al. (2009) found that while counseling was effective in maintaining abstinence at 6 months, abstinence was not sustained in the relapse prevention group, underscoring the need for better cessation and relapse prevention strategies for smokers who quit before or during pregnancy.

Postpartum and Smoking Relapse

About two-thirds of women who stop smoking during pregnancy relapse within 6 months after delivery (e.g., Martin et al., 2008; Ratner, Johnson, Bottorff, Dahinten, & Hall, 2000). Increased postpartum depressive symptoms predict a greater chance of relapse (Park et al., 2009). Park et al. (2009) found that women who relapsed at the end of 24 weeks postpartum reported a higher score of depressive, anxiety, and stress symptoms compared to nonsmokers. A qualitative study of 49 inner-city women who quit smoking before or during pregnancy showed similar results, with stress cited as the predominant reason for postpartum relapse (Letourneau et al., 2007). Women, especially those from underserved communities, might benefit from learning effective coping strategies to deal with stress. Because women who do relapse postpartum are also more likely to report a history of depression (Park et al., 2009), there is a need for clinic-level interventions to address depressive symptoms of maternal smokers during pregnancy and prepare them for mood changes, while closely monitoring the postpartum period as they cope with mood changes.

Moreover, based on the association between sleep and depressed mood (Posmontier, 2008), disturbed sleep patterns, along with parenting stress and hormonal changes during the first 3 months postpartum, could play a role in relapse to smoking during this period. Similar to prenatal smoking interventions, pediatric primary care visits are an excellent opportunity to address postpartum smoking (Collins, Nair, Shwarz, & Winick-off, in press). Also similar to prenatal clinics, pediatric providers rarely follow complete guidelines to assess, advise, refer, and follow up with identified maternal smokers for many of the same reasons as obstetrics and gynecology providers (e.g., lack of time, confidence in counseling ability, lack of reimbursement; Collins, Levin, & Bryant-Stephens, 2007; Mueller & Collins, 2008).

Sociocultural Factors

African American women initiate smoking later than Caucasian women (Moon-Howard, 2003). Although later initiation relates to better cessation outcomes in general, African Americans do not express this effect (Thompson, Moon-Howard, & Messeri, 2011). African American females have lower cessation rates compared to Caucasian female smokers (King et al., 2006) and are less successful in quitting smoking, although they have a strong desire to quit, are more confident in their ability to quit, and smoke fewer cigarettes per day than their counterparts (e.g., Ludman et al., 2000). An explanation for this disparity could be that standard cessation paradigms are less socioculturally relevant to African Americans, hence limiting their efficacy (Fernander, Bush, Goldsmith-Mason, White, & Obi, 2009). Interventions to reduce postpartum smoking among African Americans are rare, particularly in underserved populations. Multilevel strategies that include more intensive counseling integrated with community-based interventions may be the most effective solution in this population.

PUBLIC HEALTH PRIORITIES AND FUTURE DIRECTIONS

Ongoing, broad public health priorities in tobacco control persist worldwide. Of primary importance are continued efforts to improve the effectiveness of prevention and cessation treatments across multiple levels of intervention (e.g., individual- and family-level counseling, social marketing). Essential target populations include women, particularly in underserved, economically deprived areas, and racial minorities that bear disproportionate tobacco-related MM burden. The next step to considering future directions involves evaluating the advances in tobacco intervention and control over the past few decades (see Niaura & Abrams, 2002).

Present NRT and nicotine withdrawal medications increase the likelihood of achieving smoking cessation. Unfortunately, these medications demonstrate extensive variation in success rates across studies, produce side effects, and when used without counseling, demonstrate relatively low success rates. Thus, the need to develop more effective smoking cessation drugs continues. Cassella, Caponnetto, and Polosa (2010) describe potentially substantial benefits from new cessation products, such as immunopharmacotherapies (vaccines), which use specific antibodies to reduce nicotine blood levels in the brain, minimizing nicotine's reinforcing effects on brain reward pathways. Preclinical studies support hypothesized pharmacokinetic and self-administration effects of nicotine vaccines, and preliminary clinical trial data is encouraging (e.g., Cornuz et al., 2008; Moreno et al., 2010). Monoamine type B (MAO-B) inhibitors represent another novel pharmacotherapy that is likely to be available soon. Notwithstanding these advances, more development and testing needs to focus on the unique challenges women face with smoking cessation.

Future programs could capitalize on the growing evidence of efficacy of treatment matching (Niaura & Abrams, 2002). This approach uses precessation assessments to identify characteristics that benefit from specific types of treatment components. Examples include (a) genotyping and genetic counseling to identify those who could benefit from intensive treatment and/or those who are likely to respond favorably to specific classes of medication; (b) assessing self-reported weight concerns, or observing smoking urge and NA responses to smoking-related cues (Collins et al., 2011) to identify women who may benefit most from physical activity and/or targeted counseling components. Additional tools that could uncover specific treatment needs include neuroimaging (e.g., functional magnetic resonance imaging [fMRI], positron emission tomography), instruments that are currently used to improve our understanding of the neurobiological processes underlying nicotine dependence.

Most recent advances in tobacco control reflect massive efforts focused on prevention, policy, and pharmacological strategies to promote cessation. From a global perspective, these efforts are critical, because without considerable innovation in tobacco control, reductions in smoking prevalence, especially in LTMI countries, are less likely to occur. But policy and public health efforts as well as pharmacotherapies tackle only part of the challenge, and these efforts should not overshadow the importance of resources needed to improve behavioral interventions.

Counseling and behavioral interventions are necessary to enhance women's motivation to quit smoking, facilitate active quit attempts, and minimize the high relapse rates that occur well after the nicotine withdrawal phase and after discontinuation of pharmacotherapy. There are numerous ways in which behavioral science can inform and improve tobacco control efforts, such as the following:

- Inform front-line strategies within primary care clinics in which women frequently seek services (Collins et al., 2007; Mueller & Collins, 2008). Maternal and child health clinicians embody a credible source for tobacco-related education, and clinic-level interventions are known to increase maternal smokers' motivation to quit.
- Facilitate tailoring intervention components to specific individual-level needs, such as PA and weight concerns management, or broader population needs, such as strategies that assist women in managing NA without smoking. For example, cue

exposure paradigms (e.g., Collins et al., 2011) could be improved by integrating cognitive coping skills training for mood management.

- Guide innovative ways to improve the generalizability of treatment gains across temporal and environmental contexts (Collins & Brandon, 2002). For example, family-level interventions may facilitate social support and interpersonal behavioral shaping within contexts where maternal smoking and child SHSe most frequently occur (Collins et al., 2010).
- Guide novel community-level strategies that improve enrollment and retention of high-risk smokers in evidence-based cessation interventions. Without adequate participant retention in smoking trials, research cannot establish the validity or effectiveness of interventions.

By highlighting the multiple points of intervention where behavioral science can improve tobacco control efforts, it becomes apparent that the next appropriate steps to improve cessation intervention services are multilevel interventions that address individual, group, and environmental influences on tobacco use (NIHSBC, 2009). Current approaches to intervention and control are limited in their potential impact when implemented at a single level. For example, because of resource and time constraints, pediatric clinic-based interventions to reduce child SHSe and maternal smoking rates tend to be brief and lack sufficient intensity to promote lasting smoking behavior change.

Developing and testing multilevel strategies that can integrate and improve social marketing, health education, advice from clinicians, and navigation support of existing intervention services is possible, but some could argue costly to implement. However, offering this comprehensive service in communities that have the highest prevalence of tobacco use and tobacco-related MM could produce the greatest public health benefits. For example, publicly supported community-based providers of smoking cessation services and primary care clinics that serve high-risk populations could adopt this model. It would place minimal burden on clinicians, but they would remain a credible gateway to the more intensive intervention and provide longer follow-up support.

Future tobacco intervention trials should be guided by theory that frames the interplay among relevant biobehavioral and sociocultural components. Theory-driven research generates important information about why and for whom interventions work and provides direction to further advance innovation. We conceptualize the multilevel intervention-behavior change process within a behavioral ecological model (BEM) (Hovell, Wahlgren, & Gehrman, 2002), a model that integrates biological and ecological concepts grounded with principles of behavior based on associative learning theories. Behavioral interventions within this framework emphasize the importance of interacting contingencies that influence smoking behavior change across the individual-, interpersonal-, and broader group- and population/policy-levels.

REFERENCES

American Cancer Society. (2009). *Cancer facts and figures 2009*. Atlanta, GA: Author.

Amos, A., Greaves, L., Nichter, M., & Bloch, M. (2011). Women and tobacco: A call for including gender in tovbacco control research, policy and practice. *Tobacco Control, 21*(2), 236–243.

Ahluwalia, J. S., Dang, K. S., Choi, W. S., & Harris, K. J. (2002). Smoking behaviors and regular source of health care among African Americans. *Preventive Medicine*, *34*(3), 393–396.

Alexander, C., Piazza, M., Mekos, D., & Valente, T. (2001). Peers, schools, and adolescent cigarette smoking. *Journal of Adolescent Health*, *29*(1), 22–30.

Allen, S. S., Allen, A. M., Lunos, S., & Hatsukami, D. K. (2009). Patterns of self-selected smoking cessation attempts and relapse by menstrual phase. *Addictive Behaviors*, *34*(11), 928–931.

Allen, S. S., Allen, A. M., & Pomerleau, C.S. (2009). Influence of phase-related variability in premenstrual symptomology, mood, smoking withdrawal, and smoking behavior during ad libitum smoking on smoking cessation outcome. *Addictive Behaviors*, *34*(1), 107–111.

Allen, S. S., Bade, T., Center, B., Finstad, D., & Hatsukami, D. K. (2008). Menstrual phase effects on smoking relapse. *Addiction*, *103*, 809–821.

Ambrosone, C. B., & Shields, P. (2001). Smoking as a risk factor for breast cancer. In A. Bowcock (Ed.), *Breast cancer: Molecular genetics, pathogenesis, and therapeutics* (pp. 519–536). Totowa, NJ: Humana Press.

Benowitz, N. L., & Wilson, P. M. (2000). Nonnicotine pharmacotherapy for smoking cessation: Mechanisms and prospects. *CNS Drugs*, *13*, 265–285.

Berg, C. J., Park, E. R., Chang, Y., & Rigotti, N. A. (2008). Is concern about post-cessation weight gain a barrier to smoking cessation among pregnant women? *Nicotine & Tobacco Research*, *10*(7), 1159–1163.

Bjartveit, K., & Tverdal, A. (2005). Health consequences of smoking 4 cigarettes per day. *Tobacco Control*, *14*(5), 315–320.

Blitzer, P. H., Rimm, A. A., & Giefer, E. E. (1977). The effect of cessation of smoking on body weight in 57,032 women: Cross-sectional and longitudinal analyses. *Journal of Chronic Diseases*, *30*(7), 415–429.

Bock, B. C., Marcus, B. H., King, T. K., Borrelli, B., & Roberts, M. R. (1999). Exercise effects on withdrawal and mood among women attempting smoking cessation. *Addictive Behaviors*, *24*(3), 399–410.

Boden, J. M., Fergusson, D. M., & Horwood, L. J. (2010). Cigarette smoking and depression: Tests of causal linkages using a longitudinal birth cohort. *The British Journal of Psychiatry*, *196*(6), 440–446.

Boyd, T. C., Boyd, C. J., & Greenlee, T. B. (2003). A means to an end: Slim hopes and cigarette advertising. *Health Promotion Practice*, *4*(3), 266–277.

Burns, D. M. (1997, June). *Estimating the benefits of a risk reduction strategy*. Paper presented at the Society for Research on Nicotine and Tobacco, Nashville, TN.

Burton, S. L., Gitchell, J. G., & Shiffman, S. (2000). Use of FDA-approved pharmacological treatments for tobacco dependence: United States 1984–1998. *Morbidity and Mortality Weekly Report*, *49*, 665–668.

Cahill, K., Stead, L., & Lancaster, T. (2009). A preliminary benefit-risk assessment of Varinicline in smoking cessation. *Drug Safety*, *32*(2), 119–135.

Camp, D. E., Klesges, R. C., & Relyea, G. (1993). The relationship between body weight concerns and adolescent smoking. *Health Psychology*, *12*(1), 24–32.

Carpenter, M. J., Saladin, M. E., Leinbach, A. S., Larowe, S. D., & Upadhyaya, H. P. (2008). Menstrual phase effects on smoking cessation: A pilot feasibility study. *Journal of Women's Health (15409996)*, *17*(2), 293–301.

Cassella, G., Caponnetto, P., & Polosa, R. (2010). Therapeutic advances in the treatment of nicotine addiction: Present and future. *Therapeutic Advances in Chronic Disease Prevention*, *1*(3), 95–106.

Cavallo, D. A., Duhig, A. M., McKee, S., & Krishnan-Sarin, S. (2006). Gender and weight concerns in adolescent smokers. *Addictive Behavior*, *31*(11), 2140–2146.

Cawley, J., Markowitz, S., & Tauras, J. (2004). Lighting up and slimming down: The effects of body weight and cigarette prices on adolescent smoking initiation. *Journal of Health Economics*, *23*(2), 293–311.

Centers for Disease Control and Prevention. (2001). *Highlights: Health consequence of tobacco use among women.* Available at: http://www.cdc.gov/tobacco/data_statistics/sgr/2001/highlights/consequences/index.htm

Centers for Disease Control and Prevention. (2007). *Summary health statistics for U.S. adults: National health survey 2006*. Atlanta, GA: Author.

Centers for Disease Control and Prevention. (2008). *Smoking-attributable mortality, years of potential life* lost, and productivity losses—United States, 2000–2004. Atlanta, GA: Author.

Centers for Disease Control and Prevention. (2010). *Youth and tobacco use: Current estimates.* Available at: http://www.cdc.gov/tobacco/data_statistics/fact_sheets/youth_data/tobacco_use/index.htm

Cepeda-Benito, A., & Reig Ferrer, A. (2000). Smoking consequences questionnaire—Spanish. *Psychology of Addictive Behaviors, 14*(3), 219–230.

Cepeda-Benito, A., Reynoso, J. T., & Erath, S. (2004). Meta-analysis of the efficacy of nicotine replacement therapy for smoking cessation: Differences between men and women. *Journal of Consulting and Clinical Psychology, 72*(4), 712–722.

Clark, M. M., Hays, J. T., Vickers, K. S., Patten, C. A., Croghan, I. T., Berg, E., . . . Hurt, R. D. (2005). Body image treatment for weight concerned smokers: A pilot study. *Addictive Behaviors, 30*(6), 1236–1240.

Collins, B. N., & Brandon, T. H. J. (2002). Effects of extinction context and retrieval cues on alcohol cue reactivity among nonalcoholic drinkers. *Journal of Consulting and Clinical Psychology, 70,* 390–397.

Collins, B. N., DiSantis, K. I., & Nair, U. S. (2011). Longer previous smoking abstinence relates to successful breastfeeding initiation among underserved smokers. *Breastfeeding Medicine, 6*(6), 385–391.

Collins, B. N., Ibrahim, J., Hovell, M. H., Tolley, N. M., Nair, U. S., Jaffe, K., Zanis, D., & Audrain-McGovern, J. (2010). Residential smoking restrictions alone may not be sufficient to reduce child secondhand smoke exposure among low-income, urban African Americans. *Health 2*(11), 1264–1271.

Collins, B. N., Levin, K., & Bryant-Stephens, T. (2007). Pediatrician practices and attitudes about environmental tobacco smoke and parental smoking. *Journal of Pediatrics, 150*(5), 547–552.

Collins, B. N., Nair, U., Hovell, M. H., & Audrain-McGovern, J. (2009). Predictors of smoking-related weight concerns among underserved, black female smokers. *American Journal of Health Behavior, 33*(6), 699–709.

Collins, B. N., Nair, U. S., Hovell, M. H., Wileyto, E. P., Jaffe, K., & Audrain-McGovern, J. (in submission). Behavioral counseling with underserved maternal smokers reduces young children's SHS exposure and promotes smokers' quit attempts.

Collins, B. N., Nair, U. S., & Komaroff, E. A. (2011). Smoking cue reactivity across massed extinction trials: Negative affect and gender effects. *Addictive Behaviors, 36*(4), 308–314.

Collins, B. N., Nair, U. S., Swarz, M., & Winickoff, J. (in press). Pediatric sick visits linked to maternal depressive symptoms among low-income African American smokers. *Journal of Child and Family Studies.*

Collins, B. N., Wileyto, E. P., Hovell, M. H., Nair, U. S., Jaffe, K., & Audrain-McGovern, J. (2011). Proactive recruitment predicts retention to end of treatment in a secondhand smoke reduction trial with low-income maternal smokers. *Translational Behavioral Medicine, 1*(3), 394–399.

Collins, B. N., Wileyto, E. P., Patterson, F., Rukstalis, M., Audrain-McGovern, J., Kaufmann, V., . . . Lerman, C. (2004). Gender differences in smoking cessation in a placebo-controlled trial of bupropion with behavioral counseling. *Nicotine & Tobacco Research, 6,* 27–37.

Copeland, A. L., & Carney, C. E. (2003). Smoking expectancies as mediators between dietary restraint and disinhibition and smoking in college women. *Experimental and Clinical Psychopharmacology, 11*(3), 247–251.

Copeland, A. L., Martin, P. D., Geiselman, P. J., Rash, C. J., & Kendzor, D. E. (2006). Predictors of pretreatment attrition from smoking cessation among pre- and postmenopausal, weight-concerned women. *Eating Behaviors, 7*(3), 243–251.

Cornuz, J., Zwahlen, S., Jungi, W. F., Osterwalder, J., Klingler, K., van Melle, G., . . . Cerny, T. (2008). A vaccine against nicotine for smoking cessation: A randomized controlled trial. *PLoS ONE, 3*(6), e2547.

Covey, L. S. (2004). Comments on "History of depression and smoking cessation outcome: A meta-analysis," *Nicotine & Tobacco Research* (Vol. 6, pp. 743–745). Oxford, UK: Oxford University Press.

de Leon, J., Diaz, F. J., Rogers, T., Browne, D., & Dinsmore, L. (2002). Initiation of daily smoking and nicotine dependence in schizophrenia and mood disorders. *Schizophrenia Research, 56*(1–2), 47–54.

Delva, J., Tellez, M., Finlayson, T. L., Gretebeck, K. A., Siefert, K., Williams, D. R., & Ismail, A. I. (2005). Cigarette smoking among low-income African Americans: A serious public health problem. *American Journal of Preventive Medicine*, *29*(3), 218–220.

Dempsey, D., Jacob, P., & Benowitz, N. L. (2002). Accelerated metabolism of nicotine and cotinine in pregnant smokers. *Journal of Pharmacology and Experimental Therapeutics*, *301*(2), 594–598.

DiSantis, K. I., Collins, B. N., & McCoy, A. (2010). Associations among breastfeeding, smoking relapse, and prenatal factors in a brief postpartum smoking intervention. *Acta Obstetricia et Gynecologica Scandinavica*, *89*, 582–586.

Downs, S., Brandli, O., Zellweger, J. P., Schindler, C., Kunzli, N., Gerbase, M., . . . SAPALDIA Team. (2005). Accelerated decline in lung function in smoking women with airway obstruction: SAPALDIA 2 cohort study. *Respiratory Research*, *6*(1), 45.

Dransfield, M. T., Davis, J. J., Gerald, L. B., & Bailey, W. C. (2006). Racial and gender differences in susceptibility to tobacco smoke among patients with chronic obstructive pulmonary disease. *Respiratory Medicine*, *100*(6), 1110–1116.

Droomers, M., Schrijvers, C. T. M., & Mackenbach, J. P. (2002). Why do lower-educated people continue smoking? Explanations from the longitudinal GLOBE Study. *Health Psychology*, *21*(3), 263–272.

Ewart, C. K., & Suchday, S. (2002). Discovering how urban poverty and violence affect health: Development and validation of a neighborhood stress index. *Health Psychology*, *21*(3), 254–262.

Fagan, P., Moolchan, E. T., Lawrence, D., Fernander, A., & Ponder, P. K. (2007). Identifying health disparities across the tobacco continuum. *Addiction*, *102*, 5–29.

Fernander, A., Bush, H., Goldsmith-Mason, S., White, P., & Obi, B. (2009). End-of-treatment smoking cessation among African American female participants in the Breath Free for Women smoking cessation program: Results of a pilot study. *Journal of the National Medical Association*, *101*(10), 1034–1040.

Fiore, M. C., Bailey, W. C., Cohen, S. J., Dorfman, S. F., Goldstein, M. G., & Gritz, E. R. (2000). *Treating tobacco use and dependence: Clinical practice guideline.* Rockville, MD: USDHHS, Public Health Service.

Flay, B. R., Hu, F. B., Siddiqui, O., Day, L. E., Hedeker, D., Petraitis, J., . . . Sussman, S. (1994). Differential influence of parental smoking and friends' smoking on adolescent initiation and escalation and smoking. *Journal of Health and Social Behavior*, *35*(3), 248–265.

Foulds, J. (2006). The neurobiological basis for partial agonist treatment of nicotine dependence: Varenicline. *International Journal of Clinical Practice*, *60*(5), 571–576.

Franklin, T. R., Ehrman, R., Lynch, K. G., Harper, D., Sciortino, N., O'Brien, C. P., & Childress, A. R. (2008). Menstrual cycle phase at quit date predicts smoking status in an NRT treatment trial: A retrospective analysis. *Journal of Women's Health (15409996)*, *17*(2), 287–292.

Franklin, T. R., Napier, K., Ehrman, R., Gariti, P., O'Brien, C. P., & Childress, A. R. (2004). Retrospective study: Influence of menstrual cycle on cue-induced cigarette craving. *Nicotine & Tobacco Research*, *6*(1), 171–175.

Gan, W., Man, S., Postma, D., Camp, P., & Sin, D. (2006). Female smokers beyond the perimenopausal period are at increased risk of chronic obstructive pulmonary disease: A systematic review and meta-analysis. *Respiratory Research*, *7*(1), 52.

Gasperino, J., & Rom, W. N. (2004). Gender and lung cancer. *Clinical Lung Cancer*, *5*(6), 353–359.

Giovino, G. A., Sidney, S., Gfroerer, J. C., O'Malley, P. M., Allen, J. A., Richter, P. A., & Cummings, K. M. (2004). Epidemiology of menthol cigarette use. *Nicotine & Tobacco Research*, *6*(Suppl 1), S67–S81.

Goldade, K., Nichter, M., Nichter, M., Adrian, S., Tesler, L., & Muramoto, M. (2008). Breastfeeding and smoking among low-income women: Results of a longitudinal qualitative study. *Birth*, *35*(3), 230–240.

Gupta, P. C., Mehta, F. S., & Pindborg, J. J. (1984). Mortality among reverse chutta smokers in south India. *British Medical Journal (Clinical research ed.)*, *289*(6449), 865–866.

Hannover, W., Thyrian, J. R., Roske, K., Grempler, J., Rumpf, H. J., John, U., & Hapke, U. (2009). Smoking cessation and relapse prevention for postpartum women: Results from a randomized controlled trial at 6, 12, 18, and 24 months. *Addictive Behaviors*, *34*(1), 1–8.

Hitsman, B., Borrelli, B., McChargue, D. E., Spring, B., & Niaura, R. (2003). History of depression and smoking cessation outcome: A meta-analysis. *Journal of Consulting and Clinical Psychology*, *71*(4), 657–663.

Ho, M. G., Shi, Y., Ma, S., & Novotny, T. E. (2007). Perceptions of tobacco advertising and marketing that might lead to smoking initiation among Chinese high school girls. *Tobacco Control, 16*(5), 359–360.

Holtrop, J., Meghea, C., Raffo, J., Biery, L., Chartkoff, S., & Roman, L. (2009). Smoking among pregnant women with Medicaid insurance: Are mental health factors related? *Maternal and Child Health Journal, 14*(6), 971–977.

Horta, B. L., Victora, C. G., Menezes, A. M., & Barros, F. C. (1997). Environmental tobacco smoke and breastfeeding duration. *American Journal of Epidemiology, 146*(2), 128–133.

Hovell, M. F., Wahlgren, D. R., & Gehrman, C. (2002). The behavioral ecological model: Integrating public health and behavioral science. In R. J. DiClemente, R. Crosby, & M. Kegler (Eds.), *New and emerging models and theories in health promotion and health education* (pp. 347–385). San Francisco, CA: Jossey-Bass.

Hu, F. B., Flay, B. R., Hedeker, D., Siddiqui, O., & Day, L. E. (1995). The influences of friends' and parental smoking on adolescent smoking behavior: The effects of time and prior smoking. *Journal of Applied Social Psychology, 25*(22), 2018–2047.

Husky, M. M., Mazure, C. M., Paliwal, P., & McKee, S. A. (2008). Gender differences in the comorbidity of smoking behavior and major depression. *Drug and Alcohol Dependence, 93*(1–2), 176–179.

International Agency for Research on Cancer. (2008). *World cancer report.* Lyon, France: Author.

Jemal, A., Tiwari, R. C., Murray, T., Ghafoor, A., Samuels, A., Ward, E., . . . American Cancer Society. (2004). Cancer statistics, 2004. *CA: A Cancer Journal for Clinicians, 54*(1), 8–29.

Jensen, T. K., Joffe, M., Scheike, T., Skytthe, A., Gaist, D., Petersen, I., & Christensen, K. (2006). Early exposure to smoking and future fecundity among Danish twins. *International Journal of Andrology, 29*(6), 603–613.

Johnson, K. C. (2005). Accumulating evidence on passive and active smoking and breast cancer risk. *International Journal of Cancer, 1171*, 619–628.

Jonsdottir, D., & Jonsdottir, H. (2001). Does physical exercise in addition to a multicomponent smoking cessation program increase abstinence rate and suppress weight gain? An intervention study. *Scandinavian Journal of the Caring Sciences 15*, 275–282.

Kahn, R. S., Certain, L., & Whitaker, R. C. (2002). A reexamination of smoking before, during, and after pregnancy. *American Journal of Public Health, 92*(11), 1801–1808.

Kato, I., Toniolo, P., Koenig, K. L., Shore, R. E., Zeleniuch-Jacquotte, A., Akhmedkhanov, A., & Riboli, E. (1999). Epidemiologic correlates with menstrual cycle length in middle-aged women. *European Journal of Epidemiology, 15*(9), 809–814.

Kelly, A., Blair, N., & Pechacek, T. F. (2001). Women and smoking: Issues and opportunities. *Journal of Women's Health & Gender-Based Medicine, 10*(6), 515–518.

King, G., Polednak, A., Fagan, P., Gilreath, T., Humphrey, E., & Fernander, A. E. A. (2006). Heterogeneity in the smoking behavior of African American women. *American Journal of Health Behavior, 30*, 237–246.

Klesges, R. C., Winders, S. E., Meyers, A. W., Eck, L. H., Ward, K. D., Hultquist, C. M., . . . Shadish, W. R. (1997). How much weight gain occurs following smoking cessation? A comparison of weight gain using both continuous and point prevalence abstinence. *Journal of Consulting and Clinical Psychology, 65*(2), 286–291.

Kotlyar, M., Golding, M., Hatsukami, D. K., & Jamerson, B. D. (2001). Effect of non-nicotine pharmacotherapy on smoking behavior. *Pharmacotherapy, 21*(12), 1530–1548.

Lasser, K., Boyd, J. W., Woolhandler, S., Himmelstein, D. U., McCormick, D., & Bor, D. H. (2000). Smoking and mental illness. *JAMA, 284*(20), 2606–2610.

Lerman, C., Roth, D., Kaufmann, V., Audrain, J., Hawk, L., Liu, A., . . . Epstein, L. (2002). Mediating mechanisms for the impact of bupropion in smoking cessation treatment. *Drug and Alcohol Dependence, 67*(2), 219–223.

Letourneau, A. R., Sonja, B., Mazure, C. M., O'Malley, S. S., James, D., & Colson, E. R. (2007). Timing and predictors of postpartum return to smoking in a group of inner-city women: An exploratory pilot study. *Birth, 34*(3), 245–252.

Levine, M. D., Marcus, M. D., & Perkins, K. A. (2003). A history of depression and smoking cessation outcomes among women concerned about post-cessation weight gain. *Nicotine & Tobacco Research, 5*(1), 69.

Levine, M. D., Perkins, K. A., & Marcus, M. D. (2001). The characteristics of women smokers concerned about postcessation weight gain. *Addictive Behaviors, 26*(5), 749–756.

Linares Scott, T. J., Heil, S. H., Higgins, S. T., Badger, G. J., & Bernstein, I. M. (2009). Depressive symptoms predict smoking status among pregnant women. *Addictive Behaviors, 34*(8), 705–708.

Ludman, E. J., McBride, C. M., Nelson, J. C., Curry, S. J., Grothaus, L. C., Lando, H. A., & Pirie, P. L. (2000). Stress, depressive symptoms, and smoking cessation among pregnant women. *Health Psychology, 19*(1), 21–27.

Malaiyandi, V., Lerman, C., Benowitz, N. L., Jepson, C., Patterson, F., & Tyndale, R. F. (2006). Impact of CYP2A6 genotype on pretreatment smoking behaviour and nicotine levels from and usage of nicotine replacement therapy. *Molecular Psychiatry, 11*(4), 400–409.

Manfredi, C., Lacey, L., Warnecke, R., & Buis, M. (1992). Smoking-related behavior, beliefs, and social environment of young black women in subsidized public housing in Chicago. *American Journal of Public Health, 82*(2), 267–272.

Marcus, B. H., Forsyth, L. H., Stone, E. J., Dubbert, P. M., McKenzie, T. L., Dunn, A. L., & Blair, S. N. (2000). Physical activity behavior change: Issues in adoption and maintenance. *Health Psychology, 19*(1), 32–41.

Martin, L. T., McNamara, M., Milot, A., Bloch, M., Hair, E. C., & Halle, T. (2008). Correlates of smoking before, during, and after pregnancy. (Clinical report). *American Journal of Health Behavior, 32*(3), 272. (211)

Mazas, C. A., & Wetter, D. W. (2003). Smoking cessation interventions among African Americans: Research needs. *Cancer Control, 10*(5), 87–89.

Mazure, C. M., Toll, B., McKee, S. A., Wu, R., & O'Malley, S. S. (2011). Menstrual cycle phase at quit date and smoking abstinence at 6 weeks in an open label trial of Bupropion. *Drug and Alcohol Dependence, 114*(1), 68–72.

McChargue, D. E., Cohen, L. M., & Cook, J. W. (2004). The influence of personality and affect on nicotine dependence among male college students. *Nicotine & Tobacco Research, 6*(2), 287–294.

McChargue, D. E., Spring, B., Cook, J. W., & Neumann, C. A. (2004). Reinforcement expectations explain the relationship between depressive history and smoking status in college students. *Addictive Behaviors, 29*(5), 991–994.

Meireles, S. I., Esteves, G. H., Hirata, R., Peri, S., Devarajan, K., Slifker, M., . . . Clapper, M. L. (2010). Early changes in gene expression induced by tobacco smoke: Evidence for the importance of estrogen within lung tissue. *Cancer Prevention Research, 3*(6), 707–717.

Mermelstein, R. (1999). Ethnicity, gender and risk factors for smoking initiation: An overview. *Nicotine & Tobacco Research, 1*(Suppl 2), S39–S43.

Meyers, A. W., Klesges, R. C., Winders, S. E., Ward, K. D., Peterson, B. A., & Eck, L. H. (1997). Are weight concerns predictive of smoking cessation? A prospective analysis. *Journal of Consulting and Clinical Psychology, 65*(3), 448–452.

Mishra, G. D., Dobson, A. J., & Schofield, M. J. (2000). Cigarette smoking, menstrual symptoms and miscarriage among young women. *Australian and New Zealand Journal of Public Health, 24*(4), 413–420.

Mizes, J., Sloan, D., Segraves, K., Spring, B., Pingitore, R., & Kristeller, J. (1998). The influence of weight-related variables on smoking cessation. *Behavior Therapy, 29*, 371–385.

Moon-Howard, J. (2003). African American women and smoking: Starting later. *American Journal of Public Health, 93*(3), 418–420.

Moreno, A. Y., Azar, M. R., Warren, N. A., Dickerson, T. J., Koob, G. F., & Janda, K. D. (2010). A critical evaluation of a nicotine vaccine within a self-administration behavioral model. *Molecular Pharmaceutics, 7*(2), 431–441.

Mousa, K., Ostergren, P. O., Grahn, M., Kunst, A. E., Eek, F., & Essen, B. (2009). Socioeconomic differences in smoking trends among pregnant women at first antenatal visit in Sweden 1982–2001: Increasing importance of educational level for the total burden of smoking. *Tobacco Control, 18*, 92–97.

Mueller, D., & Collins, B. N. (2008). Addressing patient exposure to ETS in pediatric specialty clinics: A current practices and training implications from a national internet survey. *Otolaryngology Head and Neck Surgery, 139*(3), 348–352.

Munafò, M. R., Hitsman, B., Rende, R., Metcalfe, C., & Niaura, R. (2008). Effects of progression to cigarette smoking on depressed mood in adolescents: Evidence from the National Longitudinal Study of Adolescent Health. *Addiction, 103*(1), 162–171.

Mwenifumbo, J. C., Sellers, E. M., & Tyndale, R. F. (2007). Nicotine metabolism and CYP2A6 activity in a population of black African descent: Impact of gender and light smoking. *Drug and Alcohol Dependence, 89*(1), 24–33.

Nair, U.S., Collins, B. N., & Napolitano, M. A. (under review). Physical activity and urge to smoke among weight-concerned physically active and sedentary college-age female smokers. *Psychology of Addictive Behaviors.*

Niaura, R., & Abrams, D. B. (2002). Smoking cessation: Progress, priorities, and prospectus. *Journal of Consulting and Clinical Psychology, 70*(3), 494–509.

Nichols, T. R., Birnbaum, A. S., Birnel, S., & Botvin, G. J. (2006). Perceived smoking environment and smoking initiation among multi-ethnic urban girls. *Journal of Adolescent Health, 38*(4), 369–375.

Nichols, T. R., Graber, J. A., Brooks-Gunn, J., & Botvin, G. J. (2004). Maternal influences on smoking initiation among urban adolescent girls. *Journal of Research on Adolescence, 14*(1), 73–97.

Nielsen, K., & Fiore, M. C. (2000). Cost-benefit analysis of sustained-release bupropion, nicotine patch, or both for smoking cessation. *Preventive Medicine, 30*(3), 209–216.

National Institute of Health. (2009, June 15–16). Science of behavior change. In *NIH Science and Behavior Change Meeting*, Bethesda, MD. Available at https://commonfund.nih.gov/documents/SOBC_Meeting_Summary_2009.pdf

Olsen, J. R. (1991). Cigarette smoking, tea and coffee drinking, and subfecundity. *American Journal of Epidemiology, 133*(7), 734–739.

Otten, R., Engels, R., van de Ven, M., & Bricker, J. (2007). Parental smoking and adolescent smoking stages: The role of parents' current and former smoking, and family structure. *Journal of Behavioral Medicine, 30*(2), 143–154.

Park, E. R., Chang, Y., Quinn, V., Regan, S., Cohen, L., Viguera, A., . . . Rigotti, N. (2009). The association of depressive, anxiety, and stress symptoms and postpartum relapse to smoking: A longitudinal study. *Nicotine & Tobacco Research, 11*(6), 707–714.

Patton, G. C., Carlin, J. B., Coffey, C., Wolfe, R., Hilbert, M., & Bowles, G. (1998). Depression, anxiety, and smoking initiation: A prospective study over 3 years. *American Journal of Public Health, 88*(10), 1518–1522.

Peppone, L. J., Piazza, K. M., Mahoney, M. C., Morrow, G. R., Mustian, K. M., Palesh, O. G., & Hyland, A. (2009). Associations between adult and childhood secondhand smoke exposures and fecundity and fetal loss among women who visited a cancer hospital. *Tobacco Control, 18*(2), 115–120.

Perez-Stable, E. J., Herrera, B., Jacob, P., & Benowitz, N. L. (1998). Nicotine metabolism and intake in black and white smokers. *JAMA, 280*(2), 152–156.

Perkins, K. A., Levine, M. D., Marcus, M. D., & Shiffman, S. (1997). Addressing women's concerns about weight gain due to smoking cessation. *Journal of Substance Abuse Treatment, 14*(2), 173–182.

Perkins, K. A., Marcus, M. D., Levine, M. D., D'Amico, D., Miller, A., Broge, M., . . . Shiffman, S. (2001). Cognitive-behavioral therapy to reduce weight concerns improves smoking cessation outcome in weight-concerned women. *Journal of Consulting and Clinical Psychology, 69*(4), 604–613.

Perkins, K. A., & Scott, J. (2008). Sex differences in long-term smoking cessation rates due to nicotine patch. *Nicotine & Tobacco Research, 10*(7), 1245–1251.

Phillips, D. H., Martin, F. L., & Grover, P. L., & Williams, J. A. (2001). Toxicological basis for a possible association of breast cancer with smoking and other sources of environmental carcinogens. *Journal of Women's Cancer, 3*, 9–16.

Piasecki, T. M., Kenford, S. L., Smith, S. S., Fiore, M. C., & Baker, T. B. (1997). Listening to nicotine: Negative affect and the smoking withdrawal conundrum. *Psychological Science, 8*(3), 184–189.

Pierce, J. P., & Gilpin, E. A. (1995). A historical analysis of tobacco marketing and the uptake of smoking by youth in the United States: 1890–1977. *Health Psychology, 14*(6), 500–508.

Pinto, B. M., Borrelli, B., King, T. K., Bock, B. C., Clark, M. M., Roberts, M., & Marcus, B. H. (1999). Weight control smoking among sedentary women. *Addictive Behaviors, 24*(1), 75–86.

Pomerleau, C. S., Garcia, A. W., Pomerleau, O. F., & Cameron, O. G. (1992). The effects of menstrual phase and nicotine abstinence on nicotine intake and on biochemical and subjective measures in women smokers: A preliminary report. *Psychoneuroendocrinology, 17*(6), 627–638.

Pomerleau, C. S., Pomerleau, O. F., Namenek, R. J., & Mehringer, A. M. (2000). Short-term weight gain in abstaining women smokers. *Journal of Substance Abuse Treatment*, *18*(4), 339–342.

Pomerleau, C. S., Zucker, A. N., & Stewart, A. J. (2001). Characterizing concerns about post-cessation weight gain: Results from a national survey of women smokers. *Nicotine and Tobacco Research*, *3*(1), 51–60.

Posmontier, B. (2008). Sleep quality in women with and without postpartum depression. *Journal of Obstetric, Gynecologic, & Neonatal Nursing*, *37*(6), 722–737.

Prescott, E., Hippe, M., Schnohr, P., Hein, H. O., & Vestbo, J. (1998). Smoking and risk of myocardial infarction in women and men: Longitudinal population study. *British Medical Journal*, *316* (7137), 1043.

Rahmanian, S. D., Diaz, P. T., & Wewers, M. E. (2011). Tobacco use and cessation among women: Research and treatment-related issues. *Journal of Women's Health (15409996)*, *20*(3), 349–357.

Ratner, P. A., Johnson, J. L., Bottorff, J. L., Dahinten, S., & Hall, W. (2000). Twelve-month follow-up of a smoking relapse prevention intervention for postpartum women. *Addictive Behaviors*, *25*(1), 81–92.

Rigotti, N. A., Park, E. R., Chang, Y., & Regan, S. (2008). Smoking cessation medication use among pregnant and postpartum smokers. *Obstetrics & Gynecology*, *111* (2, Part 1), 348–355. doi: 310.1097/1001. AOG.0000297305.0000254455.0000297302e.

Rodgman, A., & Perfetti, T. A. (2009). *The chemical components of tobacco and tobacco smoke*. Boca Raton, FL: CRC Press.

Rosenberg, M. J., Waugh, M. S., & Stevens, C. M. (2006). Smoking and cycle control among oral contraceptive users. *American Journal of Obstetrics & Gynecology*, *174*(2), 628–832.

Samet, J. M., & Yoon, S. Y. (Eds.). (2010). *Gender, women, and the tobacco epidemic*. Geneva, Switzerland: World Health Organization.

Scharf, D., & Shiffman, S. (2004). Are there gender differences in smoking cessation, with and without bupropion? Pooled- and meta-analyses of clinical trials of Bupropion SR. *Addiction*, *99*(11), 1462–1469.

Schiff, I., Bell, W. R., Davis, V., Kessler, C. M., Meyers, C., Nakajima, S., & Sexton, B. J. (1999). Oral contraceptives and smoking, current considerations: Recommendations of a consensus panel. *American Journal of Obstetrics and Gynecology*, *180*(6, Supplement 1) S383–S384.

Secker-Walker, R. H., Solomon, L. J., Flynn, B. S., Skelly, J. M., & Mead, P. B. (1998). Smoking relapse prevention during pregnancy: A trial of coordinated advice from physicians and individual counseling. *American Journal of Preventive Medicine*, *15*(1), 25–31.

Shafey, O., Eriksen, M., Ross, H., & Mackay, J. (2009). *The tobacco atlas*. Atlanta, GA: American Cancer Society.

Shiffman, S., Mason, K. M., & Henningfield, J. E. (1998). Tobacco dependence treatments: Review and prospectus. *Annual Review of Public Health*, *19*, 335–358.

Snively, T. A., Ahijevych, K. L., Bernhard, L. A., & Wewers, M. E. (2000). Smoking behavior, dysphoric states and the menstrual cycle: Results from single smoking sessions and the natural environment. *Psychoneuroendocrinology*, *25*(7), 677–691.

Sonntag, H., Wittchen, H. U., Hofler, M., Kessler, R. C., & Stein, M. B. (2000). Are social fears and DSM-IV social anxiety disorder associated with smoking and nicotine dependence in adolescents and young adults? *European Psychiatry*, *15*(1), 67–74.

Stevens, S. L., Colwell, B., Smith, D. W., Robinson, J., & McMillan, C. (2005). An exploration of self-reported negative affect by adolescents as a reason for smoking: Implications for tobacco prevention and intervention programs. *Preventive Medicine*, *41*(2), 589–596.

Stotts, A. L., DiClemente, C. C., Carbonari, J. P., & Mullen, P. D. (2000). Postpartum return to smoking: Staging a "suspended" behavior. *Health Psychology*, *19*(4), 324–332.

Stroud, L. R., Paster, R. L., Papandonatos, G. D., Niaura, R., Salisbury, A. L., Battle, C., . . . Lester, B. (2009). Maternal smoking during pregnancy and newborn neurobehavior: Effects at 10 to 27 days. *The Journal of Pediatrics*, *154*(1), 10–16.

Swan, G. E., & Carmelli, D. (1995). Characteristics associated with excessive weight gain after smoking cessation in men. *American Journal of Public Health*, *85*(1), 73–77.

Talcott, G. W., Fiedler, E. R., Pascale, R. W., Klesges, R. C., Peterson, A. L., & Johnson, R. S. (1995). Is weight gain after smoking cessation inevitable? *Journal of Consulting and Clinical Psychology*, *63*(2), 313–316.

Tanko, L. B., & Christiansen, C. (2004). An update on the antiestrogenic effect of smoking: a literature review with implications for researchers and practitioners. *Menopause, 11*(1), 104–109. doi: 110.1097/1001.GME.0000079740.0000018541 .DB.

Tashkin, D. P., Kanner, R., Bailey, W., Buist, S., Anderson, P., Nides, M. A., . . . Jamerson, B. (2001). Smoking cessation in patients with chronic obstructive pulmonary disease: A double-blind, placebo-controlled, randomised trial. *The Lancet, 357*(9268), 1571–1575.

Terry, P. D., & Rohan, T. F. (2002). Cigarette smoking and the risk of breast cancer in women. *Cancer Epidemiology Biomarkers & Prevention, 11*(10), 953–971.

Thompson, A. B., Moon-Howard, J., & Messeri, P. A. (2011). Smoking cessation advantage among adult initiators: Does it apply to black women? *Nicotine & Tobacco Research, 13*(1), 15–21.

Toll, B. A., & Ling, P. M. (2005). The Virginia Slims identity crisis: An inside look at tobacco industry marketing to women. *Tobacco Control, 14*(3), 172–180.

Tomeo, C. A., Field, A. E., Berkey, C. S., Colditz, G. A., & Frazier, A. L. (1999). Weight concerns, weight control behaviors, and smoking initiation. *Pediatrics, 104*(4), 918–924.

Turner, L. R., Mermelstein, R., Hitsman, B., Warnecke, R. B. (2008). Social support as a moderator of the relationship between recent history of depression and smoking cessation among lower-educated women. *Nicotine and Tobacco Research, 28*(1), 201–212.

U.S. Department of Health and Human Services. (2001). *Women and smoking: A report of the Surgeon General.* Available at: www.cdc.gov/tobacco/ sgr/sgr_forwomen/Executive_Summary.htm.

U.S. Department of Health and Human Services. (2006). *The health consequences of involuntary exposure to tobacco smoke: A report of the Surgeon General.* Available at: http://www.surgeongeneral.gov/ librar/secondhandsmoke/

Vainio, H., Weiderpass, E., & Kleihues, P. (2001). Smoking cessation in cancer prevention. *Toxicology, 166*(1–2), 47–52.

Vogel, J. S., Hurford, D. P., Smith, J. V., & Cole, A. K. (2003). The relationship between depression and smoking in adolescents. *Adolescence, 38*(149), 57.

Voorhees, C. C., Schreiber, G. B., Schumann, B. C., Biro, F., & Crawford, P. B. (2002). Early predictors of daily smoking in young women: The National Heart, Lung, and Blood Institute Growth and Health Study. *Preventive Medicine, 34*(6), 616–624.

Voorhees, C. C., Ye, C., Carter-Pokras, O., MacPherson, L., Kanamori, M., Zhang, G., . . . Fiedler, R. (2011). Peers, tobacco advertising, and secondhand smoke exposure influences smoking initiation in diverse adolescents. *American Journal of Health Promotion, 25*(3), e1–e11.

Wack, J. T., & Rodin, J. (1982). Smoking and its effects on body weight and the systems of caloric regulation. *American Journal of Clinical Nutrition, 35*(2), 366–380.

Waldron, I., Lye, D., & Brandon, A. (1991). Gender differences in teenage smoking. *Women's Health, 17*(2), 65–90.

Webb, M. S., & Carey, M. P. (2008). Tobacco smoking among low-income Black women: Demographic and psychosocial correlates in a community sample. *Nicotine and Tobacco Research, 10*(1), 219–229.

Weekley, C. K., III, Klesges, R. C., & Reylea, G. (1992). Smoking as a weight-control strategy and its relationship to smoking status. *Addictive Behaviors, 17*(3), 259–271.

Westhoff, C., Jones, K., Robilotto, C., Heartwell, S., Edwards, S., Zieman, M., & Cushman, L. (2009). Smoking and oral contraceptive continuation. *Contraception, 79*(5), 375–378.

Wittchen, H. U., Stein, M. B., & Kessler, R. C. (1999). Social fears and social phobia in a community sample of adolescents and young adults: Prevalence, risk factors and co-morbidity. *Psychological Medicine, 29*(02), 309–323.

Wu, P., Wilson, K., Dimoulas, P., & Mills, E. J. (2006). Effectiveness of smoking cessation therapies: a systematic review and meta-analysis. *British Medical Centers Public Health, 6*, 300.

Xue, F., Willett, W. C., Rosner, B. A., Hankinson, S. E., & Michels, K. B. (2011). Cigarette smoking and the incidence of breast cancer. *Archives of Internal Medicine, 171*, 125–133.

Yamanaka, H., Nakajima, M., Fukami, T., Sakai, H., Nakamura, A., Katoh, M., . . . Yokoi, T. (2005). CYP2A6 and CYP2B6 are involved in nornicotine formation from nicotine in humans: Interindividual differences in these contributions. *Drug Metabolism and Disposition, 33* (12), 1811–1818.

Zang, E. A., & Wynder, E. L. (1996). Differences in lung cancer risk between men and women: Examination of the evidence. *Journal of the National Cancer Institute, 88*(3–4), 183–192.

Zeman, M. V., Hiraki, L., & Sellers, E. M. (2002). Gender differences in tobacco smoking: Higher relative exposure to smoke than nicotine in women. *Journal of Women's Health & Gender-Based Medicine, 11*(2), 147–153.

Zucker, A. N., Harrell, Z. A., Miner-Rubino, K., Stewart, A. J., Pomerleau, C. S., & Boyd, C. J. (2001). Smoking in college women: The role of thinness pressures, media exposure, and critical consciousness. *Psychology of Women Quarterly, 25*(3), 233–241.

7

Obesity in Women

MICHAEL R. LOWE, MEGHAN L. BUTRYN, AND ALICE V. ELY

INTRODUCTION

Obesity is a significant health problem affecting a growing number of people in the Western world. Sixty-eight percent of the population of the United States is overweight or obese (Flegal, Carroll, Ogden, & Curtin, 2010). The resultant medical and psychosocial difficulties can be debilitating and life-threatening, and extant research is only beginning to illuminate the range of causes and consequences of elevated weight. Furthermore, treatment research suggests that our ability to treat obesity remains limited, and individuals will frequently regain weight that is lost. Expanding knowledge on contributing factors and associated outcomes, particularly as related to gender, is important in developing effective care and building preventive interventions.

The purpose of this chapter is to review the causes and consequences of obesity and to provide an overview of research-based efforts to prevent and treat obesity. The chapter begins with a description of the multiple biological and environmental factors that affect weight gain and the development of obesity. This is followed by a discussion of the many consequences of obesity, which in Western cultures include psychological, social, and physical domains. Behavioral, dietary, surgical, and pharmacological treatments for weight loss are then

reviewed. Recently developed weight gain prevention research will be considered. Throughout the chapter, particular considerations for weight control in girls and women (such as during puberty, pregnancy, and menopause) are highlighted.

CAUSES OF WEIGHT GAIN AND OBESITY

Heritability

The amount of fat tissue that people accumulate in their bodies is a reflection of the long-term balance between their energy intake (from food and beverages) and their energy expenditure (from biological processes required for life as well as the energy expended in everyday activities). [Body mass index (BMI) or (weight in kgs)/(height in meters^2) is usually used to denote the level of adiposity, with a BMI of 25 to 30 denoting overweight and a BMI greater than 30 denoting obesity.] If more calories are consumed over time than are required to meet total energy needs, then weight will be gained. So-called naturally thin people can eat more calories than their bodies require because they are metabolically inefficient—their bodies are predisposed to burn off extra calories rather than to store them as body fat.

Most, if not all, of the influences that affect caloric intake and energy expenditure are partially heritable, and how much someone weighs relative to their height is also heritable. For instance, one study found that when pairs of identical twins were overfed under controlled conditions, the two members of each twin pair gained similar amounts of weight, while the average weight gain of different pairs of twins varied widely. This shows both that genes have a strong influence on how much overfeeding contributes to weight gain and how individual differences in genetic susceptibility will produce different amounts of weight change from the same level of overfeeding. However, genes are not necessarily destiny: Our gene pool as a species has not changed significantly in the past 50 years, but the prevalence of obesity has skyrocketed during the same period. Therefore, genes create a predisposition, but in the case of body weight, the environment— starting even before birth—determines whether such a predisposition will manifest in excessive weight gain (Stroebe, 2008).

Energy Balance

The process that determines whether we gain weight sounds simple: If we consume more calories than our bodies expend, then we will gain weight. Nonetheless, the biological and environmental determinants of how much we eat and much energy we burn are fiendishly complex. The obesity epidemic did not exist 50 years ago, and there has been considerable debate about how much increased caloric intake versus decreased energy expenditure (e.g., more sedentary activities) has contributed to the epidemic. Most researchers have concluded that increased caloric intake has played a more significant role than decreased caloric expenditure. However, preventing unhealthy weight gain and treating overweight should involve both

decreases in habitual caloric intake and increases in physical activity. Increased physical activity is important both because it burns calories and because it promotes health and counteracts many of the negative effects of weight gain.

The modern food environment in many developed countries has been called "toxic" because it promotes unhealthy weight gain and the many medical problems that obesity causes. Many specific aspects of the food environment promote excessive caloric intake. These include the availability of good-tasting food almost everywhere (including hardware stores, gas stations, sporting events, etc.), the optimization of the rewarding properties of food by food companies and restaurants, the high caloric density of many foods, the relatively low price of calorie-dense foods, the huge increase in portion sizes, and the increases in the variety of delicious foods available. All of these influences have been shown to increase caloric intake. At the same time, the amount of required energy expenditure from activities of daily living has decreased dramatically over the past century. People use a variety of labor-saving devices all day long, and many also spend much of their day sitting in front of computers or TVs. The resulting increase in energy intake and decrease in energy expenditure is responsible for the very high levels of overweight and obesity in most developed countries (Stroebe, 2008).

Metabolism and Obesity

Another question about the causes of obesity is how much differences in metabolism contribute to weight gain and obesity. That is, to what extent do some people have slow metabolisms that contribute to weight gain even if they don't eat an excessive amount of calories? It was once believed that many obese individuals had slow metabolisms, because studies where people kept track of their caloric intake found that obese individuals consume about the same number of calories as normal-weight individuals. However, as researchers developed tools to measure actual energy expenditure in everyday life, it became clear that overweight individuals were burning more calories than normal-weight individuals but were not losing weight. This means that the overweight individuals had to be consuming as much food energy as they were burning, which indicated that overweight individuals were underreporting their actual caloric intake in the studies where self-report was used to measure food intake. Subsequent research indeed found that overweight people are more likely to underreport their food intake. Therefore, the great majority of overweight people do not have slow metabolisms—on a pound-for-pound basis, they burn calories at the same rate as those who are not overweight. A small minority of individuals (research has estimated this to be about 15% of people) do have a sluggish metabolism and are therefore at greater risk for gaining weight over time (Ravussin, 2002).

Smoking Cessation

Smoking cessation is associated with significant weight gain over the ensuing 5 years. It has been estimated that 80% of those who quit will experience such a gain, which is greatest in the first year after quitting (at an average of 5 kg/11 lbs), but continues over the next 4 years as well (at an additional total of 3 kg/6–7 lbs). On average, women gain more weight during this period than do men. There is some evidence for nicotine replacement therapy limiting weight gain during the quitting process, but this effect has not been demonstrated to persist after treatment stops (Chandler & Rennard, 2010).

Viruses

A human adenovirus (adenovirus-36; Ad-36) has been shown to induce adiposity in experimentally infected chickens, mice, and nonhuman primates (Ginneken, Sitnya-kowsky, & Jeffery, 2009). No such causal evidence is available in a human population, but there is some correlational evidence for the possible role of Ad-36 in obesity, based on the discovery of an increased presence of antibodies for Ad-36 in obese subjects as compared to nonobese subjects (30% versus 11%, respectively).

Toxins

Endocrine-disrupting chemicals, long studied mostly for their effects on reproduction and cancer growth, may also affect weight gain and by extension obesity. Exposure to such toxins during the perinatal period might disrupt the normal functioning of homeostatic control systems later in life, making it more difficult for individuals to maintain a normal body weight. Findings from epidemiological studies have so far been inconclusive, with several finding positive associations between DDT and PCB exposures during pregnancy and later BMI, whereas others found null or negative associations (Hatch, Nelson, Stahlhut, & Webster, 2010).

Influences on Weight Related to Female Gender

Several factors specific to females affect the risk of weight gain and therefore the risk of becoming overweight or obese.

Nursing Breastfeeding has been demonstrated to reduce the risk for obesity in both children and mothers. Full-time breastfeeding, in contrast to no breastfeeding or a combination of breast and formula feeding, tends to place the child at a decreased risk for obesity and can also facilitate postpartum weight loss for mothers (Krause, Lovelady, Peterson, Chowdhury, & Ostbye, 2010).

Menarche Early menarche (younger than 12 years of age) has been related to higher adult BMI, waist circumference, fat mass index, and adulthood obesity. Late menarche, conversely, has been associated with decreased risk of adult obesity and lower BMI. Some studies have found this relationship to be partially mediated by childhood BMI and birth weight, but not by socioeconomic status (Prentice & Viner, 2010).

Pregnancy Maternal obesity places both mother and fetus at risk for a variety of complications. Risks to the mother include gestational diabetes, hypertension leading to preeclampsia during pregnancy, as well as heart disease and hypertension later in life. Increased risks for the child include stillbirth, congenital anomalies at birth, and obesity, heart disease, and diabetes in adulthood (Begum, Sachchithanantham, & De Somsubhra, 2011).

Menopause Menopause has been related to an increase in waist circumference, visceral fat, and total fat mass beginning several years before the final menstrual period. The rate of increase of visceral fat decreases significantly after the final menstrual period, although total fat mass continues to increase with age (Janssen, Powell, Kazlauskaite, & Dugan, 2010).

CONSEQUENCES OF OBESITY

A growing literature shows that obesity has pervasive public health, psychosocial, and physical costs. The medical difficulties that can result from severe overweight can be significant, and susceptibility to these health problems increases exponentially when one transitions from overweight to morbid obesity. Obesity can affect quality of life, lead to sleep difficulties, and produce hormonal changes. The stigma and discrimination experienced by obese individuals is also significant. This section outlines the various physical, psychological, and public health consequences of obesity.

Medical Consequences of Obesity

Obesity is associated with increases in disease risk and in mortality. Hypertension, diabetes, and coronary heart disease have all been shown to increase in prevalence with weight gain, in particular with abdominal and upper-body obesity. Though women are more likely to initially gain weight in the lower body, if weight gain continues, fat distribution tends to shift toward the upper body, which predisposes them to greater health risks (Pi-Sunyer, 2002). Upper-body obesity is linked with a higher incidence of many metabolic and cardiovascular abnormalities, including diabetes, insulin resistance, and hypertension (Ohlson et al., 1985; Hartz, Rupley, & Rimm, 1984).

Many studies have highlighted the association between obesity and type 2 diabetes. Diabetes is particularly strongly linked with higher BMIs in women, as shown in the Nurses' Health Study, a 14-year longitudinal study of health outcomes for 100,000 registered nurses (Colditz, Willett, Rotnitzky, & Manson, 1995). BMI was shown to be the primary risk factor predicting the development of diabetes. Those in the overweight range, between 25.0 and 28.9 kg/m^2, had markedly higher risks of developing diabetes than those whose BMI was 22 kg/m^2, while women in the study with a BMI higher than 35 kg/m^2 had 93 times the risk of developing diabetes than their normal-weight counterparts. Furthermore, body fat distribution is independently predictive of the development of the disease; holding BMI constant, a higher waist circumference (greater than 40 inches) is associated with 3.5 times the diabetes risk (Lean, Hans, & Seidell, 1998).

Cardiac abnormalities are also linked to obesity. Because of an increase in body mass (which comprises increases in both lean and adipose tissue), total body oxygen consumption is elevated, as is absolute cardiac output (Kopelman, 2000). Although this is proportional to body weight, structural changes in the heart take place resulting from increased blood volume, which can subsequently lead to increased stress to the walls of the chambers in the heart. Increased cardiac work, indicated by higher cardiac weights at higher BMIs, is suggested to produce cardiac myopathy and heart failure even when other pathology is absent (Bray, 2004). The Nurses' Health Study also found a link between coronary heart disease (CHD) and obesity (Manson et al., 1995), and between excess weight and risk of hypertension (Redon, 2001).

Overweight in women has been linked to higher rates of cancer, specifically of the gallbladder and reproductive system. Bray (2004) argues that the elevated risk in endometrial cancer is related to higher estrogen production of fat cells in overweight women, which will be discussed later in this chapter. In addition, breast cancer is, in particular, associated with central body fat (Schapira et al., 1994).

Respiratory function has also been shown to suffer with marked increases in body weight, even in the absence of pulmonary disease (Strohl, Strobel, & Parisi, 2004), because of decreased lung capacity from the pressure of excess weight on the diaphragm. Sleep apnea is linked to severe obesity as well, and is discussed in greater detail as follows.

Mortality

In the Nurses' Health Study, mortality resulting from all causes was shown to sharply increase for women with BMIs above 27 kg/m^2 (Manson et al., 1995). In those who had never smoked, the risk of dying from CHD was significantly higher in women with higher BMIs, with those with BMIs of 32 kg/m^2 and higher showing 5.8 times the risk than those with BMIs of 22 kg/m^2. Upper-body obesity was also shown to incur a greater risk of death from CHD; as compared to those in the lowest quintile of waist-to-hip ratio (a measure of body fat distribution), risk of CHD death was 8.7 times higher for women in the highest quintile. Furthermore, women who are 40% overweight are 55% more likely to die from cancer than average-weight women (Garfinkel, 1985). Cancer mortality risk increased with higher BMIs, with the death rate for women with BMIs higher than 32 kg/m^2 twice that of their average-weight counterparts, primarily from breast, colon, and endometrial cancers. Life expectancy decreases significantly with BMI, with women nonsmokers losing 3.3 years to overweight and 7.1 years to obesity (Peeters et al., 2003).

Health-Seeking Behavior

It has been shown that despite the higher risk for mortality from illnesses described previously, higher BMIs are shown to correlate with reduced health-seeking behavior. Among women working in healthcare, cancelling medical appointments is linked to BMI, frequently because of embarrassment about weight (72%; Olson, Schumaker, & Yawn, 1994). Overweight and obese women are less likely to receive preventative screenings, such as Pap smears and mammography (Wee, McCarthy, Davis, & Phillips, 2000). These results hold true even when controlling for barriers to care such as access, illness burden, and sociodemographic variables. Although obese women report more frequent physician visits than average-weight women, it has been shown that they receive preventive cancer screenings less often (Fontaine, Faith, Allison, & Cheskin, 1998).

Physician behavior also contributes to infrequency of medical care. Medical professionals report they would spend less time with obese patients and express a significantly more negative view of obese patients as compared to their normal-weight counterparts (Hebl & Xu, 2001). Most notably, physicians reported significantly less desire to help obese patients. These results highlight that physicians appear to be just as affected by stereotypes about obesity than the general public, and this could likely contribute to the reluctance of obese patients to seek medical care.

Biological and Hormonal Changes

Obesity can also affect the biological processes of the body in ways that are likely to eventually undermine health. BMI has been shown to negatively correlate with insulin sensitivity, and obese subjects require significantly higher levels of insulin to maintain normal levels of glucose tolerance (Polonsky et al., 1988). The endocrine system is further affected by increases in BMI, including increases in androgens, progesterone, cortisol, and adrenocorticotropic hormones (ACTH). Upper-body obesity has also been shown to affect the hormones that regulate the breakdown of lipids, or lipolysis, thereby contributing to further accumulation of body fat. Abdominal adipose tissue, more so than that in other body regions, is linked to increased response to noradrenaline, while cortisol may inhibit the effect of insulin on lipolysis, leading to elevated release of free fatty acids from abdominal adipose tissue (Kopelman, 2000). Increased free fatty acids in the blood, associated with obesity, have also demonstrated effects on glucose processing, resulting in hypoglycemia and impaired glucose tolerance (Pi-Sunyer, 2002).

Sexual and Reproductive Health

Reproductive hormonal changes can lead to notable abnormalities in sexual health. Irregular menses, anovulation, amenorrhea, and infertility have all been linked to obesity (Bray, 2004). Upper-body obesity in particular has been associated with lower rates of conception, with even small increases linked to a lower probability of conception in women receiving artificial insemination (Zaadstra et al., 1993), whereas weight loss is associated with improvement in pregnancy outcomes and ovulation (Clark et al., 1995). Obesity has also been linked with sexual dysfunction in women, specifically to reduced arousal and satisfaction (Esposito et al., 2007; Larson, Wagner, & Heitman, 2007). Early sexual development is associated with overweight in young girls, with higher BMI, body fat percentages, and waist circumferences at 7 years old associated with early onset of puberty at 9 years old (Davison, Susman, & Birch, 2003). However, some racial differences exist in the association between obesity and early pubertal maturation (Morrison et al., 1994).

Sleep

Sleep difficulties have been widely demonstrated in obesity, particularly sleep-related breathing difficulties and sleep apnea. As described earlier, increased body fat leads to reduced lung volume (Kopelman, 2000; Strohl et al., 2004). Risk and severity of sleep apnea is lower in women as compared to men, with prevalence around 1%, although postmenopausal women who are not undergoing hormone replacement therapy may show higher rates of sleep apnea and have lower levels of oxygen saturation (Bixler et al., 2001; Kopelman, Apps, Cope, & Empey, 1985; Millman, Carlisle, Eveloff, McGarvey, & Levinson, 1995). Weight loss has been shown to resolve many of these symptoms (Dixon, Schacter, & O'Brien, 2001).

In addition, short average sleep duration has been shown to be correlated with increased future weight gain; more than 68,000 women in the Nurses' Health Study were followed for 16 years, and the risk of obesity was significantly higher for those sleeping only 5 or 6 hours per night, as compared to those women who regularly slept at least 7 hours.

Weight Loss

Adipocytes, or fat cells, are the only type of cell whose size varies widely depending on the physiological condition of the body. Obesity is characterized either by an elevated number of adipose tissue cells, associated with early onset of overweight, or by increased size of those fat cells (Salans, Cushman, & Weismann, 1973). Furthermore, as an individual gains weight, fat cells initially expand, but if weight gain continues, new fat cells will be formed.

Weight loss is accompanied by a reduction in daily energy expenditure, and weight regain would occur if food intake reductions instituted in the process of weight loss are not strictly maintained (Dulloo, 2007). It is demonstrably difficult for individuals who have undergone significant weight loss to maintain losses, as evidenced by the high rates of regain (Brownell & Jeffrey, 1987). However, recent studies have estimated that up to 20% of weight losers are successful in maintaining their weight loss (Wing & Phelan, 2005).

Obese individuals also show brain activation substantially different from normal-weight individuals in response to food cues. These differences may make weight loss even more difficult. Although research using behavioral and self-report measures demonstrates that obese participants experience greater reward from food intake, neuroimaging studies have shown that obese individuals display decreased activation of brain regions associated with reward upon consumption of food as compared to normal-weight participants. It is theorized (Stice, Spoor, Ng, & Zald, 2009) that obese individuals anticipate greater food reward than normal-weight individuals but actually experience less reward upon receipt of food, which could make curbing energy intake particularly difficult.

Psychosocial Consequences of Obesity

It is well documented that obesity is associated with impaired quality of life, and that this impairment is magnified as BMI increases. Women show reduced health-related quality of life as compared to men, even at lower levels of obesity and younger ages (Kolotkin et al., 2008). In the Nurses' Health Study, weight gain was strongly associated with reduced physical function and increased bodily pain, independent of baseline weight (Fine et al., 1999). Weight loss, alternatively, was shown to be associated with improved vitality and physical function. Weight loss after bariatric surgery has been demonstrated to produce improvements in psychosocial measures of health-related quality of life (Kolotkin et al., 2008; Pataky, Carrard, & Golay, 2011).

Discrimination and stigma against obese individuals can also affect quality of life. Stigmatization of overweight is common among all ages, both sexes, and in multiple cultures (Ogden & Clementi, 2010). Obese individuals are frequently rated as less attractive, less successful, less ambitious, and less intelligent than individuals of normal weight (Harris, Harris, & Bochner, 1982). This stereotyping is magnified for women in comparison to men, with women judged more negatively based on their weight (Tiggemann & Rothblum, 1988). Stigma has been demonstrated even in health professionals charged with caring for the obese, as described previously. Weight-related discrimination has been linked to emotional eating and body dissatisfaction (Farrow & Tarrant, 2009) and may be a barrier to medical health treatment (Texiera & Budd, 2010).

Understandably in the face of such negative evaluation from others, reduced self-esteem and body dissatisfaction are elevated in obese individuals, especially in those who present for weight-loss treatment. Nonclinical samples suggest that obese individuals are not significantly different from normal-weight individuals on measures of psychopathology (Stunkard & Sobel, 1995), but those who seek treatment for weight loss show higher rates of psychopathology and

distress than those overweight individuals not seeking treatment, reporting higher levels of body image concern, depression, and general psychopathology (Friedman, Reichmann, Costanzo, & Musante, 2002).

Changes in Cognition

Cognitive changes have been shown to be related to higher BMIs, with a decrease in cognitive function linked to obesity. One study demonstrated lower scores on cognitive tasks in individuals with higher BMIs, and found that a higher BMI at baseline was associated with increased cognitive decline at follow-up assessment (Cournot et al., 2006). However, research is conflicting on whether this effect is gender-specific to men (Elias, Elias, Sullivan, Wolf, & D'Agostino, 2003).

Public Health Costs

The burden of healthcare costs resulting from obesity is substantial. Expenditures for healthcare attributable to obesity in 2008 alone were estimated at $147 billion (Finkelstein, Trogdon, Cohen, & Dietz, 2009), while lost productivity resulting from morbidity and mortality related to obesity was estimated to be almost as high. The obesity-related diseases described earlier are also associated with considerable economic burden; among women aged 45 to 54 years old, expected costs for treatment nearly doubles from $18,800 at a BMI of $22.5 \, kg/m^2$ to $35,300 at $37.5 \, kg/m^2$, with diabetes ranking as most costly (Thompson, Edelsberg, Colditz, Bird, & Oster, 1999). In one review, obese workers were found to miss more workdays from disability, illness, or injury, adding to the indirect costs of high BMI (Trogdon, Finkelstein, Hylands, Dellea, & Kamal-Bahl, 2008).

In sum, many adverse consequences of obesity specifically affect women. Increases in mortality and morbidity, sleep and reproductive difficulties, as well as psychosocial costs all add to the burden of obesity. Although weight loss maintenance is difficult, even small losses are associated with positive health outcomes, both physical and mental.

DESCRIPTION AND EFFECTIVENESS OF OBESITY TREATMENT FOR WOMEN

Benefits of Weight Loss

Weight loss is associated with a reduction in the risk for diabetes and cardiovascular disease, as well as marked improvements in blood pressure, triglycerides, and high-density lipoprotein (HDL) cholesterol in overweight and obese adults (Blackburn, 1995; Goldstein, 1992; Knowler et al., 2002; Tuomilehto et al., 2001; Wing et al., 1987). Professional guidelines suggest that weight control should be emphasized as a core component of treatment for women with hypertension, dyslipidemia, or type 2 diabetes (National Institutes of Health [NIH], 1995, 1997, 2001). Some studies have observed differences in the extent to which weight loss produces health benefits for women compared to men. For example, in the Diabetes Prevention Program (a randomized clinical trial comparing lifestyle modification and metformin for diabetes prevention in adults with impaired glucose tolerance) weight loss of more than 3% of body weight produced a greater reduction in serum glucose, insulin, and lipids in men than in women (Perreault et al., 2008). The body of research investigating such differences is small, and more studies need to examine how reliably such differences are

observed, the effect size of such differences, and the mechanisms of action. Because a large body of studies indicates that weight loss produces health and quality-of-life benefits for both women and men, women's weight control efforts should continue to be encouraged.

Treatment Options

Women who wish to lose weight have several options for intervention. The gold standard of weight loss treatment is behavioral therapy (also referred to as lifestyle modification). This treatment and its effectiveness are described in detail in the following section, along with various approaches to changing diet and physical activity. Weight loss surgery and medication options are also described. Finally, because the majority of women who diet choose to use a self-guided approach, rather than seeking out one of the aforementioned professionally administered programs, a description of self-guided approaches and their effectiveness is provided.

Behavioral Therapy and Lifestyle Modification The National Heart, Lung, and Blood Institute (NHLBI) recommends that a program of diet, exercise, and behavioral therapy be provided as the first line of treatment for obesity (NHLBI, 1998). Behavioral therapy is usually provided on a weekly basis for an initial period of 3 to 6 months. Programs that are focused on building weight loss maintenance skills often continue treatment after this period with several months of biweekly sessions. Treatment is provided in groups of 10 to 15 participants, because group treatment is more effective than individual sessions (it is also more cost-effective) (Renjilian et al., 2001). Each session typically lasts 60 or 90 minutes. Group leaders are professionals with degrees in nutrition, psychology, or a related field. Each session begins with private measurement of each participant's weight. Once the group has convened, each group member shares his or her progress toward the previous week's goals by, for example, reporting his or her average daily caloric intake, total minutes of physical activity, number of days in which food records were kept, and success in meeting a particular behavioral goal. Problem solving is used to address challenges, and reinforcement is provided for successful changes. A new skill is addressed in each session according to a structured curriculum. Examples of skills taught include making healthy selections when eating in restaurants, using portion control, obtaining social support for behavior changes, and managing stress.

In the dozens of studies that have examined behavioral treatment, participants have lost an average of approximately 10% of their initial weight (on average, the equivalent of 10 kg) in an average of 30 weeks of treatment (Wadden & Butryn, 2003). Participants have typically lost 0.4 to 0.5 kg per week and reached their peak weight loss by 6 months (Jeffery et al., 2000). In most studies, the rate of discontinuing treatment prematurely was approximately 20% (Wadden & Butryn, 2003). Many studies have conducted follow-up evaluations of adults who participated in behavioral treatment programs. On average, 30% to 35% of weight loss was regained in the year following treatment (Wadden, Butryn, & Byrne, 2004). By 4 to 5 years after treatment, patients maintained an average weight loss of approximately 1 to 3 kg, and many patients regained all of the weight they lost (Anderson, Konz, Frederich, & Wood, 2001; Perri & Foreyt, 2004).

These results are disappointing for many participants. However, several novel interventions have facilitated greater long-term success, such as those that used a model of continued care after initial weight loss. Data from the Look AHEAD study (a randomized clinical trial examining the effects of a lifestyle modification for adults with type 2 diabetes), found that after 4 years of continued treatment, participants maintained a weight loss of 5% of initial weight (The Look AHEAD Research Group, 2010). In the Diabetes Prevention Program (described earlier), participants who received lifestyle intervention obtained a weight loss of, on average, 7 kg at the end of 1 year, and they regained approximately one-third of their weight in the 2 to 3 years after that (Knowler et al., 2002). Even in the context of weight regain, these participants reduced their risk of developing type 2 diabetes by 58% compared to participants treated with placebo. Emphasizing the health benefits produced by modest weight losses may be helpful in increasing satisfaction with long-term results.

Some studies have found small sex differences in the outcomes of behavioral treatment. Within the lifestyle intervention of the Diabetes Prevention Program, men were significantly more physically active, lost more weight (8.0% vs. 7.0% of initial body weight), and met more of the goals of the lifestyle intervention than did women (Knowler et al., 2002). In a study in which men and women were matched for age and initial BMI and placed on programs with identical changes in diet and exercise, men lost a significantly higher percentage of initial body weight than women (5.1% vs. 4.3%) (Sartorio, Maffiuletti, Agosti, & Lafortuna, 2005). In that study, men lost equal amounts of fat mass and fat-free mass, whereas women's weight loss consisted almost entirely of fat mass. However, the body of research on sex differences in weight loss remains small, and definitive conclusions about such differences cannot be drawn.

Dietary Interventions Behavioral treatment programs typically prescribe a calorie goal of 1,200 to 1,500 calories per day, and some programs also limit fat gram intake to approximately 30% of total calories. There are many available variations on dietary intake in weight loss diets. Several randomized clinical trials have studied various dietary interventions in men and women, but the optimal macronutrient composition of weight loss diets has not been established, particularly for weight loss maintenance.

Several studies have compared long-term weight losses using a low-fat diet (with no calorie restriction) and restricted-calorie diets. One study found that participants who were instructed to consume a low-fat diet in the 2 years after initial weight loss regained significantly less weight than those who were prescribed a low-calorie diet, but two other studies found that these two interventions did not differ in long-term weight loss (Schlundt et al., 1993; Toubro & Astrup, 1997). Another approach to a low-fat diet consists of a low-energy-density diet, which is based on the principle that the volume of food consumed, not calorie content, influences satiety (Apovian et al., 2009; Bell & Rolls, 2001; Rolls et al., 1999; Schlundt et al., 1993). Energy density can be reduced by replacing fat (i.e., 9 kcal/g) with carbohydrate or protein (i.e., each 4 kcal/g) and by increasing the fiber or water content in foods (e.g., by increasing intake of fruits and vegetables). A study of this diet found that participants who followed a reduced-energy-density diet maintained significantly greater weight loss than those who

followed a low-fat diet (Ello-Martin, Roe, Ledikwe, Beach, & Rolls, 2007).

Several clinical trials have compared low-carbohydrate and low-fat diets: Two found no weight loss differences between groups at 1 year (Foster et al., 2003; Stern et al., 2004), and one found long-term support for a low-carbohydrate diet (Shai et al., 2008). In the largest long-term clinical trial (Sacks et al., 2009) conducted to date, four diets were compared. At 2 years, weight loss was similar in groups that were assigned to a diet with low- or high-protein, low- or high-fat, and low- or high-carbohydrates. Taken together, these findings indicate that calorie intake, not macronutrient composition, determines weight loss maintenance. However, the amount or type of macronutrient may have important health implications, particularly for conditions such as type 2 diabetes mellitus or cardiovascular disease. Women were well represented as participants in most of these studies, but sex differences were typically not examined, so it is largely unknown whether particular compositions of the diet produce different effects for women and men.

Evidence consistently suggests that, regardless of dietary composition, increasing the structure of the diet improves long-term outcomes in adults. Jeffery et al. (1993) found that consuming portion-controlled servings of conventional foods improved the maintenance of weight loss. Portion-controlled servings, such as frozen food entrees, eliminate the need to weigh and measure foods, save time planning and preparing meals, and reduce contact with problem foods (Wadden & Berkowitz, 2002). To the extent that they reduce dietary variety, portion-controlled meals also may better satisfy appetite (Rolls, 1986; Wing, Tate, Gorin, Raynor, & Fava, 2006). Increasing dietary structure in the form of detailed meal plans also has been found to improve weight loss maintenance (Wing et al., 1996).

Meal replacements are another method of increasing the structure of the diet. Meal replacements, which include liquid shakes, meal bars, and frozen food entrees, provide dieters with a fixed amount of food, with a known calorie content. Dieters know precisely how many calories they have consumed when eating meal replacements. By contrast, they typically underestimate their calorie intake by 40% to 50% when consuming a diet of conventional foods (Lichtman et al., 1992). In addition, meal replacements reduce dieters' contact with tempting foods and the difficulties they may experience in deciding what to eat (which may lead to overeating) (Wadden, Butryn, & Wilson, 2007). Meal replacements also are relatively inexpensive compared to conventional foods and require little preparation. A meta-analysis of six randomized clinical trials of obese adults (75% of whom were female) showed that meal replacements increased mean weight loss by 2.5 kg at 12 months, compared to a diet of conventional foods (Heymsfield, van Mierlo, van der Knapp, Heo, & Frier, 2003). A long-term study found that participants who continued to replace one meal and one snack with meal replacements after initial weight loss maintained a weight loss of 11% after 27 months and 8% after 51 months (Ditschuneit & Flechtner-Mors, 2001).

In summary, research indicates that calorie intake, rather than macronutrient composition of the diet, is the most important determinant of weight loss maintenance. The choice of a particular dietary approach depends, in large measure, on personal preference. Treatment providers also should consider whether a particular diet (e.g.,

one that is low in carbohydrates) is most likely to control comorbid conditions in a patient (type 2 diabetes). The use of portion-controlled servings and meal replacements currently has the strongest evidence of long-term efficacy. Future research should be conducted to examine sex differences in dietary interventions.

Physical Activity Interventions Many studies have found that adults who engaged in high levels of physical activity had superior weight loss maintenance compared to those with lower levels of activity (Catenacci et al., 2008; Jakicic, Marcus, Gallagher, Napolitano, & Lang, 2003; Jeffery, Wing, Sherwood, & Tate, 2003; Tate, Jeffery, Sherwood, & Wing, 2007). The mechanism of action for the possible benefit of high levels of physical activity is unclear, but candidates include maintenance of energy balance, prevention of loss of fat-free mass, and improved mood (Ballor & Poehlman, 1994; Wadden et al., 1997). Several studies have examined ways of promoting physical activity for weight control. In two studies, lifestyle activity, which involves increasing energy expenditure while completing everyday tasks, was superior to programmed activity for maintaining weight losses (Andersen et al., 1999; Epstein, Wing, Koeske, & Valoski, 1985). Additionally, daily exercise that was completed in multiple short bouts, as well as that which was completed in a single long bout, produced similar weight loss maintenance effects at 18 months (Jakicic, Winters, Lang, & Wing, 1999). Completing home-based activity also was found to be superior to on-site or group-based activity for weight loss maintenance (Perri, Martin, Leermakers, Sears, & Notelovitz, 1997).

Physical activity is one of the areas of weight control in which sex differences have most consistently been found. The association between physical activity and body weight appears stronger for men than for women (Meijer et al., 1991; Paul, Novotny, & Rumpler, 2004; Westerterp & Goran, 1997). Women who begin a program of physical activity often experience smaller weight losses and less fat loss than men. For example, in one large clinical trial for adults at high risk for cardiovascular disease, all participants received a behavioral intervention during the first 6 months of intervention and were instructed to increase moderate-intensity physical activity (Hollis et al., 2008). During that phase of the intervention, the relationship between physical activity and weight loss was stronger for men than for women, such that a given increase in physical activity had a greater effect on weight loss for men than for women. It is possible that women have a different metabolic response to exercise, that they exercise at a lower intensity than men, or that women increase their calorie intake following exercise.

In summary, strong evidence shows that high levels of physical activity are associated with the best long-term outcomes in weight control, but this relationship appears weaker in women than in men. As research continues to investigate these sex differences, physical activity should continue to be included in weight control programs for women, because it unquestionably confers benefits for cardiovascular and metabolic health (Blair & Leermakers, 2002).

Medication An expert panel convened by the NHLBI recommended that weight loss medications should be an option for adults with a BMI greater than $30 \, kg/m^2$ (or greater than $27 \, kg/m^2$ in the presence of comorbid conditions) who cannot lose 10% of initial weight with lifestyle modification alone (NIH, 1998). Several studies (Phelan & Wadden, 2002; Wadden et al., 2005) have shown that lifestyle modification and weight loss medication have additive effects, producing greater weight loss than either approach used alone.

Orlistat is the only medication approved in the United States for the induction and maintenance of weight loss (other medications are approved for short-term use only). Orlistat is a gastric and pancreatic lipase inhibitor that induces weight loss by blocking the absorption of about one-third of the fat contained in a meal (Sjöström et al., 1998). The undigested fat (i.e., oil) is excreted in stool and may be associated with gastrointestinal events that include oily stools, flatulence with discharge, and related complications (Sjöström et al., 1998). Two randomized clinical trials that examined the long-term effectiveness of orlistat found that adults who received 2 years of orlistat had significantly better weight loss maintenance than those who received placebo (Davidson et al., 1999; Sjöström et al., 1998). Sex differences were observed in one randomized clinical trial, such that the difference in weight loss for orlistat compared to placebo was larger for women than for men (Richelsen et al., 2007). In that study, after an initial period of weight loss, all participants began a 3-year lifestyle modification program and also were randomized to receive orlistat or placebo. After 3 years, women had weight losses of 8.4% versus 5.3% in orlistat and placebo, respectively, whereas men had weight losses of 8.3% versus 7.5% in orlistat and placebo, respectively. It appears that the difference in effect size was influenced by higher weight losses in the placebo group for men compared to women.

Until recently, sibutramine, a combined serotonin-norepinephrine reuptake inhibitor that is associated with increased satiation (i.e., fullness) and a resulting reduction in food intake, was approved for long-term use in the United States by the Food and Drug Administration (FDA) (James et al., 2000). Unfortunately, in 2010 a clinical trial demonstrated that patients taking sibutramine experienced an increased risk of cardiovascular events, including myocardial infarction and stroke, compared with placebo-treated patients (James et al., 2010). As a result, the FDA and the European Medicines Agency recommended withdrawal of the medication from the market, arguing that the benefits of treatment did not outweigh its risks.

Surgery Bariatric surgery may be recommended for women who have been unable to lose weight through other methods and who have severe obesity. Bariatric surgery produces weight loss by restricting food intake and, in some procedures, modifying the digestive process to prevent the absorption of some calories and nutrients. Roux-en-Y gastric bypass is the gold standard and is the most commonly performed obesity surgery (Steinbrook, 2004). After bariatric surgery, 50% to 70% of patients have lost 50% of their excess weight (Sjöström, 2008). The Swedish Obese Subjects Study provided the longest-term data on the largest sample of surgery patients, and the majority of the sample comprised women. After 10 years, the average amount of initial weight lost was 25% in gastric bypass, 16% in vertical-banded gastroplasty, and 14% in banding (Sjöström, 2008). The majority of patients who have received surgery have experienced reversal or improvement of type 2 diabetes, hypertension, sleep apnea, and dyslipidemia (Buchwald et al., 2004; Sjöström et al., 2004; Sjöström et al., 2007).

Men and women may present for bariatric surgery with somewhat different profiles. Among one sample of bariatric surgery candidates, females had significantly higher BMI, were more likely to report a history of depression or anxiety, and had higher levels of current depression and anxiety (Mahony, 2008). However, it is unclear to what extent those gender differences are predictive of weight or psychological outcomes following surgery. In fact, some research has found that women experienced better outcomes than men following bariatric surgery (Fernandez et al., 2004; Livingston et al., 2002; Poulose et al., 2005). Additional research must be conducted to establish what differences in outcomes are consistently observed and to understand what mediates such observed differences.

Self-Guided Dieting At any given time, between one-quarter and one-half of women report dieting (Bish et al., 2005; Kant, 2002; Paeratakul, York-Crowe, Williamson, Ryan, & Bray, 2002). Of those women, only a small percentage diet under the direction of a professional or structured weight loss program, whereas many more report developing their own diets; following a diet recommend by another person, book, magazine, or found on the Internet; or seeking out a minimal level of support from a community-based program (Jeffery, Adlis, & Forster, 1991; Levy & Heaton, 1993; Paeratakul et al., 2002). The body of research on self-guided dieting is small because many of these dieters are by definition not part of programs that collect information on outcomes. However, most of these dieters do not appear to achieve a meaningful weight loss (Butryn, Phelan, & Wing, 2007; Womble, Wang, & Wadden, 2002). Many self-guided dieters ultimately struggle to reduce their calorie intake in a consistent and sustained way. Low levels of physical activity also are likely contributing to the discouraging results that many self-guided dieters experience, particularly with regard to weight loss maintenance. Observational studies should prospectively identify self-guided dieters, collect information on behaviors and weight loss over long periods of follow-up, and examine mediators and moderators of success.

Prevention of Obesity

Prevention of weight gain is a critical component in addressing the obesity epidemic in women (World Health Organization, 1997). Unfortunately, research on obesity prevention is in its infancy, and few effective approaches have been identified (Lombard, Deeks, & Teede, 2009). One approach to weight gain prevention is to identify times that create a high risk for weight gain for women and then develop interventions for these times. The periods surrounding pregnancy and menopause are two examples of such times.

Pregnancy

The period surrounding pregnancy is an important opportunity for intervention for several reasons (Lombard, Deeks, Jolley, Ball, & Teede, 2010). Women of reproductive age have a rate of weight gain of approximately 0.6 kg per year (Brown, 2005). Childcare demands and the physical burden of pregnancy and delivery can make engagement in healthy eating and physical activity behaviors difficult. In addition, women in this target group who adopt healthy weight control behaviors are likely to have a positive ripple effect on their partners and children (Trost et al., 2003).

Excessive gestational weight gain has been associated with poor outcomes for women and their children. In most studies, overweight women have been much more likely than normal-weight women to gain excessive amounts of weight during pregnancy (Olson & Strawderman, 2003; Stotland, Cheng, Hopkins, & Caughey, 2006). Mothers who gained greater than 16 kg in pregnancy had children who were more likely to be overweight or obese (Moreira, Padez, Mourão-Carvalhal, & Rosado, 2007). Women who gained the most weight during pregnancy also retained the most weight following delivery (Ohlin & Rossner, 1990; Olson, Strawderman, Hinton, & Pearson, 2003; Schauberger, Rooney, & Brimer, 1992).

The relationship between gestational weight gain and later weight has been observed over periods as long as 15 years (Linne, Dye, Barkeling, & Rossner, 2004; National Research Council, Institute of Medicine, 2007; Rooney, Schauberger, & Mathiason, 2005). The relationship between pregnancy weight gain and postpartum weight retention is especially strong for low-income women (Olson et al., 2003). For example, 53% of low-income women who gained more than the Institute of Medicine recommended amounts during pregnancy weighed 4.5 kg or more at 1 year postpartum than they did in early pregnancy. Research has very recently begun to evaluate interventions that aim to prevent excessive gestational weight gain. Interventions focused on monitoring weight, providing counseling, and facilitating physical activity may be effective (Olson, 2008). The conventional wisdom regarding weight gain in pregnancy has begun to shift, so that obese pregnant women may receive some support in making lifestyle modifications during pregnancy that may limit their weight gain (Artal, Lockwood, & Brown, 2010).

Menopause

Weight gain and increases in central body fat occur in many women as they transition through the period of menopause (Lovejoy & Sainsbury, 2009; Sowers et al., 2007). Several hormonal factors increase this risk, and the decline in resting energy expenditure that occurs with age is greater for women than for men (Roubenoff et al., 2000). Physical activity may be protective for women during this period (Sternfeld, Bhat, Wang, Sharp, & Queensbury, 2005), in part because it appears to reduce insulin resistance, which increases the risk for weight gain (Brown, Moore, Korytkowski, McCole, & Hagberg, 1997; Miller et al., 1994). Unfortunately, women who have already gained weight before menopause may be least likely to engage in physical activity because of a reduced level of physical functioning and greater discomfort during physical activity (Arterburn, McDonell, Hedrick, Diehr, & Fihn, 2004; Fine et al., 1999). Interventions that facilitate physical activity during this period may have promise for weight gain prevention.

FUTURE DIRECTIONS

Several gaps in the extant research on obesity would be greatly served by additional inquiry. Considering the limited long-term effectiveness of current weight loss treatment, a primary goal in the field is to improve the capacity of treatments to translate into weight loss maintenance. There also is insufficient information about gender disparity in obesity and the extent to which sex differences exist in obesity. Future research should examine how genetic predisposition, race, ethnicity, age, menstrual status, body fat distribution, and socioeconomic status influence eating behavior, weight gain and weight loss in women, as well as how these variables interact to effect disease risk in women. More research should be conducted with women to understand the relationship between physical activity and weight. Furthermore, if certain treatments (e.g., lifestyle modification, medication, surgery) produce differential weight losses for women and men, then exploring the mechanisms of action of those differences would be necessary. Knowledge about when or if the risk of disordered eating is increased in relation to factors such as dieting behavior in obese women must also be expanded and disseminated. Lastly, additional research on weight gain prevention in women is needed. In particular, examining prevention efforts during puberty, pregnancy, and menopause would be vital to tailoring programs to women's needs.

REFERENCES

Andersen, R. E., Wadden, T. A., Bartlett, S. J., Zemel, B., Verde, T. J., & Franckowiak, S. C. (1999). Effects of lifestyle activity vs structured aerobic exercise in obese women: A randomized trial. *JAMA*, *281*(4), 335–340.

Anderson, J. W., Konz, E. C., Frederich, R. C., & Wood, C. L. (2001). Long-term weight-loss maintenance: A meta-analysis of US studies. *American Journal of Clinical Nutrition*, *74*(5), 579–584.

Apovian, C., Bigornia, S., Cullum-Dugan, D., Schoonmaker, C., Radziejowska, J., Phipps, J., . . . Lenders, C. (2009). Milk-based nutritional supplements in conjunction with lifestyle intervention in overweight adolescents. *ICAN: Infant, Child, & Adolescent Nutrition*, *1*(1), 37–44.

Artal, R., Lockwood, C. J., & Brown, H. L. (2010). Weight gain recommendations in pregnancy and the obesity epidemic. *Obstetrics & Gynecology*, *115*, 152–155.

Arterburn, D. E., McDonell, M. B., Hedrick, S. C., Diehr, P., & Fihn, S. D. (2004). Association of body weight with condition-specific quality of life in male veterans. *American Journal of Medicine*, *117*(10), 738–746.

Ballor, D. L., & Poehlman, E. T. (1994). Exercise-training enhances fat-free mass preservation during diet-induced weight loss: A meta-analytical finding. *International Journal of Obesity & Related Metabolic Disorders: Journal of the International Association for the Study of Obesity*, *18*(1), 35–40.

Begum, K. S., Sachchithanantham, K., & De Somsubhra, S. (2011). Maternal obesity and pregnancy outcome. *Clinical and Experimental Obstetrics and Gynecology*, *38*(1), 14–20.

Bell, E., & Rolls, B. (2001). Energy density of foods affects energy intake across multiple levels of fat content in lean and obese women. *American Journal of Clinical Nutrition*, *73*(6), 1010–1018.

Bish, C. L., Blanck, H. M., Serdula, M. K., Marcus, M., Kohl, H. W., & Khan, L. K. (2005). Diet and physical activity behaviors among americans trying to lose weight: 2000 behavioral risk factor surveillance system. *Obesity Research*, *13*, 296–607.

Bixler, E. O., Vgontzas, A. N., Lin, H. M., Have, T. T., Rein, J., Vela-Bueno, A., & Kales, A. (2001). Prevalence of sleep-disordered breathing in women: Effects of gender. *American Journal of Respiratory Critical Care Medicine*, *163*(3), 608–613.

Blackburn, G. L. (1995). Effect of degree of weight loss on health benefits. *Obesity Research*, *3*, 211S–216S.

Blair, S. N., & Leermakers, E. A. (2002). Exercise and weight management. In T. A. Wadden & A. J. Stunkard (Eds.), *Handbook of obesity treatment* (pp. 283–300). New York, NY: Guilford Press.

Bray, G. A. (1996). Health hazards of obesity. *Endocrinology & Metabolism Clinics of North America*, *25*(4), 907–919.

Bray, G. A. (2004). Medical consequences of obesity. *Journal of Clinical Endocrinology Metabolism*. *89*, 2583–2589.

Brown, M. D., Moore, G. E., Korytkowski, M. T., McCole, S. D., & Hagberg, J. M. (1997). Improvement of insulin sensitivity by short-term exercise training in hypertensive african american women. *Hypertension*, *30*(6), 1549–1553.

Brown, W. (2005). *Australian women and their weight: A growing problem.* Presented at a meeting of the Commonwealth Department of Health and Ageing, October 11, 2005. Canberra, Australia: Women's Health Australia.

Brownell, K. D., & Jeffrey, R. W. (1987). Improving long-term weight loss: Pushing the limits of treatment. *Behavior Therapy*, *18*, 353–374.

Buchwald, H., Avidor, Y., Braunwald, E., Jensen, M. D., Pories, W., Fahrbach, K., & Schoelles, K. (2004). Bariatric surgery: A systematic review and meta-analysis. *JAMA*, *13*, 724–737.

Butryn, M. L., Phelan, S., & Wing, R. R. (2007). Self-guided approaches to weight loss. In J. Latner & G. T. Wilson (Eds.), *Self-help approaches for obesity and eating disorders* (pp. 3–20). New York, NY: Guilford Press.

Catenacci, V. A., Ogden, L. G., Stuht, J., Phelan, S., Wing, R. R., Hill, J. O., & Wyatt, H. R. (2008). Physical activity patterns in the national weight control registry. *Obesity*, *16*, 153–161.

Chandler, M. C., & Rennard, S. I. (2010). Smoking cessation. *CHEST*, *137*(2), 428–435.

Clark, A. M., Ledger, W., Galletly, C., Tomlinson, L., Blaney, F., Wang, X., & Norman, R. J. (1995). Weight loss results in significant improvement in pregnancy and ovulation rates in anovulatory obese women. *Human Reproduction*, *10*(10), 2705–2712.

Colditz, G. A., Willett, W. C., Rotnitzky, A., & Manson J. E. (1995). Weight gain as a risk factor for clinical diabetes mellitus in women. *Annals of Internal Medicine*, *122*, 481–486.

Cournot, M., Marquié, J. C., Ansiau, D., Martinaud, C., Fonds, H., Ferrières, J., & Ruidavets, J. B. (2006). Relation between body mass index and cognitive function in healthy middle-aged men and women. *Neurology*, *67*(7), 1208–1214.

Davidson, M. H., Hauptman, J., DiGirolamo, M., Foreyt, J. P., Halsted, C. H., Heber, . . . Heymsfield, S. B. (1999). Weight control and risk factor reduction in obese subjects treated for 2 years with orlistat: A randomized controlled trial. *JAMA*, *281*(3), 235–242.

Davison, K. K., Susman, E. J., & Birch, L. L. (2003). Percent body fat at age 5 predicts earlier pubertal development among girls at age 9. *Pediatrics*, *111*(4), 815–821.

Ditschuneit, H. H., & Flechtner-Mors, M. (2001). Value of structured meals for weight management: Risk factors and long-term weight maintenance. *Obesity Research*, *9*(Suppl 4), 284S–289S.

Dixon, J. B., Schachter, L. M., & O'Brien, P. E. (2001). Sleep disturbance and obesity changes following surgically induced weight loss. *Archives of Internal Medicine, 161,* 102–106.

Dulloo, A. G. (2007). Thrifty energy metabolism in catch-up growth trajectories to insulin and leptin resistance. *Best Practice & Research Clinical Endocrinology & Metabolism, 22,* 155–171.

Elias, M. F., Elias, P. K., Sullivan, L. M., Wolf, P. A., & D'Agostino, R. B. (2003). Lower cognitive function in the presence of obesity and hypertension: The Framingham heart study. *International Journal of Obesity and Related Metabolic Disorders, 27*(2), 260–268.

Ello-Martin, J. A., Roe, L. S., Ledikwe, J. H., Beach, A. M., & Rolls, B. J. (2007). Dietary energy density in the treatment of obesity: A year-long trial comparing two weight-loss diets. *American Journal of Clinical Nutrition, 85,* 1465–1477.

Epstein, L. H., Wing, R. R., Koeske, R., & Valoski, A. (1985). A comparison of lifestyle exercise, aerobic exercise, and calisthenics on weight loss in obese children. *Behavior Therapy, 16*(4), 345–356.

Esposito, K., Ciotola, M., Giugliano, F., Bisogni, C., Schisano, B., Autorino, R., . . . Giugliano, D. (2007). Association of body weight with sexual function in women: Body weight and sexual function in women. *International Journal of Impotence Research, 19,* 353–357.

Farrow, C. V., & Tarrant, M. (2009). Weight-based discrimination, body dissatisfaction and emotional eating: The role of perceived social consensus. *Psychology Health, 24*(9), 1021–1034.

Fernandez, A. Z., DeMaria, E. J., Tichansky, D. S., Kellum, J. M., Wolfe, L. G., Meador, J., & Sugerman, H. J. (2004). Experience with over 3,000 open and laparoscopic bariatric procedures: Multivariate analysis of factors related to leak and resultant mortality *Surgical Endoscopy, 18*(2), 193–197.

Fine, J. T., Colditz, G. A., Coakley, E. H., Moseley, G., Manson, J. E., Willett, W. C., & Kawachi, I. (1999). A prospective study of weight change and health-related quality of life in women. *JAMA, 282*(22), 2136–2142.

Finkelstein, E. A., Trogdon, J. G., Cohen, J. W., & Dietz, W. (2009). Annual medical spending attributable to obesity: Payer- and service-specific estimates. *Health Affairs, 28*(5), w822–w831.

Flegal, K. M., Carroll, M. D., Ogden, C. L., & Curtin, L. R. (2010). Prevalence and trends in obesity among US adults, 1999-2008. *JAMA, 303,* 235–241.

Fontaine, K. R., Faith, M. S., Allison, D. B., & Cheskin, L. J. (1998). Body weight and health care among women in the general population. *Archives of Family Medicine, 7,* 381–384.

Foster, G. D., Wyatt, H. R., Hill, J. O., McGuckin, B. G., Brill, C., Mohammed, B. S., . . . Klein, S. (2003). A randomized trial of a low-carbohydrate diet for obesity. *New England Journal of Medicine, 348*(21), 2082–2090.

Friedman, K. E., Reichmann, S. K., Costanzo, P. R., & Musante, G. J. (2002). Body image partially mediates the relationship between obesity and psychological distress. *Obesity Research, 10,* 33–41.

Garfinkel, L. (1985). Overweight and cancer. *Annals of Internal Medcine, 103,* 1034–1036.

Ginneken, V., Sitnyakowsky, L., & Jeffery, J. E. (2009). Infectobesity: Viral infections (especially with human adenovirus-36: Ad-36) may be a cause of obesity. *Medical Hypothesis, 72*(4), 383–388.

Goldstein, D. J. (1992). Beneficial health effects of modest weight loss. *International Journal of Obesity and Related Metabolic Disorders, 16*(6), 397–415.

Harris, M. B., Harris, R. J., & Bochner, S. (1982). Fat, four-eyed and female: Stereotypes of obesity, glasses and gender. *Journal of Applied Psychology, 100,* 78–83.

Hartz, A. J., Rupley, D. C., & Rimm, A. A. (1984). The association of girth measurements with disease in 32,856 women *American Journal of Epidemiology, 119,* 71–80.

Hatch, E. E., Nelson, J. W., Stahlhut, R. W., & Webster, T. F. (2010). Association of endocrine disruptors and obesity: Perspectives from epidemiologic studies. *International Journal of Andrology, 33*(2), 324–332.

Hebl, M. R., & Xu, J. (2001). Weighing the care: Physicians' reactions to the size of a patient. *International Journal of Obesity, 25,* 1246–1252.

Heymsfield, S. B., van Mierlo, C., van der Knapp, H. C., Heo, M., & Frier, H. I. (2003). Weight management using a meal replacement strategy: Meta and pooling analysis from six studies. *International Journal of Obesity and Related Metabolic Disorders, 27*(5), 537–549.

Hollis, J. F., Gullion, C. M., Stevens, V. J., Brantley, P. J., Appel, L. J., Ard, J. D., . . . Weight Loss Maintenance Trial Research Group. (2008). Weight loss during the intensive intervention phase of the weight-loss maintenance trial. *American Journal of Preventive Medicine*, *32*(5), 118–126.

Jakicic, J. M., Marcus, B. H., Gallagher, K. I., Napolitano, M., & Lang, W. (2003). Effect of exercise duration and intensity on weight loss in overweight, sedentary women: A randomized trial. *JAMA*, *290*(10), 1323–1330.

Jakicic, J. M., Winters, C., Lang, W., & Wing, R. R. (1999). Effects of intermittent exercise and the use of home exercise equipment on adherence, weight loss, and fitness in overweight women: A randomized controlled trial. *JAMA*, *282*, 1554–1560.

James, W. P. T., Astrup, A., Finer, N., Hilsted, J., Kopelman, P., Rössner, S., . . . van Gaal, L. F. (2000). Effect of sibutramine on weight maintenance after weight loss: A randomised trial. *The Lancet*, *356*, 2119–2125.

James, W. P. T., Caterson, I. D., Coutinho, W., Finer, N., van Gaal, L. F., Maggioni, A. P., . . . SCOUT Investigators. (2010). Effect of sibutramine on cardiovascular outcomes in overweight and obese subjects. *New England Journal of Medicine*, *363*(10), 905–917.

Janssen, I., Powell, L. H., Kazlauskaite, R., & Dugan, S. A. (2010). Testosterone and visceral fat in midlife women: The study of women's health across the nation (SWAN) fat patterning study. *Obesity*, *18*(3), 604–610.

Jeffery, R. W., Adlis, S. A., & Forster, J. L. (1991). Prevalence of dieting among working men and women: The healthy worker project. *Health Psychology*, *10*(4), 274–281.

Jeffery, R. W., Drewnowski, A., Epstein, L. H., Stunkard, A. J., Wilson, G. T., Wing, R. R., & Hill, D. R. (2000). Long-term maintenance of weight loss: Current status. *Health Psychology*, *19*, 5–16.

Jeffery, R. W., Wing, R. R., Sherwood, N. E., & Tate, D. F. (2003). Physical activity and weight loss: Does prescribing higher physical activity goals improve outcome? *American Journal of Clinical Nutrition*, *78*(4), 684–689.

Jeffery, R. W., Wing, R. R., Thorson, C., Burton, L. R., Raether, C., Harvey, J., & Mullen, M. (1993). Strengthening behavioral interventions for weight loss: A randomized trial of food provision and monetary incentives. *Journal of Consulting and Clinical Psychology*, *61*(6), 1038–1045.

Kant, A. K. (2002). Weight-loss attempts and reporting of food nutrients, and biomarkers in a national cohort. *International Journal of Obesity*, *26*(1194), 1204.

Knowler, W. C., Barrett-Connor, E., Fowler, S. E., Hamman, R. F., Lachin, J. M., Walker, E. A., & Nathan, D. M. (2002). Reduction in the incidence of type 2 diabetes with lifestyle intervention or metformin. *New England Journal of Medicine*, *346*(6), 393–403.

Kolotkin, R. L., Crosby, R. D., Gress, R. E., Hunt, S. C., Engel, S. G., & Adams, T. D. (2008). Health and health-related quality of life: Differences between men and women who seek gastric bypass surgery. *Surgery for Obesity and Related Disorders*, *4*(5), 651–658.

Kopelman, P. G. (2000). Obesity as a medical problem. *Nature*, *404*, 635–643.

Kopelman, P. G., Apps, M. C. P., Cope, T., & Empey, D. W. (1985). The influence of menstrual status, body weight and hypothalamic function on nocturnal respiration in women. *Journal of the Royal College of Physicians London*, *19*, 243–247.

Krause, K. M., Lovelady, C. A., Peterson, B. L., Chowdhury, N., & Ostbye, T. (2010). Effect of breast feeding on weight retention at 3 and 6 months postpartum: Data from the North Carolina WIC Programme. *Public Health Nutrition*, *13*(12), 2019–2026.

Larson, S. H., Wagner, G., & Heitmann, B. L. (2007). Sexual function and obesity. *International Journal of Obesity*, *31*, 1189–1198.

Lean, M. E. J., Hans, T. S., & Seidell, J. C. (1998). Impairment of health and quality life in people with large waist circumference. *Lancet*, *351*, 853–856.

Levy, A. S., & Heaton, A. W. (1993). Weight control practices of U.S. adults trying to lose weight *Annals of Internal Medicine*, *119*, 661–666.

Lichtman, S. W., Pisarska, K., Berman, E., Pestone, M., Dowling, H., Offenbacher, E., . . . Heymsfield, S. B. (1992). Discrepancy between self-reported and actual caloric intake and exercise in obese subjects. *New England Journal of Medicine*, *327*(27), 1893–1898.

Linne, Y., Dye, L., Barkeling, B., & Rossner, S. (2004). Long-term weight development in women: A 15-year follow-up of the effects of pregnancy. *Obesity Research*, *12*(7), 1166–1178.

Livingston, E. H., Huerta, S., Arthur, D., Lee, S., DeShields, S., & Heber, D. (2002). Male gender is a predictor of morbidity and age a predictor of mortality for patients undergoing gastric bypass. *Annals of Surgery*, *236*(5), 576–582.

Lombard, C., Deeks, A., Jolley, D., Ball, K., & Teede, H. (2010). A low intensity, community based lifestyle programme to prevent weight gain in women with young children: Cluster randomised controlled trial. *British Medical Journal*, *341*, c3215.

Lombard, C. B., Deeks, A. A., & Teede, H. J. (2009). A systematic review of interventions aimed at the prevention of weight gain in adults. *Public Health Nutrition*, *12*, 2236–2246.

Lovejoy, J. C., & Sainsbury, A. (2009). Stock Conference 2008 Working Group: Sex differences in obesity and the regulation of energy homeostasis. *Obesity Reviews*, *10*(2), 154–167.

Mahony, D. (2008). Psychological gender differences in bariatric surgery candidates. *Obesity Surgery*, *18*(5), 607–610.

Manson, J. E., Willett, W. C., Stampfer, M. J., Colditz, G. A., Hunter, D. J., Hankinson, S. E., . . . Speizer, F. E. (1995). Body weight and mortality among women. *New England Journal of Medicine*, *333*(11), 677–685.

Meijer, G. A., Janssen, G. M., Westerterp, K. R., Verhoeven, F., Saris, W. H., & ten Hoor, F. (1991). The effect of a 5-month endurance-training programme on physical activity: Evidence for a sex-difference in the metabolic response to exercise. *European Journal of Applied Physiology and Occupational Physiology*, *62*, 11–17.

Miller, J. P., Pratley, R. E., Goldberg, A. P., Gordon, P., Rubin, M., Treuth, M. S., . . . Hurley, B. F. (1994). Strength training increases insulin action in healthy 50- to 65-yr-old men. *Journal of Applied Physiology*, *77*(3), 1122–1127.

Millman, R. P., Carlisle, C. C., Eveloff, S. E., McGarvey, S. T., & Levinson, P. D. (1995). Body fat distribution and sleep apnea severity in women. *Chest*, *107*(2), 362–366.

Moreira, P., Padez, C., Mourão-Carvalhal, I., & Rosado, V. (2007). Maternal weight gain during pregnancy and overweight in Portuguese children. *International Journal of Obesity*, *31*, 608–614.

Morrison, J. A., Barton, B., Biro, F. M., Sprecher, D. L., Falkner, F., & Obarzanek, E. (1994). Sexual maturation and obesity in 9- and 10-year-old black and white girls: The National Heart, Lung, and Blood Institute Growth and Health Study. *The Journal of Pediatrics*, *124*(6), 889–895.

National Heart, Lung, and Blood Institute (NHLBI). (1998). Clinical guidelines on the identification, evaluation and treatment of overweight and obesity in adults. The evidence report. *Obesity Research*, *6*, 51S–209S.

National Institutes of Health. (1995). *NHLBI report of the conference on socioeconomic status and cardiovascular health and disease*. Washington, DC: United States Department of Health and Human Services (USDHHS).

National Institutes of Health. (1997). The sixth report of the joint national committee on prevention, detection, evaluation, and treatment of high blood pressure. *Archives of Internal Medicine*, *157*, 2413–2416.

National Institutes of Health. (1998). Clinical guidelines on the identification, evaluation, and treatment of overweight and obesity in adults: The evidence report. *Obesity Research*, *6*(Suppl 2), 51S–209S.

National Institutes of Health. (2001). *NHLBI task force report on research in prevention of cardiovascular disease*. Washington, DC: USDHHS.

National Research Council, Institute of Medicine. (2007). *Influence of pregnancy weight on maternal and child health: Workshop report*. Washington, DC: National Academic Press.

Ogden, J., & Clementi, C. (2010). Experience of being obese and the many consequences of stigma. *Journal of Obesity*, *42*, 90–98.

Ohlin, A., & Rossner, S. (1990). Maternal weight development after pregnancy. *International Journal of Obesity*, *14*, 159–173.

Ohlson, L. O., Larsson, B., Svardsudd, K., Welin, L., Eriksson, H., Wilhelmsen, L., . . . Tibblin, G. (1985). The influence of body fat distribution on the incidence of diabetes mellitus: 13.5 years of follow up of the participants in the study of men born in 1913. *Diabetes*, *34*, 1055–1058.

Olson, C. L., Schumaker, H. D., & Yawn B. P. (1994). Overweight women delay medical care. *Archives of Family Medicine*, *3*, 888–892.

Olson, C. M. (2008). Achieving a healthy weight gain during pregnancy. *Annual Review of Nutrition, 28,* 411–423.

Olson, C. M., & Strawderman, M. S. (2003). Modifiable behavioral factors in a biopsychosocial model predict inadequate and excessive gestational weight gain. *Journal of the American Dietetic Association, 103,* 48–54.

Olson, C. M., Strawderman, M. S., Hinton, P. S., & Pearson, T. A. (2003). Gestational weight gain and postpartum behaviors associated with weight change from early pregnancy to 1 year postpartum. *International Journal of Obesity, 27,* 117–127.

Paeratakul, S., York-Crowe, E. E., Williamson, D. A., Ryan, D. H., & Bray, G. A. (2002). Americans on a diet: Results from the 1994-1996 continuing survey of food intakes by individuals. *JAMA, 102,* 1247–1251.

Pataky, Z., Carrard, I., & Golay, A. (2011). Psychological factors and weight loss in bariatric surgery. *Current Opinion in Gastroenterology, 27*(2), 167–173.

Paul, D. R., Novotny, J. A., & Rumpler, W. V. (2004). Effects of the interaction of sex and food intake on the relation between energy expenditure and body composition. *American Journal of Clinical Nutrition, 79,* 385–389.

Peeters, A., Barendregt, J. J., Willekens, F., Mackenbach J. P., Al Mamun, A., & Bonneux, L. (2003). Obesity in adulthood and its consequences for life expectancy: A life-table analysis. *Annals of Internal Medicine, 138,* 24–32.

Perreault, L., Ma, Y., Dagogo-Jack, S., Horton, E., Marrero, D., Crandall, J., & Barrett-Connor, E. (2008). Sex differences in diabetes risk and the effect of intensive lifestyle modification in the diabetes prevention program. *Diabetes Care, 31,* 1416–1421.

Perri, M. G., & Foreyt, J. P. (2004). Preventing weight regain after weight loss. In G. A. Bray & C. Bouchard (Eds.), *Handbook of obesity: Clinical applications* (pp. 185–199). New York, NY: Marcel Dekker.

Perri, M. G., Martin, A. D., Leermakers, E. A., Sears, S. F., & Notelovitz, M. (1997). Effects of group-versus home-based exercise in the treatment of obesity. *Journal of Consulting & Clinical Psychology, 65*(2), 278–285.

Phelan, S., & Wadden, T. A. (2002). Combining behavioral and pharmacological treatments for obesity. *Obesity Research, 10*(6), 560–574.

Pi-Sunyer, F. X. (2002). The obesity epidemic: Pathophysiology and consequences of obesity. *Obesity Research, 10,* 97S–104S.

Polonsky, K. S., Given, B. D., Hirsh L. J., Tillil, H., Shapiro, E. T., Beebe, C., . . . Van Cauter, E. (1988). Abnormal patterns of insulin secretion in non-insulin-dependent diabetes mellitus. *New England Journal of Medicine, 318,* 1231–1239.

Poulose, B. K., Griffin, M. R., Moore, D. E., Zhu, Y., Smalley, W., Richards, W. O., . . . Holzman, M. D. (2005). Risk factors for post-operative mortality in bariatric surgery. *Journal of Surgery Research, 127*(1), 1–7.

Prentice, P., & Viner, R. (2010). The effect of pubertal timing on later adult obesity. *British Society for Paediatric Endocrinology and Diabetes, 24,* P18.

Ravussin, E. (2002). Energy expenditure and obesity. In K. D. Brownell & C. G. Fairburn (Eds.), *Eating disorders and obesity: A comprehensive handbook* (pp. 55–62). New York, NY: Guilford Press.

Redon, J. (2001). Hypertension in obesity. *Nutrition Metabolism and Cardiovascular Disease, 11,* 344–353.

Renjilian, D. A., Perri, M. G., Nezu, A. M., McKelvey, W. F., Shermer, R. L., & Anton, S. D. (2001). Individual versus group therapy for obesity: Effects of matching participants to their treatment preferences. *Journal of Consulting and Cinical Psychology, 69*(4), 717–721.

Richelsen, B., Tonstad, S., Rössner, S., Toubro, S., Niskanen, L., Madsbad, S., . . . Rissanen, A. (2007). Effect of orlistat on weight regain and cardiovascular risk factors following a very-low-energy diet in abdominally obese patients. *Diabetes Care, 30*(1), 27–32. doi: 10.2337/dc06-0210.

Rolls, B. J. (1986). Sensory-specific satiety. *Nutrition Reviews, 44*(3), 93–101.

Rolls, B. J., Bell, E. A., Castellanos, V. H., Chow, M., Pelkman, C. L., & Thorwart, M. L. (1999). Energy density but not fat content of foods affected energy intake in lean and obese women. *American Journal of Clinical Nutrition, 69,* 863–871.

Rooney, B. L., Schauberger, C. W., & Mathiason, M. A. (2005). Impact of perinatal weight change on long-term obesity and obesity-related illnesses. *Obstetrics & Gynecology, 106,* 1349–1356.

Roubenoff, R., Hughes, V. A., Dallal, G. E., Nelson, M. E., Morganti, C., Kehayias, J. J., . . . Roberts, S. (2000). The effect of gender and body composition method on the apparent decline in lean mass-adjusted resting metabolic rate with age. *The Journals of Gerontology Series A: Biological Sciences and Medical Sciences, 55,* M575–M760.

Sacks, F. M., Bray, G. A., Carey, V. J., Smith, S. R., Ryan, D. H., Anton, S. D., . . . Williamson, D. A. (2009). Comparison of weight-loss diets with different compositions of fat, protein, and carbohydrates. *New England Journal of Medicine, 360*(9), 859–873.

Salans, L. B., Cushman, S. W., & Weismann, R. E. (1973). Studies of human adipose tissue: Adipose cell size and number in nonobese and obese patients. *The Journal of Clinical Investigation, 52*(4), 929–941.

Sartorio, A., Maffiuletti, N. A., Agosti, F., & Lafortuna, C. L. (2005). Genderrelated changes in body composition, muscle strength and power output after a short-term multidisciplinary weight loss intervention in morbid obesity. *Journal of Endocrinological Investigation, 28,* 494–501.

Schapira, D. V., Clark, R. A., Wolff, P. A., Jarrett, A. R., Kumar, N. B., & Aziz, N. M. (1994). Visceral obesity and breast cancer risk. *Cancer, 74,* 632–639.

Schauberger, C. S., Rooney, B. L., & Brimer, L. M. (1992). Factors that influence weight loss in the puerperium. *Obstetrics & Gynecology, 79,* 424–429.

Schlundt, D. G., Hill, J. O., Pope-Cordle, D., Arnold, K. L., Virts, K. L., & Katahn, M. (1993). Randomized evaluation of a low fat "ad libitum" carbohydrate diet for weight reduction. *International Journal of Obesity and Related Metabolic Disorders, 17,* 623–629.

Shai, I., Schwarzfuchs, D., Henkin, Y., Shahar, D. R., Witkow, S., Greenberg, I., . . . Stampfer, M. J. (2008). Weight loss with a low-carbohydrate, Mediterranean, or low-fat diet. *New England Journal of Medicine, 359*(3), 229–241.

Sjöström, L. (2008). Bariatric surgery and reduction in morbidity and mortality: Experiences from the SOS Study. *International Journal of Obesity, 32,* S93–S97.

Sjöström, L., Lindroos, A. K., Peltonen, M., Torgerson, J., Bouchard, C., Carlsson, B., . . . Swedish Obese Subjects Study Scientific Group. (2004). Lifestyle, diabetes, and cardiovascular risk factors 10 years after bariatric surgery. *New England Journal of Medicine, 23,* 2683–2693.

Sjöström, L., Narbro, K., Sjostrom, C. D., Karason, K., Larsson, B., Wedel, H., . . . Swedish Obese Subjects Study. (2007). Effects of bariatric surgery on mortality in Swedish obese subjects. *New England Journal of Medicine, 23*(741), 752.

Sjöström, L., Rissanen, A., Andersen, T., Boldrin, M., Golay, A., Koppeschaar, H. P. F., & Krempf, M. (1998). Randomised placebo-controlled trial of orlistat for weight loss and prevention of weight regain in obese patients. *Lancet, 352* (9123), 167–172.

Sowers, M., Zheng, H., Tomey, K., Karvonen-Guitierrez, C., Jannausch, M., Li, X., . . . Symons, J. (2007). Changes in body composition in women over six years at midlife: Ovarian and chronological aging. *Journal of Clinical Endocrinology and Metabolism, 92*(3), 895–901.

Steinbrook, R. (2004). Surgery for severe obesity. *New England Journal of Medicine, 350*(11), 1075–1079.

Stern, L., Iqbal, N., Seshadri, P., Chicano, K. L., Daily, D. A., McGrory, J., . . . Samaha, F. F. (2004). The effects of low-carbohydrate versus conventional weight loss diets in severely obese adults: One-year follow-up of a randomized trial. *Annals of Internal Medicine, 140*(10), 778–785.

Sternfeld, B., Bhat, A. K., Wang, H., Sharp, T., & Queensbury, C. P. (2005). Menopause, physical activity, and body composition/fat distribution in midlife women. *Medicine and Science in Sports and Exercise, 37*(7), 1195–1202.

Stice E., Spoor S., Ng J., & Zald D. H. (2009). Relation of obesity to consummatory and anticipatory food reward. *Physiology & Behavior, 97,* 551–560.

Stotland, N. E., Cheng, Y. W., Hopkins, L. M., & Caughey, A. B. (2006). Gestational weight gain and adverse neonatal outcome among term infants. *Obstetrics & Gynecology, 108,* 635–643.

Stroebe, W. (2008). *Dieting, overweight and obesity: Self-regulation in a food-rich environment.* Washington, DC: American Psychological Association.

Strohl, K. P., Strobel, R. J., & Parisi, R. A. (2004). Obesity and pulmonary function. In G. A. Bray, C. Bouchard, & W. P. James (Eds.), *Handbook of obesity: Etiology and pathophysiology* (2nd ed., pp. 725–739). New York, NY: Marcel Dekker.

Stunkard, A. J., & Sobal, J. (1995). Psychosocial consequences of obesity. In K. D. Brownell & C. G. Fairburn (Eds.), *Eating disorders and obesity:*

A comprehensive handbook (pp. 417–421). New York, NY: Guilford Press.

Tate, D. F., Jeffery, R. W., Sherwood, N. E., & Wing, R. R. (2007). Long-term weight losses associated with prescription of higher physical activity goals: Are higher levels of physical activity protective against weight regain? *American Journal of Clinical Nutrition, 85*(4), 954–959.

Teixeira, M. E., & Budd, G. M. (2010). Obesity stigma: A newly recognized barrier to comprehensive and effective type 2 diabetes management. *Journal of the American Academy of Nurse Practitioners, 22*(10), 527–533.

The Look AHEAD Research Group. (2010). Long-term effects of lifestyle intervention on weight and cardiovascular risk factors in individuals with type 2 diabetes: Four-year results of the Look AHEAD trial. *Archives of Internal Medicine, 170,* 1566–1575.

Thompson, D., Edelsberg, J., Colditz, G. A., Bird, A. P., & Oster, G. (1999). Lifetime health and economic consequences of obesity. *Archives of Internal Medicine, 159,* 2177–2183.

Tiggemann, M., & Rothblum, E. D. (1988). Gender differences in social consequences of perceived overweight in the United States and Australia. *Sex Roles, 18*(1–2), 75–86.

Toubro, S., & Astrup, A. (1997). Randomized comparison of diets for maintaining obese subjects' weight after major weight loss: Ad lib, low fat, high carbohydrate diet versus fixed energy intake. *British Medical Journal, 314*(7073), 29–42.

Trogdon, J. G., Finkelstein, E. A., Hylands, T., Dellea, P. S., & Kamal-Bahl, S. J. (2008). Indirect costs of obesity: A review of the current literature. *Obesity Reviews, 9*(5), 489–500.

Trost, S., Sallis, J., Pate, R., Freedson, P., Taylor, W., & Dowda, M. (2003). Evaluating a model of parental influence on youth physical activity. *American Journal of Preventive Medicine, 25,* 277–282.

Tuomilehto, J., Lindstrom, J., Eriksson, J. G., Valle, T. T., Hamalainen, H., Ilanne-Parikka, P., . . . Finnish Diabetes Prevention Study Group. (2001). Prevention of type 2 diabetes mellitus by changes in lifestyle among subjects with impaired glucose tolerance. *New England Journal of Medicine, 344*(18), 1343–1350.

Wadden, T. A., & Berkowitz, R. I. (2002). Very low-calorie diets. In C. G. Fairburn & K. D. Brownell (Eds.), *Eating disorders and obesity: A comprehensive handbook* (2nd ed., pp. 534–538). New York, NY: Guilford Press.

Wadden, T. A., & Butryn, M. L. (2003). Behavioral treatment of obesity. *Endocrinology & Metabolism Clinics of North America, 32*(4), 981–1003.

Wadden, T. A., Butryn, M. L., & Byrne, K. J. (2004). Efficacy of lifestyle modification for long-term weight control. *Obesity Research, 12*(Suppl), 151S–62S.

Wadden, T. A., Butryn, M. L., & Wilson, C. (2007). Lifestyle modification for the management of obesity. *Gastroenterology, 132*(6), 2226–2238.

Wadden, T. A., Berkowitz, R. I., Womble, L. G., Sarwer, D. B., Phelan, S., Cato, R. K., . . . Stunkard, A. J. (2005). Randomized trial of lifestyle modification and pharmacotherapy for obesity. *New England Journal of Medicine, 353*(20), 2111–2120.

Wadden, T. A., Vogt, R. A., Andersen, R. E., Bartlett, S. J., Foster, G. D., Kuehnel, R. H., . . . Steen, S. N. (1997). Exercise in the treatment of obesity: Effects of four interventions on body composition, resting energy expenditure, appetite, and mood. *Journal of Consulting & Clinical Psychology, 65*(2), 269–277.

Westerterp, K. R., & Goran, M. I. (1997). Relationship between physical activity related energy expenditure and body composition: A gender difference. *International Journal of Obesity, 21,* 184–188.

Wee, C. C., McCarthy, E. P., Davis, R. B., & Phillips, R. S. (2000). Screening for cervical and breast cancer: Is obesity an unrecognized barrier to preventative care? *Annals of Internal Medicine, 132,* 697–704.

Wing, R. R., Jeffery, R. W., Burton, L. R., Thorson, C., Nissinoff, K. S., & Baxter, J. E. (1996). Food provision vs. structured meal plans in the behavioral treatment of obesity. *International Journal of Obesity Related Metabolic Disorders, 20*(1), 56–62.

Wing, R. R., Koeske, R., Epstein, L. H., Nowalk, M. P., Gooding, W., & Becker, D. (1987). Long-term effects of modest weight loss in type II diabetic patients. *Archives of Internal Medicine, 147*(10), 1749–1753.

Wing, R. R., Tate, D. F., Gorin, A. A., Raynor, H. A., & Fava, J. L. (2006). A self-regulation program for maintenance of weight loss. *New England Journal of Medicine, 355*(15), 1563–1571.

Wing, R. R., & Phelan, S. (2005). Long-term weight loss maintenance. *American Journal of Clinical Nutrition, 82,* 2225–2255.

Wolf, A. M., & Colditz, G. A. (1998). Current estimates of the economic cost of obesity in the United States. *Obesity Research, 6,* 97–106.

Womble, L. G., Wang, S. S., & Wadden, T. A. (2002). Commercial and self-help weight loss programs. In T. A. Wadden & A. J. Stunkard (Eds.), *Handbook of obesity treatment* (pp. 395–415). New York, NY: Guilford Press.

World Health Organization (1997). *Obesity: Preventing and managing the global epidemic: Report of a WHO consultation of obesity.* Geneva, Switzerland: The Stationary Office Books.

Zaadstra, B. M., Seidell, J. C., Van Noord, P. A., te Velde, E. R., Habbema, J. D., Vrieswijk, B., . . . Norman, R. J. (1993). Fat and female fecundity: Prospective study of effect of body fat distribution on conception rates. *British Medical Journal, 306,* 484.

8

Eating and Weight-Related Disorders

Matthew Fuller-Tyszkiewicz, Ross Krawczyk, Lina Ricciardelli, and J. Kevin Thompson

INTRODUCTION

Eating disorders (EDs) are among the most common and debilitating psychological disorders, especially for young girls and women (Thompson & Smolak, 2001). Although at most 1 in 10 women will be formally diagnosed with one or another of these disorders in their lifetime, subthreshold symptoms are common in the general population (Frederick, Forbes, Grigoran, & Jarcho, 2007). Importantly, evidence suggests that both subthreshold and full-syndrome cases of ED are linked with other serious psychosocial disorders, including depression, anxiety, obesity, increased risk of self-harm, and suicidal ideation (Ben-Tovim et al., 2001; Grabe, Hyde, & Lindberg, 2007).

EDs have the highest mortality rate of any psychiatric disorder (Fairburn, Cooper, Doll, Norman, & O'Connor, 2000). Hospitalization for EDs and the need for continued long-term psychological and physical care for ED patients is a huge financial burden on public health systems (Pratt & Woolfenden, 2002). It is, therefore, not surprising to find that body image and eating disturbances have been identified by governments, researchers, and healthcare professionals alike as a key health priority area. This chapter provides an overview of current issues relevant to EDs, including diagnostic criteria and prevalence rates, evidence for environmental and genetic influences on EDs, and treatment alternatives.

DIAGNOSTIC FEATURES

The *DSM-IV-TR* (2000) describes four main classifications of eating disorders: Anorexia Nervosa, Bulimia Nervosa, Binge-Eating Disorder, and Eating Disorder Not Otherwise Specified. Binge-eating disorder is currently included in the appendix of "criteria sets and axes provided for further study," but this diagnosis will likely be integrated into the ED section in *DSM-5* (American Psychiatric Association, 2012). It is also included in this review chapter because of the increasing recognition that it is distinct from the other EDs (Wilfley, Bishop, Wilson, & Agras, 2007). We will also examine Body Dysmorphic Disorder, given that the focus of this condition is on extreme appearance concerns.

Anorexia Nervosa

The key diagnostic features of anorexia nervosa (AN) involve severe underweight, preoccupation with body image, and disordered eating. To be diagnosed with AN, an individual must have a body size that is at least

15% less than minimally normal weight for one's age and height. Individuals with AN commonly present with a body weight that is considerably thinner than 15% below the normal weight, and emaciation or cachexia is common. However, rigid adherence to the weight criterion for diagnosis is ill-advised, particularly if the individual meets all other criteria for AN (Walsh & Garner, 1997). Keel and McCormick (2010) point out that since the *DSM-IV-TR* does not provide a formal method for evaluating what a minimally normal weight is for one's age and height, a patient may be diagnosed with AN by one clinician and with EDNOS by another.

Because of the low weight range of individuals with AN and their excessive weight loss and caloric restriction, the *DSM-IV-TR* stipulates that absence of at least three consecutive menstrual cycles is another necessary precondition for diagnosis of AN. However, it has been argued that this criterion is harsh, because individuals with AN may have irregular menstrual functioning and still fail to meet the amenorrhea criterion (Keel & McCormick, 2010). It has been demonstrated that inclusion of the amenorrhea criterion fails to significantly enhance specificity of diagnosis (Andersen, Bowers, & Watson, 2001). Furthermore, disruptions to menstrual functioning are not relevant for premenarcheal or post-menopausal females, or males who otherwise meet criteria for a diagnosis of AN. For these reasons, this amenorrhea criterion is often ignored by researchers when recruiting individuals with AN to their studies.

Despite their severely low weight, individuals with AN typically exhibit an extreme level of dissatisfaction with their appearance, and they will seek to either maintain their emaciated condition or lose further weight.

Although it was initially thought that this body size overestimation may be the result of a general sensory disturbance to visual processing (and, thus, an overestimation of one's actual size), subsequent research has shown that individuals with AN are able to accurately estimate the size of other people's bodies and, with prompting, can accurately identify their own body size (Norris, 1984). Thus, it is now widely believed that this distortion has cognitive-evaluative origins (Smeets, Ingleby, Hoek, & Panhuysen, 1999).

Individuals with AN are also intensely fearful of gaining weight, and they may avoid highly caloric foods, engage in excessive exercise, and rely upon purgative methods to manage weight gain (e.g., laxative use, diuretics, self-induced vomiting). However, some individuals with AN are able to meet the weight criteria without reliance upon purgative methods. Therefore, the *DSM-IV-TR* divides AN into two subtypes: (1) *restricting subtype*, in which individuals do not engage in binge eating or purging, and (2) *binge/purge subtype* for individuals who regularly engage in binge eating and/or purging.

Bulimia Nervosa

Bulimia nervosa (BN) is characterized by recurrent (at least once per week for 3 months) episodes of binge eating and inappropriate compensatory behaviors to prevent weight gain. These binge episodes are accompanied by the feeling that one cannot stop eating (i.e., perceived loss of control) and are typically followed by feelings of guilt, shame, and increased weight concern (Elmore & De Castro, 1990). Additionally, individuals with BN make self-evaluations that are unduly influenced by body shape and weight. Individuals with BN are further divided into those who do and those who do not engage in purgative behaviors: BN-Purge subtype and BN-Nonpurging subtype, respectively. Members of the latter group attempt to control their weight by overexercising and/or fasting.

Binge-Eating Disorder

Binge-eating disorder (BED) is characterized by binge eating and distress about the occurrence and frequency of binge episodes. Whereas diagnosis for BN involves at least two binge episodes per week for a period of 3 months, the criterion is twice weekly for 6 months in BED. A further difference between BN and BED is that binge episodes for individuals with BED are not associated with purgative methods to compensate for overeating. In addition, there is no body image disturbance criterion for BED.

Despite sharing the core symptom of binge eating, the eating patterns and characteristics of a binge episode appear different for BN and BED. Individuals with BED typically consume fewer calories than individuals with BN during a binge episode, and yet consume more calories on average during nonbinge episodes than BN counterparts. Whereas individuals with BN are most likely to consume dessert foods during a binge episode, BED individuals are more varied in the foods they binge eat (Wilfley, Wilson, & Agras, 2003).

Additionally, the clinical presentation and associated demographics for BN and BED are distinct. Whereas BN is most common among adolescent to early adult white women from Western cultures, BED appears to be more evenly distributed across gender, race, and ethnicity (Streigel-Moore & Franko, 2008). Moreover, individuals with BED tend to be older than those

diagnosed with BN (Johnson, Spitzer, & Williams, 2001). Whereas the prevalence of BN appears to be stable across early and middle adulthood (roughly 1% prevalence), Johnson et al. (2001) found that the prevalence of BED steadily increased from 3% among 18- to 25-year-olds to 8.5% among 46- to 55-year-olds.

Eating Disorder Not Otherwise Specified

Individuals diagnosed with Eating Disorder Not Otherwise Specified (EDNOS) meet some, but not all, criteria for AN or BN. Despite this, sufferers' level of eating disturbance is sufficiently extreme to warrant clinical attention. Variations of EDNOS for AN include individuals meeting all criteria, except: (1) the criterion for amenorrhea, (2) the 15% below normal weight criterion, or (3) denial that one is preoccupied with body shape and weight. For BN, EDNOS individuals typically fail to meet the frequency requirement for binge eating, use of compensatory behaviors, or their binge episodes are not objectively large (Wildes & Marcus, 2010).

Body Dysmorphic Disorder

Body dysmorphic disorder (BDD) is characterized by preoccupation with an imagined or slight defect in one's appearance. This preoccupation is so severe that it causes clinically significant levels of distress and/or interferes with daily functioning. Based on observations of more than 500 clinically diagnosed individuals with BDD, Phillips (2009) identified skin, hair, and nose as the most cited areas of concern. She also observed three distinct patterns in BDD expression. Approximately 30% of cases exhibited just one area of body concern throughout the course of their condition. A further 40% initially exhibited one area of body concern and developed additional areas of concern as the disorder progressed. A third group (which accounted for roughly 30%) were initially dissatisfied with one body part, only to have that concern disappear and be supplanted by dissatisfaction with another body part.

Dual Diagnoses

A range of Axis I and II clinical disorders commonly co-occur with eating disorders. Comorbid major depression is present in approximately one-third of individuals with AN at any one time, and the lifetime diagnosis of major depression in this population is estimated at 60% (Agras, 2001). In contrast, roughly 20% of individuals with BN have current major depression, and 50% may develop depression at some point concurrent with their eating disorder (Crow & Brandenburg, 2009). Comorbid depression rates may be highest among individuals with BED; Williamson, Thaw, and Varnado-Sullivan (2001) estimated that 40% to 50% of individuals with BED also had major depression. Although these numbers are quite high, they are likely underestimates of the co-occurrence of depressive symptoms, because many individuals with an ED who do not meet full criteria for depression still have more severe depressive symptoms than nonclinical populations (Williamson et al., 2001).

A range of anxiety disorders—most notably, obsessive-compulsive disorder (OCD) and social phobia—are common among ED populations. For individuals with AN, lifetime prevalence rates range from 20% to 65% across the various anxiety disorders (Kaye et al., 2004; Williamson et al., 2001; Wonderlich & Mitchell, 1997). Onset of

anxiety disorders typically occurs in childhood and precedes development of an eating disorder. The rates of anxiety disorders among BN individuals is comparable to individuals with AN, with the exception of posttraumatic stress disorder, which seems to be more common among BN than AN individuals (Crow & Brandenburg, 2009).

Of the Axis II personality disorders, obsessive-compulsive personality disorder is most common among individuals with AN-R, whereas borderline personality disorder is more common among AN-BP individuals. The co-occurrence rate of personality disorders in BN is approximately 34% (Sansone, Levitt, & Sansone, 2005), although estimates for borderline personality disorder vary from 2% to 47% (Keel & McCormick, 2010). It is estimated that one-third of individuals with BED have a personality disorder, with OCD being the most common comorbidity.

Although these numbers are remarkably high, they may actually underestimate the extent of comorbidity in ED populations. When symptoms (rather than formal diagnosis) are used, ED populations exhibit considerably higher levels of depression, anxiety, and other symptoms than nonclinical comparison groups (Keel & McCormick, 2010). Even though many ED individuals do not meet a formal diagnosis for a second disorder, it would be a mistake to believe that symptoms of anxiety, personality disorder, or depression are absent for these individuals.

Prevalence Rates

Prevalence estimates for eating disorders typically range from approximately 0.5% for AN to approximately 1% to 3% for BN and BED (APA, 2000). Rates for EDNOS are slightly higher, with estimates ranging from 2% to 5% (Favaro, Ferrara, & Santonastaso, 2003; Wade, Bergin, Tiggemann, Bulik, & Fairburn, 2006). The majority of individuals diagnosed with an eating disorder are late adolescent or early adult women, although the gender distribution is almost equal for BED. Roughly 90% of individuals with AN and BN are female, compared with 60% for BED (APA, 2000).

Less is known about the prevalence of body dysmorphic disorder or muscle dysmorphic disorder, a form of body dysmorphic disorder in which the individual is preoccupied with her or his muscularity, believing that s/he is too lean (Pope et al., 2005). In a German community-based sample, Rief, Buhlmann, Wilhelm, Borkenhagen, and Brahler (2006) estimated that the prevalence rate for BDD was 1.7%, with a slightly higher proportion of the female population (1.9%) than male population (1.4%) meeting diagnostic criteria for the disorder. In another U.S.-based study, it was estimated that 2.5% of the female adult population and 2.2% of the male adult population had BDD (Phillips, 2009).

Although the majority of available data comes from studies of adolescent and college-aged men and women from Westernized cultures and English-speaking countries (most notably, Australia, England, and the United States), there is evidence to suggest that prevalence rates for EDs are, in many instances, similar in non-Western cultures. Nobakht and Dezhkam (2000) reported lifetime prevalence rates of 0.9% for AN, 3.2% for BN, and 6.6% for partial syndrome among adolescent girls in Iran. Similarly, Kjelsas, Bjornstrom, and Gotestam (2004) found that the point estimates and gender differences for reported lifetime prevalence of EDs in Norway were consistent with those found in English-speaking countries,

although their estimates of EDNOS were higher. They reported lifetime prevalence rates of 0.7% for AN, 1.2% for BN, 1.5% for BED, and 14.6% for EDNOS among Norwegian adolescent girls, and 0.2% for AN, 0.4% for BN, 0.9% for BED, and 5% for EDNOS among Norwegian adolescent boys. Lower prevalence rates have been reported for Hungarian high school and college students (Tolgyes & Nemessury, 2004) and Turkish adolescents (Kiziltan, Karabudak, Unver, Sezgin, & Unal, 2006), although these differences may be attributable to smaller sample sizes in these studies (300 to 500 compared with 2,000 to 3,000 participants).

Available data from samples of women beyond early adulthood (i.e., older than 25 years of age) suggests that eating disorders are less prevalent in later life (Brandsma, 2007; Peat, Peyerl, & Muehlenkamp, 2008). However, attempts to accurately estimate prevalence of EDs in later life is complicated by the limited number of studies, with fluctuating estimates due in part to small sample sizes. Estimates from many of these studies are also confounded because they include individuals who experience onset of symptoms or full diagnosis in adolescence or early adult life (Peat et al., 2008). Studies that have controlled for age of onset suggest that late-onset EDs are quite rare (Zerbe, 2003).

Despite the low prevalence rates of eating disorders in both Western and non-Western cultures for adolescents and adults, symptoms of disordered eating (such as binge eating, eating concerns, weight management, and body dissatisfaction) are quite common in the general population. A substantial proportion of women in the general population and in university samples engage in dieting behaviors (approximately 50%), although a much smaller percentage (approximately 5%) engage in these extreme weight loss techniques (Timko, Perone, & Crossfield, 2006). This has led some researchers (e.g., Fitzgibbon, Sanchez-Johnsen, & Martinovich, 2003; Lowe et al., 1996) to propose that ED symptoms occur along a continuum. This continuum model acknowledges that ED symptoms (especially, appearance concerns, binge eating, and dieting) are common in the general population, albeit with lesser severity and frequency. Moreover, this model assumes that differences across clinical and nonclinical populations in the expression of ED symptoms are quantitative rather than qualitative (as a categorical view of EDs would suggest). Importantly, evidence suggests that subclinical levels of symptomatology are one of the main risk factors for developing an ED (Herzog, Hopkins, & Burns, 1993), thus emphasizing the need to investigate disordered eating in both clinical and subclinical samples of individuals (Fitzgibbon et al., 2003).

Course and Prognosis

AN typically develops in mid- to late adolescence (APA, 2000). Prognosis for AN is greatest for individuals who are diagnosed at an early age and who commence treatment shortly after diagnosis (Steinhausen, 2002). However, of all the eating disorders, AN is associated with the greatest mortality and is the most chronic. It is estimated that individuals with AN have a ten-fold increased likelihood of mortality (relative to nonclinical populations) because of their condition (Keel et al., 2003). Even with treatment, few individuals suffering from AN reach full remission (Keel & McCormick, 2010).

The course for BN is typically more favorable than for AN. Mortality rates are considerably lower for individuals with BN (roughly two-fold increase in likelihood

relative to general community) (Keel et al., 2003). Longitudinal studies show that the majority of individuals with BN are in partial or full remission within 3 to 5 years (Crow & Brandenburg, 2009). However, the pattern of recovery from BN often involves periods of relapse and/or diagnostic crossover. Individuals with BN most commonly cross over to EDNOS or BED, which is not surprising given the overlap of symptoms for these conditions (Crow & Brandenburg, 2009).

The estimated lifetime duration for BED is 8 years as compared to 2 years for AN (Hudson, Hiripi, Pope, & Kessler, 2007). Naturalistic longitudinal studies suggest that the symptoms persist longer for individuals who meet full criteria for BED (Hudson et al., 2007), while remission appears more likely to occur for individuals who meet subthreshold levels of BED (Fairburn et al., 2000). However, mortality rates are considerably lower for BED than for AN; individuals with BED have a two-fold increase in mortality risk compared to the general population (Fichter, Quadflieg, & Hedlund, 2008).

BDD usually begins in early adolescence, with an average age of onset of 16 years (Phillips, 2009). In retrospective accounts, more than 80% of patients described their BDD as chronic. Although this figure appears inflated, it is evident from prospective studies that BDD symptoms endure for an extended period. Of the group of individuals who met criteria for BDD at baseline, only 9% of individuals were free of BDD symptoms for at least eight consecutive weeks during the 1-year testing gap, and 21% no longer met full *DSM-IV* criteria. After 2 years, 16% were free of symptoms and 28% no longer met full *DSM-IV* criteria. After 3 years, 17% were free of symptoms and 36% no longer met full criteria (Phillips, 2009).

The merits of addressing course and prognosis for EDNOS have been debated on the grounds that it is presently unclear whether EDNOS is a convenience label for a group of disorders with different symptoms, courses, and prognoses (Wildes & Marcus, 2009). Furthermore, earlier attempts to quantify the course of EDNOS were often conflated by inclusion of cases of BED (Wildes & Marcus, 2009).

Available data suggests that EDNOS remits in the majority of individuals within 1 to 2 years (Wildes & Marcus, 2009). However, this finding should be tempered with several key considerations. First, as a subthreshold classification for EDs, cases of EDNOS may remit because the symptoms are less extreme than for full EDs. Second, there is considerable cross-over into other EDs; individuals who initially failed to meet a diagnosis for BN, AN, or BED may progress to these disorders over time (Fairburn & Cooper, 2011), consistent with the continuum model for EDs.

RISK FACTORS FOR EDS

Genetic Factors

Broadly speaking, researchers have adopted one of two approaches to investigate the genetic basis for EDs. The first approach evaluates the heritability of full-ED syndromes with use of family, twin, and adoption studies. In the second approach, researchers attempt to isolate relationships between genes and specific ED symptoms (Scherag, Hebebrand, & Hinney, 2010).

Family studies suggest that the risk of developing an ED is substantially higher for individuals who have a first-degree relative who has been diagnosed with an ED. The

increased risk of developing an ED is approximately 11-fold for individuals with a relative who has AN (Strober, Freeman, Lampert, Diamond, & Kaye, 2000), four- to nine-fold for relatives with BN (Kassett et al., 1989; Strober et al., 2000), and two-fold for relatives with BED (Hudson et al., 2006; Javaras et al., 2008). Heritability has also been established for subthreshold levels of ED (Strober et al., 2000).

Findings from twin studies, which are considered a better approach for separating genetic and environmental influences on behavior, support the results of these family studies. Differences in concordance rates for EDs between monozygotic twins (i.e., twins with identical DNA barring stochastic errors in DNA replication) and dizygotic twins (those who share about half of their genes) provide a more realistic estimate of the influence of genes on ED transmission. Estimates of the gene influence on EDs have ranged from 58% to 88% for AN (Bulik, Sullivan, Wade, & Kendler, 2000; Klump, Kaye, & Strober, 2001; Wade et al., 2000), 54% to 83% for BN (Bulik, Sullivan, & Kendler, 1998; Wade et al., 1999), and 41% to 57% for BED (Javaras et al., 2008; Reichborn-Kjennerud, Bulik, Tambs, & Harris, 2004). To date, genetic influences on ED-NOS and BDD have not been evaluated.

Family and twin studies have also been used to evaluate the genetic basis for EDs at the symptom level. Klump et al. (2001) found that 32% to 72% of factors such as body dissatisfaction, eating and weight concerns, and weight preoccupation were heritable, as were 46% to 72% of dietary restraint, binge eating, and vomiting. However, other findings suggest that the heritability of drive for thinness and body dissatisfaction are considerably stronger for women than men (Keski-Rahkonen et al., 2005). Findings of a stronger genetic basis for EDs among female populations may partially explain gender differences in the prevalence of eating and weight-related disorders.

Pathways implicated in body weight regulation and eating behavior, particularly the serotonergic system, have been investigated in the hope that they may uncover genetic markers and pathways that predispose an individual to EDs. It seems likely that serotonin (5-HT) dysregulation plays a role in the pathology of EDs given that (1) there is an established link between serotonin and feeding, mood, and impulse control; (2) medication that affects serotonin levels has established efficacy in treatment of EDs; and (3) disturbances in serotonin levels persist beyond recovery from the ED (Kaye et al., 2005).

Relative to healthy control groups, individuals with BN exhibit decreased levels of the serotonin metabolite 5-hydroxyindoleacetic acid in cerebrospinal fluid (CSF) and blunted prolactin response to 5-HT receptor agonists m-chlorophenylpiperazine, 5-hydroxytrytophan, and difenfluramine (Jimerson & Wolfe, 2006). Dysfunctional serotonin functioning has also been reported among individuals with AN. Patients with AN have been found to have a blunted prolactin response to 5-HT drugs and reduced 3-H imipramine binding, as well as showing low levels of CSF 5-HIAA (a metabolite of serotonin) (Kaye et al., 2005). However, it remains unclear whether the depleted CSF 5-HIAA levels contribute to AN or whether they are a consequence of nutritional deprivation characteristic of those with AN.

Several specific genes have been identified that may explain how serotonin dysregulation occurs in ED populations. The G-143AA polymorphism in the promoter region of the 5-HT2A receptor gene has been linked to the etiology of AN (Klump & Gobrogge, 2005). 5-HTTLPR, a serotonin transporter, has also been found to be associated with AN and BN (Mazzeo, Slof'Op't, van Furth, & Bulik, 2006). Other findings suggest that the opioid delta receptor OPRD1 and the serotonin receptor HTR1D link to etiology of AN, and that regions on chromosomes 1, 10, and 14 may play a role in a range of eating pathologies (Klump & Gobrogge, 2005; Mazzeo et al., 2006).

Given the variability of ED symptom expression (both with respect to cluster and severity of symptoms), the genetic pathways for ED phenotypes are likely to involve a diffuse and complex network of associations (Scherag et al., 2010). Although the identification of single genes or alleles as sources of ED behaviors is an encouraging first step, researchers need to be aware that too narrow a focus on one or several genes rather than a network approach is liable to lead to findings that are inconsistent and more difficult to replicate, thus giving the impression that a gene may have falsely been shown to be relevant to uncovering the etiology of EDs (Scherag et al., 2010). Systematic, genome-wide studies may help identify currently ignored sources of genetic influence on EDs (Scherag et al., 2010).

Developmental Stages

Researchers have also considered how ED symptoms may be prompted by developmental milestones in the female lifespan. In particular, researchers have investigated the possibility that women who struggle with key transitional periods (i.e., puberty, pregnancy, menopause, and loss of loved ones) may be at increased risk for the development of body image concerns and/or disordered eating symptoms (Peat et al., 2008).

Although the empirical evidence supporting a direct relationship between pubertal status and development of EDs is underwhelming (Stice, 2002), there is a clear link between sexual maturation and precursors to EDs, such as body image disturbances, dieting behaviors, and depressive symptoms (O'Dea & Abraham, 1999; Stice, Presnell, & Bearman, 2001; Striegel-Moore et al., 2001). It is likely that the desire of early- and late-maturing girls to change their appearance is motivated by their experiences of public scrutiny, stigmatization, and social ostracism for having a physical appearance that is out of step with the majority of their peer group (Striegel-Moore et al., 2001).

Girls who experience early menarche tend to be shorter and heavier than girls who exhibit a more normative developmental trajectory (Garn, Labelle, Rosenberg, & Hawthorne, 1986), and their earlier increases in adipose tissue during menarche move them further from the thin ideal (Graber, Brooks-Gunn, Paikoff, & Warren, 1994). Early sexual development may also force these girls to confront new stressors before they are psychologically ready (Stice et al., 2001). In contrast, those girls who are later maturing may be less desirable to the opposite sex, and may feel awkward about their appearance.

Pregnancy is characterized by rapid physical changes in appearance that push women further away from societal norms of appearance. It is not surprising then that many pregnant women report feeling dissatisfied with their appearance (Skouteris, Carr, Wertheim, Paxton, & Duncombe, 2005). This body dissatisfaction is linked to anxiety, depressive symptoms, and low self-esteem (Clark, Skouteris, Wertheim, Paxton, & Milgrom, 2009; Duncombe, Wertheim, Skouteris, Paxton, & Kelly, 2008), and to

unhealthy eating behaviors, dieting, and smoking—all of which may be used to control weight gain (Duncombe et al., 2008).

Although body dissatisfaction is a common experience for pregnant women, the severity of body image disturbances and disordered eating symptomatology appears linked to their expectations regarding postpartum weight loss, familial and spousal support, the extent to which women retain unrealistic appearance-related ideals throughout pregnancy, and the amount of weight they gain during pregnancy (Haedt & Keel, 2007; Upton & Han, 2003).

Women continue to experience a range of changes to their physical appearance and functioning beyond age 40, including the onset of menopause, increases in body size and weight, the appearance of wrinkles and loss of skin elasticity, as well as graying and thinning of hair (Andres, 1989). Fredrickson and Roberts (1997) argue that the impact of the physical aging process on body dissatisfaction and weight management behaviors depends on the extent to which an individual is able to relinquish or modify the appearance standards she adopted throughout youth and early adulthood.

It has been shown that women aged 40 or older who continue to value physical appearance exhibit levels of body dissatisfaction comparable to younger women (Mellor, Fuller-Tyszkiewicz, McCabe, & Ricciardelli, 2010). Concern with the physical signs of aging are also related with drive for thinness and body dissatisfaction among middle-aged women (Gupta, 1995). Anecdotal evidence from case reports implicate fear of aging as a contributor to late-onset EDs (e.g., Hall & Driscoll, 1993; Kellett, Trimble, & Thorley, 1976), but this appears to be a weak predictor when one compares the low incidence of cases of late-onset EDs against the relatively high prevalence of body image concerns in middle age and beyond. Additionally, the retrospective nature of these clinical observations, and overreliance on cross-sectional designs, fail to rule out the possibility that body image issues experienced in midlife are a continuation of appearance-related concerns from youth and/or early adulthood.

The experience of loss has also been discussed as a potential risk factor for the development of body image and eating-disordered symptoms (Peat et al., 2008). For instance, it has been argued that loss of a loved one (through widowhood or divorce) means that the individual must confront single life and decide whether (and how) to seek a new partner. To the extent that women decide to re-enter the dating scene, they may experience renewed focus on their appearance, as they attempt to attract a potential mate (Brandsma, 2007). Hsu and Zimmer's (2009) case study of five women with late-onset AN suggests that loss of loved ones was a chief contributor to development of ED symptoms, although others (e.g., Hall & Driscoll, 1993) have cautioned that AN-type symptoms (such as loss of weight and reduced appetite) may instead be a function of depressive symptoms. Evidence is mixed regarding the impact of marital discord on body image and eating disorders (Abramson, 1999; Dally, 1984;Lewis & Cachelin, 2001).

Psychological/Sociocultural Factors

Thompson, Heinberg, Altabe, and Tantleff-Dunn (1999) proposed the tripartite influence model, a formal theoretical model to understand the most important sociocultural sources of pressure to conform to cultural appearance ideals. In this model, the three sources of pressure are peers, parents, and media, which ultimately predict negative outcomes such as eating disorders and body image disturbance. Specifically, people who report exposure to more messages and pressure to conform to cultural appearance ideals from their parents, their peers, and the media also tend to report more negative outcomes, such as body appearance dissatisfaction, eating disorder symptomatology, body shame, and appearance anxiety. Although the media seems to be a steady influence on appearance ideals at all ages, the importance of these various other sources for the transmission of body image ideals appears to change across the lifespan. Whereas parental comments are most influential for shaping the body image attitudes and behaviors of children, adolescents are most influenced by messages from peers (especially weight- and appearance-related teasing), and young adults by comments from partners (Thompson et al., 1999).

The tripartite influence model also proposes two factors that mediate the relationship between the sociocultural influences and negative eating and body image outcomes: appearance ideal internalization and appearance comparison. Internalization refers to a person taking cues about appearance ideals from external influences, such as their peers, their parents, and the media, and adopting them as their own internal views (Thompson & Stice, 2001). This may be thought of as a person viewing themselves from a third-person or outsider's perspective. When people view unrealistic standards and internalize them, their own standards of how they should appear can become unrealistic or even impossible to obtain. Internalization of cultural appearance ideals is related to eating pathology and body dissatisfaction in both Western (Thompson et al., 1999) and Eastern cultures (Krawczyk, Menzel, Swami, & Thompson, 2011).

Earlier findings of lower prevalence rates of disordered eating and appearance concerns among ethnic minorities within Western cultures and among individuals who reside in non-Western countries have been explained in terms of non-Western cultures having different (and perhaps more realistic) appearance-related standards that serve as a protective factor against eating-disordered symptoms. However, these cultural and ethnic differences are rapidly diminishing, a finding that is largely attributed to the effects of globalization, particularly the increased exposure to Western media and Western body ideals (Markey, 2004).

The second mediating factor in the tripartite influence model is social appearance comparison, which occurs when the girl or woman compares her own physical appearance with that of someone else. The target of comparison can be a friend, a stranger, a celebrity on television, a model in an advertisement, or any other person. Social appearance comparison is not necessarily always harmful, especially at lower frequency. However, empirical evidence shows that stimuli that portray unrealistic cultural appearance ideals, such as fashion magazines, increase the frequency of appearance comparison among girls (Martin & Kennedy, 1993) and young women (Thompson et al., 1999). Evidence also shows that social appearance comparison predicts body image and eating disturbance, acting as a mediator for the link between sociocultural influences and negative outcomes (Heinberg & Thompson, 1995). These sociocultural influences may include feedback from peers such as appearance-related teasing (Thompson, Coovert, & Stromer, 1999), media influences such as

thin ideal depictions in magazines (Tiggemann & McGill, 2004), or parental influences such as family preoccupation with weight and dieting (Keery, van den Berg, & Thompson, 2004).

Mass Media

Beyond the tripartite model, a great deal of research has examined the body image and eating outcomes related to mass media. The mass media are a reflection of the sociocultural environment and an ever-present influence that plays a major part in the lives of people of all ages (Comstock & Scharrer, 2007). Western mass media frequently portrays cultural appearance ideals (Herbozo, Tantleff-Dunn, Gokee-Larose, & Thompson, 2004; Levine & Murnen, 2009), suggesting that it potentially influences body image. As an example of the powerful and fast-acting influence of Western mass media, Becker, Burwell, Herzog, Hamburg, and Gilman (2002) and Becker (2004) found that girls and women in Fiji exhibited virtually none of the symptoms of eating disorders before the arrival of Western television. A short time after its arrival, symptoms of eating disorders had emerged, and the cultural appearance ideals had shifted from idolizing a fuller-figured body type to idolizing thinness. Despite these findings, researchers have questioned whether the relationship is actually a causal relationship, because body image and eating disorders are complex and multifaceted constructs that are determined by many factors, including genetics, biology, and sociocultural environment (Bulik, 2004;Cash & Pruzinsky, 2002). Levine and Murnen (2009) reviewed the existing evidence and concluded that it is clear that media exposure is related to negative body image and eating outcomes, but that "engagement with mass media is probably best considered a variable risk factor that might well be later shown to be a causal risk factor" (p. 32).

Not only is this emphasis increasing in media directed at adults, but it is also appearing in children's media. Mass media has also been found to be important for children. Herbozo et al. (2004) found that the majority of popular children's movies depicted female thinness and emphasized physical attractiveness. In addition, they depicted the thin ideal being related to positive attributes such as sociability, kindness, and happiness while depicting obesity as being related to evilness, stupidity, and laziness. Furthermore, approximately half of the movies depicted obesity as being related to food and eating. Children's toys also provide information about appearance ideals and attractiveness. Pope, Phillips, and Olivardia (2000) concluded that girls' toys, such as Barbie, have depicted the same unrealistic appearance ideal (very tall and thin with large breasts) for decades, whereas boys' toys, such as GI Joe, have increased in their depiction of ideals that are unrealistic (more extreme size and muscularity).

Objectification Theory

In addition to the tripartite influence model, objectification theory (Fredrickson & Roberts, 1997) provides a coherent and related theoretical framework for understanding the experience of women living in a society that frequently values them only for their physical appearance and treats them as sexual objects (Calogero, Tantleff-Dunn, & Thompson, 2011). Objectification theory is based on the ideas of sexual objectification (Bartky, 1990), an interpersonal phenomenon that occurs when a person is seen or treated as a body or collection of body parts for use or consumption by others. This occurs frequently in Western cultures and can occur in many ways, including gaze, visual inspection, sexualized evaluation, commentary, and even sexual violence. As sexual objectification occurs over time, a person may begin to adopt these external views, viewing themselves from the third-person perspective. This internalization of cultural appearance ideals leads the person to objectify themselves, a process known as self-objectification. Self-objectification has been linked to several psychological consequences, such as appearance anxiety, low self-esteem, body shame, eating disorders, depression, and sexual dysfunction (Calogero et al., 2011).

Both women and men are prompted to self-objectify by different stimuli because of differences in underlying cultural appearance ideals (Morry & Staska, 2001). Finally, women's lived experiences of sexual objectification, such as being gazed at, receiving sexually harassing comments, or being depicted in the media valued only as body parts, are very different from men's in that they are more frequent and often more severe (Calogero et al., 2011).

One of the most commonly studied outcomes of objectification is body shame, which occurs when a person compares him or herself to a cultural ideal, determines that he or she does not meet the ideal, and has the potential for social exposure (Fredrickson & Roberts, 1997). Many studies have found a relationship between increased state self-objectification and body shame (Calogero, 2004; Fredrickson, Roberts, Noll, Quinn, & Twenge, 1998; Quinn, Kallen, & Cathey, 2006; Roberts & Gettman, 2004), which is in turn linked with negative consequences such as inclination to change body weight or undergo cosmetic surgery (Forbes, Jobe, & Revak, 2006), body surveillance (Buchanan, Fischer, Tokar, & Yoder, 2008), and lower body esteem, which can be conceptualized as self-esteem relating only to the body and appearance (McKinley, 2006).

Researchers have also examined the relationship between lived interpersonal sexual objectification experiences and body shame, finding that body shame is predicted by pressure to be thin (Tylka & Hill, 2004), peer sexual harassment among adolescents (Lindberg, Hyde, & McKinley, 2006), weight criticism (Befort et al., 2001), and exposure to sexually objectifying media (Aubrey, 2007). Research has also found a link between objectification and appearance anxiety (Calogero, 2004; Roberts & Gettmann, 2004), which in turn, is related to eating-disordered symptomatology (Tiggemann & Kuring, 2004; Tiggemann & Lynch, 2001).

Despite the growing evidence in support of objectification theory, this area of research suffers from several important limitations that should be addressed in the future. For instance, the biggest limitation to this area of research is a lack of racial, ethnic, and cultural diversity among the populations studied. The vast majority of studies in this area have examined samples that were predominantly young, white, heterosexual women enrolled in colleges or universities (Moradi & Huang, 2008). Fredrickson and Roberts (1997) hypothesized that any woman with a reproductively mature body may be subject to sexual and self-objectification. However, there may be important differences among ethnicities because of differences in underlying cultural appearance ideals (Harrison & Fredrickson, 2003; Hebl, King, & Lin, 2004). Another limitation to this area of research is that there

is a lack of research examining how objectification may occur or affect women in non-Western cultures. It appears that self-objectification is more common in cultures that focus heavily on appearance and have unrealistic appearance ideals, but more empirical study is needed.

TREATMENT OPTIONS

Although a variety of options are available for treatment of eating disorders, they each have different points of emphasis. Some treatment programs focus primarily on body image disturbances, in the belief that body image disturbances are the primary trigger and maintenance factor for EDs. Other treatment programs focus on behavioral symptoms of EDs exclusively, and seek to return the individual to a normal eating pattern, which no longer includes bingeing, purging, or food restriction. A third, holistic approach seeks to treat both ED symptoms and body image. Importantly, these treatment approaches are not uniformly successful across all forms of eating disorders. This section briefly describes some of the main forms of therapy for EDs, before evaluating the empirical support from comparative studies for their use within the context of each ED.

Common Treatment Approaches

Cognitive-behavioral therapy (CBT) is a multicomponent approach to treatment of psychological disorders, which seeks to identify and challenge dysfunctional thoughts, feelings, and behaviors (Cash & Strachan, 2002). Within the context of eating disorders, CBT typically involves a range of complementary techniques, which target the (a) *cognitive-evaluative* (e.g., psychoeducation, exposure and desensitization, and monitoring and cognitive restructuring of one's appearance- and food-related cognitions), (b) *behavioral* (strategies to minimize avoidant behaviors, binge eating, dietary restraint, and purging, and appearance-checking tendencies, building skills in problem solving, and assertiveness), and (c) *perceptual* aspects of body image disturbance (training in accurate body size estimation) (Cash & Pruzinsky, 2002).

Interpersonal therapy operates on the assumption that psychological symptoms are manifestations of interpersonal difficulties that an individual is currently experiencing, and her/his inability to resolve these issues. As a consequence, interpersonal therapy involves helping patients identify and modify any current interpersonal problems they may have. It is believed that through successful change in patterns of interpersonal behaviors, psychological symptoms will also dissipate (Wilfley et al., 2002).

In family therapy, siblings and parents are asked to attend and contribute to group therapy sessions along with ED patients. In the early stages of treatment, parents are asked to take control of their child's eating and weight until a level of compliance is obtained from the patient. Gradually, as the patient begins to show signs of healthier behaviors, s/he is afforded more control over her/his own eating and weight-related behaviors (Wilson, Grilo, & Vitousek, 2007).

Behavioral therapies, such as weight restoration programs and very-low-calorie-diet treatments, primarily target problematic eating habits associated with EDs. Such therapies may also include nutrition education sessions to ensure that ED patients have an accurate understanding of the types of foods they may consume to eat healthy.

Pharmacotherapy involves prescription of medication aimed to alleviate the symptoms of EDs. These medications range from antidepressants (such as fluoxetine), which target the mood-related symptoms, to weight-reducing and satiety-based medications, which reduce one's body mass and/or restrict the amount of food s/he eats. Pharmacotherapy is generally prescribed in more severe cases of EDs, in which other therapeutic approaches have failed to improve symptoms (Allen & Hollander, 2002). It is also commonly used in inpatient treatment, but this may be a function of patients having severe ED and comorbid symptoms that require urgent attention (Wilson et al., 2007).

Anorexia Nervosa

Individuals with AN tend to be resistant to treatment, regardless of whether the treatment is individualized or offered in group sessions, and whether the treatment focus is behavioral, cognitive-behavioral, or pharmacological (Wilson et al., 2007). Treatment outcomes are most positive when initiated early in the duration of illness and when onset of illness is in childhood (Russell, Szmukler, Dare, & Eisler, 1987). In such instances, family therapy is the one method of treatment that has been endorsed for use in AN populations, as it has produced the most consistent and strongest change in symptoms when compared to other common treatment approaches (most notably, CBT and pharmacological treatment) (National Institute for Clinical Excellence, 2004). Roughly half of patients have full remission using family therapy. However, this approach has not been consistently found to improve symptoms in adult populations and/or among those with longer duration of illness (Lock, Agras, Bryson, & Kraemer, 2005).

None of the treatment options used in BN populations have consistently generalized to AN populations. For example, in many instances, CBT has been shown to improve ED symptoms without leading to full remission of AN (Ball & Mitchell, 2004; McIntosh et al., 2005), and in instances where short-term remission is achieved, relapse often follows (Meads, Gold, & Burls, 2001). Likewise, the use of antidepressants has failed to show significant improvement over placebos (Attia, Haiman, Walsh, & Flater, 1998; Walsh et al., 2006). It should be noted that attempts to appraise the merits of treatment alternatives for AN populations are complicated by high drop-out rates and resistance to treatment. For instance, Pike, Walsh, Vitousek, Wilson, and Bauer (2003) found that 22% of ANs who were treated using CBT dropped out of treatment, compared with a 73% drop-out rate for nutritional counseling. Pike and colleagues also found that AN individuals in the CBT treatment group were slower to relapse. Halmi et al. (2005) were unable to statistically compare efficacy of CBT and medication-based approaches to treatment of AN because so many individuals withdrew from the medication-only group.

Although many practitioners believe that inpatient treatment is more effective than outpatient care, attempts to evaluate this notion have been adversely affected by the paucity of available data and potential differences between those who seek inpatient versus outpatient treatment for symptoms of AN. In a review of data from randomized control trials and case studies, Meads et al. (2001) failed to find a significant difference in the efficacy of out- and inpatient treatment modalities. However, the authors acknowledge that this nonsignificant result may be a result of the paucity of studies that have evaluated treatment efficacy (outpatient or inpatient) among AN populations. Another concern is that differences in symptom severity and duration may confound attempts to compare treatment effects for individuals with AN. Inpatient treatment is often considered once other approaches have failed and/or when the severity of somatic and psychological symptoms dictates the need for monitoring by professionals (Fairburn & Harrison, 2003). Indeed, Lievers et al. (2009) found that duration of inpatient treatment of AN was longest for individuals with severe symptom expression and longer duration of illness at admission, presence of comorbid disorders, the need for use of tube feeding during stay, and failure to meet weight goals specified by staff.

Perhaps the most glaring issue in ED treatment studies is the underrepresentation of AN patients in these studies relative to BNs and BEDs. Wilson et al. (2007) attribute the paucity and inconsistency of findings for AN populations to a range of factors, including the low prevalence rates of AN and consequent small sample sizes in these efficacy studies, the co-occurrence of medical complications that require more urgent attention and that override the effectiveness of the intended treatment approach, high attrition and low compliance rates among AN populations in efficacy studies, and that treatment duration is typically longer to achieve full remission from AN than for other EDs. Given the increased mortality risks associated with AN, there is a growing need to identify treatment strategies that effectively treat the symptoms of AN.

Bulimia Nervosa

Treatment of bulimia nervosa is typically done on an outpatient basis, with routine sessions with a psychologist and psychiatrist, in order to monitor physical and psychological symptoms (Durand & King, 2003). Evidence from efficacy studies suggests that CBT is the most effective treatment approach for individuals with bulimia nervosa (NICE, 2004). CBT reduces the occurrence of problematic eating behaviors (bingeing, purging, and dietary restraint), as well as improving self-esteem and social functioning (Wilson et al., 2007). Furthermore, the success of CBT in reducing binge and purge behaviors may be mediated by earlier reductions in dietary restraint behaviors (Wilson, Fairburn, Agras, Walsh, & Kraemer, 2005).

Chen et al. (2003) demonstrated that the benefits of CBT for individuals with BN are comparable regardless of whether treatment is delivered individually or in a group setting. Both treatment modalities yielded significant improvements in ED symptoms and psychological functioning (i.e., self-esteem, anxiety, and mood). However, their findings also suggested that the two approaches may have differential effects on the various aspects of EDs. First, although the individualized care group showed the greatest improvement in binge and purge symptoms immediately following treatment, this difference was nonsignificant at subsequent follow-up periods. Second, the group approach showed a substantially greater improvement in social functioning (including reduction in social anxiety) when compared to the individualized treatment.

Given the key role that body image disturbances play in the etiology and maintenance of BN, it is not surprising that remission rates are higher when body image disturbances are a primary focus of intervention than in instances when treatment of negative body image is incidental to, or embedded within, treatment of eating-disordered symptoms (Jarry & Ip, 2005). Moreover, negative body image is a key indicator of resistance to treatment for eating-disordered symptoms, and in instances where body image is left untreated, there is an increased likelihood of patient drop-out from treatment and/or relapse into eating-disordered behaviors (Allen & Hollander, 2002).

Other treatment approaches have also shown benefit for alleviating symptoms of BN, although these effects are less impressive than the results obtained for CBT. For instance, use of antidepressant medication (such as fluoxetine) has also been shown to relieve cognitive and affective symptoms for individuals with BN (Agras et al., 1992; Walsh & Garner, 1997), although its performance in reducing bingeing and purging is less effective than CBT. Moreover, although the long-term benefits of CBT have been documented for individuals with BN, there is less evidence for sustained improvements based on treatments focusing on use of antidepressants (Wilson et al., 2007). Likewise, evidence suggests that the combined use of CBT and medication fails to make significant improvements above the individual contributions of CBT and medication for alleviation of ED symptoms (Peterson & Mitchell, 1999). Interpersonal therapy has shown efficacy comparable to CBT in long-term follow-ups, although the gains appear less immediately (Agras, Walsh, Fairburn, Wilson, & Kraemer, 2000).

Binge-Eating Disorder

CBT has shown to improve all symptoms of BED, with the exception of weight loss (Wilfley et al., 2002). It is estimated that more than half of BED sufferers reach full remission following CBT. Interpersonal therapy has also been shown to produce comparable short-term gains relative to CBT (Wilfley et al., 2002), although the sustained benefits of interpersonal therapy on BED symptoms have not been evaluated.

There is less empirical support for the use of behavioral weight loss and very-low-calorie-diet treatments (Devlin et al., 2005; Telch & Agras, 1993). Agras et al. (2000) argue that, unlike CBT and interpersonal therapy, which target the root cause of disordered eating, emphasis on behavioral symptoms alone is unlikely to lead to sustained change. Despite short-term reduction in weight and frequency of binge episodes, a substantial proportion of BED patients regain their initial weight status or become heavier than they were before commencing treatment (de Zwaan et al., 2005; Nauta, Hospers, Kok, & Jansen, 2000). Evidence from meta-analytic studies also suggests that pharmacotherapy fails to yield improvements over the use of a placebo for alleviating binge episodes or obesity (NICE, 2004).

Eating Disorder Not Otherwise Specified

Attempts to evaluate treatment efficacy for EDNOS are hampered by the heterogeneity of symptoms for patients with this diagnosis. Wildes and Marcus (2009) argue that, in the absence of a clear gold standard for treatment of EDNOS, clinicians' treatment of EDNOS has typically involved determining whether the symptom cluster most closely resembles AN or BN, and then using a treatment strategy suitable for that disorder.

Fairburn (2005) has advocated the use of individualized treatment that targets the symptoms that an individual presents with rather than a standard treatment for classic diagnostic criteria. This approach has proven beneficial in treatment of other EDs, although it has yet to be tested in EDNOS groups.

Body Dysmorphic Disorder

CBT and pharmacotherapy (particularly use of serotonin-reuptake inhibitors [SSRIs]) are often effective in treatment of BDD (Phillips, 2009). Furthermore, although a recent meta-analytic study showed that both medication and CBT lead to significant improvement in symptoms, the efficacy of CBT was significantly higher than for medication-based treatments. Despite these encouraging figures, many individuals with BDD seek alternative treatment strategies, most notably cosmetic surgery to remove their perceived physical flaws. It is estimated that 5% to 15% of individuals who seek cosmetic surgery procedures have BDD (Sarwer & Crerand, 2008). Unfortunately, it is rare for patients with BDD to experience improvement in symptoms following surgical procedures (Crerand, Franklin, & Sarwer, 2006).

In the most severe cases of BDD, CBT plus pharmacological interventions have been shown to be more effective than CBT alone (Allen & Hollander, 2002). Allen and Hollander (2002) argue that failure to treat the comorbid symptoms, such as obsessive-compulsive aspects of BDD, means that an individual may experience relief of negative body image but still experience clinically significant levels of psychological dysfunction.

Challenges to Treatment

There is growing recognition of the economic burden and healthcare service use of individuals with EDs (Simon, Schmidt, & Pilling, 2005). In response to this problem,

Crow and Brandenburg (2009) argue that healthcare professionals should use a stepped-care approach in the management of patients with eating disorders. This approach starts with mild and cost-effective treatments that may be sufficient for less-severe cases of ED (e.g., guided self-help procedures). Patients with severe symptoms that cannot be resolved by this first approach may then proceed to more intensive and costly treatments, such as use of medication and CBT. However, Mitchell et al. (2002) have argued that in moderate and extreme cases, lengthy delays between approaches are likely to lead to dropout from treatment. In such instances where the milder treatment methods are ineffective, Crow and Brandenburg argue that retention rates may be enhanced by more quickly cycling through the various levels of treatment. This view is shared by Mitchell, Raymond, and Specker (1993), who argue that more frequent sessions early in the treatment process may be beneficial to efficacy and also to reduce the likelihood of dropout.

Some individuals may be unwilling or unable to seek treatment for EDs because of the costs involved in treatment, feelings of shame and embarrassment in seeking help, aversion to one-on-one or group contact, or lack of available counseling services within a reasonable distance of one's home and/or place of work. Increasingly, researchers are looking to inexpensive, self-guided alternatives to in-person treatment. Online programs in psychoeducation or CBT have demonstrated moderate positive effects relative to nontreatment control groups (Strachan & Cash, 2002; Winzelberg, Abascal, & Taylor, 2002). However, it has also been shown that minimal contact with clinicians for CBT interventions yields clinically significant improvements over the effects of self-guided CBT, and that minimal versus consistent contact-based CBT yield comparable results (Cash & Hrabosky, 2003). Contact with a therapist is advantageous to the treatment process because it increases compliance with treatment protocols and decreases the likelihood of dropout (Strachan & Cash, 2002). However, as suggested by Winzelberg et al. (2002), self-guided therapies may be used as an initial screening strategy in a multifaceted treatment regimen. In many instances, self-guided treatment may sufficiently reduce body image concerns to the point that further treatment is unnecessary, but in cases where symptoms persist, the client may then be referred to clinician-guided therapy.

FUTURE RESEARCH

In the past 30 years, extensive research has examined classification systems, etiology, health implications, and treatment options for EDs. In this review, we have emphasized that both environmental and genetic processes influence the development and maintenance of ED symptoms. Current theories of EDs emphasize the important role that sociocultural values—transmitted via media, peers, and family—play by encouraging girls and women to adopt unrealistic physiques. Those who adopt these values are at increased risk for body image disturbances and eating pathology.

Findings from twin and family studies also provide evidence of a genetic predisposition to each of the EDs at both syndrome and symptom levels. As discussed, the genetic pathways through which EDs develop are likely to be complex and multifaceted. Available data have implicated the serotonergic pathway in the expression of

ED symptoms. However, there is a need for systematic, genome-wide investigation of genetic markers for EDs, because it is likely that multiple genes are necessary to account for the various symptoms of EDs. Additionally, these studies have focused primarily on AN and BN populations. Further research into the genetic basis for BED, EDNOS, and BDD are necessary. Such information will assist with the early detection of probable cases of EDs.

Further understanding of the genetic basis of EDs may also progress discussions of the correct classification system for the various EDs. At present, EDNOS is a convenient category to identify individuals who, while failing to meet the full criteria for AN or BN, warrant clinical attention. Because EDNOS represents a heterogeneous group, attempts to understand the determinants of, and treatment needs for, EDNOS have yielded inconsistent results. Given that EDNOS represents the largest proportion of all cases of ED, it is vital for researchers to determine whether there are other reliable ways of subclassification of EDNOS.

Overall, CBT has been shown to be the most effective treatment approach for EDs. An advantage of CBT is that it can be implemented on an individual basis or in group settings, and it has also been successfully adapted in guided self-care programs. However, CBT is most effective for BN, BDD, and BED individuals, but less successful in treating AN. Unfortunately, treatment efficacy studies have failed to find a treatment strategy that consistently leads to remission in cases of AN. At present, CBT has yielded the strongest effects, leading to some symptom relief, even though few AN individuals fully remit symptoms during the period of treatment. The paucity of treatment studies involving AN individuals is, in part, a function of high drop-out rates and low compliance for treatment within this population.

Given the severity of symptoms and the substantial risk of mortality for individuals with AN, it is important to find treatment strategies that encourage AN individuals to maintain progress in treatment settings and that also alleviate symptoms. The most promising line of evidence to date suggests that early detection is the best predictor of a successful outcome in cases of AN. The symptom-focused approach proposed by Fairburn (2005) may provide a step forward in the treatment of EDs, particularly for EDNOS, because of the heterogeneity of symptom clusters for individuals belonging to this group.

Finally, we acknowledge throughout this chapter that the majority of the ED-related literature derives from studies of adolescent to early adult, middle-class women from Western cultures. There is increasing recognition of the need to evaluate models of ED transmission and progression among more diverse samples, but gaps remain in our documentation of disordered eating and appearance-related symptoms among minority groups, non-Western cultures, individuals with lower socioeconomic status, and women in midlife and beyond. In addition to ensuring that current treatment models are equally effective for these groups who have been poorly represented in prior research, more inclusive studies may also enhance our knowledge of the protective factors that prevent the onset or duration of eating disorders.

REFERENCES

Abramson, E. E. (1999). *To have and to hold: How to take off the weight when marriage puts on the pounds.* New York, NY: Kensington Books.

Agras, S. (2001). The consequences and costs of eating disorders. *Psychiatric Clinics of North America, 24,* 371–379.

Agras, W., Rossiter, E., Arnow, B., Schneider, J., Telch, C., Raeburn, S., . . . Koran, L. (1992). Pharmacologic and cognitive-behavioral treatment for bulimia nervosa: A controlled comparison. *American Journal of Psychiatry, 149,* 82–87.

Agras, S., Walsh, T., Fairburn, G., Wilson, T., & Kraemer, C. (2000). A multi-center comparison of cognitive-behavioral therapy and interpersonal psychotherapy for bulimia nervosa. *Archives of General Psychiatry, 57,* 459–466.

Allen, A., & Hollander, E. (2002). Psychopharmacological treatments for body image disturbances. In C. Cash & T. Pruzinsky (Eds.), *Body image: A handbook of theory, research, and clinical practice* (pp. 450–459). New York, NY: Guilford Press.

American Psychiatric Association. (2000). *Diagnostic and statistical manual of mental disorders* (4th ed., text rev.). Washington, DC: Author.

American Psychiatric Association. (2012). DSM-5: The future of psychiatric diagnosis. In American Psychiatric Association DSM-5. Retrieved from http://www.dsm5.org.

Andersen, A., Bowers, W., & Watson, T. (2001). A slimming program for Eating Disorders Not Otherwise Specified: Reconceptualizing a confusing, residual diagnostic category. *Psychiatric Clinics of North America, 4,* 561–571.

Andres, R. (1989). Does the "best" body weight change with age? In A. J. Stunkard & A. Baum (Eds.), *Perspectives in behavioural medicine: Eating, sleeping, and sex* (pp. 99–107). Hillsdale, NJ: Erlbaum.

Attia, E., Haiman, C., Walsh, B., & Flater, S. (1998). Does fluoxetine augment the inpatient treatment of anorexia nervosa? *American Journal of Psychiatry, 155,* 548–551.

Aubrey, J. (2007). The impact of sexually objectifying media exposure on negative body emotions and sexual self perceptions: Investigating the mediating role of body self-consciousness. *Mass Communication and Society, 10,* 1–23.

Ball, J., & Mitchell, P. (2004). A randomized controlled study of cognitive behavior therapy and behavioral family therapy for anorexia nervosa patients. *Eating Disorders, 12,* 303–314.

Bartky, S. (1990). *Femininity and domination: Studies in the phenomenology of oppression.* New York, NY: Routledge.

Becker, A. (2004). Television, disordered eating, and young women in Fiji: Negotiating body image and identity during rapid social change. *Culture, Medicine, and Psychiatry, 28,* 533–559.

Becker, A., Burwell, R., Herzog, D., Hamburg, P., & Gilman, S. (2002). Eating behaviours and attitudes following prolonged exposure to television among ethnic Fijian adolescent girls. *British Journal of Psychiatry, 180,* 509–514.

Befort, C., Kurpius, S., Hull-Blanks, E., Nicpon, M., Huser, L., & Sollenberger, S. (2001). Body image, self esteem, and weight-related criticism from romantic partners. *Journal of College Student Development, 42,* 407–419.

Ben-Tovim, D. I., Walker, K., Gilchrist, P., Freeman, R., Kalucy, R., & Esterman, R. (2001). Outcomes in patients with eating disorders: A 5-year study. *Lancet, 357,* 1254–1257.

Brandsma, L. (2007). Eating disorders across the lifespan. *Journal of Women & Aging, 19,* 155–172.

Buchanan, T., Fischer, A., Tokar, D., & Yoder, J. (2008). Testing a culture-specific extension of objectification theory regarding African American women's body image. *The Counselling Psychologist, 36,* 697–719.

Bulik, C. (2004). Genetic and biological risk factors. In K. Thompson (Ed.), *Handbook of eating disorders and obesity* (pp. 3–16). Hoboken, NJ: Wiley.

Bulik, C., Sullivan, P., & Kendler, K. (1998). Heritability of binge eating and broadly defined bulimia nervosa. *Biological Psychiatry, 44,* 1210–1218.

Bulik, C., Sullivan, P., Wade, T., & Kendler, K. (2000). Twin studies of eating disorders: A review. *International Journal of Eating Disorders, 27,* 2–20.

Calogero, R. (2004) A test of objectification theory: The effect of the male gaze on appearance concerns in college women. *Psychology of Women Quarterly, 28,* 16–21.

Calogero, R., Tantleff-Dunn, S., & Thompson, J. (2011). *Self objectification in women: Causes, consequences and counteractions.* Washington, DC: American Psychological Association.

Cash, T., & Hrabosky, J. (2003). The effects of psychoeducation and self-monitoring in a cognitive-behavioral program for body-image improvement. *Eating Disorders: Journal of Treatment and Prevention, 11,* 255–270.

Cash, T., & Pruzinsky, P. (2002). *Body image: A handbook of theory, research and clinical practice.* New York, NY: Guilford Press.

Cash, T., & Strachan, M. (2002). Cognitive behavioral approaches to body image change. In T. Cash, & P. Pruzinsky (Eds.), *Body image: A handbook of theory, research and clinical practice* (pp. 478–486). New York, NY: Guilford Press.

Chen, E., Touyz, S. W., Beumont, P. J. V., Fairburn, C. G., Griffiths, R., Butow, P., . . . Basten, C. (2003). Comparison of group and individual cognitive-behavioral therapy for patients with bulimia nervosa. *International Journal of Eating Disorders, 33*, 241–254.

Clark, A., Skouteris, H., Wertheim, E. H., Paxton, S. J., & Milgrom, J. (2009). The relationship between depression and body dissatisfaction across pregnancy and the postpartum: A prospective study. *Journal of Health Psychology, 14*, 27–35.

Comstock, G., & Scharrer, E. (2007). *Television: What's on, who's watching, and what it means.* San Diego, CA: Academic Press.

Crerand, C., Franklin, M., & Sarwer, D. (2006). Body dysmorphic disorder and cosmetic surgery. *Plastic and Reconstructive Surgery, 118*, 167–180.

Crow, S., & Brandenburg, B. (2009). Diagnosis, assessment and treatment planning for bulimia nervosa. In C. Grilo & J. Mitchell (Eds.), *The treatment of eating disorders: A clinical handbook* (pp. 28–43). New York, NY: Guilford Press.

Dally, P. (1984). Anorexia tardive: Late-onset marital anorexia nervosa. *Journal of Psychosomatic Research, 28*, 423–428.

Devlin, M., Goldfein, J., Petkova, E., Jiang, H., Raizman, P., Wolk, S., . . . Walsh, B. (2005). Cognitive behavioral therapy and fluoxetine as adjuncts to group behavioral therapy form binge eating disorder. *Obesity Research, 13*, 1077–1088.

De Zwaan, M., Mitchell, J., Crosby, R., Mussell, M., Raymond, N., Specker, S., & Seim, H. (2005). Short-term cognitive behavioural treatment does not improve outcome of a comprehensive very-low-calorie diet program in obese women with binge eating disorder. *Behaviour Therapy, 36*, 89–99.

Duncombe, D., Wertheim, E. H., Skouteris, H., Paxton, S. J., & Kelly, L. (2008). How well do women adapt to changes in their body size and shape across the course of pregnancy? *Journal of Health Psychology, 13*, 503–515.

Durand, M. A., & King, M. (2003). Specialist treatment versus self-help for bulimia nervosa: A randomised controlled trial in general practice. *British Journal of General Practice, 53*, 371–377.

Elmore, K., & De Castro, J. (1990). Self-rated moods and hunger in relation to spontaneous eating behavior in bulimics, recovered bulimics, and normals. *International Journal of Eating Disorders, 9*, 179–190.

Fairburn, C. (2005). Evidence-based treatment of anorexia nervosa. *International Journal of Eating Disorders, 37*, S26–S30.

Fairburn, C., & Cooper, Z. (2011). Eating disorders, DSM-V, and clinical reality. *British Journal of Psychiatry, 198*, 8–10.

Fairburn, C., & Harrison, P. J. (2003). Eating disorders. *Lancet, 361*, 407–416.

Fairburn, C., Cooper, Z., Doll, H., Norman, P., & O'Connor, M. (2000). The natural course of bulimia nervosa and binge eating disorder in young women. *Archives of General Psychiatry, 57*, 659–665.

Favaro, A., Ferrara, S., & Santonastaso, P. (2003). The spectrum of eating disorders in young women: A prevalence study in a general population sample. *Psychosomatic Medicine, 65*, 701–708.

Fichter, M., Quadflieg, N., & Hedlund, S. (2008). Long-term course of binge eating disorder and bulimia nervosa: Relevance for nosology and diagnostic criteria. *International Journal of Eating Disorders, 41*, 577–586.

Fitzgibbon, M., Sanchez-Johnsen, L., & Martinovich, Z. (2003). A test of the continuity perspective across bulimic and binge eating pathology. *International Journal of Eating Disorders, 34*, 83–97.

Forbes, G., Jobe, R., & Revak, J. (2006). Relationships between dissatisfaction with specific body characteristics and the Sociocultural Attitudes toward Appearance Questionnaire-3 and Objectified Body Consciousness Scale. *Body Image, 3*, 295–300.

Frederick, D. A., Forbes, G. B., Grigoran, K. E., & Jarcho, J. M. (2007). The UCLA Body Project I: Gender and ethnic differences in self-objectification and body satisfaction among 2,206 undergraduates. *Sex Roles, 57*, 317–327.

Fredrickson, B., & Roberts, T. (1997). Objectification theory: Toward understanding women's lived experiences and mental health risks. *Psychology of Women Quarterly, 21*, 173–206.

Fredrickson, B., Roberts, T., Noll, S., Quinn, D., & Twenge, J. (1998). That swimsuit becomes you: Sex differences in self-objectification, restrained eating, and math performance. *Journal of Personality and Social Psychology*, *75*, 269–284.

Garn, S. M., Labelle, M., Rosenberg, K. R., & Hawthorne, V. M. (1986). Maturational timing as a factor in female fatness and obesity. *American Journal of Clinical Nutrition*, *43*, 879–883.

Grabe, S., Hyde, J. S., & Lindberg, S. M. (2007). Body objectification and depression in adolescents: The role of gender, shame, and rumination. *Psychology of Women Quarterly*, *31*, 164–175.

Graber, J. A., Brooks-Gunn, J., Paikoff, R. L., & Warren, M. P. (1994). Prediction of eating problems: An 8-year study of adolescent girls. *Developmental Psychology*, *30*, 823–834.

Gupta, M. A. (1995). Concerns about aging and a drive for thinness: A factor in the biopsychosocial model of eating disorders? *International Journal of Eating Disorders*, *18*, 351–357.

Haedt, A., & Keel, P. (2007). Maternal attachment, depression, and body dissatisfaction in pregnant women. *Journal of Reproductive and Infant Psychology*, *25*, 285–295.

Hall, P., & Driscoll, R. (1993). Anorexia in the elderly: An annotation. *International Journal of Eating Disorders*, *14*, 497–499.

Halmi, K., Agras, S., Crow, S., Mitchell, J., Wilson, T., Bryson, S., & Kraemer, H. (2005). Predictors of treatment acceptance and completion in anorexia nervosa: Implications for future study designs. *Archives of General Psychiatry*, *62*, 776–781.

Harrison, K., & Fredrickson, B. L. (2003). Women's sports media, self-objectification, and mental health in black and white adolescent females. *Journal of Communication*, *53*, 216–232.

Hebl, M., King, E., & Lin, J. (2004). The swimsuit becomes us all: Ethnicity, gender, and vulnerability to self objectification. *Personality and Social Psychology Bulletin*, *30*, 1322–1331.

Heinberg, L., & Thompson, J. (1995). Social comparison: Gender, target importance ratings, and relation to body image disturbance. *Journal of Social Behavior and Personality*, *7*, 335–344.

Herbozo, S., Tantleff-Dunn, S., Gokee-LaRose, J., & Thompson, J. K. (2004). Beauty and thinness messages in children's media: A content analysis. *Eating Disorders: The Journal of Treatment and Prevention*, *12*, 21–34.

Herzog, D., Hopkins, J., & Burns, C. (1993). A follow-up study of 33 subdiagnostic eating disordered women. *International Journal of Eating Disorders*, *14*, 261–267.

Hsu, L., & Zimmer, B. (2009). Eating disorders in old age. *International Journal of Eating Disorders*, *7*, 133–138.

Hudson, J., Hiripi, E., Pope, H., & Kessler, R. (2007). The prevalence and correlates of eating disorders in the national comorbidity survey replication. *Biological Psychiatry*, *61*, 348–358.

Hudson, J., Lalonde, J., Berry, J., Pindyck, L., Bulik, C., & Crow, S. (2006). Binge eating disorder as a distinct familial phenotype in obese individuals. *Archives of General Psychiatry*, *63*, 313–319.

Jarry, J., & Ip, K. (2005). The effectiveness of stand-alone cognitive-behavioural therapy for body image: A meta-analysis. *Body Image*, *2*, 317–331.

Javaras, K., Leird, N., Reichborn-Kjennerud, T., Bulik, C., Pope, H., & Hudson, J. (2008). Familiarity and heritability of binge eating disorder: Results of a case-control family study and a twin study. *International Journal of Eating Disorders*, *41*, 174–179.

Jimerson, B., & Wolfe, D. (2006). Psychobiology of eating disorders. In S. Wonderlich, J. Mitchell, M. de Zwaan, & H. Steiger (Eds.), *Annual review of eating disorders* (pp. 1–16). Oxford, UK: Radcliffe.

Johnson, W., Spitzer, R., & Williams, J. (2001). Health problems, impairment and illnesses associated with bulimia nervosa and binge eating disorder among primary care and obstetric gynaecology patients. *Psychological Medicine*, *31*, 1455–1466.

Kassett, J. A., Gershon, E. S., Maxwell, M. E., Guroff, J. J., Kazuba, D. M., Smith, A. L., . . . Jimerson, D. C. (1989). Psychiatric disorders in the first-degree relatives of probands with bulimia nervosa. *American Journal of Psychiatry*, *146*, 1468–1471.

Kaye, W., Bulik, C., Thornton, L., Barbarich, N., Masters, K., & Fichter, M. (2004). Comorbidity of anxiety disorders with anorexia and bulimia nervosa. *American Journal of Psychiatry*, *161*, 2215–2221.

Kaye, W., Frank, G., Bailer, U., Henry, S., Meltzer, C., Price, J., . . . Wagner, A. (2005). Serotonin alterations in in anorexia and bulimia nervosa: New insights from imaging studies. *Physiology and Behavior*, *85*, 73–81.

Keel, P., & McCormick, L. (2010). Diagnosis, assessment and treatment planning for anorexia nervosa. In C. Grilo & J. Mitchell (Eds.), *The treatment of eating disorders: A clinical handbook* (pp. 3–27). New York, NY: Guilford Press.

Keel, P., Dorer, D. J., Eddy, K. T., Franko, D., Charatan, D. L., & Herzog, D. B. (2003). Predictors of mortality in eating disorders. *Archives of General Psychiatry, 60,* 179–183.

Keery, H., van den Berg, P., & Thompson, K. (2004). An evaluation of the Tripartite Influence Model of body dissatisfaction and eating disturbance with adolescent girls. *Body Image, 1,* 237–251.

Kellett, J., Trimble, M., & Thorley, A. (1976). Anorexia nervosa after the menopause. *British Journal of Psychiatry, 128,* 555–558.

Keski-Rahkonen, A., Bulik, C. M., Neale, B. M., Rose, R. J., Rissanen, A., & Kaprio, J. (2005). Body dissatisfaction and drive for thinness in young adult twins. *International Journal of Eating Disorders, 37,* 188–199.

Kiziltan, G., Karabudak, E., Unver, S., Sezgin, E., & Unal, A. (2006). Prevalence of bulimic behaviours and trends in eating attitudes among Turkish late adolescents. *Adolescence, 41,* 677–689.

Kjelsas, E., Bjornstrom, C., & Gotestam, K. G. (2004). Prevalence of eating disorders in female and male adolescents (14-15 years). *Eating Behaviors, 5,* 13–25.

Klump, K., & Gobrogge, K. (2005). A review and primer of molecular genetic studies of AN. *International Journal of Eating Disorders, 37,* 43–48.

Klump, K., Kaye, W., & Strober, M. (2001). The evolving genetic foundations of eating disorders. *Psychiatric Clinics of North America, 24,* 215–225.

Krawczyk, R., Menzel, J., Swami, V., & Thompson, K. (2011). Attitudinal assessment of body image for adolescents and adults. In T. Cash & L. Smolak (Eds.), *Body image: A handbook of science, practice and prevention* (pp. 154–172). New York, NY: Guilford Press.

Levine, M., & Murnen, S. (2009). "Everybody knows that mass media (pick one) are/are not a cause of eating disorders": A critical review of evidence for a causal link between media, negative body image, and disordered eating in females. *Journal of Clinical and Social Psychology, 28,* 9–42.

Lewis, D. M., & Cachelin, F. M. (2001). Body image, body dissatisfaction, and eating attitudes in midlife and elderly women. *Eating Disorders, 9,* 29–39.

Lievers, L. S., Curt, F., Wallier, J., Perdereau, F., Rein, Z., Jeammet, P., & Godart, N. (2009). Predictive factors of length of inpatient treatment in anorexia nervosa. *European Child & Adolescent Psychiatry, 18,* 75–84.

Lindberg, S. M., Hyde, J. S., & McKinley, N. M. (2006). A measure of objectified body consciousness for pre-adolescent and adolescent youth. *Psychology of Women Quarterly, 30,* 65–76.

Lock, J., Agras, W., Bryson, S., & Kraemer, H. (2005). A comparison of short- and long-term family therapy for adolescent anorexia nervosa. *Journal of the American Academy of Child Adolescent Psychiatry, 44,* 632–639.

Lowe, M., Gleaves, D., DiSimone-Weiss, R., Furgueson, C., Gayda, C., Kolsky, P. . . . McKinney, S. (1996). Restraint, dieting and the continuum model of bulimia nervosa. *Journal of Abnormal Psychology, 105,* 508–517.

Markey, C. N. (2004). Culture and the development of eating disorders: A tripartite model. *Eating Disorders, 12,* 139–156.

Martin, M., & Kennedy, P. (1993). Advertising and social comparison: Consequences for female pre-adolescents and adolescents. *Psychology and Marketing, 10,* 513–530.

Mazzeo, S., Slof'Op't, L., van Furth, E., & Bulik, C. (2006). Genetics of eating disorders. In S. Wonderlich, J. Mitchell, M. de Zwann, & H. Steiger (Eds.), *Eating disorders review: Part 2* (pp. 17–33). Oxford, UK: Radcliffe.

McIntosh, V. V., Jordan, J., Carter, F. A., Luty, S. E., McKenzie, J. M., Bulik, C. M., . . . Joyce, P. R. (2005). Three psychotherapies for anorexia nervosa: A randomized, controlled trial. *American Journal of Psychiatry, 162,* 741–747.

McKinley, N. M. (2006). The development and cultural contexts of objectified body consciousness: A longitudinal analysis of two cohorts of women. *Developmental Psychology, 54,* 159–173.

Meads, C., Gold, L., & Burls, A. (2001). How effective is outpatient care compared to inpatient care for the treatment of anorexia nervosa? *A systematic review. European Eating Disorders Review, 9,* 229–241.

Mellor, D., Fuller-Tyszkiewicz, M., McCabe, M., & Ricciardelli, L. (2010). Body image and self-esteem across age and gender: A short-term longitudinal study. *Sex Roles, 63,* 672–686.

Mitchell, J. E., Raymond, N., & Specker, S. (1993). A review of the controlled trials of pharmacotherapy and psychotherapy in the treatment of bulimia nervosa. *International Journal of Eating Disorders*, *14*, 229–247.

Mitchell, J. E., Halmi, K., Wilson, G. T., Agras, W. S., Kraemer, H., & Crow, S. (2002). A randomized secondary treatment study of women with bulimia nervosa who fail to respond to CBT. *International Journal of Eating Disorders*, *32*, 271–281.

Moradi, B., & Huang, Y. (2008). Objectification theory and psychology of women. A decade of advances and future directions. *Psychology of Women Quarterly*, *32*, 377–398.

Morry, M., & Staska, S. (2001). Magazine exposure: Internalization, self-objectification, eating attitudes, and body satisfaction in male and female university students. *Canadian Journal of Behavioural Sciences*, *4*, 269–279.

National Institute for Clinical Excellence (2004). *Eating disorders: Core interventions in the treatment and management of anorexia nervosa, bulimia nervosa and related eating disorders*. London, UK: National Institute of Clinical Excellence.

Nauta, H., Hospers, H., Kok, G., & Jansen, A. (2000). A comparison between a cognitive and a behavioral treatment for obese binge eaters and obese non-binge eaters. *Behavior Therapy*, *31*, 441–461.

Nobakht, M., & Dezhkam, M. (2000). An epidemiological study of eating disorders in Iran. *International Journal of Eating Disorders*, *28*, 265–271.

Norris, D. L. (1984). The effects of mirror confrontation on self-estimation of body dimension in anorexia nervosa, bulimia and two control groups. *Psychological Medicine*, *14*, 835–842.

O'Dea, J., & Abraham, S. (1999). Onset of disordered eating attitudes and behaviours in early adolescence: Interplay of pubertal status, gender, weight and age. *Adolescence*, *34*, 671–680.

Peat, C. M., Peyerl, N. L., & Muehlenkamp, J. J. (2008). Body image and eating disorders in older adults: A review. *Journal of General Psychology*, *135*, 343–358.

Peterson, C. B., & Mitchell, J. E. (1999). Psychosocial and pharmacological treatment of eating disorders: A review of research findings. *Journal of Clinical Psychology*, *55*, 685–697.

Phillips, K. A. (2009). *Understanding body dysmorphic disorder*. New York, NY: Oxford University Press.

Pike, K., Walsh, T., Vitousek, K., Wilson, T., & Bauer, J. (2003). Cognitive behavior therapy in the posthositalization treatment of anorexia nervosa. *American Journal of Psychiatry*, *160*, 2046–2049.

Pope, C., Pope, H., Menard, W., Fay, C., Olivardia, R. & Phillips, K. (2005). Clinical features of muscle dysmorphia among males with body dysmorphic disorder. *Body Image*, *2*, 395–400.

Pope, H., Phillips, K., & Olivardia, R. (2000). *The Adonis complex: The secret crisis of male body obsession*. New York, NY: Free Press.

Pratt, B., & Woolfenden, S. (2002). Interventions for preventing eating disorders in children and adolescents. *Cochrane Database Systems Review*, CD002891.

Quinn, D., Kallen, R., & Cathey, C. (2006). Body on my mind: The lingering effect of state self-objectification. *Sex Roles*, *55*, 869–874.

Reichborn-Kjennerud, T., Bulik, C. M., Tambs, K., & Harris, J. R. (2004). Genetic and environmental influences on binge eating in the absence of compensatory behaviors: A population-based twin study. *International Journal of Eating Disorders*, *36*, 307–314.

Rief, W., Buhlmann, U., Wilhelm, S., Borkenhagen, A., & Brahler, E. (2006). The prevalence of body dysmorphic disorder: A population-based survey. *Psychological Medicine*, *36*, 877–885.

Roberts, T., & Gettman, J. (2004). Mere exposure: Gender differences in the negative effects of priming a state of self-objectification. *Sex Roles*, *51*, 17–27.

Russell, G., Szmukler, G., Dare, C., & Eisler, I. (1987). An evaluation of family therapy in anorexia nervosa and bulimia nervosa. *Archives of General Psychiatry*, *44*, 1047–1056.

Sansone, R., Levitt, J., & Sansone, L. (2005). The prevalence of personality disorders among those with eating disorders. *Eating Disorder: The Journal of Treatment and Prevention*, *13*, 3–5.

Sarwer, D., & Crerand, C. (2008). Body dysmorphic disorder and appearance enhancing medical treatments. *Body Image*, *5*, 50–58.

Scherag, S., Hebebrand, J., & Hinney, A. (2010). Eating disorders: The current status of molecular genetic research. *European Child and Adolescent Psychiatry*, *19*, 211–226.

Simon, J., Schmidt, U., & Pilling, S. (2005). The health service use and cost of eating disorders. *Psychological Medicine*, *35*, 1543–1551.

Skouteris, H., Carr, R., Wertheim, E. H., Paxton, S. J., & Duncombe, D. (2005). A prospective study of factors that lead to body dissatisfaction during pregnancy. *Body Image, 2,* 347–361.

Smeets, M. A. M., Ingleby, J. D., Hoek, H. W., & Panhuysen, G. E. M. (1999). Body size perception in anorexia nervosa: A signal detection approach. *Journal of Psychosomatic Research, 46,* 465–477.

Steinhausen, H. (2002). The outcome of anorexia nervosa in the 20th century. *American Journal of Psychiatry, 159,* 1284–1293.

Stice, E. (2002). Risk and maintenance factors for eating pathology: A meta-analytic review. *Psychological Bulletin, 128,* 825–848.

Stice, E., Presnell, K., & Bearman, S. K. (2001). Relation of early menarche to depression, eating disorders, substance abuse, and comorbid psychopathology among adolescent girls. *Developmental Psychology, 37,* 608–619.

Strachan, M., & Cash, T. (2002). Self-help for a negative body image: A comparison of components of a cognitive-behavioral program. *Behavior Therapy, 33,* 235–251.

Striegel-Moore, R. H., & Franko, D. L. (2008). Should binge eating disorder be included in the DSM-V? A critical review of the state of the evidence *Annual Review of Clinical Psychology, 4,* 305–324.

Striegel-Moore, R. H., McMahon, R. P., Biro, F. M., Schreiber, G., Crawford, P. B., & Voorhees, C. (2001). Exploring the relationship between timing of menarche and eating disorder symptoms in Black and White adolescent girls. *International Journal of Eating Disorders, 30,* 421–433.

Strober, M., Freeman, R., Lampert, C., Diamond, J., & Kaye, W. (2000). Controlled family study of anorexia nervosa and bulimia nervosa: Evidence of shared liability and transmission of partial syndromes. *American Journal of Psychiatry, 157,* 393–401.

Telch, C., & Agras, W. (1993). The effects of a very low calorie diet on binge eating. *Behavior Therapy, 24,* 177–193.

Thompson, J., & Smolak, L. (2001). *Body image, eating disorders and obesity in youth.* Washington, DC: American Psychological Association.

Thompson, J., & Stice, E. (2001). Thin-ideal internalization: Mounting evidence for a new risk factor for body-image disturbance and eating pathology. *Current Directions in Psychological Science, 10,* 181–183.

Thompson, J., Coovert, M., & Stromer, S. (1999). Body image, social comparison, and eating disturbance: A covariance structure modeling investigation. *International Journal of Eating Disorders, 26,* 43–51.

Thompson, J., Heinberg, L., Altabe, M., & Tantleff-Dunn, S. (1999). *Exacting beauty: Theory, assessment and treatment of body image disturbance.* Washington, DC: American Psychological Association.

Tiggemann, M., & Kuring, J. (2004). The role of body objectification in disordered eating and depressed mood. *British Journal of Clinical Psychology, 43,* 299–311.

Tiggemann, M., & Lynch, J. (2001). Body image across the life span in adult women: The role of self-objectification. *Developmental Psychology, 37,* 243–253.

Tiggemann, M., & McGill, B. (2004). The role of social comparison in the effect of magazine advertisements on women's mood and body dissatisfaction. *Journal of Social and Clinical Psychology, 23,* 23–44.

Timko, C. A., Perone, J., & Crossfield, A. (2006). Are you currently on a diet? What respondents mean when they say "yes". *Eating Disorders: The Journal of Treatment and Prevention, 14,* 157–166.

Tolgyes, T., & Nemessury, J. (2004). Epidemiological studies on the adverse dieting behaviours and eating disorders among young people in Hungary. *Social Psychiatry & Psychiatric Epidemiology, 39,* 647–654.

Tylka, T., & Hill, M. (2004). Objectification theory as it relates to disordered eating among college women. *Sex Roles, 51,* 719–730.

Upton, R. L., & Han, S. S. (2003). Maternity and its discontents: Getting the body back after pregnancy. *Journal of Contemporary Ethnography, 32,* 670–692.

Wade, T. D., Bergin, J. L., Tiggemann, M., Bulik, C. M., & Fairburn, C. G. (2006). Prevalence and long-term course of lifetime eating disorders in an adult Australian twin cohort. *The Australian and New Zealand Journal of Psychiatry, 40,* 121–128.

Wade, T., Martin, N. G., Neale, M. C., Tiggemann, M., Treloar, S. A., Bucholz, K. K., . . . Heath, A. C. (1999). The structure of genetic and environmental risk factors for three measures of disordered eating. *Psychological Medicine, 29,* 925–934.

Wade, T., Martin, N., Tiggemann, M., Abraham, S., Treloar, S., & Heath, A. (2000). Genetic and environmental risk factors shared between disordered eating, psychological and family variables. *Personality and Individual Differences, 28,* 729–740.

Walsh, B., & Garner, D. (1997). Diagnostic issues. In D. Garner & P. Garfinkel (Eds.), *Handbook of treatment for eating disorders* (pp. 25–33). New York, NY: Guilford Press.

Walsh, B. T., Kaplan, A. S., Attia, E., Olmstead, M., Parides, M., Carter, J. C., . . . Rockert, W. (2006). Fluoxetine after weight restoration in anorexia nervosa: A randomized controlled trial. *JAMA, 295,* 2605–2612.

Wildes, J., & Marcus, M. (2010). Diagnosis, assessment and treatment planning for binge-eating disorder and eating disorder not otherwise specified. In C. Grilo & J. Mitchell (Eds.), *The treatment of eating disorders: A clinical handbook* (pp. 44–65). New York, NY: Guilford Press.

Wilfley, D., Bishop, M., Wilson, T., & Agras, S. (2007). Classification of eating disorders: Toward DSM-V. *International Journal of Eating Disorders, 40,* 123–129.

Wilfley, D., Wilson, G., & Agras, A. (2003). The clinical significance of binge eating disorder. *International Journal of Eating Disorders, 34,* 96–106.

Wilfley, D. E., Welch, R. R., Stein, R. I., Spurrell, E. B., Cohen, L. R., Saelens, B. E., . . . Matt, G. E. (2002). A randomized comparison of group cognitive-behavioral therapy and group interpersonal psychotherapy for the treatment of overweight individuals with binge-eating disorder. *Archives of General Psychiatry, 59,* 713–721.

Williamson, D., Thaw, J., Varnado-Sullivan, P. (2001). Cost-effectiveness analysis of a hospital-based cognitive-behavioral treatment program for eating disorders. *Behavior Therapy, 32,* 459–477.

Wilson, T., Fairburn, C., Agras, S., Walsh, T., & Kraemer, H. (2005). Cognitive-behavioral therapy for bulimia nervosa: Time course and mechanisms of change. *Journal of Consulting and Clinical Psychology, 70,* 267–274.

Wilson, G., Grilo, C., & Vitousek, K. (2007). Psychological treatment of eating disorders. *American Psychology, 62,* 199–216.

Winzelberg, A., Abascal, L., & Taylor, C. (2002). Psychoeducational approaches to the prevention and change of negative body image. In T. Cash & T. Pruzinsky (Eds.), *Body image: A handbook of theory, research and clinical practice* (pp. 487–498). New York, NY: Guilford Press.

Wonderlich, S. A., & Mitchell, J. E. (1997). Eating disorders and comorbidity: Empirical, conceptual and clinical implications. *Psychopharmacology Bulletin, 33,* 3981.

Zerbe, K. J. (2003). Eating disorders in middle and late life: A neglected problem. *Primary Psychiatry, 10,* 80–82.

9 Cosmetic Medical Procedures and Body Adornment

Canice E. Crerand, Leanne Magee, Jacqueline Spitzer, and
David B. Sarwer

INTRODUCTION

According to the American Society of Plastic Surgeons (ASPS), approximately 13.1 million cosmetic surgical and nonsurgical cosmetic treatments were performed in the United States in 2010 (ASPS, 2011). More than 1.5 million surgical procedures were performed, including the most common procedures of breast augmentation, rhinoplasty, eyelid surgery, liposuction, and abdominoplasty. Over 11.5 million treatments were minimally invasive nonsurgical facial cosmetic procedures, including *Botulinum* toxin injections, soft tissue fillers, chemical peels, microdermabrasion, and laser skin resurfacing (ASPS, 2011). These statistics are well known to professionals who work in these areas, but the numbers are staggering to many Americans who are unaware of the popularity of cosmetic medical treatments. However, these figures are likely an underestimate, as they do not reflect procedures performed by other medical specialists, such as dermatologists, aestheticians, otorhinolaryngologists, or dentists.

As in the past, the majority of individuals who seek cosmetic procedures today are female, although increasing numbers of men now pursue these treatments as well

(ASPS, 2011). The gender difference in pursuit and receipt of cosmetic procedures is likely the result of a multitude of sociocultural, psychological, and other factors, which contribute to feminine beauty standards and motivate women to change or enhance their physical appearances. This chapter presents the motivations driving pursuit of cosmetic procedures and body adornment, as well as trends in appearance alteration throughout the lifespan and throughout history.

Type-changing cosmetic surgical procedures, designed to noticeably alter the shape or contour of an appearance feature, are described, and the literature on the psychosocial characteristics of patients who pursue such appearance changes is reviewed. Some of the more common anti-aging cosmetic surgical and minimally invasive procedures performed today are also detailed, with a review of the existing psychosocial research on the patients who seek such procedures. The role of psychiatric disorders, such as body dysmorphic disorder and eating disorders, in motivating pursuit of cosmetic procedures is also described. The chapter concludes with recommendations for screening and treatment of individuals who are experiencing psychosocial distress related to their appearance.

MOTIVATIONS FOR COSMETIC PROCEDURES

The popularity of cosmetic surgery can be understood from several perspectives, as several internal and external factors may motivate an individual to seek surgical and nonsurgical facial cosmetic treatments (Sarwer & Crerand, 2004; Sarwer & Magee, 2006; Sarwer, Magee, & Crerand, 2004). These factors include attitudes toward cosmetic procedures, body image dissatisfaction, gender, ethnicity, and age.

Increased Acceptance of Cosmetic Medical Treatments

Cosmetic procedures are quite popular and are being increasingly accepted as appropriate means of altering one's appearance. According to a 2009 Consumer Attitudes Survey of 1,000 American households, 59% of women and 51% of men reported approval of cosmetic surgery (ASAPS, 2009). Thirty-seven percent of women and 19% of men indicated that they would consider cosmetic surgery for themselves now or in the future, and 73% of women and 66% of men reported that they would not be embarrassed about having cosmetic surgery (ASAPS, 2009). Research studies also have suggested that women, more than men, are more likely to consider (Swami et al., 2008) or receive cosmetic surgery (Brown, Furnham, Glanville, & Swami, 2007). Among college-aged women, 43% agreed with the statement that people should do whatever they want to look good, and 45% approved of people surgically changing their appearance to feel better about themselves. Forty percent of respondents would consider seeking cosmetic medical treatments in the near future, and 48% would consider it in middle age (Sarwer, Cash, et al., 2005).

The increasing acceptance of cosmetic surgery as a tool for the improvement of physical appearance can be attributed to several factors (Sarwer et al., 2004). Advances in surgical techniques, including improved safety and wound care, have contributed to less risk and recovery time. The less invasive nature, reduced risk, and smaller price tag of many minimally invasive facial procedures (e.g., Botox injections) have likely contributed to the tremendous popularity of these procedures. However, the effects of these procedures typically last for a period of 3 to 6 months, thereby requiring repeated procedures to maintain the optimal result. Over time, the costs for these repeated treatments can add up and may lead some patients to pursue more permanent changes in their appearance. As such, minimally invasive treatments can end up serving as a gateway to more intensive surgical interventions.

Changes in the surgical and medical communities, including direct-to-consumer marketing and the performance of cosmetic procedures by a wide range of medical and aesthetic professionals, have also likely contributed to the growth. Though earlier generations were extremely private regarding their cosmetic surgeries, patients are increasingly open about their experiences with changing their appearance with medical treatments. The recent trend of Botox® parties highlights the decrease in secrecy about procedures, as women socialize while receiving minimally invasive procedures in spa-like settings.

The mass media and entertainment industries have a long history of directly and indirectly promoting cosmetic medicine. Consumers are bombarded by mass media images of beauty on an unprecedented scale—in advertisements, television programs, film, music, and the Internet. Mass media coverage of cosmetic surgery has introduced a wider audience to the notion of cosmetic surgery and its potential benefits while espousing an ideal of beauty that is increasingly unattainable without surgical assistance (Sarwer, Grossbart, & Didie, 2002; Sarwer et al., 2004).

These mass media messages appear to influence attitudes toward surgery. Swami and colleagues (2008) showed that media exposure, including viewing advertisements, television programs, and articles about cosmetic surgery, mediated the relationship between gender and likelihood of cosmetic surgery. Television shows featuring cosmetic surgery have been found to influence attitudes toward and interest in receiving cosmetic surgery. In a correlational study of 2,057 college-aged women, viewership of reality television shows featuring cosmetic surgery was significantly related to more favorable attitudes toward cosmetic surgery, perceived pressure to have cosmetic surgery, past experience with cosmetic surgery, decreased fear of surgery, and body image dissatisfaction, internalization of media ideals, and disordered eating (Sperry, Thompson, Sarwer, & Cash, 2009). In an experimental study of 198 young adults, participants who viewed a surgical makeover television program wanted to surgically alter their own appearance more than participants who viewed a neutral television program (Markey & Markey, 2010).

Similar studies have demonstrated that exposure to surgery among friends and family is associated with greater approval of cosmetic surgery as well as a greater likelihood of considering surgery for oneself. Among college-aged women, 3% (Delinsky, 2005) to 5% (Sarwer, Cash, et al., 2005) have undergone cosmetic surgery. One-half

(Delinsky, 2005) to two-thirds (Sarwer, Cash, et al., 2005) of these women had a friend or family member who had surgery, the experience of which was associated with greater approval of cosmetic surgery (Delinsky, 2005; Sarwer, Cash, et al., 2005). Greater vicarious experience of cosmetic surgery further increases the likelihood of undergoing surgery. Brown and colleagues (2007) have suggested that it may not be media exposure, or vicarious exposure, alone that influences attitudes toward cosmetic surgery, but rather the internalization of mass media's perpetuation of unattainable ideals of beauty and its messages about cosmetic surgery that is reflected in study findings such as these.

Other studies have looked at additional factors that may be related to increased acceptance and consideration of cosmetic surgery. More favorable attitudes toward cosmetic surgery are related to increased age (particularly for women) as well as greater use of makeup, lower social self-esteem and body esteem, higher body shame, and a greater motivation for avoidance of feared possible selves compared to pursuit of desired selves (Henderson-King & Henderson-King, 2005). Acceptance of cosmetic surgery has also been associated with appearance-based rejection sensitivity, or the tendency to anxiously expect, easily perceive, and overreact to signs of interpersonal rejection based on one's appearance (Calogero, Park, Rahemtulla, & Williams, 2010).

Body Image

Although increased exposure and access to cosmetic treatments can explain the growing popularity of surgical and nonsurgical appearance interventions, our drive for beauty is also influenced by body image and internalization of beauty standards. Body image dissatisfaction has long been thought to motivate many appearance-enhancing behaviors, from weight loss and exercise to clothing and cosmetic purchases (Sarwer & Crerand, 2004). Dissatisfaction with one's body image, comprised of the degree of investment in and satisfaction with physical appearance, is believed to be the primary motivational factor in the pursuit of cosmetic surgery (Sarwer, Wadden, Pertschuk, & Whitaker, 1998a). We have reviewed the relationship between body image and cosmetic surgery in detail elsewhere (e.g., Sarwer & Crerand, 2004; Sarwer, Wadden, Pertschuk, & Whitaker, 1998a). In brief, several studies have suggested that cosmetic surgery patients report increased body image dissatisfaction before surgery (e.g., Sarwer et al., 2003). Others have found improvements in body image postoperatively (e.g., Banbury et al., 2004; Bolton, Pruzinsky, Cash, & Persing, 2003; Dunofsky, 1997; Sarwer, Infield, et al., 2008). As discussed in detail later, extreme body image dissatisfaction in the form of body dysmorphic disorder and eating disorders is of particular concern among those who undergo cosmetic procedures.

Gender

Attractive and youthful appearance standards are most strongly held for women. Especially in popular culture, images of women's bodies have proliferated along with the idea that attractiveness and youth are linked with social power. Feminist theorists suggest that as women have gained freedoms in their roles, visibility, and contribution to the world, more subtle means of constraint have emerged, whereby a woman's value is increasingly based on her physical appearance (Gillespie, 1996). Objectification theories suggest that women are defined by their bodies and appearance as a result of gender socialization and sexual objectification experiences (Moradi, 2010).

Marketing of cosmetics and surgical procedures for women has also contributed to the medicalization of appearance, and has influenced popular beliefs that signs of normal age-related changes in appearance can and should be addressed with makeup, serums, and minimally invasive and surgical treatments. The field of cosmetic surgery is viewed by some feminists as exploiting women's appearance concerns, defining facial imperfections as medical ailments to be treated, and reinforcing narrow cultural beauty standards as a means of defining women's value in society (Gillespie, 1996). Women who opt not to buy into these standards and treatments may be viewed as deviant, unattractive, and devalued in society (Gillespie, 1996).

On the contrary, some feminist theorists argue that cosmetic surgery can be used as a tool to improve one's appearance, adhere to gender and beauty norms, and gain social power in a culture that strongly values female attractiveness (Gillespie, 1996). However, the argument remains that rather than being empowered by the surgical manipulation of appearance, women may continue to remain victims to unrealistic beauty standards and pressures from the medical community. Thus, while changing one's body through cosmetic surgery may be seen as a means of perpetuating the subordination of women, it is also paradoxically a means of attaining social power in a culture that very narrowly values women based on their physical attractiveness.

Ethnicity

Historically, the vast majority of persons seeking cosmetic surgical and nonsurgical interventions identify as Caucasian. More recently, individuals of other ethnicities are increasingly seeking cosmetic procedures (ASPS, 2011). In 2010, 12% of cosmetic procedure patients identified as Hispanic, 8% identified as African American, 6% as Asian, and 5% as other ethnicity (ASPS, 2011).

For individuals of non-Caucasian ethnicities who pursue type-changing facial procedures, such as rhinoplasty, cosmetic surgery may reinforce ethnocentric ideals of beauty, specifically Caucasian facial features. Asian American women in the United States and Asia are increasingly seeking "double eyelid" blepharoplasty to create a crease on the upper eyelid and more closely approximate a Western ideal. Similarly, many African American, Jewish, Italian, and increasing numbers of Asian persons seek rhinoplasty to alter ethnic characteristics and to better represent the highly valued Caucasian, feminine nose shape. Rhinoplasty is among the top three most commonly requested facial cosmetic surgeries among African American, Asian American, and Hispanic patients (ASPS, 2011). Asian American patients often pursue rhinoplasty to augment the nasal tip and dorsum (Nolst Trenité, 2003; Toriumi & Pero, 2010), while African American patients often request that their noses be made to appear smaller and narrower (Slupchynskyj & Gieniusz, 2008).

A retrospective study of African American rhinoplasty patients found that although patients reported a desire to alter ethnic characteristics of their nose, almost half reported no change in ethnic features postoperatively, whereas the majority reported postoperative satisfaction with the new facial proportions (Slupchynskyj & Gieniusz, 2008). High patient satisfaction with surgical outcome and the perceived preservation of ethnic characteristics is inconsistent with the idea that patients seek surgery to minimize ethnic features. More research on frequently requested type-changing surgeries among non-Caucasian patient populations is warranted to better clarify motivations for and satisfaction with surgery.

Age

Pursuit of particular cosmetic procedures and body adornment varies with age. For many adult patients, pursuit of cosmetic procedures stems from a desire to recapture a more youthful appearance. Age-related appearance changes include wrinkles, creases, frown lines, crow's feet, and loss of skin elasticity leading to sagging or drooping of skin, loss of muscle tone, and discoloration of skin. The pursuit of youthful appearance through restorative cosmetic treatments is grounded in bioevolutionary theories of attractiveness and is valued across cultures and ethnicities (Sarwer & Magee, 2006). In many cultures, aging appearance features are viewed negatively, as reflected in the use of the term "anti-aging" to describe restorative cosmetic procedures. Negative attitudes toward aging appearance features are also emphasized in the increasing medicalization of aging, which is now "treated" with injections, chemicals, and surgery.

Although the majority of cosmetic surgical and nonsurgical procedures are performed on adult patients, an increasing number of child and adolescent patients seek cosmetic procedures each year. Teens accounted for 5% of all cosmetic surgical procedures and 1% of all nonsurgical cosmetic procedures performed in 2009 (ASPS, 2011). Adolescents age 13 to 19 accounted for 29% of otoplasty (ear pinning) surgeries and 14% of rhinoplasty surgeries (ASPS, 2011).

TYPE-CHANGING COSMETIC PROCEDURES

Type-changing cosmetic procedures include surgical procedures that noticeably alter the size, shape, or contour of an appearance feature. The typical patient seeks to significantly change her appearance because of dissatisfaction with a particular feature. Almost invariably, the type-changing surgery results in a change to the overall appearance of the face or body, even though only a single feature may have been altered. Although individuals of all ages may pursue these procedures, they are frequently desired by younger individuals. The most common type-changing facial cosmetic surgeries include rhinoplasty and lip, chin, and cheek implants. Breast augmentation is the most common type-changing cosmetic surgery for the body. Major findings from the psychosocial literature for each type of surgery are presented as follows.

Rhinoplasty

Rhinoplasty is one of the most popular cosmetic surgical procedures, with more than 250,000 being performed in 2010 (ASPS, 2011). It is also the most commonly received procedure for adolescents.

The psychological characteristics of rhinoplasty patients have received as much attention as any cosmetic procedure. Early reports of the psychological characteristics of rhinoplasty patients date back to the 1940s and 1950s. Many of these investigations, as well as studies conducted into the 1960s, relied heavily on clinical interviews and observations of patients and suggested that patients were highly psychopathological (Hill & Silver, 1950; Linn & Goldman, 1949). Early authors often conceptualized the desire for rhinoplasty from a psychodynamic perspective. From this perspective, the nose was thought to symbolize the penis, and the desire for rhinoplasty was conceptualized as the patient's unconscious displacement of sexual conflicts onto his or her nose (Book, 1971; Gifford, 1973). Rhinoplasty was thought to provide resolution to these conflicts.

More recent studies, for the most part, have utilized improved methodologies, such as use of reliable and valid self-report questionnaires, clinical interviews with established diagnostic criteria, as well as pre- and postoperative assessments (e.g., Borges-Dinis, Dinis, & Gomes, 1998; Ercolani, Baldaro, Rossi, & Trombini, 1999; Goin & Rees, 1991; Hern, Rowe-Jones, & Hinton, 2003; Rankin, Borah, Perry, & Wey, 1998; Sarwer, Whitaker, Wadden, & Pertschuk, 1997). Collectively, these studies have, more or less, suggested that rhinoplasty patients are psychologically healthy individuals. These findings are also more consistent with the clinical experiences of most present-day cosmetic surgeons, who report that most rhinoplasty patients are psychologically healthy individuals who are dissatisfied with the size and shape of their noses and not presenting for surgery with significant psychopathology.

Postoperatively, improvements in quality of life; symptoms of anxiety, depression, and self-esteem; satisfaction with facial appearance; and decreased self-consciousness have been documented (deArruda Alves, Alba, Santos, & Ferreira, 2005; Litner, Rotenberg, Dennis, & Adamson, 2008; Moss & Harris, 2009). However, increased obsessive symptoms and symptoms of body dysmorphic disorder also have been noted in rhinoplasty patients (Pecorari et al., 2010; Veale, De Haro, & Lambrou, 2003; Zojaji, Javanbakht, Ghanadan, Hosien, & Sadeghi, 2007). These observations highlight the importance of preoperative psychological screening for patients who seek rhinoplasty and particularly for those who return for secondary procedures on their noses (Crerand, Gibbons, & Sarwer, 2007).

Facial Skeletal Procedures

A comparatively small number of patients seek other facial skeletal surgeries to address concerns with the shape of their faces. These procedures involve bone contouring, bone grafting, or the insertion of cheek, chin, or other facial implants to change the physical structure of the face. Approximately 12,000 chin augmentation surgeries, designed to increase the projection or size of a small or recessed chin, were performed in 2010 (ASPS, 2011). Approximately 8,000 patients sought malar augmentation, or cheek implants, to increase the projection of the cheekbones (ASPS, 2011). Chin, jaw, and cheek implants can be used to augment more than one facial region and to increase symmetry among facial features. Some individuals also pursue surgical augmentation of their lips to permanently enhance fullness. More than 17,000 surgical lip augmentations were performed in 2010 (ASPS, 2011). No studies have yet examined the psychological or body image characteristics of individuals who pursue these procedures.

Cosmetic Breast Augmentation

The American Society of Plastic Surgeons reported that 296,203 cosmetic breast augmentation surgeries were performed in 2010 (ASPS, 2011), making it the most popular of all cosmetic surgical procedures. There is a large literature on the psychological aspects of breast augmentation, including descriptive studies of the psychological characteristics of women who are interested in the procedure, as well as studies of postoperative psychological changes.

The typical breast augmentation patient is European American, in her late 20s or early 30s, and is married with children. Although these characteristics may describe the typical patient, women from their late teens to mid-40s of varying ethnic backgrounds and relationship status present for breast augmentation surgery. Furthermore, patient characteristics may vary based on region of the country, characteristics of a surgeon's practice, and other variables as well.

Women who receive breast implants differ from other women on a variety of unique characteristics. Women with breast implants are more likely to have had more sexual partners, report a greater use of oral contraceptives, be younger at their first pregnancy, and have a history of terminated pregnancies as compared to other women (e.g., Brinton, Brown, Colton, Burich, & Lubin, 2000; Cook et al., 1997; Kjoller et al., 2003). They have been found to be more frequent users of alcohol and tobacco (Cook et al., 1997; Fryzek et al., 2000; Kjoller et al., 2003). They also have a higher divorce rate (Beale, Lisper, & Palm, 1980; Schlebusch & Levin, 1983). Finally, they have been found to have a below-average body weight (e.g., Brinton et al., 2000; Fryzek et al., 2000;

Sarwer et al., 2003), leading to concern that some of these women may be experiencing eating disorders (discussed in more detail later).

Several studies have investigated the preoperative psychological status of women who are interested in breast augmentation. Early research employing clinical interviews largely characterized breast augmentation candidates as highly psychopathological and as experiencing increased symptoms of depression, anxiety, guilt, and low self-esteem (Beale et al., 1980; Ohlsen, Ponten, & Hambert, 1978; Schlebusch & Levin, 1983; Sihm, Jagd, Pers, 1978). Subsequent studies using valid and reliable psychometric assessment tools have found significantly less psychopathology than the interview-based investigations (Baker, Kolin & Bartlett, 1974; Kilmann, Sattler & Taylor, 1987; Schlebusch, 1989; Shipley, O'Donnell, & Bader, 1977).

More recently, studies have focused on the body image concerns of women who are interested in breast augmentation. Breast augmentation candidates typically report less dissatisfaction with their breasts compared to breast reduction patients (Sarwer et al., 1998). However, greater than 50% of breast augmentation patients reported significant behavioral avoidance, such as camouflaging their breasts or avoidance of being seen undressed, in response to negative feelings about their breasts. At least two studies have compared breast augmentation candidates to small-breasted women not seeking breast augmentation. Women who sought breast augmentation, as compared to controls recruited from a university community, reported greater dissatisfaction with their breasts, as well as greater investment in their overall appearance and greater concern with their appearance in social

situations (Sarwer et al., 2003). Augmentation candidates also rated their ideal breast size, as well as the breast size preferred by women, as significantly larger than did controls. Finally, prospective patients reported more frequent teasing about their physical appearance and more frequent use of psychotherapy than did controls. In the second study, breast augmentation candidates were compared to healthy women similar in age, body mass, and breast size who were recruited from a gynecology outpatient clinic (Didie & Sarwer, 2003). Women who were interested in breast augmentation again reported greater dissatisfaction with their breasts, but compared to controls, they did not report greater investment or dissatisfaction with their overall appearance.

Clinical reports suggest that the majority of women are satisfied with the outcome of breast augmentation surgery (Park, Chetty & Watson, 1996; Schlebusch & Marht, 1993; Wells et al., 1994; Young, Nemecek, & Nemeck, 1994), with satisfaction rates as high as 94% being reported postoperatively (Cash, Duel, & Perkins, 2002). Women who undergo breast augmentation experience improvements in their body image postoperatively, as suggested by clinical reports (Baker et al., 1974; Sihm et al., 1978; Young et al., 1994) and empirical studies (e.g., Banbury et al., 2004; Cash et al., 2002; Sarwer, Infield, et al., 2008). Two studies have shown that improvements in psychological functioning, specifically body image and quality of life, endure for several years after surgery for the vast majority of women (Cash et al., 2002; Murphy, Beckstrand, & Sarwer, 2008).

These benefits, however, may be tempered by the experience of a postoperative complication. Between 10% and 25% of women are reported to experience a surgical or implant-related complication (Cunningham, Lokeh & Gutowski, 2000; Gabriel et al., 1997; Kjoller et al., 2002). The most common complications are implant leakage or rupture/deflation, capsular contracture, discomfort or pain, breast asymmetry, scarring, loss of nipple sensation, and breast-feeding difficulties. At least three studies have suggested that the experience of a complication is negatively related to postoperative satisfaction (Cash et al., 2002; Fiala, Lee, & May, 1993; Handel, Wellisch, Silverstein, Jensen, & Waisman, 1993). Intuitively, women who experience a postoperative complication may be more likely to have a less positive psychological outcome. However, this issue has received very little empirical attention. A large prospective study found that while women typically report improvements in self-image and body image after breast augmentation, those who experienced postoperative complications reported less favorable changes in body image, particularly if the complication was visible to others, as in the case of significant capsular contracture (Cash et al., 2002).

In the past decade, seven epidemiological studies that investigated silicone gel-filled breast implants and all-cause mortality have found an association between cosmetic breast implants and suicide (Brinton, Lubin, Bruich, Colton, & Hoover, 2001; Brinton, Lubin, Murray, Colton, & Hoover, 2006; Jacobsen et al., 2004; Koot, Peeters, Granath, Grobbee, & Nyren, 2003; Lipworth, 2007; Pukkala et al., 2003; Villeneuve et al., 2006). Women who have undergone cosmetic breast augmentation exhibit a two- to three-fold increased rate of suicide compared to the general population, a rate that is greatest among women receiving implants after age 40 (Brinton et al., 2006; Villeneuve et al., 2006). Although one study suggested

that the occurrence of suicide among women with breast implants was more frequent than among women who underwent other forms of cosmetic surgery (Brinton, Lubin, Bruich, Colton, & Hoover, 2001), a subsequent investigation with a larger sample found no difference in the rate of suicide among breast augmentation and other cosmetic surgery patients (Villeneuve et al., 2006).

Research indicates that breast implants do not directly increase mortality in women. Rather, potential explanations of this relationship largely have focused on the preoperative functioning and psychosocial status of the patients. As noted earlier, women who undergo breast augmentation exhibit several characteristics that are, in and of themselves, risk factors for suicide, including more lifetime sexual partners and a greater use of oral contraceptives, younger age at the time of their first pregnancy, a history of terminated pregnancies, more frequent alcohol and tobacco use, and below-average body weight (Sarwer, Brown & Evans, 2007). One study has documented a higher rate of previous psychiatric hospitalizations among women with breast implants when compared with women who received other cosmetic procedures and women who underwent breast reduction, but information on diagnosis, history of illness, or other psychiatric treatments for the women was not reported (Jacobsen et al., 2004). A history of mental illness requiring psychiatric hospitalization is one of the strongest risk factors for suicide. Other studies also have shown that women with breast implants report a higher rate of outpatient psychological or psychiatric treatment compared with other women (Sarwer et al., 2003).

Nevertheless, the relationship between preoperative psychopathology and subsequent suicide following cosmetic breast augmentation remains inconclusive. In a review of these studies identifying a relationship between breast implants and suicide, an alternative explanation for the epidemiological findings suggested that improvements in body image following breast augmentation may actually produce a "protective effect" for women who may have otherwise been at increased risk for suicide because of other preexisting demographic and psychosocial risk factors (Joiner, 2003). This hypothesis, while intriguing, has yet to receive any direct empirical study.

RESTORATIVE PROCEDURES

Anti-aging cosmetic surgical procedures seek to restore or rejuvenate the appearance of facial features. Unlike type-changing surgeries, restorative procedures aim to create subtle changes to create a more youthful appearance without changing any major structures or shapes of the face. This section reviews common anti-aging procedures for the face, including facelift, eyelift, and minimally invasive procedures, as well as restorative surgical procedures for the body, such as liposuction and tummy tuck.

Rhytidectomy and Blepharoplasty

Rhytidectomy and blepharoplasty are two of the most popular cosmetic surgical procedures for those interested in restoring or maintaining a youthful appearance (ASPS, 2011). Rhytidectomy, more commonly known as facelift surgery, can address concerns with loose or sagging skin of the face and neck that result from loss of elasticity caused by aging, weight change, sun exposure, or heritable factors. Facelifts are often performed along with blepharoplasty, a surgical procedure designed to remove fat and excess skin or muscle from the upper and/or lower eyelids that often form with age. Facelift and eyelid surgeries are often performed in conjunction with a brow lift or forehead lift, which is designed to minimize the creases that form across the forehead or between the eyebrows and lift a low or sagging brow. All three procedures are also often performed with other minimally invasive anti-aging procedures.

Although facelifts have historically been one of the most popular cosmetic surgical procedures, counted among the top five between 2000 and 2004, the development of minimally invasive anti-aging procedures, which are less expensive and require less recovery time, has led to a decline in the popularity of facelifts over the past 5 years. Approximately 112,000 facelift surgeries were performed in 2010, compared to more than 130,000 in 2000, representing a 16% decline (ASPS, 2011). Similarly, forehead lifts and brow lifts dropped 65% in the same time period. Although eyelid surgeries dropped by 36% since the year 2000, blepharoplasty was still the third most popular cosmetic surgical procedure in 2010, with a total of more than 208,000 performed (ASPS, 2011).

Early studies of facelift patients, much like the initial studies of rhinoplasty patients, identified high levels of psychopathology. Patients were frequently characterized as dependent and depressed, although studies also noted postoperative improvements in well-being (Webb, Slaughter, Meyer, & Edgerton, 1965). In contrast to these interview-based investigations, studies of aging face patients that incorporated standardized self-report measures found lower rates of psychopathology (e.g., depression) (Goin, Burgoyne, Goin, & Staples, 1980) and postoperative increases in appearance satisfaction, self-confidence, social engagement, and feelings of happiness (Rankin et al., 1998).

A few studies have examined the appearance concerns of these patients (Sarwer, Wadden, Pertschuk, & Whitaker, 1998b). In one study, women seeking facelift or blepharoplasty endorsed high levels of pre-operative dissatisfaction with their aging facial appearance, but they were largely satisfied with their overall body image (Sarwer et al., 1997). Compared to a significantly younger sample of women seeking rhinoplasty, facelift and blepharoplasty patients reported greater investment in appearance and satisfaction with overall body image (Sarwer et al., 1997). Postoperatively, patients reported decreases in body image dissatisfaction for the feature that was treated, but no changes in overall body image (Sarwer, Wadden, & Whitaker, 2002).

Findings suggest that although patients seeking anti-aging surgeries may endorse greater investment in their appearance, they also experience less feature-specific body image disturbance compared to women seeking a type-changing surgery. Overall, research indicates that patients who pursue anti-aging facial surgeries are typically psychologically healthy. Additional research is needed to better understand the ways in which age may affect global and feature-specific body image among patients seeking anti-aging facial procedures, and to determine if postoperative benefits in body image and overall psychosocial functioning are maintained over time.

Minimally Invasive Cosmetic Procedures

Minimally invasive procedures make up the majority of cosmetic procedures performed in the United States. For example, more than 5.3 million botulinum toxin injections were performed in 2010, representing a 584% increase over the past 10 years, and making this the most popular of all cosmetic procedures (ASPS, 2011). Botox® and similar agents are typically injected into the face in order to reduce the appearance of wrinkling. The toxin has also been used to treat hyperhydrosis, or excessive sweating, in the face and other areas of the body such as the underarms. Injectable soft tissue fillers are used to add fullness to the lips and face, improve wrinkles and deep scars, and reduce or smooth the appearance of the nasolabial folds. Substances such as hyaluronic acids (e.g., Juvederm®, Restylane®), hydroxylapatite (e.g., Radiesse®), and polymethylmethacrylate (PMMA) are used as injectable fillers. Synthetic polylactic acids, such as Sculptra®, are also used to fill wrinkles and fine lines on the face.

Collagen is also used to support the skin and plump lips; many patients opt to use fat harvested from their own bodies through liposuction, which is then processed and reinjected to enhance facial fullness and contours. In both chemical peels and microdermabrasion, superficial skin cells are removed with the common goal of improving the appearance and texture of the skin; the former uses a chemical method, whereas the latter employs a mechanical method. Both procedures are used to improve the skin, including redness, deep wrinkles, discoloration, sun damage, facial veins, and acne scarring. Finally, laser skin resurfacing targets superficial and deeper layers of skin to improve the look of fine lines, wrinkles, scars, and irregular pigmentation.

Despite the popularity of these procedures, little is known about the psychological characteristics or body image concerns of the patients who seek these and other minimally invasive procedures. A German study of 30 patients who received Botox® injections for facial lines found that post-treatment, more than half of the sample felt more attractive, 75% felt more comfortable with their bodies, and 80% thought the treatment was beneficial; however, only one-third reported improved emotional well-being after treatment (Sommer, Azchocke, Bergfeld, Sattler & Augustin, 2003).

Few studies have investigated the psychological characteristics of patients who sought other minimally invasive facial procedures. A study of 178 patients seeking laser skin resurfacing reported that 18% received prior treatment for depression (Koch, Newman, & Safer, 2003). Significant improvements in appearance and relationship satisfaction have been noted following treatment with alphahydroxy acid chemical peel (Fried & Cash, 1998).

Lipoplasty

Lipoplasty, more commonly known as liposuction, is traditionally one of the most common cosmetic surgical procedures. More than 200,000 liposuction procedures were performed in 2010, making it the fourth most popular surgical procedure nationwide (ASPS, 2011). The areas of the body treated with lipoplasty frequently vary by gender. Not surprisingly, women often request lipoplasty for the lateral thighs and hips.

As with most cosmetic procedures, patient selection is essential for optimal outcomes. The physically best patient has a normal or slightly elevated body mass index with localized areas of fat that have been resistant to diet and exercise. Although these features paint the picture of a patient's

physicality, far less is known about the psychological characteristics of the typical liposuction patient. Many patients mistakenly believe that liposuction leads to significant weight loss. Surprisingly, the typical weight loss experienced following liposuction has not been well-documented. One pilot study of 14 moderately overweight women (BMI = 27 kg/m^2) reported a mean weight loss of 5.1 kg by 6 weeks postoperatively, with an additional 1.3 kg weight loss by 4 months (Giese, Bulan, Commons, Spear, & Yanovski, 2001). Studies investigating changes in lipids and insulin sensitivity following liposuction have been equivocal (Baxter, 1997; Klein et al., 2004; Samdal, Birkeland, Ose & Amland, 1995).

Many patients erroneously believe that fat deposits will *never* return to the treated areas. Fat can indeed return to some degree if the patient gains weight. Liposuction reduces the number of fat cells in a local area of the body, but the remaining fat cells may still expand if body weight increases. Approximately three-quarters of all liposuction patients report satisfaction with the postoperative result (Dillerud & Haheim, 1993; Rohrich et al., 2004). Almost one-third of patients, however, complained that too little fat was removed (Dillerud & Haheim, 1993). Between 40% and 50% reported weight gain after surgery, and up to 29% claimed that their fat returned to the site of the surgery (Dillerud & Haheim, 1993; Rohrich et al., 2004). Unfortunately, these studies provided no information on patients' pre- and postoperative expectations or body weight.

Individuals with excessive weight or shape concerns, or those with formal eating disorders, require particular attention before lipoplasty. Individuals with anorexia nervosa or bulimia nervosa, as discussed in detail later, may mistakenly seek lipoplasty as an inappropriate compensatory behavior to control their shape and weight. In a case report of two women with bulimia nervosa who underwent lipoplasty, the request for surgery was accompanied with an unrealistic expectation that surgery would result in an improvement of eating disorder symptoms (Willard, McDermott, & Woodhouse, 1996). Postoperatively, both women had exacerbations of their bulimic and depressive symptoms. A recent, large study of Norwegian women found that the presence of eating disorder symptoms was a significant predictor of interest in liposuction (Javo & Sorlie, 2010). Unfortunately, little else is known about the relationship between eating disorders and lipoplasty.

Abdominoplasty

In 2010, 116,000 abdominoplasties were performed in the United States (ASPS, 2011). This represents an 86% increase since 2000, making it one of the most rapidly growing surgical procedures. This increase may be partly attributed to the rising number of individuals with extreme obesity who undergo bariatric surgery for weight loss. Bariatric procedures typically result in a weight loss of approximately one-third of operative body weight; however, many patients are left with excess folds of skin and fat, which may contribute to increased body image dissatisfaction (Sarwer, Thompson, et al., 2008). This may motivate some patients to seek abdominoplasty and related body contouring procedures. In 2010, approximately 9,000 lower body lifts were performed, and following massive weight loss an additional 9,200 thigh lifts and 15,000 upper arm lifts were performed to remove loose and sagging skin (ASPS, 2011).

Case reports suggest that these individuals experience psychosocial improvements and a decrease in the physical discomfort associated with the excess skin (Rhomberg, Pulzi, & Piza-Katzer, 2003). Improvements in body image have also been reported (Pecori et al., 2007).

There is also a growing trend toward postpartum plastic surgery, also known as "Mommy Makeovers," designed to help women restore or improve their postpregnancy bodies. Such makeovers often involve multiple surgical procedures to treat stretched skin and increased or changed breast and abdominal tissue, often including lipoplasty and abdominoplasty. Exact figures for this type of surgery are difficult to estimate, as "Mommy Makeover" is a marketing rather than surgical term and can represent various combinations of surgical procedures.

To date, few studies have examined the psychosocial changes associated with abdominoplasty. One study documented significant improvements in overall body image dissatisfaction, abdominal dissatisfaction, and self-conscious avoidance of body exposure during sexual activity (Bolton et al., 2003). Patients did not report significant improvements in self-concept or general life satisfaction. These results are consistent with the other postoperative studies of cosmetic surgery patients, which found that the impact of cosmetic surgery procedures resulted in improvement in body image discontent, but not necessarily more general psychosocial functioning (Sarwer et al., 2002).

OTHER PROCEDURES

An almost limitless number of procedures can be performed to enhance the body. Many of these are relatively uncommon, but they often receive a great deal of mass media attention. We focus our discussion here on tattoos, body piercing, and genital enhancement.

Tattoos and Body Piercing

Once limited to soldiers and prison populations, tattoos are now routinely seen in mainstream culture. At the turn of the 21st century, it was estimated that up to 20 million Americans had tattoos (Greif, Hewitt, & Armstrong, 1999). A recent report found that 10% to 13% of adolescents (12 to 18 years) and 3% to 8% of the general population had tattoos (Carroll, Riffenburgh, Roberts & Myhre, 2002). More than half of tattoos are found on women (Armstrong, Stuppy, Gabriel & Anderson, 1996). Although reliable estimates are difficult to obtain, these numbers are likely much higher today. Despite the increasing popularity of tattoos, tattoo removal is believed to be on the rise as well. Similar to other cosmetic procedures, tattoo removal seems to be a consequence of a desire to improve one's self-image and not a consequence of external motivations. In a study of 105 individuals seeking tattoo removal, 61% reported embarrassment as a consequence of their tattoo(s) and 26% reported a lower body image (Armstrong et al., 1996).

Accurate estimates of the number of Americans who have undergone body piercing also are lacking. Body piercing may be even more prevalent than tattoos, as piercings are less expensive and less difficult to obtain. Furthermore, body piercings are typically considered less permanent than tattoos, as holes in the skin can close after jewelry is removed. However, piercings can result in lifelong complications such as scarring and bloodborne infectious diseases (Wright, 1995), as well as more temporary complications such as abscesses (Tweeten & Rickman, 1998). Mayers, Judelson, Moriarty, and Rundell (2002) found that 51% of 454 college students had at least one body piercing (including ear), and 17% of these individuals had experienced a medical complication (e.g. bleeding, local trauma, and bacterial infections) as a consequence of their piercing(s). Tongue piercings may be particularly prone to infection and can result in swelling, chipped or fractured teeth, speech impediment, and/or nerve damage (Farah & Harmon, 1998).

Carroll and colleagues (2002) have suggested that the presence of tattoos and/or body piercings in adolescents should be considered a marker for other risk-taking behaviors. In a sample of 484 adolescents, participants with tattoos and/or body piercings were more likely to have engaged in risky behaviors such as drug use and sexual activity and be at increased risk for disordered eating and suicide (Carroll et al., 2002). Furthermore, among college-aged women and men, Crawford and Cash (unpublished manuscript) found that pierced and/or tattooed students scored higher on a measure of excitement seeking and were more likely to smoke cigarettes and engage in binge drinking, relative to their "unmarked" peers. The pierced/tattooed students also reported more body image dissatisfaction, despite being very pleased with their "body art." Perhaps body dissatisfaction is an impetus to obtain body art to "improve" one's appearance.

Some plastic surgeons and medical aestheticians offer micropigmentation (also known as cosmetic tattooing), which entails the implantation of pigment into the skin to produce permanent makeup.

Micropigmentation is typically used to enhance or define features, including the eyebrows, eyelashes, and lips. No exact statistics are available on the number of procedures performed each year. Dissatisfaction with results is considered to be one of the most common complications, and unrealistic patient expectations and psychopathology are thought to increase the likelihood of treatment dissatisfaction (Chiang, Barsky, & Bronson, 1999).

Genital Enhancement

An unknown number of men and women are dissatisfied with the appearance of their genitalia, and some pursue what has been called "genital enhancement" or "genital beautification" procedures. Little is known about the psychological characteristics of people who undergo genital surgery for purely cosmetic reasons. Men may undergo a variety of procedures to lengthen or widen their penises. Women may seek surgery to reduce the size of the labia minora. Although these "defects" are sometimes thought of as functional (impeding urination or adversely affecting sexual functioning), there is also a significant aesthetic component. Patients typically report that they are motivated for surgery out of embarrassment, either when undressed, such as in health club locker rooms or sexual situations, or when wearing tight clothing (Choi & Kim, 2000; Perovic, Radojicic, Djordjevic & Vukadinovic, 2003).

The number of these procedures performed each year is unknown. However, many websites and Internet advertisements, typically sponsored by surgeons, are devoted to these procedures. Considering the nature of these procedures, it is possible that a significant percentage of these patients have an excessive concern with their appearance and are suffering from any number of psychiatric disorders. The plastic surgery literature includes several case reports of individuals who have performed do-it-yourself surgeries, such as injecting their genitals with various oils and substances (Behar, Anderson, Barwick, & Mohler, 1991; Bhagat, Holmes, Kulaga, Murphy, & Cockcroft, 1995; Cohen, Kreoleian, & Krull, 2001). Such procedures can result in serious and potentially life-threatening injury.

PSYCHIATRIC DISORDERS AMONG COSMETIC SURGERY PATIENTS

Understanding the psychological characteristics of patients who undergo cosmetic procedures has long been of interest to both plastic surgeons and mental health professionals. Both groups of professionals have viewed cosmetic surgery as being similar to "psychological interventions," because patients frequently report improvements in their self-esteem and body image satisfaction after receiving treatments. At the same time, the presence of psychiatric disorders may contraindicate procedures for some individuals.

Despite the longstanding interest in the psychological aspects of plastic surgery, to date, no large-scale studies on the rate of psychopathology among cosmetic surgery patients have been completed. Therefore, it is unknown if certain psychiatric disorders occur more frequently among patients who seek cosmetic procedures. However, there is evidence that one psychiatric disorder, body dysmorphic disorder (BDD), may be more common among persons who seek cosmetic procedures.

Body Dysmorphic Disorder

BDD is characterized by a preoccupation with an imagined or slight defect in physical appearance that results in significant emotional distress and/or impairment in daily functioning (APA, 2000). In the general population, the prevalence of BDD appears to range from 0.7% to 3% (Bienvenu et al., 2000; Faravelli et al., 1997; Otto, Wilhelm, Cohen, & Harlow, 2001; Rief, Buhlmann, Wilhelm, Borkenhagen, & Brähler, 2006). Studies of cosmetic populations, however, suggest much higher rates of BDD. In the United States, 7% to 8% of patients requesting cosmetic surgical procedures meet the diagnostic criteria for BDD (Crerand et al., 2004; Sarwer et al., 1998b). International studies suggest that between 3% and 17% of persons who present for cosmetic surgery have BDD (e.g., Aouizerate et al., 2003; Vulink et al., 2006).

Any body part can be a source of preoccupation, although patients typically report concerns with the skin, face, nose, and hair (Phillips, Menard, Fay, & Weisberg, 2005). BDD is characterized by obsessive thoughts about the perceived defect, as well as time-consuming, compulsive behaviors (e.g., mirror checking, excessive grooming rituals), which are performed in an attempt to reduce appearance-related distress (Phillips et al., 2005). BDD symptoms can cause significant distress and impairment in daily functioning. In severe cases, patients may become suicidal or housebound because of their appearance concerns (Phillips et al., 2005; Phillips & Menard, 2006).

Although effective psychiatric and psychological treatments (e.g., selective serotonin reuptake inhibitors, cognitive-behavioral therapy; Phillips, 2010; Veale, 2010) have been developed for BDD, many affected individuals pursue cosmetic treatments as a means of decreasing their appearance concerns (e.g., Crerand, Phillips, Menard, & Fay, 2005; Phillips, Grant, Siniscalchi, & Albertini, 2001). In the largest study of the use of cosmetic treatments among BDD patients ($n = 250$), 76% sought and 66% received treatment (Phillips et al., 2001). Dermatological and surgical procedures are among the most frequently sought and received procedures (Crerand et al., 2005; Phillips et al., 2001). Unfortunately, the majority of patients who receive these treatments experience poor outcomes (Crerand et al., 2005; Crerand, Menard, & Phillips, 2010; Phillips et al., 2001). Studies suggest that greater than 90% of cosmetic treatments typically produce no change, or even worse, an exacerbation of BDD symptoms (Crerand et al., 2005; Crerand et al., 2010). Furthermore, patients with BDD may be more likely to threaten or enact legal action and/or violence against their surgeons (Crerand, Franklin, & Sarwer, 2008). Because of these issues, the presence of BDD is often considered a contraindication for cosmetic procedures (Crerand et al., 2008; Crerand & Sarwer, 2010).

Eating Disorders

Eating disorders, such as anorexia and bulimia nervosa, are characterized by extreme body image dissatisfaction, specifically with weight and shape (APA, 2000). Given that individuals with eating disorders place excessive emphasis on their appearance, these disorders may occur with increased frequency among those who seek cosmetic surgery. Unfortunately, no studies to date have examined the prevalence of eating disorders in cosmetic surgery patients. However, the presence of eating pathology appears to predict interest in cosmetic procedures, specifically liposuction (Javo & Sorlie, 2010). Eating disorders also may be a particular concern for women who are seeking breast augmentation surgery. As noted previously, breast augmentation patients are frequently below average weight (e.g., Brinton et al., 2000; Didie & Sarwer, 2003; Sarwer et al., 2003) and report greater exercise compared to physically similar women not seeking breast augmentation (Didie & Sarwer, 2003).

Case studies have described exacerbations of eating disorder symptoms following breast augmentation, lipoplasty, rhinoplasty, and chin augmentation (McIntosh, Britt, & Bulik, 1994; Willard et al., 1996; Yates, Shisslak, Allender, & Wolman, 1988). A case report of five breast reduction patients with bulimia found that four of the women experienced an improvement in their eating disorder symptoms and reductions in emotional distress postoperatively (Losee, Serletti, Kreipe & Caldwell, 1997). The improvements in eating disorder symptoms were maintained 10 years postoperatively (Losee et al., 2004). The authors hypothesized that excessive breast tissue may have contributed to body image disturbance, which in turn served as an etiologic factor in the development of bulimia. Surgical correction may have led to improvements in body image and subsequent improvement in eating pathology. However, other factors in addition to surgery were likely responsible for symptom improvement.

PSYCHOLOGICAL ASSESSMENT OF THE COSMETIC PATIENT

The majority of patients who pursue cosmetic procedures are thought to be psychologically healthy. Thus, most do not need a psychological evaluation before undergoing a cosmetic procedure. Few, if any, cosmetic surgeons require such evaluations. However, patients who present with symptoms of psychopathology during their initial consultation, patients with a history of psychopathology, or patients who experience distress or unexpected psychological responses to surgery may be referred to mental health professionals for evaluation and/or treatment.

The literature reviewed can be used to inform the psychological assessment and management of cosmetic surgery patients. In general, a cognitive-behavioral assessment of psychosocial functioning is recommended for prospective patients. Such an evaluation should address the thoughts, behaviors, and experiences that have contributed to body image dissatisfaction and the decision to pursue cosmetic treatment. This involves the assessment of the ABCs of a patient's interest in surgery: the (A) antecedents to the decision to seek a cosmetic treatment, (B) behavioral responses to appearance concerns, and (C) consequences of the decision to seek surgery. Additionally, the assessment should be used to identify any maladaptive thoughts or behaviors that could be indicative of psychopathology such as BDD (Sarwer, Crerand, & Magee, 2011; Sarwer, 2006).

The preoperative assessment should focus on the patient's motivations and expectations for cosmetic treatment, specifically her reasons for pursuing treatment at this time and what she hopes to accomplish by having surgery. Such questions can help determine if she is motivated by internal factors, such as improving her self-esteem and confidence, or external factors, such as pleasing a current romantic partner. In general, individuals who pursue cosmetic surgery for external reasons may be at risk for poor psychological outcomes.

Body image concerns can be assessed by asking patients what specifically bothers them about their appearance, as well as how much these concerns bother them and interfere with their daily lives. Patients should also be able to articulate specific concerns that are observable with little effort (although viewing the area of concern may not always be appropriate for mental health professionals, as in the case of concerns about genitalia or breasts). There is frequently little relationship between patients' objective physical appearance and their subjective body image. However, patients who report significant distress with a relatively normal appearance, or who report preoccupation with their appearance or engage in time-consuming appearance rituals may be suffering from BDD.

Finally, a detailed psychiatric history should be obtained. It is likely that all of the major psychiatric diagnoses can be found in this patient population. However, current or past history of disorders with a body image component (e.g., eating disorders), as well as mood and anxiety disorders, should receive particular focus. The presence of these disorders, however, may not be an absolute contraindication for cosmetic surgery. In the absence of empirical data on the relationship between psychopathology and surgical outcome, appropriateness for surgery should be made on a case-by-case basis and include careful collaboration between the mental health professional and referring surgeon.

Mental health professionals may also encounter patients who already have undergone surgery and are referred for evaluation because of dissatisfaction with a technically successful procedure or an exacerbation of psychopathology that was not detected preoperatively. The evaluation of these patients should be similar to that described. Cognitive-behavioral therapy to improve body image may be useful with these individuals (Cash, 2008), although empirically supported treatments for other diagnoses (e.g., depression) may be warranted (Sarwer, Crerand, & Magee, 2011; Sarwer, 2006).

SUMMARY

Each year, millions of cosmetic treatments are performed in the United States. As a result of their popularity, there is renewed interest in understanding the motivations that underlie the pursuit of such interventions, as well as increased interest in the psychological aspects of these procedures. The literature is fairly well developed with respect to certain procedures (e.g., breast augmentation), whereas minimally invasive and body contouring procedures remain relatively underresearched despite their recent surge in popularity. Additional studies are needed to address the motivations of patients who seek cosmetic procedures and the relationships between treatment outcomes, body image, and psychopathology.

Although most individuals who pursue cosmetic procedures do so out of a desire to improve their body images, for some, psychopathology may drive their pursuit of such interventions. There is evidence that at least one psychiatric disorder, body dysmorphic disorder, should be considered a contraindication for cosmetic treatments. As a result, preoperative psychological screenings are recommended for persons who request cosmetic procedures. Given that persons with BDD and eating disorders may be more likely to seek surgical rather than psychiatric treatment, cosmetic treatment providers are well-positioned to identify such patients and to provide appropriate referrals to mental health professionals.

REFERENCES

American Psychiatric Association. (2000). *Diagnostic and statistical manual of mental disorders* (4th ed., revised). Washington, DC: Author.

American Society of Aesthetic and Plastic Surgery. (2009). *2009 Cosmetic surgery national data bank statistics.* New York, NY: Author.

American Society of Plastic Surgeons. (2010). *National clearinghouse of plastic surgery statistics.* Arlington Heights, IL: Author.

American Society of Plastic Surgeons. (2011). *Report of the 2010 plastic surgery statistics.* Arlington Heights, IL: Author.

Aouizerate, B., Pujol, H., Grabot, D., Faytout, M., Suire, K., Braud, C., . . . Tignol, J. (2003). Body dysmorphic disorder in a sample of cosmetic surgery applicants. *European Psychiatry, 18,* 365–368.

Armstrong, M. L., Stuppy, D. J., Gabriel, D. C., & Anderson, R. R. (1996). Motivation for tattoo removal. *Archives of Dermatology, 132*(4), 412–416.

Baker, J. L., Kolin, I. S., & Bartlett, E. S. (1974). Psychosexual dynamics of patients undergoing mammary augmentation. *Plastic and Reconstructive Surgery, 53,* 652–659.

Banbury, J., Yetman, R., Lucas, A., Papay, F., Graves, K., & Zins, J. E. (2004). Prospective analysis of the outcome of subpectoral breast augmentation: Sensory changes, muscle function, and body image. *Plastic and Reconstructive Surgery, 113*(2), 701–707.

Baxter, R. A. (1997). Serum lipid changes following large-volume suction lipetomy. *Aesthetic Surgery Journal, 17,* 213–215.

Beale, S., Lisper, H., & Palm, B. (1980). A psychological study of patients seeking augmentation mammaplasty. *British Journal of Psychiatry, 136,* 133–138.

Behar, T. A., Anderson, E. E., Barwick, W. J., & Mohler, J. L. (1991). Sclerosing lipogranulomatosis: A case report of scrotal injection of automobile transmission fluid and literature review of subcutaneous injection of oils. *Plastic and Reconstructive Surgery, 91,* 352–361.

Bhagat, R., Holmes, I. H., Kulaga, A., Murphy, F., & Cockcroft, D. W. (1995). Self-injection with olive oil: A cause of lipoid pneumonia. *Chest, 107,* 875–876.

Bienvenu, O. J., Samuels, J. F., Riddle, M. A., Hoehn-Saric, R., Liang, K. Y., Cullen, B.A.,

Grados, M. A., & Nestadt, G. (2000). The relationship of obsessive-compulsive disorder to possible spectrum disorders: Results from a family study. *Biological Psychiatry, 48,* 287–293.

Bolton, M. A., Pruzinsky, T., Cash, T. F., & Persing, J. A. (2003). Measuring outcomes in plastic surgery: Body image and quality of life in abdominoplasty patients. *Plastic and Reconstructive Surgery, 112,* 619–625.

Book, H. E. (1971). Sexual implications of the nose. *Comprehensive Psychiatry, 12*(5), 450–455.

Borges-Dinis, P., Dinis, M., & Gomes, A. (1998). Psychosocial consequences of nasal aesthetic and functional surgery: A controlled prospective study in an ENT setting. *Rhinology, 36,* 32–36.

Brinton, L. A., Brown, S. L., Colton, T., Burich, M. C., & Lubin, J. (2000). Characteristics of a population of women with breast implants compared with women seeking other types of plastic surgery, *Plastic and Reconstructive Surgery, 105,* 919–927.

Brinton, L. A., Lubin, J. H., Burich, M. C., Colton, T., & Hoover, R. N. (2001). Mortality among augmentation mammoplasty patients. *Epidemiology, 12*(3), 321–326.

Brinton, L. A., Lubin, J. H., Murray, M. C., Colton, T., & Hoover, R. N. (2006). Mortality rates among augmentation mammoplasty patients: An update. *Epidemiology, 17,* 162–169.

Brown, A., Furnham, A., Glanville, L., & Swami, V. (2007). Factors that affect the likelihood of undergoing cosmetic surgery. *Aesthetic Surgery Journal, 27,* 501–508.

Calogero, R. M., Park, L. E., Rahemtulla, C. K., & Williams, K. C. D. (2010). Predicting excessive body image concerns among British university students: The unique role of Appearance-based Rejection Sensitivity. *Body Image, 7,* 78–81.

Carroll, S. T., Riffenburgh, R. H., Roberts, T. A., & Myhre, E. B. (2002). Tattoos and body piercings as indicators of adolescent risk-taking behaviors. *Pediatrics, 109,* 1021–1027.

Cash, T. F. (2008). *The body image workbook* (2nd ed.). Oakland, CA: New Harbinger.

Cash, T. F., Duel, L. A., & Perkins, L. L. (2002). Women's psychosocial outcomes of breast augmentation with silicone gel-filled implants: A 2-year prospective study. *Plastic and Reconstructive Surgery, 109*(6), 2112–2121.

Chiang, J. K., Barsky, S., & Bronson, D. M. (1999). Tretinoin in the removal of eyeliner tattoo.

Journal of the American Academy of Dermatology, 40(1), 999–1001.

Choi, H. Y., & Kim, K. T. (2000). A new method for aesthetic reduction of labia minora (the deep-ithelialized reduction labioplasty). *Plastic and Reconstructive Surgery, 105,* 419–422.

Cohen, J. L., Keoleian, C. M., & Krull, E. A. (2001). Penile paraffinoma: Self-injection with mineral oil. *Journal of the American Academy of Dermology, 45,* S222–S224.

Cook, L. S., Daling, J. R., Voigt, L. F., deHart, M. P., Malone, K. E., Stanford, F J. L., . . . Brogan, D., (1997). Characteristics of women with and without breast augmentation. *JAMA, 277,* 1612–1617.

Crawford, Y., & Cash, T. F. (2001). *Tattooing and body piercing among college students: Relationships with personality and body image.* Unpublished research, Old Dominion University, Norfolk, VA.

Crerand, C. E., Franklin, M. E., & Sarwer, D. B. (2008). Patient safety: Body dysmorphic disorder and cosmetic surgery. *Plastic & Reconstructive Surgery, 122*(4S), 1–15.

Crerand, C. E., Gibbons, L. M., & Sarwer, D. B. (2007). Psychological characteristics of revision rhinoplasty patients. In D. G. Becker & S. S. Park (Eds.), *Revision rhinoplasty* (pp. 32–41). New York, NY: Thieme Medical.

Crerand, C. E., Menard, W., & Phillips, K. A. (2010). Surgical and minimally invasive cosmetic procedures among persons with body dysmorphic disorder. *Annals of Plastic Surgery, 65,* 11–16.

Crerand, C. E., Phillips, K. A., Menard, W., & Fay, C. (2005). Non-psychiatric medical treatment of body dysmorphic disorder. *Psychosomatics, 46,* 549–555.

Crerand, C. E., & Sarwer, D. B. (2010). Cosmetic treatments and body dysmorphic disorder. *Psychiatric Annals, 40,* 344–348.

Crerand, C. E., Sarwer, D. B., Magee, L., Gibbons, L. M., Lowe, M. R., Bartlett, S.P., . . . Whitaker, L. A. (2004). Rate of body dysmorphic disorder among patients seeking facial plastic surgery. *Psychiatric Annals, 34,* 958–965.

Cunningham, B. L., Lokeh, A., & Gutowski, K. A. (2000). Saline-filled breast implant safety and efficacy: A multicenter retrospective review. *Plastic and Reconstructive Surgery, 105*(6), 2143–2149.

De Arruda Alves, M. C., Abla, L. E. F., Santos, R. A. S., & Ferreira, L. M. (2005). Quality of life and self-esteem following rhytidoplasty. *Annals of Plastic Surgery, 54,* 511–514.

Delinsky, S. S. (2005). Cosmetic surgery: A common and accepted form of self-improvement? *Journal of Applied Social Psychology, 35,* 2012–2028.

Didie, E. R., & Sarwer, D. B. (2003). Factors that influence the decision to undergo cosmetic breast augmentation surgery. *Journal of Women's Health, 12,* 241–253.

Dillerud, E., & Haheim, L. L. (1993). Long-term results of blunt suction lipectomy assessed by a patient questionnaire survey. *Plastic and Reconstructive Surgery, 92,* 35–42.

Dunofsky, M. (1997). Psychological characteristics of women who undergo single and multiple cosmetic surgeries. *Annals of Plastic Surgery, 39*(3), 223–228.

Ercolani, M., Baldaro, B., Rossi, N., & Trombini, G. (1999). Five-year follow-up of cosmetic rhinoplasty. *Journal of Psychosomatic Research, 47*(3), 283–286.

Farah, C. S., & Harmon, D. M. (1998). Tongue piercing: Case report and review of current practice. *Australian Dentistry Journal, 43* (6), 387–389.

Faravelli, C., Salvatori, S., Galassi, F., Aiazzi, L., Drei, C., & Cabras, P. (1997). Epidemiology of somatoform disorders: A community survey in Florence. *Social Psychiatry and Psychiatric Epidemiology, 32,* 24–29.

Fiala, T. G., Lee, W. P. A., & May, J. W. (1993). Augmentation mammoplasty: Results of a patient survey. *Annals of Plastic Surgery, 30,* 503–509.

Fried, R. G., & Cash, T. F. (1998). Cutaneous and psychosocial benefits of alpha-hydroxyl acid use. *Perceptual Motor Skills, 86,* 137–138.

Fryzek, J. P., Weiderpass, E., Signorello, L. B., Hakelius, L., Lipworth, L., Blot, W. J., . . . Nyren, O. (2000). Characteristics of women with cosmetic breast augmentation surgery compared with breast reduction surgery patients and women in the general population of Sweden. *Annals of Plastic Surgery, 45*(4), 349–356.

Gabriel, S. E., Woods, J. E., O'Fallon, W. M., Beard, C. M., Kurland, L. T., & Melton, L. J., 3rd. (1997). Complications leading to surgery after breast implantation. *New England Journal of Medicine, 336*(10), 677–682.

Giese, S. Y., Bulan, E. J., Commons, G. W., Spear, S. L., & Yanovski, J. A. (2001). Improvements in cardiovascular risk profile with large-volume liposuction: A pilot study. *Plastic and Reconstructive Surgery, 108*(2), 510–519.

Gifford, S. (1973). Cosmetic surgery and personality change: A review and some clinical observations. In R. M. Goldwyn (Ed.), *The unfavorable result in plastic surgery: Avoidance and treatment* (pp. 11–33). New York, NY: Little, Brown.

Gillespie, R. (1996). Women, the body and brand extension in medicine: Cosmetic surgery and the paradox of choice. *Women & Health, 24*, 69 85.

Goin, M. K., Burgoyne, R. W., Goin, J. M., & Staples, F. R. (1980). A prospective psychological study of 50 female face-lift patients. *Plastic and Reconstructive Surgery, 65*, 436–442.

Goin, M. K., & Rees, T. D. (1991). A prospective study of patients' psychological reactions to rhinoplasty. *Annals of Plastic Surgery, 27*, 210–215.

Greif, J., Hewitt, W., & Armstrong, M. L. (1999). Tattooing and body piercing: Body art practices among college students. *Clinical Nursing Research, 8*(4), 368–385.

Handel, N., Wellisch, D., Silverstein, M. J., Jensen, J. A., & Waisman, E. (1993). Knowledge, concern and satisfaction among augmentation mammaplasty patients. *Annals of Plastic Surgery, 30*, 13–22.

Henderson-King, D., & Henderson-King, E. (2005). Acceptance of cosmetic surgery: Scale development and validation. *Body Image, 2*, 137–149.

Hern, J., Rowe-Jones, J., & Hinton, A. (2003). Nasal deformity and interpersonal problems. *Clinical Otolaryngology, 28*, 121–124.

Hill, G., & Silver, A. G. (1950). Psychodynamic and esthetic motivations for plastic surgery. *Psychosomatic Medicine, 12*, 345–352.

Jacobsen, P. H., Holmich, L. R., McLaughlin, J. K., Johansen, C., Olsen, J. H., Kjoller, K., & Friis, S. (2004). Mortality and suicide among Danish women with cosmetic breast implants. *Archives of Internal Medicine, 164*, 2450–2455.

Javo, I. M., & Sorlie, T. (2010). Psychosocial characteristics of young Norwegian women interested in liposuction, breast augmentation, rhinoplasty, and abdominoplasty: A population-based study. *Plastic and Reconstructive Surgery, 125*, 1536–1543.

Joiner, T. E., Jr., (2003). Does breast augmentation confer risk of protection from suicide? *Aesthetic Surgery Journal, 23*, 370–375.

Kilmann, P. R., Sattler, J. I., & Taylor, J. (1987). The impact of augmentation mammaplasty: A follow-up study. *Plastic and Reconstructive Surgery, 80*, 374–378.

Kjøller, K., Hölmich, L. R., Fryzek, J. P., Jacobsen, P. H., Friis, S., McLaughlin, J. K., . . . Olsen, J. H. (2003). Characteristics of women with cosmetic breast implants compared with women with other types of cosmetic surgery and population-based controls in Denmark. *Annals of Plastic Surgery, 50*(1), 6–12.

Kjøller, K., Hölmich, L. R., Jacobsen, P. H., Friis, S., Fryzek, J., McLaughlin, J. K., . . . Olsen, J. H. (2002). Epidemiological investigation of local complications after cosmetic breast implant surgery in Denmark. *Annals of Plastic Surgery, 48*(3), 229–237.

Klein, S., Fontana, L., Young, V. L., Coggan, A. R., Kilo, C., Patterson, B. W., & Mohammed, B. S. (2004). Absence of an effect of liposuction on insulin action and risk factors for coronary heart disease. *New England Journal of Medicine, 350*, 2549–2557.

Koch, R. J., Newman, J. P., & Safer, D. L. (2003). Psychological predictors of patient satisfaction with laser skin resurfacing. *Archives of Facial Plastic Surgery, 5*, 445–446.

Koot, V. C., Peeters, P. H., Granath, F., Grobbee, D. E., & Nyren, O. (2003). Total and cause specific mortality among Swedish women with cosmetic breast implants: A prospective study. *British Medical Journal, 326*(7388), 527–528.

Linn, L., & Goldman, I. B. (1949). Psychiatric observations concerning rhinoplasty. *Psychosomatic Medicine, 11*, 307–315.

Lipworth, L., Nyren, O., Weimin, Y., Fryzek, J. P., Tarone, R. E., & McLaughlin, J. K. (2007). Excess mortality from suicide and other external causes of death among women with cosmetic breast implants. *Annals of Plastic Surgery, 59*(2), 124–125.

Litner, J. A., Rotenberg, B. W., Dennis, M., & Adamson, P. A. (2008). Impact of cosmetic facial surgery on satisfaction with appearance and quality of life. *Archives of Facial Plastic Surgery, 10*, 79–83.

Losee, J. E., Jiang, S., Long, D. E., Kreipe, R. E., Caldwell, E. H., & Serletti, J. M. (2004). Macromastia as an etiologic factor in bulimia nervosa: 10-year follow-up after treatment with reduction mammoplasty. *Annals of Plastic Surgery, 52,* 452–457.

Losee, J. E., Serletti, J. M., Kreipe, R. E., & Caldwell, E. H. (1997). Reduction mammaplasty in patients with bulimia nervosa. *Annals of Plastic Surgery, 39,* 443–446.

Markey, C. N., & Markey, P. M. (2010). A correlational and experimental examination of reality television viewing and interest in cosmetic surgery. *Body Image, 7,* 165–171.

Mayers, L. B., Judelson, D. A., Moriarty, B. W., & Rundell, K. W. (2002). Prevalence of body art (body piercing and tattooing) in university undergraduates and incidence of medical complications. *Mayo Clinic Proceedings, 77,* 29–34.

McIntosh, V. V., Britt, E., & Bulik, C. M. (1994). Cosmetic breast augmentation and eating disorders. *New Zealand Medical Journal, 107,* 151–152.

Moradi, B. (2010). Addressing gender and cultural diversity in body image: Objectification theory as a framework for integrating theories and grounding research. *Sex Roles, 63,* 138–148.

Moss, T. P., & Harris, D. L. (2009). Psychological change after aesthetic plastic surgery: A prospective controlled outcome study. *Psychology, Health, & Medicine, 14,* 567–572.

Murphy, D. K., Beckstrand, M., & Sarwer, D. B. (2009). A prospective, multi-center study of psychosocial outcomes following augmentation with Natrelle silicone-filled breast implants. *Annals of Plastic Surgery, 62*(2), 118–121.

Nolst Trenité, G. J. (2003). Considerations in ethnic rhinoplasty. *Facial Plastic Surgery, 19,* 239–246.

Ohlsen, L., Ponten, B., & Hambert, G. (1978). Augmentation mammaplasty: A surgical and psychiatric evaluation of the results. *Annals of Plastic Surgery, 2,* 42–52.

Otto, M. W., Wilhelm, S., Cohen, L. S., & Harlow, B. L. (2001). Prevalence of body dysmorphic disorder in a community sample of women. *American Journal of Psychiatry, 158,* 2061–2063.

Park, A. J., Chetty, U., & Watson, A. C. H. (1996). Patient satisfaction following insertion of silicone breast implants. *British Journal of Plastic Surgery, 49,* 515–518.

Pecorari, G., Gramaglia, C., Garzaro, M., Abbate-Daga, G., Cavallo, G. P., Giordano, C., & Fassino, S. (2010). Self-esteem and personality in subjects with and without body dysmorphic disorder traits undergoing cosmetic rhinoplasty:

Preliminary data. *Journal of Plastic, Reconstructive, and Aesthetic Surgery, 63,* 493–498.

Pecori, L., Cervetti, G. G. S., Marinari, G. M., Migliori, F., & Adami, G. F. (2007). Attitudes of morbidly obese patients to weight loss and body image following bariatric surgery and body contouring. *Obesity Surgery, 17,* 68–73.

Perovic, S., Radojicic, Z. I., Djordjevic, M. Lj., & Vukadinovic, V. V. (2003). Enlargement and sculpturing of a small and deformed glans. *Journal of Urology, 170,* 1686–1690.

Phillips, K. A. (2010). Pharmacotherapy for body dysmorphic disorder. *Psychiatric Annals, 40,* 325–332.

Phillips, K. A., Grant, J. E., Siniscalchi, J., & Albertini, R. S. (2001). Surgical and nonpsychiatric medical treatment of patients with body dysmorphic disorder. *Psychosomatics, 42,* 504–510.

Phillips, K. A., & Menard, W. (2006). Suicidality in body dysmorphic disorder: A prospective study. *American Journal of Psychiatry, 163,* 1280–1282.

Phillips, K. A., Menard, W., Fay, C., & Weisberg, R. (2005). Demographic characteristics, phenomenology, comorbidity, and family history in 200 individuals with body dysmorphic disorder. *Psychosomatics, 46,* 317–325.

Pukkala, E., Kulmala, I., Hovi, S. L., Hemminki, E., Keskimaki, I., Pakkanen, M., . . . McLaughlin, J. K. (2003). Causes of death among Finnish women with cosmetic breast implants, 1971–2001. *Annals of Plastic Surgery, 51,* 339–342.

Rankin, M., Borah, G. L., Perry, A. W., & Wey, P. D. (1998). Quality-of-life outcomes after cosmetic surgery. *Plastic and Reconstructive Surgery, 102*(6), 2139–2145.

Rhomberg, M., Pulzi, P., & Piza-Katzer, H. (2003). Single-stage abdominoplasty and mastopexy after weight loss following gastric banding. *Obesity Surgery, 13,* 418–423.

Rief, W., Buhlmann, U., Wilhelm, S., Borkenhagen, A., & Brähler, E. (2006). The prevalence of body dysmorphic disorder: A population-based survey. *Psychological Medicine, 36,* 877–885.

Rohrich, R. J., Broughton, G., Horton, B., Lipschitz, A., Kenkel, J. M., & Brown, S. A. (2004). The key to long-term success in liposuction: A guide for plastic surgeons and patients. *Plastic and Reconstructive Surgery, 114,* 1945–1952.

Samdal, F., Birkeland, K. I., Ose, L., & Amland, P. F. (1995). Effect of large-volume liposuction on sex hormones and glucose- and lipid metabolism in females. *Aesthetic Plastic Surgery, 19*(2), 131–135.

Sarwer, D. B. (2006). Psychological assessment of cosmetic surgery patients. In D. B. Sarwer, T. Pruzinsky, T. F. Cash, R. M. Goldwyn, J. A. Persing, & L. A. Whitaker (Eds.), *Psychological aspects of reconstructive and cosmetic plastic surgery: Clinical, empirical and ethical perspectives* (pp. 267–283). Philadelphia, PA: Lippincott, Williams & Wilkins.

Sarwer, D. B., Bartlett, S. P., Bucky, L. P., LaRossa, D., Low, D. W., Pertschuk, M. J., . . . Whitaker, L. A. (1998). Bigger is not always better: Body image dissatisfaction in breast reduction and breast augmentation patients. *Plastic and Reconstructive Surgery, 101*(7), 1956–1961; discussion 1962–1963.

Sarwer, D. B., Brown, G. K., & Evans, D. L. (2007). Cosmetic breast augmentation and suicide: A review of the literature. *American Journal of Psychiatry, 164,* 1006–1013.

Sarwer, D. B., Cash, T. F., Magee, L, Williams, E. F., Thompson, J. K., Roehrig, M., . . . Romanofski, M. (2005). Female college students and cosmetic surgery: An investigation of experiences, attitudes, and body image. *Plastic and Reconstructive Surgery, 115,* 931–938.

Sarwer, D. B., & Crerand, C. E. (2004). Body image and cosmetic medical treatments. *Body Image, 1,* 99–111.

Sarwer, D. B., Crerand, C. E., & Magee, L. (2011). Cosmetic surgery and changes in body image. In T. F. Cash & L. Smolack (Eds.), *Body image: A handbook of science, practice, and prevention* (2nd ed.). New York, NY: Guilford Press.

Sarwer, D. B., Grossbart, T. A., & Didie, E. R. (2002). Beauty and society. In M. Kaminer, J. Dover, & K. Arndt (Eds.), *Atlas of cosmetic surgery* (pp. 48–59). Philadelphia, PA: WB Saunders.

Sarwer, D. B., Infield, A. L., Baker, J. L., Casas, L. A., Glat, P. M., Gold, A. H., . . . Young, V. L. (2008). Two year results of a prospective, multi-site investigation of patient satisfaction and psychosocial status following cosmetic surgery. *Aesthetic Surgery Journal, 28,* 245–250.

Sarwer, D. B., LaRossa, D., Bartlett, S. P., Low, D. W., Bucky, L. P., & Whitaker, L. A. (2003). Body image concerns of breast augmentation patients. *Plastic and Reconstructive Surgery, 112,* 83–90.

Sarwer, D. B., & Magee, L. (2006). Physical appearance and society. In D. Sarwer & T. Pruzinsky (Eds.), *Psychological aspects of reconstructive and cosmetic plastic surgery: Clinical, empirical and ethical perspectives* (pp. 23–33). Philadelphia, PA: Lippincott, Williams, & Wilkins.

Sarwer, D. B., Magee, L., & Crerand, C. E. (2004). Cosmetic surgery and cosmetic medical treatments. In J. Thompson (Ed.), *Handbook of eating disorders and obesity* (pp. 718–737). Hoboken, NJ: Wiley.

Sarwer, D. B., Thompson, J. K., Mitchell, J. E., & Rubin, J. P. (2008). Psychological considerations of the bariatric surgery patient undergoing body contouring surgery. *Plastic and Reconstructive Surgery, 121,* 423e–434e.

Sarwer, D. B., Wadden, T. A., Pertschuk, M. J., & Whitaker, L. A. (1998a). The psychology of cosmetic surgery: A review and reconceptualization. *Clinical Psychology Review, 18,* 1–22.

Sarwer, D. B., Wadden, T. A., Pertschuk, M. J., & Whitaker, L. A. (1998b). Body image dissatisfaction and body dysmorphic disorder in 100 cosmetic surgery patients. *Plastic and Reconstructive Surgery, 101*(6), 1644–1649.

Sarwer, D. B., Wadden, T. A., & Whitaker, L. A. (2002). An investigation of changes in body image following cosmetic surgery. *Plastic and Reconstructive Surgery, 109,* 363–369.

Sarwer, D. B., Whitaker, L. A., Wadden, T. A., & Pertschuk, M. J. (1997). Body image dissatisfaction in women seeking rhytidectomy or blepharoplasty. *Aesthetic Surgery Journal, 17,* 230–234.

Schlebusch, L. (1989). Negative bodily experience and prevalence of depression in patients who request augmentation mammaplasty. *South African Medical Journal, 75,* 323–326.

Schlebusch, L., & Levin, A. (1983). A psychological profile of women selected for augmentation mammaplasty. *South African Medical Journal, 64,* 481–483.

Schlebusch, L., & Marht, I. (1993). Long-term psychological sequelae of augmentation mammaplasty. *South African Medical Journal, 83,* 267–271.

Shipley, R. H., O'Donnell, J. M., & Bader, K. F. (1977). Personality characteristics of women seeking breast augmentation. *Plastic and Reconstructive Surgery, 60,* 369–376.

Sihm, F., Jagd, M., & Pers, M. (1978). Psychological assessment before and after augmentation mammaplasty. *Scandanavian Journal of Plastic Surgery*, *12*, 295–298.

Slupchynskyj, O., & Gieniusz, M. (2008). Rhinoplasty for African American patients: A retrospective review of 75 cases. *Archives of Facial Plastic Surgery*, *10*, 232–236.

Sommer, B., Zschocke, I., Bergfeld, D., Sattler, G., & Augustin, M. (2003). Satisfaction of patients after treatment with botulinum toxin for dynamic facial lines. *Dermatological Surgery*, *29*, 456–460.

Sperry, S., Thompson, J. K., Sarwer, D. B., & Cash, T. F. (2009). Cosmetic surgery reality TV viewership: Relations with cosmetic surgery attitudes, body image, and disordered eating. *Annals of Plastic Surgery*, *62*, 7–11.

Swami, V., Arteche, A., Chamorro-Premuzic, T., Furnham, A., Stieger, S., Haubner, T., & Voracek, M. (2008). Looking good: Factors affecting the likelihood of having cosmetic surgery. *European Journal of Plastic Surgery*, *30*, 211–218.

Toriumi, D. M., & Pero, C. D. (2010). Asian rhinoplasty. *Clinics in Plastic Surgery*, *37*, 335–352.

Tweeten, S. S., & Rickman, L. S. (1998). Infectious complications of body piercing. *Clinical Infectious Disease*, *26*, 735–740.

Veale, D. (2010). Cognitive behavioral therapy for body dysmorphic disorder. *Psychiatric Annals*, *40*, 333–340.

Veale, D., De Haro, L., & Lambrou, C. (2003). Cosmetic rhinoplasty in body dysmorphic disorder. *British Journal of Plastic Surgery*, *56*, 546–551.

Villeneuve, P. J., Holowaty, E. J., Brisson, J., Xie, L., Ugnat, A. M., Latulippe, L., & Mao, Y. (2006). Mortality among Canadian women with cosmetic breast implants. *American Journal of Epidemiology*, *164*, 334.

Vulink, N. C., Sigurdsson, V., Kon, M., Bruijnzeel-Koomen, C. A., Westenberg, H. G., & Denys, D. (2006). Body dysmorphic disorder in 3–8% of patients in outpatient dermatology and plastic surgery clinics. *Nederlands Tijdschrift voor Geneeskunde*, *150*, 97–100.

Webb, W. L., Slaughter, R., Meyer, E., & Edgerton, M. (1965). Mechanisms of psychosocial adjustment in patients seeking "face-lift" operation. *Psychosomatic Medicine*, *27*, 183–192.

Wells, K. E., Cruse, C. W., Baker, J. L., Jr., Daniels, S. M., Stern, R. A., Newman, C., . . . Albers, S. E. (1994). The health status of women following cosmetic surgery. *Plastic and Reconstructive Surgery*, *93*, 907–912.

Willard, S. G., McDermott, B. E., & Woodhouse, L. M. (1996). Lipoplasty in the bulimic patient. *Plastic and Reconstructive Surgery*, *98*, 276–278.

Wright, J. (1995). Modifying the body: Piercing and tattoos. *Nursing Standard*, *10*(11), 27–30.

Yates, A., Shisslak, C. M., Allender, J. R., & Wolman, W. (1988). Plastic surgery and the bulimic patient. *International Journal of Eating Disorders*, *7*, 557–560.

Young, V. L., Nemecek, J. R., & Nemecek, D. A. (1994). The efficacy of breast augmentation: Breast size increase, patient satisfaction, and psychological effects. *Plastic and Reconstructive Surgery*, *94*, 958–969.

Zojajii, R., Javanbakht, M., Ghanadan, A., Hosien, H., & Sadeghi, H. (2007). High prevalence of personality abnormalities in patients seeking rhinoplasty. *Otolaryngology-Head and Neck Surgery*, *137*, 83–87.

CHAPTER

10

Women's Sleep Throughout the Lifespan

JACQUELINE D. KLOSS AND CHRISTINA O. NASH

INTRODUCTION

The role of sleep in women's health and quality of life has garnered significant research and clinical attention over the past 10 to 15 years (Dzaja et al., 2005; Kravitz et al., 2008; Kryger, 2004; Lee & Kryger, 2008; National Sleep Foundation [NSF], 2007; Wolfson, 2001). Once considered a confound to sleep research, hormonal fluctuations of the menstrual cycle, pregnancy, and menopause are now of primary scientific inquiry. Gender disparities in sleep research further direct us toward the physiological, psychological, and sociocultural factors that contribute to sleep disturbance among women. It is well recognized that sleep is essential for health and well-being, and the consequences of acute and chronic sleep deprivation can be severe (see Bonnet, 2005; Dinges, Rogers, Baynard, 2005, for review), ranging from impaired daytime functioning to compromised physical and emotional health. Given that sleep disturbance among women is almost twice that of men (Soares, 2005; Zhang & Wing, 2006), a more comprehensive understanding of women's sleep is warranted.

Findings from the Sleep in America Poll (NSF, 2007; $n = 1,003$, American women ages 18–64) indicated that nearly half of the sample reported having sleep problems every night, and approximately 60% of women endorsed the item "I had a good night's sleep" only a few nights per week or less. Women's ratings of daytime sleepiness were correlated with high stress, less time with friends and family, work tardiness, complaints of "too tired for sex," and drowsy driving. Poor sleep also correlated with negative mood states, such as anxiety, worry, and sadness. Health-enhancing behaviors, such as sexual activity, nutrition, and exercise, were also compromised. All too often, women sacrifice sleep because of social, occupational, familial, and/or domestic demands, at the expense of such daytime sequelae; some may also find themselves, by choice or necessity, engaging in shift work, which may lead to serious health repercussions or vulnerability to disease (Shechter, James, & Boivin, 2008). Women are also predisposed to certain sleep disorders, including insomnia, restless legs syndrome (RLS), and obstructive sleep apnea (OSA), at various periods of their lives. Likewise, health conditions such as medical or psychiatric comorbidities can place women at greater risk for sleep disturbance.

After providing a cursory primer on sleep, women's sleep throughout the lifespan is explored, to include sleep variation during menstruation, pregnancy, peri- and post-menopause, and aging. Where available, literature is presented on sociocultural factors, such as race/ethnicity and socioeconomic status (SES), although these topics have only recently gained attention in the area of sleep. Considering that the literature on sleep disorders is vast, primary insomnia and OSA were selected to illustrate their pertinence to women's health. Lastly, we include empirically based strategies that can be useful in ameliorating the symptoms that contribute to or stem from sleep complaints.

Sleep Primer

Homeostatic drive (the propensity to sleep contingent on the duration of wakefulness) and circadian rhythm (our roughly 24-hour biological clock) regulate sleep and wakefulness (see Carskadon & Dement, 2005, for review). These processes provide a backdrop by which reproductive hormones, mood, beliefs, cognition, and sociocultural influences interact to yield sleep. Technologies such as polysomnography (PSG) and actigraphy (a motion sensor worn as a wristwatch that measures gross motor movements and approximates sleep and wake states) have made it possible to measure sleep objectively, whereas questionnaires or daily sleep diaries of sleep/wakefulness patterns have enabled the subjective measurement of women's sleep quantity, continuity, or quality. Sleep architecture is characterized by both non–rapid eye movement (NREM) and rapid eye movement (REM) sleep, which alternate throughout the night, with the average sleep cycle lasting between 90 and 110 minutes. Stage 1 sleep initiates the transition from wakefulness to sleepiness and is followed by Stage 2 sleep (marked by sleep spindles on electroencephalogram [EEG]) and slow–wave sleep (SWS) or deep sleep. Approximately 80 minutes from sleep initiation, REM sleep begins (composing 20% to 25% of sleep). Notably, as the night progresses, periods of REM

increase while SWS decreases. The average sleep need for adults is about eight hours per night (Van Dongen, Maislin, Mullington, & Dinges, 2003).

SLEEP AND THE MENSTRUAL CYCLE

The hormonal fluctuations of the menstrual cycle lead investigators to compare sleep during the follicular (pre-ovulatory) phase (FP) and the luteal (post-ovulatory) phase (LP) and to examine sleep in relation to estrogen, which peaks right before ovulation, and progesterone, which dominates after ovulation. The study of sleep throughout the menstrual cycle warrants attention with regard to: (a) variability in intra- and inter-individual timing of ovulation, peak levels of reproductive hormones, anovulation, cycle length, and hormonal intervals; (b) the interactive influences of mood, dysmenorrhea, pain, or other medical conditions; (c) expense of PSG, EEG studies; (d) maintaining constant environments; (e) impracticalities of enrolling women for long durations; and (f) subsequent small sample sizes (Manber & Armitage, 1999). Thus, data are limited and should be interpreted with caution.

Subjective and Objective Sleep Changes

According to the 2007 Sleep in America Poll, 33% of women reported sleep disruption coinciding with their menstrual cycle. The late LP (i.e., the 6 days leading up to menstruation) is marked by sleep complaints independent of other premenstrual symptoms. Manber & Bootzin (1997) found that among a sample of 32 healthy women, sleep-wake diaries recorded over two menstrual cycles revealed a self-reported increase in sleep-onset latency (SOL) and decrease in sleep efficiency (SE) and sleep quality in the LP, compared to the mid–FP, independent of the severity of associated premenstrual complaints. In a similar study of 26 young, healthy women over the course of one menstrual cycle, sleep quality ratings were diminished in the 3 premenstrual and first 4 days of menstruation, but SOL, sleep continuity, sleep maintenance, and sleep duration did not vary across the menstrual cycle (Baker & Driver, 2004). Despite subjective complaints of sleep disturbance, sleep architecture among asymptomatic women (women without significant premenstrual symptoms) remains fairly stable during hormonal fluctuations. Although a complete review of the nuances of sleep architecture is beyond the scope of this chapter, recent reviews indicate that decreases in REM and increased Stage 2 sleep in the LP (Driver, Werth, Dijk, & Borbely, 2008; Shechter & Boivin, 2010) have been consistently documented. SWS does not typically vary in response to menstrual cycle changes (Driver, Dijk, Werth, Biedermann, & Borbely, 1996), signifying a resilient sleep homeostat.

Premenstrual Syndrome (PMS) or Premenstrual Dysphoric Disorder (PMDD), Dysmenorrhea, Sleepiness, and Sleep

PMS and PMDD Sleep disruption—characterized by hypersomnia, insomnia, fatigue, sleep disruption, frequent arousals, and disturbing dreams—is considered a defining symptom of PMS and PMDD (Mauri, 1990). The degree to which women with severe premenstrual symptoms experience more sleep disturbance compared to their asymptomatic counterparts is questionable, and the mechanism that contributes to

premenstrual sleep disturbance has yet to be clearly defined. Similar to asymptomatic controls, increased Stage 2 (spindle activity) and reductions in REM are observed, and some differences in SWS are noted during the LP (Lamarche, Driver, Wiebe, Crawford, & DeKonnick, 2007), but robust differences in sleep architecture between PMS/PMDD sufferers have not been consistently documented. Some studies show no change in sleep-wake cycles or sleep architecture among women with premenstrual symptoms compared to controls (Chuong, Kim, Taskin, & Karacan, 1997; Parry et al., 1999). Lee, Shaver, Giblin, and Woods (1990) found that in a sample of young, healthy women, women who endorsed premenstrual symptoms marked by negative affect evidenced significantly less SWS across both the FP and LP, compared to asymptomatic individuals. Parry, Mendelson, Duncan, Sack, and Wehr (1989) found decreased REM and increased Stage 2 across the cycle among PMS sufferers compared to healthy controls.

More recently, Baker and Driver (2007) compared women with severe PMS symptoms and found that they perceived their sleep as more disturbed than asymptomatic women, although these differences were unrelated to menstrual phase. Baker, Lamarche, Iacovides, and Colrain (2008) characterized the sleep of individuals with PMS/PMDD as trait-like, with marginal differences compared to controls across the menstrual cycle. They also suggested that women with severe PMS may have a greater sensitivity to these subtle changes or exhibit a negative reporting bias. For example, women who suffered from menstrual pain or discomfort were more likely to evidence sleep disruption and report sleepiness, compared to asymptomatic women (Baker, Driver, Rogers, Paiker, & Mitchell 1999), and EEG patterns of symptomatic women differed in a trait-like fashion compared to asymptomatic controls (Baker, Kahan, Trinder, & Colrain, 2007). Limited sample sizes, limited numbers of studies, and variation in measurement of symptom severity render conclusions about the nature of PMDD sleep disturbance tentative. Moreover, Baker and colleagues (2008) point to factors beyond sleep architecture that may account for symptom complaints, such as circadian processes in PMS/PMDD.

Circadian and Hormonal Influences

Both melatonin and core body temperature (cBT) may contribute to interactive effects between circadian and menstrual processes. Progesterone is associated with a rise of cBT but a decrease in temperature rhythm amplitude (see Baker & Driver, 2007; Driver et al., 2008 for review). Recently, Shechter, Varin, and Boivin (2010) showed that REM was sensitive to the changes of the menstrual cycle coinciding with rising progesterone and cBT changes. Among asymptomatic women, data on melatonin and the menstrual cycle have been equivocal (Shechter & Boivin, 2010), although several well-controlled studies suggest that melatonin appears unaltered (Berga & Yen, 1990; Shechter et al., 2010; Shibui et al., 2000; Wright & Badia, 1999). However, women with PMDD may have underlying circadian rhythm dysregulations (see Baker et al., 2008; Shechter & Boivin, 2010 for review) compared to controls.

Interestingly, both decreased melatonin secretion and altered circadian rhythms are also characteristic of sleep patterns among individuals with major depression (Germain & Kupfer, 2008; Srinivasan et al., 2006). An increased nocturnal cBT may account for premenstrual symptom reports (Parry, LeVeau, et al., 1997; Severino et al., 1991),

as well as a trend for a phase-advanced temperature rhythm over the entire menstrual cycle (Parry et al., 1989). Hahn, Wong, and Reid (1998) also observed thermal dysregulation among reproductive women, particularly among women with more severe ratings of PMS, who indicated chills and sweats in the late LP (compared to the FP).

Dysmenorrhea and Sleepiness   Women with dysmenorrhea (painful menstruation) reported significantly worse sleep quality, compared to women without primary dysmenorrhea (Baker et al., 1999) and during pain-free phases of their cycle (e.g., during the FP and earlier LP). PSG of dysmenorrheic women revealed reduced sleep efficiency, increased time awake, reduced Stage 1 sleep, and less REM compared to both controls and pain-free phases of their cycle.

Likewise, increased severity of PMS symptoms is associated with increased sleepiness ratings during the LP (Mauri, 1990; Manber & Bootzin, 1997). Perhaps women with greater severity of PMS may require more sleep, particularly during the LP (Manber & Bootzin, 1997). Lamarche et al. (2007) showed that women with severe premenstrual symptoms evidenced greater sleepiness and less alertness compared to their less-symptomatic counterparts in the late LP. Thus, sleepiness appears more marked among women with severe PMS symptoms, yet sleep architecture does not appear to account for sleepiness (Baker et al., 2007), warranting further study of the underlying link between sleepiness and menstrual changes.

Treatments to Alleviate Premenstrual Sleep Disturbance

Iacovides, Avidon, Bently, and Baker (2009) found not only relief, but also better sleep quality and efficiency, among women with dysmenorrhea who were administered non-steroidal anti-inflammatory drugs (NSAIDs) compared to a placebo. Napping (< 30 minutes) among women with and without pre-menstrual symptoms was beneficial in alleviating negative mood and sleepiness and increasing alertness and positive mood, as well as improving attention and cognitive processing (Lamarche, Driver, Forest, & DeKonnick, 2010). Women with pre-menstrual symptoms evidenced an even greater improvement in negative mood a half hour after napping compared to women with minimal or no symptoms, with no deleterious effects on the following night's sleep observed. Although antidepressants have been used as a gold standard to treat PMDD symptoms, several alternative, nonpharmacological treatments have been tried with some success. Evening bright light therapy has shown initial success in alleviating premenstrual symptoms (Lam et al., 1999). Similar to the use of sleep deprivation to treat depression, both partial and total nights of sleep deprivation have yielded encouraging results in improving mood among premenstrual syndrome sufferers (Parry et al., 1995; Parry & Wehr, 1987). Further study is needed to better understand the efficacy and practicality of these alternative treatments.

Oral Contraceptives (OCs) and Sleep

Women who take oral contraceptives, which suppress ovulation, have often been used as control subjects given their stable hormonal profile. However, the question arises about the degree to which the sleep of women is altered as a result of OC use. The sleep architecture of women taking OCs appears to differ from that of naturally ovulating women (see Armitage, Baker, &

Parry, 2005; Baker & Driver, 2007; Baker et al., 2001; and Burdick, Hoffman, Armitage, 2002, for review). Women who take OCs may also evidence decreased deep sleep, increases in Stage 2, and changes in REM relative to women with naturally occurring cycles (Baker, Mitchell, & Driver, 2001; Burdick, Hoffmann, & Armitage, 2002). OCs containing estrogen and progestin may raise cBT, resulting in thermodysregulation, and are hypothesized to impact melatonin levels, yet prior investigations have yielded conflicting findings (Delfs et al., 1993; Wright & Badia, 1999). Sleep quality and sleep efficiency do not appear different among women taking OCs (Baker, Mitchell, & Driver, 2001; Burdick, Hoffman, & Armitage, 2002).

SLEEP DURING PREGNANCY AND POSTPARTUM

Sleep During Pregnancy

Estimates ranging from 15% to 80% of women experience altered sleep during pregnancy (Hedman, Pohjasvaara, & Tolonen, 2002). Physical, hormonal, and behavioral changes can threaten sleep quality during pregnancy (Soares & Murray, 2006). As levels of placental hormones rise, sleep becomes more vulnerable to disruption and fragmentation. Estrogen, progesterone, and prolactin are essential to the early stages of implantation and gestation (Sahota, Jain, & Dhand, 2003). In the early stages of pregnancy, progesterone has a sedative effect on women, and thus, a woman may experience fatigue and sleepiness as some of the first signs of pregnancy. During the first trimester, nausea, backaches, vomiting, and increased frequency to urinate are also associated with sleep disruption (Lee, 1998). During the second and third trimesters, sleep continuity and quality are expected to decline (Lee, Zaffke, & McEnany, 2000; Signal, Gander, & Sangalli, 2007), with 60% to 97% of women reporting disrupted sleep patterns (Mindell & Jacobson, 2000). Fatigue, shortness of breath, discomfort from increasing fetal size, and leg cramps increase and likely contribute to more frequent nighttime awakenings (Soares & Murray, 2006).

The combination of increased fetus size, high levels of progesterone during the third trimester, and supine positioning at nighttime can also lead to increased complaints of breathing difficulty, including shortness of breath and snoring (Mindell & Jacobson, 2000). The prevalence of OSA among pregnant women is about 20% (Pien, Fife, & Pack, 2005), with obesity before pregnancy and additional weight gain during pregnancy increasing the risk for OSA. Although snoring is often overlooked during the third trimester, severe OSA may be related to a significant risk for fetal complications (Sahin et al., 2008), including increased fetal heart rate, gestational hypertension, smaller-sized infants relative to gestation time, preeclampsia (Okun, Roberts, Marsland, & Hall, 2009), gestational diabetes (Qui, Enquobahrie, Fredrick, Abetew, & Williams, 2010), and infants with lower Apgar scores and birth weights.

Pregnant women are also at increased risk for leg cramps and RLS, particularly during the third trimester. Leg cramps, classified as experiencing painful muscle contractions of the foot and/or calf area (American Sleep Disorders Association, 2006), affect up to 30% of pregnant women (Hensley, 2009). Women with RLS experience an urge to move the legs that worsens in the evening, throughout the night, or while at rest (Dzaja,

Wehrie, Lancel, & Pollmacher, 2009). As many as 15% to 25% of women experience symptoms of RLS during the third trimester. Although women in general have higher reports of RLS relative to men, pregnant women experience RLS at two to three times the prevalence of the general population, which ranges from 5.5% to 10.6% (Allen et al., 2005). Lower levels of iron, folate, or ferritin and hemoglobin before pregnancy are hypothesized to contribute to increased incidence of RLS during pregnancy, and more recent evidence has suggested that estrogen may also trigger RLS symptoms (Dzaja et al., 2009). Although RLS is often a reversible syndrome during pregnancy (Wolfson & Lee, 2005) and often rescinds following delivery (Lee, Zaffke, & Baratte-Beebe, 2001), nearly 95% of RLS sufferers also experience difficulties falling asleep, fragmented sleep, and daytime sleepiness (Berger, Luedemann, Trenkwalder, John, & Kessler, 2004).

Disturbed sleep and sleep loss during the third trimester may also be linked to labor difficulties. Okun and colleagues (2009) also hypothesized that difficulties sleeping during pregnancy may be linked to preterm labor; however, this has yet to gain further empirical support. Lee and Gay (2004) found that among a sample of 131 women, those sleeping more than 6 hours had shorter labors and were less likely to give birth via cesarean section, relative to women who were sleeping less than 6 hours on average; women who slept less than 6 hours per night experienced 12-hour or longer labors and were 4.5 times more likely to require a cesarean section for delivery, relative to women sleeping more than 6 hours.

Sleep and Postpartum

Sleep problems prior to pregnancy have been associated with poor sleep quality postpartum

(Dorheim, Bondevik, Eberhard-Gran, & Bjorvatn, 2009). Empirical evidence has also linked poor sleep quality during pregnancy to an increase in depressive symptoms later in pregnancy and during the postpartum period (Skouteris, Germano, Wertheim, Paxton, & Milgrom, 2008; Wolfson, Crowley, Answer, & Bassett, 2003). Hormonal fluctuations postpartum may also explain the link between sleep and mood postpartum. Ross, Murray, and Steiner (2005) theorized that when estrogen and progesterone levels drop significantly after giving birth, a state of hyperarousal may ensue, thereby increasing insomnia and initiating a vicious cycle between disrupted sleep and mood. During the postpartum period, mothers experience poorer sleep efficiency (SE; total time asleep relative to total time in bed), less total sleep time (TST), and less REM, a key component of restorative sleep (Posmontier, 2008) and an important regulator of mood. Because the same neurotransmitters that mediate sleep quality also mediate mood, poor sleep quality may contribute to psychiatric symptomatology during the postpartum period (Ross, Murray & Steiner, 2005). However, several researchers have proposed that certain maternal behaviors may help moderate mood disturbances and be more conducive to improved sleep quality postpartum, including breastfeeding, co-sleeping, psychoeducational interventions (Stremler et al., 2006), and behavioral recommendations, such as initiating bedtime routines (Mindell, Telofski, Wiegand, & Kurtz, 2009).

Influence of Infant/Childcare on Sleep-Wake Patterns

Infant care, especially during the first month postpartum, can lead to frequent nighttime awakenings (Lee et al., 2000), especially for novice mothers (Lee, 2006). Up to 35% of parents report difficulty settling their infants and coping with nighttime awakenings (Johnson, 1991; Ramchandani, Wiggs, Webb, & Stores, 2000), thus leading to random sleep-wake cycles when sharing in newborn care (Gay, Lee, & Lee, 2004). Physical changes, caring for other children, returning to work, and social demands may also contribute to sleep deprivation. Nighttime awakenings and, in many cases, sleep deprivation and daytime fatigue may precipitate insomnia symptoms (Bayer, Hiscock, Hampton, & Wake, 2007; Ross et al., 2005). These symptoms may also impact mood and are hypothesized to increase vulnerability to postpartum depression (Munk-Olsen, Laursen, Pederson, Mors, & Mortensen, 2006). Moline, Broch, and Zak (2004) suggested that women with a history of prior sleep disturbances are predisposed to having difficulties adjusting to the inconsistent sleep patterns resulting from newborn care.

Sleep and Breastfeeding

Data on breastfeeding and sleep quality are sparse, which may be the result of the intrusiveness of objective sleep measures (e.g., actigraphy) or the burden of daily sleep logging while juggling responsibilities of caring for a newborn (Hunter, Rychnovsky, & Yount, 2009). Of the studies conducted to date, lactating women experience more SWS and fewer arousals, but no significant differences emerged for duration of REM sleep or total sleep time (Blyton, Sullivan, & Edwards, 2002). Doan, Gardiner, Gay, and Lee (2007) found that women who breastfed throughout the night averaged 40 to 45 more minutes of sleep and reported fewer sleep disturbances relative to bottle-feeding mothers. In contrast, Montgomery-Downs, Clawges, and Santy (2010) found no differences on objective, subjective, daytime sleepiness or fatigue among mothers utilizing different feeding methods. Because of the many well-established benefits of breastfeeding, such as optimal health outcomes for the infant, the American Academy of Pediatrics (AAP) made a 2005 policy statement that reflects its position as a proponent of breastfeeding. Moreover, Montgomery-Downs and colleagues (2010) have suggested that pediatricians clarify to new parents that bottle-feeding has not been shown to improve maternal sleep, which is a common misconception.

Sleep and Bed-Sharing Families from diverse cultures have practiced bed-sharing or room-sharing between mothers and infants throughout history, but co-sleeping may be controversial as women weigh the value of breastfeeding and infant and mother bonding with the risk of Sudden Infant Death Syndrome (SIDS) (McKenna & McDade, 2005). In Western cultures, such as the United States, bed-sharing/room-sharing trends have doubled since 1993 (Willinger, Ko, Hoffman, Kessler, & Corwin, 2003), and it remains a common practice and societal norm among a majority of cultures worldwide (Owens, 2004). For example, the prevalence of children bed-sharing in China was up to 58.9% with 7-year-old children, and 73.5% of mothers in Korea agreed with bed-sharing for children ages 3 to 6 years old (Yang & Hahn, 2002).

In the United States, co-sleeping appears to be more prevalent among ethnically diverse families, families with lower SES, less parental education, and higher rates of familial stress (Lozoff, Wolf, & Davis, 1984). Proponents of co-sleeping believe that it promotes breastfeeding, maternal and infant bonding, and may reduce sleep disturbance among new mothers. However, opponents of bed-sharing argue that it may increase the risk for SIDS from smothering by heavy blankets. In a policy statement written by the American Academy of Pediatrics Task Force on Sudden Infant Death Syndrome (2005), pediatricians recommend that infants can sleep in the same room as their parents to increase bonding and breastfeeding, but should not co-sleep in the same bed before the age of 12 months.

Sleep Strategies for Expecting and New Mothers

Testing the efficacy of pharmacological and behavioral regimens, while protecting fetal and maternal safety during pregnancy, can be challenging. It is noteworthy that medications, including zolpidem and diphenhydramine, are considered Class B medications (i.e., possibly harmful to fetus), and evidence is mixed regarding their potential harmful side effects on the fetus (see Pien & Schwab, 2004, for review). Although research is limited, some obstetricians have suggested prolonging hospital stays after delivery and utilizing sedatives as strategies to promote protected sleep time and reduce sleep deprivation (Soares & Murray, 2006). Mindell (2005) recommends that new mothers nap when their babies nap and hire a babysitter or request a few hours of reprieve from a family member to obtain rest if they are feeling sleep deprived. With regard to psychotherapies, an 8-week mindfulness-based intervention was associated with significantly reduced reports of anxiety by women in their third trimester (Vieten & Astin, 2008). Additionally, in a pilot investigation, Beddoe, Lee, Weiss, Powell-Kennedy, and Yang (2010) showed that mindful yoga reduced nighttime awakenings and improved SEs among women during the second trimester compared to controls.

Dietary recommendations are the first line of prevention for RLS and include iron supplements and a diet rich in folic acid (e.g., leafy greens, folate-enriched products) to be initiated ideally before conception or at the earliest sign of pregnancy. With regard to sleep-disordered breathing, all pregnant women should be assessed for snoring and sleep apnea symptoms during prenatal checkups by asking questions about snoring—or if they "wake up gasping for air"—or experience morning headaches. Continuous positive airway pressure (CPAP) therapy for pregnant women with sleep apnea is safe (Roush & Bell, 2004) and also effective at controlling blood pressure among preeclamptic pregnant women (Edwards, Blyton, & Kiravainen, 2000).

SLEEP AND MENOPAUSE

It is important to place menopausal sleep disturbance in context. Insomnia is one of the foremost complaints of peri- and post-menopausal women (NIH, 2005; Ohayon, 2006; Owens & Matthews, 1998). However, the degree to which menopause per se causes sleep disruption is questionable. Subjective and objective indices of sleep disruption as a function of menopausal status are often discrepant. Widely held assumptions implicating hot flashes as causative in midlife sleep disruption are equivocal. Multiple factors may *coincide* with menopause (e.g., aging, distressed mood, physical compromise) and contribute to sleep disturbance, yet menopause per se may not *cause* such symptoms.

Bolge and colleagues (2010) found that sleep maintenance insomnia correlated with reduced health-related quality of life ratings, increased healthcare utilization, and decreased work productivity among

symptomatic menopausal women. Shaver (2010) further acknowledges that distinctions between causal versus overlapping symptoms be made to best predict the healthcare utilization of those with insomnia symptoms during menopause. Menopause may be best understood through a biopsychosocial lens that captures the interplay between the changing hormonal milieu, concomitant physiological changes (e.g., hot flashes and night sweats, nocturnal micturition), coexisting medical or health conditions, psychological factors such as mood, perception, and beliefs about menopause, as well as sociocultural influences.

Reproductive Hormones and Sleep

In a large, multiethnic, community-based, prospective study (SWAN; Study of Women's Health Across the Nation) of midlife women, Kravitz and colleagues (2008) found that, controlling for age, hormone replacement therapies, and other health and related psychosocial variables, subjective sleep difficulties were pronounced during perimenopause, specifically noting associations with menopausal status, hormone levels (E2 and FSH), and vasomotor symptoms. Prior data from the Wisconsin Sleep Cohort Study, including primarily Caucasian women (Young, Rabago, Zgierska, Austin, & Finn, 2003), in which age and body mass index (BMI) were controlled, showed that peri- and postmenopausal women reported less satisfaction with their sleep, but PSG did not substantiate these complaints; likewise, Shaver, Giblin, and Paulsen (1991) indicated no marked objective changes in sleep. Pien, Sammel, Freeman, Lin, and DeBlasis (2008) found that among a stratified sample of Caucasians and African Americans, inhibin B—a reproductive hormone that falls in the early menopausal transition—was an indicator of reported sleep disturbance; notably, sleep quality was not readily explained by menopausal status alone but in the context of other menopausal symptoms (depression, vasomotor symptoms).

Hot Flashes and Sleep Disturbance

Numerous studies of peri- and postmenopausal women have implicated hot flashes to account for menopausal sleep disturbance (Dennerstein, Dudley, Hopper, Guthrie, & Burger, 2000; Hollander et al., 2001; Kravitz et al., 2003; 2005; Owens & Matthews, 1998; Woodward & Freedman, 1994). Reports of hot flashes often coincide with reports of poor sleep quality and continuity, with approximately 44% of women who experience severe hot flashes meeting criteria for chronic insomnia (Ohayon, 2006). According to the NSF survey, approximately 20% of women attributed poor sleep to hot flashes on at least a few nights per week. Early work (Shaver, Giblin, Lentz, & Lee, 1988; Woodward & Freedman, 1994) demonstrated that hot flashes were associated with sleep alterations as measured by PSG, with a greater frequency of hot flashes seen earlier in the night (Woodward & Freedman, 1994). However, the widely held belief that hot flashes and changes in hormonal milieu *cause* disturbed sleep is not consistently substantiated by objective data (Freedman, 2005; Freedman & Roehrs, 2004; Moe, 2004; Regestein, 2006; Sharkey et al., 2003; Thurston, Blumenthal, Babyak, & Sherwood, 2006; Young et al., 2003). Methodological limitations, such as self-report and measurement error, make conclusions about hot flashes causing sleep disturbance tentative.

Likewise, PSG over a 1- to 3-night period may be insufficient to capture causative relationships. Perhaps sleep stage (REM vs. non-REM) may moderate the effect of hot flashes and awakenings (Freedman & Roehrs, 2006), and therefore more careful measurement and attention to stage may be indicated to determine to what extent hot flashes exert an adverse effect on sleep. Even asymptomatic women (who do not endorse having nocturnal flashes) objectively evidence hot flashes during the night (Freedman & Roehrs, 2004). In addition, hyperarousal and its link to thermoregulation may also be significant contributors to sleep disturbance in midlife women (see Minarik, 2009 for review). Thus, attention to cognitive and emotional arousal and perceived stress are also relevant in explaining sleep disturbance during the menopausal transition (Woods & Mitchell, 2010).

The Role of Cognitions Hunter and Mann (2010) offer a cognitive model for menopausal hot flashes and night sweats, and contend that the experience of hot flashes and night sweats are likely an interaction of physiological and psychological processes to include symptom perception (e.g., attention, negative affectivity, somatization), cognitive appraisals (beliefs and problem-rating), and behavioral responses (help-seeking). Likewise, dysfunctional beliefs and attitudes about sleep (DBAS) mediated the relationship between hot flashes and sleep quality among perimenopausal women (Kloss, Tweedy, & Gilrain, 2004). Similarly, "flashing" women may misattribute the cause of any poor sleep to hot flashes (Regestein, 2006), when it may be more accurately explained by events or behaviors other than hot flashes, such as alcohol or caffeine use. Interestingly, Krystal, Edinger, Wohlgemuth, and Marsh (1998) suggest that hot flashes serve as an initial trigger for insomnia, but then a "behaviorally conditioned insomnia" may develop as a result of these events, and persist after the hot flashes have resolved. Given the importance of cognitive factors, Hunter and colleagues (Hunter & Liao, 1996; Hunter, Coventry, Hamed, Fentiman, & Grunfeld, 2009) describe initial support for the efficacy of cognitive and behavioral approaches toward the management of hot flashes.

Circadian Changes During Menopause

As women age, cBT and melatonin advances by about 1 hour, and consolidation and homeostatic pressure for sleep decreases (Dijk, Duffy, Czeisler, 2000). Age-related changes in melatonin depletion (Mahlberg, Tilmann, Salewski, & Kunz, 2006) may further influence the timing of the circadian rhythm in post- compared to premenopausal women, as well as the onset of sleepiness/ offset of alertness (Walters, Hampton, Ferns, & Skene, 2005). Some have associated higher cBTs with poorer PSG ratings among postmenopausal women (Murphy & Campbell, 2007). Increases in cBT may also trigger hot flashes (Freedman, 2005; Freedman, Norton, Woodwar, & Cornelissen, 1995). A dysregulation in thermoregulation is hypothesized to play a role in sleep disruption among women as they age, perhaps requiring future study between thermoregulation, hot flashes, and sleep disruption (Joffee, Massler, & Sharkey, 2010).

Mood and Sleep

Depressed mood and psychological distress are significant predictors of sleep disturbance, in general, and their comorbidity may be pronounced among perimenopausal women (see Brown, Gallicchio, Flaws, & Tracy, 2009;

Kravitz et al., 2003; Parry et al., 2006). Subjective ratings of sleep quality appear to be related to depressed or anxious mood, negative mood, or high perceived stress among midlife women (Dennerstein et al., 2000; Kravitz et al., 2003; Kravitz et al., 2005; Pien et al., 2008). Some suggest that depression is thought to accompany the menopausal transition (Freeman, Sammel, Lin, & Nelson, 2006; Rajewska & Rybakowski, 2003; Steiner, Dunn, & Born, 2003) and can, therefore, subsequently account for increased symptoms of insomnia. Brown et al. (2009) suggest that sleep disturbance may even mediate the relationship between menopausal symptoms and depressed mood. Interestingly, Woods and Mitchell (2010) suggest that severity of nighttime and early-morning awakenings was linked with depressed mood.

Perceptions of poor sleep may also account for psychological distress among midlife women, even when objective sleep measures show marginal differences (Shaver et al., 1991; Shaver & Paulsen, 1993). Burleson, Todd, and Travarthan (2010) conducted a prospective study on self-reported vasomotor symptoms, mood, and sleep disturbance. First, sleep problems accounted for more of the variance in mood ratings, compared to vasomotor symptoms. Second, their data only partially supported the model that hot flashes/night sweats resulted in sleep disruption, which then accounted for next-day mood disturbances. They also noted that, even while controlling for sleep problems, vasomotor symptoms continued to predict mood troubles the next day. In efforts to understand the relationships between sleep, hot flashes, and mood, Regestein (2010) purports a "domino hypothesis"—weakening in circadian timing that coincides with age may result in both hot flashes and decreased sleep quality, and, contingent upon predisposition to negative affect, worsened depressed mood. Independent of the cause of these symptom clusters, the interplay between mood and sleep warrants attention during midlife. Furthermore, conditions such as sleep apnea, chronic pain, or other health conditions known to disrupt sleep (Ohayon, 2006), for example, nighttime voiding (Asplund & Aberg, 1996), that may become more prevalent in midlife may also account for insomnia that arises during the transition to menopause.

Cultural and Ethnic Factors

Hunter and Mann (2010) propose that culture and ethnicity may influence the experience of hot flashes/night sweats, which may have relevance for women's sleep perception. Gupta, Sturdee, and Hunter (2006) compared peri- and postmenopausal Asian women in the UK to Asian women in Delhi to Caucasian women in the UK. Although sleep problems did not differ by subgroup, *attribution* of sleep to menopause was greatest among the Caucasian women, followed by the Asian UK and Asian Delhi women, respectively. Lock (1994) also noted a striking difference in prevalence of hot flash and night sweat reporting among Japanese women compared to Western women. In Japan, night sweats were not even related to menopausal status. Moreover, reporting of sleep problems was significantly less, as was use of sleep medicines, compared to Canadian and American samples.

Likewise, in Hsu, Chen, Jou, An, and Tsa's (2009) study of Taiwanese perimenopausal women, very few attributed sleep problems to hot flashes. Thus, the menopausual symptom experience itself and/or the attribution of sleep problems to the symptom experience may differ by ethnicity or culture.

While ethnic/racial differences are notable, other factors that may co-vary with sociocultural factors, such as climate, lifestyle, diet, and attitudes about menopause and aging, may also serve as key moderators of the hot flash/night sweat experience, thereby differentially influencing sleep (Gupta et al., 2006; Nagata, Takasuta, Inaba, Kawkami, & Shimizu, 1998). Furthermore, education or beliefs about menopause, such as positively embracing or pathologizing menopause, may vary, thereby ultimately affecting symptom reporting.

Based on SWAN study data, several multiracial and ethnic differences among menopause symptom reports were identified (see Avis et al., 2001; Gold et al., 2000). Caucasian women had significantly more difficulty staying asleep, and Hispanics had the fewest problems with sleep continuity and early-morning awakenings (Kravitz et al., 2008). Avis and colleagues (2001) found that African American women endorsed the greatest amount of vasomotor symptoms, with the least amount of vasomotor symptom reporting among Chinese and Japanese women. With regard to sleep-related variables, Caucasians reported sleeping worse than all other groups (Gold et al., 2000). In addition, lower education and self-reported inability to afford basic items were related to overall symptom reporting.

Of note, difficulty sleeping was also correlated to employment status. Hollander and colleagues (2001) conducted a longitudinal study of African American and White women in their late reproductive age over a 2-year period; African Americans and those with less employment and less education were at greater risk for worsened sleep complaints. In contrast, in Pien and colleagues (2008), racial identity (African American and Caucasian) was not related to sleep quality.

Clearly, menopause and ensuing sleep disturbance is not a universal experience. In addition to exploring women's beliefs and attributions about menopause, other factors such as SES, education, and employment could serve as potential stressors or context to poor sleep in women.

Sleep Strategies for Menopausal Women

Pharmacological Management of sleep disturbance involves multiple approaches and careful assessment to target the most beneficial regimen for each individual presentation. Empirically-based options include hormone therapies (HTs), hypnotics, behavioral strategies to address sleep (see following section), mood disturbance, and/or hot flashes, or other pharmacotherapies, such as antidepressants, that could help mood and/or hot flashes. Because of the fluctuating hormonal milieu and associated hot flashes presumed to disrupt sleep, HTs have traditionally been used to alleviate menopausal symptoms, including sleep disturbance. As reviewed by Joffee, Massler, and Sharkey (2010), use of HTs (e.g., estrogen replacement) for sleep improvement has been most successful for women whose sleep is associated with hot flashes, but they caution that because of small sample sizes, and at times, use of populations without significant sleep or symptom complaints, the degree to which HT exerts a meaningful effect on sleep is still questionable.

Results from the Women's Health Initiative associating the use of HT with increased risk for cancer, stroke, heart disease, and vascular dementia (Writing Group for the Women's Health Initiative Investigators, 2002) initiated a tempering of this practice, generally leading to recommendations to use HT for only a brief period to relieve hot flashes. More recently, Tranah and colleagues (2010) investigated long-term use of HT on objective sleep measures of postmenopausal women and found that HT users experienced significantly shorter wake after sleep onset (WASO). Another study suggested that HT may also be associated with less-severe OSA among postmenopausal women (Bixler & Kales, 2001). However, more studies are needed to determine whether HT should be recommended for postmenopausal women, particularly because of heightened risk of vascular side effects and limited research on the long-term impact of those side effects (Tranah et al., 2010). Further study on the mechanisms and formulations of HT (estrogens/progestins used alone or in combination) that exert their effect on sleep are needed, with attention to both objective as well as subjective measures of sleep quality and hot flashes. It seems to be the consensus that HT is indicated when the benefits are believed to outweigh the risks, especially when improving women's quality of life.

With regard to pharmacological, but nonhormonal treatments, several agents have been tried with some success. Eszopiclone and zolpidem have shown to improve sleep onset and sleep maintenance difficulties (see Joffee, Massler, & Sharkey, 2010, for review), perhaps in part by enabling women to sleep through nocturnal hot flashes. Initial support for ramelteon was found in one trial to treat insomnia among peri- and postmenopausal women with insomnia (Dobkin et al., 2009), without evidence of tolerance or withdrawal. Other alternatives include antidepressants, namely selective serotonin reuptake inhibitors (SSRIs), in alleviating menopausal symptoms to improve sleep (Stearns, Beebe, Iyengar, & Dube, 2003). Likewise, Yurchescn, Guttuso, McDermott,

Holloway, and Perlis (2009) found gabapentin to improve sleep quality among postmenopausal women with hot flashes. Similarly, Nelson and colleagues' (2006) meta-analysis showed some support for SSRIs and serotonin–norepinephrine reuptake inhibitors (SNRIs), clonidine, and gabapentin to alleviate the frequency and severity of hot flashes, but not for red clover isoflavone or soy. Although the findings for the former (SSRIs, clonidine, and gabapentin) were not judged to be as potent as estrogen, they may provide an alternative for women when HT is contraindicated.

Over-the-Counter Remedies In general, melatonin shows promise in an aging population, particularly when circadian rhythm sleep conditions, such as shift work and delayed sleep phase syndrome, are involved (Arendt & Skene, 2005; Gooneratne, 2008), yet its effect on primary insomnia needs to be better researched and established. Melatonin may even have the potential to lessen depressed mood and improve thyroid function among peri- and postmenopausal women (Bellipanni, Bianchi, Pierpaoli, Bulian, & Ilyia, 2001). The usefulness of soy, black cohosh, and/or other herbal remedies require further investigation. Newton et al. (2006) did not find strong substantiation for black cohosh to alleviate menopausal symptoms, whereas others found that black cohosh and other foods that contain phytoestrogens (Kronenberg & Fugh-Berman, 2002) show the potential to alleviate menopausal symptoms, such as hot flashes. Further investigation, particularly with regard to the long-term effects of these regimens, as well as the effects on sleep, is warranted.

Behavioral Strategies can be applied to reduce menopausal-associated symptoms,

although no impact on sleep is ensured. Common recommendations for women to relieve hot flashes are based on reducing cBT and include wearing multiple layers or light layers to bed at night, keeping the ambient temperature cool, consuming cold drinks, and losing weight. Wijma, Melin, Nedstrand, and Hammar (1997) found that applied relaxation strategies may help reduce the number of hot flashes among postmenopausal women. Likewise, relaxation was also found to be helpful in reducing hot flash intensity and associated tension-anxiety and depression among a sample of midlife women with daily hot flashes (Irvin, Domar, Clark, Zuttermeister, & Friedman, 1996). Interestingly, relaxation strategies are among the empirically based treatments for insomnia (Morgenthaler et al., 2006). Investigations that study the concomitant effect on both daytime and nighttime hot flashes, anxiety, and sleep would be helpful. As discussed later, CBT-I is one of the most effective treatments for chronic insomnia (Morgenthaler et al., 2006). However, to our knowledge, the targeted use of CBT-I approaches specifically among symptomatic menopausal women has not been attempted.

SLEEP AND AGING

Nearly 50% of women over the age of 60 (without chronic health conditions) report difficulties sleeping (Foley et al., 1995; Schubert et al., 2002), and women are twice as likely as men to report sleep disturbances independent of mental health conditions (Brabbins et al., 1993). Hachul, Bittencourt, Soares, Tufik, and Baracat (2009) proposed that sleep complaints may be even *more* prevalent among postmenopausal women relative to women in early menopause. While chronic medical conditions and/or medication side effects are often implicated in the increased sleep complaints, several factors may predispose an aging woman to sleep disorders, including, but not limited to, physiological, psychological and social factors.

Sleep Architecture and Circadian Rhythms

Changes in sleep architecture and circadian rhythmicity may account for some of the sleep changes that manifest as women age. They may be more likely to experience frequent nighttime awakenings, early-morning awakenings, and to a lesser extent, increased sleep-onset latencies. Perhaps the most salient change to sleep architecture as individuals age is the reduction of SWS (Lee & DeJoseph, 1992), although this is less pronounced in women than men. Stage 1 sleep *increases* with age for both men and women, thus making sleep more fragmented, with increases in nighttime awakenings and difficulties falling back to sleep (Carskadon, Brown, & Dement, 1982). Aging women also experience longer latencies to REM relative to men, but research suggests that REM sleep is more protected in women (as shown by increases in REM periods; Rediehs, Reis, & Creason, 1990). Circadian rhythm disruptions, particularly 1-hour phase-advances (Campbell, Christian, Kripke, Erikson, & Clopton, 1989; Dijk, Duffy, Czeisler, 2000), are also common among aging women and may also contribute to decreased TST.

Circadian rhythms and homeostatic sleep pressure work together to produce drive for sleep and are vulnerable to changes in both endogenous and exogenous factors (Dzaja et al., 2005). Endogenous factors include disruptions in neural connections of the suprachiasmatic nucleus (SCN), aging of the retina (i.e., where light enters the eye), and hormone production of the pineal gland (i.e., manufacturer of melatonin; Skene & Swaab, 2003). Several investigators have also found that changes in estrogen and gonadotropins and cBT likely contribute to phase-advanced changes seen in aging women relative to age-matched men (Moe, 1999; Murphy & Campbell, 2007). Nocturnal levels of estradiol and gonadotropin luteinizing hormone (LH) were associated with changes in objective measures of sleep, and higher LH levels were correlated with changes in the variation of sleep-related body temperature and greater sleep disruptions (Murphy & Campbell, 2007). Nocturnal melatonin secretion has also been observed in adults aged 65 to 80, who had nearly 43% lower levels of melatonin compared with individuals ages 20 to 35. Similarly, decreases in melatonin were observed among postmenopausal women (ages 48 to 60) (Kos-Kudla et al., 2002), and such decreases have been linked to complaints of sleep disturbance (Tuunainen et al., 2002). Taking naps during the day may also lead to changes in the homeostatic drive for sleep, decreasing pressure for sleep, and lack of a daytime routine after retirement may also contribute to shifts in sleep patterns (Dzaja et al., 2005).

Sleep Disorders and Their Correlates Among Aging Women

Comorbid medical illnesses and life changes (e.g., retirement, weight gain, more sedentary behaviors) may increase the vulnerability of elderly women to sleep complaints or disorders, such as insomnia, PLMS, sleep apnea, and circadian rhythm disorders (ASPD). Sleep disturbances may also be related to increased risk of cardiovascular disease (i.e., particularly from sleep apnea), reduced immune functioning, psycho-pathology (i.e., depression), and a decline in cognitive functioning (Tworoger, Lee, Schernhammer, & Goldstein, 2006).

Apnea Postmenopausal women are also twice as likely (47% vs. 21%) to have sleep apnea, more likely to be obese, and to have larger neck circumferences (an anatomical feature of those with a higher risk for sleep apnea) compared to premenopausal women (Dancey et al., 2003). Even when control-ling for obesity and neck circumference, postmenopausal women still reported signif-icantly more sleep apnea relative to pre- and perimenopausal women (Dancey et al., 2003). Untreated sleep apnea is likely to result in compromised daytime functioning (e.g., excessive daytime sleepiness, cognitive and memory deficits; Décary, Rouleau, & Montplaisir, 2000), increased risk for motor vehicle accidents, heightened risk for other sleep disorders, such as insomnia (Teran-Santos, Jiminez-Gomez, & Cordero-Guevara, 1999), and cardiovascular disease (Yaggi et al., 2005). However, symptoms of sleep apnea among women are often over-looked in primary care, perhaps because snoring—a symptom suggestive of sleep apnea—is often less pronounced in women compared to men (Redline, Kump, Tishler, Browner, & Ferrette, 1994). Thus, a thor-ough assessment to include PSG for sleep apnea among postmenopausal women who complain of sleep disturbance and afore-mentioned daytime symptoms is critical (Young, Hutton, Finn, Badr, & Palta, 1996).

Insomnia Between 61% and 83% of women over the age of 60 indicate symptoms of insomnia, particularly difficulties maintain-ing sleep (Campos, Bittencourp, Haider, Tufik, & Baracat, 2005; Hachul et al.,

2009). Webb and Campbell (1980) found that older women took nearly 4 times longer to return to sleep once awakened compared with their younger counterparts; this is cor-roborated with subjective ratings of increased number and length of nighttime awakenings (Morin & Grambling, 1989) and lower SEs (Baker, Simpson, & Dawson 1997). Daytime activities are hypothesized to impact insomnia prevalence during later life, with high levels of physical activity considered a protective factor against chronic insomnia (Morgan, 2003). However, older adults are more likely to lack an overall daytime routine and to spend more time napping or resting in bed during the day. These behaviors can result in reduced homeostatic pressure for sleep and sleep frag-mentation at night (Bootzin, Engle-Fried-man, & Hazelwood, 1983). In contrast, Morin and Grambling (1989) found that time napping appeared to be equivalent among both good and poor sleepers, suggest-ing that napping may not necessarily contrib-ute to insomnia. Despite mixed evidence, daytime napping is typically not recom-mended to individuals if it is compromises the homeostatic drive for sleep at night.

Periodic Limb Movements During Sleep (PLMS)
In addition, aging women are also at risk for PLMS. Among a community sample of elderly individuals, 25% to 58% experienced PLMS that impacted their sleep (Gehrman et al., 2002). Likewise, Claman and colleagues (2006) found that 73% of women with PLMS experienced poorer sleep quality and less restorative (i.e., SWS) sleep. PLMS are associated with sleep frag-mentation, daytime sleepiness, and increased risk for insomnia. When PLMS events are greater than 15 events per hour and result in daytime sleepiness, a diagnosis of PLMD is warranted.

Advanced Sleep Phase Disorder (ASPD)

ASPD is characterized by involuntary sleep and wake times that are typically more than 3 hours earlier than what society considers to be the norm. Individuals with ASPD may also experience daytime sleepiness. Although ASPD is estimated to affect approximately 1% of middle-aged adults, no gender differences have emerged.

Treatments for Advanced Rhythms

The use of bright light therapy and melatonin has been hypothesized to shift phase-advanced circadian rhythms. Although this practice is indicated in the treatment of ASPD, the evidence is inconclusive (Sack et al., 2007). It is also of important note that melatonin is considered a homeopathic treatment and is not FDA-approved for the treatment of circadian rhythm disorders. Melatonin can typically be found at drugstores and health food stores, but it is often mixed with other additives, and it is recommended that individuals consult with their physician before taking melatonin.

Polypharmacy and Sleep Among Aging Women

Aging women are more likely to be on numerous medications to manage co-occurring conditions, such as chronic pain, cancer, diabetes, cardiovascular disease (Prinz, Vitiello, Raskind, & Thorpy, 1990), Alzheimer's disease and dementia (Brabbins et al., 1993), and even sleep disorders. Taken together, these conditions and the side effects of the medications used to treat them may impact sleep and daytime symptoms of sleepiness and fatigue (Monane, 1992). For example, some chemotherapies can produce fatigue, and some medications used to treat chronic pain can have a sedative effect. These symptoms may also contribute to sedentary lifestyles, excessive napping, or erratic sleep schedules, which can thereby affect sleep quality. The prevalence of the use of hypnotics is also heightened among the elderly, and this places elderly women (and men) at an increased risk for falls and hip fractures, as hypnotics create sedation and reduce overall vigilance.

SLEEP CHALLENGES

Shift Work

The adverse health and psychosocial consequences of shift work are quite extensive and range from daytime impairments in mood and cognitive performance to grave physical health consequences, such as increased risk for motor vehicle accidents, cardiovascular disease, and breast cancer (see Boivin, Trembly, & James, 2007; Shechter, James, & Boivin, 2008 for review). The SCN, the home of the circadian pacemaker, contains receptors for estrogen and progesterone (Kruijver & Swaab, 2002). The desynchrony between the circadian cycle and typical night/day (light and dark) rhythms places women who engage in shift work at significant risk for menstrual irregularities, reproduction difficulties, and breast cancer (see Baker & Driver, 2007; Shechter et al., 2008, for review). Examples of problems include menstrual dysregularity, dysmenorrhea, decreased alertness, and worsened mood. Shift work is also hypothesized to influence fertility, pregnancy, and fetal development (see Mahoney, 2010, for review). Shift work also appears to place women at an increased risk for breast cancer, perhaps because of the suppression of melatonin as a result of the nighttime exposure to artificial light (Stevens et al., 1992).

Several strategies to counter the adverse effects of shift work (see Boivin et al., 2007; Shechter et al., 2008) have met with some success: strategic napping and/or the use of stimulants (i.e., caffeine or modafinil), or the monitored use of hypnotics or melatonin to help induce sleepiness to promote better sleep, and appropriately timed phototherapy, bright light at work, wearing sunglasses on the commute home, promoting bedroom darkness while sleeping during the day.

Chronic Insomnia in Women

Chronic primary insomnia (CPI) is a sleep disorder manifested by difficulty initiating or maintaining sleep, or waking too early without being able to fall back to sleep, and/or nonrestorative sleep despite allotting time to sleep, and daytime impairment (APA, 2000; American Sleep Disorders Association, 2005). Althoughsome individuals may experience transient (less than 1 week) or short-term (1 to 3 weeks) insomnia, CPI is recognized when the following criteria are met: (1) sleep onset 31 minutes or longer; (b) 3 or more nights per week; and (c) duration of 6 months or more (Lichstein, Durrence, Taylor, Bush, & Riedel, 2003). Although not all studies consistently operationally define *insomnia* as described, it is well documented that insomnia complaints and diagnoses are more common among women than men. Characterized as an "overlooked epidemic" (Soares, 2005), risk ratios for insomnia among women range from 1.28 among young adults (ages 15 to 30) to 1.78 in older adults (65 and older) (Zhang & Wing, 2006). Li, Wing, Ho, and Fong (2002) found similar patterns in Hong Kong, where women had 1.6 times greater risk than men.

Hormonal and psychosocial factors likely interact to produce these striking gender differences. For example, "empty nest" experiences, care for elderly or childcare and dealing with children's sleep disruptions, separation or divorce, and workforce demands (Meltzer & Mindell, 2007; Polo-Kantola & Erkola, 2004; Shaver, 2002) may place women at greater risk for sleep disruption compared to men. A Finnish study (Urponen, Vuori, Hasan, & Partinen, 1988) showed that worries, interpersonal difficulties, and regrets were more predominant risk factors among women, whereas work-related stress dominated as a risk factor among men. Li et al.'s (2002) study of Chinese women showed that insomnia risk heightened among women who were divorced or widowed, were exposed to nighttime noise, and had more frequent alcohol use.

Results from the NSF study (NSF, 2007) indicate noise (39%) childcare (20%) voiding (17%), pets (17%), "nothing" or no apparent reason (16%), pain (8%), spouse/bed partner (7%), nightmares (6%), and stress (5%) among the reasons for sleep disturbance (though notably unclear whether this is due to insomnia or other reasons for sleep disturbance). Psychiatric comorbidities, such as anxiety and depression, may also contribute to women's increased insomnia prevalence. Individuals with lower SES were also more likely to suffer from insomnia while controlling for gender, age, and ethnicity (Gellis et al., 2005). The incidence of other medical conditions, such as chronic pain, nocturnal micturition, or RLS, particularly as women (and men) age, may likely produce insomnia complaints. To illustrate, a vicious cycle between fibromyalgia, which is more common in women than men, and insomnia can ensue with decreased sleep worsening pain reports among fibromyalgia patients (Lentz, Landis, Rothermel, & Shaver, 1999).

In addition to reduced quality of life, CPI is associated with significant daytime impairment (difficulty concentrating, worsened mood, decreased cognitive functioning, general malaise; Kloss, 2003). Moreover, elderly women (and men) with insomnia have significantly increased healthcare utilization (Sarsour, Kalsekar, Swindle, Foley, & Walsh, 2011). Both women and men with untreated CPI had a greater risk of an onset of major depression, anxiety disorder, and alcohol use disorder (Ford & Kamerow, 1989); women with CPI are more likely to develop depression (Mallon, Broman, & Hetta, 2000). Moderate to severe insomnia was associated with decreased productivity and increased healthcare utilization, compared to individuals without insomnia complaints (Sarsour et al., 2011).

Pharmacologic Treatment of Chronic Insomnia in Women Several both pharmacologic and cognitive-behavioral treatments are available for treating CPI. Benzodiazepines provide both sedative and soporific effects, but they carry risks of tolerance, dependence, changes in sleep architecture, insomnia rebound after stopping use, and cognitive impairment the following day (see Davidson, 2008, for review). Nonbenzodiazepines (zolpidem and zaleplon) are considered less "risky" than benzodiazepines, as they do not produce similar addictive potential, and they alleviate sleep-onset and maintenance insomnia symptoms. Of note, benzodiazepines are contraindicated during pregnancy and nursing. Moreover, use of any hypnotic is cautioned in elderly women (and men) because of cognitive and motor impairments (e.g., dizziness and risk of falls). Antidepressants may exert their effects on sleep by

relieving other symptoms associated with menopause (vasomotor symptoms, pain, mood swings) and may provide a viable alternative to HRT (Soares & Murray, 2006). However, research on the hypnotic effects of antidepressants is limited among nondepressed individuals (Davidson, 2008).

According to the meta-analyses conducted by Brzezinski et al. (2005) and other reviews (Pandi-Perumal et al., 2005, 2007), melatonin shows promise in improving sleep quality and reducing insomnia symptoms, particularly where melatonin production may be decreased, and perhaps among individuals with comorbid insomnia and medical/psychiatric complaints. With carefully timed administration, melatonin is likely to improve sleep quality, particularly where circadian disruption occurs, such as shift work or jet lag (Arendt & Skene, 2005; Burgess, Sharkey, & Eastman, 2002). However, Gooneratne (2008) found the efficacy on melatonin for elderly populations for primary insomnia is less definitive. Ramelteon, a melatonin analogue with FDA approval for insomnia, has gained support in alleviating insomnia symptoms, with potential side effects judged to be minimal (headache, dizziness, fatigue at higher doses, stomach upset, sleepiness; Davidson, 2008, Pandi-Perumal et al., 2007). Fortunately, the use of melatonin is generally well tolerated, and the adverse effects of its short-term use are judged to be minimal, but research on its safety and long-term use is warranted (Arendt & Skene; 2005; Gooneratne, 2008; Pandi-Perumal, 2007). Because of unknown safety risk in pregnancy and potential influence on reproductive function, melatonin should only be used if the benefits are thought to outweigh the risks; also, its influence on cardiovascular and immune effects requires further study (Gooneratne, 2008).

Herbal therapies, such as lavender, valerian, chamomile, black cohosh, and kava kava, have gained popularity among women to alleviate sleep troubles, although the limited data available are inconclusive on herbal remedies for insomnia (Davidson, 2008; Soares & Murray, 2008). Although women are likely to experiment and tolerate herbal products and report beneficial effects, caution is heeded in the absence of well-constructed methodology and potential or unknown risks of some agents. Gooneratne (2008) reviewed the efficacy of valerian and showed that using valerian for at least 2 weeks yielded subjective sleep improvement, yet objective records were inconclusive. He also recommends larger sample sizes to obtain sufficient power, standardized compounds of the agent, and methodological rigor in conducting studies on herbal therapies.

Cognitive-Behavioral Therapy for Insomnia

Empirically based, cognitive behavioral therapy for insomnia (CBT-I) is considered the treatment of choice for CPI (Morgenthaler et al., 2006; Morin, 2006; Morin, Culbert, & Schwartz, 1994; Murtagh & Greenwood, 1995). Treatment is comprised of regimens such as stimulus control, sleep restriction, relaxation, cognitive therapy (see Perlis, Aloia, & Kuhn's [2011] comprehensive handbook). In contrast to hypnotics, which generally work immediately in inducing their soporific effects, CBT-I requires patient education and training, and may take several sessions to derive benefit, yet the long-term efficacy far outweighs that of pharmacological approaches. It is noteworthy that sleep restriction is contra-indicated for patients with bipolar disorder or seizure disorders, and patients need to be cautioned about the side effects of sleep deprivation, such as drowsy driving

or operating heavy machinery. For individuals with comorbid insomnia, research is encouraging and suggests that CBT-I is efficacious even in the presence of a comorbid medical or psychiatric diagnosis. CBT-I has shown promising efficacy for comorbid insomnia, with chronic pain, cancer, and other psychiatric comorbidities (Smith, Huang, & Manber, 2005). Although we would expect that CBT-I would also yield encouraging results in women who are experiencing menstrual-related or menopausal-related insomnia, CBT-I studies have yet to be conducted targeting women with these symptoms.

Obstructive Sleep Apnea

Manifestation of OSA in Women According to the *International Classification of Sleep Disorders* (ICSD-2), OSA is a result of the cessation of airflow while sleeping marked by apnea and hypopnea events on PSG, often accompanied by snoring, daytime sleepiness, morning headaches, and/or nocturia. Individuals with OSA often feel like they have "run a marathon" after sleeping, attesting to complaints of daytime fatigue and sleepiness. Patients may also report that they sleep better sitting up and experience the most difficulty lying supine, which places pressure on their airway. OSA may increase the risk for insomnia and heighten the chance of hypertension, cardiac arrhythmias, heart attack, stroke (Shepard, 1992), cognitive deficits, or pregnancy complications.

Commonly believed to affect mostly men, OSA is often overlooked in women (Lee & Kryger, 2008), which can have potentially harmful consequences. Although men may have higher reported incidence of sleep apnea relative to women (4% vs. 2%), some authors have suggested that women may clinically present symptoms for OSA differently than men (e.g., Shepertycky, Banno, & Kryger, 2004). Alarmingly, Young, Evans, Finn, and Palta (1997) found that as many as 90% of women with moderate to severe apnea were undiagnosed and that women with sleep apnea may also have an increased 5-year mortality rate. According to Kapsimalis and Kryger's (2002) review, the reduction of female hormones during menopause may be a significant risk factor for the manifestation of OSA in older women. They also concluded that females with OSA were more likely to be diagnosed with depression and COPD, and PSG findings show that women were more likely to experience more hypopnea events rather than apnea events than men, thus making their apnea appear less severe. In addition to postmenopausal status, risk factors for sleep-disordered breathing also include elevated BMI (Godfrey, 2009), the FP (vs. the LP) (Driver et al., 2005), pregnancy, especially during the third trimester (Pien et al., 2005), and polycystic ovarian syndrome (Gopal, Duntley, Uhles, & Attarain, 2002). Older women with OSA show reduced cognitive functioning, including short-term memory difficulties, deficiencies in verbal recall tests, and decreased alertness, that have not been replicated in age-matched men with OSA (Décary et al., 2000).

OSA Treatments If an individual is experiencing mild OSA, the first line of treatment is typically weight loss and sleeping on one's side rather than supine or on the stomach. Weight loss of as little as 5 to 10 pounds has been shown to reduce OSA symptoms. The most efficacious treatment for obstructive sleep apnea is the use of a continuous positive airway pressure (CPAP) machine (El-Solh, Ayyar, Akinnusi, Relia, & Akinnusi,

2010). This machine works by placing air pressure on the airway to open the airway and make it easier for patients with OSA to breathe with less obstruction and resistance. However, certain individuals may experience difficulty adapting to their CPAP machines. Among these individuals are veterans with posttraumatic stress disorder (PTSD), who may be at a higher risk for sleep-disordered breathing in comparison with nonveterans (Maher, Rego, & Asnis, 2006). El-Solh and colleagues (2010) found that frequent nightmares were a strong predictor of nonadherence of CPAP use among veterans. To our knowledge, this has not specifically been examined among women, but with the growing number of female veterans, there is an impetus to give attention to this issue.

Several types of CPAP masks are available that may reduce their invasiveness. Psychotherapists can also conduct desensitization procedures to increase adherence. Overall, CPAP machines are only effective if they are worn consistently, every time an individual is going to sleep, even while napping. Some studies have also suggested that hormone replacement therapy (HRT) may be a protective factor for OSA in postmenopausal women (e.g., Bixler & Kales, 2001), as estrogen serves as a salient hormone in the regulation of fat distribution and progesterone helps stimulate respiratory function (Avidan, 2005). However, HRT may carry its own potential risks and is not suggested as a first line of treatment for OSA.

FUTURE DIRECTIONS

Advancing the knowledge of women's sleep in the context of hormonal changes, developmental periods, and sociocultural milieu has yielded intriguing questions and find-ings, but not without methodological chal-lenges. Investigations that use longitudinal methods, actigraphy or PSG, and other objective indices (e.g., hormones, circadian), coupled with psychological measures, could better qualify what underlies and maintains women's sleep disruption. Both the exami-nation of the independent contribution of circadian, hormonal, and psychosocial fac-tors *and* their interaction will help advance our understanding. For example, how do circadian, hormonal, and lifestyle factors affect cancer risk or reproductive capacity among shift workers? What is the role of cognition, attitudes, and beliefs about sleep during pregnancy or menopause, and how might ways of cognitive or behavioral cop-ing during these periods enable better sleep?

Likewise, sleep problems comorbid with medical and psychiatric conditions are more often the norm, yet they are often understudied. Identification of moderating (and protective) factors is also increasingly recognized. For example, cognitive, emo-tional, and behavioral factors are acknowl-edged in the extant literature on insomnia, yet specific perceptions, attributions, and expectancies among women during their menstrual cycle, menopause, and postpar-tum have yet to be identified. For example, to what degree does sleep mediate mood during the postpartum period?

Critical moderators, such as SES, employment status, and racial and ethnic identity, have been relatively unexplored, yet these variables may differentially predict sleep (Mezick et al., 2008). Questions should be asked, such as: What are the protective factors in postpartum sleep? How does one's culture or beliefs about the premenstrual syndrome or menopause influence sleep-related complaints? How does the stress of

un- or underemployment, juggling work and family, or being a new mom affect sleep? Moderating variables may also account for treatment receptivity and accessibility. Who has access to behavioral sleep medicine and how do we disseminate BSM to more diverse populations?

While a strong literature base for empir-ically validated treatments for behavioral sleep medicine (e.g., CBT-I) exists among general adult samples, these strategies still need to be applied and tested in the context of the menstrual cycle, pregnancy, or men-opause. Furthermore, translational research is needed to determine efficient ways to disseminate sleep knowledge across diverse populations of women. For example, how can we help underserved women obtain proper sleep knowledge, empirically based strategies, and access sleep specialists? How could telehealth (Ritterband et al., 2009) foster the dissemination of BSM? Likewise, primary care or obstetrics and gynecology can serve as front-line resources for initial screening of sleep problems and providing referrals, yet future research and models about incorporating sleep education into these settings would be needed. Future endeavors may also look at the utility of third-wave therapies, such as acceptance and commitment therapy and mindfulness train-ing (Ong & Sholtes, 2010).

REFERENCES

Allen, R. P., Walters, A. S., Montplaisir, J., Hening, W., Myers, A., Bell, T. J., & Ferini-Stranbi, L. F. (2005). Restless legs syndrome prevalence and impact: REST general population study. *Archives of Internal Medicine, 163,* 1286–1292.

American Academy of Pediatrics Task Force on Sud-den Infant Death Syndrome. (2005). The chang-ing concept of sudden infant death syndrome:

Diagnostic coding shifts, controversies regarding infant environment, and new variables to consider reducing risk. *Pediatrics, 116*(5), 1245–1255.

American Psychiatric Association. (2000). *Diagnostic and statistical manual of mental disorders* (4th ed., text rev.). Washington, DC: Author.

American Sleep Disorders Association. (2005). *The international classification of sleep disorders: Diagnostic and coding manual* (2nd ed., ICSD-2). Westchester, IL: American Academy of Sleep Medicine.

American Sleep Disorders Association, Diagnostic Classification Steering Committee. (2006). *The international classification of sleep disorders: Diagnostic and coding manual* (2nd ed., Pocket Version). Westchester, IL: American Academy of Sleep Medicine.

Arendt, J., & Skene, D. J. (2005). Melatonin as chronobiotic. *Sleep Medicine Reviews, 9,* 25–39.

Armitage, R., Baker, F. C., & Parry, B. L. (2005). The menstrual cycle and circadian rhythms. In M. H. Kryger, T. Roth, & W. C. Dement (Eds.), *Principles and practice of sleep medicine* (pp. 1266–1277). Philadelphia, PA: Elsevier Saunders.

Asplund, R., & Aberg, H. (1996). Nocturnal micturition, sleep and well-being in women ages 40–64 years. *Maturitas,* 73–81.

Avidan, A. Y. (2005). Sleep in the geriatric patient population. *Seminars in Neurology, 25*(1), 52–63. doi: 10.1055/s-2005-867076

Avis, N. E., Stellato, R., Crawford, S., Bromberger, J., Ganz, P., Cain, V., & Kagawa-Singer, M. (2001). Is there a menopausal syndrome? Menopausal status and symptoms across racial/ethnic groups. *Social Medicine, 52,* 345–356.

Baker, F. C., & Driver, H. S. (2004). Self-reported sleep across the menstrual cycle in young, healthy women. *Journal of Psychosomatic Research, 56,* 239–243.

Baker, F. C., & Driver, H. S. (2007). Circadian rhythms, sleep, and the menstrual cycle. *Sleep Medicine,* 613–622.

Baker, F. C., Driver, H. S., Rogers, G. G., Paiker, J., & Mitchell, D. (1999). High nocturnal body temperatures and disturbed sleep in women with primary dysmenorrhea. *American Journal of Physiology, 277*(60), E1013–E1021.

Baker, F. C., Kahan, T. L., Trinder, J., & Colrain, I. M. (2007). Sleep quality and the sleep electroencephalogram in women with severe premenstrual syndrome. *Sleep, 30*(10), 1283–1291.

Baker, F. C., Lamarche, L., Iacovides, S., & Colrain, I. M. (2008). Sleep and menstrual related disorders. *Sleep Medicine Clinics, 3,* 25–35.

Baker, F. C., Mitchell, D., & Driver, H. S. (2001). Oral contraceptives alter sleep and raise body temperature in young women. *Pflugers Archives of European Journal of Physiology, 442,* 729–737.

Baker, A., Simpson, S., & Dawson, D. (1997). Sleep disruption and mood changes associated with menopause. *Journal of Psychosomatic Research, 43,* 359–369.

Baker, F. C., Waner, J. I., Vieira, E. F., Taylor, S. R., Driver, H. S., & Mitchell, D. (2001). Sleep and 24 hour body temperatures: A comparison in young men, naturally cycling women, and women taking oral contraceptives. *Journal of Physiology, 530,* 565–574.

Bayer, J. K., Hiscock, H., Hampton, A. & Wake, M. (2007). Sleep problems in young infants and maternal mental and physical health. *Journal of Pediatric Child Health, 43,* 66–73.

Beddoe, A. E., Lee, K. A., Weiss, S. J., Powell-Kennedy, H., & Yang, P. C. (2010). Effects of mindful yoga on sleep in pregnant women: A pilot study. *Biological Research for Nursing, 11*(4), 363–370.

Bellipanni, D., Bianchi, P., Pierpaoli, W., Bulian, D., & Ilyia, E. (2001). Effects of melatonin in perimenopausal and menopausal women: A randomized and placebo controlled study. *Experimental Gerontology, 36,* 297–310.

Berga, S. L., & Yen, S. S. (1990). Circadian patterns of plasma melatonin concentrations during four phases of the human menstrual cycle. *Neuroendocrinology, 51*(5), 606–612.

Berger, K., Luedemann, J., Trenkwalder, C., John, U., & Kessler, C. (2004). Sex and the risk of restless legs syndrome in the general population. *Archives Internal Medicine, 164,* 196–202.

Bixler, E. O., & Kales, A. (2001). Prevalence of sleep-disordered breathing in women: Effects of gender. *American Journal of Respiration and Critical Care Medicine, 163,* 608–613.

Blyton, D. M., Sullivan, C. E., & Edwards, N. (2002). Lactation is associated with an increase in slow-wave sleep in women. *Journal of Sleep Research, 11,* 297–303.

Boivin, D. B., Tremblay, G. M., & James, F. O. (2007). Working on atypical schedules. *Sleep Medicine, 8,* 578–589.

Bolge, S. C., Balkrishnan, R., Kannan, H., Seal, B., & Drake, C. (2010). Burden associated with chronic sleep maintenance insomnia characterized by nighttime awakenings among women with menopausal symptoms. *Menopause, 17,* 80–86.

Bonnet, M. (2005). Acute sleep deprivation. In M. H. Kryger, T. Roth, & W. C. Dement (Eds.), *Principles and practice of sleep medicine* (4th ed., pp. 51–66). Philadelphia, PA: Elsevier Saunders.

Bootzin, R. R., Engle-Friedman, M., & Hazelwood, L. (1983). Insomnia. In P. M. Lewinsohn & L. Teri (Eds.), *Clinical Geropsychology: New Directions in Assessment and Treatment* (pp. 81–115). New York, NY: Pergamon Press.

Brabbins, C. J., Dewey, M. E., Copeland, J. R. M., Davidson, I. A., McWilliam, C., Saunders, P., . . . Sullivan, C. (1993). Insomnia in the elderly: Prevalence, gender differences and relationships with morbidity and mortality. *International Journal of Geriatric Psychiatry, 8*(6), 473–480.

Brown, J. P., Gallicchio, L., Flaws, J. A., & Tracy, J. K. (2009). Relations among menopausal symptoms, sleep disturbance and depressive symptoms in midlife. *Maturitas, 62*(2), 184–189.

Brzezinski, A., Vangel, M. G., Wurtman, R. J., Norrie, G., Zhdanova, I., Ben-Shushan, A., & Ford, I. (2005). Effects of exogenous melatonin on sleep: A meta-analysis. *Sleep Medicine Review, 9*(1), 41–50. doi: S1087079204000607 [pii]

Burdick, R. S., Hoffman, R., & Armitage, R. (2002). Short note: Oral contraceptives and sleep in depressed and healthy women. *Sleep, 25,* 347–349.

Burgess, H. J., Sharkey, K. M., & Eastman, C. I. (2002). Bright light, dark, and melatonin can promote circadian adaptation in night shift workers. *Sleep Medicine Review, 6,* 407–420.

Burleson, M. H., Todd, M., & Travarthan, W. R. (2010). Daily vasomotor symptoms, sleep problems, and mood: Using daily data to evaluate the domino hypothesis in mid-aged women. *Menopause, 17,* 87–95.

Campbell, S. S., Christian, G. J., Kripke, F. F., Erikson, P., & Clopton, P. (1989). Gender differences in the circadian temperature rhythms of healthy elderly subjects: relationships to sleep quality. *Journal of Sleep Research & Sleep Medicine, 12*(6), 529–536.

Campos, H. H., Bittencourt, L. R. A., Haidar, M. A., Tufik, S., & Baracat, E. C. (2005). Disturbios do sono no climaterio. *Femina, 33*(11), 815–820.

Carskadon, M. A., Brown, E. D., & Dement, W. C. (1982). Sleep fragmentation in the elderly: Relationship to daytime sleep tendency. *Neurobiology of Aging, 3*(4), 321–327.

Carskadon, M. A., & Dement, W. C. (2005). Normal human sleep: An overview. In M. H. Kryger, T. Roth, & W. C. Dement (Eds.), *Principles and practice of sleep medicine* (4th ed., pp. 13–23). Philadelphia, PA: Elsevier Saunders.

Chuong, C. J., Kim, S. R., Taskin, O., & Karacan, I. (1997). Sleep pattern changes in menstrual cycles of women with premenstrual syndrome: A preliminary study. *American Journal of Obstetrics and Gynecology, 177*(3), 554–558.

Claman, D. M., Redline, S., Blackwell, M. A., Ancoli-Israel, S., Surovec, S., Scott, N., . . . Stone, K. L. (2006). Prevalence and correlates of periodic limb movements in older women. *Journal of Clinical Sleep Medicine, 2*(4), 438–445.

Dancey, D. R., Hanly, P. J., Soong, C., Lee, B., Shepard, J., & Hoffstein, V. (2003). Gender differences in sleep apnea: The role of neck circumference. *Chest, 123*(5), 1544–1550.

Davidson, J. R. (2008). Insomnia: Therapeutic options for women. *Sleep Medicine Clinics, 3,* 109–119.

Décary, A., Rouleau, I., & Montplaisir, J. (2000). Cognitive deficits associated with sleep apnea syndrome: A proposed neuropsychological test battery. *Sleep, 23*(3), 369–381.

Delfs, T. M., Baars, S., Fock, C., Schumacher, J. O., Olcese, J., & Zimmermann, R. C. (1993). Sex steroids do not alter melatonin secretion in the human. *Human Reproduction, 9*(1), 49–54.

Dennerstein, I., Dudley, E. C., Hopper, J. L., Guthrie, J. R., & Burger, H. G. (2000). A prospective population-based study of menopausal symptoms. *Obstetrics and Gynecology, 96,* 351–358.

Dijk, D. J., Duffy J. F., & Czeisler C. A. (2000). Contribution of circadian physiology and sleep homeostasis to age-related changes in human sleep. *Chronobiology International, 17*(3), 285–311.

Dinges, D. F., Rogers, N. L. & Baynard, M. D. (2005). Chronic sleep deprivation. In M. H. Kryger, T. Roth, & W. C. Dement (Eds.), *Principles and practice of sleep medicine* (4th ed., pp. 67–76). Philadelphia, PA: Elsevier Saunders.

Doan, T., Gardiner, A., Gay, C. L., & Lee, K. A. (2007). Breast-feeding increases sleep duration of new parents. *Journal of Perinatal & Neonatal Nursing, 21*(3), 200–206.

Dobkin, R. D., Menza, M., Bienfait, K. L., Allen, P. A., Marin, H., & Gara, M. A. (2009). Ramelteon for the treatment of insomnia in menopausal women. *Menopause International, 15*, 13–18.

Dorheim, S. K., Bondevik, G. T., Eberhard-Gran, M., & Bjorvatn, B. (2009). Sleep and depression in postpartum women: A population-based study. *Sleep, 32*(7), 847–855.

Driver, H. S., Dijk D. J., Werth, E., Biedermann, K., & Borbely A. A. (1996). Menstrual cycle effects on sleep electroencephalogram across the menstrual cycle in young healthy women. *Journal of Clinical Endocrinology and Metabolism, 81*(2), 728–735.

Driver, H., McLean, H., Kumar, D. V., Farr, N., Day, A. G., & Fitzpatrick, M. (2005). The influence of the menstrual cycle on upper airway resistance and breathing during sleep. *Sleep, 28*, 449–456.

Driver, H., Werth, E., Dijk, D., & Borbely, A. (2008). The menstrual cycle effects on sleep. *Sleep Medicine Clinics, 3*, 1–11.

Dzaja, A., Arber, S., Hislop, J., Kerkhofs, M., Kopp, C., Pollmacher, T., . . . Porkka-Heiskanen, T. (2005). Women's sleep in health and disease. *Journal of Psychiatric Research, 39*, 55–76.

Dzaja, A., Wehrie, R., Lancel, M., & Pollmacher, T. (2009). Elevated estradiol plasma levels in women with restless legs during pregnancy. *SLEEP, 32*(2), 169–174.

Edwards, N., Blyton, D. M., Kiravainen, T. (2000). Nasal continuous positive airway pressure reduces sleep induced blood pressure increments in pre-eclampsia. *American Journal of Respiratory Critical Care Medicine, 162*, 252–257.

El-Solh, A. A., Ayyar, L., Akinnusi, M., Relia, S., & Akinnusi, O. (2010). Positive airway pressure adherence in veterans with posttraumatic stress disorder. *SLEEP, 33*(11), 1495–1500.

Foley, D., Monjan, A., Broen, S., Simonsick, E., Wallace, R., & Blazer, D. (1995). Sleep complaints among elderly persons: An epidemiologic study of three communities. *Sleep, 18*, 425–432.

Ford, D. E., & Kamerow, D. B. (1989). Epidemiologic study of sleep disturbances and psychiatric disorders. An opportunity for prevention? *JAMA, 262*, 1479–1484.

Freedman, R. R. (2005). Pathophysiology and treatment of menopausal hot flashes. *Seminars in Reproductive Medicine, 23*, 117–125.

Freedman, R., R., Norton, D., Woodward, S., & Cornelissen, G. (1995). Core body temperature and circadian rhythm of hot flashes in menopausal women. *Journal of Endocrinology and Metabolism, 80*, 2354–2358.

Freedman, R. R., & Roehrs, T. A. (2004). Lack of sleep disturbance from menopausal hot flashes. *Fertility and Sterility, 82*, 138–144.

Freedman, R., & Roehrs, T. A. (2006). Effects of REM sleep and ambient temperature on hot-flash-induced sleep disturbance. *Menopause, 13*, 576–583.

Freeman, E. W., Sammel, M. D., Lin, H., & Nelson, D. B. (2006). Associations of hormones and menopausal status with depressed mood in women with no history of depression. *Archives of General Psychiatry, 63*, 375–382.

Gay, C. L., Lee, K. A., & Lee, S. Y. (2004). Sleep patterns and fatigue in new mothers and fathers. *Biological Research for Nursing, 5*(4), 311–318.

Gehrman, P., Stepnowsky, C., Cohen-Zion, M., Marler, M., Kripke, D. F., & Ancoli-Israel, S. (2002). Long-term follow-up of periodic limb movementsin sleep in older adults. *Sleep, 25*, 340–343.

Gellis, L. A., Lichstein, K. L., Scarinci, I. C., Durrence, H. H., Taylor, D. J., Bush, A. J., & Riedel, B. W. (2005). Socioeconomic status and insomnia. *Journal of Abnormal Psychology, 114*(1), 111–118. doi: 2005-01472-011 [pii]

Germain, A., & Kupfer, D.J. (2008). Circadian rhythm disturbances in depression. *Human Psychopharmacology, 23*, 571–585.

Godfrey, J. R. (2009). Toward optimal health: Diagnosis and management of disordered sleep in women. *Journal of Women's Health, 18*(2), 147–152.

Gold, E. B., Sternfield, B., Kelsey, J. L., Brown, C., Mouton, C., Reame, N., . . . Stellato, R. (2000). Relation of demographic and lifestyle factors to symptoms in a multi-racial/ethnic population of women 40-55 years of age. *American Journal of Epidemiology, 151*, 463–473.

Gooneratne, N. (2008). Complementary and alternative medicine for sleep disturbances in older adults. *Clinics in Geriatric Medicine*, 121–138.

Gopal, M., Duntley, S., Uhles, M., & Attarian, H. (2002). The role of obesity in the increased prevalence of obstructive sleep apnea syndrome in patients with polycystic ovarian syndrome. *Sleep Medicine, 3*, 401–404.

Gupta, P., Sturdee, D., & Hunter, M. S. (2006). Mid-Age Health in Women from the Indian Subcontinent (MAHWIS): General health and the experience of menopause in women. *Climicteric, 9*, 13–22.

Hachul, H., Bittencourt, L. R. A., Soares, J. M., Tufik, S., & Baracat, E. C. (2009). Sleep in post-menopausal women: Differences between early and late post-menopause. *European Journal of Obstetrics & Gynecology and Reproductive Biology, 145*, 81–84.

Hahn, P. M., Wong, J., & Reid, R. L. (1998). Menopausal-like hot flashes reported in women of reproductive age. *Fertility and Sterility, 70*(5), 913–918.

Hedman, C., Pohjasvaara, T., Tolonen, U. (2002). Effects of pregnancy on mother's sleep. *Sleep Medicine, 3*, 37–42.

Hensley, J. G. (2009). Leg cramps and restless legs syndrome during pregnancy. *Journal of Midwifery & Women's Health, 54*(3), 211–218.

Hollander, L. E., Freeman, E. W., Sammel, M. D., Berlin, J. A., Grisso, J. A., & Battistini, M. (2001). Sleep quality, estradiol levels, and behavioral factors in late reproductive age women. *Obstetrics and Gynecology, 98*, 391–397.

Hsu, H., Chen, N. H., Jou, H. J., An, C. A., & Tsa, L. I. (2009). Sleep disturbance experiences among perimenopausal women in Taiwan. *Journal of Clinical Nursing, 18*, 2116–2124.

Hunter, M. S., Coventry, S., Hamed, H., Fentiman, I., & Grunfeld, E. (2009). Evaluation of group cognitive behavioral intervention for women suffering from menopausal symptoms following breast cancer treatment. *Psycho-Oncology, 18*, 560–563.

Hunter, M. S., & Liao, K. L. M. (1996). Evaluation of a four session cognitive behavioral intervention for menopausal hot flushes. *British Journal of Health Psychology, 1*, 113–125.

Hunter, M., & Mann, E. (2010). A cognitive model of menopausal hot flushes and night sweats. *Journal of Psychosomatic Research, 69*, 491–501.

Hunter, L. P., Rychnovsky, J. D., & Yount, S. M. (2009). A selective review of maternal sleep characteristics in the postpartum period. *Journal of Obstetric, Gynecologic, and Neonatal Nursing, 38*, 60–68.

Iacovides, S., Avidon, I., Bentley, A., & Baker, F. (2009). Diclofenac potassium restores objective and subjective measures of sleep quality in women with primary dysmenorrhea. *Sleep, 32*, 1019–1026.

Irvin, J. H., Domar, A. D., Clark, C., Zuttermeister, P. C., & Friedman, R. (1996). The effects of relaxation response training on menopausal symptoms. *Journal of Psychosomatic Obstetrics and Gynecology, 17*, 202–207.

Joffe, H., Massler, A., & Sharkey, K. M. (2010). Evaluation and management of sleep disturbance during the menopause transition. *Seminars in Reproductive Medicine, 28*(5), 404–421.

Johnson, C. M. (1991). Infant and toddler sleep: A telephone survey of parents in one community. *Journal of Developmental and Behavioral Pediatrics, 12*, 108–114.

Kapsimalis, F., & Kryger, M. H. (2002). Gender and obstructive sleep apnea syndrome, Part 1: Clinical features. *SLEEP, 25*(40), 409–416.

Kloss, J. D. (2003). Daytime sequelae of insomnia. In M. P. Szuba, J. D. Kloss, & D. F. Dinges (Eds.), *Insomnia: Principles and management* (pp. 23–42). Cambridge, UK: Cambridge University Press.

Kloss, J. D., Tweedy, K., & Gilrain, K. (2004). Psychological factors associated with sleep disturbance among perimenopausal women. *Behavioral Sleep Medicine, 2*(4), 177–190.

Kos-Kudla, B., Ostrowska, Z., Marek, B., Kajdaniuk, D., Ciesielska-Kopacz, N., Kudla, M., . . . Nasiek, M. (2002). Circadian rhythm of melatonin in postmenopausal asthmatic women with hormone replacement therapy. *Neurology and Endocrinology Letters, 23*(3), 243–248. doi: NEL230302A07 [pii]

Kravitz, H. M., Ganz, P. A., Bromberger, J., Powell, L. H., Sutoon-Tyrell, K., & Meyer, P. M. (2003). Sleep difficulty in women at midlife: A community survey of sleep and the menopausal transition. *Menopause, 10*, 19–28.

Kravitz, H. M., Janssen, I., Santoro, N., Bromberger, J., Schocken, M., Everson-Rose, S., . . . Powell, L. H. (2005). Relationship of day-to-day reproductive hormone levels to sleep in midlife women. *Archives of Internal Medicine, 165*, 2370–2376.

Kravitz, H. M., Zhao, Z., Bromberger, J. T., Gold, E., Hall, M., Matthews, K., & Sowers, M. F. (2008). Sleep disturbance during the menopausal transition in a multi-ethnic community sample of women. *Sleep*, *31*, 979–990.

Kroneberg, F., & Fugh-Berman, A. (2002). Complementary and alternative medicine for menopausal symptoms: A review of randomized controlled trials. *Annals of Internal Medicine*, *137*(10), 805–813.

Kruijver, F. P., & Swaab, D. F. (2002). Sex hormone receptors are present in the human suprachiasmatic nucleus. *Neuroendocrinology*, *75*, 296–305.

Kryger, M. (2004). *A woman's guide to sleep disorders*. New York, NY: McGraw-Hill.

Krystal, A. D., Edinger, J., Wohlgemuth, W., & Marsh, G. R. (1998). Sleep in peri- and postmenopausal women. *Sleep Medicine Reviews*, *2*, 243–253.

Lam, R. W., Carter, D., Misri, S., Kuan, A. J., Latham, L. N., & Zis, A. P. (1999). A controlled study of light therapy in women with late luteal phase dysphoric disorder. *Psychiatry Research*, *86*(3), 185–192.

Lamarche, L. J., Driver, H. S., Forest, G., & DeKonnick, J. (2010). Napping during the late luteal phase improves sleepiness, alertness, mood and cognitive performance in women with and without premenstrual symptoms. *Sleep and Biological Rhythms*, *8*, 151–159.

Lamarche, L. J., Driver, H. S., Wiebe, S., Crawford, L., & DeKonnick, J. M. (2007). Nocturnal sleep, daytime sleepiness, and napping among women with significant emotional/behavioral premenstrual symptoms. *Journal of Sleep Research*, *16*(3), 262–268.

Lee, K.A. (2006). Sleep dysfunction in women and its management. *Current Treatment Options in Neurology*, *8*(5), 376–386.

Lee, K. A. (1998). Alterations in sleep during pregnancy and postpartum: A review of 30 years of research. *Sleep Medicine Review*, *2*, 231–242.

Lee, K. A., & DeJoseph, J. F. (1992). Sleep disturbances, vitality, and fatigue among a select group of employed childbearing women. *Birth*, *19*(4), 208–213.

Lee, K. A., & Kryger, M. H. (2008). Women and sleep. *Journal of Women's Health*, *17*(7), 1189–1190.

Lee, K. A., & Gay, C. L. (2004). Sleep in late pregnancy predicts length of labor and type of delivery. *American Journal of Obsterics and Gynecology*, *191*, 2041–2046.

Lee, K., Shaver, J. F., Giblin, E. C., & Woods, N. (1990). Sleep patterns related to menstrual cycle phase and premenstrual affective symptoms. *Sleep*, *13*, 403–409.

Lee, K., Zaffke, M. E., & Barratte-Beebe, K. (2001). Restless legs syndrome and sleep disturbance during pregnancy: The role of folate and iron. *Journal of Women's Health and Gender-Based Medicine*, *10*(4), 335–341.

Lee, K. A., Zaffke, M. E., & McEnany, G. (2000). Parity and sleep patterns during and after pregnancy. *Obstetrics and Gynecology*, *95*(1), 14–18.

Lentz, M. J., Landis, C. A., Rothermel, J., & Shaver, J. L. (1999). Effects of selective slow wave sleep disruption on musculoskeletal pain and fatigue in middle aged women. *Journal of Rheumatology*, *26*, 1586–1592.

Li, R. H., Wing, Y. K., Ho, S. C., & Fong, S. Y. (2002). Gender differences in insomnia: A study in the Hong Kong Chinese population. *Journal of Psychosomatic Research*, *53*(1), 601–609.

Lichstein, K. L., Durrence, H. H., Taylor, D. J., Bush, A. J., & Riedel, B. W. (2003). Quantitative criteria for insomnia. *Behavioral Research and Therapy*, *41*(4), 427–445.

Lock, M. (1994). Menopause in cultural context. *Experimental Gerontology*, *29*, 307–317.

Lozoff, B., Wolf, A. W., & Davis, N. S. (1984). Co-sleeping in urban families with young children in the United States. *Pediatrics*, *74*, 171–182.

Maher, M. J., Rego, S. A. & Asnis, G. M. (2006). Sleep disturbances in patients with posttraumatic stress disorder: Epidemiology, impact and approaches to management. *CNS Drugs*, *20*, 567–590.

Mahlberg, R., Tilmann, A., Salewski, L., & Kunz, D. (2006). Normative data on the daily profile of urinary 6-sulfatoxymelatonin in healthy subjects between the ages of 20 and 84. *Psychoneuroendocrinology*, *31*, 634–641.

Mahoney, M. M. (2010). Shift work, jet lag, and female reproduction. *International Journal of Endocrinology*, 1–9. doi: 10.1155/2010/813764

Mallon, L., Broman, J. E., & Hetta, J. (2000). Relationship between insomnia, depression, and mortality: A 12-year follow-up of older adults in the community. *International Psychogeriatrics, 46,* 295–306.

Manber, R., & Armitage, R. (1999). Sex, steroids, and sleep: A review. *Sleep, 22,* 540–555.

Manber, R., & Bootzin, R. R. (1997). Sleep and the menstrual cycle. *Health Psychology, 16*(3), 209–214.

Mauri, M. (1990). Sleep and the reproductive cycle: A review. *Health Care Women International, 11*(4), 409–421.

McKenna, J. J., & McDade, T. (2005). Why babies should never sleep alone: A review of the co-sleeping controversy in relation to SIDS, bed-sharing and breast feeding. *Paediatric Respiratory Reviews, 6,* 134–152.

Meltzer, L. J., & Mindell, J. A. (2007). Relationship between child sleep disturbances and maternal sleep, mood, and parenting stress: A pilot study. *Journal of Family Psychology, 21,* 67–73.

Mezick, E. J., Matthews, K. A., Hall, M., Strollo, P. J., Jr., Buysse, D. J., Kamarck, T. W., . . . Reis, S. E. (2008). Influence of race and socio-economic status on sleep: Pittsburgh Sleep-SCORE project. *Psychosomatic Medicine, 70*(4), 410–416. doi: 70/4/410 [pii]

Minarik, P. A. (2009). Sleep disturbance in midlife women. *Journal of Obstetric, Gynecologic, and Neonatal Nursing, 38,* 333–343.

Mindell, J. A. (2005). *Sleeping through the night: How infants, toddlers, and their parents can get a good night's sleep* (rev. ed.). New York, NY: HarperCollins, 2005.

Mindell, J. A., & Jacobson, B. J. (2000). Sleep disturbances during pregnancy. *Journal of Obstetric, Gynecologic, and Neonatal Nursing, 29,* 590–597.

Mindell, J. A., Telofski, L. S., Wiegand, B., & Kurtz, E. S. (2009). A nightly bedtime routine: Impact on sleep in young children and maternal mood. *Sleep, 32*(5), 599–606.

Moe, K. E. (1999). Reproductive hormones, aging and sleep. *Seminars in Reproductive Endocrinology, 17,* 339–348.

Moe, K. E. (2004). Hot flashes and sleep in women. *Sleep Medicine Reviews, 8,* 487–497.

Moline, M., Broch, L., & Zak, R. (2004). Sleep problems across the life cycle in women. *Current Treatment Options in Neurology, 6,* 319–330.

Monane, M. (1992). Insomnia in the elderly. *Journal of Clinical Psychiatry, 53*(Suppl), 23–28.

Montgomery-Downs, H. E., Clawges, H. M., & Santy, E. E. (2010). Infant feeding methods and maternal sleep and daytime functioning. *Pediatrics, 126*(6), 1562–1568.

Morgan, K. (2003). Daytime activity and risk factors for late-life insomnia. *Journal of Sleep Research, 12,* 231–238.

Morgenthaler, T., Kramer, M., Alessi C., Friedman, L., Boehlecke, B., Brown, T., . . . American Academy of Sleep Medicine. (2006). Practice parameters for the psychological and behavioral treatment of insomnia: An update. *Sleep, 29,* 1415–1419.

Morin, C. M. (2006). Combined therapeutics for insomnia: Should our first approach be behavioral or pharmacological? *Sleep Medicine, 7*(Suppl 1), S15–S19. doi: S1389-9457(06)00070-0 [pii]

Morin, C. M., Culbert, J. P., & Schwartz, S. M. (1994). Nonpharmacological interventions for insomnia: A meta-analysis of treatment efficacy. *American Journal of Psychiatry, 151*(8), 1172–1180.

Morin, M. C., & Grambling, S. E. (1989). Sleep patterns and aging: Comparison of older adults with and without insomnia complaints. *Psychology of Aging, 4*(3), 290–294.

Munk-Olsen, T., Laursen, T. M., Pederson, C. B., Mors, O., & Mortensen, P. B. (2006). New parents and mental disorders: A population-based register study. *JAMA, 296,* 2582–2589.

Murphy, P. J., & Campbell, S. S. (2007). Sex hormones, sleep, and core body temperature in older postmenopausal women. *Sleep, 30*(12), 1788–1794.

Murtagh, D. R., & Greenwood, K. M. (1995). Identifying effective psychological treatments for insomnia: A meta-analysis. *Journals of Consuting Clinical Psychology, 63*(1), 79–89.

Nagata, C., Takasuta, N., Inaba, S., Kawakami, N., & Shimizu, H. (1998). Association of diet and other lifestyle with onset of menopause in Japanese women. *Maturitas, 29,* 105–113.

National Institutes of Health, State of the Science Panel. (2005). National Institutes of Health State-of-the-Science conference statement: Management of menopause-related symptoms *Annals of Internal Medicine, 142,* 1003–1013.

National Sleep Foundation. (2007). *The National Sleep Foundation's 2007 Women and Sleep Poll.* Washington, DC: Author.

Nelson, H. D., Vesco, K. K., Haney, E., Rongwei, F., Nedrow, A., Nicolaidis, C., . . . Humphrey, L. (2006). Nonhormonal therapies for menopausal hot flashes. *JAMA, 295*(17), 2057–2071.

Newton, K. M., Reed, S. D., La Croix, A. Z., Grothaus, L. C., Ehrlich, K., & Guiltinan, J. (2006). Treatment of vasomotor symptoms of menopause with black cohosh, multibotanicals, soy, hormone therapy or placebo: A randomized trial. *Annals of Internal Medicine, 145*(12), 869–879.

Ohayon, M. M. (2006). Severe hot flashes are associated with chronic insomnia. *Archives of Internal Medicine, 166,* 1262–1268.

Okun, M., Roberts, J. M., Marsland, A. L., & Hall, M. (2009). How disturbed sleep may be a risk factor for adverse pregnancy outcomes: A hypothesis. *Obstetrical and Gynecological Survey, 64*(4), 273–280.

Ong, J., & Sholtes, D. (2010). A mindfulness-based approach to the treatment of insomnia. *Journal of Clinical Psychology, 66*(11), 1175–1184. doi: 10.1002/jclp.20736

Owens, J. A. (2004). Sleep in children: Cross-cultural perspectives. *Sleep and Biological Rhythms, 2*(3), 165–173.

Owens, J. F., & Matthews, K. A. (1998). Sleep disturbance in healthy middle-aged women. *Maturitas, 30,* 41–50.

Pandi-Perumal, S. R., Srinivasan, V., Spence, D. W., & Cardinali, D. P. (2007). Role of melatonin system in the control of sleep: Therapeutic implications. *CNS Drugs, 21*(12), 995–1018.

Pandi-Perumal, S. R., Zisapel, N., Srinivasan, V., & Cardinali, D. P. (2005). Melatonin and sleep in aging population. *Experimental Gerontology, 40,* 911–925.

Parry, B. L., Cover, H., Mostofi, N., LeVeau, B., Sependa, P. A., Resnick, A., . . . Gillin, C. (1995). Early vs. late partial sleep deprivation in patients with premenstrual dysphoric disorder and normal comparison subjects. *American Journal of Psychiatry, 152,* 404–412.

Parry, B., LeVeau, B., Mostofi, N., Naham, H. C., Loving, R., Clopton, P., & Gillin, C. J. (1997). Temperature circadian rhythms during the menstrual cycle and sleep deprivation in premenstrual dysphoric disorder and normal comparison subjects. *Journal of Biological Ryhtms, 12,* 34–46.

Parry, B. L., Martinez, L. F., Maurer, E. L., Lopez, A. M., Sorenson, D., & Meliska, C. (2006). Sleep rhythms and women's mood, Part II: Menopause. *Sleep Medicine Reviews, 10,* 197–208.

Parry, B., Mendelson, W. B., Duncan, W. C., Sack, D. A., & Wehr, T. (1989). Longitudinal sleep EEG, temperature, and activity measurements across the menstrual cycle in patients with premenstrual depression and in age-matched controls. *Psychiatry Research 30,* 285–303.

Parry, B. L., Mostofi, N., LeVau, B., Nahum, H. C., Golshan, S., Laughlin, G. A., & Gillin, C. (1999). Sleep EEG studies during early and late partial sleep deprivation in premenstrual dysphoric disorder and normal control subjects. *Psychiatry Research, 85,* 127–143.

Parry, B. L., & Wehr, T. A. (1987). Therapeutic effects of sleep deprivation in patients with premenstrual syndrome. *American Journal of Psychiatry, 144,* 808–810.

Perlis, M., Aloia, M., & Kuhn, B. (Eds.). (2011). *Behavioral treatments for sleep disorders: A comprehensive primer of behavioral sleep medicine interventions.* London, UK: Academic Press/Elsevier.

Pien, G. W., Fife, D., & Pack, A. (2005). Changes in symptoms of sleep-disordered breathing during pregnancy. *SLEEP, 28,* 1299–1305.

Pien, G. W., Sammel, M. D., Freeman, E. W., Lin, H., & DeBlasis, T. L. (2008). Predictors of sleep quality in women in the menopausal transition. *Sleep, 31,* 991–999.

Pien, G. W., & Schwab, R. J. (2004). Sleep disorders during pregnancy. *Sleep, 27*(7), 1405–1417.

Polo-Kantola, P., & Erkkola, R. (2004). Sleep and the menopause. *Journal of the British Menopause Society, 10,* 145–150.

Posmontier, B. (2008). Sleep quality in women with and without postpartum depression. *Journal of Obstetric, Gynecologic, and Neonatal Nursing, 37,* 722–737.

Prinz, P. N., Vitiello, M. V., Raskind, M. A., & Thorpy, M. J. (1990). Geriatrics: Sleep disorders and aging. *New England Journal of Medicine, 323*(8), 520–526. doi: 10.1056/NEJM199008233230805

Qui, C., Enquobahrie, D., Frederick, I. O., Abetew, D., & Williams, M. (2010). Glucose intolerance and gestational diabetes risk in relation to sleep duration and snoring during pregnancy: A pilot study. *BMC Women's Health, 10,* 17.

Rajewska, J., & Rybakowski, J. K. (2003). Depression in premenopausal women: Gonadal hormones and serotonergic system assessed by D-fenfluramine challenge test. *Progress in Neuro-Psychopharmacology & Biological Psychiatry*, 27, 705–709.

Ramchandani, P., Wiggs, L., Webb, V., & Stores, G. (2000). A systematic review of treatments for settling problems and night waking in young children. *British Medical Journal*, 320, 209–213.

Rediehs, M. H., Reis, J. S., & Creason, N. S. (1990). Sleep in old age: Focus on gender differences. *Sleep*, 13(5), 410–424.

Redline, S., Kump, K., Tishler, P. V., Browner, I., & Ferrette, V. (1994). Gender differences in sleep disordered breathing in a community-based sample. *American Journal of Respiratory and Critical Care Medicine*, 149, 722–726.

Regestein, Q. R. (2006). Hot flashes and sleep. *Menopause*, 13, 549–552.

Regestein, Q. R. (2010). Hot flashes, sleep, and mood. *Menopause: The Journal of the North American Menopause Society*, 17, 16–18.

Ritterband, L. M., Thorndike, F. P., Gonder-Frederick, L. A., Magee, J. C., Bailey, E. T., Saylor, D. K., & Morin, C. M. (2009). Efficacy of an internet-based behavioral intervention for adults with insomnia. *Archives of General Psychiatry*, 66(7), 692–698. doi: 66/7/692 [pii]

Ross, L. E., Murray, B. J., & Steiner, M. (2005). Sleep and perinatal mood disorders: A critical review. *Journal of Psychiatry Neuroscience*, 30(4), 247–256.

Roush, S. F., & Bell, L. (2004). Obstructive sleep apnea in pregnancy. *Journal of American Board of Family Practice*, 17, 292–294.

Sack, R. L., Auckley, D., Auger, R. R., Carskadon, M. A., Wright, K. P., Jr., Vitiello, M. V., & Zhdanova, I. V. (2007). Circadian rhythm sleep disorders: Part II, advanced sleep phase disorder, delayed sleep phase disorder, free-running disorder, and irregular sleep-wake rhythm. An American Academy of Sleep Medicine review. *Sleep*, 30(11), 1484–1501.

Sahin, F. K., Koken, G., Cosar, E., Saylan, F., Fidan, F., Yilmazer, M., & Unlu, M. (2008). Obstructive sleep apnea in pregnancy and fetal outcome. *International Journal of Gynecology and Obsterics*, 100, 141–146.

Sahota, P. K., Jain, S. S., & Dhand, R. (2003). Sleep disorders in pregnancy. *Current Opinion in Pulmonary Medicine*, 9, 477–483.

Sarsour, K., Kalsekar, A., Swindle, R., Foley, K., & Walsh, J. K. (2011). The association between insomnia severity and healthcare and productivity costs in a health plan sample. *Sleep*, 34, 443–450.

Schubert, C. R., Cruickshanks, K. J., Dalton, D. S., Klein, B. E., Klein, R., & Nondahl, D. M. (2002). Prevalence of sleep problems and quality of life in an older population. *Sleep*, 25, 889–893.

Severino, S. K., Wagner, D. R., Moline, S. W., Hurt, C., Pollack, P., & Zendell, S. (1991). High nocturnal body temperature in premenstrual syndrome and the late luteal phase dysphoric disorder. *American Journal of Psychiatry*, 148, 1329–1335.

Sharkey, K., Bearpark, H., Acebo, C., Millman, R., Cavallo, A., & Carskadon, M. (2003). Effects of menopausal status on sleep in midlife women. *Behavioral Sleep Medicine*, 1, 69–80.

Shaver, J. L. (2002). Women and sleep. *Nursing Clinics of North America*, 37, 707–718.

Shaver, J. L. F. (2010). Insomnia burden: Definition and link to the menopausal transition. *Menopause: The Journal of the North American Menopause Society*, 17, 12–15.

Shaver, J., Giblin, E., Lentz, M., & Lee, K. (1988). Sleep patterns and stability in perimenopausal women. *Sleep*, 11(6), 556–561.

Shaver, J. L. F., Giblin, E., & Paulsen, V. M. (1991). Sleep quality subtypes in midlife women. *Sleep*, 14, 18–23.

Shaver, J. L. F., & Paulsen, V. (1993). Sleep psychological distress, and somatic symptoms. *Family Practice Research Journal*, 13, 373–384.

Shechter, A., & Boivin, D. B. (2010). Sleep, hormones, and circadian rhythms throughout the menstrual cycle in healthy women and women with premenstrual dysphoric disorder. *International Journal of Endocrinology*, 1–17.

Shechter, A., James, F. O., & Boivin, D. B. (2008). Circadian rhythms and shift working women. *Sleep Medicine Clinics*, 3, 13–24.

Shechter, A., Varin, F., & Boivin, D. B. (2010). Circadian variation of sleep during the follicular and luteal phases of the menstrual cycle. *Sleep*, 33(5), 647–656.

Shepard, J. W. (1992). Hypertension, cardiac arrhythmias, myocardial infarction and stroke in relation to obstructive sleep apnea. *Clinics in Chest Medicine*, 13, 437–458.

Shepertycky, M. R., Banno, K., & Kryger, M. H. (2004). Differences between men and women in the clinical presentation of patients diagnosed with obstructive sleep apnea syndrome. *SLEEP, 28*(3), 309–314.

Shibui, K., Uchiyama, M., Okawa, M., Kudo, Y., Kim, K., Liu, X., . . . Ishibashi, K. (2000). Diurnal fluctuation of sleep propensity and hormonal secretion across the menstrual cycle. *Biological Psychiatry, 48*(11), 1062–1068.

Signal, T. L., Gander, P. H., & Sangalli, M. R. (2007). Sleep duration and quality in healthy nulliparous and multiparous women across pregnancy and post-partum. *Australian and New Zealand Journal of Obstetrics and Gynecology, 47,* 16–22.

Skene, D. J., & Swaab, D. F. (2003). Melatonin rhythmicity: Effect of age and Alzheimer's disease. *Experimental Gerontology, 38,* 199–206.

Skouteris, H., Germano, C., Wertheim, E. H., Paxton, S., & Milgrom, J. (2008). Sleep quality and depression during pregnancy: A prospective study. *Journal of Psychosomatic Research, 17,* 217–220.

Smith, M. T., Huang, M. I., & Manber, R. (2005). Cognitive behavior therapy for chronic insomnia occurring in the context of medical and psychiatric disorders. *Clinical Psychology Reviews, 25,* 559–592.

Soares, C. N. (2005). Insomnia in women: An overlooked epidemic. *Archives of Women's Mental Health, 8,* 205–213.

Soares, C. N., & Murray, B. J. (2006). Sleep disorders in women: Clinical evidence and treatment strategies. *Psychiatric Clinics of North American, 29,* 1095–1113.

Srinivasan, V., Smits, M., Spence, W., Lowe, A. D., Kayumov, L., Pandi-Perumal, S. R., . . . Cardinali, D. P. (2006). Melatonin in mood disorders. *World Journal of Biological Psychiatry, 7,* 138–151.

Stearns, V., Beebe, K. L., Iyengar, M., & Dube, E. (2003). Paroxetine controlled release in the treatment of menopausal hot flashes: A randomized controlled trial. *JAMA, 289,* 2827–2834.

Steiner, M., Dunn, E., & Born, L. (2003). Hormones and mood from menarche to menopause and beyond. *Journal of Affective Disorders, 74,* 67–83.

Stevens, R. G., Davis, S., Thomas, D. B., Anderson, L. E., & Wilson, B. (1992). Electrical power, pineal function, and the risk of breast cancer. *The FASEB Journal, 6,* 853–860.

Stremler, R., Hodneff, E., Lee, K., MacMillan, S., Mill, C., Ongcangco, L., & Willan, A. (2006). A behavioral-educational intervention to promote maternal and infant sleep: A pilot randomized, control trial. *Sleep, 29*(12), 1609–1615.

Teran-Santos, J., Jimenez-Gomez, A., & Cordero-Guevara, J. (1999). The association between sleep apnea and the risk of traffic accidents. Cooperative Group Burgos-Santander. *New England Journal of Medicine, 340*(11), 847–851. doi: 10.1056/NEJM199903183401104

Thurston, R. C., Blumenthal, J. S., Babyak, M. A., & Sherwood, A. (2006). Association between hot flashes, sleep complaints, and psychological functioning among healthy menopausal women. *Intrenational Journal of Behavioral Medicine, 13,* 163–172.

Tranah, G., Parimi, N., Blackwell, T., Ancoli-Israel, S., Ensrud, K. E., Cauley, J. A., . . . Stone, K. L. (2010). Postmenopausal hormones and sleep quality in the elderly: A population-based study. *BMC Women's Health, 10*(15), 1–8.

Tuunainen, A., Kripke, D. F., Elliott, J. A., Assmus, J. D., Rex, K. M., Klauber, M. R., & Langer, R. D. (2002). Depression and endogenous melatonin in postmenopausal women. *Journal of Affective Disorders, 69*(1–3), 149–158.

Tworoger, S. S., Lee, S., Schernhammer, E. S., & Goldstein, F. (2006). The association of self-reported sleep duration, difficulty sleeping, and snoring with cognitive function in older women. *Alzheimer Disease Association Discord, 20*(1), 41–48.

Urponen, H., Vuori, I., Hasan, J., & Partinen, M. (1988). Self-evaluations of factors promoting and disturbing sleep: An epidemiological survey in Finland. *Social Science Medicine, 26,* 443–450.

Van Dongen, H. P. A., Maislin, G., Mullington, J. M., & Dinges, D. F. (2003). The cumulative cost of additional wakefulness: Dose-response effects on neurobehavioral functions and sleep physiology from chronic sleep restriction and total sleep deprivation. *Sleep, 26,* 117–126.

Vieten, C., & Astin, J. (2008). Effects of a mindfulness-based intervention during pregnancy on prenatal stress and mood: Results of a pilot study. *Archieves of Women's Mental Health, 11,* 67–74.

Walters, J. F., Hampton, S. M., Ferns, G. A. A., & Skene, D. J. (2005). Effect of menopause on melatonin and alertness rhythms investigated in constant routine conditions. *Chronobiology International*, *22*(5), 859–872.

Webb, W., & Campbell, S. (1980). Awakenings and return to sleep in an older population. *Sleep*, *3*, 41–46.

Wijma, K., Melin, A., Nedstrand, E., & Hammar, M. (1997). Treatment of menopausal symptoms with applied relaxation: A pilot study. *Journal of Behavior Therapy and Experimental Psychiatry*, *28* (4), 251–261.

Willinger, M., Ko, C. W., Hoffman, H. J., Kessler, R. C., & Corwin, M. J. (2003). Trends in infant bed sharing in the United States, 1993–2000: The national infant sleep position study. *Archives of Pediatric and Adolescent Medicine*, *157*, 43–49.

Wolfson, A. R. (2001). *The woman's book of sleep: A complete resource guide*. Oakland, CA: New Harbinger.

Wolfson, A. R., Crowley, S. J., Answer, U., & Bassett, J. L. (2003). Changes in sleep patterns and depressive symptoms in first-time mothers: Last trimester to 1-year postpartum. *Behavioural Sleep Medicine*, *1*, 54–67.

Wolfson, A., & Lee, K. A. (2005). Pregnancy and the postpartum period. In M. H. Kryger, T. Roth, & W. C. Dement (Eds.), *Principles and practice of sleep medicine* (4th ed., pp. 1278–1286). Philadelphia, PA: Elsevier Saunders.

Woods, N. F., & Mitchell, E. S. (2010). Sleep symptoms during the menopausal transition and early postmenopause: Observations from the Seattle Midlife Women's Health Study. *Sleep*, *33*(4), 539–549.

Woodward, S., & Freedman, R. F. (1994). The thermoregulatory effects of menopausal hot flashes on sleep. *Sleep*, *17*, 497–501.

Wright, K., & Badia, P. (1999). Effects of menstrual cycle phase and oral contraceptives on alertness, cognitive performance, and circadian rhythms during sleep deprivation. *Behavioral Brain Research*, *103*, 185–194.

Writing Group for the Women's Health Initiative Investigators. (2002). Risks and benefits of estrogen plus progestin in healthy postmenopausal women. *JAMA*, *288*, 321–333.

Yaggi, H. K., Concato, J., Kernan, W. N., Lichtman, J. H., Brass, L. M., & Mohsenin, V. (2005). Obstructive sleep apnea as a risk factor for stroke and death. *New England Journal of Medicine*, *353* (19), 2034–2041. doi: 353/19/2034 [pii]

Yang, C. K., & Hahn, H. M. (2002). Cosleeping in young Korean children. *Journal of Developmental & Behavioral Pediatrics*, *23*, 151–157.

Young, T., Evans, L., Finn, L., & Palta, M. (1997). Estimation of the clinically diagnosed proportion of sleep apnea syndrome in middle-aged men and women. *Sleep*, *20*(9), 705–706.

Young, T., Hutton, R., Finn, L., Badr, S., & Palta, M. (1996). The gender bias in sleep apnea: Are women missed because they have different symptoms? *Archives of Internal Medicine*, *156*(21), 2445–2451.

Young, T., Rabago, D., Zgierska, A., Austin, D., & Finn, L. (2003). Objective and subjective sleep quality in premenopausal, perimenopausal, and postmenopausal women in the Wisconsin Cohort Study. *Sleep*, *26*, 667–672.

Yurchesen, M. E., Guttuso, T., McDermott, M., Holloway, R., & Perlis, M. (2009). Effects of Gabapentin on sleep in menopausal women with hot flashes as measured by a Pittsburgh Sleep Quality Index Factor Scoring Model. *Journal of Women's Health*, *18*, 1355–1360.

Zhang, B., & Wing, Y. K. (2006). Sex differences in insomnia: A meta-analysis. *Sleep*, *29*, 85–93.

CHAPTER

Promotion of Physical Activity for Women's Health

DORI PEKMEZI, SARAH LINKE, SHERI HARTMAN, AND BESS H. MARCUS

INTRODUCTION

The health benefits of an active lifestyle are well-documented for women and include lower risk of early death, coronary heart disease, stroke, high blood pressure, adverse blood lipid profile, type 2 diabetes, and colon and breast cancer. Regular physical activity can help reduce depression, prevent weight gain, and even result in weight loss, particularly when combined with reduced calorie intake. Furthermore, some evidence supports an association between an active lifestyle and lower risk of lung and endometrial cancer, improved sleep quality, and weight maintenance after weight loss (Physical Activity Guidelines Advisory Committee, 2008).

How much physical activity is necessary to reap these benefits? The general consensus is that some is better than none, but additional health benefits are incurred with increasing amounts (i.e., intensity, frequency, and/or duration) of physical activity. National guidelines for adults emphasize at least 150 minutes per week of moderate-intensity (e.g., brisk walking) or 75 minutes per week of vigorous-intensity (e.g., running) aerobic physical activity, along with muscle-strengthening activities on 2 or more days per week, for substantial health benefits

(Physical Activity Guidelines Advisory Committee, 2008).

Most Americans do not meet these recommendations. In fact, 39.1% of U.S. adults report being completely inactive, with more women (40.9%) than men (37%) reporting a sedentary lifestyle. Similar trends are also found among youth (Eaton et al., 2010). National guidelines for children and adolescents call for an hour or more of physical activity daily (Physical Activity Guidelines Advisory Committee, 2008), but Youth Risk Behavior Surveillance (YRBSS) data revealed that only 11.4% of the female high school students surveyed met this criteria, compared to 24.8% of the male high school students. This discrepancy may result from some physical activity barriers specific to girls, such as negative peer messages. For example, qualitative data has shown that both male and female seventh- and eighth-graders described physically active girls as "tomboys" and "too aggressive" (Vu, Murrie, Gonzalez, & Jobe, 2006). In another study, adolescent girls were more likely than boys to report feeling uncomfortable and self-conscious about the way they look when engaging in physical activity (Westerterp & Goran, 1997). Such factors likely contribute to the decline in physical activity seen during adolescence for girls. YRBSS data indicated that the rates of adolescent girls meeting physical activity recommendations steadily decreased over the high school years (13.6%, 12.7%, 10.3%, and 8.6% in 9th, 10th, 11th, and 12th grades, respectively) and corroborated similar findings from a longitudinal study conducted in Europe (Engeland, Bjorge, Sogaard, & Tverdal, 2003).

For women, these declines appear to continue into adulthood, particularly during critical periods such as during pregnancy and the postpartum period. National guidelines specifically pertaining to pregnancy and the postpartum period recommend that under-active women engage in at least 150 minutes of moderate-intensity aerobic activity per week and highly active women maintain their current level of activity as long as they stay healthy and discuss with their healthcare provider whether adjustments to their activity level are needed over time (Physical Activity Guidelines Advisory Committee, 2008). Research has demonstrated that moderate-intensity activity is safe during a healthy pregnancy (i.e., does not increase risk of low birth weight, preterm delivery, or early pregnancy loss) and may even reduce the risk of pregnancy complications (e.g., preeclampsia and gestational diabetes) and the length of labor. Furthermore, moderate-intensity physical activity during the postpartum period can help women achieve and maintain a healthy weight, and improve mood, with no apparent adverse effects in terms of breast milk volume and composition, or infant growth (Physical Activity Guidelines Advisory Committee, 2008). Much can be gained from an active lifestyle, but women in this stage of life often experience many barriers to participating in regular physical activity. For example, findings from the IMPACT

study indicated that both the number and intensity of perceived maternal stressors, such as difficulty controlling children's behavior, negatively impacted attempts to become more physically active ($n = $ 68 mothers, mean age $= 32$ years) (Urizar et al., 2005).

Unfortunately, exercise does not appear to grow any easier with age for women, as past research indicates that older women report health problems as a substantial physical activity barrier (Booth, Bauman, & Owen, 2002; Booth, Bauman, Owen, & Gore, 1997; De Bourdeaudhuij & Sallis, 2002; Juarbe, Turok, & Perez-Stable, 2002; Kowal & Fortier, 2007). Rates of inactivity are as high as 50.7% and 65.9% for women aged 65 to 74 years and 75 years or older (respectively), compared to 37% among 18- to 44-year-olds. This is concerning, considering the important role physical activity plays in healthy aging. The relationship between physical activity and lower risk of falls and better cognitive functioning for older adults has been well-established, with some support for lower risk of hip fracture, increased bone density, and better functional health for older adults (Physical Activity Guidelines Advisory Committee, 2008). Thus, for women 65 years of age and older, an active lifestyle can be the key to maintaining independence.

Physical activity is obviously essential to women's health and needs to be incorporated throughout the lifespan. Because of the breadth of literature available on this topic, this chapter focuses primarily on the research evidence related to physical activity for chronic disease prevention and management, smoking cessation, and mental health in adult women. Efforts to promote physical activity among women in underserved populations and via innovative technologies will also be highlighted.

PHYSICAL ACTIVITY AND OBESITY

Physical activity can play an important role in combating the current obesity epidemic, which has so deleteriously impacted women's health. Approximately one in four American women are overweight or obese (Centers for Disease Control and Prevention [CDC], 2010), and women generally have a higher percentage of body fat than men (De Lorenzo et al., 2003). Although physical activity alone often does not result in weight loss, perhaps due to compensatory eating in some women (Hopkins, King, & Blundell, 2010), several reviews of the literature have reported effective weight loss results when physical activity was combined with changes in diet (Donnelly et al., 2009; Physical Activity Guidelines Advisory Committee, 2008; Sweet & Fortier, 2010).

Furthermore, women who have lost weight may find physical activity helpful in terms of weight loss maintenance (Donnelly et al., 2009; Physical Activity Guidelines Advisory Committee, 2008). Jakicic and colleagues (2008) reported that women enrolled in a weight loss program ($n = 201$) who sustained a weight loss of 10% or more of their body weight at 24 months reported being more active than those who sustained less than 10% weight loss. The women who sustained the greater weight loss were engaging in, on average, more than 275 minutes of physical activity per week. Reviews (Donnelly et al., 2009; Physical Activity Guidelines Advisory Committee, 2008) support the findings of this study and indicate that women (and men) should participate in more than 250 minutes of moderate-intensity physical activity per week to maintain weight loss.

Finally, from a prevention standpoint, research indicates that 150 minutes of moderate-intensity physical activity per week can help women maintain a stable weight (Donnelly et al., 2009). Such findings may be particularly relevant to women approaching menopause, because of the increased risk for gaining weight at this time (Azarbad & Gonder-Frederick, 2010). More specifically, women are likely to gain weight around their abdomen during menopause (Azarbad & Gonder-Frederick, 2010). This is concerning because central obesity (fat on the abdomen) and visceral fat (around internal organs) are more of a health risk in terms of cardiovascular disease and diabetes than the peripheral obesity (fat on the thighs, hips, and buttocks) and subcutaneous fat (just beneath the skin) more commonly found in women prior to menopause (Nedungadi & Clegg, 2009). One review (Ohkawara, Tanaka, Miyachi, Ishikawa-Takata, & Tabata, 2007) estimated that at least 180 minutes of moderate-intensity physical activity per week is needed for reduction in central obesity. A recent study (Eriksson, Udden, Hemmingsson, & Agewall, 2010) of 50 women with central obesity found significant decreases in waist circumference, as well as improvements in blood pressure and heart functioning, after only 6 months of walking and biking and without any changes in overall weight. This research demonstrates how women receive benefits from being physically active even at lower levels of physical activity and in the absence of weight loss. These health benefits and the implications in terms of chronic disease prevention and management will be elaborated on in the following sections.

PHYSICAL ACTIVITY FOR CHRONIC DISEASE PREVENTION AND MANAGEMENT

Cardiovascular Disease

Although traditionally considered a "man's disease," cardiovascular disease (CVD), including coronary artery disease, myocardial infarction, and heart failure, is the leading cause of death among women (Lloyd-Jones et al., 2009). Increasing physical activity is one of the most controllable and effective ways to reduce CVD risk, both directly and indirectly via the positive impact it has on other CVD risk factors, such as hypertension, dyslipidemia, diabetes, and obesity. Although higher physical activity is associated with lower body mass index (BMI), which is also a protective factor against CVD risk, physical activity is an independent predictor of CVD risk among women (Hu et al., 2004; Stevens, Cai, Evenson, & Thomas, 2002; Wessel et al., 2004). Specifically, among women with a BMI in the healthy range, those who lead sedentary lives have significantly higher relative risks (1.48 [95% CI: 1.24 to 1.77]) of incident major coronary heart disease compared with those who obtain 3.5 or more hours of physical activity per week (Li et al., 2006). Similarly, physical activity may attenuate the negative impact of overweight/obesity on cardiovascular-related morbidity and mortality (Blair & Brodney, 1999; Weinstein et al., 2008), as increasing physical activity even in the absence of weight loss has been shown to decrease CVD risk among overweight/obese women (Janiszewski & Ross, 2009).

Risk reductions in CVD attributed to physical activity range from 28% to 58% (Brown et al., 2007), with even small, less intense amounts of activity decreasing CVD risk among women (Haennel & Lemire, 2002; Lee, Rexrode, Cook, Manson, & Buring, 2001; Manson et al., 2002). In fact, some research indicates that walking confers cardiovascular benefits similar to those associated with vigorous exercise among women (Manson et al., 2002). Other research suggests that more intense activity is associated with lower CVD risk. For example, better cardiorespiratory fitness, which reflects higher regular physical activity levels, has been correlated with a lower risk of CVD events and all-cause mortality among women (Gulati et al., 2003; Gulati et al., 2005; Kodama et al., 2009; Mora et al., 2003). Findings related to a dose-response relationship remain mixed (Brown et al., 2007; Kohl, 2001; Lee et al., 2001), but any amount of physical activity clearly helps reduce the risk of CVD in women of all ages, racial and ethnic backgrounds, and levels of education (Manson et al., 2002).

Physical activity can also reduce CVD severity and mortality (including both all-cause and cardiac mortality) by 20% to 32% (Taylor et al., 2004) and has been shown to be particularly effective at improving health outcomes after cardiovascular events among women (Limacher, 1998). Moreover, women with diabetes, who suffer from higher rates of cardiovascular disease, reap better cardiovascular outcomes with increasing levels of physical activity (Hu et al., 2004).

Diabetes

Regular physical activity substantially reduces women's risk of developing Type 2 diabetes mellitus. Among 68,497 women enrolled in the Nurses' Health Study who did not have diabetes at baseline, each hour per day of brisk walking was associated with a 34% (95% CI: 27% to 41%) reduction in diabetes risk (Hu et al., 2004). Based on results from that cohort, researchers estimated that approximately 43% (95% CI: 32% to 52%) of incident diabetes cases could be prevented by reducing sedentary behaviors (i.e., watching less than 10 hours per week of television) and walking briskly for at least 30 minutes per day (Hu et al., 2004). Furthermore, the combination of physical activity and modest weight loss can decrease the risk of incident diabetes by up to 58% in high-risk female populations (Knowler et al., 2002; Tuomilehto et al., 2001).

Regular physical activity also reduces the risk of gestational diabetes by approximately 50% (Dempsey, Butler, & Williams, 2005). Research has demonstrated how regular physical activity both before and during pregnancy can help prevent gestational diabetes. For example, the Nurses' Health Study II found that nulliparous women who reportedly engaged in vigorous physical activity or walked at a relatively brisk pace were significantly less likely to develop gestational diabetes when they later became pregnant; furthermore, walking more than four hours per week at a brisk or very brisk pace was associated with a lower risk of gestational diabetes (RR = 0.56 [95% CI: 0.31 to 1.00]) compared to walking fewer minutes at a casual pace (Zhang, Solomon, Manson, & Hu, 2006). Likewise, a prospective study reported that previously inactive pregnant women who adopted physical activity while pregnant had a 57% lower adjusted-odds ratio of gestational diabetes than women who remained inactive throughout pregnancy (Liu, Laditka, Mayer-Davis, & Pate, 2008). Finally, another study reported that women who engaged in recreational physical activity

throughout the year before as well as during their pregnancy had a 69% lower risk of gestational diabetes compared to women who were inactive during both time periods (Dempsey et al., 2004).

In addition to lowering the risk of incident diabetes, physical activity can also play an important role in diabetes management once women are diagnosed with diabetes. Physical activity and other lifestyle changes are effective enough to enable many women with diabetes to reduce or discontinue their diabetes medications (American College of Sports Medicine and the American Diabetes Association, 2010). In fact, physical activity plays such an integral role in blood sugar control that women with diabetes are advised not to remain inactive for more than 2 consecutive days (American College of Sports Medicine and the American Diabetes Association, 2010). However, physical activity does not need to be sustained for long periods to reap these benefits; research has shown that the recommended 150 minutes of weekly physical activity can be accumulated in shorter 10-minute bouts with the same positive effect on diabetes control (American College of Sports Medicine and the American Diabetes Association, 2010). One study reported mortality reductions of 39% and 54% among individuals with diabetes ($n = 2,896$; 52.5% women) who walked at least 2 hours and 3 to 4 hours per week, respectively (Gregg, Gerzoff, Caspersen, Williamson, & Narayan, 2003). The greatest reduction in mortality was apparent among those who walked at a perceived moderate intensity. Moreover, even in the absence of appreciable increases in exercise capacity, regular physical activity improves blood sugars and HbA1c levels among women with diabetes (Segerstrom et al., 2010). One small ($n = 9$) intervention study reported that an exercise program of twice-weekly aerobic and strength training sessions significantly improved glucose, insulin, and HbA1c levels after 4 and 16 weeks among postmenopausal women with diabetes (Tokmakidis, Zois, Volaklis, Kotsa, & Touvra, 2004). Clearly, physical activity is one of the most effective treatments for diabetes among women.

Hypertension

Lifestyle changes, including increased physical activity, can help reduce blood pressure, which along with diabetes (Kannel, Feinleib, Mcnamara, Garrison, & Castelli, 1979), is one of the leading risk factors for CVD among women (Dickey & Janick, 2001). Although blood pressure temporarily rises during and up to an hour after each bout of physical activity, regular physical activity leads to better blood pressure control and reduces the effect of each acute bout of exercise on blood pressure over time. Among hypertensive women, increased aerobic activity may result in clinically meaningful and statistically significant reductions in systolic (5.3%) and diastolic (6.9%) blood pressure (Hua, Brown, Hains, Godwin, & Parlow, 2009; Pinto et al., 2006). Moreover, a meta-analysis reported that aerobic exercise even reduced systolic and diastolic pressure among normotensive women by a modest but statistically significant 2% and 1%, respectively (Kelley, 1999).

As for which types of physical activity to recommend, research indicates that strength training is as effective as aerobic conditioning in blood pressure control among individuals with pre- and stage 1 hypertension (Collier et al., 2008) and reduces diastolic blood pressure to a greater extent among women than men (Collier, 2008). A systematic review of randomized controlled trials concluded that a combination of regular aerobic and strength training exercise offers the greatest overall health benefits, including blood pressure control, among postmenopausal women (Asikainen, Kukkonen-Harjula, & Miilunpalo, 2004).

Breast Cancer

With more than 70 studies in the area, the link between physical activity and reduced risk for breast cancer has been well-established. In fact, epidemiological studies have consistently shown an inverse relationship between physical activity and breast cancer risk (Friedenreich, 2010; Friedenreich, Courneya, & Bryant, 2001; Friedenreich, Thune, Brinton, & Albanes, 1998; Gammon, John, & Britton, 1998; International Agency for Research on Cancer, 2002; Lee & Oguma, 2006; McTiernan, 2008; Physical Activity Guidelines Advisory Committee, 2008; Reigle & Wonders, 2009). For example, in a prospective cohort study of 74,171 postmenopausal women (McTiernan et al., 2003), women who engaged in the equivalent of 1.25 to 2.5 hours per week of brisk walking had an 18% decreased risk of breast cancer compared to inactive women. Similar results were also seen when assessing premenopausal women at the 6-year follow-up of the Nurses' Health Study II (Maruti, Willett, Feskanich, Rosner, & Colditz, 2008). In this prospective cohort study of 64,777 premenopausal women, women engaging in the equivalent of 3.25 hours per week of running had a 23% lower risk of developing breast cancer before menopause than women reporting less activity.

Despite the large number of studies, it is still not clear the optimal amount, intensity, and timing of physical activity needed to reduce breast cancer risk. Reviews of the literature, however, do support a dose-response relationship for physical activity and breast cancer risk (Friedenreich, 2010; Friedenreich & Cust, 2008; Friedenreich et al., 1998; Friedenreich et al., 2001; Monninkhof et al., 2007; Physical Activity Guidelines Advisory Committee, 2008). One review of epidemiological studies that examined dose-response related to different intensities of physical activity reported a 22% risk reduction for moderate-intensity physical activity and 26% risk reduction for vigorous-intensity physical activity (Friedenreich & Cust, 2008). Another review examining the dose-response related to time spent engaged in physical activity calculated that for every 1 hour of physical activity per week, there is an additional 6% breast cancer risk reduction (Monninkhof et al., 2007).

The amount of breast cancer risk reduction from physical activity has varied across studies because of methodological differences as well as individual differences. Case control studies have generally found an average of 30% risk reduction, in contrast to cohort studies, which have found an average of 20% risk reduction (Friedenreich, 2010). Greater benefits of physical activity have also been found in women with normal BMI, compared to those who are overweight or obese (Friedenreich, 2010; Friedenreich et al., 2001; Physical Activity Guidelines Advisory Committee, 2008). With regards to other individual characteristics, such as family history of breast cancer and number of pregnancies, research has been more mixed (Physical Activity Guidelines Advisory Committee, 2008).

Several researchers have also examined whether there is a period of time when engaging in physical activity would be most beneficial for breast cancer risk reduction. Studies have found that physical activity during adolescence (Maruti et al., 2008) and adulthood (Yang, Bernstein, & Wu, 2003) is beneficial; however, there is some support for greater risk reduction for postmenopausal women rather than premenopausal women (Friedenreich, 2010; Friedenreich et al., 2001; Monninkhof et al., 2007; Physical Activity Guidelines Advisory Committee, 2008). One review (Monninkhof et al., 2007) found that recreational activity offered a 20% to 80% risk reduction for postmenopausal women and only a 15% to 20% risk reduction for premenopausal women. Other researchers have stressed long-term maintenance of physical activity as protective (Dorn, Vena, Brasure, Freudenheim, & Graham, 2003). These mixed results suggest that women of all ages could potentially reduce their risk of developing breast cancer by engaging in physical activity.

Physical activity can help decrease the risk of developing breast cancer, but it can also provide a range of benefits to women who have already been diagnosed with breast cancer. One area that has received much attention is the role of physical activity on quality of life and fatigue in breast cancer survivors. Many randomized controlled trials have examined this relationship with promising results. In fact, a meta-analysis showed small but statistically significant benefits for physical activity on quality of life and fatigue for breast cancer survivors (Courneya & Friedenreich, 1999). A more recent American College of Sports Medicine review found that, for randomized controlled trials ($n = 7$) conducted with breast cancer patients undergoing treatment (chemotherapy and radiotherapy), most studies showed improvement in quality of life ($n = 4$) and fatigue ($n = 4$) (Schmitz et al., 2010). In randomized controlled trials conducted with breast cancer survivors after treatment, 12 out of 18 studies showed improvement in quality of life and 4 out of 9 studies showed improvements in fatigue.

Another benefit that has been found for physical activity is its potential to decrease a breast cancer survivor's risk for recurrence. Although only a limited number of studies have examined the role of physical activity and breast cancer recurrence, there have been some promising results. One such study, the Nurses' Health Study, found that breast cancer survivors who engaged in the equivalent of 1 to 3 hours per week of moderate-intensity walking had a 17% reduced risk of breast cancer recurrence, and those who engaged in the equivalent of 3 to 5 hours per week of moderate-intensity walking had a 43% reduced risk of breast cancer recurrence (Holmes, Chen, Feskanich, Kroenke, & Colditz, 2005). A recent review found only four studies that assessed physical activity and breast cancer recurrence, and calculated a weighted average effect of 14% risk reduction (Patterson, Cadmus, Emond, & Pierce, 2010).

The relationship of physical activity to breast cancer mortality has been studied more extensively, generally finding a large and consistent relationship (Carmichael, Daley, Rea, & Bowden, 2010; Irwin, 2009). One review of the literature found that women who were physically active after a breast cancer diagnosis compared to those who were not active had a 24% to 67% reduction in total deaths and 50% to 53% reduction in the risk of breast cancer death (Irwin, 2009). This review found that while any amount of physical activity was beneficial, the greatest benefit was found for breast cancer survivors who were engaging in the equivalent of brisk walking 3 hours per week. For example, the Nurses' Health Study (Holmes et al., 2005) found that 3 to 5 hours per week of moderate-intensity walking reduced the risk of death for breast cancer survivors by 50% (Holmes et al., 2005). This decreased risk of death has been found in breast cancer survivors in varying stages of life (pre- and post-menopausal), weight categories (overweight and normal weight), and stages of breast cancer (Holmes et al., 2005; Irwin, 2009). One limitation of this body of research is that these studies have been observational, and it is unclear whether just the activity after the breast cancer diagnosis influences mortality or if activity before diagnosis matters. One study found increased risk of death with a decrease in physical activity after diagnosis, suggesting that activity after diagnosis may be particularly important for mortality (Irwin et al., 2008).

PHYSICAL ACTIVITY FOR SMOKING CESSATION

Recently published data from a prospective cohort study (Nurse's Health Study) indicated that active smoking ($n = 111,140$ women from 1976 and 2006) may be associated with a modest increase in the risk of breast cancer (Xue, Willett, Rosner, Hankinson, & Michels, 2011). Furthermore, the other previously mentioned chronic diseases (e.g., hypertension, cardiovascular disease, diabetes) are also related to and/or exacerbated by smoking. This particular health behavior is discussed in detail in an earlier chapter, but this section briefly highlights the beneficial impact of physical activity upon smoking cessation [see review (Ussher, Taylor, & Faulkner, 2008)] in women. For example, in a randomized controlled trial, 281 healthy sedentary female smokers received 12 cognitive-behavioral smoking cessation group sessions along with either a vigorous-intensity exercise or wellness contact control program (Marcus et al., 1998). Findings indicated that the exercise condition produced significant improvements in fitness (estimated VO^2 peak, 25 ± 6 to 28 ± 6 ml/kg/min, $p < .01$), less weight gain (3.05 vs. 5.40 kg, $p = .03$), and higher rates of continuous abstinence at end of treatment (19.4% vs. 10.2%, $p = .03$), 3 months (16.4% vs. 8.2%, $p = .03$), and 12 months (11.9% vs. 5.4%, $p = .05$) than the control group. Thus, this study demonstrated that vigorous-intensity exercise can facilitate smoking cessation with women when combined with a cognitive-behavioral smoking cessation program.

Unfortunately, many women, especially those who are sedentary and smoking, may find engaging in physical activity at such a high intensity uncomfortable and/or unappealing. Given that women are more likely to maintain moderate physical activity (Sallis et al., 1986), researchers have begun to examine the potential of moderate-intensity exercise for smoking cessation in women. In another randomized controlled trial conducted by Marcus and colleagues, sedentary female smokers ($n = 217$) received an 8-week cognitive-behavioral smoking cessation program plus either a moderate-intensity exercise program or wellness contact control condition. Both groups were equally likely to have quit smoking at the end of treatment and 12 months, but results indicated that the exercise group was more likely to report smoking cessation at the 3-month follow-up (11.9% vs. 4.6%, $p < .05$), compared with the control group. Additionally, exercise participants who reported high adherence to the exercise prescription were significantly more likely to be abstinent at the end of treatment than those reporting lower exercise adherence.

Other researchers (Kinnunen et al., 2008) have examined the efficacy of supplementing nicotine replacement therapy (gum) with a 19-week moderate-intensity exercise intervention, relative to contact control and standard care control conditions, for sedentary female smokers ($n = 182$). Results indicated higher abstinence rates in the exercise and contact control conditions, compared to the standard care condition, at the end of treatment (24.2% and 23.2% vs. 14.7%, respectively) and 12 months (9.8% and 12.5% vs. 5.9%, respectively), with no significant advantage for exercise over the contact control condition. However, results may have been impacted by the low rate of adherence to exercise. Thus, findings on studies examining moderate-intensity physical activity for smoking cessation remain mixed, and the potential mechanisms behind the relationship between exercise and smoking cessation are not yet known. Some research suggests that stress reduction could play a role. For example, Taylor and colleagues reported temporary mood improvements and craving reductions in response to acute bouts of physical activity among temporarily abstinent smokers craving cigarettes (Taylor, Ussher, & Faulkner, 2007).

PHYSICAL ACTIVITY FOR MENTAL HEALTH

Much of the recent research on physical activity's impact on mental health has focused on depression, anxiety/stress, and insomnia/sleep disorders, the most prevalent mental health problems among women (Riemann, 2007; van Mill, Hoogendijk, Vogelzangs, van Dyck, & Penninx, 2010). Evidence is mounting that regular, moderate-intensity physical activity alleviates symptoms of depression and anxiety (Daley, 2008; Dunn, Trivedi, Kampert, Clark, & Chambliss, 2005; Dunn, Trivedi, & O'Neal, 2001; Mead et al., 2009) and improves mood across the lifespan (Arent, Landers, & Etnier, 2000). One study found significant reductions in depressive symptoms among depressed women ($n = 32$) who participated in either a home- or clinic-based walking program (Craft, Freund, Culpepper, & Perna, 2007). Research indicates that physical activity may even be as effective as an antidepressant medication (sertraline, a selective serotonin reuptake inhibitor) (Blumenthal et al., 2007) and bright light therapy (Pinchasov, Shurgaja, Grischin, & Putilov, 2000) at alleviating depression among women. A systematic review and meta-analysis of five studies found that physical activity may also be an effective primary or adjunctive treatment for postpartum depression; however, relevant studies were too heterogeneous and results too mixed to draw definitive conclusions (Daley, Jolly, & MacArthur, 2009).

Similarly, a 4-month randomized controlled trial comparing the effects of walking, yoga, and no-exercise control on mental health outcomes among relatively inactive middle-aged menopausal women ($n = 164$) suggested that physical activity (both walking and yoga) may enhance positive affect and reduce negative affect; however, a causal link could not be established because of potential confounding variables, such as improvements in menopausal-related symptoms (Elavsky & McAuley, 2007). As for the amount of physical activity required to alleviate depression, a recent meta-analysis found support for as little as 30 minutes, three times per week, of moderate-intensity physical activity for at least 8 weeks (Perraton, Kumar, & Machotka, 2010).

Other mental health disorders appear to be correlated with and influenced by physical activity as well. For example, a considerable amount of evidence supports the positive effects of physical activity on insomnia and other sleep disorders (Buman & King, 2010; Montgomery & Dennis, 2002; Youngstedt, O'Connor, & Dishman, 1997). Recent studies in primarily mixed-gender samples suggest that exercise may be an effective primary or adjunctive treatment for obsessive-compulsive disorder (Brown et al., 2007) and substance use disorders (Brown et al., 2009). The limited research that has been conducted on other mental disorders (schizophrenia, bipolar disorder) indicates that physical activity may be useful for addressing illness-related symptoms (e.g., negative symptoms of schizophrenia and weight gain from treatment, neurocognitive dysfunction in bipolar disorder), but it is not touted as a cure for chronic, severe mental illnesses (Faulkner, Cohn, & Remington, 2007; Gorczynski and Faulkner, 2010; Kucyi, Alsuwaidan, Liauw, & McIntyre, 2010).

The mechanisms underlying the connection between physical activity and mental health are currently incompletely understood but appear to include biochemical/physiological (e.g., neurotransmitters, endorphins) and/or psychological (e.g., self-esteem, self-efficacy, behavioral activation, mood/affect) explanations (Daley, 2002; Ernst, Olson, Pinel, Lam, & Christie, 2006; Youngstedt, 2005). For example, physical activity could impact depression via increased self-confidence and/or levels of monoamines (noradrenaline, serotonin, dopamine) within the reward areas of the brain. Furthermore, individuals participating in physical activity may experience a release of endogenous opioids called endorphins, which can trigger an analgesic and euphoric ("runner's high"). Because scientific investigation using physical activity as medicine for mental health problems is in its infancy, many questions remain (Paluska & Schwenk, 2000; Strohle, 2009), and sex differences have yet to be extensively explored. However, current findings are likely reflective of and applicable to both sexes, as women are at least equally (if not overly) represented in most of these research studies.

INTERNET TECHNOLOGIES AND OTHER INNOVATIVE PHYSICAL ACTIVITY INTERVENTION STRATEGIES

Physical activity clearly has many benefits to offer women in terms of mental health, chronic disease prevention and management, and smoking cessation, but questions linger regarding the most effective and efficient delivery channels for providing physical activity information, resources, and support services. Modern health research strives to use technology to deliver interventions in order to reach as many individuals as possible (van den Berg, Schoones, & Vliet Vlieland, 2007; Vandelanotte, Spathonis, Eakin, & Owen, 2007). As a target population, women seek health-related information via the Internet and other technologies at higher rates than men, and thus may be particularly receptive to technology-based health behavior interventions. For example, among adults aged 18 to 64, 58% of women (vs. 43.4% of men) reportedly look up health information on the Internet, and 4.1% of women (vs. 2.5% of men) use online chat groups to learn about health topics (Cohen & Stussman, 2010). Moreover, results from a recent survey indicated that the percentage

of American adult women Internet users searching for exercise and fitness information from online resources has increased from 38% in 2002 to 52% in 2008 (Fox & Jones, 2009).

Many preexisting, theory-based physical activity interventions are relatively readily transferable via technological channels such as the Internet, cell phone applications, text messaging, and video games (Doshi, Patrick, Sallis, & Calfas, 2003; Marcus et al., 1998). Some interventions that have previously been delivered through more traditional channels such as print-based mailings or brochures, face-to-face individual and/or group sessions, and landline telephones have been translated into technology-based channels with equally efficacious results and significant cost and resource savings (Lewis, Williams, Neighbors, Jakicic, & Marcus, 2010; Marcus et al., 2007; Pinto et al., 2002). Other interventions have been developed specifically for delivery via various technologies, such as "exer-games" including the Wii-Fit (Jin, 2009; Nitz, Kuys, Isles, & Fu, 2010).

Women constitute a majority of the samples of the technology-based interventions that have been conducted to date (Marcus et al., 2007; Dinger et al., 2007). For example, in Step Into Motion ($n = 249$, 83% female), researchers compared the efficacy of three physical activity interventions (motivationally tailored Internet, motivationally tailored print, standard Internet) in a randomized trial. At 12 months, the physical activity minutes per week were 90.0, 90.0, and 80.0 for those in the tailored Internet, tailored print, and standard Internet arms, respectively ($p = .74$). Findings from this study indicated that these Web-based physical activity interventions were more efficacious than a contact control condition ($p = .01$ and $p = .004$ for the tailored and standard Internet arms, respectively) and at least as equally effective as the traditional print-based interventions.

Other technology-based interventions have been directly targeted at sedentary women. *Mobile Mums*, a randomized controlled trial comparing minimal contact control ($n = 43$) with a primarily text messaging–based physical activity intervention designed for postnatal women ($n = 45$), produced significant increases in walking and physical activity frequency (days per week) as well as trends in walking and physical activity duration (minutes per week) (Fjeldsoe, Miller, & Marshall, 2010). Benefits of mobile-based technologies such as text messaging and applications ("apps") include immediacy, frequency, and consistency. These modalities can be particularly useful for reminding women to exercise and collecting physical activity data soon after it is completed, which may increase the accuracy of self-report data and thus enable researchers to tailor their physical activity interventions appropriately (Fry & Neff, 2009; Hurling et al., 2007).

Overall, the research in this area to date is promising (Marcus et al., 2007). Additional studies are needed to determine whether individually tailoring (Carroll et al., 2010; Marcus et al., 2007; Wanner, Martin-Diener, Braun-Fahrlander, Bauer, & Martin, 2009) and/or making Website-based interventions more interactive (Hurling, Fairley, & Dias, 2006) results in greater increases in physical activity for women, compared to standard Internet-based physical activity interventions. Another emerging component that may potentially enhance modern technologies is social networking (Centola, 2010; Christakis & Fowler, 2007; Fowler & Christakis, 2010). Women may particularly benefit from physical activity interventions that incorporate social networking because of the increased social support and interaction they provide. Some challenges exist in this burgeoning field related to privacy, confidentiality, and security concerns (Atkinson & Gold, 2002), but technology-based strategies may prove particularly helpful in reaching women from underserved populations, reducing geographic limitations, and keeping pace with the fast-paced lifestyles of modern women.

PHYSICAL ACTIVITY PROMOTION IN WOMEN FROM UNDERSERVED POPULATIONS

Women from low-income and/or racial/ethnic minority groups report high rates of inactivity and suffer disproportionately from related chronic diseases (National Center for Health Statistics, 2009). Numerous physical activity intervention efforts, as well as several reviews of the available research literature in this area (Banks-Wallace & Conn, 2002; Pekmezi et al., 2009; Pekmezi et al., 2010), have been aimed at addressing these existing health disparities. One promising approach involves using computer technology to tailor physical activity interventions to the specific needs and preferences of women from underserved populations. These interventions can then be delivered via Internet, mail, and telephone and help facilitate reaching low-income, minority women who might have difficulty attending center-based exercise programs because of care-taking responsibilities and financial concerns (Richter, Wilcox, Greaney, Henderson, & Ainsworth, 2002).

In the Seamos Activas study, 93 sedentary low-income Latinas were randomly assigned to either a home-based, computer-tailored physical activity print intervention or a wellness contact control condition (Pekmezi et al., 2009). The 6-month program consisted of monthly mailings of motivation-matched physical activity manuals and computer expert system feedback reports that were individually tailored based on constructs from the Social Cognitive Theory and Transtheoretical Model, along with pedometers and physical activity logs to promote self-monitoring of exercise behavior. Moderate-intensity (or greater) physical activity increased from an average of 16.56 minutes per week (SD = 25.76) at baseline to 147.27 (SD = 241.55) at 6 months for intervention participants and from 11.88 minutes per week (SD = 21.99) to 96.79 (SD = 118.49) for wellness contact control participants. Although no between-group differences were seen in overall physical activity, intervention participants reported significantly greater increases in several related psychosocial and environmental variables, such as cognitive and behavioral processes of change and available physical activity supplies and equipment at home, compared to control participants. To corroborate these promising findings, a large, ongoing randomized controlled trial (Seamos Saludables; $n = 312$ Latinas) will test the efficacy of this home-based approach to increasing activity levels among Latinas.

Although perhaps having less potential for impacting public health, face-to-face physical activity interventions have also shown promising results with low-income and/or minority women in several studies. In a randomized trial comparing an aerobic dance intervention to a safety education control condition ($n = 151$) sedentary low-income Latinas (Hovell et al., 2008), exercise participants attended three supervised aerobic dance sessions per week for 6 months. Results indicated significantly greater increases in vigorous activity and fitness post-test, as well as some maintenance of these gains 6 months post-treatment, for exercise participants. Similarly, in a church-based study (Duru, Sarkisian, Leng, & Mangione, 2010) for underactive African American women aged 60 and older ($n = 62$), 8 weeks of group sessions with exercise classes, goal setting, and faith-based components (prayer, scripture readings), followed by monthly maintenance sessions for 6 months, produced significantly higher average increases in weekly steps than a control condition (+9883 vs. +2426, respectively, $p = .02$).

Regardless of program format, cultural sensitivity is often an important consideration when promoting physical activity among minority women. Efforts to increase the appeal and relevance of physical activity programs for the target population in the previously mentioned studies (as well as others) included incorporating the religious beliefs and practices of the community into the program, hiring bilingual/bicultural research staff, providing all program components (physical activity sessions, print materials) in the participant's preferred language (Spanish), offering childcare, and helping participants solve culture-specific barriers to exercise (i.e., childcare, social support, safety, fatigue, time constraints). Hovell and colleagues also included dance sessions to culturally popular music (e.g., salsa/merengue). Data suggests that such efforts were warmly received, as retention rates were high in all three studies. Furthermore, Seamos Activas participants reported that receiving the physical activity program in Spanish made them feel more engaged and that information regarding culture-specific barriers to physical activity was helpful, in terms of setting realistic goals and feeling understood by research staff (Pekmezi et al., 2009).

DISCUSSION

An active lifestyle is fundamental to women's health. Regular physical activity helps women achieve and maintain a healthy weight, as well as prevent and manage many of the chronic illnesses that are major causes of death and disability for women around the world, such as cardiovascular disease, diabetes, hypertension, and breast cancer. Although the connections between physical activity and chronic disease prevention and management are well-established for the most part, some questions still remain. For example, research has yet to quantify the optimal dose (i.e., frequency, intensity, duration, timing) of physical activity needed to reduce breast cancer risk and improve outcomes for women diagnosed with breast cancer. Gaps in the research literature on physical activity for mental health and smoking cessation in women were also noted. Namely, more studies are needed to determine the efficacy of moderate-intensity physical activity, as well as the relative efficacy of vigorous- versus moderate-intensity physical activity, for smoking cessation in women. Little research has been conducted on physical activity for the treatment of substance use disorders related to alcohol and illicit drugs in women, despite some promising preliminary findings in the area (Brown et al., 2009; Weinstock, Barry, & Petry, 2008).

Additionally, this review of the evidence on physical activity for women's health suggests that more emphasis should be placed on strength training. The majority of physical activity studies conducted among women are focused only on aerobic exercise, but there is a growing evidence base in support of strength training for disease prevention and management in women (Okamoto, Masuhara, & Ikuta, 2009), including diverse groups such as sedentary, older African American women (Adams et al., 2001; Rogers, Sherwood, Rogers, & Bohlken, 2002), overweight/obese women (Campbell et al., 2009; Hunter et al., 2008), women with Type 2 diabetes mellitus (Christos et al., 2009; Winnick, Gaillard, & Schuster, 2008), and breast cancer survivors (Ligibel et al., 2009; Speck et al., 2010; Waltman et al., 2010). The national guidelines recommend two strength training sessions per week (Physical Activity Guidelines Advisory Committee, 2008), but this might be a tough sell given that women have previously expressed concerns in focus groups related to physical injuries (Bopp, Wilcox, Oberrecht, Kammermann, & McElmurray, 2004; Cousins, 2000) and "bulking up" (O'Dougherty et al., 2008) as a result of strength training. Thus, when encouraging women to incorporate strength training into their lives, health professionals should consider helping women solve such potential barriers (e.g., provide brief instruction on injury prevention and education on the likelihood of bulking up, as needed).

In terms of intervention approaches, the emerging literature on technology-based strategies for promoting physical activity in women appears quite promising. Additional research is needed to tease out any additional effects gained from individually tailoring (Carroll et al., 2010; Marcus et al., 2007; Wanner et al., 2009) and/or making Website-based interventions more interactive (Hurling et al., 2006). Interactive components such as discussion boards, chat rooms, and existing, popular social networking Websites such as Twitter and Facebook remain underutilized in existing Web-based physical activity interventions and might be particularly appealing to women. Such strategies could result in enhanced social support, which has been shown to be a significant predictor of physical activity for women of various racial/ethnic backgrounds (Marquez & McAuley, 2006; Sharma, Sargent, & Stacy, 2005), by serving as a venue for connecting with potential walking partners and/or receiving physical activity encouragement and advice online.

Furthermore, interactive components could help keep women engaged and involved in the physical activity program and thus be conducive to retention (Richardson et al., 2010). Other gaps in the literature include the need for larger-scale text messaging studies with longer follow-up periods to corroborate promising preliminary findings and establish whether enduring changes to physical activity can be produced. Wii Fit has generated a great deal of enthusiasm and interest, but future studies will be needed to test the efficacy of such "exer-games" in terms of producing actual increases in fitness.

This research area has plenty of room to grow, but the potential for technology-based interventions to access and appeal to difficult-to-reach, at-risk groups is exciting. For example, Latinas report high rates of inactivity and related medical conditions (e.g., obesity, diabetes; National Center for Health Statistics, 2009), as well as numerous barriers (i.e., care-taking responsibilities, ethic of care, gender roles) that could interfere with attending traditional face-to-face physical activity counseling and classes (Pekmezi et al., 2009). Furthermore, most physical activity information and resources in the United States are available only in English, which can also impede access and participation for this group. Thus, given recent increases in Internet access and interest among Latinas, Marcus and colleagues have already begun to develop and test a Website-based intervention that offers individually tailored physical activity counseling for Latinas (the Pasos Hacia La Salud study). This format allows the women to access the program at their convenience, with respect to time and place, without interfering with care-taking or family responsibilities. Furthermore, this program is likely to be well received, because women from the Latino community played a key role in guiding the Website development and determining aesthetics and features (i.e., colorful graphics, Spanish-language text, dance video clips, salsa/merengue music) during the extensive formative research process.

Although this particular line of research is currently focused on adult women between the ages of 18 and 65, such technology-based interventions might be even more intriguing to younger generations. Adolescent girls, particularly minorities, are highly sedentary (Saxena, Borzekowski, & Rickert, 2002) and often report preferring activities such as talking on the phone, playing video games, and using the computer (Ford, Kohl, Mokdad, & Ajani, 2005). In fact, according to Pew Research Center data, most girls call friends on their cell phone every day (59%) and send and receive 80 texts per day, with minority adolescents using cell phones and accessing the Internet from mobile devices at even higher rates than other groups (Lenhart, Ling, Campbell, & Purcell, 2010). Thus, these technology-based delivery channels most likely constitute familiar and appealing approaches for providing physical activity information and counseling for this age group, particularly to the minority girls who are at greatest risk for sedentary lifestyles.

Physical activity health disparities crop up early, with significantly lower levels of habitual activity *already* found in African American girls by 9 or 10 years of age (Kimm et al., 2002). Data indicating longitudinal declines in physical activity in 100% of African American girls between the ages of 9 and 19 years (vs. 64% of White girls, $p <$ 0.001) are particularly disturbing and require further investigation and intervention (Kimm et al., 2002). In order to see real change in these rates of physical activity, related health disparities, and an overall impact on women's health, multiple levels of influence, including intrapersonal (knowledge, attitudes), interpersonal (cultural norms), institutional (school, work), and environmental and policy factors, will need to be addressed, with concern for cost-effectiveness. Furthermore, future researchers should continue to examine the physical activity barriers salient to different age groups of women and show sensitivity to such issues as the health-related needs and abilities of older women and care-taking stressors of mothers when designing physical activity programs.

REFERENCES

Adams, K. J., Swank, A. M., Berning, J. M., Sevene-Adams, P. G., Barnard, K. L., & Shimp-Bowerman, J. (2001). Progressive strength training in sedentary, older African American women. *Medicine and Science in Sports and Exercise, 33*(9), 1567–1576.

American College of Sports Medicine and the American Diabetes Association. (2010). Joint position statement: Exercise and type 2 diabetes. *Medicine and Science in Sports and Exercise, 42*(12), 2282–2303.

Arent, S. M., Landers, D. M., & Etnier, J. L. (2000). The effects of exercise on mood in older adults: A meta-analytic review. *Journal of Aging and Physical Activity, 8*(4), 407–430.

Asikainen, T. M., Kukkonen-Harjula, K., & Miilunpalo, S. (2004). Exercise for health for early postmenopausal women: A systematic review of randomised controlled trials. *Sports Medicine, 34*(11), 753–778.

Atkinson, N. L., & Gold, R. S. (2002). The promise and challenge of eHealth interventions. *American Journal of Health Behavior, 26*(6), 494–503.

Azarbad, L., & Gonder-Frederick, L. (2010). Obesity in women. *Psychiatry Clinics of North America, 33*(2), 423–440.

Banks-Wallace J., & Conn, V. (2002, September–October). Interventions to promote physical activity among African American women. *Public Health Nursing, 19*(5), 321–335.

Blair, S. N., & Brodney, S. (1999). Effects of physical inactivity and obesity on morbidity and mortality: Current evidence and research issues. *Medicine and Science in Sports and Exercise, 31*(11 Suppl), S646–S662.

Blumenthal, J. A., Babyak, M. A., Doraiswamy, P. M., Watkins, L., Hoffman, B. M., Barbour, K. A., . . . Sherwood, A. (2007). Exercise and pharmacotherapy in the treatment of major depressive disorder. *Psychosomatic Medicine, 69* (7), 587–596.

Booth, M. L., Bauman, A., & Owen, N. (2002). Perceived barriers to physical activity among older Australians. *Journal of Aging and Physical Activity, 10*(3), 271–280.

Booth, M. L., Bauman, A., Owen, N., & Gore, C. J. (1997). Physical activity preferences, preferred sources of assistance, and perceived barriers to increased activity among physically inactive Australians. *Preventive Medicine, 26*(1), 131–137.

Bopp, M., Wilcox, S., Oberrecht, L., Kammermann, S., & McElmurray, C. T. (2004). Correlates of strength training in older rural African American and Caucasian women. *Women & Health, 40*(1), 1–20.

Brown, R. A., Abrantes, A. M., Read, J. P., Marcus, B. H., Jakicic, J., Strong, D. R., . . . Gordon, A. A. (2009). Aerobic exercise for alcohol recovery rationale, program description, and preliminary findings. *Behavior Modification, 33*(2), 220–249.

Brown, R. A., Abrantes, A. M., Strong, D. R., Mancebo, M. C., Menard, J., Rasmussen, S. A., & Greenberg, B. D. (2007). A pilot study of moderate-intensity aerobic exercise for obsessive compulsive disorder. *Journal of Nervous and Mental Disease, 195*(6), 514–520.

Buman, M. P., & King, A. C. (2010). Exercise as a treatment to enhance sleep. *American Journal of Lifestyle Medicine, 4*, 500–514.

Campbell, W. W., Haub, M. D., Wolfe, R. R., Ferrando, A. A., Sullivan, D. H., Apolzan, J. W., & Iglay, H. G. (2009). Resistance training preserves fat-free mass without impacting changes in protein metabolism after weight loss in older women. *Obesity, 17*(7), 1332–1339.

Carmichael, A. R., Daley, A. J., Rea, D. W., & Bowden, S. J. (2010). Physical activity and breast cancer outcome: A brief review of evidence, current practice and future direction. *European Journal of Surgical Oncology, 36*(12), 1139–1148.

Carroll, J. K., Lewis, B. A., Marcus, B. H., Lehman, E. B., Shaffer, M. L., & Sciamanna, C. N. (2010). Computerized tailored physical activity reports. A randomized controlled trial. *American Journal of Preventive Medicine, 39*(2), 148–156.

Centers for Disease Control and Prevention. (2010). Vital signs: State-specific obesity prevalence among adults—United States, 2009. *MMWR, 59*, 1–5. Available at http://www.cdc.gov/mmwr/preview/mmwrhtml/mm59e0803a1.htm

Centola, D. (2010). The spread of behavior in an online social network experiment. *Science, 329*(5996), 1194–1197.

Christakis, N. A., & Fowler, J. H. (2007). The spread of obesity in a large social network over 32 years. *New England Journal of Medicine, 357*(4), 370–379.

Christos, Z. E., Tokmakidis, S. P., Volaklis, K. A., Kotsa, K., Touvra, A. M., Douda, E., & Youvas, I. G. (2009). Lipoprotein profile, glycemic control and physical fitness after strength and aerobic training in post-menopausal women with type 2 diabetes. *European Journal of Applied Physiology, 106*(6), 901–907.

Cohen, R. A., & Stussman, B. (2010). Health information technology use among men and women aged 18–64: Early release of estimates from the National Health Interview Survey, January–June 2009. *Health E-Stats.*

Collier, S. R. (2008). Sex differences in the effects of aerobic and anaerobic exercise on mood pressure and arterial stiffness. *Gender Medicine, 5*(2), 115–123.

Collier, S. R., Kanaley, J. A., Carhart, R., Frechette, V., Tobin, M. M., Hall, A. K., Luckenbaugh, A. N., & Fernhall, B. (2008). Effect of 4 weeks of aerobic or resistance exercise training on arterial stiffness, blood flow and blood pressure in pre- and stage-1 hypertensives. *Journal of Human Hypertension, 22*(10), 678–686.

Courneya, K. S., & Friedenreich, C. M. (1999). Physical exercise and quality of life following cancer diagnosis: A literature review. *Annals of Behavioral Medicine, 21*(2), 171–179.

Cousins, S. O. (2000). "My heart couldn't take it": Older women's beliefs about exercise benefits and risks. *Journals of Gerontology Series B—Psychological Sciences and Social Sciences, 55*(5), P283–P294.

Craft, L. L., Freund, K. M., Culpepper, L., & Perna, F. M. (2007). Intervention study of exercise for depressive symptoms in women. *Journal of Womens Health, 16*(10), 1499–1509.

Daley, A. J. (2002). Exercise therapy and mental health in clinical populations: Is exercise therapy a worthwhile intervention? *Advances in Psychiatric Treatment, 8*, 262–270.

Daley, A. J. (2008). Exercise and depression: A review of reviews. *Journal of Clinical Psychology in Medical Settings, 15*(2), 140–147.

Daley, A. J., Jolly, K., & MacArthur, C. (2009). The effectiveness of exercise in the management of post-natal depression: Systematic review and meta-analysis. *Family Practice, 26*(2), 154–162.

De Bourdeaudhuij, I., & Sallis, J. (2002). Relative contribution of psychosocial variables to the explanation of physical activity in three population-based adult samples. *Preventive Medicine, 34*(2), 279–288.

De Lorenzo, A., Deurenberg, P., Pietrantuono, M., Di Daniele, N., Cervelli, V., & Andreoli, A. (2003). How fat is obese? *Acta Diabetologica, 40*, S254–S257.

Dempsey, J. C., Butler, C. L., & Williams, M. A. (2005). No need for a pregnant pause: Physical activity may reduce the occurrence of gestational diabetes mellitus and preeclampsia. *Exercise and Sport Sciences Reviews, 33*(3), 141–149.

Dempsey, J. C., Sorensen, T. K., Williams, M. A., Lee, I. M., Miller, R. S., Dashow, E. E., & Luthy, D. A. (2004). Prospective study of gestational diabetes mellitus risk in relation to maternal recreational physical activity before and during pregnancy. *American Journal of Epidemiology*, *159*(7), 663–670.

Dickey, R. A., & Janick, J. J. (2001). Lifestyle modifications in the prevention and treatment of hypertension. *Endocrine Practice*, *7*(5), 392–399.

Dinger, M. K., Heesch, K. C., Cipriani, G., & Qualls, M. (2007). Comparison of two email-delivered, pedometer-based interventions to promote walking among insufficiently active women. *Journal of Science and Medicine in Sport*, *10*(5), 297–302.

Donnelly, J. E., Blair, S. N., Jakicic, J. M., Manore, M. M., Rankin, J. W., & Smith, B. K. (2009). American College of Sports Medicine Position Stand. Appropriate physical activity intervention strategies for weight loss and prevention of weight regain for adults. *Medicine and Science in Sports and Exercise*, *41*(2), 459–471.

Dorn, J., Vena, J., Brasure, J., Freudenheim, J., & Graham, S. (2003). Lifetime physical activity and breast cancer risk in pre- and postmenopausal women. *Medicine and Science in Sports and Exercise*, *35*(2), 278–285.

Doshi, A., Patrick, K., Sallis, J. F., & Calfas, K. (2003). Evaluation of physical activity Web sites for use of behavior change theories. *Annals of Behavioral Medicine*, *25*(2), 105–111.

Dunn, A. L., Trivedi, M. H., Kampert, J. B., Clark, C. G., & Chambliss, H. O. (2005). Exercise treatment for depression: Efficacy and dose response. *American Journal of Preventive Medicine*, *28*(1), 1–8.

Dunn, A. L., Trivedi, M. H., & O'Neal, H. A. (2001). Physical activity dose-response effects on outcomes of depression and anxiety. *Medicine and Science in Sports and Exercise*, *33*(6), S587–S597.

Duru, O. K., Sarkisian, C. A., Leng, M., & Mangione, C. M. (2010). Sisters in motion: A randomized controlled trial of a faith-based physical activity intervention. *Journal of the American Geriatrics Society*, *58*(10), 1863–1869.

Eaton, D. K., Kann, L., Kinchen, S., Shanklin, S., Ross, J., Hawkins, J., & Centers for Disease Control and Prevention. (2010). Youth risk behavior surveillance—United States, 2009.

Morbidity and Mortality Weekly Report Surveillance Summaries, *59*(5), 1–142.

Elavsky, S., & McAuley, E. (2007). Physical activity and mental health outcomes during menopause: A randomized controlled trial. *Annals of Behavioral Medicine*, *33*(2), 132–142.

Engeland, A., Bjorge, T., Sogaard, A. J., & Tverdal, A. (2003). Body mass index in adolescence in relation to total mortality: 32-year follow-up of 227,000 Norwegian boys and girls. *American Journal of Epidemiology*, *157*(6), 517–523.

Eriksson, M., Udden, J., Hemmingsson, E., & Agewall, S. (2010). Impact of physical activity and body composition on heart function and morphology in middle-aged, abdominally obese women. *Clinical Physiology Functional Imaging*, *30*(5), 354–359.

Ernst, C., Olson, A. K., Pinel, J. P., Lam, R. W., & Christie, B. R. (2006). Antidepressant effects of exercise: Evidence for an adult-neurogenesis hypothesis? *Journal of Psychiatry and Neuroscience*, *31*(2), 84–92.

Faulkner, G., Cohn, T., & Remington, G. (2007). Interventions to reduce weight gain in schizophrenia. *Cochrane Database of Systematic Reviews*, *1*, CD005148.

Fjeldsoe, B. S., Miller, Y. D., & Marshall, A. L. (2010). MobileMums: A randomized controlled trial of an SMS-based physical activity intervention. *Annals of Behavioral Medicine*, *39*(2), 101–111.

Ford, E. S., Kohl, H. W., Mokdad, A. H., & Ajani, U. A. (2005). Sedentary behavior, physical activity, and the metabolic syndrome among US adults. *Obesity Research*, *13*(3), 608–614.

Fowler, J. H., & Christakis, N. A. (2010). Cooperative behavior cascades in human social networks. *Proceedings of the National Academy of Sciences, USA*, *107*(12), 5334–5338.

Fox, S., & Jones, S. (2009). *The social life of health information*. Pew Internet and American Life Project. Washington, DC: Pew Research Center.

Friedenreich, C. M. (2010). The role of physical activity in breast cancer etiology. *Seminars in Oncology*, *37*(3), 297–302.

Friedenreich, C. M., Courneya, K. S., & Bryant, H. E. (2001). Relation between intensity of physical activity and breast cancer risk reduction. *Medicine Scientific Sports Exercise*, *33*(9), 1538–1545.

Friedenreich, C. M., & Cust, A. E. (2008). Physical activity and breast cancer risk: Impact of timing, type and dose of activity and population subgroup effects. *British Journal of Sports Medicine, 42*(8), 636–647.

Friedenreich, C. M., Thune, I., Brinton, L. A., & Albanes, D. (1998). Epidemiologic issues related to the association between physical activity and breast cancer. *Cancer, 83*(3 Suppl), 600–610.

Fry, J. P., & Neff, R. A. (2009). Periodic prompts and reminders in health promotion and health behavior interventions: Systematic review. *Journal of Medical Internet Research, 11*(2), e16.

Gammon, M. D., John, E. M., & Britton, J. A. (1998). Recreational and occupational physical activities and risk of breast cancer. *Journal of the National Cancer Institute, 90*(2), 100–117.

Gorczynski, P., & Faulkner, G. (2010). Exercise therapy for schizophrenia. *Cochrane Database System Reviews, 5*, CD004412.

Gregg, E. W., Gerzoff, R. B., Caspersen, C. J., Williamson, D. F., & Narayan, K. M. V. (2003). Relationship of walking to mortality among US adults with diabetes. *Archives of Internal Medicine, 163*(12), 1440–1447.

Gulati, M., Black, H. R., Shaw, L. J., Arnsdorf, M. F., Merz, C. N. B., Lauer, M. S., . . . Thisted, R. A. (2005). The prognostic value of a nomogram for exercise capacity in women. *New England Journal of Medicine, 353*(5), 468–475.

Gulati, M., Pandey, D. K., Arnsdorf, M. F., Lauderdale, D. S., Thisted, R. A., Wicklund, R. H., . . . Black, H. R. (2003). Exercise capacity and the risk of death in women. The St James Women Take Heart Project. *Circulation, 108*(13), 1554–1559.

Haennel, R. G., & Lemire, F. (2002). Physical activity to prevent cardiovascular disease: How much is enough? *Canadian Family Physician, 48*, 65–71.

Holmes, M. D., Chen, W. Y., Feskanich, D., Kroenke, C. H., & Colditz, G. A. (2005). Physical activity and survival after breast cancer diagnosis. *JAMA, 293*(20), 2479–2486.

Hopkins, M., King, N. A., & Blundell, J. E. (2010). Acute and long-term effects of exercise on appetite control: is there any benefit for weight control? *Current Opinion in Clinical Nutrition and Metabolism Care, 13*(6), 635–640.

Hovell, M. F., Mulvihill, M. M., Buono, M. J., Liles, S., Schade, D. H., Washington, T. A., . . . Sallis, J. F. (2008). Culturally tailored aerobic exercise intervention for low-income Latinas. *American Journal of Health Promotion, 22*(3), 155–163.

Hu, F. B., Willett, W. C., Li, T., Stampfer, M. J., Colditz, G. A., & Manson, J. E. (2004). Adiposity as compared with physical activity in predicting mortality among women. *New England Journal of Medicine, 351*(26), 2694–2703.

Hua, L. P. T., Brown, C. A., Hains, S. J. M., Godwin, M., & Parlow, J. L. (2009). Effects of low-intensity exercise conditioning on blood pressure, heart rate, and autonomic modulation of heart rate in men and women with hypertension. *Biological Research for Nursing, 11*(2), 129–143.

Hunter, G. R., Byrne, N. M., Sirikul, B., Fernandez, J. R., Zuckerman, P. A., Darnell, B. E., & Gower, B. A. (2008). Resistance training conserves fat-free mass and resting energy expenditure following weight loss. *Obesity, 16*(5), 1045–1051.

Hurling, R., Fairley, B. W., & Dias, M. B. (2006). Internet-based exercise interventions: Are more interactive designs better? *Psychology and Health, 21*(6), 757–772.

Hurling, R., Catt, M., Boni, M. D., Fairley, B. W., Hurst, T., Murray, P., . . . Sodhi, J. S. (2007). Using internet and mobile phone technology to deliver an automated physical activity program: Randomized controlled trial. *Journal of Medical Internet Research, 9*(2), e7.

International Agency for Research on Cancer. (2002). *International Agency for Research on Cancer Handbooks of Cancer Prevention: Weight Control and Physical Activity* (Vol. 6) Lyon, France: IARC Press.

Irwin, M. L. (2009). Physical activity interventions for cancer survivors. *British Journal of Sports Medicine, 43*(1), 32–38.

Irwin, M. L., Smith, A. W., McTiernan, A., Ballard-Barbash, R., Cronin, K., Gilliland, F. D., . . . Bernstein, L. (2008). Influence of pre- and post-diagnosis physical activity on mortality in breast cancer survivors: The Health, Eating, Activity, and Lifestyle Study. *Journal of Clinical Oncology, 26*(24), 3958–3964.

Jakicic, J. M., Marcus B. H., Lang, W., & Janney, C. (2008). Effect of exercise on 24-month weight loss maintenance in overweight women. *Archives of Internal Medicine, 168*(14), 1550–1559; discussion, 1559–1560.

Janiszewski, P. M., & Ross, R. (2009). The utility of physical activity in the management of global cardiometabolic risk. *Obesity, 17*, S3–S14.

Jin, S. A. A. (2009). Avatars mirroring the actual self versus projecting the ideal self: The effects of self-priming on interactivity and immersion in an exergame, Wii Fit. *Cyberpsychology & Behavior*, *12*(6), 761–765.

Juarbe, T., Turok, X. P., & Perez-Stable, E. J. (2002). Perceived benefits and barriers to physical activity among older Latina women. *Western Journal of Nursing Research*, *24*(8), 868–886.

Kannel, W. B., Feinleib, M., Mcnamara, P. M., Garrison, R. J., & Castelli, W. P. (1979). Investigation of coronary heart-disease in families: Framingham Offspring Study. *American Journal of Epidemiology*, *110*(3), 281–290.

Kelley, G. A. (1999). Aerobic exercise and resting blood pressure among women: A meta-analysis. *Preventive Medicine*, *28*(3), 264–275.

Kimm, S. Y. S., Glynn, N. W., Kriska, A. M., Barton, B. A., Kronsberg, S. S., Daniels, S. R., . . . Liu, K. (2002). Decline in physical activity in black girls and white girls during adolescence. *New England Journal of Medicine*, *347*(10), 709–715.

Kinnunen, T., Leeman, R. F., Korhonen, T., Quiles, Z. N., Terwal, D. M., Garvey, A. J., & Hartley, H. L. (2008). Exercise as an adjunct to nicotine gum in treating tobacco dependence among women. *Nicotine & Tobacco Research*, *10*(4), 689–703.

Knowler, W. C., Barrett-Connor, E., Fowler, S. E., Hamman, R. F., Lachin, J. M., Walker, E. A., . . . Diabetes Prevention Program Research Group. (2002). Reduction in the incidence of type 2 diabetes with lifestyle intervention or metformin. *New England Journal of Medicine*, *346*(6), 393–403.

Kodama, S., Saito, K., Tanaka, S., Maki, M., Yachi, Y., Asumi, M., . . . Sone, H. (2009). Cardiorespiratory fitness as a quantitative predictor of all-cause mortality and cardiovascular events in healthy men and women: A meta-analysis. *JAMA*, *301*(19), 2024–2035.

Kohl, H. W. (2001). Physical activity and cardiovascular disease: Evidence for a dose response. *Medicine and Science in Sports and Exercise*, *33*(6), S472–S483.

Kowal, J., & Fortier, M. S. (2007). Physical activity behavior change in middle-aged and older women: The role of barriers and of environmental characteristics. *Journal of Behavioral Medicine*, *30*(3), 233–242.

Kucyi, A., Alsuwaidan, M. T., Liauw, S. S., & McIntyre, R. S. (2010). Aerobic physical exercise as a possible treatment for neurocognitive dysfunction in bipolar disorder. *Postgraduate Medicine*, *122*(6), 107–116.

Lee, I.-M., & Oguma, Y. (2006). Physical activity. In D. F. Schottenfeld & F. Joseph (Eds.), *Cancer epidemiology and prevention* (Vol. 3) New York, NY: Oxford University Press.

Lee, I. M., Rexrode, K. M., Cook, N. R., Manson, J. E., & Buring, J. E. (2001). Physical activity and coronary heart disease in women: Is "no pain, no gain" passe? *JAMA*, *285*(11), 1447–1454.

Lenhart, A., Ling, R., Campbell, S., & Purcell, K. (2010). Teens and mobile phones. Pew Internet Research Center. Available at http://pewinternet.org/Reports/2010/Teens-and-Mobile-Phones/Summary-of-findings.aspx

Lewis, B. A., Williams, D. M., Neighbors, C. J., Jakicic, J. M., & Marcus, B. H. (2010). Cost analysis of Internet vs. print interventions for physical activity promotion. *Psychology of Sport and Exercise*, *11*(3), 246–249.

Li, T. Y., Rana, J. S., Manson, J. E., Willett, W. C., Stampfer, M. J., Colditz, G. A., . . . Hu, F. B. (2006). Obesity as compared with physical activity in predicting risk of coronary heart disease in women. *Circulation*, *113*(4), 499–506.

Ligibel, J. A., Giobbie-Hurder, A., Olenczuk, D., Campbell, N., Salinardi, T., Winer, E. P., & Mantzoros, C. S. (2009). Impact of a mixed strength and endurance exercise intervention on levels of adiponectin, high molecular weight adiponectin and leptin in breast cancer survivors. *Cancer Causes Control*, *20*(8), 1523–1528.

Limacher, M. C. (1998). Exercise and rehabilitation in women: Indications and outcomes. *Cardiology Clinics*, *16*(1), 27–36.

Liu, J., Laditka, J. N., Mayer-Davis, E. J., & Pate, R. R. (2008). Does physical activity during pregnancy reduce the risk of gestational diabetes among previously inactive women? *Birth-Issues in Perinatal Care*, *35*(3), 188–195.

Lloyd-Jones, D., Adams, R., Carnethon, M., De Simone, G., Ferguson, T. B., Flegal, K., . . . Hong, Y. (2009). Heart disease and stroke statistics—2009 update: A report from the American Heart Association Statistics Committee and Stroke Statistics Subcommittee. *Circulation*, *119* (3), 480–486.

Manson, J. E., Greenland, P., LaCroix, A. Z., Stefanick, M. L., Mouton, C. P., Oberman, A., &

Siscovick, D. S. (2002). Walking compared with vigorous exercise for the prevention of cardiovascular events in women. *New England Journal of Medicine, 347*(10), 716–725.

Marcus, B. H., Lewis, B. A., Williams, D. M., Dunsiger, S., Jakicic, J. M., Whiteley, J. A., . . . Parisi, A. F. (2007). A comparison of Internet and print-based physical activity interventions. *Archives of Internal Medicine, 167*(9), 944–949.

Marcus, B. H., Owen, N., Forsyth, L. H., Cavill, N. A., & Fridinger, F. (1998). Physical activity interventions using mass media, print media, and information technology. *American Journal of Preventive Medicine, 15*(4), 362–378.

Marquez, D. X., & McAuley, E. (2006). Social cognitive correlates of leisure time physical activity among Latinos. *Journal of Behavioral Medicine, 29*(3), 281–289.

Maruti, S. S., Willett, W. C., Feskanich, D., Rosner, B., & Colditz, G. A. (2008). A prospective study of age-specific physical activity and premenopausal breast cancer. *Journal of the National Cancer Institute, 100*(10), 728–737.

McTiernan, A. (2008). Mechanisms linking physical activity with cancer. *Nature Reviews Cancer, 8*(3), 205–211.

McTiernan, A., Kooperberg, C., White, E., Wilcox, S., Coates, R., Adams-Campbell, L. L., . . . Ockene, J. (2003). Recreational physical activity and the risk of breast cancer in postmenopausal women: The Women's Health Initiative Cohort Study. *JAMA, 290,* 1331–1336.

Mead, G. E., Morley, W., Campbell, P., Greig, C. A., McMurdo, M., & Lawlor, D. A. (2009). Exercise for depression. *Cochrane Database of Systematic Reviews, 3,* CD004366.

Monninkhof, E. M., Elias, S. G., Vlems, F. A., van der Tweel, I., Schuit, A. J., Voskuil, D. W., & van Leeuwen, F. E. (2007). Physical activity and breast cancer: A systematic review. *Epidemiology, 18*(1), 137–157.

Montgomery, P., & Dennis, J. (2002). Physical exercise for sleep problems in adults aged 60+. *Cochrane Database System Reviews, 4,* CD003404.

Mora, S., Redberg, R. F., Cui, Y. D., Whiteman, M. K., Flaws, J. A., Sharrett, A. R., & Blumenthal, R. S. (2003). Ability of exercise testing to predict cardiovascular and all-cause death in asymptomatic women: A 20-year follow-up of the lipid

research clinics prevalence study. *JAMA, 290*(12), 1600–1607.

National Center for Health Statistics. (2010). *Health, United States, 2009: With special feature on medical technology.* Hyattsville, MD: Author.

Nedungadi, T. P., & Clegg, D. J. (2009). Sexual dimorphism in body fat distribution and risk for cardiovascular diseases. *Journal of Cardiovascular Translational Research, 2*(3), 321–327.

Nitz, J. C., Kuys, S., Isles, R., & Fu, S. (2010). Is the Wii Fit (TM) a new-generation tool for improving balance, health and well-being? A pilot study. *Climacteric, 13*(5), 487–491.

O'Dougherty, M., Dallman, A., Turcotte, L., Patterson, J., Napolitano, M. A., & Schmitz, K. H. (2008). Barriers and motivators for strength training among women of color and Caucasian women. *Women & Health, 47*(2), 41–62.

Ohkawara, K., Tanaka, S., Miyachi, M., Ishikawa-Takata, K., & Tabata, I. (2007). A dose-response relation between aerobic exercise and visceral fat reduction: Systematic review of clinical trials. *International Journal of Obesity, 31*(12), 1786–1797.

Okamoto, T., Masuhara, M., & Ikuta, K. (2009). Home-based resistance training improves arterial stiffness in healthy premenopausal women. *European Journal of Applied Physiology, 107*(1), 113–117.

Paluska, S. A., & Schwenk, T. L. (2000). Physical activity and mental health: Current concepts. *Sports Medicine, 29*(3), 167–180.

Patterson, R. E., Cadmus, L. A., Emond, J. A., & Pierce, J. P. (2010). Physical activity, diet, adiposity and female breast cancer prognosis: A review of the epidemiologic literature. *Maturitas, 66*(1), 5–15.

Pekmezi, D. W., Neighbors, C. J., Lee, C. S., Gans, K. M., Bock, B. C., Morrow, K. M., . . . Marcus, B. H. (2009). Randomized trial of a culturally adapted physical activity intervention for Latinas. *American Journal of Preventive Medicine, 37*(6), 495–500.

Pekmezi, D. W., Williams, D. M., Dunsinger, S., Jennings, E. G., Lewis, B. A., Jakicic, J. M., & Marcus, B. H. (2010). Feasibility of using computer-tailored and internet-based interventions to promote physical activity in underserved populations. *Telemedicine Journal and E-health: The Official Journal of the American Telemedicine Association, 16*(4), 498–503.

Perraton, L. G., Kumar, S., & Machotka, Z. (2010). Exercise parameters in the treatment of clinical depression: A systematic review of randomized controlled trials. *Journal of Evaluation in Clinical Practice*, *16*(3), 597–604.

Physical Activity Guidelines Advisory Committee. (2008). *Physical Activity Guidelines Advisory Committee Report, 2008*. Washington, DC: Department of Health and Human Services.

Pinchasov, B. B., Shurgaja, A. M., Grischin, O. V., & Putilov, A. A. (2000). Mood and energy regulation in seasonal and non-seasonal depression before and after midday treatment with physical exercise or bright light. *Psychiatry Research*, *94*(1), 29–42.

Pinto, A., Di Raimondo, D., Tuttolomondo, A., Fernandez, P., Arna, V., & Licata, G. (2006). Twenty-four hour ambulatory blood pressure monitoring to evaluate effects on blood pressure of physical activity in hypertensive patients. *Clinical Journal of Sport Medicine*, *16*(3), 238–243.

Pinto, B. M., Friedman, R., Marcus, B. H., Kelley, H., Tennstedt, S., & Gillman, M. W. (2002). Effects of a computer-based, telephone-counseling system on physical activity. *American Journal of Preventive Medicine*, *23*(2), 113–120.

Reigle, B. S., & Wonders, K. (2009). Breast cancer and the role of exercise in women. *Methods in Molecular Biology*, *472*, 169–189.

Richardson, C. R., Buis, L. R., Janney, A. W., Goodrich, D. E., Sen, A., Hess, M. L., . . . Piette, J. D. (2010). An online community improves adherence in an Internet-mediated walking program. Part 1: Results of a randomized controlled trial. *Journal of Medical Internet Research*, *12*(4), 138–153.

Richter, D. L., Wilcox, S., Greaney, M. L., Henderson, K. A., & Ainsworth, B. E. (2002). Environmental, policy, and cultural factors related to physical activity in African American women. *Women & Health*, *36*(2), 91–109.

Riemann, D. (2007). Insomnia and comorbid psychiatric disorders. *Sleep Medicine*, *8*, S15–S20.

Rogers, M. E., Sherwood, H. S., Rogers, N. L., & Bohlken, R. M. (2002). Effects of dumbbell and elastic band training on physical function in older inner-city African-American women. *Women & Health*, *36*(4), 33–41.

Sallis, J. F., Haskell, W. L., Fortmann, S. P., Vranizan, K. M., Taylor, C. B., & Solomon, D. S. (1986). Predictors of adoption and maintenance of physical activity in a community sample. *Preventive Medicine*, *15*(4), 331–341.

Saxena, R., Borzekowski, D. L. G., & Rickert, V. I. (2002). Physical activity levels among urban adolescent females. *Journal of Pediatric and Adolescent Gynecology*, *15*(5), 279–284.

Schmitz, K. H., Courneya, K. S., Matthews, C., Demark-Wahnefried, W., Galvao, D. A., Pinto, B. M., . . . Schwartz, A. L. (2010). American College of Sports Medicine roundtable on exercise guidelines for cancer survivors. *Medicine and Science in Sports Exercise*, *42*(7), 1409–1426.

Segerstrom, A. B., Glans, F., Eriksson, K. F., Holmback, A. M., Groop, L., Thorsson, O., & Wollmer, P. (2010). Impact of exercise intensity and duration on insulin sensitivity in women with T2D. *European Journal of Internal Medicine*, *21*(5), 404–408.

Sharma, M., Sargent, L., & Stacy, R. (2005). Predictors of leisure-time physical activity among African American women. *American Journal of Health Behavior*, *29*(4), 352–359.

Speck, R. M., Gross, C. R., Hormes, J. M., Ahmed, R. L., Lytle, L. A., Hwang, W. T., & Schmitz, K. H. (2010). Changes in the Body Image and Relationship Scale following a one-year strength training trial for breast cancer survivors with or at risk for lymphedema. *Breast Cancer Research and Treatment*, *121*(2), 421–430.

Stevens, J., Cai, J. W., Evenson, K. R., & Thomas, R. (2002). Fitness and fatness as predictors of mortality from all causes and from cardiovascular disease in men and women in the Lipid Research Clinics Study. *American Journal of Epidemiology*, *156*(9), 832–841.

Strohle, A. (2009). Physical activity, exercise, depression and anxiety disorders. *Journal of Neural Transmission*, *116*(6), 777–784.

Sweet, S. N., & Fortier, M. S. (2010). Improving physical activity and dietary behaviours with single or multiple health behaviour interventions? A synthesis of meta-analyses and reviews. *International Journal of Environmental Research and Public Health*, *7*(4), 1720–1743.

Taylor, A. H., Ussher, M. H., & Faulkner, G. (2007). The acute effects of exercise on cigarette cravings, withdrawal symptoms, affect and smoking behaviour: A systematic review. *Addiction*, *102*(4), 534–543.

Taylor, R. S., Brown, A., Ebrahim, S., Jolliffe, J., Noorani, H., Rees, K., . . . Oldridge, N. (2004).

Exercise-based rehabilitation for patients with coronary heart disease: Systematic review and meta-analysis of randomized controlled trials. *American Journal of Medicine, 116*(10), 682–692.

Tokmakidis, S. P., Zois, C. E., Volaklis, K. A., Kotsa, K., & Touvra, A. M. (2004). The effects of a combined strength and aerobic exercise program on glucose control and insulin action in women with type 2 diabetes. *European Journal of Applied Physiology, 92*(4–5), 437–442.

Tuomilehto, J., Lindstrom, J., Eriksson, J. G., Valle, T. T., Hamalainen, H., Ilanne-Parikka, P., . . . Uusitupa, M. (2001). Prevention of type 2 diabetes mellitus by changes in lifestyle among subjects with impaired glucose tolerance. *New England Journal of Medicine, 344*(18), 1343–1350.

Urizar, G. G., Hurtz, S. Q., Albright, C. L., Ahn, D. K., Atienza, A. A., & King, A. C. (2005). Influence of maternal stress on successful participation in a physical activity intervention: The IMPACT project. *Women & Health, 42*(4), 63–82.

Ussher, M. H., Taylor, A., & Faulkner, G. (2008). Exercise interventions for smoking cessation. *Cochrane Database System Reviews, 4,* CD002295.

Van den Berg, M. H., Schoones, J. W., & Vliet Vlieland, T. P. (2007). Internet-based physical activity interventions: A systematic review of the literature. *Journal of Medical Internet Research, 9*(3), e26.

Van Mill, J. G., Hoogendijk, W. J. G., Vogelzangs, N., van Dyck, R., & Penninx, B. W. (2010). Insomnia and sleep duration in a large cohort of patients with major depressive disorder and anxiety disorders. *Journal of Clinical Psychiatry, 71*(3), 239–246.

Vandelanotte, C., Spathonis, K. M., Eakin, E. G., & Owen, N. (2007). Website-delivered physical activity interventions a review of the literature. *American Journal of Preventive Medicine, 33*(1), 54–64.

Vu, M. B., Murrie, D., Gonzalez, V., & Jobe, J. B. (2006). Listening to girls and boys talk about girls' physical activity behaviors. *Health Education & Behavior, 33*(1), 81–96.

Waltman, N. L., Twiss, J. J., Ott, C. D., Gross, G. J., Lindsey, A. M., Moore, T. E., . . . Kupzyk, K. (2010). The effect of weight training on bone mineral density and bone turnover in post-menopausal breast cancer survivors with bone loss: A 24-month randomized controlled trial. *Osteoporosis International, 21*(8), 1361–1369.

Wanner, M., Martin-Diener, E., Braun-Fahrlander, C., Bauer, G., & Martin, B. W. (2009). Effectiveness of active-online, an individually tailored physical activity intervention, in a real-life setting: Randomized controlled trial. *Journal of Medical Internet Research, 11*(3), e23.

Weinstein, A. R., Sesso, H. D., Lee, I. M., Rexrode, K. M., Cook, N. R., Manson, J. E., . . . Gaziano, J. M. (2008). The joint effects of physical activity and body mass index on coronary heart disease risk in women. *Archives of Internal Medicine, 168*(8), 884–890.

Weinstock, J., Barry, D., & Petry, N. M. (2008). Exercise-related activities are associated with positive outcome in contingency management treatment for substance use disorders. *Addictive Behaviors, 33*(8), 1072–1075.

Wessel, T. R., Arant, C. B., Olson, M. B., Johnson, B. D., Reis, S. L., Sharaf, B. L., . . . Merz, N. B. (2004). Relationship of physical fitness vs. body mass index with coronary artery disease and cardiovascular events in women. *JAMA, 292*(10), 1179–1187.

Westerterp, K. R., & Goran, M. I. (1997). Relationship between physical activity related energy expenditure and body composition: A gender difference. *International Journal of Obesity, 21*(3), 184–188.

Winnick, J. J., Gaillard, T., & Schuster, D. P. (2008). Resistance training differentially affects weight loss and glucose metabolism of White and African American patients with type 2 diabetes mellitus. *Ethnicity & Disease, 18*(2), 152–156.

Xue, F., Willett, W. C., Rosner, B. A., Hankinson, S. E., & Michels, K. B. (2011). Cigarette smoking and the incidence of breast cancer. *Archives of Internal Medicine, 171*(2), 125–133.

Yang, D., Bernstein, L., & Wu, A. H. (2003). Physical activity and breast cancer risk among Asian-American women in Los Angeles: A case-control study. *Cancer, 97*(10), 2565–2575.

Youngstedt, S. D. (2005). Effects of exercise on sleep. *Clinical Journal of Sports Medicine, 24*(2), 355–365, xi.

Youngstedt, S. D., O'Connor, P. J., & Dishman, R. K. (1997). The effects of acute exercise on sleep: A quantitative synthesis. *Sleep, 20*(3), 203–214.

Zhang, C. L., Solomon, C. G., Manson, J. E., & Hu, F. B. (2006). A prospective study of pregravid physical activity and sedentary behaviors in relation to the risk for gestational diabetes mellitus. *Archives of Internal Medicine, 166*(5), 543–548.

REPRODUCTIVE HEALTH

CHAPTER 12

Women's Sexual Health

PATRICIA J. MOROKOFF AND MAGGIE L. GORRAIZ

INTRODUCTION

In this chapter we present a model for women's sexual health and discuss the relevant research literature supporting components of this model. We begin by considering barriers to healthy sexuality for women, then present the research literature relating to each dimension of healthy sexuality, and finally consider the balance between relational and individual goals with respect to sexuality. To evaluate this model we draw on the work of feminist theorists in identifying what constitutes healthy sexuality for women and examine the influences of sexual development and culture.

Do We Need a Model for Healthy Sexuality?

Sexual desire, the physical changes that comprise the sexual response cycle, and sexual behaviors are fundamental to what it means to be human. A satisfying sex life is one of life's joys, and women who are satisfied with their sex lives tend to report greater well-being (Davison, Bell, LaChina, Holden, & Davis, 2009). As with other aspects of human functioning, expectations for sexual behavior are closely intertwined with cultural expectations, especially in the area of gender role expectations. Before outlining

our view of healthy sexuality, it may be relevant to think about whether we even need such a model for women. Alternatively put, why do we think that women's sexuality has the potential to be unhealthy? Part of the answer, as will be documented in this chapter, is that for women, the potential negative consequences of sex in real life are extensive, including unwanted pregnancy, sexually transmitted disease, sexual victimization, engaging in unwanted sexual behaviors, emotional distress or trauma, and adverse effects on an intimate relationship.

Socialized gender expectations encourage women to value relatedness and nurturance of others. This valuing is enacted in many spheres of a relationship, including cooking, cleaning, and emotionally caring for a partner. It extends to the area of sexuality, in which women, who are socialized to put the needs of others ahead of their own, may engage in sexual care-taking of a partner's needs with less attention to their own sexual desires or even lack of desire. The sexual goals of experiencing one's own desires, owning and acting on these desires, and focusing on one's own pleasure are in sharp contrast to the ideals of femininity with its emphasis on self-sacrifice. Gender socialization has been found to influence sexual satisfaction in lesbian and bisexual women as well as heterosexual women (Henderson, Levahot, & Simoni, 2009).

From the standpoint of sexual ideals, sex should be maximally gratifying with minimal negative consequences. Yet, many women report sexual dysfunctions, including low sexual desire, difficulty becoming aroused, difficulty reaching orgasm, sexual pain, and sexual anxiety. Overall, 43% of women compared to 31% of men report sexual dysfunction (Laumann, Paik, & Rosen, 1999). In this study, African American women reported a higher rate of low sexual desire and less sexual pleasure compared to White women, although White women were more likely to report sexual pain. Hispanic/Latina women reported fewer sexual problems than other ethnic groups. Clearly, many women do not achieve the concept of ideal sexuality.

The goal of sexual satisfaction for women is of recent origin. In previous eras, women were not expected to achieve personal goals, including goals of ideal or healthy sexuality. The challenge in conceptualizing healthy sex for women is in integrating traditional gender expectations for women with a new set of sexual ideals. Therefore, we assert that a model for healthy sexuality is needed. However, before proposing the following characteristics of healthy sexuality, we note that barriers based on traditional ideals for femininity must be overcome in order to actualize these characteristics in the lives of women.

Characteristics of Healthy Sexuality

We propose that healthy sexuality will have the following characteristics:

- Active
- Consensual
- Wanted/Liked
- Safe

ACTIVE SEX

Research literatures over several domains strongly support the notion that healthy sexuality requires women to play an active, nonsubmissive role in the sexual relationship. We consider active sexuality to include avoiding a submissive sexual role in relation to the partner, focusing on one's own internal sexual feelings rather than thinking of oneself from another's perspective, and having the ability to assert one's sexual desires and preferences to a partner.

Dominance and Submission

Themes of dominance and submission are core elements of Western sexuality, as frequently depicted in myth (e.g., the rape of Persephone), literature (e.g., Shakespeare's *The Rape of Lucretia; The Girl with the Dragon Tattoo*), sculpture (e.g., *Rape of the Sabine Women*), painting (e.g., Titian's *Rape of Europa*), and film (rape revenge movies, e.g., *Thelma and Louise*). A component of the traditional feminine role is sexual passivity. Gendered expectations for sex allow and encourage men to take an active, dominant role in initiating sexual activity, whereas women are not encouraged to directly initiate sex (although they may signal receptivity). Once engaged in sex, the traditional woman acquiesces to her partner's desires rather than imposing her own desire for specific sexual acts (Morokoff, 2000). Because an intuitive expectation for healthy sex is that it be satisfying, the question immediately arises whether sexual satisfaction can be obtained through the passive role rather than requiring the active or dominant role. In discussing a passive role, we are not referring here to sexual role-play in which a partner may role-play sexual submission, but rather referencing an internalization of the submissive role in relation to sexuality.

The question has been addressed in an elegant series of studies (Kiefer, Sanchez, Kalinka, & Ybarra, 2006; Sanchez, Kiefer, & Ybarra, 2006), in which sexual passivity and submissiveness are demonstrated to be internalized at a nonconscious level in heterosexual women. These studies, using a reaction time test, show that heterosexual women respond more quickly to sex-primed passivity-related words compared to neutral-primed passivity-related words. Examples of sex-primed words were *sex, climax, oral, naked, caress*, and *bed*; the neutral words included *oven, brick, chalk, clock, table*, and *house*. Passivity-related words were *comply, submit, slave, yield, concede*, and *weaken*. Facilitation of response by sex-primed passivity-related words was not found for men. Furthermore, the extent to which sex primes facilitated response to passivity-related words predicted submissive behavior. Kiefer and colleagues (2006) demonstrate that women's adoption of a submissive sexual role predicted lower reported sexual arousal. Sanchez et al. (2006) report that extent of reaction time response to sex-primed submissive words predicted reported orgasm.

This finding has also been demonstrated in Hispanic/Latina women (Rodriguez, Morokoff & Gorraiz, 2012). Hispanic/Latino culture may promote the expectation that men should be strong, sexually experienced, independent, and unemotional, whereas women should be submissive, dependent, and emotional (Raffaelli & Suarez, 1998). Compared to White women, Hispanic/Latina women have been shown to have less knowledge of human immunodeficiency virus (HIV), less sexual power in relationships, and less self-efficacy to use condoms (Gómez & VanOss Marin, 1996).

Rodriguez et al. (2012) demonstrated the same results previously found for White women: Faster reaction time responses to sex-primed submission words than to neutral-primed submission words with slower times for sex-primed dominance words compared to neutral-primed dominance words indicating that the Hispanic/Latina women associate sex with submission just as White women do. The hypothesis that Hispanic/Latina women in this college-educated sample would demonstrate a different pattern because of cultural differences was not supported.

An additional study (Kiefer & Sanchez, 2007) demonstrated that passive sexual behavior (in which male and female participants rated items such as "I tend to take on a submissive role during sexual activity") was associated with lower sexual satisfaction for both men and women. However, women reported engaging in more sexual passivity than men. Endorsement of traditional roles (passivity for women; dominance for men) was associated with greater sexual passivity for women but less for men. Again, passivity was found to be negatively related to reported sexual arousal, ability to reach orgasm, and sexual satisfaction. Furthermore, sexual autonomy, defined as feeling that one's actions in sexual contexts are authentic expressions of the self, was found to function as a mediator between sexual passivity and sexual outcomes. According to the authors, "these findings suggest that women engage in sexual passivity largely because sexual scripts dictate such behavior and that sexual passivity adversely affects subjective sexual experiences for both men and women" (Kiefer & Sanchez, 2007, p. 285). These results were supported by Rodriguez et al.'s (2012) finding that for both Hispanic/Latina and White women, implicit sex-submission associations significantly predicted the level of women's perceptions of control over their own sexuality and identification with female gender roles. The stronger the sex-submission association, the less control over their own sexuality women reported and the stronger the identification with traditional female gender roles.

The implication is that in order to feel able to genuinely express and act upon one's sexual desires—a direct predictor of sexual arousal, orgasm, and satisfaction—one must take an active, assertive sexual role. Adherence to traditional sex roles lowers women's but not men's sexual activity. It is not clear whether this is predicated on a heterosexual relationship in which gender roles prescribe levels of sexual activity. These studies demonstrate that (a) in women, sexual satisfaction is inversely related to sexual passivity (measured by self-reported sexual arousal, orgasm, or sexual satisfaction) and (b) gendered expectations for women's sexual passivity present a barrier to sexual satisfaction. It is an interesting question requiring further research, how such themes manifest in lesbian sexual relationships.

Internal Focus

Internal focus refers to paying attention to one's own thoughts, feelings, and sensations. It is a concept closely related to the idea of *flow*, which has been defined as complete absorption in the present moment (Nakamura & Csikszentmihalyi, 2009). It has been hypothesized that this internal focus leads to a self-directed, active sexuality and is in contrast to a preoccupation with how one is perceived by others (Frederickson & Roberts, 1997). A barrier to this internal focus is the social phenomenon of sexualization and its counterpart sexual objectification.

Sexualization and Sexual Objectification The Report of the American Psychological Association (APA) Task Force on the Sexualization of Girls (2010) indicates that sexualization occurs when

> (1) A person's value comes only from his or her sexual appeal or behavior, to the exclusion of other characteristics; (2) a person is held to a standard that equates physical attractiveness (narrowly defined) with being sexy; (3) a person is sexually objectified—that is, made into a thing for others' sexual use, rather than seen as a person with the capacity for independent action and decision making; and (4) sexuality is inappropriately imposed upon a person.

One consequence of this emphasis on appearance is that girls may begin to focus on how they look to the external observer. According to Fredrickson and Roberts' (1997) objectification theory, repeated subjection to physical inspection and evaluation causes women to adopt an observer's perspective on their bodies. As a result, women come to treat themselves as objects, or a collection of parts, to be looked at and evaluated by others. This internalization of an observer's perspective is referred to as *self-objectification*.

Numerous studies have demonstrated a relationship between sexual objectification (e.g., through exposure to sexualized media images) and self-objectification (Aubrey, 2006b; Morry & Staska, 2001; Roberts & Gettman, 2004). Hill and Fischer (2008) examined the relationship between sexualized gaze/harassment and self-objectification in lesbian and heterosexual women and found that both groups reported similar levels of harassment and that for both groups harassment was associated with self-objectification. Self-objectification can in turn cause further preoccupation with physical appearance, manifesting as habitual body monitoring or body surveillance (McKinley & Hyde, 1996; Moradi, Dirks, & Matteson, 2005). If a woman evaluates herself and feels she does not measure up to societal standards for attractiveness, she may feel body shame. Self-objectification is further related to body shame and impaired sexual functioning (Calogero & Thompson, 2009; Sanchez & Kiefer, 2007). Sanchez and Kiefer (2007) found that feeling body shame during sexual interactions decreased sexual functioning in both heterosexual men and women. In a comparison of lesbian and heterosexual samples, Kozee and Tylka (2006) found that for lesbian women there was evidence that sexual objectification directly influenced body surveillance, which in turn predicted body shame, whereas in heterosexual women, self-objectification was a mediating link.

In summary, sexual objectification of women is prevalent and often leads to self-objectification. Both objectification and self-objectification have been shown to be associated with body shame, anxiety, and disrupted flow, all of which may reduce focus on internal sensations, negatively affecting sexual satisfaction. The more that a woman focuses on how she appears to her partner, especially when she feels shame concerning her body, the less easily she can maintain the kind of internal focus associated with flow and positive sexual experiences.

Sexual Assertiveness

Sexual assertiveness is conceptualized as the self-perceived ability to engage in wanted sexual activity, refuse unwanted sexual activity, communicate effectively concerning sex, and engage in protected, safe sexual behaviors (Morokoff et al., 1997). A study of young women in family planning clinics revealed that close to 20% believed that they never have the right to make decisions about contraception, to tell a partner that they do not want to have intercourse without protection, or to stop foreplay at any time (Rickert, Sanghvi, & Wiemann, 2002). Several instruments have been developed to measure sexual assertiveness (e.g., Morokoff et al., 1997). Lower sexual assertiveness has been associated with more risky sexual behavior, lower condom self-efficacy, and lower stage of change for condom use (Harlow, Quina, Morokoff, Rose, & Grimley, 1993; Morokoff et al., 1997). Sexual communication in intimate relationships has also been identified as a predictor of safer sex behaviors (Quina, Harlow, Morokoff, Burkholder & Dieter, 2000). DiClemente and Wingood (1995) designed a social skills HIV sexual risk reduction intervention for African American women based on community and focus group input. Because community members identified a relative lack of power in sexual relationships experienced by African American women, one of the components of the program was sexual assertiveness. The intervention was successful in comparison to an HIV education control in increasing sexual assertiveness.

Hyperfemininity, defined as adherence to traditional attitudes about the rights and roles of women in society, is related to lower sexual assertiveness (Williams, Morokoff, & Rossi, 2011). The study found that women who maintain traditional views of femininity are less likely to assert themselves in sexual situations, in both initiating and refusing sex. Moreover, women who strongly endorse hyperfemininity may engage in risky sexual behaviors such as an increase in frequency of casual sex.

Sexual assertiveness has been shown to be inversely predicted by abuse experiences. For example, past sexual victimization was found to predict sexual assertiveness in refusing unwanted sexual advances. In this longitudinal study, sexual assertiveness in refusing unwanted sex measured at baseline was found to predict subsequent victimization 12 and 24 months later (Livingston, Testa, & VanZile-Tamsen, 2007). The authors conceptualize a reciprocal relationship between sexual victimization and sexual assertiveness, in which the victimization experience diminishes women's beliefs about their rights to refuse unwanted sex, which in turn makes revictimization more likely.

A review of the evidence across the domains of dominance/submission, flow, and sexual assertiveness leads to a clear conclusion that an active expression of sexuality is important for healthy sexuality in promoting sexual satisfaction, positive sexual functioning, and safe sexual behavior. Furthermore, in all studies examined, active sexuality appeared equally important across ethnic/racial groups. This construct requires further study in women's same-sex relationships.

CONSENSUAL SEX

Consensual sex requires an ongoing, active process of communication that is the responsibility of both partners. Nonconsensual sex can be conceptualized on a continuum ranging from verbal pressure to threats and intimidation to physical coercion. Such coercion can be used against girls as well as women. The research literature reviewed as follows presents a clear case that there are multiple sexual and general health sequelae to coerced participation in sex.

Childhood Sexual Abuse (CSA)

Definition and Prevalence   As a form of child maltreatment, CSA has been defined within the federal Child Abuse Prevention and Treatment Act (Public Law 93 247 originally enacted in 1974). According to this statute, CSA includes

> (A) the employment, use, persuasion, inducement, enticement, or coercion of any child to engage in, or assist any other person to engage in, any sexually explicit conduct or simulation of such conduct for the purpose of producing a visual depiction of such conduct; or (B) the rape, molestation, prostitution, or other form of sexual exploitation of children or incest with children. (Child Welfare Information Gateway, 2008)

In research, the operationalization of CSA varies across studies, with some definitions including the frequency of specific behaviors (e.g., exhibition, genital touching, and penetration). The breadth of the definition used will affect prevalence rates. Some investigators define CSA as sex between an underage girl and a partner more than a certain number of years older. Some researchers simply ask participants whether they have experienced sexual abuse, allowing participants to interpret this according to their own standards. This approach typically results in a lower rate of reported abuse than when participants are asked to report their experience of specific behaviors (Rellini &

Meston, 2007). Data collection methods also influence rates of any type of reported abuse. For example, research has demonstrated that anonymous reporting produces higher rates than face-to-face data collection methods (Watts & Zimmerman, 2002).

Most studies using nonclinical populations demonstrate that between one-fifth and one-third of women report a history of childhood sexual abuse (Zwickl & Merriman, 2011). For example, CSA was reported by approximately one-third of women in a national stratified random sample (compared to 14% of men) (Briere & Elliott, 2003). CSA was reported in approximately one in four girls (National Center for Victims of Crime, 2008). In a meta-analysis of 65 articles covering 22 countries, 19.7% of women had suffered some form of sexual abuse before the age of 18 (Pereda, Guilera, Forns, & Gómez-Benito, 2009). Comparing women by sexual orientation, Balsam, Rothblum, and Beauchaine (2005) found higher rates of CSA in lesbian women (44%) and bisexual women (48%) compared to heterosexual women (30%). The rate of reported CSA can be much higher in clinical populations. Polusny and Follete (1995) indicate that up to 75% of women in clinical populations report a history of some form of sexual abuse during childhood. These high rates for maltreatment of children suggest a systemic, cross-cultural problem that goes beyond individual misconduct.

Sexual Health Consequences of CSA

A large body of literature associates CSA with sexual behaviors that put one at risk for sexually transmitted infections (STIs) (see review by Senn, Carey, & Vanable, 2008). Risk behaviors include younger age of first consensual sex, number of lifetime sexual partners, unprotected sex, and exchanging sex for money or drugs. A meta-analysis of studies conducted through 1996 found a relationship between CSA and sexual promiscuity (Paolucci, Genuis, & Violato, 2001). A more recent meta-analysis exploring the relationship between CSA and HIV risk behavior in women found relationships between CSA and unprotected sex, sex with multiple partners, and using sex for money or drugs (Arriola, Louden, Doldren, & Fortenberry, 2005). Similar results were found with patients recruited from a clinic treating sexually transmitted diseases (STDs) (Senn, Carey, Vanable, Coury-Doniger, & Urban, 2006). A longitudinal prospective study of sexually abused women and a comparison group revealed that 10 years after disclosure, abused participants were more preoccupied with sex, younger at first voluntary intercourse, and younger at the birth of their first child (Noll, Trickett, & Putnam, 2003). Early and chronic sexual abuse was associated with a seven-fold increase in HIV-risk behaviors in a population-based study (Bensley, Eenwyk, & Simmons, 2000).

Among African American women, CSA was associated with a younger age of first consensual intercourse, younger age of first pregnancy (Fiscella, Kitzman, Cole, Sidora, & Olds, 1998), greater likelihood to report having had an STI, and greater likelihood of having a partner who was physically abusive when asked to use condoms (Wingood & DiClemente, 1997). However, Wyatt and colleagues (2002) found that race/ethnicity was not an independent predictor of HIV-related risk, and few racial/ethnic differences in risk behaviors were observed.

In addition to engaging in riskier sex, CSA is associated with reproductive health difficulties, including adult pelvic pain and a series of gynecological disorders such as painful intercourse, irregular menstruation, and vaginal infections (Leserman, 2005). Further-more, survivors of CSA may experience problems with sexual functioning. In Shearer and Herbert's (1987) seminal review, women with a history of CSA or sexual trauma reported an increased aversion to sex, diffi-culty reaching orgasm, and decreased trust in their sexual partners. A more recent review of the literature indicated that the sexual sequelae of CSA may include lack of sexual desire, difficulty becoming aroused, sexual aversion, orgasm difficulty, dyspareunia, vaginismus, and lower sexual satisfaction (Leonard & Follete, 2002).

Not all studies have found a relationship between CSA and sexual difficulties. Fur-thermore, in an investigation of differences in sexual functioning, women identifying as CSA survivors reported less sexual satisfaction and personal sexual distress, but did not differ in measures of sexual dysfunction from those who did not self-identify as CSA survivors (Rellini & Meston, 2007). Schloredt and Heiman (2003) found that abuse survivors did not differ from women who had not been abused on sexual desire, arousal/orgasm, sex-ual pain, or masturbation. However, women with abuse histories reported more negative affect during sexual arousal.

As previously discussed, a history of nonconsensual sex may impede one's ability to be assertive in a sexual decision-making situation, which may in turn result in unprotected sex or sexual victimization. Sexually abused women reported signifi-cantly more negative attitudes about sexual-ity, less assertiveness about birth control or in refusing unwanted sex, less efficacy concern-ing HIV prevention, more anticipation for negative partner response concerning safer sex, more substance use, and more sexual victimization in adulthood (Johnsen & Harlow, 1996).

In sum, research indicates that women with a history of CSA are more likely to engage in risky sex, have an increased likeli-hood of reproductive health problems, and often report poorer sexual functioning and satisfaction than nonvictimized women. Clearly, nonconsensual sex that forms the basis of CSA is not consistent with the development of healthy sexuality; the pre-vention of CSA is of the highest priority in promoting women's sexual health. Evidence suggests that this pattern is the case across racial/ethnic groups.

Rape

Definition and Prevalence Sexual assault includes a range of unwanted behaviors up to, but not including, penetration. The issue of consent is critical. Several factors are recognized as precluding victim consent, including age, disability, or the influence of alcohol and/or drugs. According to the National Institute of Justice (2010), most state laws currently define *rape* as "noncon-sensual oral, anal, or vaginal penetration of the victim by body parts or objects using force, threats of bodily harm, or by taking advantage of a victim who is incapacitated or otherwise incapable of giving consent." A large, nationally representative sample of 16,507 adults completed the National Intimate Partner and Sexual Violence Survey. Nearly one in five women surveyed said they had been raped or had experienced an attempted rape at some point in their lives. About half of the female victims reported they had been raped before age 18 (Black et al., 2011). The data suggest that 1.3 million American women annually may be victims of rape or attempted rape.

The National Violence Against Women Survey is a large nationally representative telephone survey of women and men, which found that 17.6% of surveyed women, compared to 3% of men, reported having been raped at some point in their lifetimes. Of those women who had been raped, 54% experienced the first occurrence of rape under the age of 18. An additional 29.4% of women reported their first rape occurrence between the ages of 18 and 24 (Tjaden & Thoennes, 2006). Almost one-third of female rape victims were injured during the assault, which was about double the rate for male victims. No statistically significant differences between minority and non-minority women in lifetime experience of rape were found overall. However, examined separately, American Indian/Alaska native women were more likely than women from any other backgrounds to have been raped. Examining rates by sexual orientation, Balsam et al. (2005) found that completed rape was more prevalent among those women identifying as lesbian (15.5%) and bisexual women (16.9%) than heterosexual women (7.5%). The authors acknowledge that this finding needs further study, indicating it would have been reasonable to hypothesize that "women who partner primarily or exclusively with other women would be at lower risk of rape."

Sexual Health Sequelae of Rape

One consequence of rape is genital injury or STIs. Golding, Wilsnack, and Learman (1998) report that women with a history of sexual assault display numerous gynecological complaints including menstrual difficulties. In a review of this literature, Weaver (2009) found moderately high rates of these problems and a greater incidence of dyspareunia, endometriosis, menstrual irregularities, and chronic pelvic pain in women who had been raped compared to women who had not.

Sexual assault may also affect the survivor's sexual functioning. For example, several studies have shown that sexual contact decreases following sexual assault (see review by van Berlo & Ensink, 2000). However, there is also evidence that a subgroup of women engage in more sexual activity following sexual assault (Deliramich & Gray, 2008). In her review, Weaver (2009) found that raped women engaged in significantly more high-risk sexual behaviors. Shapiro and Schwartz (1997) found that women who were date-raped reported a higher number of sexual partners and greater frequency of sexual intercourse than women who had not been date-raped.

Another consequence of rape may be sexual dysfunction. More than half of women who experience rape report sexual dysfunction, compared to 17% of nonassaulted women, and 70% of these women attributed the dysfunction to the sexual assault (Becker, Skinner, Abel, & Cichon, 1986). Golding and colleagues (1998) report an increased odds ratio for sexual dysfunction among sexual assault survivors. Van Berlo and Ensink (2000) note that rape survivors developed sexual problems, including sexual inhibition, impaired sexual desire, and arousal difficulties. Immediate emotional reactions post-assault predicted long-term sexual problems. Emotions focused on the self, such as shame, guilt, and anger, felt during or immediately after the assault are predictors of sexual dysfunction in women. Having a relationship with a safe partner is protective against sexual dysfunction, helping to reduce aversive feelings that might lead a survivor to avoid future sexual contact. Additional research is needed in this area to determine to what extent post-traumatic stress disorder (PTSD)–related symptoms mediate the role between sexual assault or victimization and sexual problems or cognitions.

Many women with a history of sexual assault have significant general psychological and physical health sequelae, including PTSD, depression, sexual problems, substance abuse, difficulty in interpersonal relationships, poor self-esteem, somatization, anxiety, physical health problems, and eating disorders (see Browne & Finkelhor, 1986; Golding, 1999; Polusny & Follete, 1995; and Resick, 1993, for reviews).

The type of tactic used by the rapist may impact the consequences for women's mental health outcomes. Zinzow et al. (2010) conceptualized three types of rape tactics. *Forcible rape*, in which force, threats of force, or injury are employed, was the strongest predictor of PTSD and major depressive episodes, where victimized women were three times as likely as nonvictims to meet lifetime criteria for both psychiatric disorders. *Incapacitated rape*, involving rape that occurs after a victim voluntarily uses drugs or alcohol to the point that she is incapacitated, was not associated with either PTSD or major depressive episodes. *Drug- or alcohol-facilitated rape*, involving the perpetrator deliberately giving the victim drugs without her permission or trying to get her drunk, was significantly associated with PTSD. In another study, lifetime experience of incapacitated rape and drug- or alcohol-facilitated rape were predictors of substance abuse and binge drinking within the past year, but lifetime experience of forcible rape was not associated with substance abuse (McCauley, Ruggiero, Resnick, Conoscenti, & Kilpatrick, 2009). This helps disentangle previous research that links rape to alcohol use. When in isolation and defined as such, forcible rape is not associated with substance abuse.

Whether or not the victim reports the rape may help protect against any adverse sexual health outcomes and mental health symptomatology. Resnick et al. (2000) found that only one in five women reported their rape, but that women who reported an adult rape to authorities or police were nine times more likely to receive timely medical care. The timeliness of treatment is important, because women can receive emergency contraception up to 72 hours after the rape, and they may benefit from prophylactic treatments that help prevent STI transmission. Moreover, timely medical care following any sort of sexual assault has the potential to reduce psychological sequelae and other medical care utilization. In a national sample of college women, a sexual assault by an unknown stranger is more likely to be reported than a sexual assault with an acquaintance or partner (Wolitzky-Taylor et al., 2011a).

Barriers to reporting rape include societal attitudes, socioeconomic inequities, gender inequities, unwanted disclosure, and fear of being blamed (Wolitzky-Taylor et al., 2011b). Women who did not report rape indicated a fear of reprisal by the offender as the biggest obstacle. Results of this national sample demonstrated that the prevalence of women reporting rape (15.8%) has not increased since the 1990s.

The high prevalence and serious consequences of rape make it an important public health issue. Sanday (1981) has identified that the prevalence of rape varies from one society to another and that higher prevalence of rape is associated with a cultural configuration that includes interpersonal violence, male dominance, and gender separation. She has done anthropological work in American fraternities to identify the characteristics of a rape-prone social setting and has more generally examined differences across college campuses, categorizing some as rape-prone (Sanday, 1996; Sanday, 2007). This research suggests that gender and other cultural issues must be included in designing programs to prevent rape.

Sexual Revictimization

Sexual revictimization is the experience of both CSA and later sexual or physical abuse as an adult (Messman & Long, 1996). A large body of evidence supports the hypothesis that women with a history of CSA are at an increased risk for sexual revictimization. A review of this literature (Classen, Palesh, & Aggarwal, 2005) found more than 30 studies suggesting that CSA is a risk factor for sexual revictimization.

One-third of CSA victims report repeated sexual victimization, with a 2 to 3 times greater risk of adult revictimization than women with no history of CSA (Arata, 2002). In a review of the literature, studies across general, clinical, and college-aged samples provide statistics of revictimization. Results overall suggest that between 16% and 72% of women who experience CSA are likely to be revictimized as adults (Messman & Long, 1996). Some research suggests that African American CSA victims may be more likely than women of other race/ethnicities to be revictimized (Urquiza & Goodlin-Jones, 1994). In a prospective study of 113 African American women who had been treated at a city hospital for CSA as children, 30% were found to have been sexually revictimized (West, Williams, & Siegel, 2000). The revictimized women reported more partner violence, involvement in prostitution, STIs, difficulty conceiving, and dyspareunia. The authors note that survivors may be reluctant to seek assistance, perceiving doctors to be condescending and unhelpful. They recommend that helping professionals should assess CSA when treating women for STIs or partner violence and should make an effort to establish rapport, explain medical and therapeutic procedures, and ask permission before touching their clients. It has also been reported that women who identify as bisexual are more likely to be revictimized than women who identify as lesbian (Heidt, Marx, & Gold, 2005).

Several studies have identified sexual behavior and attitudes toward sexuality that mediate between CSA and adult victimization (Arata, 2002, for review). Women with a history of CSA and revictimization displayed more intrusive sexual thoughts and behaviors, lower sexual self-esteem, and poorer sexual adjustment than women with no abuse history (Van Bruggen, Runtz, & Kadlec, 2006). Revictimization has been associated with higher levels of emotional problems, prostitution, HIV risk, and lack of contraceptive use than childhood- or adult-only victimization (Miner, Flitter, & Robinson, 2006). Researchers have attempted to determine whether CSA is an independent risk factor for revictimization, separate from other forms of child maltreatment. Messman-Moore and Brown (2004) found that CSA is a risk factor for adult victimization independent of family functioning, although experiencing multiple forms of child maltreatment increased the risk of adult rape.

In summary, women who have experienced CSA are at risk for multiple sexual and general health problems, including a higher risk for adult sexual victimization. Healthcare professionals have an important role in helping to identify women who may be victimized to offer a variety of treatment options, including psychological assistance, substance abuse treatment, safety from domestic violence, medical treatment for STIs and other disorders, and treatment for sexual dysfunction.

SEX THAT IS WANTED AND LIKED

Because of the extensive literature on sexual and emotional health hazards associated with coercive sex, it is easy to agree that sex must be consensual to be considered healthy. It is not as clear a case that healthy sex must be *wanted* sex. Women may voluntarily acquiesce to unwanted sex for a variety of reasons. The term *sexual compliance* refers to unwanted yet consensual acquiescence to sex despite a lack of sexual desire. Significant portions of women and men report having consented to unwanted sexual activity: O'Sullivan and Allgeier (1998), in their seminal study, reported that one-half of college women and one-quarter of college men engaged in sexual compliance. Participants reported consenting to unwanted sexual activity to satisfy the partner's needs, promote relationship intimacy, and avoid relationship tension. It should be noted that these reasons are all consistent with the feminine gender role expectation to facilitate relationships. The authors report that most participants reported positive outcomes associated with these motives. This is plausible, because one can imagine a committed relationship in which partners are sensitive to each other's needs and agree to sex to please the partner and facilitate relationship goals despite not (perhaps initially) being in the mood for sex or experiencing sexual desire.

Katz and Tirone (2009) tested the hypothesis that sexually compliant women would both be more invested in ideal womanhood (adherence to traditional norms) and report higher relationship satisfaction and commitment, especially for those who expressed positive motives for compliance (relationship and self-enhancement) versus negative motives (avoidance of conflict). In this study of college women, more than one-third reported engaging in compliant behavior. Compliant women in this sample showed greater investment in ideal womanhood; however, contrary to the hypothesis, they reported less relationship satisfaction. Interestingly, most women identified motives for compliance that were categorized as positive. In other words, women were engaging in unwanted sex in order to enhance the relationship; unfortunately, it did not have this effect for them, as it was associated with less relationship satisfaction. It is possible that if male partners had been included in the study, results would have shown that the women's sexual compliance enhanced her partner's sexual satisfaction, given the strong relationship between sexual frequency and relationship satisfaction in men. However, for women it did not.

The authors describe sexual compliance as a form of self-sacrifice and express concern that it may be an unrecognized and therefore unreciprocated sacrifice. Women may conceal their lack of desire and therefore their partners may be unaware of the extent of this sacrifice. O'Sullivan and Allegier (1998) argue that an individual may consent to unwanted sexual activity, referring to situations in which an individual feigns sexual desire or interest. They found that satisfying a partner's needs, promoting intimacy, and avoiding relationship tension were some of the most prevalent reasons. This analysis focuses on women in heterosexual relationships. The issue of sexual compliance in same-sex relationships has not been fully investigated and would aid in our understanding of the impact of compliance on relationship satisfaction.

An additional issue of importance is the potential interaction of sexual compliance with prior sexual trauma or experience of nonconsensual sex. Given the high rate at which women experience nonconsensual sex, this poses a significant concern. Although women may freely choose to engage in sex in order to satisfy a partner's needs or otherwise enhance their relationships, this behavior may evoke feelings of being coerced into unwanted sex. Especially in the case of women who have been victimized by CSA or rape, the ability to differentiate between wanted and unwanted sex may be reduced. This is an important area for further research. A woman cannot control whether she has been the victim of coerced sex. She can control whether she is compliant to unwanted sex. It is important for women and their treatment providers to be aware of this recent research demonstrating the potential negative relationship (and associated health) consequences of sexual compliance.

Engaging in Disliked Sexual Activities

The concept of *wanted* sexual activity becomes more complex when we explore specific sexual acts within the sexual repertoire. One can imagine a situation in which a woman is sexually desirous, but she finds that once involved in the sexual activity, her partner expects her to engage in sexual activities that she dislikes. According to Kaestle (2009), results from Wave 3 of the National Longitudinal Study of Adolescent Health demonstrate that 12% of women compared to 3% of men report engaging

repeatedly in sexual activities they disliked, primarily fellatio and anal sex. She found that this was primarily an issue for women: 81% of those who engaged even once in a disliked activity were women. For women, having a partner who had insisted on sex was associated with repeated disliked sexual activities, and married women were more likely than dating women to have repeatedly engaged in sexual activities that were disliked. The author concludes that:

> young adults may need education on the importance of accepting a partner's sexual desires and being sensitive to both a partner's unwillingness to engage in an activity and the true extent of a partner's dislike of certain activities. They may also need guidance on how to voice their own preferences and dislikes. (Kaestle, 2009, p. 33)

As previously noted, active sexuality conflicts with gender role expectations and proscriptions for women and may therefore not be easy to achieve. Sexual assertiveness training has not always demonstrated successful results. In fact, in one study, sexual assertiveness scores decreased following sexual assertiveness training, presumably because women became more aware of ways in which they were not being sexually assertive (Deiter, 1994). The solution to this problem is probably a long-term one in which women increasingly take the risk of communicating their true feelings to their partners. In order to feel comfortable doing so, women will want to feel secure that their partners will not abandon them if they do not comply sexually, including engaging in disliked sexual activities. The impact of such issues in same-sex relationships for women needs further exploration. As noted by Henderson, Levahot, and Simoni (2009), gender socialization is a significant predictor of sexual satisfaction in lesbian relationships. More research is needed to determine whether this results in engaging in disliked sexual behavior to please a partner in these relationships.

SAFE SEX

Sex for women (and to a lesser extent, men) has the potential to be physically unsafe even if it is consensual. The most common unsafe consequences for consensual sexual activity are STDs and unwanted pregnancy. The risks are less for men because women are more susceptible to STIs acquired through heterosexual sex (European Study Group on Heterosexual Transmission of HIV, 1992) and experience far more immediate sequelae from pregnancy than do men. Protection from both pregnancy and STIs may require dual methods of protection. Correct and consistent use of latex condoms is a highly effective barrier method to prevent STIs (CDC, 2011c). However, data indicate that although condom use has increased over recent decades, still only 20% or fewer of men and women consistently use condoms (CDC, 2011c; Shlay, McClung, Patnaik, & Douglas, 2004).

There are many reasons why women do not use contraceptives, including fear of side effects (e.g., weight gain), previous difficulties with a contraceptive, financial barriers, perception that pregnancy is unlikely, or having unexpected sex when not prepared. In addition, women who are young, single, living in poverty, and less educated are more likely to experience an unplanned pregnancy (Chandra, Martinez, Mosher, Abma, & Jones, 2005; Finer & Henshaw,

2006). In cases of intimate partner violence (i.e., physical or emotional abuse in a romantic relationship), women are less likely to use their preferred contraceptive method. However, compared to nonabused women, they are more likely to use condoms than oral contraceptives (Williams, Larsen, & McCloskey, 2008).

Much research has examined predictors of consistent condom use. The more negative a woman's attitudes toward condoms were, the more likely she was to engage in risky sex, according to a study by Sterk, Klein, and Elifson (2004). These authors also found that women who were younger, had higher self-esteem, did not have a history of neglect, and had fewer drug-related problems displayed more positive attitudes toward condoms. Other research shows that contraceptive use is predicted by shared decision making with partners. Women who communicated their contraceptive use and pregnancy views, while taking into account their partner's views, were more likely to be consistent and effective contraceptive users (Kraft et al., 2010).

In a longitudinal study of African American women, compared with inconsistent condom users, women who were consistent condom users were more likely to (a) have high assertive communication skills, (b) desire not becoming pregnant, (c) have high sexual self-control over condom use, (d) perceive having control over their partners' use of condoms, (e) be younger, and (f) report having a partner who was not committed to the relationship (Wingood & DiClemente, 1998). Utilizing a high-risk sample, Morokoff et al. (2009) found a good fit for a model in which CSA was mediated by sexual assertiveness for condom use in predicting unprotected sex, a composite measure including protected sex ratio, frequency of unprotected sex, and stage of condom use.

Among Hispanic/Latina women, acculturation is a significant factor in risky sexual behavior. For example, Van Oss Marin, Gomez, and Hearst (1993) found that moderately or highly acculturated women are more likely to have multiple partners than are less-acculturated women. Furthermore, about half of acculturated women reported always using condoms with secondary heterosexual partners. In a study of mostly Latina women, women with high levels of relationship power were 5 times as likely as women with low levels of power to report consistent condom use, after controlling for sociodemographic and psychosocial variables. It was suggested that 52% of the lack of consistent condom use among women can be attributed to low sexual relationship power (Pulerwitz, Amaro, De Jong, Gortmaker, & Rudd, 2002).

According to the Centers for Disease Control and Prevention (CDC), an unintended pregnancy is one that is mistimed or unwanted at the time of conception, which accounts for about half of the pregnancies in the United States each year. There are several associated risks for women who have unintended pregnancies, such as delayed prenatal care (CDC, 2011b). Many young women do not use contraceptives consistently, despite their intentions to avoid unintended pregnancies or STIs. In a national sample of adult women at risk for unintended pregnancy, 5.6% of those who did not want to be pregnant did not use contraceptives, and 16.6% displayed inconsistent use within the past year (Frost, Singh, & Finer, 2007).

STIs are another consequence of inconsistent contraceptive use. One of the most common STIs is human papillomavirus (HPV). Although infected persons usually don't show signs or symptoms, long-term health consequences are genital warts and cervical cancer. The virus is passed on through sexual contact, either genital to genital or via oral sex. The CDC estimates that each year approximately 6 million people become infected with HPV, and that 20 million Americans are currently affected (CDC, 2011a). Two vaccines are currently available and have been shown to be effective in preventing specific strains of the virus that may lead to cervical cancer (e.g., Gardasil and Cervarix). However, there may be barriers to vaccination, such as lack of awareness or knowledge about HPV, parents' beliefs about condoning and consenting to a vaccine that surrounds sexual activity, and misperceptions about the safety of the vaccination (Dempsey & Davis, 2006). In addition, access to healthcare and cultural beliefs across race/ethnicity may impede an individual from inquiring about and obtaining the vaccination (Downs, Scarinci, Einstein, Collins, & Flowers, 2010).

Women involved in same-sex sexual relationships may be at risk for STIs including HPV (Marrazzo, Koutsky, Kiviat, Kuypers, & Stine, 2001). Despite this risk, many lesbians do not feel at risk for STIs (Power, McNair, & Carr, 2009). Most women in same-sex relationships do not use condoms. Sexual practices involving digital-vaginal or digital-anal contact, particularly with shared penetrative sex toys, have been frequently reported among female sex partners, which according to Marrazzo, Coffey, and Bingham (2005) present a plausible means for STI transmission. In one study, a higher percentage of women in same-sex relationships had bacterial vaginosis (27%) than did heterosexual women (23%) (Marrazzo et al., 2002).

Early sexual debut has shown to have many reproductive health consequences, such as unplanned pregnancies (Manlove, Terry-Humen, & Ikramullah, 2006; Raine, Minnis, & Padian, 2003), vaginal infections, and risky behavior like unprotected sex. Early sexual debut has also been linked to an increased risk for STIs (Greenberg, Magder, & Aral, 1992; Kaestle, Halpern, Miller & Ford, 2005). Leval and colleagues (2011) examined a national population-based sample in Sweden to investigate sexual habits, such as condom use, sexual partners, and STI risk perceptions, and found that early sexual debut was associated with non-condom use later in life. Sexual risk behaviors in gay, lesbian, and bisexual youths was found to be related to initiation of sex during early adolescence (Rosario, Meyer-Bahlburg, Hunter, & Gwadz, 1999).

Early sexual debut is also associated with an increased number of sexual partners (Cavazos-Rehg et al., 2007). A secondary data analysis on the 1996 National Sexual Health Survey suggested that early initiation of sexual intercourse was associated with sexual risk factors such as an increased number of sexual partners and higher probability of engaging in sexual intercourse under the influence of alcohol or drugs as opposed to those engaging in sexual intercourse for the first time at a later age (Sandfort, Orr, Hirsch, & Santelli, 2008). Finally, early sexual debut has been associated with susceptibility for vaginal infections. Westrom and Eschenbach (1999) found that young women who engage in sexual intercourse at an early age have an underdeveloped cervix, creating more susceptibility to HPV infection, the most common cause of cervical cancer.

It is important to investigate early risk factors for increased risk for STIs because of significant reproductive health consequences, such as pelvic inflammatory disease or preterm births. In addition, educating girls and women about the importance of gynecological exams, regular Pap smears, STI testing, and condom use would be beneficial.

INTEGRATING RELATIONSHIP AND INDIVIDUAL SEXUAL GOALS

The traditional approach underlying theories and research in the area of sexuality assumes that capacities for desire and sexual response are physiologically based and reside in the individual. This approach is consistent with traditional gendered expectations for male sexuality but not for female sexuality (Morokoff, 2000). It has taken some effort on the part of feminist theorists to introduce the concept that women's sexual behaviors may be motivated by relational concerns rather than the desire to simply satisfy one's own autonomous desires. However, the model for healthy female sexuality frequently proposed transfers such individual imperatives to women. A significant change over recent decades is the recognition of individual sexual goals for women; that is, that women are entitled to sexual satisfaction, are entitled to initiate sex when desired, and are entitled to ask partners to perform particular sexual acts.

As noted by Lamb (2010) in a discussion of healthy female adolescent sexuality, feminist theorists frequently emphasize the need for young women to focus on desire, pleasure, and their own subjectivity (as opposed to objectivity or objectification). She asserts that there is a problem with using these qualities as a marker for healthy sexuality, although they appear to address three historically problematic areas: (1) objectification; (2) abuse and victimization; and (3) stereotypes of female passivity. She reminds us that a straightforward focus on these qualities is really a replication of the traditional model of sexuality, which is principally focused on intrinsic and autonomous sexual experience and ignores sex in the context of relationship. Of course, an exclusive focus on sex in the context of a relationship is what these qualities are selected to avoid, and research discussed here demonstrates that addressing relationship goals through a passive approach to sex without autonomy is associated with lower sexual satisfaction, as is the experience of sexual abuse or victimization.

The solution to this quandary is in the balance of individual and relational needs. McHugh's (2006) answer to the question "What do women want? A new view of women's sexual problems," is instructive. Based on diaries read in her 25 years of teaching Psychology of Women—a sort of long-term qualitative study—she presents the issues most often identified by the young women in her courses. According to McHugh, women want consensual sex, mutually satisfying sex, sexual agency, relationships, self-love, time and rest, sexual health, and liberation. McHugh says,

> According to my classes, a sexually liberated woman is a woman who: is knowledgeable about sex and her own body; feels comfortable or good about her body; is comfortable touching or pleasing herself sexually; is knowledgeable and responsible about reproduction; understands her own sexual orientation and respects the orientation and choices of others; makes her own choices; is able to say "yes" and is able to say "no"; can communicate her sexual feelings to her partner(s); avoids exploitative or abusive relationships and situation; protects herself against sexually transmitted diseases; attends to her health; develops and maintains meaningful relationships; and expresses love and affection in appropriate ways. (p. 368)

This list clearly focuses both on the personal and the relational. A sexual relationship occurs within an interpersonal relationship, regardless of the length of that relationship. Therefore, a larger question of what constitutes healthy sexuality is what constitutes a healthy relationship. These young women would answer that a healthy relationship is one free from exploitation and abuse, where each partner has agency and there is mutual respect. The sex part of the healthy relationship might be expected to correspond in just this way. For example, Kaestle's (2009) data indicate that 7% to 8% of women reported that their partner victimized them by insisting on sex or a specific sexual behavior (the proportion of men reporting this was the same). *Sexual insistence* was defined to include any method of making or insisting that a reluctant partner engage in unwanted sexual relations. Note that this is different from voluntarily acquiescing to sex with a noninsistent partner. Each partner's experience of agency in the relationship—authority to make decisions and act on them—would equally apply to the sexual relationship. This, of course, does not mean that a woman would always get her way—as in the general relationship, decisions sometimes need to be negotiated. Finally, mutual respect in a relationship really more broadly encompasses freedom from exploitation and agency. It is virtually impossible to think of a sexual relationship wherein a woman experiences no exploitation or abuse, where she is an equal partner in sexual decision making and where she and her partner exchange mutual respect for which this would not also be true of the relationship as a whole.

The model of healthy sexuality proposed here identifies four components: (1) that a woman's sexual role be active; (2) that all sex be consensual; (3) that sex women engage in be wanted and liked; and (4) that it be safe. These requirements set the stage for meeting individual sexual goals of fully experienced sexual desire, pleasure, and internal focus. When a woman fully chooses the sexual activity she engages in, when it is not likely to lead to disease or unwanted pregnancy, when she is empowered to not be submissive, is assertive, and has an internal focus, she has an excellent opportunity to experience full pleasure and sexual satisfaction. At the same time, there is no conflict with relational goals if the relationship is characterized by equality of opportunity and decision making and mutual respect. If, on the other hand, a woman is in a subordinate position in her relationship such that she does not have the opportunity to participate fully in sexual decision making, these characteristics of healthy sexuality will not fit easily in the relationship. The characteristics of healthy sexuality outlined here, therefore, require an egalitarian relationship marked by mutual respect.

However, more than the characteristics of any one given relationship, healthy sexuality requires that throughout her life, a woman is treated as (and perceives herself as) an autonomous sexual decision maker. As

has been seen, CSA can have devastating lifelong negative implications for sexuality. As has further been seen, CSA increases the likelihood for women of engaging in behaviors that put women at risk for STDs and sexual revictimization. We also note that the roles women are allowed to play in society are correlated to the prevalence of CSA and rape. The existence of rape-prone societies—characterized by higher levels of violence, male domination, and gender separation—stack the deck against the goals of healthy sexuality for women. For women to be more active in sex, they will need assurance that this will be permissible to a partner and that they will not find themselves and their children abandoned if they turn down sex when they wish or refuse to engage in disliked sexual activities. Unsafe sexual activities are frequently coerced sexual activities, when women exchange sex for money or drugs or agree to sex without a condom to meet relationship goals.

Social change evolves slowly, and as we look back, we see much change even as we see many problems at present. Women's sexual health will be facilitated by:

- Education for women ensuring that women are able to obtain good jobs to support themselves and not be financially forced into risky relationships or behaviors
- Sex education teaching women and men the correlates of sexual satisfaction such as sexual assertiveness; the consequences for their own health and sexual satisfaction of being overly compliant; and information about prevention of disease and unwanted pregnancy
- Education for men such as the rape-prevention programs that have been

instituted on college campuses (e.g., Foubert, 2000)

- Programs to address child sexual abuse
- Home visitation programs to identify child maltreatment (see Putnam, 2003, for a discussion)
- Awareness by health providers of the need to assess for CSA and rape sequelae
- A legal system that offers support to victims and legal procedures that prevent bias
- Efforts by individual women and their relationship partners to create a climate for healthy sexuality

In this list we recommend educational interventions that can be delivered by federal or state government programs, medical school curricula, university student services, and local school systems. We recommend programs to address child abuse that falls in the domain of state or municipal departments of health. We identify the need for further reform of our legal system. Finally, we acknowledge that individual partners bear responsibility for creating healthy, supportive relationships. It is clear that many facets of our society are permissive for unhealthy sexual relationships and that efforts at multiple levels are needed to change this situation.

Sexual health is a strong contributor to overall health and satisfying relationships. Achievements that women have made in the recognition of the importance of individual sexual goals (satisfaction and sexual autonomy) must be matched by respect for these phenomena in relationships with partners. The elements of a healthy sexual relationship proposed here lay a framework for achieving a space in which women's sexual goals can be achieved.

REFERENCES

American Psychological Association, Task Force on the Sexualization of Girls. (2010). *Report of the APA Task Force on the Sexualization of Girls.* Retrieved from http://www.apa.org/pi/women/programs/girls/report-full.aspx

Arata, C. M. (2002). Child sexual abuse and sexual revictimization. *Clinical Psychology: Science and Practice, 9*(2), 135–164.

Arriola, K. R. J., Louden, T., Doldren, M. A., & Fortenberry, R. M. (2005). A meta-analysis of the relationship of child sexual abuse to HIV risk behavior among women. *Child Abuse & Neglect, 29*(6), 725–746.

Aubrey, J. S. (2006a). Effects of sexually objectifying media on self-objectification and body surveillance in undergraduates: Results of a 2-year panel study. *Journal of Communication, 56*(2), 366–386.

Aubrey, J. S. (2006b). Exposure to sexually objectifying media and body self-perceptions among college women: An examination of the selective exposure hypothesis and the role of moderating variables. *Sex Roles, 55*(3–4), 159–172.

Balsam, K. F., Rothblum, E. D., & Beauchaine, T. P. (2005). Victimization over the life span: A comparison of lesbian, gay, bisexual, and heterosexual siblings. *Journal of Consulting and Clinical Psychology, 73*(3), 477–487.

Becker, J. V., Skinner, L. J., Abel, G. G., & Cichon, J. (1986). Level of postassault sexual functioning in rape and incest victims. *Archives of Sexual Behavior, 15*(1), 37–49.

Bensley, L. S., Eenwyk, J. V., & Simmons, K. W. (2000). Self-reported childhood sexual and physical abuse and adult HIV-risk behaviors and heavy drinking. *American Journal of Preventive Medicine, 18*(2), 151–158.

Black, M. C., Basile, K. C., Breiding, M. J., Smith, S. G., Walters, M. L., Merrick, M. T., . . . Stevens, M. R. (2011). *The National Intimate Partner and Sexual Violence Survey (NISVS): 2010 summary report.* Atlanta, GA: National Center for Injury Prevention and Control, Centers for Disease Control and Prevention.

Briere, J., & Elliott, D. M. (2003). Prevalence and psychological sequelae of self-reported childhood physical and sexual abuse in a general population sample of men and women. *Child Abuse & Neglect, 27*(10), 1205–1222.

Browne, A., & Finkelhor, D. (1986). Impact of child sexual abuse: A review of the research. *Psychological Bulletin*, *99*(1), 66–77.

Calogero, R. M., & Thompson, J. K. (2009). Potential implications of the objectification of women's bodies for women's sexual satisfaction. *Body Image*, *6*(2), 145–148.

Cavazos-Rehg, P. A., Spitznagel, E. L., Bucholz, K. K., Norberg, K., Reich, W., Nurnberger, J., . . . Bierut, L. J. (2007). The relationship between alcohol problems and dependence, conduct problems and diagnosis, and number of sex partners in a sample of young adults. *Alcoholism: Clinical and Experimental Research*, *31*(12), 2046–2052.

Centers for Disease Control and Prevention. (2011a). Human papillomavirus (HPV). Retrieved from http://www.cdc.gov/hpv/WhatIsHPV.html

Centers for Disease Control and Prevention. (2011b). Unintended pregnancy prevention. Retrieved from http://www.cdc.gov/reproductivehealth/UnintendedPregnancy/index.htm

Centers for Disease Control and Prevention. (2011c). Male latex condoms and sexually transmitted diseases. Retrieved from http://www.cdc.gov/condomeffectiveness/brief.html

Chandra, A., Martinez, G. M., Mosher, W. D., Abma, J. C., & Jones, J. (2005). Fertility, family planning, and reproductive health of U.S. women: Data from the 2002 National Survey of Family Growth. *Vital Health Statistics*, *23*(25), 1–160.

Child Welfare Information Gateway. (2008). *Definitions of child abuse and neglect*. Washington, DC: U.S. Department of Health and Human Services, Children's Bureau.

Classen, C. C., Palesh, O. G., & Aggarwal, R. (2005). Sexual revictimization: A review of the empirical literature. *Trauma, Violence, & Abuse*, *6*(2), 103–129.

Davison, S. L., Bell, R. J., LaChina, M., Holden, S. L., & Davis, S. R. (2009). The relationship between self-reported sexual satisfaction and general well-being in women. *Journal of Sexual Medicine*, *6*(10), 2690–2697.

Deiter, P. (1994). *Sexual assertiveness training for college women: An intervention study*. Unpublished doctoral dissertation, University of Rhode Island.

Deliramich, A. N., & Gray, M. J. (2008). Changes in women's sexual behavior following sexual assault. *Behavior Modification*, *32*(5), 611–621.

Dempsey, A. F., & Davis, M. M. (2006). Overcoming barriers to adherence to HPV vaccination recommendations. *American Journal of Managed Care*, *12*(17), 484–491.

DiClemente, R. J., & Wingood, G. M. (1995). A randomized controlled trial of an HIV sexual risk—Reduction intervention for young African-American women. *Journal of the American Medical Association*, *274*(16), 1271–1276.

Downs, L. S., Scarinci, I., Einstein, M. H., Collins, Y., & Flowers, L. (2010). Overcoming barriers to HPV vaccination in high-risk populations in the U.S. *Gynecologic Oncology*, *117*(3), 488–490.

European Study Group on Heterosexual Transmission of HIV. (1992). Comparison of female to male and male to female transmission of HIV in 563 stable couples. *British Medical Journal*, *304*, 809–813.

Finer, L. B., & Henshaw, S. K. (2006). Disparities in rates of unintended pregnancy in the United States, 1994 and 2001. *Perspectives on Sexual and Reproductive Health*, *38*(2), 90–96.

Fiscella, K., Kitzman, H. J., Cole, R. E., Sidora, K. J., & Olds, D. (1998). Does child abuse predict adolescent pregnancy? *Pediatrics*, *101*(4), 620–624.

Foubert, J. D. (2000). The longitudinal effects of a rape-prevention program on fraternity men's attitudes, behavioral intent, and behavior. *Journal of American College Health*, *48*(4), 158–163.

Fredrickson, B. L., & Roberts, T. (1997). Objectification theory: Toward understanding womens lived experiences and mental health risks. *Psychology of Women Quarterly*, *21*(2), 173–206.

Frost, J. J., Singh, S., & Finer, L. (2007). U.S. women's one-year contraceptive use patterns, 2004. *Perspectives on Sexual and Reproductive Health*, *39*(1), 48–55.

Golding, J. M. (1999). Sexual assault history and medical care seeking: The roles of symptom prevalence and illness behavior. *Psychology & Health*, *14*(5), 949–957.

Golding, J. M., Wilsnack, S. C., Learman, L. A. (1998). Prevalence of sexual assault history among women with common gynecologic symptoms. *American Journal of Obstetrics and Gynecology*, *179*(4), 1013–1019.

Gómez, C. A., & VanOss Marín, B. (1996). Gender, culture, and power: Barriers to HIV-prevention strategies for women. *Journal of Sex Research, 33* (4), 355–362.

Greenberg, J., Magder, L., Aral, S. (1992). Age at first coitus: A marker for risky sexual behavior in women. *Sexually Transmitted Disease, 19,* 331–334.

Harlow, L. L., Quina, K., Morokoff, P. J., Rose, J. S., & Grimley, D. M. (1993). HIV risk in women: A multifaceted model. *Journal of Applied Biobehavioral Research, 1*(1), 3–38.

Heidt, J. M., Marx, B. P., & Gold, S. D. (2005). Sexual revictimization among sexual minorities: A preliminary study. *Journal of Traumatic Stress, 18*(5), 533–540.

Henderson, A. W., Lehavot, K., & Simoni, J. M. (2009). Ecological models of sexual satisfaction among lesbian/bisexual and heterosexual women. *Archives of Sexual Behavior, 38*(1), 50–65.

Hill, M. S., & Fischer, A. R. (2008). Examining objectification theory: Lesbian and heterosexual women's experiences with sexual- and self-objectification. *The Counseling Psychologist, 36* (5), 745–776.

Johnsen, L. W., & Harlow, L. L. (1996). Childhood sexual abuse linked with adult substance use, victimization, and AIDS risk. *AIDS Education and Prevention, 8*(1), 44–57.

Kaestle, C. E. (2009). Sexual insistence and disliked sexual activities in young adulthood: Differences by gender and relationship characteristics. *Perspectives on Sexual and Reproductive Health, 41*(1), 33–39.

Kaestle, C. E., Halpern, C. T., Miller, W. C., & Ford, C. A. (2005). Young age at first sexual intercourse and sexually transmitted infections in adolescents and young adults. *American Journal of Epidemiology, 161*(8), 774–780.

Katz, J., & Tirone, V. (2009). Women's sexual compliance with male dating partners: Associations with investment in ideal womanhood and romantic well-being. *Sex Roles, 60*(5–6), 347–356.

Kiefer, A. K., & Sanchez, D. T. (2007). Scripting sexual passivity: A gender role perspective. *Personal Relationships, 14*(2), 269–290.

Kiefer, A. K., Sanchez, D. T., Kalinka, C. J., & Ybarra, O. (2006). How women's nonconscious association of sex with submission relates to their subjective sexual arousability and ability to reach orgasm. *Sex Roles, 55*(1–2), 93–94.

Kozee, H. B., & Tylka, T. L. (2006). A test of objectification theory with lesbian women. *Psychology of Women Quarterly, 30*(4), 348–357.

Kraft, J. M., Harvey, S. M., Hatfield-Timajchy, K., Beckman, L., Farr, S. L., Jamieson, D. J., & Thorburn, S. (2010). Pregnancy motivations and contraceptive use: Hers, his, or theirs? *Women's Health Issues, 20*(4), 234–241.

Lamb, S. (2010). Feminist ideals for a healthy female adolescent sexuality: A critique. *Sex Roles, 62*(5–6), 294–306.

Laumann, E. O., Paik, A., & Rosen, R. C. (1999). Sexual dysfunction in the United States: Prevalence and predictors. *JAMA, 281*(6), 537–544.

Leonard, L. M., & Follette, V. M. (2002). Sexual functioning in women reporting a historing a history of child sexual abuse: Review of the empirical literature and clinical implications. *Annual Review of Sex Research, 13,* 346–388.

Leserman, J. (2005). Sexual abuse history: Prevalence, health effects, mediators, and psychological treatment. *Psychosomatic Medicine, 67*(6), 906–915.

Leval, A., Sundström, K., Ploner, A., Arnheim Dahlström, L., Widmark, C., & Sparén, P. (2011). Assessing perceived risk and STI prevention behavior: A national population-based study with special reference to HPV. *PLoS ONE, 6*(6), e20624.

Livingston, J. A., Testa, M., & VanZile-Tamsen, C. (2007). The reciprocal relationship between sexual victimization and sexual assertiveness. *Violence Against Women, 13*(3), 298–313.

Manlove, J., Terry-Humen, E., & Ikramullah, E. (2006). Young teens and older sexual partners: Correlates and consequences for males and females. *Perspectives on Sexual and Reproductive Health, 38*(4), 439–519.

Marrazzo, J. M., Coffey, P., & Bingham, A. (2005). Sexual practices, risk perception and knowledge of sexually transmitted disease risk among lesbian and bisexual women. *Perspectives on Sexual Reproductive Health, 37*(1), 6–12.

Marrazzo, J. M., Koutsky, L. A., Eschenbach, D. A., Agnew, K., Stine, K., & Hiller, S. (2002). Characterization of vaginal flora and bacterial vaginosis in women who have sex with women. *Journal of Infectious Diseases, 185,* 1307–1313.

Marrazzo, J. M., Koutsky, L. A., Kiviat, N. B., Kuypers, J. M., & Stine, K. (2001). Papanicolaou test screening and prevalence of genital human papillomavirus among women who have sex with women. *American Journal of Public Health*, *91*(6), 947–952.

McCauley, J., Ruggiero, K. J., Resnick, H. S., Conoscenti, L. M., & Kilpatrick, D. G. (2009). Forcible, drug-facilitated, and incapacitated rape in relation to substance use problems: Results from a national sample of college women. *Addictive Behaviors*, *34*(5), 458–462.

McHugh, M. C. (2006). What do women want? A new view of women's sexual problems. *Sex Roles*, *54*(5–6), 361–369.

McKinley, N. M., & Hyde, J. S. (1996). The objectified body consciousness scale: Development and validation. *Psychology of Women Quarterly*, *20*(2), 181–215.

Messman, T. L., & Long, P. J. (1996). Child sexual abuse and its relationship to revictimization in adult women: A review. *Clinical Psychology Review*, *16*(5), 397–420.

Messman-Moore, T. L., & Brown, A. L. (2004). Child maltreatment and perceived family environment as risk factors for adult rape: Is child sexual abuse the most salient experience? *Child Abuse & Neglect*, *28*(10), 1019–1034.

Miner, M. H., Flitter, J. M. K., & Robinson, B. E. (2006). Association of sexual revictimization with sexuality and psychological function. *Journal of Interpersonal Violence*, *21*(4), 503–524.

Moradi, B., Dirks, D., & Matteson, A. V. (2005). Roles of sexual objectification experiences and internalization of standards of beauty in eating disorder symptomatology: A test and extension of objectification theory. *Journal of Counseling Psychology*, *52*(3), 420–428.

Morokoff, P. J. (2000). A cultural context for sexual assertiveness in women. In C. B. Travis & J. W. White (Eds.), *Sexuality, society, and feminism* (pp. 299–319). Washington, DC: American Psychological Association.

Morokoff, P. J., Quina, K., Harlow, L. L., Whitmire, L., Grimley, D. M., Gibson, P. R., & Burkholder, G. J. (1997). Sexual assertiveness scale (SAS) for women: Development and validation. *Journal of Personality and Social Psychology*, *73*(4), 790–804.

Morokoff, P. J., Redding, C. A., Harlow, L. L., Cho, S., Rossi, J. S., Meier, K. S., . . . Brown-Peterside, P. (2009). Associations of sexual victimization, depression, and sexual assertiveness with unprotected sex: A test of the multifaceted model of HIV risk across gender. *Journal of Applied Biobehavioral Research*, *14*(1), 30–54.

Morry, M. M., & Staska, S. L. (2001). Magazine exposure: Internalization, self-objectification, eating attitudes, and body satisfaction in male and female university students. *Canadian Journal of Behavioural Science/Revue Canadienne Des Sciences Du Comportement*, *33*(4), 269–279.

Nakamura, J., & Csikszentmihalyi, M. (2009). Flow theory and research. In S. J. Lopez & C. R. Snyder (Eds.), *The Oxford handbook of positive psychology* (2nd ed., pp. 195–206). New York, NY: Oxford University Press.

National Center for Victims of Crime. (2008). Child sexual abuse. Retrieved from http://www.ncvc .org/ncvc/main.aspx?dbName=Document Viewer&DocumentID=32315

National Institute of Justice. (2010, October). Rape and sexual violence. Retrieved from http:// www.nij.gov/topics/crime/rape-sexual-violence/ welcome.htm

Noll, J. G., Trickett, P. K., & Putnam, F. W. (2003). A prospective investigation of the impact of childhood sexual abuse on the development of sexuality. *Journal of Consulting and Clinical Psychology*, *71*(3), 575–586.

O'Sullivan, L. F., & Allegier, E. R. (1998). Feigning sexual desire: Consenting to unwanted sexual activity in heterosexual dating relationships. *Journal of Sex Research*, *35*(3), 234–243.

Paolucci, E. O., Genuis, M. L., & Violato, C. (2001). A meta-analysis of the published research on the effects of child sexual abuse. *Journal of Psychology: Interdisciplinary and Applied*, *135*(1), 17–36.

Pereda, N., Guilera, G., Forns, M., & Gómez-Benito, J. (2009). The prevalence of child sexual abuse in community and student samples: A meta-analysis. *Clinical Psychology Review*, *29*(4), 328–338.

Polusny, M. A., & Follette, V. M. (1995). Long-term correlates of child sexual abuse: Theory and review of the empirical literature. *Applied & Preventive Psychology*, *4*(3), 143–166.

Power, J., McNair, R., & Carr, S. (2009). Absent sexual scripts: Lesbian and bisexual womens knowledge, attitudes and action regarding safer sex and sexual health information. *Culture, Health & Sexuality*, *11*(1), 67–81.

Pulerwitz, J., Amaro, H., De Jong, W., Gortmaker, S. L., & Rudd, R. (2002). Relationship power, condom use and HIV risk among women in the USA. *AIDS Care*, *14*(6), 789–800.

Putnam, F. W. (2003). Ten-year research update review: Child sexual abuse. *Journal of the American Academy of Child & Adolescent Psychiatry*, *42*(3), 269–278.

Quina, K., Harlow, L. L., Morokoff, P. J., Burkholder, G., & Deiter, P. J. (2000). Sexual communication in relationships: When words speak louder than actions. *Sex Roles*, *42*(7–8), 523–549.

Rafaelli, M., & Suarez, M. (1998). Reconsidering the HIV/AIDS prevention needs of Latino women in the United States. In N. L. Roth & L. K. Fuller (Eds.), *Women and AIDS: Negotiating safer practices, care, and representation* (pp. 7–40). New York, NY: Haworth Press.

Raine, T., Minnis, A. M., & Padian, N. S. (2003). Determinants of contraceptive method among young women at risk for intended pregnancy and sexually transmitted infections. *Contraception*, *68*, 19–25.

Rellini, A., & Meston, C. (2007). Sexual function and satisfaction in adults based on the definition of child sexual abuse. *Journal of Sexual Medicine*, *4*(5), 1312–1321.

Resick, P. A. (1993). The psychological impact of rape. *Journal of Interpersonal Violence*, *8*(2), 223–255.

Resnick, H. S., Holmes, M. M., Kilpatrick, D. G., Clum, G., Acierno, R., Best, C. L., & Saunders, B. E. (2000). Predictors of post-rape medical care in a national sample of women. *American Journal of Preventive Medicine*, *19*(4), 214–219.

Rickert, V. I., Sanghvi, R., & Wiemann, C. M. (2002). Is lack of sexual assertiveness among adolescent and young adult women a cause for concern? *Perspectives on Sexual and Reproductive Health*, *34*(4), 178–183.

Roberts, T., & Gettman, J. Y. (2004). Mere exposure: Gender differences in the negative effects of priming a state of self-objectification. *Sex Roles*, *51*(1–2), 17–27.

Rodriguez, M. B., Morokoff, P. M., & Gorraiz, M. L. (2012). Relationship between psychosocial, interpersonal factors and implicit sex-submission associations in Hispanic/Latina and White women. Manuscript submitted for publication.

Rosario, M., Meyer-Bahlburg, H., Hunter, J., & Gwadz, M. (1999). Sexual risk behaviors of gay, lesbian, and bisexual youths in New York City: Prevalence and correlates. *AIDS Education and Prevention*, *11*(6), 476–496.

Sanchez, D. T., & Kiefer, A. K. (2007). Body concerns in and out of the bedroom: Implications for sexual pleasure and problems. *Archives of Sexual Behavior*, *36*, 808–820.

Sanchez, D. T., Kiefer, A. K., & Ybarra, O. (2006). Sexual submissiveness in women: Costs for sexual autonomy and arousal. *Personality and Social Psychology Bulletin*, *32*(4), 512–524.

Sanday, P. R. (1981). The socio-cultural context of rape: A cross-cultural study. *Journal of Social Issues*, *37*(4), 5–27.

Sanday, P. R. (1996). Rape-prone versus rape-free campus cultures. *Violence Against Women*, *2*, 191–208.

Sanday, P. R. (2007). *Fraternity gang rape: Sex, brotherhood, and privilege on campus* (2nd ed.). New York: New York University Press.

Sandfort, T. G. M., Orr, M., Hirsch, J. S., & Santelli, J. (2008). Long-term health correlates of timing of sexual debut: Results from a national US study. *American Journal of Public Health*, *98*(1), 155–161.

Schloredt, K. A., & Heiman, J. R. (2003). Perceptions of sexuality as related to sexual functioning and sexual risk in women with different types of childhood abuse histories. *Journal of Traumatic Stress*, *16*(3), 275–284.

Senn, T. E., Carey, M. P., & Vanable, P. A. (2008). Childhood and adolescent sexual abuse and subsequent sexual risk behavior: Evidence from controlled studies, methodological critique, and suggestions for research. *Clinical Psychology Review*, *28*(5), 711–735.

Senn, T. E., Carey, M. P., Vanable, P. A., Coury-Doniger, P., & Urban, M. A. (2006). Childhood sexual abuse and sexual risk behavior among men and women attending a sexually transmitted disease clinic. *Journal of Consulting and Clinical Psychology*, *74*(4), 720–731.

Shapiro, B. L., & Schwarz, J. C. (1997). Date rape: Its relationship to trauma symptoms and sexual self-esteem. *Journal of Interpersonal Violence*, *12*(3), 407–419.

Shearer, S. L., & Herbert, C. A. (1987). Long-term effects of unresolved sexual trauma. *American Family Physician*, *36*(4), 169–175.

Shlay, J. C., McClung, M. W., Patnaik, J. L. & Douglas, J. M. (2004). Comparison of sexually transmitted disease prevalence by reported level of condom use among patients attending an urban sexually transmitted disease clinic. *Sexually Transmitted Diseases, 31*(3), 154–60.

Sterk, C. E., Klein, H., & Elifson, K. W. (2004). Predictors of condom-related attitudes among at-risk women. *Journal of Women's Health, 13*(6), 676–688.

Tjaden, P., & Thoennes, N. (2006). *Extent, nature, and consequences of rape victimization: Findings from the National Violence Against Women Survey.* Washington, DC: National Institute of Justice.

Urquiza, A. J., & Goodlin-Jones, B. L. (1994). Child sexual abuse and adult revictimization with women of color. *Violence and Victims, 9*(3), 223–232.

van Berlo, W., & Ensink, B. (2000). Problems with sexuality after sexual assault. *Annual Review of Sex Research, 11*, 235–257.

Van Bruggen, L. K., Runtz, M. G., & Kadlec, H. (2006). Sexual revictimization: The role of sexual self-esteem and dysfunctional sexual behaviors. *Child Maltreatment, 11*(2), 131–145.

Van Oss Marin, B., Gomez, C.A., & Hearst, N. (1993). Multiple heterosexual partners and condom use among Hispanics and non-Hispanic Whites. *Family Planning Perspectives, 25*, 170–174.

Watts, C., & Zimmerman, C. (2002). Violence against women: Global scope and magnitude. *The Lancet, 359*(9313), 1232–1237.

Weaver, T. L. (2009). Impact of rape on female sexuality: Review of selected literature. *Clinical Obstetrics and Gynecology, 52*(4), 702–711.

West, C. M., Williams, L. M., & Siegel, J. A. (2000). Adult sexual revictimization among black women sexually abused in childhood: A prospective examination of serious consequences of abuse. *Child Maltreatment, 5*(1), 49–57.

Westrom, L., & Eschenbach, D. (1999). Pelvic inflammatory disease. In K. K. Holmes, P. Mardh, & P. F. Sparling (Eds.), *Sexually transmitted diseases* (pp. 783–810). New York, NY: McGraw-Hill.

Williams, C. M., Larsen, U., & McCloskey, L. A. (2008). Intimate partner violence and women's contraceptive use. *Violence Against Women, 14*(12), 1382–1396.

Williams, P., Morokoff, P., & Rossi, J. (2011). Predictors of sex frequency and partners. Manuscript submitted for publication.

Wingood, G. M., & DiClemente, R. J. (1997). Child sexual abuse, HIV sexual risk, and gender relations of African-American women. *American Journal of Preventive Medicine, 13*(5), 380–384.

Wingood, G. M., & DiClemente, R. J. (1998). Partner influences and gender-related factors associated with noncondom use among young adult African American women. *American Journal of Community Psychology, 26*(1), 29–51.

Wolitzky-Taylor, K. B., Resnick, H. S., Amstadter, A. B., McCauley, J. L., Ruggiero, K. J., & Kilpatrick, D. G. (2011a). Reporting rape in a national sample of college women. *Journal of American College Health, 59*(7), 582–587.

Wolitzky-Taylor, K. B., Resnick, H. S., McCauley, J. L., Amstadter, A. B., Kilpatrick, D. G., & Ruggiero, K. J. (2011b). Is reporting of rape on the rise? A comparison of women with reported versus unreported rape experiences in the national women's study replication. *Journal of Interpersonal Violence, 26*(4), 807–832.

Wyatt, G. E., Myers, H. F., Williams, J. K., Kitchen, C. R., Loeb, T., Carmona, J. V., . . . Presley, N. (2002). Does a history of trauma contribute to HIV risk for women of color? Implications for prevention and policy. *American Journal of Public Health, 92*(4), 660–665.

Zinzow, H. M., Resnick, H. S., Amstadter, A. B., McCauley, J. L., Ruggiero, K. J., & Kilpatrick, D. G. (2010). Drug- or alcohol-facilitated, incapacitated, and forcible rape in relationship to mental health among a national sample of women. *Journal of Interpersonal Violence, 25*(12), 2217–2236.

Zwickl, S., & Merriman, G. (2011). The association between childhood sexual abuse and adult female sexual difficulties. *Sexual and Relationship Therapy, 26*(1), 16–32.

CHAPTER

13 Premenstrual Dysphoric Disorder

SIMONE N. VIGOD AND MEIR STEINER

INTRODUCTION

The menstrual cycle is a unique aspect of women's health, and women have reported mood fluctuations across the menstrual cycle since antiquity (Delaney, Lupton, & Toth, 1976). Historically, the concept of mood fluctuations across the menstrual cycle provides a distinct example of how biological differences between men and women may have impacted social trajectories. Premenstrual mood exacerbations were seen as "confirmation" that women were in no position to assume roles of importance and responsibility (Chrisler & Johnston-Robledo, 2002). However, the myth of premenstrual mood disturbance as evidence for the inferiority of women has largely been obliterated in the scientific community. The negative impacts of premenstrual mood disturbance on quality of life, daily function, and economic burden have been well-established (Chawla, Swindle, Long, Kennedy, & Sternfeld, 2002; Yang et al., 2008), generating urgency for researchers to understand this phenomenon and provide effective options for treatment.

In recent years, there has been an explosion of research into the biological determinants of premenstrual mood disturbance and into how these interact with social and psychological factors to precipitate, perpetuate, and protect women against potentially debilitating premenstrual symptoms. This chapter reviews this research and presents a multipronged approach to the management of severe premenstrual mood disturbance, with specific focus on the most severe premenstrual mood disturbance, known as premenstrual dysphoric disorder (PMDD).

DIAGNOSIS OF PREMENSTRUAL DYSPHORIC DISORDER

To illustrate a common presentation of a woman presenting for diagnosis and treatment of premenstrual mood disturbance, we begin with the case of Krista P. Ms. P is a 33-year-old actress with no children who lives with her male partner. She complains of a pattern of mood disturbance, anxiety, and irritability that starts 4 to 5 days before her period and remits with the onset of menstruation. Prior to menstruation, she becomes easily overwhelmed and experiences "negative" thinking (e.g., she questions decisions about her job and her relationships). She finds herself becoming very tearful, and she worries a lot. She also complains of decreased interest, concentration difficulties, increased appetite, and a desire to sleep all the time. She reports low self-image and reduced sex drive during this period. From a physical perspective, she has bloating. She has not had to take time off work because of her symptoms, but she often feels that she "cannot cope." These symptoms began when she was an adolescent. However, she was taking oral contraceptive pills for several years and found that the symptoms were not as bad then. The length of her bleeding is 4 to 5 days, and she has a regular cycle every 28 days. She is currently using condoms for birth control. She denies having any depressive symptoms for the remainder of the month. She tends to be somewhat anxious and interpersonally sensitive at baseline, but the exacerbation of these characteristics prior to menstruation is severe. She does not have any history of medical problems.

As with most psychiatric and many physical syndromes, there is no existing laboratory or imaging test that can ascertain a diagnosis of premenstrual mood disturbance. Therefore, clinical criteria are required to diagnose and classify premenstrual mood disturbances for research and treatment purposes. Currently, premenstrual dysphoric disorder (PMDD) is classified in the American Psychiatric Association's *Diagnostic and Statistical Manual of Mental Disorders IV—Text Revision* (*DSM-IV-TR*) as an example of a "Depressive Disorder Not Otherwise Specified," with research diagnostic criteria specified in Appendix B (Axes Provided for Further Study) (American Psychiatric Association, 2000). It is important to note that the *DSM-IV-TR* specifically separates PMDD from premenstrual syndrome (PMS). PMS is considered a syndrome that includes mild psychological and/or physical discomfort in the premenstrual period, but does not markedly impair a woman's ability to function in her daily life. PMS is not considered to be "disordered" because up to 80% of women report some type of physical or emotional discomfort prior to menstruation that does not necessarily impact function to a great degree (American

Psychiatric Association, 2000). Although premenstrual syndrome shares the feature of symptom expression during the premenstrual phase of the menstrual cycle, PMDD is a more severe form of premenstrual disturbance that specifically requires the presence of at least one psychiatric symptom and must be associated with a marked disturbance in function (i.e., social, occupational, academic performance) (Figure 13.1).

Individuals who experience physical symptoms premenstrually, without the required psychological symptoms, likely meet criteria for PMS and not for PMDD. As such, treatment implications for PMS and PMDD may differ markedly, with increased focus on mental health and functioning for women with PMDD. In accordance with the *DSM-IV-TR*, the International Society for Premenstrual Disorders Consensus Statement supports the concept of PMDD as a core premenstrual disorder that is held distinct from PMS for the same reasons identified here. In addition, this group specifies the importance of distinguishing PMDD from other "variant" premenstrual disorders, including premenstrual exacerbation of underlying physical and psychiatric disorders, for research and treatment purposes (O'Brien et al., 2011).

The sub-work group for PMDD for the development of the fifth edition of the *DSM* (*DSM-5*) has recommended that PMDD be placed in its own category in the mood disorders section of the new manual (Epperson et al., 2012). This would lend further credence to the existence of PMDD as distinct from major depressive disorder without cyclical menstrual changes. Better identification of women with premenstrual mood disturbance may have key implications for treatment—allowing earlier detection and introduction of PMDD-specific treatment strategies. The proposed criteria for

A. In most menstrual cycles during the past year, five (or more) of the following symptoms were present for most of the time during the last week of the luteal phase, began to remit within a few days after the onset of the follicular phase, and were absent in the week postmenses, with at least one of the symptoms being either (1), (2), (3), or (4):

1. markedly depressed mood, feelings of hopelessness, or self-deprecating thoughts
2. marked anxiety, tension, feelings of being "keyed up," or "on edge"
3. marked affective lability (e.g., feeling suddenly sad or tearful or increased sensitivity to rejection)
4. persistent and marked anger or irritability or increased interpersonal conflicts
5. decreased interest in usual activities (e.g., work, school, friends, hobbies)
6. subjective sense of difficulty in concentrating
7. lethargy, easy fatigability, or marked lack of energy
8. marked change in appetite, overeating, or specific food cravings
9. hypersomnia or insomnia
10. a subjective sense of being overwhelmed or out of control
11. other physical symptoms, such as breast tenderness or swelling, headaches, joint or muscle pain, a sensation of "bloating," weight gain

Note: In menstruating females, the luteal phase corresponds to the period between ovulation and the onset of menses, and the follicular phase begins with menses. In nonmenstruating females (e.g., those who have had a hysterectomy), the timing of luteal and follicular phases may require measurement of circulating reproductive hormones.

B. The disturbance markedly interferes with work or school or with usual social activities and relationships with others (e.g., avoidance of social activities, decreased productivity and efficiency at work or school).

C. The disturbance is not merely an exacerbation of the symptoms of another disorder, such as Major Depressive Disorder, Panic Disorder, Dysthymic Disorder, or a Personality Disorder (although it may be superimposed on any of these disorders).

D. Criteria A, B, and C must be confirmed by prospective daily ratings during at least two consecutive symptomatic cycles. (The diagnosis may be made provisionally prior to this confirmation.)

(American Psychiatric Association, 2000, p. 774)

Figure 13.1 *DSM-IV-TR* **Research Criteria for Premenstrual Dysphoric Disorder**

premenstrual dysphoric disorder in the *DSM-5* are similar to the *DSM-IV-TR* Appendix B criteria, with some minor changes to Criteria A, B, and D, as well as the addition of a Criterion E that ensures symptoms are not caused by the direct physiological effects of a substance or general medical condition (see bolded areas in Figure 13.2).

Physical Disorders as Differential Diagnoses

Some physical disorders can be accompanied by premenstrual exacerbation of somatic and psychological symptoms. These include auto-immune disorders, such as rheumatoid arthritis and systemic lupus erythematosus, as well as other systemic disorders, including diabetes mellitus, anemia, hypothyroidism, epilepsy, and migraine headache (Steiner, Peer, & Soares, 2006). Premenstrual exacerbations of gynecological disorders, such as endometriosis and dysmenorrhea are also common (Steiner et al., 2006). It is important to distinguish these disorders from PMDD, because management of the underlying disorder is indicated. These disorders can most often be distinguished from PMDD by careful history taking, physical exam, and laboratory or other relevant investigations.

Psychiatric Disorders as Differential Diagnoses

Distinguishing PMDD from premenstrual exacerbations of underlying psychiatric

A. In most menstrual cycles during the past year, five (or more) of the following symptoms were present in the final week before the onset of menses, started to *improve* within a few days after the onset of menses, and were *minimal or* absent in the week postmenses, with at least one of the symptoms being either (1), (2), (3), or (4)*:

   1. marked affective lability (e.g., mood swings; feeling suddenly sad or tearful or increased sensitivity to rejection)
   2. marked irritability or anger or increased interpersonal conflicts
   3. markedly depressed mood, feelings of hopelessness, or self-deprecating thoughts
   4. marked anxiety, tension, feelings of being "keyed up," or "on edge"
   5. decreased interest in usual activities (e.g., work, school, friends, hobbies)
   6. subjective **difficulty** in concentration
   7. lethargy, easy fatigability, or marked lack of energy
   8. marked change in appetite, overeating, or specific food cravings
   9. hypersomnia or insomnia
   10. **a sense** of being overwhelmed or out of control
   11. **physical** symptoms such as breast tenderness or swelling, joint or muscle pain, a sensation of "bloating," weight gain

   *Symptoms (1), (2), (3), and (4) were ordered differently in *DSM-IV-TR* Research Criteria

B. The **symptoms are associated with clinically significant distress** or interference with work, school, usual social activities or relationships with others (e.g. avoidance of social activities, decreased productivity and efficiency at work, school, or home).

C. The disturbance is not merely an exacerbation of the symptoms of another disorder, such as Major Depressive Disorder, Panic Disorder, Dysthymic Disorder, or a Personality Disorder (although it may be superimposed on any of these disorders).

D. **Criteria A should** be confirmed by prospective daily ratings during at least two symptomatic cycles. (The diagnosis may be made provisionally prior to this confirmation.)

E. The symptoms are not due to the direct physiological effects of a substance (e.g., a drug of abuse, a medication or other treatment) or a general medical condition (e.g., hyperthyroidism).

(Epperson et al., 2012)

Figure 13.2   Proposed Criteria for Premenstrual Dysphoric Disorder

disorders is often complex, and women who report premenstrual mood disturbance should be screened for psychiatric symptoms across the menstrual cycle. Some women with PMDD do report psychiatric symptoms in the follicular phase of their menstrual cycle. However, when criteria are met for another major psychiatric disorder throughout the menstrual cycle, then this should be considered the primary diagnosis (Kornstein et al., 2005). PMDD can be diagnosed concurrently with other psychiatric disorders. However, it should not be diagnosed when the symptoms can be accounted for by another primary diagnosis. Premenstrual exacerbation of symptoms may represent undertreatment of the primary disorder,

and when the primary disorder is appropriately treated, symptoms will often remit across the menstrual cycle (Kornstein et al., 2005). Specifically, women with major depressive disorder, dysthymic disorder, anxiety disorders, bipolar disorder, and various personality disorders commonly report premenstrual exacerbation of symptoms (Critchlow, Bond, & Wingrove, 2001; Hartlage, Brandenburg, & Kravitz, 2004; Kim et al., 2004; Kornstein et al., 2005).

For example, in the National Institutes of Mental Health Sequenced Treatment Alternatives to Depression (STAR-D) trial, 64% of 433 women with major depressive disorder reported worsening of their symptoms 5 to 10 days prior to menstruation

(Kornstein et al., 2005). With respect to bipolar disorder, a systematic review of the literature examining comorbidity of premenstrual mood disturbance with other psychiatric disorders identified five retrospective cohort studies examining the relationship between bipolar disorder and premenstrual mood disturbance. These studies, using varying methods of measuring premenstrual mood disturbance, reported that between 11% and 60% of women with bipolar disorder may suffer premenstrual exacerbation of depression, mood lability, anger, and irritability (Kim et al., 2004). Women with personality disorders may also experience premenstrual exacerbation of their symptoms, including increased irritability and interpersonal difficulties (Critchlow et al., 2001).

Prospective Symptom Assessment and Rating Scales

The requirement of the *DSM-IV-TR* research diagnostic criteria for PMDD that symptoms be documented prospectively over at least two cycles is considered important for two main reasons. First, there is concern about bias inherent in retrospective ratings by women being assessed for PMDD that may result in overdiagnosis of the disorder (Rubinow, Roy-Byrne, Hoban, Gold, & Post, 1984). Second, women's retrospective reports may be influenced by the phase of the menstrual cycle during which she reports her symptoms (Lane & Francis, 2003; Meaden, Hartlage, & Cook-Karr, 2005). For example, women who are acutely symptomatic may be more likely to report symptoms than women who are not acutely symptomatic because of the cognitive and mood changes associated with these symptomatic periods. Many rating scales have been used over the years to document premenstrual mood disturbance. Most of these use either a visual analog or Likert rating scale (e.g., Daily Record of Severity of Problems; DRSP), where the patient can self-report and record symptoms over the 2-month period (ideally prior to consultation with a healthcare professional regarding treatment; Pearlstein & Steiner, 2008).

The DRSP is likely the most widely used system in both research and clinical practice (Endicott, Nee, & Harrison, 2006). This scale has 21 items that correspond to the 11 symptoms outlined in the *DSM-IV-TR* criterion. Women are asked to rate the severity of these items on a six-point Likert rating scale. Three additional items assess functional impairment. Women make daily ratings across the menstrual cycle (see example in Figure 13.3), and ratings can be scored using a standardized summary score sheet. In addition, clinicians are urged to examine the pattern of symptoms and impairment across the cycle to assist with making a clinical diagnosis. This system has good internal consistency as well as good test-retest reliability and is sensitive to change in symptoms after treatment (Endicott et al., 2006). It should be noted that women are not required to be completely asymptomatic during the follicular phase of their cycle in order to be diagnosed with PMDD. However, an increase in severity of symptoms between 30% to 50% in the luteal phase is generally preferred for diagnostic purposes (Smith, Schmidt, & Rubinow, 2003). When prospective ratings are unavailable or not feasibly collected, the Premenstrual Symptoms Screening Tool (PSST)—a retrospective rating scale intended for completion during clinical consultation with the patient—has potential utility in identifying women who are likely

Each evening the woman notes the degree to which she experiences each of the listed problems. She puts an "x" in the box which corresponds to symptom severity: 1—not at all, 2—minimal, 3—mild, 4—moderate, 5—severe, 6—extreme.

Month: *October*		Day (Mark Menses with an X)																														
													X	X	x	x	x	X														
Item (Severity)																																
Sad or down"	1	x	x	x	x	x	x											x	X	x	x	X	x	x	X	x	x	x	x	x	x	x
	2							x	x							x	x															
	3									X					X																	
	4										X	x	x	X																		
	5																															
	6																															
Tense or "on edge"	1					x	x	x								x	x	x			x	X	x	x		x	x		x	x	x	x
	2	x	x																													
	3			x	x														X	x					X							
	4								x																			x				
	5									X	X	x																				
	6												x	X	X																	

∗ Adapted from Daily Record of Severity of Problems (Endicott et al., 2006).

Figure 13.3 Two Items From Krista P.'s Cycle Chart∗

PREVALENCE AND DEMOGRAPHIC CORRELATES

Historically, prevalence estimates for premenstrual mood disturbance were mainly based on retrospective diagnoses, and the definition of "severe" premenstrual mood disturbance varied significantly. Given the strict diagnostic criteria for PMDD, it has been difficult to obtain population prevalence estimates. Therefore, most prevalence estimates generated using *DSM-IV-TR* criteria differ depending on the population being studied. Studies in clinical and volunteer populations tend to report higher prevalence estimates than samples that are more representative of the general population. Studies in which full *DSM-IV-TR* criteria are applied (i.e., prospective charting over two cycles) tend to generate lower prevalence estimates. For example, Rivera-Tovar and Frank (1990) reported a prevalence of 4.6% in a sample of 217 female university students charting prospectively over 90 days (Rivera-Tovar & Frank, 1990); a Kuwaiti study of 110 nursing students reported a prevalence of 5.6% using the DSRP over two cycles (Omu, Al-Marzouk, Delles, Oranye, & Omu, 2011); and a Croatian study of young women (aged 18 to 30) found a prevalence of 5.8% using daily prospective rating scales (Rojnic Kuzman & Hotujac, 2007). The Harvard Study for Moods and Cycles reported a PMDD prevalence of 6.4% among women aged 36 to 44 (although these women only completed 1 month of prospective ratings) (Cohen et al., 2002). There have been two population-based studies (one in Iceland and one in the United States). In a group of 83 women sampled from the National Registry of Iceland, the prevalence of PMDD was estimated at 2% to 6% based on 1 month of prospective mood charting (Sveindottir & Backstrom, 2000). The lowest population-based prevalence estimate was generated in a U.S. sample of 1,246 women ages 13 to 55, where psychiatric interviews were conducted and 2 months of prospective rating scales were analyzed (Gehlert, Song, Chang, & Hartlage, 2009). The prevalence of PMDD was only 1.6% in this sample.

The risk of PMDD may be increased for women who have a family history of the disorder, with studies indicating that between 42% to 54% of the variance of premenstrual symptoms may be explained by heritable factors (Kendler, Karkowski, Corey, & Neale, 1998; Treloar, Heath, & Martin, 2002). In addition, personal history of depression, particularly in the context of pregnancy and the postpartum period, may also be associated with an increased risk of PMDD (Payne, Palmer, & Joffe, 2009). Both day-to-day life stress and history of traumatic life experiences appear to be strongly associated with premenstrual mood disturbance, with up to 40% of women with PMDD reporting previous sexual abuse (Beck, Gevirtz, & Mortola, 1990; Fontana & Palfai, 1994; Friedman, Hurt, Clarkin, Corn, & Aronoff, 1982; Paddison et al., 1990; Pilver, Desai, Kasl, & Levy, 2011; Pilver, Levy, Libby, & Desai, 2011; Warner & Bancroft, 1990).

Other demographic correlates of PMDD have not been as well-established. Although one published study of 332 women in the United States reported that women aged 20 to 35 had more severe symptoms of premenstrual dysphoria than women aged 36 to 44 (Freeman, Rickels,

Schweizer, & Ting, 1995), other studies have suggested that women appear to have increased severity of symptoms later in life. Tschudin, Bertea, and Zemp (2010) found that the prevalence of PMS (although not PMDD) was higher among women aged 35 to 44 in a Swiss population-based sample of 3,913 women than among women in a younger age group. Data is equally conflicting with respect to education level. Although some studies suggest that women with higher levels of education tend to report more premenstrual symptoms overall, a recent Polish study of 1,540 women found that tertiary education was protective against the development of PMDD (Skrzypulec-Plinta, Drosdzol, Nowosielski, & Plinta, 2010). The Harvard Study of Moods and Cycles also reported that women with PMDD had lower educational levels than women without PMDD. This latter result, however, may have been a result of the high comorbidity of PMDD and major depressive disorder (Cohen et al., 2002).

There is some evidence that risk of PMDD varies with acculturation in developed countries. For example, nativity status, duration of residence in the United States, and age at immigration were significantly associated with PMDD among 3,856 English-speaking, premenopausal Asian, Latina, and Black women from the National Latino and Asian American Survey and the National Survey of American Life (Pilver, Kasl, Desai, & Levy, 2011). Women born outside of the United States (Odds Ratio [OR] = 0.38; 95% Confidence Interval [CI] = 0.21–0.68) were less likely to have PMDD than U.S.-born women. Immigrants who arrived to the United States after age 6 (OR = 0.33, 95% CI = 0.18–0.62) were less likely than U.S.-born women/immigrants

who arrived before age 6 to have PMDD. Prevalence of PMDD increased with longer duration of U.S. residence.

IMPACT

The impact of PMDD on psychosocial function has been widely studied. Women repeatedly report impairments in two main areas of psychosocial function: (1) interpersonal relationships and (2) work productivity and absenteeism (Chawla et al., 2002; Heinemann, Minh, Filonenko, & Uhl-Hochgraber, 2010; Pearlstein et al., 2000). The level of psychosocial functioning impairment in the symptomatic phase of the illness appears to be similar to the level of impairment suffered by women with chronic depressive (i.e., dysthymic) disorders (Pearlstein et al., 2000). Women with PMDD report physical and emotional health-related quality of life scores that are far lower than U.S. general population norms and comparable to other chronic illnesses, including chronic back pain, osteoarthritis, rheumatoid arthritis, diabetes mellitus, and hypertension. Impairments in work productivity appear to extend even into the follicular (i.e., postmenstrual) phase of the illness (Chawla et al., 2002). In one study following women with PMDD for 1 year, nearly half of the women missed work once per month, and 6.5% missed work two to three times per month because of menstrual-related mood symptoms (Robinson & Swindle, 2000).

In an attempt to quantify the impairment suffered by women with PMDD, researchers have calculated psychosocial impairment in women with PMDD using the World Health Organization (WHO) Global Burden of Disease concept of disability-adjusted life years (DALY) (Halbreich, Borenstein, Pearlstein, & Kahn, 2003; Murray & Lopez, 1996). This measure incorporates the years of life lost to premature death and the length and severity of disability, where one DALY is equivalent to one lost year of healthy life. Given the length and severity of disability related to PMDD alone (because years of life lost to premature death such as suicide has not been evaluated but is presumably low), the authors calculated that each woman afflicted with PMDD would experience 3.84 DALYs (or years of disability) (Halbreich et al., 2003). The authors further calculated that this would correspond to a burden of 14,492,465 DALYs for the United States alone given a 5% prevalence of PMDD among women ages 14 to 51 (Halbreich et al., 2003).

POTENTIAL ETIOLOGIC FACTORS

The underlying basis for the development of PMDD has not been fully elucidated. There is evidence for the role of both biological and psychosocial factors, and it is likely that multiple factors interact to predispose women to this disorder, to precipitate onset, and perpetuate the symptoms.

We use the case of Andrea F. to illustrate potential contributing factors in the onset and maintenance of PMDD. Andrea is a 36-year-old married accountant with three children ages 6, 8, and 11. She complains of relatively severe psychological and physical symptoms in the premenstrual period since she stopped breastfeeding her youngest daughter. A trial of oral contraceptive pills last year improved her physical symptoms such as menorrhagia and cramping to a great extent, but not the psychological symptoms. She has since stopped the oral contraceptives because of

severe headaches, but the physical symptoms have not recurred. Prospective charting reveals fatigue, anxiety, restlessness, irritability, interpersonal sensitivity, concentration difficulty, hypersomnia, and physical symptoms that appear to onset 1 to 2 days prior to menstruation and persist several days into the follicular phase. Throughout the menstrual cycle, she reports mildly depressed mood, mild insomnia, fatigue, and decreased concentration. However, these symptoms are significantly worse prior to menstruation. She has a good relationship with her husband, but reports that she is "stressed on a daily basis" by the pressure to keep up with the demands of her children and work. Her cycles are regular, and there are no perimenopausal symptoms. She reports a previous major depressive episode after the birth of her first child. She did not seek treatment. Her maternal grandmother suffered major depressive disorder and postpartum depression. Her mother suffered from premenstrual mood disturbances and depression at menopause, and her sister became depressed while undergoing assisted reproductive technology (fertility treatments).

Biological Factors

Heritability The etiology of PMDD is complex, but there is clearly evidence for a distinct contribution of familial heritability in the onset of the disorder. Twin studies suggest that premenstrual mood disturbance is a heritable phenomenon, as illustrated by the following studies. Kendler et al. (1998) studied 1,312 twins from a U.S. population-based twin register (Kendler et al., 1998). They found that genetic factors accounted for 56% of the variance in premenstrual exacerbation of fatigue, sadness, and irritability when assessed at two time points over a 6-year period. In a study of 722 Australian female twin pairs (63% monozygotic), 44% of the variance in premenstrual symptoms was explained by additive genetic factors (Treloar et al., 2002). Evidence for the heritability of premenstrual mood disturbance has sparked investigation into biological mechanisms important in the pathophysiology of PMDD.

Hormones   Most of the research into the biological mechanisms underlying the pathophysiology of PMDD has focused on sex hormones. It has been hypothesized that some women may be uniquely vulnerable to the hormonal changes, with resultant emergence of premenstrual mood disturbance (Payne et al., 2009). This hypothesis has been supported by two small but well-conducted studies. In a study of 20 women with PMS and 20 controls, women with PMS whose symptoms abated when ovarian function was suppressed had a significant recurrence in symptoms when hormones were reinstated, while women without PMS were unaffected (Schmidt, Nieman, Danaceau, Adams, & Rubinow, 1998). Furthermore, Eriksson, Backstrom, Stridsberg, Hammarlund-Udenaes, and Naessen (2006) found that women with premenstrual mood dysphoria ($n = 13$) exhibited an exaggerated luteinizing hormone (LH) response when given exogenous estrogen after pharmacological estrogen depletion (i.e., a standard estrogen challenge test) compared to controls without premenstrual mood dysphoria ($n = 12$), and that the level of the physiological response was correlated with symptom levels in the premenstrual mood dysphoria group. Huo et al., (2007) identified a genetic variation in the estrogen receptor alpha gene (ESR-1) among

women with PMDD that may partly explain the genetic mechanism underlying differential responses to hormones by women with PMDD.

The other major sex hormone that has been investigated in the pathophysiology of PMDD is the progesterone metabolite allopregnanolone. In the central nervous system, allopregnanolone affects GABA-A receptors (Kim, Cho, Choi, Lee, & Jang, 2011; Sundstrom et al., 1998). Normally, positive GABA-A modulators (such as allopregnanolone) induce sedative and anxiety-reducing effects. However, women with PMDD appear to have a paradoxical response to allopregnanolone, whereby GABA-A modulators may induce the opposite effect, generating premenstrual symptoms in the context of increased allopregnanolone premenstrually (Backstrom et al., 2011). This has been confirmed via imaging studies as well as in clinical studies demonstrating these paradoxical effects to other compounds with GABA-A activity, such as flumazenil and benzodiazepines, among women with PMDD (Le Melledo, Van Driel, Coupland, Lott, & Jhangri, 2000; Sundstrom, Ashbrook, & Backstrom, 1997; Sundstrom, Nyberg, & Backstrom, 1997).

Neurotransmitters   The genetic mechanism underlying differential responses to sex steroids in some women has yet to be fully elucidated. However, attention has been focused on the neurotransmitter serotonin because of the known influence of sex hormones on the serotonergic pathway and because PMDD can often be successfully treated with selective serotonin reuptake inhibitor medications (see Management section). Evidence that serotonergic neurotransmitter pathways may be involved is supported by research demonstrating that sensitivity to GABA-A steroids among women with PMDD appears to normalize when women are treated with serotonin reuptake inhibitors, possibly because the drugs modulate allopregnanolone levels via their activity at the GABA-A receptor (Sundstrom & Backstrom, 1998). Other evidence for the involvement of serotonergic pathways includes a positron emission tomography study that demonstrated differences between women with PMDD and controls with respect to brain serotonergic function across the menstrual cycle (Jovanovic et al., 2006). Furthermore, serotonergic agents, such as buspirone, l-tryptophan, and fenfluramine, have induced serotonergic dysfunction when given to women with severe premenstrual mood disturbance (Bancroft, Cook, Davidson, Bennie, & Goodwin, 1991; FitzGerald et al., 1997; Rasgon et al., 2001). Particular variants (polymorphisms) of the serotonin transporter gene have been studied as emerging factors in the etiology of major depressive disorder (Kuzelova, Ptacek, & Macek, 2010). More recently, several studies have reported associations between serotonin transporter polymorphisms and PMDD (Gingnell, Comasco, Oreland, Fredrikson, & Sundstrom-Poromaa, 2010).

Psychosocial Factors

Sociocultural Factors There are those who argue that premenstrual mood disturbance is a culturally bound syndrome specific to Western cultures (Halbreich et al., 2007). Proponents of this concept of "menstrual socialization" argue that Western society (and North American society in particular) has socialized women into having negative expectations about the premenstrual period and that women therefore interpret "normal" physiological changes with a negative, instead of a neutral, valence (Johnson, 1987). It is difficult to attribute PMDD solely to "menstrual socialization," as more studies are emerging that identify premenstrual dysphoria in non-Western societies and more evidence emerges for biological determinants of the disorder (as discussed in the Biological Factors section). However, there is some support for the hypothesis that acculturation plays a role.

As discussed previously, a recent U.S. study showed that the prevalence of PMDD (retrospectively reported) increased in premenopausal Asian, Latina, and Black women based on the amount of time they had lived in America (Pilver, Kasl, et al., 2011). Another study comparing American women to women in Bahrain and Italy found that although physical premenstrual symptoms were reported in more than 30% of women in all three cultures, irritability and mood swings were significantly more prevalent in the U.S. sample than either the Italian or Bahraini groups (Dan & Monagle, 1994). This finding is consistent with other reports that populations of women outside of the United States tend to report more somatic than affective symptoms in general (Chang, Holroyd, & Chau, 1995; Merikangas, Foeldenyi, & Angst, 1993). Taken together, these findings suggest that culture may play a role in the symptoms that women attend to or determine to be problematic, as well as the way that women report symptoms, during the premenstrual period.

Furthermore, the concept of menstrual socialization may be important, because there is some evidence that cognitive framing might be an important point of intervention for both prevention and treatment. A small experimental study demonstrated that women who watched a video that negatively portrayed premenstrual mood symptoms were later more likely to report severe premenstrual mood symptoms than women who had watched a more neutral video (Marvan & Escobedo, 1999). Furthermore, a group intervention focused on positively reframing menstruation experiences was able to reduce PMDD-associated functional impairment (Morse, 1999).

Potential Impact of Life Stress and Sexual Abuse

Psychological factors important to the etiology of PMDD have also been studied. As noted earlier, there is a relatively well-established relationship between life stress and premenstrual dysphoria, whereby premenstrual mood disturbances appear to be associated with high levels of daily stress (Beck et al., 1990; Fontana & Palfai, 1994; Warner & Bancroft, 1990). However, it is not likely that the stress itself "causes" PMDD. Experts have hypothesized that the relationship may be mediated by the tendency for women with premenstrual dysphoria to demonstrate coping styles that rely heavily on relatively ineffective behaviors to mitigate stress, such as avoidance or wishful thinking (Ornitz & Brown, 1993).

Such findings lead us to question the underlying basis for the development of these coping behaviors. There is evidence that premenstrual dysphoria is associated not only with daily life stress, but also with a history of stressful life events. Specifically, a history of sexual abuse appears to be particularly common among women with premenstrual mood and physical symptoms (Friedman et al., 1982; Paddison et al., 1990). This may generate clues as to the mechanism underlying PMDD, because childhood (as well as adult) interpersonal trauma and stress has lasting psychological and physiological effects that specifically include dysfunctional responses to stress. For example, research into the pathophysiology of major depression has shown that hypothalamic–pituitary–adrenal (HPA) axis changes that occur in childhood persist into adulthood; these changes may partially explain why depression is triggered in some people by apparently minor events, whereas other people do not become depressed under even more difficult circumstances (Heim et al., 2000).

Two independent studies have now shown that women with PMDD have dysregulated neuroendocrine and cardiovascular responses to stress (Bunevicius et al., 2005; Matsumoto, Ushiroyama, Kimura, Hayashi, & Moritani, 2007). Furthermore, differences in brain function related to processing of stressful stimuli have also been observed. A functional neuroimaging study showed that women with PMDD have selectively enhanced processing of negative stimuli and decreases in cortical control of limbic responses in the premenstrual phase (Protopopescu et al., 2008). Results from this emergent research clearly suggest that there are interactions among social, psychological, and biological factors in the development of PMDD. Additional research is needed to more fully understand the interplay between these factors.

MANAGEMENT OF PREMENSTRUAL DYSPHORIC DISORDER

The approach to the treatment of PMDD is based on the concept that the etiology of PMDD is multidetermined. A stepwise

1. Psychoeducation: education about the disorder, validation of symptoms and support about symptoms of PMDD, identification of symptom triggers*
2. Lifestyle modification* and dietary supplementation
3. Relaxation skills
4. Psychotherapy
5. Pharmacotherapy
6. Hormone manipulation
7. Complementary and alternative treatments (please see text for examples) may be used at any time during other interventions.

   *Should be recommended for every woman diagnosed with PMDD and continued during other interventions.
   (Adapted from *Approach to Premenstrual Dysphoria for the Mental Health Practitioner* [Vigod, Frey, Soares, & Steiner, 2010])

Figure 13.4   Stepwise Approach to the Management of PMDD

approach to the management of PMDD is outlined in Figure 13.4. For women with less-severe symptoms, lifestyle interventions, dietary supplements, and psychoeducation are appropriate and may ameliorate symptoms. In women with more-severe functional impairment, or for whom lifestyle interventions are insufficient, management strategies that include more intensive intervention, such as psychotherapy and pharmacotherapy, may be warranted. When psychiatric issues, physical symptoms, and/or functional impairment are persistent and resistant to less-invasive treatments, pharmacological and even surgical suppression of ovarian function may be required. For all patients, a thorough clinical assessment is required to establish the diagnosis and identify and treat medical and psychiatric comorbidity. Throughout the treatment process, symptoms and functional impairment should be consistently reassessed (see Diagnosis section).

Psychoeducation

Women with PMS and PMDD may benefit from education about the disorder, validation of symptoms, and support (Morse, 1999; Seideman, 1990; Taylor, 1999).

Women can be encouraged to try to identify symptom triggers and modify their environments to reduce stressful activities during the premenstrual phase. There is some evidence that group psychoeducation that includes positive reframing of the menstrual cycle experience can be beneficial for reducing premenstrual symptoms and impairment (Morse, 1999).

Healthy Lifestyle and Dietary Supplementation

Modifications to diet, exercise routine, and sleep may be effective in ameliorating symptoms for some women with PMDD, particularly for those with mild symptoms (Jarvis, Lynch, & Morin, 2008). Women can be advised to increase their consumption of fruit, vegetables, and whole grains and keep well-hydrated with increased water consumption throughout the menstrual cycle. Frequent, smaller meals, as well as reduced intake of salty foods, sugar, caffeine, and alcohol, are also recommended to reduce bloating and associated irritability. To our knowledge, no trials of dietary supplements have been conducted in women with strictly diagnosed PMDD. However, dietary supplements for which there is some evidence of efficacy in improving symptoms of PMS include calcium, vitamin B_6 (pyridoxine), and specially formulated carbohydrate-rich beverages. A large double-blind, randomized, controlled trial demonstrated superiority of calcium supplementation (1,200 mg) over placebo, with a significant reduction in overall premenstrual symptom scores by the third menstrual cycle in women taking calcium (Thys-Jacobs, Starkey, Bernstein, & Tian, 1998). With respect to vitamin B_6 supplementation, a systematic review of four randomized controlled trials representing 541 patients found an improvement in depressive symptoms relative to placebo (OR = 1.69, 95% CI = 1.39–2.06; Wyatt, Dimmock, Jones, & Shaughn O'Brien, 1999). A subsequent randomized controlled trial also found that women with PMS who took vitamin B_6 (80 mg) had a greater reduction in psychiatric symptom scores compared to placebo (Kashanian, Mazinani, & Jalalmanesh, 2007). Vitamin B_6 should be recommended with caution, however, because higher doses have been associated with neurological complications such as peripheral neuropathy.

Recommendations to eat carbohydrate-rich meals are often made based on the theory that increasing intake of the serotonin precursor, tryptophan, could improve mood. However, these recommendations are based on two small studies of women with PMS who showed improvement in self-reported symptoms of anger and depression after ingesting a specially formulated carbohydrate-rich beverage (Freeman, Stout, Endicott, & Spiers, 2002; Sayegh et al., 1995).

Whether regular exercise has a specific effect on symptoms in women with PMDD has not been explored, but regular aerobic exercise (i.e., 20 to 30 minutes per day, three to four times per week) is often recommended for women with physical and psychological premenstrual symptoms (Frackiewicz & Shiovitz, 2001). In a nonclinical population, women who performed regular aerobic exercise demonstrated significantly less negative mood states and fewer clinical symptoms across the menstrual cycle (Aganoff & Boyle, 1994).

Although there is no evidence to support weight loss as an intervention for PMDD, there is some evidence that women with a high percentage of body fat may be more likely to develop PMS. In the United States Nurses' Health Study, more than 3,000 women were assessed every 2 years over a 13-year period (1989–2001) to investigate the relationship between body mass index (BMI) and the development of PMS. For every 1 kg per month increase in BMI, women were 3% more likely to develop PMS over the follow-up period. The mechanisms for this relationship are unknown, but it may be related to the influence of adipose tissue (i.e., body fat) on hormonal and neurochemical factors that are important in the pathophysiology of premenstrual mood disturbance (Bertone-Johnson, Hankinson, Willett, Johnson, & Manson, 2010).

There is increasing evidence that women with PMDD have abnormal circadian rhythm patterns, particularly during the premenstrual period (Shechter & Boivin, 2010). Premenstrual mood may be improved by adopting a regular sleep-wake pattern across the menstrual cycle with consistent bedtime and waking times. Although, in some women, additional clinical intervention may be needed to regulate sleep.

Relaxation Skills and Structured Psychotherapies

Relaxation skills may be beneficial, possibly because they help reduce levels of daily life stress (Goodale, Domar, & Benson, 1990; Morse, Dennerstein, Farrell, & Varnavides, 1991). Cognitive-behavioral therapy (CBT), which includes both cognitive reframing and behavioral relaxation strategies in a short-term structured treatment program, has also been investigated for its efficacy in PMDD. A systematic review by Lustyk, Gerrish, Shaver, and Keys (2009) found that CBT may provide some benefit with respect to reducing symptoms of PMDD. The amount and quality of the evidence for CBT (seven studies, among them three randomized controlled trials) is limited, so it is difficult to make definitive recommendations on the utility of CBT for women with PMDD. However, the efficacy of CBT in managing other affective and somatic disorders that share symptoms in common with PMDD (e.g., anxiety and pain) does provide a theoretical justification for its use in managing premenstrual mood symptoms. Justification for the recommendation of CBT with this population may become stronger as more empirical support becomes available.

Herbal, Complementary, and Other Treatments

Complementary and alternative treatments have also been explored as management options for PMS and PMDD. With respect to herbal treatments, *Vitex Agnus Castus* (Chasteberry) has been shown to improve premenstrual symptoms in randomized controlled trials, although it may have more impact on physical than psychological symptoms (Whelan, Jurgens, & Naylor, 2009). Small randomized trials provide support for the use of saffron, Qi therapy, massage therapy, biofeedback, and chiropractic treatment (Agha-Hosscini et al., 2008; Jang, Lee, Kim,

& Chong, 2004). Open trials provide limited evidence for acupuncture, yoga, and guided imagery (Pearlstein & Steiner, 2008). As previously discussed, emerging evidence shows that women with PMDD have altered circadian rhythms, so bright light therapy has been explored as a treatment option. A recent systematic review of four randomized trials suggests that this treatment option may be effective at reducing PMDD symptoms (Krasnik, Montori, Guyatt, Heels-Ansdell, & Busse, 2005).

Pharmacotherapy

Pharmacotherapy is indicated for women who either do not respond to nonpharmacological treatments or for women whose symptoms are severe enough to require immediate treatment. The mainstays of treatment for the symptoms of PMDD are the medications that increase the reuptake of serotonin in the central nervous system. These medications include selective serotonin reuptake inhibitors (SSRIs), serotonin-norepinephrine reuptake inhibitors (SNRIs), and serotonergic tricyclic antidepressants. A meta-analysis of randomized controlled studies published by the Cochrane Database for Systematic Reviews (Brown, O'Brien, Marjoribanks, & Wyatt, 2009) supports the efficacy of fluoxetine, sertraline, paroxetine, citalopram, and fluvoxamine (all SSRIs), as well as clomipramine (a serotonergic tricyclic antidepressant; Brown et al., 2009). Randomized controlled trials also support the efficacy of the SNRIs venlafaxine extended-release and duloxetine for PMDD (Freeman et al., 2001; Ramos, Hara, & Rocha, 2009).

In contrast to the 1- to 2-week delay in onset of therapeutic efficacy seen when antidepressants are used for the treatment of major depressive disorder, the effect of these medications on PMDD symptoms are seen immediately (Halbreich et al., 2002; Landen et al., 2007). The mechanism of action behind the rapid efficacy is not completely understood. It is hypothesized that it is related to the immediate repletion of serotonin in women with PMDD who are sensitive to hormonally related serotonin depletion. These medications can be given daily throughout the menstrual cycle, or cyclically in the luteal (i.e., premenstrual) phase of the cycle for women who do not experience follicular phase symptoms. Women do not appear to experience withdrawal effects from intermittent dosing (possibly because the use of the drug is not sustained). Unfortunately, PMDD symptom relapse is common upon medication discontinuation, particularly in women with the most severe symptoms (Freeman, Rickels, Sammel, Lin, & Sondheimer, 2009; Lopez, Kaptein, & Helmerhorst, 2009).

Manipulation of Menstruation

Because of the clear relationship between the menstrual cycle and PMDD symptoms, hormonal treatments have been widely investigated in the treatment of PMDD. In general, ovulation-suppression treatments should only be considered when other treatments have failed, because of the potential for adverse effects, including thromboembolic complications from oral contraceptives (e.g., deep-vein thrombosis, pulmonary embolism), osteoporosis and androgenization from gonadotropin-releasing hormone (GnRH) agonists, and permanent sterilization if the ovaries are removed.

Oral contraceptives have been widely used in attempts to suppress ovulation and alleviate symptoms of PMS and PMDD. Because many women also desire contraception, this has been viewed as a reasonable strategy, despite minimal evidence for efficacy in relieving psychological symptoms of PMDD. A systematic review of the literature supports the efficacy of a combination of ethinyl estradiol and drospirenone (Lopez et al., 2009). This combination has been approved by the U.S. Food and Drug Administration (FDA) for women with PMDD who also wish to use the medication for contraceptive purposes. However, post-marketing analysis of adverse drug effects appears to suggest that the risk of venous thromboembolic complications for this combination may be more than twice that of traditional oral contraceptives (Jick & Hernandez, 2011; Parkin, Sharples, Hernandez, & Jick, 2011). Women wishing to pursue this option should take these risks into account.

In more extreme cases, ovulation-suppression agents (such as GnRH agonists) have been used in the treatment of PMS and PMDD, although they appear to be more efficacious for physical than psychological symptoms (Freeman, Sondheimer, & Rickels, 1997; Muse, Cetel, Futterman, & Yen, 1984). Unfortunately, they also induce a low-estrogen state that can present with clinical signs of androgenization (e.g., hirsutism) and over the long term can cause osteoporosis. Danazol is a synthetic steroid that can also inhibit ovulation, and it has been shown to reduce the psychological symptoms of PMS and PMDD (O'Brien & Abukhalil, 1999). However, its use is also accompanied by significant risk. At low doses (e.g., 200 mg per day), pregnancy may still be possible, but danazol can lead to androgenization of the fetus. At higher doses (600–800 mg per day), ovulation may be completely inhibited, but other undesirable side effects can occur, including weight gain, acne, and mood changes. Removal of the ovaries can be highly effective at eliminating symptoms of PMDD, but it will cause permanent sterilization and should be reserved only for very extreme cases (Cronje, Vashisht, & Studd, 2004).

CASE FOLLOW-UPS

Krista P.

Krista was given information about her diagnosis of PMDD and elected to begin her treatment with lifestyle modification. She continued to track her symptoms over the course of several cycles, during which she modified her diet, participated in regular exercise (including yoga), and used calcium and vitamin B supplementation. She also attended an 8-week course in relaxation skills therapy. She noted that her symptoms improved somewhat throughout the menstrual cycle, with reduced severity of her premenstrual exacerbations. Although she was not symptom-free, she felt that she was able to function much better. As she and her partner were planning to conceive, she elected to defer further treatment with medication, knowing that other treatment options, such as cognitive-behavioral therapy and/or medication, were available, if her symptoms became more problematic in the future.

Andrea F.

Andrea was given a diagnosis of major depressive disorder with severe premenstrual exacerbation. She indicated that despite walking to work daily (60 minutes) and a healthy diet with no alcohol intake, her symptoms limited her ability to function effectively. She was given education about relaxation techniques and suggestions for setting limits to decrease her daily stress levels (particularly at times when her symptoms were severe). She elected to begin therapy with a selective serotonin reuptake inhibitor to be taken throughout the month because of her daily symptoms. She continued to monitor her cycles and began to see significant improvement in the premenstrual exacerbation of symptoms quickly. She continues to work on maintaining effective coping strategies to manage her level of daily stress.

FUTURE DIRECTIONS

Over the past 20 to 30 years, significant advancements have been made in the field of premenstrual mood disturbance. However, there is still more work to be done, both to understand the etiology of premenstrual mood disturbance and to optimize treatment. One significant question that remains unanswered is why SSRI/SNRI medications work to alleviate symptoms of premenstrual dysphoria when used cyclically in the luteal phase of the menstrual cycle. This is particularly interesting, because these medications often require 2 weeks of treatment or longer to take effect for the treatment of other mood and anxiety disorders. Researchers have hypothesized that the immediate action on premenstrual symptoms might have to do with sensitivity to acute serotonin depletion among women with PMDD, such that symptoms resolve immediately when brain serotonin levels increase, whereas in other mood and anxiety disorders, symptom remission only occurs after time because of the need for modification of neuronal circuitry. This hypothesis is still awaiting further research. Because the etiology of premenstrual dysphoria has not been completely elucidated, our treatment options are limited. When lifestyle modification, antidepressant medication, and/or an oral contraceptive pill do not remit symptoms, women are faced with choices that have serious side effects (e.g., pharmacological and/or surgical menopause). Additional treatment options for this population are urgently required.

SUMMARY

Severe premenstrual mood disturbance (PMDD) affects a significant proportion of women, with a substantial impact on quality of life and productivity. Although biology plays a large role in predisposing women to severe PMS/PMDD, there is clear evidence for the interplay of biological and psychosocial factors in the onset and persistence of this disorder. With that complexity in mind, a multifaceted approach to treatment is required, with attention to biological, psychological, and social factors.

REFERENCES

Aganoff, J. A., & Boyle, G. J. (1994). Aerobic exercise, mood states and menstrual cycle symptoms. *Journal of Psychosomatic Research*, *38*(3), 183–192.

Agha-Hosseini, M., Kashani, L., Aleyaseen, A., Ghoreishi, A., Rahmanpour, H., Zarrinara, A. R., & Akhandzadeh, S. (2008). Crocus sativus L. (saffron) in the treatment of premenstrual syndrome: a double-blind, randomised and placebo-controlled trial. *British Journal of Obstetrics and Gynaecology*, *115*(4), 515–519.

American Psychiatric, Association. (2000). *Diagnostic and statistical manual of mental disorders* (4th ed., text rev.). Washington, DC: American Psychiatric Association.

Backstrom, T., Haage, D., Lofgren, M., Johansson, I. M., Stromberg, J., Nyberg, S., . . . Bengtsson,

S. K. (2011). Paradoxical effects of GABA-A modulators may explain sex steroid induced negative mood symptoms in some persons. *Neuroscience*, *15*(191), 46–54.

Bancroft, J., Cook, A., Davidson, D., Bennie, J., & Goodwin, G. (1991). Blunting of neuroendocrine responses to infusion of L-tryptophan in women with perimenstrual mood change. *Psychological Medicine*, *21*(2), 305–312.

Beck, L. E., Gevirtz, R., & Mortola, J. F. (1990). The predictive role of psychosocial stress on symptom severity in premenstrual syndrome. *Psychosomatic Medicine*, *52*(5), 536–543.

Bertone-Johnson, E. R., Hankinson, S. E., Willett, W. C., Johnson, S. R., & Manson, J. E. (2010). Adiposity and the development of premenstrual syndrome. *Journal of Women's Health*, *19*(11), 1955–1962.

Brown, J., O'Brien, P. M., Marjoribanks, J., & Wyatt, K. (2009). Selective serotonin reuptake inhibitors for premenstrual syndrome. *Cochrane Database Systems Review*, *2*, CD001396.

Bunevicius, R., Hinderliter, A. L., Light, K. C., Leserman, J., Pedersen, C. A., & Girdler, S. S. (2005). Histories of sexual abuse are associated with differential effects of clonidine on autonomic function in women with premenstrual dysphoric disorder. *Biological Psychology*, *69*(3), 281–296.

Chang, A. M., Holroyd, E., & Chau, J. P. (1995). Premenstrual syndrome in employed Chinese women in Hong Kong. *Health Care for Women International*, *16*(6), 551–561.

Chawla, A., Swindle, R., Long, S., Kennedy, S., & Sternfeld, B. (2002). Premenstrual dysphoric disorder: Is there an economic burden of illness? *Medical Care*, *40*(11), 1101–1112.

Chrisler, J. C., & Johnston-Robledo, I. (2002). Raging hormones? Feminist perspectives on premenstrual syndrome and postpartum depression. In M. Ballou & L. S. Brown (Eds.), *Rethinking mental health and disorder: Feminist perspectives* (pp. 174–197). New York, NY: Guilford Press.

Cohen, L. S., Soares, C. N., Otto, M. W., Sweeney, B. H., Liberman, R. F., & Harlow, B. L. (2002). Prevalence and predictors of premenstrual dysphoric disorder (PMDD) in older premenopausal women: The Harvard Study of Moods and Cycles. *Journal of Affective Disorders*, *70*(2), 125–132.

Critchlow, D. G., Bond, A. J., & Wingrove, J. (2001). Mood disorder history and personality assessment in premenstrual dysphoric disorder. *Journal of Clinical Psychiatry, 62*(9), 688–693.

Cronje, W. H., Vashisht, A., & Studd, J. W. (2004). Hysterectomy and bilateral oophorectomy for severe premenstrual syndrome. *Human Reproduction, 19*(9), 2152–2155.

Dan, A. J., & Monagle, L. (1994). Sociocultural influences on women's experiences of perimenstrual symptoms. In J. H. Gold & S. K. Severino (Eds.), *Premenstrual dysphorias: Myths and realities* (pp. 201–212). Washington, DC: American Psychiatric Press.

Delaney, J., Lupton, M. J., & Toth, E. (1976). *The curse: A cultural history of menstruation.* New York, NY: E. P. Dutton.

Endicott, J., Nee, J., & Harrison, W. (2006). Daily Record of Severity of Problems (DRSP): Reliability and validity. *Archives of Women's Mental Health, 9*(1), 41–49.

Epperson, C. N., Steiner, M., Hartlage, S. A., Eriksson, E., Schmidt, P. J., Jones, I., & Yonkers, K. A. (2012). Premenstrual dysphoric disorder: Evidence for a new category for the DSM-5. *American Journal of Psychiatry, 169*(5), 465–475.

Eriksson, O., Backstrom, T., Stridsberg, M., Hammarlund-Udenaes, M., & Naessen, T. (2006). Differential response to estrogen challenge test in women with and without premenstrual dysphoria. *Psychoneuroendocrinology, 31*(4), 415–427.

FitzGerald, M., Malone, K. M., Li, S., Harrison, W. M., McBride, P. A., Endicott, J., . . . Mann, J. J. (1997). Blunted serotonin response to fenfluramine challenge in premenstrual dysphoric disorder. *American Journal of Psychiatry, 154*(4), 556–558.

Fontana, A. M., & Palfai, T. G. (1994). Psychosocial factors in premenstrual dysphoria: Stressors, appraisal, and coping processes. *Journal of Psychosomatic Research, 38*(6), 557–567.

Frackiewicz, E. J., & Shiovitz, T. M. (2001). Evaluation and management of premenstrual syndrome and premenstrual dysphoric disorder. *Journal of the American Pharmacists Association, 41*(3), 437–447.

Freeman, E. W., Rickels, K., Sammel, M. D., Lin, H., & Sondheimer, S. J. (2009). Time to relapse after short- or long-term treatment of severe premenstrual syndrome with sertraline. *Archives of General Psychiatry, 66*(5), 537–544.

Freeman, E. W., Rickels, K., Schweizer, E., & Ting, T. (1995). Relationships between age and symptom severity among women seeking medical treatment for premenstrual symptoms. *Psychological Medicine, 25*(2), 309–315.

Freeman, E. W., Rickels, K., Yonkers, K. A., Kunz, N. R., McPherson, M., & Upton, G. V. (2001). Venlafaxine in the treatment of premenstrual dysphoric disorder. *Obstetrics and Gynecology, 98* (5, Pt. 1), 737–744.

Freeman, E. W., Sondheimer, S. J., & Rickels, K. (1997). Gonadotropin-releasing hormone agonist in the treatment of premenstrual symptoms with and without ongoing dysphoria: A controlled study. *Psychopharmacology Bulletin, 33*(2), 303–309.

Freeman, E. W., Stout, A. L., Endicott, J., & Spiers, P. (2002). Treatment of premenstrual syndrome with a carbohydrate-rich beverage. *International Journal of Gynaecology and Obstetrics, 77*(3), 253–254.

Friedman, R. C., Hurt, S. W., Clarkin, J., Corn, R., & Aronoff, M. S. (1982). Sexual histories and premenstrual affective syndrome in psychiatric inpatients. *American Journal of Psychiatry, 139*(11), 1484–1486.

Gehlert, S., Song, I. H., Chang, C. H., & Hartlage, S. A. (2009). The prevalence of premenstrual dysphoric disorder in a randomly selected group of urban and rural women. *Psychological Medicine, 39*(1), 129–136.

Gingnell, M., Comasco, E., Oreland, L., Fredrikson, M., & Sundstrom-Poromaa, I. (2010). Neuroticism-related personality traits are related to symptom severity in patients with premenstrual dysphoric disorder and to the serotonin transporter gene-linked polymorphism 5-HTTPLPR. *Archives of Women's Mental Health, 13*(5), 417–423.

Goodale, I. L., Domar, A. D., & Benson, H. (1990). Alleviation of premenstrual syndrome symptoms with the relaxation response. *Obstetrics and Gynecology, 75*(4), 649–655.

Halbreich, U., Alarcon, R. D., Calil, H., Douki, S., Gaszner, P., Jadresic, E., . . . Trivedi, J. K. (2007). Culturally-sensitive complaints of depressions and anxieties in women. *Journal of Affective Disorders, 102*(1–3), 159–176.

Halbreich, U., Bergeron, R., Yonkers, K. A., Freeman, E., Stout, A. L., & Cohen, L. (2002).

Efficacy of intermittent, luteal phase sertraline treatment of premenstrual dysphoric disorder. *Obstetrics and Gynecology, 100*(6), 1219–1229.

Halbreich, U., Borenstein, J., Pearlstein, T., & Kahn, L. S. (2003). The prevalence, impairment, impact, and burden of premenstrual dysphoric disorder (PMS/PMDD). *Psychoneuroendocrinology, 28* (Suppl 3), 1–23.

Hartlage, S. A., Brandenburg, D. L., & Kravitz, H. M. (2004). Premenstrual exacerbation of depressive disorders in a community-based sample in the United States. *Psychosomatic Medicine, 66*(5), 698–706.

Heim, C., Newport, D. J., Heit, S., Graham, Y. P., Wilcox, M., Bonsall, R., . . . Nemeroff, C. B. (2000). Pituitary-adrenal and autonomic responses to stress in women after sexual and physical abuse in childhood. *JAMA, 284*(5), 592–597.

Heinemann, L. A., Minh, T. D., Filonenko, A., & Uhl-Hochgraber, K. (2010). Explorative evaluation of the impact of severe premenstrual disorders on work absenteeism and productivity. *Women's Health Issues, 20*(1), 58–65.

Huo, L., Straub, R. E., Roca, C., Schmidt, P. J., Shi, K., Vakkalanka, R., . . . Rubinow, D. R. (2007). Risk for premenstrual dysphoric disorder is associated with genetic variation in ESR1, the estrogen receptor alpha gene. *Biological Psychiatry, 62*(8), 925–933.

Jang, H. S., Lee, M. S., Kim, M. J., & Chong, E. S. (2004). Effects of Qi-therapy on premenstrual syndrome. *International Journal of Neuroscience, 114* (8), 909–921.

Jarvis, C. I., Lynch, A. M., & Morin, A. K. (2008). Management strategies for premenstrual syndrome/premenstrual dysphoric disorder. *Annals of Pharmacotherapy, 42*(7), 967–978.

Jick, S. S., & Hernandez, R. K. (2011). Risk of non-fatal venous thromboembolism in women using oral contraceptives containing drospirenone compared with women using oral contraceptives containing levonorgestrel: Case-control study using United States claims data. *British Medical Journal, 342*, d2151.

Johnson, T. M. (1987). Premenstrual syndrome as a western culture-specific disorder. *Culture, Medicine, and Psychiatry, 11*(3), 337–356.

Jovanovic, H., Cerin, A., Karlsson, P., Lundberg, J., Halldin, C., & Nordstrom, A. L. (2006). A PET study of 5-HT1A receptors at different phases of

the menstrual cycle in women with premenstrual dysphoria. *Psychiatry Research, 148*(2–3), 185–193.

Kashanian, M., Mazinani, R., & Jalalmanesh, S. (2007). Pyridoxine (vitamin B6) therapy for premenstrual syndrome. *International Journal of Gynaecology and Obstetrics, 96*(1), 43–44.

Kendler, K. S., Karkowski, L. M., Corey, L. A., & Neale, M. C. (1998). Longitudinal population-based twin study of retrospectively reported premenstrual symptoms and lifetime major depression. *American Journal of Psychiatry, 155* (9), 1234–1240.

Kim, B. G., Cho, J. H., Choi, I. S., Lee, M. G., & Jang, I. S. (2011). Modulation of presynaptic GABA (A) receptors by endogenous neurosteroids. *British Journal of Pharmacology, 164*(6), 1698–1710.

Kim, D. R., Gyulai, L., Freeman, E. W., Morrison, M. F., Baldassano, C., & Dube, B. (2004). Premenstrual dysphoric disorder and psychiatric co-morbidity. *Archives of Women's Mental Health, 7*(1), 37–47.

Kornstein, S. G., Harvey, A. T., Rush, A. J., Wisniewski, S. R., Trivedi, M. H., Svikis, D. S., . . . & Harvey, R. (2005). Self-reported premenstrual exacerbation of depressive symptoms in patients seeking treatment for major depression. *Psychological Medicine, 35*(5), 683–692.

Krasnik, C., Montori, V. M., Guyatt, G. H., Heels-Ansdell, D., & Busse, J. W. (2005). The effect of bright light therapy on depression associated with premenstrual dysphoric disorder. *American Journal of Obstetrics and Gynecology, 193* (3, Pt. 1), 658–661.

Kuzelova, H., Ptacek, R., & Macek, M. (2010). The serotonin transporter gene (5-HTT) variant and psychiatric disorders: Review of current literature. *Neurology and Endocrinology Letters, 31*(1), 4–10.

Landen, M., Nissbrandt, H., Allgulander, C., Sorvik, K., Ysander, C., & Eriksson, E. (2007). Placebo-controlled trial comparing intermittent and continuous paroxetine in premenstrual dysphoric disorder. *Neuropsychopharmacology, 32*(1), 153–161.

Lane, T., & Francis, A. (2003). Premenstrual symptomatology, locus of control, anxiety and depression in women with normal menstrual cycles. *Archives of Women's Mental Health, 6*(2), 127–138.

Le Melledo, J. M., Van Driel, M., Coupland, N. J., Lott, P., & Jhangri, G. S. (2000). Response to flumazenil in women with premenstrual dysphoric disorder. *American Journal of Psychiatry*, *157*(5), 821–823.

Lopez, L. M., Kaptein, A. A., & Helmerhorst, F. M. (2009). Oral contraceptives containing drospirenone for premenstrual syndrome. *Cochrane Database Systems Review*, *2*, CD006586.

Lustyk, M. K., Gerrish, W. G., Shaver, S., & Keys, S. L. (2009). Cognitive-behavioral therapy for premenstrual syndrome and premenstrual dysphoric disorder: A systematic review. *Archives of Women's Mental Health*, *12*(2), 85–96.

Marvan, M. L., & Escobedo, C. (1999). Premenstrual symptomatology: Role of prior knowledge about premenstrual syndrome. *Psychosomatic Medicine*, *61*(2), 163–167.

Matsumoto, T., Ushiroyama, T., Kimura, T., Hayashi, T., & Moritani, T. (2007). Altered autonomic nervous system activity as a potential etiological factor of premenstrual syndrome and premenstrual dysphoric disorder. *Biopsychosocial Medicine*, *1*, 24.

Meaden, P. M., Hartlage, S. A., & Cook-Karr, J. (2005). Timing and severity of symptoms associated with the menstrual cycle in a community-based sample in the Midwestern United States. *Psychiatry Research*, *134*(1), 27–36.

Merikangas, K. R., Foeldenyi, M., & Angst, J. (1993). The Zurich Study. XIX. Patterns of menstrual disturbances in the community: Results of the Zurich Cohort Study. *European Archives of Psychiatry and Clinical Neuroscience*, *243*(1), 23–32.

Morse, C. A., Dennerstein, L., Farrell, E., & Varnavides, K. (1991). A comparison of hormone therapy, coping skills training, and relaxation for the relief of premenstrual syndrome. *Journal of Behavioral Medicine*, *14*(5), 469–489.

Morse, G. (1999). Positively reframing perceptions of the menstrual cycle among women with premenstrual syndrome. *Journal of Obstetric, Gynecological, and Neonatal Nursing*, *28*(2), 165–174.

Murray, C. J. L., & Lopez, A. D. (1996). The global burden of disease: A comprehensive assessment of mortality and disability from diseases, injuries, and risk factors in 1990 and projected to 2020. *Global Burden of Disease and Injury Series*. Boston, MA: The Harvard School of Public Health, on behalf of the World Health Organization and the World Bank.

Muse, K. N., Cetel, N. S., Futterman, L. A., & Yen, S. C. (1984). The premenstrual syndrome: Effects of "medical ovariectomy." *New England Journal of Medicine*, *311*(21), 1345–1349.

O'Brien, P. M., & Abukhalil, I. E. (1999). Randomized controlled trial of the management of premenstrual syndrome and premenstrual mastalgia using luteal phase-only danazol. *American Journal of Obstetrics and Gynecology*, *180* (1, Pt. 1), 18–23.

O'Brien, P. M., Backstrom, T., Brown, C., Dennerstein, L., Endicott, J., Epperson, C. N., . . . Yonkers, K. (2011). Towards a consensus on diagnostic criteria, measurement and trial design of the premenstrual disorders: The ISPMD Montreal consensus. *Archives of Women's Mental Health*, *14*(1), 13–21.

Omu, F. E., Al-Marzouk, R., Delles, H., Oranye, N. O., & Omu, A. E. (2011). Premenstrual dysphoric disorder: Prevalence and effects on nursing students' academic performance and clinical training in Kuwait. *Journal of Clinical Nursing*, *20* (19–20), 2915–2923.

Ornitz, A. W., & Brown, M. A. (1993). Family coping and premenstrual symptomatology. *Journal of Obstetric, Gynecological, and Neonatal Nursing*, *22*(1), 49–55.

Paddison, P. L., Gise, L. H., Lebovits, A., Strain, J. J., Cirasole, D. M., & Levine, J. P. (1990). Sexual abuse and premenstrual syndrome: Comparison between a lower and higher socioeconomic group. *Psychosomatics*, *31*(3), 265–272.

Parkin, L., Sharples, K., Hernandez, R. K., & Jick, S. S. (2011). Risk of venous thromboembolism in users of oral contraceptives containing drospirenone or levonorgestrel: Nested case-control study based on UK General Practice Research Database. *British Medical Journal*, *342*, d2139.

Payne, J. L., Palmer, J. T., & Joffe, H. (2009). A reproductive subtype of depression: conceptualizing models and moving toward etiology. *Harvard Review of Psychiatry*, *17*(2), 72–86.

Pearlstein, T., & Steiner, M. (2008). Premenstrual dysphoric disorder: Burden of illness and treatment update. *Journal of Psychiatry and Neuroscience*, *33*(4), 291–301.

Pearlstein, T. B., Halbreich, U., Batzar, E. D., Brown, C. S., Endicott, J., Frank, E., . . . Yonkers, K. A. (2000). Psychosocial functioning in women with premenstrual dysphoric disorder before and after treatment with sertraline or placebo. *Journal of Clinical Psychiatry*, *61*(2), 101–109.

Pilver, C. E., Desai, R., Kasl, S., & Levy, B. R. (2011). Lifetime discrimination associated with greater likelihood of premenstrual dysphoric disorder. *Journal of Women's Health*, *20*(6), 923–931.

Pilver, C. E., Kasl, S., Desai, R., & Levy, B. R. (2011). Exposure to American culture is associated with premenstrual dysphoric disorder among ethnic minority women. *Journal of Affective Disorders*, *130*(1–2), 334–341.

Pilver, C. E., Levy, B. R., Libby, D. J., & Desai, R. A. (2011). Posttraumatic stress disorder and trauma characteristics are correlates of premenstrual dysphoric disorder. *Archives of Women's Mental Health*, *14*(5), 383–393.

Protopopescu, X., Tuescher, O., Pan, H., Epstein, J., Root, J., Chang, L., . . . Silbersweig, D. (2008). Toward a functional neuroanatomy of premenstrual dysphoric disorder. *Journal of Affective Disorders*, *108*(1–2), 87–94.

Ramos, M. G., Hara, C., & Rocha, F. L. (2009). Duloxetine treatment for women with premenstrual dysphoric disorder: A single-blind trial. *International Journal of Neuropsychopharmacology*, *12*(8), 1081–1088.

Rasgon, N., Serra, M., Biggio, G., Pisu, M. G., Fairbanks, L., Tanavoli, S., & Rapkin, A. (2001). Neuroactive steroid-serotonergic interaction: Responses to an intravenous L-tryptophan challenge in women with premenstrual syndrome. *European Journal of Endocrinology*, *145*(1), 25–33.

Rivera-Tovar, A. D., & Frank, E. (1990). Late luteal phase dysphoric disorder in young women. *American Journal of Psychiatry*, *147*(12), 1634–1636.

Robinson, R. L., & Swindle, R. W. (2000). Premenstrual symptom severity: Impact on social functioning and treatment-seeking behaviors. *Journal of Women's Health and Gender-Based Medicine*, *9*(7), 757–768.

Rojnic Kuzman, M., & Hotujac, L. (2007). Premenstrual dysphoric disorder—A neglected diagnosis? *Preliminary study on a sample of Croatian students. Collegium Antropologicum*, *31*(1), 131–137.

Rubinow, D. R., Roy-Byrne, P., Hoban, M. C., Gold, P. W., & Post, R. M. (1984). Prospective assessment of menstrually related mood disorders. *American Journal of Psychiatry*, *141*(5), 684–686.

Sayegh, R., Schiff, I., Wurtman, J., Spiers, P., McDermott, J., & Wurtman, R. (1995). The effect of a carbohydrate-rich beverage on mood, appetite, and cognitive function in women with premenstrual syndrome. *Obstetrics and Gynecology*, *86* (4, Pt. 1), 520–528.

Schmidt, P. J., Nieman, L. K., Danaceau, M. A., Adams, L. F., & Rubinow, D. R. (1998). Differential behavioral effects of gonadal steroids in women with and in those without premenstrual syndrome. *New England Journal of Medicine*, *338*(4), 209–216.

Seideman, R. Y. (1990). Effects of a premenstrual syndrome education program on premenstrual symptomatology. *Health Care for Women International*, *11*(4), 491–501.

Shechter, A., & Boivin, D. B. (2010). Sleep, hormones, and circadian rhythms throughout the menstrual cycle in healthy women and women with premenstrual dysphoric disorder. *International Journal of Endocrinology*, *2010*, 259345.

Skrzypulec-Plinta, V., Drosdzol, A., Nowosielski, K., & Plinta, R. (2010). The complexity of premenstrual dysphoric disorder—Risk factors in the population of Polish women. *Reproductive and Biological Endocrinology*, *8*, 141.

Smith, M. J., Schmidt, P. J., & Rubinow, D. R. (2003). Operationalizing DSM-IV criteria for PMDD: Selecting symptomatic and asymptomatic cycles for research. *Journal of Psychiatric Research*, *37*(1), 75–83.

Steiner, M., Macdougall, M., & Brown, E. (2003). The Premenstrual Symptoms Screening Tool (PSST) for clinicians. *Archives of Women's Mental Health*, *6*(3), 203–209.

Steiner, M., Peer, M., & Soares, C. N. (2006). Comorbidity and premenstrual syndrome. *Gynecology Forum*, *11*, 13–16.

Sundstrom, I., Andersson, A., Nyberg, S., Ashbrook, D., Purdy, R. H., & Backstrom, T. (1998). Patients with premenstrual syndrome have a different sensitivity to a neuroactive steroid during the menstrual cycle compared to control subjects. *Neuroendocrinology*, *67*(2), 126–138.

Sundstrom, I., Ashbrook, D., & Backstrom, T. (1997). Reduced benzodiazepine sensitivity in patients with premenstrual syndrome: A pilot study. *Psychoneuroendocrinology*, *22*(1), 25–38.

Sundstrom, I., & Backstrom, T. (1998). Citalopram increases pregnanolone sensitivity in patients with premenstrual syndrome: An open trial. *Psychoneuroendocrinology*, *23*(1), 73–88.

Sundstrom, I., Nyberg, S., & Backstrom, T. (1997). Patients with premenstrual syndrome have reduced sensitivity to midazolam compared to control subjects. *Neuropsychopharmacology*, *17*(6), 370–381.

Sveindottir, H., & Backstrom, T. (2000). Prevalence of menstrual cycle symptom cyclicity and premenstrual dysphoric disorder in a random sample of women using and not using oral contraceptives. *Acta Obstetricia et Gynecologica Scandinavica*, *79*(5), 405–413.

Taylor, D. (1999). Effectiveness of professional–peer group treatment: Symptom management for women with PMS. *Research in Nursing Health*, *22*(6), 496–511.

Thys-Jacobs, S., Starkey, P., Bernstein, D., & Tian, J. (1998). Calcium carbonate and the premenstrual syndrome: Effects on premenstrual and menstrual symptoms. Premenstrual Syndrome Study Group. *American Journal of Obstetrics and Gynecology*, *179*(2), 444–452.

Treloar, S. A., Heath, A. C., & Martin, N. G. (2002). Genetic and environmental influences on premenstrual symptoms in an Australian twin sample. *Psychological Medicine*, *32*(1), 25–38.

Tschudin, S., Bertea, P. C., & Zemp, E. (2010). Prevalence and predictors of premenstrual syndrome and premenstrual dysphoric disorder in a population-based sample. *Archives of Women's Mental Health*, *13*(6), 485–494.

Vigod, S. N., Frey, B. N., Soares, C. N., & Steiner, M. (2010). Approach to premenstrual dysphoria for the mental health practitioner. *Psychiatric Clinics of North America*, *33*(2), 257–272.

Warner, P., & Bancroft, J. (1990). Factors related to self-reporting of the pre-menstrual syndrome. *British Journal of Psychiatry*, *157*, 249–260.

Whelan, A. M., Jurgens, T. M., & Naylor, H. (2009). Herbs, vitamins and minerals in the treatment of premenstrual syndrome: A systematic review. *Canadian Journal of Clinical Pharmacology*, *16*(3), e407–e429.

Wyatt, K. M., Dimmock, P. W., Jones, P. W., & Shaughn O'Brien, P. M. (1999). Efficacy of vitamin B-6 in the treatment of premenstrual syndrome: Systematic review. *British Medical Journal*, *318*(7195), 1375–1381.

Yang, M., Wallenstein, G., Hagan, M., Guo, A., Chang, J., & Kornstein, S. (2008). Burden of premenstrual dysphoric disorder on health-related quality of life. *Journal of Women's Health*, *17*(1), 113–121.

CHAPTER

14

The Stress of Infertility

Lauren B. Prince and Alice D. Domar

TOPIC INTRODUCTION AND SIGNIFICANCE

Infertility is estimated to affect 10% to 15% of couples in the United States. It is defined by the Centers for Disease Control and Prevention (CDC) as the failure to become pregnant after 1 year or more of unprotected intercourse, or 6 months if over 35 years old (CDC, 2011a). The definition of infertility also includes women who are able to get pregnant but unable to stay pregnant or carry the pregnancy to full term. The American Society for Reproductive Medicine (ASRM) regards infertility as a disease, not simply a quality-of-life issue. Furthermore, a U.S. Supreme Court opinion recently determined that conditions that interfere with reproduction should be regarded as disabilities, as defined under the Americans with Disabilities Act, because reproduction is a major life activity, the disturbance of which can be severely debilitating.

Primary infertility is the inability to conceive and carry to term a first biological child. Secondary infertility is more common than primary and refers to a woman or couple who already have at least one biological child but are unable to have another. There are several contributing factors to secondary infertility, including the fact that both members of the couple are older than when they conceived their first child.

Infertility affects people across the globe and, contrary to public opinion, also occurs in developing countries. A recent study of the prevalence of infertility worldwide, across 25 populations and sampling 172,412 women, found the overall median prevalence of infertility to be 9%. In the United States, it is estimated that about 6.1 million women ages 15 to 44 have difficulty getting or staying pregnant. According to the worldwide investigation, it is estimated that 72.4 million women across the globe are currently infertile (Boivin, Bunting, Collins, & Nygren, 2007). It is clear that infertility is a common condition.

Infertility can be the result of male factors, female factors, a combination of the two, or unexplainable factors. Organic causes are those that are biologically evident upon examination, including abnormalities of sperm production, ovulation, or structural issues. The most common cause of female infertility is polycystic ovarian syndrome (PCOS), a hormone imbalance that disrupts normal ovulation. Other common causes include primary ovarian insufficiency (when a woman's ovaries stop functioning normally before age 40), pelvic inflammatory disease (which scars the fallopian tubes), and endometriosis (the growth of uterine tissue outside of the uterus, which can lead to severe pain and scarring of the female reproductive organs). Environmental causes, such as exposure to certain chemicals and toxins, have been shown to adversely impact reproductive function. Infertility can also be the result of cancer or HIV treatments, such as chemotherapy, that damage eggs and sperm. In many cases, unexplained causes can be a very difficult reality for many couples and physicians to accept.

Male-factor infertility is caused by problems with the sperm. In order for sperm to inseminate an egg successfully, they have to be produced in large numbers, be normally shaped, and be able to move quickly. The most common cause of male-factor infertility is varicocele, when the veins in the testicles are enlarged, leading to pooling of blood, which causes heating of the testicles and affects the viability of sperm. Blockages in the male reproductive tract are also possible, whereby normal sperm are produced but are unable to make it into the ejaculate.

Recently, lifestyle factors have been examined as potential causes of infertility. It has been shown that for both men and women, being underweight or obese, smoking, and using alcohol can disrupt reproductive function, making it more difficult to achieve a pregnancy. More controversial is the idea that stress or other psychological factors, such as depression or anxiety, cause infertility. Although it is indubitable that stress and infertility coexist, the relationship between them is unclear. Some believe that psychological disorders disrupt brain functioning, which disrupts the production of reproductive hormones and leads to infertility. However, as pointed out by Brkovich and Fisher (1998), the assumption of a link between psychological distress and infertility is controversial, because it has the potential to blame women for their infertility. As of now, it is unclear whether stress can cause infertility, but the issue has received much attention and will be covered in depth later in this chapter.

Many treatment choices are available for infertility patients, including medical, surgical, or psychological options. Common medical treatments include drug therapy, surgery, artificial insemination, and assisted reproductive technology (ART). Psychological treatments focus on coping with infertility and reducing the stress associated with it. This can include individual or couples therapy, group therapy, or mind–body techniques such as yoga or acupuncture. The treatment course will differ for every couple and is determined by the cause of infertility, age of the partners, health of the partners, financial issues, and their preferences.

Many medications available for the treatment of infertility in women induce ovulation by acting on the brain centers responsible for controlling reproductive hormones. Common fertility drugs are follicle-stimulating hormone (FSH), which stimulates ovulation, and gonadotropin-releasing hormone (GnRH), which acts on the pituitary gland to regulate ovulation.

Some surgeries are able to correct physical problems with male or female reproductive organs and can increase the likelihood of conception. In addition to medication and surgery, another treatment for infertility is intrauterine insemination (IUI), also known as artificial insemination. In this procedure, specially prepared sperm are delivered via catheter directly into the uterus.

A more complex class of treatments for infertility is ART. The most common and effective method of ART is in vitro fertilization (IVF), whereby a woman is treated with drugs to stimulate her ovaries' production of eggs, the eggs are removed and fertilized with sperm outside of the body, and viable embryos are transferred into the woman's uterus several days later.

Whether infertility can be treated successfully, there are concomitant psychological effects. The process of identifying, coping with, and treating infertility is highly stressful and emotionally draining, making anxiety and depression common. One study found that 25% of women and 9% of men referred to an infertility clinic had clinically elevated scores on a measure of anxiety (Anderson, Sharpe, Rattray, & Irvine, 2003). Another study found that 40% of women entering an assisted reproduction clinic had a diagnosable psychiatric disorder; 23.3% of them had generalized anxiety disorder, 17% had major depressive disorder, and 9.8% had dysthymic disorder (Chen, Shang, Tsai, & Juang, 2004). In another study, 50% of women reported that infertility was the most stressful experience of their life (Freeman, Boxer, Rickels, Tureck, & Mastroianni, 1985). In addition to anxiety and depression, women dealing with infertility can suffer with respect to self-esteem, memory, and concentration abilities (Oddens, de Tonkelaar, & Nieuwenhuyse, 1999).

Infertility can affect every area of an individual or couple's life, including their relationship, sex life, relationships with family and friends, jobs/career, financial stability, and faith. Infertility treatment is a psychological trigger because, irrespective of treatment type, the success rate per cycle is less than 50% and can be far lower depending on the patients' age, prognosis, and the kind of treatment. Thus, it is not surprising that infertility poses such a unique psychological challenge. This chapter discusses the impact of multiple factors on fertility, including acupuncture, nutrition, body mass index (BMI), exercise, alcohol, and nicotine, and examines the effects of infertility on psychological well-being. It covers the impact of mind-body interventions, incorporating stress reduction, relaxation, and social support on fertility. Furthermore, we address whether these issues function the same way for various cultural and ethnic groups and people of differing income levels and social backgrounds. We close by covering the future directions in the study of the psychological impact of infertility and identifying the gaps that remain in our understanding of the nature of the condition.

CRITICAL REVIEW

Lifestyle Factors That Impact Infertility and Its Treatment

Exercise, BMI, and Nutrition Modern culture is inundated with advice about diet and exercise, with a focus on decreasing the prevalence of obesity, an epidemic currently plaguing Western society. Obesity is defined as a BMI greater than 30 kg/m^2. More than one-third of adults and 17% of children in the United States are obese (CDC, 2011b). Obesity is associated with numerous health problems, and the reproductive system is not exempt from the adverse impact of being morbidly overweight. Several studies have shown that obesity is associated with an increased risk of infertility. One study found that 25% of ovulatory infertility in the United States might be attributable to being overweight (Rich-Edwards et al., 2002). Severe obesity (i.e., a BMI greater than 35) is associated with significant reductions in clinical pregnancy rates and successful implantation in ART cycles. It is estimated that 40% of women with PCOS are obese, and it has been shown that even modest weight loss can lead to increased reproductive functioning (Balen, 2006). Obese women with PCOS are less likely to respond to treatment with metformin, which serves the dual function of treating PCOS and increasing fertility (Tang et al., 2006). For obese women with PCOS, therefore, weight loss may be a successful way to improve ovulatory functioning and the chance of conception. This issue is not confined to females; obesity in men compromises their reproductive capacity as well (Pauli et al., 2008).

Being underweight also hinders successful pregnancy. The relationship between weight and reproductive capacity can be viewed as an inverse U-shaped curve, whereby individuals with either a very low or a very high BMI have the most trouble achieving pregnancy. One study found that those at the highest risk for ovulatory infertility have a BMI below 20.0 or above 24.0 kg/m^2 and that 12% of ovulatory infertility in the United States can be attributed to being underweight (Rich-Edwards et al., 2002). One study found that 16.7% of women presenting at infertility clinics had an eating disorder (Stewart, Robinson, Goldbloom, & Wright, 1990). These women are at heightened risk for infertility, as severely disordered eating can lead to amenorrhea, failure to ovulate, and reduced sex drive (Stewart, 1992). Therefore, it is important to collect nutritional information and assess all women suffering from infertility for eating disorders, as these factors may be a major cause contributing to their inability to conceive.

Nutrition and exercise share a complex relationship with fertility. Unhealthy foods and chemicals in one's dietary supply have been shown to have a negative effect on reproductive function. One study found that a diet rich in trans-fatty acids increased the odds of fetal loss, with each one-unit increase in percent of calories from trans-fatty acids associated with a 10% increase in the odds of fetal loss (Morrison, Glueck, & Wang, 2008). Studies have also shown an adverse impact of high caffeine consumption on IVF outcomes, with caffeine intake displaying a negative relationship to number of live births and gestational age in those undergoing IVF treatment (Klonoff-Cohen, Lam-Kruglick, & Gonzalez, 2002). However, the failure to eat *enough* also has undesirable consequences with respect to fertility. One study showed that when overweight and obese patients undergoing IVF treatment were exposed to a low-calorie diet for a short period before and during treatment, IVF outcomes were lower than in women who did not diet before their cycle (Tsagareli, Noakes, & Norman, 2006).

Suboptimal nutrition, be it the result of overeating, a diet high in chemicals and preservatives, or insufficient caloric intake, has a detrimental effect on reproductive functioning. Hormones that aid in reproduction, such as leptin, are released according to body composition and dietary habits. Conditions characterized by inconsistent and unhealthy caloric intake and suboptimal body composition are associated with abnormal leptin levels, and thus abnormal reproductive function. These conditions include eating disorders such as anorexia nervosa, exercise-induced amenorrhea, and PCOS, which includes obesity among its symptoms (Pinelli & Tagliabue, 2007).

Disorders or diet patterns that are characterized by a tipped energy balance, either caloric intake greater than caloric expenditure or vice versa, seem to consistently have detrimental effects on reproductive health. Indeed, high levels of exercise and low nutritional intake have been shown to suppress reproductive function. One study measured levels of reproductive hormones and quality of reproductive function in a sample of athletes who partook in extensive recreational running as compared to non-athlete controls. Although 11 of the 13 controls had normal levels of progesterone, estrogen, and normal luteal phase length, only 10 of the 17 athletes satisfied these criteria (Broocks et al., 1990).

A second study calculated the odds of several unfavorable IVF outcomes for women who participated in varying levels of exercise. Participants were given a survey prior to embarking on the IVF process regarding several of their behaviors, including physical exercise patterns. The outcomes they investigated were successful live birth, cycle cancellation, implantation failure, pregnancy loss, and failed fertilization. Interestingly, they found that women who reported participating in four or more hours per week of exercise for one to nine years before their IVF attempt were 40% less likely to have a live birth and twice as likely to have implantation failure or pregnancy loss than women who did not report exercise (Morris et al., 2006). These results remained despite control for BMI, smoking, age, and other possible confounding variables.

Furthermore, the researchers found cardiovascular exercise to be associated with the poorest IVF outcomes, with this exercise category being 30% less likely than nonexercisers to have a successful pregnancy. This effect was most severe for those cardiovascular exercisers in the duration group of 4 or more hours per week for 1 to 9 years, as they had a 50% lower likelihood of successful pregnancy than nonexercisers. The authors provide the explanation for these surprising findings that women who exercise in this manner "exercise long enough to alter their endogenous hormonal environment and affect the outcome of their first cycle of IVF" but not long enough to "have achieved an equilibrium or create a different hormonal environment" that promotes conception (Morris et al., 2006, p. 944).

These provocative initial findings regarding exercise and IVF outcome need to be replicated before providing the basis for clinical recommendations. Future studies investigating the same phenomena could refine the design of this study by stratifying the exercise categories more sensitively (i.e., by using metabolic equivalents per week, which would account for the intensity and duration of reported exercise) and controlling for diet and stress. This study was strong, however, in its utilization of a large sample size.

Despite findings such as these, it should be mentioned that, as is the case with most aspects of health, exercise could also confer salutary effects on the reproductive system. One study found that "women who reported frequent, high-intensity activity during the 2 years prior to the reference date had a 76% reduced endometrioma risk compared with women who engaged in no physical activity" (Dhillon & Holt, 2003, p. 156). So while physical exercise can suppress reproductive function if it is highly strenuous and not offset by increased nutritional intake, it can be associated with a lower risk of endometriosis.

The chemical relationship between underweight and fertility is simple. Mircea, Lujan, and Pierson (2007) claim that the primary metabolic cue that modulates reproduction is the availability of oxidizable fuel. The body and brain detect our level of available oxidizable fuel, the energy we get from calories and fat, and when the levels become low, the brain inhibits the release of gonadotropin-releasing hormone and luteinizing hormone, which in turn suppresses reproductive capacity.

The mechanisms through which obesity adversely affects fertility are not as intuitive as the mechanisms relating underweight and fertility. If we adopt the viewpoint that fertility is suppressed when the body detects that environmental conditions are suboptimal, it would be expected that having lots of extra fat available and leading a sedentary lifestyle would encourage conception. However, hormonal changes associated with obesity can lead to suppressed fertility. Hyperinsulinemia, or excess insulin existing in the blood, is a condition that commonly accompanies obesity. Hyperinsulinemia affects the production of androgens, like estrogen and testosterone, in the ovaries. Hyperandrogenism (excess androgens) results, which causes the maturation of anovulatory follicles, premature luteinization, and follicular arrest. Insulin is just one culprit linking obesity and infertility; leptin is another. Elevated leptin levels disrupt the normal release of reproductive hormones and can lead to infertility.

Through several complex mechanisms involving interactions between hormones and ovarian functions, being underweight or overweight may adversely impact reproductive capacity. Women of a healthy BMI with a relatively stable energy balance are in the best condition to conceive. Excessive exercise coupled with a lack of compensation by increased caloric intake puts individuals in a state of negative energy balance and inhibits normal reproductive function, whereas overweight and obesity trigger the overproduction of hormones, which in turn disrupts fertility. As is the case with most aspects of health, a healthy weight and a nutritious diet are critical for achieving optimal reproductive function.

Acupuncture and Complementary Medicine Complementary and alternative medicine approaches (CAM) are widely available to infertility patients. Smith et al. (2010) observed the use of CAM among individuals facing infertility and how this use differed by age, education, income, religion, and infertility diagnosis. The participants in the study were couples recruited from eight reproductive endocrinology clinics, in which the woman presented for infertility treatment but had not yet begun IVF attempts.

The researchers found that the highest use of CAM was among women age 35 to 39, who were college graduates, had a high household income, had a female-factor infertility diagnosis, and among couples pursuing IVF (Smith et al., 2010). The most common CAM treatment reported was acupuncture, with 22.4% of subjects reporting use. Seventeen percent of subjects utilized herbal therapy, 4.7% utilized bodywork (i.e., yoga), and 1.2% utilized meditation (Smith et al., 2010).

The most frequently used CAM is acupuncture, an ancient Chinese practice of inserting needles into specific acupoints on the body that are related to various psychological and biological functions. The idea behind the treatment is that the operation of our organs and bodily systems are governed by energy channels through which Qi flows. Qi can be understood as the body's source of "vital force and energy" (Westergaard et al., 2006, p. 1342). By targeting points on the body, acupuncture is intended to restore Qi, and thus improve ailing physical and psychological systems.

The effectiveness of acupuncture as a treatment for infertility is debatable. The assumption is that acupoints can be targeted to increase blood flow to the uterus and ovaries, regulate the functioning of the reproductive system, and increase the likelihood of pregnancy. According to Manheimer et al. (2007), as outlined in their meta-analysis of acupuncture-infertility research, three potential mechanisms mediate the effects of acupuncture on the reproductive system:

> Firstly, acupuncture may mediate the release of neurotransmitters, which may in turn stimulate secretion of gonadotrophin releasing hormone, thereby influencing the menstrual cycle, ovulation, and fertility. Secondly, acupuncture may stimulate blood flow to the uterus by inhibiting uterine central sympathetic nerve activity. Thirdly, acupuncture may stimulate the production of endogenous opioids, which may inhibit the central nervous system outflow and the biological stress response. (Manheimer et al., 2007, p. 2)

Chen (1997) showed that electroacupuncture could regulate the functioning of the hypothalamic-pituitary-ovarian axis, the connection between our brain and reproductive system and the pathway through which hormone release and thus reproductive functioning is mediated. They posited that acupuncture could normalize the release of several hormones, including gonadotropin-releasing hormone, luteinizing hormone, and estrogen, thereby curing anovulation and restoring fertility (Chen, 1997).

These proposed mechanisms are controversial, and the scientific community is divided on the issue of whether acupuncture can have a meaningful effect on reproductive health and wellness. Most studies of the acupuncture–infertility link specifically have looked at the effects of acupuncture on women undergoing assisted reproductive treatments such as IVF or intra-cytoplasmic sperm injection (ICSI). The results have been inconsistent, with some studies finding a highly significant impact of acupuncture and an equal amount of others finding no such results.

Paulus, Zhang, Strehler, El-Danasouri, and Sterzik (2001) recruited 160 women who were undergoing ART and randomly divided them into two groups. On the day of embryo transfer (ET), acupuncture was performed on half of the women 25 minutes before and after transfer. The remaining women simply underwent ET and lay quietly for the equivalent amount of time. They found that clinical pregnancy was achieved in 42.5% of the patients in the acupuncture group and only 26.2% of control patients. They thus concluded that acupuncture was an effective treatment for increasing successful outcomes in ART (Paulus et al., 2001). Other studies have found similar results. Omodei et al. (2010) found that the pregnancy rate per transfer was 50% in an acupuncture group compared with 34.6% in a control group, and concluded that acupuncture performed on the day of ET appears to increase pregnancy rates in women undergoing IVF (Omodei et al., 2010).

Despite these promising findings, the efficacy of acupuncture is unknown because of several studies that have found the opposite result. In one such study, Wang, Check, Liss, and Chloe (2007) matched 64 women on age, BMI, and other factors, and assigned one of the pair to receive acupuncture and the other to receive no supportive treatment on the day of IVF ET. They found ultrasound evidence of pregnancy in 13 of the 32 women receiving acupuncture and 17 of the 32 women receiving no acupuncture. Furthermore, there were more ongoing and delivered pregnancies in the control group compared to the treatment group (Wang et al., 2007). Utilizing a larger sample size, Madaschi, Braga, de Figueira, Iaconelli, and Borges (2010) randomly assigned women undergoing ICSI cycles for the first time to a control group or an experimental group that received acupuncture. The researchers found no difference between the two groups with regards to implantation rate, pregnancy, spontaneous abortion, or live birth rate (Madaschi et al., 2010).

A major problem with many of the currently available studies of acupuncture in relation to ART outcomes lies in their flawed designs. These studies fail to control for the placebo effect, whereby the simple act of undergoing a treatment that you think will be effective can make it effective. In order to control for results confounded by this, it is important to have groups blinded to whether or not they are receiving treatment. In acupuncture, this can be done by using "sham needles" or by applying acupuncture to points other than those specified for the condition to be treated. As such, in fertility studies, half of the group would undergo acupuncture targeting the relevant points while the other half would undergo acupuncture targeting points for, perhaps, headaches or nausea, or would undergo acupuncture with the use of sham needles. If a consistent difference in ART outcomes emerged between the two groups, the efficacy of acupuncture for the treatment of infertility would be supported.

However, several studies that have used these controls have found that significant differences fail to persist with the implementation of these necessary controls. Moy et al. (2010) randomly assigned women to a true-acupuncture group (treatment) or a sham-acupuncture group (control). Both groups underwent their assigned treatment 25 minutes before and 3 days after ET, and completed an ET pain questionnaire. Doctors

and patients were both blinded, with the acupuncturist the only one aware of group membership. Although they found no differences in clinical pregnancy rates between the treatment and control groups, they did find that women in the treatment group described their ET as more fearful, tiring, and painful (Moy et al., 2010).

Given these reports, we conclude that while acupuncture has been shown to be an effective treatment for several ailments, whether this is the case for infertility is still unclear. Regardless, acupuncture is a relatively inexpensive treatment with few side effects, and several of the studies on IVF patients have shown lower stress and higher optimism levels in the acupuncture patients, with a preference for including acupuncture in future cycles.

Alcohol The CDC estimates that 6 in 10 women of childbearing age consume alcohol, and 18.3% of American women over the age of 18 smoke cigarettes (CDC, 2010; CDC, 2011c). The detrimental health impacts of excessive drinking and smoking have been repeatedly documented over the past 20 years, particularly for women.

It is estimated that about 7% of women drink while pregnant. Doing so has been shown to increase the risk of miscarriage, especially if more than seven drinks per week are consumed and in the first trimester of pregnancy (Kesmodel, Wisborg, Olsen, Henriksen, & Secher, 2002). The CDC asserts that no amount of alcohol consumption is risk-free during pregnancy, and therefore should be avoided completely.

Studies have shown that excessive female alcohol consumption during childbearing years can lead to subfertility. A 2002 study examined the impact of alcohol consumption during the year prior to an ART attempt on pregnancy outcomes. Using a sample that was representative of couples enrolling for IVF programs with regards to age, race, and education level, and controlling for caffeine, nicotine, and prescription and illicit drug use, they found that female alcohol consumption was related to a 13% decrease in the amount of eggs aspirated, with a 2% to 23% decrease for each additional drink reported per day. Consumption was also associated with an increase in the risk of not achieving pregnancy by 2.86 times and an increased risk of miscarriage by 2.21 times compared with women consuming no alcohol (Klonoff-Cohen, Bleha, & Lam-Kruglick, 2002).

Grodstein, Goldman, and Cramer (1994) compared alcohol use in a large representative sample of women presenting with infertility to a sample of women who recently gave birth. They separated women based on their alcohol consumption into three groups: heavy drinkers (those consuming more than 100 grams of alcohol per week, or roughly 10 or more drinks), moderate drinkers (those consuming between 0 and 100 grams of alcohol per week), and nondrinkers (those reporting no alcohol consumption). After adjusting for possible confounders including education status, age, and smoking, they found significantly increased odds of infertility for women reporting heavy and moderate alcohol consumption; women with ovulatory factor infertility were 30% more likely to be moderate drinkers and 60% more likely to be heavy drinkers compared with fertile women. The dose-response relationship of increasing ovulatory infertility risk with increasing alcohol intake was also significant. Women who were moderate or heavy drinkers were also 50% more likely than nondrinkers to have been diagnosed with

endometriosis, an additional infertility risk factor (Grodstein et al., 1994).

Because a causal relationship linking alcohol use to higher infertility and endometrioma risk cannot be confirmed by relative risk data, we cannot be certain whether alcohol use causes reproductive problems or increased alcohol consumption is used as a self-medication by women suffering from the pain and stress associated with these conditions. It is possible that a third variable is causing both heavy alcohol consumption and reproductive disorder, and that the two simply co-occur frequently but are not the result of one another. For example, women suffering from anxiety or stress disorders may be at a high risk for alcohol abuse as well as compromised fertility. Future studies into the alcohol–fertility link may elucidate some of these remaining issues.

One factor implicated in the alcohol–fertility relationship is age. A 2003 study followed more than 7,000 Danish women for a mean of 5 years, collecting data on health behaviors including alcohol consumption and fertility problems. They found that alcohol consumption at baseline was unrelated to a later infertility diagnosis for younger women, but it was a significant predictor of fertility problems for women over age 30 (Tolstrupp et al., 2003). The authors conclude that younger women may be protected from some of the harmful impacts of alcohol on reproductive function, but older women trying to conceive should be especially cautious regarding alcohol use.

Studies have shown that alcohol intake in men can also lead to subfertility. Muthusami & Chinnaswamy (2005) found that heavy alcohol use adversely affects the viability of sperm. They included a sample of alcoholic men and a sample of nonalcoholic men and assessed reproductive hormones and general sexual functioning. They found that 71% of alcoholics and 7% of controls had erectile dysfunction. Alcoholics also had lower testosterone levels, lower sperm count, a decreased percentage of rapidly motile sperm, and a lower percentage of morphologically normal sperm as compared with controls. Other researchers have looked at drinking in nonalcoholic men and found that, similar to women, any alcohol intake can adversely affect fertility (Rossi, Hornstein, Cramer, & Missmer, 2009; Klonoff-Cohen et al., 2002).

Research has found that, in women, alcohol use is associated with decreased ovarian weight, decreased estrogen and progesterone secretion, and higher frequencies of menstrual disturbance and anovulation (Grodstein et al., 1994; Van Thiel, Gavaler, Lester, & Sherins, 1978). In men, it is postulated that alcohol use leads to male-factor infertility by inhibiting sperm and testosterone production through a direct toxic effect on the testes (Muthusami & Chinnaswamy, 2005). Alcohol also increases levels of "feminine" sex hormones in the male through its effects on the brain centers responsible for reproductive functioning, thus leading to male-factor subfertility and sterility. A review of the literature suggests that high levels of alcohol consumption should be avoided in men and women trying to conceive, as it frequently leads to reproductive disturbance. Pregnant women should unequivocally avoid alcohol consumption to ensure the health of fetus and mother.

Nicotine Cigarette smoking during pregnancy, while attempting to conceive, or while undergoing ART treatment is another lifestyle behavior that decreases chances of pregnancy and can harm both mother and fetus. Several studies have noted an association between smoking and infertility. A meta-analysis by Augood, Duckitt, and Templeton (1998) found that women smokers were 60% more likely than nonsmokers to be diagnosed as infertile, and women smokers undergoing IVF had a 35% decrease in odds of pregnancy per IVF cycle compared with nonsmokers (Augood et al., 1998). A second meta-analysis found that women smokers were almost 50% less likely than nonsmokers to conceive after an IVF cycle. These women also had an increased risk of spontaneous abortion (Hughes & Brennan 1996).

A unique study in Germany measured smoking not by self-report, which is common in most studies, but by blood plasma levels of cotinine, the principle metabolite of nicotine. Cotinine concentration in follicular fluid has been shown to be directly related to the amount of cigarette smoking, and is thus a more reliable measure of smoking behavior than self-report, which can be subject to lying or bias. Based on cotinine levels, the 197 female participants with tubal infertility in this study were separated into three categories: nonsmokers, passive smokers (those with cotinine levels high enough to suggest frequent exposure to cigarettes via second-hand smoke), or active smokers. Although no differences among groups in fertilization and pregnancy rates were observed, estrogen serum levels were much lower in active smokers than in passive or nonsmokers. Overall, there was a negative correlation between cotinine and estrogen levels, lending insight into the possible mechanism through which smoking could lead to infertility. The fact that passive smokers did not have significantly different estrogen levels than nonsmokers supports the idea that moderate or light smoking could have more minimal effects on reproductive hormones and thus fertility (Sterzik et al., 1996). However, it is important to note that all of the subjects in this study suffered from tubal factor infertility only and all had apparently normal ovulatory cycles. Based on these results alone, we cannot conclude that other types of infertility caused by non-tubal factors share the same relationship to smoking.

Other studies have found that the effects of cigarette smoking on reproductive health can be minimized when smoking is infrequent or reversed when smoking is ceased. Researchers (Jensen et al., 1998) followed 423 Danish couples who were trying to conceive and stopped using contraception for six menstrual cycles or until pregnancy was achieved. All participants reported on cigarette smoking, alcohol and caffeine consumption, reproductive disorders, and if their mother smoked while pregnant with them. The sample was divided into three groups: exposure in utero, current exposure, or both, with those experiencing neither serving as the reference group. A total of 51.2% of smokers and 63% of nonsmokers conceived. After adjustment for BMI, alcohol and caffeine use, reproductive diseases, duration of menstrual cycle and seminal quality, the authors determined that smokers were one-third less likely than nonsmokers to achieve pregnancy. They also found that women who quit smoking within a year prior to the pregnancy attempt had odds of pregnancy similar to that of nonsmokers, lending support to the idea that the effects of smoking on fertility are reversible. Furthermore, they found that maternal smoking impaired male fertility, but current smoking was not associated with fertility in males (Jensen et al., 1998).

Many studies have found inconsistent results concerning the effects of male smoking on fertility (Hughes & Brennan, 1996; Jensen et al., 1998). However, female smoking has been consistently displayed to be detrimental to reproductive capacity. Zavos (1989) summarized the mechanisms through which female smoking compromises fertility:

> In general, studies in women and animals confirm the possible alteration of physiological characteristics of the tubes in smokers, resulting in a disturbance of intratubal transport of the embryo, a premature or delayed arrival of the blastocyst in the uterus, and alterations of the immune system that could explain the epidemiologic association of smoking and lowered fertility. (Zavos, 1989, p. 43)

In addition, nicotine can destroy oocytes and decrease their viability, leading to an early decline in the ability to reproduce. Female smokers have also been shown to experience amenorrhea, vaginal bleeding, changes in cycle timing, and lowered estrogen levels in the luteal phase. Although the evidence regarding the effects of male smoking on fertility are still inconclusive, some studies have found that male smokers are more likely to have sperm with morphological abnormalities, lowered density and mobility, and fluctuations in levels of androgens and gonadotropins (Zavos, 1989).

Psychiatric Disorders The inflated hopes and subsequent disappointment, feelings of isolation and inadequacy, and feelings of a loss of control that characterize a couple's experience of infertility culminate over time and can increase their vulnerability to psychological disorder. In the following subsections, we cover the evidence surrounding the issue of psychological distress following an infertility diagnosis and the evidence for and against the idea that psychological factors can produce infertility.

Psychiatric Disorders Secondary to Infertility

In a recent study, 30.8% of females and 10.2% of males undergoing IVF treatment were found to have a psychiatric disorder. Anxiety disorders were the most common diagnosis: 14.8% of females and 4.9% of males were determined to suffer from anxiety. Major depression was also common, with 10.9% of females and 5.1% of males affected. Most surprising was the finding that only 21% of the subjects with a diagnosable psychiatric disorder were receiving treatment (Volgsten, Svanberg, Ekselius, Lundkvist, & Poromaa, 2008). Many couples report that their mental health is neglected amidst the obsession with their physical health. In reality, infertility impacts psychological well-being perhaps more severely than physical well-being and thus demands assessment and possible treatment of both mind and body.

Chen et al. (2004) found that, of 112 women visiting an infertility clinic with the intention of beginning an ART course, 23% had generalized anxiety disorder and 17% had major depressive disorder as indicated by scores on the Mini International Psychiatric Interview (MINI). Furthermore, 9.8% of these women had dysthymic disorder. Women who had previously undergone ART treatments did not differ from new patients concerning depression and anxiety (Chen et al., 2004).

Depression and anxiety are not the only psychiatric disorders commonly found in individuals dealing with infertility. A study by Sbaragli et al. (2008) involved the psychological assessment of 70 fertile and 81 infertile couples. They found that several types of

pathology were much more common in the infertile sample than the control sample, including obsessive-compulsive disorder and panic disorder. Although the percentage of people suffering from these disorders was higher in the infertile sample, the only statistically significant difference between the case and control groups were in adjustment disorder with anxiety and depression mixed, and, somewhat unexpectedly, binge-eating disorder. While 3% of fertile subjects suffered from adjustment disorder with anxiety and depression, 28% of the infertile subjects were diagnosed with an adjustment disorder. Also, while none of the fertile subjects had diagnosable binge-eating disorder, 18% of the infertile subjects did (Sbaragli et al., 2008). However, because the BMI of the participants was not measured, we cannot be sure if this finding could be explained by the effects of BMI or caloric dysregulation on fertility, or if people suffering from infertility are subsequently at a higher risk for developing a binge-eating disorder.

Another study by Freizinger, Franko, Dacey, Okun, and Domar (2010) found the prevalence of eating disorders (ED) in an infertile sample to be higher than expected: 20.7% of the participants in this study met the criteria for a past or current eating disorder, which is 5 times higher than the general population prevalence. However, BMI did not differ significantly between the ED and non-ED groups. One troubling finding of this study was that none of the participants with an eating disorder had discussed their current or past ED with their infertility health provider (Freizinger et al., 2010).

It makes sense that the prevalence of past or current EDs would be high in an infertile population; they could be the cause or the result of infertility. We know that unstable body mass and nutritional intake leads to problems with reproductive hormone release and functioning and can thus lead to subfertility. It is also possible that women respond to the experience of infertility, defined by a lack of control, by trying to reign in control of other areas of their lives—in this case, eating. This is one area, along with the problem of disclosure to fertility specialists, that should be explored in future research.

It is clear that depression and anxiety are highly prevalent in individuals experiencing infertility relative to their fertile counterparts. These results have been replicated several times with samples from around the world. Mahajan et al. (2009) compared a sample of women in India who were experiencing infertility to a control group. They found that the infertile women underwent significant increases in negative affect and anxiety as the period of infertility continued, while the fertile controls showed no such pattern (Mahajan et al., 2009). Similar results were found in Taiwan (Chang & Mu, 2008). We can assume that, for most humans, infertility is a profoundly stressful experience.

Endless blood tests, frequent appointments, questions about intimate processes, scheduled intercourse, and painful procedures are inevitable parts of the infertility treatment process. These activities are also highly time-consuming and financially costly, and thus may detract from the rewarding aspects of life. King (2003) found that sterility is not associated with generalized anxiety disorder but infertility is, suggesting that one of the greatest stressors of infertility is the uncertainty surrounding the fertility outcome.

Psychological Factors Primary to Infertility

When stress, depression, or anxiety follow the realization of infertility, these are referred to as psychological factors *secondary* to infertility. When these conditions precede and thus potentially contribute to infertility, they are referred to as psychological factors *primary* to infertility. Unfortunately, the issue of whether stress produces infertility has not been sufficiently examined and remains inconclusive. In order to establish a causal connection between stress and infertility, longitudinal or prospective studies would need to be conducted. Obviously, studies such as these are large undertakings that require sufficient funding and time on the part of the investigators and participants. Several studies of this nature that repeatedly show an association between women with high initial stress levels reproducing at a lower rate than women without high stress could offer a consensus on the issue. For the present, we cannot say conclusively whether stress causes infertility.

The limited evidence regarding this question was assessed by Nakamura, Sheps, and Arck in a 2008 meta-analysis of all the epidemiological literature on the link between stress and reproductive success from 1980 to 2007. The mixed evidence they found led them to conclude that, while general trends can be observed, every woman is different in the way her reproductive system responds to stress (Nakamura, Sheps, & Arck, 2008, p. 57).

Historically, women have been blamed for their infertility. Although society has progressed in this view, the myth that a woman could "bring about" a state of infertility by failing to maintain her mental and physical health still abounds. An interesting study by Brand, Roos, and van der Merwe (1982) actually refuted the notion that infertile women brought on their condition as a result of maladaptive personalities or an inability to cope effectively with stress. Fifty-nine women referred to an infertility clinic were separated into three groups with respect to the cause of their infertility: (1) functional infertility (no identifiable organic causes), (2) organic infertility, and (3) those who were fertile but unable to conceive due to male factors. They found that, between the three groups of women, there were no significant differences in physiological measures of inherent stress, such as pulse volume, heart rate, and muscle tension. All of the women were dealing with infertility, but those who were the source of the condition (functional and organic groups) were not any more stressed than those who were not the source of the condition. They also found that the three groups of women were no different with regards to social integration, ego strength, paranoid behavior, sense of guilt, frustration, self-esteem, self-behavior, or self-identity (Brand et al., 1982). The results of this study support the notion that infertility, whether it is caused by male or female factors, is what produces stress in women, and it is not the other way around. It is possible, however, that these women had differential stress levels prior to encountering a fertility problem but that the experience of infertility at the time of assessment produced equal amounts of stress in all groups, obscuring any preexisting differences. These results therefore fail to completely rule out the possibility of stress causing infertility. However, the fact that personality variables (like self-esteem or social integration), which we usually view as stable and unchanging, were not different between the groups is at odds with the idea that the women had drastically different personalities prior to their infertility diagnosis that somehow exacerbated or protected them from the condition.

Although the notion is controversial, researchers posit how the causal connection linking stress and infertility would play out

biologically. Prolonged stress leads to chemical changes in the brain. Stress increases the release of adrenaline and epinephrine in the brain and blood stream. These hormones exist to help us employ the fight-or-flight response. Adrenaline and epinephrine mediate the release of gonadotropin-releasing hormone (GnRH), the now-familiar hormone that mediates reproductive functions. Increases in stress lead to increases in adrenaline and epinephrine, and thus disruption in the release of GnRH from the hypothalamus, and ultimately disruption in reproductive function, and possible anovulation and infertility.

Other chemicals and hormones are involved in the stress–infertility connection. Stress leads to elevation in not only adrenaline and epinephrine, but in endorphins as well. Endorphins regulate hormones that are responsible for normal menstrual cycles. Elevation in endorphins may thus disturb reproductive function. Melatonin is a hormone released from the pineal gland in our brain that modulates our sleep-wake cycle and whose secretion is disrupted by stress. Prolonged increases in melatonin can lead to infertility by altering the release of luteinizing hormone and suppressing GnRH secretion. Lastly, stress could conceivably lead to infertility by the fact that female reproductive organs are innervated by the autonomic nervous system (that which carries out the fight-or-flight response and subsequent relaxation and return to homeostasis). When the autonomic nervous system is constantly activated for a prolonged period, female reproductive organs can suffer the consequences. Autonomic innervations control blood supply to the ovaries, the size of follicles, and the process of ovulation (Schenker, Meirow, & Schenker, 1992).

Whether or not stress does lead to infertility, the physiological pathways present in our bodies make the connection possible. However, other psychological factors primary to the infertility diagnosis can impact the course of infertility treatment. Preexisting personality factors, if they do not produce infertility, can moderate a woman's psychological and emotional response to infertility. Verhaak, Smeenk, van Minnen, Kremer, and Kraaimaat (2005) looked at 187 women undergoing IVF treatment to determine which women were going to have the most severe negative reaction to an unsuccessful outcome. Specifically, the researchers wanted to know which personality traits and lifestyle factors were best able to predict which women would fail to respond well to fertility-related disappointment. They determined that women with higher levels of neuroticism were more vulnerable to a severe emotional reaction, as were those with elevated feelings of helplessness and marital dissatisfaction. The results of this study indicate that neuroticism, helplessness, and marital dissatisfaction are risk factors for the experience of severe emotional distress when dealing with the process of infertility treatment. The authors recommend identifying women who are most likely to have a serious negative emotional reaction to fertility disappointment and devoting resources to these women, rather than supplying psychotherapy and support services to every woman presenting for infertility treatment (Verhaak et al., 2005).

Social Support and Relationship Quality

In addition to dispositional factors, relationship quality and level of social support can predict women's response to infertility. The aforementioned study found that, despite all of the risk factors for a poor emotional response to the diagnosis of infertility, women with higher perceived social support were less likely to respond poorly to an unsuccessful IVF outcome (Verhaak et al., 2005). Social support, in this sense, can be viewed as a protective factor against a severely negative event in infertile women. Men are also affected by social support in their struggle with their partners' infertility. Lund, Sejbaek, Christensen, and Schmidt (2009) found that, among men, low emotional support, low appreciation, and high excessive demands from the partner were significant determinants of the incidence of severe depressive symptoms. Among women and men, low appreciation by family, many conflicts, and high excessive demands from family, friends, and neighbors were significant determinants of severe depressive symptoms following failed IVF treatment (Lund et al., 2009).

Peterson, Newton, and Rosen (2003) found that couples experiencing infertility were more likely to have marital satisfaction if they perceived that they had equal levels of infertility stress. A lack of agreement over relationship concerns and the need for parenthood between partners was associated with low marital satisfaction and depression in women (Peterson et al., 2003). It is easy to see how incongruence in stress between partners could lead to distress: If the woman desperately wants a child and agonizes over her condition while her male partner is less emotionally invested and less deeply affected, relationship difficulty is likely to emerge. This study lends initial support to the idea that communication about stress levels between couples experiencing infertility could help maintain marital satisfaction.

In fact, some studies have found that the experience of infertility could actually have benefits for marital quality. Schmidt, Holstein, Christensen, and Boivin (2005) found that 25.9% of women and 21.1% of men dealing with infertility reported marital benefits from the process. Those with healthy coping styles and communication patterns were most likely to realize these benefits, while couples who chose to keep their infertility a secret, had difficulty communicating, and used maladaptive coping strategies were likely to have low marital benefit (Schmidt et al., 2005).

The current literature and the personal testaments of women suffering from infertility reinforce the notion that the condition of infertility is associated with psychological distress and various psychiatric disorders. A significant percentage of women presenting with infertility have diagnosable mental disorders, the most common of which are anxiety, depression, and eating disorders. Whether psychological factors can be considered among the causes of infertility still remains unclear, several studies have investigated the issue with mixed results. Other psychological factors primary to infertility are dispositional personality factors, coping style, and relationship quality. It seems that individuals with healthy coping styles and a low level of initial trait neuroticism are able to cope best with the diagnosis of infertility. Furthermore, those women engaged in healthy and communicative relationships with their partners and integrated into meaningful social support networks seem to be protected from some of the psychological distress produced by the experience of infertility.

IMPACT OF PSYCHOLOGICAL INTERVENTIONS FOR INFERTILITY

Since a strong association between psychological distress and the experience of infertility has been displayed, recent research has examined whether psychological treatments can have a meaningful impact on the condition. Some interventions are meant to simply reduce the stress, anxiety, and depression associated with infertility, whereas others seek to achieve the former *and* increase pregnancy rates. Several different kinds of psychological treatments are used with this specific population, some more popular and reputable than others. Common therapies include cognitive-behavioral therapy, behavioral modification, relaxation training, and group support.

Perhaps the most commonly employed psychological intervention for individuals with infertility is cognitive-behavioral therapy (CBT). A common negative thought in individuals with infertility is "I will never get pregnant." People allow these thoughts to grip them and shape their reality. They begin to only pay attention to events that confirm their preconceived notion, such as a negative pregnancy test or a failed IVF attempt, and discredit those pieces of information that are at odds with the notion, such as a doctor's hopeful prognosis or multiple healthy-looking embryos. Patients can then deteriorate into a state of despair and depression, and CBT can be useful at alleviating these unpleasant mental states. Through several sessions of examining and restructuring negative thought patterns, patients can change the notion "I will never get pregnant" to something more positive, such as "I am hopeful about the possibility of having a child." CBT has been shown to be an effective treatment for infertility-related depression. Faramarzi et al. (2007) randomized 89 depressed infertile women in Iran to receive CBT, antidepressant therapy, or no intervention. The patients in the CBT group received relaxation training, cognitive restructuring, and elimination of negative automatic thoughts and dysfunctional attitudes for 10 sessions. At the end of the study, 79.3% of the women in the CBT group were free of depression, while only 50% in the drug therapy group and 10% in the control group had the same result (Faramarzi et al., 2007).

Other psychological treatments for infertility are behavioral modification, relaxation training, and group support. These three modalities are sometimes delivered together and referred to as "psychosocial intervention." Many studies have examined the effects of two or more of them on distress and pregnancy rates. Behavioral modification can consist of changing diet and exercise habits or quitting smoking and drinking alcohol. Relaxation training consists of a series of methods used to reduce stress, including meditation, deep breathing, guided imagery, and muscle relaxation. Studies of these two techniques have produced results that are encouraging in terms of decreasing psychological distress and increasing pregnancy rates.

Hosaka, Matsubayashi, Sugiyama, Izumi, and Makino (2002) randomized 100 infertile Japanese women into a control group or an intervention group receiving five weekly 90-minute sessions focused on behavioral education, problem-solving skill development, psychological support, and relaxation training. Participants were administered measures of depression and mood states prior to and following treatment, and plasma samples were taken to measure their levels of natural killer cell (NK-cell) activity. NK-cells are implicated in the immune responses associated with reproduction, and levels have been found to be higher in infertile than fertile women. After the fifth session, the authors found that scores on depression, lack-of-vigor, aggression–hostility, fatigue, and total mood disturbance were decreased in the intervention group. NK-cell activity was also significantly decreased in comparison to the study inception. No such significant changes were found in the control group. The women were followed for 1 year following the study conclusion, and it was found that 34.8% of women in the intervention group became pregnant, compared with only 13.5% of women in the control group (Hosaka et al., 2002).

The promising results of this study have been replicated in other settings with other populations. Domar et al. (2000) studied the effects of psychosocial intervention in a group of 184 women in the United States who were all in the second or third year of infertility, the point at which psychological symptoms tend to appear. Women were assigned to a mind-body group, a support group, or a routine-care control group. The mind-body group underwent relaxation-response training, cognitive restructuring, emotional expression, and education on nutrition and exercise issues related to infertility for 2 hours per week for 10 weeks. The support group met at the same intervals for the same duration but simply shared their infertility experiences from the previous week and discussed topics relevant to infertility. The researchers found that women in the mind-body and support groups both improved with regards to stress management, anxiety, marital distress, and total mood disturbance, whereas the psychological state of the control group deteriorated significantly over the course of the 10 weeks.

In a comparison of the two intervention groups, CBT participants fared better, with higher scores on measures of stress-management skills. Along with positive psychological effects, the psychosocial treatment groups also showed higher pregnancy rates. Domar et al. reported that 55% of the initial mind-body participants became pregnant within 6 months, as did 54% of the support group participants, while only 20% of the control patients became pregnant (Domar et al., 2000). This study shows that while any kind of psychosocial support can be more effective than none at reducing infertility-related distress, CBT coupled with relaxation-training and behavioral modification can provide infertile women with important coping skills to further improve their psychological health.

Despite these promising results, we are still unable to comment decisively on the efficacy of psychological interventions for infertility, because some studies have found the treatments to be ineffective. De Klerk et al. (2005) administered a psychosocial intervention to a group of infertile women in the Netherlands and found that, when compared to a control group receiving no such treatment, distress was unaffected by the intervention.

A comprehensive review article considered the effects of various psychological interventions on various outcome measures. Boivin (2003) divided the interventions into three classes: counseling, focused-educational, or comprehensive-educational. The outcome measures were negative affect (depression, anxiety, psychiatric disorder), nonaffect measures (interpersonal functioning, infertility distress, target behaviors), and pregnancy rates. Of the studies focusing on negative affect, half showed a positive effect of psychosocial interventions, with more reductions in anxiety than depression levels. The studies that measured interpersonal functioning generally failed to demonstrate consistent positive intervention effects. Studies measuring infertility-specific distress, on the other hand, showed universally positive effects of intervention. It was thus concluded that interventions were most effective in reducing negative affect and infertility-specific distress. The author asserted that psychosocial interventions do not appear to influence pregnancy rates, because only 3 of 15 studies showed a positive effect of intervention on pregnancy. With regards to the interventions themselves, the author found that educational interventions, which focused on information provision and skill development, were generally more effective than counseling interventions, which emphasized emotional expression, but this was only the case for psychological improvement and not for pregnancy rates (Boivin, 2003).

It seems reasonable to conclude that psychological interventions can have a positive impact on infertility-related distress and on mental state in general. Whether these interventions can meaningfully impact pregnancy rates has not been supported and is the subject of increasing scientific studies: One very recent study found promising results demonstrating a positive impact of psychosocial intervention on IVF success rate. Domar et al. (2011) randomized women undergoing their first IVF cycle to participate in a 10-week mind-body group or to undergo routine treatment. There were no significant differences in IVF success rate between the two groups of women after cycle 1 (both had a 43% pregnancy rate), but at this point, only half of the participants in the experimental group had attended any mind-body sessions, and a mere 9% had attended 6 to 10 sessions. After cycle 2, however, when 76% of the mind-body participants had attended 6 to 10 sessions, significant differences in pregnancy rates following IVF emerged: 52% of the women who received the mind-body intervention achieved pregnancy, while only 20% of women in the control group did (Domar et al., 2011).

The causal connection linking psychological factors and subsequent fertility, and thus the efficacy of treating psychological factors to treat infertility, is an issue within the field that warrants further investigation before a sound conclusion can be reached. Despite some of the evidence for the efficacy of psychosocial interventions, they are underutilized by women with infertility, suggesting a treatment gap (Boivin, 1997). The limited research up to this point leads us to believe that psychosocial intervention can affect pregnancy rates, but that at least five sessions (Hammerli, Znoj, & Barth, 2009) that focus on skills acquisition and information provision (Boivin, 2003) are necessary to have a meaningful benefit.

RACE, ETHNIC, AND SOCIOECONOMIC DIFFERENCES IN THE PSYCHOLOGICAL ASPECT OF INFERTILITY

There exist very real differences between women of different races, ethnicities, and socioeconomic status concerning fertility and reproductive health. These differences can be categorized as (a) differences in biological factors impacting fertility, (b) differences in access to and use of infertility care, and (c) differences in the psychosocial experience of infertility.

Biological Differences Across the Lifespan

Statistics show that ART outcomes are less favorable for Blacks than Whites on average. Compared with Whites, Black women presenting for infertility treatment are more likely to have tubal factor infertility, a higher BMI, and have waited longer before seeking treatment. Implantation and ongoing pregnancy rates were also much lower in Black than White women. In fact, it has been shown that ART outcomes are less favorable for every ethnic group other than Whites. A recent study found that Asian women had a 14% lower likelihood of achieving pregnancy and a 10% lower rate of live birth than White women. Hispanic women, though having clinical pregnancy rates similar to Whites, were 13% less likely to have a live birth after ART. Black women were 38% less likely than White women to have a live birth. Furthermore, all ethnic groups studied had higher rates of miscarriage in comparison to Whites. The reasons for these troubling findings are uncertain. It likely has to do with an interaction between genetic, socioeconomic, environmental, and behavioral factors (Fujimoto et al., 2008).

Studies have found inconsistent results concerning hormonal differences among women of different racial groups. The Study of Women Across the Nation (SWAN) found that mean follicular-stimulating hormone (FSH) levels were higher in Blacks and Hispanics than in other ethnic groups, but that estrogen did not differ among groups. In all ethnic groups, BMI was associated with reproductive hormone levels. The Penn Ovarian Aging Study, however, found that estrogen levels were lower in Blacks than in Whites, and that there were no differences between the two groups in FSH levels. Although the Women's Interagency IVF Study found that anti-Müllerian hormone (AMH) level, which signals ovarian reserve and is arguably the most accurate biomarker of ovarian age, was 25% lower in Black than White women, the Penn study found comparable AMH levels in these two groups.

Differences in Access to and Use of Care

In addition to reproductive differences among racial and ethnic groups based on biological factors, others are based in cultural and social divergences. There are glaring differences between racial groups in the utilization of ART for infertility. Although White women are not the ethnic group most at risk for infertility, they are the group using the majority of the services. A recent study utilized the Society for Assisted Reproductive Technology (SART) data for the years 1999 and 2000 and found that 83.5% of women using ART were White, while only 4.6% were Black and 11.9% were of other ethnicities (Seifer et al., 2009).

This discrepancy is thought to be the result of financial factors. However, a study by Jain (2006) found that non-White groups were still reluctant to use IVF, even when mandatory state health insurance fully covered the procedure. The author examined Massachusetts, which mandates full coverage of IVF, to see if racial discrepancies in utilization still persisted. IVF patients were predominantly White, educated, and wealthy. African American and Hispanic women were underrepresented and Asian American women were overrepresented, a finding that is likely the result of the Asian Americans in this sample being highly educated and wealthy. So why, although IVF care is essentially free under Massachusetts health insurance, are Hispanics and African Americans not utilizing care? The author posits that it involves a lack of appropriate information and education among these groups, coupled with a possible lack of referrals by primary care physicians or a cultural bias against infertility treatment (Jain, 2006).

Differences in the Psychosocial Experience of Infertility

Cultural factors have been shown to play a large role in the different feelings expressed by women suffering from infertility. Although nearly all infertile women across the world are likely to experience some level of psychological distress, the reported source of this distress is different depending on cultural affiliation. The most obvious discrepancy in the response to an infertility diagnosis is between women from independent versus interdependent cultures (traditionally Western versus Eastern, respectively). Many individuals in Western societies, upon reaching childbearing age, have made themselves independent from their parents. In many Asian countries, however, family and community closeness is a much more valued element of life, even as individuals reach adulthood. Therefore, a lot of the distress experienced by women dealing with infertility from Eastern cultures has to do with family and community factors. For example, a study of infertile women in Taiwan found the five most common themes expressed by these women in describing their infertility distress were the stress of carrying on the ancestral line, the psychological reactions of the couple, disordering of family life, reorganization of family life, and external family support (Chang & Mu, 2008). In contrast, a study that sought to assess the most difficult aspects of infertility in a sample of U.S. women found them to be, in order of rated difficulty, uncertainty and lack of control, family and social pressures, impact on self and spouse, treatment-induced problems, and treatment-related procedures (Benyamini, Gozlan, & Kokia, 2005). Therefore, while almost all of the themes identified by

Taiwanese women had to do with family factors, only two of those identified by the U.S. women as most difficult did. This highlights the fact that the sources of infertility distress can vary greatly as a function of cultural values.

A large study of South Asian couples dealing with infertility highlighted some of the difficulties specific to this Eastern population. Although childlessness has become an acceptable option for couples in Western culture, voluntary childlessness in South Asian culture is blatantly admonished. Women withstand the worst of the stress of infertility, and the failure to conceive can lead to painful questioning, criticism by family and community, social stigma, and is acceptable grounds for a man to divorce his wife. It was acknowledged that views are changing, but many participants claimed that older and more traditional members of society still see infertility as the result of divine retribution, and the medicalization of infertility that has occurred in the West has not developed to the same degree in their culture. Despite some of these differences between the South Asian and Western experience of infertility, several aspects were the same: Women reported severe distress and anxiety, avoidance of social or family events where they would have to be surrounded by couples with children, and an adverse impact on their marriage, social life, and career (Culley, Johnson, Hudson, Rapport, & Katbamna, 2004).

In their study conducted on Iranian couples dealing with infertility, Noorbala et al. (2008) found that relatives' comments and opinions about their infertility was a major stressor (Noorbala et al., 2008). Adoption is seldom an option in Iranian society, thus the stress of infertility can be magnified

by the feeling that the only way to raise a child is through conception. The authors found that housewives were more depressed at the study outset than were working women, which is likely because housewives have "few roles to support identity and self-esteem besides motherhood" (Noorbala et al., 2008, p. 251).

In conclusion, ethnic, socioeconomic, and cultural differences play an undeniably large role in the reproductive experience of the world's female population. More research should explore why ethnic minorities are underutilizing infertility treatments, whether the psychological interventions effective in some racial and cultural populations prove effective in others, and how to better understand and treat the sources of distress for infertile women based on their various cultural backgrounds.

CRITICAL FUTURE DIRECTIONS

Despite the undeniable progress that has been made in examining the psychological aspects of infertility, unanswered questions still remain. As the medical treatment of infertility improves with new discoveries and more advanced methods, so will our understanding of the psychological aspect of infertility continue to evolve. The final section of this chapter outlines some of the areas that currently warrant further research and highlights ways in which studies of this particular issue could be improved.

Improved Methodological Rigor

Many studies of the psychological reactions to and psychosocial treatments for infertility are flawed from a design perspective. For example, studies that seek to answer the question "Does stress cause infertility?" need to be prospective in design. Rather than taking a sample of women already diagnosed as infertile and a sample of women without infertility and measuring them on psychological factors, women of early childbearing years need to be followed and periodically assessed with respect to psychological factors and pregnancy rates. This type of design will allow for a temporal sequence linking psychological factors to fertility, and will thus provide a credible basis for a causal connection between the two. Brkovich & Fisher (1998) agree that because current research includes women who already have an infertility diagnosis, it is impossible to determine causality.

Studies also need to ensure adequate sample sizes and randomization into treatment conditions to allow for sufficient statistical power and control for confounding variables (Boivin, 2003). Lastly, studies should utilize psychometrically validated measures of psychological factors such as stress or psychological disorders. After a review of intervention-based literature, Boivin (2003) concludes that too many studies use in-house measures of distress that are not necessarily valid and reliable assessments. Measurement of stress could be advanced by the use of physiological measure, such as pulse rate, salivary cortisol levels, and galvanic skin response, rather than self-report measures, which are subject to human manipulation and potential bias.

More Study of Ethnically and Culturally Diverse Populations

Although there is ample research on infertility in world populations, there remains a dearth of knowledge regarding the experience of infertility for ethnic and cultural minorities residing in the United States. Racial minorities, especially Hispanic and African Americans, are under-utilizing infertility treatments, despite controlling for financial variables (Jain, 2006). Further investigation is needed to explain this discrepancy, and the information gleaned could allow us to develop ways to increase use of infertility care by minorities.

It is also important that psychosocial treatments for infertility are validated for various ethnic and cultural groups. While upper-middle-class White women may respond positively to group therapy or CBT, this may not be most effective for different socioeconomic or ethnic groups. Limited research in this area implies that reactions to psychological treatment differ as a function of social factors and ethnic identity. For example, Noorbala et al. (2008) found that levels of depression in infertile couples varied according to education level. While depression was most prevalent in participants with only a primary school education, a psychological intervention involving psychotherapy and medication had the most effect on this group. The authors speculate that explaining the biological cause of infertility may help women with limited education to cease self-blame. They further found that treatment efficacy varied according to employment and age (Noorbala et al., 2008). The various studies reviewed in the previous section demonstrated that the sources of distress for infertile women were different depending on cultural affiliation (Chang & Mu, 2008; Culley et al., 2004). This evidence indicates that psychosocial interventions need to be adjusted for each woman based on her ethnic and cultural background.

More Study of the Physician-Patient Relationship

Becker and Nachtigall (1991) describe the physician-patient relationship in the case of infertility as ambiguous and complex. There is negotiation over who assumes responsibility for a pregnancy, and both patient and physician participate in treatment. Patients are expected to maintain healthy behaviors and chart their cycles, while physicians are expected to use their training advantage to "cure" the infertility problem (Becker & Nachtigall, 1991). The dynamics of this relationship can lead to frustration and disappointment, and it is an important factor contributing to a couple's experience of infertility treatment. However, there is little research on the impact of the physician-patient relationship and how it can be improved to ameliorate some of the stress associated with the treatment process, decrease treatment drop-out rates, and increase overall satisfaction with the medicalized aspect of fertility. Future research will need to examine this issue more critically so empirically based recommendations can be made to physicians in regards to their mode of interaction with their patients to ensure patient comfort and satisfaction with the process.

More Opportunities for Psychological Treatments

We have seen that infertility and its treatment are associated with high levels of distress, anxiety, and depression, but we have also seen that the use of psychological and counseling services for infertility patients is remarkably low. For example, Volgsten et al. (2008) found that while 30% of women undergoing IVF treatment had a diagnosable psychiatric disorder, only 21% of those women were receiving psychological

treatment. In a study of 50 South Asian individuals experiencing infertility, only 16% were using psychological treatment (Culley et al., 2004). A study of dropout rates of IVF patients showed the most common reason for terminating treatment was stress, with 39% of the respondents citing this cause. Participants were also asked to give suggestions on how to make the IVF experience better, and the two most frequent answers were "written information on how to deal with stress/psychological issues" and "easy immediate access to a psychologist or social worker" (Domar, Smith, Conboy, Iannone, & Alper, 2006, p. 1459). One of the most critical future directions in the treatment of the psychological aspect of infertility will be the adequate provision of psychological counseling and treatment to those who need it, mental-health monitoring of infertility patients, and the availability of infertility-related stress information to women of childbearing age. It is important that medical students considering OB/GYN and fertility treatment as their specialization are sufficiently informed about the psychological impact that infertility will have on their patients, and that they are prepared to deal with this aspect of infertility treatment.

REFERENCES

Anderson, K. M., Sharpe, M., Rattray, A., & Irvine, D. S. (2003). Distress and concerns in couples referred to an infertility specialist. *Journal of Psychosomatic Research, 54*(4), 353–355.

Augood, C., Duckitt, K., & Templeton, A. A. (1998). Smoking and female infertility: A systematic review and meta-analysis. *Human Reproduction, 13*(6), 1532–1539.

Balen, A. H. (2006). Should obese women with polycystic ovary syndrome receive treatment for infertility? *British Medical Journal, 332*, 434–435.

Becker, G., & Nachtigall, R. D. (1991). Ambiguous responsibility in the doctor-patient relationship: The case of infertility. *Social Science and Medicine, 32*(8), 875–885.

Benyamini, Y., Gozlan, M., & Kokia, E. (2005). Variability in the difficulties experienced by women undergoing infertility treatments. *Fertility and Sterility, 83*(2), 275–283.

Boivin, J. (1997). Is there too much emphasis on psychosocial counseling for infertile patients? *Journal of Assisted Reproduction and Genetics, 14*(4), 184–186.

Boivin, J. (2003). A review of psychosocial interventions in infertility. *Social Science & Medicine, 57*(12), 2325–2341.

Boivin, J., Bunting, L., Collins, J. A., & Nygren, K. G. (2007). International estimates of infertility prevalence and treatment-seeking: Potential need and demand for infertility medical care. *Human Reproduction, 22*(6), 1506–1512.

Brand, H. J., Roos, S. S., & van der Merwe, A. B. (1982). Psychological stress and infertility. Part 1: Psychophysiological reaction patterns. *Journal of Medical Psychology, 55*, 379–384.

Brkovich, A. M., & Fisher, W. A. (1998). Psychological distress and infertility: Forty years of research. *Journal of Psychosomatic Obstetrics, 19*(4), 218–228.

Broocks, A., Pirke, K. M., Schweiger, U., Tuschl, R. J., Laessle, R. G., Strowitzki, T., . . . Jeschke, D. (1990). Cyclic ovarian function in recreational athletes. *Journal of Applied Physiology, 68*(5), 2083–2086.

Centers for Disease Control and Prevention. (2010). Excessive alcohol use and women's health. Retrieved from www.cdc.gov/alchohol/fact-sheets/womens-health.htm

Centers for Disease Control and Prevention. (2011a). Infertility FAQs. Retrieved from www.cdc.gov/reproductivehealth/Infertility

Centers for Disease Control and Prevention. (2011b). Overweight and obesity. Retrieved from www.cdc.gov/Obesity

Centers for Disease Control and Prevention. (2011c). Adult cigarette smoking in the United States: Current estimate. Retrieved from www.cdc.gov/tobacco/data_statistics/fact_sheets/adult_data/cig_smoking/index.htm

Chang, S.-N., & Mu, P.-F. (2008). Infertile couples' experience of family stress while women are hospitalized for Ovarian Hyperstimulation Syndrome during infertility treatment. *Journal of Clinical Nursing 17*(4), 531–538.

Chen, B. Y. (1997). Acupuncture normalizes dysfunction of hypothalamic-pituitary-ovarian axis. *International Journal of Acupuncture and Electro-Therapeutics Research, 22*, 97–108.

Chen, T.-H., Shang, S.-P., Tsai, C.-F., & Juang, K.-D. (2004). Prevalence of depressive and anxiety disorders in an assisted reproductive technique clinic. *Human Reproduction, 19*(10), 2313–2318.

Culley, L., Johnson, M., Hudson, N., Rapport, F., & Katbamna, S. (2004). A study of the provision of infertility services to South Asian communities: Final report. May 2004, De Montfort University, Leicester, UK.

de Klerk, C., Hunfeld, J. A. M., Duivenvoorden, H. J., den Outer, M. A., Fauser, B. C. J. M., Passchier, J., & Macklon, N. S. (2005). Effectiveness of a psychosocial counselling intervention for first-time IVF couples: A randomized controlled trial. *Human Reproduction, 20*(5), 1333–1338.

Dhillon, P. K., & Holt, V. L. (2003). Recreational physical activity and endometrioma risk. *American Journal of Epidemiology, 158*(2), 156–164.

Domar, A. D., Clapp, D., Slawsby, E., Kessel, B., Orav, J., & Freizinger, M. (2000). The impact of group psychological interventions on distress in infertile women. *Health Psychology, 19*(6), 568–575.

Domar, A. D., Rooney, K. L., Wiegand, B., Orav, E. J., Alper, M. M., Berger, B. M., & Niklovski, J. (2011). Impact of a group mind/body intervention on pregnancy rates in IVF patients. *Fertility and Sterility, 95*(7), 2269–2273.

Domar, A. D., Smith, K., Conboy, L., Iannone, M., & Alper, M. (2006). A prospective investigation into the reasons why insured United States patients drop out of in vitro fertilization treatment. *Fertility and Sterility, 94*(4), 1457–1459.

Faramarzi, M., Alipor, A., Esmaelzadeh, S., Kheirkhah, F., Poladi, K., & Pash, H. (2007). Treatment of depression and anxiety in infertile women: Cognitive behavioral therapy versus fluoxetine. *Journal of Affective Disorders, 108*(1), 159–164.

Freeman, E. W., Boxer, A. S., Rickels, K., Tureck, R., & Mastroianni, L., Jr. (1985). Psychological evaluation and support in a program of in vitro fertilization and embryo transfer. *Fertility and Sterility, 43*(1), 48–53.

Freizinger, M., Franko, D. L., Dacey, M., Okun, B., & Domar, A. D. (2010). The prevalence of eating disorders in infertile women. *Fertility and Sterility*, *93*(1), 72–78.

Fujimoto, V. Y., Luke, B., Brown, M. B., Jain, T., Armstrong, A., Grainger, D. A., & Hornstein, M. D. (2008). Racial and ethnic disparities in assisted reproductive technology outcomes in the United States. *Fertility and Sterility*, *93*(2), 382–390.

Grodstein, F., Goldman, M. B., & Cramer, D. W. (1994). Infertility in women and moderate alcohol use. *American Journal of Public Health*, *84*(9), 1429–1432.

Hammerli, K., Znoj, H., & Barth, J. (2009). The efficacy of psychological interventions for infertile patients: A meta-analysis examining mental health and pregnancy rate. *Human Reproduction*, *15*(3), 279–295.

Hosaka, T., Matsubayashi, H., Sugiyama, Y., Izumi, S., & Makino, T. (2002). Effect of psychiatric group intervention on natural-killer cell activity and pregnancy rate. *General Hospital Psychiatry*, *24*(5), 353–356.

Hughes, E. G., & Brennan, B. G. (1996). Does cigarette smoking impair natural or assisted fecundity? *Fertility and Sterility*, *66*(5), 679–689.

Jain, T. (2006). Socioeconomic and racial disparities among infertility patients seeking care. *Fertility and Sterility*, *85*(4), 876–881.

Jensen, T. K., Henriksen, T. B., Hjolland, N. H. I., Scheike, T., Kolstad, H., Giwercman, A., . . . Olsen, J. (1998). Adult and prenatal exposures to tobacco smoke as risk indicators of fertility among 430 Danish couples. *American Journal of Epidemiology*, *148*(10), 992–997.

Kesmodel, U., Wisborg, K., Olsen, S. F., Henriksen, T. B., & Secher, N. J. (2002). Moderate alcohol intake in pregnancy and the risk of spontaneous abortion. *Alcohol and Alcoholism*, *37*(1), 87–92.

King, R. B. (2003). Subfecundity and anxiety in a nationally representative sample. *Social Science & Medicine*, *56*(4), 739–751.

Klonoff-Cohen, H., Bleha, J., & Lam-Kruglick, P. (2002). A prospective study of the effects of female and male caffeine consumption on the reproductive endpoints of IVF and gamete intrafallopian transfer. *Human Reproduction*, *17*(7), 1746–1754.

Klonoff-Cohen, H., Lam-Kruglick, P., & Gonzalez, C. (2002). Effects of maternal and paternal alcohol consumption on the success rate of in vitro fertilization and gamete intrafallopian transfer. *Fertility and Sterility*, *79*(2), 330–339.

Lund, R., Sejbaek, C. S., Christensen, U., & Schmidt, L. (2009). The impact of social relations on the incidence of severe depressive symptoms among infertile women and men. *Human Reproduction*, *24*(11), 2810–2820.

Madaschi, C., Braga, D. P., de Figueira, C. R., Iaconelli, A., Jr., & Borges, E., Jr. (2010). Effect of acupuncture on assisted reproductive treatment outcomes. *Acupuncture in Medicine*, *28*, 180–184.

Mahajan, N. N., Turnbull, D. A., Davies, M. J., Jindal, U. N., Briggs, N. E., & Taplin, J. E. (2009). Adjustment to infertility: The role of intrapersonal and interpersonal resources/vulnerabilities. *Human Reproduction*, *24*(4), 906–912.

Manheimer, E., Zhang, G., Udoff, L., Haramati, A., Langenberg, P., Berman, B. M., & Bouter, L. M. (2007). Effects of acupuncture on rates of pregnancy and live birth among women undergoing in vitro fertilisation: Systematic review and meta-analysis. *British Medical Journal*, *336*, 545–549.

Mircea, C. N., Lujan, M. E., & Pierson, R. A. (2007). Metabolic fuel and clinical implications for female reproduction. *Journal of Obstetrics and Gynaecology Canada*, *29*(11), 887–902.

Morris, S. N., Missmer, S. A., Cramer, D. W., Powers, R. D., McShane, P. M., & Hornstein, M. D. (2006). Effect of lifetime exercise on the outcome of in vitro fertilization. *Obstetrics and Gynecology*, *108*(4), 938–945.

Morrison, J. A., Glueck, C. J., & Wang, P. (2008). Dietary trans fatty acid intake is associated with increased fetal loss. *Fertility and Sterility*, *90*(2), 385–390.

Moy, I., Milad, M. P., Barnes, R., Confino, E., Kazer, R. R., & Zhang, X. (2010). Randomized controlled trial: Effects of acupuncture on pregnancy rates in women undergoing in vitro fertilization. *Fertility and Sterility*, *95*(2), 583–587.

Muthusami, K. R., & Chinnaswamy, P. (2005). Effect of chronic alcoholism on male fertility hormones and semen quality. *Fertility and Sterility*, *84*(4), 919–924.

Nakamura, K., Sheps, S., & Arck, P. C. (2008). Stress and reproductive failure: Past notions, present insights, and future directions. *Journal of Assisted Reproduction and Genetics, 25*(2–3), 47–62.

Noorbala, A. A., Ramazanzadeh, F., Malekafzali, H., Abedinia, N., Forooshani, A. R., Shariat, M., & Jafarabadi, M. (2008). Effects of a psychological intervention on depression in infertile couples. *International Journal of Gynecology and Obstetrics, 101*(3), 248–252.

Oddens, B. J., de Tonkelaar, I., & Nieuwenhuyse, H. (1999). Psychosocial experiences in women facing fertility problems: A comparative survey. *Human Reproduction, 14*(1), 255–261.

Omodei, U., Piccioni, G., Tombesi, S., Dordoni, D., Fallo, L., & Ghilardi, F. (2010). Effect of acupuncture on rates of pregnancy among women undergoing in vitro fertilization. *Fertility and Sterility, 94*(4), 1.

Pauli, E. M., Legro, R. S., Demers, L. M., Kunselman, A. R., Dodson, W. C., & Lee, P. A. (2008). Diminished paternity and gonadal function with increasing obesity in men. *Fertility and Sterility, 90* (2), 346–351.

Paulus, W. E., Zhang, M., Strehler, E., El-Danasouri, I., & Sterzik, K. (2001). Influence of acupuncture on the pregnancy rate in patients who undergo assisted reproduction therapy. *Fertility and Sterility, 77*(4), 721–724.

Peterson, B. D., Newton, C. R., & Rosen, K. H. (2003). Examining congruence between partners' perceived infertility-related stress and its relationship to marital adjustment and depression in infertile couples. *Family Process, 42*(1), 59–70.

Pinelli, G., & Tagliabue, A. (2007). Nutrition and fertility. *Minerva Gastroenterology & Dietology, 53*(4), 375–382.

Rich-Edwards, J. W., Spiegelman, D., Garland, M., Hertzmark, E., Hunter, D. J., Colditz, G. A., . . . Manson, J. E. (2002). Physical activity, body mass index, and ovulatory disorder infertility. *Epidemiology, 13*(2), 184–190.

Rossi, B. V., Hornstein, M. D., Cramer, D. W., & Missmer, S. A. (2009). The effect of alcohol on in vitro fertilization (IVF) live birth rates. *Fertility and Sterility, 92*(3), S51–S52.

Sbaragli, C., Morgante, G., Goracci, A., Hofkens, T., De Leo, V., & Castrogiovanni, P. (2008). Infertility and psychiatric morbidity. *Fertility and Sterility, 90*(6), 2107–2111.

Schenker, J. G., Meirow, D., & Schenker, E. (1992). Stress and human reproduction. *European Journal of Obstetrics & Gynecology and Reproductive Biology, 45*(1), 1–8.

Schmidt, L., Holstein, B. E., Christensen, U., & Boivin, J. (2005). Communication and coping as predictors of fertility problem stress: Cohort study of 816 participants who did not achieve a delivery after 12 months of fertility treatment. *Human Reproduction, 20*(11), 3248–3256.

Seifer D. B., Golub, E. T., Lambert-Messerlian, G., Benning, L., Anastos, K., Watts, D. H., . . . Greenblatt, R. M. (2009). Variations in serum mullerian inhibiting substance between White, Black, and Hispanic women. *Fertility and Sterility, 92*, 1674–1678.

Smith, J. F., Eisenberg, M. L., Millstein, S. G., Nachtigall, R. D., Shindel, A. W., Wing, H., . . . Katz, P. P. (2010). The use of complementary and alternative fertility treatment in couples seeking fertility care: Data from a prospective cohort in the United States. *Fertility and Sterility, 93*(7), 2169–2174.

Sterzik, K., Strehler, E., De Santo, M., Trumpp, N., Abt, M., Rosenbusch, B., & Schneider, A. (1996). Influence of smoking on fertility of women attending an in vitro fertilization program. *Fertility and Sterility, 65*(4), 810–814.

Stewart, D. E. (1992). Reproductive functions in eating disorders. *Annals of Medicine, 24*(4), 287–291.

Stewart, D. E., Robinson, E., Goldbloom, D. S., & Wright, C. (1990). Infertility and eating disorders. *American Journal of Obstetrics and Gynecology, 163*, 1196–1199.

Tang, T., Glanville, J., Hayden, C. J., White, D., Barth, J. H., & Balen, A. H. (2006). Combined life-style modification and metformin in obese patients with polycystic ovary syndrome (PCOS): A randomised, placebo-controlled, double-blind multi-centre study. *Human Reproduction, 21*, 80–89.

Tolstrupp, J. S., Kruger Kjaer, S., Holst, C., Sharif, H., Munk, C., Osler, M., . . . Gronbaek, M. (2003). Alcohol use as a predictor for infertility in a representative population of Danish women. *Acta Obstetrica et Gynecologica Scandinavica, 82*(8), 744–749.

Tsagareli, V., Noakes, M., & Norman, R. J. (2006). Effect of a very low calorie diet on in vitro fertilization outcomes. *Fertility and Sterility, 86*(1), 227–229.

Van Thiel, D., Gavaler, J. H., Lester, R., & Sherins, R. J. (1978). Alcohol-induced ovarian failure in the rat. *The Journal of Clinical Investigation, 61*(3), 624–632.

Verhaak, C. M., Smeenk, J. M. J., van Minnen, A., Kremer, J. A. M., & Kraaimaat, F. W. (2005). A longitudinal, prospective study on emotional adjustment before, during and after consecutive fertility treatment cycles. *Human Reproduction, 20* (8), 2253–2260.

Volgsten, H., Skoog Svanberg, A., Ekselius, L., Lundkvist, O., & Sundström Poromaa, I. (2008). Prevalence of psychiatric disorders in infertile women and men undergoing in vitro fertilization treatment. *Human Reproduction, 23*(9), 2056–2063.

Wang, W., Check, J. H., Liss, J. R., & Chloe, J. K. (2007). A matched controlled study to evaluate the efficacy of acupuncture for improving pregnancy rates following in vitro fertilization–embryo transfer. *Clinical and Experimental Obstetrics & Gynecology, 34*(3), 137–138.

Westergaard, L. G., Mao, Q., Krogslund, M., Sandrini, S., Lenz, S., & Grinsted, J. (2006). Acupuncture on the day of embryo transfer significantly improves the reproductive outcome in infertile women: A prospective, randomized trial. *Fertility and Sterility, 85*(5), 1341–1346.

Zavos, P. M. (1989). Cigarette smoking and human reproduction: Effects on female and male fecundity. *Infertility, 12*(1), 35–46.

The Psychology of Agency in Childbearing

PAMELA A. GELLER, ALEXANDRA R. NELSON, AND EFRAT EICHENBAUM

INTRODUCTION

Changing societal expectations regarding women's reproduction and increasing acceptance of a range of paths toward parenthood, along with advances in reproductive technology and maternal-fetal medicine, are affording women tremendous agency in relation to childbearing. Many women become pregnant without medical assistance and go on to have successful births, while some women choose to remain child-free. In some cases, pregnancy may be achieved, but for various reasons it may terminate—either by choice or by chance. For other women, a variety of circumstances may complicate their ability to become pregnant and give birth, introducing many decisions regarding possible paths surrounding childbearing and becoming a parent. Although not typically discussed under the purview of health psychology, decisions surrounding reproductive health events can be quite stressful for women and their partners, and there can be significant emotional responses associated with the decisions or events themselves. With an increasing presence of clinical health psychologists in primary care and within settings more specific to women, such as obstetrics and gynecology and reproductive endocrinology (Geller,

Nelson, Kornfield, & Silverman, 2013), it is important that healthcare professionals understand these issues.

This chapter provides an overview of women's decision making surrounding pregnancy and childbearing and associated maternal mental health consequences, with a focus on women within the United States. We begin with a brief discussion of trends that have expanded the need for decision making, followed by a discussion of decisions related to the initation of pregnancy or parenting, including voluntary childlessness, the use of assisted reproductive technology (ART), and adoption. Agency around pregnancy termination—both voluntary and involuntary—is discussed next. We then address childbearing-related options that assist others to become mothers, including egg donation, surrogacy, and relinquishing a child for adoption.

FACTORS ASSOCIATED WITH EXPANDED DECISION MAKING

Societal changes, along with notable advances in medical technology, have introduced choices that were nearly nonexistent several decades ago. Such trends are allowing women greater agency in the arena of childbearing and motherhood.

Societal Changes

Greater societal acceptance of a range of family units and diversity in life choices have resulted in a growing number of parenting arrangements beyond the traditional married heterosexual couple (e.g., Thornton & Young-DeMarco, 2001). Same-sex marriage is legal in some states, as are adoptions to same-sex couples. Deliberate childbearing and rearing by single mothers also has increased (Abma & Martinez, 2006). Fertility treatment has allowed such women, as well as lesbian couples, the option to bear biological children in the absence of a male partner.

Another societal trend is the increasing delay of childbearing into women's later reproductive years, particularly for those with greater educational attainment and work experience and of higher socioeconomic status (Livingston & Cohn, 2010). There are myriad reasons that women may delay (e.g., establishing a career, waiting to find an appropriate mate). Postponing childbearing may be a decision in itself, but it also can give rise to other decisions. Fertility declines with age, with women 35 years or older considered of "advanced maternal age" and their pregnancies classified as "high risk." Decisions regarding fertility treatment may come into play, which may involve the retrieval and freezing of eggs at an earlier age for later use, as well as a range of options to initiate pregnancy. Once women become pregnant, prenatal screening or genetic testing can necessitate decision making described as follows.

Advances in Reproductive Medicine

The tremendous expansion of knowledge and technology in women's reproductive medicine, such as genetics and reproductive endocrinology, has resulted in greater decision making around childbearing. First, safe and effective contraceptive options for women are greatly expanded (Wasik & Kim, 2011), allowing women greater control over childbearing. Second, significant developments in fertility treatments have expanded options for those who otherwise may be unable to conceive, while the success of treatments involving ovulation induction and embryo transfer simultaneously contribute to the need for decision making. For example, multiple gestations have risen dramatically in recent decades, with more than 70% of all twins and 99% of higher-order multiples resulting from fertility treatment (Evans, Ciorica, Britt, & Fletcher, 2005), presenting decisions related to fetal reduction, as discussed later.

Next, there is increased accuracy and accessibility of prenatal screening and diagnostic tests to detect fetal abnormality prior to birth. The American College of Obstetricians and Gynecologists (ACOG) recommends that all pregnant women, regardless of maternal age, be offered first- and second-trimester screening tests and invasive diagnostic testing (ACOG, 2007a, 2007b). In addition to ultrasound to measure fetal nuchal translucency, the quad marker screening test identifying four substances in the blood suggestive of fetal abnormalities is most commonly used, given its relatively low false-positive rate (American Pregnancy Association, 2009), with risk calculated in conjunction with other factors (e.g., ethnicity and maternal age). Diagnostic tests include (a) chorionic villus sampling (CVS), typically conducted between 10 and 13 weeks' gestation, and involving transcervical or transabdominal removal of placental tissue (ACOG, 2007b; March of Dimes, 2011b); (b) amniocentesis, performed between 15 and 20 weeks' gestation, where fluid is removed from the amniotic sac transabdominally (ACOG, 2007b; March of Dimes, 2011a); and (c) cordocentesis, performed less frequently and later in pregnancy as a follow-up to CVS or amniocentesis, and involving puncturing the umbilical vein (ACOG, 2007b). Ultrasound techniques such as pulsed-wave and color Doppler imaging have improved the ability to detect and help in the management of clinical problems (Dias & Thilaganathan, 2009).

Such technology requires that women make decisions about whether to participate in screening as well as subsequent diagnostic testing, and then how and when they might act (or not) on positive results. Each stage in this process can evoke heightened worry and anxiety. In the case of positive evidence of genetic abnormality or other anomaly, critical decisions regarding termination are necessary. Intrauterine fetal surgery to correct certain congenital issues has become available in certain facilities within the United States (Adzick, 2010), which also involves decision making.

The more routine use of ultrasound may promote attachment (sooner), adding additional complexity to already difficult decisions. Asch (1999) cautions against the unconditional acceptance of disability as precluding life satisfaction, which in turn may promote social endorsement of diagnostic testing as a routine means to identify and end pregnancies in which a disabling trait is evident.

DECISIONS RELATED TO THE INITIATION OF PREGNANCY OR PARENTING

The most fundamental decision regarding childbearing is whether or not to bear children. For many women, the experiences of becoming pregnant and giving birth are longstanding and deeply valued goals. Many women become pregnant without incident and continue on to have successful pregnancies and births. Conversely, a growing number of women choose to remain child-free. For some women who desire children, a variety of circumstances may complicate their ability to become pregnant or carry a pregnancy to term, and they may seek options, including the use of ART or adoption. This section highlights decision making regarding the choice to bear children and trends in utilization, associated stressors, emotional experiences, and decision-making considerations of fertility treatments and adoption.

Choosing To Be Child-Free

Approximately 20% of women in the United States end their childbearing years never having borne a child. This represents a shift from the 1970s, where 10% of women were child-free at the cessation of their childbearing years (Livingston & Cohn, 2010). White, never-married, highly educated women have been most likely to remain child-free, but changing sociodemographic trends are emerging. Between 1994 and 2008, rates of childlessness rose 11% for White women and more than 30% for Black and Hispanic women (Livingston & Cohn, 2010). Marital status and race appear to interact: For married women, rates of childlessness for Blacks and Whites are the same; however, never-married White women are twice as likely to be childless than never-married Black women. Regardless of marital status, Hispanic women have lower rates of childlessness than non-Hispanic women (Livingston & Cohn, 2010). Level of education also influences rates of childlessness;

historically, highly educated women have been most likely to be child-free. Yet, in recent years, rates of childlessness have risen dramatically for the least educated women, with the rate for women with less than a high school diploma rising 66% between 1994 and 2008 (Livingston & Cohn, 2010).

Voluntarily childless refers to women with no known fertility problems who do not wish to bear or raise children at any point in their life. This contrasts with women who may be *temporarily child-free* by choice—that is, those delaying childbearing who have intentions to bear children in the future, and women with impaired fecundity who are *involuntarily childless*. Little research exists on the experiences and decisions of women who choose to live child-free. Varied inclusion criteria regarding birth expectations and biological ability make it challenging to compare results across studies.

Factors Contributing to Choice

The increasingly wider range and availability of effective contraceptive options (e.g., Wasik & Kim, 2011), including female-controlled methods, contribute to women's ability to remain child-free voluntarily. Such access allows women the freedom to make reproductive decisions based on other factors. A host of individual circumstances in women's lives may contribute to this decision. In addition to satisfaction with being child-free, these circumstances might involve their relationship with a life partner; personal, social, or economic resources; medical or health conditions; or competing priorities, to name but a few. In addition, the drive to reproduce and the salience of motherhood just may not be evident. Cost-benefit analyses are employed in decision making around childbearing (Abma & Martinez, 2006). In addition, religious exposure in early life appears to influence childbearing decisions (Pearce, 2002), and lower levels of religiosity in adulthood are connected with being voluntarily childless (Abma & Martinez, 2006).

Personal values regarding the meaning and importance of motherhood, as well as perceptions of societal attitudes and familial pressures, also may influence decision making. Socialization within typical Western culture identifies motherhood as essential to the adult female identity (e.g., Gerson, Posner, & Morris, 1991). Living child-free by choice, therefore, has been stigmatized as deviant and unnatural, and those who choose this lifestyle may be viewed as selfish, cold, immature, and excessively ambitious, yet unfulfilled and unhappy—stereotypes that are unfounded (see Lee, 1998). Ironically, lesbian and single women who *do* choose to become mothers have been similarly stereotyped as selfish and unnatural (Lee, 1998).

In recent decades, society has become increasingly accepting of childlessness and more tolerant of individual choice, placing less social pressure on women to bear children (Thornton & Young-DeMarco, 2001). Approximately 60% of adults in the United States completing the General Social Survey in 2002 disagreed that individuals without children "lead empty lives," and a Pew Research Center poll in 2009 revealed that nearly 50% of individuals believe "it makes no difference one way or the other that a growing share of women do not ever have children" (Livingston & Cohn, 2010). Women's attitudes toward childlessness appear to be more positive than men's (Koropeckyj-Cox & Pendell, 2007). Increasingly, children are seen as less essential for a good marriage (Livingston & Cohn, 2010). Other opportunities, such as improved job and career options for women, seem to have reduced the need to view motherhood as a woman's primary adult role (McQuillan, Greil, Shreffler, & Tichenor, 2008). With greater availability of childcare and family-friendly policies within work settings, such as flexible work hours and institution of the Family and Medical Leave Act of 1993, having a career and childbearing may be more compatible and feasible (Abma & Martinez, 2006), thereby allowing women the choice to develop and maintain a successful career with or without children.

Socioeconomic and Health Considerations

Although the impact of these factors on individual decision making varies, being child-free appears to garner some advantages as well as impose some consequences. For example, married couples and older unmarried women without children tend to have somewhat greater income and wealth than those with children (Plotnick, 2009). In terms of health consequences, nulliparous women (and women with advanced age at first birth) have increased breast cancer incidence (e.g., Simpson et al., 2002; Soerjomataram, Pukkala, Brenner, & Coebergh, 2008). Research has found that childless women report lower life satisfaction than women with children (Hansen, Slagsvold, & Moum, 2009), but that depression levels do not differ between these groups (Bures, Koropeckyj-Cox, & Loree, 2009), suggesting that mental health outcomes may vary according to individual, interpersonal, and cultural factors. Elderly individuals without children are more likely than those with children to either live alone or in an institution (Koropeckyj-Cox & Call, 2007).

Use of ART to Become Pregnant

Several circumstances may contribute to a woman's or couple's decision to undertake fertility treatment, including both medical and nonmedical reasons. Infertility—or an inability to become pregnant within 1 year of regular intercourse without contraception (or within 6 months for women over age 35)—is a primary indication for fertility treatment; however, women may pursue fertility treatment for reasons other than infertility. Such circumstances include threats to fertility imposed by medical circumstances, such as illness, cancer treatment, or premature ovarian failure. Furthermore, women who are single or in same-sex couples may elect to pursue fertility treatments using donor insemination to experience pregnancy or biological parenthood in the absence of a male reproductive partner. For instance, nationally representative data indicate that one-third of lesbian women have given birth (Gates, Badgett, Macomber, & Chambers, 2007), and 69% of female, same-sex households have only biological children living in the household (Krivickas & Lofquist, 2011).

Historically, medical communities have raised ethical concerns regarding provision of fertility treatments to single or lesbian women, including concerns about absence of male father figures, social intolerance and stigma, and child developmental outcomes (Baetens & Brewaeys, 2001; Englert, 1994); however, a review of empirical studies investigating outcomes of reproductive technologies wherein a genetic link exists between only one parent and the child found no evidence of negative parenting or child development outcomes. In fact, some benefits were suggested compared to naturally conceived families, including parent-child relational functioning (Bos & van Balen, 2010). Given the lack of substantiated evidence for concerns about the social well-being of children reared in lesbian households, along with a changing climate of acceptance of diverse lifestyles and family structures, ACOG and the Ethics Committee of the American Society for Reproductive Medicine (ASRM) have issued statements of support for nondiscrimination and equal access to fertility treatment regardless of marital status or sexual orientation (ASRM, 2009).

Within the United States, 12% of married women of reproductive age received at least one fertility-related medical service, and 8.3% received medical assistance to become pregnant in their lifetimes (Chandra, Martinez, Mosher, Abma, & Jones, 2005). Such services included ovulation-inducing medications (used by 3.8% of women), intra-uterine insemination (IUI; used by 1.1% of women), and ART (used by 0.3% of women). White women who are married, without children, over the age of 30, and with higher income and education levels most commonly receive fertility treatments (Chandra et al., 2005). Notable sociodemographic differences exist between populations most commonly receiving fertility services compared to those most likely to experience infertility, which include Hispanic and non-Hispanic Black women and those who have not completed college (Stephen & Chandra, 2006).

Treatment Options The decision to initiate fertility treatment presents many choices, stressors, and challenges for women and couples. Such decisions involve interactions between patients and providers; a review of patient perspectives on fertility treatment highlighted the importance of patient involvement in decision making, personalized care, and respect from providers, as well as the perceived importance and potential shortcomings of information and communication from providers, including information about treatment planning and treatment alternatives (Dancet et al., 2010). Treatment

options include surgeries to repair tubal damage, hormonal ovulation stimulation treatments, IUI, and ART (most commonly, in vitro fertilization [IVF]), each with patient-specific indications. Fertility preservation options, such as ovarian tissue cryopreservation or ovarian stimulation with oocyte or embryo cryopreservation, are also available for women facing threats to their future fertility, including women undergoing cancer treatment, women with certain medical conditions, and adolescents with premature ovarian failure (Centers for Disease Control and Prevention [CDC], 2010; Jensen, Morbeck, & Coddington, 2011). Decisions then must be made regarding unused cryopreserved materials.

Additionally, women may choose to use donor eggs and/or sperm when pursuing IUI or ART; such approaches are commonly utilized by single or lesbian women undergoing fertility treatment. Gametes may be donated anonymously or openly, carrying different considerations regarding treatment costs and decision making; for example, an altruistic "known" sperm donor may influence disclosure-related decisions or desired relationships with the future child, and "open" sperm donors can allow sperm banks to enable communication with future offspring seeking information about their parentage (Amato & Jacob, 2004). Use of donated gametes can present disclosure-related decisions, which can include parents' concerns about stigma and negative psychological consequences for the child (e.g., Murray, MacCallum, & Golombok, 2006; Shehab et al., 2008). Among lesbian couples, ART can involve "co-maternity," in which one woman's egg is fertilized with donor sperm and transferred to the other's uterus. Additionally, options for partial or full surrogacy can enable couples with infertility, lesbian couples, and single women to become parents (as discussed later).

Treatment-Related Stressors/ Decision-Making Considerations

Treatment Outcome Numerous stressors impacting treatment-related decision making are associated with the process of fertility treatment. First, various treatment methods have differential outcomes; for instance, IVF appears to be more efficacious than IUI, with reports that a course of two IUI cycles resulted in fewer live births than just one IVF cycle (27.6% compared to 39.2%), although wide variability is impacted by age, number of follicles, and use of additional ovarian stimulation medications (Chambers et al., 2010; Karuppaswamy, Smedley, & Carter, 2009). Multiple births are not uncommon in either of these treatments (13.3% in IUI and 10.1% in IVF; Chambers et al., 2010). Of note, treatment results may vary among women who elect fertility treatment for medical reasons compared to those who elect fertility treatment for circumstances in the absence of a medical problem (e.g., no male partner). Furthermore, medical and psychosocial circumstances may interact to impact treatment outcome; single women who seek fertility treatment may be older than lesbian or heterosexual, partnered women, having delayed childbearing in the absence of a male partner and consequently pursuing fertility treatment later in life (Leiblum, Palmer, & Spector, 1995), when outcomes tend to be less favorable (CDC, 2010).

Financial Considerations Fertility treatments are very expensive and may be cost prohibitive for many, contributing significant stress and impacting medical decision making related to fertility treatment. In 2011, median per-patient costs ranged from $1,182 for treatment with medication only to $24,373 for IVF and $38,015 for IVF with donor eggs, with much higher cost estimations for successful outcomes when accounting for failed treatment cycles (Katz et al., 2011). Insurance coverage is not mandated in most states (Henne & Bundorf, 2008), and Medicaid does not cover fertility treatment (King & Meyer, 1997). Insurance limitations may partly explain the disparity in fertility treatment access noted among socioeconomically disadvantaged populations.

Several financial options may be available to those struggling to afford fertility treatment, including pursuing less expensive fertility treatments (e.g., ovulation stimulation medications), which may not fully meet their needs (Mundy, 2003). Other options include obtaining loans from fertility financing companies or charitable grants, participating in gamete donation programs with shared cycles in which the donor and recipient both pursue fertility treatment while the donor is compensated for donating a portion of her eggs, or participating in clinical trials with reduced treatment costs (www.resolve .org). Future research should examine the impact of financial resources by which fertility services may become available to less-advantaged populations.

Psychosocial Stressors The experience of receiving fertility treatment is marked by significant stress, particularly among women (e.g., Freeman, Boxer, Rickels, Tureck, & Mastroianni, 1985). Such stress may be related to a woman's valuation of motherhood, relational strain related to infertility and treatment (e.g., necessity to time intercourse, mood swings caused by hormonal treatments), social challenges and perceived stigma, and attributions of infertility to a personal failure (Abbey, Halman, & Andrews, 1992; Newton, Sherrard, & Glavac, 1999; Slade, O'Neill, Simpson, & Lashen, 2007; Whiteford & Gonzalez, 1995). The significant psychosocial consequences of infertility are described by Prince and Domar in Chapter 14 of this volume. Distinguishing the negative impact of fertility treatment from that of the infertility condition is challenging, because most studies assess a sample that has experienced both of these stressors, and methodological characteristics vary widely across studies. However, one review reported that despite mixed findings, many studies have found that women are psychologically well-adjusted upon entering fertility treatment, but they become significantly depressed during or after treatment (Eugster & Vingerhoets, 1999), suggesting that treatment experiences contribute unique, deleterious effects on psychosocial well-being.

Specific circumstances may contribute additional stress and decision-making challenges for some women seeking treatment, including those pursuing treatment for non-medical reasons, who have received less attention in the literature. For example, for lesbian women, pursuing fertility treatment can prompt considerations about whether and how to "come out" to treatment providers, which can accompany concerns about homophobia and its impact on treatment (McManus, Hunter, & Renn, 2006). Evidence suggests that sufficient social support and encouragement might be particularly salient in the decision to initiate fertility treatment among lesbian women, who were found to be more likely than single women to report this support at treatment initiation (Leiblum et al., 1995). Other considerations

for lesbian women and couples can include selection of a known or anonymous sperm donor, decisions about which partner will carry the child, and negotiation of each partner's role in parenting (for a review, see McManus et al., 2006). Given the specific stressors and decision-making challenges for lesbian women seeking fertility treatment, healthcare providers should be knowledgeable about their unique experiences, be open, nonjudgmental, and nonheteronormative, and acknowledge the important role of the co-mother (Werner & Westerstahl, 2008). Single women pursuing fertility treatment may experience similar concerns related to social stigma, concerns about rejection from medical providers, and concerns about selection of sperm donors. Additionally, single women were more likely than lesbian women to report the feeling that "time was running out" at the time of treatment initiation (Leiblum et al., 1995).

The use of donated gametes in fertility treatment also presents several decision-making challenges. For instance, heterosexual couples who have been unable to conceive with their own gametes may face decisions regarding whether to pursue gamete donation or to terminate fertility treatment. Women may consider the importance of procreating with their own genetic material and/or that of their partner's, the importance of experiencing pregnancy and childbirth, and the importance of becoming a parent through any possible means (e.g., adoption), which might involve conflicting emotions and cognitions within and between partners. Furthermore, women utilizing donated gametes typically face a decision of whether and/or how to disclose this information to others, including to the conceived child. Opinions regarding disclosure may differ between partners, requiring extensive negotiation; factors such as social and cultural climates surrounding the couple, religious and cultural backgrounds, ethical belief systems, counseling, and professional opinions may influence disclosure decisions (Shehab et al., 2008). Counseling appears to be well-received by donor oocyte recipients, particularly counseling addressing disclosure and future interactions between the donor and offspring (Hammarberg, Carmichael, Tinney, & Mulder, 2008). Literature exploring such issues is in its infancy, with the majority utilizing retrospective, descriptive, and exploratory designs (Hershberger, 2004).

Questions have been raised regarding potential differences between psychosocial experiences of women conceiving through fertility treatments compared to those conceiving spontaneously, both during and after pregnancy. A comprehensive review of literature related to these experiences in heterosexual couples receiving ART (see Hammarberg, Fisher, & Wynter, 2008) revealed variable findings. Generally, studies suggested similar, low rates of depressive symptoms during ART and spontaneous pregnancies, with mixed reports of elevated anxiety during ART pregnancies. Specific anxieties might relate to fetal health or pregnancy stability. ART might impact adjustment to pregnancy, with some reporting delayed fetal attachment or delayed belief of pregnancy status because of a desire for emotional self-preservation. Several studies indicated that postpartum depressive symptoms and distress are similar between mothers conceiving with ART or spontaneously (e.g., Glazebrook, Sheard, Cox, Oates, & Ndukwe, 2004). Such findings suggest that stresses of infertility and fertility treatment do not necessarily dissipate with a successful pregnancy or birth, informing clinical considerations for couples managing the outcomes of fertility treatment.

Psychosocial stressors and reactions can impact women's treatment-related decision making. For instance, women with elevated depressive symptomatology appear less likely to initiate fertility treatment (Eisenberg et al., 2010), and psychological distress is a leading reason for treatment attrition when controlling for poor prognosis or financial hardship (e.g., Domar, 2004). Emotional distress can relate to cycles of hope and disappointment and perceptions of loss of control. Conversely, one survey found that three-quarters of women reported that their desire for a child eclipsed other life domains, and many providers indicated that such overwhelming desires have impacted women's decision-making capacity regarding when to terminate fertility treatment (Rauprich, Berns, & Vollmann, 2011). If and when a woman decides to terminate treatment without a successful outcome, she may face additional decisions regarding whether to pursue alternative family-building solutions through adoption or to remain child-free and consequently face significant psychosocial experiences and decision-making considerations.

Adoption

Adoption is the process by which children are brought into families by legalizing a relationship between adults and nonbiological children. In 2008, approximately 136,000 adoptions occurred in the United States, a 6% increase from 2000 (Child Welfare Information Gateway [CWIG], 2011; Flango & Flango, 1995). Approximately three-quarters of U.S. adoptions are domestic (Vandivere, Malm, & Radel, 2009). Over the past 30 years, availability of domestic adoption has declined, because of decreases in the adolescent birthrate, increases in the number of women choosing to raise children born from unwanted pregnancies, and government policies designed to keep biological families intact and increase adoptions by relatives (CWIG, 2011). While demand for inter-country adoptions in the United States consequently has risen (Jones, 2007), the rate of international adoptions has been declining since 2004 because changes in several nations' policies have created significant obstacles to international adoptions to the United States (Vandivere et al., 2009). Forty percent of adopted children in the United States are adopted by parents of a different race, culture, or ethnicity, primarily as a result of international adoption (CWIG, 2010).

Characteristics of Women Who Adopt

Among women aged 18 to 44 in the United States, 1.1% adopted a child and 1.6% (1 million women) sought to adopt in 2002 (CWIG, 2011). Several factors may motivate women's decisions to adopt. Adoptive parents most frequently cite "wanting to provide a permanent home for a child in need" (81%), followed by wanting to add to their family (69%), fertility difficulties (52%), desiring a sibling for a child (24%), and having already adopted the child's sibling (7%). Parents adopting from foster care are more likely to report being motivated by having previously adopted the child's sibling, and they are least likely to have been motivated by infertility (Vandivere et al., 2009).

One-third of all women in the United States of reproductive age have considered adoption at some point. This proportion does not vary by age or parity. Overall, 4.7% of women in the United States have ever taken steps to adopt a child. Women who seek to adopt are typically 30 to 44 years old and married. Hispanic or non-Hispanic Black women with other children are also more likely to seek adoption. Neither income nor education appears to affect women's choice to seek adoption (Jones, 2007).

A smaller proportion, representing approximately 1.6% of women in the United States, has completed an adoption. Women who adopt are typically between 40 to 44 years old, nulliparous, and have a history of fertility service usage. Age, income, race, and marital status are also factors in completed adoption rates; women who are older, with income between 150% and 299% above the poverty level, who are non-Hispanic White, and in their second marriage or later, are more likely to complete adoption. However, 17% of women who have adopted have never been married (CWIG, 2011; Jones, 2007). Fecundity status substantially impacts many women's adoption decisions. Seven out of 10 women who have considered adoption have also used fertility services. History of fertility services is associated with both considering and seeking adoption. One-fourth of nulliparous women aged 40 to 44 who have used infertility services have adopted a child (Jones, 2007).

Stressors Related to Adoption

The adoption process can be complex and is associated with stressors both before and after completing adoption. The majority of published literature reports on adoptive parents in general; therefore, we use the term "parents" unless the cited research reports a gender distinction.

Prospective adoptive parents must comply with adoption laws as well as applicable international regulations, and they may have to undergo a home study to evaluate their eligibility for adoption. Prospective parents may struggle with deciding whether to adopt, their preferred type of adoption, whether to use an adoption service provider, and how to prepare for a home study. An additional challenge is the uncertain and often lengthy nature of the adoption process (CWIG, 2010). Cost can be a major factor, particularly in private and international adoptions (Vandivere et al., 2009). Given these potential stressors, prospective adoptive parents may experience anxiety or a disruption in routine during the adoption process. When an adoption is not successfully completed, prospective parents may experience significant distress, and a sense of loss and grief, particularly if they already met the child (CWIG, 2010).

Following adoption, parents commonly experience a honeymoon period with their adopted child. However, adjustment following adoption can be complicated by several factors. Physical, emotional, and developmental difficulties in adoptive children, all of which are more likely in children adopted from foster care, can be stressors to parents (Vandivere et al., 2009). Adoption type can influence stressors. In open adoptions, parents may have concerns about adoptive children becoming confused about their role within the family, or they may be anxious about interactions with the children's biological family. In international adoptions, parents may struggle with lack of sufficient background about the child's life prior to adoption, or they may have distressing encounters with individuals disapproving of transcultural adoptions. In adoptions from foster care, adoptive children may begin demonstrating aversive behaviors to "test" their relationship with their parents. Parents may also struggle with conflicting feelings about their child's biological family (CWIG, 2010). Lack of postadoption support is another potential stressor.

Approximately 30% of adoptive parents report not receiving at least one needed adoption-related support (e.g., parent trainings, online resources, meetings with agency staff; Vandivere et al., 2009).

Adoptive Parents' Well-Being and Mental Health

Most parents fare well following adoption, reporting high relationship quality; 53% of adoptive parents report coping "very well" with adoptive parenting (Vandivere et al., 2009). Distress rates in adoptive parents appear to be lower compared with biological parents (McKay, Ross, & Goldberg, 2010). Adoptive mothers report lower rates of anxiety and higher levels of well-being, compared with biological mothers (Mott, Schiller, Richards, O'Hara, & Stuart, 2011).

Parental stress and mental health problems do sometimes occur. Parents of adopted children, particularly those who adopted from foster care, are somewhat more likely to report experiencing parental stress than the general parent population in the United States (11% versus 6%; Vandivere et al., 2009). Some adoptive parents also may experience post-adoption depression syndrome (PADS), possibly caused by tedium, lack of sleep, and pressure of parental responsibilities that can accompany adoption. PADS has been characterized by mothers' difficulties becoming attached to the adopted child and doubts about their parental efficacy (CWIG, 2010). Rates of depressive symptomology in adoptive parents range from 8% to 32%, depending on how depression is assessed (McKay et al., 2010).

Factors associated with post-adoption maternal depression include preexisting depressive symptoms and sleep difficulties, mothers' expectations (or actual presence) of behavioral or emotional problems in the adoptive child, and more children in the family before adoption (Gair, 1999; Viana & Welsh, 2010). Additionally, adoptive mothers with histories of infertility, previous mental health problems, and lower marital satisfaction may be more likely to experience depression in the first year following adoption. Of note, mothers' preadoption perceived social support predicts lower rates of post-adoption stress (Viana & Welsh, 2010).

Adoptive parents may also struggle adjusting to their new identity and role, as some adoptive parents report doubts about being "legitimate" parents or not loving their child "quickly enough." The lack of role models in adoption may exacerbate these identity difficulties (CWIG, 2010). Relationship quality may also suffer in some parents following adoption. A study of 125 adoptive couples revealed that relationship quality tends to decline in the first year post-adoption, regardless of sexual orientation (Goldberg, Smith, & Kashy, 2010). Parents reporting higher preadoption depression levels, relationship maintenance behaviors, and confrontative coping were at greatest risk for post-adoption declines in relationship quality. Despite obstacles sometimes present with adoption, most adoptive mothers are satisfied with their decision to adopt. Eighty-seven percent of adopted children have parents who reported they would "definitively" decide again to adopt their child, while 3% of adoptive children's parents reported they would "probably" or "definitely" not have adopted their child (Vandivere et al., 2009).

Adoptions among Sexual Minorities and Same-Sex Couples
The number of adoptive parents in the United States identifying as gay and lesbian continues to rise. National adoption data demonstrated that 2 million gay and lesbian individuals are interested in adoption, 14,100 foster children live with parents who are sexual minorities, and 65,000 adopted children (4% of the total adopted population) live with a parent identifying as either gay or lesbian (Gates et al., 2007).

Sexual minorities may face additional adoption-related obstacles resulting from stigma and discrimination. For example, state policies are highly varied in the degree to which they allow sexual minorities to adopt (Gates et al., 2007). Even in states that do not ban such adoptions, preferences and biases of adoption agencies and social workers may obstruct sexual minorities from adopting. Other adoption-related stressors include difficulties identifying gay-friendly adoption agencies and lack of family support, and stigma regarding transracial adoptions (Kinkler & Goldberg, 2011). Lesbian and bisexual women may experience multiple, intersecting stigmas when they adopt, given that their sexual orientation, adoptive parent status, and the race of their adoptive child may be considered "non-normative" (Richardson & Goldberg, 2010).

Research about mental health outcomes of sexual minority adoptive mothers is limited. However, a recent study revealed that higher perceived workplace support, social support, neighborhood "gay friendliness," and lower internalized homophobia are associated with lower anxiety or depression in this population, while living in areas with stricter gay adoption policies is associated with greater depression and anxiety (Goldberg & Smith, 2011). It should also be noted that, compared with heterosexual women, lesbians report less commitment to having a biological child, and they may experience a less-challenging transition from fertility treatment to adoption (Goldberg, Downing, & Richardson, 2009).

AGENCY SURROUNDING THE ENDING OF PREGNANCIES

Pregnancy is not a positive event for all women (see Geller, 2004). Sometimes pregnancies are unplanned or occur at times, under circumstances or with information that warrant decisions about the continuation of the pregnancy. In addition, positive pregnancy outcomes do not occur for all women or for all pregnancies. This section reviews decision-making with regard to pregnancy termination, as well as spontaneous adverse outcomes where decision-making options are limited.

Induced Abortion

Induced abortion involves the deliberate termination of a pregnancy and has been subcategorized into *therapeutic*, where decisions center on the health of the mother or the fetus, and *elective*, which is voluntary termination for any other reason. Both surgical and medical procedures are available. Surgical procedures, including dilation and curettage (D&C), dilation and evacuation (D&E), and vacuum aspiration, account for the vast majority of elective abortions and are most commonly performed at or prior to 13 weeks' gestation, but they may also be performed later in a pregnancy. Nonsurgical procedures, such as medical abortion with mifepristone, are safe for use in early-term abortions and account for 13.1% of abortions (Pazol et al., 2011). Since mifepristone was introduced in 2000, its utilization for early-term abortions has increased, while utilization of curettage procedures has declined, except in abortions performed beyond 13 weeks' gestation. Dilation and extraction (D&X; or Intra-uterine Cranial Decompression), which is

performed after 21 weeks, is not permitted in the United States per the *Partial-Birth Abortion Ban Act of 2003*, except under certain circumstances. Most states stipulate a specific gestational age limit for abortion procedures, which is most typically that of fetal viability (Guttmacher Institute, 2011); late-stage abortion remains controversial.

Therapeutic Abortion Therapeutic abortion is performed following medical advisement for reasons impacting maternal and/or fetal health. Specifically, abortion may be recommended in order to save the life of the pregnant woman, preserve the woman's physical or mental health, or prevent the birth of a child with a congenital disorder that otherwise would be fatal or associated with significant morbidity. Another type of therapeutic abortion is fetal reduction in multiple pregnancies, which involves the selective abortion of one (or more) fetus(es) identified with severe anomaly, or reducing the number of fetuses to lessen health risks of multiple conceptions; these include perinatal morbidity and loss associated with preterm birth, intrauterine growth restriction, and respiratory complications and maternal risks, such as gestational diabetes, preeclampsia, and postpartum hemorrhage (e.g., Evans et al., 2005). When therapeutic abortion is recommended because of an abnormality in a fetus (as opposed to selective reduction of multiples derived from fertility treatment, where women may be somewhat prepared for this possibility), the news may be especially shocking.

Women and their partners face decisions after being informed of medical circumstances prompting the recommendation of therapeutic abortion. The primary decision is whether to take action (e.g., induce labor or termination; selectively reduce), as opposed to allowing the pregnancy to follow its natural course despite risks of maternal or perinatal morbidity and mortality. In addition to contextual factors similar to those surrounding elective abortion (as discussed later), considerations that may influence women's decision making include the types of procedures available given the woman's or fetus's medical condition and the stage of the pregnancy. For women receiving a positive prenatal diagnosis of Down syndrome, considerations also include anticipated burden and reward of parenting, quality of life for the child, attitude toward and comfort with people with disabilities, and social support (Choi, Van Riper, & Thoyre, 2012).

With fetal reduction, the implications of risk for the mother and the remaining fetus(es) if reduction does not occur is also a critical consideration. Although outcomes are generally good, the potential consequences of the procedure itself, such as pregnancy loss, possible morbidity with the surviving fetus(es), and an additional risk of premature ruptured membranes and preterm delivery, also are important considerations (Morris & Kilby, 2010). That pregnancies may be planned, strongly desired, and possibly difficult to achieve in the first place may exacerbate feelings of uncertainty, grief, and despair as parents struggle with decision making (Garel et al., 1997). Moral, religious, and ethical issues are complex, and clearly may contribute to the stress and struggle surrounding decision making.

Following therapeutic abortion, psychological responses can be similar to those following perinatal loss; however, feelings of regret, shame, and secrecy also may arise. The experience of the procedure as traumatic, as well as the perception that others may pass judgment about their "decision," may add to distress, especially when a woman or her partner's attitude toward abortion may not be favorable. Although acute emotional pain has been shown to lessen with time (see Garel et al., 1997), genetic and grief counseling may help limit the severity of the grief reaction.

Elective Abortion   Elective abortion has been legal in the United States since the 1973 Supreme Court ruling in the case of *Roe v. Wade*. Roughly half of pregnancies in the United States are unintended, 42% of which end in elective abortion (Finer & Henshaw, 2006). In 2007, the CDC reported more than 827,000 elective abortions, occurring in 16 out of every 1,000 women of reproductive age. The substantial majority are performed in younger women, with more than half of abortions in 2007, and historically, performed for women aged 20 to 29 and 16.5% performed for adolescents aged 15 to 19. The overall abortion rate has declined in recent years, reflecting a decrease in younger women but an increase among women older than 35. Racial and ethnic disparities are observed in abortion rates; non–Hispanic Black women represent the highest abortion rate relative to other groups. Unmarried women account for nearly 84% of all abortions (Pazol et al., 2011).

Contextual   Considerations   Decision making related to elective abortion is complicated by contextual factors that may influence women's choices. The emotional experiences surrounding elective abortion have been pivotal topics of debate among various political, religious, and scientific communities over the past several decades, with significant clinical and practical consequences, as beliefs regarding psychological outcomes have the potential to influence legislative policy. Furthermore, the scientific literature addressing psychological consequences and experiences may be biased by subjective beliefs, underscoring the need for well-designed, methodologically rigorous studies to elucidate women's experiences (Kornfield & Geller, 2010). It is therefore important to note these potential influences on both patients and providers in their decision making surrounding elective abortion.

It is also critical to consider decisions regarding elective abortion within the broader psychosocial context, which may be influential in many ways. First, the context of the pregnancy is inextricable from elective abortion; circumstances surrounding conception and psychosocial coping resources influence both the impact of an unwanted pregnancy and the impact of aborting an unwanted pregnancy, which could reduce or exacerbate stress (Adler et al., 1990, 1992). Additionally, the emotional and mental health consequences of abortion for unwanted pregnancies are best understood in the context of possible alternative resolutions, underscoring the importance of appropriate comparisons against which to evaluate the impact of abortion—evaluating abortion in the context of an alternative "state of nonpregnancy" is erroneous (Major et al., 2009, p. 865).

Also contextually relevant is the setting of stigma in which abortion is commonly experienced (Major et al., 2009), which might impact decision making and emotional experiences after abortion. Perceived stigma may relate to attributions of personhood to the fetus, placement of legal restrictions on access to abortion, content of anti–abortion campaigns, and perceptions that abortion is dirty or unhealthy; stigma is perpetuated by the privacy surrounding the abortion experience for many women (Norris et al., 2011). Stigma has also been discussed in relation to perceived "transgressions" of cultural feminine

ideals, including fertility, motherhood, and nurturance (Kumar, Hessini, & Mitchell, 2009). Stigma has been associated with psychological distress via its association with increased secrecy, which in turn leads to increased thought suppression and decreased emotional disclosure (Major & Gramzow, 1999). Preliminary results from an intervention developed to provide a "culture of support" for women following abortion suggest a protective effect against the impact of social stigma (Littman, Zarcadoolas, & Jacobs, 2009), providing some evidence that stigmatization is malleable.

Decision-Making Considerations Given these many contextual variables, women considering abortions are faced with what may be a difficult decision involving multiple factors related to the woman, the unborn child, existing children, the partner and other significant relationships, and financial considerations (Bankole, Susheela, & Haas, 1998; Kirkman, Rosenthal, Mallett, Rowe, & Hardiman, 2010; Kirkman, Rowe, Hardiman, Mallett, & Rosenthal, 2009). An early study exploring the decision-making process surrounding abortion found that it is often conflicted and may be influenced by attitudes about abortion ethics, knowledge of role models for single parenthood, and abortion histories among friends and relatives (Bracken, Klerman, & Bracken, 1978). Women may experience ambivalence when they recognize reasons to continue the pregnancy yet choose abortion because its benefits are assessed to outweigh its harms (Kirkman et al., 2009). Emotional factors such as denial and fear may contribute to delays in obtaining abortion care (Foster et al., 2008), but fewer than 40% of women cite difficulty making the decision to undergo abortion as a factor in delaying the procedure (Finer, Frohwirth, Dauphinee, Singh, & Moore, 2006).

Reasons for choosing abortion also reflect the context in which abortion-related decisions are made. The most common reasons have been reported as interference of having a child with other commitments, such as education, work, or other childcare responsibilities (74%), inability to afford a baby (73%), and not wanting to be a single mother or presence of relationship problems (48%). Among this sample, one-quarter reported having completed their childbearing, while one-third were not yet ready to have a child (Finer, Frohwirth, Dauphinee, Singh, & Moore, 2005). Other reasons include inappropriate timing, being too young, not wanting children, problematic relationship with the intimate partner, concern for the well-being of the potential child or existing children, the influence of others, and less commonly, violence or sexual assault (Kirkman et al., 2009).

Psychosocial Consequences The psychosocial consequences of elective abortion have been explored in numerous empirical studies. When interpreting outcomes, it is important to consider limitations of this body of research, particularly common methodological variability and flaws. These include inappropriate comparison groups failing to account for critical variables (e.g., wantedness of pregnancy); sampling bias resulting from reliance on volunteers; timing of assessment (e.g., lack of baseline data against which to compare post-abortion status; short-term assessment windows); insufficient attention to contextual and individual historical factors (e.g., reproductive history; psychological history); and lack of control for co-occurring risk factors (Adler et al., 1990; Major et al., 2009).

Furthermore, Major et al. (2009) emphasized significant contextual frameworks influencing the study and interpretation of abortion experiences, such as the influence of stigma on negative emotions and risk factors co-occurring with abortion, such as systemic, behavioral, and personality factors, which can pose independent risk for mental health problems.

While the experiences of individual women vary greatly and may include emotions ranging from grief, regret, guilt, and loss to relief and happiness, broad-based reviews have noted that overall, adult women who have received abortions do not report significant psychological distress and uncommonly experience severe, negative reactions (Adler et al., 1990, 1992; Major et al., 2009). Bradshaw and Slade (2003) concluded that the mental health of women who have had abortions is comparable to those who have given birth to both wanted and unwanted children. Of note, an alternative option to abortion would be to carry an unwanted pregnancy to term, which may result in other serious, negative outcomes for both the mother and child (see Kornfield & Geller, 2010).

Overall, critical reviews of the scientific literature produced in the past 50 years have agreed that rigorously designed studies utilizing appropriate samples, comparison groups, assessment techniques, and controls indicate a lack of pervasive, deleterious psychosocial consequences of elective abortion (e.g., Adler et al., 1990, 1992; Major et al., 2009; Romans-Clarkson, 1989). In response to claims that elective abortion may result in post-abortion syndrome, a traumatic emotional reaction presenting months or years after an abortion, Charles, Polis, Sridhara, and Blum (2008) reviewed studies assessing long-term emotional consequences, finding that studies of the highest quality produced the most neutral results, indicating few differences between the mental health sequelae of women receiving abortions and appropriate comparison groups. Conversely, lower-quality studies reported more negative psychosocial sequelae of elective abortion. Importantly, existing literature does not support causal conclusions between abortion and negative psychological experiences when they are detected (Major et al., 2009).

However, negative post-abortion experiences have been reported. Risk factors for negative emotion following abortion are typically noted, including prior depression, history of psychiatric instability, younger age, first pregnancy, termination of a pregnancy that is wanted and meaningful to the woman, decisional coercion, decisional conflict, self-blame for the pregnancy, perceptions of poor support from partner or parents, perceptions of stigma and need to maintain secrecy, poor coping self-efficacy, ambivalence about the procedure, delay of abortion until the second trimester, and negative attitudes about abortion (Adler et al., 1992; Andrews & Boyle, 2003; Major et al., 2009; Major et al., 2000; Romans-Clarkson, 1989). Past history of mental health problems appears to be the strongest predictor of negative mental health sequelae following elective abortion (Major et al., 2009).

Engaging in preabortion decision making and locating post-abortion social support have been identified as primary challenges in qualitative analysis of interviews with women experiencing emotional distress following abortion. Decision-making experiences tended to be distressing when women perceived external pressure related to the decision and tended to be improved when women felt autonomous and empowered to make an independent choice. Following abortion, women perceiving an absence of available social support or unsupportive social reactions demonstrated worse emotional outcomes (Kimport, Foster, & Weitz, 2011).

Perinatal Loss

When women experience spontaneous adverse events during pregnancy or within the 30 days following childbirth, there is a distinct lack of agency. Such events can be extremely stressful and impact not only women's parenting status but also women's mental health. The umbrella term "pregnancy loss" refers to fetal mortality, defined as "the intrauterine death of a fetus at any gestational age" (MacDorman & Kirmeyer, 2009). An estimated 1 million fetal deaths occur per year in the United States, the majority occurring prior to 20 weeks completed gestation (Ventura, Abma, Mosher, & Henshaw, 2008). Following a 1.4% annual decline of fetal deaths between 1999 and 2003, the fetal mortality rate has recently plateaued (MacDorman & Kirmeyer, 2009).

Fetal mortality is typically classified into two major categories: miscarriage and stillbirth. The definitions of these terms are not consistent across studies, and they tend to overlap. Miscarriage is defined as the unintended termination of pregnancy before 20 weeks' gestation in clinical practice (ACOG, 2005) and prior to 27 weeks in research studies (e.g., Neugebauer et al., 1992). Miscarriage is estimated to occur in 30% to 50% of conceptions and in 10% to 15% of clinically recognized pregnancies (ACOG, 2005; Michels & Tiu, 2007; Stephenson & Kutteh, 2007). Rates vary by maternal age, ranging from 9% for women between the ages of 20 and 24 to 75% for women over 45 (Andersen, Wohlfahrt, Christens, Olsen, & Melbye, 2000). The rate of miscarriage is difficult to calculate, because many women do not realize they are pregnant at the time of miscarriage, and the U.S. Department of Health does not record fetal losses that occur earlier than 20 weeks' completed gestation. Approximately 26,000 stillbirths (i.e., fetal death occurring at or after the 20th week of gestation; ACOG, 2009) are reported in the United States every year; in 2005, the stillbirth rate in the United States was 6.22 per 1,000 live births (MacDorman & Kirmeyer, 2009). In 2009, neonatal death, defined as the death of an infant in the first 28 days of life, occurred in approximately 4.19 per 1,000 live births (Kochanek, Xu, Murphy, Miniño, & Kung, 2011). Approximately 19,000 neonatal deaths (a rate of 4.42 per 1,000 live births) occurred in the United States in 2007 (Xu, Kochanek, Murphy, & Tejada-Vera, 2010).

Risk Factors and Etiology Many pregnancy losses are medically unexplained. Among the most common known causes of fetal loss is chromosomal abnormality (e.g., Down syndrome, Turner syndrome), which is responsible for approximately 50% of fetal deaths (ACOG, 2005; Jacobs & Hassold, 1987). Although not routinely investigated until multiple miscarriages occur, some miscarriages are caused by maternal infections (e.g., HPV, streptococcus, uterine infection) or other maternal health problems, including hormonal imbalance and thrombophilia (ACOG, 2005). Uterine fibroids and anatomical defects of the cervix or uterus are linked to second-trimester and recurrent miscarriages (ACOG, 2005; March of Dimes, 2008).

Fetal growth restriction (FGR), a common cause of stillbirth, is often associated with fetal genetic defects, infection, smoking, or certain maternal diseases (ACOG, 2009). Placental abruption, potentially caused by tobacco and illicit drug use, hypertension, and preeclampsia, is also a common cause of stillbirth (ACOG, 2005).

Additional potential risk factors for pregnancy loss include maternal use of caffeine and exposure to certain toxins (e.g., second-hand smoke), previous pregnancy complications (e.g., preeclampsia), polycystic ovary syndrome, congenital and karyotic anomalies, obesity, some maternal diseases (e.g., diabetes, severe kidney disease, lupus), and stressful life events (ACOG, 2005, 2009; March of Dimes, 2008). Multiple gestation is also a risk factor for fetal loss. In 2005, the likelihood of fetal loss in twin pregnancies was 2.7 times greater than for single gestation; fetal loss was 4.6 times more likely in triplet and higher-order pregnancies (MacDorman & Kirmeyer, 2009), which may be due to higher rates of preterm labor, restricted fetal growth, maternal hypertension, and problems with the placental cord (Goldenberg, Kirby, & Dulhane, 2004). Several groups experience higher rates of fetal mortality. Women who are non-Hispanic Black, teenagers, over the age of 35, unmarried, and who have experienced two or more previous pregnancies are at higher risk of pregnancy loss (MacDorman & Kirmeyer, 2009).

The leading cause of neonatal mortality is premature birth (i.e., delivery before 37 weeks of gestation), causing 25% of neonatal deaths (Matthews, Menacker, & MacDorman, 2004). Survival increases with gestational age. Women who have experienced previous preterm deliveries, have certain cervical or uterine problems, and who are pregnant with multiples are at greater risk of premature delivery (March of Dimes, 2010).

The leading causes of death for preterm infants, particularly those born before 32 weeks of pregnancy, are respiratory distress syndrome, intraventricular hemorrhage, necrotizing enterocolitis, and certain infections (e.g., pneumonia, sepsis, meningitis), with birth defects accounting for an additional 20% of neonatal deaths (March of Dimes, 2010; Xu et al., 2010).

Emotional Aspects of Perinatal Loss

Given both the physical and psychological aspects, pregnancy loss has been identified as a traumatic event for nearly five decades (Cain, Erikson, Fast, & Vaughan, 1964; Saraiya et al., 1999). Pregnancy loss can be a rapid and unexpected event that is potentially life-threatening to the mother, involving severe physical pain (Grimes, 2006) and the delivery of a dead or terminally ill infant. For many mothers, the unexpected termination of pregnancy is associated with several profound losses: the loss of the baby and the imagined life with the child, the end of an envisioned dream of motherhood, and the loss of an identity as a "normal," healthy parent (Brier, 1999; Diamond, Diamond, & Jaffe, 2005; Worden, 2000). The often medically unexplained nature of spontaneous pregnancy loss can also be distressing (Klier, Geller, & Ritsher, 2002).

Consequently, pregnancy loss is associated with several adverse psychological outcomes. Women who experience miscarriage are at greater risk for depressive symptoms (e.g., Janssen, Cuisinier, Hoogduin, & De Graauw, 1996), as well as minor and major depressive disorder (MDD; Klier et al., 2002; Neugebauer et al., 1997). Women who miscarry have a 5.2 times greater risk of developing MDD than comparable community women, with previous history of MDD as a predisposing factor. Neither gestational age at time of loss nor the woman's attitude toward the pregnancy (i.e., whether the pregnancy was wanted) are identified risk factors for depression (Klier, Geller, & Neugebauer, 2000; Neugebauer et al., 1997). Fetal loss is also a risk factor for elevated anxiety symptoms and development or recurrence of certain anxiety disorders, including obsessive-compulsive disorder and post-traumatic stress disorder (PTSD; e.g., Brier, 2004; Engelhard, van den Hout, & Arntz, 2001; Geller, Klier, & Neugebauer, 2001; Lee & Slade, 1996). Stillbirth also is a risk factor for depression and anxiety (Hughes, Turton, & Evans, 1999), and long-term consequences can include PTSD and relationship difficulties (Turton, Evans, & Hughes, 2008).

An intense grief reaction, which can involve guilt, self-blame, and lower self-esteem, often follows pregnancy loss (Brier, 1999, 2008; Worden, 2000). Many women also worry about subsequent pregnancies and possible infertility (Gaudet, Sejourne, Camborieux, Rogers, & Chabrol, 2010; Geller, Woodland & Daetwyler, 2008). Women with limited social support may experience more severe grief and greater risk of psychological symptoms following loss (Cacciatore, Schnebly, & Froen, 2009; Lancaster et al., 2010). Women experiencing multiple losses may decide to attempt fertility treatment, which is associated with further challenges. Following stillbirth, women must make difficult decisions regarding whether to view, hold, and photograph their stillborn child, which potentially may impact emotional responses during subsequent pregnancies (Hughes, Turton, Hopper, & Evans, 2002).

Neonatal death is associated with many of the same emotional experiences (e.g., grief, stress, coping) as pregnancy loss (Boyle, Vance, Najman, & Thearle, 1996; Dyer, 2005; Romesberg, 2004). However, unique factors related to neonatal death also can cause distress, including the "rollercoaster" of hope and despair that frequently characterizes the acute period prior to the newborn infant's death in the neonatal intensive care unit (NICU), choosing when and how to deliver following a diagnosis of fetal demise, and making decisions regarding the infant's remains (Davis & Stein, 2004; Sears, Sears, Sears, & Sears, 2004).

Subsequent Pregnancies As many as half of women experiencing perinatal loss become pregnant again within a year, with such subsequent pregnancies involving heightened maternal anxiety (e.g., Armstrong, 2004; Bergner, Beyer, Klapp, & Rauchfuss, 2008). Risk for developing depression and anxiety in subsequent pregnancies may be associated with time since loss, requiring women to decide when to attempt conception again (Hughes et al., 1999; Janssen et al., 1996; Turton, Hughes, Evans, & Fainman, 2001). Although some women may have difficulty with attachment, subsequent pregnancies may have a beneficial effect, with post-loss pregnancies associated with reduced grief and despair (Armstrong & Hutti, 1998; Franche & Bulow, 1999). The pattern of elevated symptoms during subsequent pregnancy, followed by a rapid decrease in symptoms following delivery, may suggest that this symptomology may be self-limiting, or that having a healthy baby following loss may be healing (Turton et al., 2001). Given that many factors likely contribute to women's well-being following loss and the decision to initiate subsequent pregnancies (e.g., maternal personality, age, advice from relatives; Hughes et al., 1999), providers are encouraged to consider women's individual psychosocial contexts in advising about when to conceive again.

Coping Following Loss Women may choose among several techniques to cope with grief and distress following pregnancy loss. Of note, the extent to which women's coping following loss is an intentional choice is often unclear. A wide range of coping techniques have been used by women who experienced pregnancy loss; these strategies vary in the extent to which they appear to be active, deliberate choices (e.g., seeking social support, religious activity) as opposed to "natural" coping reactions following loss (e.g., anxious or depressive coping, wishful thinking) or avoidance (i.e., not dealing with the loss; Bergner et al., 2008).

Among the more active coping strategies are keeping busy at work, focusing on the positive, and engaging in wishful thinking (Allen & Marks, 1993; McGreal, Evans, & Burrows, 1997). Some women also engaged in self-improvement (e.g., weight loss) and pampering activities (e.g., shopping) to cope with pregnancy loss (Allen & Marks, 1993).

Many women reach out to their social networks following the loss, and "talking about it" is a frequently identified coping technique (Allen and Marks, 1993; Worden, 2000). Religious coping (e.g., seeking a stronger connection with God, praying) is a common coping strategy following perinatal loss (e.g., Cowchock, Lasker, Toedter, Skumanich, & Koenig, 2009; McGreal et al., 1997). Some women also attend support groups and seek information about the loss (Kavanaugh, 1997; McGreal et al., 1997). Several rituals, including gathering mementos of the lost pregnancy (e.g., a lock of hair, ultrasound pictures), naming the baby, having a funeral or memorial service, and writing letters or poems, may facilitate coping following a pregnancy loss (Brier, 1999; Worden, 2000).

Receiving contact and information from medical professionals, both immediately and in the months following the loss, may mitigate women's post-loss psychological symptoms and increase satisfaction with providers' care following loss (Dunn, Goldbach, Lasker, & Toedter, 1991; Geller, Psaros, & Kornfield, 2010; Jind, 2003). ACOG recommends that after-loss care professionals provide emotional support and clear communication about the fetal loss (e.g., autopsy results, cytogenic studies; 2009). Sharing medical information, even if it is inconclusive, with women and their families in a prompt, clear fashion may be helpful (ACOG, 2009; Rushton, 1994). In addition, referral to support resources, including mental health professionals, religious leaders, and peer groups, is recommended (ACOG, 2009).

An emerging trend is the use of online groups and social media networks to cope with pregnancy loss. Women using these resources report valuing the anonymous and convenient nature of online support group use and feeling less isolated in their grief (Gold, Boggs, Mugisha, & Palladino, 2012). A systematic review of online pregnancy loss resources is available (Geller, Psaros, & Kerns, 2006).

Cultural Considerations Fetal mortality in non-Hispanic black women in 2005 was 11.13 per 1,000 live births, a rate 2.3 times greater than non-Hispanic White women. American Indian or Alaska Native women's fetal mortality rates were 29% higher than non-Hispanic White women. Fetal mortality in Hispanic women was 14% higher compared with non-Hispanic White women (MacDorman & Kirmeyer, 2009).

Given the disparity between African American women's rates of loss relative to

any other racial/ethnic groups in the United States, this population has received increased attention by researchers (e.g., Kavanaugh & Hershberger, 2005; Van & Meleis, 2010). African American women's pregnancy loss rates persist even after controlling for age, marital status, education, and income (MacDorman & Kirmeyer, 2009; Schoendorf, Hogue, Kleinman, & Rowley, 1992); the cause of this disparity is not yet determined, but potential contributing factors include differential rates of use and entry into prenatal care, stress, exposure to racism, and maternal depression (Arias, MacDorman, Strobino, & Guyer, 2003; Dominiguez, 2008; Orr, James, & Prince, 2002).

Research regarding other ethnic/racial minority groups' experiences following pregnancy loss is extremely limited. A small-sample qualitative study with a diverse group of women revealed that having a strong social support network and positive relationships with aftercare providers was beneficial to coping following pregnancy loss (Abboud & Liamputtong, 2005). Further research is warranted in this area, particularly given the increasing diversity of the U.S. population.

AGENCY AROUND CHILDBEARING THAT ASSISTS OTHERS TO HAVE CHILDREN

Agency in childbearing includes options that a woman possesses, for various reasons, to assist others who may be unable to bear their own biological children. Third-party reproduction refers to fertility treatments that use donated gametes or embryos or involve traditional or gestational surrogacy (ASRM, 2006). Relinquishment refers to offering one's biological child for adoption to another. The following sections highlight decision-making considerations and psycho-social experiences related to use of third-party reproduction or relinquishment of biological offspring, from the perspective of those assisting others to have children.

Egg Donation

Egg donation, also called oocyte donation, enables women to become pregnant using another woman's eggs. There are several indications for use of donor eggs, including diminished ovarian reserve, advanced reproductive age, history of repeated ART failures or poor oocyte or embryo quality, and concerns that the mother might carry a significant genetic defect. Egg donors may be anonymous or known to the recipient and might be recruited through egg donation programs or agencies, advertisements, or IVF programs obtaining donated eggs from other patients (2008 Guidelines for gamete and embryo donation: A Practice Committee report, 2008). In 2009, roughly 12% of ART treatment cycles utilized fresh or frozen donated eggs or embryos and had better outcomes than nondonor eggs (CDC, 2010), with recipients most often being between the ages of 34 and 41, White, educated, and financially secure. Women and couples may choose to use donated eggs for reasons including a desire for genetically related offspring, a mistrust of adoption, and a desire to conceive and experience pregnancy (Hershberger, 2004).

Use of egg donation is psychologically complex for both the donor and recipient, and research in this area is limited and largely exploratory. Egg donation has raised ethical concerns related to several factors, including concerns that financial compensation might lead donors to minimize the medical or psychological risks of donation and concerns about valuation and commodification of human life and differential compensation for specific donor characteristics (see Financial compensation of oocyte donors, 2007). Donor motives and willingness to donate have been a topic of research interest, with reports indicating that women are fairly evenly divided in expressing potential intentions, uncertain intentions, and unwillingness to donate; positive attitudes surrounding oocyte donation, support and positive attitudes from others, perceived decisional control, less conventional reasons for parenthood, altruistic tendencies, lower religiosity, and existence of a relationship with the recipient (Purewal & van den Akker, 2006, 2009a). Motives supporting decisions to donate vary (e.g., pass on one's genes, compensate for a past abortion), but they appear most commonly to be altruistic and/or financial in nature (Klock, Stout, & Davidson, 2003; Soderstrom-Anttila, 1995; Yee, Hitkari, & Greenblatt, 2007), and donors reporting initial financial motives may later develop altruistic motives (Kalfoglou & Gittelsohn, 2000).

Overall, most donors report positive and satisfying experiences with donation, including feeling supported, perceiving themselves as helpful, and denying regret (Kalfoglou & Gittelsohn, 2000; Purewal & van den Akker, 2009b; Soderstrom-Anttila, 1995). However, negative experiences may be associated with poor treatment outcomes for the recipient or for patient donors themselves, or with medical aspects of donation, including medical risks, time investment, or dissatisfaction with medical care (Ahuja, Mostyn, & Simons, 1997; Ahuja, Simons, Nair, Rimington, & Armar, 2003; Blyth, 2004; Kalfoglou & Gittelsohn, 2000; Klock, et al., 2003; Pearson, 2006). Donors may also experience disappointment about unknown recipient treatment outcomes, have concerns about the implications of resulting offspring, or experience difficulties with relationship boundaries, including feelings of attachment and responsibility to the resulting child if a relationship is maintained (Ahuja et al., 1997; Soderstrom-Anttila, 1995; Yee, Hitkari, & Greenblatt, 2007). Ahuja et al. (1997) found that nearly two-thirds of patient donors and one-third of nonpatient, uncompensated donors would donate again, citing emotional and lifestyle disruption as reasons against donating again, and others have reported that women who were willing to donate again were quicker in their donation decision making, had less donation-related ambivalence, and had higher satisfaction with medical aspects of donation (Klock et al., 2003). Parenting and child developmental outcomes among families created through egg donation tend to be similar to those created with natural conception (Bos & van Balen, 2010; Murray et al., 2006). Given the small body of literature, there remains a need for additional research with larger samples, appropriate comparison groups, and long-term follow-up to better elucidate the experience of egg donation (see Purewal & van den Akker, 2009b, for a discussion).

Surrogacy

Surrogacy refers to arrangements in which one woman carries a pregnancy for another woman or couple, including "traditional surrogacy" (also known as "partial surrogacy") arrangements in which the surrogate's own oocytes are inseminated, and "gestational surrogacy" (also known as "full surrogacy") in which the surrogate carries an embryo created with the gametes of the intended recipients. Indications

may include history of hysterectomy, repeated miscarriages, repeated IVF failure, and medical conditions that are contraindicated with pregnancy (e.g., severe heart disease; Brinsden, 2003). In 2009, roughly 1% of fertility treatment cycles using fresh nondonor eggs used a gestational carrier (CDC, 2010). Surrogacy arrangements generally reflect a contractual agreement in which the surrogate is commissioned to carry a pregnancy for the intended recipient, often receiving financial compensation for the arrangement.

Surrogacy has been referred to as "the most controversial of reproductive innovations," despite its documented utilization dating back to at least the Old Testament (Ciccarelli & Beckman, 2005). Ethical, legal, psychological, and religious concerns have been raised regarding possible coercion and exploitation of the surrogate, distinctions between altruistic and commercial surrogacy arrangements, informed consent, commodification of women and motherhood, and commodification of infants and children, as well as issues of motivation, relationships between surrogates and recipients, relinquishment of the resulting child, and the child's development (Ber, 2000; Blyth, 1994; Brinsden, 2003; Edelmann, 2004; van Niekerk & van Zyl, 1995). Some support surrogacy on the grounds of women's reproductive freedom, whereas others invoke concerns about possible harm to the surrogate, her family, and society, as well as the potential for disputed parentage of the resulting child (Sharma, 2006; van Niekerk & van Zyl, 1995). Public attitudes toward surrogacy appear generally supportive, with more supportive attitudes toward gestational than traditional surrogacy (Constantinidis & Cook, 2012).

Of note, a review of 27 studies of surrogacy indicated that surrogates tended to be married, White women with children, of "modest" but not socioeconomically disadvantaged status, perhaps in part resulting from screening and selection to reduce risk of exploitation, which might help dispel some concerns about coercion and exploitation in decision making to become a surrogate (Ciccarelli & Beckman, 2005); additionally, interviews with surrogates were found to suggest that decisions were self-generated and free of coercion (Blyth, 1994). Altruistic motivations, along with empathy, a sense of achievement, self-fulfillment, and enjoyment of pregnancy, are among reported motives to offer surrogacy (Ciccarelli & Beckman, 2005; Jadva, Murray, Lycett, MacCallum, & Golombok, 2003). Importantly, there remains a need to engage more surrogates in research to enhance the representativeness of research findings (Ciccarelli & Beckman, 2005), as current literature may not capture experiences of all women who serve as surrogates.

Surrogates and commissioning couples appear to report generally positive experiences (MacCallum, Lycett, Murray, Jadva, & Golombok, 2003). Surrogates and commissioning couples are faced with decisions about managing their relationship, and qualitative data suggest that relationships between surrogates and commissioning couples are typically harmonious, with regular contact throughout the pregnancy and at least some involvement of the commissioning couple that was generally perceived as satisfactory (Jadva et al., 2003; MacCallum et al., 2003). For some surrogates, relinquishment of the child can be emotionally distressing, particularly among those who knew the commissioning couple prior to surrogacy (Blyth, 1994; Jadva et al., 2003). In many arrangements, surrogates choose to maintain contact with the child, which has been found to be generally satisfying to both

the surrogate and the commissioning family (MacCallum et al., 2003). Commissioning families appear to have positive psychosocial outcomes, with no differences in familial bonding between families using traditional and gestational surrogacy or those using known or unknown surrogates, with generally positive family adjustment for both parents and children (Golombok, MacCallum, Murray, Lycett, & Jadva, 2006).

As with egg donation recipients, commissioning couples in surrogacy arrangements are faced with decisions regarding disclosure, including disclosure to friends and family as well as disclosure to their child in the future, with all couples interviewed in one study indicating intentions to disclose to their child, citing the child's right to the information, desire to avoid disclosure from someone else, and no perceived reasons to maintain secrecy (MacCallum et al., 2003). With empirical study of experiences and outcomes of surrogacy still in its infancy and the majority of studies relying on anecdotal evidence and qualitative data with small sample sizes and no comparison groups, much remains to be learned, particularly in the areas of child outcomes with third-party reproduction, complex interpersonal relationships created during surrogacy arrangements, and potential for regret following relinquishment (Ciccarelli & Beckman, 2005; Edelmann, 2004).

Relinquishment of a Biological Child

Relinquishment of a biological child refers to the planned adoption of a woman's offspring within the first month following birth. Women's decision to relinquish biological children has become increasingly uncommon in the United States, dropping from 8.7% in 1973 to 1% in 2002 (Jones,

2007; Vandivere et al., 2009). Factors associated with relinquishment may indicate women's motivation to make this decision: Women who place a child for adoption tend to have a higher education and income, a greater level of future career and educational aspirations, and previous experience with the adoption system (i.e., either knowing someone who was adopted or being adopted themselves; CWIG, 2005; Miller & Coyl, 2000). However, women's mothers or the birth father appear most strongly influential in relinquishment decisions (CWIG, 2005).

Research addressing the experiences of women who relinquish children for adoption is limited but reveals several themes. Stress related to relinquishment can start during the pregnancy: Birth mothers may struggle with the decision to relinquish the child, worry about the child's future adoptive home, and manage a relationship with several parties involved in the adoption (e.g., adoption agency, adoptive parents; CWIG, 2004).

Once the child is born, a central theme for biological mothers can be loss and grief. Women relinquishing a child may lose their role as a parent, relationships with friends and family who are unsupportive of their decision, and the dream of who their children may have become, as well as their imagined involvement in their offspring's life (CWIG, 2004). In addition, birth mothers may experience a sense of "disenfranchised grief" resulting from stigma surrounding relinquishment, lack of societal recognition or social support, and shortage of role models (Aloi, 2009; CWIG, 2004; Doka, 2002). Women may experience guilt and identity concerns resulting from feelings of incompetence or "illegitimacy" as a parent or encounters with individuals who do not understand or support their decision to relinquish. Long-term grief is associated with

the birth mother's perception of being pressured to relinquish, maternal feelings of guilt or shame, and the absence of opportunities for the birth mother to discuss her feelings (CWIG, 2004). Women experiencing persistent grief and loss following relinquishment may experience difficulties forming relationships, decide to avoid future pregnancy or marriage, or feel overprotective of subsequent children (Askren & Bloom, 1999).

Women's experiences of relinquishment may be influenced by their degree of social support, the extent to which the adoption is closed or open, and the quality of the birth mother's relationship with others involved in the adoption process (CWIG, 2004). Open adoptions are generally associated with better post-adoption outcomes for birth mothers, including well-being and mental health (CWIG, 2010; Leve, Neiderhiser, Scaramella, & Reiss, 2008).

A process of "resolution and control" following relinquishment, involving the utilization of several coping strategies, has been described in adoption literature (CWIG, 2004). Romanchik (1999) described birth mothers' use of entrustment ceremonies in which children are "entrusted" to adoptive parents, as a possible coping mechanism. Other traditions can include planting a tree or writing letters, taking time to grieve and gain resolution, seeking support (both formal and informal), obtaining education about relinquishment, and getting professional help (CWIG, 2004; Roles, 1989).

CONCLUSIONS

In the face of greater societal acceptance of historically less-traditional lifestyle options and advances in reproductive medicine and technology, women's choices regarding childbearing and motherhood have clearly expanded. Although options certainly are available to women regarding *childbirth*, such as the type of provider who will deliver the baby, the setting in which the birth will take place, and potentially even electing a cesarean birth, decision making surrounding pregnancy and childbearing were the focus of this chapter. Agency, as we have discussed it, relates to choices surrounding how women respond to reproductive events that may not necessarily be within their control or of their choosing (e.g., infertility, unplanned pregnancy). For a particular woman, consideration of the individual *context* in which decisions must be made, as well as the psychological stressors and psychosocial settings that precede or coexist with these decisions, is critical to truly understanding, empowering, and assisting her in navigating her unique reproductive journey and managing the associated emotional responses.

REFERENCES

Abbey, A., Halman, L. J., & Andrews, F. M. (1992). Psychosocial, treatment, and demographic predictors of the stress associated with infertility. *Fertility and Sterility, 57*(1), 122–128.

Abboud, L., & Liamputtong, P. (2005). When pregnancy fails: Coping strategies, support networks and experiences with health care of ethnic women and their partners. *Journal of Reproductive and Infant Psychology, 23*(1), 3–18.

Abma, J. C., & Martinez, G. M. (2006). Childlessness among older women in the United States: Trends and profiles. *Journal of Marriage and Family, 68*(4), 1045–1056.

Adler, N. E., David, H. P., Major, B. N., Roth, S. H., Russo, N. F., & Wyatt, G. E. (1990). Psychological responses after abortion. *Science, 248*(4951), 41–44.

Adler, N. E., David, H. P., Major, B. N., Roth, S. H., Russo, N. F., & Wyatt, G. E. (1992). Psychological factors in abortion: A review. *The American Psychologist, 47*(10), 1194–1204.

Adzick, N. S. (2010). Open fetal surgery for life-threatening fetal anomalies. *Seminars in Fetal and Neonatal Medicine, 15*(1), 1–8.

Ahuja, K. K., Mostyn, B. J., & Simons, E. G. (1997). Egg sharing and egg donation: Attitudes of British egg donors and recipients. *Human Reproduction, 12*(12), 2845–2852.

Ahuja, K. K., Simons, E. G., Nair, S., Rimington, M. R., & Armar, N. A. (2003). Minimizing risk in anonymous egg donation. *Reproductive Biomedicine Online, 7*(5), 504–505.

Allen, M., & Marks, S. (1993). *Miscarriage: Women sharing from the heart.* New York, NY: Wiley.

Aloi, J. A. (2009). Nursing the disenfranchised: Women who have relinquished an infant for adoption. *Journal of Psychiatric and Mental Health Nursing, 16*, 27–31.

Amato, P., & Jacob, M. C. (2004). Providing fertility services to lesbian couples: The lesbian baby boom. *Sexuality, Reproduction and Menopause, 2*(2), 83–88.

American College of Obstetricians and, Gynecologists. (2005). Repeated Miscarriage (AP100). Patient Education Pamphlets. Retrieved from www.acog.org/publications/patient_education/bp100.cfm

American College of Obstetricians and, Gynecologists. (2007a). ACOG Practice Bulletin No. 77, January 2007: Screening for fetal chromosomal abnormalities. *Obstetrics & Gynecology, 109*(1), 217–227.

American College of Obstetricians and Gynecologists. (2007b). ACOG Practice Bulletin No. 88, December 2007: Invasive prenatal testing for aneuploidy. *Obstetrics & Gynecology, 110*(6), 1459–1467.

American College of Obstetricians and Gynecologists (2009). Management of stillbirth: ACOG Practice Bulletin No. 102. *Obstetrics and Gynecology, 113*, 748–761.

American Pregnancy Association. (2009). Quad screen. Retrieved from http://www.americanpregnancy.org/prenataltesting/quadscreen.html

American Society for Reproductive Medicine (2006). *Third party reproduction: A guide for patients.* Birmingham, AL: Author.

American Society for Reproductive Medicine (2009). Access to fertility treatment by gays, lesbians, and unmarried persons. *Fertility and Sterility, 92*(4), 1190–1193.

Andersen, A. M. N., Wohlfahrt, J., Christens, P., Olsen, J., & Melbye, M. (2000). Maternal age and fetal loss: Population-based register linkage study. *British Medical Journal, 320*(7251), 1708.

Andrews, J. L., & Boyle, J. S. (2003). African American adolescents' experiences with unplanned pregnancy and elective abortion. *Health Care for Women International, 24*(5), 414–433.

Arias, E., MacDorman, M. F., Strobino, D. M., & Guyer, B. (2003). Annual summary of vital statistics—2002. *Pediatrics, 112*(6), 1215–1230.

Armstrong, D., & Hutti, M. (1998). Pregnancy after perinatal loss: The relationship between anxiety and prenatal attachment. *Journal of Obstetric, Gynecologic, & Neonatal Nursing, 27* (2), 183–189.

Armstrong, D. S. (2004). Impact of prior perinatal loss on subsequent pregnancies. *Journal of Obstetric, Gynecologic, & Neonatal Nursing, 33*(6), 765–773.

Asch, A. (1999). Prenatal diagnosis and selective abortion: A challenge to practice and policy, *American Journal of Public Health, 89*(11), 1649–1657.

Askren, H. A., & Bloom, K. C. (1999). Postadoptive reactions of the relinquishing mother: A review. *Journal of Obstetric, Gynecologic, & Neonatal Nursing, 28*(4), 395–400.

Baetens, P., & Brewaeys, A. (2001). Lesbian couples requesting donor insemination: An update of the knowledge with regard to lesbian mother families. *Human Reproduction Update, 7*(5), 512–519.

Bankole, A., Susheela, S., & Haas, T. (1998). Reasons why women have induced abortions: Evidence from 27 countries. *International Family Planning Perspectives, 24*(3), 117–127.

Ber, R. (2000). Ethical issues in gestational surrogacy. *Theoretical Medicine and Bioethics, 21*(2), 153–169.

Bergner, A., Beyer, R., Klapp, B. F., & Rauchfuss, M. (2008). Pregnancy after early pregnancy loss: A prospective study of anxiety, depressive symptomatology and coping. *Journal of Psychosomatic Obstetrics & Gynecology, 29*(2), 105–113.

Blyth, E. (1994). "I wanted to be interesting. I wanted to be able to say 'I've done something interesting with my life'": Interviews with surrogate mothers in Britain. *Journal of Reproductive and Infant Psychology, 12*(3), 189–198.

Blyth, E. (2004). Patient experiences of an "egg sharing" programme. *Human Fertility, 7*(3), 157–162.

Bos, H., & van Balen, F. (2010). Children of the new reproductive technologies: Social and genetic parenthood. *Patient Education and Counseling, 81*(3), 429–435.

Boyle, F. M., Vance, J. C., Najman, J. M., & Thearle, M. J. (1996). The mental health impact of stillbirth, neonatal death or SIDS: Prevalence and patterns of distress among mothers. *Social Science & Medicine, 43*(8), 1273–1282.

Bracken, M. B., Klerman, L. V., & Bracken, M. (1978). Abortion, adoption, or motherhood: An empirical study of decision-making during pregnancy. *American Journal of Obstetrics and Gynecology, 130*(3), 251–262.

Bradshaw, Z., & Slade, P. (2003). The effects of induced abortion on emotional experiences and relationships: A critical review of the literature. *Clinical Psychology Review, 23*(7), 929–958.

Brier, N. (1999). Understanding and managing the emotional reactions to a miscarriage. *Obstetrics & Gynecology, 93*(1), 151–155.

Brier, N. (2004). Anxiety after miscarriage: A review of the empirical literature and implications for clinical practice. *Birth, 31*(2), 138–142.

Brier, N. (2008). Grief following miscarriage: A comprehensive review of the literature. *Journal of Women's Health, 17*(3), 451–464.

Brinsden, P. R. (2003). Gestational surrogacy. *Human Reproduction Update, 9*(5), 483–491.

Bures, R. M., Koropeckyj-Cox, T., & Loree, M. (2009). Childlessness, parenthood, and depressive symptoms among middle-aged and older adults. *Journal of Family Issues, 30*, 670–687.

Cacciatore, J., Schnebly, S., & Froen, J. F. (2009). The effects of social support on maternal anxiety and depression after stillbirth. *Health & Social Care in the Community, 17*(2), 167–176.

Cain, A. C., Erikson, M. E., Fast, I., & Vaughan, R. A. (1964). Children's disturbed reaction to their mothers' miscarriage. *Psychosomatic Medicine, 24*, 58–66.

Centers for Disease Control and Prevention, American Society for Reproductive Medicine. (2010). 2009 assisted reproductive technology success rates: National summary and fertility clinic reports. Atlanta, GA: U.S. Department of Health and Human Services.

Chambers, G. M., Sullivan, E. A., Shanahan, M., Ho, M. T., Priester, K., & Chapman, M. G. (2010). Is in vitro fertilisation more effective than stimulated intrauterine insemination as a first-line therapy for subfertility? A cohort analysis. *Australian and New Zealand Journal of Obstetrics and Gynaecology, 50*(3), 280–288.

Chandra, A., Martinez, G. M., Mosher, W. D., Abma, J. C., and Jones, J. (2005). Fertility, family planning, and reproductive health of U.S. women: Data from the 2002 National Survey of Family Growth. National Center for Health Statistics. (DHHS Publication No. 2006-1977, Vital and Health Statistics, Series 23, Number 25). Hyattsville, MD: U.S. Department of Health and Human Services.

Charles, V. E., Polis, C. B., Sridhara, S. K., & Blum, R. W. (2008). Abortion and long-term mental health outcomes: A systematic review of the evidence. *Contraception, 78*(6), 436–450.

Child Welfare Information Gateway. (2004). *Impact of adoption on birth parents.* Washington, DC: U.S. Department of Health and Human Services, Children's Bureau.

Child Welfare Information Gateway. (2005). *Voluntary relinquishment for adoption.* Washington, DC: U.S. Department of Health and Human Services, Children's Bureau.

Child Welfare Information Gateway. (2010). *Impact of adoption on adoptive parents: Factsheet for families.* Washington, DC: Department of Health and Human Services, Children's Bureau.

Child Welfare Information Gateway. (2011). *How many children were adopted in 2007 and 2008?* Washington, DC: U.S. Department of Health and Human Services, Children's Bureau.

Choi, H., Van Riper, M., & Thoyre, S. (2012). Decision making following a prenatal diagnosis of Down syndrome: An integrative review. *Journal of Midwifery & Women's Health, 57*(2), 156–164.

Ciccarelli, J. C., & Beckman, L. J. (2005). Navigating rough waters: An overview of psychological aspects of surrogacy. *The Journal of Social Issues, 61*(1), 21–43.

Constantinidis, D., & Cook, R. (2012). Australian perspectives on surrogacy: The influence of cognitions, psychological and demographic characteristics. *Human Reproduction, 27*(4), 1080–1087.

Cowchock, F., Lasker, J., Toedter, L., Skumanich, S., & Koenig, H. (2009). Religious beliefs affect grieving after pregnancy loss. *Journal of Religion and Health,* 1–13.

Dancet, E. A. F., Nelen, W. L. D. M., Sermeus, W., De Leeuw, L., Kremer, J. A. M., & D'Hooghe, T. M. (2010). The patients' perspective on fertility care: A systematic review. *Human Reproduction Update, 16*(5), 467–487.

Davis, D. L., & Stein, M. T. (2004). *Parenting your premature baby and child: The emotional journey.* Golden, CO: Fulcrum.

Diamond, M., Diamond, D., & Jaffe, J. (2005). Reproductive trauma: The psychology of infertility and pregnancy loss: GYN/OB-4. *Southern Medical Journal, 98*(10), S57.

Dias, T., & Thilaganathan, B. (2009). The role of ultrasound in obstetrics, Sri Lanka. *Journal of Obstetrics and Gynaecology, 31,* 76–83.

Doka, K. J. (Ed.). (2002). *Disenfranchised grief: New directions, challenges, and strategies for practice.* Champaign, IL: Research Press.

Domar, A. D. (2004). Impact of psychological factors on dropout rates in insured infertility patients. *Fertility and Sterility, 81*(2), 271–273.

Dominiguez, T. P. (2008). Race, racism, and racial disparities in adverse birth outcomes. *Clinical Obstetrics and Gynecology, 51*(2), 360–379.

Dunn, D. S., Goldbach, K. R., Lasker, J. N., & Toedter, L. J. (1991). Explaining pregnancy loss: Parents' and physicians' attributions. *Journal of Death and Dying, 23,* 13–23.

Dyer, K. A. (2005). Identifying, understanding, and working with grieving parents in the NICU, Part I: Identifying and understanding loss and the grief response. *Neonatal Network: The Journal of Neonatal Nursing, 24*(3), 35–46.

Edelmann, R. J. (2004). Surrogacy: The psychological issues. *Journal of Reproductive and Infant Psychology, 22*(2), 123–136.

Eisenberg, M. L., Smith, J. F., Millstein, S. G., Nachtigall, R. D., Adler, N. E., Pasch, L. A., & Katz, P. P. (2010). Predictors of not pursuing infertility treatment after an infertility diagnosis: Examination of a prospective U. S. cohort. *Fertility and Sterility, 94*(6), 2369–2371.

Engelhard, I. M., van den Hout, M. A., & Arntz, A. (2001). Posttraumatic stress disorder after pregnancy loss. *General Hospital Psychiatry, 23* (2), 62–66.

Englert, Y. (1994). Artificial insemination of single women and lesbian women with donor semen. Artificial insemination with donor semen:

Particular requests. *Human Reproduction, 9*(11), 1969–1971.

Eugster, A., & Vingerhoets, A. J. (1999). Psychological aspects of in vitro fertilization: A review. *Social Science and Medicine, 48*(5), 575–589.

Evans, M. I., Ciorica, D., Britt, D. W., & Fletcher, J. C. (2005). Update on selective reduction. *Prenatal Diagnosis, 25*(9), 807–813.

Financial compensation of oocyte, donors. (2007). *Fertility and Sterility, 88*(2), 305–309.

Finer, L. B., Frohwirth, L. F., Dauphinee, L. A., Singh, S., & Moore, A. M. (2005). Reasons U. S. women have abortions: Quantitative and qualitative perspectives. *Perspectives on Sexual and Reproductive Health, 37*(3), 110–118.

Finer, L. B., Frohwirth, L. F., Dauphinee, L. A., Singh, S., & Moore, A. M. (2006). Timing of steps and reasons for delays in obtaining abortions in the United States. *Contraception, 74*(4), 334–344.

Finer, L. B., & Henshaw, S. K. (2006). Disparities in rates of unintended pregnancy in the United States, 1994 and 2001. *Perspectives on Sexual and Reproductive Health, 38*(2), 90–96.

Flango, V., & Flango, C. (1995). How many children were adopted in 1992? *Child Welfare, 74,* 1018–1032.

Foster, D. G., Jackson, R. A., Cosby, K., Weitz, T. A., Darney, P. D., & Drey, E. A. (2008). Predictors of delay in each step leading to an abortion. *Contraception, 77*(4), 289–293.

Franche, R.-L., & Bulow, C. (1999). The impact of a subsequent pregnancy on grief and emotional adjustment following a perinatal loss. *Infant Mental Health Journal, 20*(2), 175–187.

Freeman, E. W., Boxer, A. S., Rickels, K., Tureck, R., & Mastroianni, L., Jr. (1985). Psychological evaluation and support in a program of in vitro fertilization and embryo transfer. *Fertility and Sterility, 43*(1), 48–53.

Gair, S. (1999). Distress and depression in new motherhood: Research with adoptive mothers highlights important contributing factors. *Child and Family Social Work, 4,* 55–66.

Garel, M., Stark, C., Blondel, B., Lefebvre, G., Vauthier-Brouzes, D., & Zorn, J. R. (1997). Psychological reactions after multifetal pregnancy reduction: A 2-year follow-up study. *Human Reproduction, 12*(3), 617–622.

Gates, G. J., Badgett, M. V., Macomber, J. E., & Chambers, K. (2007). Adoption and foster care by gay and lesbian parents in the United States. *E-Scholarship, University of California.* Retrieved from http://escholarship.org/uc/item/2v4528cx

Gaudet, C., Sejourne, N., Camborieux, L., Rogers, R., & Chabrol, H. (2010). Pregnancy after perinatal loss: Association of grief, anxiety, and attachment. *Journal of Reproductive and Infant Psychology, 28*(3), 249–251.

Geller, P. A. (2004). Pregnancy as a stressful life event. *CNS Spectrums: The International Journal of Neuropsychiatric Medicine, 9*(3), 188–197.

Geller, P. A., Klier, C. M., & Neugebauer, R. (2001). Anxiety disorders following miscarriage. *Journal of Clinical Psychiatry, 62*(6), 432–438.

Geller, P. A., Nelson, A. R., Kornfield, S. L., & Silverman, D. G. (2013). Women's health: Obstetrics and gynecology. In C. M. Hunter, C. L. Hunter, & R. Kessler (Eds.), *Handbook of clinical psychology in medical settings: Evidence-based assessment and intervention.* New York, NY: Springer.

Geller, P. A., Psaros, C., & Kerns, D. (2006). Web-based resources for health care providers and women following pregnancy loss. *Journal of Obstetric, Gynecologic, & Neonatal Nursing, 35*(4), 523–532.

Geller, P. A., Psaros, C., & Kornfield, S. L. (2010). Satisfaction with pregnancy loss aftercare: Are women getting what they want? *Archives of Women's Mental Health, 13*(2), 111–124.

Geller, P. A., Woodland, M. B., & Daetwyler, C. (2008). Psychological and medical aspects of pregnancy loss. Retrieved from http://webcampus.drexelmed.edu/interactive/pregloss

Gerson, M.-J., Posner, J. A., & Morris, A. M. (1991). The value of having children as an aspect of adult development. *Journal of Genetic Psychology, 152,* 327–339.

Glazebrook, C., Sheard, C., Cox, S., Oates, M., & Ndukwe, G. (2004). Parenting stress in first-time mothers of twins and triplets conceived after in vitro fertilization. *Fertility and Sterility, 81*(3), 505–511.

Gold, K. J., Boggs, M. E., Mugisha, E., & Palladino, C. L. (2012). Internet message boards for pregnancy loss: Who's on-line and why? *Women's Health Issues, 22*(1), e67–e72.

Goldberg, A. E., Downing, J. B., & Richardson, H. B. (2009). The transition from infertility to adoption: Perceptions of lesbian and heterosexual couples. *Journal of Social and Personal Relationships, 26*(6–7), 938–963.

Goldberg, A. E., & Smith, J. A. Z. (2011). Stigma, social context, and mental health: Lesbian and gay couples across the transition to adoptive parenthood. *Journal of Counseling Psychology, 58* (1), 139–150.

Goldberg, A. E., Smith, J. A. Z., & Kashy, D. A. (2010). Preadoptive factors predicting lesbian, gay, and heterosexual couples' relationship quality across the transition to adoptive parenthood. *Journal of Family Psychology, 24*(3), 221–232.

Goldenberg, R. L., Kirby, R., & Dulhane, J. F. (2004). Stillbirth: A review. *Journal of Maternal Fetal Neonatal Medicine, 16,* 79–94.

Golombok, S., MacCallum, F., Murray, C., Lycett, E., & Jadva, V. (2006). Surrogacy families: Parental functioning, parent–child relationships and children's psychological development at age 2. *Journal of Child Psychology and Psychiatry, and Allied Disciplines, 47*(2), 213–222.

Grimes, D. A. (2006). Estimation of pregnancy-related mortality risk by pregnancy outcome, United States, 1991 to 1999. *American Journal of Obstetrics and Gynecology, 194*(1), 92–94.

Guttmacher Institute. (2011). *State policies in brief as of May 1, 2011: An overview of abortion laws.* Washington, DC: Guttmacher Institute.

Hammarberg, K., Carmichael, M., Tinney, L., & Mulder, A. (2008). Gamete donors' and recipients' evaluation of donor counselling: A prospective longitudinal cohort study. *Australian and New Zealand Journal of Obstetrics and Gynaecology, 48*(6), 601–606.

Hammarberg, K., Fisher, J. R., & Wynter, K. H. (2008). Psychological and social aspects of pregnancy, childbirth and early parenting after assisted conception: a systematic review. *Human Reproduction Update, 14*(5), 395–414.

Hansen, T., Slagsvold, B., Moum, T. (2009). Childlessness and psychological well-being in midlife and old age: An examination of parental status effects across a range of outcomes. *Social Indicators Research, 94*(2), 343–362.

Henne, M. B., & Bundorf, M. K. (2008). Insurance mandates and trends in infertility treatments. *Fertility and Sterility, 89*(1), 66–73.

Hershberger, P. (2004). Recipients of oocyte donation: An integrative review. *Journal of Obstetric, Gynecologic, and Neonatal Nursing, 33*(5), 610–621.

Hughes, P. M., Turton, P., & Evans, C. D. H. (1999). Stillbirth as risk factor for depression and anxiety in the subsequent pregnancy: Cohort study. *British Medical Journal, 318*(7200), 1721–1724.

Hughes, P., Turton, P., Hopper, E., & Evans, C. D. H. (2002). Assessment of guidelines for good practice in psychosocial care of mothers after stillbirth: A cohort study. *The Lancet, 360*(9327), 114–118.

Jacobs, P. A., & Hassold, T. (1987). Chromosome abnormalities: Origin and etiology in abortions and livebirths. In F. Vogel & K. Sperling (Eds.), *Human genetics* (pp. 233–244). Berlin, Germany: Springer-Verlag.

Jadva, V., Murray, C., Lycett, E., MacCallum, F., & Golombok, S. (2003). Surrogacy: The experiences of surrogate mothers. *Human Reproduction, 18*(10), 2196–2204.

Janssen, H., Cuisinier, M., Hoogduin, K., & De Graauw, K. (1996). Controlled prospective study on the mental health of women following pregnancy loss. *American Journal of Psychiatry, 153*(2), 226–230.

Jensen, J. R., Morbeck, D. E., & Coddington, C. C., 3rd (2011). Fertility preservation. Mayo Clinic proceedings. *Mayo Clinic, 86*(1), 45–49.

Jind, L. (2003). Parents' adjustment to late abortion, stillbirth or infant death: The role of causal attributions. *Scandinavian Journal of Psychology, 44*(4), 383–394.

Jones, J. (2007). Adoption experiences of women and men and demand for children to adopt by women 18-44 years of age in the United States, 2002. *Vital Health Statistics, 23*(27), 1–36.

Kalfoglou, A. L., & Gittelsohn, J. (2000). A qualitative follow-up study of women's experiences with oocyte donation. *Human Reproduction, 15*(4), 798–805.

Karuppaswamy, J., Smedley, M., & Carter, L. (2009). Intra-uterine insemination: Pregnancy rate in relation to number, size of pre-ovulatory follicles and day of insemination. *Journal of the Indian Medical Association, 107*(3), 141-143, 147.

Katz, P., Showstack, J., Smith, J. F., Nachtigall, R. D., Millstein, S. G., Wing, H., . . . Adler, N. (2011). Costs of infertility treatment: Results from an 18-month prospective cohort study. *Fertility and Sterility, 95*(3), 915–921.

Kavanaugh, K. (1997). Parents' experience surrounding the death of newborn whose birth is at the margin of viability. *Journal of Obstetric, Gynecologic, & Neonatal Nursing, 26*(1), 43–51.

Kavanaugh, K., & Hershberger, P. (2005). Perinatal loss in low-income African American parents. *Journal of Obstetric, Gynecologic, & Neonatal Nursing, 34*(5), 595–605.

Kimport, K., Foster, K., & Weitz, T. A. (2011). Social sources of women's emotional difficulty after abortion: Lessons from women's abortion narratives. *Perspectives on Sexual and Reproductive Health, 43*(2), 103–109.

King, L., & Meyer, M. H. (1997). The politics of reproductive benefits: U.S. insurance coverage of contraceptive and infertility treatments. *Gender and Society, 11*(1), 8–30.

Kinkler, L. A., & Goldberg, A. E. (2011). Working with what we've got: Perceptions of barriers and supports among small-metropolitan-area same-sex adopting couples. *Family relations, 60*(4), 387–403.

Kirkman, M., Rosenthal, D., Mallett, S., Rowe, H., & Hardiman, A. (2010). Reasons women give for contemplating or undergoing abortion: A qualitative investigation in Victoria, Australia. *Sexual & Reproductive Healthcare: Official Journal of the Swedish Association of Midwives, 1* (4), 149–155.

Kirkman, M., Rowe, H., Hardiman, A., Mallett, S., & Rosenthal, D. (2009). Reasons women give for abortion: A review of the literature. *Archives of Women's Mental Health, 12*(6), 365–378.

Klier, C. M., Geller, P. A., & Neugebauer, R. (2000). Minor depressive disorder in the context of miscarriage. *Journal of Affective Disorders, 59*(1), 13–21.

Klier, C. M., Geller, P., & Ritsher, J. (2002). Affective disorders in the aftermath of miscarriage: A comprehensive review. *Archives of Women's Mental Health, 5*(4), 129–149.

Klock, S. C., Stout, J. E., & Davidson, M. (2003). Psychological characteristics and factors related to willingness to donate again among anonymous oocyte donors. *Fertility and Sterility, 79*(6), 1312–1316.

Kochanek, K. D., Xu, J., Murphy, S. L., Miniño, A. M., & Kung, H. (2011). Deaths: Preliminary data for 2009. *National Vital Statistics Reports, 59*(4), 1–69.

Kornfield, S. L., & Geller, P. A. (2010). Mental health outcomes of abortion and its alternatives:

Implications for future policy. *Womens Health Issues, 20*(2), 92–95.

Koropeckyj-Cox, T., & Call, V. R. A. (2007). Characteristics of older childless persons and parents: Cross-national comparisons. *Journal of Family Issues, 28*(10), 1362–1414.

Koropeckyj-Cox, T., & Pendell, G. (2007). The gender gap in attitudes about childlessness in the United States. *Journal of Marriage and Family, 69*, 899–915.

Krivickas, K. M., & Lofquist, D. (2011). *Demographics of same-sex couple households with children.* SEHSD Working Paper Number 2011-11. Washington, DC: U.S. Census Bureau, Fertility & Family Statistics Branch.

Kumar, A., Hessini, L., & Mitchell, E. M. (2009). Conceptualising abortion stigma. *Culture, Health & Sexuality, 11*(6), 625–639.

Lancaster, C. A., Gold, K. J., Flynn, H. A., Yoo, H., Marcus, S. M., & Davis, M. M. (2010). Risk factors for depressive symptoms during pregnancy: A systematic review. *American Journal of Obstetrics and Gynecology, 202*(1), 5–14.

Lee, C. (1998). *Women's health: Psychological and social perspectives.* London, UK: SAGE Publications.

Lee, C., & Slade, P. (1996). Miscarriage as a traumatic event: A review of the literature and new implications for intervention. *Journal of Psychosomatic Research, 40*(3), 235–244.

Leiblum, S. R., Palmer, M. G., & Spector, I. P. (1995). Non-traditional mothers: Single heterosexual/lesbian women and lesbian couples electing motherhood via donor insemination. *Journal of Psychosomatic Obstetrics and Gynaecology, 16*, 11–20.

Leve, L. D., Neiderhiser, J. M., Scaramella, L. V., & Reiss, D. (2008). The Early Growth and Development Study: Using the prospective adoption design to examine genotype–environment interplay. *Xin Li Xue Bao. Actapsychologica Sinica, 40* (10), 1106–1115.

Littman, L. L., Zarcadoolas, C., & Jacobs, A. R. (2009). Introducing abortion patients to a culture of support: A pilot study. *Archives of Women's Mental Health, 12*(6), 419–431.

Livingston, G., & Cohn, D. (2010). *Childlessness up among all women; Down among women with advanced degrees.* Retrieved from http://www.pewsocialtrends.org/2010/06/25/childlessness-up-among-all-vwomen-down-among-women-with-advanced-degrees/

MacCallum, F., Lycett, E., Murray, C., Jadva, V., & Golombok, S. (2003). Surrogacy: The experience of commissioning couples. *Human reproduction*, *18*(6), 1334–1342.

MacDorman, M. F., & Kirmeyer, S. (2009). Fetal and perinatal mortality, United States, 2005. *National Vital Statistics Reports*, *57*(8), 1–20.

Major, B., Appelbaum, M., Beckman, L., Dutton, M. A., Russo, N. F., & West, C. (2009). Abortion and mental health: Evaluating the evidence. *American Psychologist*, *64*(9), 863–890.

Major, B., Cozzarelli, C., Cooper, M. L., Zubek, J., Richards, C., Wilhite, M., & Gramzow, R. H. (2000). Psychological responses of women after first-trimester abortion. *Archives of General Psychiatry*, *57*(8), 777–784.

Major, B., & Gramzow, R. H. (1999). Abortion as stigma: Cognitive and emotional implications of concealment. *Journal of Personality and Social Psychology*, *77*(4), 735–745.

March of Dimes. (2008). Miscarriage: Loss and grief. Retrieved from http://www.marchofdimes .com/loss_miscarriage.html

March of Dimes. (2010). Neonatal death: Loss and grief. Retrieved from http://www.marchofdimes .com/baby/loss_neonataldeath.html

March of Dimes. (2011a). Prenatal care: Amniocentesis. Retrieved from http://www .marchofdimes.com/pregnancy/prenatalcare_ amniocentesis.html

March of Dimes. (2011b). Prenatal care: Chorionic villus sampling. Retrieved from http://www .marchofdimes.com/pregnancy/prenatalcare_ chorionicvillus.html

Matthews, T. J., Menacker, F., & MacDorman, M. F. (2004). Infant mortality statistics from the 2002 period linked birth/infant death data set. *National Vital Statistics Reports*, *53*(10), 1–29.

McGreal, D., Evans, B. J., & Burrows, G. D. (1997). Gender differences in coping following pregnancy loss of a child through miscarriage or stillbirth: A pilot study. *Stress Medicine*, *13*, 159–165.

McKay, K., Ross, L. E., & Goldberg, A. E. (2010). Adaptation to parenthood during the post-adoption period: A review of the literature. *Adoption Quarterly*, *13*(2), 125–144.

McManus, A. J., Hunter, L. P., & Renn, H. (2006). Lesbian experiences and needs during childbirth: Guidance for health care providers. *Journal of Obstetric, Gynecologic, and Neonatal Nursing*, *35* (1), 13–23.

McQuillan, J., Greil, A. L., Shreffler, K. M., & Tichenor, V. (2008). The importance of motherhood among women in the contemporary United States. *Gender & Society*, *22*(4), 477–496.

Michels, T. C., & Tiu, A. Y. (2007). Second trimester pregnancy loss. *American Family Physician*, *76*(9), 1341–1346.

Miller, B. C., & Coyl, D. D. (2000). Adolescent pregnancy and childbearing in relation to infant adoption in the United States. *Adoption Quarterly*, *4*, 3–25.

Morris, R. K., & Kilby, M. D. (2010). Fetal reduction. *Obstetrics, Gynaecology & Reproductive Medicine*, *20* (11), 341–343.

Mott, S. L., Schiller, C. E., Richards, J. G., O'Hara, M. W., & Stuart, S. (2011). Depression and anxiety among postpartum and adoptive mothers. *Archives of Women's Mental Health*, *14*(4), 335–343.

Mundy, L. (2003). A special kind of poverty; The poor get used to going without. But going without a baby is hard to get used to. *The Washington Post*, available at http://www.highbeam.com/doc/ 1P2-269379.html

Murray, C., MacCallum, F., & Golombok, S. (2006). Egg donation parents and their children: Follow-up at age 12 years. *Fertility and Sterility*, *85*(3), 610–618.

Neugebauer, R., Kline, J., O'Connor, P., Shrout, P., Johnson, J., Skodol, A., . . . Susser, M. (1992). Determinants of depressive symptoms in the early weeks after miscarriage. *American Journal of Public Health*, *82*(10), 1332–1339.

Neugebauer, R., Kline, J., Shrout, P., Skodol, A., O'Connor, P., Geller, P. A., . . . Susser, M. (1997). Major depressive disorder in the 6 months after miscarriage. *JAMA*, *277*(5), 383–388.

Newton, C. R., Sherrard, W., & Glavac, I. (1999). The Fertility Problem Inventory: Measuring perceived infertility-related stress. *Fertility and Sterility*, *72*(1), 54–62.

Norris, A., Bessett, D., Steinberg, J. R., Kavanaugh, M. L., De Zordo, S., & Becker, D. (2011). Abortion stigma: A reconceptualization of constituents, causes, and consequences. *Women's Health Issues*, *21* (3, Supplement), S49–S54.

Orr, S. T., James, S. A., & Prince, C. B. (2002). Maternal prenatal depressive symptoms and spontaneous preterm births among African-American women in Baltimore, Maryland. *American Journal of Epidemiology, 156*(9), 797–802.

Pazol, K., Zane, S. B., Parker, W. Y., Hall, L. R., Gamble, S. B., Hamdan, S., . . . Cook, D. A. (2011). Abortion surveillance—United States, 2007. *MMWR Surveillance Series, 60*(1), 1–42.

Pearce, L. (2002). The influence of early life course religious exposure on young adults' dispositions toward childbearing. *Journal for the Scientific Study of Religion, 41*, 325–340.

Pearson, H. (2006). Health effects of egg donation may take decades to emerge. *Nature, 442*(7103), 607–608.

Plotnick, R. D. (2009). Childlessness and economic well-being of older Americans. *The Journal of Gerontology, 64*(6), 767–776.

Purewal, S., & van den Akker, O. B. (2006). British women's attitudes towards oocyte donation: Ethnic differences and altruism. *Patient Education and Counseling, 64*(1–3), 43–49.

Purewal, S., & van den Akker, O. B. (2009a). Attitudes and intentions towards volunteer oocyte donation. *Reproductive Biomedicine Online, 19* (Suppl 1), 19–26.

Purewal, S., & van den Akker, O. B. (2009b). Systematic review of oocyte donation: Investigating attitudes, motivations and experiences. *Human Reproduction Update, 15*(5), 499–515.

Rauprich, O., Berns, E., & Vollmann, J. (2011). Information provision and decision-making in assisted reproduction treatment: Results from a survey in Germany. *Human Reproduction, 26*(9), 2382–2391.

Richardson, H. B., & Goldberg, A. E. (2010). The intersection of multiple minority identities: Perspectives of white lesbian couples adopting racial/ethnic minority children. *The Australian and New Zealand Journal of Family Therapy, 31*(4), 340–353.

Roles, P. (1989). *Saying goodbye to a baby. Volume I: The birthparent's guide to loss and grief in adoption.* Washington, DC: Child Welfare League of America.

Romanchik, B. (1999). *Your rights and responsibilities: A guide for expectant parents considering adoption.* Royal Oak, MI: R-Squared Press.

Romans-Clarkson, S. E. (1989). Psychological sequelae of induced abortion. *The Australian and New Zealand Journal of Psychiatry, 23*(4), 555–565.

Romesberg, T. L. (2004). Understanding grief: A component of neonatal palliative care. *Journal of Hospice & Palliative Nursing, 6*(3), 161–170.

Rushton, D. (1994). Prognostic role of the perinatal postmortem. *British Journal of Hospital Medicine, 52*(9), 450–454.

Saraiya, M., Green, C. A., Berg, C. J., Hopkins, F. W., Koonin, L. M., & Atrash, H. K. (1999). Spontaneous abortion-related deaths among women in the United States, 1981-1991. *Obstetrics & Gynecology, 94*(2), 172–176.

Schoendorf, K. C., Hogue, C. J., Kleinman, J. C., & Rowley, D. (1992). Mortality among infants of Black as compared to White college-educated parents. *New England Journal of Medicine, 326*(23), 1522–1526.

Sears, W., Sears, R., Sears, M., & Sears, J. (2004). *The premature baby book: Everything you need to know about your premature baby from birth to age one.* Boston, MA: Little, Brown.

Sharma, B. R. (2006). Forensic considerations of surrogacy—An overview. *Journal of Clinical Forensic Medicine, 13*(2), 80–85.

Shehab, D., Duff, J., Pasch, L. A., Mac Dougall, K., Scheib, J. E., & Nachtigall, R. D. (2008). How parents whose children have been conceived with donor gametes make their disclosure decision: Contexts, influences, and couple dynamics. *Fertility and Sterility, 89*(1), 179–187.

Simpson, H. W., McArdle, C. S., George, W. D., Griffiths, K., Turkes, A., & Pauson, A. W. (2002). Pregnancy postponement and childlessness leads to chronic hypervascularity of the breasts and cancer risk. *British Journal of Cancer, 87*, 1246–1252.

Slade, P., O'Neill, C., Simpson, A. J., & Lashen, H. (2007). The relationship between perceived stigma, disclosure patterns, support and distress in new attendees at an infertility clinic. *Human Reproduction, 22*(8), 2309–2317.

Soderstrom-Anttila, V. (1995). Follow-up study of Finnish volunteer oocyte donors concerning their attitudes to oocyte donation. *Human Reproduction, 10*(11), 3073–3076.

Soerjomataram, I., Pukkala, E., Brenner, H., & Coebergh, J. W. (2008). On the avoidability of breast cancer in industrialized societies: Older mean age at first birth as an indicator of excess breast cancer risk. *Breast Cancer Research and Treatment, 111*(2), 297–302.

Stephen, E. H., & Chandra, A. (2006). Declining estimates of infertility in the United States: 1982-2002. *Fertility and Sterility, 86*(3), 516–523.

Stephenson, M., & Kutteh, W. (2007). Evaluation and management of recurrent early pregnancy loss. *Clinical Obstetrics and Gynecology, 50*(1), 132–145.

Thornton, A., & Young-DeMarco, L. (2001). Four decades of trends in attitudes toward family issues in the United States: The 1960s through the 1990s. *Journal of Marriage and Family, 63*(4), 1009–1037.

Turton, P., Evans, C. D. H., & Hughes, P. (2009). Long-term psychosocial sequelae of stillbirth: Phase II of a nested case-control cohort study. *Archives of Women's Mental Health, 12*(1), 35–41.

Turton, P., Hughes, P., Evans, C. D. H., & Fainman, D. (2001). Incidence, correlates and predictors of post-traumatic stress disorder in the pregnancy after stillbirth. *The British Journal of Psychiatry, 178* (6), 556–560. doi: 10.1192/bjp.178.6.556

2008 Guidelines for gamete and embryo donation: A Practice Committee report. (2008). *Fertility and Sterility, 90* (5 Suppl), S30–S44.

Van, P., & Meleis, A. (2010). Factors related to dimensions of grief intensity among African-American women after pregnancy loss. *Journal of National Black Nurses' Association, 21*(2), 1–8.

Van, P., & Meleis, A. I. (2003). Coping with grief after involuntary pregnancy loss: Perspectives of African American women. *Journal of Obstetric, Gynecologic, & Neonatal Nursing, 32*(1), 28–39.

Vandivere, S., Malm, K., & Radel, L. (2009). *Adoption USA: A chartbook based on the 2007 National Survey of Adoptive Parents.* Washington, DC: The U.S. Department of Health and Human Services, Office of the Assistant Secretary for Planning and Evaluation.

van Niekerk, A., & van Zyl, L. (1995). The ethics of surrogacy: Women's reproductive labour. *Journal of Medical Ethics, 21*(6), 345–349.

Ventura, S. J., Abma, J. C., Mosher, W. D., & Henshaw, S. K. (2008). Estimated pregnancy rates by outcome for the United States, 1990-2004. *National Vital Statistics Reports, 15*(56), 1–26.

Viana, A. G., & Welsh, J. A. (2010). Correlates and predictors of parenting stress among internationally adopting mothers: A longitudinal investigation. *International Journal of Behavioral Development, 34*(4), 363–373.

Wasik, S. L., & Kim, M. (2011). Contraceptive treatments: A review of current hormone options and newer agents for women. *Formulary, 46*, 54–63.

Werner, C., & Westerstahl, A. (2008). Donor insemination and parenting: Concerns and strategies of lesbian couples. A review of international studies. *Acta Obstetricia et Gynecologica Scandinavica, 87*(7), 697–701.

Whiteford, L. M., & Gonzalez, L. (1995). Stigma: The hidden burden of infertility. *Social Science and Medicine, 40*(1), 27–36.

Worden, J. W. (2000). *Grief counseling and grief therapy: A handbook for the mental health practitioner* (3rd ed.). New York, NY: Springer.

Xu, J., Kochanek, K. D., Murphy, S. L., & Tejada-Vera, B. (2010). Deaths: Final data for 2007. *National Vital Statistics Reports, 58*(19), 1–135.

Yee, S., Hitkari, J. A., & Greenblatt, E. M. (2007). A follow-up study of women who donated oocytes to known recipient couples for altruistic reasons. *Human Reproduction, 22*(7), 2040–2050.

16

Psychiatric Symptoms and Pregnancy

DANIELLE M. NOVICK AND HEATHER A. FLYNN

INTRODUCTION

Many women experience a spectrum of psychiatric symptoms around the time of childbearing, the puerperal period. These puerperal symptoms may occur both during and following pregnancy (the antenatal and postnatal periods, respectively). For a minority of these women, symptoms will move beyond the normative and into the pathological experience, warranting the need for safe and efficacious treatment. Both syndromal and subsyndromal puerperal psychiatric disorders, such as mood and anxiety, are burdensome and costly—not only to the mothers but also to their infants and family members.

Women and their health professionals face difficult cost-benefit decisions about how to best manage or prevent recurrences of these disorders during childbearing years. Psychoeducation and assessment are necessary, and acute and prophylactic (i.e., preventive or maintenance) treatments are often essential. Accordingly, understanding for whom to intervene, how to intervene, and how to engage is of enormous significance to health professionals. Luckily, there is a surging recognition of the importance for understanding these puerperal issues and an accompanying research literature.

In this chapter, we provide a summary of these empirical investigations and their limitations. We discuss the practical and clinical implications of existing research findings for health professionals, especially in regards to providing and timing psychoeducation, assessment, and treatment. First, we present the disease burden of psychiatric symptoms during and following pregnancy that are especially common or deleterious and provide recommendations for basic clinical practice. Then, we briefly discuss the sociodemographic and environmental factors that contribute to risk and the potential consequences of these puerperal problems. Next, we focus on intervention delivery, including identifying and engaging women who are at increased risk for antenatal and postnatal psychopathology. We conclude with an explication of recommendations for general clinical practice and future research. Of note, throughout this chapter, we pay particular attention to depression and issues most relevant to women living in the United States. Additionally, we do not provide detailed information about specific interventions, but rather refer readers to other publications, including treatment guidelines published online from the American Psychiatric Association (APA; http://www.psych.org) and the American College of Obstetricians and Gynecologists (ACOG; http://www.acog.org).

THE BURDEN OF ANTENATAL AND POSTNATAL PSYCHIATRIC SYMPTOMS

Reproductive events are associated with substantial hormonal, psychosocial, and quality-of-life changes, and some women may be especially vulnerable, biologically and/or psychologically, to these repercussions (Barrett & Fleming, 2011; Bloch et al., 2000; Gale & Harlow, 2003; Glover, 2011; National Research Council and Institute of Medicine [NRC], 2009; Yonkers et al., 2009). Accumulating evidence suggests that reproductive events are not necessarily protective against psychiatric symptoms. In fact, several psychiatric disorders may emerge or worsen during the antenatal and postnatal periods, especially mood and anxiety (Ross & Mclean, 2006; Vesga-Lopez et al., 2008).

Yet, the true prevalence, or rate of all cases in any given period, of puerperal psychiatric disorders is unclear (Beck & Gable, 2001; Gaynes et al., 2005). Epidemiological estimates are influenced by methodological and assessment heterogeneity, including timing of assessment. Researchers report higher rates when utilizing self-report instruments and longer timeframes, and lower rates when using clinician-administered diagnostic instruments and shorter timeframes (O'Hara & Swain, 1996). As is the case in general, estimates relying on screening tools (e.g., self-report instruments) probably either over- or underestimate the true prevalence of antenatal and postnatal psychiatric disorders. For instance, screening measures implemented in the general population typically identify only 75% of individuals with any depressive disorder and 25% to 40% of individuals with a major depressive episode (MDE; Evins, Theofrastous, & Galvin, 2000; Kroenke, 2006; U.S. Preventive Task Force, 2002).

Although psychiatric disorders may emerge or worsen during the antenatal and postnatal periods, in the *Diagnostic and Statistical Manual of Mental Disorders, Fourth Edition, Text Revision* (*DSM-IV-TR*), there is no distinct puerperal psychiatric disorder classification (APA, 2000a). This reflects the existing evidence that puerperal psychiatric disorders are nosologically similar to psychiatric disorders occurring at nonreproductive times (Cooper et al., 2007; Jones, 2010; Jones & Cantwell, 2010; Wisner, Peindl, & Hanusa, 1994). That is, the etiology (cause), pathogensis (mechanism or pathway by which the disease is caused), and symptoms are similar. In the *DSM-IV-TR*, a woman's current or recent pregnancy or reproductive event (e.g., miscarriage) is captured in the multiaxial assessment, on Axis III: General Medical Conditions, and, in some instances, by the addition of a postpartum course specifier. In *DSM-IV-TR*, if onset of the current or most recent depressive, manic, or mixed episode or brief psychotic disorder is within 4 weeks postpartum, then a postpartum course specifier should be added to the diagnosis. In *DSM-5*, the use of the postpartum course specifier will remain restricted to symptom onset within 4 weeks postpartum except for depressive episodes, which will be extended to 6 months. This extended window may more accurately reflect a woman's sustaining risk as she adjusts to the hormonal, psychosocial, and quality-of-life changes that accompany caring for an infant (Forty et al., 2006; Jones, 2010).

Notably, in both *DSM-IV-TR* and *DSM-5*, the postpartum course specifier is not applicable to a hypomanic episode. Sharma and Burt (2011) maintain that this division is unsupported. They argue that modifying the postpartum course specifier to include hypomanic episodes might increase recognition of hypomanic symptoms during the postnatal period (which are often underdetected) (Glover, Liddle, Taylor, Adams, & Sandler, 1994; Heron, Craddock, & Jones, 2005), improve diagnosis of bipolar II and bipolar spectrum disorders (which are often underdiagnosed) (Benazzi, 2007), and, in turn, better manage the elevated suicide risk associated with these disorders (which is often underestimated) (Novick, Swartz, & Frank, 2010).

We briefly review the clinical presentation or noteworthy characteristics, epidemiology, psychiatric risk factors, and treatment needs associated with common or severe puerperal psychiatric symptoms.

MOOD SYMPTOMS

Antenatal Depressive Symptoms

Based on the existing research literature, the phenomenology of nonpsychotic depression in pregnant women seems to be similar to that documented in nonpregnant women and similarly heterogeneous (Koleva, O'Hara, Stuart, & Bowman-Reif, 2011; Shaw, 2011; Wisner et al., 1994). Although a few investigations report that pregnant women experience less suicidal ideation than do nonpregnant women (Stallones, Leff, Canetto, Garrett, & Mendelson, 2007), most investigations find no difference, suggesting that pregnancy is not inherently protective against suicidal ideation (Gavin, Tabb, Melville, Guo, & Katon, 2011; Lindhal, Pearson, & Cople, 2005). Antenatal depression is distinct from depressions occurring at nonreproductive times because of the potential adverse consequences to pregnancy health, fetal development, birth outcomes, and postnatal health (Berle et al., 2005; Littleton, Breitkopf, & Berenson, 2007). For example,

about 50% of women who experience antenatal depressive symptoms will also experience postnatal depressive symptoms (Flynn, 2005; NRC, 2009; Vesga-Lopez et al., 2008).

Prevalence estimates for major or minor depression during pregnancy range between 8.5% and 11.0%, indicating that the prevalence of depression during pregnancy is neither higher nor lower than it is among similarly aged nonchildbearing women (Bennett, Einarson, Taddio, Koren, & Einarson, 2004; Evans, Heron, Francomb, Oke, & Golding, 2001; Gaynes et al., 2005; Koleva et al., 2011). The prevalence of severe major depression with or without psychotic features appears to be lower during pregnancy than it is following pregnancy (Evans et al., 2001; Jones & Cantwell, 2010). Among women with a personal history of a mood disorder, pregnancy is a time of increased risk (Flynn, 2005; Jones & Craddock, 2001; NRC, 2009; Viguera et al., 2007, 2011). This is especially true for women who discontinue maintenance antidepressant pharmacotherapy during pregnancy (Cohen et al., 2004, 2006). For instance, among women with any past depression, about 25% will experience some antenatal depressive symptoms. Among women with a past unipolar MDE, about 5% will experience a syndromal recurrence. Among women with bipolar disorder, the risk is even higher, with around 23% expected to experience a syndromal recurrence.

Epidemiological investigations across trimesters are few and somewhat inconsistent. Some investigations show risk for both initial illness onset and illness relapse following maintenance treatment discontinuation to be highest during the first trimester (Cohen et al., 2004, 2006; Gavin et al., 2005; Viguera et al., 2000, 2007). Other investigations find greater risk for depressive symptoms during the second and third trimesters than in the first trimester (Bennett et al., 2004; Heron, O'Conner, Evans, Golding, & Glover, 2004), whereas others find no difference (Yonkers, Vigod, & Ross, 2011). Despite a somewhat inconsistent literature, it is evident that neither pregnancy overall nor any specific trimester inherently protects against depressive symptoms.

Intervention Recommendations for Antenatal Depressive Symptoms

Health professionals should inform all women and their families that depression during pregnancy is a serious complication, and not a normal, expected experience of pregnancy. They should evaluate pregnant women for risk factors and depression at least once every trimester. For women with several risk factors, including a personal history of a mood disorder and pregnancy-related discontinuation of psychotropic pharmacotherapy, health professionals should discuss prophylactic treatment and evaluate more frequently. For women experiencing subsyndromal or syndromal depressive symptoms, health professionals should assess their needs and present treatment options. Additionally, health professionals should screen any woman with depressive symptoms for a personal or family history of bipolarity, especially before initiating pharmacotherapy. Overall, providing early and frequent psychoeducation, assessment, and treatment may reduce the complications associated with antenatal depressive symptoms (APA, 2000b; Gossler, 2010; Kuehn, 2010; Sockol, Epperson, & Barber, 2011; Yonkers et al., 2009, 2011).

Antenatal Hypomanic and Manic Symptoms

The phenomenology and prevalence of hypomanic and manic symptoms during pregnancy are unclear for several reasons (Chessick & Dimidjian, 2010; Heron, Haque, Oyebode, Craddock, & Jones, 2009; Littleton et al., 2007; Sharma, Burt, & Ritchie, 2010). One, there are simply fewer investigations of antenatal psychopathology compared to postnatal psychopathology. Two, most investigations have focused on antenatal anxiety and depressive symptoms, not anxiety and *mood* symptoms. Three, hypomanic or mild manic symptoms are often underdetected, typically attracting clinical attention only when they co-occur with worrisome behaviors, lead to depression, or escalate into acute mania.

Against this background, based on a limited number of reports, it seems that antenatal hypomanic symptoms are less common than both antenatal depressive symptoms and postnatal hypomanic symptoms (Heron et al., 2009; Jones & Craddock, 2001; Sharma, 2009; Smith et al., 2009; Viguera et al., 2007, 2011). Antenatal manic symptoms seem to be the least common affective experience. For instance, using a retrospective life charting design, Viguera and colleagues (2011) compared rates of affective episodes during pregnancy among women with a diagnosis of unipolar, bipolar I, or bipolar II disorder. Among women with a unipolar diagnosis, 2.8% experienced an MDE. Among women with a bipolar I diagnosis, 8.9% experienced an MDE, 2.7% experienced a hypomanic episode, 8.1% experienced a mixed episode, and 2.3% experienced a manic episode. Among women with a bipolar II diagnosis, 10.4% experienced an MDE, 2.8% experienced a hypomanic episode, and 3.6% experiencing a mixed episode. Thus, across diagnostic groups, the most common antenatal psychopathology was depression, followed by mixed episodes (characterized by co-occurring symptoms of depression and mania). Likewise, Heron and colleagues (2009) investigated the prevalence of hypomanic symptoms among women (selected for pregnancy, not psychiatric diagnosis) receiving care at midwifery clinics. They found that the rates of positive screens for antenatal versus postnatal hypomanic "highs" to be 1.4% versus 11.7%, respectively. Comparatively, rates of positive screens for antenatal versus postnatal depression were 19.0% and 14.6%, respectively.

Notably, abrupt discontinuation of antimanic medication most often precedes antenatal manic symptoms and manias (Newport et al., 2008; Viguera, Cohen, Boufford, Whitfield, & Baldessarini, 2002; Viguera et al., 2007, 2011). Findings suggest that recurrence is common among women who stop antimania pharmacotherapy, and that recurrence rates are similar for pregnant and nonpregnant women but higher for postnatal than for nonpostnatal women (Viguera et al., 2011). Although much is unknown about hypomania and mania during pregnancy, the implications of these experiences are serious and potentially life-threatening. Bipolarity is the most robust predictor of severe postnatal mental health complications, including psychosis (Heron, Robertson Blackmore, McGuinness, Craddock, & Jones, 2007; Kim, Choi, & Ha, 2008; Sit, Rothschild, & Wisner, 2006).

Intervention Recommendations for Hypomanic and Manic Symptoms During Pregnancy

Health professionals should broach mental health history as early as possible, including during preconception planning and prenatal care visits. They should screen for suspected or confirmed personal or family history of bipolar or bipolar spectrum disorders. When symptoms are present, health professionals should assess illness history and reproductive risks of acute and maintenance treatments. For women engaged in maintenance treatment, health professionals should discourage abrupt changes in treatment regimen, even in the context of an unplanned pregnancy. The management of bipolar disorder during and following pregnancy can be complex, especially given the severity of the illness, potential teratogenicity of pharmacotherapy, and other treatment issues. Health professionals may prefer collaborating care with a specialty perinatal mood disorders clinic, when accessible and based on the woman's preference. Overall, providing early and frequent psychoeducation, assessment, and treatment may reduce the substantial postnatal morbidity associated with bipolarity. For additional reading, see Yonkers et al. (2011) and Chessick and Dimidjian (2010).

Postnatal Depressive Symptoms

Postnatal Baby Blues By definition, the postnatal baby blues is a transient condition where depressive and other mood symptoms are present but of insufficient duration or severity to meet diagnostic criteria for an MDE (Henshaw, 2003; O'Hara, 2009). During the baby blues, women often experience mood lability, depressed or irritable mood, interpersonal hypersensitivity, tearfulness, and preoccupation with infant wellbeing (Altshuler, Hendrick, & Cohen, 2000; Flynn, 2005; Wisner, Parry, & Piontek, 2002). Symptoms may peak in severity 5 days following delivery. Generally, the symptoms resolve within 7 to 14 days following delivery and do not require treatment. Severe baby blues may increase risk for postnatal psychiatric disorders (Beck, 2001; Henshaw, Foreman, & Cox, 2004). An incidence rate—that is, the rate of new cases in a specified period—of up to 75% has been observed across cultures (Austin et al., 2010; Henshaw, 2003).

Intervention Recommendations for Postnatal Baby Blues

Health professionals should provide psychoeducation before childbirth to women and their families about the baby blues. During a woman's baby blues experience, health professionals should offer reassurance and normalization to both her and her family, and monitor for clinical worsening or persistence. Additionally, health professionals should provide clear guidance to women and their families about signs and symptoms that signal the need for additional assessment and possible treatment. These include presence of suicidal ideation, severe insomnia, severe anxiety, confusion, thoughts about harming the baby, and duration of any symptoms lasting more than 2 weeks. In general, the postnatal baby blues are a typical experience that remits without intervention. When symptoms are severe or do not remit, health professionals should conduct a comprehensive psychiatric assessment.

Major Depressive Episode With Postpartum Onset (MDE-PP)

Based on the existing literature, a nonpsychotic MDE with postpartum onset (MDE-PP) is similar to an MDE occurring at nonreproductive times (Wisner et al., 1994). The clinical presentation, however, may be somewhat different. Some depressive symptoms or features occur with greater frequency in MDE-PP than in MDE, including anxiety, somatic complaints, and sleep disturbances (Cooper et al., 2007; Gale & Harlow, 2003; Miller, 2002; Swanson, Flynn, Wilburn, Marcus, & Armitage, 2010; Yonkers et al., 2011). The overall experience

of having and caring for a new baby may better explain symptomatic differences than does some underlying nosological difference. For example, a woman's sleep is likely to be disrupted by an infant's sleeping and feeding schedules. Or, she may suffer physical changes, discomfort, or pain associated with delivery and breastfeeding. During MDE-PP, a woman may have distressing, intrusive thoughts about infant safety or parenting competency and guilt. She may experience difficulty falling or staying asleep, even when the infant is sleeping or outside her care. These symptoms, especially when at syndromal significance, may lead to negative mother, infant, and mother–infant dyad outcomes (Moses-Kolko & Roth, 2004; NRC, 2009).

An incidence of up to 54% has been observed for nonpsychotic major or minor MDE-PP, with higher rates found in postnatal samples comprising primarily economically disadvantaged women (Flynn, 2005; Gaynes et al., 2005; Kessler, McGonagle, Swartz, Blazer, & Nelson, 1993; O'Hara & Swain, 1996; Viguera et al., 2011). Community-based epidemiological studies suggest a prevalence rate of 13%. Although these rates are similar to rates observed in women without reproductive events, between 45% and 65% of women will experience their first MDE during the postnatal year. Furthermore, among women with a personal history of a mood disorder, between 30% and 50% will experience a recurrence during the postnatal year. Among women with a personal or family history of an antenatal or postnatal affective episode, the recurrence risk is even higher. For instance, Robertson, Jones, Haque, Holder, and Craddock (2005) found that women with bipolar disorder and a previous postnatal affective episode had a 60% risk of experiencing a recurrence following another pregnancy compared to 25% of women with bipolar disorder and no past postnatal affective episode. Forty and colleagues (2006) reported that 42% of women with a family history of MDE-PP, compared to 15% of women without such a history, experienced MDE-PP.

Intervention Recommendations for MDE-PP Health professionals should assess women's risk for MDE-PP before childbirth, during prenatal visits. For women with several risk factors, such as a personal history of a mood disorder or a personal or family history of a postnatal recurrence, health professionals should discuss prophylactic treatment and develop a postnatal assessment and treatment plan. At the 6-week postnatal obstetrical visit and pediatric well visits, health professionals should identify, engage, and treat women suffering from moderate to severe MDE-PP. When MDD-PP is severe, health professionals should frequently assess for deterioration, suicide risk, and psychotic features, and provide clear guidance to women and their families about when to seek urgent care.

For women experiencing subsyndromal or syndromal MDE-PP of mild severity or impairment, health professionals should assess their needs and monitor until remission of symptoms. During any assessment of postnatal depressive symptoms, when possible, health professionals should observe mother–infant interaction to gauge impairments in attachment and bonding. Overall, providing early psychoeducation, coupled with developing a postnatal assessment and treatment plan, may reduce the burden and cost associated with postnatal depressive symptoms. For additional reading, see Yonkers et al. (2011), Kuehn (2010), and APA (2000b).

Postnatal Hypomanic Symptoms

What is true about the antenatal hypomania and mania literature is also true about the postnatal hypomania literature: We know relatively little, and much of what we do know is about full-blown acute mania (see Psychotic Symptoms section). Nonetheless, the available evidence supports a strong relationship between childbirth and onset of hypomanic symptoms (Heron et al., 2005, 2009; Sharma, 2009; Sharma et al., 2010).

Whereas the clinical presentation of postnatal hypomania appears to be similar to hypomanias occurring at nonreproductive times, it may be more difficult to detect for several reasons (Chessick & Dimidijian, 2010; Smith et al., 2009). One, childbirth is typically associated with a high level of elation. Two, sleep disturbances or changes are also common following childbirth. One way to distinguish a pathological from a normative experience may be to assess sleep need and other symptoms of hypomania, including energy. Among women who do experience postnatal hypomania, symptoms typically emerge immediately after delivery, peak between 1 and 5 days after delivery, and gradually remit within 1 week of delivery (Heron et al., 2004, 2005, 2009; Sharma, 2009). Prevalence estimates of postnatal hypomania in nonclinical populations range between 9.6% and 20.4%, indicating that there is about a 10% increase in the prevalence of hypomanic symptoms from during to following pregnancy.

There are two major implications of postnatal hypomania (Benazzi, 2007; Chessick & Dimidijian, 2010; Sharma, Burt, & Ritchie, 2010). One is its role in increasing risk for the development of postnatal depressive symptoms. The other is its importance for accurate diagnosis. An incorrect diagnosis may lead to subsequent use of antidepressant pharmacotherapy for later postnatal depressive symptoms or an underestimation of risk for postpartum psychosis, both of which are associated with increased risk for suicide and infanticide (Heron et al., 2007; Kim et al., 2008; Sit et al., 2006).

Intervention Recommendations for Postnatal Hypomanic Symptoms

Health professionals should assess women's experience of hypomania, especially if the woman has a suspected or confirmed personal or family history of bipolar or bipolar spectrum disorders. Typically, hypomanic symptoms are associated with little to no impairment in functioning. Nonetheless, when present, it is important for health professionals to record a bipolar diagnosis and provide psychoeducation to women and their families. Psychoeducation should include information about the diagnosis and associated risk for postnatal depressive symptoms and postpartum psychosis. For some women, hypomanic symptoms may be an early symptom of postpartum psychosis (see Psychotic Symptoms section). At the 6-week postnatal obstetrical visit and pediatric well visits, health professionals should assess for any postnatal mood symptoms. Overall, increasing recognition of postnatal hypomanic symptoms may improve the accuracy of psychiatric diagnoses and reduce the burden and cost associated with undetected bipolarity. For additional reading, see Sharma et al. (2010) and Yonkers et al. (2011).

PSYCHOTIC SYMPTOMS

In *DSM-IV-TR* and *DSM-5*, postnatal psychotic symptoms may be diagnosed as MDE severe with psychotic features with postpartum onset (MDE-PP-S), manic episode severe with psychotic features with postpartum onset (M-PP-S), or brief psychotic disorder with postpartum onset (PD-PP). These disorders are often grouped together and collectively referred to as postpartum psychosis (Jones & Cantwell, 2010; Yonkers et al., 2011). Postpartum psychosis is most often accounted for by bipolar disorder, followed by schizoaffective disorder and, least often, schizophrenia (Jones & Craddock, 2001; Jones, 2010; Ruggero et al., 2011; Sit et al., 2006).

In postpartum psychosis, symptom onset is often rapid, and there is a dramatic change in the woman's functioning (Attia, Downey, & Oberman, 1999; Kim et al., 2008; Sit et al., 2006). In one retrospective chart review, Heron and colleagues (2007) documented initial onset of symptoms within 1 to 3 days of delivery. Nonetheless, risk may persist beyond the first few days or weeks. In postpartum psychosis, a woman may experience severe mood lability, marked cognitive disturbance and impairment (especially confusion), delusional beliefs about her infant, bizarre behavior, hallucinations, "unusual" psychotic symptoms, such as tactile or olfactory hallucinations, and, less often, command hallucinations to kill her infant. Importantly, homicidality is rare. In one study of hospitalized women with postnatal psychosis, 35% described delusions about their infant, but only 9% had thoughts of harming their infant (Kumar, Marks, Platz, & Yoshida, 1995). Nonetheless, in postpartum psychosis, insight and judgment may be absent, placing both the woman and her infant's security at incredible risk.

Postpartum psychosis is relatively rare; the incidence is about 1 in 500 for MDE-PP-S and 1 or 2 in 1,000 women for PD-PP (Jones et al., 2011; Ruggero et al., 2011; Sit et al., 2006). Among women with a personal history of bipolar disorder, risk is estimated to be between 25% and 50%. Among women with a personal history of bipolar disorder and a personal or family history of postpartum psychosis, risk is about 60%. Importantly, although women with postpartum psychosis usually experience a rapid treatment response and remission of psychotic symptoms, suicide risk remains elevated 70-fold during the first postnatal year.

Intervention Recommendations for Postpartum Psychosis

Health professionals should assess women's risk for postnatal psychosis before childbirth, during prenatal visits. Risk factors include a personal or family history of postnatal psychosis, a personal history of bipolar disorder, a personal history of unipolar psychotic depression, and current or planned discontinuation of maintenance antimanic pharmacotherapy. For women with any risk factor, health professionals should provide psychoeducation to women and their families, discuss prophylactic treatment, and develop a postnatal assessment and treatment plan. Psychoeducation should include instructions to a woman and her family to seek emergency care if any psychotic or manic symptom surfaces. A postnatal assessment and treatment plan should center on early identification of symptoms and rapid referral for treatment and, most likely, urgent care. Health professionals should coordinate symptom assessment during a woman's hospital stay and at her 6-week postnatal obstetrical visit. In the presence of psychotic or manic symptoms, hospitalization is often necessary. Overall, providing rapid intervention may reduce the potentially devastating cost associated with postpartum psychosis. For additional reading, see Doucet, Jones, Letourneau, Dennis, and Blackmore (2011), Ruggero et al. (2011), and Sit et al. (2006).

ANXIETY SYMPTOMS

The antenatal and postnatal periods may be a time of increased risk for general anxiety symptoms and the onset or relapse of specific anxiety disorders (Altshuler et al., 2000; Austin et al., 2010; Mauri et al., 2010; Ross & McClean, 2006). Increasingly, there is evidence that anxiety is as common and deleterious as is depression, especially during the postnatal period. Yet, less attention has been paid to puerperal anxiety disorders, and to a lesser extent, anxiety symptoms, compared to puerperal mood disorders and mood symptoms. In part, this may be explained by the frequent co-occurrence of these disorders and symptoms. Traditionally, when depressive and anxiety symptoms are present, a depression diagnosis has primacy over an anxiety diagnosis. Consequently, epidemiological estimates of puerperal anxiety disorders likely underestimate the burden of anxiety. Because of the limited nature of this literature, we present only a brief discussion of anxiety across the antenatal and postnatal periods, with particular focus on general anxiety symptoms and obsessive-compulsive disorder (OCD).

General anxiety symptoms during pregnancy are common, especially for first-time mothers (Austin et al., 2010; Buist, Gotman, & Yonkers, 2011). General anxiety symptoms seem to be highest during the first and third trimesters of pregnancy, and higher during compared to following pregnancy (Field et al., 2010; Figueiredo & Conde, 2011; Teixeira, Figueiredo, Conde, Pacheco, & Costa, 2009; Wenzel, Haugen, Jackson, &

Robinson, 2003). Unlike general anxiety symptoms, specific anxiety disorders, including OCD and panic disorder, appear to be more frequent in the postnatal than in the antenatal period, and more frequent in postnatal women than in the general population (Abramowitz, Schwartz, & Moore, 2003; Heron et al., 2004; Ross & McLean, 2006; Wisner, Peindl, Gigliotti, & Hanusa, 1999; Zambaldi et al., 2009).

Obsessive-Compulsive Disorder (OCD)

Prevalence estimates of OCD during pregnancy are lower during than following pregnancy, ranging between 0.2% and 1.2% and 2.3% and 3.9%, respectively (Abramowitz et al., 2003; Ross & McLean, 2006; Zambaldi et al., 2009). Postnatal OCD prevalence is estimated to be higher than is the lifetime prevalence in the general population. In antenatal or postnatal OCD, a woman's intrusive thoughts often center on causing harm to her fetus or infant. Importantly, OCD thoughts are often distinguished from disturbed or delusional thoughts, characterizing postpartum psychosis by the preservation of rational thought (e.g., the woman recognizes the thoughts as unreasonable), absence of acting on the thoughts (e.g., the woman exerts great effort to avoid action), and co-occurrence of fear or anxiety (e.g., the woman identifies the thoughts as unwanted) (Ross & McLean 2006; Ruggero et al., 2011; Sit et al., 2006). Yet, obsessional thoughts about harming the fetus or infant may not be indicative of either OCD or postpartum psychosis; more than 40% of women with postnatal depression and between 34% and 65% of new parents in healthy community samples report experiencing such thoughts (Abramowitz et al., 2010; Jennings, Ross, Popper, & Elmore, 1999; Wisner et al., 1999).

One major complication of postnatal OCD is that the woman, fearing she will harm her newborn, may avoid or refuse to care for him or her. Another major complication is that onset of antenatal or postnatal OCD is typically followed by onset of depressive symptoms. Risk factors for puerperal OCD include a personal history of a psychiatric disorder and suffering childbirth complications (e.g., preterm delivery, unexpected cesarean section without labor, etc.) (Abramowitz et al., 2010; Zambaldi et al., 2009).

Intervention Recommendations for Antenatal and Postnatal Anxiety Symptoms

Health professionals should educate women and their families that some general anxiety during and following pregnancy is normal, but that anxiety that is of moderate or greater severity, or impairs functioning, is a serious complication. Pregnant women should be evaluated for risk factors, including a personal history of a psychiatric disorder. For women with any risk factors, health professionals should discuss prophylactic treatment and evaluate more often. An assessment of anxiety should occur in concert with other mental health assessments at least once every trimester, at the 6-week postnatal obstetrical visit, and at pediatric well visits. For women experiencing syndromal anxiety, health professionals should assess their needs and present treatment options. Based on available evidence, puerperal anxiety disorders are best managed in the same manner as anxiety disorders occurring during nonreproductive times. Overall, providing early and frequent psychoeducation, assessment, and treatment may reduce the complications associated with antenatal and postnatal anxiety. For additional reading, see Buist et al., (2011),

Austin et al. (2010), and Ross and McLean (2006).

even in the presence of *every* documented risk factor.

SOCIODEMOGRAPHIC AND ENVIRONMENTAL RISK FACTORS

Pregnancy is not inherently protective against psychiatric disorders, and some women are at increased risk for experiencing antenatal and postnatal onset, recurrence, or relapse. In addition to a personal or family history of psychiatric or puerperal disorders, some sociodemographic and environmental factors also confer risk, especially for depression. In fact, there is a robust, positive association between depression, at any time, and social disadvantage, such that women of poor sociodemographic or environmental circumstances account for a greater proportion of depression cases than do women of social advantage (NRC, 2009; Segre, O'Hara, Arndt, & Stuart, 2007). Some of these factors also contribute to risk during and following pregnancy, and include poverty, unintended pregnancy, single relationship status, good to poor overall health, marital or partner-related conflict, limited social support, childhood adversity, negative life events, intimate partner violence before or during pregnancy, and childcare stress (Beck, 2001; Koleva et al., 2011; O'Hara, 2009; Rudolph et al., 2000; Sajatovic, Sanders, Alexeenko, & Madhusoodanan, 2010). Variables inconsistently associated with increased risk include smoking, alcohol use, parity, obstetric complications, maternal race/ethnicity, and maternal age. Whereas the presence of multiple risk factors may confer cumulative risk, no single or combination of variables reliably and consistently predicts which women will suffer. Moreover, some women will show resiliency—

EFFECTS ON WOMEN AND THEIR FAMILIES

Psychiatric disorders are periods of biological dysregulation further complicated by pregnancy, childbirth, and postnatal recovery (Barrett & Fleming, 2011; Miller & LaRusso, 2011; NRC, 2009). Empirical investigations demonstrate that these disorders, especially when present in women with a history of childhood adversity, interrupt optimal mothering, even before birth, through complex physiological and behavioral systems (Barrett & Fleming, 2011; Leibenluft & Yonkers, 2010; Shaw, 2011). Although these risks are documented, much is unknown. We summarize some of the empirical findings as follows. For a discussion of key issues regarding the effect of depression on parenting (see NRC, 2009).

Consequences of Antenatal Mood and Anxiety Symptoms

Antenatal mood and anxiety symptoms, at both the syndromal and subsyndromal level, are risk factors for adverse pregnancy, childbirth, and neonatal outcomes (Berle et al., 2005; Coelho, Murray, Royal-Lawson, & Cooper, 2011; Field, Diego, & Hernandez-Reif, 2006; Glover, 2011; Grote et al., 2010; Littleton et al., 2007; Righetti-Veltma, Conne-Perreard, Bousquet, & Manzano, 2002). Investigations show that a woman with antenatal depression, especially if she is an adolescent, may delay or seek less prenatal care, obtain inadequate sleep or nutrition, and use drugs, alcohol, or cigarettes. The consequences of the interaction between psychiatric symptoms and these health behaviors may include higher incidence of preeclampsia, increased fetal activity, preterm birth and lower birth weight, and newborn neurobehavioral dysregulation, including greater inconsolability and more crying (Broth, Goodman, Hall, & Raynor, 2004; Dieter et al., 2001; Field et al., 2007, 2010; Grote et al., 2010; Kurki, Hiilesmaa, Raitasalo, Mattila, & Ylikorkala, 2000; Marcus et al., 2011; Rondo et al., 2003). Similarly, for a woman experiencing antenatal anxiety, her infant may be born premature, weigh less, and receive a lower Apgar score (Berle et al., 2005; Field et al., 2010; Kelly et al., 2002; Rondo et al., 2003).

Adverse pregnancy, childbirth, and neonatal outcomes may have long-term consequences for both the woman and her infant (Coelho et al., 2011; Davies, Winter, & Ciccetti, 2006; Reay, Matthey, Ellwood, & Scott, 2011). For example, antenatal depression and anxiety are the most robust predictors of postnatal mental health complications. Children of women who experience antenatal depression are at increased risk for developing childhood depression (Lundy et al., 1999). Similarly, children of women who experience antenatal anxiety are at increased risk for developing general anxiety at 1 year of age and childhood attentional, behavioral, and anxiety disorders (Gerardin et al., 2011; Glover, 2011; West & Newman, 2003).

Consequences of Postnatal Mood and Anxiety Symptoms

Postnatal mood and anxiety symptoms are associated with impairments in mothering, poor mother–infant interactions, disrupted infant behavior and development, and inadequate infant health management (NRC, 2009). Investigations show that, compared to women without mental health complications, women experiencing postnatal mood and/or anxiety symptoms are less likely to breastfeed and more likely to stop breastfeeding early in infancy (Field et al., 2010; Field, Hernandez-Reif, & Larissa, 2002; Watkins, Meltzer-Brody, Zolnoun, & Stuebe, 2011). They are more likely to delay or not vaccinate their infants (Turner, Boyle, & O'Rourke, 2003). They are more likely to miss their infants' outpatient healthcare visits and access acute outpatient or emergency room care (Flynn, Davis, Marcus, Cunningham, & Blow, 2004). Women with postnatal depression and/or anxiety are more likely to assess themselves as having poor competency as a mother (Teti & Gelfand, 1991). They are more likely to have difficulty accurately perceiving their infants' emotional expressions and identify their infants as difficult (Broth et al., 2004). In turn, the infants are more likely to have an insecure attachment, emotion regulatory difficulties, and eating or sleeping difficulties (Davies et al., 2006; Righetti-Veltema et al., 2002; Swanson et al., 2010; Verduyn, Barrowclough, Roberts, Tarrier, & Harrington, 2003; West & Newman, 2003).

INTERVENTION DELIVERY

For some women, antenatal and postnatal mood and anxiety symptoms will be brief and remit without intervention. For others, symptoms will persist, throughout pregnancy, the first postnatal year, or beyond. Depending on the duration and intensity of symptoms, and other complex factors, some women will be able to maintain functioning as a parent, whereas others will experience severe and chronic impairment. To date, the literature is relatively uninformative for predicting women's likely symptom and functioning trajectories. Therefore, the decision to initiate prophylactic or acute treatment or continue maintenance treatment largely depends on a women's history, risk, and, if present, symptom severity and duration (Kuehn, 2010; Yonkers et al., 2009).

Fortunately, preliminary research indicates that evidence-based treatment for antenatal and postnatal psychiatric disorders improves or restores overall maternal functioning, prevents negative infant outcomes, and improves mother–infant interactions immediately postpartum and at 18-month and 5-year follow-up (Logsdon, Wisner, Hanusa, & Phillips, 2003; Moses-Kolko & Roth, 2004; Murray, Cooper, & Hipwell, 2003; Verduyn et al., 2003). Yet, few women are receiving any of the prophylactic, acute, or maintenance care that they need during or following pregnancy. For instance, women with antenatal or postnatal depression seem to be accessing treatment at a rate lower than is the national rate of depression treatment in the general population, which ranges between 30% and 50% (Van Hook, 1999; Woolhouse, Brown, Krastev, Perlen, & Gunn, 2009; Young, Klap, Sherbourne, & Wells, 2001). For example, in one study, our group prospectively examined the incidence and treatment of depression in obstetric settings among pregnant women (Marcus, Flynn, Blow, & Barry, 2003). Whereas 20% of the sample met a screening threshold for significant depressive symptomatology, only 14% received any treatment. Similarly, in another study, our group documented that only 33% of pregnant women with a confirmed diagnosis of MDE received any treatment (Flynn, Marcus, & Blow, 2006). Much of the recent research literature suggests that interventions that target improving mother–infant attachment and dyadic factors, and not necessarily maternal depression outcomes, lead to improved mother–infant functioning (NRC, 2009).

Psychiatric symptoms during and following pregnancy are underrecognized and undertreated. Thus, effective intervention, resulting in the amelioration of symptoms and restoration of optimal mothering, depends on not only having effective evidence-based treatments, but also in identifying women in need, connecting women to care, *and* decreasing barriers to accessing care. We discuss the empirical evidence for identifying women who are at elevated risk and engaging these women in treatment as follows. For a review of evidence-based somatic and nonsomatic treatment strategies, see Kuehn (2011). For a discussion of complementary and alternative therapies, see Gossler (2010). Additionally, treatment guidelines are available online from the American Psychiatric Association (http://www.psych.org) and the American College of Obstetricians and Gynecologists (http://www.acog.org).

IDENTIFYING WOMEN IN NEED

Health professionals have several contact points to identify women who are at increased risk for or who are experiencing mood and anxiety symptoms, to provide psychoeducation, and to connect to treatment (NRC, 2009). These include preconception planning visits, prenatal clinical visits, hospitalization during childbirth, the 6-week postnatal obstetrical visit, and pediatric well visits (Buist, 2006; Buist et al., 2005; Chaudron, Szilagyi, Kitzman, Wadkins, & Conwell, 2004; Earls & Committee, 2010; Hewitt et al., 2009; Leddy, Haaga, Gray, & Schulkin, 2011; Marcus et al., 2003, 2005). The most likely opportunities may be at prenatal clinical visits and pediatric well visits, because more than 80% of women present for prenatal care at some point during their pregnancy, and pediatricians provide care for about 80% of children under age 5 (Flynn, 2005; NRC, 2009).

Several investigations have evaluated the feasibility and acceptability of depression screening during prenatal care, showing that screening can be feasibly conducted but has little or no impact on depression outcomes. In general, health professionals recognize depression as a serious antenatal and postnatal health issue, and they view screening during prenatal and postnatal care as largely feasible and acceptable (Buist, 2003, 2006; Buist et al., 2005; Flynn et al., 2006; Kelly, Zatzick, & Anders, 2001; LaRocco-Cockburn, Melville, Bell, & Katon, 2003). Yet, it is not routine practice, and outcomes are insufficient (Gaynes et al., 2005; Hewitt et al., 2009). For example, the rate of screening at the 6-week postnatal obstetrical visit ranges between 3.7% and 6.3% (Evins et al., 2000; Georgiopoulos, Bryan, Wollan, & Yawn, 2001; Leddy et al., 2011). Health professionals in obstetric settings identify screening barriers including time constraints, lack of training to identify or treat depression, discomfort with discussing mental health issues, uncertainty that screening improves outcomes, and lack of infrastructure for responding to positive screens.

A less-investigated screening contact point is at pediatric well visits. Pediatricians interact with postnatal women and their infants several times during the postnatal year. Thus, pediatric well visits provide multiple opportunities to assess symptoms and parenting (Earls & Committee, 2010; Kuehn, 2011). Yet, results about women and pediatricians' acceptability of screening during these visits are mixed. For instance, Chaudron and colleagues (2004) reported that when a screening measure was added to the routine paperwork at pediatric well visits, 88% of women completed the screen. Moreover, pediatricians' rate of detecting postnatal depression improved from 1.6% to 8.5%. In contrast, when Tam and colleagues (2002) approached two urban and one suburban pediatric clinics to be study sites, the suburban clinic declined participation, stating concerns about medical-legal responsibility for women who are identified as depressed. Recruiting at only the two urban clinics, Tam and colleagues approached 160 women during their infants' first pediatric well visit. Fewer than 5% agreed to complete the screening measures and none agreed to a structured diagnostic clinical interview. One explanation for the dramatically different results might be that women accepted mental health screening when it was part of routine clinical care but not when it was identified as separate or part of research.

Screening Measures

Ideally, health professionals would use self-report assessment measures in concert with face-to-face conversations about past and current mental health. Realistically, self-report assessment measures may be the "only conversation." Thus, if screening during prenatal visits is to become routine clinical practice, then screening procedures must be brief and must produce easily interpretable results (Earls & Committee, 2010; Gaynes et al., 2005; U.S. Preventive Task Force, 2002).

Generally, screening measures assess type, severity, and duration of symptoms. Based on what a woman endorses, a total score is calculated. This total score can then be compared to a specified cut point. Cut points for "positive screens" are determined based on comparing the screening measure and a gold standard, typically a validated diagnostic interview. A screening measure's accuracy of prediction is based on three indices of accuracy: sensitivity, specificity, and positive predictive value (PPV). *Sensitivity* is the ability of the measure to correctly identify women with the disorder, the true positive rate. *Specificity* is the ability of the measure to correctly identify women without the disorder, the true negative rate. *PPV* is the probability that a woman with a positive screen is suffering from the disorder. Based on ratings of sensitivity, specificity, and PPV, a screening measure is assessed as psychometrically valid or invalid.

Psychometrically valid screening measures for women during and following pregnancy include the Edinburgh Postnatal Depression Scale (EPDS) (Cox, 1983), the Postpartum Depression Screening Scale (PDSS) (Beck & Gable, 2001), and the Highs Scale (Glover et al., 1994). Generally, women can complete any of these measures in less than 10 minutes.

The EPDS is a 10-item questionnaire that was designed to detect depressive symptoms, excluding somatic symptoms that may be confounded by pregnancy (Cox, 1983). However, the EPDS also asks women about symptoms of anxiety. Items assess ability to laugh and enjoy oneself, sad and anxious mood, self-blame, sleep difficulties not resulting from childbirth, coping, and suicidality (i.e., suicidal thoughts and suicidal behaviors). Total scores range from 0 to 30. The most commonly used cut point of 13 has excellent sensitivity and specificity. A cut point of 10 has excellent sensitivity and good specificity.

The PDSS is a 35-item questionnaire that also asks women about symptoms of depression (Beck & Gable, 2001). The first seven items can be used as a short questionnaire. Items assess sleeping and eating disturbances, feelings of anxiety and insecurity, emotional lability (i.e., unstable, quick to change, or disproportionate emotions), cognitive and thought difficulties, loss of self (i.e., feeling abnormal), feelings of guilt and shame, and suicidality. Total scores range from 35 to 175. A cut point of 80 has excellent sensitivity and specificity. A cut point of 60 has excellent sensitivity and good specificity.

The Highs Scale is a seven-item questionnaire that asks women about symptoms of hypomania and mania (Glover et al., 1994). Items assess feelings of elation, talkativeness, activation, racing thoughts, grandiosity, sleep need, and concentration/distractibility. Total scores range from 0 to 12. A cut point of 8 has fair sensitivity and specificity.

Screening Recommendations Health professionals should screen for mood and anxiety symptoms or psychiatric risk during preconception planning visits, prenatal clinical visits, hospitalization during childbirth, the 6-week postnatal obstetrical visit, and pediatric visits. Screening measures should be part of routine clinical paperwork, psychometrically valid for puerperal populations, and cover the full spectrum of symptoms. Given that prior history of psychiatric illness is a strong predictor of subsequent episodes, screening should also take into account the personal history of depression, mania, and anxiety. One option may be the EPDS or PDSS *and* Highs, combined with lifetime history items. Generally, health professionals should use lower cut points, decreasing specificity and increasing sensitivity, and thus, casting a wider net for detection of illness. The downside of this approach is increased false-positive rates, especially in clinic settings where follow-up assessment and access to treatments are scarce. At a minimum, an assessment for bipolarity is needed among women who screen positive for depressive symptoms or who are considering antidepressant pharmacotherapy. Importantly, health professionals should not substitute a positive screen for a comprehensive diagnostic assessment. If this assessment is unavailable at the screening location, health professionals should arrange for women with a positive screen a follow-up assessment with their primary care physician or a mental health specialist. The referring health professionals should confirm women's attendance to the follow-up appointments and address nonadherence.

ENGAGING WOMEN IN TREATMENT

Unfortunately, simply screening women and providing a treatment referral, regardless of obstetric or pediatric setting, is unlikely to improve antenatal and postnatal outcomes dramatically (Earls et al., 2010). Among women detected by screening procedures, between 41% and 87% decline or do not attend treatment (Reay et al., 2011; Smith et al., 2009; Thio, Browne, Coverdale, & Argyle, 2006; Woolhouse et al., 2009). Worse, for women who do connect with mental

health services, most receive inadequate treatment or discontinue prematurely (Flynn et al., 2006; Marcus, Flynn, Blow, & Barry, 2005).

Poor treatment engagement and adherence during and following pregnancy are complex phenomenon involving barriers across many levels (NRC, 2009). Barriers include both system-level (healthcare policy, clinician training and reimbursement, healthcare system resources) and individual-level (motivational, practical/logistical, stigma, and treatment and venue preferences) barriers. We discuss individual-level barriers to treatment engagement and adherence among women with puerperal psychiatric disorders as follows.

Motivational and Practical Barriers to Care

The emotional and biological dysregulation associated with psychiatric disorders, coupled with the substantial hormonal, psychosocial, and quality-of-life changes that occur during and following pregnancy, may be barriers to care for several reasons (Barrett & Fleming, 2011; Buist, 2003). One, the features of puerperal psychiatric disorders may create motivational deficits. These include loss of motivation and energy, hopelessness, difficulty concentrating or making decisions, and anxiety. Two, during pregnancy, hormonal changes and fetal development may lead to practical barriers, including pregnancy-related fatigue, nausea, physical discomfort, and bed rest. Three, following childbirth, hormonal changes and caring for a new baby may lead to new logistical and motivational barriers, including new time or childcare demands, insufficient or poor quality of sleep, and low energy. Four, the financial demands of caring for a new baby, potentially amplified by high insurance copayments or loss of prenatal healthcare coverage (e.g.,

Medicaid), may lead to financial barriers. Any one or a combination of these factors may present substantial motivational or practical barriers to care, potentially discouraging treatment engagement or adherence among antenatal and postnatal women. Yet, one investigation by our group demonstrated that even in a clinic site where transportation, childcare, access, and payment barriers were absent, fewer than one-third of women attended their scheduled mental health appointment (Flynn et al., 2006). This finding suggests a key role for other factors, including stigma and treatment acceptability.

Stigma

One major reason most women detected by screening do not attend treatment or decline a treatment referral is stigma and negative beliefs about mental health and treatment (Brown et al., 2001; Mojtabai, Olfson, & Mechanic, 2002; O'Mahen & Flynn, 2008; Reay et al., 2011; Satcher, 2001; U.S. DHHS, 2011). Positive attitudes about mental health and treatment are strongly associated with engaging in treatment. Unfortunately, mental health treatment continues to be mired in stigma and incorrect information, including the belief that depression signifies a weakness or personal failing, treatment is ineffective, and pharmacotherapy is dangerous. In turn, stigma and poor social responses may aggravate motivational barriers, further reducing treatment engagement. This may be particularly salient for African-American women. Investigations by our group and others have found that, compared to White women, African-American women endorse greater stigma and fear about mental health treatment, less knowledge about and different conceptualizations of depression, and less confidence in antidepressant pharmacotherapy.

Treatment Acceptability

The majority of women's mental health treatment is provided in general medical settings, such as obstetrics and gynecology or primary care clinics (Scholle, Haskett, Hanusa, Pincus, & Kupfer, 2003). In these settings, antidepressant pharmacotherapy is the most frequently provided psychiatric treatment, and evidence-based psychotherapy frequently is unavailable or inaccessible (McGowen & Miller, 2004). Yet, many pregnant and breastfeeding women, especially African-American women, are simply unwilling to take these medications, and they report a strong preference for psychotherapy and nonsomatic treatments (Alvidrez & Azocar, 1999; Cohen et al., 2004; Marcus et al., 2005; van Schaik et al., 2004). Nonetheless, despite these women's stated preferences for psychosocial interventions, a substantial proportion of them who begin treatment discontinue prematurely, citing dissatisfaction with the treatment. One reason might be that current psychosocial interventions are not as relevant or tailored to the specific difficulties associated with pregnancy and caring for a new baby, including interpersonal conflicts. For example, Zayas, McKee, and Jankowski (2004) offered cognitive-behavioral therapy (CBT) to minority women who were experiencing depression in their third trimester of pregnancy. They reported that only one-third of women completed the full course of treatment, and women said that they chose to miss sessions in which the content seemed irrelevant to their needs.

Another reason that antenatal and postnatal women prematurely discontinue treatment might be that practical barriers interfere with women's ability to adhere to traditional weekly face-to-face psychotherapy.

Delivering treatment through alternative modalities, such as telephone or Internet-based, and providing treatment at health-care settings where women already are presenting for care, such as obstetrics or pediatric clinics, might diminish these practical barriers and improve treatment acceptability (Kuehn, 2011; O'Mahen & Flynn, 2008). Based on a qualitative study of mostly poor women with varying degrees of depression, the extent to which the clinical engagement interaction was patient-centered and flexible was found to be highly important in referral follow-through and engagement (Flynn, Henshaw, O'Mahen, & Forman, 2010; Henshaw et al., 2011).

RECOMMENDATIONS FOR GENERAL CLINICAL PRACTICE

Despite increased awareness about the frequency and seriousness of antenatal and postnatal psychiatric symptoms, health professionals are underdetecting and undertreating puerperal psychiatric disorders. Health professionals cite several barriers to understanding for whom to intervene, how to intervene, and how to engage. Moreover, women experience barriers to communicating their experiences and connecting with care. To dramatically improve outcomes and reduce the burden and cost of puerperal psychiatric disorders, the field must take action to conquer barriers. Although optimal strategies for doing so require further investigation, the existing literature illuminates some promising approaches as follows:

> *Health professionals need to increase their knowledge about and comfort with mental health.* Health professionals need

to be comfortable initiating conversations about a woman's mental health history. At a minimum, they need to be able to provide basic psychoeducation about symptoms and options to women and their families. Training programs need to better prepare health professionals for these tasks.

> *Health professionals need to incorporate mood and anxiety screening into their routine clinical practice.* Routine use of brief and easily interpretable screening measures will increase detection of pathological experiences. Additionally, it may improve women's comfort with and perceptions about mental health and treatment.

> *Health professionals need to develop a basic infrastructure for addressing positive mood and anxiety screens.* Health professionals need to be able to provide guidance about initiating or continuing treatment, and connect women with mental healthcare.

> *Health professionals need to be listeners.* Health professionals need to elicit from women their concerns about treatment and help women connect with treatment that is consistent with their values and personalized for their situation.

> *Health professionals need to be flexible.* Health professionals need to consider alternative treatment delivery modalities and settings.

> *Health professionals need to be determined.* Women, especially those who are most in need of intervention, may not accept or continue with treatment. Health professionals should be persistent and continually evaluate women's symptoms and

engagement with treatment. If a woman's treatment seems to be inconsistent with best practices or treatment guidelines, health professionals need to voice their concerns.

Clearly, these recommendations give more burden to health professionals and add to already long lists of responsibilities. Yet, the management of psychiatric issues during and following pregnancy is just as important as the management of physical issues in women and their infants. Moreover, robust evidence shows that psychiatric and physical health are intimately interwoven, as is maternal and fetal/infant health (NRC, 2009). Thus, to not only reduce the potentially detrimental consequences of puerperal disorders, but also to improve overall pregnancy, childbirth, neonatal, and infant outcomes, health professionals must incorporate into routine clinical practice psychiatric psychoeducation, assessment, and treatment.

CONCLUSION

Puerperal psychiatric disorders are of great clinical and public health importance, and connecting women in need with existing and effective evidence-based treatments remains a major public health challenge. Although health professionals may be best suited to bridge this gap during their multiple points of contact with women and their families, further study of strategies for understanding for whom to intervene, how to intervene, and how to engage is needed. Moreover, further exploration of these disorders is necessary, including investigating whether there is a risk threshold for illness duration and severity, and whether there are sensitive periods when susceptibility and impact peak.

REFERENCES

Abramowitz, J. S., Melzer-Brody, S., Leserman, J., Killenberg, S., Rinaldi, K., Mahaffey, B., & Pedersen, C. (2010). Obsessional thoughts and complusive behaviors in a sample of women with postpartum mood symptoms. *Archives of Women's Health, 13*(6), 523–530.

Abramowitz, J. S., Schwartz, S. A., & Moore, K. M. (2003). Obsessive-compulsive symptoms in pregnancy and the puerperium: A review of the literature. *Journal of Anxiety Disorders, 17,* 521–526.

Altshuler, L. L., Hendrick, V., & Cohen, L. S. (2000). An update on mood and anxiety disorders during pregnancy and the postpartum period. *Primary Care Companion to the Journal of Clinical Psychiatry, 2*(6), 217–222.

Alvidrez, J., & Azocar, F. (1999). Distressed women's clinic patients: Preferences for mental health treatments and perceived obstacles. *General Hospital Psychiatry, 21*(5), 340–347.

American Psychiatric Association. (2000a). *Diagnostic and statistical manual of mental disorders* (4th ed., text rev.). Washington DC: Author.

American Psychiatric Association. (2000b). *Practice guidelines for the treatment of patients with major depressive disorder* (3rd ed.). Washington DC: Author.

Attia, E., Downey, G., & Oberman, M. (1999). Postpartum psychoses. In L. Miller (Ed.), *Postpartum mood disorders* (p. 101). Washington DC: American Psychiatric Press.

Austin, M. P., Hadzi-Pavlovic, D., Priest, S. R., Reilly, N., Wilhelm, K., Saint, K., & Parker, G. (2010). Depressive and anxiety disorders in the postpartum period: How prevalent are they and can we improve their detection? *Archives of Women's Mental Health, 13*(5), 395–401.

Barrett, J., & Fleming, A. (2011). All mothers are not created equal: Neural and psychobiological perspectives on mothering and the importance of individual differences. *Journal of Child Psychology and Psychiatry, 52*(4), 368–397.

Beck, C. T. (2001). Predictors of postpartum depression: An update. *Journal of Nursing Research, 50*(5), 275–285.

Beck, C. T., & Gable, R. K. (2001). Comparative analysis of the performance of the Postpartum Depression Screening Scale with two other depression instruments. *Nursing Research*, *50*(4), 242–250.

Benazzi, F. (2007). Bipolar II disorder: Epidemiology, diagnosis and management. *CNS Drugs*, *21*(9), 727–740.

Bennett, H. A., Einarson, A., Taddio, A., Koren, G., & Einarson, T. R. (2004). Prevalence of depression during pregnancy: Systematic review. *Obstetrics and Gynecology*, *103*(4), 698–709.

Berle, J. O., Mykletun, A., Daltveit, A. K., Rasmussen, S., Holsten, F., & Dahl, A. A. (2005). Neonatal outcomes in offspring of women with anxiety and depression during pregnancy. *Archives of Women's Mental Health*, *8*(3), 181–189.

Bloch, M. S., Schmidt, P. J., Danaceau, M., Murphy, J., Nieman, L., & Rubinow, D. R. (2000). Effects of gonadal steroids in women with a history of postpartum depression. *American Journal of Psychiatry*, *157*, 924–930.

Broth, M. R., Goodman, S. H., Hall, C., & Raynor, L. C. (2004). Depressed and well mothers' emotion interpretation accuracy and the quality of mother-infant interaction. *Infancy*, *6*(1), 37–55.

Brown, C., Dunbar-Jacob, J., Palenchar, D. R., Kelleher, K. J., Bruehlman, R. D., Sereika, S., & Thase, M. E. (2001). Primary care patients' personal illness models for depression: A preliminary investigation. *Family Practice*, *18*(3), 314–320.

Buist, A. (2003). Promoting positive parenthood: Emotional health in pregnancy. *Australian Journal of Midwifery*, *16*(1), 10–14.

Buist, A. (2006). Perinatal depression: Assessment and management. *Australian Family Physician*, *35*(9), 670–673.

Buist, A., Bilszta, J. Barnett, B., Milgrom, J., Ericksen, J., Condon, J., . . . Brooks, J. (2005). Recognition and management of perinatal depression in general practice: A survey of GPs and postnatal women. *Australian Family Physician*, *34*(9), 787–790.

Buist, A., Gotman, N., & Yonkers, K. A. (2011). Generalized anxiety disorder: Course and risk factors in pregnancy. *Journal of Affective Disorders*, *131*(1–3), 277–283.

Chaudron, L. H., Szilagyi, P. G., Kitzman, H. J., Wadkins, H. I., & Conwell, Y. (2004). Detection of postpartum depressive symptoms by screening at well-child visits. *Pediatrics*, *113*(3), 551–558.

Chessick, C. A., & Dimidjian, S. (2010). Screening for bipolar disorder during pregnancy and the postpartum period. *Archives of Women's Mental Health*, *13*, 233–248.

Coelho, H. F., Murray, L., Royal-Lawson, M., & Cooper, P. J. (2011). Antenatal anxiety disorders as a predictor of postnatal depression: A longitudinal study. *Journal of Affective Disorders*, *129*(1–3), 348–353.

Cohen, L. S., Altshuler, L. L., Harlow, B. L., Nonacs, R., Newport, J. D., Viguera, A. C., . . . Stowe, Z. N. (2006). Relapse of major depression during pregnancy in women who maintain or discontinue antidepressant treatment. *Journal of the American Medical Association*, *295*(5), 499–507.

Cohen, L. S., Nonacs, R. M., Bailey, J. W., Viguera, A. C., Reminick, A. M., Altshuler, L. L., . . . Faraone, S. V. (2004). Relapse of depression during pregnancy following antidepressant discontinuation: A preliminary prospective study. *Archives of Women's Mental Health*, *7*, 217–221.

Cooper, C., Jones, L., Dunn, E., Forty, L., Haque, S., Oyebode, F., . . . Jones, I. (2007). Clinical presentation of postnatal and non-postnatal depressive episodes. *Psychological Medicine*, *37*(9), 1273–1280.

Cox, J. L. (1983). Postnatal depression: A comparison of African and Scottish women. *Social Psychiatry*, *18*(1), 25–28.

Davies, P. T., Winter, M. A., & Ciccetti, D. (2006). The implications of emotional security theory for understanding and treating childhood psychopathology. *Development and Psychopathology*, *18*(3), 707–735.

Dieter, J. N., Field, T., Herdandez-Reif, M., Jones, N. A., Lecanuet, J. P., Salman, F. A., Redzepi, M. (2001). Maternal depression and increased fetal activity. *Journal of Obstetrics and Gynecology*, *21*(5), 468–473.

Doucet, S., Jones, I., Letourneau, N., Dennis, C. L., & Blackmore, E. R. (2011). Interventions for the prevention and treatment of postpartum psychosis: A systematic review. *Archives of Women's Mental Health*, *14*(2), 89–98.

Earls, M. F., & Committee on Psychosocial Aspects of Child and Family Health American Academy of Pediatrics. (2010). Incorporating recognition and management of perinatal and postpartum depression into pediatric practice. *Pediatrics*, *126*(5), 1032–1039.

Evans, J., Heron, J., Francomb, H., Oke, S., & Golding, J. (2001). Cohort study of depressed mood during pregnancy and after childbirth. *British Medical Journal, 323*, 257–260.

Evins, G. G., Theofrastous, J. P., & Galvin, S. L. (2000). Postpartum depression: A comparison of screening and routine clinical evaluation. *American Journal of Obstetrics & Gynecology, 182*(5), 1080–1082.

Field, T., Diego, M., & Hernandez-Reif, M. (2006). Prenatal depression effects on the fetus and newborn: A review. *Infant Behavior and Development, 29*, 445–455.

Field, T., Diego, M., Hernandez-Reif, M., Figueiredo, B., Deeds, O., Ascencio, A., . . . Kuhn, C. (2010). Comorbid depression and anxiety effects on pregnancy and neonatal outcome. *Infant Behavior and Development, 33*, 23–29.

Field, T., Diego, M., Hernandez-Reif, M., Figueiredo, B., Schanberg, S., & Kuhn, C. (2007). Sleep disturbances in depressed pregnant women and their newborns. *Infant Behavior and Development, 30*, 127–133.

Field, T., Hernandez-Reif, M., & Larissa, F. (2002). Breastfeeding in depressed mother-infant dyads. *Early Child Development and Care, 172*(6), 539–545.

Figueiredo, B. C., & Conde, A. (2011). Anxiety and depression in women and men from early pregnancy to 3 months postpartum. *Archives of Women's Mental Health, 14*(3), 247–255.

Flynn, H. A. (2005). The phenomenology and epidemiology of postpartum mood disorders. *Psychiatric Annals, 35*(7), 544–551.

Flynn, H. A., Davis, M., Marcus, S. M., Cunningham, R., & Blow, F. C. (2004). Rates of maternal depression in pediatric emergency department and relationship to child service utilization. *General Hospital Psychiatry, 26*, 316–322.

Flynn, H. A., Henshaw, E., O'Mahen, H., & Forman, J. (2010). Patient perspectives on improving the depression referral processes in obstetrics settings: A qualitative study. *General Hospital Psychiatry, 32*(1), 9–16.

Flynn, H. A., Marcus, S. M., & Blow, F. C. (2006). Rates and predictors of depression treatment among women seeking prenatal care. *General Hospital Psychiatry, 28*(4), 289–295.

Forty, L., Jones, L., Macgregor, S., Caesar, S., Cooper, C., Hough, A., . . . Jones, I. (2006). Familiality of postpartum depression in unipolar disorder: Results of a family study. *American Journal of Psychiatry, 163*(9), 1549–1553.

Gale, S., & Harlow, B. L. (2003). Postpartum mood disorders: A review of clinical and epidemiological factors. *Journal of Psychosomatic Obstetrics & Gynecology, 24*(4), 257–266.

Gavin, A. R., Tabb, K. M., Melville, J. L., Guo, Y., & Katon, W. (2011). Prevalence and correlates of suicidal ideation during pregnancy. *Archives of Women's Mental Health, 14*(3), 239–246.

Gavin, N. I., Gaynes, B. N., Lohr, K. N., Meltzer-Brody, S., Gartlehner, G., & Swinson, T. (2005). Perinatal depression: A systematic review of prevalence and incidence. *Obstetrics and Gynecology, 106*(5, Pt. 1), 1071–1083.

Gaynes, B. N., Gavin, N., Meltzer-Brody, S., Lohr, K. N., Swinson, T., Gartlehner, G., . . . Willer, W. C. (2005). *Perinatal depression: Prevalence, screening accuracy, and screening outcomes.* Agency for Healthcare Research and Quality Report, U.S. Department of Health and Human Services, (119), 1–8.

Georgiopoulos, A. M., Bryan, T. L., Wollan, P., & Yawn, B. P. (2001). Routine screening for postpartum depression. *Journal of Family Practice, 50*(2), 117–122.

Gerardin, P., Wendland, J., Bodeau, N., Galin, A., Bialobos, S., Tordjman, S., . . . Cohen, D. (2011). Depression during pregnancy: Is the developmental impact earlier in boys? *A prospective case-control study. Journal of Clinical Psychiatry, 72*(3), 378–387.

Glover, V. (2011). Prenatal stress and the origins of psychopathology: An evolutionary perspective. *Journal of Child Psychology and Psychiatry, 52*(4), 356–367.

Glover, V., Liddle, P., Taylor, A., Adams, D., & Sandler, M. (1994). Mild hypomania (the highs) can be a feature of the first postpartum week. *British Journal of Psychiatry, 164*(4), 517–521.

Gossler, S. M. (2010). Use of complementary and alternative therapies during pregnancy, postpartum, and lactation. *Journal of Psychosocial Nursing and Mental Health Services, 48*(11), 30–36.

Grote, N. K., Bridge, J. A., Gavin, A. R., Mellville, J. L., Iyengar, S., & Katon, W. J. (2010). A meta-analysis of depression during pregnancy and the risk of preterm birth, low birth weight, and intrauterine growth restriction. *Archives of General Psychiatry, 67*, 1012–1024.

Henshaw, C. (2003). Mood disturbance in the early puerperium: A review. *Archives of Women's Mental Health, 6*(Suppl. 2), S33–S42.

Henshaw, C., Foreman, D., & Cox, J. (2004). Post-natal blues: A risk factor for postnatal depression. *Journal of Psychosomatic Obstetrics & Gynecology*, *25*(3–4), 267–272.

Henshaw, E. J., Flynn, H. A., Himle, J. A., O'Mahen, H. A., Forman, J., & Fedock, G. (2011). Patient preferences for clinician interactional style in treatment of perinatal depression. *Qualitative Health Research*, *21*(7), 936–951.

Heron, J., Craddock, N., & Jones, I. (2005). Postnatal euphoria: Are "the highs" an indicator of bipolarity? *Bipolar Disorder*, 7, 103–110.

Heron, J., Haque, S., Oyebode, F., Craddock, N., & Jones, I. (2009). A longitudinal study of hypo-mania and depression symptoms in pregnancy and the postpartum period. *Bipolar Disorders*, *11*(4), 410–417.

Heron, J., O'Conner, T. G., Evans, J., Golding J., & Glover, V. (2004). The course of anxiety and depression through pregnancy and the postpar-tum in a community sample. *Journal of Affective Disorders*, *80*(1), 65–73.

Heron, J., Robertson Blackmore, E., McGuinness, M., Craddock, N., & Jones, I. (2007). No "latent period" in the onset of bipolar affective puerperal psychosis. *Archives of Women's Mental Health*, *10*(2), 79–81.

Hewitt, C. E., Gilbody, S. M., Brealey, S., Paulden, M., Palmer, S., Mann, R., . . . Richards, D. (2009). Methods to identify postnatal depression in primary care: An integrated evidence synthesis and value of information analysis. *Health Technol-ogy Assessment*, *13*(36), 147–230.

Jennings, K. D., Ross, S., Popper, S., & Elmore, M. (1999). Thoughts of harming infants in depressed and nondepressed mothers. *Journal of Affective Disorders*, *5*(1–2), 21–28.

Jones, I. (2010). DSM-V: The perinatal onset specifier for mood disorders. Online publication retrieved from dsm5.org

Jones, I., & Cantwell, R. (2010). The classification of perinatal mood disorder—Suggestions for DSM-V and ICD-11. *Archives of Womens Mental Health*, *13*(1), 33–36.

Jones, I., & Craddock, N. (2001). Familiality of the puerperal trigger in bipolar disorder: Results of a family study. *American Journal of Psychiatry*, *158*, 913–917.

Kelly, R., Zatzick, D., & Anders, T. F. (2001). The detection and treatment of psychiatric disorders and substance use among pregnant women cared for in obstetrics. *American Journal of Psychiatry*, *158* (2), 213–219.

Kelly, R. H., Russo, J., Holt, V. L., Danielsen, B. H., Zatzick, D. F., Walker, E., & Katon, W. (2002). Psychiatric and substance use disorders as risk factors for low birth weight and preterm delivery. *Obstetrics and Gynecology*, *100*(2), 297–304.

Kessler, R. C., McGonagle, K. A., Swartz, M., Blazer, D. G., & Nelson, C. B. (1993). Sex and depres-sion in the National Comorbidity Survey I: Life-time prevalence, chronicity and recurrence. *Journal of Affective Disorders*, *29*(2–3), 85–96.

Kim, J. H., Choi, S. S., & Ha, K. (2008). A closer look at depression in mothers who kill their children: Is it unipolar or bipolar depression? *Journal of Clinical Psychiatry*, *69*(10), 1625–1631.

Koleva, H., O'Hara, M. W., Stuart, S., & Bowman-Reif, J. (2011). Risk factors for depressive symp-toms during pregnancy. *Archives of Women's Men-tal Health*, *14*(2), 99–105.

Kroenke, K. (2006). Minor depression: Midway between major depression and euthymia. *Annals of Internal Medicine*, *144*, 528–530.

Kuehn, B. M. (2010). Depression guidelines highlights choices, care for hard-to-treat or pregnant patients. *Journal of the American Medical Association*, *304*(22), 2465–2466.

Kuehn, B. M. (2011). Report promotes depression screening for mothers during pediatric visits. *Journal of the American Medical Association*, *305* (1), 26–27.

Kumar, R., Marks, M., Platz, C., & Yoshida, K. (1995). Clinical survey of a psychiatric mother and baby unit: Characteristics of 100 consecutive admissions. *Journal of Affective Disorders*, *33*(1), 11–22.

Kurki, T., Hiilesmaa, V., Raitasalo, R., Mattila, H., & Ylikorkala, O. (2000). Depression and anxiety in early pregnancy and risk for preeclampsia. *Obstet-rics and Gynecology*, *95*(4), 487–490.

LaRocco-Cockburn, A., Melville, J., Bell, M., & Katon, W. (2003). Depression screening attitudes and practices among obstetrician-gynecologists. *Obstetrics and Gynecology*, *101*, 892–898.

Leddy, M., Haaga, D., Gray, J., & Schulkin, J. (2011). Postpartum mental health screening and diagnosis by obstetrician-gynecologists. *Journal of Psychosomatic Obstetrics & Gynecology*, *32*(1), 27–34.

Leibenluft, E., & Yonkers, K. (2010). The ties that bind: Maternal-infant interactions and the neural circuitry of postpartum depression. *American Journal of Psychiatry, 167*(11), 1294–1296.

Lindhal, V., Pearson, J. L., & Cople, L. (2005). Prevalence of suicidality during pregnancy and the postpartum. *Archives of Women's Mental Health, 8*(2), 77–87.

Littleton, H. L., Breitkopf, C. R., & Berenson, A. B. (2007). Correlates of anxiety symptoms during pregnancy and association with perinatal outcomes: A meta-analysis. *American Journal of Obstetrics & Gynecology, 196*(5), 424–432.

Logsdon, M. C., Wisner, K., Hanusa, B. H., & Phillips, A. (2003). Role functioning and symptom remission in women with postpartum depression after antidepressant treatment. *Archives of Psychiatric Nursing, 17*(6), 276–283.

Lundy, B. L., Jones, N. A., Field, T., Nearing, G., Davalos, M., Pietro, P. A., & Kuhn, A. (1999). Prenatal depression effects on neonates. *Infant Behavior and Development, 22*(1), 119–129.

Marcus, S. M., Flynn, H. A., Blow, F. C., & Barry, K. L. (2003). Depressive symptoms among pregnant women screened in obstetrics settings. *Journal of Women's Health, 12*(4), 373–380.

Marcus, S. M., Flynn, H. A., Blow, F., & Barry, K. (2005). A screening study of antidepressant treatment rates and mood symptoms in pregnancy. *Archives of Women's Mental Health, 8*(1), 25.

Marcus, S. M., Lopez, J. F., McDonough, S., MacKenzie, M. J., Flynn, H., Neal, C. R. Jr., . . . Vazquez, D. M. (2011). Depressive symptoms during pregnancy: Impact on neuroendocrine and neonatal outcomes. *Infant Behavior & Development, 34*(1), 26–34.

Mauri, M., Oppo, A., Montagnani, M. S., Borri, C., Banti, S., . . . Cassano, G. B. (2010). Beyond "postpartum depressions": Specific anxiety diagnosis during pregnancy predict different outcomes: Results from PND-ReScU. *Journal of Affective Disorders, 127*(1–3), 177–184.

McGowen, K. R., & Miller, M. N. (2004). Depression treatment during pregnancy. *American Journal of Psychiatry, 161,* 2137–2138.

Miller, L., & LaRusso, E. M. (2011). Preventing postpartum depression. *Psychiatric Clinics of North America, 34*(1), 53–65.

Miller, L. J. (2002). Postpartum depression. *Journal of American Medical Association, 13*(6), 762–765.

Mojtabai, R., Olfson, M., & Mechanic, D. (2002). Perceived need and help-seeking in adults with mood, anxiety, or substance abuse disorders. *Archives of General Psychiatry, 59*(1), 77–84.

Moses-Kolko, E. L., & Roth, E. K. (2004). Antepartum and postpartum depression: Healthy mom, healthy baby. *Journal of the American Medical Women's Association, 59*(3), 181–191.

Murray, L., Cooper, P., & Hipwell, A. (2003). Mental health of parents caring for infants. *Archives of Women's Mental Health, 6*(Supplement 2), S71–77.

National Research Council and Institute of Medicine (NRC). (2009). *Depression in parents, parenting, and children: Opportunities to improve identification, treatment, and prevention.* Washington, DC: The National Academies Press.

Newport, D. J., Stowe, Z. N., Viguera, A. C., Calamaras, M. R., Juric, S., Knight, B., . . . Baldessarini, R. J. (2008). Lamotrigine in bipolar disorder: Efficacy during pregnancy. *Bipolar Disorder, 10,* 432–436.

Novick, D., Swartz, H., & Frank, E. (2010). Suicide attempts in bipolar I and bipolar II disorder: A review and meta-analysis of the evidence. *Bipolar Disorders, 12*(1), 1–9.

O'Hara, M. W. (2009). Postpartum depression: What we know. *Journal of Clinical Psychology, 65*(12), 1258–1269.

O'Hara, M. W., & Swain, A. M. (1996). Rates and risk of postpartum depression: A meta-analysis. *International Review of Psychiatry, 8,* 37–54.

O'Mahen, H. A., & Flynn, H. F. (2008). Preferences and perceived barriers to depression treatment among women in low income prenatal care clinics. *Journal of Women's Health, 17*(8), 1301–1309.

Reay, R., Matthey, S., Ellwood, D., & Scott, M. (2011). Long-term outcomes of participants in a perinatal depression early detection program. *Journal of Affective Disorders, 129*(1–3), 94–103.

Righetti-Veltema, M., Conne-Perreard, E., Bousquet, A., & Manzano, J. (2002). Postpartum depression and mother–infant relationship at 3 months old. *Journal of Affective Disorders, 70*(3), 291–306.

Robertson, E., Jones, I., Haque, S., Holder, R., & Craddock, N. (2005). Risk of puerperal and nonpuerperal recurrence of illness following bipolar affective puerperal (postpartum) psychosis. *British Journal of Psychiatry, 186,* 258–259.

Rondo, P. H., Ferreira, R. F., Nogueira, F., Ribeiro, M. C., Lobert, H., & Artes, R. (2003). Maternal psychological stress and distress as predictors of low birth weight, prematurity and intrauterine growth retardation. *European Journal of Clinical Nutrition*, *57*(2), 266–272.

Ross, L. E., & Mclean, L. M. (2006). Anxiety disorders during pregnancy and the postpartum period: A systematic review. *Journal of Clinical Psychiatry*, *67*(8), 1285–1298.

Rudolph, K. D., Hammen, C., Burge, D., Lindberg, N., Herzberg, D., & Daley, S. E. (2000). Toward an interpersonal life-stress model of depression: The developmental context of stress generation. *Development and Psychopathology*, *12*, 215–234.

Ruggero, C. J., Kotov, R., Carlson, G. A., Tanenberg-Karant, K., Gonzalez, D. A., & Bromet, E. J. (2011). Diagnostic consistency of major depression with psychosis across 10 years. *Journal of Clinical Psychiatry*, *72*(9), 1207–1213.

Sajatovic, M., Sanders, R., Alexeenko, L., & Madhusoodanan, S. (2010). Primary prevention of psychiatric illness in special populations. *Annals of Clinical Psychiatry*, *22*(4), 262–273.

Satcher, S. (2001). Executive summary: A report of the Surgeon General on mental health. *Public Health Report*, *11*, 89–101.

Scholle, S. H., Haskett, R. F., Hanusa, B. H., Pincus, H. A., & Kupfer, D. J. (2003). Addressing depression in obstetrics/gynecology practice. *General Hospital Psychiatry*, *25*(2), 83–90.

Segre, L., O'Hara, M. W., Arndt, S., & Stuart, S. (2007). The prevalence of postpartum depression: The relative significance of three social status indices. *Social Psychiatry and Psychiatric Epidemiology*, *42*(4), 316–321.

Sharma, V. (2009). Management of bipolar II disorder during pregnancy and the postpartum period. *Canadian Journal of Clinical Pharmacology*, *16*(1), e33–e41.

Sharma, V., & Burt, V. K. (2011). DSM-V: Modifying the postpartum-onset specifier to include hypomania. *Archives of Women's Mental Health*, *14*(1), 67–69.

Sharma, V., Burt, V. K., & Ritchie, H. L. (2010). Assessment and treatment of bipolar II postpartum depression: A review. *Journal of Affective Disorders*, *125*(1–3), 18–26.

Shaw, D. (2011). Diagnosis and treatment of depression during pregnancy and lactation. In D. Ciraulo (Ed.), *Pharmacotherapy of depression*, (pp. 309–354). Totowa, NJ: Humana Press.

Sit, D. K., Rothschild, A. K., & Wisner, K. (2006). A review of postpartum psychosis. *Journal of Women's Health*, *15*(4), 352–368.

Smith, S., Heron, J., Haque, S., Clarke, P., Oyebode, F., & Jones, I. (2009). Measuring hypomania in the postpartum: A comparison of the Highs Scale and the Altman Mania Rating Scale. *Archives of Women's Mental Health*, *12*, 323–331.

Sockol, L. E., Epperson, N. C., & Barber, J. P. (2011). A meta-analysis of treatments for perinatal depression. *Clinical Psychology Review*, *31*, 839–849.

Stallones, L., Leff, M., Canetto, S. S., Garrett, C. J., & Mendelson, B. (2007). Suicidal ideation among low-income women on family assistance programs. *Women & Health*, *45*(4), 65–83.

Swanson, L. M., Flynn, H. A., Wilburn, K., Marcus, S., & Armitage, R. (2010). Maternal mood and sleep in children of women at risk for perinatal depression. *Archives of Women's Health*, *13*(6), 531–534.

Tam, L. W., Newton, R. P., Dern, M. & Parry, B. L. (2002). Screening women for postpartum depression at well baby visits: Resistance encountered and recommendations. *Archives of Women's Mental Health*, *5*, 79–82.

Teixeira, C., Figueiredo, B., Conde, A., Pacheco, A., & Costa, R. (2009). Anxiety and depression during pregnancy in women and men. *Journal of Affective Disorders*, *11*(1–3), 142–148.

Teti, D. M., & Gelfand, D. M. (1991). Behavioral competence among mothers of infants in the first year: The mediational role of maternal self-efficacy. *Child Development*, *62*(5), 918–929.

Thio, I. M., Browne, M. A., Coverdale, J. H., & Argyle, N. (2006). Postnatal depressive symptoms go largely untreated: A probability study in urban New Zealand. *Social Psychiatry and Psychiatric Epidemiology*, *41*(10), 814–818.

Turner, C., Boyle, F., & O'Rourke, P. (2003). Mothers' health post-partum and their patterns of seeking vaccination for their infants. *International Journal of Nursing Practice*, *9*(2), 120–126.

U.S. Department of Health and Human Services Agency (U.S. DHHS) for Healthcare Research and Quality (UDHHS AHRQ). (2011). Perinatal depression: Prevalence, screening accuracy, and screening outcomes. *Evidence Report/Technology Assessment*, 119.

U.S. Preventive Task Force. (2002). Screening for depression: Recommendations and rationale. *Annals of Internal Medicine, 136,* 760–764.

Van Hook, M. P. (1999). Women's help-seeking patterns for depression. *Social Work in Health Care, 29*(1), 15–34.

van Schaik, D. J., Klijn, A. F., van Hout, H. P., van Marwijk, H. W., Beekman, A. T., de Haan, M., & van Dyck, R. (2004). Patients' preferences in the treatment of depressive disorder in primary care. *General Hospital Psychiatry, 26*(3), 184–189.

Verduyn, C., Barrowclough, C., Roberts, J., Tarrier, T., & Harrington, R. (2003). Maternal depression and child behaviour problems: Randomised placebo-controlled trial of a cognitive-behavioural group intervention. *British Journal of Psychiatry, 183,* 342–348.

Vesga-Lopez, O., Blanco, C., Keyes, K., Olfson, M., Grant, B., & Hasin, D. (2008). Psychiatric disorders in pregnant and postpartum women in the United States. *Archives of General Psychiatry, 65*(7), 805–815.

Viguera, A. C., Cohen, L. S., Bouffard, S., Whitfield, T. H., & Baldessarini, R. J. (2002). Reproductive decisions by women with bipolar disorder after pregnancy psychiatric consultation. *American Journal of Psychiatry, 159,* 2102–2104.

Viguera, A. C., Nonacs R., Cohen, L. S., Tondo, L., Murray, A., & Baldessarini, R. J. (2000). Risk of recurrence of bipolar disorder in pregnancy and nonpregnant women after discontinuing lithium maintenance. *American Journal of Psychiatry, 157,* 179–184.

Viguera, A. C., Tondo, L., Koukopoulos, A. E., Reginaldi, D., Lepri, B., & Baldessarini, R. J. (2011). Episodes of mood disorders in 2,252 pregnancies and postpartum periods. *American Journal of Psychiatry, 168,* 1179–1185.

Viguera, A. C., Whitfield, T., Baldessarini, R. J., Newport, D. J., Stowe, Z., Remick, A., . . . Cohen, L. S. (2007). Risk of recurrence in women with bipolar disorder during pregnancy: Prospective study of mood stabilizer discontinuation. *American Journal of Psychiatry, 164*(12), 1817–1824.

Watkins, S., Meltzer-Brody, S., Zolnoun, D., & Stuebe, A. (2011). Early breastfeeding experiences and postpartum depression. *Obstetrics & Gynecology, 118*(2), 214–221.

Wenzel, A., Haugen, E. N., Jackson, L. C., & Robinson, K. (2003). Prevalence of generalized anxiety at eight weeks postpartum. *Archives of Women's Health, 6*(1), 43–49.

West, A. E., & Newman, D. L. (2003). Worried and blue: Mild parental anxiety and depression relation to the development of young children's temperament and behavior problems. *Parenting-Science and Practice, 3*(2), 133–154.

Wisner, K., Peindl, K., Gigliotti, T., & Hanusa, B. (1999). Obsessions and compulsions in women with postpartum depression. *Journal of Clinical Psychiatry, 60*(3), 176–180.

Wisner, K. L., Parry, B. L., & Piontek, C. M. (2002). Postpartum depression. *New England Journal of Medicine, 347,* 194–199.

Wisner, K. L., Peindl, K., & Hanusa, B. H. (1994). Symptomatology of affective and psychotic illnesses related to childbearing. *Journal of Affective Disorders, 30*(2), 77–87.

Woolhouse, H., Brown, S., Krastev, A., Perlen, S., & Gunn, J. (2009). Seeking help for anxiety and depression after childbirth: Results of the Maternal Health Study. *Archives of Women's Mental Health, 12*(2), 75–83.

Yonkers, K. A., Vigod, S., & Ross, L. E. (2011). Diagnosis, pathophysiology and management of mood disorders in pregnant and postpartum women. *Obstetrics and Gynecology, 117*(4), 961–977.

Yonkers, K. A., Wisner, K. L., Stewart, D. E., Oberlander, T. F., Dell, D. L., Stotland, N., . . . Lockwood, C. (2009). The management of depression during pregnancy: A report from the American Psychiatric Association and the American College of Obstetricians and Gynecologists. *General Hospital Psychiatry, 31*(5), 403–413.

Young, A. S., Klap, R., Sherbourne, C., & Wells, K. B. (2001). The quality of care for depressive and anxiety disorders in the United States. *Archives of General Psychiatry, 58*(1), 55–61.

Zambaldi, C. F., Cantilinoa, A., Montenegroa, A. C., Paesb, J. A., de Albuquerqueb, T. L., & Sougeya, E. B. (2009). Postpartum obsessive-compulsive disorder: Prevalence and clinical characteristics. *Comprehensive Psychiatry, 50*(6), 503–509.

Zayas, L. H., McKee, M. D., & Jankowski, K. R. B. (2004). Adapting psychosocial intervention research to urban primary care environments: A case example. *Annals of Family Medicine, 2*(5), 504–508.

Breastfeeding and Maternal Mental and Physical Health

JENNIFER HAHN-HOLBROOK, CHRIS DUNKEL SCHETTER,
AND MARTIE HASELTON

INTRODUCTION

Expectant mothers are inundated with information about the benefits of breastfeeding for their babies but are often poorly informed about the consequences breastfeeding has for their own mental and physical health. Women know about the potential benefits of breastfeeding for the baby's immune function and intellect (Kramer et al., 2001; Kramer et al., 2008), but mothers could also be asking themselves: What about me? A deep desire to breastfeed an infant is not shared by every mother. In fact, even before the advent of bottles and formula, many affluent women avoided breastfeeding altogether by paying poorer women to do it for them in an arrangement called *wet-nursing*. As the anthologist Sarah Hrdy (1992) noted, "during the heyday of wet-nursing at the end of the 18th century . . . up to ninety percent of infants born in urban centers such as Paris and Lyon were nursed by women *other* than their biological mother" (p. 415).

Today, the World Health Organization (2009) recommends exclusive breastfeeding for the first 6 months postpartum and the use of breast milk as a supplementary form of feeding for up to 2 years in order to confer optimal health benefits to the mother and child. Despite these guidelines, recent estimates are that while 70% of mothers initiate breastfeeding after the birth of their child, only 13.5% of infants in the United States are exclusively breastfed for 6 months (Centers for Disease Control and Prevention, 2011a).

Deciding how an infant will be fed is a complex decision involving various social, psychological, emotional, and environmental factors (Arora, McJunkin, Wehrer, & Kuhn, 2000). In order of importance, the top five reasons women give for deciding to breastfeed are (1) its benefits for the infant's health, (2) that it is "natural," (3) to strengthen bonding with their infant, (4) convenience, and (5) benefits for their own health (Arora et al., 2000). By contrast, the top five factors that discourage breastfeeding are (1) opposition by the baby's father, (2) concerns that the baby is not getting enough milk, (3) the need to return to work, (4) discomfort while breastfeeding, and (5) the misconception that breastfeeding will adversely change the appearance of the breasts (Arora et al., 2000). Given the level of commitment that breastfeeding requires, and the number of factors that mothers take into account when making this complex decision, it is important for mothers to have good information about what breast-feeding can and cannot offer them in return.

This chapter presents the state of the evidence concerning the advantages and disadvantages of breastfeeding for mothers.[1] Questions addressed include: Does breast-feeding really help mothers bond with their infants? Are there health benefits of breast-feeding for mothers? Will breastfeeding change the appearance of the breasts? We use the term *breastfeeding* to refer to any amount of breastfeeding, whether it is the infant's sole nutritional source or only a supplemental form of feeding. We use *exclusive breastfeeding*, by contrast, to refer to when infants are only given breast milk and are not given any other liquid, solid, or vitamins (Labbok and Krasovec, 1990). This chapter starts with an overview of the biology of breastfeeding, which forms the basis of many of the consequences of breastfeeding discussed.

The core of the chapter summarizes the evidence suggesting that breastfeeding aids mothers in weight loss and reduces their risk for ovarian and breast cancers, along with a discussion of the influence of breastfeeding on maternal stress, postpartum depression, and maternal bonding. We approach many of these topics using the lenses of anthropology and comparative research, highlighting the ways that breastfeeding mothers are sometimes very similar and sometimes very different from their mammalian counterparts. The chapter also presents information on the physical, economic, and social costs associated with breastfeeding for mothers. Finally, we conclude by discussing

options women have in navigating the minefields associated with choosing an infant feeding method.

THE BIOLOGY OF BREASTFEEDING

Background on the biology of breastfeeding is important for understanding how breast-feeding can have a widespread impact on maternal psychology and health. Here, we present a brief overview. For a more detailed account of the biological underpinnings of breastfeeding, see Riordan (2005).

The two most important hormones associated with lactation are oxytocin and prolactin (see Riordan, 2005). Oxytocin, named after the Greek word for "speedy birth," acts in the body as a smooth muscle contractor, facilitating contractions during labor and the release of milk during lacta-tion. Prolactin is the primary hormone responsible for milk production. Prolactin levels increase slowly during pregnancy, triggering changes in the breast tissue that stimulate milk production. Oxytocin also increases during pregnancy, although more rapidly, quadrupling in volume to stimulate labor (Riordan, 2005). Before a breastfeed-ing session begins, the mother's body releases oxytocin into the blood stream to aid in milk ejection (White-Traut et al., 2009). Mothers separated from their infants before a feeding session do not show this prefeeding oxytocin release; therefore, it appears that infant cues drive this effect (McNeilly, Robinson, Houston, & Howie, 1983). During the feed-ing session, when tactile stimulation is received from the nipple, oxytocin and prolactin are released in pulsating patterns, controlled by nerve fibers linked to the hypothalamus (Gimpl & Fahrenholz,

---

[1]The majority of studies on the impacts of breastfeed-ing have been conducted in the United States; for this reason, studies discussed in this review were U.S.-based unless otherwise noted.

2001). Prolactin levels are generally heightened in women who are breastfeeding as compared to women who are not breastfeeding, although prolactin levels are proportionate to breastfeeding frequency and the infant's milk demands (Battin, Marrs, Fleiss, & Mishell, 1985).

Estrogen and progesterone are also suppressed during lactation, resulting in a period of postpartum infertility, called lactational amenorrhea. This natural form of birth control remains 98% effective throughout the first 6 months of exclusive breastfeeding, as long as breast milk is given to the child from the breast at least every 4 hours during the day and every 6 hours during the night (Peterson et al., 2000; Valdes, Labbok, Pugin, & Perez, 2000). Lactational amenorrhea becomes a less effective form of contraception (94.6%) if mothers use a breast pump or are separated from their infant for long periods (Valdes et al., 2000). This amenorrheic state has been observed to last years in malnourished populations seemingly because of elevated levels of prolactin (Lunn, Austin, Prentice, & Whitehead, 1984).

Until recently, scientists thought that the functions of oxytocin and prolactin were limited to birth and lactation, but they now recognize the impact these hormones have on psychological states. Oxytocin and prolactin circulate in the brain and act on their own receptors distributed widely across different brain regions (Freeman, Kanyicska, Lerant, & Nagy, 2000; Gimpl & Fahrenholz, 2001). Animal research has implicated oxytocin and prolactin in critical maternal behaviors such as grooming, protection, and sensitivity to infant cues (Freeman et al., 2000; Gimpl & Fahrenholz, 2001). As we discuss later, studies in humans have revealed that breastfeeding mothers experience lower levels of stress and negative mood than do mothers who do not breastfeed, perhaps aiding in the transition to motherhood.

PHYSICAL HEALTH BENEFITS OF BREASTFEEDING

A large research literature suggests that women who breastfeed experience an array of health benefits (Bernier, Plu-Bureau, Bossard, Ayzac, & Thalabard, 2000; Rea, 2004). In the short term, breastfeeding helps mothers lose weight gained during pregnancy (Garza & Rasmussen, 2000; Kramer & Kakuma, 2004) and helps the uterus contract after pregnancy (Negishi et al., 1999). Over the long term, breastfeeding is associated with reduced risk of reproductive cancers (Bernier et al., 2000), metabolic syndrome (Ford, Giles, & Dietz, 2002; Kramer & Kakuma, 2004), type 2 diabetes (Stuebe & Rich-Edwards, 2009), and cardiovascular disease (Schwarz et al., 2009). The literature linking breastfeeding to improved health has been reviewed elsewhere (Bernier et al., 2000; Rea, 2004). Here, we provide a general overview.

Weight Loss and Metabolic Syndrome

Breastfeeding is calorically costly and is therefore associated with weight loss after pregnancy. Human mothers devote an estimated 525 to 625 calories per day producing the 750 mL of milk infants require daily over the first year of life (Garza & Ramussen, 2000). A caloric shortfall is experienced in most breastfeeding women, who often do not report more hunger than nonbreastfeeding women (Heck & de Castro, 1993). In a study that followed more than 20,000 Danish women from pregnancy to

18 months postpartum, women who exclusively breastfed for the recommended 6 months after birth lost an additional 2 kgs (4.4 pounds) of pregnancy-related weight by 6 months postpartum than women who breastfed for shorter durations (Baker et al., 2008). In line with this result, a systematic review of 20 studies showed that exclusive feeding with breast milk for the first 6 months postpartum predicts significantly greater postpregnancy weight loss than with mixed forms of breastfeeding (breastfeeding while introducing other foods or liquids) (Kramer & Kakuma, 2004).

Studies have also shown that women with a history of breastfeeding have a reduced risk of developing metabolic syndrome, a combination of medical disorders, such as obesity, insulin resistance, and high blood pressure, which increases the risk of cardiovascular disease and diabetes (Ford et al., 2002). A cross-sectional analysis of 2,516 midlife women found a 20% reduction in the risk of developing metabolic syndrome for every additional year of breastfeeding women reported (Ram et al., 2008). The authors noted that, although weight loss associated with breastfeeding accounted for a significant portion of the reduced risk in their sample, breastfeeding was associated with reductions in metabolic syndrome risk above and beyond weight loss, even when health behaviors and sociodemographic variables were statistically controlled. These additional benefits could owe to the observation that breastfeeding primes the body to become more metabolically efficient. This idea, dubbed the "reset hypothesis," proposes that breastfeeding reverses gestational increases in fat accumulation, insulin resistance, and lipid and tryglicerin levels more quickly and completely (Stuebe & Rich-Edwards, 2009).

According to the hypothesis, the reset process causes long-term positive impacts on women's health, reducing the risk for metabolic syndrome, and, consequently, reducing the risk of type 2 diabetes and cardiovascular disease.

New research indicates that breastfeeding may reduce the risk of developing both type 2 diabetes and cardiovascular disease. For example, Schwarz and colleagues (2009) found that among 139,681 postmenopausal women, those who reported a lifetime history of breastfeeding of more than 1 year were less likely to develop postmenopausal diabetes, hypertension, and cardiovascular disease than women who never breastfed. Likewise, another large study found that women who breastfed over their lifetime for 2 years or more were 23% less likely to develop coronary heart disease than women who never breastfed, even after controlling for parental history, early adult adiposity, and various lifestyle factors (Stuebe et al., 2009). Interestingly, some evidence suggests that longer durations of breastfeeding the same child, rather than total time spent breastfeeding over one's lifetime, has the greatest protective benefit against coronary heart disease (Stuebe, Rich-Edwards, Willett, Manson, & Michels, 2005).

A study that investigated the relationship between type 2 diabetes and breastfeeding in two cohorts of more than 70,000 women found that, although the total lifetime duration of breastfeeding was associated with reduced risk of type 2 diabetes, it was longer durations of breastfeeding involving the same child, as opposed to the combined duration of breastfeeding across multiple children, that conferred the greatest protective benefits (Stuebe et al., 2005). In this sample, a year of continuously breastfeeding one child was associated with a 44% decrease in risk of developing later diabetes, while a year of breastfeeding spread across two children was only associated with a 24% decrease. Whether this finding can be attributed to the reset hypothesis is unclear, although it seems possible that women's bodies could require more than half a year of breastfeeding after any given pregnancy to completely reset metabolic action.

Breast and Ovarian Cancer

Breastfeeding may also protect against breast and ovarian cancers by suppressing ovulation, and thus limiting lifetime estrogen exposure (Clemons & Goss, 2001; Key & Pike, 1988). Theoretically, reductions in total estrogen exposure may reduce the risk of breast cancer, because estrogen increases rates of breast cell proliferation and differentiation, giving more opportunities for mutations to occur and, when they do, fueling cancer growth (Clemons & Goss, 2001; Key & Pike, 1988). In support of this model, a meta-analysis of 23 case-control studies found a small protective effect of breastfeeding on breast cancer: Any lifetime history of breastfeeding, regardless of duration, yielded a benefit, although this effect was small compared to other known biological risk factors (Bernier et al., 2000). This effect was strongest in nonmenopausal women and in women who had breastfed for longer than 12 months.

Recent research has also begun to examine the impact of breastfeeding on women with hereditary predispositions to develop breast cancers, with mixed results. Jernström and colleagues (2004), for example, evaluated the role of breastfeeding in women who carried the genetic mutations BRCA1 or BRCA2, which are known to raise the lifetime risk of breast cancer by

approximately 80% (King, Marks, & Mandell, 2003). In this study, 685 carriers of BRCA1 and 280 carriers of BRCA2 were compared to 965 women with no history of ovarian or breast cancer. They found that cumulative breastfeeding for longer than a year reduced the risk of hereditary breast cancer in women with the BRCA1 mutation, but not the BRCA2 mutation. By contrast, neither Lee et al. (2008) nor Andrieu et al. (2006) observed an association between breastfeeding and breast-cancer risk in women with BRCA1 or BRCA2.

Studies suggest that the risk of ovarian cancer is reduced by breastfeeding behaviors as well. A review by Shoham (1994) revealed that 6 of 11 studies found that breastfeeding was related to reduced risk of ovarian cancer. More recently, researchers analyzed 391 cases of epithelial ovarian cancer among 149,693 women in the Nurses' Health Study (Danforth et al., 2007). They found that for each month of additional breastfeeding, the risk of epithelial ovarian cancer was reduced by 2%. Another study documented a similar 1.4% reduction in ovarian cancer risk for every additional month of breastfeeding (Jordan, Siskind, Green, Whiteman, & Webb, 2010), although the reduction in risk did not continue to accrue beyond the first 12 months. Breastfeeding has been found not only to reduce the risk of developing ovarian cancer, but also to improve the chances of surviving in women who do develop it. One study found that women diagnosed with ovarian cancer lived longer if they had ever breastfed than if they had never breastfed (Nagle, Bain, Green, & Webb, 2008). In this same study, there was no relationship between duration or frequency of breastfeeding and improved ovarian cancer outcomes.

Evidence continues to accumulate demonstrating an association between breastfeeding and reduced risk of ovarian and breast cancers, diabetes, and cardiovascular disease. Breastfeeding is a biologically complex phenomenon, involving changes in hormone levels that act on receptors throughout the brain and the body. Although the links to maternal health are not yet fully known, these hormone dynamics may exert long-term impacts on women's health. Reductions in diseases related to metabolic syndrome may owe, in part, to weight loss and improved metabolic function associated with breastfeeding. Breastfeeding also reduces lifetime estrogen exposure, potentially accounting for reduced risk of reproductive cancers among women with a history breastfeeding. Some studies find dose–response relationships between increased total duration of lifetime breastfeeding and better health outcomes.

MENTAL HEALTH BENEFITS OF BREASTFEEDING

Stress Regulation

Being a new parent is as stressful as it is rewarding. Sources of maternal stressors range from worries about being a "good" mother (Mercer, 1986) to physical stressors, such as sleep deprivation, body changes, and sexual dysfunction (Gjerdingen, Froberg, Chaloner, & McGovern, 1993). New mothers struggle to find time for their baby while trying to meet the needs of partners, other children, and themselves (Gruis, 1977). The vigilance required to be a good parent is also a stressor for new mothers (Hahn-Holbrook, Holbrook, & Haselton, 2011). Given all the stressful demands and challenges parenthood

brings, it is perhaps unsurprising that approximately one in five women self-report depressive symptoms within the first year after birth (Gavin et al., 2005). However, nature may also have provided mothers with a stress-buffer: breastfeeding (Carter & Altemus, 1997; Groer, Davis, & Hemphill, 2002).

Only recently have scientists begun to recognize the ways that lactation alters a mother's stress responses (Groer et al., 2002; Lonstein, 2007; Mezzacappa, 2004). The earliest studies done on rodents revealed that lactating dams were remarkably resistant to stress. Lactating rodents exposed to stressors, such as electric shocks, fierce predators, or complex mazes, displayed fewer hormonal and cardiovascular signs of anxiety than their nonlactating female counterparts (see Neumann, 2001, for a review).

Corresponding research in humans has shown a similar association between breastfeeding and reduced stress. The first study conducted in humans showed that breastfeeding women had significantly lower hormonal stress responses (as evidence by lower cortisol and ACTH) during exercise stress than nonbreastfeeding mothers or women without children (Altemus, Deuster, Galliven, Carter, & Gold, 1995). Several follow-up studies have since examined women's cardiovascular and hormonal stress responses to the classic Treir Social Stress Task, which involves giving a public speech and doing difficult mental arithmetic in front of a critical audience. Although these studies tend not to find evidence of lower stress reactivity using hormonal markers of stress, such as cortisol, they consistently find that breastfeeding women have lower cardiovascular markers of stress than do formula-feeding women.

For example, one study detected lower cardiovascular markers of stress (as evidence by lower basal systolic blood pressures, higher levels of cardiac parasympathetic control, and modulation of heart rate reactivity) during the task in breastfeeders compared with nonbreastfeeding mothers and women without children (Altemus et al., 2001). Another study found similar cardiovascular patterns for breastfeeding mothers during the anticipation of the public-speaking stressor (Light et al., 2000). It is possible that any stress-buffering effects of breastfeeding are more potent directly after the act. Mothers randomly assigned to breastfeed before this public-speaking stressor have blunted cortisol responses when compared to breastfeeding women who were instructed to hold their infants (Heinrichs et al., 2001).

The stress-reducing effects of breastfeeding may extend to other stressors as well. Mezzacappa, Kelsey, and Katkin (2005), for example, compared the cardiovascular responses to difficult mental arithmetic (verbal serial subtractions) and immersion of one's hand into ice water in four groups of women—those exclusively breastfeeding, exclusively formula-feeding, mixed feeding (breast and formula), and women without children. In response to the challenging mental arithmetic, mothers who breastfed exclusively displayed attenuated heart-rate reactivity and shortened preejection period (PEP; an indicator of the reduced cardiac stress related to the sympathetic nervous system) compared to all other groups. Moreover, this study found a dose-response relationship between breastfeeding frequency and stress reduction. Women who breastfed more times per day had lower heart rates in reaction to doing the difficult mental arithmetic and reduced sympathetic reactivity to the cold water task than women who breastfed less frequently. In this study,

the stress buffering effects of breastfeeding appeared to fade as children grew older. Breastfeeding mothers with very young infants derived greater stress-buffering from breastfeeding than women who had 1-year-old children.

Preliminary research suggests links between breastfeeding and reduced stress in women's daily lives outside of the laboratory. Breastfeeding mothers are more likely to report positive mood states, less anxiety, and increased calm as compared to formula-feeding mothers (Altshuler, Hendrick, & Cohen, 2000; Carter & Altemus, 1997; Fleming, Ruble, Flett, & Van Wagner, 1990; Ford et al., 2002; Heinrichs et al., 2001). These differences between breastfeeding and formula-feeding mothers remain after controls for possible confounds, including maternal age, work status, income, and health behaviors (Mezzacappa, Guethlein, & Katkin, 2002; Mezzacappa, Guethlein, Vaz, & Bagiella, 2000; Mezzacappa & Katlin, 2002).

While studies in rodents indicate that the stress reduction associated with lactation is mediated by the hormones oxytocin (Neumann, Torner, & Wigger, 2000; Windle, Shanks, Lightman, & Ingram, 1997) and prolactin (Bole-Feysot, Goffin, Edery, Binart, & Kelly, 1998; Freeman et al., 2000), data in humans are more limited. We do know that women with higher plasma oxytocin and prolactin in the early postpartum period report less anxiety than do women with lower levels of these hormones (Nissen, Gustavsson, Widstrom, & Uvnas-Moberg, 1998; Uvnas-Moberg, Widstrom, Werner, Matthiesen, & Winberg, 1990). Furthermore, breastfeeding women who release more oxytocin during infant suckling have lower levels of cortisol than women who release less oxytocin during infant feedings (Chiodera et al., 1991). In addition, breastfeeding women with higher oxytocin show reduced markers of stress while preparing for a public-speaking stressor relative to those with lower oxytocin (Light et al., 2000).

Research in humans and other species has shown that physiological responses to stressors are reduced among lactating relative to nonlactating females. In studies with human mothers, the stress-buffering effects of breastfeeding appear to be stronger in the early postpartum period and soon after a feeding session. Cardiovascular measures of stress, which tap into sympathetic and para-sympathetic nervous system activity, are more likely to reveal differences in stress reactivity between breast- and formula-feeding women than hypothalamic-pituitary-adrenal (HPA) axis hormones like cortisol. Breastfeeding mothers also report less perceived stress in their daily lives than formula-feeding mothers. The stress-buffering effect of lactation appears to result from the hormones oxytocin and prolactin in nonhumans, although direct evidence in humans in lacking. Collectively, nonhuman and human evidence strongly suggests that breastfeeding is an important regulator of maternal stress in the postpartum period.

Postpartum Depression

Although the birth of a child typically conjures images of joy and fulfillment, many women experience feelings of hopelessness and despair instead. Postpartum depression is a devastating mental illness affecting approximately 13% of women worldwide within the first 12 weeks after giving birth (O'Hara & Swain, 1996), and roughly one in five women within the first postpartum year (Gaynes et al., 2005). Postpartum depression is distinct from other postpartum mood disorders like the common and transient "postpartum blues," which affects 50% to 80% of mothers worldwide (Pitt, 1973; Yalom, Lunde, Moos, & Hamburg, 1968), or the very serious, although rare, occurrence of postpartum psychosis (Herzog & Detre, 1976). The effects of postpartum depression are insidious because they can disrupt parenting behaviors (Field, 2010), resulting in long-term negative consequences on the cognitive, emotional, and behavioral development of children (Grace, Evindar, & Stewart, 2003). Because of the serious negative consequences of this disorder, there has been much research identifying predictors of postpartum depression.

A recent systematic review identified 12 studies that reported that breastfeeding women had lower rates of postpartum depression in comparison to formula-feeding women (Dennis & McQueen, 2009). However, there is an important question that few studies explicitly address: Does less breastfeeding lead to more depression, or does more depression lead to less breastfeeding? The vast majority of research on this topic to date has focused solely on the ways that depression can lead to less breastfeeding.

It is easy to imagine why depression might interfere with breastfeeding. Symptoms of depression commonly include decreased motivation, increased anxiety, and, for new mothers, avoidance of the infant (Beck, 1992). Breastfeeding is an intimate behavior demanding sustained periods of direct mother–infant contact, which many depressed mothers may find difficult. Formula-feeding then might seem the more attractive option for depressed mothers, because it can be performed by other caregivers. Furthermore, anxiety associated with depression can interfere with the maternal milk supply (Riordan, 2005), leading depressed mothers to feel that they have insufficient milk and need to switch to formula to ensure that their infant receives adequate nutrition. Finally, many antidepressant medications are not recommended for breastfeeding mothers, because the active ingredients can be transferred to the baby through breast milk and could have adverse impacts on infant development (Riordan, 2005). It is not surprising, then, that studies find depressed mothers are less likely to breastfeed.

Depressed mothers commonly report more difficulties with breastfeeding (Edhborg, Friberg, Lundh, & Widstrom, 2005; Tamminen, 1988), lower levels of breastfeeding self-efficacy (Dai & Dennis, 2003), and more failed breastfeeding attempts (Fergerson, Jamieson, & Lindsay, 2002). One study found that depressive symptoms seven weeks after delivery predicted higher rates of weaning by 24 weeks postpartum (Galler, Harrison, Biggs, Ramsey, & Forde, 1999). Similarly, another study found that women who were depressed at 2 weeks postpartum were more likely to wean before 2 months postpartum than women who were not depressed at 2 weeks postpartum (Taveras et al., 2003). Researchers have found that women who experience depression in pregnancy are less likely to initiate breastfeeding (Seimyr, Edhborg, Lundh, & Sjögren, 2004). These studies show that decreased breastfeeding behavior follows depression during pregnancy and in the early postpartum period. However, the existence of this relationship does not preclude the possibility that breastfeeding may also exert protective effects against postpartum depressive symptoms.

There are reasons to think that breastfeeding could protect mothers against depression. The act of breastfeeding releases oxytocin, which has been found in lower levels in depressed mothers than in nondepressed mothers (Skrundz, Bolten, Nast, Hellhammer, & Meinlschmidt, 2011). Women currently using both breastfeeding and formula-feeding methods report lower levels of negative mood if they are randomly assigned to breastfeed their infant in the laboratory than if they are randomly assigned to formula-feed (Mezzacappa & Katlin, 2002), perhaps from the oxytocin released by breastfeeding. Breastfeeding is also associated with reduced stress (Mezzacappa, 2004), and because stress is one of the strongest risk factors in the development of depression (Hammen, 2005), breastfeeding could buffer women against depression. Breastfed infants tend to have easier temperaments (Jones, McFall, & Diego, 2004) and fewer health problems over the long term (Ip et al., 2007), which could also have positive downstream consequences for maternal mental health. Taken together, these findings suggest that breastfeeding could confer protective benefits against depression.

Very few studies have investigated the possibility that breastfeeding might be protective against postpartum depression. Two studies found that never having breastfed versus having breastfed was associated with subsequent postpartum depression (Chaudron et al., 2001; Hannah, Adams, Lee, Glover, & Sandler, 1992), and one study found that discontinuing breastfeeding versus continuing to breastfeed was also associated with subsequent depression (Nishioka et al., 2011). Critically, however, none of these studies controlled for baseline levels of depression during pregnancy, leaving open the possibility that women who engaged in breastfeeding were simply less depressed from the outset.

Only one published study was identified that explicitly set out to test the hypothesis that breastfeeding is protective against the development of postpartum depression (Dennis & McQueen, 2007). This study found that women who exclusively breastfed at one week postpartum were equivalently likely to become depressed at 4 or 8 weeks postpartum as women who exclusively formula-fed (Dennis & McQueen, 2007), suggesting that there is no protective benefit of exclusive breastfeeding at one week against the development of depressive symptoms at 4 and 8 weeks postpartum. Importantly, however, this study may have been limited in its ability to detect the mental health benefits of breastfeeding, because the mothers in the sample had only been breastfeeding for a very short time. Furthermore, the time frame within which depression was assessed (between 1 and 8 weeks postpartum) may have been too narrow to detect the downstream effects of breastfeeding on depression.

Breastfeeding is clearly related to postpartum depression; however, the nature of that relationship remains somewhat unclear. On the one hand, much research has shown that depression predicts lower rates of breastfeeding initiation and shorter durations of breastfeeding. These effects likely result from the increased problems depressed women encounter while breastfeeding. On the other hand, very little research has assessed the possibility that breastfeeding might also be protective against postpartum depression. Given the theoretical reasons to think that breastfeeding might be protective against depression, further research using longitudinal or experimental designs is clearly needed before conclusions can be drawn about whether the relationship between depression and breastfeeding is bidirectional (depression leading to less breastfeeding and less breastfeeding leading to depression) or simply unidirectional (depression leading to less breastfeeding).

Maternal Bonding

Conventional wisdom holds that breastfeeding helps mothers bond with their babies. In fact, one of the most common reasons given by women for wanting to breastfeed is the opportunity to bond with their children (Arora et al., 2000). In the scientific literature as well, breastfeeding is often assumed to aid in maternal–infant attachment, without necessarily giving reference to direct evidence (for examples, see Jansen, Weerth, & Riksen-Walraven, 2008). Given this, it is surprising that only a few studies have actually tested this hypothesis in humans, and even fewer have found significant results. Here, we review the small literature on the impact of breastfeeding on the mother–child bond (for a more in-depth review, see Jansen et al., 2008). Although the mother–infant relationship is bidirectional—in that the mother can bond with the infant and the infant can bond with the mother—our primary focus is maternal bonding. Briefly, however, we found no studies with evidence that breastfed infants are more securely attached to their mothers than formula-fed infants (see Jansen et al., 2008, for a review). Like the data linking lactation and stress, most of what we have learned about breastfeeding and bonding comes from animal studies.

Lactation is critical for inciting maternal behaviors in many mammalian species, because it releases the hormones oxytocin and prolactin, which facilitate maternal behavior (see Kendrick, 2000, for a review). For example, female rats will suddenly display maternal behaviors if oxytocin (Pedersen, Caldwell, Peterson, Walker, & Mason, 1992) or prolactin (Bridges, DiBiase, Loundes, & Doherty, 1985) is injected into their brains. If a chemical that blocks the actions of oxytocin or prolactin is injected into the brain of a rat shortly after birth, a rodent's mothering behavior is significantly impaired (Bridges, Rigero, Byrnes, Yang, & Walker, 2001; van Leengoed, Kerker, & Swanson, 1987). In nonhuman primates, however, hormonal changes linked to lactation play a smaller role in the onset of maternal behaviors, with early learning and social experience making up the difference (Pedersen, 2004). For example, administration of an oxytocin antagonist into the brain of a female rhesus monkey reduces certain caregiving behaviors, while leaving others fully intact (Boccia, Goursaud, Bachevalier, Anderson, & Pedersen, 2007). Years of observations by primatologists also tell us that maternal behaviors routinely emerge in female primates without the influence of lactation. For example, female primates who do not have offspring of their own often seek out caregiving opportunities, such as carrying and grooming infants (Hrdy, 1999).

Breastfeeding is certainly not necessary for parental bonding to occur in humans, as adoptive mothers, formula-feeding mothers, and fathers can attest. However, might breastfeeding give mothers, especially if they are reluctant or are experiencing mothering challenges, extra incentives to care for their infant?

Recent studies in humans suggest that oxytocin is important for maternal bonding. For instance, plasma oxytocin levels during pregnancy and the postpartum period predict more maternal bonding behaviors, such as eye gaze, vocalizations, positive affect, and affectionate touch, and more attachment-related thoughts (Feldman, Weller, Zagoory-Sharon, & Levine, 2007). Also, mothers who provide high levels of affectionate touch during a play session with their children have higher levels of oxytocin after the encounter than mothers who provide low levels of affectionate touch (Feldman, Gordon, Schneiderman, Weisman, & Zagoory-Sharon, 2010). Given this evidence, one might predict breastfeeding, which gives women extra bursts of oxytocin, would lead to greater levels of maternal bonding.

Three out of four studies investigating whether breastfeeding promotes maternal bonding have found supportive evidence (see Martone & Nash, 1988, for the null result). In the largest study on the topic, mother–infant interactions were observed at 4 and 12 months postpartum in women who had either breastfed for at least a week ($n = 439$) versus women who had not initiated breastfeeding ($n = 94$) (Else-Quest, Hyde, & Clark, 2003). The researchers found that mothers who had breastfed for at least 1 week showed higher-quality interactions with their babies at 12 months, but not at 4 months postpartum. In another study of 405 women, mothers who were supplying over half of their infant's diet though breastfeeding at 5 months postpartum reported that they were more emotionally bonded to their infant at that time than women who were supplying less than half of their infant's diet through breast milk or were not breastfeeding at all (Nishioka et al., 2011).

Similarly, Britton, Britton, and Gronwaldt (2006) found that mothers who were breastfeeding at 3 months reported that they felt they were more sensitive to their child's needs than women who were not currently breastfeeding. The findings of the previous two studies should be interpreted with caution, however, because maternal behavior was not rated by objective observers. In fact, Britton et al. (2006) found women who intended to breastfeed in pregnancy also reported higher sensitivity toward their infants at 3 months, suggesting that women who choose to breastfeed may just be more sensitive (or report being more sensitive) from the outset. In fact, other studies suggest that the quality of the maternal–infant bond predicts a mother's willingness to breastfeed. A study found that better bonding behavior 48 hours after birth predicted higher rates of exclusive breastfeeding at 6 months in a sample of more than 500 women (Cernadas, Noceda, Barrera, Martinez, & Garsd, 2003).

At this early stage of the research, it is too soon to tell whether breastfeeding increases bonding between mothers and infants as compared to other forms of feeding. This topic deserves additional research attention with prospective or experimental designs and objective measures of bonding, especially given that many women worry that not breastfeeding will interfere with their ability to bond with their babies. One important observation in the largest of the studies noted (Else-Quest et al., 2003) was that women who had never breastfed at all exhibited maternal sensitivity well within the normal range defined by clinicians. Oxytocin could still facilitate maternal bonding for mothers who do not breastfeed. For example, direct skin-to-skin contact with the infant and affectionate touch likely increases maternal oxytocin levels (Uvnäs-Moberg, 1998). These alternative mechanisms may be partly responsible for bonding in mothers of adopted infants, fathers, and other caretakers.

POTENTIAL MATERNAL COSTS OF LACTATION

Breastfeeding has many possible benefits for mothers, but it can also clash with other goals for women, such as having a full-time career. Some of the costs associated with breastfeeding are probably overstated, like sagging breasts, whereas others are likely understated, for example, the social stigma associated with breastfeeding in some societies. Breastfeeding can also be problematic for women with certain physical or health conditions. Furthermore, many women find breastfeeding very difficult because of work constraints or physical pain. Here, we review the potential physical, economic, and social costs associated with breastfeeding for mothers.

Physical Costs

Breastfeeding does have some physical costs for women. Most mothers will have some nipple discomfort during the first 10 days of breastfeeding (Riordan, 2005). If pain is prolonged, a medical assessment by a lactation consultant or nurse is usually required to identify the source of the problem. The most common causes of severe nipple pain are nonideal positioning of the infant at the breast or poor suckling technique on the part of the infant (Morland-Schultz & Hill, 2005). Both of these can usually be identified and remedied by a trained lactation consultant or nurse (Riordan, 2005). Severe nipple pain can sometimes be a sign of a more serious breastfeeding-related infection. Common infections include mastitis, a usually benign infection that is easily treatable by increasing breast milk expression and antibiotics, and candidiasis (or thrush), a yeast infection transferred from the baby's mouth into the nipple that is treatable with antifungal medications (Riordan, 2005). Women can reduce their risk for these and other breastfeeding-related infections by employing good positioning and latching techniques, and by massaging their breasts to facilitate milk flow (Riordan, 2005).

Beyond the potential for discomfort, breastfeeding restricts the types of medications a mother can take. A Scandinavian study found that up to 25% of women took some form of medication while they were breastfeeding, and uncertainty regarding the drug's safety was a major reason for the discontinuation of breastfeeding (Matheson, Kristensen, & Lunde, 1990). There are often alternative forms of a drug within the same drug class (e.g., antibiotics, selective serotonin reuptake inhibitors, oral contraceptives) that are safe for breastfeeding women. For example, a women who requires medication to treat depression but who also wants to breastfeed could talk to her doctor about taking Paxil (paroxetine) instead of Prozac (fluoxetine) or Trilafon (perphenazine) instead of Nardil (phenelzine), both of which are considered safe for breastfed infants (Riordan, 2005). Mothers and healthcare professionals can find advice about the safety of medications for breastfeeding mothers online at LactMed (http://toxnet.nlm.nih.gov/cgi-bin/sis/htmlgen?LACT), the U.S. National Library of Medicine's drugs and breastfeeding database (U.S. National Library of Medicine, 2001).

Nutrients to synthesize breast milk are often mobilized from maternal stores at the mother's expense (Dewey, 1997). To offset these costs, the body generally has mechanisms in place that help the mother rebound from the nutritional stores used during breastfeeding. For example, by producing 600 to 1,000 mL of breast milk per day, a mother

loses 200 mg of calcium daily (Rea, 2004); however, calcium absorption becomes more efficient during pregnancy and after weaning often resulting in net calcium gains over the long term (Riordan, 2005). However, in women who are malnourished or immunologically compromised, the nutrients required for breastfeeding can overwhelm the mother's body and lead to health problems. For example, a randomized clinical trial found that breastfeeding among HIV-infected women increased maternal death by threefold at a 2-year follow-up as compared to formula feeding (Nduati et al., 2001). The investigators postulated that the nutritional demands posed by breastfeeding may be too great for HIV-infected women. With the exception of malnourished women or women with HIV, the nutritional costs of breastfeeding can usually be met by simply increasing caloric intake of nutrient-rich foods by 200 to 700 calories per day, depending on the frequency of breastfeeding (Riordan, 2005). Mothers are often advised to take a multivitamin with 100 mg of iron, along with a calcium and omega-3 fatty acid supplement, to ensure proper nutrition for the mother and breastfed infant (Riordan, 2005).

A common reason that women give for not breastfeeding is the belief that it will adversely affect the appearance of the breasts (Arora et al., 2000). Fathers also commonly worry that breastfeeding will have these effects, leading some men to discourage their partners from breastfeeding (Bar-Yam & Darby, 1997). These concerns, however, are not supported by empirical evidence. For example, a study of 93 women who were seeking plastic surgery to improve the shape of their breasts found no significant relationship between objective ratings of breast ptosis (drooping or sagging) and breastfeeding initiation or duration (Rinker,

Veneracion, & Walsh, 2008). The notion that breastfeeding makes breasts sag likely stems from the fact that pregnancy does lead to changes in breast tissue. This same study found that number of pregnancies, along with age, body mass index, larger prepregnancy bra cup size, and smoking history were positively related to breast ptosis. Similarly, a prospective Italian study found that mothers frequently reported that the size and the shape of their breasts had changed after childbirth, but these changes were not different as a function of infant feeding behaviors (Pisacane & Continisio, 2004).

Breastfeeding appears to have some clear physical costs for mothers, although these are usually transitory, and most can be ameliorated by proper breastfeeding techniques and nutrition during breastfeeding. With the exception of women with HIV or severely malnourished women, there is little evidence for any long-term physical costs associated with breastfeeding.

Labor and Economic Costs

Breastfeeding can place a burden on women's time and freedom from childcare responsibilities. A woman providing breast milk exclusively to her child has to breastfeed her child or express milk approximately 8 to 12 times per day during the first 6 months of exclusive breastfeeding (U.S. Department of Health and Human Services' Office on Women's Health [OWH], 2011). Each breastfeeding or expression session takes approximately 15 to 20 minutes, meaning that women will spend an estimated 2 to 4 hours per day breastfeeding (OWH, 2011). Actual time spent feeding is lessened by formula-feeding because the infant drinks milk from a bottle more quickly and formula is digested more slowly;

therefore, feedings can be performed faster and less frequently. In addition, because feeding responsibilities can be shared by other caregivers, feeding with formula may also give the mother more freedom.

The time commitment associated with breastfeeding can place a burden on women in the workplace. A breastfeeding mother needs to allocate approximately 45 to 75 minutes per workday to express breast milk (Mohler, 2011). In addition, breastfeeding women need a private place to express milk, a place to store breast milk, and the ability to take several breaks per day. It is also possible that women who need to make these arrangements are perceived as less serious about their jobs, or are stigmatized by co-workers who are uncomfortable with breastfeeding (Smith, Hawkinson, & Paull, 2011). Given the burden that pumping breast milk at work places on women, it is not surprising that women who return to work within 12 weeks after birth wean sooner than those who do not return to work within 12 weeks (Callen & Pinelli, 2004).

In a cross-cultural comparison, the United States was found to have the lowest breastfeeding initiation rates compared to other industrialized nations such as Canada, Sweden, and Australia (Callen & Pinelli, 2004), a fact that may be related to American maternity leave policies (Guendelman et al., 2009). In the United States, the Family and Medical Leave Act allows mothers only 12 weeks of unpaid maternity leave. Compare this to Sweden, where parents are entitled to approximately 16 months of paid leave after the birth of a child (Galtry, 2003). As a result of this, approximately one-third of American women return to work within 3 months of giving birth, as compared to in Sweden, where only about 5% return to work within 3 months (Klerman & Leibowitz, 1999). It should not be surprising that breastfeeding initiation is nearly universal in Sweden (97% of mothers), with approximately 40% of infants still breastfeeding exclusively at 6 months (Galtry, 2003). The possible link between breastfeeding rates and maternity leave policies highlights the role of structural factors in shaping infant feeding decisions, which are normally thought to simply reflect personal choices.

Recently, the U.S. government has taken steps that might increase rates of breastfeeding initiation and its duration. In 2010, President Obama signed the Patient Protection and Affordable Care Act, which includes a provision requiring employers to provide a place other than the bathroom and reasonable break time for female employees to express breast milk for the first year after a child's birth. Some employers are exempted, however, because they have fewer than 60 employees or because allowing breaks would cause an unreasonable burden for the business.

Although breastfeeding does require substantial time commitments for the mother, which may reduce the time available for work, there may be some economic benefits of breastfeeding. The increased cost of formula as compared with breastfeeding is between $1,000 and $4,000 per year per baby (Mohler, 2011). Additional indirect cost savings include the possibility that there will be fewer medical bills related to infant illness and fewer absences from paid work time for doctor visits with sick infants (Mohler, 2011). Because there are possible health benefits of breastfeeding, such as reduced risk of type 2 diabetes in mothers (Stuebe & Rich-Edwards, 2009) or reduced risk of gastrointestinal infection in infants (Kramer et al., 2001), breastfeeding is associated with reductions in medical costs (Mohler, 2011). Breastfeeding also does not require

environmental waste from formula production and packaging. Furthermore, breastfeeding women may save some time that would otherwise be spent preparing formula and sterilizing bottles.

Breastfeeding poses significant burdens on women's time and freedom during the postpartum period. Feeding with formula allows mothers more freedom, because other caregivers can care for the infant more readily. Pumping breast milk for feedings when the mother is absent is also not feasible for many women who do not have access to adequate support. These costs, however, may be offset to some extent by the fact that breastfeeding is less expensive than formula-feeding, and may lead to considerable reductions in healthcare costs and time taken from work because of child and maternal illness over the long term. Future research might address whether women gain equivalent health benefits from breast pumping and breastfeeding, given that this question has important implications for women who are in the workforce and need to pump regularly.

Social Costs

Breastfeeding can have some social costs for women. For example, women often feel embarrassed about breastfeeding in public, although it is legal in 45 states in the United States. A study found that low-income pregnant women in Missouri felt that discreetly breastfeeding in one's home in front of visitors was acceptable, but that it was less acceptable to breastfeed in public, especially if people were embarrassed by it or if the breastfeeding was not discrete (Libbus & Kolostov, 1994). Similarly, women often reported feeling "vulnerable" while breastfeeding in public and expect to receive negative attention for it (Sheeshka et al., 2001). These feelings can lead women to remain housebound or restrict their movements during exclusive breastfeeding to avoid the social stigma of breastfeeding in public (Sheeshka et al., 2001).

In cultures where breastfeeding is widely accepted, women often have more freedom to breastfeed in public places. For example, Dettwyler (1995b) asserts that in places such as Mali or Nepal, women are able to breastfeed their infants in public freely and without stigmatization. Dettwyler (1995b) argues that the sexualization of the breast in many Western cultures accounts for much of the taboo surrounding breastfeeding in public, noting that in Mali and Nepal, where breastfeeding in public is completely socially acceptable, breasts do not have the same sexual connotation for men or women that they do elsewhere in the world. In cultures where the primary function of the breast is thought to be sexual, the sight of a women breastfeeding is often considered "perverted" or "obscene." For example, the popular social networking website, Facebook, officially banned pictures of women breastfeeding their infants, claiming that these photos violated their decency code by showing an exposed breast (Worthman, 2009). Women who breastfeed in cultures where breastfeeding is taboo often face continual pressure from friends and family to use formula, have low breastfeeding confidence, feel intense stigma around breastfeeding in public, and have very little access to breastfeeding information outside of medical professionals (Scott & Mostyn, 2003).

The social acceptability of breastfeeding varies by culture and ethnicity, which has implications for breastfeeding rates (see Kelley, Watt, and Nazoo, 2006, for a review). Women who immigrate to the United States from cultures where breastfeeding is more common have higher rates of breastfeeding than the U.S. population. For example, Black women who immigrate to the United States from West Indian Counties—where breastfeeding is the norm—are more likely to intend to breastfeed exclusively after birth than are African American women (Bonuck, Freeman, & Trombley, 2005). Among Puerto Rican women, length of residence in the continental United States is inversely associated with breastfeeding initiation (Pérez-Escamilla et al., 1998), indicating that living in a culture like the United States where breastfeeding is less common than in Puerto Rico can alter breastfeeding practices.

There is also variation across cultures in beliefs about the appropriate age to wean a child. Women who violate their local norms can face social stigma. Although the average duration of breastfeeding in traditional societies is approximately 2.5 years (Dettwyler, 1995a), many women in the United States report that they receive negative reactions from others if they breastfeed past the first few months postpartum (Kendall-Tackett & Sugarman, 1995). In a survey conducted in the United States, the percentage of mothers citing "social stigma" as a negative aspect of breastfeeding was strongly related to the age of the child: 29% of women breastfeeding past 6 months and 61% of women breastfeeding past 24 months reported feeling stigma as a result of breastfeeding (Kendall-Tackett & Sugarman, 1995).

Recent research also suggests that breastfeeding women face social stigma in the United States regardless of where or how long they choose to feed their infants. In a series of studies conducted with college students, breastfeeding mothers were rated as less competent and less likely to be hired for a hypothetical job compared to mothers who were not breastfeeding or women without children (Smith et al., 2011). In this research, the negative effects of breast-feeding were comparable, in terms of the negative perceptions evoked in the minds of both male and female students, to a woman's decision to purposefully sexualize her breasts (Smith et al., 2011). These results suggest that although breastfeeding may have many benefits for the mother, mothers who choose to breastfeed may also suffer social costs.

Moving into the private realm, mothers may also be concerned that breastfeeding will have negative consequences for their social relationships. Breastfeeding is an inti-mate experience between a mother and her child that can sometimes lead the other parent to feel left out. Fathers sometimes report that breastfeeding interrupts their ability to form a relationship with the new infant (Bar-Yam & Darby, 1997). Even when fathers are supportive of their partners' breastfeeding, many also admit to feelings of jealousy at their inability to contribute dur-ing the feeding process (Rempel & Rempel, 2011). In-depth interviews with fathers sug-gest that these feelings can lead fathers to postpone the forming of a relationship with the child until after the infant is weaned or to compensate by becoming more involved in other aspects of caring for the infant (i.e., baths, diapers) (Gamble & Morse, 1993). Presumably, the feeling of being left out of the parenting process can also extend to families in which two women co-parent, but only one breastfeeds the baby.

Families can sometimes alleviate these negative feelings in co-parents by framing breastfeeding as a team effort, discussing with co-parents the benefits of breastfeeding for their child, involving co-parents in breast-feeding decisions, and having co-parents provide instrumental support (like helping with chores or entertaining company) (Gamble & Morse, 1993). Additionally, co-parents may participate in infant feeding directly if breastfeeding mothers use a breast-pump to express milk that can be fed to the infant in a bottle.

Another factor that can lead partners to have negative attitudes toward breastfeeding is its impact on women's sexuality (Rempel & Rempel, 2011). Breastfeeding lowers women's estrogen levels in the early post-partum period (Battin et al., 1985), which can lead to decreases in sexual desire and cause vaginal dryness for a subset of women, making sex painful (Brown & McDaniel, 2008). For example, breastfeeding women report more vaginal pain during intercourse at 3 months postpartum than formula-feeding women, although there was no difference at 6 months postpartum (Con-nolly, Thorp, & Pahel, 2005). Another study found that breastfeeding at 3 months (but not 6 months) was related to reduced fre-quency of sex, sexual desire, and sexual satisfaction as compared to women who were not breastfeeding (Judicibus & McCabe, 2002). Overall, women perceive that breastfeeding has a slightly negative impact on the physiological aspects of sexu-ality; however, most report that it does not greatly affect the sexual relationship with their partner (Avery, Duckett, & Frantzich, 2000). In one study, the majority of women (60.3%) perceived that the baby's father thought breastfeeding made them neither more nor less sexually desirable than before pregnancy, while 12.7% thought it made them less sexually attractive, and 27% thought it made them more attractive to their partner.

Although there are social costs associated with breastfeeding for mothers, there can also be social costs associated with *not* breast-feeding (Hauck & Irurita, 2003). Because of the widespread beliefs about the positive effects of breastfeeding on a child, women sometimes feel extensive social pressure to breastfeed. Although most mothers (approximately 96%; Simopoulos & Grave, 1984) are physically capable of breastfeeding, other barriers—just as real—can make breastfeeding nearly impossible. If women do not have access to accurate information regarding proper breastfeeding techniques, they may not produce enough milk to support the needs of their infant or may develop physical problems that make breastfeeding painful. Furthermore, many mothers must work to financially support the needs of their children and are not allowed convenient or flexible breaks to breast pump, nor are they given the space necessary to pump and store their breast milk.

Whatever the reasons behind the decision not to breastfeed, many women feel that this decision will lead to the perception that they are "bad mothers" (Ladd–Taylor & Umansky, 1998). As one mother recounts, "I was feeling very guilty [for stopping breastfeeding] and I didn't know what to do" (Hauck & Irurita, 2003, p. 70). There have even been select reports of medical professionals pushing the "breast is best" message, regardless of the mother's circumstances and choices, leading some mothers to report they are breastfeeding "just to keep the nurses happy" (Bauer, 2000, p. 15). These overt instances of pressure from health professionals are likely extreme, rare examples. For many years, physicians, breastfeeding consultants, nurses, and clinical experts have been aware that encouraging mothers to breastfeed by supporting them is helpful, but that pressuring them or creating guilt for lack of success is not (Dillaway &

Douma, 2004). Nonetheless, even when healthcare professionals are sensitive in their approach, family, friends, and even strangers share their advice about best practices for breastfeeding initiation, duration, and weaning. Interviews with new mothers have revealed that when the expectations of others do not match the choices of the mother, mothers can often feel guilt (Hauck & Irurita, 2003).

Breastfeeding is associated with some social costs. Mothers can become socially restricted by breastfeeding because they do not feel comfortable breastfeeding in public places. Furthermore, breastfeeding mothers are stigmatized and perceived as less competent than nonbreastfeeding mothers, a fact that could have negative consequences for women in the workplace or for women who breastfeed for periods beyond the cultural norm. Finally, some women find that breastfeeding reduces their sex drive for a time or makes their partners feel left out of the childcare experience. There are, however, also social costs associated with not breastfeeding, such as being branded a "bad mother" or being made to feel guilty.

CONCLUSIONS

This chapter reviewed the scientific research on the benefits and costs associated with breastfeeding for mothers. Many studies point out that breastfeeding is associated with many health benefits for mothers, including reduced risk for metabolic syndrome and certain reproductive cancers. Furthermore, evidence suggests that breastfeeding could buffer women against biological and psychosocial stressors during the postpartum period. Little evidence is available examining whether breastfeeding reduces the risk of postpartum depression or increases maternal bonding to the infant. More research is needed in each of these areas.

Although research has often focused on the benefits of breastfeeding for mothers, there is also evidence of substantial costs associated with breastfeeding. Mothers must devote several hours per day to breast-feeding if it is the sole feeding method, and some mothers feel confined to their homes because they are uncomfortable breastfeed-ing in public. Breastfeeding mothers also face significant logistical and professional challenges in the workplace. Finally, the majority of women will experience some discomfort during breastfeeding, particularly early in the postpartum period, which can sometimes develop into painful conditions requiring medical attention.

More studies are needed to evaluate these many trade-offs in the benefits and costs of breastfeeding at both the population and individual level. Even if studies demon-strate that the benefits of breastfeeding out-weigh the costs for women as a group, decisions for individual mothers need to be made based on their personal circum-stances, which will vary in the many com-plex and multifaceted trade-offs described in this chapter. Because of the growing evi-dence of the health benefits of breastfeeding for infants and their mothers, it makes sense for social policies to attempt to reduce bar-riers to breastfeeding. Policy makers and healthcare professionals have made strides in breastfeeding promotion in recent years (Centers for Disease Control and Preven-tion, 2011b). Educating mothers, partners, families, and communities about the health benefits of breastfeeding, along with how to overcome the challenges, have proven to be particularly effective (Centers for Disease Control and Prevention, 2011b). However, policy makers and medical professionals should also realize that variation in mothers' circumstances—both personal and struc-tural—affect whether breastfeeding is the best choice for a particular woman and her child.

REFERENCES

Altemus, M., Deuster, P. A., Galliven, E., Carter, C. S., & Gold, P. W. (1995). Suppression of hypo-thalmic-pituitary-adrenal axis responses to stress in lactating women. *Journal of Clinical Endocrinol-ogy & Metabolism, 80*(10), 2954–2959. doi: 10.1210/jc.80.10.2954

Altemus, M., Redwine, L. S., Leong, Y. M., Frye, C. A., Porges, S. W., & Carter, C. S. (2001). Responses to laboratory psychosocial stress in postpartum women. *Psychosomatic Medicine, 63*(5), 814–821.

Altshuler, L. L., Hendrick, V., & Cohen, L. S. (2000). An update on mood and anxiety disorders during pregnancy and the postpartum period. *Primary Care Companion Journal of Clinical Psychiatry, 2*(6), 217–222.

Andrieu, N., Goldgar, D. E., Easton, D. F., Rookus, M., Brohet, R., Antoniou, A. C., . . . Chang-Claude, J. (2006). Pregnancies, breast-feeding, and breast cancer risk in the International BRCA1/2 Carrier Cohort Study (IBCCS). *Jour-nal of the National Cancer Institute, 98*(8), 535–544. doi: 10.1093/jnci/djj132

Arora, S., McJunkin, C., Wehrer, J., & Kuhn, P. (2000). Major factors influencing breastfeeding rates: Mother's perception of father's attitude and milk supply. *Pediatrics, 106*(5), E67.

Avery, M. D., Duckett, L., & Frantzich, C. R. (2000). The experience of sexuality during breastfeeding among primiparous women. *The Journal of Midwifery & Women's Health, 45*(3), 227–237. doi: 10.1016/s1526-9523(00)00020-9

Baker, J. L., Gamborg, M., Heitmann, B. L., Lissner, L., Sorensen, T. I., & Rasmussen, K. M. (2008). Breastfeeding reduces postpartum weight retention. *American Journal of Clinical Nutrition, 88*(6), 1543–1551. doi: 10.3945/ajcn.2008 .26379

Bar-Yam, N. B., & Darby, L. (1997). Fathers and breastfeeding: A review of the literature. *Journal of Human Lactation, 13*(1), 45–50. doi: 10.1177/089033449701300116

Battin, D. A., Marrs, R. P., Fleiss, P. M., & Mishell, D. R., Jr. (1985). Effect of suckling on serum prolactin, luteinizing hormone, follicle-stimulating hormone, and estradiol during prolonged lactation. *Obstetrics and Gynecology, 65*(6), 785–788.

Bauer, C. (2000). Pressure to breastfeed. *AJN: The American Journal of Nursing, 100*(11), 15.

Beck, C. T. (1992). The lived experience of postpartum depression: A phenomenological study. *Nursing Research, 41*(3), 166–170. doi: 10.1097/00006199-199205000-00008

Bernier, M. O., Plu-Bureau, G., Bossard, N., Ayzac, L., & Thalabard, J. C. (2000). Breastfeeding and risk of breast cancer: A metaanalysis of published studies. *Human Reproduction Update, 6*(4), 374–386.

Boccia, M. L., Goursaud, A.-P. S., Bachevalier, J., Anderson, K. D., & Pedersen, C. A. (2007). Peripherally administered non-peptide oxytocin antagonist, L368,899®, accumulates in limbic brain areas: A new pharmacological tool for the study of social motivation in non-human primates. *Hormones and Behavior, 52*(3), 344–351. doi: 10.1016/j.yhbeh.2007.05.009

Bole-Feysot, C., Goffin, V., Edery, M., Binart, N., & Kelly, P. A. (1998). Prolactin (PRL) and its receptor: Actions, signal transduction pathways and phenotypes observed in PRL receptor knockout mice. *Endocrine Reviews, 19*(3), 225–268.

Bonuck, K. A., Freeman, K., & Trombley, M. (2005). Country of origin and race/ethnicity: Impact on breastfeeding intentions. *Journal of Human Lactation, 21*, 320–326. doi: 10.1177/0890334405278249

Bridges, R. S., DiBiase, R., Loundes, D. D., & Doherty, P. C. (1985). Prolactin stimulation of maternal behavior in female rats. *Science, 227*(4688), 782–784.

Bridges, R. S., Rigero, B. A., Byrnes, E. M., Yang, L., & Walker, A. M. (2001). Central infusions of the recombinant human prolactin receptor antagonist, S179D-PRL, delay the onset of maternal behavior in steroid-primed, nulliparous female rats. *Endocrinology, 142*(2), 730–739. doi: 10.1210/en.142.2.730

Britton, J. R., Britton, H. L., & Gronwaldt, V. (2006). Breastfeeding, sensitivity, and attachment. *Pediatrics, 118*(5), e1436–e1443. doi: 10.1542/peds.2005-2916

Brown, H., & McDaniel, M. (2008). A review of the implications and impact of pregnancy on sexual function. *Current Sexual Health Reports, 5*(1), 51–55. doi: 10.1007/s11930-008-0009-6

Callen, J., & Pinelli, J. (2004). Incidence and duration of breastfeeding for term infants in Canada, United States, Europe, and Australia: A literature review. *Birth, 31*(4), 285–292. doi: 10.1111/j.0730-7659. 2004.00321.x

Carter, C. S., & Altemus, M. (1997). Integrative functions of lactational hormones in social behavior and stress management. *Annals of the New York Academy of Sciences, 807*, 164–174.

Centers for Disease Control and Prevention. (2011a). Breastfeeding among U.S. children born 2000–2008. *CDC National Immunization Survey.* Retrieved from http://www.cdc.gov/breastfeeding/data/nis_data/

Centers for Disease Control and Prevention. (2011b). *Breastfeeding report card—United States, 2011.* Retrieved from http://www.cdc.gov/breastfeeding/pdf/2011breastfeedingreportcard.pdf

Cernadas, J. M., Noceda, G., Barrera, L., Martinez, A. M., & Garsd, A. (2003). Maternal and perinatal factors influencing the duration of exclusive breastfeeding during the first 6 months of life. *Journal of Human Lactation, 19*(2), 136–144.

Chaudron, L. H., Klein, M. H., Remington, P., Palta, M., Allen, C., & Essex, M. J. (2001). Predictors, prodromes and incidence of postpartum depression. *Journal of Psychosomatic Obstetrics & Gynecology, 22*, 103–112.

Chiodera, P., Salvarani, C., Bacchi-Modena, A., Spallanzani, R., Cigarini, C., Alboni, A., . . . Coiro, V. (1991). Relationship between plasma profiles of oxytocin and adrenocorticotropic hormone during suckling or breast stimulation in women. *Hormone Research, 35*(3–4), 119–123.

Clemons, M., & Goss, P. (2001). Estrogen and the risk of breast cancer. *New England Journal of Medicine, 344*(4), 276–285. doi: 10.1056/NEJM200101253440407

Connolly, A., Thorp, J., & Pahel, L. (2005). Effects of pregnancy and childbirth on postpartum sexual function: A longitudinal prospective study. *International Urogynecology Journal, 16*(4), 263–267. doi: 10.1007/s00192-005-1293-6

Dai, X., & Dennis, C. L. (2003). Translation and validation of the Breastfeeding Self-Efficacy Scale into Chinese. *Journal of Midwifery and Women's Health, 48*(5), 350–356.

Danforth, K. N., Tworoger, S. S., Hecht, J. L., Rosner, B. A., Colditz, G. A., & Hankinson, S. E. (2007). Breastfeeding and risk of ovarian cancer in two prospective cohorts. *Cancer Causes Control, 18*(5), 517–523. doi: 10.1007/s10552-007-0130-2

Dennis, C. L., & McQueen, K. (2007). Does maternal postpartum depressive symptomatology influence infant feeding outcomes? *Acta Paediatrica, 96*(4), 590–594. doi: 10.1111/j.1651-2227.2007.00184.x

Dennis, C. L., & McQueen, K. (2009). The relationship between infant-feeding outcomes and postpartum depression: A qualitative systematic review. *Pediatrics, 123*(4), e736–e751. doi: 10.1542/peds.2008-1629

Dettwyler, K. A. (1995a). A time to wean: The hominid blueprint for the natural age of weaning in modern human populations. In P. Stuart-Macadam & K. A. Dettwyler (Eds.), *Breastfeeding: Biocultural perspectives* (pp. 39–73). New York, NY: Aldinde Gruyter.

Dettwyler, K. A. (1995b). Beauty and the breast: The cultural context of feeding in the United States. In P. Stuart-Macadam & K. A. Dettwyler (Eds.), *Breastfeeding: Biocultural perspectives* (pp. 167–215). New York, NY: Aldine deGruyter.

Dewey, K. G. (1997). Energy and protein requirements during lactation. *Annual Review of Nutrition, 17*, 19–36. doi: 10.1146/annurev.nutr.17.1.19

Dillaway, H. E., & Douma, M. E. (2004). Are pediatric offices "supportive" of breastfeeding? Discrepancies of mothers' and healthcare providers' reports. *Clinical Pediatrics, 43*(5), 417–430. doi: 10.1177/000992280404300502

Edhborg, M., Friberg, M., Lundh, W., & Widstrom, A. M. (2005). "Struggling with life": Narratives from women with signs of postpartum depression. *Scandinavian Journal of Public Health, 33*(4), 261–267. doi: 10.1080/14034940510005725

Else-Quest, N. M., Hyde, J. S., & Clark, R. (2003). Breastfeeding, bonding and the mother-infant relationship. *Merrill-Palmer Quarterly, 49*, 495–517.

Feldman, R., Gordon, I., Schneiderman, I., Weisman, O., & Zagoory-Sharon, O. (2010). Natural variations in maternal and paternal care are associated with systematic changes in oxytocin following parent-infant contact. *Psychoneuroendocrinology, 35*(8), 1133–1141. doi: 10.1016/j.psyneuen.2010.01.013

Feldman, R., Weller, A., Zagoory-Sharon, O., & Levine, A. (2007). Evidence for a neuro-endocrinological foundation of human affiliation: Plasma oxytocin levels across pregnancy and the postpartum period predict mother-infant bonding. *Psychological Science, 18*, 965–970.

Fergerson, S. S., Jamieson, D. J., & Lindsay, M. (2002). Diagnosing postpartum depression: Can we do better? *American Journal of Obstetrics and Gynecology, 186*(5), 899–902.

Field, T. (2010). Postpartum depression effects on early interactions, parenting, and safety practices: A review. *Infant Behavior and Development, 33*(1), 1–6. doi: 10.1016/j.infbeh.2009.10.005

Fleming, A. S., Ruble, D. N., Flett, G. L., & Van Wagner, V. (1990). Adjustment in first-time mothers: Changes in mood and mood content during the early postpartum months. *Developmental Psychology, 26*(1), 137–143. doi: 10.1037/0012-1649.26.1.137

Ford, E. S., Giles, W. H., & Dietz, W. H. (2002). Prevalence of the metabolic syndrome among US adults: Findings from the third National Health and Nutrition Examination Survey. *JAMA, 287*(3), 356–359.

Freeman, M. E., Kanyicska, B., Lerant, A., & Nagy, G. (2000). Prolactin: Structure, function, and regulation of secretion. *Physiological Reviews, 80*(4), 1523–1631.

Galler, J. R., Harrison, R. H., Biggs, M. A., Ramsey, F., & Forde, V. (1999). Maternal moods predict breastfeeding in Barbados. *Journal of Developmental and Behavioral Pediatrics, 20*(2), 80–87.

Galtry, J. (2003). The impact on breastfeeding of labour market policy and practice in Ireland, Sweden, and the USA. *Social Science & Medicine, 57*(1), 167–177. doi: 10.1016/s0277-9536(02)00372-6

Gamble, D., & Morse, J. M. (1993). Fathers of breastfed infants: Postponing and types of involvement. *Journal of Obstetric, Gynecologic, & Neonatal Nursing, 22*(4), 358–369. doi: 10.1111/j.1552-6909.1993.tb01816.x

Garza, R., & Ramussen, K. M. (2000). Pregnancy and lactation. In J. S. Garrow, W. P. T. James, & A.

Ralph (Eds.), *Human nutrition and dietetics* (10th ed., pp. 437–448). Edinburgh, Scotland: Churchill-Livingstone.

Gavin, N. I., Gaynes, B. N., Lohr, K. N., Meltzer-Brody, S., Gartlehner, G., & Swinson, T. (2005). Perinatal depression: A systematic review of prevalence and incidence. *Obstetrics and Gynecology, 106*(5, Pt. 1), 1071–1083. doi: 10.1097/01 .AOG.0000183597.31630.db

Gaynes, B. N., Gavin, N., Meltzer-Brody, S., Lohr, K. N., Swinson, T., Gartlehner, G., . . . Miller, W. C. (2005). Perinatal depression: Prevalence, screening accuracy, and screening outcomes. *Evidence Report—Technology Assessment (Summary), 119*, 1–8.

Gimpl, G., & Fahrenholz, F. (2001). The oxytocin receptor system: Structure, function, and regulation. *Physiological reviews, 81*(2), 629–683.

Gjerdingen, D. K., Froberg, D. G., Chaloner, K. M., & McGovern, P. M. (1993). Changes in women's physical health during the first postpartum year. *Archives of Family Medicine, 2*(3), 277–283.

Grace, S. L., Evindar, A., & Stewart, D. E. (2003). The effect of postpartum depression on child cognitive development and behavior: A review and critical analysis of the literature. *Archives of Women's Mental Health, 6*(4), 263–274. doi: 10.1007/s00737-003-0024-6

Groer, M. W., Davis, M. W., & Hemphill, J. (2002). Postpartum stress: Current concepts and the possible protective role of breastfeeding. *Journal of Obstetric, Gynecologic, & Neonatal Nursing, 31*(4), 411–417. doi: 10.1111/j.1552-6909.2002.tb00063.x

Gruis, M. (1977). Beyond maternity: Postpartum concerns of mothers. *American Journal of Maternal Child Nursing, 2*, 182–188.

Guendelman, S., Kosa, J. L., Pearl, M., Graham, S., Goodman, J., & Kharrazi, M. (2009). Juggling work and breastfeeding: Effects of maternity leave and occupational characteristics. *Pediatrics, 123*(1), e38–e46. doi: 10.1542/peds.2008-2244

Hahn-Holbrook, J., Holbrook, C., & Haselton, M. G. (2011). Parental precaution: Neurobiological means and adaptive ends. *Neuroscience & Biobehavioral Reviews, 35*(4), 1052–1066. doi: 10.1016/j.neubiorev.2010.09.015

Hammen, C. (2005). Stress and depression. *Annual Review of Clinical Psychology, 1*(1), 293–319. doi: 10.1146/annurev.clinpsy.1.102803.143938

Hannah, P., Adams, D., Lee, A., Glover, V., & Sandler, M. (1992). Links between early postpartum mood and post-natal depression. *The British Journal of Psychiatry, 160*(6), 777–780. doi: 10.1192/bjp.160.6.777

Hauck, Y., & Irurita, V. (2003). Incompatible expectations: The dilemma of breastfeeding mothers. *Health Care for Women International, 24*(1), 62–78. doi: 10.1080/07399330390170024

Heck, H., & de Castro, J. M. (1993). The caloric demand of lactation does not alter spontaneous meal patterns, nutrient intakes, or moods of women. *Physiology & Behavior, 54*(4), 641–648. doi: 10.1016/0031-9384(93)90071-m

Heinrichs, M., Meinlschmidt, G., Neumann, I., Wagner, S., Kirschbaum, C., Ehlert, U., & Hellhammer, D. H. (2001). Effects of suckling on hypothalamic-pituitary-adrenal axis responses to psychosocial stress in postpartum lactating women. *Journal of Clinical Endocrinology and Metabolism, 86*(10), 4798–4804.

Herzog, A., & Detre, T. (1976). Psychotic reactions associated with childbirth. *Diseases of the Nervous System, 37*(4), 229–235.

Hrdy, S. B. (1992). Fitness tradeoffs in the history and evolution of delegated mothering with special reference to wet-nursing, abandonment, and infanticide. *Ethology and Sociobiology, 13*(5–6), 409–442. doi: 10.1016/0162-3095(92)90011-r

Hrdy, S. B. (1999). *Mother nature: A history of mothers, infants, and natural selection*. New York, NY: Pantheon Books.

Ip, S., Chung, M., Raman, G., Chew, P., Magula, N., DeVine, D., . . . Lau, J. (2007). Breastfeeding and maternal and infant health outcomes in developed countries. *Evidence Report—Technology Assessment (Full Report), 153*, 1–186.

Jansen, J., Weerth, C. D., & Riksen-Walraven, J. M. (2008). Breastfeeding and the mother-infant relationship—A review. *Developmental Review, 28*(4), 503–521. doi: 10.1016/j.dr.2008.07.001

Jernström, H., Lubinski, J., Lynch, H. T., Ghadirian, P., Neuhausen, S., Isaacs, C., . . . Narod, S. A. (2004). Breast-feeding and the risk of breast cancer in BRCA1 and BRCA2 mutation carriers. *Journal of the National Cancer Institute, 96*(14), 1094–1098. doi: 10.1093/jnci/djh211

Jones, N. A., McFall, B. A., & Diego, M. A. (2004). Patterns of brain electrical activity in infants of depressed mothers who breastfeed and bottle feed: The mediating role of infant temperament. *Biological Psychology*, *67*(1–2), 103–124. doi: 10.1016/j.biopsycho.2004.03.010

Jordan, S. J., Siskind, V., Green, C. A., Whiteman, D. C., & Webb, P. M. (2010). Breastfeeding and risk of epithelial ovarian cancer. *Cancer Causes Control*, *21*(1), 109–116. doi: 10.1007/s10552-009-9440-x

Judicibus, M. A. D., & McCabe, M. P. (2002). Psychological factors and the sexuality of pregnant and postpartum women. *The Journal of Sex Research*, *39*(2), 94–103.

Kelley, Y. J., Watt, R. G., & Nazoo, J. Y. (2006). Racial/ethnic differences in breastfeeding initiation and continuation in the United Kingdom and comparison with findings in the United States. *Pediatrics*, *118*, 1428–1435. doi: 10.1542/peds.2006-0714\

Kendall-Tackett, K. A., & Sugarman, M. (1995). The social consequences of long-term breastfeeding. *The Journal of Human Lactation*, *11*, 179–183. doi: 10.1177/089033449501100316

Kendrick, K. M. (2000). Oxytocin, motherhood and bonding. *Experimental Physiology*, *85*(Spec), 111S–124S.

Key, T. J., & Pike, M. C. (1988). The role of oestrogens and progestagens in the epidemiology and prevention of breast cancer. *European Journal of Cancer and Clinical Oncology*, *24*(1), 29–43.

King, M. C., Marks, J. H., & Mandell, J. B. (2003). Breast and ovarian cancer risks due to inherited mutations in BRCA1 and BRCA2. *Science*, *302*(5645), 643–646. doi: 10.1126/science.1088759

Klerman, J. A., & Leibowitz, A. (1999). Job continuity among new mothers. *Demography*, *36*(2), 145–155.

Kramer, M. S., Aboud, F., Mironova, E., Vanilovich, I., Platt, R. W., Matush, L., . . . For The Promotion of Breastfeeding Intervention Trial Study Group. (2008). Breastfeeding and child cognitive development: New evidence from a large randomized trial. *Archives of General Psychiatry*, *65*(5), 578–584. doi: 10.1001/archpsyc.65.5.578

Kramer, M. S., Chalmers, B., Hodnett, E. D., Sevkovskaya, Z., Dzikovich, I., Shapiro, S., . . . For The Promotion of Breastfeeding Intervention Trial Study Group. (2001). Promotion of Breastfeeding Intervention Trial (PROBIT): A randomized trial in the Republic of Belarus. *JAMA*, *285*(4), 413–420. doi: 10.1001/jama.285.4.413

Kramer, M. S., & Kakuma, R. (2004). The optimal duration of exclusive breastfeeding: A systematic review. *Advances in Experimental Medicine and Biology*, *554*, 63–77.

Labbok, M., & Krasovec, K. (1990). Toward consistancy in breastfeeding definitions. *Studies in Family Planning*, *21*, 226–230.

Ladd-Taylor, M., & Umansky, L. (1998). *"Bad" mothers: The politics of blame in twentieth-century America*. New York, NY: New York University Press.

Lee, E., Ma, H., McKean-Cowdin, R., Van Den Berg, D., Bernstein, L., Henderson, B. E., & Ursin, G. (2008). Effect of reproductive factors and oral contraceptives on breast cancer risk in BRCA1/2 mutation carriers and noncarriers: Results from a population-based study. *Cancer Epidemiology Biomarkers & Prevention*, *17*(11), 3170–3178. doi: 10.1158/1055-9965. epi-08-0396

Libbus, M. K., & Kolostov, L. S. (1994). Perceptions of breastfeeding and infant feeding choice in a group of low-income mid-Missouri women. *Journal of Human Lactation*, *10*(1), 17–23. doi: 10.1177/089033449401000123

Light, K. C., Smith, T. E., Johns, J. M., Brownley, K. A., Hofheimer, J. A., & Amico, J. A. (2000). Oxytocin responsivity in mothers of infants: A preliminary study of relationships with blood pressure during laboratory stress and normal ambulatory activity. *Health Psychology*, *19*(6), 560–567.

Lonstein, J. S. (2007). Regulation of anxiety during the postpartum period. *Frontiers in Neuroendocrinology*, *28*(2–3), 115–141. doi: 10.1016/j.yfrne.2007.05.002

Lunn, P., Austin, S., Prentice, A., & Whitehead, R. (1984). The effect of improved nutrition on plasma prolactin concentrations and postpartum infertility in lactating Gambian women. *The American Journal of Clinical Nutrition*, *39*(2), 227–235.

Martone, D. J., & Nash, B. R. (1988). Initial differences in postpartum attachment behavior in breastfeeding and bottle-feeding mothers. *Journal of Obstetric, Gynecologic, & Neonatal Nursing*, *17*(3), 212–213. doi: 10.1111/j.1552-6909.1988.tb00427.x

Matheson, I., Kristensen, K., & Lunde, P. K. (1990). Drug utilization in breast-feeding women. A survey in Oslo. *European Journal of Clinical Pharmacology*, *38*(5), 453–459.

McNeilly, A. S., Robinson, I. C., Houston, M. J., & Howie, P. W. (1983). Release of oxytocin and prolactin in response to suckling. *British Medicine Journal (Clinical Research Ed.)*, *286*(6361), 257–259.

Mercer, R. T. (1986). *First-time motherhood*. New York, NY: Springer.

Mezzacappa, E. S. (2004). Breastfeeding and maternal stress response and health. *Nutrition Reviews*, *62*(7, Pt. 1), 261–268.

Mezzacappa, E. S., Guethlein, W., & Katkin, E. S. (2002). Breast-feeding and maternal health in online mothers. *Annals of Behavioral Medicine*, *24*(4), 299–309.

Mezzacappa, E. S., Guethlein, W., Vaz, N., & Bagiella, E. (2000). A preliminary study of breast-feeding and maternal symptomatology. *Annals of Behavioral Medicine*, *22*(1), 71–79.

Mezzacappa, E. S., & Katlin, E. S. (2002). Breast-feeding is associated with reduced perceived stress and negative mood in mothers. *Health Psychology*, *21*(2), 187–193.

Mezzacappa, E. S., Kelsey, R. M., & Katkin, E. S. (2005). Breast feeding, bottle feeding, and maternal autonomic responses to stress. *Journal of Psychosomatic Research*, *58*(4), 351–365. doi: 10.1016/j.jpsychores.2004.11.004

Mohler, B. (2011). Is the breast best for business? The implications of the breastfeeding promotion act. *William and Mary Business Law Review*, *2*(1), 155–184.

Morland-Schultz, K., & Hill, P. D. (2005). Prevention of and therapies for nipple pain: A systematic review. *Journal of Obstetric, Gynecologic, and Neonatal Nursing*, *34*(4), 428–437. doi: 10.1177/0884217505276056

Nagle, C. M., Bain, C. J., Green, A. C., & Webb, P. M. (2008). The influence of reproductive and hormonal factors on ovarian cancer survival. *International Journal of Gynecological Cancer*, *18*(3), 407–413. doi: 10.1111/j.1525-1438.2007.01031.x

Nduati, R., Richardson, B. A., John, G., Mbori-Ngacha, D., Mwatha, A., Ndinya-Achola, J., . . . Kreiss, J. (2001). Effect of breastfeeding on mortality among HIV-1 infected women: A randomised trial. *Lancet*, *357*(9269), 1651–1655. doi: 10.1016/S0140-6736(00)04820-0

Negishi, H., Kishida, T., Yamada, H., Hirayama, E., Mikuni, M., & Fujimoto, S. (1999). Changes in uterine size after vaginal delivery and cesarean section determined by vaginal sonography in the puerperium. *Archives of Gynecology and Obstetrics*, *263*, 13–16.

Neumann, I. D. (2001). Alterations in behavioral and neuroendocrine stress coping strategies in pregnant, parturient and lactating rats. *Progress in Brain Research*, *133*, 143–152.

Neumann, I. D., Torner, L., & Wigger, A. (2000). Brain oxytocin: Differential inhibition of neuroendocrine stress responses and anxiety-related behaviour in virgin, pregnant and lactating rats. *Neuroscience*, *95*(2), 567–575.

Nishioka, E., Haruna, M., Ota, E., Matsuzaki, M., Murayama, R., Yoshimura, K., & Murashima, S. (2011). A prospective study of the relationship between breastfeeding and postpartum depressive symptoms appearing at 1–5 months after delivery. *Journal of Affective Disorders*, *133*(3), 553–559. doi: 10.1016/j.jad.2011.04.027

Nissen, E., Gustavsson, P., Widstrom, A. M., & Uvnas-Moberg, K. (1998). Oxytocin, prolactin, milk production and their relationship with personality traits in women after vaginal delivery or Cesarean section. *Journal of Psychosomatic Obstetrics and Gynecology*, *19*(1), 49–58.

O'Hara, M. W., & Swain, A. M. (1996). Rates and risk of postpartum depression—A meta-analysis. *International Review of Psychiatry*, *8*(1), 37–54. doi: 10.3109/09540269609037816

Pedersen, C. A. (2004). Biological aspects of social bonding and the roots of human violence. *Annals of the New York Academy of Sciences*, *1036*(1), 106–127. doi: 10.1196/annals.1330.006

Pedersen, C. A., Caldwell, J. D., Peterson, G., Walker, C. H., & Mason, G. A. (1992). Oxytocin activation of maternal behavior in the rat. *Annals of the New York Academy of Sciences*, *652*(1), 58–69. doi: 10.1111/j.1749-6632.1992.tb34346.x

Pérez-Escamilla, R., Himmelgreen, D., Segura-Millán, S., González, A., Ferris, A. M., Damio, G., & Bermúdez-Vega, A. (1998). Prenatal and perinatal factors associated with breast-feeding initiation among inner-city Puerto-Rican women. *Journal of the American Dietetic Association*, *98*, 657–663.

Peterson, A. E., Pérez-Escamilla, R., Labbok, M. H., Hight, V., von Hertzen, H., & Van Look,

P. (2000). Multicenter study of the lactational amenorrhea method (LAM) III: Effectiveness, duration, and satisfaction with reduced client-provider contact. *Contraception, 62*(5), 221–230.

Pisacane, A., & Continisio, P. (2004). Breastfeeding and perceived changes in the appearance of the breasts: A retrospective study. *Acta Paediatrica, 93*(10), 1346–1348.

Pitt, B. (1973). Maternity blues. *British Journal of Psychiatry, 122*(569), 431–433.

Ram, K. T., Bobby, P., Hailpern, S. M., Lo, J. C., Schocken, M., Skurnick, J., & Santoro, N. (2008). Duration of lactation is associated with lower prevalence of the metabolic syndrome in midlife: SWAN, the Study of Women's Health Across the Nation. *American Journal of Obstetrics and Gynecology, 198*(3), 268 e261–e266. doi: 10.1016/j.ajog.2007.11.044

Rea, M. F. (2004). Benefits of breastfeeding and women's health. *Journal of Pediatrics (Rio J), 80*(5 Suppl), S142–S146.

Rempel, L. A., & Rempel, J. K. (2011). The breast-feeding team: The role of involved fathers in the breastfeeding family. *Journal of Human Lactation, 27* (2), 115–121. doi: 10.1177/0890334410390045

Rinker, B., Veneracion, M., & Walsh, C. P. (2008). The effect of breastfeeding on breast aesthetics. *Aesthetic Surgery Journal, 28*(5), 534–537. doi: 10.1016/j.asj.2008.07.004

Riordan, J. (2005). *Breastfeeding and human lactation* (3rd ed.). Sudbury, MA: Jones & Bartlett.

Scott, J. A., & Mostyn, T. (2003). Women's experiences of breastfeeding in a bottle-feeding culture. *Journal of Human Lactation, 19*, 270–277.

Schwarz, E. B., Ray, R. M., Stuebe, A. M., Allison, M. A., Ness, R. B., Freiberg, M. S., & Cauley, J. A. (2009). Duration of lactation and risk factors for maternal cardiovascular disease. *Obstetrics and Gynecology, 113*(5), 974–982. doi: 10.1097/01.AOG.0000346884.67796.ca

Seimyr, L., Edhborg, M., Lundh, W., & Sjögren, B. (2004). In the shadow of maternal depressed mood: Experiences of parenthood during the first year after childbirth. *Journal of Psychosomatic Obstetrics & Gynecology, 25*(1), 23–34. doi: 10.1080/01674820410001737414

Sheeshka, J., Potter, B., Norrie, E., Valaitis, R., Adams, G., & Kuczynski, L. (2001). Women's experiences breastfeeding in public places. *Journal of Human Lactation, 17*(1), 31–38.

Shoham, A. (1994). Epidemiology, etiology, and fertility drugs in ovarian epithelial carcinoma: Where are we today? *Fertility and Sterility, 62*, 433–438.

Simopoulos, A. P., & Grave, G. D. (1984). Factors associated with the choice and duration of infant-feeding practice. *Pediatrics, 74*(4), 603–614.

Skrundz, M., Bolten, M., Nast, I., Hellhammer, D. H., & Meinlschmidt, G. (2011). Plasma oxytocin concentration during pregnancy is associated with development of postpartum depression. *Neuropsychopharmacology, 36*(9), 1886–1893. doi: 10.1038/npp.2011.74

Smith, J. L., Hawkinson, K., & Paull, K. (2011). Spoiled milk: An experimental examination of bias against mothers who breastfeed. *Personality and Social Psychology Bulletin, 37*(7), 867–878. doi: 10.1177/0146167211401629

Stuebe, A. M., Michels, K. B., Willett, W. C., Manson, J. E., Rexrode, K., & Rich-Edwards, J. W. (2009). Duration of lactation and incidence of myocardial infarction in middle to late adulthood. *American Journal of Obstetrics and Gynecology, 200*(2), 138.e131–138.e138. doi: 10.1016/j.ajog.2008.10.001

Stuebe, A. M., & Rich-Edwards, J. W. (2009). The reset hypothesis: Lactation and maternal metabolism. *American Journal of Perinatology, 26*(1), 81–88. doi: 10.1055/s-0028-1103034

Stuebe, A. M., Rich-Edwards, J. W., Willett, W. C., Manson, J. E., & Michels, K. B. (2005). Duration of lactation and incidence of type 2 diabetes. *JAMA, 294*(20), 2601–2610. doi: 10.1001/jama.294.20.2601

Tamminen, T. (1988). The impact of mother's depression on her nursing experiences and attitudes during breastfeeding. *Acta Pædiatrica, 77*, 87–94. doi: 10.1111/j.1651-2227.1988.tb10864.x

Taveras, E. M., Capra, A. M., Braveman, P. A., Jensvold, N. G., Escobar, G. J., & Lieu, T. A. (2003). Clinician support and psychosocial risk factors associated with breastfeeding discontinuation. *Pediatrics, 112(1, Pt. 1)*, 108–115.

U.S. Department of Health and Human Services, Office on Women's Health (OWH). (2011). *Your guide to breastfeeding*. Washington, DC: Author.

U.S. National Library of Medicine. (2001). LactMed. Retrieved from http://toxnet.nlm.nih.gov/cgi-bin/sis/htmlgen?LACT

Uvnäs-Moberg, K. (1998). Oxytocin may mediate the benefits of positive social interaction and emotions. *Psychoneuroendocrinology*, *23*(8), 819–835. doi: 10.1016/s0306-4530(98)00056-0

Uvnas-Moberg, K., Widstrom, A. M., Werner, S., Matthiesen, A. S., & Winberg, J. (1990). Oxytocin and prolactin levels in breast-feeding women: Correlation with milk yield and duration of breast-feeding. *Acta Obstetricia et Gynecologica Scandinavia*, *69*(4), 301–306.

Valdes, V., Labbok, M. H., Pugin, E., & Perez, A. (2000). The efficacy of the lactational amenorrhea method (LAM) among working women. *Contraception*, *62*(5), 217–219.

van Leengoed, E., Kerker, E., & Swanson, H. H. (1987). Inhibition of post-partum maternal behaviour in the rat by injecting an oxytocin antagonist into the cerebral ventricles. *Journal of Endocrinology*, *112*(2), 275–282. doi: 10.1677/joe.0.1120275

White-Traut, R., Watanabe, K., Pournajafi-Nazarloo, H., Schwertz, D., Bell, A., & Carter, C. S. (2009). Detection of salivary oxytocin levels in lactating women. *Developmental Psychobiology*, *51*(4), 367–373. doi: 10.1002/dev .20376

Windle, R. J., Shanks, N., Lightman, S. L., & Ingram, C. D. (1997). Central oxytocin administration reduces stress-induced corticosterone release and anxiety behavior in rats. *Endocrinology*, *138*(7), 2829–2834.

World Health Organization. (2009). *Infant and young child feeding: Model chapter for textbooks for medical students and allied heath professionals.* Washington, DC: Author.

Worthman, J. (2009, January 2). Facebook won't budge on breastfeeding photos. *New York Times.* Retrieved from http://bits.blogs.nytimes.com/ 2009/01/02/breastfeeding-facebook-photos/

Yalom, I. D., Lunde, D. T., Moos, R. H., & Hamburg, D. A. (1968). "Postpartum blues" syndrome: A description and related variables. *Archives of General Psychiatry*, *18*(1), 16–27.

18

Rethinking Menopause

PAULA S. DERRY AND HEATHER E. DILLAWAY

INTRODUCTION

Menopause and the transition to menopause are associated with many health issues. Women need accurate information about the normal course of reproductive aging. All too often, this information is presented as a list of symptoms, uncomfortable experiences, or health hazards, rather than as a description of what menopause is and what to expect. If distressing experiences do occur, women need information about how to successfully cope with them. Furthermore, the end of menstruation is intertwined with personal, societal, and biomedical appraisals of midlife, femininity, and aging. In arriving at a personal concept of themselves as midlife or mature women, it is useful for women to understand their appraisals of menopause, whether positive, negative, or neutral, and the implicit meanings that underlie biomedical discourse and cultural messages.

Menopause is biopsychosocial. In this chapter, we emphasize physiological, psychological, and sociocultural factors that contribute to health, and psychological and sociocultural contexts within which personal experience and scientific study are framed and interpreted. We emphasize that the scientific knowledge base is limited and incomplete, and "expert opinion" is relied on when facts are simply not known. Ambiguity, uncertainty, and diversity characterize the discipline, ranging from disagreements about how to define menopause and the stages surrounding it, what constitutes a normal transition, and what symptoms and experiences are associated with it to the meaning of menopause scientifically, developmentally, and experientially.

DEFINITIONS

All women will naturally stop menstruating during midlife, aside from those who stop earlier for reasons such as surgery or medical conditions. The final menstrual period (FMP) is one point in a much longer physiological process (Harlow et al., 2008). Understanding menopausal physiology requires understanding the dynamics of this underlying process and how physiology is intertwined with psychology and the social and physical context.

Professionals do not agree about how to conceptualize and define reproductive aging and menopause. In this chapter, the term *menopause* refers to the FMP. *Perimenopause* refers to the transitional time surrounding the end of menstruation (including the year following the FMP). *Premenopause* is the time before perimenopause; *postmenopause*, the time following the FMP. These are common definitions (Soules et al., 2001), but in the literature the same terms may be defined differently or other terms may be used (Harlow et al., 2008; Prior, 1998). Other common terms for the entire transitional process are *reproductive aging*, the *climacteric*, the *change*, or the *change of life*, and the word *menopause* may be used to refer to the entire transitional process.

The Stages of Reproductive Aging Workshop (STRAW) (Harlow et al., 2008; Soules et al., 2001) was a recent attempt to articulate uniform menopause-related definitions based on objective criteria. Perimenopause begins with an increase of at least 7 days in variability between one cycle and the next, progresses to a separate stage characterized by skipped periods (a 60-day gap), and ends a year following the FMP. Stages of premenopause and postmenopause are also defined. The STRAW staging system has been useful in providing clear operational definitions for researchers and in predicting time to menopause. However, others (Harlow et al., 2008; Mansfield, Carey, Anderson, Barsom, & Koch, 2004) argue that the stages are not universal or invariant. For other professionals, criteria that are subjective or vary from woman to woman are important. For Prior (1998, 2005), perimenopause begins with subjective experiences like hot flashes and increased breast tenderness. She argues that subjective changes precede changes in menstrual flow and are clinically important when women have distressing perimenopause-related experiences. For other researchers (e.g., Dennerstein et al., 1993; Lock, 1993), sociopsychological definitions are important, such as how a woman defines her stage. Physiological definitions do not capture cross-cultural variability in how women define menopause or information important to understanding definitions of self or coping techniques.

BIOLOGY OF PERIMENOPAUSE/ MENOPAUSE

Physiology

The menstrual cycle involves a complicated set of feedback relationships among ovarian (e.g., estrogen, progesterone), pituitary [e.g., follicle-stimulating hormone (FSH) and luteinizing hormone (LH)], and hypothalamic hormones, as well as additional hormones, other chemicals and brain structures, and other factors. These feedback relationships change during late premenopause, perimenopause, and postmenopause, in ways that scientists have not explained or even fully described.

After menopause, far lower amounts of the hormone estrogen and far higher amounts of FSH are found in a woman's body. As recently as the late 1990s, research was guided by a common-sense idea (e.g., Rubinow, Schmidt, & Roca, 1998) that there would be a linear change: During perimenopause estrogen would be declining, FSH on the rise, and the perimenopause was therefore a low-estrogen state. Symptoms like hot flashes, for example, might be attributed to low estrogen levels. However, as research began accumulating, especially since the 1980s and 1990s, the underlying physiological patterning was not what was expected (see summaries in Hale & Burger, 2005; Prior, 1998, 2005). Perhaps the most unexpected finding was that perimenopause is not, as had been assumed, a low-estrogen state. Estrogen levels are on average higher, and they fluctuate and can remain unchanged or spike above rather than below those found earlier in life (Hale et al., 2007; Prior, 1998). FSH levels are on average higher, but not predictably higher, and they can be elevated one month and return to premenopausal levels the next. Changes are not progressive and consistent; a change might be found one cycle but not the next. Feedback relationships among hormones found earlier in life are no longer reliably found. For example, FSH and estrogen levels might not be inverse, as is usual earlier in life, and regular periods may be observed even when FSH and estrogen levels have changed. Furthermore, a surprising and inexplicable variety exists throughout, with these unexpected and unpredictable hormone levels and altered feedback relationships varying from one woman to the next. Menstrual cycles are more likely to be anovulatory (Prior, 2005). Increased cycle variability is a key characteristic of the transition to menopause, rather than linear and straightforward change in one particular direction (e.g., Harlow, Lin, & Ho, 2000; Lisabeth, Harlow, & Qaqish, 2004).

Postmenopause is a low-estrogen state. Estrogen levels will become low and FSH levels high for the rest of a woman's life. Hormonal changes do not stop abruptly; they continue to change, especially in the years immediately after the FMP. There is no fundamental understanding of how much estrogen is needed to maintain overall bodily health if the high levels that support pregnancy and reproduction are not needed. The ovaries and adrenal glands continue to produce androgens, which are converted into estrogens in a variety of body tissues. Estrogens are a family of hormones; the dominant form after menopause is estrone; before menopause, estradiol. While dismissed as a weak estrogen, estrone is more potent, in the sense that it is less likely to be found in a biologically inactive form.

One theory (e.g., Burger, Hale, Dennerstein, & Robertson, 2008) is that perimenopause begins when ovarian follicles (an immature egg surrounded by a ball of cells)

reach a critical low number. Most of the 300,000 to 500,000 follicles in an average girl's body at puberty do not become active and simply die. By postmenopause, follicles are essentially depleted. This atresia (programmed cell death) begins prenatally and continues throughout life, including prior to puberty. However, during each menstrual cycle, a small number of follicles briefly become active. One then becomes the "primary follicle," the source of the egg ovulated that month and the primary site for manufacturing hormones. One theory is that when follicle number becomes too low, other changes follow. For example, inhibin B, another ovarian hormone, decreases, which then affects other hormones. Perhaps aging follicles respond abnormally to chemical signals. Another theory suggests that the aging central nervous system (CNS) becomes less responsive to chemical signals or that CNS set points that establish relationships among these signals are altered. Derry and Derry (2012) suggest that the surprising pattern of results obtained is what would be expected if the reproductive endocrine system is a nonlinear, dynamical, chaotic system.

Biomedical Model

The physiology of menopause cannot be understood apart from psychological, sociological, and cultural factors. Sociocultural and psychological variables shape scientific and medical discourse, in terms of what topics are researched, how facts are interpreted, and how decisions are made about what health implications may or may not exist for menopause and what interventions are justified and make sense.

Utian (2003) reported that 40 years earlier, menopause was "no more than a one-liner in a general textbook of gynecology." Inferences and judgments about the nature of menopause have therefore been based on many factors aside from empirical knowledge. A metatheory based on the biomedical model has been especially important, as have culturally dominant, seemingly common sense, ideas about aging and gender (e.g., see Hyde, Nee, Howlett, Drennan, & Butler, 2010; Kaufert & Gilbert, 1986; Voda, 1997). The biomedical model influences or underlies much practical decision making about research and clinical practice. For example, the idea that menopause causes or exacerbates chronic illnesses has a limited research base (e.g., see Barrett-Connor & Stuenkel, 1999; Grady & Cummings, 2001; Writing Group for the Women's Health Initiative Investigators, 2002; Yaffe, Sawaya, Lieberburg, & Grady, 1998), but an inherent plausibility if this model is accepted (Derry, 2004a, 2008).

A common metatheory expressed in work guided by the biomedical model has been that menopause is unpleasant, unnatural, or unhealthy, even a "deficiency disease" caused by the "failure" of women's bodies to produce constant amounts of estrogen across the lifespan (Kaufert & Gilbert, 1986; MacPherson, 1981; Voda, 1997). Menopause is senescence—the reproductive system stops working because the ovary has aged and stops functioning. Instead of assuming that women become infertile at menopause with few ramifications for other biological systems, the traditional biomedical model assumes that premenopausal levels of estrogen are needed for general physical and psychological health. Postmenopausal estrogen levels cause health problems, even constitute an "estrogen deficiency." A further assumption is that menopause is the central event of midlife physically and psychologically; it is "the change in life."

Professionals have disagreed about the nature of the "unhealthiness," and concepts of what is unhealthy have changed over time, but the underlying idea has remained (MacPherson, 1981; Voda, 1992, 1997). An earlier stereotype was that premenopausal estrogen levels not only kept a woman healthy, but they kept her a woman, as stated perhaps most infamously by the gynecologist Robert Wilson (1966) when he wrote that menopausal women "witness the death of their own womanhood" (p. 15) and suffer "the horror of this living decay" (p. 43). As this older stereotype was discredited, a newer one replaced it: Estrogen is crucial to the physical health of women. In this view, when estrogen levels decline below those of the reproductive years, a woman becomes vulnerable to a range of chronic illnesses, including heart, bone, and brain disease (Murtaugh & Hepworth, 2003). This newer stereotype dovetailed with a decoupling of menopause with the entry into old age, and promised to aid women in keeping themselves young with prescriptions for estrogens.

Critics have suggested (e.g., Kaufert & Gilbert, 1986; MacPherson, 1981; Voda, 1992) that the idea that fertility is central to women's physical and psychological health reflects stereotypes about gender and aging rather than science. Many authors have pointed out scientific descriptions of menopause that were nonobjective. The ovaries, along with other body parts, were said to "atrophy," become "senile," and in other ways break down and stop working properly (e.g., Lyons & Griffin, 2003; Martin, 1992). Increased menstrual cycle variability or increased numbers of anovulatory cycles might be defined as "abnormal" (e.g., Santoro, 2005; Sherman, West, & Korenman, 1975) during perimenopause but not during adolescence. The World

Health Organization (WHO Scientific Group, 1996) defines menopause as the "loss" of ovarian activity, rather than a "completion" or "change."

Diversity of medical opinion with regard to the traditional biomedical model has always existed (e.g., see Barrett-Connor & Stuenkel, 1999; Grady & Cummings, 2001) and in recent years has gained strength and acceptance. For example, a National Institutes of Health (NIH) state-of-the-science conference (2005) concluded that menopause is natural, healthy, and overly medicalized; for many health problems, the effects of aging and menopause have been conflated. It has become more common among health professionals to state that menopause is "perfectly natural," although professionals remain divided about whether menopause, although natural, is unfortunately related to negative health effects.

Alternative Perspectives

Why menopause is a human universal does not yet have an answer based in scientific fact. Anthropologists, behavioral biologists, and others with an evolutionary or adaptational perspective provide a scientific metatheoretical alternative to the assumptions of the traditional biomedical model. Here, physiological processes can only be understood by their place within the body plan and life history of a species (Bogin, 1999).

Menopause is a human universal, yet an oddity in nature. Humans, unlike other primates, have a complete shutdown of the reproductive system that occurs decades before any other body system exhibits advanced signs of aging. This change is universal and is under genetic control (Pavelka & Fedigan, 1991). Humans thus have a life stage during which women are postreproductive and healthy that precedes old age; this may reflect the working of evolutionary forces (Derry, 2006; Hawkes, O'Connell, Burton Jones, Alvarez, & Charnov, 1998; Kaplan, Gurven, Winking, Hooper, & Stieglitz, 2010; Pavelka & Fedigan, 1991). Although a smaller percentage than now, women lived past menopause before the advent of modern medical care. Researchers of contemporary hunter-gatherers, for example, typically find postmenopausal women are important members of their social groups (Lee, 1985). Perhaps natural selection created a long lifespan rather than an early menopause (Bogin, 1999); perhaps a postmenopausal life stage was adaptive because human groups benefited from older members with social and technical skills (e.g., Kaplan et al., 2010) or older "grandmothers" who aided younger women (Hawkes, O'Connell, & Burton Jones, 1997).

The idea that menopause is part of the human body plan and life course, decoupling the end of reproduction from the senescence of other bodily systems, and defining a life stage of mature adulthood, all lead metatheoretically to different basic assumptions and speculations from those of a traditional biomedical model. How much estrogen is needed for health when the high levels underlying reproduction are no longer needed? For example, menopause would not be expected, a priori and in the absence of strong evidence, to cause cognitive decline if postreproductive women are important, skilled members of their social groups (Kaplan et al., 2010). Gass (2010), a physician and menopause expert, speculates that bone loss around the time of menopause could be an adjustment if higher bone mass, needed during the reproductive years, no longer has a function and is shed.

PERIMENOPAUSE/MENOPAUSE AND LIFE STAGE

One role for health psychologists is to help women find positive personal definitions of what it means to be a menopausal and a midlife/mature woman. For some women, these identities are interrelated; for others, they are not. Biomedical knowledge carries great weight because of its connection to science, and therefore "fact," but, as discussed earlier, it also intertwines physiological facts with assumptions about the nature of aging and femininity. Social meanings and personal experiences also are important in the creation of meaning. As cultural changes redefine the nature of womanhood and midlife, implicit assumptions that underlie normative ideas about aging and gender are also in flux.

Women are more likely to feel confused, uncertain, or negative about menopause during early perimenopause, but, over time, they gradually develop a self-image of what it means to be a midlife or a menopausal woman and a sense of what symptoms mean. Quinn (1991) suggests that the process of integrating a changing sense of self as a perimenopausal woman includes the following stages: (a) tuning into me, my body, and moods (awareness of physical and emotional changes), (b) facing a paradox of feelings and contrasting impressions (assimilation of information and formulation of a woman's personal meaning), and (c) making adjustments. Other authors similarly suggest that a period of introspection and developmental change occur during either the transition to menopause or a more general transition to

midlife as a developmental stage (see Derry, 2004b, for a review). Individual women regard menopause, as they do most life changes, in a variety of ways. For some women, menopause is intertwined with a transition to midlife/mature adulthood; for others, these are separate processes. Some women experience a transition to deep wisdom. Others regard menopause as the gateway to old age. Many report neutral or indifferent feelings about reaching menopause (Avis & McKinlay, 1991; Gannon, 1999; Gullette, 1997).

There is no cultural consensus about what it means to be a midlife or mature woman. Some women do not define themselves as midlife women; they may avoid being "old" by continuing to be "young," maintaining a youthful appearance, activity level, and so on (e.g., Ballard, Elston, & Gabe, 2005). If personal health or a family member's health falters, feeling old, and negative feelings about menopause as a marker of aging, may result (Kaufert, Gilbert, & Tate, 1992; Winterich, 2003). Others experience a life stage with distinctive characteristics, like a changing sense of time (from "time since birth" to "time left") or a self experienced as more centered, autonomous, or concerned for the common good (see Derry, 2004b). Menopause may be perceived to be closely related to this transition or unimportant.

In the United States, broad cultural attitudes toward older women have been negative, and menopause has been a marker of aging and decreased sexual appeal (Avis & Crawford, 2008). However, most women do not have an illness or disease orientation toward menopause (Kaufert & Gilbert, 1986; Lock, 1993; Voda, 1992). Regardless of the bodily changes they may experience, some women view menopause as ushering in a "good" life stage—one that is better and more carefree than the one before it (Dillaway, 2005). Some women welcome menopause as relief from the prospect of pregnancy and the burdens of menstruation and contraception (Gannon & Ekstrom, 1993). However, negativity is often found around problematic symptoms (e.g., hot flashes, irregular bleeding), long-term health concerns (e.g., osteoporosis, heart disease), sexual difficulties (e.g., vaginal dryness), and gendered appearance concerns (e.g., weight gain). In addition, masking the visible manifestations of perimenopause and aging, because of negative cultural attitudes, is a stressor for some women. For example, an employed woman may fear that she will be respected less if she appears old or if she is sweating profusely from a hot flash (Kittell, Mansfield, & Voda, 1998).

Currently, in the United States, cultural definitions of menopause and aging are in flux. As the average expected lifespan for women approaches 80 years, and as people are healthier for a longer period, menopause no longer signals old age. In addition, women are increasingly in the paid labor force and have other meaningful social roles during midlife, so that menopause has less potency as a cultural marker of entry into an anomic or negative life stage.

Women are less likely to feel "old" at midlife (Cremin, 1992). If they are worried about aging, they might be worried about the bodily changes related to physical appearance (e.g., graying hair, sagging skin, weight gain) that make them feel less feminine or attractive or that might suggest health problems in the future (Ballard et al., 2005; Markson, 2003). There are also fewer sociocultural markers of a transition into a separate stage of old age in contemporary times. For example, as Baby Boomers age,

they may identify and behave in the same ways they did when they were chronologically younger. For example, they participate in similar leisure activities, wear similar clothing, and are physically and socially active (Featherstone & Hepworth, 1991). Work and family trends can also make the menopausal transition seem inconsequential or positive within women's lives. As contemporary women delay childbearing, take on elderly caregiving, and continue to engage fully in paid work, they may not attach a great deal of significance to this transition (Gannon & Ekstrom, 1993; Komesaroff, Rothfield, & Daly, 1997; Lyons & Griffin, 2003). In fact, menopause may parallel women's greatest accomplishments in paid work in contemporary times.

Women's feelings about menopause cannot be separated from decisions that women and their partners make about whether to become parents. In some social contexts, menopause may take on more negative meanings, as seen in trends toward delayed marriage, divorce, and remarriage; delayed childbearing; and rising concerns about infertility (Greil, 1991). Loss of fertility may be an important issue for a woman who has delayed childbearing until her thirties or forties and discovers that she is having trouble becoming pregnant. These women do not want to be finished with childbearing, both emotionally and in terms of life goals. Other women may have never actively made the decision to stop having children (even if, in some cases, it has been more than 10 or 15 years since their last childbearing experience). For these women, the onset of menopause may make it feel like they never had the choice to finalize their decision themselves—the onset of menopause took that final decision out of their hands. Some lesbians desire biological motherhood despite forgoing heterosexual partnerships and experience some of the same feelings as heterosexual women about the loss of fertility (Dillaway, 2012).

Other women with fertility difficulties may feel that menopause has robbed them of their final chances to become biological parents. In cases of divorce and remarriage, or delayed first marriage (especially if a new intimate partner desires children), women's menopause may also take on a negative light. Conversely, some women who assume they are no longer fertile become pregnant accidentally during perimenopause, especially if they have stopped using birth control. Menopause can be neutral or positive for women in light of earlier reproductive difficulties. Coping with menopause may not seem difficult when compared to coping with infertility or miscarriage, and menopause may be a relief for a woman with a long history of difficulty becoming pregnant, who now has closure and can put decisions about infertility treatment and hopes for a family to rest (Dillaway, 2012).

Different women experience sexuality, another important psychosocial context for menopause, very differently. Freed from the threat of pregnancy, birth control, and menstruation, women's ideas and experiences of sexuality may become more positive during menopause than in previous life stages. For others, sexual interest wanes, and physical changes like vaginal atrophy may make intercourse more painful. The stereotypic association of aging with loss of sexual attractiveness is also experienced in a variety of ways. For lesbians or heterosexual women who were never comfortable with sexual objectification and sexual harassment by men, sexual invisibility may be freeing and represent a "better" time of life; others may mourn their perceived loss of sexual attractiveness (Cole & Rothblum, 1990; Trethewey, 2001).

NORMAL COURSE OF PERIMENOPAUSE/MENOPAUSE

One role of health psychologists is to provide information about the normal course of reproductive aging. When surveyed (e.g., Mansfield, Theisen, & Boyer, 1992), women report that they want accurate information about what to expect during the transition to menopause, including information about what is normal; what the course of the transition, including that of distressing or uncomfortable experiences, might be; what is potentially a health problem; and what to do about distressing experiences and problems if they occur. Uncertainty about what to expect and about what is normal are stressors (Mansfield et al., 1992), while information can provide a sense of mastery with regard to understanding and coping with changes. Kaufert (1994) found that the majority of visits to doctors were for evaluation of whether perimenopausal menstrual bleeding changes, common at this time, were a problem, rather than for distresses like hot flashes.

Accurate information also provides a baseline for understanding when changes are occurring at an appropriate chronological age. For example, most women have heard that they are "supposed to be done" with menopause around age 51, and they may experience frustration when menstruation (or a symptom such as a hot flash) does not cease completely by this age (Dillaway & Burton, 2011). A woman who experiences hot flashes or other symptoms while she is in her late thirties or early forties, especially if her cycles have not increased in irregularity, might be told by her physician or think to herself that she is "too young to be entering menopause." Yet experiencing hot flashes after 50 or before 40 is not in fact unusual.

The average age of menopause is 51 years in industrialized Western cultures. Most women reach menopause between 45 and 55; 40 to 60 is often defined as the normal age range. Although women typically skip periods during perimenopause for shorter amounts of time—in one study, 50% of women who had not menstruated for 6 months had another period before stopping permanently—a gap as long as a year is usually permanent. Some experts state that any bleeding after a 1-year gap is abnormal. However, while a woman who menstruates again after a year should be evaluated medically to make sure this is not a symptom of a medical problem, 5% to 10% of women in fact do bleed again after technically reaching menopause (Treloar, 1981; Treloar, Boynton, Behn, & Brown, 1967). As a practical matter, sometimes the FMP, and thus menopause, is not defined as having occurred until after a 2-year gap, because timing this requires that women remember their exact menstrual history, which is especially difficult when irregular periods come first or if periods were never regular (Rostosky & Travis, 1996).

Menopause is the absolute end of fertility. However, it does not coincide with the perceived end of fertility for many women who have ended their childbearing through birth control. Furthermore, fertility declines over the course of many years prior to menopause, and many women are infertile prior to the FMP. On the one hand, women still need birth control prior to menopause to avoid unwanted pregnancies, because only at menopause is there an absolute impossibility of conception. On the other hand, difficulty or an inability to get pregnant can be a problem for women who have delayed childbearing until their late thirties or beyond.

Paradoxically, while perimenopause is understood to be an important time, professionals disagree about what exactly perimenopause is, when it begins and ends, and what its associated signs/symptoms are. However defined, perimenopause is variable: Some women do not appear to have any transition between regular periods and menopause (i.e., they do not notice menstrual cycle or other changes); other women transition for many years (up to 10 years, depending on the definition of perimenopause). Perimenopause is important because this is when (a) many women begin to wonder how to make sense of changes in their body like alterations in menstrual flow; (b) troublesome signs/symptoms like hot flashes are most likely to occur; and (c) women are most likely to begin considering what it means to them, if anything, to be a "midlife," "mature," or "menopausal" woman (Ballard et al., 2005; Hyde et al., 2010). Some women report and are bothered by many symptoms, whereas others are not aware of or significantly affected by any (Matthews et al., 1990).

Changes in menstrual flow typify perimenopause. Women first might notice subtle changes in flow (such as heavier or lighter periods); in some definitions (e.g., STRAW), these changes precede perimenopause proper. STRAW (Soules et al., 2001) assumes a typical sequence from irregular to skipped periods. However, Mansfield and colleagues (2004) found 8 to 20 patterns. Some women remained in one stage for numerous years and then moved on quickly, some alternated between stages over many years, and some progressed quickly through stages. Irregular periods do not herald the imminent arrival of menopause, which may be many years off. In one study, increased variability of more than 6 days predicted the LMP in 4 to 6 years (the range was not reported); a 45-day gap, in 4 to 5 years (Harlow et al., 2008). The quality of menstrual flow may change. Periods with clots, very heavy flow, gushing flow, unfamiliar patterns (e.g., a flow that stops for a day and starts again) may occur and tend to be especially worrisome. Unpredictable periods may be annoying or distressing. For many women, a change from their regular cyclicity is significant, even worrisome. Kittell, Mansfield, Morse, and Voda (1997) suggest that women may go through four stages: (1) noticing changes (losing one's baseline, searching for validation), (2) relinquishing familiar patterns, (3) taking precautions (e.g., if flow is very heavy or unpredictable), and (4) wanting it to end. Periods shorter than 14 days apart and spotting between periods are indications for medical evaluation. Women who seek medical advice about worrisome patterns may find that medical opinion is divided with regard to which changes need to be evaluated or treated. Heavy periods may be medically treated with hormones, hysterectomy, or watchful waiting, whereas irregular periods might be addressed with hormone medications to make them more predictable.

A woman who lives to the current average life expectancy of almost 80 will spend approximately half of her life in the peri- and postmenopausal years. The assumption seems to be that women will be "in postmenopause" for the rest of their lives, but then what does this mean? Biomedical definitions fall short of explaining to women what the true "end" of reproductive aging might be, if indeed there

is one. The only "end" that is fairly well documented in biomedical research is the end of perimenopause—if it is defined solely by the cessation of menstruation.

SIGNS/SYMPTOMS

Perimenopause/menopause has been portrayed primarily in terms of negative, confusing, and stressful bodily changes that require medical definition, attention, monitoring, and treatment (Dickson, 1990; Hyde et al., 2010). Health psychologists can provide a normalizing, positive, noncatastrophic perspective on experienced bodily changes, a realistic idea of how likely distressing symptoms are, and to encourage active coping when problems arise.

Medical websites and other authoritative sources, as well as women themselves, often assume the existence of a syndrome of symptoms that typify perimenopause, including mood changes, memory problems (especially with retrieving words), fatigue, hot flashes, insomnia, sexual changes, weight gain, fatigue, heart palpitations, headaches, and joint pain (Avis et al., 2001). Mood changes range from depression and anxiety to irritability. Cobb (1993) includes more than 100 items in her list of symptoms reported by midlife women. Because many of these experiences occur during many different life stages, it is perhaps not surprising that ambiguity and disagreement exist about when these are directly related to the hormonal changes of perimenopause, and it can be difficult for women to appraise their own experiences. Women may or may not feel an inner certainty that their experiences are caused by hormone changes.

Epidemiological studies have not found evidence for a menopausal syndrome. Only bleeding changes, hot flashes, vaginal atrophy, and perhaps insomnia are more common in perimenopausal and/or menopausal, as compared with premenopausal, women (e.g., Holte, 1992; Kaufert et al., 1992; NIH, 2005). In Europe and the United States, approximately 70% of women will experience a hot flash (Ayers, Forshaw, & Hunter, 2010). Insomnia becomes more frequent during the forties and fifties, but appears related to many factors, such as depression, anxiety, and hot flashes, with a small possible effect of estrogen levels (Hollander et al., 2001; McKinlay, Brambilla, & Posner, 1992). Premenstrual symptoms may become more common during a woman's thirties or forties. Menstrual migraines may become more severe. Breast tenderness and other signs of high estrogen levels may be found. Apart from these changes, symptoms do not become more common or form a syndrome (i.e., co-occur) as a function of menopause status, although it is possible that future research could uncover such evidence or identify subgroups of women for whom such relationships exist.

Subjective well-being is associated with the same psychological variables that are important at other times of life, not menopause status per se (Dennerstein, 1996). Research has established that clinical depression is not, as was once assumed, widespread during perimenopause or menopause, and the strongest predictors of depression during midlife are life stress and a history of previous depression (Kaufert et al., 1992; McKinlay, McKinlay, & Brambilla, 1987). A small increase in depression rates occurs during perimenopause but decrease after menopause (Bromberger et al., 2007); however, the extent to which this is caused by hormone changes, symptoms like hot flashes, or other factors remains controversial (Nicole-Smith, 1999). It is still common for sub-clinical changes in feeling moody, anxious, or angry to be included on lists of common symptoms of perimenopause/menopause, notwithstanding the lack of a research base for this assertion. As stated above, epidemiological studies have not found evidence for a menopausal syndrome.

A small subset of women and their doctors (10% to 15%) report severe, debilitating symptoms that develop abruptly during perimenopause (Miller & Daniels-Brady, 2005). Some women who learn that perimenopause can be associated with a constellation of symptoms like debilitating fatigue, depression, and problems with memory have a sudden realization that what they have been feeling has finally been explained in a way that makes sense to them. Such a woman may feel exhausted/weak or unable to cope. Some women fear they may never function well again. For example, they may wonder whether their professional life is effectively over. Many women in this group find relief when they are prescribed hormone therapy. However, some women are disappointed when symptoms do not remit with hormone treatment or they develop medication side effects such as depression, headache, or odd bodily sensations. The etiology of such severe symptoms remains unknown.

Women with surgical or medical menopause should be considered separately from those with natural menopause in research and practice. They have no estrogen production, unlike women with a natural menopause, who have low but continuing levels of endogenous estrogen. They may be many years younger than women experiencing natural menopause, a time when higher hormone levels are normal. They are more likely to have distressing symptoms like hot flashes, which may respond differently to pharmacologic or other interventions. They may have a unique set of psychological issues, ranging from relief at a hysterectomy eliminating troubling symptoms, to infertility when they still want to have children, to the co-occurrence of a serious illness like cancer. In addition, a woman with a hysterectomy but not oophorectomy has ovaries that continue to produce estrogen and other reproductive hormones. She is endocrinologically not menopausal although she cannot menstruate, and determining when she does reach menopause can be difficult.

Menopause has been considered to create physical health risks. However, putative increases in risk for cardiovascular and brain disease remain controversial, as research remains inconclusive and increased rates may result from aging. Even with osteoporosis, where measurable decreases in bone density are found in the years surrounding the FMP, the relative importance of menopause, aging, lifelong nutrition, and activity levels to bone disease are disputed. (See Love, 2003, and Voda, 1997, for summaries of these issues.)

Hot Flashes

Hot flashes (or flushes) have been described by many authors (e.g., Hanisch, Hantsoo, Freeman, Sullivan, & Coyne, 2008; Voda, 1997). They are most common in the years immediately surrounding the FMP, although some women will continue to flash for many years after menopause. They appear to be a family of experiences, varying in frequency, intensity, meaning, and the amount of distress they cause. They are often described as a transient feeling of heat, sometimes accompanied by visible reddening or sweating.

They most typically begin in the head or upper back, although they can be felt anywhere in the body and can travel from the point of origin to other body parts. A chilled feeling sometimes follows. Flashes can last up to an hour, but most typically are 5 minutes or less. Frequency varies from several each day to monthly or less; women may have them for up to a year to 5 years or more. Some women who experience flashes for many years find that the severity decreases over time. For some women the flash is purely a feeling of heat; some women report other associated sensations such as a racing heart, nausea, and breathlessness; other women experience cognitions and feelings such as anxiety and catastrophic thoughts. The majority of women rate flashes as creating mild to moderate discomfort and will cope well with them, but approximately 15% to 20% will find them troublesome.

Hot flashes are physiologically based. Sternal and fingertip conductance both change during a flash, as do core and peripheral body temperature (Freedman, 2001). The most common physiological explanation (Freedman, 2001) is that fluctuating (rather than low) estrogen levels cause a narrowing of the thermoregulatory zone, a control center in the hypothalamus that maintains body temperature within a normal range. As a result, small changes in temperature lie outside the normal range, triggering a response that is experienced as a hot flash. However, there is no understanding of why the thermoregulatory zone narrows. Furthermore, many experiences associated with hot flashes are not a simple response to thermoregulation. A woman might feel like she is on fire, or feel so only in an isolated body part like her arms or earlobes. The experience might feel like anxiety. For some, there is a sharp physical shock, unrelated to psychological factors. Some women may not realize their feeling of gentle warmth is caused by a flash until later.

Before the 1970s, there was little research on hot flashes, and a woman was more likely to be told that her experience was "all in her head" (Voda, 1997). That flashes are physiologically "real" is a relief to many women. However, it has become clear that the hot flash experience is a complex combination of physiology with psychological and sociocultural appraisals. The frequency of flashes has a low correlation with self-ratings of severity and seems to measure a different dimension, while severity correlates with flashes being experienced as troublesome or problematic (Hunter & Mann, 2010). Hunter and Liao (1996) found that psychological variables were more predictive of distress than flash frequency. Drawing on theories of symptom perception and self-regulation and cognitive-behavioral models, Hunter and Mann (2010) present a model of the factors contributing to the perception of hot flash severity, including cognitive representatives of menopause (as having symptoms and negative consequences); individual differences in tendencies to attend to the body or somatize; negative affect including anxiety, depression, and stress; coping mechanisms; sociocultural messages and context.

In a series of studies, Reynolds (1997, 2000) found factors that distinguished women who were highly distressed by flashes from others, which included a greater number of shaming self-labels (social embarrassment and challenges to self-image), catastrophic cognitions (e.g., that flashes would never end or would be unbearable), social isolation, and passive coping mechanisms (e.g., "grin and bear it").

An important part of the experience is whether and how others perceive a hot flash and, therefore, how women feel like they have to handle its visibility. A menopausal body that leaks (sweats) or changes color (becomes red or flushed), or that is calling public attention to a menstruation-related phenomenon, may be seen as uncontrollable, embarrassing, or disruptive (Dillaway, 2011; Kittell et al., 1998) and may challenge a woman's self-concept (Reynolds, 1997). A felt need to hide hot flashes can be a significant stressor (Kittell et al., 1998). Negative attitudes toward menopause correlate with symptom experience (Avis & McKinlay, 1991).

Cross-Cultural and Social Class Variations

When social class, racial, and cultural variations are studied, great variation exists within groups (Avis & Crawford, 2008). Therefore, to understand an individual woman's experience, her personal experience must be ascertained. However, there are also general differences across these social groups.

Cross-cultural differences in symptom reporting and the meaning of menopause have been well documented (Avis & Crawford, 2008). The frequency of hot flashes varies among cultures and is not a physiological universal (Avis & Crawford, 2008). For example, Lock (1993) studied differences among menopausal women in North America and Japan. The "menopausal syndrome" was differently constituted: Japanese women were far less likely to report hot flashes (25% vs. 75% of Canadian/U.S. women ever experienced a flash) but more likely to report shoulder pain (more than 50%). The FMP was only a small part of *konenke*, a transition to a more authoritative midlife social status. How aversive women find symptoms also varies. In Wales, women welcomed hot flashes, based on a belief that flashes made for a swifter and safer transition to menopause (Skulkans, 1970). Japanese women (Lock, 1993) were far less likely to be distressed by flashes when they did occur. It is unclear what factors, in addition to genetics, might account for these differences. Positive or negative attitudes toward menopause, positive or negative social roles for postmenopausal women, lifestyle factors like diet and reproductive history, and methodological research issues like reporting bias may all play a role (Crawford, 2007). An additional factor may be the amount of contact diverse groups of women have with biomedical definitions of menopause (or with doctors in general). Thus, more recent research with Japanese women has found higher rates of hot flashes, possibly because of increasing medicalization of menopause in Japan (Melby, 2005).

There is limited research about racial-ethnic and social class differences in menopause in the United States. Quantitative studies that concentrate on symptom reporting often report that racial/ethnic minorities experience higher rates of menopausal symptoms and/or more intense symptoms. Yet, some research also suggests that they may report more positive (or at least more neutral) attitudes toward reproductive aging than their European American counterparts may. Thus, physiologically some groups may appear more distressed, but psychologically they seem more resilient (Avis et al., 2001; Bromberger et al., 2001; Dillaway, Byrnes, Miller, & Rehan, 2008; Gold et al., 2006; Green & Santoro, 2009; Im, Lee & Chee, 2010, 2011; Nixon, Mansfield, Kittell, & Faulkner, 2001; Sommer et al., 1999). In their survey of almost 15,000 U.S. women,

Avis et al. (2001) discovered that Caucasian women report the largest number of symptoms when compared to Hispanic, African American, Japanese, and Chinese women. Yet African American women were more likely to report vasomotor symptoms (e.g., hot flashes, night sweats, and vaginal dryness) than other racial/ethnic groups. Black women in general have more positive attitudes toward menopause being a natural process. Nixon et al. (2001) found that low-income, rural African American women valued "staying strong," enduring by relying on inner resources (like prayer) and the support of others. They may be more likely to be open in talking with friends.

Social class differences among women in the United States have been rarely studied. Women in lower socioeconomic status groups are more likely to report troublesome symptoms (Avis & Crawford, 2008), but they, like African American women, are more likely to value "staying strong." The intersection of race and social class has been little studied. With regard to gender diversity, Winterich (2003) infers that lesbian women may not be that different from heterosexual women in how they interpret menopausal symptoms or how they think about menopause overall.

What underlies racial and social class differences in symptom reporting is unknown, but could include lifestyle factors (e.g. smoking, hormone therapy use) and other background characteristics (e.g., education levels) (Avis et al., 2001). Medicalization could play a role. African American and lower social class women have less contact with physicians, and are therefore less exposed to biomedical definitions, but on the other hand receive less treatment when experiencing distress (e.g., Brumberg, 1997; Nixon et al., 2001). African Americans are less likely than White women are to receive a physician recommendation of hormone therapy (Weng et al., 2001) and to discuss menopausal management with their doctors (Grisso, Freeman, Maurin, Garcia-Espana, & Berlin, 1999). However, they have hysterectomy rates 2 to 3 times higher than Caucasian women do in the United States (Elson, 2004). Varying rates of hysterectomy could contribute to differences in symptoms and attitudes (Bromberger et al., 2001). Possible effects of stress caused by racism or social class differences on rates of symptoms or consequent distress is unknown.

COPING WITH DISTRESS

Coping with distress at this time, perhaps like coping with any distressing event, is likely to be facilitated by a positive self-concept and sense of mastery, a positive regard for and comfort with one's body, a positive concept of one's life stage, as well as accurate information about health problems and health-promoting practices. The experience of distress during perimenopause or postmenopause involves a psychological component, in which there is appraisal of physiological experiences based on both individual psychology and cultural messages. An expectation that she is experiencing a change that is culturally determined to be negative, unalterable because it is physiological, or that has negative implications for self-image, facilitates catastrophizing, anxiety, annoyance, distress, and a passive stance toward immediate experience (see Derry, 2004b; Hunter & Mann, 2010; Reynolds, 1997, 2000). Some research has linked catastrophizing—expecting that the worst will occur—and passive coping to more distress (Reynolds, 1997). Cultural attitudes that overestimate the

likelihood of very troubling symptoms and underestimate the possibility of coping may make the situation more difficult (Gullette, 1997; Lyons & Griffin, 2003).

Women engage in a variety of self-help techniques to cope with distress. With regard to hot flashes, self-help techniques include dressing in layers, carrying a fan, identifying and avoiding individual triggers, and talking with friends. Common triggers include stress, physical exertion like running, caffeine, wine, and spicy foods. A woman who identifies her personal triggers and avoids them can reduce the likelihood of having a flash. Women can moderate temperature changes via wearing layers of clothing that can be removed or carrying a fan. Deep abdominal breathing has also been suggested.

Proactive, health-promoting behaviors of women between the ages of 40 and 70 years old have increased dramatically in the last 5 to 10 years. Diet, exercise, multivitamins and minerals, herbal/dietary supplements, home remedies, and various complementary/alternative medicine (CAM) strategies are preferred by many women for perimenopause/menopause-related distress (Brett & Keenan, 2007; Eisenberg et al., 1998). Research and clinical guidelines indicate that some relief might be gained from dietary modification and lifestyle changes, such as reduction in smoking, caffeine, and alcohol use, management of stress, and increase in exercise (Fiona & Davis, 2010). Studies of dietary supplements and herbs, mind-body therapies, acupuncture, and Eastern medicine have had incomplete or inconclusive results, but some women report benefits, and these practices tend to involve little harm (for overviews, see Borud & White, 2010; Innes, Selfe, & Vishnu, 2010; Low Dog, 2005; Scheid, Ward, Cha, Watanabe, & Liao, 2010; WHO, 2002). Concerns about harm have been articulated most with regard to dietary supplements and herbs, about such issues as harmful interactions with other medications and adulterated products (Low Dog, 2005).

Cognitive-behavioral, narrative, and other psychological approaches have been underutilized with regard to perimenopausal distress, compared to the common use of these techniques for other physically based distress like pain. As noted previously, psychological approaches have been proposed (see Hunter & Mann, 2010; Trembley, Sheeran, & Aranda, 2008, for overviews). Women may need to sort through whether their assumption that troubling symptoms are related to hormonal changes comes from the reality of their personal experience or from overestimating the likelihood of this because of stereotypes about perimenopause/menopause. The belief that menopause symptoms are unwanted intrusions ("This shouldn't be happening to me") may amplify the psychological experience of distress or make active coping less likely. Women should not expect to develop problems that cannot be overcome. Furthermore, the onset of troubling symptoms like severe hot flashes does not necessarily mean that they will continue indefinitely; they may or may not end spontaneously.

For postmenopausal women with severe symptoms, hormone therapy (HT, a prescription estrogen combined with another hormone called a progestin if women have not had a hysterectomy) provides the most reliable relief (Hunter & Mann, 2010). The effectiveness of HT for perimenopausal women is less evidence-based, and it raises questions because estrogen levels are already high or erratic, not low (Prior, 1998). Some women with distressing symptoms would prefer a CAM or a cognitive-behavioral treatment if these were available (e.g., see

Hunter & Liao, 1996). For professionals working with very distressed women, a careful individualized diagnosis is important. Women should be encouraged to examine their individual, personal experience and to take an active problem-solving stance. Very distressed women need validation of their experiences. However, while validating the experience of distress, women should also be encouraged to find solutions, whether these are an active decision to use a hormone medication or other medications, cognitive-behavioral changes, or CAM. Because many interventions tend to work for some women but not others, a woman might be advised that she approach them with an open mind until she finds one that works for her, rather than that she expect a given option should be effective. Mood changes like depression should be explored, as is the case during other life stages, for its meaning in the overall context of a woman's life.

Instead of emphasizing discrete stages of an aging reproductive system that is in the process of shutting down, it might be useful to emphasize to women that continuity and a life course to menstruation also exist. For example, perimenopausal menstrual irregularity may simply be the state of the system for many years rather than best understood as a time-limited transitional state (no longer "normal" or "as expected," evidence of a system breaking down or becoming unreliable, which "should" be over soon), directly leading to a predictable menopause.

POSTMENOPAUSAL HORMONE THERAPY

Beginning in the 1980s, professionals argued that prescription estrogen supplements (postmenopausal hormone therapy or HT), either estrogen alone (ET) or estrogen combined with a progestin (EPT), were important for preventing chronic diseases like heart, bone, and brain disease, for all postmenopausal women (see Derry, 2004a, 2008, for reviews). Although chronic illnesses are caused by a multitude of factors, the assumption was that menopause did not simply contribute a small amount to these diseases; its impact was primary. There was, for example, pessimism about the prospect that lifestyle changes rather than hormones could significantly affect coronary heart disease (CHD). Furthermore, women were said to "feel better" on estrogen, being less mentally foggy, more energized, and less moody.

This expression of the estrogen deficiency metatheory was reflected in the name originally given to prescription estrogen supplements: hormone replacement therapy (HRT). It was expressed in the popular as well as the professional press. For example, *New York Times* health columnist Jane Brody (1997) wrote "A 50-year-old woman can expect to live another 35 years in a state of hormonal deficiency," and she compared hormone therapy to insulin used by a diabetic. Beginning in the 1990s, professional guidelines increasingly recommended offering HT to all postmenopausal women for disease prevention. For example, the National Committee for Quality Assurance (NCQA, 2001), which creates standards of care, recommended that all women be counseled on HT use and created a questionnaire to evaluate whether health plans offered this service. Prescriptions for HT rose during this time. For example, in the United States, prescriptions increased from 58 million in 1995 to 90 million in 1999 (Hersh, Stefanick, & Stafford, 2004).

The conviction that HT prevents chronic illnesses developed in the absence of a firm research base. Clinical trial evidence of a medication's safety and effectiveness is the "gold standard" required for approval by the Food and Drug Administration (FDA). Aside from bone disease, where sufficient evidence does exist, using HT for prevention has not been FDA-approved, which is especially notable with regard to CHD prevention, where such approval was sought by pharmaceutical companies and denied.

It was asserted by many professionals that the research that did exist, namely epidemiological studies supported by laboratory studies of biological mechanisms, made a strong case even without clinical trial data. The majority of professionals concluded that as a practical matter, enough evidence existed to warrant recommending medication. This conviction, however, was based on a reading of the literature that overlooked or discounted contradictory data and explanations. This is seen clearly in the literature on CHD prevention (see Barrett-Connor & Grady, 1998; Barrett-Connor & Stuenkel, 1999; and Derry, 2004a, for reviews). Women's health advocates and some professionals disagreed with advocating widespread use of a medication, especially one that might have negative health effects, without clinical trial evaluation.

This was the context within which the Women's Health Initiative (WHI) clinical trials were designed to put to the test whether hormone therapies are safe and effective for preventing heart disease in postmenopausal women (Women's Health Initiative Steering Committee, 2004; Writing Group for the Women's Health Initiative Investigators, 2002). Twin studies were designed in 1991 and 1992. Women who had a uterus received EPT or a placebo; women who had had a hysterectomy received ET or a placebo. The dependent variables were measures of actual heart disease—either myocardial infarction (MI, or heart attack) or death. Other major outcomes included breast cancer, thought to be the major potential adverse outcome from HT, and, since HT has a variety of effects on a variety of body systems, a "global index" measured whether the overall effect of HT was helpful or harmful when several diseases were considered simultaneously. Secondary outcomes were also measured, including hip fracture, other fracture, other cardiovascular diseases, and certain cancers.

The main result was that, contrary to epidemiological studies supported by laboratory studies of biological mechanisms and the common wisdom of the day, HT did not prevent heart disease. Furthermore, overall harm outweighed overall benefit in the global index. A possible increase in breast cancer risk was especially worrisome. (For more detailed results, see Chlebowski et al., 2003; Hsia et al., 2006; Manson et al., 2003; Women's Health Initiative Steering Committee, 2004; Writing Group for the Women's Health Initiative Investigators, 2002.) WHI had weaknesses as well as strengths. For example, about half the participants had dropped out of the study by the time it ended, weakening the conclusions that could be drawn. However, the major conclusions of the study—that HT has no benefit for CHD risk and that overall harm outweighed benefits—could reliably be drawn even given these limitations.

Prescription rates fell, in part because of individual decisions by women and their doctors. The FDA concluded that HT should be used only for treatment of hot flashes, vaginal dryness, and possibly osteoporosis, at the lowest dose and for the shortest period of time (FDA, 2003). Furthermore, an FDA advisory stated that

hormone medications should not be referred to as "hormone replacement therapy" since no evidence exists that HT is a replacement of needed hormones (Federal Register, 2002).

Use of HT by symptomatic women has remained a complex issue. The WHI researched disease prevention; symptom relief is a separate issue. As noted, HT is effective for relief of hot flashes and other severe, distressing symptoms. The original WHI research reports and the FDA guidelines both concluded that the risk of harm is small enough to warrant use for symptomatic women who will gain a clear benefit. However, the WHI results, especially as portrayed in some professional articles and the popular media, have led many women to stop using HT, make more complex decisions about whether their symptoms warrant HT, or look for an alternative treatment.

Continuing results from the WHI project have appeared, as have continuing disputes among professionals about what conclusions can legitimately be drawn. From the time the first CHD trial results were reported, some professionals maintained that methodological flaws in the WHI were so serious that conclusions could not be confidently drawn (e.g., as reported in NIH, 2002). One major critique is the "timing hypothesis," which asserts that estrogen protects against chronic illness only when started immediately around the time of menopause, before illness begins; once women are older and illness exists, estrogen is no longer protective and may even be harmful. This argument logically leads to broadening indications for hormone use and an assertion that continuing research on hormones and disease prevention is needed. The timing hypothesis has quickly gained credence as a legitimate and plausible possibility. Yet the hypothesis relies on epidemiological evidence and plausible biological mechanisms—the same kinds of evidence that before WHI were relied on to prove that all women would benefit from HT. It also draws heavily on statistical analyses of experimental data that are methodologically weak or incorrect, such as reporting as results data that are post-hoc, underpowered, or not statistically significant (see Derry, 2008, for an analysis of this research literature). The timing hypothesis appears to draw its plausibility, in part, on the estrogen deficiency metatheory, again showing practical implications of this metatheory.

CONCLUSION

Menopause and the transition to menopause are associated with a wide range of health issues, ranging from understanding the normal course of reproductive aging to coping with uncomfortable or distressing physical symptoms to the adult-developmental task of forming a self-concept as a menopausal or mature woman. An accurate understanding of the underlying physiology is crucial. However, this is a biopsychosocial process in which psychological and cultural processes are intimately involved. Cultural stereotypes and cognitive-behavioral processes influence definitions of midlife as a life stage, appraisals of distressing experiences, and how to cope with them.

Many women look to biomedical information to understand the realities of perimenopause and menopause. The reality they must understand is based in part on their individual physical experiences, such as if they are experiencing severe symptoms or none at all. However, the meaning of the end of menstruation ultimately represents an individual woman's appraisal of the transition that she is experiencing, not an absolute reality. Furthermore, the state-of-the-art with regard to scientific information is limited rather than authoritative, with many ambiguities, and reflects the influence of cultural presuppositions.

Health psychologists can contribute interdisciplinary perspectives that combine an accurate understanding of physiology with cultural, cognitive-behavioral, and narrative factors to emphasize positive paradigms of a woman's life stage and coping ability. Key points include that (a) perimenopause/menopause differs from woman to woman physiologically and psychologically; (b) biomedical information provides important anchors, but women should not expect a predictable course; (c) women should not expect a priori that debilitating symptoms are likely or that they will not be able to cope with distress if it occurs; (d) cultural stereotypes have encouraged negative views of menopause and midlife; and (e) a woman's own definition of her life stage is key. A woman's task, ultimately, is to find and define her personal inner reality.

REFERENCES

Avis, N., & Crawford, S. (2008). Cultural differences in symptoms and attitudes toward menopause. *Menopause Management, 17,* 8–12.

Avis, N., & McKinlay, S. (1991). A longitudinal analysis of women's attitudes toward the menopause: Results from the Massachusetts Women's Health Study. *Maturitas, 13,* 65–79.

Avis, N., Stellato, R., Crawford, S., Bromberger, J., Ganz, P., Cain, V., & Kagawa-Singer, M. (2001). Is there a menopausal syndrome? *Menopausal status and symptoms across racial/ethnic groups. Social Science and Medicine, 52,* 345–356.

Ayers, B., Forshaw, M., & Hunter, M. (2010). The impact of attitudes towards the menopause on women's symptom experience: A systematic review. *Maturitas, 65,* 28–36.

Ballard, K., Elston, M. A., & Gabe, J. (2005). Beyond the mask: Women's experiences of public and private ageing during midlife and their use of age-resisting activities. *Health: An Interdisciplinary Journal for the Social Study of Health, Illness and Medicine, 9*(2), 169–187.

Barrett-Connor, E., & Grady, D. (1998). Hormone replacement therapy, heart disease, and other considerations. *Annual Review of Public Health, 19,* 55–72.

Barrett-Connor, E., & Stuenkel, C. (1999). Hormones and heart disease in women: Heart and estrogen/progestin replacement study in perspective. *Journal of Clinical Endocrinology and Metabolism, 84,* 1848–1853.

Bogin, B. (1999). *Patterns of human growth.* Cambridge, UK: Cambridge University Press.

Borud, E., & White, A. (2010). A review of acupuncture for menopausal problems. *Maturitas, 66,* 131–134.

Brett, K. M., and Keenan, N. L. (2007). Complementary and alternative medicine use among midlife women for reasons including menopause in the United States: 2002. *Menopause, 14*(2), 300–307.

Brody, J. (1997). Personal health column. *New York Times* Health Section, August 28, 1997.

Bromberger, J. T., Matthews, K. A., Schott, L. L., Brockwell, S., Avis, N. E., Kravitz, H. M., . . . Randolph, J. F., Jr., (2007). Depressive symptoms during the menopausal transition: The Study of Women's Health Across the Nation (SWAN). *Journal of Affective Disorders, 103,* 267–272.

Bromberger, J. T., Meyer, P. M., Kravitz, H. M., Sommer, B., Cordal, A., Powell, L., . . . Sutton-Tyrrell, K. (2001). Psychologic distress and natural menopause: A multi-ethnic community study. *American Journal of Public Health, 91,* 1435–1442.

Brumberg, J. J. (1997). *The body project: An intimate history of American girls.* New York, NY: Random House.

Burger, H., Hale, G., Dennerstein, L., & Robertson, D. (2008). Cycle and hormone changes during the perimenopause: The key role of ovarian function. *Menopause, 15,* 603–612.

Chlebowski, R., Hendrix, S., Langer, R., Stefanick, M., Gass, M., Lane, D., . . . WHI Investigators. (2003). Influence of estrogen plus progestin on breast cancer and mammography in healthy postmenopausal women. *Journal of the American Medical Association, 289,* 3243–3253.

Cobb, J. (1993). *Understanding menopause.* New York, NY: Penguin.

Cole, E., & Rothblum, E. (1990). Commentary on 'sexuality and the midlife woman.' *Psychology of Women Quarterly, 14,* 509–512.

Crawford, S. (2007). The roles of biologic and non-biologic factors in cultural differences in vasomotor symptoms measured by surveys. *Menopause, 14,* 725–733.

Cremin, M. C. (1992). Feeling old versus being old: Views of troubled aging. *Social Science & Medicine, 34,* 1305–1315.

Dennerstein, L. (1996). Well-being, symptoms, and the menopausal transition. *Maturitas, 23,* 147–157.

Dennerstein, L., Smith, A., Morse, C., Burger, H., Green, A., Hopper, J., & Ryan, M. (1993). Menopausal symptoms in Australian women. *The Medical Journal of Australia, 159,* 232–236.

Derry, P. (2004a). Hormones, menopause, and heart disease: Making sense of the Women's Health Initiative. *Women's Health Issues, 14,* 212–219.

Derry, P. (2004b). Coping with distress during perimenopause. *Women and Therapy, 27,* 165–177.

Derry, P. (2006). A lifespan biological model of menopause. *Sex Roles, 54,* 393–399.

Derry, P. (2008). Update on hormones, menopause, and heart disease: Evaluating professional responses to the Women's Health Initiative. *Health Care for Women International, 29,* 720–737.

Derry, P., & Derry, G. (2012). Menstruation, perimenopause, and chaos theory. *Perspectives in Biology and Medicine, 55,* 26–42.

Dickson, G. (1990). A feminist poststructuralist analysis of the knowledge of menopause. *Advanced Nursing Science, 12,* 15–31.

Dillaway, H. (2005). Menopause is the "good old": Women's thoughts about reproductive aging. *Gender & Society, 19,* 398–417.

Dillaway, H. (2011). Menopausal and misbehaving: When women "flash" in front of others. In C. Bobel & S. Kwan (Eds.), *Embodied resistance: Breaking the rules in public spaces* (pp. 197–208). Nashville, TN: Vanderbilt University Press.

Dillaway, H. (2012). Reproductive history as social context: Exploring how women converse about menopause and sexuality at midlife.

In J. DeLamater & L. Carpenter (Eds.), *Sex for life: From virginity to Viagra, how sexuality changes throughout our lives* (pp. 217–235). New York, NY: New York University Press.

Dillaway, H., & Burton, J. (2011). "Not done yet?! How women discuss the "end" of menopause. *Women's Studies: An Interdisciplinary Journal, 40*(2), 149–176.

Dillaway, H., Byrnes, M., Miller, S., & Rehan, S. (2008). Talking among us: How women from different racial ethnic groups define and discuss menopause. *Healthcare for Women International, 29*(7), 766–781.

Eisenberg, D. M., Davis, R. B., Ettner, S. L., Appel, S., Wilkey, S., Van Rompay, M., & Kessler, R. C. (1998). Trends in alternative medicine in the US, 1990-1997: Results of a follow-up national survey. *Journal of the American Medical Association, 7*, 30–49.

Elson, J. (2004). *Am I still a woman? Hysterectomy and gender identity.* Philadelphia, PA: Temple University Press.

Featherstone, M., & Hepworth, M. (1991). The mask of ageing and the postmodern life course. In M. Featherstone, M. Hepworth, & B. Turner (Eds.), *The body: Social process and cultural theory.* London, UK: Sage.

Federal Register. (2002). Food and Drug Administration Draft guidance for clinical evaluation of combination estrogen/progestin-containing drug products. Vol. *68*, January 31, 2002.

Fiona, J., & Davis, S. (2010). Menopause. In L. Borgelt, M. B. O'Connell, J. Smith, & K. Calis (Eds.), *Women's health across the life span* (pp. 249–265). Bethesda, MD: American Society of Health-System Pharmacists.

Food and Drug Administration. (2003). Menopause and hormones. Retrieved from www. fda. gov/womens/menopause/mht-FS.html

Freedman, R. (2001). Physiology of hot flashes. *American Journal of Human Biology, 13*, 453–464.

Gannon, L. (1999). *Women and aging: Transcending the myths.* New York, NY: Routledge.

Gannon, L., & Ekstrom, B. (1993). Attitudes toward menopause: The influence of sociocultural paradigms. *Psychology of Women Quarterly, 17*, 275–288.

Gass., M. (2010). Broadening the perspective on bone. *Menopause Management, 19*, 8, 16.

Gold, E., Colvin, A., Avis, N., Bromberger, J., Greendale, G., Powell, L., . . . Matthews, K. (2006). Longitudinal analysis of the association between vasomotor symptoms and race/ethnicity across the menopausal transition: Study of Women's Health across the Nation. *American Journal of Public Health, 96*, 1226–35.

Grady, D., & Cummings, S. (2001). Postmenopausal hormone therapy for prevention of fractures: How good is the evidence? *Journal of the American Medical Association, 285*, 2909–2910.

Green, R., & Santoro, N. (2009). Menopausal symptoms and ethnicity: The Study of Women's Health Across the Nation. *Women's Health, 5*, 127–133.

Greil, A. L. (1991). *Not yet pregnant: Infertile couples in contemporary America.* New Brunswick, NJ: Rutgers University Press.

Grisso, J. A., Freeman, E. W., Maurin, E., Garcia-Espana, B., & Berlin, J. (1999). Racial differences in menopause information and the experience of hot flashes. *Journal of General Internal Medicine, 14*, 98–103.

Gullette, M. M. (1997). Menopause as magic marker: Discursive consolidation in the United States, and strategies for cultural combat. In P. Komesaroff, P. Rothfield, & J. Daly (Eds.), *Reinterpreting menopause: Cultural and philosophical issues* (pp. 176–199). New York, NY: Routledge.

Hale, G., & Burger, H. (2005). Perimenopausal reproductive endocrinology. *Endocrinology and Metabolism Clinics of North America, 34*, 907–922.

Hale, G., Zhao, X., Hughes, C., Burger, H., Robertson, D., & Fraser, I. (2007). Endocrine features of menstrual cycles in middle and late reproductive age and the menopausal transition classified according to the Stages of Reproductive Aging Workshop (STRAW) staging system. *Journal of Clinical Endocrinology and Metabolism, 92*, 3060–3067.

Hanisch, L., Hantsoo, L., Freeman, E., Sullivan, G., & Coyne, J. (2008). Hot flashes and panic attacks: A comparison of symptomatology, neurobiology, treatment, and a role for cognition. *Psychological Bulletin, 134*, 247–269.

Harlow, S., Lin, X., & Ho, M. (2000). Analysis of menstrual diary data across the reproductive life span: Applicability of the bipartite model approach and the importance of within-woman variance. *Journal of Clinical Epidemiology, 53*, 722–733.

Harlow, S., Mitchell, E., Crawford, S., Nan, B., Little, R., & Taffe, J. (2008). The ReSTAGE collaboration: Defining optimal bleeding criteria for onset of early menopausal transition. *Fertility and Sterility, 89,* 129–140.

Hawkes, K., O'Connell, J., & Burton Jones, N. (1997). Hadza women's time allocation, offspring provisioning, and the evolution of long post-menopausal life spans. *Current Anthropology, 38,* 551–577.

Hawkes, K., O'Connell, J., Burton Jones, N., Alvarez, H., & Charnov, E. (1998). Grandmothering, menopause, and the evolution of human life histories. Proceedings of the National Academy of Sciences, *95,* 1336–1339.

Hersh, A., Stefanick, M., & Stafford, R. (2004). National use of postmenopausal hormone therapy: annual trends and response to recent evidence. *Journal of the American Medical Association, 291,* 47–53.

Hollander, L., Freeman, E., Sammel, M., Berlin, J., Grisso, J., & Battistini, M. (2001). Sleep quality, estradiol levels, and behavioral factors in late reproductive women. *Obstetrics & Gynecology, 98,* 391–397.

Holte, A. (1992). Influences of natural menopause on health complaints. *Maturitas, 14,* 127–141.

Hsia, J., Langer, R., Manson, J., Kuller, L., Johnson, K., & Hendrix, S. (2004). Conjugated equine estrogens and coronary heart disease. *Archives of Internal Medicine, 166,* 357–365.

Hunter, M., & Liao, K. (1996). Evaluation of a four-session cognitive-behavioural intervention for menopausal hot flushes. *British Journal of Health Psychology, 1,* 113–125.

Hunter, M., & Mann, E. (2010). A cognitive model of menopausal hot flushes and night sweats. *Journal of Psychosomatic Research, 69,* 491–501.

Hyde, A., Nee, J., Howlett, E., Drennan, J., & Butler, M. (2010). Menopause narratives: The interplay of women's embodied experiences with biomedical discourses. *Qualitative Health Research, 20(6)* 805–815.

Im, E., Lee, S. H., & Chee, W. (2010). Black women in menopausal transition. *Journal of Obstetric, Gynecologic, & Neonatal Nursing, 39,* 435–443.

Im, E., Lee, S. H., & Chee, W. (2011). "Being conditioned, yet becoming strong": Asian American women in menopausal transition. *Journal of Transcultural Nursing, 22*(3), 290–299.

Innes, K., Selfe, T., & Vishnu, A. (2010). Mind-body therapies for menopausal symptoms: A systematic review *Maturitas, 66,* 135–149.

Kaplan, H., Gurven, M., Winking, J., Hooper, P., & Stieglitz, J. (2010). Learning, menopause, and the human adaptive complex. *Annals of the New York Academy of Sciences, 1204,* 30–42.

Kaufert, P. (1994). A health and social profile of the menopausal woman. *Experimental Gerontology, 29,* 343–350.

Kaufert, P., & Gilbert, P. (1986). Women, menopause, and medicalization. *Culture, Medicine and Psychiatry, 10,* 7–21.

Kaufert, P., Gilbert, P., & Tate, R. (1992). The Manitoba Project: A reexamination of the link between menopause and depression. *Maturitas, 14,* 143–155.

Kittell, L., Mansfield, P., Morse, J., & Voda, A. (1997). Experiencing changes in menstrual bleeding during the menopausal transition. *Menopause, 4,* 173–183.

Kittell, L., Mansfield, P., & Voda, A. (1998). Keeping up appearances: The basic social process of the menopausal transition. *Qualitative Health Research, 8,* 618–633.

Komesaroff, P., Rothfield, P., & Daly, J. (Eds.). (1997). *Reinterpreting menopause: Cultural and philosophical issues.* New York, NY: Routledge.

Lee, R. (1985). Work, sexuality, and aging among! Kung women. In J. Brown & V. Kerns (Eds.), *In her prime* (pp. 23–35). South Hadley, MA: Bergin & Garvey.

Lisabeth, L., Harlow, S., & Qaqish, B. (2004). A new statistical approach demonstrated menstrual patterns during the menopausal transition did not vary by age at menopause. *Journal of Clinical Epidemiology, 57,* 484–496.

Lock, M. (1993). *Encounters with aging: Mythologies of menopause in Japan and North America.* Berkeley: University of California Press.

Love, S. (2003). *Dr. Susan Love's menopause & hormone book.* New York, NY: Three Rivers Press.

Low Dog, T. (2005). Menopause: a review of botanical dietary supplements. *American Journal of Medicine, 118*(12B): 98S–108S.

Lyons, A. C., & Griffin, C. (2003). Managing menopause: A qualitative analysis of self-help literature for women at midlife. *Social Science & Medicine, 56,* 1629–1642.

MacPherson, K. (1981). Menopause as disease: The social construction of a metaphor. *Advanced in Nursing Research*, *3*, 95–113.

Mansfield, P., Carey, M., Anderson, A., Barsom, S. H., & Koch, P. B. (2004). Staging the menopausal transition: Data from the Tremin research program on women's health. *Women's Health Issues*, *14*, 220–226.

Mansfield, P., Theisen, S., & Boyer, B. (1992). Midlife women and menopause: A challenge for the mental health counselor. *Journal of Mental Health Counseling*, *14*, 73–83.

Manson, J., Hsia, J., Johnson, K., Rossouw, J., Assaf, A., Lasser, N., . . . WHI Investigators. (2003). Estrogen plus progestin and the risk of coronary heart disease. *New England Journal of Medicine*, *349*, 523–534.

Markson, E. W. (2003). The female aging body through film. In C. Faircloth (Ed.), *Aging bodies: Images and everyday experiences* (pp. 77–102). Walnut Creek, CA: AltaMira Press.

Martin, E. (1992). *The woman in the body: A cultural analysis of reproduction* (2nd ed.). Boston, MA: Beacon Press.

Matthews, K. A., Wing, R. R., Kuller, L. H., Meilahn, E. N., Kelsey, S. F., Costello, E. J., & Caggiula, A. W. (1990). Influences of natural menopause on psychological characteristics and symptoms of middle-aged healthy women. *Journal of Consulting and Clinical Psychology*, *58*(3), 345–351.

McKinlay, J., McKinlay, S., & Brambilla, D. (1987). The relative contributions of endocrine changes and social circumstances to depression in mid-aged women. *Journal of Health and Social Behavior*, *28*, 345–356.

McKinlay, S., Brambilla, D., & Posner, J. (1992). The normal menopause transition. *Maturitas*, *14*, 103–115.

Melby, M. (2005). Vasomotor symptom prevalence and language of menopause in Japan. *Menopause*, *12*, 250–257.

Miller, L., & Daniels-Brady, C. (2005). Depression during perimenopause. *Menopause Management*, 10–16.

Murtagh, M. J., & Hepworth, J. (2003). Menopause as a long-term risk to health: Implications of general practitioner accounts of prevention for women's choice and decision-making. *Sociology of Health & Illness*, *25*, 185–207.

National Committee for Quality Assurance. (2001). *HEDIS 2001: Specifications for survey measures* (Vol. 3). Washington, DC: Author.

National Institutes of Health. (2002). *Scientific workshop on menopausal hormone therapy*. October 23–24, 2002, Bethesda, MD.

National Institutes of Health. (2005). NIH state-of-the-science conference statement on management of menopause-related symptoms. *NIH Consensus Statements Scientific Statements, March 21-23, 2005 22*, 1–38.

Nicole-Smith, L. (1999). Causality, menopause, and depression: A critical review of the literature. *British Medical Journal*, *313*, 1229–1232.

Nixon, E., Mansfield, P. K., Kittell, L. A., & Faulkner, S. A. (2001). "Staying strong": How low-income rural African American women manage their menopausal changes. *Women & Health*, *34*(2), 81–95.

Pavelka, M., & Fedigan, L. (1991). Menopause: A comparative life history perspective. *Yearbook of Physical Anthropology*, *34*, 13–38.

Prior, J. (1998). Perimenopause: The complex endocrinology of the menopausal transition. *Endocrine Reviews*, *19*, 397–428.

Prior, J. (2005). Ovarian aging and the perimenopausal transition. *Endocrine*, *26*, 297–300.

Quinn, A. (1991). A theoretical model of the perimenopausal process. *Journal of Nurse-Midwifery*, *36*, 25–29.

Reynolds, F. (1997). Psychological responses to menopausal hot flushes: Implications of a qualitative study for counseling interventions. *Counseling Psychology Quarterly*, *10*, 309–321.

Reynolds, F. (2000). Relationships between catastrophic thoughts, perceived control and distress during menopausal hot flushes: Exploring the correlates of a questionnaire measure. *Maturitas*, *36*, 113–122.

Rostosky, S., & Travis, C. (1996). Menopause research and the dominance of the biomedical model 1984–1994. *Psychology of Women Quarterly*, *20*, 285–312.

Rubinow, D., Schmidt, P., & Roca, C. (1998). Hormone measures in reproductive endocrine-related mood disorders: Diagnostic issues. *Psychopharmacology Bulletin*, *34*, 289–290.

Santoro, N. (2005). The menopausal transition. *American Journal of Medicine*, *118*, 8S–13S.

Scheid, V, Ward, T., Cha, W., Watanabe, K., & Liao, X. (2010). The treatment of menopausal symptoms by traditional East Asian medicines: Review and perspectives. *Maturitas, 66,* 111–130.

Sherman, B., West, J., & Korenman, S. (1975). The menopausal transition: Analysis of LH, FSH, estradiol, and progesterone concentrations during menstrual cycles of older women. *Journal of Clinical Endocrinology and Metabolism, 42,* 629–636.

Skulkans, V. (1970). The symbolic significance of menstruation and menopause. *Man, 5,* 639–651.

Sommer, B., Avis, N., Meyer, P., Ory, M., Madden, T., Kagawa-Singer, M., . . . Adler, S. (1999). Attitudes towards menopause and aging across ethnic/racial groups. *Psychosomatic Medicine, 16,* 868–875.

Soules, M., Sherman, S., Parrott, E., Rebar, R., Santoro, N, Utian, W., & Woods, N. (2001). Stages of Reproductive Aging Workshop (STRAW). *Journal of Women's Health and Gender-Based Medicine, 10,* 843–848.

Treloar, A. (1981). Menstrual cyclicity and the premenopause. *Maturitas, 3,* 249–264.

Treloar, A., Boynton, R., Behn, B., & Brown, B. (1967). Variation of the human menstrual cycle through reproductive life. *International Journal of Fertility, 12,* 77–126.

Tremblay, A., Sheeran, L., & Aranda, S. (2008). Psychoeducational interventions to alleviate hot flashes: A systematic review. *Menopause, 15,* 193–202.

Trethewey, A. (2001). Reproducing and resisting the master narrative of decline: Midlife professional women's experiences of aging. *Management Communication Quarterly, 15,* 183–226.

Utian, W. (2003). *Textbook of perimenopausal gynecology.* New York, NY: Parthenon.

Voda, A. (1992). Menopause: A normal view. *Clinical Obstetrics and Gynecology, 35,* 923–933.

Voda, A. (1997). *Menopause, me and you.* Binghamton, NY: Haworth.

Weng, H. H., McBride, C. M., Bosworth, H. B., Grambow, S. C., Siegler, I. C., & Bastian, L. (2001). Racial differences in physician recommendation of hormone replacement therapy. *Preventive Medicine, 33*(6), 668–673.

WHO Scientific Group. (1996). *Research on the menopause in the 1990s. A report of the WHO Scientific Group.* Geneva, Switzerland: WHO.

Wilson, R. (1966). *Feminine forever.* New York, NY: M. Evans.

Winterich, J. (2003). Sex, menopause and culture: Sexual orientation and the meaning of menopause for women's sex lives. *Gender & Society, 17,* 627–642.

Women's Health Initiative Steering Committee. (2004). Effects of conjugated equine estrogen in postmenopausal women with hysterectomy: The Women's Health Initiative randomized controlled trial. *Journal of the American Medical Association, 291,* 1701–1712.

World Health Organization (WHO). (2002). *Monographs on selected medicinal plants.* (Vol 2). Geneva, Switzerland: Author.

Writing Group for the Women's Health Initiative Investigators. (2002). Risks and benefits of estrogen plus progestin in healthy postmenopausal women: Principal results from the Women's Health Initiative randomized controlled trial. *Journal of the American Medical Association, 288,* 321–333.

Yaffe, K., Sawaya, G., Lieberburg, I., & Grady, D. (1998). Estrogen therapy in postmenopausal women: Effects on cognitive function and dementia. *Journal of the American Medical Association, 279,* 688–695.

DISABILITY AND CHRONIC CONDITIONS

19

Women's Responses to Disability

Rhoda Olkin

Disability is a rich topic that encompasses a wide range of issues, from very specific topics to the basic question of what it means to be human.

(Olkin, 2002)

How does one tackle the issues faced by women with disabilities? First is to acknowledge the complexity of the topic. The terms *women*, *disability*, and *adjustment* all require parsing. There is tremendous diversity among women, and I don't need to convince readers of this point. The diversity of disabilities merits some attention, and the issue of adjustment will be discussed in the section on language.

Although I want to spend most of this chapter on factors of clinical importance, and providing disability-affirmative therapy (Olkin, 2008) in a health psychology context, to do so I first have to introduce several critical conceptual issues. These include how disability differentially affects populations, the dimensions on which disabilities differ from each other, the language we use to talk about disability, how disability is conceptualized, and consideration of disability in the context of other demographic variables. Then I can turn to the more clinical topics, such as responses to disability, and seven factors of clinical importance common to clients with disabilities. Finally, I make a few recommendations for health psychologists. My goal is to frame how you think about disability, such

that you can make independent clinical decisions that are informed by a solid foundation from the field of disability studies.

WHAT IS A DISABILITY?

Disability is socially determined and can be defined variously for different purposes. The current legal definition comes from the *Rehabilitation Act* (1973) and was repeated in the *Americans with Disabilities Act* (1990). The context in which the legal definition is key is in employment for adults. (Definitions regarding disabilities in children, especially those that affect learning, are codified in the *Individuals with Disabilities Education Act*.) Two other codifications of disability appear in the *International Classification of Functioning, Disability and Health* (ICF; World Health Organization, 2001) and the *Diagnostic and Statistical Manual (DSM)* for (mostly, but not exclusively) mental disorders. From this partial list of sources of definitions we see the complexity of defining disability and the importance of the purpose of definition in developing the parameters.

Despite these varying purposes and definitions, it can be useful to think of broad categories of disabilities. These categories include (a) physical disabilities (e.g., spinal cord injury [SCI], polio), (b) sensory disabilities (e.g., hearing loss, deafness, low vision, blindness), (c) systemic disabilities (e.g., multiple sclerosis [MS], insulin-dependent diabetes), (d) cognitive disabilities (e.g., stroke, traumatic brain injury, intellectual disabilities), (e) psychiatric disabilities (e.g., bipolar disorder), (f) learning disabilities (e.g., attention deficit hyperactivity disorder [ADHD], specific learning disabilities), and (g) functional disabilities (e.g., alcoholism or substance abuse). These categories are not discrete; for example, MS can be a physical and a cognitive disability. Nor do they mirror the definitions outlined here; codification systems often lag behind practice. For example, many school districts still define learning disabilities by discrepancy scores (ability versus accomplishment) and thus overlook students who do well on standardized tests.

The *DSM-IV-TR* and the upcoming *DSM-5* still include as one criterion for intellectual disability (therein called mental retardation) as a score on IQ tests, whereas the more useful ARC definition defines it by functioning in various activities of daily living (ADL). The World Health Organization (WHO), however, has demonstrated more awareness of the social context of disability and notes the interplay between personal conditions and the environment: "The International Classification of Functioning, Disability and Health . . . is a classification of health and health-related domains. . . . Since *an individual's functioning and disability occurs in a context, the ICF also includes a list of environmental factors*" (http://www.who.int/classifications/icf/en/; emphasis added).

If social context is important, then disability might be defined in part by the reaction of others to the condition (i.e., the stigma engendered by some physical conditions). Some authors have made this argument, asserting that by this definition being fat is a disability (Brandon & Pritchard, 2011).

For health psychology, it is probably most useful to consider (a) the effects of the condition on overall health; (b) the nature of the impairment in the context of the person's environment; (c) the cultural meanings attached to the condition; and (d) the degree of stigma associated with the condition. Health psychology encompasses a conceptualization of a wellness–illness continuum. Disability does not fit neatly onto this continuum, nor is it orthogonal to it. Rather, disability overlaps and diverges from wellness and illness. Differentiating disability from illness is difficult but conceptually important. For some disabilities (e.g., arthritis or polio), health can be unaffected directly by the disability and can range from poor to excellent just as it would for someone without the disability. For other disabilities (e.g., SCI or muscular dystrophy), secondary conditions are common, such that disability indirectly affects health. And for yet other disabilities (e.g., acquired immunodeficiency syndrome [AIDS] or insulin-dependent diabetes), health is directly affected by the disability.

For clinicians and practitioners, the take-home messages are that disability has multiple definitions, depending on the purpose of the definition; disability and health are related but not completely overlapping, and disability is not conceptualized as a chronic health condition; and disability is always an interplay between functioning and the environment.

DISABILITY IN CONTEXT

Disability is not random; it follows patterns affected by geographic location, socioeconomic status, gender, ethnicity, and age. Regarding ethnicity, rates are generally highest for American Indians and Aleuts, followed by African Americans, and lower for Hispanics and Asian Americans, with Whites generally in the middle range. Disability increases with age, and onset of disability tends to follow a bimodal pattern, occurring either at birth or shortly thereafter and then again in later adulthood. Although boys are more likely than girls to have a disability, by adulthood the ratio reverses; for women ages 16 to 64, 12.4% have a disability, compared to 11.7% for men (U.S. Census Bureau, 2010). Longer life expectancy is one factor, as the incidence of disabilities increases with age (5% for ages 5 to 17; 10% for ages 18 to 64; 38% for those 65 or older). But longer life expectancy of women does not entirely explain the higher rates (Guralnik & Simonsick, 1993). Some disabilities are more common in women, such as MS, and even though rates of arthritis increase with age for both genders, the rate is higher for women at every age (Verbrugge, 1995; Zinc, Braun, Listing, & Wollenhaupt, 2000).

Disability and socioeconomic status are intertwined. The proportion of persons with disabilities varies across the United States, roughly corresponding inversely to mean income levels. Thus in the United States there are great differences in rates of disability between the poorest states (cutting a swath through the South and up Appalachia) and the richest states (in the Northeast and Alaska), not because of anything inherent in those environments, but because of their respective rates of poverty. Poverty begets disability through malnutrition, vitamin deficiencies, exposure to toxins, increased stressors and violence, and other environmental factors. Conversely, disability affects income and is associated with higher rates of living below the poverty level. Despite laws designed to reduce discrimination, the employment rate of men and women

with disabilities fell over the 1990s, at a time of increasing employment for nondisabled women and steady rates for nondisabled men (Bound & Waidmann, 2002). Only 35% of working-age persons with disabilities are working, compared to 74% of those without disabilities, a 39% gap that has been virtually unchanged over the past three decades (AAPD, 2011). However, employment rates vary tremendously by disability type. For example, those with polio are about as likely to be working as their nondisabled peers, whereas persons with MS have one of the lowest employment rates of all disabilities. These two disabilities may seem to have surface commonalities (e.g., fatigue, weakness, mobility limitations), but they have more subtle differences such that the effects on employment are quite different.

Rates of employment tend to be slightly higher for those with early-onset disabilities versus those with adult onset. For example, the rate of employment for those with an SCI from childhood is about 42% to 69%, compared with a rate of about 19% to 23% for those with adult onset of SCI (Vogel, Chlan, Zebracki, & Anderson, 2011). Studies show consistently higher rates of employment for Whites with disabilities compared with African Americans with disabilities (Anderson & Vogel, 2002; Krause, Saunders, & Staten, 2010; Yasuda, Wehman, Targett, Cifu, & West, 2002). Employment is a key outcome variable, because it is associated with higher reports of satisfaction with life and other positive measures (Chapin & Holbert, 2010; Fadyl & McPherson, 2010). This is to be expected, because employment has many side benefits, such as income, insurance, social opportunities, and meaningful work. However, at least one study on girls with SCI suggests that social participation also was important in positive outcomes, along with job opportunities (Gorzkowski, Kelly, Klaas, & Vogel, 2010).

What do we know about the differences between women and men with disabilities? In thinking about employment for women with disabilities it is helpful to consider the greater context of trends for women in general. The rate of women who are working has risen over the past decades, from 33% in 1955 to 61% in 1999 (and remained at about that level since). Still, women earn only about 75% of what their male counterparts earn (Bianchi, 1995), and they are more likely than men to live in poverty and to be single parents (Belle, 1990). The combination of being female and having a disability disadvantages women even more. They are less likely than their nondisabled counterparts to be in the workforce, are more likely to earn less, more likely to be single mothers, and more likely to live in poverty, compared to women without disabilities.

Despite being more likely to hold a college degree than are men with disabilities (15.2% versus 12.8%), this rate is still below that of nondisabled women or men. Despite the advantage of being more likely to have a college degree, White women with disabilities are less likely to be employed than are White men with disabilities (34.2% versus 41.1%), and their median income is less ($25,700 versus $27,600). However, African American women with disabilities are more likely to be employed than are African American men with disabilities. But for all ethnicities, women with disabilities are more likely to live below the poverty line (estimates range from 23% to 31%, depending on the definition of disability used) than are men with disabilities (18% to 25%), and well above the proportion for nondisabled women and men (10%). (The data in this paragraph are from the U.S. Bureau of Labor Statistics, 2011, and U.S. Census Data, 2008.)

Although in some studies people with disabilities are less likely to report being satisfied with life than are people without disabilities, other studies do not show this difference (e.g., Vogel et al., 2011). However, age at disability onset, time since disability onset, as well as the definition of disability used would affect results. Data comparing men and women with disabilities on life satisfaction are absent. However, people with disabilities are much less likely to be married than the general population, and women with disabilities are less likely than men with disabilities to be married. This is in part a function of their lower participation in the workforce, because those not in the workforce generally have fewer social contacts, and fewer social contacts means less romantic contacts. If marriage affects life satisfaction, then we would expect the differential marriage rates for men and women with disabilities to moderate life satisfaction.

Women handle disabilities differently than men, and in particular are less likely to use surgical procedures. For example, although women have a higher prevalence of hip and knee arthritis, have worse symptoms, and are more functionally impaired, they are three times less likely than men to have surgical repairs (Hawker et al., 2000). Additionally women seem to have more disability associated with impairments (Gregg et al., 2000; Pinsky, Jette, Branch, Kannel, & Feinleib, 1990) and may not recover as quickly (Oman, Reed, & Ferrara, 1999).

DIMENSIONS OF DISABILITY

Understanding a person's disability requires in part knowing many factors about both the

Table 19.1   Psychosocial Dimensions of Disability

Factor	Dimensions[a]
Onset Speed:	Acute . . . . Gradual
Onset Type:	Benign . . . . Traumatic
Course:	Progressive, Constant, Relapsing
Outcome:	Life expectancy wnl[b] . . . . Shortened Lifespan . . . . Terminal
Degree of Impairment:	None . . . . Mild . . . . Moderate . . . . Severe
Degree of Uncertainty:	Mostly predictable . . . . Mostly unpredictable
Pain Level:	None . . . . Mild . . . . Moderate . . . . Severe
Pain Frequency:	None . . . . Occasional . . . . Frequent . . . . Constant
Individual's Overall Health:	Excellent . . . . Compromised . . . . Poor
Disability Phase:	Diagnosis; Remission; Exacerbation; Chronic
Individual Developmental Phase:	Dependence; Emancipating; Interdependence
Family's Life Stage:	Centripetal (joining); Centrifugal (separating)
Degree of Stigma:	Low Stigma Moderate Stigma High Stigma
Person's Model of Disability:	Moral; Medical; Social; Combined
Socioenvironmental Factors:	Accommodating . . . . Some . . . . Mostly Inhospitable

[a]Dimensions with dots connecting the descriptors are on a continuum; those separated by a semicolon are not on a continuum, and are not mutually exclusive.
[b]Within normal limits.

disability and the person. There are multiple ways to understand disability. In medicine disabilities are categorized by diagnosis (e.g., asthma; cerebral palsy) or by the system affected (e.g., nervous, musculoskeletal, cardiovascular, pulmonary, visual, and auditory systems). Other ways to consider disabilities is by a description of the bodily impairment (e.g., left hemiplegia, paraplegia) or by the functional limitations (e.g., mobility impairment, low vision). But to understand disability, all of these factors, plus others, should be considered. These factors include age of onset, the way in which onset occurred (e.g., accident, war, medical event) and the speed of onset (suddenly, incrementally), and the course of the disability and the degree of certainty about the course.

Table 19.1 shows various dimensions of disability that can be evaluated. As can be seen, two disabilities may appear functionally similar but be quite different in important ways. For example, a woman using a wheelchair might have MS, a disorder that has gradual onset, a course that is almost completely unpredictable, and virtually no effect on lifespan. Another woman using a wheelchair might have amyotrophic lateral sclerosis (ALS), a disorder that also has a gradual onset but that is unfortunately fairly predictable and life threatening (most die within 5 years of diagnosis; Sejvar, Holman, Bresee, Kochanek, & Schonberger, 2005). By viewing disabilities in all their complexity, we see that even seemingly simple questions such as *severity of disability* are difficult to determine.

LANGUAGE OF DISABILITY

Language shapes and is shaped by conceptualizations and meanings attached to conditions. Older words associated with disability, such as *crippled*, *retarded*, and *lunatic*, have mostly been discarded. Yet the language used to describe disability still tends to connote a negative valence (e.g., inflicted with, suffers from, burdened by, confined to). People continue to be described by their conditions (e.g., schizophrenics, an epileptic, the autistic), and the metaphor of disability is still used in daily language (e.g., traffic was snarled by a disabled big rig; turning a blind eye to; falling on deaf ears). To address this, the American Psychological Association's publication manual (6th edition, 2010) devotes a section to reducing bias in language. In the two paragraphs on disability, it asserts the overriding principle of "nonhandicapping" language (p. 76) and suggests people-first language (person who uses a wheelchair). It also suggests avoiding euphemisms that are condescending, as these can be patronizing, and suggests that the real words are too awful to say. Additionally, people with disabilities should not be referred to as patients unless it is a hospital or clinical setting.

These suggestions are useful guidelines, but there are more subtleties to the language of disability. Two words deserve special discussion: *burden* and *adjustment*. *Burden* is a word that is so often linked with disability in the literature that readers may fail to question the association. Titles focus on the burden of children's disabilities on mothers, the burden of costs of accommodations on businesses, the burden of caregiving, the financial burden of autism, and so on. Unfortunately, the burden of the disability generalizes too readily to the person with the disability.

Adjustment is a word that is often associated with disability (e.g., he has adjusted to the disability, or she has not adjusted to the

disability). There are at least three problems with this terminology. First, it places the burden of disability solely on the person with the disability, when we have just seen that disability is an interface of person and context. Second, it implies stages of adjustment to disability (most commonly those promulgated by Kubler-Ross, i.e., denial, bargaining, depression, anger, and acceptance), although numerous studies have shown that people do not follow stages of adjustment and the notion of stages should be discarded. Furthermore, depression is not a normal, modal, or expected response to disability; embracing a stage model of adjustment implies that it is. And third, adjustment connotes completion of the task—that is, one reaches adjustment and is done.

I prefer the term *response* to disability. Response implies fluidity and change; one's response can change often, markedly, radically, or almost imperceptibly, minutely, and subtly, but it is always changing. Response to disability is likely to be affected by changes in relationship status, becoming a parent, growing older, starting a new job, finding an appropriate assistive device, incurring an additional medical condition. Thus we expect the response to disability to be protean, and at times more or less negative or positive than at other times. By thinking of it in this way, we are less prone to pathologize those who may be experiencing more negative emotions, but also to see depression for what it is—namely, a treatable condition.

CONCEPTUALIZING DISABILITY

Elsewhere, Olkin (1999, 2002) has discussed three models of disability, namely the moral, medical, and social models. These models

Table 19.2 Comparison of the Moral, Medical, and Social Models of Disability

	Moral	Medical	Social
Meaning of disability	A defect caused by moral lapse or sins, failure of faith, evil, test of faith	A defect in or failure of a bodily system, which is inherently abnormal and pathological	A social construct; problems reside in the interaction of person and environment, and the failure of society to accommodate people with disabilities.
Moral implications	The disability brings shame to the person and his or her family.	A medical abnormality caused by genetics, bad health habits, and behavior	Society has failed a segment of its citizens and oppresses them.
Sample ideas	"God gives us only what we can bear" or "There's a reason I was chosen to have this disability."	Clinical descriptions of "patients" in medical terminology; isolation of body parts	"Nothing about us without us." "Civil rights, not charity."
Origins	Oldest model and still most prevalent worldwide	Mid-19th century; most common model in U.S.; entrenched in most rehabilitation clinics and journals	Early 1900s, then revived in 1975 with the demonstrations by people with disabilities in support of the then-unsigned Rehabilitation Act
Goals of intervention	Spiritual or divine; acceptance	"Cure" or amelioration of the disability to the greatest extent possible; "adjustment"	Political, economic, social, and policy systems, increased access and inclusion
Benefits of model	An acceptance of being selected, a special relationship with God, a sense of greater purpose to the disability	A lessened sense of shame and stigma; faith in medical intervention; spurs medical and technological advances	Promotes integration of the disability into the self; a sense of community and pride; depathologizing of disability
Negative effects	Shame, ostracization, need to conceal the disability or person with the disability	Paternalistic, promotes benevolence and charity; services for but not by people with disabilities	Powerlessness in the face of broad social and political changes needed; challenges to prevailing ideas

differ along multiple dimensions, including the meanings and moral implications of the disability, the target and goals of interventions, and the benefits versus negative effects of the model on the person with a disability and his or her family (see Table 19.2). These models may seem abstract, but they are clinically important. The language a client uses, the beliefs about causes of the disability and therefore appropriate interventions, and the relationship to the medical establishment will be greatly influenced by the model of disability. Additionally, the match or mismatch between the client and the clinician in language and approach will either facilitate or impair the relationship and hence the outcomes.

Although Olkin (1999) argued that clinicians should hold the social model, she cautions against imposing any model on clients. Furthermore, clinicians must be able to work effectively within any model of the family, helping to minimize the negative effects and maximize the benefits of the model.

Of course, clients rarely fall neatly into only one coherent set of beliefs. How might the three models interact? Theoretically, any one person could hold more than one model simultaneously, but intuitively it would seem that some models are more compatible than others. Unfortunately, there are scant empirical data on client beliefs about their own disabilities and the models they espouse.

However, one qualitative study (Wong, 2007) with monolingual Chinese immigrant parents of children with autism indicated that parents easily hold the moral and social models simultaneously, despite the seeming contradiction between these two sets of beliefs. For example, a father might attribute his son's autism to the mother's evil thoughts or deeds during pregnancy, yet be aware of his son's legal entitlements and emphatic about his need to ensure those rights for his son. But note that this study was limited by the fact that no measure of individuals' models of disability exists, and thus was based on a rubric (Olkin, 1999) that was modified (Wong, 2007) but has not yet been validated.

The discipline of health psychology often encompasses the medical model by linking behaviors and health outcomes. Because there can be both a correlation and a causal link between behavior and health, it is easy to lay the blame for negative health outcomes solely on the individual, though recent health psychology texts generally include information about global conditions affecting health (e.g., lack of clean drinking water). To take one example, obesity and heart problems are more common in poor areas (Wang, 2001; Zhang & Wang, 2004). Some of the individual behaviors that help account for this are eating more foods high in fat and fewer fresh fruits and vegetables. But the social level of the problem lies in part in the higher cost of healthier foods and the ready availability and lower costs of less-healthy foods. As practitioners we can focus on the individual level, or the socioeconomic level, or both levels. The danger is in focusing only on the individual level as the cause of health problems, without acknowledgement of larger social forces and constraints. Furthermore, there is a danger of overgeneralizing the relationship between

behaviors and health: It is an easy step from believing that diabetes is caused by poor eating habits, to smoking causes cancer, to incurring an SCI because of risky behaviors. This tendency to find causes and lay blame on the individual is protective in that it maintains a belief in a just and fair world (Dion, Berscheid, & Walster, 1972; Walster, 1966; Walster, Berscheid, & Walster, 1972), and facilitates belief in one's own immunity from disability. Because some of the correlations do imply causation (e.g., smoking and cancer), it is easy to mistakenly believe that other correlations do as well.

There is general understanding that demographic, economic, social, and cultural factors play a large role in health. For example, a current health psychology textbook asserts that "there is substantial evidence linking poor social conditions with ill-health" (Marks, Murray, Evans, & Vida Estacio, 2011, p. 1). These factors not only contribute to wellness or ill health, but they also influence how people understand health and illness, how they react to illness in themselves and others, and how they shape their belief systems (Marks et al., 2011). One belief system is about the relationship between mind and body. Culture greatly contributes to beliefs about this relationship. Traditionally Eastern cultures have viewed these as interdependent parts of a whole, and Western culture has made more of a binary split. But such distinctions recently have been more blurred. To use the various editions of the DSM as an example, the first edition listed epilepsy, a clearly neurological disorder, as a mental condition. Subsequent editions have gone back and forth about inclusion and exclusion of physiological disorders. The fourth edition underscored the relationship between mind and body by including as a rule-out diagnoses resulting from general medical conditions. Although it no longer included epilepsy, it did include dementias, another neurological disorder.

Greater integration of mind and body has been one force within health psychology, and it is here that the culture of the disability community can conflict with health psychology. In the disability community one might hear the phrase *I am not my body*, or *Do not judge me by my outside*. When the body carries conditions such as blindness, spasmodic movements, or drooling, the images these create in others tend to be negatively valenced. Although the person with that disability might integrate the body features into a self-concept that is whole (i.e., both mind and body), the prejudice of others gives rise to a disavowal of the body as an advertisement of the self.

Health psychology literature has seen the rise of the stress and coping model of health and wellness. A seemingly objective methodology (such as factor analysis) has been used to define good and bad, or useful and counterproductive, coping. How does this model apply to disability (as opposed to illness)? As discussed previously, response to disability can vary among many choices in a fluid way. Responses need to be viewed in the long term, and therefore ways of coping should not be considered in the short term. If one type of coping is associated with, say, depression, the depression is problematic, not the coping. The coping and depression may have circular causality, and it may be true that by changing the coping the depression will lift (and undoubtedly as the depression lifts, dormant types of coping will emerge). An important principle to keep in mind is that no one gives up a strategy, even one that isn't very effective, unless a different strategy is available.

One major stressor of living with a disability is not included in most of these stress and coping models, which is the barrage of micro-aggressions that people with disabilities encounter on a daily basis. These micro-aggressions could range in severity from minor (having to ask someone to reach something on a high shelf in a grocery store) to medium (a new acquaintance tells you about another person with a disability they know) to major (being rejected as a potential romantic partner because of the disability). Research indicates that the effects of micro-aggressions can affect health (Sue, 2010), although micro-aggressions specific to people with disabilities have not been studied.

Consider one common example to see how the idea of good and bad coping is complicated. Suppose a person who uses a wheelchair sees the last handicapped parking place taken by someone who does not have a handicapped placard and who does not appear disabled. Options for coping could include yelling at the person getting out of the car, politely asking that person if he or she has a handicapped parking placard, parking one's own car behind the illegally parked car such that the latter car cannot get out, parking elsewhere, or going home. What makes one of these a good or bad strategy? The answer might lie in the effects of the coping on the person, but those effects might vary from day to day. One day it might be beneficial to barely register the micro-aggression (unintended slights or social cues about one's disability status) and simply go about one's day, but on a different day it might be more beneficial to vent some of the anger that such behaviors engender. Furthermore, the disability community might value certain actions over others; generally, assertive responses to micro-aggressions are encouraged. But the ubiquity of micro-aggressions might make it imperative that a large portion of them become almost invisible, for the sake of one's personal mental health. Therefore, the benefits or deficits associated with any type of coping are malleable. Again, this puts disability culture and health psychology somewhat at odds in perspectives.

Disability culture and community (Olkin, 2005) has several norms and values that do integrate well with health psychology. One such value is *agency*, the idea of taking control of and being an active participant in your health and well-being. Being in partnership with one's medical service delivery system is a desirable goal. This goal is often thwarted heavily by insurance constraints, which tend to take choices out of consumers' hands. Compared with persons without disabilities, persons with disabilities are more likely to use government insurance and less likely to have private insurance, meaning that they tend to encounter decision-making models based on cost saving rather than on consumer choice.

The constrictions on choice can affect what is referred to as compliance and adherence on one hand, or noncompliance, assistive technology abandonment, or resistance on the other. Health psychology must of necessity consider how to best help individuals adopt healthy habits. The disability community might not view compliance in the same way. For example, among polio survivors, falling and its potential for injury is a problem. One study showed that the incidence of falling within the past 12 months was about 74%, and that most falls occur in the home (Bickerstaffe, Beelen, & Nollet, 2010). One question that arises is whether the person was using an assistive device or an orthotic at the time of the fall. Assistive devices and orthotics might

minimize the risk of falling (though their effects on the severity of the fall are less clear). Health psychology might view this as a compliance issue: If compliance with wearing an orthotic was higher, falling might be reduced. Furthermore, if polio survivors could be persuaded that falling is not inevitable, perhaps they would take more measures to prevent falling.

I see the problem very differently (I am a polio survivor). My house is 90%, but not 100%, wheelchair accessible. Most people with disabilities have to pay for housing modifications out of pocket, despite earning less than their neighbors (Olkin, Abrams, Preston, & Kirshbaum, 2006). Thus it is likely that assistive devices cannot go to all parts of the household. Furthermore, orthotics can irritate, especially in heat or cold. Thus not wearing it in the house is common. Taking off an orthotic when a foot is swollen or not using the wheelchair in the inaccessible bathroom may seem necessary. These decisions are ways of balancing out contradictory needs and making choices about immediate physical priorities. I would call that agency (i.e., asserting personal power and choice), rather than noncompliance with orthotic use.

RESPONSES TO DISABILITY

In addition to the difficulties with the language and conceptualization of *adjustment* versus *response* to disability, there have been numerous methodological problems in studies examining outcomes of disability. In brief, these include inexact definitions of terms (e.g., not specifying whether depression met diagnostic criteria), inappropriate control groups, cross-sectional designs, and biased sampling (e.g., clinical populations). Thus good data on basic questions, such as whether rates of clinical syndromes are higher in people with disabilities, are lacking. Furthermore, although the past decade has seen some research on positive outcomes to disability (c.f., Kennedy, Lude, Elfstrom, & Smithson, 2010; Kortte, Gilbert, Gorman, & Wegener, 2010; White, Driver, & Warren, 2010), most of the research is pathology focused, depriving us of potentially useful information on resilience and hardiness. Researchers and clinicians should include measures of positive outcomes and not just the absence of negative outcomes. Empirically, the opposite of depression is not-depressed, which is different than happiness or satisfaction. Studies that measure both ends of the spectrum can inform us better about how to not only diminish negative outcomes but increase positive outcomes.

That said, three negative responses could be problematic and require professional intervention. These are clinical depression, anxiety, and posttraumatic stress disorder (PTSD). Regarding *depression*, there cannot be a simple answer to whether people with disabilities have higher rates of clinical depression (Olkin, 2004). First, the definition of disability changes from study to study. Second, the array of disabilities is too varied; how could we lump together a child with muscular dystrophy with an adult with osteoporosis, or a man with late-onset hearing loss with a congenitally Deaf mother? Third, age and gender are associated with depression, such that rates increase with age, and women are twice as likely to experience clinical depression as men (Nolen-Hoeksema, 2001); therefore, disabilities affecting more women than men and older versus younger populations may be more associated with depression, but not caused by the disability. Fourth, models of coping, social support, and depression would seem to vary by ethnicity, and models tested

on one ethnicity should not be generalized to other ethnicities (c.f., Zea, Belgrave, Townsend, Jarama, & Banks, 1996). Fifth, some disabilities may directly physically influence rates of depression (e.g., MS seems to increase depression; in trisomy 21 [Down syndrome] the rates are lower than in the general population). Sixth, selecting the appropriate comparison group is not simple. If the disability is early onset, perhaps the comparison group would be other children experiencing adversity, rather than just nondisabled children. If the disability is later onset, perhaps the control group should be people who have experienced other stressors. Studies have tended to use the absence of disability as the appropriate comparison without controlling for other factors. Seventh, studies have focused on variables such as coping, family support, and time since disability, but have not well-delineated sources and effects of stigma, discrimination, prejudice, and microaggressions. Lastly, the higher incidence of being a victim of abuse (see later section) increases the chances of psychiatric difficulties.

Although empirical research discredits it, there is still a pervasive belief that onset of a disability requires mourning of a loss. In fact, an episode of clinical depression is the best predictor of future depression, and most people who incur a disability do not become depressed (Olkin, 2004; Pollard & Kennedy, 2007). Although some women may perceive the disability as a loss (of health, or former abilities), mourning does not seem to be the modal response, nor is mourning a necessary stage (Olkin, 2004). Furthermore, finding meaning in the disability may not be necessary for adjustment (Davis, Wortman, Lehman, & Cohen Silver, 2000).

Despite several studies suggesting that people with disabilities have a higher lifetime risk of depression than the general nondisabled population (Neese & Finlayson, 1996; Turner & Beiser, 1990; Turner & Noh, 1988), it seems that only about 30% (plus or minus 5%) of persons with acquired disability will experience depression in the year after disability onset (Frank, Elliott, Corcoran, & Wonderlich, 1987; Heinrich & Tate, 1996; Lichtenberg, 1997; Turner & McLean, 1989; Weissman & Myers, 1978). Furthermore, depression after disability onset is still the best predictor of subsequent episodes of depression, meaning that episodes of depression are predictors of future episodes, rather than disability per se. But the caveats in the previous paragraphs should be kept in mind when reading this research. Generally, it is better to examine rates of depression for specific disabilities than to try to compare people with and without disabilities. (For a review of depression in six specific disabilities—three physical disabilities, one intellectual disability, and two sensory disabilities—see Olkin, 2004.)

Regarding *anxiety*, the aforementioned issues apply, along with some additional ones. Later-onset disability can be associated with great disruptions of family and partner relationships, parenting, transportation abilities, employment and hence income and insurance, and activities of daily living (ADL). These interruptions, separately or synergistically, may well be expected to affect levels of anxiety. Studies of anxiety in persons with disabilities generally have not included these variables, and there are no reviews of rates of anxiety disorders (except PTSD) among people with disabilities. There are studies on specific disabilities, especially SCI (Hancock, Craig, Dickson, Chang, & Martin, 1993; Kennedy & Rogers, 2000) and stroke (Burvill et al., 1995; Langhorne et al., 2000), but it is premature to make generalizations about approximate rates of anxiety disorders among

people with disabilities. However, screening for anxiety is important, as is not assuming a causal link between disability and anxiety. As with disability and depression, pain is a complicating factor associated with negative mood states.

Several studies over the past two decades have examined rates of PTSD in certain groups of people with later-onset disabilities, usually SCI (Agar, Kennedy, & King, 2006; Chung, Preveza, Papandreou, & Preveza, 2006) or traumatic brain injury (TBI) (King, 2008; Klein, Gaspi, & Gill, 2003). SCI and TBI are often associated with a traumatic onset, such as gunshots, accidents, or wartime conflict, which in themselves could lead to PTSD. Additionally, onset of SCI or TBI requires incredible reconfiguring of basic ADL, as well as prolonged hospitalization and rehabilitation. Thus it is not surprising to see higher rates of PTSD in people with these two disabilities, but we should be quite cautious in generalizing from SCI and TBI to persons with other types of disabilities.

Women with disabilities might be expected to have higher rates of negative outcomes compared with men with disabilities, not because of the disability per se, but because of factors associated with being female, such as histories of sexual abuse, lower rates of employment, lower incomes, lower rates of marriage, and cognitive styles more associated with depression. Studies of women with disabilities should include these types of background and demographic variables, so that outcomes are not misattributed to disability status. Additionally, the ways in which a woman with a disability views her situation (appraisal) may be more informative than her stress and coping scores (c.f., Lequerica et al., 2010).

In the past decade, research looking at *positive outcomes* associated with various disabilities has increased somewhat. There has been a recognition that absence of negative outcomes is not the same thing as positive outcomes, and quality of life (QOL) has become an important outcome variable in health psychology. Most of the research on QOL and people with disabilities has focused on disabilities acquired later in life and health conditions such as stroke and heart attacks. Most studies of children with disabilities focus on the effects on family and do not examine QOL for the children. Thus, not much is known about the life course and its quality for adults with early-onset disabilities.

Regarding women with disabilities, a few studies suggest factors that would be important for clinicians to know. Ever since Wright, in her seminal book on physical disabilities (1963), wrote about realignment of values as a factor in response to disability, surprisingly few studies have examined whether people do, in fact, adjust their values after disability onset. One such study compared chronically ill women to women without a chronic disease 7 years apart, when the women were a mean age of 42 and 58, respectively (Chen, Kasen, & Cohen, 2009). Although both groups of women showed significant changes in life values with age, those with chronic disease showed more change, with increased valuation of health and love and decreased valuation of extrinsic values (power, fame, attractiveness). These changes were associated with better mental health for the women with chronic illnesses but not for those without.

It may be that a woman's style of cognitions are important in her well-being. A study on stress appraisal used interviews with 50 women with SCI regarding their experiences of stress and coping (Lequerica et al., 2010). They found that appraisal of stress could affect life satisfaction apart from the coping strategies used. They suggested that interventions to facilitate coping with loss and enhancing problem-solving skills, as well as education about available resources, could change how stressors are perceived and thus diminish the negative impact of stressors. An intriguing idea related to appraisal comes from a study on persons with SCI incurred through a motor vehicle accident or violence, in which forgiveness (of self and of others) was associated with positive outcomes (Webb, Toussaint, Kalpakjian, & Tate, 2010).

Another study of mental health in women with physical disabilities showed that seven weekly sessions focusing on health issues increased scores in several areas, including self-efficacy for diet, medical decision making, social interaction, and physical functioning. Additionally, the impact of physical limitations on role activities was reduced, and overall vitality increased (Hughes, Nosek, Howland, Groff, & Dolan Mullen, 2003). Self-efficacy and agency are similar ideas, and both seem related to the well-being of women with disabilities.

Women with a new-onset disability could benefit from being given information about options open to them. A simple example is to give a woman the toll-free number for the national association related to her disability; from that resource she can find local support groups, brochures, and suggested readings. But it is unclear how much information beyond medical data women are given. For example, one study found that women with physical disabilities who participated in sports did not learn about the possibility for wheelchair sports from medical professionals (Ruddell & Shinew, 2006). Similarly, women with later-onset disabilities are unlikely to receive information about the impact of their disability on sexuality or any specific suggestions for sexual activities (Nosek, Howland, Rintala, Young, & Chanpong, 2001). Although there is a lot of information to impart when a woman has a new disability, the psychosocial aspects of the disability tend to receive less attention.

FACTORS OF CLINICAL IMPORTANCE

So far I have emphasized the variability of disability and the need to see disability in the context of the woman (e.g., ethnicity, age, religion, socioeconomic status), the model of disability she holds (moral, medical, social, or combined), and the woman's culture (family, community, and society). Nonetheless, there are a few issues common across many disabilities, and for which some special training is helpful. These include common physical effects of disability (fatigue, pain, and falling and the fear of falling) and the increased probability of violence (sexual abuse, physical abuse, and neglect) and different forms of violence that people with disabilities experience. Additionally, encountering stigma and micro-aggressions are common across most, if not all, disabilities. I briefly discuss these issues in the following sections.

Physical Concomitants of Disability

Several physical concomitants of disability are sufficiently frequent and disruptive that they merit attention: pain, fatigue, and falling. These issues may bring women to a clinic, or they may complain about them to a medical professional.

Fatigue is a misleading word, because it is used in common language to denote the effects of a few days of intense activity and/or decreased sleep. The remedy for this type of fatigue is a good night's rest and perhaps a day of taking it easy. In contrast, the fatigue associated with disability is usually chronic and not equated with sleepiness. The remedy is careful management of activities—not just over the day but over the week and month. It requires avoiding getting overfatigued, because doing so can mandate several days or even weeks of reduced activity. Every decision to do one activity affects whether one can decide to do another activity. So a one-hour commute to and from work may mean that Saturdays are days of imposed rest. Attending a dinner party on Friday night might mean not going grocery shopping that weekend. These are the trade-offs that women with disabilities must contend with on a daily basis. If we add parenting to the activity list, then it becomes apparent that other compromises must be made. It is not surprising, therefore, that several studies have shown that even educated women with disabilities who hold advanced degrees tend to opt out of the workforce when they become parents (Cohen, 1998; Conley-Jung & Olkin, 2001; Olkin et al., 2006).

Women with disabilities who live in poorer communities have additional challenges. The physical environment is less likely to be accessible (e.g., fewer curb cuts, more housing and stores that are inaccessible), public transportation is not as good, and services are farther away. Additionally poorer women with disabilities are less likely to have their own transportation, less likely to have flexible health insurance, and more likely to have to travel farther to work and clinics. These factors combine with fatigue to make daily life more difficult to manage.

Pain is not a concomitant of all disabilities, but of many of them. (See Siddall, 2009, for a review of pain after SCI.) Coping with pain, especially on a daily basis, requires energy. In some cases, pain can serve as a signal (e.g., to rest, to use an assistive device, to change position), and in some cases it serves no purpose at all (neuropathic pain). Differentiating these two types of pain puts demands on the person to monitor, evaluate, ignore, or act, all of which takes psychoemotional and physical energy. Thus pain interacts with fatigue and is one cause of fatigue.

People with disabilities who experience pain may not be referred to pain clinics as often as nondisabled persons with pain of unknown origins, because the pain is of known origin. That doesn't mean the pain is easily treatable. Additionally, it may not be a part of routine exams; that is, medical professionals may not inquire about pain or its management in outpatient settings (though this has become more routine in inpatient settings). Furthermore, the physician who is expert in the disability may not have corollary knowledge of pain management, and the language the medical profession uses is not how people with disabilities or chronic conditions talk about pain (Zelman et al., 2004). Physicians and drug companies generally use a numbered pain scale, whereas persons with disability or chronic conditions think about the impact of the pain and whether the pain was manageable or whether it significantly interfered with activity and/or attention. For various reasons, on one day a pain level of six might be manageable, but on another day it may put the person out of commission. Reasons could include how long the pain has been experienced, what the tasks of the day are, other psychosocial stressors, the location of pain, availability of assistive devices, and

so on. Thus a scale of manageability may be a better barometer than a scale of intensity.

People with disabilities tend to see a variety of professionals, such as a general practitioner, a specialist in their disability, a specialist in assistive devices, and a physician who manages their pain medication. If they have a secondary condition, even more professionals are involved. This segments the person into body parts or functions. An important role for health psychologists is to collate the information from various sources into one place and help clients navigate through the medical labyrinth. It is important that pain and fatigue are seen as relevant not just by the specialist but with each healthcare provider. Without this coordination it is easy to assume that another professional is handling an issue and to overlook other (nondisability) causes of symptoms. Asking about pain, taking it seriously, and having pain management ideas is important for virtually every professional who works with people with disabilities. This seems simple enough, but it is something people with disabilities complain about.

For example, one study showed that most people with SCI are dissatisfied with the level of knowledge about SCI pain their health providers have (Norman et al., 2010). Conversely, from the perspective of the professional, it can be difficult to differentiate a legitimate need for high doses of pain medication from drug seeking by patients. For later onset of disability, there is the advantage of being able to inquire about predisability substance use, which is the best predictor of postdisability substance use. But the ability to evaluate and treat chronic pain in women with disabilities needs more attention.

Falls can be a complicating factor for many disabilities. Falling, like pain, is underevaluated and treated (or, in this case, prevented). Falls in older persons with some types of disabilities are associated with depression (direction of causality has not been determined; Olkin, 2004). Falls may be much more common than professionals believe. For example, in one study of persons with polio, 74% had fallen at least once in the past year (most more than once; Bickerstaffe et al., 2010). In another study, 62% of persons with SCI who could walk some had fallen in the past 6 months (Wirz, Muller, & Bastiaenen, 2010). It may be that many people with disabilities expect to fall and see it as a necessary part of living with the disability. This expectation is problematic for several reasons. First, and obviously, falls can lead to secondary injuries (16% of those who had fallen, in the Bickerstaffe et al., 2010 study, sustained a major injury). As people age, falls can cause more serious damage and are more likely to lead to broken bones. Thus preventing falls prevents other injuries, hitting the head, or even accidental death. Second, this perception of falling as normal may impede a search for solutions to prevent falling, such as putting up ramps and grab bars, using an assistive device more often, resting more frequently, and other such measures. Third, the fear of falling may impact activity levels even more than falling itself, as those who fall are more likely to reduce ambulation more than those who don't fall (Bickerstaffe et al., 2010).

Violence

People with disabilities are more likely to be victims of violence, abuse, and rape. Although tracking down how much more likely is difficult for all the expected reasons (definitions of disability, sampling problems), most studies consistently show higher

exposure to violence of all sorts (Brownridge, 2006; Chang et al., 2003; Horner-Johnson & Drum, 2006; Nosek, Foley, Hughes, & Howland, 2001; Sobsey, 2000; Ticoll, 1994). The problem is not limited to any one country and may be greater in countries in which disability is even more highly stigmatized. For example, a survey from the state of Orissa, India, found that virtually all of the women and girls with disabilities were beaten at home, 25% of the women with intellectual disabilities had been raped, and 6% of the women with disabilities had been forcibly sterilized (Mohapatra & Mohanty, 2004). Studies on children with disabilities likewise show consistently higher rates of physical and sexual abuse compared to their nondisabled peers (Bonner, Crow, & Hensley, 1997; Crosse, 1992; Kvam, 2000; Putnam, 2003; Sullivan & Knutson, 2000). Additionally, data support the idea that people with disabilities are targets of hate crimes (Grattet & Jenness, 2001; McMahon, West, Lewis, Armstrong, & Conway, 2004; Petersilia, 2001; Putnam, 2003; Teplin, McClelland, Abram, & Weiner, 2005; Waxman, 1991).

In addition to the higher rates, other factors about abuse of people with disabilities are important. First is that the abusers are more likely to be people in their daily lives, such as family or caregivers. Second, the nature of the abuse may include vulnerabilities specific to the disability, such as disconnecting a wheelchair battery to immobilize a person, leaving someone on the toilet for long stretches, not fixing an automatic door opener, or removing door openers. Third, some studies indicate that the abuse continues for a longer period for women with disabilities, perhaps in part because of dependence on others for assistance (Nosek, Foley, et al., 2001; Nosek,

Howland, et al., 2001). Other types of abuse could be called social abuse, such as stereotypes (e.g., of asexuality or passivity), lack of access to adaptive equipment, inaccessibility of homes (one's own and one's neighbors'), increased experiences of being the one provided help in medical or other service settings, and diminished employment options. Assessment of abuse should be a routine part of screening.

Substance Abuse

Some disabilities are closely associated with accidents, such as traumatic brain injury and SCI. Such accidents are more likely when the person abuses substances. Drug tests at hospital admission show a high rate of positive tests for drugs or alcohol use for TBI (Taylor, Kreutzer, Demm, & Meade, 2003). However, it would not be appropriate to generalize from one type of disability, especially one so closely linked to accidents, to other disabilities, especially those with congenital or early onset. Although I do not review the rates of substance abuse among people with varying disabilities here, the main point to take away is that substance use prior to disability onset is the best predictor of substance use after disability onset. Furthermore, those medicines used for control of major pain (e.g., oxycontin, vicodin, percoset) unfortunately are those more prone to substance abuse. Screening for substance use and abuse is an important part of clinical assessment.

Medical Trauma

Adults with early-onset disabilities may have experienced one or more traumas as children with disabilities, and these may have lasting psychoemotional effects. So it is important

not to attribute effects to disability per se, but to the sequelae of disability. For example, children with disabilities may have experienced hospitalizations, one or more surgeries, multiple doctor visits, physical rehabilitation, fittings for orthotics, and other interactions with professionals related to their disability. These experiences may have involved separation from family at early ages or repeated separations (this is especially true for older persons, before outpatient surgeries were more common). *Medical stripping* is a common experience—when a doctor leads a group of interns/residents in a discussion of the patient's case, often when the patient is partially or completely nude. Some people with disabilities may report feeling abandoned or being yelled at by nurses, and even sexual abuse. One small qualitative study of gay men with disabilities found a 40% rate of sexual abuse during childhood hospitalizations (Olkin & Loewy, 2011); data are difficult to find on this phenomenon, but it should be routinely asked about in clinical interviews.

Although experiences with medical professionals will vary widely, it is likely that children with disabilities have had at least one or more unpleasant medical experiences. This is not to blame the professionals; rather, professionals are associated with unpleasant events, such as shots, cutting of casts with scary spinning wheels, pain after surgery, and so on. Sometimes it is the fault of the professionals who are, after all, not immune to pervasive negative stereotypes about people with disabilities and who most commonly encounter such people as patients rather than peers. Additionally, the office personnel and environment can reawaken earlier trauma in the initial and subsequent interactions with patients. As discussed in the section on micro-aggressions, simple environmental factors (counter heights) and interactions (the nurse not telling you the results of the blood pressure reading) can be experienced very negatively by someone with a history of medical traumas. In light of these negative experiences, some people with disabilities have a negative stance toward the medical establishment. Health psychologists may not see themselves as part of the medical establishment, but their clients likely do. Thus feelings toward doctors will be conferred on health psychologists. Rather than distancing oneself from medicine, it may be more helpful in the long run to accept the label and provide a positive experience, thereby positively affecting the core beliefs about medical professionals.

Stigma and Micro-Aggressions

The stigma attached to disability is indisputable (Bagenstos, 2000; Yuker, 1994). Nonetheless, stigma does vary with type of disability (Olkin & Howson, 1994). Family is an important source of anti-stigma, an environment that can foster resilience against stigma. Of course, not all families are uniformly affirming, and children with disabilities usually grow up surrounded by mixed messages about their disabilities. Children in the U.S. educational system quickly learn what it means to be in resource room, to have an aide, to be pulled out of the classroom for individual tutoring, or to be in the slower math group. Derogatory words are still prevalent on the playground (e.g., *spazz, moron, retarded*). Thus it is not possible for even the most accepting family to shield a child with a disability from these messages, or for the child to come of age without internalizing some of the negativity.

That negativity gets played out throughout life in the form of micro-aggressions (Sue, 2010). Sue defines *micro-aggressions* as unintended slights or social cues by members of a dominant group that demean members of minority groups because of their minority status. He notes that micro-aggressions have become less apparent and more subtle over time, making them harder to identify and acknowledge. In his book he documents the negative consequences of micro-aggressions on the targets, including psychological, emotional, and health outcomes. Although he limited his topic to people of color, women, and gays, the concept can be extended to people with disabilities. Like these other groups, people with disabilities are likely to encounter multiple micro-aggressions in education, work, social interactions, and healthcare. But unlike these groups, people with disabilities also encounter micro-aggressions in the environment, through inaccessibility of housing, neighborhoods, public places, and work sites. Furthermore, people with disabilities are the only group where it is still legal to segregate (e.g., special seating in theaters, separate entrances, transportation, drinking fountains, and bathrooms). Although this segregation may be one way to ensure accessibility, it is also a daily reminder of one's disability status.

As discussed in the section on medical traumas, healthcare can be one of the venues of micro-aggressions. Attitudes toward disability are no better, and may in some cases be even worse, among healthcare providers (Basnett, 2001; Rainville, Bagnall, & Phalen, 1995; Streiner, Saigal, Burrows, Stoskopf, & Rosenbaum, 2001; Tervo & Palmer, 2004). Importantly, clients with disabilities may perceive health psychologists as medical personnel and generalize some negative feelings and cognitions to them. Because health psychologists do work with health professionals and often in healthcare environments, they may need to be aware of the physical and personnel environment from a disability perspective and take extra efforts to make their office a welcoming and accessible place. This includes how phone calls are handled, whether there is ample handicapped parking, whether the environment is clearly marked and easily accessible even when crowded, if signs and other materials are in Braille and large print, and if language used is simple and straightforward.

An appointment can impose multiple micro-aggressions even before the person is seen by the health psychologist if the physical and psychosocial environment contains barriers. Even simple acts (such as holding a door open, commenting on someone's shoes, giving overly detailed instructions about where you are headed) can carry different meanings for people with disabilities. For example, when a woman uses a wheelchair, her feet are more on display than if she were walking, so commenting on her shoes is a subtle reminder of her seated status. It is simply not possible to anticipate all of these interactions or the variations in people's responses to them. Therefore, attention to basic etiquette guidelines (APA, no date; Olkin, 1999) is advised. But most important is to be so genuinely comfortable with a variety of types of disabilities that your behaviors—even those subtle behaviors such as eye contact and smiling—are not unconsciously influenced by the presence of a disability.

CONCLUSIONS AND RECOMMENDATIONS

For Clinicians

1. Working with people with disabilities requires some specialized knowledge. Being culturally appropriate implies learning about the culture of disability, the experiences that are more common for people with disabilities, the ways of conceptualizing disability, and the language to use when talking with people with disabilities who espouse particular beliefs.

2. The cultures of health psychology and disability have some important commonalities—namely the goals of agency, of integrating the self into one whole, and the attention to culture and diversity in interactions. They differ in some respects with regard to integration of mind and body.

3. Models of disability are important; interactions and treatment should be consistent with the client's model. Even within a model, ethnicity may play a large role in views of disability, family, community, employment, and participation. Interactions have to be tailored to the model, the culture, and the individual.

4. Several experiences should be routine in screenings, namely any history of physical or sexual abuse, substance use/abuse, falling, and pain. Many factors will affect a person's responses to being touched, being unclothed, and displaying parts of the body to others.

5. Do your homework. People with disabilities are experts about their own responses to disability, but they should not be expected to teach you about the disability in general, their ethnicity, or their culture.

6. You are part of a medical service delivery system, and feelings about that system will be transferred to

you. Therefore, it is important that you contribute to a welcoming environment that is as free of micro-aggressions as possible. This might include training staff regarding interactions with persons with disabilities and altering the physical environment to be more user friendly.

For Researchers

7. The term *disability* is too broad, and researchers should be careful to focus more specifically on either a diagnosis or, as appropriate, functional impairments.

8. It is important to assess variables besides disability, such as history of trauma and abuse, substance use, and socioeconomic factors, so that conclusions are not erroneously attributed solely to disability status.

9. Using nondisability as a criterion for control groups is not sufficient. Doing so may mean that the two groups (those with and without disabilities) differ not just on disability, but on other sequelae of disability (e.g., violence, trauma, experiences of micro-aggressions, pain).

10. Differences across disabilities could illuminate variables in responses to disability. For example, comparing persons with mobility limitations caused by different disabilities (such as polio, MS, SCI) could help explain the variables influencing adjustment.

11. Responses to disability should not be pathologized, but rather conceptualized as variable responses to the ongoing factors inherent in being a stigmatized person.

12. Persons with disabilities should be involved in all levels of research, from question generation to data interpretation and dissemination.

REFERENCES

Agar, E., Kennedy, P., & King, N. S. (2006). The role of negative cognitive appraisals in PTSD symptoms following spinal cord injuries. *Behavioural and Cognitive Psychology, 34*, 437–452.

American Association of People with Disabilities (AAPD). (2011). Annual Disability Statistics Compendium. Retrieved from http://www.aapd.com/site/apps/nlnet/content2.aspx?c=pvI1IkNWJqE&b=5818457&ct=8848455&notoc=1

American Psychological Association. (2010). *Publication manual of the American Psychological Association.* Washington, DC: Author.

American Psychological Association. (no date). Enhancing your interactions with people with disabilities. Retrieved from http://www.apa.org/pi/disability/resources/publications/enhancing.aspx

Americans with Disabilities Act of 1990, Public Law 101-336, 42 U.S.C. 12111, 12112.

Anderson, C. J., & Vogel, L. C. (2002). Employment outcomes of adults who sustained spinal cord injuries as children or adolescents. *Archives of Physical Medicine and Rehabilitation, 83*, 791–801.

Bagenstos, S. R. (2000). Subordination, stigma, and "disability." *Virginia Law Review, 86*(3), 398–534.

Basnett, I. (2001). Health care professionals and their attitudes toward and decisions affecting disabled people. In G. L. Albrecht, K. Seelman, & M. Bury (Eds.), *Handbook of disability studies* (pp. 450–464) Thousand Oaks, CA: Sage.

Belle, D. (1990). Poverty and women's mental health. *American Psychologist, 45*(3), 385–389.

Bianchi, S. M. (1995). Changing economic roles of women and men. In R. Farley (Ed.), *State of the union: American in the 1990s, Volume I: Economic trends* (pp. 107–154). New York, NY: Russell Sage Foundation.

Bickerstaffe, A., Beelen, A., & Nollet, F. (2010). Circumstances and consequences of falls in polio survivors. *Journal of Rehabilitation Medicine, 42*(10), 908–915.

Bonner, B. L., Crow, S. M., & Hensley, L. D. (1997). State efforts to identify maltreated children with disabilities: A follow-up study. *Child Maltreatment*, *2*(1), 52–60.

Bound, J., & Waidmann, T. (2002). Accounting for recent declines in employment rates among working-aged men and women with disabilities. *The Journal of Human Resources*, *37*(2), 231–250.

Brandon, T., & Pritchard, G. (2011). "Being fat": A conceptual analysis using three models of disability. *Disability and Society*, *26*(1), 79–92.

Brownridge, D. A. (2006). Partner violence against women with disabilities: Prevalence, risks, and explanations. *Violence Against Women*, *12*(9), 805–822.

Burvill, P. W., Johnson, G. A., Jamrozik, K. D., Anderson, C. S., Stewart-Wynne, E. G., & Chakera, T. M. (1995). Anxiety disorders after stroke: Results from the Perth Community Stroke Study. *The British Journal of Psychiatry*, *166*, 328–332.

Chang, J. C., Martin, S. L., Moracco, K. E., Dulli, L., Scandlin, D., Loucks-Sorrel, M. B., . . . Bou-Saada, I. (2003). Helping women with disabilities and domestic violence: Strategies, limitations, and challenges of domestic violence programs and services. *Journal of Women's Health*, *12*(7), 699–708.

Chapin, M. H., & Holbert, D. (2010). Employment at closure is associated with enhanced quality of life and subjective well-being for persons with spinal cord injuries. *Rehabilitation Counseling Bulletin*, *54*(1), 6–14.

Chen, H., Kasen, S., & Cohen, P. (2009). Life values and mental health: A longitudinal study comparing chronically ill women to women without chronic disease. *Psychology and Health*, *24*(4), 395–405.

Chung, M. C., Preveza, E., Papandreou, K., & Preveza, N. (2006). The relationship between post-traumatic stress disorder following spinal cord injury and locus of control. *Journal of Affective Disorders*, *93*(1), 229–232.

Cohen, L. J. (1998). *Mothers' perceptions of the influence of their physical disabilities on the developmental tasks of children*. Unpublished doctoral dissertation, California School of Professional Psychology, Alameda, CA.

Conley-Jung, C., & Olkin, R. (2001). Mothers with visual impairments or blindness raising young children. *Journal of Visual Impairments or Blindness*, *91*(1), 14–29.

Crosse, S. B. (1992). A report on the maltreatment of children with disabilities. Washington, DC: National Center on Child Abuse and Neglect. Retrieved from http://eric.ed.gov/PDFS/ED365089.pdf

Davis, C. G., Wortman, C. B., Lehman, D. R., & Cohen Silver, R. (2000). Searching for meaning in loss: Are clinical assumptions correct? *Death Studies*, *24*, 497–540.

Dion, K., Berscheid, E., & Walster, E. (1972). What is beautiful is good. *Journal of Personality and Social Psychology*, *24*(3), 285–290.

Fadyl, J. K., & McPherson, K. M. (2010). Understanding decisions about work after spinal cord injury. *Journal of Occupational Rehabilitation*, *20*, 69–80.

Frank, R. G., Elliott, T. R., Corcoran, J. R., & Wonderlich, S. A. (1987). Depression after SCI: Is it necessary? *Clinical Psychology Review*, *7*, 611–630.

Gorzkowski, J. A., Kelly, E. H., Klaas, S. J., & Vogel, L. (2010). Girls with spinal cord injury: Social and job related participation and psychosocial outcomes. *Rehabilitation Psychology*, *55*(1), 58–67.

Grattet, R., & Jenness, V. (2001). Examining the boundaries of hate crime law: Disabilities and the "dilemma of difference." *The Journal of Criminal Law and Criminology*, *91*(30), 653–698.

Gregg, E. W., Beckles, G. L., Williamson, D. F., Leveille, S. G., Langlois, J. A., Engelgau, M. M., & Narayan, K. M. (2000). Diabetes and physical disability among older U.S. adults. *Diabetes Care*, *23*(9), 1272–1277.

Guralnik, J. M., & Simonsick, E. M. (1993). Physical disability in older Americans. *Journal of Gerontology*, *48*, 3–10.

Hancock, K. M., Craig, A. R., Dickson, H. G., Chang, E., & Martin, J. (1993). Anxiety and depression over the first year of spinal cord injury: A longitudinal study. *Paraplegia*, *31*, 349–357.

Hawker, G., A., Wright, J. G., Coyte, P. C., Williams, J. I., Harvey, B., Glazier, R., & Badley, E. M. (2000). Differences between men and women in the rate of use of hip and knee arthroplasty. *New England Journal of Medicine*, *342*, 1016–1022.

Heinrich, R., & Tate, D. (1996). Latent variable structure of the Brief Symptom Inventory in a sample of persons with spinal cord injuries. *Rehabilitation Psychology*, *41*, 131–148.

Horner-Johnson, W., & Drum, C. E. (2006). Prevalence of maltreatment of people with intellectual disabilities: A review of recently published research. *Mental Retardation and Developmental Disabilities Research Reviews*, 12(1), 57–69.

Hughes, R. B., Nosek, M. A., Howland, C. A., Groff, J. Y., Dolan Mullen, P. (2003). Health promotion for women with physical disabilities: A pilot study. *Rehabilitation Psychology*, 48(3), 182–188.

Kennedy, P., Lude, P., Elfstrom, M. L., & Smithson, E. (2010). Sense of coherence and psychological outcomes in people with spinal cord injury: Appraisals and behavioural responses. *British Journal of Health Psychology*, 15, 611–621.

Kennedy, P., & Rogers, B. A. (2000). Anxiety and depression after spinal cord injury: A longitudinal analysis. *Archives of Physical Medicine and Rehabilitation*, 81(7), 932–937.

King, N. S. (2008). PTSD and traumatic brain injury: Folklore and fact? *Brain Injury*, 22(1), 1–5.

Klein, E., Gaspi, Y., & Gill, S. (2003). The relation between memory of the traumatic event and PTSD: Evidence from studies of traumatic brain injury. *The Canadian Journal of Psychiatry*, 48, 28–33.

Kortte, K. B., Gilbert, M., Gorman, P., & Wegener, S. (2010). Positive psychological variables in the prediction of life satisfaction after spinal cord injury. *Rehabilitation Psychology*, 55(1), 40–47.

Krause, J. S., Saunders, L., & Staten, D. (2010). Race-ethnicity, education, and employment after spinal cord injury. *Rehabilitation Counseling Bulletin*, 53(2), 78–86.

Kvam, M. H. (2000). Is sexual abuse of children with disabilities disclosed? A retrospective analysis of child disability and the likelihood of sexual abuse among those attending Norwegian hospitals. *Child Abuse and Neglect*, 24(8), 1073–1084.

Langhorne, P., Stott, D. J., Robertson, L., MacDonald, J., Jones, L., McAlpine, C., . . . Murray, G., (2000). Medical complications after stroke: A multicenter study. *Stroke*, 31, 1223–1229.

Lequerica, A. H., Forchheimer, M., Albright, K. J., Tate, D. G., Duggan, C., & Rahman, R. O. (2010). Stress appraisal in women with spinal cord injury: Supplementary findings through mixed methods. *International Journal of Stress Management*, 17(3), 259–275.

Lichtenberg, P. (1997). The DOUR project: A program of depression research in geriatric rehabilitation

minority inpatients. *Rehabilitation Psychology*, 42, 103–114.

Marks, D., Murray, M., Evans, B., & Vida Estacio, E. (2011). *Health psychology: Theory, research and practice* (3rd ed.). Thousand Oaks, CA: Sage.

McMahon, B. T., West, S. L., Lewis, A. N., Armstrong, A. J., & Conway, J. P. (2004). Hate crimes and disability in America. *Rehabilitation Counseling Bulletin*, 47(2), 66–75.

Mohapatra, S., & Mohanty, M. (2004). Abuse and activity limitation: A study on domestic violence against disabled women in Orissa, India. Retrieved from http://www.swabhiman.org/Domestic%20%20Violence.pdf

Neese, R. E., & Finlayson, F. E. (1996). Management of depression in patients with coexisting medical illness. *American Family Physician*, 53, 2125–2133.

Nolen-Hoeksema, S. (2001). Gender differences in depression. *Current Directions in Psychological Science*, 10(5), 173–176.

Norman, C., Bender, J., MacDonald, J., Dunn, M., Dunne, S., Siu, B., . . . Hunter, J. (2010). Questions that individuals with spinal cord injury have regarding their chronic pain: A qualitative study. *Disability and Rehabilitation*, 32(2), 114–124.

Nosek, M. A., Foley, C. C., Hughes, R. B., & Howland, C. A. (2001). Vulnerabilities for abuse among women with disabilities. *Sexuality and Disability*, 19(3), 177–189.

Nosek, M. A., Howland, C., Rintala, D. H., Young, M. E., & Chanpong, G. F. (2001). National study of women with disabilities: Final report. *Sexuality and Disability*, 19(1), 5–40.

Olkin, R. (1999). *What psychotherapists should know about disability*. New York, NY: Guilford Press.

Olkin, R. (2002). Could you hold the door for me? Including disability in diversity. *Cultural Diversity & Ethnic Minority Psychology*, 8(2), 130–137.

Olkin, R. (2004). Disability and depression. In S. L. Welner & F. Haseltine (Eds.), *Welner's guide to the care of women with disabilities* (pp. 279–300). Philadelphia, PA: Lippincott Williams & Wilkins.

Olkin, R. (2005). *Disability culture: A baker's dozen*. Newsletter of the Contra Costa County Psychological Association.

Olkin, R. (2008). Disability-Affirmative Therapy and case formulation: A template for understanding disability in a clinical context. *Counseling & Human Development*, 39(8), 1–20.

Olkin, R., Abrams, K., Preston, P., & Kirshbaum, M. (2006). Comparison of parents with and without disabilities raising teens: Information from the NHIS and two national surveys. *Rehabilitation Psychology, 51*(1), 43–49.

Olkin, R., & Howson, L. (1994). Attitudes toward and images of physical disability. *Journal of Social Behavior and Personality, 9*(5), 81–96.

Olkin, R., & Loewy, M. (2011). *The lived experiences of gay men with disabilities.* Unpublished manuscript, Clinical Psychology, California School of Professional Psychology at Alliant International University, San Francisco, CA.

Oman, D., Reed, D., & Ferrara, A. (1999). Do elderly women have more disability than men do? *American Journal of Epidemiology, 150*(8), 834–842.

Petersilia, J. R. (2001). Crime victims with developmental disabilities. *Criminal Justice and Behavior, 28*(6), 655–694.

Pinsky, J. L., Jette, A. M., Branch, L. G., Kannel, W. B., & Feinleib, M. (1990). The Framingham disability study: Relationship of various coronary heart disease manifestations to disability in older persons living in the community. *American Journal of Public Health, 80*(11), 1363–1367.

Pollard, C., & Kennedy, P. (2007). A longitudinal analysis of emotional impact, coping strategies and post-traumatic psychological growth following spinal cord injury: A ten-year review. *British Journal of Health Psychology, 12,* 347–362.

Putnam, F. W. (2003). Ten-year research update review: Child sexual abuse. *Child and Adolescent Psychiatry, 42*(3), 269–278.

Rainville, J., Bagnall, D., & Phalen, L. (1995). Health care providers attitudes and beliefs about functional impairments and lower back pain. *The Clinical Journal of Pain, 11*(4), 287–295.

Rehabilitation Act of 1973, Public Law 93-112.

Ruddell, J. L, & Shinew, K. J. (2006). The socialization process for women with physical disabilities: The impact of agents and agencies in the introduction to an elite sport. *National Recreation and Park Association, 38*(3), 421–444.

Sejvar, J. J., Holman, R. C., Bresee, J. S., Kochanek, K. D., & Schonberger, L. B. (2005). Amyotrophic lateral sclerosis mortality in the United States, 1979–2001. *Neuroepidemiology, 25*(3), 1444–1452.

Siddall, P. J. (2009). Management of neuropathic pain following spinal cord injury: Now and in the future. *Spinal Cord, 47,* 352–359.

Sobsey, D. (2000). Faces of violence against women with developmental disabilities. *Impact, 13*(3).

Streiner, D. L., Saigal, S., Burrows, E., Stoskopf, B., & Rosenbaum, P. (2001). Attitudes of parents and health care professionals toward active treatment of extremely premature infants. *Pediatrics, 108*(1), 152–157.

Sue, D. W. (2010). *Micro-aggressions in everyday life: Race, gender, and sexual orientation.* Hoboken, NJ: Wiley.

Sullivan, P. M., & Knutson, J. F. (2000). Maltreatment and disabilities: A population-based epidemiological study. *Child Abuse and Neglect, 24*(10), 1257–1273.

Taylor, L. A., Kreutzer, J. S., Demm, S. R., & Meade, M. A. (2003). Traumatic brain injury and substance abuse: A review and analysis of the literature. *Neurological Rehabilitation, 13*(1/2) 165–188.

Teplin, L. A., McClelland, G., Abram, K. M., & Weiner, D. A. (2005). Crime victimization in adults with severe mental illness: Comparison with the national crime victimization survey. *Archives of General Psychiatry, 62*(8), 911–921.

Tervo, R. C., & Palmer, G. (2004). Health professional student attitudes toward people with disabilities. *Clinical Rehabilitation, 18*(8), 908–915.

Ticoll, M. (1994). Violence and people with disabilities: A review of the literature. *National Criminal Justice Reference Service,* publication # ISBN 0-662-22712-3.

Turner, R. J., & Beiser, M. (1990). Major depression and depressive symptomatology among the physically disabled: Assessing the role of chronic stress. *The Journal of Nervous and Mental Disease, 178*(6), 343–350.

Turner, R. J., & McLean, P. D. (1989). Physical disability and distress. *Rehabilitation Psychology, 34,* 225–242.

Turner, R. J., & Noh, S. (1988). Physical disability and depression: A longitudinal analysis. *Journal of Health and Social Behavior, 29,* 23–37.

U.S. Bureau of Labor Statistics. (2011). Labor force statistics. Retrieved from http://data.bls.gov/cgi-bin/print.pl/news.release/empsit.t06.htm and http://data.bls.gov/cgi-bin/print.pl/webapps/legacy/cpsatab6.htm

U.S. Census Bureau. (2010). Americans with disabilities: 2010. http://www.census.gov/people/disability/publications/sipp2010.html

U.S. Census Data. (2008). Retrieved from http://www.census.gov/prod/2008pubs/p70-117.pdf

Verbrugge, L. (1995). Women, men and osteo-arthritis. *Arthritis and Rheumatism, 8*(4), 212–220.

Vogel, L. C., Chlan, K. M., Zebracki, K., & Anderson, C. J. (2011). Long-term outcomes of adults with pediatric onset spinal cord injuries as a function of neurological impairment. *The Journal of Spinal Cord Medicine, 34*(1), 60–66.

Walster, E. (1966). Assignment of responsibility for an accident. *Journal of Personality and Social Psychology, 3*, 73–79.

Walster, E., Berscheid, E., & Walster, G. W. (1972). New directions in equity research. *Journal of Personality and Social Psychology, 25*, 151–176.

Wang, Y. (2001). Cross-national comparison of childhood obesity: The epidemic and the relationship between obesity and socioeconomic status. *International Journal of Epidemiology, 30*(5), 1129–1136.

Waxman, B. F. (1991). Hatred: The unacknowledged dimension of violence against disabled people. *Sexuality and Disability, 9*(3), 185–199.

Webb, J. R., Toussaint, L., Kalpakjian, C. Z., & Tate, D. G. (2010). Forgiveness and health-related outcomes among people with spinal cord injury. *Disability and Rehabilitation, 32*(5), 360–366.

Weissman, M. M., & Myers, J. K. (1978). Affective disorders in a U.S. urban community: The use of Research Diagnostic Criteria in an epidemiological survey. *Archives of General Psychiatry, 35*, 1304–1311.

White, B., Driver, S., & Warren, A. M. (2010). Resilience and indicators of adjustment during rehabilitation from a spinal cord injury. *Rehabilitation Psychology, 55*(1), 23–32.

Wirz, M, Muller, R., & Bastiaenen, C. (2010). Falls in persons with spinal cord injury: Validity and reliability of the Berg Balance Scale. *Neurorehabilitation and Neural Repair, 24*(1), 70–77.

Wong, D. (2007). *Attitudes and beliefs of immigrant Chinese parents of children with disabilities: How they fit into the theoretical models of disability.* Unpublished doctoral dissertation, California School of Professional Psychology at Alliant International University, San Francisco.

World Health Organization (2001). *International Classification of Functioning, Disability and Health (ICF).* Geneva: Author.

Wright, B. (1963). *Physical disability: A psychological approach.* New York, NY: Harper & Row.

Yasuda, S., Wehman, P., Targett, P., Cifu, D. X., & West, M. (2002). Return to work after spinal cord injury: A review of recent research. *NeuroRehabilitation, 17*, 177–186.

Yuker, H. (1994). Variables that influence attitudes toward persons with disabilities: Conclusions from the data. *Psychosocial perspectives on disability, A special issue of the Journal of Social Behavior and Personality, 9*, 3–22.

Zea, M. C., Belgrave, F. Z., Townsend, T. G., Jarama, S. L., & Banks, S. R. (1996). The influence of social support and active coping on depression among African Americans and Latinos with disabilities. *Rehabilitation Psychology, 41*(3), 225–242.

Zelman, D.C., Smith, M., Hoffman, D., Reed, P., Edwards, L., Levine, E., & Dukes, E. (2004). Acceptable, manageable, and tolerable days: Patient daily goals for medication management of persistent pain. *Journal of Pain and Symptom Management, 28*, 474–489.

Zhang, Q., & Wang, Y. (2004). Trends in the association between obesity and socioeconomic status in U.S. adults: 1971–2000. *Obesity Research, 12*(10), 1622–1632.

Zinc, A., Braun, J., Listing, J., & Wollenhaupt, J. (2000). Disability and handicap in rheumatoid arthritis and ankylosing spondylitis: Results from the German rheumatological database. *Journal of Rheumatology, 27*(3), 613–622.

The Experience of Cancer in Women

ANNETTE L. STANTON AND BETINA YANEZ

INTRODUCTION

Every day in the United States, more than 2,000 women are diagnosed with cancer. Although numerous cancer-related psychosocial and physical demands are common across women and men, some demands are more prevalent in women (e.g., compromise of reproductive capacity) as a function of undergoing cancer diagnosis and treatment. Characterizing the experience of women who confront a cancer diagnosis, as well as elucidating the process of adjustment to cancer and the factors that facilitate and hinder adjustment and quality of life, can improve the experience of undergoing cancer diagnosis and treatment and enhance salutary outcomes among women. In this chapter, we offer a background on the epidemiology of cancer and its treatment in women. We then provide brief reviews of several attendant psychosocial, behavioral, and physical consequences and describe contributors to the substantial variability in these consequences. We also highlight effective interventions for improving women's well-being and health in light of a cancer diagnosis and treatment, as well as directions for research and application.

The focus of the chapter is on the experience of nonmetastatic breast cancer, which has received the majority of empirical attention, although we attempt to incorporate relevant literature on other cancers. We refer the reader to other sources for the important areas of cancer screening in women (e.g., Hay, McCaul, & Magnan, 2006; Pasick & Burke, 2008), the impact on women of genetic testing for cancer risk (e.g., Hamilton, Lobel, & Moyer, 2009), and biobehavioral contributors to cancer initiation and progression (e.g., Antoni, Lutgendorf, et al., 2006; McTiernan, Irwin, & VonGruenigen, 2010; Park & Gaffey, 2007).

EPIDEMIOLOGY

Among women, cancer is the second leading cause of death in the United States, exceeded only by heart disease. In 2011, an estimated 774,370 women were diagnosed with cancer, and 271,520 women died from the disease (Siegel, Ward, Brawley, & Jemal, 2011). Breast cancer is expected to account for 30% of all new cancers among women, followed by cancers of the lung/bronchus, colon/rectum, and uterus. However, lung/bronchus cancers lead in cancer-related deaths in women, trailed by cancers of the breast, colon/rectum, and pancreas. In women, cancer incidence rates have declined annually by 0.6% since 1993. Moreover, improvements in detection, diagnosis of cancer at an early stage, and medical treatments have contributed to an increase in survival. The current 5-year relative survival rate for all cancers, across men and women, between 1999 and 2005 is 68%, an improvement from 50% in 1975 to 1977 (American Cancer Society, 2010).

Progress in reducing women's cancer incidence and mortality is inconsistent across socioeconomic strata, race/ethnicity, and particular cancers, however. For example, mortality rates for the least-educated women are more than twice those of the most-educated women, and African American women have a lower cancer incidence rate but a 17% higher mortality rate than White women in the United States (Siegel et al., 2011). The 5-year relative survival is lower among African American women than Whites for every stage for most cancers (Jemal, Siegel, Xu, & Ward, 2010). Explanatory mechanisms for these disparities (e.g., Siegel et al., 2011) include sociodemographic factors, which restrict access to cancer-related information, high-quality screening, and medical care; biological explanations (e.g., higher rate of hormone receptor-negative breast cancer in African American women; distinct patterns of co-morbid conditions); and cultural differences in beliefs and attitudes about cancer (e.g., Perez-Stable, Sabogal, Otero-Sabogal, Hiatt, & McPhee, 1992). It is estimated that elimination of educational and racial disparities could have prevented 30% of all premature cancer deaths in 2007 in women aged 25 to 64 years (Siegel et al., 2011).

CANCER STAGING AND TREATMENT

Cancers are staged according to tumor size and localization of tumor relative to the initial site of diagnosis (e.g., localized to the site, regional, distant). For most cancers, tumors are categorized into four stages based on the size of the tumor(s) and the extent of its spread (e.g., spread to the lymph nodes and other parts of the body), with Stage I connoting early-stage cancer and Stage IV indicating advanced or metastatic disease (i.e., cancer that has spread to organs in other parts of the body).

In some cases, medical treatment begins with neoadjuvant treatments (chemotherapy or radiotherapy administered prior to surgery), which may be used to shrink tumors and clean boundaries around the tumor to make them more operable. Except for advanced disease and other specific indications, however, treatment for cancer typically commences with surgical intervention for tumor removal. Due to the equivalent survival rates conferred by mastectomy (complete removal of breast) and lumpectomy (breast-conserving surgery) in early-stage breast cancer, women are provided with surgical options. Not all women diagnosed with early-stage breast cancer prefer involvement in the treatment decision-making process; the scope of preferred involvement ranges from delegating the decision about treatment preference to the physician or family members to desiring complete involvement in the process (Bruera, Willey, Palmer, & Rosales, 2002; Janz et al., 2004). Surgical treatment decision-making preferences are influenced by numerous factors, including concerns about body image, fears about cancer recurrence, and others (Degner et al., 1997). Among women diagnosed with gynecological cancers, surgical interventions include oophorectomy (removal of ovaries) and hysterectomy (removal of uterus).

Following surgical treatment, adjuvant treatments such as radiation, chemotherapy, and hormonal therapy can be indicated, which are targeted toward the eradication of cancer cells remaining in the area of the primary tumor site (radiation), eradication of cells that may have traveled to other areas of the body (chemotherapy), or suppression of additional cancer cells (hormonal therapy). Although treatment approaches to cancer vary considerably, women with nonmetastatic cancer typically will undergo excision of the tumor, which may be supplemented with adjuvant treatment. Each of these treatments can have concomitant acute effects, including postsurgical pain, body disfigurement, marked fatigue, hair loss, and nausea/vomiting, among others.

CANCER AND QUALITY OF LIFE IN WOMEN

Quality of life is a multidimensional construct that encompasses various areas of functioning, including emotional, physical, work-related, social, and sexual domains. These domains are not orthogonal but rather interrelated, in that functional decrements in one domain will likely affect function across one or several other domains. For example, experiencing pain and fatigue following cancer treatment can contribute to depressive symptoms and social withdrawal. In this section, we review some of the most prominent areas of impact of cancer on women in each domain.

Psychological Domain

To assess the psychological domain, researchers in this area employ indicators of positive and negative mood (e.g., vitality, anxiety, cancer-related distress), psychological disorder (e.g., depression, anxiety disorder), and perceived limitations resulting from emotional problems. A diagnosis of

cancer threatens multiple life domains, and thus it is not surprising that it can be accompanied by periods of elevated cancer-related distress, depressive symptoms, and anxiety. Undergoing diagnosis and treatment for breast cancer provokes significant and enduring distress in some women (Millar, Purushotham, McLatchie, George, & Murray, 2005; van't Spijker, Trijsburg, & Duivenvoorden, 1997).

Major depressive disorder and depressive symptoms are prevalent in individuals with cancer. Diagnosing depression in the context of cancer is complicated by the fact that the diagnostic criteria for depression often overlap with side effects of cancer treatments, such as fatigue, weight loss, and sleep disturbance; thus, controversy exists over how much attention should be paid to somatic symptoms of depression among cancer patients (see Vodermaier, Linden, & Siu, 2009, for a review of distress assessment in cancer patients). In the general population, cancer types that are more strongly associated with depression are head and neck, pancreatic, breast, and lung cancer, whereas cancers less likely to be associated with depression are colon and gynecological cancers (Massie, 2004). The literature on gender differences in depressive symptoms among individuals with cancer yields conflicting findings (Massie, 2004; Miaskowski, 2004; Mitchell et al., 2011); research is needed to clarify the relationship between gender and depression following cancer, as well as the prominent contributors to depression in women and men diagnosed with cancer.

The prevalence estimate of depression among women with early-stage breast cancer is double that in the general population of women, particularly during the first year after diagnosis (Burgess et al., 2005), with estimates indicating that up to one-quarter of women with breast cancer meet criteria for depression (Reich, Lesur, & Perdrizet-Chevallier, 2008). For example, of 3,343 breast cancer patients at 12 to 16 weeks after surgery, 14% had major depressive disorder (MDD) based on diagnostic interview (Christensen et al., 2009). Note that the MDD point prevalence for women in the general population is estimated at 5% to 9% and lifetime prevalence at 21% (Kessler, Chiu, Demler, & Walters, 2005). Assessments of women diagnosed with ovarian cancer also indicate that close to one-quarter of women report levels of symptoms suggestive of clinical depression (Bodurka-Bevers et al., 2000).

Depression can have profound consequences during the experience of cancer. In the general cancer population, individuals with cancer endorsing clinically significant levels of depressive symptoms are 3 times less likely to be adherent to general medical treatment than are nondepressed patients (DiMatteo, Lepper, & Croghan, 2000). Among breast cancer patients, women who had elevated depressive symptoms 2 to 4 years after surgery requested more medical testing and medical care than did nondepressed women (de Bock et al., 2004). Elevated depressive symptoms predict lower arm mobility on the side where breast cancer surgery was performed (Caban et al., 2006), as well as lower satisfaction with medical care over time in breast cancer patients (Bui, Ostir, Kuo, Freeman, & Goodwin, 2005). Medicare beneficiaries diagnosed with cancer are at least twice as likely to use emergency departments and medical inpatient services if they have significant depressive symptoms than if they do not (Himelhoch, Weller, Wu, Anderson, & Cooper, 2004).

In addition to depressive symptoms, the experience of cancer diagnosis and treatment can prompt anxiety. The psychological burden of waiting for diagnostic results and fears of cancer progression and recurrence is a source of significant concern. Clinically significant anxiety occurs when worrying becomes excessive, is associated with somatic symptoms such as fatigue or muscle tension, and leads to impairment in functioning. Although few studies have examined gender differences in anxiety following cancer, some evidence suggests that women are more likely than men to report anxiety (Massie, 2004). The prevalence of anxiety in the year after breast cancer diagnosis has been reported to be 48%, which is approximately twice that of women in the general population (Burgess et al., 2005). Among patients diagnosed with ovarian cancer, 29% of women report levels of symptoms suggestive of clinical anxiety (Bodurka-Bevers et al., 2000). In light of the prevalence estimates of depression and anxiety in women diagnosed with cancer relative to the general population and potential negative implications of those disorders for important outcomes, psychosocial interventions designed to reduce psychological distress and enhance emotional well-being may carry numerous benefits for women.

Despite the significant emotional burden of cancer, women diagnosed with cancer generally adjust well over time. Approximately two years following completion of treatment, women diagnosed with cancer generally report equivalent quality of life relative to the general population (e.g., Burgess et al., 2005). However, it is important to note that adjustment to cancer varies considerably, and women diagnosed with cancer may experience elevated levels of distress during particular phases in the cancer trajectory (Andersen, Anderson, & DeProsse, 1989), which we address later in the chapter.

Physical Domain

The construct of quality of life encompasses the subjective evaluation of health status and bodily functioning, as well as perceived impact of physical problems on maintenance of somatic function and independence. Treatments for most cancers are associated with numerous physical changes and disruptions to bodily functioning. Common side effects of treatment that may affect quality of life include fatigue, sleep disturbance, nausea/vomiting, hair loss, and pain. The large, prospective Nurses' Health Study revealed that women diagnosed with cancer during the 4-year study period experienced a decline in physical functioning and increases in fatigue and pain relative to women who did not receive a cancer diagnosis (Michael, Kawachi, Berkman, Holmes, & Colditz, 2000; also see Trentham-Dietz et al., 2008).

Cancer-related fatigue is one of the most common and debilitating adverse effects of treatment, especially among women treated with chemotherapy and radiation (Bower, 2008), and fatigue may persist for many years after medical treatments (Bower et al., 2000). An estimated 25% to 99% of women with breast cancer report fatigue during treatment, with 25% to 30% reporting fatigue after completion of treatment (Bower, 2008). Long-term cancer-related fatigue can negatively affect mood, activities of daily living, social relationships, and work (Bower, 2008).

Insomnia is a common complaint following a diagnosis and treatment of cancer. Although also reported in patients with other cancers, sleep disturbances are most commonly studied in patients with breast cancer because of the increased severity of hot flashes associated with hormone-suppressing treatments. Research on sleep disturbance among breast cancer patients suggests that approximately 20% of women with nonmetastatic breast cancer meet diagnostic criteria for insomnia (Fiorentino & Ancoli-Israel, 2006).

Chemotherapy for cancer often causes nausea. Despite the increase in use of preventive antiemetic medications, chemotherapy-induced nausea and vomiting are still considered by patients to be severe side effects of treatment (Booth et al., 2007). In a study of breast cancer patients (Booth et al., 2007), treatment-related nausea was reported by 37% of the sample within 24 hours of chemotherapy infusion and by 70% of the sample within 2 to 5 days after infusion.

Beginning in the 1990s, systematic research began to document the effects of undergoing chemotherapy on cognitive functioning, with the majority of studies focused on women with breast cancer (for reviews, see Ahles & Saykin, 2007; Janelsins et al., 2011; Vardy, 2009). Women often report that cognitive problems are most obvious when they are attempting multiple tasks simultaneously, and their self-reported problems typically exceed those detectable upon objective testing (Vardy, 2009). Documented in neuropsychological testing, decrements in cognitive function are often subtle and most consistently evident in tests of working memory, executive function, processing speed, and attention (Ahles & Saykin, 2007; Vardy, 2009). Problems are most likely during the course of chemotherapy, although they linger for up to 35% of women (McDonald Conroy, Ahles, West, & Saykin, 2010). Several mechanisms for these cognitive changes are being investigated (Ahles & Saykin, 2007; McDonald et al., 2010).

Pain is a common complaint following surgical treatment for cancer. Women experience pain caused by nerve, tissue, and organ damage or removal during surgery. A study of a multiethnic sample of women with breast cancer who were diagnosed and treated within the past 2 years reported a pain prevalence of 79% (Eversley et al., 2005). For women who undergo mastectomy, complaints of stiffness, limited range of movement, and loss of sensation may persist. Also present after mastectomy is phantom breast syndrome, the sometimes painful false sensation of a breast, which has been estimated to occur in approximately 20% of women 2 years following mastectomy (Dijkstra, Rietman, & Geertzen, 2007). Among the approximately 16% of breast cancer patients who have axillary lymph node dissection, pain accompanying lymphedema (i.e., accumulation of interstitial fluid in soft tissue) can be a particular problem (McLaughlin et al., 2008). Among women treated for ovarian cancer, lingering pain can occur in the bowel, pelvis, bladder, and groin areas. One survey of ovarian cancer survivors 2 years after treatment revealed that approximately 50% reported pain related to the cancer or its treatment (Stewart, Wong, Duff, Melancon, & Cheung, 2001). Cancer-related pain can lead to functional impairments, and women who experience severe cancer-related pain are more likely to endorse depressive symptoms (McCorkle, Tang, Greenwald, Holcombe, & Lavery, 2006).

Sexual and Reproductive Domains

The sexual consequences of cancer treatment can be significant and enduring. Surgery and adjuvant treatment (e.g., chemotherapy-induced menopause) can lead to permanent bodily changes and decrements in sexual functioning. Furthermore, women may experience concerns about the effect of diagnosis and treatment on partners' reactions and sexual intimacy. Although gynecologic cancer patients may continue intercourse following treatment, they report diminished sexual responsiveness, lower sexual satisfaction, and evidence higher rates of sexual dysfunction compared to healthy controls (Andersen et al., 1989; Carpenter, Andersen, Fowler & Maxwell, 2009). In a longitudinal study of breast cancer patients, sexual problems were significantly greater following surgery compared to retrospective reports of the period prior to diagnosis, and gradually decreased over a 12-month period (Andersen, Carpenter, Yang, & Shapiro, 2007). However, women's perceptions of sexual problems were still greater at 1 year after surgery compared to before diagnosis. Furthermore, sexual intercourse frequency declined more over a 12-month period among younger women compared to older women (greater than 52 years). Sexual well-being declines further after a recurrence of breast cancer, although couples often aim to maintain intimacy (Andersen, 2009).

The topic of cancer-related infertility has received mounting attention in the past decade, especially in light of the increasing number of younger women receiving a diagnosis of cancer (Howard-Anderson, Ganz, Bower, & Stanton, 2012). By age 39, one in 51 women will have received a diagnosis of cancer (Altekruse et al., 2010). Furthermore, the increasing trend of postponing pregnancy until women's thirties and forties may further complicate childbearing plans for young women diagnosed with cancer (Canada & Schover, 2012). The risk of infertility with cancer treatments increases with age of the woman as well as the type of treatment received (Abusief, Missmer, Ginsburg, Weeks, & Partridge, 2010). Surgical treatments that remove the reproductive organs in gynecological cancers generally result in infertility, because standard treatment involves total hysterectomy with oophorectomy. Among women who continue to menstruate after chemotherapy for cancer, reduced ovarian reserve and high rates of premature ovarian failure can affect fertility. Although several options exist for achieving parenthood (e.g., in vitro fertilization, embryo cryopreservation), such options are not always available or successful in preserving fertility.

A diagnosis of cancer at a young age may threaten adult identity and developmental goals throughout a woman's reproductive years, such as building relationships and bearing children. Infertility is an important long-term survivorship issue among women of childbearing age who are diagnosed with breast cancer (Ganz, Greendale, Petersen, Kahn, & Bower, 2003). Cancer treatment-related infertility is associated with significant psychological distress, with levels of depression twice that of the general population of women, as well as reduced quality of life in areas of emotional well-being, relationships, and sexuality among women diagnosed with gynecologic cancers (Carter et al., 2005). Among women diagnosed with various types of cancer, having more reproductive concerns is associated with compromised quality of life and higher cancer-specific distress (Wenzel et al., 2005). Furthermore, women who are left infertile after cancer treatment report significantly more reproductive concerns, poorer mental health, and lower psychological and physical well-being than women who are able to conceive (Wenzel et al., 2005).

Long-term female survivors of cancer who are unable to conceive after cancer treatment report significantly poorer mental health and lower psychological well-being

than women who were able to have children (Canada & Schover, 2012). Among long-term cancer survivors, women who experienced an interruption in childbearing continued to report significant distress about cancer-related infertility, but not elevated general emotional distress, and women who viewed themselves as infertile demonstrated lower sexual and relationship satisfaction 10 years following diagnosis (Canada & Schover, 2012). Even when women do not experience menstrual changes during cancer treatments, they may have concerns about having children following diagnosis of a life-threatening illness and about subsequent pregnancies increasing the risk of recurrence (Avis, Crawford, & Manuel, 2005).

The psychological sequelae of cancer-related infertility can be grave. In addition to the stress imposed by diagnosis and treatment of cancer, women may be forced to confront yet another profound life stressor if the threat of infertility is superimposed on the cancer context. A sense of loss of control, anger, grief, and a yearning to give birth can accompany infertility induced by cancer treatments (Carter et al., 2005; Cousineau & Domar, 2007). Discussion of fertility preservation is essential prior to the initiation of adjuvant therapy (Kim, Klemp, & Fabian, 2011).

Social Domain

The exigencies of managing cancer diagnosis and treatment can interfere with women's social worlds. The Nurses' Health Study demonstrated that women diagnosed with cancer during the study period experienced a decline in social functioning relative to women who did not receive a cancer diagnosis, with a particularly pronounced decline in women aged 40 and younger compared to older women diagnosed with cancer (Kroenke, Rosner, Chen, Colditz, & Holmes, 2004; Michael et al., 2000). Although making the transition from the often more familiar role of support provider to support recipient is not easy for women, informational and emotional support can be vitally important to women diagnosed with cancer. During the acute phase of diagnosis and treatment, women diagnosed with cancer typically report receiving helpful informational support from the medical team and helpful emotional support from the medical team, family, and friends (e.g., Arora, Finney Rutten, Gustafson, Moser, & Hawkins, 2007). Such support may erode over time, however, leaving women with unmet informational and emotional needs (Arora et al., 2007; Chen & Siu, 2001; Luker, Beaver, Leinster, & Owens, 1996). For example, breast cancer patients report getting useful informational support from medical professionals during treatment, but they report discomfort in requesting information from healthcare professionals and unmet information needs at 21-month follow-up (Luker et al., 1996).

Cancer rarely affects the woman alone, but rather also her interpersonal nexus. One body of literature in this area characterizes the experience of cancer on women and their intimate partners (e.g., Manne & Badr, 2008), with nearly all research pertaining to heterosexual couples. A meta-analysis of the experience of cancer in couples demonstrated that, whether in the role of cancer patient or partner, women report more distress than do men (Hagedoorn, Sanderman, Bolks, Tuinstra, & Coyne, 2008). While taking care of women with breast cancer at the end of life, however, partners and other caregivers are likely to experience more distress than are women diagnosed

with the disease (Grunfeld et al., 2004). It is important to note that many couples find that the experience of cancer enhances intimacy. For example, both members of the couple, interviewed individually, reported that the breast cancer experience had brought them closer in 42% of 282 couples at 12 months after initiation of medical treatment (e.g., Dorval et al., 2005).

A substantial literature also documents the experience of primary caregivers (e.g., partner, family member, friend) for individuals with cancer, typically as nominated by the diagnosed person. A review of 164 studies revealed that 63.5% of the caregivers were women and were most frequently the partner, adult child, or parent (Stenberg, Ruland, & Miaskowski, 2010). Research documents the multiple challenges of caregiving, particularly during the acute phase of diagnosis and treatment and the advanced and terminal periods (Kim & Given, 2008; Stenberg et al., 2010).

Employment Domain

Over recent decades, legal protections, improvement in medical treatments, and other resources have aided the substantial majority of employed women who maintain or return to their work after cancer diagnosis (Hoffman, 2005; Short & Vargo, 2006). In a large interview study of 1,433 cancer survivors 1 to 5 years after diagnosis, 39% of women stopped work during medical treatments (41% men), and the projected rate of return to work at 4 years was 84% across women and men, with the large majority returning in the first year after diagnosis (Short, Vasey, & Tunceli, 2005). However, 21% of women who were employed at diagnosis reported cancer-related limitations in their ability to work (16% men).

Additional research documents challenges regarding employment for women. A meta-analysis of unemployment rates in adult cancer survivors revealed that the rate of unemployment was 1.28 times higher for women with breast or gynecologic cancers compared to healthy controls (de Boer, Taskila, Ojajärvi, van Dijk, & Verbeek, 2009), and a study of Canadian women with breast cancer documented wage losses in the year after diagnosis (Lauzier et al., 2008). Furthermore, few controlled trials are available to document whether interventions can promote women's return to work (Hoving, Broekhuizen, & Frings-Dresen, 2009), although a small literature suggests that multidisciplinary approaches (e.g., physical exercise, education, counseling) show promise (de Boer et al., 2011). In light of the centrality of employment to health in social, financial, and psychological domains for the majority of women, effective interventions are needed to promote welcoming work environments and to increase women's preparedness to return to work.

Finding Benefit in the Experience of Cancer

Despite the variety of psychosocial threats and losses associated with a diagnosis of cancer, many women report positive life changes from the experience of cancer, a psychological phenomenon commonly referred to in the literature as *benefit finding* or *posttraumatic growth* (e.g., Calhoun & Tedeschi, 2006; Park, Lechner, Antoni, & Stanton, 2009). Over the past decade, psychologists increasingly have emphasized the important contribution of benefit finding to quality of life following the experience of traumatic and stressful life events, especially in the context of cancer.

Review of the empirical literature reveals that the majority of individuals with cancer report finding some benefit following a diagnosis of cancer (Stanton, Bower, & Low, 2006). Commonly reported areas of benefit include increases in the intimacy of relationships, spirituality, sense of personal strength, appreciation of life, and commitment to life priorities (Sears, Stanton, & Danoff-Burg, 2003; Tedeschi & Calhoun, 1996). Such positive psychological consequences have been widely investigated and reported among women with breast cancer (Tomich & Helgeson, 2004) and, although rarely investigated in women with gynecological malignancies, also reported in women diagnosed with ovarian cancer (Wenzel et al., 2002). Some evidence indicates that finding benefit in the experience of cancer increases over time, as documented by Manne et al. (2004) in both breast cancer patients and their partners from approximately four months after diagnosis through 18 months later. Furthermore, women diagnosed with breast cancer report significantly greater benefit finding in some areas compared to healthy controls, suggesting that the experience of cancer affords a unique opportunity to catalyze psychological growth (Cordova, Cunningham, Carlson, & Andrykowski, 2001). Results from a meta-analysis on benefit finding associated with a variety of stressors revealed a gender difference, such that women engaged in more benefit finding than men (Helgeson, Reynolds, & Tomich, 2006), which is consistent with the literature suggesting that women engage in more positive reappraisal coping and positive self-talk than men (Tamres, Janicki, & Helgeson, 2002).

Studies examining the relationship between benefit finding and psychological adjustment reveal mixed findings. Noteworthy positive findings include the observations that perceived positive meaning in the cancer experience at 1 to 5 years after diagnosis predicted an increase in positive affect 5 years later in a sample of 763 breast cancer patients (Bower et al., 2005) and that finding benefit in the year after surgery predicted lower distress and depressive symptoms 4 to 7 years later in another sample of women diagnosed with breast cancer (Carver & Antoni, 2004). In a meta-analysis of 87 cross-sectional studies in individuals experiencing a variety of stressful or traumatic events, Helgeson et al. (2006) concluded that perceptions of growth were related to lower depressive symptoms and greater well-being, but also more stressor-related intrusive and avoidant thoughts. Perhaps reports of benefits arising from the cancer experience serve distinct motivational functions for different women. For some survivors, reporting cancer-related benefits might be akin to wishful thinking, which is linked with negative psychological consequences, whereas citing benefits might signify profound and sustained positive shifts in worldviews, emotions, or behaviors for others, with accompanying salutary psychological and health-related consequences (e.g., Stanton, Danoff-Burg, & Huggins, 2002).

CONTRIBUTORS TO QUALITY OF LIFE IN WOMEN WITH CANCER

Responses to cancer vary greatly across women, and researchers have sought to specify determinants of women's diverse responses across the cancer trajectory. Understanding risk and protective factors for psychological adjustment and quality of life is crucial to developing effective strategies for prevention and intervention among women diagnosed with cancer. To that end, we review several key contributors to

psychological adjustment and quality of life among women with cancer.

Medical Factors

Undergoing medical treatments for cancer affects women's quality of life, although the impact of surgical intervention often is confined to a negative influence on body image for women undergoing mastectomy compared to breast-conserving surgery (e.g., Janz et al., 2005). Relative to other treatments, receipt of chemotherapy is associated with a greater number of toxic side effects, which can persist after treatment (e.g., Ganz, Kwan, Stanton, Bower, & Belin, 2011), decrements in quality of life in several domains (e.g., Janz et al., 2005), and less rapid return to work (e.g., Johnsson et al., 2009). Women's experience of medical treatment also can affect psychological adjustment after treatment completion. The number of physical symptoms/side effects experienced during treatment predicts cancer-related distress and general distress 4 months after treatment completion in women with early-stage breast cancer (Jim, Andrykowski, Munster, & Jacobsen, 2007).

Interestingly, studies do not consistently demonstrate significant relationships between objective disease-related factors and adjustment. Bardwell et al. (2006) examined the relative relationship of early-stage breast cancer parameters (e.g., treatment type, time elapsed since diagnosis, cancer stage; note that the research did not include women with metastatic disease), health behaviors, and psychosocial variables (e.g., stressful life events, optimism) to depressive symptoms in a large sample ($n = 2,595$) of women within 4 years after treatment completion. Although psychosocial variables evidenced significant relationships with depressive symptoms, disease and treatment factors did not. The meanings women attach to disease-related factors, as well as personal and environmental resources for managing the disease and its treatment, may have more impact on psychological adjustment than do objective disease indicators.

Women diagnosed with cancers of poorer prognosis, such as metastatic breast cancer or ovarian cancer, which most often is diagnosed at an advanced stage, confront life threat and often invasive and shifting treatments alongside tests to monitor the status of the cancer. These demands can leave women feeling consumed by the management of the disease and encumbered by limited energy and other physical problems. Women with advanced cancers also may struggle with accepting a shift in treatment goals from eliminating disease to reducing tumor size or additional spread of cancer. Feeling concerned about the well-being of loved ones, modifying valued career and family-focused goals, and managing uncertainty are among the numerous tasks posed by advanced disease for women. In a 5-year study of women diagnosed with early-stage breast cancer within 5 months of study entry (Burgess et al., 2005), depression and anxiety were more prevalent (45%) in the 3 months following diagnosis of cancer recurrence (i.e., return of the cancer to the initial site, lymph nodes, or other organs) than after initial breast cancer diagnosis (36%).

Phase of the Cancer Trajectory

Each phase of the cancer continuum affords unique psychological challenges. Upon a cancer diagnosis, women may struggle with uncertainty about the future, confront their mortality, make multiple treatment decisions, and manage reactions of their interpersonal network. Throughout the active treatment phase (i.e., receipt of surgery, chemotherapy, and/or radiotherapy), women can experience distress as they await updates regarding treatment progress amidst dealing with the side effects of surgical intervention and adjuvant treatment and as they manage changes in central roles (e.g., partner, mother, worker). During the reentry phase (i.e., the months following treatment completion; Costanzo et al., 2007; Stanton et al., 2005), women contend with lingering side effects of treatment. Moving past the active treatment phase also is associated with a sense of loss of a safety net of medical staff and active treatment regimens. Treatment completion may signal to patients a time to process losses and life changes associated with cancer diagnosis and treatment, such as permanent changes to appearance or impact on life priorities, intimate relationships, and self-perceptions.

Longitudinal studies suggest that women diagnosed with cancer follow variable patterns of adjustment. A longitudinal study of distress within the first year following breast cancer diagnosis, which began prior to surgery and concluded 6 months after treatment completion, indicated four distinct distress trajectories: 36% of women reported no or minimal distress across the five assessment points, 33% experienced distress from the point of diagnosis through medical treatment and then declined in distress, 15% experienced distress at treatment completion and through 6 months following treatment (i.e., re-entry phase), and 15% experienced high distress throughout the study period (Henselmans et al., 2010). A similar study of 398 women with breast cancer also identified four trajectories of depressive symptoms, with assessment beginning after diagnosis but prior to surgery and continuing through 6 months after surgery (Dunn et al., 2011). The largest group of women (45%) reported depressive symptoms just above the clinically relevant cut-off point for depression, which increased slightly over the course of the study. More than one-third of women (39%) reported a low level of depressive symptoms, which decreased slightly over the course of the study. Smaller groups reported a level suggestive of clinical depression prior to surgery, which decreased and then increased to clinically suggestive levels in the fifth and sixth month (11%), or had scores below the cutoff prior to surgery (4.5%), which increased sharply over 3 months and then declined to the presurgery level at 6 months (Dunn et al., 2011). In a study of women with breast cancer beginning at 4 months after diagnosis and extending through 4 years (Helgeson, Snyder, & Seltman, 2004), the largest proportions of women evidenced positive psychological (43%) and physical (55%) health-related quality of life, which changed little over the 4 years. Other groups demonstrated somewhat compromised functioning, which evidenced no change, gradual improvement, or rapid improvement over time, and the smallest proportions (less than 15%) evidenced declines in mental and physical quality of life over the 4 years.

With the caveat that findings to date are limited to relatively nondiverse samples of women diagnosed primarily with early-stage breast cancer, the research suggests that a large proportion of women can expect relatively stable, positive functioning or marked recovery over time in psychological and physical domains upon diagnosis of cancer. Continued investigation of factors that contribute to chronically compromised psychological and physical health, peaks of life disruption at particular phases (e.g., reentry), and declines

in function after diagnosis without recovery is essential. Within the context of generally positive adjustment, it is also important to note that specific problems can persist into longer-term survivorship (e.g., 5 years beyond diagnosis) for women. Reviews highlight problems with arm lymphedema and pain, sexual health (e.g., decreased desire, menopause-induced vaginal dryness), fatigue, and fear of cancer recurrence (Alfano & Rowland, 2006; Bloom, Petersen, & Kang, 2007; Mols, Vingerhoets, Coebergh, & van de Poll-Franse, 2005).

Sociodemographic Factors

Having low socioeconomic status can place women at a disadvantage by limiting social and psychological resources (Gallo & Matthews, 2003) and put women at risk for ongoing life stressors, which may reduce their ability to manage the stress associated with a cancer diagnosis. Women with lower socioeconomic status have been shown to evidence poorer adjustment to cancer, especially in the months following the diagnosis (Simon & Wardle, 2008). Although findings are not completely consistent, perceived global stress, stressful life events, and cancer-related stress assessed at initial cancer diagnosis have been shown to predict poor psychological and physical quality of life among women with breast cancer (Golden-Kreutz et al., 2005).

The relations of ethnic minority status with psychological and physical health, as well as mechanisms for observed associations, are active topics of inquiry. A review of quality of life research among African American breast cancer survivors included only three quantitative studies, highlighting the need for additional research (Powe et al., 2007). Recent studies present a mixed picture, with African American women evidencing some decrements (e.g., physical functioning) and some advantages (e.g., cancer-related benefits) in quality of life relative to their White counterparts (e.g., Bellizzi et al., 2010; Janz et al., 2009; Paskett et al., 2008). A review of 20 quantitative studies revealed poorer mental, physical, and social functioning among Latinas diagnosed with breast cancer compared to their White counterparts (Yanez, Thompson, & Stanton, 2011; also see Ashing-Giwa et al., 2009 for similar findings in Latina and White cervical cancer survivors). Ethnicity and race, however, are atheoretical constructs that in themselves provide little insight into psychological and physical phenomena. More important than assessing ethnic-racial differences is examining underlying explanatory mechanisms that may elucidate ethnic disparities in cancer, such as low income and education, as well as limited access to healthcare, all of which have been shown to predict poor physical health (Janz et al., 2007). Cultural differences in perceptions of disease may also influence the cancer experience. For example, a diagnosis of breast cancer might be especially disruptive for Latinas in light of culturally specific causal attributions about cancer, including the notion that cancer represents punishment for one's sins, as well as fatalistic beliefs about cancer (Buki et al., 2008; Ramirez, Suarez, Laufman, Barroso, & Chalela, 2000).

Age is another important correlate of quality of life and psychological adjustment. Younger breast cancer patients evidence greater decrements in mood and quality of life than older women (Avis et al., 2005; Baucom, Porter, Kirby, Gremore, & Keefe, 2005, 2006; Howard-Anderson et al., 2012; Kroenke et al., 2004) and poorer quality of life years after the diagnosis (Härtl et al., 2010).

Cancer may pose a greater threat to younger women's psychological and physical well-being for many reasons. Younger women may have higher expectations for their emotional, social, and physical status than older women. They also are likely to have several developmentally understandable concerns following cancer diagnosis and treatment, including concerns about a foreshortened future, treatment-induced premature menopause, fertility, and impact on social and employment-related roles (Avis et al., 2005).

Personality Attributes

Personality traits have been associated with women's adjustment to cancer. The most frequently investigated is dispositional optimism (i.e., generalized favorable expectancies for positive outcomes), which predicts salutary adjustment to breast cancer over time (for a review, see Carver, Scheier, & Segerstrom, 2010). Optimism also carries long-term significance in that it predicts more favorable adjustment 5 to 13 years after surgical treatment for breast cancer (Carver et al., 2005). One explanation for the utility of optimism is that it incites and sustains effort toward desired goals, including more approach-oriented coping with the experience of cancer, resulting in more favorable behavioral outcomes. There also is evidence that a constellation of psychosocial resources, including such factors as optimism, perceived social support, a sense of personal control, and self-esteem, predict enhanced quality of life in women with cancer (e.g., Helgeson et al., 2004).

Coping Processes

The effectiveness of specific coping strategies has been studied extensively in women with cancer. Coping is conceptualized as cognitive and behavioral efforts initiated in the context of situations that are appraised as personally significant and as taxing or exceeding the individual's resources for managing them (Lazarus & Folkman, 1984) or blocking pathways toward desired goals (Carver, Scheier, & Pozo, 1992). Coping varies as a function of the environmental context and is sensitive to personality attributes and cognitive appraisals of stressful situations (Folkman & Moskowitz, 2004). Active forms of coping that focus on addressing the problem, accepting the reality of the situation, or expressing cancer-related emotions are generally linked to declines in distress among women (e.g., Carver et al., 1993; Epping-Jordan et al., 1999; Stanton et al., 2000; Stanton et al., 2002). Women's coping with cancer through avoidance typically is associated with elevated distress (Carver et al., 1993; Stanton & Snider, 1993) and predicts fear of cancer recurrence among women with breast cancer across the first year following diagnosis (Stanton et al., 2002).

The Social Context

A large body of research establishes the centrality of the woman's interpersonal milieu in her adjustment to cancer. Of the various types of social support (i.e., emotional, informational, instrumental), emotional support evidences the strongest relation with positive adjustment in individuals with cancer (e.g., Helgeson & Cohen, 1996). The absence of support or presence of unsupportive behaviors also affects quality of life. For example, social isolation prior to a breast cancer diagnosis in the Nurses' Health Study cohort predicted poorer quality of life 4 years after diagnosis, accounting for more

variance than did cancer- and treatment-related factors (Michael, Berkman, Colditz, Holmes, & Kawachi, 2002). In women with gynecologic cancer, perceptions of unsupportive behaviors, involving avoidance and criticism, by family and friends predicted women's depressive symptoms over time (Manne et al., 2008).

Multiple Contributors to Women's Cancer-Related Adjustment

Although we have organized this section to describe discrete classes of factors that influence quality of life and functioning during women's experience of cancer, the empirical literature demonstrates that multiple and interacting factors shape adjustment. A good example comes from the body of research on women's return to employment after cancer diagnosis. Predictors of women's not returning to work or less rapid return include employment in a physically demanding job (Bouknight, Bradley, & Luo, 2006; Spelten et al., 2003), low perceived employer accommodation and high perceived employer discrimination regarding cancer (Bouknight et al., 2006), and the presence of depressive symptoms, comorbid diseases, advanced cancer, and cancer treatment-related physical complaints (Short et al., 2005; Spelten et al., 2003). Thus, the work environment, the disease-related context, and intra- and interpersonal parameters contribute to women's ability to return to work.

INTERVENTIONS FOR WOMEN DIAGNOSED WITH CANCER

In light of the negative psychosocial and physical consequences following diagnosis and treatment of cancer, it is crucial to develop effective interventions targeted at reducing psychological and physical morbidity and enhancing well-being and health. The substantial majority of research in this area focuses on women with breast cancer. Among the psychotherapies, the most extensively studied is cognitive-behavioral therapy (CBT). CBT seeks to improve behavioral, cognitive, and affective functioning through an array of strategies including cognitive restructuring, behavioral activation, relaxation training, and problem solving. The extant literature suggests that CBT is efficacious in women diagnosed with cancer. For example, Antoni, Lechner, et al. (2006) tested a 10-week group cognitive-behavioral stress management intervention among women newly treated for nonmetastatic breast cancer, following them for 1 year after recruitment. The intervention reduced reports of social disruption and increased emotional well-being, positive states of mind, cancer-related benefit finding, positive lifestyle change, and positive affect for up to 12 months. A meta-analysis revealed that cognitive-behavioral techniques are effective for reducing distress and pain in women with breast cancer (Tatrow & Montgomery, 2006). There is some evidence that CBT and similar interventions for women with breast cancer also influence neuroendocrine and immune function (McGregor & Antoni, 2009). Limited evidence suggests that CBT can be effective for women with gynecological cancers (Hersch, Juraskova, Price, & Mullan, 2008).

Several other intervention approaches to bolster quality of life and ameliorate specific sequelae of cancer treatment have been tested in randomized, controlled trials. Meta-analyses demonstrate the effectiveness of psychological interventions targeted toward the couple contending with cancer or toward the caregiver on such outcomes as quality of life and caregiver burden (Martire, Schulz, Helgeson, Small, & Saghafi, 2010; Northouse, Katapodi, Song, Zhang, & Mood, 2010). Research also indicates that physical exercise, such as cardiovascular exercise, progressive weight lifting, and targeted exercises (e.g., arm and shoulder), can be useful for improving both psychological (e.g., depressive symptoms, quality of life) and physical (e.g., physical functioning, fatigue, arm range of motion, lymphedema) outcomes in breast cancer patients (Duijts, Faber, Oldenburg, van Beurden, & Aaronson, 2011; McNeely et al., 2006; McNeely et al., 2010; Schmitz et al., 2010). Both nonpharmacologic (e.g., yoga) and pharmacologic approaches evidence some success for managing menopausal symptoms in women treated for breast cancer (e.g., Carson, Carson, Porter, Keefe, & Seewaldt, 2009; Cella & Fallowfield, 2008).

DIRECTIONS FOR APPLICATION AND RESEARCH

The past two decades of research have produced considerable progress in specification of psychosocial and physical consequences of cancer and its treatment for women, identification of contributors to those consequences, and development of evidence-based interventions to address them. Progress is uneven, however. The volume of research on the experience of breast cancer is strikingly large compared with that on other cancers of women, and generalization of findings across cancers experienced by women, particularly those with relatively high prevalence or poor prognosis (i.e., lung, colorectal, gynecologic cancers), is underexplored. With notable exceptions, the knowledge base primarily pertains to highly educated, White women. Research on ethnically, racially, and socio-economically diverse samples, as well as on other understudied groups (e.g., rural women: Bettencourt, Schlegel, Talley, & Molix, 2007; lesbians: Arena et al., 2006) is needed. Increased attention to groups that might be most at risk for untoward psycho-social and physical outcomes (e.g., young women, women with advanced cancer) also is warranted. Although effective inter-ventions for psychosocial and behavioral sequelae of cancer diagnosis and treatment in women are available, evidence-based refinement and dissemination are needed, so that they can be delivered most efficiently and effectively to diverse groups. The research base on contributors to psychosocial and physical concomitants of women's cancer experience can help guide such refinement of interventions.

As the number of cancer survivors con-tinues to rise, the necessity of long-term management of psychological and physical health following medical treatment comple-tion has drawn attention (e.g., Hewitt, Greenfield, & Stovall, 2006). The challenges faced by women treated for cancer are not solely confined to the active treatment phase and may extend years beyond treatment completion. Some problems and treatment side effects such as fatigue, sleep disruption, and fear of cancer recurrence may persist, whereas others such as cardiovascular com-plications of chemotherapy and lymph-edema can appear months later. The presence of long-term effects and late effects can serve as a constant reminder of the cancer experience to women looking to move beyond their experience with cancer, affecting psychological adjustment.

Upon completion of active treatment, cancer survivors may be uncertain about what follow-up care involves and which professionals will provide care. Despite the exponential growth of cancer survivors, there is a dearth of adult cancer survivorship programs in the United States. Continued investigation of long-term and late effects of cancer and of approaches to providing high-quality follow-up care for cancer survivors is essential. Recommendations from the Insti-tute of Medicine for adult cancer survivor-ship programs include raising awareness of the medical, functional, and psychosocial consequences of cancer and its treatment and identifying strategies to improve quality of life (Hewitt et al., 2006). Understudied issues of particular relevance to women include management of adherence to long-term endocrine therapies and side effects of treatment, sexual health, and fer-tility following cancer diagnosis and treat-ment (Niemasik et al., 2012). Ultimately, provision of effective preventive strategies and evidence-based care in both medical and psychosocial realms to women and their loved ones who confront a cancer diagnosis is a vitally important goal.

REFERENCES

Abusief, M. E., Missmer, S. A., Ginsberg, E. S., Weeks, J. C., & Partridge, A. H. (2010). The effects of paclitaxel, dose density, and trastuzu-mab on treatment-related amenorrhea in preme-nopausal women with breast cancer. *Cancer, 116,* 791–798.

Ahles, T. A., & Saykin, A. J. (2007). Candidate mechanisms for chemotherapy-induced cogni-tive changes. *Nature Reviews Cancer, 7,* 192–201.

Alfano, C. M., & Rowland, J. H. (2006). Recovery issues in cancer survivorship: A new challenge for supportive care. *The Cancer Journal, 12,* 432–443.

Altekruse, S. F., Kosary, C. L., Krapcho, M., Neyman, N., Aminou, R., & Waldron, W. (2010). *SEER cancer statistics review, 1975–2007*. Bethesda, MD: National Cancer Institute.

American Cancer Society. (2010). *Cancer facts & figures 2010*. Atlanta, GA: Author.

Andersen, B. L. (2009). In sickness and in health: Maintaining intimacy after breast cancer recurrence. *Cancer Journal, 15*, 70–73.

Andersen, B. L., Anderson, B., & DeProsse, C. (1989). Controlled prospective longitudinal study of women with cancer: II. Psychological outcomes. *Journal of Consulting and Clinical Psychology, 57*, 692–697.

Andersen, B. L., Carpenter, K. M., Yang, H.-C., & Shapiro, C. L. (2007). Sexual well-being among partnered women with breast cancer recurrence. *Journal of Clinical Oncology, 25*, 3151–3157.

Antoni, M. H., Lechner, S. C., Kazi, A., Wimberly, S. R., Sifre, T., Urcuyo, K. R., . . . Carver, C. S. (2006). How stress management improves quality of life after breast cancer. *Journal of Consulting and Clinical Psychology, 74*, 1143–1152.

Antoni, M. H., Lutgendorf, S. K., Cole, S. W., Dhabhar, F. S., Sephton, S. E., McDonald, P. G., . . . Sood, A. K. (2006). The influence of bio-behavioural factors on tumour biology: Pathways and mechanisms. *Nature Reviews Cancer, 6*, 240–248.

Arena, P. L., Carver, C. S., Antoni, M. H., Weiss, S., Ironson, G., & Durán, R. E. (2006). Psychosocial responses to treatment for breast cancer among lesbian and heterosexual women. *Women's Health, 44*, 81–102.

Arora, N. K., Finney Rutten, L. J., Gustafson, D. H., Moser, R., & Hawkins, R. P. (2007). Perceived helpfulness and impact of social support provided by family, friends, and health care providers to women newly diagnosed with breast cancer. *Psycho-Oncology, 16*, 474–486.

Ashing-Giwa, K. T., Tejero, J. S., Kim, J., Padilla, G. V., Kagawa-Singer, M., Tucker, M. B., & Lim, J. W. (2009). Cervical cancer survivorship in a population-based sample. *Gynecologic Oncology, 112*, 358–364.

Avis, N. E., Crawford, S., & Manuel, J. (2005). Quality of life among younger women with breast cancer. *Journal of Clinical Oncology, 23*, 3322–3330.

Bardwell, W. A., Natarajan, L., Dimsdale, J. E., Rock, C. L., Mortimer, J. E., Hollenbach, K., & Pierce, J. P. (2006). Objective cancer-related variables are not associated with depressive symptoms in women treated for early-stage breast cancer. *Journal of Clinical Oncology, 24*, 2420–2427.

Baucom, D. H., Porter, L. S., Kirby, J. S., Gremore, T. M., & Keefe, F. J. (2005, 2006). Psychosocial issues confronting young women with breast cancer. *Breast Disease, 23*, 103–113.

Bellizzi, K. M., Smith, A. W., Reeve, B. B., Alfano, C. M., Bernstein, L., Meeske, K., . . . Ballard-Barbash, R. R. (2010). Posttraumatic growth and health-related quality of life in a racially diverse cohort of breast cancer survivors. *Journal of Health Psychology, 15*, 615–626.

Bettencourt, B. A., Schlegel, R. J., Talley, A. E., & Molix, L. A. (2007). The breast cancer experience of rural women: A literature review. *Psycho-Oncology, 16*, 875–887.

Bloom, J. R., Petersen, D. M., & Kang, S. H. (2007). Multi-dimensional quality of life among long-term (5+ years) adult cancer survivors. *Psycho-Oncology, 16*, 691–706.

Bodurka-Bevers, D., Basen-Engquist, K., Carmack, C. L., Fitzgerald, M. A., Wolf, J. K., de Moor, C., & Gershenson, D. M. (2000). Depression, anxiety, and quality of life in patients with epithelial ovarian cancer. *Gynecologic Oncology, 78*, 302–308.

Booth, C. M., Clemons, M., Dranitsaris, G., Joy, A., Young, S., Callaghan, W., . . . Petrella, T. (2007). Chemotherapy-induced nausea and vomiting in breast cancer patients: A prospective observational study. *Journal of Supportive Oncology, 5*, 374–80.

Bouknight, R. R., Bradley, C. J., & Luo, Z. (2006). Correlates of return to work for breast cancer survivors. *Journal of Clinical Oncology, 24*, 345–353.

Bower, J. E. (2008). Behavioral symptoms in patients with breast cancer and survivors. *Journal Clinical Oncology, 26*, 768–77.

Bower, J. E., Ganz, P. A., Desmond, K. A., Rowland, J. H., Meyerowitz, B. E., & Belin, T. R. (2000). Fatigue in breast cancer survivors: Occurrence, correlates, and impact on quality of life. *Journal of Clinical Oncology, 18*, 743–753.

Bower, J. E., Meyerowitz, B. E., Desmond, K. A., Bernaards, C. A., Rowland, J. H., & Ganz, P. A.

(2005). Perceptions of positive meaning and vulnerability following breast cancer: Predictors and outcomes among long-term breast cancer survivors. *Annals of Behavioral Medicine, 29,* 236–245.

Bruera E., Willey J. S., Palmer J. L., & Rosales M. (2002). Treatment decisions for breast carcinoma: Patient preferences and physician perceptions. *Cancer, 94,* 2076–2080.

Bui, Q. U., Ostir, G. V., Kuo, Y. F., Freeman, J., & Goodwin, J. S. (2005). Relationship of depression to patient satisfaction: Findings from the barriers to breast cancer study. *Breast Cancer Research and Treatment, 89,* 23–28.

Buki, L. P., Garces, D. M., Hinestrosa, M. C., Kogan, L., Carrillo, I. Y., & French, B. (2008). Latina breast cancer survivors' lived experiences: Diagnosis, treatment and beyond. *Cultural Diversity and Ethnic Minority Research, 14,* 163–167.

Burgess, C., Cornelius, V., Love, S., Graham, J., Richards, M., & Ramirez, A. (2005). Depression and anxiety in women with early breast cancer: Five-year observational cohort study. *British Medical Journal, 330,* 702–705.

Caban, M. E., Freeman, J. L., Zhang, D. D., Jansen, C., Ostir, G., Hatch, S. S., & Goodwin, J. S. (2006). The relationship between depressive symptoms and shoulder mobility among older women: Assessment at one year after breast cancer diagnosis. *Clinical Rehabilitation, 20,* 513–522.

Calhoun, L. G., & Tedeschi, R. G. (2006). *Handbook of posttraumatic growth: Research and practice.* Mahwah, NJ: Erlbaum.

Canada, A. L., & Schover, L. R. (2012). The psychosocial impact of interrupted child-bearing in long-term female cancer survivors. *Psycho-Oncology, 21*(2), 134–143.

Carpenter, K. M., Andersen, B. L, Fowler, J., & Maxwell, L. (2009). Sexual self schema as a moderator of sexual and psychological outcomes for gynecologic cancer survivors. *Archives of Sexual Behavior, 38,* 828–841.

Carson, J. W., Carson, K. M., Porter, L. S., Keefe, F. J., & Seewaldt, V. L. (2009). Yoga of Awareness program for menopausal symptoms in breast cancer survivors: Results from a randomized trial. *Supportive Care in Cancer, 17,* 1301–1309.

Carter, J., Rowland, K., Chi, D., Brown, C., Abu-Rustum, N., Castiel, M., & Barakat, R.

(2005). Gynecologic cancer treatment and the impact of cancer-related infertility. *Gynecologic Oncology, 97,* 90–95.

Carver, C. S., & Antoni, M. H. (2004). Finding benefit in breast cancer during the year after diagnosis predicts better adjustment 5 to 8 years after cancer. *Health Psychology, 23,* 595–598.

Carver, C. S., Pozo, C., Harris, S. D., Noriega, V., Scheier, M. F., Robinson, D. S., . . . Clark, K. C. (1993). How coping mediates the effect of optimism on distress: A study of women with early stage breast cancer. *Journal of Personality and Social Psychology, 65,* 375–390.

Carver, C. S., Scheier, M. F., & Pozo, C. (1992). Conceptualizing the process of coping with health problems. In H. S. Friedman (Ed.), *Hostility, coping, and health* (pp. 167–187). Washington, DC: American Psychological Association.

Carver, C. S., Scheier, M. F., & Segerstrom, S. C. (2010). Optimism. *Clinical Psychology Review, 30,* 879–889.

Carver, C. S., Smith, R. G, Antoni, M. H., Petronis, V. M., Weiss, S., & Derhagopian, R. P. (2005). Optimistic personality and psychosocial well-being during treatment predict psychosocial well-being among long-term survivors of breast cancer. *Health Psychology, 24,* 508–516.

Cella, D., & Fallowfield, L. J. (2008). Recognition and management of treatment-related side effects for breast cancer patients receiving adjuvant endocrine therapy. *Breast Cancer Research and Treatment, 107,* 167–180.

Chen, X., & Siu, L. L. (2001). Impact of the media and the Internet on oncology: Survey of cancer patients and oncologists in Canada. *Journal of Clinical Oncology, 19,* 4291–4297.

Christensen, S., Zachariae. R., Jensen, A., Væth, M., Møller, S., Ravnsbæk, J., & von der Maase, H. (2009). Prevalence and risk of depressive symptoms 3-4 months post-surgery in a nationwide cohort study of Danish women treated for early stage breast-cancer. *Breast Cancer Research and Treatment, 113,* 339–355.

Cordova, M. J., Cunningham, L. L., Carlson, C. L., & Andrykowski, M. A. (2001). Posttraumatic growth following breast cancer: A controlled comparison study. *Health Psychology, 20,* 176–185.

Costanzo, E. S., Lutgendorf, S. K., Mattes, M. L, Trehan, S., Robinson, C. B., Tewfik, F., & Roman, S. L. (2007). Adjusting to life after treatment: Distress and quality of life following treatment for breast cancer. *British Journal of Cancer, 97,* 1625–1631.

Cousineau, T. M., & Domar, A. D. (2007). Psychological impact of infertility. *Best Practice & Research Clinical Obstetrics & Gynaecology, 21,* 293–308.

de Bock, G. H., Bonnema, J., Zwaan, R. E., van de Velde, C. J., Kievit, J., & Stiggelbout, A. M. (2004). Patients' needs and preferences in routine follow-up after treatment for breast cancer. *British Journal of Cancer, 90,* 1144–1150.

de Boer, A. G., Taskila, T., Ojajärvi, A., van Dijk, F. J., & Verbeek, J. H. (2009). Cancer survivors and unemployment: A meta-analysis and meta-regression. *Journal of the American Medical Association, 301,* 753–762.

de Boer, A. G., Taskila, T., Tamminga, S. J., Frings-Dresen, M. H., Feuerstein, M., & Verbeek, J. H. (2011). Interventions to enhance return-to-work for cancer patients. *Cochrane Database of Systematic Reviews, 2,* No. CD007569. doi: 10.1002/14651858.CD007569.pub2

Degner L. F., Kristjanson L. J., Bowman D., Sloan, J. A., Carriere, K. C., O'Neil, J., . . . Mueller, B. (1997). Information needs and decisional preferences in women with breast cancer. *Journal of the American Medical Association, 277,* 1485–1492.

Dijkstra, P. U., Rietman, J. S., & Geertzen, J. H. (2007). Phantom breast sensations and phantom breast pain: A 2-year prospective study and a methodological analysis of literature. *European Journal of Pain, 11,* 99–108.

DiMatteo, M. R., Lepper, H. S., & Croghan, T. W. (2000). Depression is a risk factor for non-compliance with medical treatment. Meta-analysis of the effects of anxiety and depression on patient adherence. *Archives of Internal Medicine, 160,* 2101–2107.

Dorval, M., Guay, S., Mondor, M., Mondor, M., Mâsse, B., Falardeau, M., . . . Maunsell, E. (2005). Couples who get closer after breast cancer: Frequency and predicators in a prospective investigation. *Journal of Clinical Oncology, 23,* 3588–3596.

Duijts, S. F. A., Faber, M. M., Oldenberg, H. S. A., van Beurden, M., & Aaronson, N. K. (2011). Effectiveness of behavioral techniques and physical exercise on psychosocial functioning and health-related quality of life in breast cancer

patients and survivors—A meta-analysis. *Psycho-Oncology, 20,* 115–126.

Dunn, L. B., Cooper, B. A., Neuhaus, J., West, C., Paul, S. Aouizerat, B., . . . Miaskowski, C. (2011). Identification of distinct depressive symptom trajectories in women following surgery for breast cancer. *Health Psychology, 30*(6), 683–692.

Epping-Jordan, J. E., Compas, B. E., Osowiecki, D. M., Oppedisano, G., Gerhardt, C., Primo, K., & Krag, D. N. (1999). Psychological adjustment in breast cancer: Processes of emotional distress. *Health Psychology, 18,* 315–326.

Eversley, R., Estrin, D., Dibble, S., Wardlaw, L., Pedrosa, M., & Favila-Penney, W. (2005). Post-treatment symptoms among ethnic minority breast cancer survivors. *Oncology Nursing Forum, 32,* 250–256.

Fiorentino, L., & Ancoli-Israel, S. (2006). Insomnia and its treatment in women with breast cancer. *Sleep Medicine Reviews, 10,* 419–429.

Folkman, S., & Moskowitz, J. T. (2004). Coping: Pitfalls and promise. *Annual Review of Psychology, 55,* 745–774.

Gallo, L. C., & Matthews, K. A. (2003). Understanding the association between socioeconomic status and physical health: Do negative emotions play a role? *Psychological Bulletin, 129,* 10–51.

Ganz, P. A., Greendale, G. A., Petersen, L., Kahn, B., & Bower, J. E. (2003). Breast cancer in younger women: Reproductive and late health effects of treatment. *Journal of Clinical Oncology, 21,* 4184–4193.

Ganz, P. A., Kwan, L., Stanton, A. L., Bower, J. E., & Belin, T. R. (2011). Physical and psychosocial recovery in the year after primary treatment of breast cancer. *Journal of Clinical Oncology, 29,* 1101–1109.

Golden-Kreutz, D. M., Thornton, L. M., Wells-Di Gregorio, S., Frierson, G. M., Jim, H. S., . . . Andersen, B. L. (2005). Traumatic stress, perceived global stress, and life events: Prospectively predicting quality of life in breast cancer patients. *Health Psychology, 24,* 288–294.

Grunfeld, E., Coyle, D., Whelan, T., Clinch, J., Reyno, L., Earle, C. C., . . . Glossop, R. (2004). Family caregiver burden: Results of a longitudinal study of breast cancer patients and their principal caregivers. *Canadian Medical Association Journal, 170,* 1795–1801.

Hagedoorn, M., Sanderman, R., Bolks, H. N., Tuinstra, J., & Coyne, J. C. (2008). Distress in couples coping with cancer: A meta-analysis and critical review of role and gender effects. *Psychological Bulletin, 134,* 1–30.

Hamilton, J. G., Lobel, M., & Moyer, A. (2009). Emotional distress following genetic testing for hereditary breast and ovarian cancer: A meta-analytic review. *Health Psychology, 28,* 510–518.

Härtl, K., Engel, J., Herschbach, P., Reinecker, H., Sommer, H., & Friese, K. (2010). Personality traits and psychosocial stress: Quality of life over 2 years following breast cancer diagnosis and psychological impact factors. *Psycho-Oncology, 19,* 160–169.

Hay, J. L., McCaul, K. D., & Magnan, R. E. (2006). Does worry about breast cancer predict screening behaviors? A meta-analysis of the prospective evidence. *Preventive Medicine, 42,* 401–408.

Helgeson, V. S., & Cohen, S. (1996). Social support and adjustment to cancer: Reconciling descriptive, correlational, and intervention research. *Health Psychology, 15,* 135–148.

Helgeson, V. S., Reynolds, K. A. & Tomich, P. (2006). A meta-analytic review of benefit finding and growth. *Journal of Consulting and Clinical Psychology, 74,* 797–816.

Helgeson, V. S., Snyder, P., & Seltman, H. (2004). Psychological and physical adjustment to breast cancer over 4 years: Identifying distinct trajectories of change. *Health Psychology, 23,* 3–15.

Henselmans, I., Helgeson, V. S., Seltman, H., de Vries, J., Sanderman, R., & Ranchor, A. V. (2010). Identification and prediction of distress trajectories in the first year after a breast cancer diagnosis. *Health Psychology, 29,* 160–168.

Hersch, J., Juraskova, I., Price, M., & Mullan, B. (2008). Psychosocial interventions and quality of life in gynaecological cancer patients: A systematic review. *Psycho-Oncology, 18,* 795–810.

Hewitt, M., Greenfield, S., & Stovall, E. (2006). *From cancer patient to cancer survivor: Lost in transition.* Washington, DC: Committee on Cancer Survivorship: Improving Care and Quality of Life, National Cancer Policy Board, Institute of Medicine, and National Research Council, National Academies Press.

Himelhoch, S., Weller, W. E., Wu, A. W., Anderson, G. F., & Cooper, L. A. (2004). Chronic medical illness, depression, and use of acute medical services among Medicare beneficiaries. *Medical Care, 42,* 512–521.

Hoffman, B., (2005). Cancer survivors at work: A generation of progress. *CA: A Cancer Journal for Clinicians, 55,* 271–280.

Hoving, J. L., Broekhuizen, M. L. A., & Frings-Dresen, M. H. W. (2009). Return to work of breast cancer survivors: A systematic review of intervention studies. *BMC Cancer, 9,* 117. doi: 10.1186/1471-2407-9-117

Howard-Anderson, J., Ganz, P. A., Bower, J. E., & Stanton, A. L. (2012). Quality of life, fertility concerns, and behavioral health outcomes in younger breast cancer survivors: A systematic review. *Journal of the National Cancer Institute, 104,* 386–405.

Janelsins, M. C., Kohli, S., Mohile, S. G., Usuki, K., Ahles, T. A., & Morrow, G. R. (2011). An update on cancer- and chemotherapy-related cognitive dysfunction: Current status. *Seminars in Oncology, 38,* 431–438.

Janz, N. K., Mujahid, M., Chung, L. K., Lantz, P. M., Hawley, S. T., Morrow, M., . . . Katz, S. J. (2007). Symptom experience and quality of life of women following breast cancer treatment. *Journal of Women's Health, 16,* 1348–1361.

Janz, N. K., Mujahid, M., Hawley, S. T., Griggs, J. J., Alderman, A., Hamilton, A. S., . . . Katz, S. J. (2009). Racial/ethnic differences in quality of life after diagnosis of breast cancer. *Journal of Cancer Survivorship, 3,* 212–222.

Janz, N. K., Mujahid, M., Lantz, P. M., Fagerlin, A., Salem, B., Morrow, M., . . . Katz, S. (2005). Population-based study of the relationship of treatment and sociodemographics on quality of life after breast cancer. *Quality of Life Research, 14,* 1467–1479.

Janz, N. K., Wren, P. A., Copeland, L. A., Lowery, J. C., Goldfarb, S. L., & Wilkins, E. G. (2004). Patient-physician concordance: Preferences, perceptions, and factors influencing the breast cancer surgical decision. *Journal of Clinical Oncology, 22,* 3091–3098.

Jemal, A., Siegel, R., Xu, J., & Ward, E. (2010). Cancer statistics, 2010. *CA: A Cancer Journal for Clinicians, 60,* 277–300.

Jim, H. S., Andrykowski, M. A., Munster, P. N., & Jacobsen, P. B. (2007). Physical symptoms/side effects during breast cancer treatment predict posttreatment distress. *Annals of Behavioral Medicine, 34,* 200–208.

Johnsson, A., Fornander, T., Rutqvist, L. E., Vaez, M., Alexanderson, K., & Olsson, M. (2009). Predictors of return to work ten months after primary breast cancer surgery. *Acta Oncologica, 48,* 93–98.

Kessler, R. C., Chiu, W. T., Demler, O., & Walters, E. E. (2005). Prevalence, severity, and comorbidity of 12-month DSM-IV disorders in the National Comorbidity Survey replication. *Archives of General Psychiatry, 62,* 617–627.

Kim, Y., & Given, B. A. (2008). Quality of life of family caregivers of cancer survivors across the trajectory of the illness. *Cancer, 112*(Suppl. 11), 2556–2568.

Kim, S. S., Klemp, J., & Fabian, C. (2011). Breast cancer and fertility preservation. *Fertility & Sterility, 95,* 1535–1543.

Kroenke, C. H., Rosner, B., Chen, W. Y., Colditz, G. A., & Holmes, M. D. (2004). Functional impact of breast cancer by age at diagnosis. *Journal of Clinical Oncology, 22,* 1849–1856.

Lauzier, S., Maunsell, E., Drolet, M., Coyle, D., Hébert-Croteau, N., Brisson, J., . . . Robert, J. (2008). Wage losses in the year after breast cancer: Extent and determinants among Canadian women. *Journal of the National Cancer Institute, 100,* 321–332.

Lazarus, R. S., & Folkman, S. (1984). *Stress, appraisal, and coping.* New York, NY: Springer.

Luker, K. A., Beaver, K., Leinster, S. J., & Owens, R. G. (1996). Information needs and sources of information for women with breast cancer: A follow-up study. *Journal of Advanced Nursing, 23,* 487–495.

Manne, S., & Badr, H. (2008). Intimacy and relationship processes in couples' psychosocial adaptation to cancer. *Cancer, 112*(Suppl. 11), 2541–2555.

Manne, S., Ostroff, J., Winkel, G., Goldstein, L., Fox, K., & Grana, G. (2004). Posttraumatic growth after breast cancer: Patient, partner, and couple perspectives. *Psychosomatic Medicine, 66,* 442–454.

Manne, S., Rini, C., Rubin, S., Rosenblum, N., Bergman, C., Edelson, M., . . . Rocereto, T. (2008). Long-term trajectories of psychological adaptation among women diagnosed with gynecological cancers. *Psychosomatic Medicine, 70,* 677–687.

Martire, L. M., Schulz, R., Helgeson, V. S., Small, B. J., & Saghafi, E. M. (2010). Review and meta-analysis of couple-oriented interventions for chronic illness. *Annals of Behavioral Medicine, 40,* 325–342.

Massie, M. J. (2004). Prevalence of depression in patients with cancer. *Journal of the National Cancer Institute Monographs, 32,* 57–71.

McCorkle, R., Tang, S. T., Greenwald, H., Holcombe, G., & Lavery, M. (2006). Factors related to depressive symptoms among long-term survivors of cervical cancer. *Health Care for Women International, 27,* 45–58.

McDonald, B. C., Conroy, S. K., Ahles, T. A., West, J. D., & Saykin, A. J. (2010). Gray matter reduction associated with systemic chemotherapy for breast cancer: A prospective MRI study. *Breast Cancer Research and Treatment, 123,* 819–828.

McGregor, B. A., & Antoni, M. H. (2009). Psychological intervention and health outcomes among women treated for breast cancer: A review of stress pathways and biological mediators. *Brain, Behavior, and Immunity, 23,* 159–166.

McLaughlin, S. A., Wright, M. J., Morris, K. T., Giron, G. L., Sampson, M. R., Brockway, J. P., . . . Van Zee, K. J. (2008). Prevalence of lymphedema in women with breast cancer 5 years after sentinel lymph node biopsy or axillary dissection: Objective measurements. *Journal of Clinical Oncology, 26,* 5213–5219.

McNeely, M. L., Campbell, K. L., Ospina, M., Rowe, B. H., Dabbs, K., Klassen, T. P., Mackey, J., & Courneya, K. (2010). Exercise interventions for upper-limb dysfunction due to breast cancer treatment. *Cochrane Database Systematic Reviews, 16*(6), CD005211.

McNeely, M. L., Campbell, K. L., Rowe, B. H., Klassen, T. P., Mackey, J. R., & Courneya, K. S. (2006). Effects of exercise on breast cancer patients and survivors: A systematic review and meta-analysis. *Canadian Medical Association Journal, 175,* 34–41.

McTiernan, A., Irwin, M., & VonGruenigen, V. (2010). Weight, physical activity, diet, and prognosis in breast and gynecologic cancers. *Journal of Clinical Oncology, 28,* 4074–4080.

Miaskowski, C. (2004). Gender differences in pain, fatigue, and depression in patients with cancer.

Journal of the National Cancer Institute Monographs, 32, 139–143.

Michael, Y. L., Berkman, L. F., Colditz, G. A., Holmes, M. D., & Kawachi, I. (2002). Social networks and health-related quality of life in breast cancer survivors: A prospective study. *Journal of Psychosomatic Research, 52,* 285–293.

Michael, Y. L., Kawachi, I., Berkman, L. F., Holmes, M. D., & Colditz, G. A. (2000). The persistent impact of breast carcinoma on functional health status. Prospective evidence from the Nurses' Health Study. *Cancer, 89,* 2176–2186.

Millar, K., Purushotham A. D., McLatchie, E., George, W. D., & Murray, G. (2005). A 1-year prospective study of individual variation in distress, and illness perceptions, after treatment for breast cancer. *Journal of Psychosomatic Research, 58,* 335–342.

Mitchell, A. J., Chan, M., Bhatti, H., Halton, M., Grassi, L., Johansen, C., & Meader, N. (2011). Prevalence of depression, anxiety, and adjustment disorder in oncological, haematological, and palliative-care settings: A meta-analysis of 94 interview-based studies. *Lancet Oncology, 12,* 160–174.

Mols, F., Vingerhoets, A. J. J. M., Coebergh, J. W., & van de Poll-Franse, L. V. (2005). Quality of life among long-term breast cancer survivors: A systematic review. *European Journal of Cancer, 41,* 2613–2619.

Niemasik, E. E., Letourneau, J., Dohan, D., Katz, A., Melisko, M., Rugo, H., & Rosen, M. (2012). Patient perceptions of reproductive health counseling at the time of cancer diagnosis: A qualitative study of female California cancer survivors. *Journal of Cancer Survivorship, 6,* 324–332.

Northouse, L. L., Katapodi, M. C., Song, L., Zhang, L., & Mood, D. W. (2010). Interventions with family caregivers of cancer patients: Meta-analysis of randomized trials. *CA: A Cancer Journal for Clinicians, 60,* 317–339.

Park, C. L., & Gaffey, A. E. (2007). Relationships between psychosocial factors and health behavior change in cancer survivors: An integrative review. *Annals of Behavioral Medicine, 34,* 115–134.

Park, C. L., Lechner, S. C., Antoni, M. H., & Stanton, A. L. (Eds.). (2009). *Medical illness and positive life change: Can crisis lead to personal transformation?* Washington, DC: American Psychological Association.

Pasick, R. J., & Burke, N. J. (2008). A critical review of theory in breast cancer screening promotion across cultures. *Annual Review of Public Health, 29,* 351–368.

Paskett, E. D., Alfano, C. M., Davidson, M. A., Andersen, B. L., Naughton, M. J., Sherman, A., McDonald, P., & Hays, J. (2008). Breast cancer survivors' health-related quality of life: Racial differences and comparisons to non-cancer controls. *Cancer, 113,* 3222–3230.

Perez Stable E. J., Sabogal, F., Otero-Sabogal, R., Hiatt, R. A., & McPhee, S. J. (1992). Misconceptions about cancer among Latinos and Anglos. *Journal of the American Medical Association, 268,* 3219–3223.

Powe, B. D., Hamilton, J., Hancock, N., Johnson, N., Finnie, J., Ko, J., . . . Boggan, M. (2007). Quality of life of African American cancer survivors: A review of the literature. *Cancer, 109,* 435–445.

Ramirez, A. G., Suarez, L., Laufman, L., Barroso, C., & Chalela, P. (2000). Hispanic women's breast and cervical cancer knowledge, attitudes, and screening behaviors. *American Journal of Health Promotion, 14,* 292–300.

Reich, M., Lesur, A., & Perdrizet-Chevallier, C. (2008). Depression, quality of life, and breast cancer: A review of the literature. *Breast Cancer Research and Treatment, 110,* 9–17.

Schmitz, K. H., Ahmed, R. L., Troxel, A. B., Cheville, A., Lewis-Grant, L., Smith, R., . . . Chittams, J. (2010). Weight lifting for women at risk of breast cancer-related lymphedema: A randomized trial. *Journal of the American Medicine Association, 304,* 2699–2705.

Sears, S. R., Stanton, A. L., & Danoff-Burg, S. (2003). The Yellow Brick Road and the Emerald City: Benefit finding, positive reappraisal coping, and posttraumatic growth in women with early-stage breast cancer. *Health Psychology, 22,* 487–497.

Short, P. F., & Vargo, M. M. (2006). Responding to employment concerns of cancer survivors. *Journal of Clinical Oncology, 24,* 5138–5141.

Short, P. F., Vasey, J. J., & Tunceli, K. (2005). Employment pathways in a large cohort of adult cancer survivors. *Cancer, 103,* 1292–1301.

Siegel, R., Ward, E., Brawley, O., & Jemal, A. (2011). Cancer statistics, 2011: The impact of eliminating socioeconomic and racial disparities on premature cancer deaths. *CA: A Cancer Journal for Clinicians, 61*(4), 212–236.

Simon, A. E., & Wardle, J. (2008). Socioeconomic disparities in psychosocial well-being in cancer patients. *European Journal of Cancer, 44*, 572–578.

Spelten, E. R., Verbeek, J. H. A. M., Uitterhoeve, A. L. J., Ansink, A. C., van der Lelie, J., de Reijke, T. M., . . . Sprangers, M. A. G. (2003). Cancer, fatigue, and the return of patients to work—A prospective cohort study. *European Journal of Cancer, 39*, 1562–1567.

Stanton, A. L., Bower, J. E., & Low, C. A. (2006). Posttraumatic growth after cancer. In L. G. Calhoun & R. G. Tedeschi (Eds.), *Handbook of posttraumatic growth: Research and practice* (pp. 138–175). Mahwah, NJ: Erlbaum.

Stanton, A. L., Danoff-Burg, S., Cameron, C. L., Bishop, M. M., Collins, C. A., Kirk, S. B., & Twillman, R. (2000). Emotionally expressive coping predicts psychological and physical adjustment to breast cancer. *Journal of Consulting and Clinical Psychology, 68*, 875–882.

Stanton, A. L., Danoff-Burg, S., & Huggins, M. E. (2002). The first year after breast cancer diagnosis: Hope and coping strategies as predictors of adjustment. *Psycho-Oncology, 11*, 93–102.

Stanton, A. L., Ganz, P. A., Rowland, J. H., Meyerowitz, B. E., Krupnick, J. L., & Sears, S. R. (2005). Promoting adjustment after treatment for cancer. *Cancer, 104*, 2608–2613.

Stanton, A. L., & Snider, P. R. (1993). Coping with a breast cancer diagnosis: A prospective study. *Health Psychology, 12*, 16–23.

Stenberg, U., Ruland, C. M., & Miaskowski, C. (2010). Review of the literature on the effects of caring for a patient with cancer. *Psycho-Oncology, 19*, 1013–1025.

Stewart, D. E., Wong, F., Duff, S., Melancon, C. H., & Cheung, A. M. (2001). "What doesn't kill you makes you stronger": An ovarian cancer survivor survey. *Gynecologic Oncology, 83*, 537–542.

Tamres, L. K., Janicki, D., & Helgeson, V. S. (2002). Sex differences in coping behavior: A meta-analytic review and an examination of relative coping. *Personality and Social Psychology Review, 6*, 2–30.

Tatrow, K., & Montgomery, G. H. (2006). Cognitive behavioral therapy techniques for distress and pain in breast cancer patients: A meta-analysis. *Journal of Behavioral Medicine, 29*, 17–27.

Tedeschi, R. G., & Calhoun, L. G. (1996). The posttraumatic growth inventory: Measuring the positive legacy of trauma. *Journal of Traumatic Stress, 9*, 455–471.

Tomich, P. L., & Helgeson, V. S. (2004). Is finding something good in the bad always good? Benefit finding among women with breast cancer. *Health Psychology, 23*, 16–23.

Trentham-Dietz, A., Sprague, B. L., Klein, R., Klein, B. E. K., Cruickshanks, K. J., Fryback, D. G., & Hampton, J. M. (2008). Health-related quality of life before and after a breast cancer diagnosis. *Breast Cancer Research and Treatment, 109*, 379–387.

van't Spijker, A., Trijsburg, R. W., & Duivenvoorden, H. J. (1997). Psychological sequelae of cancer diagnosis: A meta-analytical review of 58 studies after 1980. *Psychosomatic Medicine, 59*, 280–293.

Vardy, J. (2009). Cognitive function in breast cancer survivors. *Cancer Treatment and Research, 151*, 387–419.

Vodermaier, A., Linden, W., & Siu, C. (2009). Screening for emotional distress in cancer patients: A systematic review of assessment instruments. *Journal of the National Cancer Institute, 101*, 1464–1488.

Wenzel, L., Dogan-Ates, A., Habbal, R., Berkowitz, R., Goldstein, D. P., Bernstein, M., . . . Cella, D. (2005). Defining and measuring reproductive concerns of female cancer survivors. *Journal of the National Cancer Institute Monographs, 34*, 94–98.

Wenzel, L. B., Donnelly, J. P., Fowler, J. M., Habbal, R., Taylor T. H., Aziz, N., & Cella, D. (2002). Resilience, reflection, and residual stress in ovarian cancer survivorship: A gynecologic oncology group study. *Psycho-Oncology, 11*, 142–153.

Yanez, B., Thompson E. H., & Stanton, A. L. (2011). Quality of life among Latina breast cancer patients: A systematic review of the literature. *Journal of Cancer Survivorship, 5*, 191–197.

21

The Psychology of Irritable Bowel Syndrome

SARAH K. BALLOU AND LAURIE KEEFER

INTRODUCTION

Irritable bowel syndrome (IBS) is a functional disorder of the gastrointestinal tract that affects approximately 10% to 15% of the population (Hungin, Chang, Locke, Dennis, & Barghout, 2005; Saito, Schoenfeld, & Locke, 2002). It is characterized by abdominal pain/discomfort and is associated with diarrhea, constipation, or a mixture of both (Longstreth et al., 2006; Remes-Troche et al., 2009). In the absence of a reliable biomarker, the diagnosis of IBS is based on reported symptom experience, clinical presentation, and the absence of "alarm features," which might include bleeding, unexplained weight loss, a family history of colorectal cancer, fever, or anemia (Longstreth et al., 2006; Remes-Troche et al., 2009).

The diagnostic criteria for IBS has undergone several modifications from its original version in 1989, with the most updated version, the ROME III Criteria, published in 2006. In order to meet criteria for IBS, a patient must have abdominal pain that is relieved with defecation or associated with a change in frequency, form, and/or appearance of stool on a recurring basis for at least 3 months (Longstreth et al., 2006). IBS is further classified by predominant bowel patterns, which include diarrhea-predominant (IBS-D); constipation-predominant (IBS-C);

or mixed-type (IBS-M). Due to the sometimes unpredictable nature of IBS symptoms, a diagnosis of one of these three subtypes is not always absolute, and patients may fluctuate between two or three different subtypes in the course of their IBS. Although studies regarding the prevalence of each IBS subtype have been largely inconclusive, a credible estimate for the prevalence of IBS-D, IBS-C, and IBS-M may be 30.9%, 57% to 66%, and 63%, respectively (Guilera, Balboa, & Mearin, 2005). Prevalence rates of IBS are remarkably similar across various ethnic groups around the world (Sperber, 2009).

The majority of IBS patients (60%) are women, which is likely a reflection of socially defined gender differences in healthcare-seeking behavior rather than true biological gender differences in gastrointestinal functioning (Drossman, Camilleri, Mayer, & Whitehead, 2002). Unfortunately, due to the predominance of female patients, IBS has been pejoratively labeled a "career woman's" disease (Toner & Akman, 2000), implying a relationship between IBS presentation and nonconformity to traditional gender roles. IBS is most prevalent among 40- to 50-year-old women, but can occur at any time during the lifespan (Hungin et al., 2005; Hungin,

Whorwell, Tack, & Mearin, 2003). Indeed, adolescent women in the community frequently report severe abdominal pain (Hyams, Burke, Davis, Rzepski, & Andrulonis, 1996), and younger women with IBS are a growing patient population that will likely continue to expand as healthcare becomes increasingly available and social stigmas around bowel symptoms and psychological stress decrease.

Due in part to a lack of effective medical treatments, healthcare utilization among IBS patients is comparable to that of patients with diabetes and heart disease (Shih et al., 2002). It is one of the most frequently diagnosed and costly gastrointestinal (GI) conditions in the United States (Sandler et al., 2002), accounting for up to 13.8 hours per 40-hour workweek in lost work productivity alone (Pare et al., 2006). Patients with IBS also report poor health-related quality of life, especially in the areas of diet, mood, daily activities, and sleep (Groll et al., 2002; Longstreth et al., 2005; Patrick, Drossman, Frederick, DiCesare, & Puder, 1998). One study recently showed that, on average, IBS patients would be willing to give up 15.1 years of their lives if they could find a treatment to completely eliminate symptoms (Drossman et al., 2009). Many IBS patients cope with the limitations of their disease by incorporating related stress and worry into their everyday lives (Farndale & Roberts, 2011).

Biopsychosocial Model of IBS

IBS is best understood in the context of the biopsychosocial model. Research has demonstrated that IBS is a multifactorial disease and reflects the complex interplay among biology, early life experiences, psychological processes, and societal influences.

BIOLOGICAL FACTORS

The physiological basis for IBS involves multiple symptoms and processes and, unfortunately, most research is limited by the use of all-female samples. As a result, most gender-based conclusions about IBS are invalid. The following section briefly outlines the underlying physiology of IBS in both men and women.

The *central nervous system* (CNS) interacts directly with the digestive system through neurons that begin in the gut and travel through the spinal cord to the brain. This interaction is bidirectional, with signals traveling from the brain to the gut and, opposite, from the gut to the brain. Patients with IBS may have disrupted functioning of this pathway (Drossman, Whitehead, et al., 2000; Levine, Jarrett, Cain, Heitkemper, 1997), leading to the amplification of pain and stress responses to normal bowel stimuli. This process is known as *visceral hypersensitivity*. When compared to healthy controls and patients with other GI diseases, brain imaging studies have revealed heightened visceral sensitivity in IBS patients in response to a variety of GI and extraintestinal stimuli (Murray et al., 2004). Increased visceral sensitivity may also be associated with heightened reactivity of smooth muscle fibers in the GI tract, suggesting abnormal *autonomic nervous system* (ANS) regulation in IBS patients.

The *limbic system* likely plays a role in the symptom experience of IBS. As in many pain syndromes, it is in the limbic system and particularly in the anterior cingulate cortex (ACC) where emotional experience is linked to pain perception. For example, when patients with IBS feel pain or discomfort, they also exhibit increased ACC activity when compared to individuals without IBS. One explanation for this increased

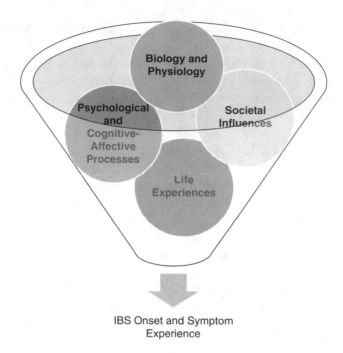

IBS Onset and Symptom
Experience

Figure 21.1   Factors Affecting the Onset and Maintenance of IBS in Women: The Biopsychosocial Model.

ACC activation is that IBS patients are unable to prepare appropriately on a neural level when anticipating pain or stress, resulting in higher sensitivity and responsiveness to such undesirable stimuli. Finally, the *hypothalamic-pituitary adrenal (HPA) axis* secretes hormones that regulate stress, digestion, emotion, and mood. Specifically, corticotropic-releasing hormone (CRH) modulates gut motility, levels of stress, and sensitivity to pain and is, therefore, an important physiological factor in the symptoms of IBS (Fukudo, 2007).

Medical Comorbidity

The biological underpinnings of IBS are further evidenced by the increased prevalence of certain medical comorbidities within this population. About 65% of IBS patients report comorbid extraintestinal (non-GI) symptoms, which is significantly higher than patients with other functional GI diseases

(Riedl et al., 2008). IBS patients with more medical comorbidities tend to report lower quality of life, take more sick days, use more health resources, and generate higher health-related costs (Johansson, Farup, Bracco, & Vandvik, Williams, Kalilani, & Cook, 2010; Riedl, 2008); this does not seem to be gender specific. The following section outlines the most prevalent symptoms and comorbidities associated with IBS.

Bloating   The most significant intestinal comorbidity in IBS is bloating, which includes visible swelling of the abdomen and a subjective feeling of distention. Bloating is described in 76% of patients with IBS, with women reporting bloating and distension more frequently than men (Chang, Lee, Naliboff, Schmulson, & Mayer, 2001; Ringel, Williams, Kalilani, & Cook, 2009). Despite the high prevalence of bloating among IBS patients, it is not included in the ROME III diagnostic criteria as an essential symptom, because previous research has suggested that it does not adequately differentiate IBS from other GI disorders and may obscure the importance of abdominal pain and discomfort as a central feature of IBS (Spiller, Camilleri, & Longstreth, 2010). This decision is controversial, and future diagnostic criteria for IBS may include bloating.

Bloating and abdominal distention seem to be particularly distressing for women because it pertains to their body image and the cultural association of thinness with attractiveness (Toner & Akman, 2000). Distorted body image caused by symptoms of bloating in addition to other IBS factors can influence awareness of body size, resulting in an increased risk for disordered eating including diet restriction (Tang et al., 1998). In women with IBS, more severe bloating is correlated with higher levels of distress (Park, Jarrett, Cain, & Heitkemper, 2008). The direction of this relationship, however, has not been determined.

Physical explanations of bloating symptoms in IBS patients have been attributed to both abnormal transit of intestinal gas as well as impaired tolerance of intestinal gas (Heitkemper et al., 2004; Serra, Azpiroz, & Malagelada, 2001). This explanation reveals that not only may IBS patients have increased amounts of gas in their intestines, but they may also be more sensitive to *any* amount of gas. Increased sensitivity to even normal levels of intestinal gas can be explained by heightened reactivity of the ANS and increased visceral sensitivity. Smooth muscle in the GI tract contains fibers belonging to both the sympathetic and parasympathetic nervous systems. Patients with IBS may have disrupted functioning of the ANS fibers in the gut, leading to increased sensitivity to certain stimuli,

such as gas in the intestines, which may contribute to the sensation of bloating (Drossman, Whitehead, et al., 2000; Levine et al., 1997; Murray et al., 2004).

Fibromyalgia Fibromyalgia, which is also more prevalent in women, is diagnosed in about 32% of patients with IBS (Riedl et al., 2008; Sperber et al., 1999; Sperber & Dekel, 2010), and the two syndromes share many symptoms. IBS patients who also suffer from fibromyalgia tend to experience increased severity of functional symptoms, including sleep problems, psychological distress, and generally impaired well-being (Sperber et al., 2000). Although these two syndromes often occur together, it remains unclear whether there is some common underlying pathophysiology. While fibromyalgia is attributed to somatic hypersensitivity, IBS is attributed to visceral hypersensitivity (Chang, Mayer, Johnson, FitzGerald, & Naliboff, 2000), and the degree of overlap is not yet clearly understood.

Back Pain In women with IBS (especially older women), the number of GI symptoms is directly correlated with the presence of lower back pain (Smith, Russell, & Hodges, 2008). Possible explanations for this association include emotional and physical factors, such as comorbid depression, hypersensitivity to pain, and/or increased spinal load during bowel movements (Smith et al., 2008).

Urogenital and Gynecological Symptoms Lower urinary tract symptoms (LUTS), such as increased frequency and nocturia (frequent urination during the night), have also been associated with IBS patients in comparison to non-IBS controls (Francis, Duffy, Whorwell, & Morris, 1997; Guo et al., 2010). Women with IBS are believed to overuse antibiotics prescribed for possible recurrent urinary infections, which are associated with significant GI side effects in addition to their public health implications (Agrawal & Whorwell, 2006). Other gynecological syndromes, including chronic pelvic pain, dysmenorrhea, and sexual dysfunction, have all been found to have high coincidence in women with IBS (Riedl et al., 2008), further raising the question of a common pathophysiology among certain functional symptoms and IBS.

Notably, many patients with IBS are inappropriately referred to gynecologists for their abdominal symptoms, which can lead to a host of unnecessary and invasive diagnostics (i.e., exploratory laparoscopy for endometriosis) or even hysterectomy. Eighteen percent to 33% of women with IBS have had a hysterectomy, compared to 12% to 17% of women without IBS who have had this same surgery (Hasler & Schoenfeld, 2003; Longstreth & Yao, 2004). Similarly, women with IBS are at increased risk for other unnecessary abdominopelvic and gallbladder surgeries (Cole et al., 2005) and back surgery (Talley, 2004). Abdominal surgeries are associated with poor outcome in IBS and should be avoided in most cases (Longstreth, 2007).

Sleep Problems   Patients with IBS report more sleep problems than do individuals without IBS (Elsenbruch, Harnish, & Orr, 1999; Goldsmith & Levin, 1993; Heitkemper et al., 2005). Women with IBS who do report sleep disturbances also report more IBS symptoms the day following a poor night's sleep (Jarrett, Heitkemper, Cain, Burr, & Hertig, 2000). Research has shown a discrepancy between self-reported sleep disturbances and actual changes in sleep architecture in patients with IBS (Keefer, Stepanski, Ranjbaran, Benson, & Keshavarzian, 2006). Although some studies

demonstrate that there is no objective difference in sleep between IBS and non-IBS patients (Elsenbruch et al., 1999; Heitkemper et al., 2005), other researchers are compelled by findings indicating increased rapid eye movement (REM) patterns in IBS patients (Kumar, Thompson, Wingate, Vesselinova-Jenkins, & Libby, 1992; Orr, Crowell, Lin, Harnish, & Chen, 1997). Whether there is an actual objective difference in sleep quality of IBS patients remains to be determined. The fact that a large percentage of patients with IBS report sleep problems, however, is of clinical significance and, similar to conditioned insomnia, may indicate hypersensitivity to normal amounts of sleep disturbance.

The search for a common pathophysiology between IBS and other comorbidities has produced variable results. One literature review found that IBS patients were not more likely to report specific constellations of comorbid syndromes, but rather showed amplified incidence in the same patterns as the general population (Whitehead et al., 2007). This may indicate that IBS and other functional syndromes do not share physiological causes but may be characterized by hypervigilance or hypersensitivity to certain symptoms. Another important consideration regarding IBS comorbidities involves the influence of psychiatric factors on symptom experience. IBS patients with psychiatric diagnoses are significantly more likely to report comorbid somatic disorders than are IBS patients without psychiatric diagnoses (Riedl et al., 2008; Vandvik, Wilhelmsen, Ihlebaek, & Farup, 2004; Whitehead et al., 2007), further supporting the hypothesis that comorbid somatic syndromes may be a result of hypervigilance or hypersensitivity in this population.

Arguments for physiologic causes of functional somatic syndromes such as IBS should not be overlooked. For example, because the neurotransmitter serotonin is associated with motility, bloating, pain, and nausea (Chang & Talley, 2010), one hypothesis suggests that IBS may be characterized by altered serotonin signaling between the brain and the gut. Diarrhea-predominant IBS (IBS-D) has been associated with an overproduction of serotonin, whereas inadequate serotonin availability seems to be common amongst constipation-predominant IBS (IBS-C). Recent studies have shown that some selective serotonin reuptake inhibitors (SSRIs), commonly used as antidepressants, are effective in treating IBS-D symptoms (Friedrich, Grady, & Wall, 2010). There is little data identifying sex differences associated with serotonin or serotonin-based therapies. Hypotheses involving the role of estrogen and the HPA axis on symptom experience are also being considered (Warnock & Clayton, 2003).

PSYCHOLOGICAL FACTORS

Although brain imaging and other technological advances in the last decade have informed our understanding of the physiological factors underlying IBS, they have also bolstered support for the consideration of cognitive-affective processes in the etiology of IBS; certain processes, described in the following sections, have a direct impact on GI physiology and motility.

Comorbid Psychiatric Disorders

A typical profile of a patient with IBS is associated with increased psychological distress, decreased reported interpersonal support, and exacerbation of IBS symptoms in response to psychosocial factors (Jones,

Wessinger, & Crowell, 2006; Pinto, Lele, Joglekar, Panwar, & Dhavale, 2000).

Anxiety   Anxiety disorders are present in as many as 58% of patients with IBS (Canavan, Bennett, Feely, O'Morain, & O'Connor, 2009; Gros, Antony, McCabe, & Swinson, 2009; Whitehead, Palsson, & Jones, 2002). These conditions tend to remain stable over time and are believed to precede IBS (Sykes, Blanchard, Lackner, Keefer, & Krasner, 2003). GAD in these patients often presents as worry about GI symptoms. For example, IBS patients with GAD may worry that their symptoms are attributable to something more serious, or they may worry about their IBS in the context of other responsibilities (e.g., "What if I am sick for my daughter's wedding?") (Crane & Martin, 2002). Worry and intolerance of uncertainty independent of GAD have also been associated with IBS (Keefer et al., 2006). Panic disorder can affect up to 41% of patients with IBS, with a slightly increased prevalence in IBS-D (Lydiard et al., 1994); these patients have the poorest quality of life, likely caused by social isolation associated with both conditions (Maunder, 1998).

GI-Specific Anxiety   As noted earlier, some patients with IBS have disrupted functioning of the CNS brain–gut pathway (Drossman, Whitehead, et al., 2000; Levine et al., 1997), resulting in visceral hypersensitivity or amplification of painful responses to physical and psychological stimuli. When coupled with anxiety, patients with high visceral sensitivity can become preoccupied with GI sensations, symptoms, or the contexts in which they may appear. Patients may then mislabel these symptoms and contexts as dangerous and modify their behavior accordingly (e.g., a patient may not attend a social gathering due to fear of having symptoms). Unfortunately, this cycle can disrupt interpersonal relationships, including those with a healthcare provider.

Mood Depression, which is more prevalent in women over the lifespan, has been reported in about 34% of patients with IBS. Dysthymia has been reported in about 7% of patients with IBS (Canavan et al., 2009; Lydiard et al., 1994). Consistent with other research on somatization (Chioqueta & Stiles, 2004), a recent survey study found that 38% of treatment-seeking IBS patients had seriously considered suicide because of their bowel problems; this appeared to be mediated by hopelessness around obtaining relief for IBS, not because of depression or personality disorder (Miller, Hopkins, & Whorwell, 2004). Finally, these coping concerns may vary among the three subtypes of IBS. Women with IBS-A report higher psychological distress and lower quality of life than women with diarrhea- or constipation-predominant IBS (Cain et al., 2006; Coffin, Dapoigny, Cloarec, Comet, & Dyard, 2004; Tillisch et al., 2005). This may be because of decreased predictability of GI symptoms associated with IBS-A when compared to IBS-C or IBS-D and, therefore, increased frustration and feelings of hopelessness.

Somatization Between 15% and 48% of IBS patients meet diagnostic criteria for a somatization disorder (Lydiard et al., 1993; Miller et al., 2001); this may be overinflated because, in the absence of good diagnostic tools and treatment, IBS patients utilize a substantial amount of healthcare prior to diagnosis.

Psychological Stress Psychological stressors in the form of daily hassles or major life events are associated with changes in GI motility, regardless of whether a person has IBS. This is not surprising in that the release of stress hormones mediates a host of autonomic, behavioral, immunological, and visceral responses in the gut (Chang, 2011). However, for individuals with IBS, stressors may affect them more readily or more severely, or they may be predisposed to higher reactivity to stress (Sapolsky, 1996a, 1996b, 2004). It is not clear whether patients with IBS experience more stressors than others (Blanchard et al., 2008), but, when present, stress is associated with higher symptom intensity and poorer response to IBS treatment (Bennett, Tennant, Piesse, Badcock, & Kellow, 1998).

Women with IBS show significantly higher levels of reported stress (often associated with anxiety and/or depression) when compared to women without any bowel dysfunction (Whitehead, Crowell, Robinson, Heller, & Schuster, 1992). Furthermore, reported daily stress in women is positively correlated with reported daily IBS symptoms (Levy, Cain, Jarrett, & Heitkemper, 1997), indicating an association between stress and symptom severity in women with IBS. Underscoring the impact of ongoing life stress is the example of postinfectious IBS, which accounts for up to 32% of new cases (Thabane & Marhall, 2009). Increased life stress within the past year and negative illness beliefs may predispose a person to postinfectious IBS long after the acute gastritis has resolved (Thabane & Marhall, 2009).

Coping How a patient thinks about her disease can affect her health. Women who demonstrate maladaptive coping skills in response to IBS pain are more likely to have a poor health outcome (Drossman, Leserman, et al., 2000). Maladaptive coping often results from catastrophic thinking, during which a patient exaggerates the negative consequences of her disease, feels unable to control onset and duration of symptoms, and fails to use positive reappraisal when pain occurs (Lackner & Quigley, 2005). Some data suggests that individuals with IBS may use confrontative, escape-avoidant, and self-controlling coping strategies to manage both stress and IBS symptoms (Jones et al., 2006). Women who employ such maladaptive coping skills are more likely to feel helpless and out-of-control in the setting of their IBS, which may increase catastrophization, stress levels, and symptom severity. Many women who feel anxious and/or powerless in the treatment of their IBS frequently seek medical attention, leading to more medical visits and often more diagnostic procedures. These treatment-seeking women are characterized by increased stress and a low self-perceived ability to decrease their discomfort (Drossman, Leserman, et al., 2000).

SOCIAL FACTORS

IBS has many characteristics that make it susceptible to stigmatization, including its unalterable course, limited treatment options, lack of clear etiology, unpredictability and uncontrollability, social disruption, and an association with psychopathology. Patients report feelings that IBS is not taken seriously and is poorly understood, and they perceive that others imply that their symptoms are their fault or are "all in their heads." Approximately half of patients with IBS perceive themselves as being stigmatized because of their condition, with the most perceived stigma coming from co-workers and employers, followed by healthcare providers and friends (Jones et al., 2009). Although not

previously examined, social support groups may help with reducing shame and stigma associated with a chronic bowel disorder. There is also a societal tendency for others to view individuals with IBS as beneficiaries of the "sick role," with IBS symptoms reflecting malingering behavior or at least secondary gain (Levy, Langer, & Whitehead, 2007; Levy et al., 2004). For example, an IBS patient may report that their co-workers are complaining to their boss that they are not "pulling their weight" because of a perception of increased sick leave or time in the bathroom during work hours. These negative consequences of illness behavior can affect self-esteem and self-efficacy, which in turn can further exacerbate the IBS patient's condition.

IBS ACROSS THE FEMALE LIFESPAN

The symptom experiences of women with IBS change across the female life cycle and are influenced by a host of social factors that are disproportionately prevalent among women. These social factors include physical/sexual abuse, social and economic disparities, mental health problems, and reproductive health needs (Leslie & Swider, 1986; Raikes, Shoo, & Brabin, 1992). In the following sections, we consider IBS in the context of female development, discussing some commonly shared experiences and developmental milestones from birth through old age.

Early Life Experiences

Although IBS tends to run in families, and a genetic link has been examined (Kalantar, Locke, Zinsmeister, Beighley, & Talley, 2003; Levy et al., 2001; Morris-Yates, Talley, Boyce, Nandurkar, & Andrews, 1998; Saito

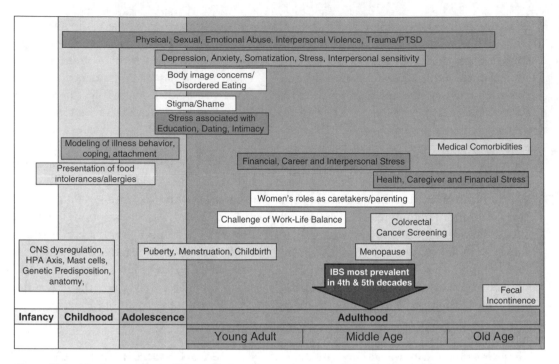

Figure 21.2   The Intersection of Women's Experiences Across the Lifespan and Risk Factors for IBS

& Talley, 2008), data more strongly supports the role that modeling of illness behavior plays in the onset and maintenance of IBS. In a rich study of IBS patients and their families, individuals who grew up in a household where a parent (particularly a mother) had IBS or "stomach problems" and who received excessive attention for somatic symptoms were more likely to develop IBS themselves (Levy et al., 2001; Levy et al., 2007; Levy, Whitehead, Von Korff, & Feld, 2000). Another study suggested that early learning around pain, bowel habits, coping, and healthcare seeking influenced the onset or maintenance of IBS (Chitkara et al., 2009; Chitkara, van Tilburg, Blois-Martin, & Whitehead, 2008; Levy et al., 2007). Psychological processes including dysfunctional core beliefs, overly negative cognitive appraisals, maladaptive coping, suppression of emotion, and alexithymia can also be transmitted

within the family environment and contribute to IBS (Chitkara et al., 2008; Levy et al., 2000; Levy et al., 2007). As primary caregivers, women with IBS have an increased chance of transmitting IBS to their offspring.

Violence Against Women: Physical, Sexual, and Emotional Abuse

Women with histories of physical and sexual abuse, especially in childhood, are more likely to have many different health problems, including psychiatric disorders, functional somatic syndromes, increased healthcare utilization, more lifetime surgeries, and more hospitalizations (Arnow, 2004; Leserman & Drossman, 2007; McCauley et al., 1997). The relationship between abuse history and reported GI symptoms has been extensively researched (Drossman et al., 1990; Hulme, 2000; Leserman, 2007; Leserman

& Drossman, 2007; Leserman, Drossman, & Hu, 1998). Not only are women with a history of abuse 1.5 to 2 times more likely to report GI complaints than their nonabused counterparts (Leserman, 2007), but women with GI disorders who report a history of abuse are also more likely than nonabused controls to experience extraintestinal symptoms such as panic, depression, musculoskeletal disorders, respiratory illnesses, and sleep disturbances (Leserman et al., 1998; Park, Jarrett, & Heitkemper, 2010).

Severity of reported abuse may mediate the relationship between abuse history and future health problems. For example, the severity of physical and/or sexual abuse is positively correlated with the number of reported somatic symptoms and the number of scheduled healthcare visits in women with GI disorders. Women with GI disorders who report severe abuse have been found to have an average of eight more medical visits per year than women with no history of abuse. This can be compared to women with GI disorders and a history of moderate abuse, who have an average of three more medical visits per year than controls (Leserman et al., 1998). Finally, there is a significant difference between abuse reporting in patients with IBS versus patients with organic GI diseases such as Crohn's disease or ulcerative colitis (Delvaux, Denis, & Allemand, 1997; Drossman et al., 1990), indicating that abuse may be more closely associated with the expression of functional symptoms. In fact, patients with other functional somatic syndromes also report high levels of abuse history (Paras et al., 2009); this may be linked to the impact of negative psychosocial factors on abnormal illness behavior (Drossman et al., 1990) and the possibility of increased sensitivity to visceral pain documented among abuse survivors (Ringel et al., 2008).

Considerably less is known about emotional abuse, but women with IBS have been found to score higher on measures of emotional abuse than women with inflammatory bowel diseases (Ali et al., 2000). Because emotional abuse may be more prevalent and may have different psychological outcomes than physical or sexual abuse (Wright, Crawford, & Del Castillo, 2009), this line of research is valuable for further understanding of possible related health outcomes.

IBS Among Women Veterans

Given the high comorbidity of physical and sexual abuse history with IBS, it is not surprising that there is also a high prevalence (8% to 38%) of IBS patients who have comorbid posttraumatic stress disorder (PTSD) (Cohen et al., 2006; Irwin et al., 1996). This relationship has become increasingly relevant from a woman's health perspective as the number of female veterans in the United States increases. Approximately 21% of female veterans screen positive for PTSD (Dobie et al., 2004), and 48% screen positive for depression (Dobie et al., 2004; Haskell et al., 2010); both disorders are known risk factors for the development of IBS (Savas et al., 2009). Military trauma history is associated with a 50% to 115% excess risk of developing IBS in women veterans (White et al., 2010), and women veterans have a higher prevalence of IBS than the general population (38% compared to 5% to 27%, respectively) (Savas et al., 2009). Women veterans who have IBS report lower health-related quality of life (HRQOL) than do women veterans without IBS, although women veterans overall report lower HRQOL than the general population (Graham et al., 2010). As women continue to expand their role within the military, their risk for developing psychiatric and physical health concerns should be evaluated.

Hormones, Menstrual Cycle, Menopause

Perhaps one of the most obvious gender-specific factors regarding women and IBS is the influence of reproductive hormones and the menstrual cycle on IBS symptom experience. IBS often presents for the first time in the context of other gynecological concerns or childbirth (Crowell et al., 1994). Regardless of IBS subtype or use of oral contraceptives, women with IBS report different levels and severity of symptoms depending on their current phase of the menstrual cycle (Heitkemper et al., 2003; Kane, Sable, & Hanauer, 1998; Whitehead et al., 1990). Specifically, it seems that GI transit is slowest and pain is highest during the luteal and menses phases of the menstrual cycle (Heitkemper & Jarrett, 2008; Wald et al., 1981). One hypothesis for the variation of symptoms with the menstrual cycle is that symptoms are the worst when ovarian hormones are the lowest, and pain is the lowest when ovarian hormones are elevated (Heitkemper & Chang, 2009). This hypothesis is supported by the fact that during pregnancy, when ovarian hormones are high, somatic pain thresholds are also high (Cogan & Spinnato, 1986), whereas during menopause and certain phases of the menstrual cycle, when ovarian hormones are low, somatic pain and symptom severity are more intense (Heitkemper & Chang, 2009). From a physiological stand point, women with IBS demonstrate variations in autonomic arousal, which appear to be mediated by menstrual cycle phases and are different from women without IBS (Houghton, Lea, Jackson, & Whorwell, 2002).

Interpersonal Relationships and Family

Interpersonal relationships are an important part of female development, and they have been included in conceptual models of IBS (Toner et al., 2000b). Interpersonal difficulties have been identified as a risk factor for the development of IBS, particularly after exposure to an acute infection (Grover, Herfarth, & Drossman, 2009). This issue can be particularly salient for women in the context of both familiar and professional relationships. Traditionally, the female gender role is expected to be relationship-oriented, intuitive, and even submissive (Toner, 1994). This is juxtaposed with a modern requirement for independence and assertiveness and can lead to conflicting expectations and increased stress.

Individuals with IBS have been found to have a pattern of interpersonal problems when compared to those without IBS. Specifically, difficulties with assertiveness and social inhibition have been noted in IBS patients more than in healthy controls (Lackner & Gurtman, 2004, 2005). As a result, IBS patients may perceive themselves to have inadequate interpersonal support (Jones et al., 2006), and this perception may exacerbate symptoms by limiting patients' ability to respond positively to life stressors (Lackner, Brasel, et al., 2010). Treatments that target interpersonal relationships have demonstrated considerable success, cost effectiveness, and durability in IBS (Creed et al., 2003; Hyphantis, Guthrie, Tomenson, & Creed, 2009), especially in cases where abuse has occurred (Creed et al., 2005).

Considerably less is known about the impact of IBS on intimate relationships or domestic functioning, but one study suggested that sexual functioning is a complaint in 80% of women with IBS, with painful intercourse being the most reported symptom. Possible explanations for this reveal that sexual intercourse may cause abdominal pain in women with IBS, although this has not been shown to be true for women with other GI diseases such as inflammatory bowel disease (Guthrie, Creed, & Whorwell, 1987). Ongoing domestic stress may also limit treatment response in women with IBS (Bennett et al., 1998).

Issues Unique to Middle and Advanced Age

Colorectal Cancer As women enter middle age and beyond, their risk for colorectal cancer increases (Menees & Fenner, 2007). Although adherence to these recommendations is poor, current guidelines advise adults to be screened via colonoscopy beginning at age 50 and then at regular intervals to reduce the risk of colorectal cancer and/or decrease mortality through early detection (Menees & Fenner, 2007). Colonoscopy is aversive to many patients because of the intrusive nature of the test and the inconvenience and discomfort of the preparation (Levin et al., 2008). Another important barrier for colorectal cancer screening among women is the shortage of female gastroenterologists, who women typically prefer to perform the procedure (Menees, Inadomi, Korsnes, & Elta, 2005). The rate of screening compliance among adults varies by gender, race, ethnicity, and socioeconomic status (Beydoun & Beydoun, 2008; Geiger et al., 2008). African American women are more likely to die of colorectal cancer than are women of any other racial or ethnic group, potentially because of low adherence to screening recommendations. Research in this area has suggested that faith-based campaigns to raise awareness may be more suitable in this group of women (Frank, Swedmark, & Grubbs, 2004).

Constipation Fifty percent of community-dwelling elderly and 74% of nursing home residents report constipation caused by medical factors, including medication side effects and underlying illnesses (Rao & Go, 2010). The experience of constipation can affect reported mood and quality of life in these patients (Glia & Lindberg, 1997).

Fecal Incontinence Fecal incontinence (the involuntary loss of stool) is a common but potentially embarrassing health issue for elderly patients. One out of 10 women in the United States report fecal incontinence, and 1 out of 15 women report severe incontinence (Bharucha et al., 2005). Fecal incontinence has many different etiologies, but it almost always results in decreased quality of life and decreased functional status in elderly patients (Bharucha et al., 2005; Crane & Talley, 2007). As the population ages, there has been increased focus on the psychological and physiological risk factors for this problem (Dunivan et al., 2010; Whitehead, 2005; Whitehead et al., 2009) and the development of behavioral treatments such as biofeedback (Karling et al., 2009; Palsson, Heymen, & Whitehead, 2004) in order to reduce the need for nursing home institutionalization (Grover & Whitehead, 2011; Heymen et al., 2009; Norton, Whitehead, Bliss, Harari, & Lang, 2010).

MANAGEMENT OF IBS

Current treatment options for IBS are largely ineffective, at least for its full range of symptoms (Camilleri & Mayer, 2009; Schmulson et al., 2009). However, a few medical therapies have demonstrated modest efficacy in randomized controlled trials, including antispasmodics (e.g., hyoscine) (Ford et al., 2008), peppermint oil (Ford et al., 2008), the antidiarrheal loperamide (Schmulson et al., 2009), and short courses of nonabsorbable antibiotics such as Rifaximin (Fumi & Trexler, 2008; Pimentel, Park, Mirocha, Kane, & Kong, 2006) when bloating is also present (Schmulson et al., 2009). Tricyclic antidepressants and SSRIs are prescribed for abdominal pain as a second-line therapy (Ford, Talley, Schoenfeld, Quigley, & Moayyedi, 2009). Notably, laxatives are not indicated for the treatment of IBS, and the potential for laxative abuse should be strongly considered when patients with IBS are using them regularly (DiPalma, DeRidder, Orlando, Kolts, & Cleveland, 2000). Laxative abuse is particularly concerning for women with IBS, because it has been associated with specific psychopathology such as suicidality, anger, and feelings of emptiness among women with diagnosed eating disorders (Tozzi et al., 2006). To date, lifestyle interventions, particularly dietary considerations and stress management, have been at the core of IBS management for women.

Dietary Management

Food intolerances have been implicated in IBS, despite limited evidence to support this claim (Nanda, James, Smith, Dudley, & Jewell, 1989). As many as 60% of IBS patients report a wide range of foods to which they are intolerant, particularly dairy products and wheat (Atkinson, Sheldon, Shaath, & Whorwell, 2004; King, Elia, & Hunter, 1998; Nanda et al., 1989). New data suggests that fructose intolerance may also contribute to the presence of IBS symptoms studies (Choi, Kraft, Zimmerman, Jackson, & Rao, 2008; Shepherd & Gibson, 2006). However, true food allergies are uncommon (Dainese, Galliani, De Lazzari, Di Leo, & Naccarato, 1999).

There are still no empirically supported dietary guidelines for IBS despite a host of websites and trade books devoted to this topic

(Alpers, 2006; Heizer, Southern, & McGovern, 2009). Exclusion diets have been used in this population; between 12.5% and 67% of patients had a response to an exclusion diet, although the majority of these diet studies were uncontrolled. Emerging evidence shows that dairy and large quantities of fiber can trigger abdominal discomfort or diarrhea in a subset of patients with IBS. Constipation can be associated with a lack of adequate fiber intake (approximately 25 to 35 grams per day) (Whorwell, 2009). Carbonated beverages, foods with high methane such as lentils, beans, broccoli, and cabbage, and foods high in carbohydrates or in artificial sugars can increase intestinal gas production. Caffeine, found in coffee or teas, and alcohol can also be problematic in this group (Saito, Locke, Weaver, Zinsmeister, & Talley, 2005). Low-carbohydrate diets have been modestly effective for diarrhea in overweight patients (Austin et al., 2009), and fructose-restricted diets have also shown some benefit (Choi et al., 2008; Shepherd & Gibson, 2006); however, both diets are difficult to sustain. Despite the established effects of high physical activity (e.g., marathon running) on gas clearance and GI motility (Lampe, Slavin, & Apple, 1991), there are virtually no studies examining the effects of physical activity on IBS. However, many women may choose to restrict physical activity to avoid exacerbation of symptoms. A newer approach to dietary management of IBS includes the probiotic *Bifidobacterium infantis 35624*, which has demonstrated superiority to placebo in five randomized controlled trials (Brenner & Chey, 2009).

Notably, between 4% and 8% of IBS patients have anorexia nervosa or bulimia nervosa (Porcelli, Leandro, & De Carne, 1998); this is slightly increased from the general population, which is currently about

1% (Baker, Mitchell, Neale, & Kendler, 2010; Striegel-Moore et al., 2009). However, it is unclear as to whether IBS may be preceded by or initiate disordered eating. Many patients utilize dietary changes in an attempt to control IBS symptoms, and these behavioral changes may lead to selective reinforcement of maladaptive eating habits.

Psychological Management

Women with IBS have reported the loss of bodily functions (incontinence, passing gas), the trivialization of their disease by health-care providers, and the fear of being viewed as "needy" among their top concerns when seeking psychotherapy for IBS (Toner et al., 1998; Toner, Segal, Emmott, & Myran, 2000). IBS has also been associated with perceived stigma, particularly with respect to the belief that IBS is a "waste basket" diagnosis and that employers, physicians, friends, and family of the patients believe it to be "all in their head" (Jones et al., 2009). Furthermore, IBS patients report a variety of educational needs that are currently not met by reassurance or standard care (Halpert et al., 2006; Halpert et al., 2007).

Cognitive-behavioral therapy (CBT) is the most well-supported psychological treatment for IBS to date (Blanchard et al., 2007; Drossman et al., 2003; Lackner, Gudleski, et al., 2010; Lackner et al., 2008). Placing an emphasis on relaxation, decatastrophizing symptoms and their triggers, and increasing the use of flexible problem-solving skills, CBT has demonstrated efficacy against inert and active control conditions across many modes of delivery (Lackner, Mesmer, Morley, Dowzer, & Hamilton, 2004).

Hypnotherapy is a technique that focuses on deep physical relaxation and altered awareness, attention, and concentration. Gut-directed hypnotherapy, which targets bowel symptoms through very specific post-hypnotic suggestions, is one of the first empirically supported therapies for IBS that seems to be particularly successful in refractory cases (Miller & Whorwell, 2009), with response rates above 85% (Gonsalkorale, Miller, Afzal, & Whorwell, 2003; Lea et al., 2003; Miller & Whorwell, 2009; Palsson, Turner, Johnson, Burnett, & Whitehead, 2002; Palsson, Turner, & Whitehead, 2006; Palsson & Whitehead, 2002; Whorwell, Prior, & Colgan, 1987).

Brief psychodynamic therapy, also referred to as interpersonal psychotherapy (IPT), has been successfully employed in IBS. Focused around the patient developing insight into her experiences with IBS, including relationships with others, and to identify feelings about her illness, IPT has substantial empirical support (Guthrie, Creed, Dawson, & Tomenson, 1993; Hislop, 1980; Svedlund, 1983; Svedlund et al., 1983), especially in the case of interpersonal difficulties (Hyphantis et al., 2009) or if there is a history of sexual abuse (Creed et al., 2005).

Finally, nurse-led patient education groups and community support groups have increases in popularity, as self-management of IBS in this form has demonstrated efficacy in randomized controlled trials (Colwell, Prather, Phillips, & Zinsmeister, 1998; Hungin, 2006; Saito et al., 2004). Social support is a key component of these programs, many of which are women-centered.

CONCLUSION AND FUTURE DIRECTIONS

In this chapter we have reviewed the literature in the area of irritable bowel syndrome, emphasizing what we know to date about its intersection with gender, age, ethnicity, and experience across the female life cycle. Although significant progress has been made in the past decade in gastrointestinal health among women, there are several important limitations.

First and most importantly, the vast majority of studies that report on gender issues were published much earlier in this history of IBS literature. This is problematic because, until the late 1990s, IBS was considered a psychosomatic disorder. Since the widespread acceptance of the biopsychosocial model of IBS, considerably less gender-driven research has been published. We suspect that this oversight may be reflective of the strongly held view that women are no longer underrepresented in clinical research (Holden, 2008) and that gender-driven research is no longer necessary.

IBS is unique from other medical conditions in which men have historically been the primary focus in clinical research (e.g., heart disease, cancer, etc.). IBS is more prevalent in women and, therefore, it has been acceptable to consider it a "women's disease." Unfortunately, this may not be an accurate assumption; most studies on IBS have excluded men completely or have had inadequate statistical power to be able to appropriately report on gender differences. In the future, oversampling of men and arranging trials to include *a priori* hypothesis around potential gender differences are critical to the advancement of IBS care.

That said, IBS is an important women's health concern in that it is associated with significant impairment and reduced quality of life and can present at numerous points during the female lifespan. Similarly, although IBS affects men to a lesser degree, GI symptoms such as bloating and its associated body image disturbance may result in

disordered eating patterns, exacerbating a problem to which women are already susceptible. Stigma and shame are present for a portion of women with IBS, perhaps in part because of the socially unacceptable nature of discussions of bowel habits among women. Sexual abuse, which occurs more often in women, is also associated with IBS, although there is a limited understanding as to the nature of this association or how to effect change in IBS if abuse is present.

Finally, in the absence of effective medications for IBS, it is important that we continue to consider sex/gender as potential mediators or moderators of disease outcomes. For example, few clinical trials have controlled for the effects of hormones and age on IBS symptoms in women, nor have they considered these variables with respect to treatment response, and this is critical for drug trials in particular, where safety concerns and side effects may be impacted by such parameters.

We still know very little about the impact of ethnicity and race on the experience of IBS. This may be partly because of the low rate of racial and ethnic minorities seeking medical care for gastrointestinal symptoms and their participation in colorectal cancer screening more generally (Carlos, Fendrick, Patterson, & Bernstein, 2005; Frank et al., 2004; Wang et al., 2006). Women's preference for women physicians, who are more prevalent in primary care settings than in gastroenterology, may also limit whether patients obtain an IBS diagnosis (Menees et al., 2005). Finally, cultural and gender differences in the expression of pain may impact the diagnosis and management of IBS.

There are some important developments on the horizon for women with bowel concerns. In this chapter, we focused on gender in the context of IBS; however, newer research in the area of inflammatory bowel diseases (e.g., ulcerative colitis and Crohn's disease) and pelvic floor disorders/fecal incontinence are emerging.

REFERENCES

Agrawal, A., & Whorwell, P. J. (2006). Irritable bowel syndrome: Diagnosis and management. *British Medical Journal, 332*(7536), 280–283.

Ali, A., Toner, B. B., Stuckless, N., Gallop, R., Diamant, N. E., Gould, M. I., & Vidins, E. I. (2000). Emotional abuse, self-blame, and self-silencing in women with irritable bowel syndrome. *Psychosomatic Medicine, 62*(1), 76–82.

Alpers, D. H. (2006). Diet and irritable bowel syndrome. *Current Opinion in Gastroenterology, 22*(2), 136–139.

Arnow, B. A. (2004). Relationships between childhood maltreatment, adult health and psychiatric outcomes, and medical utilization. *Journal of Clinical Psychiatry, 65*(Suppl 12), 10–15.

Atkinson, W., Sheldon, T. A., Shaath, N., & Whorwell, P. J. (2004). Food elimination based on igg antibodies in irritable bowel syndrome: A randomised controlled trial. *Gut, 53*(10), 1459–1464.

Austin, G. L., Dalton, C. B., Hu, Y., Morris, C. B., Hankins, J., Weinland, S. R., . . . Drossman, D. A. (2009). A very low-carbohydrate diet improves symptoms and quality of life in diarrhea-predominant irritable bowel syndrome. *Clinical Gastroenterology and Hepatology, 7*(6), 706–708 e701.

Baker, J. H., Mitchell, K. S., Neale, M. C., & Kendler, K. S. (2010). Eating disorder symptomatology and substance use disorders: Prevalence and shared risk in a population based twin sample. *International Journal of Eating Disorders, 43*(7), 648–658.

Bennett, E. J., Tennant, C. C., Piesse, C., Badcock, C. A., & Kellow, J. E. (1998). Level of chronic life stress predicts clinical outcome in irritable bowel syndrome. *Gut, 43*(2), 256–261.

Beydoun, H. A., & Beydoun, M. A. (2008). Predictors of colorectal cancer screening behaviors among average-risk older adults in the united states. *Cancer Causes Control, 19*(4), 339–359.

Bharucha, A. E., Zinsmeister, A. R., Locke, G. R., Seide, B. M., McKeon, K., Schleck, C. D., & Melton, L. J. (2005). Prevalence and burden of fecal incontinence: A population-based study in women. *Gastroenterology, 129*(1), 42–49.

Blanchard, E., Lackner, J. M., Jaccard, J., Rowell, D., Carosella, A. M., Powell, C., . . . Kuhn, E. (2008). The role of stress in symptom exacerbation among IBS patients. *Journal of Psychosomatic Research, 64*(2), 119–128.

Blanchard, E. B., Lackner, J. M., Sanders, K., Krasner, S., Keefer, L., Payne, A., . . . Dulgar-Tulloch, L. (2007). A controlled evaluation of group cognitive therapy in the treatment of irritable bowel syndrome. *Behaviour Research and Therapy, 45*(4), 633–648.

Brenner, D. M., & Chey, W. D. (2009). Bifidobacterium infantis 35624: A novel probiotic for the treatment of irritable bowel syndrome. *Reviews in Gastroenterological Disorders, 9*(1), 7–15.

Cain, K. C., Headstrom, P., Jarrett, M. E., Motzer, S. A., Park, H., Burr, R. L., Surawicz, C. M., & Heitkemper, M. M. (2006). Abdominal pain impacts quality of life in women with irritable bowel syndrome. *American Journal of Gastroenterology, 101*(1), 124–132.

Camilleri, M., & Mayer, E. A. (2009). Developing irritable bowel syndrome guidelines through meta-analyses: Does the emperor really have new clothes? *Gastroenterology, 137*(3), 766–769.

Canavan, J. B., Bennett, K., Feely, J., O'Morain, C. A., & O'Connor, H. J. (2009). Significant psychological morbidity occurs in irritable bowel syndrome: A case-control study using a pharmacy reimbursement database. *Alimentary Pharmacology and Therapeutics, 29*(4), 440–449.

Carlos, R. C., Fendrick, A. M., Patterson, S. K., & Bernstein, S. J. (2005). Associations in breast and colon cancer screening behavior in women. *Academic Radiology, 12*(4), 451–458.

Chang, J. Y., & Talley, N. J. (2010). Current and emerging therapies in irritable bowel syndrome: From pathophysiology to treatment. *Trends in Pharmacological Sciences, 31*(7), 326–334.

Chang, L. (2011). The role of stress on physiologic responses and clinical symptoms in irritable bowel syndrome. *Gastroenterology, 140*(3), 761–765. doi: S0016-5085(11)00087-4

Chang, L., Lee, O. Y., Naliboff, B., Schmulson, M., & Mayer, E. A. (2001). Sensation of bloating and visible abdominal distension in patients with irritable bowel syndrome. *American Journal of Gastroenterology, 96*(12), 3341–3347.

Chang, L., Mayer, E. A., Johnson, T., FitzGerald, L. Z., & Naliboff, B. (2000). Differences in somatic perception in female patients with irritable bowel syndrome with and without fibromyalgia. *Pain, 84*(2–3), 297–307.

Chioqueta, A.P., & Stiles, T. C. (2004). Suicide risk in patients with somatization disorder. *Crisis, 25*(1), 3–7.

Chitkara, D. K., Talley, N. J., Schleck, C., Zinsmeister, A. R., Shah, N. D., & Locke, G. R., 3rd. (2009). Recollection of childhood abdominal pain in adults with functional gastrointestinal disorders. *Scandinavian Journal of Gastroenterology, 44*(3), 301–307.

Chitkara, D. K., van Tilburg, M. A., Blois-Martin, N., & Whitehead, W. E. (2008). Early life risk factors that contribute to irritable bowel syndrome in adults: A systematic review. *American Journal of Gastroenterology, 103*(3), 765–774; quiz 775.

Choi, Y. K., Kraft, N., Zimmerman, B., Jackson, M., & Rao, S. S. (2008). Fructose intolerance in IBS and utility of fructose-restricted diet. *Journal Clinical Gastroenterology, 42*(3), 233–238.

Coffin, B., Dapoigny, M., Cloarec, D., Comet, D., & Dyard, F. (2004). Relationship between severity of symptoms and quality of life in 858 patients with irritable bowel syndrome. *Gastroenterology and Clinical Biology, 28*(1), 11–15.

Cogan, R., & Spinnato, J. A. (1986). Pain and discomfort thresholds in late pregnancy. *Pain, 27*(1), 63–68.

Cohen, H., Jotkowitz, A., Buskila, D., Pelles-Avraham, S., Kaplan, Z., Neumann, L., & Sperber, A. D. (2006). Post-traumatic stress disorder and other co-morbidities in a sample population of patients with irritable bowel syndrome. *European Journal of Internal Medicine, 17*(8), 567–571.

Cole, J. A., Yeaw, J. M., Cutone, J. A., Kuo, B., Huang, Z., Earnest, D. L., & Walker, A. M. (2005). The incidence of abdominal and pelvic surgery among patients with irritable bowel syndrome. *Digestive Diseases and Sciences, 50*(12), 2268–2275.

Colwell, L. J., Prather, C. M., Phillips, S. F., & Zinsmeister, A. R. (1998). Effects of an irritable bowel syndrome educational class on health-promoting behaviors and symptoms. *American Journal of Gastroenterology, 93*(6), 901–905.

Crane, C., & Martin, M. (2002). Perceived vulnerability to illness in individuals with irritable bowel syndrome. *Journal of Psychosomatic Research, 53*(6), 1115–1122.

Crane, S. J., & Talley, N. J. (2007). Chronic gastrointestinal symptoms in the elderly. *Clinics in Geriatric Medicine, 23*(4), 721–734.

Creed, F., Fernandes, L., Guthrie, E., Palmer, S., Ratcliffe, J., Read, N., . . . Tomenson, B. (2003). The cost-effectiveness of psychotherapy and paroxetine for severe irritable bowel syndrome. *Gastroenterology, 124*(2), 303–317.

Creed, F., Guthrie, E., Ratcliffe, J., Fernandes, L., Rigby, C., Tomenson, B., Read, N., & Thompson, D. G. (2005). Reported sexual abuse predicts impaired functioning but a good response to psychological treatments in patients with severe irritable bowel syndrome. *Psychosomatic Medicine, 67*(3), 490–499.

Crowell, M. D., Dubin, N. H., Robinson, J. C., Cheskin, L. J., Schuster, M. M., Heller, B. R., & Whitehead, W. E. (1994). Functional bowel disorders in women with dysmenorrhoea. *American Journal of Gastroenterology, 89*, 1973–1977.

Dainese, R., Galliani, E. A., De Lazzari, F., Di Leo, V., & Naccarato, R. (1999). Discrepancies between reported food intolerance and sensitization test findings in irritable bowel syndrome patients. *American Journal of Gastroenterology, 94*(7), 1892–1897.

Delvaux, M., Denis, P., & Allemand, H. (1997). Sexual abuse is more frequently reported by IBS patients than by patients with organic digestive diseases or controls: Results of a multicentre inquiry. French Club of Digestive Motility. *European Journal of Gastroenterology and Hepatology, 9*(4), 345–352.

DiPalma, J. A., DeRidder, P. H., Orlando, R. C., Kolts, B. E., & Cleveland, M. B. (2000). A randomized, placebo-controlled, multicenter study of the safety and efficacy of a new polyethylene glycol laxative. *American Journal of Gastroenterology, 95*(2), 446–450.

Dobie, D. J., Kivlahan, D. R., Maynard, C., Bush, K. R., Davis, T. M., & Bradley, K. A. (2004). Posttraumatic stress disorder in female veterans: Association with self-reported health problems and functional impairment. *Archives of Internal Medicine, 164*(4), 394–400.

Drossman, D. A., Camilleri, M., Mayer, E. A., & Whitehead, W. E. (2002). AGA technical review on irritable bowel syndrome. *Gastroenterology, 123*(6), 2108–2131.

Drossman, D. A., Leserman, J., Li, Z., Keefe, F., Hu, Y. J., & Toomey, T. C. (2000). Effects of coping on health outcome among women with gastro-intestinal disorders. *Psychosomatic Medicine, 62*(3), 309–317.

Drossman, D. A., Leserman, J., Nachman, G., Li, Z. M., Gluck, H., Toomey, T. C., & Mitchell, C. M. (1990). Sexual and physical abuse in women with functional or organic gastrointestinal disorders. *Annals of Internal Medicine, 113*(11), 828–833.

Drossman, D. A., Morris, C. B., Schneck, S., Hu, Y. J., Norton, N. J., Norton, W. F., . . . Bangdiwala, S. I. (2009). International survey of patients with IBS: Symptom features and their severity, health status, treatments, and risk taking to achieve clinical benefit. *Journal of Clinical Gastroenterology, 43*(6), 541–550.

Drossman, D. A., Toner, B. B., Whitehead, W. E., Diamant, N. E., Dalton, C. B., Duncan, S., . . . Bangdiwala, S. I. (2003). Cognitive-behavioral therapy versus education and desipramine versus placebo for moderate to severe functional bowel disorders. *Gastroenterology, 125*(1), 19–31.

Drossman, D. A., Whitehead, W. E., Toner, B. B., Diamant, N., Hu, Y. J., Bangdiwala, S. I., & Jia, H. (2000). What determines severity among patients with painful functional bowel disorders? *American Journal of Gastroenterology, 95*(4), 974–980.

Dunivan, G. C., Heymen, S., Palsson, O. S., von Korff, M., Turner, M. J., Melville, J. L., & Whitehead, W. E. (2010). Fecal incontinence in primary care: Prevalence, diagnosis, and health care utilization. *American Journal of Obstetrics and Gynecology, 202*(5), 493, e491–496.

Elsenbruch, S., Harnish, M. J., & Orr, W. C. (1999). Subjective and objective sleep quality in irritable bowel syndrome. *American Journal of Gastroenterology, 94*(9), 2447–2452.

Farndale, R., & Roberts, L. (2011). Long-term impact of irritable bowel syndrome: A qualitative study. *Primary Health Care Research and Development, 12*(1), 52–67.

Ford, A. C., Talley, N. J., Schoenfeld, P. S., Quigley, E. M., & Moayyedi, P. (2009). Efficacy of anti-depressants and psychological therapies in irritable bowel syndrome: Systematic review and meta-analysis. *Gut, 58*(3), 367–378.

Ford, A. C., Talley, N. J., Spiegel, B. M., Foxx-Orenstein, A. E., Schiller, L., Quigley, E. M., & Moayyedi, P. (2008). Effect of fibre, antispas-modics, and peppermint oil in the treatment of irritable bowel syndrome: Systematic review and meta-analysis. *British Medical Journal, 337*, a2313.

Francis, C. Y., Duffy, J. N., Whorwell, P. J., & Morris, J. (1997). High prevalence of irritable bowel syndrome in patients attending urological outpatient departments. *Digestive Diseases and Sciences, 42*(2), 404–407.

Frank, D., Swedmark, J., & Grubbs, L. (2004). Colon cancer screening in African American women. *The ABNF Journal, 15*(4), 67–70.

Friedrich, M., Grady, S. E., & Wall, G. C. (2010). Effects of antidepressants in patients with irritable bowel syndrome and comorbid depression. *Clinical Therapy, 32*(7), 1221–1233.

Fukudo, S. (2007). Role of corticotropin-releasing hormone in irritable bowel syndrome and intestinal inflammation. *Journal of Gastroenterology, 42*(Suppl 17), 48–51.

Fumi, A. L., & Trexler, K. (2008). Rifaximin treat-ment for symptoms of irritable bowel syndrome. *Annals of Pharmacotherapy, 42*(3), 408–412.

Geiger, T. M., Miedema, B. W., Geana, M. V., Thaler, K., Rangnekar, N. J., & Cameron, G. T. (2008). Improving rates for screening colonoscopy: Analysis of the health information national trends survey (Hints I) data. *Surgical Endoscopy, 22*(2), 527–533.

Glia, A., & Lindberg, G. (1997). Quality of life in patients with different types of functional consti-pation. *Scandinavian Journal of Gastroenterology, 32*(11), 1083–1089.

Goldsmith, G., & Levin, J. S. (1993). Effect of sleep quality on symptoms of irritable bowel syn-drome. *Digestive Diseases and Sciences, 38*(10), 1809–1814.

Gonsalkorale, W. M., Miller, V., Afzal, A., & Whorwell, P. J. (2003). Long-term benefits of hypnotherapy for irritable bowel syndrome. *Gut, 52*(11), 1623–1629.

Graham, D. P., Savas, L., White, D., El-Serag, R., Laday-Smith, S., Tan, G., & El-Serag, H. B. (2010). Irritable bowel syndrome symptoms and health related quality of life in female veterans. *Alimentary Pharmacology and Therapeutics, 31*(2), 261–273.

Groll, D., Vanner, S. J., Depew, W. T., DaCosta, L. R., Simon, J. B., Groll, A., Roblin, N., & Paterson, W. G. (2002). The IBS-36: A new quality of life measure for irritable bowel syndrome. *American Journal of Gastroenterology*, *97*(4), 962–971.

Gros, D. F., Antony, M. M., McCabe, R. E., & Swinson, R. P. (2009). Frequency and severity of the symptoms of irritable bowel syndrome across the anxiety disorders and depression. *Journal of Anxiety Disorders*, *23*(2), 290–296.

Grover, M., Herfarth, H., & Drossman, D. A. (2009). The functional-organic dichotomy: Postinfectious irritable bowel syndrome and inflammatory bowel disease-irritable bowel syndrome. *Clinical Gastroenterology and Hepatology*, *7*(1), 48–53.

Grover, M., & Whitehead, W. E. (2011). Is fecal incontinence a risk factor for institutionalization in the elderly? *American Journal of Gastroenterology*, *106*(2), 366–367; author reply 367.

Guilera, M., Balboa, A., & Mearin, F. (2005). Bowel habit subtypes and temporal patterns in irritable bowel syndrome: Systematic review. *American Journal of Gastroenterology*, *100*(5), 1174–1184.

Guo, Y. J., Ho, C. H., Chen, S. C., Yang, S. S., Chiu, H. M., & Huang, K. H. (2010). Lower urinary tract symptoms in women with irritable bowel syndrome. *International Journal of Urology*, *17*(2), 175–181.

Guthrie, E., Creed, F., Dawson, D., & Tomenson, B. (1993). A randomised controlled trial of psychotherapy in patients with refractory irritable bowel syndrome. *British Journal of Psychiatry*, *163*, 315–321.

Guthrie, E., Creed, F. H., & Whorwell, P. J. (1987). Severe sexual dysfunction in women with the irritable bowel syndrome: Comparison with inflammatory bowel disease and duodenal ulceration. *British Journal of Medicine*, *295*, 577–578.

Halpert, A., Dalton, C. B., Palsson, O., Morris, C., Hu, Y., Bangdiwala, S., . . . Drossman, D. (2007). What patients know about irritable bowel syndrome (IBS) and what they would like to know. National survey on patient educational needs in IBS and development and validation of the patient educational needs questionnaire (PEQ). *American Journal Gastroenterology*, *102*(9), 1972–1982.

Halpert, A. D., Thomas, A. C., Hu, Y., Morris, C. B., Bangdiwala, S. I., & Drossman, D. A. (2006). A survey on patient educational needs in irritable bowel syndrome and attitudes toward participation

in clinical research. *Journal of Clinical Gastroenterology*, *40*(1), 37–43.

Haskell, S. G., Gordon, K. S., Mattocks, K., Duggal, M., Erdos, J., Justice, A., & Brandt, C. A. (2010). Gender differences in rates of depression, PTSD, pain, obesity, and military sexual trauma among connecticut war veterans of Iraq and Afghanistan. *Journal of Womens Health*, *19*(2), 267–271.

Hasler, W. L., & Schoenfeld, P. (2003). Systematic review: Abdominal and pelvic surgery in patients with irritable bowel syndrome. *Alimentary Pharmacology and Therapeutics*, *17*(8), 997–1005. doi: 1499 [pii]

Heitkemper, M., & Jarrett, M. (2008). Irritable bowel syndrome: Does gender matter? *Journal of Psychosomatic Research*, *64*(6), 583–587.

Heitkemper, M., Jarrett, M., Burr, R., Cain, K. C., Landis, C., Lentz, M., & Poppe, A. (2005). Subjective and objective sleep indices in women with irritable bowel syndrome. *Neurogastroenterology Motility*, *17*(4), 523–530.

Heitkemper, M. M., Cain, K. C., Jarrett, M. E., Burr, R. L., Crowell, M. D., & Woods, N. F. (2004). Relationship of bloating to other gi and menstrual symptoms in women with irritable bowel syndrome. *Digestive Diseases and Sciences*, *49*(1), 88–95.

Heitkemper, M. M., Cain, K. C., Jarrett, M. E., Burr, R. L., Hertig, V., Bond, E. F. (2003). Symptoms across the menstrual cycle in women with irritable bowel syndrome. *American Journal of Gastroenterology*, *98*(2), 420–430.

Heitkemper, M. M., & Chang, L. (2009). Do fluctuations in ovarian hormones affect gastrointestinal symptoms in women with irritable bowel syndrome? *Gender Medicine*, *6*(Suppl 2), 152–167.

Heizer, W. D., Southern, S., & McGovern, S. (2009). The role of diet in symptoms of irritable bowel syndrome in adults: A narrative review. *Journal of the American Dietetic Association*, *109*(7), 1204–1214.

Heymen, S., Scarlett, Y., Jones, K., Ringel, Y., Drossman, D., & Whitehead, W. E. (2009). Randomized controlled trial shows biofeedback to be superior to pelvic floor exercises for fecal incontinence. *Diseases of the Colon and Rectum*, *52*(10), 1730–1737.

Hislop, I. G. (1980). Effect of very brief psychotherapy on the irritable bowel syndrome. *Medical Journal of Australia*, *2*(11), 620–623.

Holden, C. (2008). Women abound in NIH trials. *Science, 322*(5899), 219.

Houghton, L. A., Lea, R., Jackson, N., & Whorwell, P. J. (2002). The menstrual cycle affects rectal sensitivity in patients with irritable bowel syndrome but not healthy volunteers. *Gut, 50*(4), 471–474.

Hulme, P. A. (2000). Symptomatology and health care utilization of women primary care patients who experienced childhood sexual abuse. *Child Abuse and Neglect, 24*(11), 1471–1484.

Hungin, A. P. (2006). Self-help interventions in irritable bowel syndrome. *Gut, 55*(5), 603–604.

Hungin, A. P., Chang, L., Locke, G. R., Dennis, E. H., & Barghout, V. (2005). Irritable bowel syndrome in the United States: Prevalence, symptom patterns and impact. *Alimentary Pharmacology and Therapeutics, 21*(11), 1365–1375.

Hungin, A. P., Whorwell, P. J., Tack, J., & Mearin, F. (2003). The prevalence, patterns and impact of irritable bowel syndrome: An international survey of 40,000 subjects. *Alimentary Pharmacology and Therapeutics, 17*(5), 643–650.

Hyams, J. S., Burke, G., Davis, P. M., Rzepski, B., & Andrulonis, P. A. (1996). Abdominal pain and irritable bowel syndrome in adolescents: A community-based study. *Journal of Pediatrics, 129*(2), 220–226. doi: S0022-3476(96)70246-9

Hyphantis, T., Guthrie, E., Tomenson, B., & Creed, F. (2009). Psychodynamic interpersonal therapy and improvement in interpersonal difficulties in people with severe irritable bowel syndrome. *Pain, 145*(1–2), 196–203.

Irwin, C., Falsetti, S. A., Lydiard, R. B., Ballenger, J. C., Brock, C. D., & Brener, W. (1996). Comorbidity of posttraumatic stress disorder and irritable bowel syndrome. *Journal of Clinical Psychiatry, 57*(12), 576–578.

Jarrett, M., Heitkemper, M., Cain, K. C., Burr, R. L., & Hertig, V. (2000). Sleep disturbance influences gastrointestinal symptoms in women with irritable bowel syndrome. *Digestive Diseases and Sciences, 45*(5), 952–959.

Johansson, P. A., Farup, P. G., Bracco, A., & Vandvik, P. O. (2010). How does comorbidity affect cost of health care in patients with irritable bowel syndrome? A cohort study in general practice. *BioMed Central Gastroenterology, 10*, 31.

Jones, M. P., Keefer, L., Bratten, J., Taft, T. H., Crowell, M. D., Levy, R., & Palsson, O.

(2009). Development and initial validation of a measure of perceived stigma in irritable bowel syndrome. *Psychology Health Medicine, 14*(3), 367–374. doi: 911194998

Jones, M. P., Wessinger, S., & Crowell, M. D. (2006). Coping strategies and interpersonal support in patients with irritable bowel syndrome and inflammatory bowel disease. *Clinical Gastroenterology and Hepatology, 4*(4), 474–481. doi: S1542-3565(05)01183-3

Kalantar, J. S., Locke, G. R., 3rd, Zinsmeister, A. R., Beighley, C. M., & Talley, N. J. (2003). Familial aggregation of irritable bowel syndrome: A prospective study. *Gut, 52*(12), 1703–1707.

Kane, S. V., Sable, K., & Hanauer, S. B. (1998). The menstrual cycle and its effect on inflammatory bowel disease and irritable bowel syndrome: A prevalence study. *American Journal of Gastroenterology, 93*(10), 1867–1872. doi: S0002927098004213

Karling, P., Abrahamsson, H., Dolk, A., Hallbook, O., Hellstrom, P. M., Knowles, C. H., . . . Walter, S. (2009). Function and dysfunction of the colon and anorectum in adults: Working team report of the Swedish Motility Group (SMOG). *Scandinavian Journal of Gastroenterology, 44*(6), 646–660.

Keefer, L., Stepanski, E. J., Ranjbaran, Z., Benson, L. M., & Keshavarzian, A. (2006). An initial report of sleep disturbance in inactive inflammatory bowel disease. *Journal of Clinical Sleep Medicine, 2*(4), 409–416.

King, T. S., Elia, M., & Hunter, J. O. (1998). Abnormal colonic fermentation in irritable bowel syndrome. *Lancet, 352*(9135), 1187–1189.

Kumar, D., Thompson, P. D., Wingate, D. L., Vesselinova-Jenkins, C. K., & Libby, G. (1992). Abnormal REM sleep in the irritable bowel syndrome. *Gastroenterology, 103*(1), 12–17.

Lackner, J. M., Brasel, A. M., Quigley, B. M., Keefer, L., Krasner, S. S., Powell, C., Katz, L. A., & Sitrin, M. D. (2010). The ties that bind: Perceived social support, stress, and IBS in severely affected patients. *Neurogastroenterol Motility, 22*(8), 893–900.

Lackner, J. M., Gudleski, G. D., Keefer, L., Krasner, S. S., Powell, C., & Katz, L. A. (2010). Rapid response to cognitive behavior therapy predicts treatment outcome in patients with irritable bowel syndrome. *Clinical Gastroenterology and Hepatology, 8*(5), 426–432.

Lackner, J. M., & Gurtman, M. B. (2004). Pain catastrophizing and interpersonal problems: A circumplex analysis of the communal coping model. *Pain, 110*(3), 597–604.

Lackner, J. M., & Gurtman, M. B. (2005). Patterns of interpersonal problems in irritable bowel syndrome patients a circumplex analysis. *Journal of Psychosomatic Research, 58*(6), 523–532.

Lackner, J. M., Jaccard, J., Krasner, S. S., Katz, L. A., Gudleski, G. D., & Holroyd, K. (2008). Self-administered cognitive behavior therapy for moderate to severe irritable bowel syndrome: Clinical efficacy, tolerability, feasibility. *Clinical Gastroenterology and Hepatology, 6*(8), 899–906.

Lackner, J. M., Mesmer, C., Morley, S., Dowzer, C., & Hamilton, S. (2004). Psychological treatments for irritable bowel syndrome: A systematic review and meta-analysis. *Journal of Consulting Clinical Psychology, 72*(6), 1100–1113.

Lackner, J. M., & Quigley, B. M. (2005). Pain catastrophizing mediates the relationship between worry and pain suffering in patients with irritable bowel syndrome. *Behaviour Research and Therapy, 43*(7), 943–957. doi: S0005-7967(04)00177-9

Lampe, J. W., Slavin, J. L., & Apple, F. S. (1991). Iron status of active women and the effect of running a marathon on bowel function and gastrointestinal blood loss. *International Journal of Sports Medicine, 12*(2), 173–179.

Lea, R., Houghton, L. A., Calvert, E. L., Larder, S., Gonsalkorale, W. M., Whelan, V., . . . Whorwell, P. J. (2003). Gut-focused hypnotherapy normalizes disordered rectal sensitivity in patients with irritable bowel syndrome. *Alimentary Pharmacology and Therapeutics, 17*(5), 635–642.

Lee, S., Wu, J., Ma, Y. L., Tsang, A., Guo, W. J., & Sung, J. (2009). Irritable bowel syndrome is strongly associated with generalized anxiety disorder: A community study. *Alimentary Pharmacology and Therapeutics, 30*(6), 643–651.

Leserman, J. (2007). Association of sexual and physical abuse with functional gastrointestinal and pelvic pain. *Primary Psychiatry, 14*(4), 58–63.

Leserman, J., & Drossman, D. A. (2007). Relationship of abuse history to functional gastrointestinal disorders and symptoms: Some possible mediating mechanisms. *Trauma Violence and Abuse, 8*(3), 331–343.

Leserman, J., Li, Z., Drossman, D. A., & Hu, Y. J. (1998). Selected symptoms associated with sexual and physical abuse history among female patients with gastrointestinal disorders: The impact on subsequent health care visits. *Psychological Medicine, 28*(2), 417–425.

Leslie, L. A., & Swider, S. M. (1986). Changing factors and changing needs in women's health care. *Nursing Clinics of North America, 21*(1), 111–123.

Levin, B., Lieberman, D. A., McFarland, B., Andrews, K. S., Brooks, D., Bond, J., . . . Winawer, S. J. (2008). Screening and surveillance for the early detection of colorectal cancer and adenomatous polyps, 2008: A joint guideline from the American Cancer Society, the US Multi-society Task Force on Colorectal Cancer, and the American College of Radiology. *Gastroenterology, 134*(5), 1570–1595.

Levine, B. S., Jarrett, M., Cain, K. C., & Heitkemper, M. M. (1997). Psychophysiological response to a laboratory challenge in women with and without diagnosed irritable bowel syndrome. *Research in Nursing and Health, 20*(5), 431–441.

Levy, R., Langer, S. L., Whitehead, W. E. (2007). Social learning contributions to the etiology and treatment of functional abdominal pain and inflammatory bowel disease in children and adults. *World Journal of Gastroenterology, 13*(17), 2397–2403.

Levy, R. L., Cain, K. C., Jarrett, M., & Heitkemper, M. M. (1997). The relationship between daily life stress and gastrointestinal symptoms in women with irritable bowel syndrome. *Journal of Behavioral Medicine, 20*(2), 177–193.

Levy, R. L., Jones, K. R., Whitehead, W. E., Feld, S. I., Talley, N. J., & Corey, L. A. (2001). Irritable bowel syndrome in twins: Heredity and social learning both contribute to etiology. *Gastroenterology, 121*(4), 799–804.

Levy, R. L., Whitehead, W. E., Von Korff, M. R., & Feld, A. D. (2000). Intergenerational transmission of gastrointestinal illness behavior. *American Journal of Gastroenterology, 95*(2), 451–456.

Levy, R. L., Whitehead, W. E., Walker, L. S., Von Korff, M., Feld, A. D., Garner, M., & Christie, D. (2004). Increased somatic complaints and healthcare utilization in children: Effects of parent IBS status and parent response to gastrointestinal symptoms. *American Journal of Gastroenterology, 99*(12), 2442–2451.

Longstreth, G. F. (2007). Avoiding unnecessary surgery in irritable bowel syndrome. *Gut, 56*(5), 608–610. doi: 56/5/608

Longstreth, G. F., Bolus, R., Naliboff, B., Chang, L., Kulich, K. R., Carlsson, J., . . . Wiklund, I. K. (2005). Impact of irritable bowel syndrome on patients' lives: Development and psychometric documentation of a disease-specific measure for use in clinical trials. *European Journal of Gastroenterology and Hepatology, 17*(4), 411–420.

Longstreth, G. F., Thompson, W. G., Chey, W. D., Houghton, L. A., Mearin, F., & Spiller, R. C. (2006). Functional bowel disorders. *Gastroenterology, 130,* 1480–1491.

Longstreth, G. F., & Yao, J. F. (2004). Irritable bowel syndrome and surgery: A multivariable analysis. *Gastroenterology, 126*(7), 1665–1673.

Lydiard, R. B., Greenwald, S., Weissman, M. M., Johnson, J., Drossman, D. A., & Ballenger, J. C. (1994). Panic disorder and gastrointestinal symptoms: Findings from the NIMH Epidemiologic Catchment Area project. *American Journal of Psychiatry, 151*(1), 64–70.

Maunder, R. G. (1998). Panic disorder associated with gastrointestinal disease: Review and hypotheses. *Journal of Psychosomatic Research, 44*(1), 91–105.

McCauley, J., Kern, D. E., Kolodner, K., Dill, L., Schroeder, A. F., DeChant, H. K., . . . Bass, E. B. (1997). Clinical characteristics of women with a history of childhood abuse: Unhealed wounds. *Journal of the American Medical Association, 277*(17), 1362–1368.

Menees, S. B., & Fenner, D. E. (2007). Colon cancer screening in women. *Women's Health, 3*(2), 163–172. doi: 10.2217/17455057.3.2.163

Menees, S. B., Inadomi, J. M., Korsnes, S., & Elta, G. H. (2005). Women patients' preference for women physicians is a barrier to colon cancer screening. *Gastrointestinal Endoscopy, 62*(2), 219–223.

Miller, V., Hopkins, L., & Whorwell, P. J. (2004). Suicidal ideation in patients with irritable bowel syndrome. *Clinical Gastroenterology and Hepatology, 2*(12), 1064–1068.

Miller, A. R., North, C. S., Clouse, R. E., Wetzel, R. D., Spitznagel, E. L., & Alpers, D. H. (2001). The association of irritable bowel syndrome and somatization disorder. *Annals of Clinical Psychiatry, 13*(1), 25–30.

Miller, V., & Whorwell, P. J. (2009). Hypnotherapy for functional gastrointestinal disorders: A review. *International Journal of Clinical and Experimental Hypnosis, 57*(3), 279–292.

Morris-Yates, A., Talley, N. J., Boyce, P. M., Nandurkar, S., & Andrews, G. (1998). Evidence of a genetic contribution to functional bowel disorder. *American Journal of Gastroenterology, 93*(8), 1311–1317.

Murray, C. D., Flynn, J., Ratcliffe, L., Jacyna, M. R., Kamm, M. A., & Emmanuel, A. V. (2004). Effect of acute physical and psychological stress on gut autonomic innervation in irritable bowel syndrome. *Gastroenterology, 127*(6), 1695–1703.

Nanda, R., James, R., Smith, H., Dudley, C. R., & Jewell, D. P. (1989). Food intolerance and the irritable bowel syndrome. *Gut, 30*(8), 1099–1104.

Norton, C., Whitehead, W. E., Bliss, D. Z., Harari, D., & Lang, J. (2010). Management of fecal incontinence in adults. *Neurourology and Urodynamics, 29*(1), 199–206.

Orr, W. C., Crowell, M. D., Lin, B., Harnish, M. J., & Chen, J. D. (1997). Sleep and gastric function in irritable bowel syndrome: Derailing the brain-gut axis. *Gut, 41*(3), 390–393.

Palsson, O. S., Heymen, S., & Whitehead, W. E. (2004). Biofeedback treatment for functional anorectal disorders: A comprehensive efficacy review. *Applied Psychophysiology Biofeedback, 29*(3), 153–174.

Palsson, O. S., Turner, M. J., Johnson, D. A., Burnett, C. K., & Whitehead, W. E. (2002). Hypnosis treatment for severe irritable bowel syndrome: Investigation of mechanism and effects on symptoms. *Digestive Diseases and Sciences, 47*(11), 2605–2614.

Palsson, O. S., Turner, M. J., & Whitehead, W. E. (2006). Hypnosis home treatment for irritable bowel syndrome: A pilot study. *International Journal of Clinical and Experimental Hypnosis, 54*(1), 85–99.

Palsson, O. S., & Whitehead, W. E. (2002). The growing case for hypnosis as adjunctive therapy for functional gastrointestinal disorders. *Gastroenterology, 123*(6), 2132–2135.

Paras, M. L., Murad, M. H., Chen, L. P., Goranson, E. N., Sattler, A. L., Colbenson, K. M., . . . Zirakzadeh, A. (2009). Sexual abuse and lifetime diagnosis of somatic disorders: A systematic review and meta-analysis. *Journal of the American Medical Association, 302*(5), 550–561.

Pare, P., Gray, J., Lam, S., Balshaw, R., Khorasheh, S., Barbeau, M., Kelly, S., & McBurney, C. R.

(2006). Health-related quality of life, work productivity, and health care resource utilization of
subjects with irritable bowel syndrome: Baseline
results from logic (longitudinal outcomes study of
gastrointestinal symptoms in canada), a naturalistic study. *Clinical Therapy*, *28*(10), 1726–1735;
discussion 1710–1721.

Park, H. J., Jarrett, M., Cain, K., & Heitkemper, M.
(2008). Psychological distress and GI symptoms
are related to severity of bloating in women with
irritable bowel syndrome. *Research in Nursing and
Health*, *31*(2), 98–107.

Park, H. J., Jarrett, M., & Heitkemper, M. (2010).
Quality of life and sugar and fiber intake in
women with irritable bowel syndrome. *Western
Journal of Nursing Research*, *32*(2), 218–232.

Patrick, D. L., Drossman, D. A., Frederick, I. O.,
DiCesare, J., & Puder, K. L. (1998). Quality of
life in persons with irritable bowel syndrome:
Development and validation of a new measure.
Digestive Diseases and Sciences, *43*(2), 400–411.

Pimentel, M., Park, S., Mirocha, J., Kane, S. V., &
Kong, Y. (2006). The effect of a nonabsorbed
oral antibiotic (rifaximin) on the symptoms of the
irritable bowel syndrome: A randomized trial.
Annals of Internal Medicine, *145*(8), 557–563.

Pinto, C., Lele, M. V., Joglekar, A. S., Panwar, V. S.,
& Dhavale, H. S. (2000). Stressful life-events,
anxiety, depression and coping in patients of
irritable bowel syndrome. *Journal of the Association
of Physicians of India*, *48*(6), 589–593.

Porcelli, P., Leandro, G., & De Carne, M. (1998).
Functional gastrointestinal disorders and eating
disorders. Relevance of the association in clinical
management. *Scandinavian Journal of Gastroenterology*, *33*(6), 577–582.

Raikes, A., Shoo, R., & Brabin, L. (1992). Gender-
planned health services. *Annals of Tropical Medicine and Parasitology*, *86*(Suppl 1), 19–23.

Rao, S. S., & Go, J. T. (2010). Update on the
management of constipation in the elderly:
New treatment options. *Journal of Clinical Interventions in Aging*, *5*, 163–171.

Remes-Troche, J., Bernal-Reyes, R., Valladares-
Lepine, M., Alonso-Larraga, O., Gomez-
Escudero, O., & Melendez-Mena, D. (2009).
[Gastroenterology diagnosis and treatment
guidelines of irritable bowel syndrome: Clinical
features and diagnostic criteria.] *Revista de Gastro-
enterologóa de Mexico*, *74*(1), 58–62.

Riedl, A., Schmidtmann, M., Stengel, A., Goebel, M.,
Wisser, A. S., Klapp, B. F., & Monnikes, H.
(2008). Somatic comorbidities of irritable bowel
syndrome: A systematic analysis. *Journal of
Psychosomatic Research*, *64*(6), 573–582.

Ringel, Y., Drossman, D. A., Leserman, J. L., Suye-
nobu, B. Y., Wilber, K., Lin, W., . . . Mayer, E.
A. (2008). Effect of abuse history on pain reports
and brain responses to aversive visceral stimulation: An FMRI study. *Gastroenterology*, *134*(2),
396–404.

Ringel, Y., Williams, R. E., Kalilani, L., & Cook, S. F.
(2009). Prevalence, characteristics, and impact of
bloating symptoms in patients with irritable
bowel syndrome. *Clinical Gastroenterology and
Hepatology*, *7*(1), 68–72; quiz 63.

Saito, Y. A., Locke, G. R., 3rd, Weaver, A. L.,
Zinsmeister, A. R., & Talley, N. J. (2005).
Diet and functional gastrointestinal disorders: A
population-based case-control study. *American
Journal of Gastroenterology*, *100*(12), 2743–2748.

Saito, Y. A., Prather, C. M., Van Dyke, C. T., Fett, S.,
Zinsmeister, A. R., & Locke, G. R., 3rd. (2004).
Effects of multidisciplinary education on outcomes
in patients with irritable bowel syndrome. *Clinical
Gastroenterology and Hepatology*, *2*(7), 576–584.

Saito, Y. A., Schoenfeld, P., & Locke, G. R., 3rd.
(2002). The epidemiology of irritable bowel
syndrome in North America: A systematic
review. *American Journal of Gastroenterology*,
97(8), 1910–1915.

Saito, Y. A., & Talley, N. J. (2008). Genetics of
irritable bowel syndrome. *American Journal of
Gastroenterology*, *103*(8), 2100–2104; quiz 2105.

Sandler, R. S., Everhart, J. E., Donowitz, M., Adams,
E., Cronin, K., Goodman, C., . . . Rubin, R.
(2002). The burden of selected digestive diseases
in the United States. *Gastroenterology*, *122*(5),
1500–1511.

Sapolsky R. M. (1996a). Stress, glucocorticoids, and
damage to the nervous system: The current state
of confusion. *Stress 1*(1), 1–19

Sapolsky, R. M. (1996b). Why stress is bad for your
brain. *Science*, *273*(5276), 749–750.

Sapolsky, R. M. (2004). Organismal stress and telo-
meric aging: An unexpected connection. *Proceedings of the National Academy of Sciences, USA*,
101(50), 17323–17324.

Savas, L. S., White, D. L., Wieman, M., Daci, K.,
Fitzgerald, S., Laday Smith, S., . . . El-Serag,

H. B. (2009). Irritable bowel syndrome and dyspepsia among women veterans: Prevalence and association with psychological distress. *Alimentary Pharmacology and Therapeutics, 29*(1), 115–125.

Schmulson, M., Noble-Lugo, A., Valenzuela-de la Cueva, V., De Arino-Suarez, M., Guillermo-Denis, L., & Ramos-Narvaez, F. (2009). [Gastroenterology diagnosis and treatment guidelines of irritable bowel syndrome: Treatment.] *Revista de Gastroenterologíte;a Mexico, 74*(1), 63–70.

Serra, J., Azpiroz, F., & Malagelada, J. R. (2001). Impaired transit and tolerance of intestinal gas in the irritable bowel syndrome. *Gut, 48*(1), 14–19.

Shepherd, S. J., & Gibson, P. R. (2006). Fructose malabsorption and symptoms of irritable bowel syndrome: Guidelines for effective dietary management. *Journal of the American Dietetic Association, 106*(10), 1631–1639.

Shih, Y. C., Barghout, V. E., Sandler, R. S., Jhingran, P., Sasane, M., Cook, S., . . . Halpern, M. (2002). Resource utilization associated with irritable bowel syndrome in the United States 1987-1997. *Digestive Diseases and Sciences, 47*(8), 1705–1715.

Smith, M. D., Russell, A., & Hodges, P. W. (2008). How common is back pain in women with gastrointestinal problems? *The Clinical Journal of Pain, 24*(3), 199–203.

Sperber, A. D. (2009). The challenge of cross-cultural, multi-national research: Potential benefits in the functional gastrointestinal disorders. *Neurogastroenterology and Motility, 21,* 351–360.

Sperber, A. D., Atzmon, Y., Neumann, L., Weisberg, I., Shalit, Y., Abu-Shakrah, M., Fich, A., & Buskila, D. (1999). Fibromyalgia in the irritable bowel syndrome: Studies of prevalence and clinical implications. *American Journal of Gastroenterology, 94*(12), 3541–3546.

Sperber, A. D., Carmel, S., Atzmon, Y., Weisberg, I., Shalit, Y., Neumann, L., . . . Buskila, D. (2000). Use of the functional bowel disorder severity index (FBDSI) in a study of patients with the irritable bowel syndrome and fibromyalgia. *American Journal of Gastroenterology, 95*(4), 995–998.

Sperber, A. D., & Dekel, R. (2010). Irritable bowel syndrome and co-morbid gastrointestinal and extra-gastrointestinal functional syndromes. *Journal of Neurogastroenterology and Motility, 16*(2), 113–119. doi: 10.5056/jnm.2010.16.2.113

Spiller, R., Camilleri, M., & Longstreth, G. F. (2010). Do the symptom-based, Rome criteria of irritable bowel syndrome lead to better diagnosis and treatment outcomes? *Clinical Gastroenterology and Hepatology, 8*(2), 125–129; discussion 129-136.

Striegel-Moore, R. H., Rosselli, F., Perrin, N., DeBar, L., Wilson, G. T., May, A., & Kraemer, H. C. (2009). Gender difference in the prevalence of eating disorder symptoms. *International Journal of Eating Disorders, 42*(5), 471–474.

Svedlund, J. (1983). Psychotherapy in irritable bowel syndrome: A controlled outcome study. *Acta Psychiatrica Scandinavica, Suppl 306,* 1–86.

Svedlund, J., Sjodin, I., Ottosson, J. O., & Dotevall, G. (1983). Controlled study of psychotherapy in irritable bowel syndrome. *Lancet, 2*(8350), 589–592.

Sykes, M. A., Blanchard, E. B., Lackner, J., Keefer, L., & Krasner, S. (2003). Psychopathology in irritable bowel syndrome: Support for a psychophysiological model. *Journal of Behavioral Medicine, 26*(4), 361–372.

Talley, N. J. (2004). Unnecessary abdominal and back surgery in irritable bowel syndrome: Time to stem the flood now? *Gastroenterology, 126*(7), 1899–1903.

Tang, T. N., Toner, B. B., Stuckless, N., Dion, K. L., Kaplan, A. S., & Ali, A. (1998). Features of eating disorders in patients with irritable bowel syndrome. *Journal of Psychosomatic Research, 45*(2), 171–178.

Thabane, M., & Marshall, J. K. (2009). Post-infectious irritable bowel syndrome. *World Journal of Gastroenterology, 15*(29), 3591–3596.

Tillisch, K., Labus, J. S., Naliboff, B. D., Bolus, R., Shetzline, M., Mayer, E. A., & Chang, L. (2005). Characterization of the alternating bowel habit subtype in patients with irritable bowel syndrome. *American Journal of Gastroenterology, 100*(4), 896–904.

Toner, B. B. (1994). Cognitive-behavioral treatment of functional somatic syndromes: Integrating gender issues. *Cognitive and Behavioral Practice, 1*(1), 157–178.

Toner, B. B., & Akman, D. (2000). Gender role and irritable bowel syndrome: Literature review and hypothesis. *American Journal of Gastroenterology, 95*(1), 11–16.

Toner, B. B., Segal, Z. V., Emmott, S., Myran, D., Ali, A., DiGasbarro, I., & Stuckless, N. (1998).

Cognitive-behavioral group therapy for patients with irritable bowel syndrome. *International Journal of Group Psychotherapy, 48*(2), 215–245.

Toner, B. B., Segal, Z. V., Emmott, S. D., & Myran, D. (2000a). *Cognitive-behavioral treatment of irritable bowel syndrome: Treatment manual for practitioners.* New York, NY: Guilford Press.

Toner, B. B., Segal, Z. V., Emmott, S. D., & Myran, D. (2000b). Considerations of stigma and gender role in treating IBS. In *Cognitive-behavioral treatment of irritable bowel syndrome. The brain-gut connection* (pp. 42–58). New York, NY: Guilford Press.

Tozzi, F., Thornton, L. M., Mitchell, J., Fichter, M. M., Klump, K. L., Lilenfeld, L. R., . . . Bulik, C. M. (2006). Features associated with laxative abuse in individuals with eating disorders. *Psychosomatic Medicine, 68*(3), 470–477.

Vandvik, P. O., Wilhelmsen, I., Ihlebaek, C., & Farup, P. G. (2004). Comorbidity of irritable bowel syndrome in general practice: A striking feature with clinical implications. *Alimentary Pharmacology and Therapeutics, 20*(10), 1195–1203.

Wald, A., Van Thiel, D. H., Hoechstetter, L., Gavaler, J. S., Egler, K. M., Verm, R., Scott, L., & Lester, R. (1981). Gastrointestinal transit: The effect of the menstrual cycle. *Gastroenterology, 80*(6), 1497–1500.

Wang, J. H., Liang, W., Chen, M. Y., Cullen, J., Feng, S., Yi, B., Schwartz, M. D., & Mandelblatt, J. S. (2006). The influence of culture and cancer worry on colon cancer screening among older Chinese-American women. *Ethnic Diseases, 16*(2), 404–411.

Warnock, J. K., & Clayton, A. H. (2003). Chronic episodic disorders in women. *Psychiatric Clinics of North America, 26*(3), 725–740.

White, D. L., Savas, L. S., Daci, K., Elserag, R., Graham, D. P., Fitzgerald, S. J., . . . El-Serag, H. B. (2010). Trauma history and risk of the irritable bowel syndrome in women veterans. *Alimentary Pharmacology and Therapeutics, 32*(4), 551–561.

Whitehead, W. E. (2005). Diagnosing and managing fecal incontinence: If you don't ask, they won't tell. *Gastroenterology, 129*(1), 6.

Whitehead, W. E., Borrud, L., Goode, P. S., Meikle, S., Mueller, E. R., Tuteja, A., . . . Ye, W. (2009). Fecal incontinence in US adults: Epidemiology and risk factors. *Gastroenterology, 137*(2), 512–517, 517 e511–e512.

Whitehead, W. E., Cheskin, L. J., Heller, B. R., Robinson, J. C., Crowell, M. D., Benjamin, C., & Schuster, M. M. (1990). Evidence for exacerbation of irritable bowel syndrome during menses. *Gastroenterology, 98*(6), 1485–1489.

Whitehead, W. E., Crowell, M. D., Robinson, J. C., Heller, B. R., & Schuster, M. M. (1992). Effects of stressful life events on bowel symptoms: Subjects with irritable bowel syndrome compared with subjects without bowel dysfunction. *Gut, 33*(6), 825–830.

Whitehead, W. E., Palsson, O., & Jones, K. R. (2002). Systematic review of the comorbidity of irritable bowel syndrome with other disorders: What are the causes and implications? *Gastroenterology, 122*(4), 1140–1156.

Whitehead, W. E., Palsson, O. S., Levy, R. R., Feld, A. D., Turner, M., & Von Korff, M. (2007). Comorbidity in irritable bowel syndrome. *American Journal of Gastroenterology, 102*(12), 2767–2776.

Whorwell, P. J. (2009). The problem of insoluble fibre in irritable bowel syndrome. *British Medical Journal, 338*, a3149.

Whorwell, P. J., Prior, A., & Colgan, S. M. (1987). Hypnotherapy in severe irritable bowel syndrome: Further experience. *Gut, 28*(4), 423–425.

Wright, M. O., Crawford, E., & Del Castillo, D. (2009). Childhood emotional maltreatment and later psychological distress among college students: The mediating role of maladaptive schemas. *Child Abuse and Neglect, 33*(1), 59–68.

CHAPTER

22

Stress and Resilience in Women With Rheumatic Disease

SHARON DANOFF-BURG

INTRODUCTION

The term *rheumatic disease*, which sometimes is used interchangeably with *arthritis*, refers to more than 100 different types of illnesses and conditions affecting the joints, the tissues that surround joints, and other connective tissue. Although important medical factors differentiate these illnesses and conditions, from a psychosocial perspective they share several coping tasks that are discussed here. With regard to particular diagnoses, the focus in this chapter is on rheumatoid arthritis (RA) and systemic lupus erythematosus (SLE), both of which are more common among women than men. SLE occurs 10 times more frequently in females than males, typically developing during young adulthood (Hampton, 2007). More than 70% of patients with RA are middle-aged women, and women with RA tend to report more severe symptoms and greater levels of disability than do men; however, this gender difference may be partly because of the way that disease activity is measured (Sokka et al., 2009). Both SLE and RA are chronic, inflammatory, and thought to be autoimmune in origin. This chapter explores how these illnesses relate to gender and to women's lives. The topics of reproductive choices, sexuality, and social roles are covered first, followed by consideration of differences across demographics and culture. Next, stress and resilience in women with rheumatic disease is discussed, concluding with recommendations for future directions.

REPRODUCTIVE CHOICES, SEXUALITY, AND SOCIAL ROLES

Reproductive Choices

Like patients with other chronic illnesses, patients with RA or SLE can experience flares without warning. This aspect of chronic illness can make it difficult to plan for the future and therefore can have an impact on many different important life decisions. The initial onset of rheumatic symptoms most often occurs between the ages of 15 and 40, a time of life during which reproductive choices are important to many individuals.

When making decisions related to childbearing, female patients must consider medical concerns. Some medical treatments can compromise women's ability to conceive, and in some cases pregnancy may put women at risk for disease flares and increase the likelihood of serious fetal complications. Years ago, women with SLE were simply advised not to get pregnant. Although outcomes have improved over the past two decades, pregnancy is still categorized as a high-risk period for women with SLE, particularly among patients with active disease (Marker-Hermann & Fischer-Betz, 2010). Interestingly, women with RA typically experience a reduction in disease activity or even remission during pregnancy, followed later by relapse; however, the mechanisms underlying this disease modulation effect are not fully understood (Marker-Hermann & Fischer-Betz, 2010). The optimal situation is one in which pregnancy is planned in accordance with medical consultation, allowing patients to be fully informed of risks and advice such as which medications might need to be discontinued for a period of time prior to conception or added at the time of pregnancy or postpartum (Andreoli et al., 2010). Ideally, pregnancy also would be planned to occur during a time of disease quiescence, along with medical attention to the management of any comorbid conditions, such as diabetes or hypertension (Elliott & Chakravarty, 2010).

Clowse (2010) noted that contraception counseling is essential for adolescent and adult women with rheumatic disease. Women with rheumatic disease generally do not have a higher rate of infertility than the healthy population, yet unprotected intercourse among those with no intention of pregnancy is not unusual. Estrogen-based birth control may be contraindicated for women with SLE, leading some women to the erroneous belief that contraception in general is not an option for them. Therefore, education should be made available about barrier methods, progestin-only methods, and intrauterine devices.

Sexuality

During adolescence, rheumatic disease can affect evolving sexuality (Siegel & Baum, 2004). As discussed in a review article (Tristano, 2009), the reasons why rheumatic disease may interfere with sexual health are multifactorial, relating to the illness as well as the effects of treatment. Some studies have found that, compared to samples of healthy women, adult women with rheumatic disease experience more gynecological problems, lower sexual functioning, poorer body image, and greater depression, pain, and fatigue (e.g., Curry, Levine, Corty, Jones, & Kurit, 1994). For instance, in one study (Curry, Levine, Jones, & Kurit, 1993), 26% of SLE patients abstained from sexual activities compared to only 4% of a healthy comparison sample. A more recent study (Abdel-Nasser & Ali, 2006) of women with RA found that 62% had difficulties related to sexual performance, 17% of whom reported inability to engage in sexual intercourse because of arthritis.

It is important to keep in mind, however, that even if some aspects of sexual *functioning* are altered as a result of illness, it does not necessarily follow that sexual *satisfaction* is lower. Research indicates that sexual dissatisfaction is most likely to occur when levels of fatigue, depression, or pain are high (Curry et al., 1993; Majerovitz & Revenson, 1994; Seawell & Danoff-Burg, 2005). It also should be noted that sexual problems—which certainly are not uncommon in the general population—may in some cases be attributed to the illness by default, rather than being perceived as linked to other factors or to complex sets of causes. In contrast, some women perceive benefits in their intimate relationships as a result of rheumatic disease, such as gains in self-acceptance (Karlen, 2002) and love and support from partners (Danoff-Burg & Revenson, 2005).

Social Roles

As with other chronic illnesses or disabilities, major lifestyle changes may occur for patients with rheumatic disease and their family members. The division of household responsibilities and activities may need to be shifted or in some cases may need to change dramatically if individuals are no longer able to fulfill roles they assumed previously. Changes in this aspect of family structure may carry extra meaning if the activities had been aligned with traditional gender roles or other roles that may be central to identity. An early study of Latinas with arthritis (Abraído-Lanza, 1997) found that negative affect increased as a function of intrusions into valued identities. Similarly, a later study by the same author (Abraído-Lanza & Revenson, 2006), which examined a more diverse sample and different roles (spouse, homemaker, parent, worker), found that the effects of illness intrusion on psychological well-being were moderated by whether the patient with rheumatic disease valued particular roles.

Acceptance and flexibility may be key factors in adapting to changing roles and may have important implications for mental health. This point is underscored by a study in which the ability to balance multiple roles was found to be the sole unique predictor of psychological well-being in women with RA (Coty & Wallston, 2008). In families that are resistant to change, women with rheumatic disease may end up carrying a double burden of managing chronic illness and managing the household. Whether in the role of patient or caregiver, women typically take on a disproportionate share of the responsibility for maintaining their family's organization and functioning. These responsibilities may be logical extensions of women's traditional roles, but they can take a personal toll and add strain to relationships (Danoff-Burg & Revenson, 2000).

DIFFERENCES ACROSS DEMOGRAPHICS AND CULTURE

Ethnicity and Socioeconomic Status

International studies indicate that women of African, Asian, and Hispanic descent are more likely than Caucasian women to have SLE and are more likely to have serious disease-related complications such as renal and neurological involvement (Pons-Estel, Alarcon, Scofield, Reinlib, & Cooper, 2010). There are many physical illnesses about which practically nothing is known regarding differences across demographics and culture. Thanks to the Lupus in Minorities: Nature versus Nurture (LUMINA) study, SLE is not one of those illnesses. Patient enrollment began in 1994, and by 2008 the cohort included 220 Hispanics, 234 African Americans, and 181 Caucasians and had resulted in 75 published original research papers. A recent article (Alarcon, 2011) about the LUMINA study summarized its major findings. These include the fact that the disease tends to be more severe among ethnic minority individuals, and some of the ethnic differences can be accounted for by socioeconomic factors. Numerous studies of this cohort have indicated that poverty, not ethnicity, is an independent contributor to diminished survival. Poverty also may contribute to depression and other negative mental health outcomes in patients with

SLE (Trupin et al., 2008) and RA (Margaretten et al., 2011).

An interesting variable related to ethnicity that has received some research attention is acculturation. Acculturation may include facets such as language, self-identity, neighborhood, and length of stay in the United States. One study (Alarcon et al., 1999) found that among Hispanic patients with SLE, lower levels of acculturation were associated with lower levels of disease activity. However, in a study of Hispanic patients with RA (Escalante, del Rincon, & Mulrow, 2000), lower levels of acculturation were associated with psychological distress. These inconsistent findings may reflect lack of rigor in the measurement of acculturation. Hunt, Schneider, and Comer (2004) raised strong concerns that research on acculturation "may be based more on ethnic stereotyping than on objective representations of cultural difference" (p. 973). Researchers interested in health disparities must be aware of this critique and sensitive to bias when examining variables related to ethnicity. At the same time, it is important that researchers not shy away from exploring these variables by ignoring them or simply controlling for them in statistical analyses, which can obscure findings.

Religion and Spirituality

Religion is an important component of culture that for many people functions as an important source of social support and coping resource. Abraído-Lanza and colleagues have explored the importance of religion and prayer for Latinas with rheumatic disease. For example, Latinas reported engagement in activities to be the most common strategy for coping with rheumatic disease, followed by religion and prayer (Abraído-Lanza, Guier, & Revenson, 1996). A later study of Latina women and Latino men with rheumatic disease highlighted the relationship between religious activities and active coping strategies, indicating that religious coping is not passive (Abraído-Lanza, Vásquez, & Echeverría, 2004). This point is consistent with previous research suggesting that although religious coping is often thought of as passive, it may be better conceptualized as an active coping process among African Americans, for whom religion, spirituality, and faith have been used historically to preserve culture, family, and identity (Mattis & Jagers, 2001). Religious beliefs were also identified as an important coping strategy in a study of Jamaican patients with SLE (Chambers et al., 2008).

A review (Lin, Gau, Lin, & Lin, 2011) of spiritual well-being in people with RA examined 10 studies conducted in the United States, the United Kingdom, Canada, South Korea, and Sweden. These authors defined *spirituality* as "the behavioral expression and perception of life experience which includes personal faith, relationships with others, and religious belief" (Lin et al., 2011, p. 2). They identified four themes (living with the disease, reclaiming control, reframing the situation, bolstering courage) and concluded that spirituality should be integrated into quality-of-life evaluations of patients. In a study of adults aged 50 or older (McCauley, Tarpley, Haaz, & Bartlett, 2008), 80% of the people with arthritis reported turning to spirituality on a daily basis for comfort or strength. This was particularly true for African-American women and less common among White men. A longitudinal study using a daily diary method (Keefe et al., 2001) provided support for the effectiveness of this type of coping: Patients with RA who strongly endorsed their ability to manage pain through spiritual coping were less likely to have joint pain and more likely to report positive mood and better social support. The authors mentioned the possibility of gender differences but did not evaluate them in this study, presumably because of the small number of male participants ($n = 4$).

STRESS AND RESILIENCE

Women with rheumatic disease face a wide range of stressors and challenges. These include pain, stiffness, fatigue, changes in lifestyle and appearance, changes in valued relationships and roles, adhering to treatment regimens that may include adverse side effects, interacting with the healthcare system, and in some cases concerns about mortality. Coping tasks may change over time as symptoms, disease course, and prognosis may change over time. Tolerating unpredictable aspects of the illness and uncertainty about the future can be frustrating and frightening. Stress has an impact on quality of life and can exacerbate disease activity (Bricou et al., 2006).

Stress has been observed empirically as a factor in worsening symptoms and is also recognized as a possible pathogenetic risk factor in autoimmune rheumatic diseases, along with genetic aspects, infections, and hormones (Cutolo & Straub, 2006). Experimental research has shown that, relative to healthy women, women with RA and SLE differ in their immune response to stress, and that changes in cytokine patterns might be responsible for stress-induced exacerbation of disease activity (Jacobs et al., 2001). A longitudinal study (Wekking, Vingerhoets, van Dam, Nossent, & Swaak, 1991)

conducted in the Netherlands found that the number and intensity of daily stressors were more strongly related to physical and psychosocial status in patients with SLE than in those with RA. A Swedish study (Burckhardt, Archenholtz, & Bjelle, 1993) found that women with SLE, compared to women with RA, had more concerns about their illness and how to manage it; however, the groups were comparable with regard to their self-rated quality of life, with the best predictor of quality of life being level of psychological distress.

Interpersonal stress in particular has been identified as an important variable in the study of women with rheumatic disease. A longitudinal study (Pawlak et al., 2003), in which women with SLE used handheld computer diaries to report stress levels, concluded that daily hassles associated with social duties and relationships predicted disease flares (measured by an increase in steroid medication). Similarly, other studies (Zautra, Burleson, Matt, Roth, & Burrows, 1994; Zautra & Smith, 2001) have documented high levels of psychological and physiological reactivity to interpersonal stress among women with RA relative to those with osteoarthritis. Peralta-Ramírez, Jiménez-Alonso, and Pérez-García (2009) found both interpersonal and work-related stressors to be associated with symptom worsening among Spanish patients with SLE. Although a small number of the participants were men, the authors did not report or discuss gender differences.

Another line of stress research focuses on the relative contribution of major and minor life stressors to physical and psychological outcomes. A prospective study of women with SLE (DaCosta et al., 1999) found that major life stress predicted functional disability at an 8-month follow-up, whereas another longitudinal study (Adams, Dammers, Saia, Brantley, & Gaydos, 1994) found that minor rather than major life events best predicted increases in SLE symptoms. A more recent study (Nery et al., 2007) found that both life stressors and hassles were significantly associated with major depressive disorder in women with SLE.

Individual-Level Stress and Implications for Intervention

Chronic illness can cause stress and diminish quality of life, yet most patients with RA (Bruce, 2008) or SLE (Segui et al., 2000) do not experience clinical depression. As in the general population, however, women are more likely than men to be depressed (Dowdy, Dwyer, Smith, & Wallston, 1996). Women with RA appear to attend more to their emotions and experience them more intensely than do men with RA (van Middendorp et al., 2005).

What helps? Several meta-analyses (Astin, Beckner, Soeken, Hochberg, & Berman, 2002; Dixon, Keefe, Scipio, Perri, & Abernethy, 2007; Knittle, Maes, & de Gucht, 2010) of randomized controlled trials (RCTs) have concluded that psychological interventions for patients with RA can influence mental health outcomes and objective clinical indices of disease activity such as joint tenderness but typically do not alter biological markers. For example, one meta-analytic review (Astin et al., 2002) examined 25 studies that compared psychosocial interventions for RA to nonintervention controls (wait-list, usual care, or attention placebo). The interventions often were multimodal and included components such as cognitive-behavioral therapy (CBT), psychoeducation, emotional disclosure, group counseling, stress management, and

biofeedback. Results indicated small but significant average posttreatment effect sizes for pain, functional disability, depression, coping, and self-efficacy. At follow-up, which averaged 8.5 months posttreatment, effect sizes for depression, coping, and tender joints remained significant.

Unfortunately, RCTs examining psychological interventions for SLE are much less common. Dobkin et al. (2002) compared brief supportive-expressive group psychotherapy to standard medical care for women with SLE and found that the psychological intervention was not efficacious; both groups showed some improvement, but there were no clinically important group differences. Greco, Rudy, and Manzi (2004) randomized SLE patients to one of three groups: biofeedback-assisted CBT, symptom monitoring, or usual medical care. Biofeedback-assisted CBT participants showed the greatest posttreatment reductions in symptoms of stress, depression, and pain. At a nine-month follow-up, the effect of treatment on psychological functioning, but not on pain, remained significant relative to usual care.

A recent study (Navarrete-Navarrete et al., 2010) of CBT compared to standard medical care for SLE found improvement in mood, quality of life, and somatic symptoms, but no significant change in disease activity. Clearly, RCTs focused on CBT should be a priority in psychosocial SLE research, as interventions that are grounded in a cognitive-behavioral orientation seem most effective in managing painful chronic illnesses (Martire, 2005; Mazzuca, 1982). In addition, it would be helpful to investigate factors predicting treatment adherence, such as patient–provider communication (Seawell & Danoff-Burg, 2004). For example, a qualitative study (Salt & Peden, 2011) about decision making concerning medication use emphasized the importance of a trusting relationship between women with RA and their healthcare providers. Quantitative research (Martin et al., 2008) has yielded similar findings.

Cognitive-behavioral techniques are part of the Arthritis Self-Management Program (ASMP; Lorig & Fries, 2006), also known as the Arthritis Self-Help Course, a widely used educational program sponsored by the Arthritis Foundation. A similarly structured program for SLE patients is the Systemic Lupus Erythematosus Self-Help Course (SLESH; Braden, Brodt-Weinberg, Depka, McGlone, & Tretter, 1987). These programs provide disease-related information and teach self-management skills such as relaxation and problem solving, improving a variety of patient outcomes as well as saving costs (Bodenheimer, Lorig, Holman, & Grumbach, 2002); however, the positive treatment effects may not be long-lasting (Riemsma, Taal, Kirwan, & Rasker, 2004). Some research has focused on modifying these programs to meet the needs of ethnically diverse populations (Lorig, Gonzalez, & Ritter, 1999; Robbins, Allegrante & Paget, 1993) and those who prefer an Internet-based format (Lorig, Ritter, Laurent, & Plant, 2008).

Arthritis is one of the foremost chronic illnesses for which patients seek complementary and alternative medicine (CAM) options, and female arthritis patients are more likely to do so than male arthritis patients (Efthimiou, Kukar, & MacKenzie, 2010; Quandt et al., 2005). CAM includes a wide range of practices and mind-body approaches. For example, hatha yoga has been tested in women with RA, resulting in improved balance and decreases in pain, disability, and depression, but no changes in cortisol levels (Bosch, Traustadóttir, Howard, & Matt, 2009). A systematic review of t'ai chi for RA (Lee, Pittler, & Ernst, 2007) concluded that it may enhance quality of life and other psychological outcomes, but findings were mixed regarding the effects of t'ai chi on pain and fatigue. Researchers interested in rheumatic diseases (Pradhan et al., 2007; Rosenzweig et al., 2010; Zautra et al., 2008) also have begun to examine the benefits of mindfulness-based interventions, some of which are part of what is considered to be the third wave of cognitive-behavioral therapy (Öst, 2008). To date, there have been no published trials evaluating yoga, t'ai chi, or mindfulness in patients with SLE.

Interpersonal-Level Stress and Implications for Intervention

As discussed earlier in this chapter, interpersonal stress experienced by women with rheumatic disease has been shown to predict negative adjustment outcomes. Women with rheumatic disease frequently have needs related to their illness that remain unmet (Danoff-Burg & Friedberg, 2009), and they tend to be dissatisfied with their levels of social support (Archenoltz, Burckhardt, & Segesten, 1999). This has implications for adjustment to illness, particularly for women, who tend to spend more time than men thinking about relationships and who in general feel more upset than men by stressors within the family (Berg & Upchurch, 2007). Accordingly, researchers have examined how interactions between patients and their partners affect adjustment.

For instance, rheumatic disease patients' degree of satisfaction with the responses of their spouses has been correlated with mood and with the likelihood of feeling helpless or overwhelmed in dealing with pain (Holtzman & DeLongis, 2007). Patients are likely to become frustrated when family members underestimate their level of fatigue or misunderstand (either by underestimating or overestimating) their functional limitations. This can lead to what researchers have labeled "problematic social support." Problematic support can occur when well-intended attempts at support do not match what the patient needs or wants, or it can take the form of criticism or lack of empathy (Lehman et al., 2011; Revenson, Schiaffino, Majerovitz, & Gibofsky, 1991). Fortunately, social support is a potentially modifiable factor, which is important in light of its potential influence on health status (Sutcliffe et al., 1999).

What helps? Psychological, supportive, and educational interventions are usually aimed at individual-level change and do not include the participation of family members. However, involving close others in psychosocial interventions may improve communication and clarify which types of social support are most helpful in which situations and for which individuals. This may, in turn, enhance adherence to medical regimens and other aspects of adaptation to chronic illness. For example, involving close others in interventions may help improve family members' understanding of the illness. This is especially important for chronic illnesses such as SLE that often are referred to as invisible because patients do not necessarily "look sick." In addition, the cyclical nature of chronic illness can sometimes be difficult for family members to understand; for instance, they may question why particular activities (e.g., household chores) can be performed by the patient on some days but not others.

Sterba et al. (2008) found that women with RA fared better when their husbands shared their perceptions about the degree of controllability of the illness and its unpredictable nature. However, shared illness perceptions are not necessarily needed for optimal adjustment; incongruent perceptions and dissimilar coping strategies can in some cases be complementary (Revenson, 2003). When partners' coping strategies are congruent, it may indicate that a couple is working well together toward shared goals. When partners' coping strategies are incongruent, their coping efforts may be undermining or cancelling out one another. Alternatively, incongruence could mean that as a unit the couple has access to a wider repertoire of adaptive coping strategies. In the best case scenario, different coping strategies could be used to enhance each other's efforts or fill in coping gaps. Revenson (2003) studied heterosexual couples in which one partner had rheumatic disease, providing data supporting the theory that partners' dissimilar coping strategies do not necessarily signify poor psychological or marital adjustment.

Several studies have investigated the effectiveness of incorporating partner or family support into psychological or educational interventions for rheumatic disease. An early study by Radojevic, Nicassio, and Weisman (1992) examined whether a family support component would improve CBT for RA. The CBT with family involvement group was superior to the other groups (CBT without family support, education with family support, no-treatment control) with regard to severity and number of swollen joints, although there were no group differences in distress or pain. However, the two CBT groups did not differ from each other at a 2-month follow-up. Dutch researchers (van Lankveld, van Helmond, Näring, de Rooij, & van den Hoogen, 2004) found that having spouses participate in a CBT-oriented group for RA was not superior to the same intervention without spouse participation in terms of positive effects on disease activity, coping, cognitions, or physical and psychological functioning. Patients in the spouse participation group did, however, report more improvement in disease-related communication with the spouse at follow-up compared to patients in the group that did not include spouse participation. Along the same lines, a study of group education for RA patients (Riemsma, Taal, & Rasker, 2003) did not support the hypothesis that participation of significant others would lead to improved effects relative to group education without a partner.

As mentioned earlier, RCTs of psychosocial interventions for SLE are scarce. With regard to the inclusion of family members in treatment, Karlson et al. (2004) studied a psychoeducational intervention for SLE patients and their partners. The partner could be either a spouse or another family member, and the intervention was designed to enhance self-efficacy, problem solving, communication, and social support. Unlike the studies discussed in the previous paragraph, this study did not include a comparison group in which the same intervention was administered without partner participation. Rather, the control group in this particular RCT was an attention placebo condition in which patients and partners watched a video about SLE together and then received follow-up telephone calls. Six months posttreatment, the intervention group showed improvement in mental health status, self-efficacy, fatigue, social support, and couples' illness-related communication. Disease activity also was measured but did not change in response to the intervention.

Taken together, these studies do not provide unequivocal evidence for including family members in psychosocial interventions for rheumatic disease, and one of the studies (Riemsma et al., 2003) even indicated some deleterious effects. Still, the involvement of loved ones in treatment can be of critical value to individuals whose family interactions are interfering with adaptation to the illness. These types of interventions may be most successful when family members are trained to reinforce adaptive behaviors (Keefe et al., 1996, 1999). There also may be cultural reasons to include family members; for example, a study of how to best modify SLESH for Latino patients (Robbins et al., 1993) identified the importance of focusing on family roles rather than individual needs and emphasizing the interdependency of family members. Furthermore, research conducted with other chronic illness samples has documented benefits to having family members participate in psychosocial interventions.

A meta-analytic review (Martire, Lustig, Schulz, Miller, & Helgeson, 2004) of family member participation in psychosocial interventions for a variety of chronic illnesses (including arthritis) concluded that the strongest evidence of efficacy was for the family members. Specifically, the interventions resulted in the patients' family members feeling less depressed and less burdened. As noted by Martire (2005), future research on this topic should explore contextual factors such as gender. The importance of this point is illustrated by a study (Wing, Marcus, Epstein, & Jawad, 1991) of behavioral weight loss for obese patients with Type 2 diabetes. The participants, all of whom had obese spouses, were each randomly assigned to attend the 20-week program either alone or with their spouse. Results revealed that the effect of partner involvement varied as a function of patient gender. Men benefitted more when treated in a group without their spouses, whereas women benefitted more from the same program when accompanied by their spouses.

Resilience

The psychology of positive human functioning (Seligman & Csikszentmihalyi, 2000) increasingly is receiving attention not only from clinicians but also from scientists who realize that focusing exclusively on negative emotions and impaired functioning results in an incomplete picture. For example, a growing body of research is revealing the complex pathways through which positive affect influences physical health and even longevity (Cohen & Pressman, 2006). When considering the subject of positive versus negative emotion, it is essential to keep in mind that people do not feel all good or all bad at any given moment. Individuals experience co-occurring positive and negative emotions when coping with any stressful life experience, be it bereavement, parenthood, or chronic illness (Folkman, 2008). In fact, the presence of positive feelings in the midst of adversity can buffer against a downward negative spiral (Algoe & Stanton, 2009) or help individuals bounce back from negativity (Tugade & Frederickson, 2004).

These theories have direct relevance for the lives of women with rheumatic disease. For instance, positive affect has been found to reduce the distress associated with fluctuations in pain from RA, leading Zautra and colleagues (Smith & Zautra, 2008; Strand, Zautra, & Thoresen, 2006; Zautra, Johnson, & Davis, 2005; Zautra, Smith, Affleck, & Tennen, 2001) to describe positive affect as a source of resilience for women who live with chronic pain. Sinclair and Wallston (2004) sought to quantify resilience in patients living with RA and identified the following themes: tenacity, optimism, creativity, an aggressive approach to problem solving, and a commitment to extract positive growth from difficult situations.

Related to resilience is the ability to find benefits in adverse experiences, a topic that was discussed earlier in this chapter with regard to sexuality and intimate relationships. In a study of couples coping with one partner's rheumatic disease (Revenson, 2003), even the most psychologically distressed couples reported high levels of personal growth because of the illness. This process of benefit-finding has been associated with enhanced psychological and health-related functioning in both SLE and RA patients (Affleck, Pfeiffer, Tennen, & Fifield, 1988; Danoff-Burg, Agee, Romanoff, Kremer, & Strosberg, 2006; Danoff-Burg & Revenson, 2005; Katz, Flasher, Cacciapaglia, & Nelson, 2001). Commonly reported benefits include awareness of deepened interpersonal relationships; enhanced spirituality; identification of purpose or meaning in life; greater personal strength, compassion, or empathy; and an overall increased appreciation for life.

Understanding patients' perceptions of possible benefits and growth in response to their illness may help identify protective factors and targeted intervention goals. As this line of research continues, it will be important to consider contextual variables such as culture and gender. A few studies have already contributed to the literature in this regard. Abraído-Lanza, Guier, and Colón (1998) conducted a 3-year longitudinal study exploring factors that promote thriving in Latina women coping with poverty and arthritis. Using qualitative methods, the investigators identified enhanced appreciation of life as an important example of the participants' experiences of thriving. In a quantitative study of women and men with RA in Japan (Sato, Yamazaki, Sakita, & Bryce, 2008), female gender was an independent predictor of perceiving benefits resulting from the illness. Finally, in an exploratory study using both qualitative and qualitative methods, Wittmann et al. (2009) developed a phenomenological model of suffering and posttraumatic growth in Swiss women with SLE.

Most of the previous research regarding positive changes in response to adversity has not addressed issues of gender, and the results of the studies that have done so are inconsistent (Linley & Joseph, 2004). Some studies found no significant gender differences, such as in samples of patients with RA (Danoff-Burg & Revenson, 2005) or cancer (Collins, Taylor, & Skokan, 1990). In contrast, some studies found that women reported higher levels of posttraumatic growth than did men, as in the aforementioned Japanese study of RA (Sato et al., 2008) and a study of cancer patients and their spouses (Weiss, 2002). A meta-analytic review (Helgeson, Reynolds, & Tomich, 2006) that examined whether gender moderates the relationship between benefit-finding or perceptions of growth and adjustment outcomes was inconclusive, partly because many of the studies were conducted with samples that were all male or all female. As noted earlier, this topic should be investigated further in future research, and complex models may be needed. For example, women's experience of trauma and growth may be better explained by a curvilinear model, whereas men's experience following adverse events may be better characterized by a linear relation in which greater symptom severity predicts greater growth (Hwang,

Danoff-Burg, Hickling, Barnett, & Sison, 2010).

FUTURE DIRECTIONS

Studying not only pathology and vulnerability but also growth and protective factors will help psychologists and other health professionals understand and promote positive adjustment to rheumatic disease. In conducting this line of research, attention must be devoted to contextual variables such as gender and culture. An ecological, illness-in-context perspective (Revenson, 1990) conceptualizes health as a function not only of individual characteristics but also of broader social and cultural contexts.

Understanding the contribution of gender is important, but it can be challenging, especially when studying diseases that are much more prevalent among women. When samples of patients with rheumatic disease include only a few or no men, it can be difficult to disentangle the effects of gender from the effects of being in the role of medical patient. Theory-based, biopsychosocial research ultimately will help us develop interventions to enhance the resilience of patients and their families as they cope with rheumatic disease. Viewing illness in its broader ecological context requires thoughtful research design and sophisticated data analysis. Such efforts on the part of researchers will be needed in order to capture the complexity of the illness experience, which does not occur in isolation from an individual's relationships and environment. In the words of a 69-year-old woman with RA, "It's this whole picture, this well-being. It's like a frame into which you fit a lot of other various things about your life" (Sanderson, Morris, Calnan, Richards, & Hewlett, 2010, p. 236).

REFERENCES

Abdel-Nasser, A. M., & Ali, E. I. (2006). Determinants of sexual disability and dissatisfaction in female patients with rheumatoid arthritis. *Journal of Clinical Rheumatology*, *25*, 822–830.

Abraído-Lanza, A. F. (1997). Latinas with arthritis: Effects of illness, role identity, and competence on psychological well-being. *American Journal of Community Psychology*, *25*, 601–627.

Abraído-Lanza, A. F., Guier, C., & Colón, R. M. (1998). Psychological thriving among Latinas with chronic illness. *Journal of Social Issues*, *54*, 405–424.

Abraído-Lanza, A. F., Guier, C., & Revenson, T. A. (1996). Coping and social support resources among Latinas with arthritis. *Arthritis Care & Research*, *9*, 501–508.

Abraído-Lanza, A. F., & Revenson, T. A. (2006). Illness intrusion and psychological adjustment to rheumatic diseases: A social identity framework. *Arthritis & Rheumatism*, *55*, 224–232.

Abraído-Lanza, A. F., Vásquez, E., & Echeverría, S. E. (2004). En las manos de Dios [in God's hands]: Religious and other forms of coping among Latinos with arthritis. *Journal of Consulting and Clinical Psychology*, *72*, 91–102.

Adams, S. G., Dammers, P. M., Saia, T. L., Brantley, P. J., & Gaydos, G. R. (1994). Stress, depression, and anxiety predict average symptom severity and daily symptom fluctuation in systemic lupus erythematosus. *Journal of Behavioral Medicine*, *17*, 459–477.

Affleck, G., Pfeiffer, C., Tennen, H., & Fifield, J. (1988). Social support and psychosocial adjustment to rheumatoid arthritis. *Arthritis Care and Research*, *1*, 71–77.

Alarcon, G. S. (2011, May). The LUMINA study: Impact beyond lupus in U.S. Hispanics. *The Rheumatologist*. Retrieved from http://www.the-rheumatologist.org

Alarcon, G. S., Rodriguez, J., Benavides, G., Brooks, K., Kurusz, H., & Reveille, J. D. (1999). Systemic lupus erythematosus in three ethnic groups, Part V: Acculturation, health-related attitudes and behaviors, and disease activity in Hispanic patients from the LUMINA cohort. *Arthritis Care & Research*, *12*, 267–274.

Algoe, S. B., & Stanton, A. L. (2009). Is benefit finding good for individuals with chronic disease? In C. Park, S. Lechner, A. L. Stanton, & M. H. Antoni (Eds.), *Medical illness and positive life change: Can crisis lead to personal transformation?* (pp. 173–193). Washington, DC: American Psychological Association.

Andreoli, L., Bazzani, C., Taraborelli, M., Reggia, R., Lojacono, A., Brucato, A., Meroni, P. L., & Tincani, A. (2010). Pregnancy in autoimmune rheumatic diseases: The importance of counselling for old and new challenges. *Autoimmunity Reviews*, *10*, 51–54.

Archenholtz, B., Burckhardt, C. S., & Segesten, K. (1999). Quality of life of women with systemic lupus erythematosus or rheumatoid arthritis: Domains of importance and dissatisfaction. *Quality of Life Research*, *8*, 411–416.

Astin, J. A., Beckner, W., Soeken, K., Hochberg, M. C., & Berman, B. (2002). Psychological interventions for rheumatoid arthritis: A meta-analysis of randomized controlled trials. *Arthritis & Rheumatism*, *47*, 291–302.

Berg, C. A., & Upchurch, R. (2007). A developmental-contextual model of couples coping with chronic illness across the adult life span. *Psychological Bulletin*, *133*, 920–954.

Bodenheimer, T., Lorig, K., Holman, H., & Grumbach, K. (2002). Patient self-management of chronic disease in primary care. *JAMA*, *288*, 2469–2475.

Bosch, P. R., Traustadóttir, T., Howard, P., & Matt, K. S. (2009). Functional and physiological effects of yoga in women with rheumatoid arthritis: A pilot study. *Alternative Therapies*, *15*, 24–31.

Braden, C. J., Brodt-Weinberg, R., Depka, L., McGlone, K., & Tretter, S. (1987). *Systemic lupus erythematosus (SLE) self-help course, leader's manual*. Atlanta, GA: Arthritis Foundation.

Bricou, O., Taïeb, O., Baubet, T., Gal, B., Guillevin, L., & Moro, M. R. (2006). Stress and coping strategies in systemic lupus erythematosus: A review. *Neuroimmunomodulation*, *13*, 283–293.

Bruce, T. (2008). Comorbid depression in rheumatoid arthritis: Pathophysiology and clinical implications. *Current Psychiatry Reports*, *10*, 258–264.

Burckhardt, C. S., Archenholtz, B., & Bjelle, A. (1993). Quality of life of women with systemic lupus erythematosus: A comparison with women with rheumatoid arthritis. *Journal of Rheumatology*, *20*, 977–981.

Chambers, S., Raine, R., Rahman, A., Hagley, K., De Ceulaer, K., & Isenberg, D. (2008). Factors influencing adherence to medications in a group of patients with systemic lupus erythematosus in Jamaica. *Lupus, 17,* 761–769.

Clowse, M. E. B. (2010). Managing contraception and pregnancy in the rheumatologic diseases. *Best Practice & Research Clinical Rheumatology, 24,* 373–385.

Cohen, S., & Pressman, S. D. (2006). Positive affect and health. *Current Directions in Psychological Science, 15,* 122–125.

Collins, R. L., Taylor, S. E., & Skokan, L. A. (1990). A better world or a shattered vision? Changes in life perspective following victimization *Social Cognition, 8,* 263–285.

Coty, M. B., & Wallston, K. (2008). Roles and well-being among healthy women and women with rheumatoid arthritis. *Journal of Advanced Nursing, 63,* 189–198.

Curry, S., Levine, S., Corty, E., Jones, P., & Kurit, D. (1994). The impact of systemic lupus erythematosus on women's sexual functioning. *Journal of Rheumatology, 21,* 2254–2260.

Curry, S. L., Levine, M. N., Jones, P. K., & Kurit, D. M. (1993). Medical and psychosocial predictors of sexual outcome among women with systemic lupus erythematosus. *Arthritis Care & Research, 6,* 23–30.

Cutolo, M., & Straub, R. H. (2006). Stress as a risk factor in the pathogenesis of rheumatoid arthritis. *Neuroimmunomodulation, 13*(5–6), 277–282.

Da Costa, D., Dobkin, P. L., Pinard, L., Fortin, P. R., Danoff, D. S., Esdaile, J. M., & Clarke, A. E. (1999). The role of stress in functional disability among women with systemic lupus erythematosus: A prospective study. *Arthritis Care and Research, 2,* 112–119.

Danoff-Burg, S., Agee, J. D., Romanoff, N. R., Kremer, J. M., & Strosberg, J. M. (2006). Benefit finding and expressive writing in adults with lupus or rheumatoid arthritis. *Psychology and Health, 21,* 651–665.

Danoff-Burg, S., & Friedberg, F. (2009). Unmet needs of patients with systemic lupus erythematosus. *Behavioral Medicine, 35,* 5–13.

Danoff-Burg, S., & Revenson, T. A. (2000). Rheumatic illness and relationships: Coping as a joint venture. In K. B. Schmaling & T. G. Sher (Eds.), *The psychology of couples and illness: Theory, research,* *and practice* (pp. 105–133). Washington, DC: American Psychological Association.

Danoff-Burg, S., & Revenson, T. A. (2005). Benefit-finding among patients with rheumatoid arthritis: Positive effects on interpersonal relationships. *Journal of Behavioral Medicine, 28,* 91–103.

Dixon, K. E., Keefe, F. J., Scipio, C. D., Perri, L. M., & Abernethy, A. P. (2007). Psychological interventions for arthritis pain management in adults: A meta-analysis. *Health Psychology, 26,* 241–250.

Dobkin, P. L., Da Costa, D., Joseph, L., Fortin, P. R., Edworthy, S., Barr, S., . . . Clarke, A. E. (2002). Counterbalancing patient demands with evidence: Results from a pan-Canadian randomized clinical trial of brief supportive-expressive group psychotherapy for women with systemic lupus erythematosus. *Annals of Behavioral Medicine, 24,* 88–99.

Dowdy, S. W., Dwyer, K. A., Smith, C. A., & Wallston, K. A. (1996). Gender and psychosocial well-being of persons with rheumatoid arthritis. *Arthritis Care and Research, 9,* 449–456.

Efthimiou, P., Kukar, M., & MacKenzie, C. R. (2010). Complementary and alternative medicine in rheumatoid arthritis: No longer the last resort! *HSS Journal, 6,* 108–111.

Elliott, A., & Chakravarty, E. F. (2010). Management of rheumatic diseases during pregnancy. *Postgraduate Medicine, 122,* 213–221.

Escalante, A., del Rincon, I., & Mulrow, C. D. (2000). Symptoms of depression and psychological distress among Hispanics with rheumatoid arthritis. *Arthritis Care & Research, 13,* 156–167.

Folkman, S. (2008). The case for positive emotions in the stress process. *Anxiety, Stress, & Coping, 21,* 3–14.

Greco, C. M., Rudy, T. E., & Manzi, S. (2004). Effects of a stress-reduction program on psychological function, pain, and physical function of systemic lupus erythematosus patients: A randomized controlled trial. *Arthritis & Rheumatism, 51,* 625–634.

Hampton, T. (2007). Researchers probe lupus causes, treatments. *JAMA, 297,* 141–142.

Helgeson, V. S., Reynolds, K. A., & Tomich, P. L. (2006). A meta-analytic review of benefit finding and growth. *Journal of Consulting and Clinical Psychology, 74,* 797–816.

Holtzman, S., & Delongis, A. (2007). One day at a time: The impact of daily satisfaction with spouse responses on pain, negative affect and catastrophizing among individuals with rheumatoid arthritis. *Pain, 131,* 202–213.

Hunt, L. M., Schneider, S., & Comer, B. (2004). Should "acculturation" be a variable in health research? A critical review of research on US Hispanics. *Social Science & Medicine, 59*, 973–986.

Hwang, V. S., Danoff-Burg, S., Hickling, E. J., Barnett, S., & Sison, G. F. (2010, August). *Curvilinear effects and gender differences in post-traumatic growth and stress.* Paper presented at the annual meeting of the American Psychological Association, San Diego, CA.

Jacobs, R., Pawlak, C. R., Mikeska, E., Meyer-Olson, D., Martin, M., Heijnen, C. J., Schedlowski, M., & Schmidt. R. E. (2001). Systemic lupus erythematosus and rheumatoid arthritis patients differ from healthy controls in their cytokine pattern after stress exposure. *Rheumatology, 40*, 868–875.

Karlen, A. (2002). Positive sexual effects of chronic illness: Case studies of women with lupus (SLE). *Sexuality and Disability, 20*, 191–208.

Karlson, E. W., Liang, M. H., Eaton, H., Huang, J., Fitzgerald, L., Rogers, M. P., & Daltroy, L. H. (2004). A randomized clinical trial of a psychoeducational intervention to improve outcomes in systemic lupus erythematosus. *Arthritis & Rheumatism, 50*, 1832–1841.

Katz, R. C., Flasher, L., Cacciapaglia, H., & Nelson, S. (2001). The psychosocial impact of cancer and lupus: A cross-validation study that extends the generality of "benefit-finding" in patients with chronic disease. *Journal of Behavioral Medicine, 24*, 561–571.

Keefe, F. J., Affleck, G., Lefebvre, J., Underwood, L., Caldwell, D. S., Drew, J., . . . Pargament, K. (2001). Living with rheumatoid arthritis: The role of daily spirituality and daily spiritual and religious coping. *Journal of Pain, 2*, 101–110.

Keefe, F. J., Caldwell, D. S., Baucom, D., Salley, A., Robinson, E., Timmons, K., . . . Helms, M. (1996). Spouse-assisted coping skills training in the management of osteoarthritic knee pain. *Arthritis Care and Research, 9*, 279–291.

Keefe, F. J., Caldwell, D. S., Baucom, D., Salley, A., Robinson, E., Timmons, K., . . . Helms, M. (1999). Spouse-assisted coping skills training in the management of knee pain in osteoarthritis: Long-term follow-up results. *Arthritis Care & Research, 12*, 101–111.

Knittle, K., Maes, S., & de Gucht, V. (2010). Psychological interventions for rheumatoid arthritis: Examining the role of self-regulation with a systemic review and meta-analysis of randomized controlled trials. *Arthritis Care & Research, 62*, 1460–1472.

Lee, M. S., Pittler, M. H., & Ernst, E. (2007). Tai chi for rheumatoid arthritis: Systematic review. *Rheumatology, 46*, 1648–1651.

Lehman, A. J., Pratt, D. D., DeLongis, A., Collins, J. B., Shojania, K., Koehler, B., . . . Esdaile, J. M. (2011). Do spouses know how much fatigue, pain, and physical limitation their partners with rheumatoid arthritis experience? Implications for social support. *Arthritis Care & Research, 63*, 120–127.

Lin, W. C., Gau, M. L., Lin, H. C., & Lin, H. R. (2011). Spiritual well-being in patients with rheumatoid arthritis. *Journal of Nursing Research, 19*, 1–11.

Linley, P. A., & Joseph, S. (2004). Positive change following trauma and adversity: A review. *Journal of Traumatic Stress, 17*, 11–21.

Lorig, K., & Fries, J. F. (2006). *The arthritis helpbook* (6th ed.). Cambridge, MA: Da Capo Press.

Lorig, K., Gonzalez, V. M., & Ritter, P. (1999). Community-based Spanish language arthritis education program: A randomized trial. *Medical Care, 37*, 957–963.

Lorig, K. R., Ritter, P. L., Laurent, D. D., & Plant, K. (2008). The Internet-based arthritis self-management program: A one-year randomized trial for patients with arthritis or fibromyalgia. *Arthritis & Rheumatism, 59*, 1009–1017.

Majerovitz, S. D., & Revenson, T. A. (1994). Sexuality and rheumatic disease: The significance of gender. *Arthritis Care & Research, 7*, 29–34.

Margaretten, M., Barton, J., Julian, L., Katz, P., Trupin, L., Tonner, C., . . . Yelin, E. (2011). Socioeconomic determinants of disability and depression in patients with rheumatoid arthritis. *Arthritis Care & Research, 63*, 240–246.

Marker-Hermann, E., & Fischer-Betz, R. (2010). Rheumatic diseases and pregnancy. *Current Opinion in Obstetrics and Gynecology, 22*, 458–465.

Martin, R. W., Head, A. J., René, J., Swartz, T. J., Fiechtner, J. J., McIntosh, B. A., & Holmes-Rovner, M. (2008). Patient decision-making related to antirheumatic drugs in rheumatoid arthritis: The importance of patient trust of physician. *Journal of Rheumatology, 35*, 618–624.

Martire, L. M. (2005). The "relative" efficacy of involving family in psychosocial interventions for chronic illness: Are there added benefits to patients and family members? *Families, Systems & Health, 23,* 312–328.

Martire, L. M., Lustig, A. P., Schulz, R., Miller, G. E., & Helgeson, V. S. (2004). Is it beneficial to involve a family member? A meta-analytic review of psychosocial interventions for chronic illness. *Health Psychology, 23,* 599–611.

Mattis, J. S., & Jagers, R. J. (2001). A relational framework for the study of religiosity and spirituality in the lives of African Americans. *Journal of Community Psychology, 29,* 519–539.

Mazzuca, S. A. (1982). Does patient education in chronic disease have therapeutic value? *Journal of Chronic Disease, 35,* 521–529.

McCauley, J., Tarpley, M., Haaz, S., & Bartlett, S. (2008). Daily spiritual experiences of older adults with and without arthritis and the relationship to health outcomes. *Arthritis & Rheumatism, 59,* 122–128.

Navarrete-Navarrete, N., Peralta-Ramírez, M. I., Sabio-Sánchez, J. M., Coín, M. A., Robles-Ortega, H., Hidalgo-Tenorio, C., . . . Jiménez-Alonso, J. (2010). Efficacy of cognitive behavioural therapy for the treatment of chronic stress in patients with lupus erythematosus: A randomized controlled trial. *Psychotherapy and Psychosomatics, 79,* 107–115.

Nery, F. G., Borba, E. F., Hatch, J. P., Soares, J. C., Bonfá, E., & Neto, F. L. (2007). Major depressive disorder and disease activity in systemic lupus erythematosus. *Comprehensive Psychiatry, 48,* 14–19.

Öst, L. (2008). Efficacy of the third wave of behavioral therapies: A systematic review and meta-analysis. *Behaviour Research and Therapy, 46,* 296–321.

Pawlak, C. R., Witte, T., Heiken H., Hundt, M., Schubert, J., Wiese, B., . . . Schedlowski, M. (2003). Flares in patients with systemic lupus erythematosus are associated with daily psychological stress. *Psychotherapy and Psychosomatics, 72,* 159–165.

Peralta-Ramírez, M. I., Jiménez-Alonso, J., & Pérez-García, M. (2009). Which stressors are responsible for the worsening in the clinical symptomatology of lupus? *Health, 1,* 313–319.

Pons-Estel, G. J., Alarcon, G. S., Scofield, L., Reinlib, L., & Cooper, G. S. (2010). Understanding the epidemiology and progression of systemic lupus erythematosus. *Seminars in Arthritis and Rheumatism, 39,* 257–268.

Pradhan, E. K., Baumgarten, M., Langenberg, P., Handwerger, B., Gilpin, A. K., Magyari, T., . . . Berman, B. M. (2007). Effect of mindfulness-based stress reduction in rheumatoid arthritis patients. *Arthritis & Rheumatism, 57,* 1134–1142.

Quandt, S. A., Chen, H., Grzywacz, J. G., Bell, R. A., Lang, W., & Arcury, T. A. (2005). Use of complementary and alternative medicine by persons with arthritis: Results of the National Health Interview Survey. *Arthritis Care and Research, 53,* 748–755.

Radojevic, V., Nicassio, P. M., & Weisman, M. H. (1992). Behavioral intervention with and without family support for rheumatoid arthritis. *Behavior Therapy, 23,* 13–30.

Revenson, T. A. (1990). Not all things are equal: An ecological approach to personality and disease. In H. S. Friedman C (Ed.), *Personality and disease* (pp. 65–94). New York, NY: Wiley.

Revenson, T. A. (2003). Scenes from a marriage: Examining support, coping, and gender within the context of chronic illness. In J. Suls & K. Wallston (Eds.), *Social psychological foundations of health and illness* (pp. 530–559). Oxford, UK: Blackwell.

Revenson, T. A., Schiaffino, K. M., Majerovitz, S. D., & Gibofsky, A. (1991). Social support as a double-edged sword: The relation of positive and problematic support to depression among rheumatoid arthritis patients. *Social Science and Medicine, 7,* 807–813.

Riemsma, R. P., Taal, E., Kirwan, J. R., & Rasker, J. J. (2004). Systematic review of rheumatoid arthritis patient education. *Arthritis Care & Research, 51,* 1045–1059.

Riemsma, R. P., Taal, E., & Rasker, J. J. (2003). Group education for patients with rheumatoid arthritis and their partners. *Arthritis Care & Research, 493,* 556–566.

Robbins, L., Allegrante, J., & Paget, S. (1993). Adapting the Systemic Lupus Erythematosus Self-Help (SLESH) course for Latino SLE patients. *Arthritis Care and Research, 6,* 97–103.

Rosenzweig, S., Greeson, J. M., Reibel, D. K., Green, J. S., Jasser, S. A., & Beasley, D. (2010). Mindfulness-based stress reduction for chronic pain conditions: Variation in treatment outcomes and role of home meditation practice. *Journal of Psychosomatic Research, 68,* 29–36.

Salt, E., & Peden, A. (2011). The complexity of the treatment: The decision-making process among women with rheumatoid arthritis. *Qualitative Health Research*, *21*, 214–222.

Sanderson, T., Morris, M., Calnan, M., Richards, P., & Hewlett, S. (2010). "It's this whole picture, this well-being?": Patients' understanding of "feeling well" with rheumatoid arthritis. *Chronic Illness*, *6*, 228–240.

Sato, M., Yamazaki, Y., Sakita, M., & Bryce, T. J. (2008). Benefit-finding among people with rheumatoid arthritis in Japan. *Nursing & Health Sciences*, *10*, 51–58.

Seawell, A. H., & Danoff-Burg, S. (2004). Psychosocial research on systemic lupus erythematosus: A literature review. *Lupus*, *13*, 891–899.

Seawell, A. H., & Danoff-Burg, S. (2005). Body image and sexuality in women with and without systemic lupus erythematosus. *Sex Roles*, *53*, 865–876.

Segui, J., Ramos-Casals, M., Garcia-Carrasco, M., de Flores, T., Cervera, R., Valdes, M., Font, J., & Ingelmo, M. (2000). Psychiatric and psychosocial disorders in patients with systemic lupus erythematosus: A longitudinal study of active and inactive stages of disease. *Lupus*, *9*, 584–588.

Seligman, M. E., & Csikszentmihalyi, M. (2000). Positive psychology: An introduction. *American Psychologist*, *55*, 5–14.

Siegel, D. M., & Baum, J. (2004). Rheumatic disease and sexuality. In D. Isenberg, P. Maddison, P. Woo, D. Glass, & F. Breedveld (Eds.), *Oxford textbook of rheumatology* (3rd ed., pp. 279–285). New York, NY: Oxford University Press.

Sinclair, V. G., & Wallston, K. A. (2004). The development and psychometric evaluation of the Brief Resilient Coping Scale. *Assessment*, *11*, 94–101.

Smith, B. W., & Zautra, A. J. (2008). Vulnerability and resilience in women with arthritis: Test of a two-factor model. *Journal of Consulting and Clinical Psychology*, *76*(5), 799–810.

Sokka, T., Toloza, S., Cutolo, M., Kautiainen, H., Makinen, H., Gogus, F., . . . Pincus, T. (2009). Women, men, and rheumatoid arthritis: Analyses of disease activity, disease characteristics, and treatments in the QUEST-RA Study. *Arthritis Research & Therapy*, *11*, R7.

Sterba, K. R., DeVellis, R. F., Lewis, M. A., DeVellis, B. M., Jordan, J. M., & Baucom, D. H. (2008). Effect of couple illness perception congruence on psychological adjustment in women with rheumatoid arthritis. *Health Psychology*, *27*, 221–229.

Strand, E. B., Zautra, A. J., & Thoresen, M. (2006). Positive affect as a factor of resilience in the pain-negative affect relationship in patients with rheumatoid arthritis. *Journal of Psychosomatic Research*, *60*, 477–484.

Sutcliffe, N., Clarke, A. E., Levinton, C., Frost, C., Gordon, C., & Isenberg, A. (1999). Associates of health status in patients with systemic lupus erythematosus. *Journal of Rheumatology*, *26*, 2352–2356.

Tristano, A. G. (2009). The impact of rheumatic diseases on sexual function. *Rheumatology International*, *29*, 853–860.

Trupin, L., Tonner, M. C., Yazdany, J., Julian, L. J., Criswell, L. A., Katz, P. P., & Yelin, E. (2008). The role of neighborhood and individual socioeconomic status in outcomes of systemic lupus erythematosus. *Journal of Rheumatology*, *35*, 1782–1788.

Tugade, M. M., & Fredrickson, B. L. (2004). Resilient individuals use positive emotions to bounce back from negative emotional experiences. *Journal of Personality and Social Psychology*, *86*, 320–333.

van Lankveld, W., van Helmond, T., Näring, G., de Rooij, D. J., & van den Hoogen, F. (2004). Partner participation in cognitive-behavioral self-management group treatment for patients with rheumatoid arthritis. *Journal of Rheumatology*, *31*, 1738–1745.

van Middendorp, H., Geenen, R., Sorbi, M. J., Hox, J. H., Vingerhoets, A. J. J. M., van Doornen, L. J. P., & Bijlsma, J. W. J. (2005). Gender differences in emotion regulation and relationships with perceived health in patients with rheumatoid arthritis. *Women and Health*, *42*, 75–97.

Weiss, T. (2002). Posttraumatic growth in women with breast cancer and their husbands: An intersubjective validation study. *Journal of Psychosocial Oncology*, *20*, 65–80.

Wekking, E. M., Vingerhoets, A. J., van Dam, A. P., Nossent, J. C., & Swaak, A. J. (1991). Daily stressors and systemic lupus erythematosus: A longitudinal analysis—First findings. *Psychotherapy and Psychosomatics*, *55*, 108–113.

Wing, R. R., Marcus, M. D., Epstein, L. H., & Jawad, A. (1991). A "family-based" approach to the treatment of obese Type II diabetic patients. *Journal of Consulting and Clinical Psychology*, *59*, 156–162.

Wittmann, L., Sensky, T., Meder, L., Michel, B., Stoll, T., & Buchi, S. (2009). Suffering and posttraumatic growth in women with systemic lupus erythematosus (SLE): A qualitative/quantitative case study. *Psychosomatics, 50*, 362–374.

Zautra, A. J., Burleson, M. H., Matt, K. S., Roth, S., & Burrows, L. (1994). Interpersonal stress, depression, and disease activity in rheumatoid arthritis and osteoarthritis patients. *Health Psychology, 13*, 139–148.

Zautra, A. J., Davis, M. C., Reich, J. W., Nicassario, P., Tennen, H., Finan, P., . . . Irwin, M. R. (2008). Comparison of cognitive behavioral and mindfulness meditation interventions on adaptation to rheumatoid arthritis for patients with and without history of recurrent depression. *Journal of Consulting and Clinical Psychology, 76*, 408–421.

Zautra, A. J., Johnson, L. M., & Davis, M. C. (2005). Positive affect as a source of resilience for women in chronic pain. *Journal of Consulting and Clinical Psychology, 73*(2), 212–220.

Zautra, A. J., & Smith, B. W. (2001). Depression and reactivity to stress in older women with rheumatoid arthritis and osteoarthritis. *Psychosomatic Medicine, 63*, 687–696.

Zautra, A. J., Smith, B., Affleck, G., & Tennen, H. (2001). Examinations of chronic pain and affect relationships: Applications of a dynamic model of affect. *Journal of Consulting and Clinical Psychology, 69*, 785–796.

CHAPTER 23

Neurological Disorders in Women

M. Meredith Gillis, Kara R. Douglas-Newman, and Mary V. Spiers

INTRODUCTION

Women and men show variation in the development and expression of several neurological disorders. For example, the incidence of multiple sclerosis (Knudsen, 2009) and headache is higher in women, though men suffer more traumatic brain injury. Women have a higher lifetime risk of stroke (Bushnell, 2011), as well as a higher incidence of Alzheimer's disease in the oldest old (Haaxma et al., 2007; Sinforiana et al., 2010), while prevalence of Parkinson's disease is higher in men (Haaxma et al., 2007). Reasons for sex differences in susceptibility and progression of neurological disorders may include sex-based biological variation (e.g., genetic and hormonal, metabolic), gender-based psychosocial factors (e.g., manifestation of stress, depression, and anxiety), and cultural interactions with sex and gender issues. In this and the following chapter, neurological disorders in women are discussed. In this chapter we begin with a brief overview of structural and functional brain differences between men and women and focus on two neurological disorders that affect women more than men during younger and middle adulthood: migraines and multiple sclerosis. In the next chapter, strokes and Alzheimer's disease are discussed.

FACTORS RELATED TO BRAIN VARIATION IN MEN AND WOMEN

The past few decades have witnessed a revolution in the understanding of women's brain functioning. Neurological disorders in women were originally considered through the lens of men's brain functioning. The most reliable relationships between brain and behavior occur in right-handed men, because male brains tend to be more strongly lateralized with speech in the left hemisphere. Women's brains can also show opposite or bilateral organization and may be more subject to changes related to hormonal variation. Therefore, women's brains were seen as having more possible variance in comparison to men's brains in an era when an emphasis was on understanding general structure-function relationships in the brain.

At first, the study of dimorphisms in male and female brains centered around the hypothalamic-pituitary region of the brain, which is responsible for the regulation of reproductive hormones and mating behaviors. However, it is now clear that variations in receptors for sex steroids, such as estrogen, progesterone, and testosterone, are found in many other brain regions and impact wide areas of cognition and emotion (Gillies & McArthur, 2010). These receptors are particularly responsive to the activational or reversible effects of circulating sex hormones. In women, the cyclic ebb and flow of estrogens to the brain between puberty and menopause may then affect several behaviors. Giving opposite sex hormones (e.g., androgens) to females can masculinize some behaviors. However, this stops short of reversing sex-related brain morphology because of the organizational effect of sex steroids that sculpt the brain during development. It is generally established that without exposure to testosterone in utero, brains show female development. Moreover, genetic factors can also interact with the brain's receptiveness to hormonal and environmental stimulation. Finally, the plasticity of the brain, or its ability to modify itself through learning and experience, is influenced by a wide array of biological, developmental, and environmental factors. These considerations highlight the complexity involved in studying the brain in general and represent the challenge in considering sex and gender differences in the contribution to neurological disorders.

Clinically, neuropsychologists are most likely to focus on the behavioral impact attributable to brain disorder (e.g., memory, attention, inability to understand emotion), whereas clinical or health psychologists may focus more on the psychological risk factors and impact or sequelae of a disorder. Increasingly, both approaches are necessary in order to gain a more complete picture of how neurological disorders may affect women.

MIGRAINE HEADACHES

Migraine headaches represent one of the most common neurological problems experienced by younger women. Approximately 20% of women in the United States experience migraine each year (Breslau & Rasmussen,

2001; Waters & O'Connor, 1971), and women are more susceptible than men to developing migraine by a 3:1 ratio (Guidetti, Alberton, Galli, Mittica, & Salvi, 2009). For chronic sufferers, the experience of migraine extends beyond severe headache pain; it can be associated with disability, reduced quality of life, and a range of psychiatric issues, including irritability, depression, and anxiety.

Migraine Epidemiology

The World Health Organization ranks migraine headache as number 19 on the list of diseases causing disability worldwide (Headache Classification Committee of the International Headache Society [IHS], 2004). In Europe and North America, 1-year migraine prevalence is estimated to be between 10% and 12% (Breslau & Rasmussen, 2001). However, because headaches are evaluated based on the subjective report of the sufferer, the extent to which a person reports symptoms may depend on the method of data collection (Manzoni & Stovner, 2010). Data from the American Migraine Prevalence and Prevention Study indicates that the prevalence of migraine in the United States is high: 43% for women and 18% for men (Stewart et al., 2008). This figure is likely a conservative estimate, as the study used strict diagnostic criteria to define migraine. Notably, the preponderance of migraine in women exists only in adulthood. Prepubescent boys and girls are affected in roughly equal proportions (Tepper, 2004). This statistic is consistent with evidence that hormonal changes, particularly estrogenic variations, are partially responsible for women's increased susceptibility to migraine. Prevalence increases with age and is at its highest in the fourth and fifth decades of life (Breslau & Rasmussen, 2001; Tepper, 2004).

Migraine prevalence also varies across cultures and geographic regions. For example, studies conducted in Denmark replicated the finding of female preponderance of migraine observed in the United States, but reported a much lower overall rate. In the Danish study, 5% and 11% of women experienced migraine with or without aura, respectively, compared with 3% and 2% of men (Breslau & Rasmussen, 2001). As summarized in a review by Breslau and Rasmussen (2001), migraine prevalence is also lower in Asian and African countries, with prevalence estimates of 1.5% in Hong Kong, 2.6% in Saudi Arabia, 3% in Ethiopia, 8.4% in Japan, and 9% in Malaysia. Likewise, within the United States, prevalence of migraine is higher for Caucasians than for African-American and Asian individuals (Breslau & Rasmussen, 2001; Stewart, Lipton, & Liberman, 1996). It should be noted that the difference in prevalence rates between the United States and other nations may also be partly related to methodological variations, such as inconsistencies in classification, diagnosis, and methods of reporting, as well as cultural variation.

Given its relatively high prevalence and potential interference with activities of daily living, migraine headache is a significant consideration in the context of women's health psychology. Moreover, because migraine often occurs among women in their twenties and thirties, it may impact the reproductive years and may be modulated by hormonal fluctuations (e.g., menstrual cycle, hormonal contraceptives) (Nappi & Berga, 2010). Along with the influences of sex and gender, as well as race/ethnicity and culture, other psychological factors may be important determinants of who is affected by migraine, and these topics are reviewed later in this chapter.

Migraine Diagnosis and Disability

Of the three types of primary headaches with a neurological basis, tension-type headaches, cluster headaches, and migraine (IHS, 2004), migraine is especially likely to be underdiagnosed and subsequently undertreated (Lipton, Goadsby, Sawyer, Blakeborough, & Stewart, 2000). Providers may fail to recognize migraine or misdiagnose it as another type of headache (e.g., sinus or tension headache) (Diamond, 2002). Both types of diagnostic errors are problematic in that they can lead to suboptimal treatment and follow-up. Important considerations for migraine diagnosis include ruling out other potential causes of headache, assessing frequency of occurrence, and establishing migraine-related level of disability.

Migraine is classified as a "syndrome" because of its complex neurological presentation that may cause a wide variety of symptoms, which can precede, coincide with, or follow the headache pain (Manzoni & Torelli, 2009; Tepper, 2004). According to "The International Classification of Headache Disorders," 2nd Edition (IHS, 2004), hallmarks of migraine include headache pain with a pulsating quality, pain on one side of the head, worsening of pain with physical exertion, and moderate or severe pain intensity (two of these four criteria are necessary for diagnosis). Either sensitivity to light/sound or nausea/vomiting must also be present for a formal diagnosis of migraine. It is estimated that one out of every five individuals affected by migraine will experience pseudoneurological symptoms known as "aura," which generally occur about 30 to 60 minutes before headache pain. An aura may include visual changes (e.g., seeing wavy lines or spots) or unusual bodily sensations (e.g., numbness or tingling in the hands or face, dizziness) that, when consistent, can signal an imminent migraine. Migraines with and without aura may represent distinct conditions with different underlying mechanisms. The duration of migraine headache pain is variable, ranging from several hours up to two to three days (IHS, 2004). To receive a clinical diagnosis of migraine based on IHS criteria, the affected person must have had at least five headaches of a similar nature lasting from 4 to 72 hours.

Some people also report a migraine prodrome, separate from an aura, which precedes migraine and can last a few days before the onset of headache pain. Individuals who are well-attuned to these sensory changes report being able to sense an oncoming migraine days in advance. Prodrome symptoms may consist of bodily disturbances, such as joint pain, neck pain, sensitivity to light and sound, euphoria, depression, fatigue, or cognitive changes. The time course of the prodrome phase is unpredictable; it may indicate that a headache is anywhere from an hour to a few days away.

Although the symptom profile of cluster headaches is distinct from migraine with an acute onset of intense localized pain and reoccurrence or "clustering" within a period of time, the similarities between migraine without aura and tension-type headaches make them the most difficult types of primary headache to differentially diagnose (Manzoni & Torelli, 2009). Tension-type headaches were once regarded as a psychogenic condition; however, these headaches are now theorized to have a neurological basis, although their exact pain mechanism is poorly understood. Secondary headaches (i.e., those caused by an underlying medical condition) can also look similar to migraine. Therefore, a medical workup, including computed axial tomography (CAT) scan of the brain or magnetic resonance imaging (MRI), is typically recommended for individuals reporting migraine symptoms to rule out underlying pathology.

With regard to migraine frequency, a "chronic" specifier is used if an individual experiences migraine 15 or more days per month, for a period lasting more than 3 months (IHS, 2004). Migraine occurring less frequently is considered "episodic." The progression from episodic migraine to chronic daily headache is often observed, and the underlying neurobiology of this transformation has been an active area of research (Moschiano, D'Amico, Schieroni, & Bussone, 2003). The distinction between episodic and chronic migraine can have implications for medication management. Pharmacological treatments must be closely monitored by physicians, particularly because overuse of certain types of migraine medication has been associated with increased risk of migraine chronicity (Moschiano et al., 2003).

Migraine-related disability is also an important factor to consider. The development of the Migraine Disability Assessment (MIDAS; Stewart, Lipton, Dowson, & Sawyer, 2001) has facilitated physicians' ability to rate the degree of impairment associated with a person's migraine pain. The MIDAS is a seven-item self-report questionnaire that measures headache-related disability based on five disability questions, in which persons are asked to evaluate their impairment caused by migraine in the past three months (Stewart et al., 2001). The questionnaire assesses days of productivity lost because of migraine in the domains of school/work, household work, and family, social, or leisure activities. Scoring is based on the summation of days lost, with clinical cutoffs as follows: *0 to 5, Grade I:* little or no disability; *6 to 10, Grade II:* mild disability; *11-20, Grade III*: moderate disability, and *21 or over, Grade IV*: severe disability. Empirical study of the MIDAS has demonstrated that it is both a reliable and valid assessment, and it tends to correlate well with the clinical judgments of physicians (Stewart et al., 2001). These findings support the use of the MIDAS as a brief and effective clinical tool to improve communication between persons and physicians and help determine appropriate treatment for migraine headaches.

Biological Factors

Serotonin Migraine pain is a complex phenomenon whose biological mechanisms are still being worked out. Longstanding notions of a vascular etiology to migraine are currently being questioned. In particular, vasodilation (relaxation of cranial blood vessels) was originally implicated as an underlying cause of migraine pain by Wolff in the 1940s and 1950s. This finding was seemingly supported by the vasoconstricting triptans medications that have been successful in treating migraine pain (Panconesi, Bartolozzi, & Guidi, 2009). However, vasodilation is not reliably associated with migraine pain across all situations, and it is regarded as insufficient to explain the collection of symptoms associated with migraine (Goadsby, 2009). Furthermore, it has been argued that the efficacy of triptans is not because of their activity as vasoconstrictors but rather their action in blocking serotonin transmission.

Abnormal serotonin transmission in the brain has been implicated in migraine pain since the 1950s. During the acute attack phase of migraine, a cascade of events results in increased serotonin release. Although the exact mechanism is not fully understood, altered serotonin transmission is believed

to result in a failure to inhibit pain systems in the brain. A third and relatively new theory relating to migraine involves a chemical called calcitonin gene-related peptide (CGRP), which is shown to be elevated in acute, severe migraine attacks and likely plays a significant role in migraine pathogenesis (Goadsby, 2009; Stucky et al., 2011). Medications that block and/or reduce levels of CGRP are a new target for migraine intervention. Preliminary research with an animal model of migraine suggests that there may be baseline sex differences in the expression of CGRP and its receptor, although this finding has yet to be confirmed (Stucky et al., 2011).

Sex Steroid Hormones In understanding migraines in women, the fluctuation of sex hormones is one of the most widely accepted explanations for the 3:1 female-to-male ratio of migraine prevalence that manifests after the onset of puberty (Guidetti et al., 2009). The role of estrogen in migraine is suggested in women who experience a reduction in (or total relief of) migraine headaches during pregnancy, when the body is no longer subjected to the cyclical variation of estrogen associated with menstruation (Rasmussen, 1993), and in women whose onset of menstruation is a precipitant of migraine (Rasmussen, 2001).

Onset of menstrual periods is a known risk factor for migraine (de Tommaso et al., 2009; Johannes et al., 1995). Because this point in the menstrual cycle is characterized by a steep decrease in plasma estrogen levels, the finding suggests that estrogen withdrawal may be a trigger for migraine in women. Yet estrogen *increases*, such as those associated with using estrogen supplements, may contribute to the aura associated with migraine (Nappi & Berga, 2010). To date, the exact molecular mechanisms underlying such findings have not been uncovered. Part of the complexity stems from the fact that estrogen variation has widespread influence in the body, especially within the brain. One hypothesis is that hormone levels can alter the excitability of brain cells and affect cerebral blood flow, which may exacerbate headache symptoms by influencing sensitivity to pain (Nappi & Berga, 2010). More research is needed to validate this hypothesis. From a clinical perspective, it is recommended that women utilize "headache diaries" to record the timing and characteristics of each migraine attack to help establish whether there is a clear link with the menstrual cycle.

Genetic Factors Hormonal variation alone appears insufficient to explain the notable gender difference in migraine rates. The difference persists even in older adult populations, including postmenopausal women (Breslau & Rasmussen, 2001). Hence, other factors must also be involved. The field of genetics has been an active research area in attempting to further explain the female preponderance of migraine. Through human and animal studies, researchers have identified genetic factors that may lower the threshold for a migraine to be "set off" in the brain (Shyti, de Vries, & van den Maagdenberg, 2011). Individuals carrying these factors would be more likely to experience migraine in their lifetime and/ or experience more severe symptoms. The study of familial hemiplegic migraine (FHM), a rare type of migraine with aura that shows heritability within families, has also yielded evidence of genetic influence on migraine. Genetic mutations associated with FHM alter the brain systems responsible for balancing neurotransmitter levels (e.g., glutamate) (Shyti et al., 2011). This dysfunction may play a causal role in migraine headaches. The extent to which this may differ between men and women has yet to be determined.

Finally, evidence suggests fundamental neurological differences between men and women who experience migraine. In a sophisticated study by Liu et al. (2011), researchers used graph theory analysis to map the brain networks of 38 migraine sufferers, 20 of whom were women. They then compared the networks to 38 healthy controls. The results indicated that persons suffering from chronic migraine had functional damage to the networks examined, exhibiting disrupted connections and poor resilience to pathological disruptions. Notably, these differences varied between males and females, with female migraine sufferers demonstrating abnormalities to a greater extent than males. The authors concluded that migraine may have an additional influence on females and lead to more dysfunctional organization in neural networks. Although the clinical implications of this finding are not yet clear, it nonetheless helps improve our understanding of the differing impact of migraine between men and women.

Understanding the experience of migraine in women is likely to be an active area of future research, a notion summarized particularly well by Peterlin, Gupta, Ward, and Macgregor (2011) in their article published in the journal *Headache*: "[E]nhanced recognition and . . .attention to sex differences throughout the hormonal and life-cycle phase in both human and animal research will only help to strengthen and further our understanding of migraine and may help guide the direction of future headache research." Moreover, from a clinical perspective, a better understanding of migraine's biological factors may lead to improved understanding of their interaction with psychosocial factors and appropriate treatments for affected individuals.

Behavioral, Environmental, and Psychosocial Factors in Migraine

The influence of behavioral, environmental, and psychosocial factors is an important issue to consider in relation to understanding migraine headaches in women. The lens through which one experiences migraine can be influenced by lifestyle factors, psychiatric well-being and mental health issues, stress, household income, access to medical care, and many other factors. We describe some of these elements as follows, focusing on three psychosocial categories as they relate to migraine: mental health issues, socioeconomic status, and stress.

Generally speaking, some environmental and behavioral contributors to migraine have been well-documented. Sleep disturbances, changes in weather, mental tension, alcohol overuse, and caffeine withdrawal have all been associated with migraine and other types of headache pain (Moschiano et al., 2003; Rasmussen, 1993). Wine, cheese, chocolate, and other processed foods containing nitrates and/or tyramine are examples of foods that have been implicated as triggers for migraine (e.g., Savi et al., 2002). For individuals who keep headache diaries, a listing of meals consumed prior to the onset of migraine may be helpful in identifying potential triggers that can be avoided by a change in diet.

Mental Health Issues   The cognitive and psychological symptoms of migraines have long been recognized. These include depression, anxiety, irritability, fatigue, and problems with memory and attention.

Investigations of psychological variables and migraine have confirmed a strong association between migraine and depression, as well as migraine and anxiety disorders (Mathew, Stubita, & Nigam, 1982; Radat et al., 1999). Several studies have shown that people with migraines suffer from anxiety and depression more often than those without migraines. Moreover, these studies have established that persons with chronic migraine exhibit anxiety and depression more often than those with episodic migraine (Juang, Wang, Fuh, Lu, & Su, 2000). In an evaluation of 261 persons with chronic daily headache, including 152 with migraine, it was found that women with migraine exhibited the highest frequency of anxiety disorders.

In a French study of 1,957 individuals with migraine headache, 50.6% of subjects with active migraine were anxious and/or depressive: 28.0% were diagnosed with anxiety alone, 3.5% with depression alone, and 19.1% with both anxiety and depression. Rates of anxiety alone and combined depression/anxiety were significantly higher for the migraine group than the nonmigraine group (Lanteri-Minet, Radat, Chautart, & Lucas, 2005). These findings suggest that psychiatric factors comorbid with migraine represent important clinical considerations. They may require individually tailored treatment methods, as anxiety and depression can add to the disability level and reduced productivity associated with migraine (Holmes, MacGregor, & Dodick, 2001). Moreover, there is evidence that individuals exhibiting symptoms of depression and/or anxiety are less likely to view their migraine treatment regimen as effective or satisfactory (Lanteri-Minet et al., 2005). This finding may reflect the general negative cognitions and perceptions that can occur in the context of mood and anxiety disorders (e.g., fear, hopelessness), but it may also reflect that typical migraine treatments are actually less efficacious for individuals with migraine and co-occurring psychiatric symptoms

From these correlational studies, although an association between migraine and affective disorders does exist, the exact nature of the relationship is not clear (Guidetti et al., 2009). One hypothesis for the frequent co-occurrence of depression and migraine is that the neurological triggers for migraine are part of a pathway that can also produce depressive symptoms such as irritability, fatigue, and loss of appetite (Burstein & Jakubowski, 2009). If migraine attacks begin to occur in chronic fashion, it is possible that repeated activation of these pathways could eventually lead to short-term depressive symptoms during migraine to progress to a full-fledged depressive episode. This explanation, however, merits further research before it can be confirmed.

Depression and anxiety are not the only disorders associated with migraine. In recent years, a potential link between migraine and eating disorders has also come to light (D'Andrea et al., 2009). Specifically, it has been hypothesized that migraine headaches reflect a shared etiology with eating disorders. D'Andrea et al. (2009) investigated this hypothesis by evaluating migraine history in a group of young adult women diagnosed with bulimia or anorexia. They found that more than 75% of the women in their sample had a history of migraine—a prevalence much higher than that of the general population. They also reported that, for most persons, migraine preceded the emergence of eating disorder symptoms. Does migraine truly constitute a risk factor for developing an eating disorder? Improved understanding of the underlying genetic and neurological mechanisms of both conditions will be a key step toward answering this question.

Income and Socioeconomic Status

Several studies have reported that lower socioeconomic status (SES), as measured by income, is related to a higher prevalence of migraines. In an early study with participants classified by income, migraine prevalence in the group with the lowest income (less than $10,000) was over 60% higher than in groups with income greater than or equal to $30,000 (Stewart, Lipton, Celentano, & Reed, 1992). The lowest income group was also most likely to utilize emergency care for migraine treatment.

Similar findings were reported from a representative sample of adolescents living in the United States. Most notably, the prevalence of migraine was found to be significantly higher in adolescents whose family's annual income was lower than $22,500 (Bigal et al., 2007). However, among adolescents who had a parental history of migraine, the difference in prevalence rates between income groups was not present. The authors concluded that household income is associated with migraine prevalence only for individuals without a strong biological predisposition to migraine. These findings suggest that environmental risk factors for migraine may be related to low income.

In 2012, a study of more than 12,000 women examined the influence of SES on migraine. SES was defined based on annual household income and level of education. Consistent with previous results, women with low SES were at greater risk for *all* forms of headache, not just migraine (Winter, Berger, Buring, & Kurth, 2012). Among active migraineurs, low SES was associated with a greater frequency of migraine attacks.

It is challenging to identify clear explanations for these findings. Why would individuals of a lower SES have a higher risk of experiencing migraine? It is possible that migraine rates could be a product of poor living conditions or reduced access to regular, preventive healthcare. To the latter point, Stewart et al. (1992) found that the lowest income group in their study was more likely to use emergency services for migraine. This may indicate that such persons are not in regular treatment with a primary care physician or neurologist, and they do not seek medical help until severe symptoms emerge. Alternatively, the relationship between migraine and income may operate in the opposite direction; chronic migraine may lead to difficulties with work or career advancement, which in turn leads to low economic status.

One study of disability resulting from migraine showed that, on average, individuals with migraine who were in paid employment missed 4.4 days of work per year and, further, lost the equivalent of 12 days of work time per year because of reduced productivity from attacks (Von Korff, Stewart, Simon, & Lipton, 1998). Migraine sufferers often fear the long-term consequences of their health-related needs: They may worry about losing their jobs or being passed over for promotions because of their time away or reduced productivity (Clarke, MacMillan, Sondhi, & Wells, 1996; Holmes et al., 2001). Migraineurs may also be less likely to be hired for a job. A study from a health maintenance organization in Seattle, Washington, reported that the unemployment rate among severely affected individuals with migraine was 2 to 4 times higher than that of the general population (Holmes et al., 2001). In the long term, these types of factors could lead to a downward drift in SES for migraine sufferers.

Based on the current literature, the exact relationship between SES and migraine remains to be determined. Intuitively, one could argue that the most obvious risk factor faced by individuals with low income is the experience of *stress* related to economic hardship. Although stress can be a complex phenomenon to define and study systematically, there is convincing evidence that it plays a role in migraine.

Stress In a 2001 study, self-reported "stress and mental tension" was the most apparent precipitating factor of migraine (Rasmussen, 2001). Stress can also have an adverse impact on sleep pattern, which is problematic for many migraineurs, because disruptions to the sleep pattern are a common migraine trigger. Significantly, the impact of stress is not just psychological or related to mood alone. It has a widespread physical influence in the body, especially in cases of chronic stress.

In response to a stressful event, the hypothalamic-pituitary-adrenal (HPA) axis allows for the body's energy resources to be mobilized to handle threats (i.e., "fight or flight") while nonessential functions are temporarily halted. This response is highly adaptive in evolutionary terms, but it can produce adverse effects (including migraine) when chronic stressors cause the HPA axis to operate in a perpetual state of high activation (Sauro & Becker, 2009). It is unclear how the stress response acts specifically as a trigger for migraine, but the relationship continues to be actively investigated.

With the repeated experience of migraine, some persons report that the attacks begin to act as a stressor, which could thereby lead to a vicious cycle of increasing migraine frequency (Sauro & Becker, 2009). Fortunately for individuals suffering from stress-induced migraine, training in stress management techniques can result in physiological changes in the body that may reduce risk for future migraine episodes. Aside from the use of medication, stress management is one of the most helpful therapeutic approaches for migraineurs. Interventions are considered in the next section.

Interventions and Treatment Methods for Migraine Headaches

Treating migraine headaches includes both pharmacological and behavioral methods. Medication is typically prescribed to help prevent or alleviate migraine symptoms, especially in individuals who are chronic sufferers. Prophylactic measures may include beta-blockers, antidepressants, or anticonvulsants (D'Amico & Tepper, 2009; Lampl et al., 2009). To treat migraine pain, persons may use over-the-counter pain relievers or be prescribed a triptan medication (Panconesi et al., 2009). These medications can be highly effective in relieving pain, but it is crucial for individuals taking prescription migraine medication to be counseled on the potential dangers of medication overuse (Andrasik, Grazzi, Usai, Buse, & Bussone, 2009). Clinical researchers have pointed out that chronic and excessive use of pain medication can cause a depletion of serotonin and a recurrence of severe headache (Hering, Glover, Pattichis, Catarci, & Steiner, 1993). In a study of medication withdrawal in chronic migraine sufferers, Usai, Grazzi, D'Amico, Andrasik, and Bussone (2009) found that 1 year after medication withdrawal, the persons reported fewer migraines and less pain associated with their migraines. Levels of disability also improved, as did reports of anxiety and depression symptoms. Because of the potential risks of medication overuse, psychological and/or behavioral interventions are often worthy additions to long-term migraine treatment. Behavioral stress management and biofeedback are two such treatment techniques.

A key aspect of migraine treatment is to educate people about their own personal triggers for migraine. Although migraines are a biological condition, efforts can be made to control psychosocial risks for migraine. For example, individuals suffering with chronic migraine should be encouraged to consider their eating habits, sleeping patterns, and stress as potential triggers to be addressed. Healthier responses to stress can also be taught to migraineurs through a variety of techniques commonly referred to as "behavioral stress management." Most of these techniques share the ultimate goal of utilizing mind-body exercises to increase control over one's bodily sensations in response to stressful situations and negative emotions (Nezu, Nezu, & Jain, 2005). Several different techniques have been utilized to this end, including deep breathing, progressive muscle relaxation, meditation, hypnosis, autogenic training, and more. These strategies allow individuals to keep the stress response in check, which in turn can reduce the frequency or severity of migraine headache. Self-help books are available in this realm, but mastery of behavioral stress management techniques requires effortful practice, and thus best results are often achieved with the help of a well-trained psychologist (Nezu et al., 2005).

A second intervention utilized in migraine headache treatment is biofeedback. Like behavioral stress management, biofeedback trains the individual to exert control over a biological process. During a biofeedback procedure, a person can be trained to recognize and subsequently control certain internal physiological processes that occur involuntarily, such as heart rate, respiratory rate, blood pressure, muscle tension, neural activity, and skin conductance (Barker, 2004). An individual is provided feedback via an easily perceived stimulus, such as the sound of a tone, the blinking of a light, or a video simulation, which is directly linked to the particular autonomic process in question. In this manner, a person can learn to "voluntarily" modify an internal function that was previously beyond his or her conscious control. Types of biofeedback include the electromyogram (EMG), which monitors muscle tension, the electroencephalogram (EEG), which monitors the frequency of brain waves, and thermal biofeedback, which measures skin temperature and conductance (Denis, 1996). Interestingly, persons that successfully modify a physiological process using biofeedback frequently report, "I don't know how I'm doing it!" Biofeedback utilizing the EEG (typically called neurofeedback) has been evaluated in the context of migraine. Abnormalities in electrophysiological activity have commonly been found in the brains of migraine persons, making it possible that neurofeedback interventions may be beneficial. A study by Tansey (1991) that showed that four migraineurs could eliminate their migraines after neurofeedback training provided early support for this idea.

Hemoencephalography (HEG) is a new addition to neurofeedback training that targets the frontal lobe. HEG involves increasing the forehead temperature by watching a movie for feedback. The movie plays when measured forehead temperature rises and stops when the temperature drops. One report demonstrated that 100 migraineurs could reduce the frequency of their headaches using this form of biofeedback (Carmen, 2004). In a 2010 study, neurofeedback and HEG were combined to treat 37 migraineurs in a clinical outpatient setting. Participants completed an average of 40 neurofeedback sessions (two to three times per week for 6 months) and all were on at least one type of medication for migraine. Participants kept daily headache diaries before and during treatment to record symptom frequency, severity, and duration. Based on headache diaries and clinical interview, 26 people (70%) experienced at least a 50% reduction in the frequency of their headaches at the conclusion of treatment (Stokes & Lappin, 2010). Notably, these improvements were sustained up to 14 months after treatments were discontinued. Findings like these suggest that neurofeedback is helpful in the treatment of migraine. One notable disadvantage of this method is a continuous treatment process that requires complex equipment, which may necessitate a substantial time and financial commitment.

Summary for Migraine

Migraine headache is a significant concern in women's health psychology. Prevalence rates in women are 3 times greater than those of men. Research indicates that Caucasians are more likely to suffer migraine, as are individuals with lower socioeconomic status. Neuroscience continues to move toward an improved explanation of the underlying neurological mechanism of migraine, and evidence thus far implicates abnormal transmission of serotonin, as well as estrogenic variations associated with the menstrual cycle and possible genetic factors. Environmental, behavioral, and psychosocial influences warrant consideration as risk factors for migraine. Because of the high degree of disability and psychiatric symptoms associated with severe migraine, the cycle of stress and migraine may be self-perpetuating. Fortunately, both pharmacological and psychological/behavioral treatments are available for migraine. Individuals may be able to identify personal migraine triggers by keeping a headache diary and avoiding situations that often trigger an attack. Although there is no "cure" per se, proper clinical management of migraine headaches at their early stages can prevent the progression of episodic attacks to a more chronic and debilitating condition.

MULTIPLE SCLEROSIS

Multiple sclerosis (MS) is a neurological illness that disproportionately impacts younger women. Similar to migraines, MS is associated with extreme physical symptoms that can cause a large psychological impact. Unfortunately, MS is also similar to migraines in that there are treatments to manage symptoms but no definitive known cause or cure.

MS is a progressive autoimmune disease of the central nervous system (CNS) that can affect both the brain and the spinal cord. In MS, recurring immune attacks result in inflammation and destruction of supporting cells within the CNS that create the protective insulation (myelin) that encases neurons. Myelin is essential to the efficiency of communication among neurons. Furthermore, the destruction of myelin can result in destruction of neighboring neurons. The aftermath of these immune attacks are lesions or plaques in the brain and spinal cord that can be observed using neuroimaging technologies such as MRI (DeLuca, Ebers, & Esiri, 2004). In fact, these plaques are the hallmark of MS, and the term *multiple sclerosis* means "many plaques."

Damage from an MS attack can occur in a widespread fashion throughout the CNS, so the symptoms of MS also tend to be varied and can affect women physically, cognitively, and psychologically. As the disease progresses, symptoms can interfere with an individual's relationships with others and her ability to work, which can result in diminished quality of life and major financial burden on the individual and her family.

MS Epidemiology and Theories of Etiology

The prevalence rates of MS vary by geographic region, but they generally range from 1 in 100,000 to 120 in 100,000 (Debouverie, Pitton-Vouyovitch, Louis, Roederer, & Guillemin, 2007). The risk of developing MS relies on a combination of factors. It can develop in individuals across the lifespan, but the typical age of onset is during the primary productive and reproductive years (20 to 40 years of age). In addition, autoimmune disorders in general tend to be more common in women. This is also true for MS, as women are 2 to 4 times more likely to acquire the disease than men (Knudsen, 2009). Recent evidence has also demonstrated that the prevalence in MS has increased over the past five decades. This increase seems to be caused by an increase in prevalence in women, specifically (Jobin, Larochelle, Parpal, Coyle, & Duquette, 2010).

The specific cause of the autoimmune response in MS is unknown; however, ongoing research suggests contributions of environmental and genetic factors. Evidence for genetic factors in MS comes from epidemiologic/population studies and risk-studies of different racial groups and in families (e.g., twins, siblings). These studies indicate that genetic contributions can include family-specific genes, sex, and race. For example, first-degree relatives are

10 to 25 times more likely to develop MS as compared to prevalence rates in the general population (Robertson et al., 1996). With regard to racial differences, there is a significantly higher prevalence rate of MS in individuals of European descent than in individuals of African, Native American, and Asian descent (Kurtzke, Beebe, & Norman, 1979). The susceptibility to the disease is thought to be inherited; however, the risk of developing MS also relies heavily on environmental factors. That is, there is not one gene or set of genes that causes the disorder. Rather, a variety of genes, when they occur together, can result in a higher likelihood of developing MS, particularly if the right environmental factors are present (Kahana, 2000).

Environmental factors that are known to be associated with MS include the Epstein-Barr virus and other viruses, decreased vitamin D, smoking, geographic latitude and altitude, and month of birth. All of these environmental factors have been shown to influence immune system functioning and may trigger the onset of MS in individuals who are genetically predisposed to the disease. For example, vitamin D generally promotes immune system functioning, and epidemiological studies indicated that populations with more natural vitamin D production, like those who originate near the equator, are less likely to acquire the disease (Ramagopalan, Dobson, Meier, & Giovannoni, 2010). In contrast, incidence of MS has actually increased over the past decade or so in countries that are far north of the equator (e.g., northern European/Scandanavian countries), particularly in women, which may be associated with environmental risk factors such as a vitamin D deficit, low lifelong ultraviolet radiation, and the high-latitude geographic location

(Krokki, Bloigu, Reunanen, & Remes, 2011).

When considering the prevalence of developing MS in women with other diseases, research suggests that the prevalence of many diseases is equivalent when comparing individuals with MS to other women in the general population. This includes the prevalence of breast cancer (Catala-Lopez & Tobias, 2010) and coronary heart disease (Slawta et al., 2003). However, women with MS are more likely to develop osteoporosis (Khachanova, Demina, Smirnov, & Gusev, 2006).

MS Diagnosis and Symptoms

The type and onset of symptoms of MS varies among individuals, which makes reaching a definitive diagnosis of MS an ongoing challenge for medical professionals and a source of frustration for persons, particularly for women. This is due to the course that MS typically takes in women, onset with vague symptoms that appear and remit over the course of weeks, months, or years without clear indication of the cause or positive neuroimaging tests. The symptoms of MS fall within three general categories: physical, cognitive, and psychosocial. Any of these symptoms can affect a woman's personal, social, and occupational functioning, and ultimately, her overall well-being and quality of life.

Physical Symptoms   Some symptoms are ubiquitous for MS, and some depend primarily on the location and extent of plaques and lesions within the CNS (dysfunction in different areas of the brain affect different functions). For example, fatigue is the most commonly reported symptom in MS, but the specific cause of fatigue in MS is not well understood, and there have not been effective treatments for it in this population (Braley & Chervin, 2010). Fatigue is thought of as a generalized physical symptom that arises from the disease's general effects on the central CNS. In contrast, another physical symptom is visual disturbances or impairment, which can occur if there is a specific autoimmune response involving the optic nerve. As noted, physical symptoms are usually the first to be experienced by someone with MS and can include fatigue, pain, changes in sensation (e.g., visual impairment, numbness/tingling), muscle weakness or spasticity, problems with balance, bladder/urinary difficulties, constipation, and sexual dysfunction.

In addition, onset of symptoms can be caused by internal or environmental triggers. Heat, both internal body temperature and external temperature, is one of the most common triggers reported, which may be associated with the adverse effects of heat on the functioning of neurons with myelin damage (Marino, 2009). Although physical symptoms can begin as mild in nature, they can progress over the course of the disease, over years, and can result in disability because of damage to areas of the brain that are involved in movement (e.g., spinal cord, cerebellum).

Although MS is not typically thought of as a terminal illness, men and women with MS do have a shorter life expectancy than their counterparts. Some estimates put the figure at a 10-year difference. Age of onset may be one predictor of poorer outcome, with a younger age of onset being protective. Life expectancy can also depend on the individual's particular course and severity of MS (Bronnum-Hansen, Koch-Henriksen, & Stenager, 2004).

Cognitive Symptoms Cognitive symptoms of MS refer to difficulties with the brain's ability to perceive and process information, which can include abilities such as attention, memory, visual perception, and executive functioning (i.e., problem solving, organizing information, mental flexibility, mental manipulation of information). Cognitive problems are fairly common in people with MS, with a prevalence rate at about 50%. Symptoms can vary as a function of the course of MS, so that those experiencing a secondary-progressive course may experience greater difficulty with memory and processing speed than those with a relapsing-remitting course (Benedict et al., 2006). Although it is possible for people to experience dementia (i.e., a significant deterioration in mental functioning), these cases are rare. Typically, individuals with MS retain their general intelligence. This means that information that people have learned over the course of their lives through formal education and life experience remains largely intact. The symptoms that people most often present with and the most common clinical presentation is one of specific and subtle cognitive deficits, including problems with complex attention, efficiency of information processing, executive functioning, processing speed, and long-term memory (Genova, Sumowski, Chiaravalloti, Voelbel, & Deluca, 2009).

Mental Health Issues The most common psychiatric symptoms of MS are mood disorders. Bipolar disorder is 13 times more prevalent in people with MS. People with MS are also at increased risk for anxiety disorders such as generalized anxiety disorder, obsessive-compulsive disorder, and panic disorder. However, depression is the most common reported psychiatric consequence of MS (Jobin et al., 2010). Women can react very differently to the MS diagnosis and the associated challenges and unpredictability (Kirkpatrick Pinson, Ottens, & Fisher, 2009). Recent research suggests that risk for depression begins with the onset of MS, but the cause of the depression is probably a complex combination of the neurological changes associated with the disease, as well as psychosocial factors, including social support, coping, conceptions of the self and illness, changes in body image, and stress (Arnett, Barwick, & Beeney, 2008). The consequences of depression can include things like social withdrawal, loneliness, sadness, and changes in sleep or appetite (Williamson, 2000). Depression in MS is often associated with loneliness, which is an often underrecognized part of the experience of chronic illness and disability. Women with MS may be at risk for loneliness resulting from social network changes and functional limitations that occur in the course of chronic illness (Beal & Stuifbergen, 2007).

Disease Course   The onset of symptoms and disease progression in MS takes several different forms. The names of the forms describe the occurrence and increasing severity of symptoms. Symptoms can occur in discrete episodes (relapsing forms), or they may slowly increase in amount and severity over time (progressive forms). Women are two times more likely than men to have *relapsing-remitting MS*, which means that symptoms occur in discrete periods, often called "attacks," "exacerbations," or "flare-ups," when old symptoms return and new symptoms may emerge. These attacks can last for days, weeks, or months, and recovery time is just as variable. Between attacks, symptoms may resolve completely, but permanent neurological problems can persist, especially as the disease advances. After 10

years, 50% of people with relapsing-remitting MS will have developed another form of MS called *secondary progressive*, which means that instead of experiencing attacks, as they were before, they begin experiencing symptoms all of the time that progressively get worse. After 25 to 30 years, up to 90% of people initially diagnosed with relapsing-remitting MS will transition to secondary-progressive MS (Runmarker & Anderson, 1993).

A small minority of people display a progressive disease course from onset, termed *primary-progressive MS*. This type differs in that onset is typically in the late thirties or early forties, men are as likely as women to develop it, and initial disease activity usually occurs in the spinal cord rather than the brain (Runmarker & Anderson, 1993). Although this type of MS is easier to diagnose, the progression of symptoms is usually more severe.

Diagnosis of MS for women often comes after months or years of doctor's visits for symptoms. Although different methods for diagnosing MS have been used historically, the current gold standard for diagnosis is using a combination of taking a thorough medical history, description and tracking of symptoms over time, neuroimaging (e.g., MRI) of the brain and spinal cord, and other diagnostic tests (e.g., cerebrospinal fluid collection) (Schaffler et al., 2011). In order to be given a diagnosis of MS, a person must have experienced two separate episodes of distinctive symptoms separated by one month. The person must also demonstrate significant MRI findings, which would involve visible lesions in more than one area of the brain or spinal cord (Polman et al., 2011). It is often challenging to diagnose MS with certainty because of the variety of symptoms involved and the varying disease courses.

Taking all of this into consideration, there are several reasons why diagnosing MS is difficult in women. First, because women are more likely to suffer from relapsing-remitting forms, the first symptoms they experience often include things like fatigue, generalized pain, numbness or tingling in hands, headaches, and visual disturbances (like blurriness) that last for a few weeks. From a medical perspective, these vague symptoms can be caused by a multitude of disorders, which is why women experiencing their first attack are sometimes misdiagnosed with other disorders such as migraines, lupus, or fibromyalgia. Another reason why diagnosing MS is so difficult is because plaques in the CNS often do not appear on MRI scans until the individual has experienced multiple symptom episodes, which means that women can experience symptoms for months or years before they receive a definitive diagnosis of MS.

Reproductive Issues

MS is the most common progressive neurological disorder that is acquired by younger adults, with initial onset occurring in women during their childbearing years. MS is known to cause autonomic, urinary, and sexual dysfunction. Women with MS also experience changes in MS symptoms in relation to cyclical hormonal changes and changes in hormones throughout life (pregnancy, postpartum period, menopause, use of oral contraception, postmenopausal hormone therapy). During high-estrogen states (like pregnancy), some women with MS experience a decrease in symptoms, whereas during low-estrogen states (like menopause), some women experience worsening symptoms, although most women do not experience significant changes in relation to hormone variations (Holmqvist, Wallberg, Hammar, Landtblom, & Brynhildsen, 2006). Some women experience relief of their symptoms when taking oral contraceptives, suggesting a positive effect of the steroids on the manifestations of MS (Holmqvist et al., 2006).

Sexual Functioning Sexual dysfunction in women is an often-overlooked disability in MS. Genitourinary and sexual problems in women with MS have only recently been studied. Problems with sexual functioning (e.g., vaginal dryness, low libido, less intense or delayed orgasm) can interfere with a woman's overall quality of life and romantic relationships. Sexuality is a complex construct that can include physical sexual responses, body image and sense of attractiveness, interpersonal relationships, and self-esteem. Sexuality varies greatly from one woman to another; however, what is common among them in MS is often a change from previous sexual experiences and expectations. For example, in women who are newly diagnosed with MS, sexual functioning is a concern often expressed (Tzortzis et al., 2008), and women are much less likely to be sexually active or think about their sexuality during an MS attack (Koch, Kralik, & Eastwood, 2002).

Research in this area indicates that for men with MS, sexual dysfunction is often caused by lower-limb disability, bladder dysfunction, and problems with erection and ejaculation. For women with MS, sexual dysfunction is often associated with generalized symptoms (e.g., fatigue) (Fraser, Mahoney, & McGurl, 2008). Research also suggests that when women do experience changes in sexuality, they are usually associated with severity of neurological problems and whether a woman had a stable sexual partner (Borello-France et al., 2004). Interventions for women experiencing sexual dysfunction include education and counseling, which have been demonstrated to help women cope with sexual dysfunction (Christopherson, Moore, Foley, & Warren, 2006).

Conception, Pregnancy, and Birth The majority of individuals obtaining the diagnosis of MS are women of childbearing age. So naturally, many women with MS become concerned as to how the disease may affect the course of pregnancy and the developing fetus. When considering motherhood, women with MS often take their diagnosis into consideration when planning whether to get pregnant, the number of children they have, and how to space their pregnancies (Smeltzer, 2002). They also worry about their health and their child's health, their ability to handle child-rearing, and what others might think of their decision, all of which can put pressure on the decision-making process. Some research suggests that when women are given decision aids from organizations like the MS Society, they experience less decision-related conflict, increased self-efficacy and knowledge of MS and pregnancy, and feel more certain when making decisions about having children (Prunty, Sharpe, Butow, & Fulcher, 2008).

Although substantially more women than men develop MS, information about the effects of MS and gender-specific issues, such as pregnancy, breastfeeding, menstruation, and hormone use, has only recently been addressed in the literature. During pregnancy women often experience slower disease progression and lower rates of exacerbation. These beneficial effects are often reversed in the postpartum period. This phenomenon may be caused by a pregnancy-related change in immune system functioning, which has been found to be protective for MS disease progression (Al-Shammri et al., 2004).

During previous decades, women with MS were discouraged from having children, as pregnancy was deemed dangerous for the baby's outcome. However, today it is established that women with MS are generally no more likely to have pregnancy or delivery complications compared to healthy women, with the important caveat that treatments for MS, such as immunomodulatory therapies, should be avoided during pregnancy and while breastfeeding (Argyriou & Makris, 2008), as they can lead to birth defects (Fernandez-Liguori et al., 2009). When compared to women without MS, those with MS may have a relatively more difficult time with conception and may require assisted vaginal delivery (e.g., with the use of forceps) (Jalkanen, Alanen, & Airas, 2010). In addition, some studies have found that birth weight may be smaller for these babies (Dahl, Myhr, Daltveit, Hoff, & Gilhus, 2005). However, as noted, when the pregnant mother stops her treatments during pregnancy, the frequency of birth defects is no higher than in the general population (Dahl et al., 2005).

Women with MS also must decide whether or not to breastfeed. Many women forgo breastfeeding to start their MS treatment again, but women who breastfeed exclusively often see a reduction in postpartum relapses of their MS (Langer-Gould et al., 2009). Neurologists generally leave the decision to breastfeed up to the woman, and women trying to make this decision often benefit from counseling from their obstetrician/gynecologists on the benefits of breastfeeding, beginning oral contraception, or hormone replacement therapy (Coyle et al., 2004).

Psychosocial Factors Influencing the Experience of MS

As fatigue and other physical symptoms increase in number and severity during MS progression, we often see a decline in physical activity, body composition, and sometimes nutrition, which can result in changes in mood and overall quality of life. Therefore, some interventions for MS have focused on education and implementation of health-promoting behaviors, such as good nutrition, stress management, physical activity, positive interpersonal relations, and spiritual growth. Such interventions are associated with improved quality of life and greater participation in functional roles (Tyszka & Farber, 2010).

Quality of Life and Disability Physical, cognitive, and psychological symptoms do not occur in a vacuum. They are interconnected and can influence each other. For example, more than half of women with MS experience problems with bladder control (Borello-France et al., 2004). This can greatly disrupt a woman's functioning at work, at home, and her overall self-concept. In women with MS, changes in body image are associated with increased depression (Kindrat, 2007). Research also suggests that women with chronic pain and fatigue are more likely to have problems concentrating and experience more symptoms of depression. In fact, the relationship between MS symptoms and physical activity is influenced by the degree of fatigue and depression an individual experiences (Motl et al., 2010). Pain and fatigue are also associated with women's changes in self-esteem, self-concept toward their bodies, poor sleep, and overall quality of life (Newland, Naismith, & Ullione, 2009; Olsson, Lexell, & Soderberg, 2005).

All of these symptoms influence how well someone is able to participate in daily activities, and the term *disability* is used to describe these limitations. Once MS has been diagnosed, disability and disease severity (severity of symptoms) is often measured using rating forms such as the Expanded Disability Status Scale (Kurtzke, 1983). Disability in MS is associated with functional limitations, lower economic adequacy, less social support, and higher depressive symptoms (Phillips & Stuifbergen, 2010). Research on the interaction between MS symptoms and disability indicates that people with MS who have both physical and cognitive impairments are less likely to be employed, they engage in fewer social activities, they are less likely to work full time, they have more problems managing their household tasks, and they are typically more vulnerable to depression, which ultimately results in heavy psychological and functional burden on the individuals, their loved ones, and society (Naci, Fleurence, Birt, & Duhig, 2010). In addition, the amount of social support people have can also influence how much disability limits their ability to function in day-to-day life (Phillips & Stuifbergen, 2009). Other resources, such as employment and financial stability, can affect how women perceive their limitations and functional abilities (Clingerman, Stuifbergen, & Becker, 2004).

Stress Although flare-ups and progressive symptom severity were traditionally thought of as being a biologically driven part of the disease, recent research suggests that some behaviors and psychological factors can significantly impact a woman's symptoms of MS, which may benefit from various interventions. One of the biggest triggers or factors is stress, and there is thought to be a relationship between stressful life events and increased risk for flare-ups or attacks. Stress is a complex concept, and even for women without MS, uncontrolled or chronic stress is associated with diminished immune system functioning, changes in mood, and problems with cognitive skills like attention and memory. Several stress factors can result in increased risk for an attack, including how long a particular stressful event lasts, how often stressful events occur, and severity and type of stress. In addition, the effect of stress on the disease course can depend on other factors, such as presence of depression, anxiety, social support, and coping strategies (Mitsonis, Potagas, Zervas, & Sfagos, 2009). For example, in one study, researchers asked women with relapsing-remitting MS to keep a journal of stressful life events for about one year. They found that experiencing three or more stressful life events within 1 month was associated with a five-fold increase of MS relapses (Mitsonis et al., 2008), suggesting a need for stress management interventions for women with MS.

Coping Strategies   Compared to men, women with MS tend to experience greater self-efficacy—or their belief that they can manage their disease. However, poor coping in women can result in depression, anxiety, and resulting greater disability. One successful intervention for increasing coping skills in MS is cognitive-behavioral therapy. This type of psychotherapy can involve individual sessions with a psychotherapist and group therapy sessions that focus on psychoeducation (e.g., teaching women how MS can impact their psychological well-being) and teaching and practicing coping skills in session and in everyday life. This type of therapy may have lasting benefits for women with MS (Sinclair & Scroggie, 2005). Other

approaches to help individuals improve coping include providing education and support of the person and family or introducing a woman with MS to a role model with MS (Fraser & Polito, 2007).

Physical Activity   One target for healthcare professionals treating women with MS is to promote physical activity to break the cycle of fatigue, pain, and resulting inactivity. Physical training with trained professionals and increased physical activity is useful in reducing MS-related symptoms (Levy, Li, Cardinal, & Maddalozzo, 2009) and can result in an increase in a person's ability to perform daily self-care activities (Yates, Vardy, Kuchera, Ripley, & Johnson, 2002), improve self-efficacy, and reduce functional limitations (Morris, McAuley, & Motl, 2008).

Interventions and Treatment Methods for MS

Unfortunately, a cure for MS has not yet been found, and progression of symptoms can lead to significant disability. The current treatments for the disease include pharmacological agents (i.e., drugs), which act to treat specific symptoms, and behavioral therapies (e.g., physical therapy, cognitive rehabilitation), which help rehabilitate physical and cognitive deficits.

A wide variety of medications are used to treat the physical symptoms. The most commonly prescribed drugs are steroids, interferons, and muscle relaxers. Steroid drugs, like adrenocorticotropic hormone (ACTH) and prednisone, act by suppressing immune and inflammatory responses that destroy myelin. Steroids are typically only given during an exacerbation and not for chronic use, as they directly treat the inflammation brought on by an auto-immune attack. Another drug, interferon (e.g., Interferon beta, Avonex, Rebif), helps regulate the immune system, dampen the immune response, and has been shown to slow the progression of the disease, which reduces frequency of attacks. Other drugs, like Baclofen, decrease muscle spasticity.

Cognitive symptoms are also sometimes treated with drugs. Some disease-modifying therapies, like Avonex and Rebif, have been shown to have benefits for processing speed and memory. Other drugs, like acetylcho-linesterase inhibitors (e.g., physostigmine, donepezil/Aricept), have shown modest effect on cognition. Furthermore, stimulant drugs, like amantadine hydrochloride (e.g., Symmetrel), have been used to treat fatigue.

People with MS often seek comple-mentary and alternative medicines to man-age their disease symptoms. These can include exercise, vitamins, herbal and min-eral supplements, relaxation techniques, acupuncture, cannabis, and massage. The major symptoms treated by such treatments are pain, fatigue, and stress (Olsen, 2009).

Another intervention for people with MS includes rehabilitation for physical and cognitive deficits. Physical deficits may be treated with physical therapy, which focuses on strengthening muscles and improving bal-ance and coordination. Occupational therapy is often used to teach individual strategies to improve daily functioning, such as help with managing finances, cooking, and so on. Cog-nitive rehabilitation is designed to enhance a person's capacity to process and interpret information through training of specific cog-nitive tasks. These training exercises typically include paper-and-pencil or computer exer-cises that teach strategies or involve practice of a specific skill. Many rehabilitation programs available for MS aim to improve attention,

communication skills, and memory with the use of compensatory devices and mnemonic approaches (O'Brien, Chiaravalloti, Gover-over, & Deluca, 2008). As the use of technol-ogy in research increases, more recent evidence in the study of MS using functional MRI (measuring brain activity while a task is performed) suggests that after cognitive reha-bilitation, persons with MS show increased brain activation in areas associated with atten-tion, and in some cases, were associated with improved performances on some cognitive tasks (O'Brien et al., 2008; Penner, Kappos, Rausch, Opwis, & Radu, 2006).

CHAPTER SUMMARY

Neurological illnesses in women in their reproductive years, particularly migraines and MS, are concerns in women's health psychology. Women are at greater risk for both of these disorders, although the specific factors underlying this difference have yet to be determined conclusively. Genetic and environmental factors are thought to con-tribute to the development and course of these disorders. The role of sex hormones is also implicated, with researchers continuing to investigate the nature of these differences between men and women. For now, women's physical symptoms of both MS and migraine can be managed, but a cure remains out of reach.

The impact of these disorders is difficult to quantify for affected individuals. In addi-tion to the debilitating physical symptoms women experience with these disorders, a host of psychosocial consequences can result, including diminished quality of life, dis-ability, and psychopathology. Women and their healthcare providers should be made aware of the psychosocial impact of these neurological disorders, as pharmacological and behavioral interventions can ameliorate the psychological symptoms and perhaps reduce the overall impact of physical symptoms.

REFERENCES

Al-Shammri, S., Rawoot, P., Azizieh, F., AbuQoora, A., Hanna, M., Saminathan, T. R., & Raghupathy, R. (2004). Th1/Th2 cytokine patterns and clinical profiles during and after pregnancy in women with multiple sclerosis. *Journal of the Neurological Sciences, 222*(1–2), 21–27.

Andrasik, F., Grazzi, L., Usai, S., Buse, D. C., & Bussone, G. (2009). Non-pharmacological approaches to treating chronic migraine with medication overuse. *Neurological Sciences, 30* (Suppl. 1), S89–S93.

Argyriou, A. A., & Makris, N. (2008). Multiple sclerosis and reproductive risks in women. *Reproductive Sciences, 15*(8), 755–764.

Arnett, P. A., Barwick, F. H., & Beeney, J. E. (2008). Depression in multiple sclerosis: Review and theoretical proposal. *Journal of the International Neuropsychological Society, 14*(5), 691–724.

Barker, L. M. (2004). *Learning & behavior: Biological, psychological, and sociocultural perspectives.* Boston, MA: Pearson.

Beal, C. C., & Stuifbergen, A. (2007). Loneliness in women with multiple sclerosis. *Rehabilitation Nursing, 32*(4), 165–171.

Benedict, R. H., Cookfair, D., Gavett, R., Gunther, M., Munschauer, F., Garg, N., & Weinstock-Guttman, B. (2006). Validity of the minimal assessment of cognitive function in multiple sclerosis (MACFIMS). *Journal of the International Neuropsychological Society, 12*(4), 549–558.

Bigal, M. E., Lipton, R. B., Winner, P., Reed, M. L., Diamond, S., Stewart, W. F., & AMPP Advisory Group. (2007). Migraine in adolescents: Association with socioeconomic status and family history. *Neurology, 69*(1), 16–25.

Borello-France, D., Leng, W., O'Leary, M., Xavier, M., Erickson, J., Chancellor, M. B., & Cannon, T. W. (2004). Bladder and sexual function among women with multiple sclerosis. *Multiple Sclerosis, 10*(4), 455–461.

Braley, T. J., & Chervin, R. D. (2010). Fatigue in multiple sclerosis: Mechanisms, evaluation, and treatment. *Sleep, 33*(8), 1061–1067.

Breslau, N., & Rasmussen, B. K. (2001). The impact of migraine: Epidemiology, risk factors, and comorbidities. *Neurology, 56*(6, Suppl. 1), S4–S12.

Bronnum-Hansen, H., Koch-Henricksen, N., & Stenager, E. (2004). Trends in survival and cause of death in Danish patients with multiple sclerosis. *Brain, 127*(Pt.4), 844–850.

Burstein, R., & Jakubowski, M. (2009). Neural substrate of depression during migraine. *Neurological Sciences, 30*(Suppl. 1), S27–S31.

Bushnell, C. D. (2011). Depression and the risk of stroke in women: An identification and treatment paradox. *Stroke, 42*(10), 2718–2719.

Carmen, J. (2004). Passive infrared hemoencephalography: Four years and 100 migraines. *Journal of Neurotherapy, 8*(1), 23–51.

Catala-Lopez, F., & Tobias, A. (2010). [Incidence of breast cancer in women with multiple sclerosis: Systematic review and meta-analysis of observational cohort studies]. *Revista de Neurologia, 51*(9), 513–519.

Christopherson, J. M., Moore, K., Foley, F. W., & Warren, K. G. (2006). A comparison of written materials vs. materials and counselling for women with sexual dysfunction and multiple sclerosis. *Journal of Clinical Nursing, 15*(6), 742–750.

Clarke, C. E., MacMillan, L., Sondhi, S., & Wells, N. E. (1996). Economic and social impact of migraine. *QJM: An International Journal of Medicine, 89*, 77–84.

Clingerman, E., Stuifbergen, A., & Becker, H. (2004). The influence of resources on perceived functional limitations among women with multiple sclerosis. *Journal of Neuroscience Nursing, 36*(6), 312–321.

Coyle, P. K., Christie, S., Fodor, P., Fuchs, K., Giesser, B., Gutierrez, A., . . . Women Neurologists MS Initiative. (2004). Multiple sclerosis gender issues: Clinical practices of women neurologists. *Multiple Sclerosis, 10*(5), 582–588.

Dahl, J., Myhr, K. M., Daltveit, A. K., Hoff, J. M., & Gilhus, N. E. (2005). Pregnancy, delivery, and birth outcome in women with multiple sclerosis. *Neurology, 65*(12), 1961–1963.

D'Amico, D., & Tepper, S. J. (2009). Key points in migraine prophylaxis: Patient perspective. *Neurological Sciences, 30*(Suppl. 1), S39–S42.

D'Andrea, G., Ostuzzi, R., Francesconi, F., Musco, F., Bolner, A., d'Onofrio, F., & Colavito, D. (2009). Migraine prevalence in eating disorders and pathophysiological correlations. *Neurological Sciences*, *30*(Suppl. 1), S55–S59.

Debouverie, M., Pittion-Vouyovitch, S., Louis, S., Roederer, T., & Guillemin, F. (2007). Increasing incidence of multiple sclerosis among women in Lorraine, Eastern France. *Multiple Sclerosis*, *13*(8), 962–967.

DeLuca, G. C., Ebers, G. C., & Esiri, M. M. (2004). Axonal loss in multiple sclerosis: A pathological survey of the corticospinal and sensory tracts. *Brain*, *127*(Pt. 5), 1009–1018.

Denis, P. (1996). Methodology of biofeedback. *European Journal of Gastroenterology and Hepatology*, *8*, 530–533.

de Tommaso, M., Valeriani, M., Sardaro, M., Serpino, C., Di Fruscolo, O., Vecchio, E., . . . Livrea, P. (2009). Pain perception and laser evoked potentials during menstrual cycle in migraine. *The Journal of Headache and Pain*, *10*(6), 423–429.

Diamond, M. L. (2002). The role of concomitant headache types and non-headache co-morbidities in the underdiagnosis of migraine. *Neurology*, *58*(9 Suppl. 6), S3–S9.

Fernandez Liguori, N., Klajn, D., Acion, L., Caceres, F., Calle, A., Carra, A., . . . Villa, A. (2009). Epidemiological characteristics of pregnancy, delivery, and birth outcome in women with multiple sclerosis in Argentina (EMEMAR study). *Multiple Sclerosis*, *15*(5), 555–562.

Fraser, C., Mahoney, J., & McGurl, J. (2008). Correlates of sexual dysfunction in men and women with multiple sclerosis. *Journal of Neuroscience Nursing*, *40*(5), 312–317.

Fraser, C., & Polito, S. (2007). A comparative study of self-efficacy in men and women with multiple sclerosis. *Journal of Neuroscience Nursing*, *39*(2), 102–106.

Genova, H. M., Sumowski, J. F., Chiaravalloti, N., Voelbel, G. T., & Deluca, J. (2009). Cognition in multiple sclerosis: A review of neuropsychological and fMRI research. *Frontiers in Bioscience*, *14*, 1730–1744.

Gillies, G. E., & McArthur, S. (2010). Estrogen actions in the brain and the basis for differential action in men and women: A case for sex-specific medicines. *Pharmacological Reviews*, *62*(2), 155–198.

Goadsby, P. (2009). The vascular theory of migraine—A great story wrecked by the facts. *Brain*, *132*, 6–7.

Guidetti, V., Alberton, S., Galli, F., Mittica, P., & Salvi, E. (2009). Gender, migraine and affective disorders in the course of the life cycle. *Functional Neurology*, *24*(1), 29–40.

Haaxma, C. A., Bloem, B. R., Borm, G. F., Oyen, W. J., Leenders, K. L., Eshuis, S., . . . Horstink, M. W. (2007). Gender differences in Parkinson's disease. *Journal of Neurology, Neurosurgery, and Psychiatry*, *78*(8), 819–824.

Headache Classification Committee of the International Headache Society. (2004). The international classification of headache disorders (2nd ed.). *Cephalalgia*, *24*(Suppl. 1), 19–28.

Hering, R., Glover, V., Pattichis, K., Catarci, T., & Steiner, T. J. (1993). 5HT in migraine patients with medication induced headache. *Cephalalgia*, *13*, 410–412.

Holmes, W. F., MacGregor, E. A., & Dodick, D. (2001). Migraine-related disability: Impact and implications for sufferers' lives and clinical issues. *Neurology*, *56*(6, Suppl. 1), S13–S19.

Holmqvist, P., Wallberg, M., Hammar, M., Landtblom, A. M., & Brynhildsen, J. (2006). Symptoms of multiple sclerosis in women in relation to sex steroid exposure. *Maturitas*, *54*(2), 149–153.

Jalkanen, A., Alanen, A., & Airas, L. (2010). Pregnancy outcome in women with multiple sclerosis: Results from a prospective nationwide study in Finland. *Multiple Sclerosis*, *16*(8), 950–955.

Jobin, C., Larochelle, C., Parpal, H., Coyle, P. K., & Duquette, P. (2010). Gender issues in multiple sclerosis: an update. *Women's Health*, *6*(6), 797–820.

Johannes, C. B., Linet, M. S., Stewart, W. F., Celentano, D. D., Lipton, R. B., & Szklo, M. (1995). Relationship of headache to phase of the menstrual cycle among young women: A daily diary study. *Neurology*, *45*, 1076–1082.

Juang, K. D., Wang, S. J., Fuh, J. L., Lu, S. R., & Su, T. P. (2000). Comorbidity of depressive and anxiety disorders in chronic daily headache and its subtypes. *Headache*, *40*, 818–823.

Kahana, E. (2000). Epidemiologic studies of multiple sclerosis: A review. *Biomedicine and Pharmacotherapy*, *54*(2), 100–102.

Khachanova, N. V., Demina, T. L., Smirnov, A. V., & Gusev, E. I. (2006). [Risk factors of osteoporosis in women with multiple sclerosis]. *Zhurnal Nevrologii i Psikhiatrii Imeni S. S. Korsakova, Spec. No. 3*, 56–63.

Kindrat, S. (2007). The relationship between body image and depression in women diagnosed with relapsing remitting multiple sclerosis. *Canadian Journal of Neuroscience Nursing, 29*(1), 8–13.

Kirkpatrick Pinson, D. M., Ottens, A. J., & Fisher, T. A (2009). Women coping successfully with multiple sclerosis and the precursors of change. *Qualitative Health Research, 19*(2), 181–193.

Knudsen, G. P. (2009). Gender bias in autoimmune diseases: X chromosome inactivation in women with multiple sclerosis. *Journal of the Neurological Sciences, 286*(1–2), 43–46.

Koch, T., Kralik, D., & Eastwood, S. (2002). Constructions of sexuality for women living with multiple sclerosis. *Journal of Advanced Nursing, 39*(2), 137–145.

Krokki, O., Bloigu, R., Reunanen, M., & Remes, A. (2011). Increasing incidence of multiple sclerosis in women in Northern Finland. *Multiple Sclerosis, 17*(2), 133–138.

Kurtzke, J. F. (1983). Rating neurologic impairment in multiple sclerosis: An Expanded Disability Status Scale (EDSS). *Neurology, 33*(11), 1444–1452.

Kurtzke, J. F., Beebe, G. W., & Norman, J. E., Jr., (1979). Epidemiology of multiple sclerosis in U.S. veterans, Part 1: Race, sex, and geographic distribution. *Neurology, 29*(9 Pt. 1), 1228–1235.

Lampl, C., Huber, G., Adl, J., Luthringshausen, G., Franz, G., Marecek, S., . . . Mueller, T. (2009). Two different doses of Amitriptyline ER in the prophylaxis of migraine: Long-term results and predictive factors. *European Journal of Neurology, 16*, 943–948.

Langer-Gould, A., Huang, S. M., Gupta, R., Leimpeter, A. D., Greenwood, E., Albers, K. B., . . . Nelson, M. (2009). Exclusive breastfeeding and the risk of postpartum relapses in women with multiple sclerosis. *Archives of Neurology, 66*(8), 958–963.

Lanteri-Minet, M., Radat, F., Chautart, M. H., & Lucas, C. (2005). Anxiety and depression associated with migraine: Influence on migraine subjects' disability and quality of life, and acute migraine management. *Pain, 118*, 319–326.

Levy, S. S., Li, K. K., Cardinal, B. J., & Maddalozzo, G. F. (2009). Transitional shifts in exercise behavior among women with multiple sclerosis. *Disabilty and Health Journal, 2*(4), 216–223.

Lipton, R. B., Goadsby, P. J., Sawyer, J. P. C., Blakeborough, P., & Stewart, W. F. (2000). Migraine: Diagnosis and assessment of disability. *Reviews in Contemporary Pharmacotherapy, 11*, 63–73.

Liu, J., Qin, W., Nan, J., Li, J., Yuan, K., Zhao, L., . . . Tian, J. (2011). Gender-related differences in the dysfunctional resting networks of migraine sufferers. *PLoS One, 6*(11), e27049.

Manzoni, G. C., & Stovner, L. J. (2010). Epidemiology of headache. *Handbook of Clinical Neurology, 97*, 3–22.

Manzoni, G. C., & Torelli, P. (2009). Chronic migraine and chronic tension-type headache: Are they the same or different? *Neurological Sciences, 30*(Suppl. 1), S81–S84.

Marino, F. E. (2009). Heat reactions in multiple sclerosis: An overlooked paradigm in the study of comparative fatigue. *International Journal of Hyperthermia, 25*(1), 34–40.

Mathew, N. T., Stubita, E., & Nigam, M. P. (1982). Transformation of episodic migraine into daily headache: Analysis of factors. *Headache, 22*, 66–68.

Mitsonis, C. I., Potagas, C., Zervas, I., & Sfagos, K. (2009). The effects of stressful life events on the course of multiple sclerosis: A review. *International Journal of Neuroscience, 119*(3), 315–335.

Mitsonis, C. I., Zervas, I. M., Mitropoulos, P. A., Dimopoulos, N. P., Soldatos, C. R., Potagas, C. M., & Sfagos, C. A. (2008). The impact of stressful life events on risk of relapse in women with multiple sclerosis: A prospective study. *European Psychiatry, 23*(7), 497–504.

Morris, K. S., McAuley, E., & Motl, R. W. (2008). Self-efficacy and environmental correlates of physical activity among older women and women with multiple sclerosis. *Health Education Research, 23*(4), 744–752.

Moschiano, F., D'Amico, D., Schieroni, F., & Bussone, G. (2003). Neurobiology of chronic migraine. *Neurological Sciences, 24*(Suppl. 2), S94–S96.

Motl, R. W., McAuley, E., Wynn, D., Suh, Y., Weikert, M., & Dlugonski, D. (2010). Symptoms and physical activity among adults with relapsing-remitting multiple sclerosis. *Journal of Nervous and Mental Disease, 198*(3), 213–219.

Naci, H., Fleurence, R., Birt, J., & Duhig, A. (2010). Economic burden of multiple sclerosis: A systematic review of the literature. *Pharmacoeconomics, 28*(5), 363–379.

Nappi, R. E., & Berga, S. L. (2010). Migraine and reproductive life. *Handbook of Clinical Neurology, 97*, 303–322.

Newland, P. K., Naismith, R. T., & Ullione, M. (2009). The impact of pain and other symptoms on quality of life in women with relapsing-remitting multiple sclerosis. *Journal of Neuroscience Nursing, 41*(6), 322–328.

Nezu, A. M., Nezu, C. M., & Jain, D. (2005). *The emotional wellness way to cardiac health.* Oakland, CA: New Harbinger.

O'Brien, A. R., Chiaravalloti, N., Goverover, Y., & Deluca, J. (2008). Evidence-based cognitive rehabilitation for persons with multiple sclerosis: A review of the literature. *Archives of Physical Medicine and Rehabilitation, 89*(4), 761–769.

Olsen, S. A. (2009). A review of complementary and alternative medicine (CAM) by people with multiple sclerosis. *Occupational Therapy International, 16*(1), 57–70.

Olsson, M., Lexell, J., & Soderberg, S. (2005). The meaning of fatigue for women with multiple sclerosis. *Journal of Advanced Nursing, 49*(1), 7–15.

Panconesi, A., Bartolozzi, M. L., & Guidi, L. (2009). Migraine pain: Reflections against vasodilatation. *The Journal of Headache and Pain, 10*(5), 317–325.

Penner, I. K., Kappos, L., Rausch, M., Opwis, K., & Radu, E. W. (2006). Therapy-induced plasticity of cognitive functions in MS patients: Insights from fMRI. *Journal of Physiology—Paris, 99*(4–6), 455–462.

Peterlin, B. L., Gupta, S., Ward, T. N., & Macgregor, A. (2011). Sex matters: Evaluating sex and gender differences in migraine and headache research. *Headache, 51*(6), 839–842.

Phillips, L. J., & Stuifbergen, A. K. (2009). Structural equation modeling of disability in women with fibromyalgia or multiple sclerosis. *Western Journal of Nursing Research, 31*(1), 89–109.

Phillips, L. J., & Stuifbergen, A. K. (2010). The relevance of depressive symptoms and social support to disability in women with multiple sclerosis or fibromyalgia. *International Journal of Rehabilitation Reseasrch, 33*(2), 142–150.

Polman, C. H., Reingold, S. C., Banwell, B., Clanet, M., Cohen, J. A., Filippi, M., . . . Wolinsky, J. S. (2011). Diagnostic criteria for multiple sclerosis: 2010 revisions to the McDonald criteria. *Annals of Neurology, 69*(2), 292–302.

Prunty, M. C., Sharpe, L., Butow, P., & Fulcher, G. (2008). The motherhood choice: A decision aid for women with multiple sclerosis. *Patient Education and Counseling, 71*(1), 108–115.

Radat, F., Sakh, D., Lutz, G., El Amrani, M., Ferreri, M., & Bousser, M. G. (1999). Psychiatric comorbidity is related to headache induced by chronic substance use in migraineurs. *Headache, 39*, 477–480.

Ramagopalan, S. V., Dobson, R., Meier, U. C., & Giovannoni, G. (2010). Multiple sclerosis: Risk factors, prodromes, and potential causal pathways. *Lancet Neurology, 9*(7), 727–739.

Rasmussen, B. K. (1993). Migraine and tension-type headache in a general population: Precipitating factors, female hormones, sleep pattern and relation to lifestyle. *Pain, 63*, 65–72.

Rasmussen, B. K. (2001). Epidemiology of headache. *Cephalalgia, 21*(7), 774–777.

Robertson, N. P., Fraser, M., Deans, J., Clayton, D., Walker, N., & Compston, D. A. (1996). Age-adjusted recurrence risks for relatives of patients with multiple sclerosis. *Brain, 119*(Pt. 2), 449–455.

Runmarker, B., & Andersen, O. (1993). Prognostic factors in a multiple sclerosis incidence cohort with twenty-five years of follow-up. *Brain, 116* (Pt. 1), 117–134.

Sauro, K. M., & Becker, W. J. (2009). The stress and migraine interaction. *Headache, 49*(9), 1378–1386.

Savi, L., Rainero, I., Valfre, W., Gentile, S., Lo Giudice, R., & Pinessi, L. (2002). Food and headache attacks: A comparison of patients with migraine and tension-type headache. *Panminerva Medicine, 44*(1), 27–31.

Schaffler, N., Kopke, S., Winkler, L., Schippling, S., Inglese, M., Fischer, K., & Heesen, C. (2011). Accuracy of diagnostic tests in multiple sclerosis: A systematic review. *Acta Neurologica Scandanavica, 124*(3), 151–164.

Shyti, R., de Vries, B., & van den Maagdenberg, A. (2011). Migraine genes and the relation to gender. *Headache, 51*(6), 880–890.

Sinclair, V. G., & Scroggie, J. (2005). Effects of a cognitive-behavioral program for women with multiple sclerosis. *Journal of Neuroscience Nursing,* *37*(5), 249–257, 276.

Sinforiani, E., Citterio, A., Zucchella, C., Bono, G., Corbetta, S., Merlo, P., & Mauri, M. (2010). Impact of gender differences on the outcome of Alzheimer's disease. *Dementia and Geriatric Cognitive Disorders, 30*(2), 147.

Slawta, J. N., Wilcox, A. R., McCubbin, J. A., Nalle, D. J., Fox, S. D., & Anderson, G. (2003). Health behaviors, body composition, and coronary heart disease risk in women with multiple sclerosis. *Archives of Physical Medicine and Rehabilitation, 84*(12), 1823–1830.

Smeltzer, S. C. (2002). Reproductive decision making in women with multiple sclerosis. *Journal of Neuroscience Nursing, 34*(3), 145–157.

Stewart, W. F., Lipton, R. B., Celentano, D. D., & Reed, M. L. (1992). Prevalence of migraine headache in the United States: Relation to age, income, race, and other sociodemographic factors. *JAMA, 267,* 64–69.

Stewart, W. F., Lipton, R. B., Dowson, A. J., & Sawyer, J. (2001). Development and testing of the Migraine Disability Assessment (MIDAS) Questionnaire to assess headache-related disability. *Neurology, 56*(6, Suppl. 1), S20–S28.

Stewart, W. F., Lipton, R. B., & Liberman J. (1996). Variation in migraine prevalence by race. *Neurology, 47,* 52–59.

Stewart, W. F., Wood, C., Reed, M. L., Roy, J., Lipton, R. B., & AMPP Advisory Group. (2008). Cumulative lifetime migraine incidence in women and men. *Cephalalgia, 28,* 1170–1178.

Stokes, D. A., & Lappin, M. S. (2010). Neurofeedback and biofeedback with 37 migraineurs: A clinical outcome study. *Behavioral and Brain Functions, 6*(9), 1–10.

Stucky, N. L., Gregory, E., Winter, M. K., He, Y. Y., Hamilton, E. S., McCarson, K. E., & Berman, N. E. (2011). Sex differences in behavior and CGRP-related genes in a rodent model of chronic migraine. *Headache, 51*(5), 674–692.

Tansey, M. A. (1991). A neurobiological treatment for migraine: The response of four cases of migraine to EEG biofeedback training. *Headache Quarterly—Current Treatment and Research,* 90–96.

Tepper, S. J. (2004). *Understanding migraine and other headaches.* Jackson: University Press of Mississippi.

Tyszka, A. C., & Farber, R. S. (2010). Exploring the relation of health-promoting behaviors to role participation and health-related quality of life in women with multiple sclerosis: A pilot study. *American Journal of Occupational Therapy, 64*(4), 650–659.

Tzortzis, V., Skriapas, K., Hadjigeorgiou, G., Mitsogiannis, I., Aggelakis, K., Gravas, S., . . . Melekos, M. D. (2008). Sexual dysfunction in newly diagnosed multiple sclerosis women. *Multiple Sclerosis, 14*(4), 561–563.

Usai, S., Grazzi, L., D'Amico, D., Andrasik, F., & Bussone, G. (2009). Psychological variables in chronic migraine with medication overuse before and after inpatient withdrawal: Results at 1-year follow-up. *Neurological Sciences, 30*(Suppl. 1), S125–S127.

Von Korff, M. R., Stewart, W. F., Simon, D. J., & Lipton, R. B. (1998). Migraine and reduced work performance: A population-based diary study. *Neurology, 50,* 1741–1745.

Waters, W. E., & O'Connor, P. J. (1971). Epidemiology of headache and migraine in women. *Journal of Neurology, Neurosurgery & Psychiatry, 34*(2), 148–153.

Williamson, K. (2000). A review of the psychosocial aspect of multiple sclerosis. *British Journal of Community Nursing, 5*(3), 132–138.

Winter, A. C., Berger, K., Buring, J. E., & Kurth, T. (2012). Associations of socioeconomic status with migraine and non-migraine headache. *Cephalalgia, 32*(2), 159–170.

Yates, H. A., Vardy, T. C., Kuchera, M. L., Ripley, B. D., & Johnson, J. C. (2002). Effects of osteopathic manipulative treatment and concentric and eccentric maximal-effort exercise on women with multiple sclerosis: A pilot study. *Journal of American Osteopathic Association, 102*(5), 267–275.

24

Converging Issues in Heart Disease, Stroke, and Alzheimer's Disease in Women

MARY V. SPIERS

INTRODUCTION

In women over age 65 in the United States, three of the leading causes of death are cardiovascular disease (CVD; first), stroke (third), and Alzheimer's disease (AD; fifth) (CDC, 2007a). These conditions are considered together here not only because they represent three of the most common disorders of aging in women, but also because they share aspects of risk profiles and disability, which, when examined together in comparison and contrast, may lead to greater understanding of prevention and treatment strategies. Although each disorder may be characterized by its own risk profile, course, and approach to treatment, an emerging question of interest pertains to the degree of commonality among these three disorders in women. To what degree are there similarities in epidemiology, sex-specific risk profiles, and modifiable risk factors? Similarities in risk profiles are potentially important when considering that common strategies for prevention and intervention may lessen risk for more than one disorder of aging. Likewise, any commonalities in how these conditions are identified and treated may serve multiple purposes if issues specific to women can be identified across disorders.

In this chapter, epidemiology of heart disease, stroke, and AD are first compared, focusing on sex and ethnic risk profiles. Following this, lifestyle-related modifiable risk factors, selected psychosocial factors, and hormonal risk factors are examined among the three disorders. Then commonalities and differences related to course and disability are considered. Because stroke and AD result in cognitive impairment, the consideration of these conditions present added issues when dealing with disability. Throughout the chapter, variation related to racial and ethnic diversity is considered. Finally, although these disorders are most likely to manifest in women over age 65, risk factors emerge earlier in life, so various stages of a woman's life (e.g., pregnancy and vascular risk) are also important to consider and are interwoven throughout.

COMMONALITIES IN THE EPIDEMIOLOGY OF HEART DISEASE, STROKE, AND ALZHEIMER'S DISEASE

In women over age 65, diseases of the vascular system (e.g., heart disease and stroke) represent the top health threat and account for 35.4% of deaths (27.9% HD, 7.5% stroke) (Centers for Disease Control and Prevention [CDC], 2007a). Each year, about 785,000 Americans suffer a new coronary attack and about 610,000 experience a first stroke (Roger et al., 2012b). Alzheimer's disease (AD) represents the fifth leading cause of death for women over age 65 in the United States (CDC, 2007a; Thies & Bleiler, 2011). While the onset of AD does not present suddenly, as in a heart attack or stroke, eventually an estimated 5.4 million Americans suffer from AD (Thies & Bleiler, 2011). While deaths from heart disease and stroke declined in women and men from 1980 to 2008 (Ford et al., 2007; Thies & Bleiler, 2011), deaths from AD rose 66% (Thies & Bleiler, 2011).

The estimated 2008 combined dollar cost for direct and indirect costs of cardiovascular disease, stroke, and related vascular conditions was $297.7 billion (Roger et al., 2012b). Heart disease accounts for the largest expense at more than $190 billion (Roger et al., 2012b) and is projected to increase by more than 200% over the next 20 years (Roger et al., 2012b). Many people with any of these three conditions may be left with permanent and severe disability. In addition, the cost of care for those with long-term cognitive disability from stroke or AD in dollars and in physical and psychological toll is also enormous.

The dollar cost for Alzheimer's healthcare, long-term care, and hospice (not including unpaid caregiving) in the United States was estimated at $183 billion in 2011 (Thies & Bleiler, 2011), which rivals the cost of heart disease. While the median survival rate is between 3 and 4 years after AD diagnosis, the rate of survival can range between 2 and 20 years (Helmer, Joly, Letenneur, Commenges, & Dartigues, 2001; Wolfson

et al., 2001), making it difficult for families and caregivers to anticipate what they will bear in terms of monetary, physical, and psychosocial costs (Vitaliano, Zhang, & Scanlan, 2003).

Sex Difference Comparisons

Although women and men share several risk factors for these three disorders, there are sex-specific variations in terms of risk profile and age of onset. First cardiovascular events, stroke, and a diagnosis of AD generally occur at later ages in women than men. The average age of a first heart attack is 64.5 years for men and 70.3 years for women (Roger et al., 2012b). The mean age of stroke for men is 70.3 years and 75.1 years for women (Bushnell, 2008), and more women than men over age 85 develop AD (Andersen et al., 1999). While men and women are equally likely to die of heart disease, before age 75 men have more vascular risk factors for heart disease (Roger et al., 2012b). After age 75 women carry high risks of both cardiovascular and cerebrovascular disease (Roger et al., 2012b). In general, women have a higher lifetime risk of stroke than men and are more likely than men to die of a stroke (Bushnell, 2008; Roger et al., 2012b). In some studies, stroke risk factors are evident in women between 55 and 75 years of age (Seshadri et al., 2006), whereas in other investigations, a woman's increased risk may not be evident until the eighth decade of life (Petrea et al., 2009; Reeves et al., 2008). Regarding sex differences in AD, population-based prospective studies have reported mixed results related to women's increased lifetime incidence, with slightly more suggesting that women show a greater overall risk than men for developing AD (for review, see Barnes et al., 2005); however, after age 85 women do show a higher incidence of AD (Andersen et al., 1999).

Hypertension, a risk factor for both vascular diseases (Roger et al., 2012b) and AD (Azad, Al Bugami, & Loy-English, 2007), is more prevalent in men under age 65 and increases in women over age 65 (Azad et al., 2007). As many as 25% of women over age 65 may have hypertension (Kearney et al., 2005), and this becomes a greater risk factor for women as they age. Women over 75 also have higher rates of diabetes and hyperlipidemia than do same-aged men (Sowers, 2004), which are also risk factors in common for AD (Azad et al., 2007) and vascular diseases (Roger et al., 2012b).

The later onset of these conditions in women has been hypothesized to be related to general factors related to aging and a longer life expectancy (Barnes et al., 2005), as well as a release from the protective effects of endogenous estrogens that women experience post menopause (Bushnell, 2008; Członkowska, Ciesielska, Gromadzka, & Kurkowska-Jastrzębska, 2006; Matthews, Kuller, Sutton-Tyrrell, & Chang, 2001; Pike, Carroll, Rosario, & Barron, 2009). Women have about a 5 year advantage in life expectancy (CDC, 2011), which is the sex difference latency noted previously for first heart attack and stroke. Therefore, a question of interest across these three disorders is concerned with knowing whether women's bodies and brains age in a similar trajectory, but slower, or if they age in a qualitatively different manner than men?

Ethnic Comparisons

As the number of seniors in the U.S. population increases, so does the proportion of ethnic minority elders. Between 1990 and 2050, it is estimated that the proportion of White non-Hispanics in older age groups will decrease from 87% to 67% (Manly & Mayeux, 2004). This is notable because, for both heart disease and stroke, Black women have the highest prevalence when compared to White women, while Mexican-American women have the lowest prevalence (Roger et al., 2012a).

In terms of AD, the incidence and prevalence rates among various ethnic groups are not as clear. Most studies in the United States find higher rates of dementia and AD among African Americans and Hispanics as compared to non-Hispanic Whites, and lower rates among Native Americans, Nigerian Americans, and Japanese Americans (Manly & Mayeux, 2004). As opposed to heart attack and stroke, which are diagnosed medically around a defined event, a definitive diagnosis of AD requires the behavioral presence of dementia symptoms and the identification of specific neuropathological markers. No single medical test, imaging procedure, or behavioral measure, short of brain biopsy, can currently positively identify AD (e.g., Mayeux, 2003), via the characteristic neurofibrillary tangles and neuritic plaques. Unfortunately for diagnosis, however, these microscopic tangles and plaques are also present to some degree in normal aging and in other dementias; it is the pattern of plaques that predominate in the hippocampus and cortical association areas of the brain that identifies AD. Therefore, the clinical diagnosis of AD often depends on reports by family and significant others that trigger attention by professionals.

In addition, the diagnoses of "probable" and "possible" AD reflect, in large measure, the certainty with which other causes of dementia can be excluded (Zillmer, Spiers, & Culbertson, 2008). Not all people suspected of AD go through the extensive medical and neuropsychological workup necessary to rule out other dementias. It is possible that in geographic regions where there are fewer specialists in geriatric neurology or neuropsychology, if families don't have the means or knowledge to pursue extensive diagnostic studies, or if the identified person does not have an advocate seeking services on her behalf, then individuals may not be properly identified. Even when a problem is suspected, a diagnosis of possible or probable AD is often dependent on memory and cognitive testing validated on a largely White U.S. population, so some ethnic groups and recent immigrants may be more likely to have lower scores and therefore lead to a heightened suspicion of dementia (Manly & Mayeux, 2004). In addition, other factors of socialization, acculturation, and cultural history may also influence people of some ethnic groups to be less likely to identify cognitive decline as dementia or AD (Manly & Mayeux, 2004). Because the diagnosis of AD depends on many behavioral and cognitive factors related to identification of symptoms, until sufficient imaging and autopsy-confirmed evidence is widely available, the true ethnic picture will remain in doubt (Manly & Mayeux, 2004).

Psychosocial Risk Factors

As previously mentioned, several lifestyle-related modifiable risk factors are common to both men and women across heart disease, stroke, and AD. In addition, psychosocial risk factors such as stress and depression may be associated with poor health behaviors such as poor diet, physical inactivity, or smoking. Then, as a consequence, poor diet and physical inactivity may lead to the risk factors of obesity, as well as high cholesterol/lipid levels, diabetes, and hypertension,

which have been well documented in HD, stroke, and AD (Azad et al., 2007; Roger et al., 2012b). The metabolic syndrome, which refers to a cluster of symptoms that predict future atherosclerotic disease related to heart attack and stroke, showed an 11-fold increase in risk in women who have the combination of diabetes, hypertension, and low-HDL cholesterol (Hanefeld, Koehler, Gallo, Benke, & Ott, 2007). For both heart attack and stroke in women, many risk factors, such as coronary artery disease and high blood pressure, are identifiable well before an attack (Bushnell, 2008; Roger et al., 2012b) and are targets for preventive intervention. The general issues related to various health behaviors and pathways to disease are all vitally important and have been discussed at length earlier in this book and by others. In this section, the most-investigated psychosocial factors in women for these conditions are reviewed, particularly stress and depression, and what is known of their possible independent contributions in incident and recurrent heart disease, stroke, and Alzheimer's disease.

Stress Stress has been identified as a risk factor in the development of coronary heart disease (CHD) (Low, Thurston, & Matthews, 2010), stroke (Tsutsumi, Kayaba, Kario, & Ishikawa, 2009), and AD (Bloss, Morrison, & McEwen, 2011). However, stress as a precursor to later disorders of aging may need to be differentially understood in women, both in terms of psychosocial qualities and physiological manifestation. Psychosocially, stressors may be defined differently for women and men. For example, work-related stress related to high demand and low control has often been linked with risk for heart disease in men (Karasek, Baker, Marxer, Ahlbom, & Theorell, 1981; Siegrist,

Peter, Junge, Cremer, & Seidel, 1990) and stroke (Tsutsumi et al., 2009). However, this measure of job strain is less predictive for women in studies of risk factors for heart disease. In a review of 15 studies related to women's risk of heart disease (Low et al., 2010), it was found that women are more at risk if they have both high demand and high control at work, or if they experience both work and home stress (Low et al., 2010).

A woman's relationship to work, as well as a consideration of her multiple roles related to work and family, is an area of women's health research that considers the multi-dimensional exchange between family and work organization in the context of changing roles throughout life (see Chapter 3, Marshall). In a recent examination of the effect of multiple roles on 2-year coronary artery calcification in middle-aged Black and White women, whereas White women reported higher reward from their multiple roles, Black women showed greater cardio-vascular benefit from their rewarding roles (Janssen et al., 2012). This illustrates that the operationalization of women's stress and the path to manifestation of disease warrants more research across various ethnic groups and developmental milestones of a woman's life. Since the majority of stress research in women has been in heart disease, more work is needed in the areas of stroke and AD to determine if the psychosocial stress factors being identified in cardiovascular disease will be similar in these conditions.

In addition to different psychosocial experiences of stress, women may manifest different biological stress responses than men. Stress leading to abnormal hypothalamic-pituitary-adrenal (HPA) axis reactivity is a modulator of the aging process. It has been suggested that stress is a predisposing factor to age-related cognitive dysfunction and

disease by influencing abnormal HPA axis reactivity and increasing vulnerability to maladaptive responses in the brain (Bloss et al., 2011). Stress-induced glucocorticoid (GC) responses (e.g., cortisol) interact with other aspects of the neuroendocrine stress response. Aged animals tend to have less efficient and prolonged (GC) responses to stress (Sapolsky, Krey, & McEwen, 1983). In men, the normal circadian cycle of cortisol rhythms can also be "flattened" by stress-related factors such as financial insecurity and low occupational status (Kumari et al., 2010). Also, in humans, this inefficient response is linked to poorer hippocampal function and memory dysfunction and is particularly evident in women. A 5-year longitudinal study linked elevated cortisol levels with a decline in hippocampal volume and declarative memory in a general population (Lupien et al., 1996; Lupien et al., 1998). In a follow-up study that considered gender variation, only women showed a significant association between high cortisol levels and poor memory as well as a dynamic association, indicating that those whose cortisol levels increased showed a further decrement in delayed verbal recall, whereas those whose cortisol levels declined demon-strated memory improvement (Seeman, McEwen, Singer, Albert, & Rowe, 1997). Most importantly, higher cortisol levels are linked to AD (Martignoni et al., 1992). This hypercortisolemia in AD is also related to lower neuropsychological test performance (Elgh et al., 2006).

Although the mechanisms of stress on the HPA axis and the progression toward disease are not completely worked out, it has been hypothesized that a more responsive or sensitive HPA reaction to stress, as seen in younger animals and humans, as opposed to a more flattened and/or chronic response, may provide neuroprotection (Bloss et al., 2011). The study of this mechanism and other stress mechanisms throughout life may together lead to a better understanding of how stress may factor into diseases of aging. In women, the "tend and befriend" response (Taylor et al., 2000) may occur following hypervigilance to threat and result in a focus on close social networks and a release of oxytocin, known for its behavioral actions in bonding and maternal behavior. In addition, women show a heightened sensitivity to stress that appears post-puberty, which may be tied to hormonal (rather than chromosomal) factors and appears to contribute to making women more prone to stress-related disease (Becker et al., 2007). Because these various stress responses may contribute to disease throughout a woman's adult life, they also merit investigation for their contribution toward diseases of aging in women.

The ramifications for women are that stress may be perceived and experienced differently than it is in men, both psychologically and physiologically. Women may experience work and family stress differently than men, and there may be ethnic and life stage variation in how stressful or rewarding various roles are perceived. Women may also show a different physiological response to stress. Although there are indications that women may be more reactive to stress and more prone to stress-related diseases, there may also be protective effects of hormones such as oxytocin and estrogen. The type and impact of stress on heart disease, stroke, and AD in women, while beginning to be fleshed out, will benefit from future research to be fully understood.

Depression   Depression has been identified as an independent risk factor in incident heart disease (Lett et al., 2004; Low et al., 2010), stroke (Bushnell, 2011; Pan, Sun, Okereke, Rexrode, & Hu, 2011), and AD (Green et al., 2003; Ownby, Crocco, Acevedo, John, & Loewenstein, 2006), as well as a factor in recurrent cardiac events (Low et al., 2010) and stroke (Bushnell, 2011). Women have a lifetime prevalence of major depression that is 1.7 to 2.7 times greater than that of men (Kessler, McGonagle, Swartz, Blazer, & Nelson, 1993; Weissman et al., 1993), with this difference beginning in puberty (Kessler et al., 1993) and again heightened around the menopausal transition in a subgroup of women (Maki et al., 2010).

In cardiac research, which has received the most thorough investigation of depression in the three conditions in women, more studies show a depression and heart disease link in women than in men (Low et al., 2010). In prospective studies of women only, depressive symptoms also predicted cardiac mortality among initially healthy women (for review, see Low et al., 2010). In stroke research, fewer studies have examined the relationship between depression and stroke. However, recent reports have suggested a link between depression in women and incident stroke, particularly for middle-aged women who take antidepressant medications (Pan, Okereke, et al., 2011). In addition, a study that examined the effect of mood disorders and anxiety on any vascular disease (i.e., heart disease, heart attack, and stroke) in women and men found depression was more strongly associated across vascular disease in men, whereas bipolar disorder was more strongly associated in women when controlling for obesity, high blood pressure, smoking, and diabetes (Fiedorowicz, He, & Merikangas, 2011). Finally, in AD research, a history of depression diagnosed earlier in life presents an independent risk factor for AD (Green et al., 2003; Ownby et al., 2006) and appears distinct from prodromal AD depression (Ownby et al., 2006).

As in the study of stress, questions related to both the psychological manifestation and physiological mechanisms of depression and mood disorders and how they contribute to these disorders of aging in women need much investigation. Depression may be associated to disease via a variety of mechanisms and may show some variation among the disorders discussed here. For example, in relation to AD and brain functioning, depression is known to lead to poorer performance on memory and attention tests. In a sample of middle-aged community-dwelling women, increased symptoms of depression were associated with poorer performance on neuropsychological tests (Yaffe et al., 1999). Cognitive symptoms and mood symptoms have both been associated with polymorphisms on an estrogen receptor (ERα receptor) (Sundermann, Maki, & Bishop, 2010), so depression and cognitive symptoms may have some genetic correspondence. Other work has suggested that the menopausal transition presents a "window of vulnerability" for depression (Maki et al., 2010), as earlier menopausal transitions are associated with greater late life depression, especially in those with lower socioeconomic status (Ryan, Carriere, Scali, Ritchie, & Ancelin, 2008). Because of the relationship among depression, endogenous and exogenous hormonal status, and risk for the development of AD, further exploration is warranted in this area. In addition, the mechanisms whereby depression may also be related to heart attack need to be investigated.

Other Psychological Factors

In addition to stress and depression, other psychological factors that have received some attention across these three disorders include anxiety/distress and anger/hostility. Anxiety has been identified as a more consistent factor in heart disease for men than women (Low et al., 2010). Additionally, psychological distress, as measured by neuroticism, is a risk factor for mild cognitive impairment (MCI) and has a slightly stronger association in men (Wilson, Schneider, et al., 2007). Neuroticism was also associated with the development and progression of AD in a largely male sample but is not correlated with the neurobiologic markers (e.g., plaques and tangles) of AD, and so may contribute to cognitive decline via an alternate mechanism (Wilson, Arnold, Schneider, Li, & Bennett, 2007; Wilson et al., 2006). Although there are hints that anxiety may be a more critical factor in men, the anxiety/neuroticism construct merits further research related to sex and gender differences.

Anger and hostility, particularly as part of the "Type A" profile, have received extensive research attention in cardiovascular disease in men, and more recently, in women, but they have received little attention in stroke or AD. In women, hostility appears to be a stronger factor in predicting heart disease onset in African-American women and in predicting recurrent problems in all women with existing CHD (Low et al., 2010). Related to the construct of anger suppression or anger-in, the research has not been conclusive related to the predictive nature of this construct in women (Low et al., 2010).

In sum, the psychological factors of stress and depression have received the most research attention in women. Given that there are apparent commonalities pointing to stress and depression as risk factors for all three conditions, the understanding of all three disorders would benefit from collaboration and cross-talk among investigators. Understanding of the psychological mechanisms contributing to disease may benefit from the more sophisticated methodologies developed in cardiovascular research (e.g., going beyond self-reports). In addition, the research on the pathways to disease in AD research (e.g., depression and memory) may also provide some useful methodological paradigms in the understanding of physiological mechanisms in heart disease and stroke.

Hormonal Factors   In women, sex steroid hormones appear to afford protection against the development of heart disease (Matthews et al., 2001), stroke (Bushnell, 2008), and AD (Członkowska et al., 2006; Pike et al., 2009), until the drop in circulating endogenous estrogen (i.e., 17ß estradiol) that occurs with the menopausal transition. In addition, conditions specific to women that may also have a link to hormonal factors include increased stroke risk with oral contraception (Roger et al., 2012b) and pregnancy (Kittner et al., 1996; Kuklina, Tong, Bansil, George, & Callaghan, 2011). Absolute risk of stroke associated with oral contraceptives, although very small, carries a higher odds ratio than for those not taking oral contraceptives (Bushnell, 2008). Stroke related to pregnancy is most likely to occur either right around delivery or in the first few weeks postpartum and may be linked to a hormonal and vascular hemodynamic interaction (Kittner et al., 1996). In addition, reports of increased incidence of stroke in middle-aged women (Towfighi, Saver, Engelhardt, & Ovbiagele, 2007) may also be linked to the menopausal transition (Bushnell, 2008) as well as menopause before age 42 (Lisabeth et al., 2009).

Estradiol is a mild vasodilator (Shepherd, 2001), thereby increasing blood flow and decreasing vascular tone. In addition, brachial artery and cerebral blood flow velocities and vasomotor reactivity vary in response to physiologic levels of estradiol associated with the menstrual cycle, with highest reactivity occurring at ovulation (Diomedi et al., 2001; Hashimoto et al., 1995). Estrogens have also been shown to protect cerebral endothelial cells (Krause, Duckles, & Pelligrino, 2006), guard against inflammatory reactions that are important to vascular and AD pathology (Shepherd, 2001), and improve lipoprotein profiles and cholesterol levels (Haines et al., 1996). During the menopausal transition in women, changes in lipid profiles appear to be among the key indicators of cardiovascular risk (Matthews et al., 2001).

Estrogen receptors are found throughout the body and brain. They are not confined to areas responsible for reproduction as was previously thought. Estrogen receptor subtypes ERα and ERß have been of particular interest in both vascular and AD research in women. The association between estrogen levels and vascular health has long been linked, although the mechanisms of protection are yet to be fully understood. In one mode of action, estrogen may help prevent blood clotting, as well as the narrowing of blood vessel walls, through the prostacyclin receptor linked to ERα (Turner & Kinsella, 2010). Estradiol is also important to brain functioning in women (Craig et al., 2010; McEwen, Alves, Bulloch, & Weiland, 1997), and both subtypes of estrogen receptors (ERα and ERß) play a role in cognition. For example, ERα is involved in mood and emotional memory processing (e.g., amygdala), and ERß is involved in new declarative learning (e.g., hippocampal formation). Finally, increased estrogen at the neuronal level is associated with neuronal growth and connectivity, neurotransmitter regulation, and protection against oxidative stress (McEwen & Alves, 1999; McEwen et al., 1997; Osterlund, 2010).

In sum, there is converging evidence that naturally circulating estradiol supports both vascular and neuronal health through several mechanisms, and its decline with menopause is associated with multiple risk factors related to heart disease, stroke, and AD. In the next section, the issue of replacing or supplementing estrogen through hormone therapy (HT) is considered.

Hormone Therapy

In the mid-1990s, 38% of postmenopausal women were using HT (Keating, Cleary, Rossi, Zaslavsky, & Ayanian, 1999). HT was recommended for women with coronary heart disease (Grady et al., 1992) and was being actively investigated as a method to prevent disease and prolong life in women, largely because of the suspected protective effects of estrogen discussed previously. Early research also suggested that those taking certain types of hormone therapy may be less likely to develop AD (Gaugler, Yu, Krichbaum, & Wyman, 2009; Kawas et al., 1997; Lupien et al., 1998; Shumaker et al., 2004), and they may perform better on cognitive and memory tests (Doraiswamy et al., 1997; Yaffe, Sawaya, Lieberburg, & Grady, 1998). Also, the selective estrogen receptormodulator (SERM) Tamoxifen, used to lower estrogen levels in breast cancer treatment, has been associated with small but adverse effects on cognition in older women (Espeland et al., 2010). In contrast to general evidence of the benefits of naturally occurring estrogens and initial evidence of benefit of HT, the Women's Health Initiative

(WHI) and its associated studies (i.e., Women's Health Initiative Memory Study [WHIMS] and Women's Health Initiative Study on Cognitive Aging [WHISCA]) were halted because of increased risk of adverse effects, including cardiovascular, stroke events, and dementia in women over age 65 who were taking HT (Rossouw et al., 2002; Shumaker et al., 2003; Shumaker et al., 2004). This disconnect between the positive benefits of endogenous estrogen versus possible adverse effects of HT containing certain combinations of conjugated equine estrogen (CEE with medroxyprgesterone acetate) in women who were well past menopause has led to a drop in prescriptions for HT and a surge in research aimed at reconciling these differences.

Some of the interesting possibilities include tailoring hormonal treatments to the individual and the possibility that there may be a "window of opportunity" such that the right combination of steroid hormones taken around the time of the menopausal transition may afford the best protection against later cognitive decline (Resnick et al., 2009). Methods to determine who may benefit from HT, and under what conditions and dosages, as well as who may be at risk, need to be developed. In sum, the role of estrogens as cardio- and neuroprotective in the younger system seems robust. Further research is needed to see if HT will be most effective at the time of menopause as a protective factor against AD, HD and stroke. Additionally, it is not clear if HT can be effective in women well past menopause, so it is not clear if replacing hormones will benefit older women (Gouva & Tsatsoulis, 2004).

Genetic Factors

Although heritability factors can play a part in the vascular disorders of heart disease and stroke, AD has received the most scrutiny related to specific genetic risk factors in women. Interestingly, some of the genes at issue in AD may also interact with the functioning of estrogen and thereby also play a role in heart disease and stroke.

AD is a genetically complex disorder and does not have one dominant genetic pattern (Pericak-Vance & Haines, 1995). However, several specific genetic risk factors for AD have been identified, and women appear to suffer greater impact in comparison to men when certain genetic markers are considered (Sundermann et al., 2010). In the small percentage of cases (about 7%) of those with familial and usually early-onset (i.e., before age 65) AD dementia, no sex differences in inheritance patterns have been reported (Campion et al., 1999; Nussbaum & Ellis, 2003). However, in both sexes, having a first-degree relative increases the risk of AD by 10% to 30%.

The presence of the ApoE4 allele of chromosome 19 is associated with both higher serum cholesterol and shifting the risk of late-onset AD up to 5-10 years earlier for one allele and 10 to 20 years earlier for two alleles (Isbir et al., 2001). Notably, this allele appears to be an important marker for women. Women show a stronger association between the presence of ApoE4 and the development of both MCI (Fleisher et al., 2005) and AD (Corder et al., 2004; Duara et al., 1996) than do men. Women with this allele who develop AD also show greater memory impairments related to greater hippocampal damage (Fleisher et al., 2005). Another marker that increases the odds ratio for the development of AD in women worldwide is a genetic variation (Val66Met) of the brain-derived neurotrophic factor gene (BDNF) (Fukumoto et al., 2010). BDNF is important in supporting the function and healing of neurons. In sum, women who carry one or more of these genetic susceptibilities carry a higher risk for the development of AD.

Interestingly, ApoE4 may also interact with estrogen's anti-inflammatory properties via the ERα and ERß receptors. In mice, those with the ApoE3 allele showed the expected anti-inflammatory response to estrogen in the brain, but those with the ApoE4 allele did not (Brown, Choi, Xu, Vitek, & Colton, 2008). From this, it has been suggested that postmenopausal women with the ApoE4 allele may not benefit from the anti-inflammatory effects of estrogen replacement, and furthermore, that the ApoE4 allele could contribute to inflammatory factors known to be present in heart disease and stroke (Brown et al., 2008). In support of this finding, only ApoE3-positive (but not ApoE4) women taking HT had less internal and carotid wall thickening related to vascular atherosclerosis (Yaffe, Haan, Byers, Tangen, & Kuller, 2000). As research continues in this area, both basic science and clinical research efforts may benefit from studying estrogen–gene interactions, as well as how these will be influenced by environmental factors.

Considering the risk factors reviewed in this section, there appear to be several identified and potential commonalities in the risk factors for disease across heart disease, stroke, and Alzheimer's disease in women. Initial cardiovascular events, stroke, and a diagnosis of AD generally occur at later ages in women than men, even though many physiological and psychological risk factors may be shared. Therefore, it seems imperative to study the general question of aging in women. Do women's bodies and brains age in a similar trajectory, but slower, or do they age in a qualitatively different manner than men? In addition to lifestyle-related modifiable risk factors common to both men and women across heart disease, stroke, and AD, the psychosocial risk factors of stress and depression discussed here suggest that women may perceive and experience aspects of their own daily psychological milieu differently than men. In turn, there is some evidence that certain pathways of disease may differ from those of men.

Also, ethic differences in experience and developmental changes in a woman's life, as well as hormonal status, may interact with the psychological and physiological pathway to disease. The consideration of psychosocial factors in these diseases appears to have largely been investigated in one disorder at a time, most notably heart disease, or at times, between heart disease and stroke. Although methods of investigation are becoming more sophisticated, investigations of different disease states may benefit from sharing methodologies. In addition investigations into common factors between these conditions is likely to result in a better understanding of each individual condition.

AFTERMATH, DISABILITY, AND COURSE

In this section, the aftermath of heart attack, stroke, and diagnosis of AD are considered, with particular attention to converging issues related to reasons for increased disability suffered by women. Issues of education/awareness, physical frailty, psychosocial functioning, and formal and informal caregiving are considered.

Women often fare worse than men after heart attack (Roger et al., 2012b), stroke (Bushnell, 2008; Roger et al., 2012b), and diagnosis of AD (Sinforiani et al., 2010).

Considering all vascular events, women are more likely to die or suffer more disability than men. Of all deaths after a myocardial infarction (MI) over age 45, women are also more likely than men to have a recurrent MI, subsequent heart failure or stroke, and to die (Roger et al., 2012b). Of all stroke deaths, 60% occur in women (Roger et al., 2012b). Between 1980 and 2005, there was a greater decline in stroke death rates among men than women (Roger et al., 2012b). In addition, women over age 65 account for a larger proportion of the hospital stays related to cardiac conditions and stroke in comparison to men, and this difference widens with age (Elixhauser & Jiang, 2006). Even with a higher number of hospital stays and more comorbidities in women, they are less likely to participate in cardiac rehabilitation (Roger et al., 2012b). Post-stroke, women are only half as likely to be independent in activities of daily living, even when controlling for age, race, and other factors (Gargano & Reeves, 2007; Whitson et al., 2010), and they are more likely to suffer prestroke and poststroke disability (Di Carlo et al., 2003). The reasons for poor outcomes in women are likely multifactorial.

Lack of Education and Awareness as Contributors to Disability

Increased disability because of a lack of education and awareness includes issues related to knowledge of signs and symptoms, as well as seeking and obtaining treatment at the appropriate time, and may be related to both personal awareness as well as formal and informal caregiver awareness. Women's awareness of heart disease as the leading cause of death in women grew and nearly doubled between 1997 and 2006, with 57%

of women having this knowledge in more recent years, while Black and Hispanic women consistently showed lower awareness (Christian, Rosamond, White, & Mosca, 2007; Mosca et al., 2006). In addition, twice as many women felt more uninformed about stroke than heart disease (Christian et al., 2007). Despite this knowledge, less than half of the women were aware of the risk factors leading to heart disease (Mosca et al., 2006) and stroke (CDC, 2008; Zerwic, Hwang, & Tucco, 2007). However, if women were told that their own cardiovascular risk factors were in the unhealthy range, they were more likely to take steps to lower their risk, as well as that of their families (Mosca et al., 2006).

At the onset of a heart attack or stroke, speed at which symptoms are recognized and treatment is received is essential in saving lives and reducing damage and disability. For both heart attack and stroke, getting to the emergency room (ER) quickly is crucial. Studies indicate that many stroke patients fail to arrive at the ER within 2 hours (Smith, Lisabeth, Bonikowski, & Morgenstern, 2010; Zerwic et al., 2007), and women were likely to present later than men (Smith et al., 2010). The inability to identify stroke symptoms in about 45% of patients, particularly nonmotor symptoms, may have been partly responsible for a median time of 16 hours to be admitted to the ER in one study with a large proportion of women (Zerwic et al., 2007). Cognitive symptoms of stroke may also be better detected by others. If one is living alone, as many older women do, they may be less likely to self-identify and be able to seek help. In the case of strokes, someone other than the identified patient made the decision to seek treatment in 66% of the cases (Zerwic et al., 2007).

Although it is considered general knowledge among health professionals that heart disease is the leading cause of death in women, fewer than 20% of physicians in a recent study knew that more women than men died each year of cardiovascular disease (Mosca et al., 2005). Furthermore, when asked to rate the risk level for CVD in men and women with identical risk profiles, primary care physicians were more likely to assign women a lower risk profile (Mosca et al., 2005). Additionally, in studies of stroke in both the United States and Europe, diagnostic and imaging tests were less likely to be ordered for women than for men (CDC, 2007b; Di Carlo et al., 2003). Therefore, important etiological information might be missed.

In regard to Alzheimer's disease, in which symptoms unfold more slowly and progressively over time than with heart disease or stroke, women also show greater disability and appear to lose autonomy at a faster rate than men (Sinforiani et al., 2010). The fact that women appear to be more impaired may, again, result from several factors. Initial symptoms may go unnoticed for similar reasons as discussed previously regarding heart attack and stroke, because women are often older and likely to live alone (Sinforiani et al., 2010). In addition, the memory and executive functioning issues presenting in AD are often not recognized or acknowledged by the individual because of the nature of the disease. AD often results in a loss of metacognitive awareness, or the ability to self-monitor behavior, so that some AD patients have little insight into their own deficits (Zillmer et al., 2008).

Additionally, older women living alone do not have the external cognitive supports afforded by a significant other who can help compensate for memory difficulties and mental lapses in areas of daily living, such as medication taking and financial management. Any significant errors may quickly put a cognitively compromised person at medical or other personal risk. Therefore, the interaction of living alone and cognitive compromise in AD can compound the problem of recognition of symptoms beyond the issues discussed related to heart attack and first stroke. The disease may progress for a period of time until a critical juncture, which may result in an acute crisis that involves the healthcare system. When women present with AD, they may do so with more advanced disease and greater disability.

In sum, it appears that more women are aware of issues related to risk factors for heart disease than for other disorders, and increased awareness of personal risk appears to be related to risk-lowering behaviors. However, many individuals may not be aware of symptoms of heart attack, stroke, or AD. Unfortunately, some physicians may also downplay women's risk of CVD and also be less likely to treat symptoms of stroke. Symptoms of AD, which appear in a more insidious manner, also rely on recognition by others. Therefore, the incidence of increased mortality and morbidity may be partly because risk factors, as well as signs and symptoms, of these disorders go unrecognized and untreated. While the near doubling of the rate of awareness of heart disease as the leading cause of death in women between 1997 and 2006 is encouraging, as is the fact that cardiovascular deaths have decreased, it is not clear that these two facts are linked causally, nor has increased awareness resulted in improved clinical outcomes for women (Mosca, Barrett-Connor, & Wenger, 2011). More research is needed to disentangle the factors that lead to both greater awareness and behavioral change.

Age of Onset and Disability

Disability across all three disorders may be worse in women because they are older at age of onset, are likely to have more comorbid conditions, and may therefore be less likely to recover as well. However, disability may be worse in women because the path to disease may directly impact women to a greater degree than men. The issues of how women may age differently than men warrant further attention. For example, beginning in late middle age, routine autopsies of "normal" women show more neuropathological markers of AD than in men (Corder et al., 2004). These neuropathological signs, although not specific to AD, may also be more likely to clinically and behaviorally manifest as AD in women. For example, women with AD may be more affected in language areas than men, specifically in verbal fluency and naming (Henderson & Buckwalter, 1994). Also, lower scores on the Mini Mental State Exam, a screening of cognitive function, are correlated with low levels of the ERα receptor in the frontal cortex in women with AD (Kelly et al., 2008) and may again implicate the role of estrogen in diseases of aging in women. In a postmortem study of men and women in religious orders, each unit of AD pathology was associated with a 20-fold increase in AD diagnosis in women, but only a three-fold increase in men (Barnes et al., 2005). Researchers face the challenge of disentangling issues of age and associated increased comorbid conditions from disease processes as reasons for increased disability following heart attack, stroke, and AD diagnosis in women.

Emotional Psychosocial Issues: Focus on Depression

As with risk factors for disease, psychosocial factors after onset may interact differently in women's and men's responses to heart disease, stroke, and AD. While depression, anxiety, stress, and suppressed negative emotion have been studied to some degree in one or more of these disorders, depression following a heart attack (Low et al., 2010), stroke (Bushnell, 2011), or diagnosis of AD (Wragg & Jeste, 1989) is the psychosocial factor that has received most attention across these three disorders related to gender differences and women's health. Depression following heart attack increases the risk for cardiac morbidity and mortality (Lett et al., 2004). While depression leading to recurrence of stroke has not received the same level of research attention as in heart disease, the implication from the stroke literature is that treatment of depression may also reduce the possibility of another stroke (Bushnell, 2011). Across studies it has been reported that about one-third (30%) of heart attack (Thombs et al., 2006) as well as one-third of stroke survivors develop depressive symptoms (Hackett, Yapa, Parag, & Anderson, 2005). Post-event depression is prevalent in both women and men, but in a recent review of the literature, it was reported that depression was more prevalent in women than men in both heart attack (Low et al., 2010) and stroke (Poynter et al., 2009) in the majority of studies. Variation in findings in poststroke depression may, for example, be a direct consequence of the stroke or may result as a reaction to disability. Left-hemisphere stroke is more associated with increased depression (Bolla-Wilson, Robinson, Starkstein, Boston, & Price, 1989), so at first glance it may appear that men and women are equally likely to suffer poststroke-related depression if they suffer a left-hemisphere stroke. However, in one study, poststroke depression in women was associated more with left-hemisphere stroke, prior psychiatric diagnosis, and cognitive impairment, whereas in men depression was more associated with activities of daily living and social functioning (Paradiso & Robinson, 1998).

Several studies have suggested that treatment combinations of behavioral and medication-based treatments for depression may be useful to improve depressive symptoms poststroke (Williams et al., 2007), and that depression management may also indirectly affect cardiovascular outcomes related to medication and treatment adherence (Mosca, Benjamin, et al., 2011). However, in a review of heart disease in women, Low and colleagues (Low et al., 2010) suggest that many treatments for depression in women, as compared to men, may not benefit them in regard to cardiovascular outcomes to the same degree. Low and colleagues suggest that treatments for women, in general, may benefit more from a focus on emotional expression and social support rather than directive advice and interventions aimed at symptom reduction. It will be important to fine-tune investigations of depression treatment in both heart disease and stroke to better understand factors that may be direct effects of the disorder, such as somatic symptoms of fatigue, or frank brain damage in the case of stroke, versus reactions to the disability and the contribution of preexisting depression or mood disorders. Also, the approach to depression treatment with an eye toward the most effective psychological methods for women is an important area for development.

More than 40% of people with AD may also have depressive symptoms, and 10% to 20% may meet the criteria for a depressive disorder (Wragg & Jeste, 1989). As discussed earlier, because depression may compound memory and attention problems, those with AD and depression may suffer increased cognitive disability. Among AD patients, strategies to decrease frailty, including exercise and improved behavioral management, reduced depressive symptomology in a group of community-dwelling AD patients (Teri et al., 2003).

In sum, depressive symptoms in women following heart attack, stroke, or the onset of AD may lead to negative consequences, which may include increased risk of recurrent events or quicker decline. The fleshing out of the direct or indirect effects of depression on the various disorders requires greater research attention and more attention to tailored treatments. The effect of treatments that result in lower levels of depressive symptoms in women may lead to less disability. The effect of other psychosocial variables that have received less attention, such as stress, anxiety, and hostility, also merit further research as to the role they may play in women's health following onset of these disorders.

Aftermath and Caregiving

Informal caregiving is also an important wider sociocultural issue to consider in the aftermath of heart attack, stroke, or AD, as higher caregiver burden is associated with poorer outcomes for patients, including poorer quality of life and early nursing home placement (Gaugler, Kane, Kane, & Newcomer, 2005; Yaffe et al., 2002). In a review of the literature by Gaugler (Gaugler et al., 2009), caregiver distress indicators,

particularly stress and depression, were just as consistently predictive of nursing home placement as care recipient indicators related to behavior problems. Sociodemographic factors among caregivers related to nursing home placement have indicated that being male, Caucasian, older, Medicaid eligible, and living alone are among the leading predictors of placing a cared-for individual in a nursing home (Gaugler, Kane, Kane, Clay, & Newcomer, 2003); however, these factors may not be consistently predictive across studies (Gaugler et al., 2009).

Many caregivers care for a loved one at home in an attempt to avoid or delay nursing home placement. This may be done at the expense of employment. Nearly one-fourth of all caregivers of frail elderly in one study reduced their hours or quit work, and those who were more likely to do so were African American or Hispanic daughters or daughters-in-law caring for those with dementia (Covinsky et al., 2001). Additional research suggests that there are differences among ethnic groups in the manner in which formal and informal supports and attitudes toward disease and caregiving may manifest. Ethnic minority groups, including African Americans and Hispanics, are more likely to rely on extended family systems for caregiving (Anderson, Williams, & Gibson, 2002). More informal caregiving in minority groups may reflect cultural values and norms related to a sense of family loyalty and reciprocity, but these caregivers may also benefit from extended social support systems that may buffer some of the negative aspects of providing care, such as depression and strain, that are often experienced by those who are spending extended time in caregiving (Anderson et al., 2002). In fact, while women caregivers in general report more health problems than men, the tendency for women to seek social affiliation and adopt a "tend and befriend" style of dealing with stress may also serve as a protective factor against certain negative cardiac outcomes suffered by caregivers (Vitaliano et al., 2003).

Caring for someone with cognitive issues such as may be experienced with AD or repeated strokes typically involves more hours, has greater impact on employment, and can result in more mental and physical strain for the caregiver (Ory, Hoffman, Yee, Tennstedt, & Schulz, 1999). Dementia is considered more burdensome than many other types of caregiving because of the unique and complex challenges of dealing with someone with cognitive impairment (Covinsky et al., 2001; Schulz & Martire, 2004). In addition to the financial toll, caregiving strain also contributes to higher caregiver stress, depression, or depressive symptoms (Parks & Novielli, 2000). Nearly two-thirds of dementia caregivers rate their stress as high, and one-third report symptoms of depression (Thies & Bleiler, 2011). In regard to physical health, many report a decline in health following caregiving onset (Vitaliano et al., 2003), and this is borne out in reduced immune system functioning, slower wound healing, and the onset of hypertension and heart disease (Thies & Bleiler, 2011), as well as higher mortality among spouses (Schulz & Beach, 1999).

The behaviors considered most upsetting to caregivers include the daily hassles of the care recipient refusing or resisting care, repetitive questioning, arguing and verbal aggressiveness, waking up at night, toileting problems, wandering, inappropriate behaviors, agitation, safety issues, and delusions (Dennis, Hauck, Winter, Hodgson, & Gitlin, 2010). For caregivers it can be difficult to differentiate symptoms that appear to be part of cognitive decline from those that

appear volitional. In caring for an elderly person, the relationship between informal caregivers and the person may also need to be reconfigured if, for example, a more parental role must be assumed by a child. The stress-process model of caregiving considers aspects of strain, burden, and depression that are shared in many caregiving situations, but dementia also presents significant issues of loss and grief that may also affect caregivers' coping abilities (Noyes et al., 2010).

Taken together, there appear to be some common reasons why women fare worse after heart attack, stroke, and diagnosis of AD that need further investigation and collaboration among investigators studying different disorders. Lack of awareness of signs and symptoms of disease among women, and especially in some ethnic groups, may contribute to poor self-care behaviors and uninformed actions at critical times. In addition, lack of awareness among physicians to take critical action needs to be further addressed. Increased awareness among women regarding personal heath profiles has shown some association to better self-care in heart disease, so this is a promising avenue of investigation. Also, the fact that many women are older and live alone cuts across explanations of disability in all three disorders. This may interact in various ways with awareness, cognition, biological aging, and frailty, as well as psychological conditions such as depression. The issue of whether women may age and manifest disease in the same manner as men, which was discussed earlier, is also relevant in discussions of disability and course of a disease. Further investigations into the qualitative nature of possible differences will hopefully lead to a more tailored approach to treatment once a disorder is recognized.

CONCLUSIONS AND FUTURE DIRECTIONS

In this chapter, converging issues across heart disease, stroke, and AD in women were identified. Risk profiles related to sex and gender, and ethnicity, were discussed as well as psychosocial risk factors related to stress and depression, hormonal factors, potential hormonal genetic interactions, and outcomes. Although women and men share many similarities in risk profiles in heart disease, stroke, and AD, the 5-year difference in life expectancy may not be a simple quantitative measure that is able to account for the difference between men and women. In this comparison across disorders, there appear to be several instances in which women may show different risk patterns than men and which may lead both to a different pathway to disease as well as interact with outcome and disability differently.

It appears that much investigation is needed to understand not only how to target interventions between women and men, but also to understand the similarities and differences in these disorders of aging within women. Some of the established strategies for primary prevention in women and men appear to be similar and may lessen risk across disorders. Interventions targeted at primary prevention and that lead to behavior change regarding the risk factors of these disorders are some of the greatest challenges facing caregivers in all three of these disorders. Interventions particularly aimed at subgroups of the population where there are disparities in knowledge or treatment are also crucial. In cardiovascular disease, which has received the most research pertaining to psychosocial factors and interventions, there are calls for increased cultural competency to provide culturally sensitive care (Mosca, Barrett-Connor, et al., 2011). Well-established approaches to behavior change will need to be evaluated for their effectiveness with a variety of groups as well as across disorders.

REFERENCES

Andersen, K., Launer, L. J., Dewey, M. E., Letenneur, L., Ott, A., Copeland, J. R., . . . Hofman, A. (1999). Gender differences in the incidence of AD and vascular dementia: The EURODEM Studies. EURODEM Incidence Research Group. *Neurology, 53*(9), 1992–1997.

Anderson, P. D., Williams, I. C., & Gibson, B. E. (2002). Issues of race, ethnicity, and culture in caregiving research: A 20-year review (1980–2000). *The Gerontologist, 42*(2), 237.

Azad, N. A., Al Bugami, M., & Loy-English, I. (2007). Gender differences in dementia risk factors. *Gender Medicine, 4*(2), 120–129.

Barnes, L., L., Wilson, R. S., Bienias, J. L., Schneider, J. A., Evans, D. A., & Bennett, D. A. (2005). Sex differences in the clinical manifestations of Alzheimer disease pathology. *Archives of General Psychiatry, 62*(6), 685.

Becker, J. B., Monteggia, L. M., Perrot-Sinal, T. S., Romeo, R. D., Taylor, J. R., Yehuda, R., & Bale, T. L. (2007). Stress and disease: Is being female a predisposing factor? *Journal of Neuroscience, 27*(44), 11851–11855.

Bloss, E. B., Morrison, J. H., & McEwen, B. S. (2011). Stress and aging: A question of resilience with implications for disease. In C. D. Conrad (Ed.), *The handbook of stress: Neuropsychological effects on the brain* (pp. 349–366). New York, NY: Wiley-Blackwell.

Bolla-Wilson, K., Robinson, R. G., Starkstein, S. E., Boston, J., & Price, T. R. (1989). Lateralization of dementia of depression in stroke patients. *American Journal of Psychiatry, 146*(5), 627–634.

Brown, C. M., Choi, E., Xu, Q., Vitek, M. P., & Colton, C. A. (2008). The APOE4 genotype alters the response of microglia and macrophages to 17beta-estradiol. *Neurobiolology of Aging, 29*(12), 1783–1794.

Bushnell, C. D. (2008). Stroke and the female brain. *Nature Clinical Practice Neurology, 4*(1), 22(12).

Bushnell, C. D. (2011). Depression and the risk of stroke in women: An identification and treatment paradox. *Stroke, 42*(10), 2718–2719.

Campion, D., Dumanchin, C., Hannequin, D., Dubois, B., Belliard, S., Puel, M., . . . Frebourg, T. (1999). Early-onset autosomal dominant Alzheimer disease: prevalence, genetic heterogeneity, and mutation spectrum. *American Journal of Human Genetics, 65*(3), 664–670.

Centers for Disease Control and Prevention. (2007a). *Leading causes of death by age group, all females—United States.* Retrieved from http://www.cdc .gov/women/lcod/07_all_females.pdf

Centers for Disease Control and Prevention. (2007b). Prehospital and hospital delays after stroke onset—United States, 2005–2006. *Morbidity and Mortality Weekly Report, 56,* 474–478.

Centers for Disease Control and Prevention. (2008). Awareness of stroke warning symptoms—13 states and the District of Columbia, 2005. *Morbidity and Mortality Weekly Report, 57,* 481–485.

Centers for Disease Control and Prevention. (2011). *National Vital Statistics Reports.* Retrieved from http://www.cdc.gov/nchs/data/statab/lewk3_ 2007.pdf

Christian, A. H., Rosamond, W., White, A. R., & Mosca, L. (2007). Nine-year trends and racial and ethnic disparities in women's awareness of heart disease and stroke: An American Heart Association national study. *Journal of Womens Health 16*(1), 68–81.

Corder, E. H., Ghebremedhin, E., Taylor, M. G., Thal, D. R., Ohm, T. G., & Braak, H. (2004). The biphasic relationship between regional brain senile plaque and neurofibrillary tangle distributions: Modification by age, sex, and APOE polymorphism. *Annals of the New York Academy of Sciences, 1019*(1), 24–28.

Covinsky, K. E., Eng, C., Lui, L. Y., Sands, L. P., Sehgal, A. R., Walter, L. C., . . . Yaffe, K. (2001). Reduced employment in caregivers of frail elders: Impact of ethnicity, patient clinical characteristics, and caregiver characteristics. *Journal of Gerontolology: Medical Science, 56*(11), M707–M713.

Craig, M. C., Brammer, M., Maki, P. M., Fletcher, P. C., Daly, E. M., Rymer, J., . . . Murphy, D. G. (2010). The interactive effect of acute ovarian suppression and the cholinergic system on visuospatial working memory in young women. *Psychoneuroendocrinology, 35*(7), 987–1000.

Członkowska, A., Ciesielska, A., Gromadzka, G., & Kurkowska-Jastrzębska, I. (2006). Gender differences in neurological disease. *Endocrine, 29*(2), 243–256.

Dennis, M. P., Hauck, W. W., Winter, L., Hodgson, N., & Gitlin, L. N. (2010). Targeting and managing behavioral symptoms in individuals with dementia: A randomized trial of a nonpharmacological intervention. *Journal of the American Geriatrics Society, 58*(8), 1465.

Di Carlo, A., Lamassa, M., Baldereschi, M., Pracucci, G., Basile, A. M., Wolfe, C. D., . . . European BIOMED Study of Stroke Care Group. (2003). Sex differences in the clinical presentation, resource use, and 3-month outcome of acute stroke in Europe: Data from a multicenter multinational hospital-based registry. *Stroke, 34*(5), 1114–1119.

Diomedi, M., Cupini, L. M., Rizzato, B., Ferrante, F., Giacomini, P., & Silvestrini, M. (2001). Influence of physiologic oscillation of estrogens on cerebral hemodynamics. *Journal of the Neurological Sciences, 185*(1), 49–53.

Doraiswamy, P. M., Bieber, F., Kaiser, L., Krishnan, K. R., Reuning-Scherer, J., & Gulanski, B. (1997). The Alzheimer's Disease Assessment Scale: Patterns and predictors of baseline cognitive performance in multicenter Alzheimer's disease trials. *Neurology, 48*(6), 1511–1517.

Duara, R., Barker, W. W., Lopez-Alberola, R., Loewenstein, D. A., Grau, L. B., Gilchrist, D., . . . St. George-Hyslop, S. (1996). Alzheimer's disease: Interaction of apolipoprotein E genotype, family history of dementia, gender, education, ethnicity, and age of onset. *Neurology, 46*(6), 1575–1579.

Elgh, E., Lindqvist Astot, A., Fagerlund, M., Eriksson, S., Olsson, T., & Näsman, B. (2006). Cognitive dysfunction, hippocampal atrophy and glucocorticoid feedback in Alzheimer's disease. *Biological Psychiatry, 59*(2), 155–161.

Elixhauser, A., & Jiang, H. J. (2006). *Hospitalizations for women with circulatory disease, 2003: HCUP statistical brief no. 5.* Retrieved from http://www .hcup-us.ahrq.gov/reports/statbriefs/sb5.pdf

Espeland, M. A., Shumaker, S. A., Limacher, M., Rapp, S. R., Bevers, T. B., Barad, D. H., . . .

Resnick, S. M. (2010). Relative effects of tamoxifen, raloxifene, and conjugated equine estrogens on cognition. *Journal of Women's Health, 19*(3), 371–379.

Fiedorowicz, J. G., He, J., & Merikangas, K. R. (2011). The association between mood and anxiety disorders with vascular diseases and risk factors in a nationally representative sample. *Journal of Psychosomatic Research, 70*(2), 145–154.

Fleisher, A., Grundman, M., Jack, C. R., Jr., Petersen, R. C., Taylor, C., Kim, H. T., . . . Alzheimer's Disease Cooperative Study. (2005). Sex, apolipoprotein E epsilon 4 status, and hippocampal volume in mild cognitive impairment. *Archives of Neurology, 62*(6), 953–957.

Ford, E. S., Ajani, U. A., Croft, J. B., Critchley, J. A., Labarthe, D. R., Kottke, T. E., . . . Capewell, S. (2007). Explaining the decrease in U.S. deaths from coronary disease, 1980–2000. *The New England Journal of Medicine, 356*(23), 2388–2398.

Fukumoto, N., Fujii, T., Combarros, O., Kamboh, M. I., Tsai, S. J., Matsushita, S., . . . Kunugi, H. (2010). Sexually dimorphic effect of the Val66-Met polymorphism of BDNF on susceptibility to Alzheimer's disease: New data and meta-analysis. *American Journal of Medical Genetics. Part B, Neuropsychiatric Genetics, 153B*(1), 235–242.

Gargano, J. W., & Reeves, M. J. (2007). Sex differences in stroke recovery and stroke-specific quality of life: Results from a statewide stroke registry. *Stroke, 38*(9), 2541–2548.

Gaugler, J. E., Kane, R. L., Kane, R. A., Clay, T., & Newcomer, R. (2003). Caregiving and institutionalization of cognitively impaired older people: Utilizing dynamic predictors of change. *The Gerontologist, 43*(2), 219–229.

Gaugler, J. E., Kane, R. L., Kane, R. A., & Newcomer, R. (2005). Unmet care needs and key outcomes in dementia. *Journal of the American Geriatrics Society, 53*(12), 2098–2105.

Gaugler, J. E., Yu, F., Krichbaum, K., & Wyman, J. F. (2009). Predictors of nursing home admission for persons with dementia. *Medical Care, 47*(2), 191–198.

Gouva, L., & Tsatsoulis, A. (2004). The role of estrogens in cardiovascular disease in the aftermath of clinical trials. *Hormones, 3*(3), 171–183.

Grady, D., Rubin, S. M., Petitti, D. B., Fox, C. S., Black, D., Ettinger, B., . . . Cummings, S. R. (1992). Hormone therapy to prevent disease and prolong life in postmenopausal women. *Annals of Internal Medicine, 117*(12), 1016–1037.

Green, R. C., Cupples, L. A., Kurz, A., Auerbach, S., Go, R., Sadovnick, D., . . . Farrer, L. (2003). Depression as a risk factor for Alzheimer disease: The MIRAGE study. *Archives of Neurology, 60*(5), 753–759.

Hackett, M. L., Yapa, C., Parag, V., & Anderson, C. S. (2005). Frequency of depression after stroke: A systematic review of observational studies. *Stroke, 36*(6), 1330–1340.

Haines, C., Chung, T., Chang, A., Masarei, J., Tomlinson, B., & Wong, E. (1996). Effect of oral estradiol on Lp(a) and other lipoproteins in postmenopausal women. A randomized, double-blind, placebo-controlled, crossover study. *Archives of Internal Medicine, 156*(8), 866–872.

Hanefeld, M., Koehler, C., Gallo, S., Benke, I., & Ott, P. (2007). Impact of the individual components of the metabolic syndrome and their different combinations on the prevalence of atherosclerotic vascular disease in type 2 diabetes: The Diabetes in Germany (DIG) study. *Cardiovascular Diabetology, 6*, 13.

Hashimoto, M., Akishita, M., Eto, M., Ishikawa, M., Kozaki, K., Toba, K., . . . Ouchi, Y. (1995). Modulation of endothelium-dependent flow-mediated dilatation of the brachial artery by sex and menstrual cycle. *Circulation, 92*(12), 3431–3435.

Helmer, C., Joly, P., Letenneur, L., Commenges, D., & Dartigues, J. F. (2001). Mortality with dementia: Results from a French prospective community-based cohort. *American Journal of Epidemiology, 154*(7), 642–648.

Henderson, V. W., & Buckwalter, J. G. (1994). Cognitive deficits of men and women with Alzheimer's disease. *Neurology, 44*(1), 90–96.

Isbir, T., Agachan, B., Yilmaz, H., Aydin, M., Kara, I., Eker, E., & Eker, D. (2001). Apolipoprotein-E gene polymorphism and lipid profiles in Alzheimer's disease. *American Journal of Alzheimer's Disease and Other Dementias, 16*(2), 77–81.

Janssen, I., Powell, L., Jasielec, M., Matthews, K., Hollenberg, S., Sutton-Tyrrell, K., & Everson-Rose, S. A. (2012). Progression of coronary artery calcification in black and white women: Do the stresses and rewards of multiple roles matter? *Annals of Behavioral Medicine, 43*(1), 39–49.

Karasek, R., Baker, D., Marxer, F., Ahlbom, A., & Theorell, T. (1981). Job decision latitude, job demands, and cardiovascular disease: A prospective study of Swedish men. *American Journal of Public Health*, 71(7), 694–705.

Kawas, C., Resnick, S., Morrison, A., Brookmeyer, R., Corrada, M., Zonderman, A., . . . Metter, E. (1997). A prospective study of estrogen replacement therapy and the risk of developing Alzheimer's disease: The Baltimore Longitudinal Study of Aging. *Neurology*, 48(6), 1517–1521.

Kearney, P. M., Whelton, M., Reynolds, K., Muntner, P., Whelton, P. K., & He, J. (2005). Global burden of hypertension: Analysis of worldwide data. *Lancet*, 365(9455), 217–223.

Keating, N. L., Cleary, P. D., Rossi, A. S., Zaslavsky, A. M., & Ayanian, J. Z. (1999). Use of hormone replacement therapy by postmenopausal women in the United States. *Annals of Internal Medicine*, 130(7), 545–553.

Kelly, J. F., Bienias, J. L., Shah, A., Meeke, K. A., Schneider, J. A., Soriano, E., & Bennett, D. A. (2008). Levels of estrogen receptors alpha and beta in frontal cortex of patients with Alzheimer's disease: Relationship to Mini-Mental State Examination scores. *Current Alzheimer Research*, 5(1), 45–51.

Kessler, R. C., McGonagle, K. A., Swartz, M., Blazer, D. G., & Nelson, C. B. (1993). Sex and depression in the National Comorbidity Survey, Part I: Lifetime prevalence, chronicity and recurrence. *Journal of Affective Disorders*, 29(2–3), 85–96.

Kittner, S. J., Stern, B. J., Feeser, B. R., Hebel, R., Nagey, D. A., Buchholz, D. W., . . . Wozniak, M. A. (1996). Pregnancy and the risk of stroke. *The New England Journal of Medicine*, 335(11), 768–774.

Krause, D. N., Duckles, S. P., & Pelligrino, D. A. (2006). Influence of sex steroid hormones on cerebrovascular function. *Journal of Applied Physiology*, 101(4), 1252–1261.

Kuklina, E. V., Tong, X., Bansil, P., George, M. G., & Callaghan, W. M. (2011). Trends in pregnancy hospitalizations that included a stroke in the United States from 1994 to 2007: Reasons for concern? *Stroke*, 42(9), 2564–2570.

Kumari, M., Badrick, E., Chandola, T., Adler, N. E., Epel, E., Seeman, T., Kirschbaum, C., & Marmot, M. G. (2010). Measures of social position and cortisol secretion in an aging population: Findings from the Whitehall II study. *Psychosomatic Medicine*, 72(1), 27–34.

Lett, H. S., Blumenthal, J. A., Babyak, M. A., Sherwood, A., Strauman, T., Robins, C., & Newman, M. F. (2004). Depression as a risk factor for coronary artery disease: Evidence, mechanisms, and treatment. *Psychosomatic Medicine*, 66(3), 305–315.

Lisabeth, L. D., Beiser, A. S., Brown, D. L., Murabito, J. M., Kelly-Hayes, M., & Wolf, P. A. (2009). Age at natural menopause and risk of ischemic stroke: The Framingham Heart Study. *Stroke*, 40(4), 1044–1049.

Low, C. A., Thurston, R. C., & Matthews, K. A. (2010). Psychosocial factors in the development of heart disease in women: Current research and future directions. *Psychosomatic Medicine*, 72(9), 842–854.

Lupien, S. J., de Leon, M., de Santi, S., Convit, A., Tarshish, C., Nair, N. P., . . . Meaney, M. J. (1998). Cortisol levels during human aging predict hippocampal atrophy and memory deficits. *Nature Neuroscience*, 1(1), 69–73.

Lupien, S. J., Lecours, A. R., Schwartz, G., Sharma, S., Hauger, R. L., Meaney, M. J., & Nair, N. P. (1996). Longitudinal study of basal cortisol levels in healthy elderly subjects: Evidence for subgroups. *Neurobiology of Aging*, 17(1), 95–105.

Maki, P. M., Freeman, E. W., Greendale, G. A., Henderson, V. W., Newhouse, P. A., Schmidt, P. J., . . . Soares, C. N. (2010). Summary of the National Institute on Aging-sponsored conference on depressive symptoms and cognitive complaints in the menopausal transition. *Menopause*, 17(4), 815–822.

Manly, J. J., & Mayeux, R. (2004). Ethnic differences in dementia and Alzheimer's disease. In N. B. Anderson, R. A. Bulatao, & B. Cohen (Eds.), *Critical perspectives on racial and ethnic differences in health in late life*. Washington DC: National Academies Press.

Martignoni, E., Costa, A., Sinforiani, E., Liuzzi, A., Chiodini, P., Mauri, M., . . . Nappi, G. (1992). The brain as a target for adrenocortical steroids: Cognitive implications. *Psychoneuroendocrinology*, 17(4), 343–354.

Matthews, K. A., Kuller, L. H., Sutton-Tyrrell, K., & Chang, Y. F. (2001). Changes in cardiovascular risk factors during the perimenopause and postmenopause and carotid artery atherosclerosis in healthy women. *Stroke*, 32(5), 1104–1111.

Mayeux, R. (2003). Epidemiology of neurodegeneration. *Annual Review of Neuroscience*, *26*, 81–104.

McEwen, B. S., & Alves, S. E. (1999). Estrogen actions in the central nervous system. *Endocrine Reviews*, *20*(3), 279–307.

McEwen, B. S., Alves, S. E., Bulloch, K., & Weiland, N. G. (1997). Ovarian steroids and the brain: Implications for cognition and aging. *Neurology*, *48*(5, Suppl. 7), S8–S15.

Mosca, L., Barrett-Connor, E., & Wenger, N. K. (2011). Sex/gender differences in cardiovascular disease prevention: What a difference a decade makes. *Circulation*, *124*(19), 2145–2154.

Mosca, L., Benjamin, E. J., Berra, K., Bezanson, J. L., Dolor, R. J., Lloyd-Jones, D. M., . . . Wenger, N. K. (2011). Effectiveness-based guidelines for the prevention of cardiovascular disease in women—2011 update: A guideline from the American Heart Association. *Circulation*, *123*(11), 1243–1262.

Mosca, L., Linfante, A. H., Benjamin, E. J., Berra, K., Hayes, S. N., Walsh, B. W., . . . Simpson, S. L. (2005). National study of physician awareness and adherence to cardiovascular disease prevention guidelines. *Circulation*, *111*(4), 499–510.

Mosca, L., Mochari, H., Christian, A., Berra, K., Taubert, K., Mills, T., . . . Simpson, S. L. (2006). National study of women's awareness, preventive action, and barriers to cardiovascular health. *Circulation*, *113*(4), 525–534.

Noyes, B. B., Hill, R. D., Hicken, B. L., Luptak, M., Rupper, R., Dailey, N. K., & Bair, B. D. (2010). Review: The role of grief in dementia caregiving. *American Journal of Alzheimer's Disease and Other Dementias*, *25*(1), 9–17.

Nussbaum, R. L., & Ellis, C. E. (2003). Alzheimer's disease and Parkinson's disease. *New England Journal of Medicine*, *348*(14), 1356–1364.

Ory, M. G., Hoffman, R. R., 3rd, Yee, J. L., Tennstedt, S., & Schulz, R. (1999). Prevalence and impact of caregiving: A detailed comparison between dementia and nondementia caregivers. *The Gerontologist*, *39*(2), 177–185.

Osterlund, M. K. (2010). Underlying mechanisms mediating the antidepressant effects of estrogens. *Biochimica et Biophysica Acta*, *1800*(10), 1136–1144.

Ownby, R. L., Crocco, E., Acevedo, A., John, V., & Loewenstein, D. (2006). Depression and risk for Alzheimer disease: Systematic review, meta-analysis, and metaregression analysis. *Archives of General Psychiatry*, *63*(5), 530–538.

Pan, A., Okereke, O. I., Sun, Q., Logroscino, G., Manson, J. E., Willett, W. C., . . . Rexrode, K. M. (2011). Depression and incident stroke in women. *Stroke*, *42*(10), 2770–2775.

Pan, A., Sun, Q., Okereke, O. I., Rexrode, K. M., & Hu, F. B. (2011). Depression and risk of stroke morbidity and mortality: A meta-analysis and systematic review. *JAMA*, *306*(11), 1241–1249.

Paradiso, S., & Robinson, R. G. (1998). Gender differences in poststroke depression. *Journal of Neuropsychiatry and Clinical Neurosciences*, *10*(1), 41–47.

Parks, S. M., & Novielli, K. D. (2000). A practical guide to caring for caregivers. *American Family Physician*, *62*(12), 2613–2622.

Pericak-Vance, M. A., & Haines, J. L. (1995). Genetic susceptibility to Alzheimer disease. *Trends in Genetics*, *11*(12), 504–508.

Petrea, R. E., Beiser, A. S., Seshadri, S., Kelly-Hayes, M., Kase, C. S., & Wolf, P. A. (2009). Gender differences in stroke incidence and poststroke disability in the Framingham Heart Study. *Stroke*, *40*(4), 1032–1037.

Pike, C. J., Carroll, J. C., Rosario, E. R., & Barron, A. M. (2009). Protective actions of sex steroid hormones in Alzheimer's disease. *Frontiers in Neuroendocrinology*, *30*(2), 239–258.

Poynter, B., Shuman, M., Diaz-Granados, N., Kapral, M., Grace, S. L., & Stewart, D. E. (2009). Sex differences in the prevalence of post-stroke depression: A systematic review. *Psychosomatics*, *50*(6), 563–569.

Reeves, M. J., Bushnell, C. D., Howard, G., Gargano, J. W., Duncan, P. W., Lynch, G., . . . Lisabeth, L. (2008). Sex differences in stroke: Epidemiology, clinical presentation, medical care, and outcomes. *Lancet Neurology*, *7*(10), 915–926.

Resnick, S. M., Espeland, M. A., An, Y., Maki, P. M., Coker, L. H., Jackson, R., . . . Women's Health Initiative Study of Cognitive Aging Investigators. (2009). Effects of conjugated equine estrogens on cognition and affect in postmenopausal women with prior hysterectomy. *Journal of Clinical Endocrinology and Metabolism*, *94*(11), 4152–4161.

Roger, V. L., Go, A. S., Lloyd-Jones, D. M., Benjamin, E. J., Berry, J. D., Borden, W. B., . . . Turner, M. B. (2012a). Executive summary:

Heart disease and stroke statistics—2012 update: A report from the American Heart Association. *Circulation*, *125*(1), 188–197.

Roger, V. L., Go, A. S., Lloyd-Jones, D. M., Benjamin, E. J., Berry, J. D., Borden, W. B., . . . Turner, M. B. (2012b). Heart disease and stroke statistics—2012 update: A report from the American Heart Association. *Circulation*, *125*(1), e2–e220.

Rossouw, J. E., Anderson, G. L., Prentice, R. L., LaCroix, A. Z., Kooperberg, C., Stefanick, M. L., . . . Writing Group for the Women's Health Initiative Investigators. (2002). Risks and benefits of estrogen plus progestin in healthy postmenopausal women: Principal results from the Women's Health Initiative randomized controlled trial. *JAMA*, *288*(3), 321–333.

Ryan, J., Carriere, I., Scali, J., Ritchie, K., & Ancelin, M. L. (2008). Lifetime hormonal factors may predict late-life depression in women. *International Psychogeriatrics*, *20*(6), 1203–1218.

Sapolsky, R. M., Krey, L. C., & McEwen, B. S. (1983). The adrenocortical stress-response in the aged male rat: Impairment of recovery from stress. *Experimental Gerontology*, *18*(1), 55–64.

Schulz, R., & Beach, S. R. (1999). Caregiving as a risk factor for mortality: The Caregiver Health Effects Study. *JAMA*, *282*(23), 2215–2219.

Schulz, R., & Martire, L. M. (2004). Family caregiving of persons with dementia: Prevalence, health effects, and support strategies. *American Journal of Geriatric Psychiatry*, *12*(3), 240–249.

Seeman, T. E., McEwen, B. S., Singer, B. H., Albert, M. S., & Rowe, J. W. (1997). Increase in urinary cortisol excretion and memory declines: MacArthur studies of successful aging. *Journal of Clinical Endocrinology and Metabolism*, *82*(8), 2458–2465.

Seshadri, S., Beiser, A., Kelly-Hayes, M., Kase, C. S., Au, R., Kannel, W. B., & Wolf, P. A. (2006). The lifetime risk of stroke: Estimates from the Framingham Study. *Stroke*, *37*(2), 345–350.

Shepherd, J. E. (2001). Effects of estrogen on congnition mood, and degenerative brain diseases. *Journal of the American Pharmacological Association*, *41*(2), 221–228.

Shumaker, S. A., Legault, C., Kuller, L., Rapp, S. R., Thal, L., Lane, D. S., . . . Coker, M. H. (2004). Conjugated equine estrogens and incidence of probable dementia and mild cognitive impairment in postmenopausal women: Women's

Health Initiative Memory Study. *JAMA*, *291*(24), 2947–2958.

Shumaker, S. A., Legault, C., Rapp, S. R., Thal, L., Wallace, R. B., Ockene, J. K., . . . Wactawski-Wende, J. (2003). Estrogen plus progestin and the incidence of dementia and mild cognitive impairment in postmenopausal women: The Women's Health Initiative Memory Study: A randomized controlled trial. *JAMA*, *289*(20), 2651–2662.

Siegrist, J., Peter, R., Junge, A., Cremer, P., & Seidel, D. (1990). Low status control, high effort at work and ischemic heart disease: Prospective evidence from blue-collar men. *Social Science Medicine*, *31*(10), 1127–1134.

Sinforiani, E., Citterio, A., Zucchella, C., Bono, G., Corbetta, S., Merlo, P., & Mauri, M. (2010). Impact of gender differences on the outcome of Alzheimer's disease. *Dementia and Geriatric Cognitive Disorders*, *30*(2), 147.

Smith, M. A., Lisabeth, L. D., Bonikowski, F., & Morgenstern, L. B. (2010). The role of ethnicity, sex, and language on delay to hospital arrival for acute ischemic stroke. *Stroke*, *41*(5), 905–909.

Sowers, J. R. (2004). Diabetes in the elderly and in women: Cardiovascular risks. *Cardiology Clinics*, *22*(4), 541–551, vi.

Sundermann, E. E., Maki, P. M., & Bishop, J. R. (2010). A review of estrogen receptor alpha gene (ESR1) polymorphisms, mood, and cognition. *Menopause*, *17*(4), 874–886.

Taylor, S. E., Klein, L. C., Lewis, B. P., Gruenewald, T. L., Gurung, R. A., & Updegraff, J. A. (2000). Biobehavioral responses to stress in females: Tend-and-befriend, not fight-or-flight. *Psychological Review*, *107*(3), 411–429.

Teri, L., Gibbons, L. E., McCurry, S. M., Logsdon, R. G., Buchner, D. M., Barlow, W. E., . . . Larson, E. B. (2003). Exercise plus behavioral management in patients with Alzheimer disease: A randomized controlled trial. *JAMA*, *290*(15), 2015–2022.

Thies, W., & Bleiler, L. (2011). 2011 Alzheimer's disease facts and figures. *Alzheimers and Dementia*, *7*(2), 208–244.

Thombs, B. D., Bass, E. B., Ford, D. E., Stewart, K. J., Tsilidis, K. K., Patel, U., . . . Ziegelstein, R. C. (2006). Prevalence of depression in survivors of acute myocardial infarction. *Journal of General Internal Medicine*, *21*(1), 30–38.

Towfighi, A., Saver, J. L., Engelhardt, R., & Ovbiagele, B. (2007). A midlife stroke surge among women in the United States. *Neurology, 69*(20), 1898–1904.

Tsutsumi, A., Kayaba, K., Kario, K., & Ishikawa, S. (2009). Prospective study on occupational stress and risk of stroke. *Archives of Internal Medicine, 169*(1), 56–61.

Turner, E. C., & Kinsella, B. T. (2010). Estrogen increases expression of the human prostacyclin receptor within the vasculature through an ERalpha-dependent mechanism. *Journal of Molecular Biology, 396*(3), 473–486.

Vitaliano, P. P., Zhang, J., & Scanlan, J. M. (2003). Is caregiving hazardous to one's physical health? A meta-analysis. *Psychological Bulletin, 129*(6), 946–972.

Weissman, M. M., Bland, R., Joyce, P. R., Newman, S., Wells, J. F., & Wittchen, H. U. (1993). Sex differences in rates of depression: Cross-national perspectives. *Journal of Affective Disorders, 29*(2–3), 77–84.

Whitson, H. E., Landerman, L. R., Newman, A. B., Fried, L. P., Pieper, C. F., & Cohen, H. J. (2010). Chronic medical conditions and the sex-based disparity in disability: The Cardiovascular Health Study. *The Journals of Gerontology. Series A, Biological Sciences and Medical Sciences, 65*(12), 1325–1331.

Williams, L. S., Kroenke, K., Bakas, T., Plue, L. D., Brizendine, E., Tu, W., & Hendrie, H. (2007). Care management of poststroke depression: A randomized, controlled trial. *Stroke, 38*(3), 998–1003.

Wilson, R. S., Arnold, S. E., Schneider, J. A., Kelly, J. F., Tang, Y., & Bennett, D. A. (2006). Chronic psychological distress and risk of Alzheimer's disease in old age. *Neuroepidemiology, 27*(3), 143–153.

Wilson, R. S., Arnold, S. E., Schneider, J. A., Li, Y., & Bennett, D. A. (2007). Chronic distress, age-related neuropathology, and late-life dementia. *Psychosomatic Medicine, 69*(1), 47–53.

Wilson, R. S., Schneider, J. A., Boyle, P. A., Arnold, S. E., Tang, Y., & Bennett, D. A. (2007). Chronic distress and incidence of mild cognitive impairment. *Neurology, 68*(24), 2085–2092.

Wolfson, C., Wolfson, D. B., Asgharian, M., M'Lan, C. E., Ostbye, T., Rockwood, K., & Hogan, D. B. (2001). A reevaluation of the duration of survival after the onset of dementia. *New England Journal of Medicine, 344*(15), 1111–1116.

Wragg, R., & Jeste, D. (1989). Overview of depression and psychosis in Alzheimer's disease. *American Journal of Psychiatry, 146*(5), 577–587.

Yaffe, K., Blackwell, T., Gore, R., Sands, L., Reus, V., & Browner, W. S. (1999). Depressive symptoms and cognitive decline in nondemented elderly women: A prospective study. *Archives of General Psychiatry, 56*(5), 425–430.

Yaffe, K., Fox, P., Newcomer, R., Sands, L., Lindquist, K., Dane, K., & Covinsky, K. E. (2002). Patient and caregiver characteristics and nursing home placement in patients with dementia. *JAMA, 287*(16), 2090–2097.

Yaffe, K., Haan, M., Byers, A., Tangen, C., & Kuller, L. (2000). Estrogen use, APOE, and cognitive decline: Evidence of gene-environment interaction. *Neurology, 54*(10), 1949–1954.

Yaffe, K., Sawaya, G., Lieberburg, I., & Grady, D. (1998). Estrogen therapy in postmenopausal women: Effects on cognitive function and dementia. *JAMA, 279*(9), 688–695.

Zerwic, J., Hwang, S. Y., & Tucco, L. (2007). Interpretation of symptoms and delay in seeking treatment by patients who have had a stroke: Exploratory study. *Heart and Lung: The Journal of Acute and Critical Care, 36*(1), 25–34.

Zillmer, E., Spiers, M. V., & Culbertson, W. C. (2008). *Principles of neuropsychology* (2nd ed.). Belmont, CA: Thomson/Wadsworth.

Author Index

Aaronson, N. K., 505
Abascal, L., 190
Abbey, A., 106, 362
Abboud, L., 375
Abdel-Nasser, A. M., 540
Abel, G., 106
Abel, G. G., 289
Abeles, R. P., 51
Aberg, H., 234
Abernethy, A. P., 544
Abetew, D., 228
Abma, J. C., 294, 356, 358, 359, 360, 371
Abraham, S., 181
Abraído-Lanza, A. F., 541, 542, 548
Abram, K. M., 482
Abramowitz, J. S., 398
Abrams, D. B., 112, 134, 135, 137, 138
Abrams, K., 476
Abramson, E. E., 182
Abukhalil, I. E., 320
Abusief, M. E., 496
Acevedo, A., 586
Acierno, R. E., 106
Adams, D., 391, 422
Adams, K. J., 268
Adams, L. F., 314
Adams, S. G., 544
Adamson, P. A., 205
Adler, N. E., 35, 37, 369, 370, 371
Adlis, S. A., 162
Adzick, N. S., 357
Affleck, G., 548
Afzal, A., 527
Aganoff, J. A., 318
Agar, E., 478
Agee, J. D., 548
Agewall, S., 257
Aggarwal, R., 291
Aggen, S. H., 103
Agha-Hosseini, M., 319
Agosti, F., 158
Agras, A., 173, 175
Agras, S., 176, 188
Agras, W., 187, 189
Agrawal, A., 103, 518
Ahijevych, K. L., 134
Ahlbom, A., 584
Ahles, T. A., 495
Ahluwalia, J. S., 127, 128
Ahrens, C. E., 35

Ahuja, K. K., 376, 377
Ainsworth, B. E., 266
Airas, L., 572
Ajani, U. A., 269
Ajzen, I., 29
Akinnusi, M., 243
Akinnusi, O., 243
Akman, D., 514, 517
Alanen, A., 572
Alarcon, G. S., 541, 542
Alba, L. E., 205
Albanes, D., 260
Albarracin, D., 29
Albert, M. S., 585
Albertini, R. S., 214
Alberton, S., 557
Al Bugami, M., 583
Alexander, C., 129
Alexeenko, L., 399
Alfano, C. M., 502
Algoe, S. B., 548
Ali, A., 523
Ali, E. I., 540
Allegier, E. R., 292
Allegrante, J., 545
Allemand, H., 523
Allen, A., 134, 186, 188, 189
Allen, E. D., 7, 8
Allen, M., 374
Allen, N. E., 99, 100
Allen, R. P., 228
Allen, S. S., 134
Allen, T. D., 52
Allender, J. R., 215
Allison, D. B., 154
Al-Marzouk, R., 311
Aloi, J. A., 379
Aloia, M., 242
Alper, M., 350
Alpers, D. H., 526
Al-Shammri, S., 572
Alsuwaidan, M. T., 264
Altabe, M., 182
Altekruse, S. F., 496
Altemus, M., 419, 420
Altshuler, L. L., 393, 397, 420
Alvarez, H., 444
Alves, S. E., 588, 589
Alvidrez, J., 405
Amaro, H., 31, 33, 34, 295
Amato, P., 360

Ambrosone, C. B., 126
American Academy of Pediatrics (AAP), 230
American Association of People with Disabilities (AAPD), 469
American Cancer Society (ACS), 125, 492
American College of Obstetricians and Gynecologists (ACOG), 356, 357, 371, 372, 375, 389
American College of Sports Medicine, 259
American Diabetes Association, 259
American Institute for Cancer Research, 100
American Pregnancy Association, 356
American Psychiatric Association (APA), 96–97, 98, 102, 173, 176, 177, 178, 240, 306, 389, 390, 392, 395
American Psychological Association (APA), 472, 485
American Sleep Disorders Association (ASDA), 228, 240
American Society for Reproductive Medicine (ASRM), 360, 375
American Society of Plastic Surgeons (ASPS), 199, 200, 203, 204, 205, 208, 209, 210, 211, 214
Amland, P. F., 210
Amos, A., 124
An, C. A., 234
Ancelin, M. L., 587
Ancoli-Israel, S., 495
Anders, T. F., 402
Andersen, A., 174, 372
Andersen, B. L., 494, 496
Andersen, K., 582, 583
Andersen, O., 570
Andersen, R. E., 160
Anderson, A., 441
Anderson, B., 494
Anderson, C. J., 469
Anderson, C. L., 102
Anderson, C. S., 594
Anderson, E. E., 213
Anderson, G. F., 494
Anderson, J. W., 158
Anderson, K. D., 424
Anderson, K. M., 330
Anderson, N. B., 37

Anderson, P. D., 595
Anderson, R. R., 212
Andrasik, F., 565
Andreoli, L., 540
Andres, R., 181
Andrews, F. M., 362
Andrews, G., 521
Andrews, J. L., 371
Andrieu, N., 418
Andrulonis, P. A., 515
Andrykowski, M. A., 499, 500
Angst, J., 315
Answer, U., 229
Anthenelli, R. M., 106
Anton, R. F., 113
Antoni, M. H., 491, 499, 500, 505
Antony, M. M., 519
Aouizerate, B., 214
Apovian, C., 159
Apple, F. S., 526
Apple, R., 3
Apps, M. C. P., 155
Aral, S., 296
Aranda, S., 455
Arata, C. M., 291
Archenholtz, B., 543, 545
Arck, P. C., 340
Arena, P. L., 506
Arendt, J., 236, 241
Arent, S. M., 264
Argyle, N., 404
Argyriou, A. A., 572
Arias, E., 375
Armar, N. A., 376
Armitage, R., 224, 227, 394
Arms, S., 17
Armstrong, D., 374
Armstrong, M. L., 212
Arndt, S., 399
Arnett, P. A., 570
Arnold, S. E., 587
Arnow, B. A., 522
Arntz, A., 373
Aronoff, M. S., 311
Arora, N. K., 498
Arora, S., 414, 423, 426
Arriola, K. R. J., 287
Artal, R., 163
Arterburn, D. E., 164
Asch, A., 357
Asdigian, N. L., 67
Ashbrook, D., 314
Ashing-Giwa, K. T., 503
Asikainen, T. M., 260
Askren, H. A., 379
Asnis, G. M., 243
Asplund, R., 234
Astin, J., 230, 544
Astrup, A., 159
Atienza, A. A., 56
Atkinson, N. L., 266
Atkinson, W., 526
Attarian, H., 243

Attia, E., 187, 396
Aubrey, J., 185, 284
Audrain-McGovern, J., 130
Augood, C., 337
Augustin, M., 210
Austin, D., 231
Austin, G. L., 526
Austin, M. P., 394, 397, 399
Austin, S., 416
Avery, B., 31
Avery, M. D., 430
Avidan, A. Y., 243
Avidon, I., 226
Avis, N., 234, 445, 449, 452, 453, 497, 503
Ayala, G., 38
Ayanian, J. Z., 589
Ayers, B., 450
Ayyar, L., 243
Ayzac, L., 416
Azad, N. A., 583, 584
Azarbad, L., 257
Azchocke, I., 210
Azocar, F., 405
Azpiroz, F., 517
Azziz-Baumgartner, E., 67

Babor, T. F., 108
Babyak, M. A., 232
Bachevalier, J., 424
Bachman, J. C., 105
Bachrach, C. A., 51
Bachu, A., 46
Back, S. E., 77, 106
Backstrom, T., 311, 314, 315
Badcock, C. A., 520
Bade, T., 134
Bader, K. F., 206
Badger, G. J., 136
Badgett, M. V., 359
Badia, P., 226, 227
Badr, H., 498
Badr, S., 238
Baetens, P., 359
Bagenstos, S. R., 484
Bagiella, E., 420
Bagnall, D., 484
Bagnardi, V., 99, 100
Bailey, B., 7
Bailey, W. C., 126
Bain, C. J., 418
Bair-Merritt, M. H., 77
Baker, A., 238
Baker, D., 47, 584
Baker, F. C., 225, 226, 227, 239
Baker, J. H., 527
Baker, J. L., 206, 417
Baker, S. A., 34
Baker, T. B., 134
Balboa, A., 514
Baldaro, B., 204
Balen, A. H., 331
Ball, J., 187

Ball, K., 163
Ballard, K., 445, 446, 448
Ballor, D. L., 160
Ballou, S. K., 514–538
Balsam, K. F., 287, 289
Baltes, B., 56
Banbury, J., 202, 206
Bancroft, J., 311, 315, 316
Bandura, A., 29, 30
Bankole, A., 369
Banks, S. R., 477
Banks-Wallace, J., 266
Banno, K., 243
Bansil, P., 588
Baracat, E. C., 236, 238
Baratte-Beebe, K., 228
Barber, J. P., 392
Bardwell, W. A., 500
Barghout, V., 514
Barkeling, B., 163
Barker, L. M., 566
Barnes, G. M., 53
Barnes, L. L., 582, 583, 593
Barnett, R. C., 48, 52, 53, 54, 55
Barnett, S., 549
Barr, H. M., 101
Barrah, J. L., 56
Barrera, L., 425
Barrett, J., 390, 399, 404
Barrett-Connor, E., 443, 444, 456, 593, 597
Barron, A. M., 583
Barros, F. C., 127
Barroso, C., 503
Barrowclough, C., 400
Barry, D., 268
Barry, K., 401
Barsky, S., 213
Barsom, S. H., 441
Barth, J., 346
Bartky, S., 184
Bartlett, E. S., 206
Bartlett, S., 542
Bartolozzi, M. L., 560
Baruah, J., 99
Baruch, G. K., 48
Barwick, F. H., 570
Barwick W. J., 213
Bar-Yam, N. B., 426, 430
Basile, K. C., 65, 77
Basnett, I., 484
Bass, M., 22
Bassett, L., 229
Bastiaenen, C., 482
Bates, D. A., 50
Batt, R., 55
Battin, D. A., 416, 430
Baucom, D. H., 503
Bauer, C., 431
Bauer, D. J., 35
Bauer, G., 266
Bauer, J., 187
Baum, J., 540

Bauman, A., 256
Baxter, R. A., 210
Bayer, J. K., 229
Baynard, M. D., 223
Beach, A. M., 159
Beach, S. R., 596
Beadnell, B., 34
Beal, C. C., 570
Beale, S., 205, 206
Bearman, S. K., 181
Beauchaine, T. P., 287
Beaver, K., 498
Beck, C. T., 390, 393, 399, 403, 421
Beck, L. E., 311, 316
Beck, S. H., 55
Becker, A., 183
Becker, G., 350
Becker, H., 573
Becker, J., 106
Becker, J. B., 586
Becker, J. V., 289
Becker, M. H., 29
Becker, W. J., 564
Beckman, L. J., 377, 378
Beckner, W., 544
Beckstrand, M., 206
Beddoe, A. E., 230
Beebe, G. W., 568
Beebe, K. L., 235
Beelen, A., 476
Beeney, J. E., 570
Befort, C., 185
Begum, K. S., 152
Behar, T. A., 213
Behn, B., 448
Beighley, C. M., 521
Bein, E., 38
Beiser, M., 478
Belgrave, F. Z., 477
Belin, T. R., 500
Belkic, K. L., 47
Bell, E., 159
Bell, L., 231
Bell, M., 402
Bell, R. J., 281
Belle, D., 470
Bellipanni, D., 236
Bellizzi, K. M., 503
Benazzi, F., 391, 395
Benedict, R. H., 569
Benjamin, E. J., 594
Benke, I., 584
Bennett, D. A., 587
Bennett, E. J., 520, 525
Bennett, H. A., 391, 392
Bennie, J., 315
Benowitz, N. L., 128, 132, 136
Bensley, L. S., 287
Benson, H., 318
Benson, L. M., 518
Bentley, A., 226
Ben-Tovim, D. I., 173
Benyamini, Y., 348

Ber, R., 377
Berdahl, J. L., 50
Berenson, A. B., 391
Berg, C. A., 545
Berg, C. J., 136
Berga, S. L., 226, 558, 560, 561
Berger, K., 228, 563
Bergfeld, D., 210
Bergin, J. L., 177
Bergner, A., 374
Berkey, C. S., 129
Berkman, L. F., 495, 504
Berkowitz, R. I., 159
Berle, J. O., 391, 399, 400
Berlin, J., 454
Berman, B., 544
Bernal, G., 82
Bernards, S., 102
Bernhard, L. A., 134
Bernier, M. O., 416, 418
Berns, E., 363
Bernstein, D., 318
Bernstein, I. M., 136
Bernstein, L., 261
Bernstein, S. J., 528
Berscheid, E., 474
Bertea, P. C., 312
Bertone-Johnson, E. R., 318
Best, C. L., 106
Bethea, L., 72
Bettencourt, B. A., 506
Bevacqua, M., 20
Beydoun, H. A., 525
Beydoun, M. A., 525
Beyer, R., 374
Beynon, C., 76
Bhagat, R., 213
Bharucha, A. E., 525
Bhat, A. K., 164
Bianchi, P., 236
Bianchi, S. M., 51, 53, 470
Bickerstaffe, A., 476, 482
Biddle-Higgins, J. C., 108
Biederman, K., 225
Bienvenu, O. J., 214
Bigal, M. E., 563
Binart, N., 420
Bingham, A., 295
Birch, L. L., 154
Bird, A. P., 156
Birkeland, K. I., 210
Birnbaum, A. S., 129
Birnel, S., 129
Biro, F., 130
Birt, J., 573
Bish, C. L., 162
Bishop, J. R., 587
Bishop, M., 173
Bittencourt, L. A., 236
Bittencourt, L. R. A., 238
Bixler, E. O., 155, 235, 243
Bjartveit, K., 126
Bjelle, A., 543

Bjorge, T., 256
Bjornstrom, C., 177
Bjorvatn, B., 229
Black, M. C., 68, 288
Black, S. E., 77
Blackburn, G. L., 157
Blair, N., 123
Blair, S. N., 161, 258
Blanchard, E., 519, 520, 527
Blangiardo, M., 99
Blasco-Ros, C., 65, 75
Blazer, D. G., 394, 586
Bleha, J., 336
Bleiler, L., 582, 596
Bliss, D. Z., 525
Blitzer, P. H., 131
Bloch, M., 124, 390
Bloigu, R., 568
Blois-Martin, N., 522
Bloom, J. R., 502
Bloom, K. C., 379
Bloss, E. B., 584, 585, 586
Blow, F., 400, 401
Blum, R. W., 370
Blumenthal, J. A., 264
Blumenthal, J. S., 232
Blundell, J. E., 257
Blyth, E., 376, 377, 378
Blyton, M., 229, 231
Boaz, R. F., 56
Boccia, M. L., 424
Bochner, S., 156
Bock, B. C., 135
Boden, J. M., 129
Bodenheimer, T., 545
Bodurka-Bevers, D., 494
Bogart, L. M., 68
Bogat, G. A., 71
Boggs, M. E., 375
Bogin, B., 444
Bohlken, R. M., 268
Boivin, D. B., 223, 225, 226, 239, 240, 318
Boivin, J., 328, 342, 345, 346, 349
Bole-Feysot, C., 420
Bolge, S. C., 231
Bolks, H. N., 498
Bolla-Wilson, K., 594
Bolten, M., 422
Bolton, M. A., 202, 211
Bond, A. J., 308
Bondevik, G. T., 229
Bongers, I. M. B., 105
Bongers, P. M., 47
Bonikowski, F., 592
Bonner, B. L., 482
Bonnet, M., 223
Bonuck, K. A., 429
Book, H. E., 204
Booth, B. M., 107
Booth, C. M., 495
Booth, M. L., 256
Booth, S., 40

Bootzin, R. R., 224, 226, 238
Bopp, M., 268
Borah, G. L., 204
Borbely, A., 225
Borello-France, D., 572, 573
Borenstein, J., 313
Borges–Dinis, P., 204
Borkenhagen, A., 177, 214
Born, L., 233
Borrelli, B., 135
Borsari, B., 96
Borud, E., 454
Borzekowski, D. L. G., 269
Bos, H., 359, 377
Bosch, P. R., 545
Bosron, W. F., 99
Bossard, N., 416
Boston, J., 594
Bostrom, A., 100
Bottorff, J. L., 136
Botvin, G. J., 129
Boudreau, J., 53
Bouknight, R. R., 504
Bound, J., 469
Bousquet, A., 399
Bowden, S. J., 262
Bower, J. E., 495, 496, 497, 499, 500
Bowers, W., 174
Bowes-Sperry, L., 50
Bowleg, L., 25–45
Bowman-Reif, J., 391
Boxer, A. S., 330, 361
Boyce, P. M., 521
Boyce, W. T., 35
Boyd, C. J., 105, 128
Boyd, S. L., 56
Boyd, T. C., 128
Boyd-Wickizer, J., 108
Boyer, B., 447
Boyle, F., 373, 400
Boyle, G. J., 318
Boyle, J. S., 371
Boynton, R., 448
Brabbins, C. J., 236, 239
Brabin, L., 521
Bracken, M. B., 369
Braden, C. J., 545
Bradley, C. J., 504
Bradley, K. A., 108
Bradshaw, Z., 370
Brady, K. T., 106
Brähler, E., 177, 214
Braley, T. J., 569
Brambilla, D., 450
Branch, L. G., 470
Brand, H. J., 340, 341
Brandenburg, B., 176, 178, 190
Brandenburg, D. L., 308
Brandon, A., 129
Brandon, T., 468
Brandon, T. H. J., 139
Brandsma, L., 177, 182
Brantley, P. J., 544

Brasel, A. M., 524
Brasure, J., 261
Braun, J., 469
Braun-Fahrlander, C., 266
Brawley, O., 491
Bray, G. A., 153, 154, 162
Breiding, M. J., 68
Breitkopf, C. R., 391
Bremer, D. A., 105
Brennan, B. G., 337, 338
Brenner, D. M., 526
Brenner, H., 359
Bresee, J. S., 471
Breslau, N., 557, 558, 561
Breslow, R. A., 99
Brett, K. M., 454
Bretz, R., 53
Brewaeys, A., 359
Bricker, J., 129
Bricou, O., 543
Bridges, R. S., 424
Brienza, R. S., 107
Brier, N., 373, 374
Briere, J., 287
Brimer, L. M., 163
Brinsden, P. R., 377
Brinton, L. A., 205, 207, 215, 260
Britt, D. W., 356
Britt, E., 215
Britton, H. L., 424, 425
Britton, J. A., 260
Britton, J. R., 424, 425
Brkovich, A. M., 329, 349
Broch, L., 229
Brodney, S., 258
Brodt-Weinberg, R., 545
Brody, J., 20, 456
Broekhuizen, M. L. A., 499
Broman, J. E., 241
Bromberger, J. T., 450, 453, 454
Bronfenbrenner, U., 51
Bronnum-Hansen, H., 569
Bronson, D. M., 213
Broocks, A., 332
Brooks-Gunn, J., 129, 181
Broth, M. R., 400
Brown, A., 200, 201, 291
Brown, B., 448
Brown, C., 405
Brown, C. A., 260
Brown, C. M., 590
Brown, E. D., 237, 311
Brown, G. K., 207
Brown, H., 163, 430
Brown, J., 233, 319
Brown, M. A., 316
Brown, M. D., 164
Brown, R. A., 258, 264, 268
Brown, S., 205, 401
Brown, W., 163
Browne, A., 290
Browne, D., 130
Browne, M. A., 404

Brownell, K. D., 155
Browner, I., 238
Brownmiller, S., 18, 20
Brown-Peterside, P., 35
Brownridge, D. A., 482
Bruce, T., 544
Bruera E., 492
Brumberg, J. J., 5, 453
Brush, L. D., 69
Bryan, T. L., 402
Bryant, H. E., 260
Bryant-Stephens, T., 137
Bryce, T. J., 549
Brynhildsen, J., 571
Bryson, S., 187
Brzezinski, A., 241
Buchanan, T., 185
Buchwald, H, 162
Buck, P. O., 106
Buckwalter, J. G., 593
Budd, G. M., 156
Buhlmann, U., 177, 214
Bui, Q. U., 494
Buis, M., 131
Buist, A., 397, 398, 402, 404
Buki, L. P., 503
Bulan, E. J., 210
Bulian, D., 236
Bulik, C., 177, 179, 180, 183, 215
Bulloch, K., 588
Bullock, L., 82
Bulow, C., 374
Buman, M. P., 264
Bundorf, M. K., 361
Bunevicius, R., 316
Bunting, L., 328
Burckhardt, C. S., 543, 545
Burdick, R. S., 227
Bureau of Labor Statistics, 46, 49, 54, 55
Bures, R. M., 359
Burger, H., 232, 441, 442
Burgess, C., 493, 494, 501
Burgess, H. J., 241
Burgoyne, R. W., 208
Burich, M. C., 205, 207
Buring, J. E., 258, 563
Burke, G., 515
Burke, J., 39
Burke, N. J., 491
Burke, R. J., 52, 53
Burkholder, G., 285
Burleson, M. H., 233, 543
Burls, A., 187
Burman, M. L., 108
Burnett, C. K., 527
Burns, C., 178
Burns, D. M., 134
Burns, E., 108
Burr, R. L., 518
Burrows, E., 484
Burrows, G. D., 374
Burrows, L., 543

Burstein, R., 563
Burt, V. K., 390, 392, 395
Burton, J., 447
Burton, S. L., 132
Burton Jones, N., 444
Burvill, P. W., 478
Burwell, R., 183
Buse, D. C., 565
Bush, A. J., 240
Bush, H., 137
Bushnell, C. D., 556, 582, 583, 584, 586, 588, 594
Busse, J.W., 319
Bussone, G., 559, 565
Butler, C. L., 259
Butler, M., 443
Butow, P., 572
Butryn, M. L., 149–172
Byers, A., 590
Byrne, K. J., 158
Byrnes, E. M., 424
Byrnes, M., 453
Byron, K., 51

Caban, M. E., 494
Cacciapaglia, H., 548
Cacciatore, J., 373
Cachelin, F. M., 182
Cadmus, L. A., 262
Caetano, R., 99, 101, 102, 104
Cahill, K., 133
Cai, J. W., 258
Cain, A. C., 373
Cain, K., 515, 517, 518, 520
Caldwell, E. H., 215
Caldwell, J. D., 424
Calfas, K., 265
Calhoun, L. G., 499
Call, V. R. A., 359
Callaghan, W. M., 588
Callen, J., 427
Calnan, M., 549
Calogero, R., 184, 185, 201, 285
Camarigg, V., 52
Camborieux, L., 373
Cameron, O. G., 134
Camilleri, M., 514, 517, 525
Camp, D. E., 130
Camp, P., 126
Campbell, J. C., 71, 72, 73, 74, 75, 77
Campbell, R., 35
Campbell, S., 233, 237, 238, 269
Campbell, W. W., 268
Campion, D., 590
Campos, H. H., 238
Canada, A. L., 496, 497
Canavan, J. B., 519, 520
Canetto, S. S., 391
Cantor, D., 54
Cantwell, R., 390, 391
Caplan, L., 55
Caplan, R. D., 47
Caponnetto, P., 138

Carbonari, J. P., 131
Cardinal, B. J., 574
Carey, M., 287, 441
Carlisle, C. C., 155
Carlos, R. C., 528
Carlson, C. L., 499
Carmelli, D., 131
Carmen, J., 566
Carmichael, A. R., 262
Carmichael, M., 363
Carney, C. E., 130
Carpenter, K. M., 496
Carpenter, M. J., 134
Carr, R., 181
Carr, S., 295
Carrard, I., 156
Carriere, I., 587
Carroll, J. C., 583
Carroll, J. K., 266, 268
Carroll, M. D., 32, 149
Carroll, S. T., 212
Carskadon, M. A., 224, 237
Carson, G., 102
Carson, J. W., 505
Carson, K. M., 505
Carter, C. S., 419, 420
Carter, J., 497
Carter, L., 361
Carver, C. S., 500, 503, 504
Cash, T., 183, 185, 186, 190, 200, 201, 202, 206, 207, 210, 212, 216
Casper, M. J., 7
Caspersen, C. J., 259
Cassella, G., 138
Castelli, W. P., 260
Castro, J. M., 416
Catala-Lopez, F., 568
Catarci, T., 565
Catenacci, V. A., 160
Cathey, C., 184
Caton, D., 16
Caughey, A. B., 163
Cavallo, D. A., 135
Cavazos-Rehg, P. A., 296
Cawley, J., 129
Celentano, D. D., 563
Cella, D., 505
Center, B., 134
Center for Substance Abuse Treatment, 113
Centers for Disease Control and Prevention (CDC), 26, 32, 36, 65, 93, 124, 125, 127, 128, 257, 295, 328, 330, 335, 360, 361, 376, 377, 414, 431, 432, 581, 582, 583, 592
Cepeda-Benito, A., 132
Cernadas, J. M., 425
Certain, L., 131
Cetel, N. S., 320
Cha, W., 454
Chabrol, H., 373
Chakravarty, E. F., 540
Chalela, P., 503

Chaloner, K. M., 55, 419
Chambers, G. M., 361
Chambers, K., 359
Chambers, S., 542
Chambliss, H. O., 264
Chambliss, L. R., 71
Chan, D. K.-S., 50
Chandler, M. C., 151
Chandra, A., 294, 360
Chang, A. M., 315
Chang, C. H., 311
Chang, E., 478
Chang, J., 76, 80
Chang, J. C., 482
Chang, J. Y., 519
Chang, L., 514, 516, 517, 520, 524
Chang, S.-N., 340, 347, 349
Chang, Y., 136, 583
Chanpong, G. F., 480
Chapin, M. H., 469
Charles, V. E., 370
Charnov, E., 444
Charo, R. A., 9
Chatterji, P., 55
Chau, J. P., 315
Chaudron, L. H., 402, 422
Chautart, M. H., 562
Chawla, A., 305, 312
Check, J. H., 334
Chee, W., 453
Chen, B. Y., 334
Chen, C. M., 93, 94, 95, 104
Chen, E., 188
Chen, H., 479
Chen, J. D., 518
Chen, J. T., 31
Chen, N. H., 234
Chen, T.-H., 330, 339
Chen, W. Y., 262, 498
Chen, X., 498
Cheng, Y. W., 163
Chervin, R. D., 569
Cheskin, L. J., 154
Chesler, E., 9, 10
Chesney, M. A., 35
Chessick, C. A., 392, 393, 395
Chetty, U., 206
Cheung, A. M., 496
Cheung, S. F., 50
Chey, W. D., 526
Chiang, J. K., 213
Chiaravalloti, N., 569, 575
Chiasson, M. A., 35
Chikritzhs, T., 100
Child Welfare Information Gateway (CWIG), 286, 363, 364, 365, 366, 379
Chilton, M., 40
Chin, M. H., 107
Chinnaswamy, P., 336, 337
Chiodera, P., 421
Chioqueta, A. P., 520
Chitkara, D. K., 522

Chiu, W. T., 494
Chlan, K. M., 469
Chlebowski, R., 457
Chloe, J. K., 334
Cho, J. H., 314
Choi, E., 590
Choi, H., 368
Choi, H. Y., 213
Choi, I. S., 314
Choi, K. H., 38
Choi, S. S., 393
Choi, W. S., 127
Choi, Y. K., 526
Chong, E. S., 319
Chou, S. P., 102
Chouaf, K. L., 71
Chow, S. Y., 50
Chowdhury, N., 152
Chrisler, J. C., 305
Christens, P., 372
Christensen, K. E., 52
Christensen, S., 494
Christensen, U., 342
Christian, A. H., 592
Christian, G. J., 237
Christiansen, C., 126
Christie, B. R., 264
Christopher, P. J., 111
Christopherson, J. M., 572
Christos, Z. E., 268
Chu, S. Y., 71
Chung, M. C., 478
Chuong, C. J., 225
Ciccarelli, J. C., 377, 378
Ciccetti, D., 400
Cichon, J., 106, 289
Ciesielska, A., 583
Cifu, D. X., 469
Ciorica, D., 356
Cismaru, M., 82
Claman, D. M., 238
Clark, A., 154, 181
Clark, C., 236, 264
Clark, M. M., 130, 135
Clark, R., 55, 424
Clarke, A., 7, 38
Clarke, C. E., 564
Clarkin, J., 311
Clarren, S., 101
Classen, C. C., 291
Clawges, H. M., 229
Clay, T., 595
Clayton, A. H., 519
Cleary, P. D., 589
Clegg, D. J., 257
Clementi, C., 156
Clemons, M., 418
Cleveland, M. B., 526
Clingerman, E., 573
Clinton, A. M., 106
Cloarec, D., 520
Clopton, P., 237
Clowse, M. E. B., 540

Cobb, J., 449
Cobb, S., 47
Cochran, S. D., 31, 33, 34, 37
Cockcroft, D. W., 213
Coddington, C. C., 3rd, 360
Coebergh, J. W., 359, 502
Coelho, H. F., 399, 400
Coffey, P., 295
Coffin, B., 520
Cogan, R., 524
Cohen, H., 523
Cohen, J. L., 213
Cohen, J. W., 156
Cohen, L. J., 480
Cohen, L. M., 130
Cohen, L. S., 214, 311, 312, 391, 393, 405, 420
Cohen, P., 479
Cohen, R. A., 265
Cohen, S., 5, 6, 504, 548
Cohen Silver, R., 477
Cohn, D., 356, 357, 358
Cohn, T., 264
Coker, A. L., 72, 73, 74
Colditz, G. A., 129, 152, 156, 260, 262, 495, 498, 504
Cole, A. K., 129
Cole, E., 28, 37, 38, 447
Cole, J. A., 518
Cole, P., 69, 70
Cole, R. E., 287
Colgan, S. M., 527
Collier, S. R., 260
Collins, B. N., 123–148
Collins, J. A., 328
Collins, P. H., 27
Collins, R. L., 104, 549
Collins, Y., 295
Colón, R. M., 548
Colrain, I. M., 225, 226
Colton, C. A., 590
Colton, T., 205, 207
Colwell, B., 130
Colwell, L. J., 527
Comasco, E., 315
Comer, B., 542
Comet, D., 520
Commenges, D., 582
Committee on Psychosocial Aspects of Child and Family Health, 402, 403
Commons, G. W., 210
Comstock, G., 183
Conboy, L., 350
Conde, A., 397
Conley-Jung, C., 480
Conn, V., 266
Conne-Perreard, E., 399
Conner, P. D., 81
Connolly, A., 430
Connors, G. J., 112
Conoscenti, L. M., 290
Conroy, S. K., 495
Constantinidis, D., 377

Continisio, P., 427
Conwell, Y., 402
Cook, A., 315
Cook, J. W., 129, 130
Cook, L. S., 205
Cook, N. R., 258
Cook, R., 377
Cook-Karr, J., 309
Cooney, N. L., 112
Coontz, S., 46
Cooper, C., 390, 394
Cooper, G. S., 541
Cooper, L. A., 494
Cooper, M. L., 52
Cooper, P., 399, 401
Cooper, Z., 173, 179
Coovert, M., 183
Cope, T., 155
Copeland, A. L., 130, 131
Cople, L., 391
Corcoran, J. R., 478
Corder, E. H., 590, 593
Cordero-Guevara, J., 238
Cordova, M. J., 499
Corey, L. A., 311
Corn, R., 311
Cornelissen, G., 233
Cornuz, J., 138
Corrao, G., 99
Corty, E., 540
Corwin, M. J., 230
Cosgrove, C., 5, 6
Costa, R., 397
Costanzo, E. S., 501
Costanzo, P. R., 156
Coty, M. B., 541
Coulthard, P., 72, 73, 78
Coupland, N. J., 314
Courneya, K. S., 260, 261
Cournot, M., 156
Coury-Doniger, P., 287
Cousineau, T. M., 497
Cousins, S. O., 268
Coventry, S., 233
Coverdale, J. H., 404
Covey, L. S., 135
Covinsky, K. E., 595, 596
Cowchock, F., 374
Cox, J., 393
Cox, S., 363
Cox, W. M., 111
Coyl, D. D., 379
Coyle, P. K., 567, 572
Coyne, J., 451
Coyne, J. C., 498
Craddock, N., 391, 392, 394, 396
Craft, L. L., 264
Craig, A. R., 478
Craig, M. C., 588
Cramer, D. W., 101, 336, 337
Cramer, E., 71
Crane, S. J., 525
Crawford, E., 523

Crawford, L., 225
Crawford, P. B., 130
Crawford, S., 445, 452, 453, 497
Crawford, Y., 212
Creason, N. S., 237
Creed, F., 524, 525, 527
Cremer, P., 585
Cremin, M. C., 446
Crenshaw, K. W., 27, 28
Crerand, C. E., 189, 199–222
Critchlow, D. G., 308, 309
Crocco, E., 586
Croghan, T. W., 494
Cronje, W. H., 321
Cropanzano, R., 53
Crosby, R. D., 93, 97
Crosse, S. B., 482
Crossfield, A., 178
Crow, S., 176, 178, 190, 482
Crowell, M. D., 518, 519, 520, 524
Crowley, S. J., 229
Csikszentmihalyi, M., 284, 548
Cuadraz, G. H., 39
Cuisinier, M., 373
Culbert, J. P., 242
Culbertson, W. C., 583
Cullen, F. T., 68
Culley, L., 348, 349, 350
Culpepper, L., 264
Cummings, S., 443, 444
Cunningham, B. L., 207
Cunningham, L. L., 499
Cunningham, R., 400
Cunradi, C. B., 102
Curran, G. M., 104, 105
Curry, S. L., 540
Curtin, L. R., 32, 149
Cushman, S. W., 155
Cust, A. E., 261
Cutolo, M., 543
Czeisler, C. A., 233, 237
Członkowska, A., 583, 588

Dacey, M., 339
Da Costa, D., 543
Daetwyler, C., 373
D'Agostino, R. B., 156
Dahinten, S., 136
Dahl, J., 572
Dai, X., 422
Dainese, R., 526
Daley, A. J., 262, 264
Dally, P., 182
Daltveit, A. K., 572
Daly, J., 446
D'Amico, D., 559, 565
Dammers, P. M., 544
Dan, A. J., 315
Danaceau, M. A., 314
Dancet, E. A. F., 360
Dancey, D. R., 238
D'Andrea, G., 563
Danforth, K. N., 418

Dang, K. S., 127
Dang, Q., 67
D'Angelo, D. V., 71
Daniels-Brady, C., 450
Danoff-Burg, S., 499, 500, 539–555
Dapoigny, M., 520
Darby, L., 426, 430
Dare, C., 186
Dartigues, J. F., 582
Dauphinee, L. A., 370
Davidson, D., 315
Davidson, J. R., 241, 242
Davidson, M. H., 161, 376
Davies, P. T., 400
Davila, Y., 77
Davis, C. G., 477
Davis, D. A., 69, 70
Davis, D. L., 374
Davis, J. J., 126
Davis, K., 27, 40
Davis, M., 400
Davis, M. C., 548
Davis, M. M., 295
Davis, M. W., 419
Davis, N. S., 230
Davis, P. M., 515
Davis, R. B., 154
Davis, S., 281, 454
Davison, K. K., 154
Davison, S. L., 281
Dawson, D., 105, 110, 238, 527
Day, L. E., 129
deArruda Alves, M. C., 205
DeBlasis, T. L., 231
de Bock, G. H., 494
de Boer, A. G., 499
De Bourdeaudhuij, I., 256
Debouverie, M., 567
De Carne, M., 526
Décary, A., 238, 243
De Castro, J., 174
Deeks, A., 163
Degner L. F., 492
De Graauw, K., 373
de Gucht, V., 544
De Haro, L., 205
de Heck, H., 416
Deiter, P. J., 285, 293
DeJong, W., 34, 295
DeJoseph, J. F., 237
Dekel, R., 517
DeKeseredy, W., 65
de Klerk, C., 345
DeKonnick, J., 225, 227
Delaney, J., 305
de Lange, A. H., 47
De Lazzari, F., 526
Del Castillo, D., 523
Delclos, G. L., 49
de Leon, J., 130
Delfs, T. M., 227
Delinsky, S. S., 201
Deliramich, A. N., 289

Dellea, P. S., 156
Delles, H., 311
Delongis, A., 546
De Lorenzo, A., 257
del Rincon, I., 542
DeLuca, G. C., 567
Deluca, J., 569, 575
Delva, J., 131
Delvaux, M., 523
Dement, W. C., 224, 237
D'Emilio, J., 19
Demina, T. L., 568
Demler, O., 494
Demm, S. R., 483
Dempsey, A. F., 295
Dempsey, D., 136
Dempsey, J. C., 259
Dempster-McClain, D., 54
Denis, P., 523, 566
Dennerstein, I., 232, 233
Dennerstein, L., 319, 441, 442, 450
Denning, P., 36
Dennis, C. L., 421, 422, 423
Dennis, E. H., 514
Dennis, J., 264
Dennis, M., 205, 596
Denny, C. H., 107
Depka, L., 545
deProsse, C., 494
DeRidder, P. H., 526
de Rooij, D. J., 546
Derry, G., 442
Derry, P. S, 440–463
Desai, R., 311, 312
De Somsubhra, S., 152
de Tommaso, M., 560
de Tonkelaar, I., 330
Detre, T., 421
Dettwyler, K. A., 429
Deuster, P. A., 419
Devlin, M., 189
de Vries, B., 561
Dewey, K. G., 426
Dezhkam, M., 177
de Zwaan, M., 189
Dhand, R., 227
Dhavale, H. S., 519
Dhillon, P. K., 332
Diamond, D., 373
Diamond, J., 179
Diamond, M., 71, 373, 558
Dias, M. B., 266
Dias, T., 357
Diaz, F. J., 130
Diaz, P. T., 126
Diaz, R. M., 38
DiBiase, R., 424
Di Carlo, A., 591, 592
DiCesare, J., 515
Dickey, R. A., 260
Dickson, G., 449
Dickson, H. G., 478
DiClemente, C. C., 29, 30, 131

DiClemente, R. J., 31, 33, 34, 285, 287, 294
Didie, E. R., 201, 206, 215
Diego, M., 399, 422
Diehr, P., 164
Dieter, J. N., 400
Dietz, W., 156, 416
Dijk, D., 225, 233, 237
Dijkstra, P. U., 496
Di Leo, V., 526
Dillaway, H., 431, 440–463
Dillerud, E., 210
DiMatteo, M. R., 494
Dimidjian, S., 392, 393, 395
Dimmock, P. W., 318
Dimoulas, P., 133
DiNenno, E., 36
Dinges, D. F., 223, 224
Dinis, M., 204
Dinsmore, L., 130
Diomedi, M., 588
Dion, K., 474
DiPalma, J. A., 526
Dirks, D., 285
DiSantis, K. I., 127
Dishman, R. K., 264
Ditschuneit, H. H., 160
Dixon, J. B., 155
Dixon, K. E., 544
Djordjevic, M., 213
Doan, T., 229
Dobie, D. J., 523
Dobkin, P. L., 544
Dobkin, R. D., 235
Dobson, A. J., 126
Dobson, R., 568
Dodick, D., 562
Doherty, P. C., 424
Doka, K. J., 379
Doldren, M. A., 287
Doll, H., 173
Domar, A. D., 236, 318, 328–354, 363, 497
Dominiguez, T. P., 375
Donat, P. L. N., 19
Donnelly, J. E., 257
Doraiswamy, P. M., 589
Dorheim, S. K., 229
Dorn, J., 261
Dorval, M., 498
Doshi, A., 265
Doucet, S., 397
Douglas, J. M., 294
Douglas-Newman, K. R., 556–580
Douma, M. E., 431
Dowdall, G. W., 102
Dowdy, S. W., 544
Downey, G., 396
Downing, J. B., 366
Downing-Matibag, T. M., 29
Downs, L. S., 295
Downs, S., 126
Downs, W. R., 105

Dowson, A. J., 559
Dowzer, C., 527
Drabble, L., 104
Dransfield, M. T., 126
Drasgow, F., 50
Drennan, J., 443
Driscoll, R., 181, 182
Driver, H., 225, 226, 227, 239, 243
Driver, S., 477
Droomers, M., 131
Drosdzol, A., 312
Drossman, D. A., 514, 515, 517, 519, 520, 521, 522, 523, 527
Drum, C. E., 482
Duara, R., 590
Dube, E., 235
Dubois, J., 69
Duckett, L., 430
Duckitt, K., 337
Duckles, S. P., 588
Dudley, C. R., 526
Dudley, D. R., 80
Dudley, E. C., 232
Duel, L. A., 206
Duff, S., 496
Duffy, J. F., 233, 237
Duffy, J. N., 517
Dufour, M. C., 95
Dugan, S. A., 152
Duhig, A. M., 135, 573
Duijts, S. F. A., 505
Duivenvoorden, H. J., 493
Dulhane, J. F., 372
Dulloo, A. G., 155
Duncan, G. J., 104
Duncan, W. C., 225
Duncombe, D., 181
Dunivan, G. C., 525
Dunkle, K. L., 35
Dunn, A. L., 264
Dunn, D., 48, 375
Dunn, E., 233
Dunn, L. B., 502
Dunofsky, M., 202
Duntley, S., 243
Duquette, P., 567
Durand, M. A., 188
Durrence, H. H., 240
Duru, O. K., 267
Dutton, M. A., 72, 73, 75
Duxbury, L., 54
Dworkin, S. L., 31, 33
Dwyer, D. J., 47
Dwyer, K. A., 544
Dyard, F., 520
Dye, L., 163
Dyer, K. A., 373
Dzaja, A., 223, 228, 237

Eakin, E. G., 265
Earls, M. F., 402, 403, 404
Eastman, C. I., 241
Eastwood, S., 571

Eaton, D., 68, 255
Eaton, W. W., 48
Eaves, L. J., 103
Ebama, M. S., 99
Eberhard-Gran, M., 229
Ebers, G. C., 567
Echeverría, S. E, 542
Eckhardt, C., 82
Edelmann, R. J., 377, 378
Edelsberg, J., 156
Edery, M., 420
Edgerton, M., 208
Edhborg, M., 422
Edinger, J., 232
Edlund, M. J., 107
Edwards, N., 229, 231
Eenwyk, J. V., 287
Efthimiou, P., 545
Eggert, J., 101
Ehrhardt, A. A., 31, 33
Eichenbaum, E., 355–388
Einarson, A., 391
Einarson, T. R., 391
Einstein, M. H., 295
Eisenberg, D. M., 454
Eisenberg, M. L., 363
Eisler, I., 186
Ekselius, L., 339
Ekstrom, B., 446
Elavsky, S., 264
El-Danasouri, I., 334
Elfstrom, M. L., 477
Elgh, E., 585
Elia, M., 526
Elias, M. F., 156
Elias, P. K., 156
Elifson, K. W., 294
Elixhauser, A., 591
Elkind, M. S. V., 100
Elliot, M. N., 68
Elliott, A., 540
Elliott, D. M., 287
Elliott, T. R., 478
Ellis, C. E., 590
Ellis, D., 54
Ello-Martin, J. A., 159
Ellwood, D., 400
Elmore, K., 174
Elmore, M., 398
El-Sabbagh, S., 75
Elsenbruch, S., 518
Else-Quest, N. M., 424, 425
El-Solh, A. A., 243
Elson, J., 454
Elston, M. A., 445
Elta, G. H., 525
Ely, A. V., 149–172
Emanuele, M. A., 101
Emanuele, N. V., 101
Emmott, S., 527
Emond, J. A., 262
Empey, D. W., 155
Endicott, J., 309, 318

Engeland, A., 256
Engelhard, I. M., 373
Engelhardt, R., 588
Engels, R., 128
Engfeldt, P., 101
England, P., 104
Engle-Friedman, M., 238
Englert, Y., 359
Enquobahrie, D., 228
Ensink, B., 289
Epperson, C. N., 306
Epperson, N. C., 392
Epping-Jordan, J. E., 504
Epstein, J. N., 106
Epstein, L. H., 160, 547
Erath, S., 132
Ercolani, M., 204
Eriksen, M., 123
Erikson, M., 373
Erikson, P., 237
Eriksson, M., 257
Eriksson, O., 314
Erkkola, R., 240
Ernst, C., 264
Ernst, E., 545
Escalante, A., 542
Eschenbach, D., 296
Escobedo, C., 316
Esiri, M. M., 567
Espeland, M. A., 589
Esposito, K., 154
Essex, M. J., 55
Etnier, J. L., 264
Ettner, S. L., 51
Eugster, A., 362
European Study Group on
    Heterosexual Transmission of
    HIV, 294
Evans, B., 374, 474
Evans, C. D. H., 373, 374
Evans, D. L., 207
Evans, H. H., 19
Evans, J., 391, 392
Evans, L., 243
Evans, M. I., 356, 367
Evans, S. M., 14, 15
Eveloff, S. E., 155
Evenson, K. R., 258
Eversley, R., 496
Evindar, A., 421
Evins, G. G., 390, 402
Ewart, C. K., 131

Faber, M. M., 505
Fabian, C., 497
Fadyl, J. K., 469
Fagan, P., 124, 128
Fahrenholz, F., 415, 416
Fainman, D., 374
Fairburn, C., 173, 177, 178, 179, 187,
    188, 189, 191
Fairley, B. W., 266
Faith, M. S., 154

Fallowfield, L. J., 505
Fanslow, J. L., 65, 66
Farah, C. S., 212
Faramarzi, M., 343, 344
Faravelli, C., 214
Farber, R. S., 573
Farmer, A., 81
Farndale, R., 515
Farr, J. L., 55
Farrell, E., 319
Farrow, C. V., 156
Farup, P. G., 518
Fast, I., 373
Faulkner, G., 262, 263, 264
Faulkner, S. A., 453
Fausto-Sterling, A., 22
Fava, J. L., 159
Favaro, A., 177
Fay, C., 214
Featherstone, M., 446
Feder, L., 82
Federal Interagency Forum on Aging
    Related Statistics, 56
Federal Register, 457
Fedigan, L., 444
Feinleib, M., 46, 260, 470
Feld, A. D., 522
Feldman, R., 424
Feldman, Z. L., 107
Fendrick, A. M., 528
Fenner, D. E., 525
Fentiman, I., 233
Fenwick, R., 54
Fergerson, S. S., 422
Fergusson, D. M., 129
Fernander, A., 124, 137
Fernandez, A., 162
Fernandez Liguori, N., 572
Ferns, G. A., 233
Ferrara, A., 470
Ferrara, S., 177
Ferreira, L. M., 205
Ferrette, V., 238
Ferris, M., 52
Feskanich, D., 260, 262
Fiala, T. G., 207
Fichter, M., 178
Fiedorowicz, J. G., 586
Field, A. E., 129
Field, T., 397, 399, 400, 421
Fife, D., 228
Fifield, J., 548
Figueiredo, B. C., 397
Fihn, S. D., 164
Fillmore, K., 100
Filonenko, A., 312
Fine, J. T., 156, 164
Finer, L. B., 294, 295, 368, 370
Finkelhor, D., 67, 290
Finkelstein, E. A., 156
Finlayson, F. E., 478
Finn, L., 231, 238, 243
Finney, J. W., 111

Finney Rutten, L. J., 498
Finstad, D., 134
Fiona, J., 454
Fiore, M. C., 132, 134, 136
Fiorentino, L., 495
Fiscella, K., 287
Fischer, A., 185, 284
Fischer-Betz, R., 540
Fishbein, M., 29
Fisher, B. S., 68
Fisher, J. R., 363
Fisher, T. A., 570
Fisher, W. A., 329, 349
Fitzgerald, L. F., 50
FitzGerald, L. Z., 517
FitzGerald, M., 315
Fitzgibbon, M., 178
Fjeldsoe, B. S., 266
Flango, C., 363
Flango, V., 363
Flasher, L., 548
Flater, S., 187
Flaws, J. A., 233
Flay, B. R., 128, 129
Flechtner-Mors, M., 160
Flegal, K. M., 32, 149
Fleisher, A., 590
Fleiss, P. M., 416
Fleming, A., 390, 399, 404, 420
Fleming, M. F., 108, 111
Fletcher, J. C., 356
Flett, G. L., 420
Fleurence, R., 573
Flitter, J. M. K., 291
Flowers, L., 295
Floyd, R., 101
Flynn, B. S., 131
Flynn, H. A., 389–413
Foeldenyi, M., 315
Foley, C. C., 482
Foley, D., 231, 236
Foley, F. W., 572
Foley, K., 241
Folkman, S., 35, 504, 548
Follette, V. M., 287, 288, 290
Fong, D., 82
Fong, S. Y., 240
Fontaine, K. R., 154
Fontana, A. M., 311, 316
Fontes, L., 70
Food and Drug Administration (FDA),
    457
Forbes, G., 173, 185
Ford, A. C., 525, 526
Ford, C. A., 296
Ford, D. E., 241
Ford, E. S., 269, 416, 417, 420, 582
Ford, K., 29
Fore, M. E., 31, 38
Foreman, D., 393
Forest, G., 227
Foreyt, J. P., 158
Forman, J., 406

Forns, M., 287
Forshaw, M., 450
Forster, J. L., 162
Fortenberry, R. M., 287
Fortier, M. S., 256, 257
Forty, L., 390, 395
Foshe, V. A., 82
Foster, D. G., 369
Foster, G. D., 159
Foster, K., 371
Foubert, J. D., 299
Foulds, J., 133
Fowler, J., 496
Fox, J. A., 66, 67
Fox, S., 265
Frackiewicz, E. J., 318
Franche, R.-L., 374
Francis, A., 309
Francis, C. Y., 517
Francomb, H., 391
Frank, D., 525, 528
Frank, E., 311, 391
Frank, R. G., 478
Franklin, M., 189, 214
Franklin, T. R., 134
Franko, D. L., 175, 339
Franks, M. M., 56
Frantzich, C. R., 430
Fraser, C., 571, 574
Fraser, J. S., 81
Frazier, A. L., 129
Frederich, R. C., 158
Frederick, D. A., 173
Frederick, I. O., 228, 515
Fredrickson, B., 181, 184, 185, 284,
    548
Fredrikson, M., 315
Freedman, R., 232, 451
Freedman, R. R., 233
Freeman, E., 451
Freeman, E. W., 231, 233, 311, 318,
    319, 320, 330, 361, 454
Freeman, J., 494
Freeman, K., 429
Freeman, M. E., 416, 420
Freeman, R., 179
Freeman, S. K., 8, 9
Freizinger, M., 339
French, J. R., 47
Frese, M., 48
Freudenheim, J., 261
Freund, K. M., 264
Friberg, M., 422
Fried, R. G., 210
Friedberg, F., 545
Friedenreich, C. M., 260, 261
Friedman, K. E., 156
Friedman, P. D., 107
Friedman, R., 236, 311, 316
Friedrich, M., 519
Friend, K. B., 112
Frier, H. I., 160
Fries, J. F., 545

Frings-Dresen, M. H. W., 499
Froberg, D. G., 419
Froen, J. F., 373
Frohwirth, L. F., 370
Frone, M. R., 52, 53
Frost, J. J., 295
Fry, J. P., 266
Frye, V., 35
Fryzek, J. P., 205
Fu, S., 265
Fugh-Berman, A., 236
Fuh, J. L., 562
Fujimoto, V. Y., 346
Fukudo, S., 516
Fukumoto, N., 590
Fulcher, G., 572
Fuller-Tyszkiewicz, M., 173–198
Fumi, A. L., 526
Furnham, A., 200
Futterman, L. A., 320

Gabe, J., 445
Gable, R. K., 390, 403
Gabriel, D. C., 212
Gabriel, S. E., 207
Gaffey, A. E., 491
Gaillard, T., 268
Gair, S., 366
Gale, S., 390, 394
Galinsky, E., 52
Gallagher, K. I., 160
Gallant, S. J., 72
Galler, J. R., 422
Galli, F., 557
Galliani, E. A., 526
Gallicchio, L., 233
Galliven, E., 419
Gallo, L. C., 502
Gallo, S., 584
Galtry, J., 427, 428
Galvez, G., 82
Galvin, S. L., 390
Gamble, D., 430
Gammon, M. D., 260
Gan, W., 126
Gander, P. H., 228
Gannon, L., 445, 446
Ganster, D. C., 47, 53
Ganz, P. A., 496, 497, 500
Garcia, A. W., 134
Garcia-Espana, B., 454
Gardiner, A., 229
Gardner, D., 64
Gareis, K. C., 54
Garel, M., 368
Garfinkel, L., 153
Gargano, J. W., 591
Garn, S. M., 181
Garner, D., 174, 188
Garretsen, H. F. L., 105
Garrett, C. J., 391
Garrison, R., 48
Garrison, R. J., 260

Garrow, D. J., 11
Garsd, A., 425
Garza, R., 416
Gasperino, J., 125
Gaspi, Y., 478
Gass., M., 444
Gates, G. J., 359, 366
Gau, M. L., 542
Gaudet, C., 373
Gaugler, J. E., 589, 595
Gavaler, J. H., 337
Gavin, A. R., 391
Gavin, N. I., 419
Gay, C. L., 228, 229
Gaydos, G. R., 544
Gaynes, B. N., 390, 391, 394, 402,
    403, 421
Geertzen, J. H., 496
Gefou-Madianou, D., 103
Gehlert, S., 311
Gehrman, C., 139
Gehrman, P., 238
Geiger, T. M., 525
Geiselman, P. J., 131
Geisinger, B., 29
Gelfand, D. M., 400
Gelfand, M. J., 50
Geller, P. A., 355–388
Gellis, L. A., 240
Genkinger, J. M., 100
Genova, H. M., 569
Genuis, M. L., 287
George, M. G., 588
George, W. D., 493
Georgiopoulos, A. M., 402
Gerald, L. B., 126
Gerardin, P., 400
Gerber Fried, M., 19
Germain, A., 226
Germano, C., 229
Gerrish, W. G., 319
Gerson, K., 47
Gerson, M.-J., 358
Gerzoff, R. B., 259
Gettman, J., 184, 185, 284
Gevirtz, R., 311
Ghanadan, A., 205
Giardini, A., 48
Gibbons, L. M., 205
Giblin, E., 225, 231, 232
Gibofsky, A., 546
Gibson, B. E., 595
Gibson, P. R., 526
Giefer, E. E., 131
Gieniusz, M., 203
Giese, S. Y., 210
Gifford, S., 204
Gigliotti, T., 398
Gilbert, M., 477
Gilbert, P., 443, 445
Giles, W. H., 416
Gilhus, N. E., 572
Gill, S., 478

Gillespie, R., 202
Gillies, G. E., 556
Gillin, C., 237
Gillis, M. M., 556–580
Gilman, S., 183
Gilpin, E. A., 128
Gilrain, K., 232
Gimpl, G., 415, 416
Gingnell, M., 315
Ginneken, V., 151
Ginsberg, E. S., 496
Giovannoni, G., 568
Giovino, G. A., 128
Gitchell, J. G., 132
Gitlin, L. N., 596
Gittelsohn, J., 376
Given, B. A., 498
Gjerdingen, D. K., 55, 419
Glanville, L., 200
Glass, J., 52
Glass, N., 82
Glavac, I., 362
Glazebrook, C., 363
Glia, A., 525
Glover, V., 390, 391, 392, 399, 400, 403, 422, 565
Glueck, C. J., 331
Gmel, G., 99, 102
Go, J. T., 525
Goadsby, P., 560
Gobrogge, K., 180
Godfrey, J. R., 243
Godwin, M., 260
Goffin, V., 420
Goin, J. M., 208
Goin, M. K., 204, 208
Gokee-LaRose, J., 183
Golay, A., 156
Gold, E., 234, 453
Gold, K. J., 375
Gold, L., 187
Gold, P. W., 309, 419
Gold, R. S., 266
Gold, S. D., 291
Goldade, K., 127
Goldbach, K. R., 375
Goldberg, A. E., 365, 366
Goldbloom, D. S., 331
Goldenberg, R. L., 372
Golden-Kreutz, D. M., 502
Golding, J., 289, 290, 391
Golding, M., 132
Golding, J., 392
Goldman, I. B., 204
Goldman, M. B., 101, 336
Goldsmith, G., 518
Goldsmith-Mason, S., 137
Goldstein, D. J., 157
Goldstein, F., 238
Golombok, S., 360, 378
Gomes, A., 204
Gómez, C. A., 283, 295
Gómez-Benito, J., 287

Gonder-Frederick, L., 257
Gonsalkorale, W. M., 527
Gonzalez, C., 331
Gonzalez, L., 362
Gonzalez, V., 255
Gonzalez, V. M., 545
Goodale, I. L., 318
Goode, W. J., 46, 51
Goodlin-Jones, B. L., 291
Goodman, P. E., 71
Goodman, S. H., 400
Goodwin, G., 315
Goodwin, J. S., 494
Goodwin, M. M., 71, 76
Gooneratne, N., 236, 241, 242
Gopal, M., 243
Goran, M. I., 161, 255
Gorczynski, P., 264
Gordon, I., 424
Gordon, J. R., 112
Gordon, L., 11
Gore, C. J., 256
Gorin, A. A., 159
Gorman, P., 477
Gorraiz, M. L., 281–304
Gortmaker, S. L., 34, 295
Gorzkowski, J. A., 470
Goss, P., 418
Gossler, S. M., 392, 401
Gotestam, K. G., 177
Gotman, N., 397, 398
Goursaud, A.-P. S., 424
Gouva, L., 589
Goverover, Y., 575
Goyder, E., 107
Gozlan, M., 348
Grabe, S., 173
Graber, J. A., 129, 181
Grace, S. L., 421
Grady, D., 443, 444, 456, 589
Grady, S. E., 519
Graham, D. P., 523
Graham, K., 102
Graham, S., 261
Graham-Bermann, S., 74, 82
Grambling, S. E., 238
Gramzow, R. H., 369
Granath, F., 207
Grandey, A. A., 53
Grant, B. F., 92, 93, 98, 99, 102, 104, 105, 110, 114, 115
Grant, J. D., 105
Grant, J. E., 214
Grant, M., 20
Grattet, R., 482
Graubard, B. I., 99
Grave, G. D., 431
Gray, J., 402
Gray, M. J., 289
Gray, R., 108
Grazzi, L., 565
Greaney, M. L., 266
Greaves, L., 124

Grebennikov, I., 49
Greco, C. M., 544
Green, A. C., 418
Green, C. A., 107, 110, 418
Green, R., 453, 586, 587
Greenberg, J., 296
Greenblatt, E. M., 376, 377
Greendale, G. A., 497
Greene, G. W., 29
Greenfield, S., 99, 110, 113, 506
Greenfield, T., 107
Greenglass, E. R., 53
Greenlee, T. B., 128
Greenwald, H., 496
Greenwood, K. M., 242
Gregg, E. W., 259, 470
Greif, J., 212
Greil, A. L., 359, 446
Gremore, T. M., 503
Griffin, C., 443, 446, 454
Grigoran, K. E., 173
Grigsby, N., 64, 69, 76, 80, 81
Grilo, C., 186
Grimes, D. A., 373
Grimley, D. M., 285
Grischin, O. V., 264
Grisso, J. A., 454
Grobbee, D. E., 207
Grodstein, F., 101, 336, 337
Groer, M. W., 419
Groff, J. Y., 479
Groh, D. R., 112
Groll, D., 515
Gromadzka, G., 583
Gronwaldt, V., 424, 425
Gros, D. F., 519
Grossbart, T. A., 201
Grote, N. K., 399, 400
Grover, M., 524, 525
Grover, P. L., 127
Grubbs, L., 525
Gruis, M., 419
Grumbach, K., 545
Grunfeld, E., 233, 498
Gruskin, L., 35
Grzywacz, J. G., 51, 53, 55
Gudleski, G. D., 527
Guendelman, S., 427
Guethlein, W., 420
Guidetti, V., 557, 560, 563
Guidi, L., 560
Guier, C., 542, 548
Guilera, G., 287
Guilera, M., 514
Guillaume, L., 107
Guillemin, F., 567
Gulati, M., 258
Gullette, M. M., 445, 454
Gunn, J., 401
Guo, Y., 391
Guo, Y. J., 517
Gupta, M. A., 181, 234
Gupta, P., 124, 234

Guralnik, J. M., 469
Gurtman, M. B., 524
Gurven, M., 444
Gusev, E. I., 568
Gustafson, D. H., 498
Gustavsson, P., 420
Guthrie, E., 524, 525, 527
Guthrie, J. R., 232
Gutierrez, E. R., 19
Gutmanis, I., 76, 77, 79
Gutowski, K. A., 207
Guttmacher Institute, 367
Guttuso, T., 235
Guyatt, G. H., 319
Guyer, B., 375
Gwadz, M., 296

Ha, K., 393
Haaga, D., 402
Haan, M., 590
Haas, T., 369
Haaxma, C. A., 556
Haaz, S., 542
Habermann, B., 54
Hachul, H., 236, 238
Hackett, M. L., 594
Haedt, A., 181
Haennel, R. G., 258
Hagberg, J. M., 164
Hagedoorn, M., 498
Haheim, L. L., 210
Hahn, H. M., 230
Hahn, P. M., 226
Hahn-Holbrook, J., 414–439
Haidar, M., 238
Haiman, C., 187
Haines, C., 588
Haines, J. L., 590
Haines, V. Y., 53
Hains, S. J. M., 260
Halbreich, U., 313, 315, 320
Hale, G., 441, 442
Hall, C., 400
Hall, E. M., 48
Hall, J. E., 65
Hall, M., 228
Hall, P., 181, 182
Hall, W., 136
Hallfors, D. D., 35
Halman, L. J., 362
Halmi, K., 187
Halpern, C. T., 296
Halpert, A., 527
Hambert, G., 206
Hamburg, D. A., 421
Hamburg, P., 183
Hamburger, M. E., 35
Hamby, S., 67
Hamed, H., 233
Hamilton, J. G., 491
Hamilton, S., 527
Hammar, M., 236, 571
Hammarberg, K., 363

Hammarlund-Udenaes, M., 314
Hammen, C., 422
Hammerli, K., 346
Hampton, A., 229
Hampton, S. M., 233
Hampton, T., 539
Han, S., 55, 181
Hanauer, S. B., 524
Hancock, K. M., 478
Handel, N., 207
Hanefeld, M., 584
Hanisch, L., 451
Hankinson, S. E., 262, 318
Hannah, P., 422
Hannover, W., 136
Hans, T. S., 153
Hansen, T., 359
Hantsoo, L., 451
Hanusa, B. H., 390, 398, 401, 405
Haque, S., 392, 394
Hara, C., 319
Harari, D., 525
Hardiman, A., 369
Harlow, B. L., 214, 390, 394
Harlow, L. L., 29, 285, 288
Harlow, S., 440, 441, 442, 449
Harmon, D. M., 212
Harnish, M. J., 518
Harrell, F., 71
Harrington, R., 400
Harris, D. L., 205
Harris, J. R., 179
Harris, K. J., 127
Harris, M. B., 156
Harris, R. J., 156
Harris, T. R., 105
Harrison, K., 185
Harrison, P. J., 187
Harrison, W., 309
Härtl, K., 503
Hartlage, S. A., 308, 309, 311
Hartman, S., 255–277
Hartz, A. J., 152
Hasan, J., 240
Haselton, M., 414–439
Hashimoto, M., 588
Hasin, D. S., 98, 102, 104, 106
Haskell, S. G., 523
Haskett, R. F., 405
Hasler, W. L., 518
Hassold, T., 372
Hatch, E. E., 151
Hatsukami, D. K., 132, 134
Hattery, A. J., 52
Hauck, W. W., 596
Hauck, Y., 431
Haugen, E. N., 397
Hauserman, N., 50
Hausser, J. A., 48
Hawker, G. A., 470
Hawkes, K., 444
Hawkins, A. J., 52
Hawkins, R. P., 498

Hawkinson, K., 427
Hawthorne, V. M., 181
Hay, J. L., 491
Hayashi, T., 316
Hayman, C. R., 20
Haynes, S. G., 46
Hazelwood, L., 238
He, J., 586
Headache Classification Committee of
    the International Headache Society
    (IHS), 557
Hearst, N., 295
Heath, A. C., 103, 311
Heaton, A. W., 162
Hebebrand, J., 179
Hebl, M., 154, 185
Hedeker, D., 129
Hedlund, S., 178
Hedman, C., 227
Hedrick, S. C., 164
Heels-Ansdell, D., 319
Heeren, T., 102
Heidt, J. M., 291
Heil, S. H., 136
Heim, C., 316
Heiman, J. R., 288
Hein, H. O., 126
Heinberg, L., 182, 183
Heinemann, L. A., 312
Heinrich, R., 478
Heinrichs, M., 420
Heitkemper, M., 515, 517, 518, 520,
    523, 524
Heitman, B. L., 154
Heizer, W. D., 526
Helgeson, V. S., 499, 500, 502, 503,
    504, 505, 547, 549
Heller, B. R., 520
Hellhammer, D. H., 422
Helmer, C., 582
Helmerhorst, F. M., 320
Hemmingsson, E., 257
Hemphill, J., 419
Henderson, A. W., 281, 294
Henderson, K. A., 266
Henderson, V. W., 593
Henderson-King, D., 201
Henderson-King, E., 201
Hendrick, V., 393, 420
Henne, J., 38
Henne, M. B., 361
Henningfield, J. E., 133
Henriksen, T. B., 101, 335
Henselmans, I., 501
Henshaw, C., 393, 394
Henshaw, E., 406
Henshaw, S. K., 294, 368, 371
Hensley, J. G., 228
Hensley, L. D., 482
Heo, M., 160
Hepworth, J., 443
Hepworth, M., 446
Herbert, C. A., 288

Herbozo, S., 183, 184
Hering, R., 565
Herman, A. A., 31
Hern, J., 204
Hernandez, R. K., 320
Hernandez-Reif, M., 399, 400
Herold, J., 48
Heron, J., 391, 392, 393, 395, 396, 398
Herrera, B., 128
Hersch, J., 505
Hersh, A., 456
Hershberger, P., 363, 375, 376
Hertig, V., 518
Hertz, M. F., 77
Hertz, R., 58
Hertz, T., 47
Herzog, A., 421
Herzog, D., 178, 183
Hessini, L., 369
Hester, R. K., 108, 112
Hetta, J., 241
Hewitt, C. E., 402
Hewitt, M., 506
Hewitt, R., 54
Hewitt, W., 212
Hewlett, S., 549
Heyman, R. E., 81
Heymen, S., 525
Heymsfield, S. B., 160
Hiatt, R. A., 492
Hickling, E. J., 549
Higgins, C., 54
Higgins, S. T., 136
Hiilesmaa, V., 400
Hill, E. J., 52, 55
Hill, G., 204
Hill, M., 185, 284
Hill, P. D., 425
Himelhoch, S., 494
Hingson, R. W., 102
Hinney, A., 179
Hinterlong, J., 56
Hinton, A., 204
Hinton, P. S., 163
Hippe, M., 126
Hipwell, A., 401
Hiraki, L., 132
Hiripi, E., 178
Hirsch, A. E., 69, 70
Hirsch, J. S., 296
Hiscock, H., 229
Hislop, I. G., 527
Hitkari, J. A., 376, 377
Hitsman, B., 129, 135
Ho, M. G., 124, 442
Ho, S. C., 240
Ho, T., 69
Hoban, M. C., 309
Hochberg, M. C., 544
Hodges, P. W., 517
Hodgson, N., 596
Hoek, H. W., 174
Hoff, J. M., 572

Hoffman, B., 498
Hoffman, H. J., 230
Hoffman, R., 227
Hoffman, R. R., 3rd, 596
Hogue, C. J., 375
Holbert, D., 469
Holbrook, C., 419
Holcombe, G., 496
Holden, C., 528
Holden, S. L., 281
Holder, R., 394
Hollander, E., 186, 188, 189
Hollander, L., 232, 234, 450
Hollis, J. F., 161
Holloway, R., 236
Holman, H., 545
Holman, R. C., 471
Holmes, I. H., 213
Holmes, M. D., 262, 495, 498, 504
Holmes, W. F., 562, 564
Holmgren, P., 66
Holmqvist, P., 571
Holroyd, E., 315
Holstein, B. E., 342
Holt, V. L., 332
Holte, A., 450
Holtrop, J., 125
Holtzman, D., 107
Holtzman, S., 546
Homish, G. G., 105
Hoogduin, K., 373
Hoogendijk, W. J. G., 263
Hooper, P., 444
Hoover, R. N., 207
Hopkins, J., 178
Hopkins, L., 163, 520
Hopkins, M., 257
Hopper, E., 373
Hopper, J. L., 232
Horner-Johnson, W., 482
Hornstein, M. D., 337
Horta, B. L., 127
Horwood, L. J., 129
Hosaka, T., 344
Hosien, H., 205
Hosier, S. G., 111
Hospers, H., 189
Hotujac, L., 311
Houck, J. M., 111
Houghton, L. A., 524
Houry, D., 65, 69
House, A., 82
House, J. S., 47, 48
Houston, M. J., 415
Houtman, I. L., 47
Hovell, M. F., 139, 267
Hovell, M. H., 130
Hoving, J. L., 499
Howard, P., 545
Howard-Anderson, J., 496, 503
Howell, K., 74
Howes, J., 22
Howie, P. W., 415

Howland, C. A., 479, 480, 482
Howlett, E., 443
Howson, L., 484
Hrabosky, J., 190
Hrdy, S., 414, 424
Hsia, J., 457
Hsu, H., 234
Hsu, L., 182
Hu, F. B., 129, 258, 259, 586
Hu, J., 56
Hu, Y. J., 523
Hua, L. P. T., 260
Huang, M. I., 242
Huang, Y., 185
Hudson, J., 178, 179
Hudson, N., 348
Huggins, M. E., 500
Hughes, E. G., 337, 338
Hughes, P., 373, 374
Hughes, P. M., 373, 374
Hughes, R., 479, 482
Hughes, T., 105, 106
Hulin, C. L., 50
Hulme, P. A., 522
Humphreys, C., 69
Humphreys, J., 82
Hungin, A. P., 514, 527
Hunt, L. M., 542
Hunter, G. R., 268
Hunter, J., 296, 526
Hunter, L. P., 229, 362
Hunter, M., 232, 233, 234, 450, 452, 454, 455
Huo, L., 314
Hurford, D. P., 129
Hurling, R., 266, 268
Hurt, S. W., 311
Husky, M. M., 130, 134
Huss, M. T., 64
Hussey, D., 64–87
Huth-Bocks, A. C., 71
Hutti, M., 374
Hutton, R., 238
Hwang, S. Y., 592
Hwang, V. S., 549
Hyams, J. S., 515
Hyde, A., 443, 448, 449
Hyde, J. S., 55, 173, 185, 285, 424
Hylands, T., 156
Hyphantis, T., 524, 527

Iacovides, S.., 225, 226
Iannone, M., 350
Ihlebaek, C., 518
Ikramullah, E., 296
Ikuta, K., 268
Ilies, R., 50
Ilyia, E., 236
Im, E., 453
Inaba, S., 234
Inadomi, J. M., 525
Infield, A. L., 202, 206
Ingleby, J. D., 174

Ingram, C. D., 420
Innes, K., 454
Institute of Medicine (IOM), 95, 101, 114, 163
International Agency for Research on Cancer (IARC), 125, 127, 260
International Headache Society (IHS), 557, 558, 559
Ip, K., 188
Ip, S., 422
Iritani, B. J., 35
Irurita, V., 431
Irvin, J. H., 236
Irvine, D. S., 330
Irwin, C., 523
Irwin, M., 262, 491
Isbir, T., 590
Ishikawa, S., 584
Ishikawa-Takata, K., 257
Isles, R., 265
Iyengar, M., 235
Izumi, S., 344

Jackson, J. S., 37
Jackson, L. C., 397
Jackson, M., 526
Jackson, N., 524
Jackson, P. B., 35
Jackson, R., 107
Jacob, J. I., 55
Jacob, M. C., 360
Jacob, P., 128, 136
Jacob, T., 105
Jacobs, A. R., 369
Jacobs, J. A., 47
Jacobs, P. A., 372
Jacobs, R., 543
Jacobsen, P. B., 500
Jacobsen, P. H., 207
Jacobson, B. J., 228
Jacobson, J. L., 101
Jacobson, S. W., 101
Jadva, V., 378
Jaffe, J., 373
Jagd, M., 206
Jagers, R. J., 542
Jain, D., 565
Jain, S. S., 227
Jain, T., 347, 349
Jakicic, J. M., 160, 257, 265
Jakubowski, M., 563
Jalalmanesh, S., 318
Jalkanen, A., 572
Jamerson, B. D., 132
James, F. O., 223, 239
James, R., 526
James, S. A., 375
James, W. P. T., 162
Jamieson, D. J., 422
Janelsins, M. C., 495
Jang, H. S., 319
Jang, I. S., 314
Janick, J. J., 260

Janicki, D., 499
Janiszewski, P. M., 258
Jankowski, K. R. B., 405
Jansen, A., 189
Jansen, J., 423
Janssen, H., 373, 374
Janssen, I., 152, 585
Janz, N. K., 29, 492, 500, 503
Jarama, S. L., 477
Jarcho, J. M, 173
Jarrett, M., 54, 515, 517, 518, 520, 523, 524
Jarry, J., 188
Jarvis, C. I., 317
Jason, L. A., 112
Javanbakht, M., 205
Javaras, K., 179
Javo, I. M., 211, 215
Jawad, A., 547
Jeffery, J. E., 151, 158, 159
Jeffery, R. W., 155, 160, 162, 165
Jemal, A., 125, 491, 492
Jenness, V., 482
Jennings, J. M., 77
Jennings, K. D., 398
Jensen, G., 82
Jensen, J. A., 207
Jensen, J. R., 360
Jensen, T. K., 127, 338
Jernström, H., 418
Jeste, D., 594, 595
Jette, A. M., 470
Jewell, D. P., 526
Jhangri, G. S., 314
Jiang, H. J., 591
Jick, S., 320
Jim, H. S., 500
Jiménez-Alonso, J., 543
Jimenez-Gomez, A., 238
Jimerson, B., 180
Jin, S. A. A., 265
Jind, L., 375
Jobe, J. B., 255
Jobe, R., 185
Jobin, C., 567, 569
Joffe, H., 311
Joffee, H., 233, 235
Joglekar, A. S., 519
Johannes, C. B., 560
Johansson, P. A., 516
John, E. M., 260
John, U., 228
John, V., 586
Johnsen, L. W., 288
Johnson, A. A., 52
Johnson, B. T., 29
Johnson, C. M., 229
Johnson, D., 82, 527
Johnson, J. C., 574
Johnson, J. L., 136
Johnson, J. V., 48
Johnson, J. W., 11

Johnson, K. C., 127
Johnson, L. M., 548
Johnson, M., 107, 108, 348
Johnson, R. W., 56
Johnson, S. R., 318
Johnson, T., 315, 517
Johnson, W., 175
Johnsson, A., 500
Johnston, L. D., 105
Johnston-Robledo, I., 305
Joiner, T. E., Jr., 208
Jolley, D., 163
Jolly, K., 264
Joly, P., 582
Jones, I., 390, 391, 392, 394, 396
Jones, J., 294, 360, 364, 378
Jones, K. R., 519
Jones, L., 390
Jones, M. P., 519, 521, 524, 527
Jones, N. A., 422
Jones, P., 318, 540
Jones, S., 265
Jonsdottir, D., 135
Jonsdottir, H., 135
Jonsson, E., 101
Jordan, S. J., 418
Jose, A., 68
Joseph, G., 56
Joseph, S., 549
Jou, H. J., 234
Jovanovic, H., 315
Juang, K. D., 562
Juang, K.-D., 330
Juarbe, T., 256
Judelson, D. A., 212
Judge, T., 53
Judicibus, M. A. D., 430
Junge, A., 585
Juraskova, I., 505
Jurgens, T. M., 319

Kadden, R. M., 112
Kadlec, H., 291
Kaestle, C. E., 293, 296, 297
Kahan, T. L., 226
Kahana, E., 568
Kahn, B., 497
Kahn, L. S., 313
Kahn, R. S., 131
Kakuma, R., 416, 417
Kalantar, J. S., 521
Kales, A., 235, 243
Kalfoglou, A. L., 376
Kalinka, C. J., 283
Kallen, R., 184
Kalpakjian, C. Z., 479
Kalsekar, A., 241
Kamal-Bahl, S. J., 156
Kamerow, D. B., 241
Kammermann, S., 268
Kamo, T., 75
Kampert, J. B., 264
Kandel, D. B., 105

Kane, R. A., 595
Kane, R. L., 595
Kane, S. V., 524, 526
Kang, S. H., 502
Kannel, W. B., 260, 470
Kant, A. K., 162
Kanyicska, B., 416
Kaplan, H., 444
Kaplan, L., 18
Kappos, L., 575
Kapsimalis, F., 243
Kaptein, A. A., 320
Karabudak, E., 177
Karacan, I., 225
Karam, E. G., 75
Karasek, R., 47, 584
Kario, K., 584
Karkowski, L. M., 311
Karlen, A, 541
Karling, P., 525
Karlson, E. W., 547
Karuppaswamy, J., 361
Kasen, S., 479
Kashanian, M., 318
Kashy, D. A., 366
Kaskutas, L. A., 113
Kasl, S., 311, 312, 315
Kassett, J. A., 179
Katapodi, M. C., 505
Katbamna, S., 348
Katkin, E. S., 420, 422, 437
Kato, I., 126
Katon, W., 391, 402
Katz, J., 292
Katz, M. H., 38, 40
Katz, P., 361
Katz, R. C., 548
Kaufert, P., 443, 445, 447, 450
Kavanaugh, K., 374, 375
Kawachi, I., 495, 504
Kawas, C., 589
Kawkami, N., 234
Kayaba, K., 584
Kaye, W., 176, 179, 180
Kazlauskaite, R., 152
Kearney, P. M., 583
Keating, N. L., 589
Keefe, F. J., 503, 505, 542, 544, 547
Keefer, L., 514–538
Keel, P., 174, 176, 178, 181
Keenan, N. L., 454
Keery, H., 183
Keita, G. P., 72
Kellett, J., 181
Kelley, G. A., 260
Kelley, M., 82
Kelley, Y. J., 429
Kellow, J. E., 520
Kelly, A., 123, 124
Kelly, E. H., 470
Kelly, J. F., 593
Kelly, L., 181

Kelly, P. A., 420
Kelly, R., 400, 402
Kelly, Y. J., 101
Kelsey, R. M., 420
Kendall-Tackett, K. A., 429
Kendler, K., 179
Kendler, K. S., 103, 311, 313, 527
Kendrick, K. M., 423
Kendzor, D. E., 131
Kenford, S. L., 134
Kennedy, P., 183, 477, 478
Kennedy, S., 305
Kerker, E., 424
Kerns, D., 375
Kerr, W. C., 100
Keshavarzian, A., 518
Keski-Rahkonen, A., 180
Kesmodel, U., 101, 335
Kessler, C., 228
Kessler, R., 178, 230
Kessler, R. C., 103, 130, 394, 494, 586
Key, T. J., 418
Keyes, K. M., 98, 104
Keys, C. B., 112
Keys, S. L., 319
Khachanova, N. V., 568
Kiefer, A. K., 283, 285
Kilby, M. D., 368
Killien, M. G., 54
Kilmann, P. R., 206
Kilpatrick, D. G., 106, 290
Kim, B. G., 314
Kim, D. R., 308, 309
Kim, J. H., 393, 396
Kim, K. T., 213
Kim, M., 319, 356, 358
Kim, S. R., 225
Kim, S. S., 497
Kim, Y., 498
Kimm, S. Y. S., 270
Kimport, K., 371
Kimura, T., 316
Kindrat, S., 573
King, A. C., 264
King, E., 185
King, G., 135, 137
King, L., 361
King, M., 188
King, M. C., 418
King, M. R., 72
King, N. A., 257
King, N. S., 478
King, R. B., 340
King, T. K., 135
King, T. S., 526
Kinkler, L. A., 366
Kinnunen, T., 263
Kinsella, B. T., 588
Kinsey, A. C., 7
Kiravainen, T., 231
Kirby, J. S., 503
Kirby, R., 372
Kirkman, M., 369

Kirkpatrick Pinson, D. M., 570
Kirmeyer, S., 371, 372, 375
Kirshbaum, M., 476
Kirwan, J. R., 545
Kittell, L., 446, 449, 452, 453
Kittner, S. J., 588
Kitzman, H. J., 287, 402
Kiviat, N. B., 295
Kiziltan, G., 177
Kjelsas, E., 177
Kjoller, K., 205, 207
Klaas, S. J., 470
Klap, R., 401
Klapp, B. F., 374
Klassen, A. D., 105, 106
Kleihues, P., 126
Klein, A., 69
Klein, E., 478
Klein, H., 294
Klein, J., 107
Klein, M. H., 55
Klein, S., 55, 210
Kleinman, J. C., 375
Klemp, J., 497
Klerman, J. A., 428
Klerman, L. V., 369
Klesges, R. C., 130, 131
Klier, C. M., 373
Kline, W., 3–24
Klock, S. C., 376, 377
Klonoff-Cohen, H., 331, 336, 337
Kloss, J., 223–254
Klosterman, K., 82
Kluchin, R., 11, 18, 19
Klumb, P. L., 47
Klump, K., 179, 180
Knittle, K., 544
Knobler, H., 32
Knowler, W. C., 157, 158, 259
Knox, K., 34–35
Knudsen, G. P., 556, 567
Knutson, J. F., 482
Ko, C. W., 230
Koblin, B. A., 35
Koch, P. B., 441
Koch, R. J., 210
Koch, T., 571
Kochanek, K. D., 372, 471
Koch-Henricksen, N., 569
Kodama, S., 258
Koehler, C., 584
Koenig, H., 374
Koeske, R., 160
Kohl, H. W., 258, 269
Kohn, M., 47
Kok, G., 189
Kokia, E., 348
Koleva, H., 391, 399
Kolin, I. S., 206
Kolostov, L. S., 429
Kolotkin, R. L., 156
Kolts, B. E., 526
Komaroff, E. A., 130, 132

Komesaroff, P., 446
Kompier, M. A., 47
Kong, Y., 526
Konz, E. C., 158
Koot, V. C., 207
Kopelman, P. G., 153, 154, 155
Kopstein, A., 102
Koren, G., 391
Korenman, S., 443
Kornfield, S. L., 355, 369, 370, 375
Kornstein, S. G., 308, 309
Koropeckyj-Cox, T., 358, 359
Korsnes, S., 525
Kortte, K. B., 477
Korytkowski, M. T., 164
Kos-Kudla, B., 237
Koss, M., 102
Kotlyer, M., 132
Kotsa, K., 260
Koutsky, L. A., 295
Kowal, J., 256
Kozee, H. B., 285
Koziol-McLain, J., 76
Kraaimaat, F. W., 342
Kraemer, C., 188
Kraemer, H., 187, 188
Kraft, J. M., 294
Kraft, N., 526
Kralik, D., 571
Kramer, M. S., 414, 416, 417, 428
Krasner, S., 519
Krasnik, C., 319
Krasovec, K., 415
Krastev, A., 401
Krause, D. N., 588
Krause, J. S., 469
Krause, K. M., 152
Kravitz, H. M., 223, 231, 232, 233, 234, 308
Krawchuk, S. A., 102
Krawczyk, R., 173–198
Kreipe, R. E., 215
Kremer, J. A. M., 342
Kremer, J. M., 548
Kreoleian, C. M., 213
Kreutzer, J. S., 483
Krey, L. C., 585
Krichbaum, K., 589
Krieger, N., 31, 35, 36, 37, 38, 39
Kripke, F. F., 237
Krishnan-Sarin, S., 135
Kristensen, K., 426
Kristjanson, A. F., 93, 97, 104
Krivickas, K. M., 359
Kroenke, C. H., 262, 498, 503
Kroenke, K., 390
Krokki, O., 568
Kronenberg, F., 236
Kruijver, F. P., 239
Krull, E. A., 213
Kryger, M., 223, 242, 243
Krystal, A. D., 232
Kuchera, M. L., 574

Kucyi, A., 264
Kuehn, B. M., 392, 395, 401, 402, 406
Kuhn, B., 242
Kuhn, P., 414
Kukar, M., 545
Kukkonen-Harjula, K., 260
Kuklina, E. V., 588
Kulaga, A., 213
Kulig, A., 91–122
Kuller, L., 590
Kuller, L. H., 583
Kumar, A., 369
Kumar, D., 518
Kumar, R., 396
Kumar, S., 264
Kumari, M., 585
Kump, K., 238
Kung, H., 372
Kunz, D., 233
Kuo, Y. F., 494
Kupfer, D. J., 226, 405
Kuring, J., 185
Kurit, D., 540
Kurki, T., 400
Kurkowska-Jastrzębska, I., 583
Kurth, T., 563
Kurtz, E. S., 229
Kurtzke, J. F., 568, 573
Kustron, D. A., 80
Kutteh, W., 371
Kuypers, J. M., 295
Kuys, S., 265
Kuzelova, H., 315
Kvam, M. H., 482
Kwan, L., 500
Kwo, P. Y., 99

Labbok, M., 415, 416
Labelle, M., 181
Labouvie, E., 106
Lacey, L., 131
LaChina, M., 281
Lackner, J., 519, 521, 524, 527
Ladd-Taylor, M., 431
Laditka, J. N., 259
Laforge, R. G., 29
Lafortuna, C. L., 158
Lam, C. B., 50
Lam, R. W., 227, 264
Lamarche, L., 225, 226, 227
Lamb, S., 296
Lambrou, C., 205
Lam-Kruglick, P., 331, 336
Lampe, J. W., 526
Lampert, C., 179
Lampert, T., 47
Lampl, C., 565
Lancaster, C. A., 373
Lancel, M., 228
Landen, M., 320
Landers, D. M., 264
Landis, C. A., 241
Landsbergis, P. A., 47

Landtblom, A. M., 571
Lane, T., 309
Lang, J., 525
Lang, W., 160
Langenbucher, J. W., 106
Langer, S. L., 521
Langer-Gould, A., 572
Langhorne, P., 478
Lanteri-Minet, M., 562
Lappin, M. S., 566
Larissa, F., 400
LaRocco-Cockburn, A., 402
Larochelle, C., 567
Larowe, S. D., 134
Larsen, U., 294
Larson, S. H., 154
LaRusso, E. M., 399
Lashen, H., 362
Lasker, J., 374, 375
Lasser, K., 130
Laufman, L., 503
Laumann, E. O., 282
Laurent, D. D., 545
Laursen, T. M., 229
Lavack, A., 82
La Vecchia, C., 99
Lavery, M., 496
LaVite, C. M., 50
Lawrence, D., 124
Lazarus, R. S., 504
Lea, R., 524, 527
Lean, E. R., 50
Lean, M. E. J., 153
Leandro, G., 526
Learman, L. A., 289
Leavitt, J. W., 17
Lechner, S. C., 499
Leddy, M., 402
Ledikwe, J. H., 159
Lee, A., 422
Lee, C., 54, 358, 373
Lee, E., 56, 418
Lee, I. M., 258, 260
Lee, K., 50, 223, 228, 229, 230, 232, 237, 242
Lee, M. G., 314
Lee, M. S., 319, 545
Lee, O. Y., 516
Lee, R., 444
Lee, S., 238, 453
Lee, W. P. A., 207
Leermakers, E. A., 160, 161
Leff, M., 391
Legg, M., 68
Lehavot, K., 281, 294
Lehman, A. J., 546
Lehman, D. R., 477
Leibenluft, E., 399
Leiblum, S. R., 361, 362
Leibowitz, A., 428
Leinbach, A. S., 134
Leinster, S. J., 498
Lele, M. V., 519

Le Melledo, J. M., 314
Lemire, F., 258
Leng, M., 267
Lenhart, A., 269
Lentz, M., 232, 241
Leonard, K. E., 105
Leonard, L. M., 288
Lepper, H. S., 494
Lequerica, A. H., 478, 479
Lerant, A., 416
Lerman, C., 134
Leserman, J., 288, 520, 521, 522, 523
Leslie, L. A., 521
Lester, R., 337
Lesur, A., 494
Letenneur, L., 582
Letourneau, A. R., 137
Lett, H. S., 586, 594
Leval, A., 296
Leve, L. D., 379
LeVeau, B., 226
Levendosky, A. A., 71
Levesque, D. A., 29
Levin, A., 205, 206
Levin, B., 525
Levin, J. S., 518
Levin, K., 137
Levine, A., 424
Levine, B. S., 515, 517, 519
Levine, M., 183
Levine, M. D., 131, 135
Levine, M. N., 540
Levinson, P. D., 155
Levitt, J., 176
Levy, A. S., 162
Levy, B. R., 311, 312
Levy, R., 521
Levy, R. L., 520, 521, 522
Levy, S. S., 574
Lewis, B. A., 265
Lewis, D. M., 182
Lewis, F. R., 20
Lexell, J., 573
Li, K. K., 574
Li, Q., 104
Li, R. H., 240
Li, T. K., 99
Li, T. Y., 258
Li, Y., 587
Li, Z., 523
Liamputtong, P., 375
Liao, K., 233, 452, 455
Liao, X., 454
Liauw, S. S., 264
Libbus, M. K., 428
Libby, D. J., 311
Libby, G., 518
Liberman, J., 558
Lichstein, K. L., 240
Lichtenberg, P., 478
Lichtenstein, B., 35
Lichtman, S. W., 160
Liddle, P., 391

Lieber, C. S., 99
Lieberburg, I., 443, 589
Lievers, L. S., 187
Light, K. C., 420, 421
Lightman, S. L., 420
Ligibel, J. A., 268
Lilienthal, K., 91–122
Lilly, M., 82
Limacher, M. C., 258
Lin, B., 518
Lin, H., 231, 233, 320
Lin, H. C., 542
Lin, H. R., 542
Lin, J., 185
Lin, W. C., 542
Lin, X., 442
Linares Scott, T. J., 136
Lindberg, G., 525
Lindberg, S. M., 173, 185
Linden, W., 493
Lindhal, V., 391
Lindsay, J., 12
Lindsay, M., 422
Ling, P. M., 128
Ling, R., 269
Link, B. G., 38, 40
Linke, S., 255–277
Linley, P. A., 549
Linn, L., 204
Linne, Y., 163
Lipton, R. B., 558, 559, 563
Lipworth, L., 207
Lisabeth, L., 442, 588, 592
Lisper, H., 205
Liss, J. R., 334
Listing, J., 469
Litner, J. A., 205
Littleton, H. L., 391, 392, 399
Littman, L. L., 369
Liu, J., 259, 561
Livingston, E. H., 162
Livingston, G., 356, 357, 358
Livingston, J. A., 286
Lloyd, A. K., 81
Lloyd-Jones, D., 258
Lobel, M., 491
Lock, J., 187
Lock, M., 234, 441, 445, 452, 453
Locke, G. R., 514, 521, 526
Lockwood, C. J., 163
Loewenstein, D., 586
Loewy, M., 483
Lofquist, D., 359
Logan, J. R., 56
Logsdon, M. C., 401
Lokeh, A., 207
Lombard, C., 163
Long, P. J., 291
Long, S., 305
Longabaugh, R., 112
Longstreth, G. F., 514, 515, 517, 518
Lonstein, J. S., 419

Look AHEAD Research Group, The, 158
Lopez, A. D., 313
Lopez, L. M., 320
Loree, M., 359
Lorig, K., 545
Lo Sasso, A. T., 56
Loscocco, K. A., 48
Losee, J. E., 215
Lott, B., 36
Lott, P., 314
Louden, T., 287
Louis, S., 567
Loundes, D. D., 424
Love, S., 451
Lovejoy, J. C., 164
Lovelady, C. A., 152
Low, C. A., 499, 584, 585, 586, 587, 594
Low Dog, T., 454, 455
Lowe, M., 149–172, 178
Loy-English, I., 583
Lozoff, B., 230
Lu, S. R., 562
Lubin, J., 205, 207
Lucas, C., 562
Lucas, K., 33
Lude, P., 477
Ludman, E. J., 137
Luedemann, J., 228
Lujan, M. E., 332
Luker, K. A., 498
Lunbeck, E., 7
Lund, R., 342
Lunde, D. T., 421
Lunde, P. K., 426
Lundh, W., 422
Lundkvist, O., 339
Lundy, B. L., 400
Lunn, P., 416
Lunos, S., 134
Luo, Z., 504
Lupien, S. J., 585, 589
Lupton, M. J., 305
Lustig, A. P., 547
Lustyk, M. K., 319
Lycett, E., 378
Lydiard, R. B., 519, 520
Lye, D., 129
Lynch, A. M., 317
Lynch, J., 185
Lyons, A. C., 443, 446, 454

Ma, S., 124
MacArthur, C., 264
MacCallum, F., 360, 378
MacDorman, M. F., 371, 372, 375
Macdougall, M., 311
Macek, M., 315
MacGregor, E. A., 562
Machotka, Z., 264
Mackay, J., 123
Mackenbach, J. P., 131

MacKenzie, C. R., 545
Mackey, S. N., 81
MacMillan, H. L., 76
Macomber, J. E., 359
MacPherson, K., 443
Madaschi, C., 335
Maddalozzo, G. F., 574
Madhusoodanan, S., 399
Maes, S., 544
Maffiuletti, N. A., 158
Magder, L., 296
Magee, L., 199–222
Magill, M., 112
Magley, V. J., 50
Magnan, R. E., 491
Mahajan, N. N., 340
Maher, M. J., 243
Mahlberg, R., 233
Mahoney, J., 571
Mahoney, M. M., 239
Mahony, D., 162
Maier, S. E., 101
Maislin, G., 224
Majerovitz, S. D., 540, 546
Major, B., 369, 370, 371
Maki, P. M., 586, 587
Makino, T., 344
Makris, N., 572
Malagelada, J. R., 517
Malaiyandi, V., 131
Mallett, S., 369
Mallon, L., 241
Malloy, K., 64, 69
Malm, K., 363, 379
Malnick, S. D., 32
Man, S., 126
Man, W., 76
Manber, R., 224, 226, 242
Mandell, J. B., 418
Manfredi, C., 131
Mangione, C. M., 267
Manheimer, E., 334
Mankowski, E. S., 82
Manley, H., 7, 8
Manlove, J., 296
Manly, J. J., 583, 584
Mann, E., 232, 234, 452, 454, 455
Manne, S., 498, 499, 504
Mansfield, P., 441, 446, 447, 448, 449, 453
Manson, J., 457
Manson, J. E., 152, 153, 258, 259, 318, 417
Manuel, J., 497
Manzano, J., 399
Manzi, S., 544
Manzoni, G. C., 557, 558, 559
Marchand, A., 53
March of Dimes, 356, 357, 372, 373
Marcus, B. H., 135, 160, 255–277
Marcus, M., 131, 135, 175, 179, 189
Marcus, M. D., 547
Marcus, S., 394, 400, 401, 402, 404, 405

Marcussen, K., 104
Margaretten, M., 542
Marht, I., 206
Marin, B. V., 38
Marino, F. E., 569
Marjoribanks, J., 319
Marker-Hermann, E., 540
Markey, C. N., 183, 201
Markey, P. M., 201
Markowitz, S., 55, 129
Marks, D., 474
Marks, J. H., 418
Marks, M., 396
Marks, N. F., 51, 52
Marks, S., 46, 374
Markson, E. W., 446
Marlatt, G. A., 112
Marquez, D. X., 269
Marrazzo, J. M., 295
Marrs, R. P., 416
Marsh, G. R., 232
Marshall, A. L., 266
Marshall, J. K., 520
Marshall, N. L., 46–63
Marsland, A. L., 228
Martignoni, E., 585
Martin, A. D., 160
Martin, B. W., 266
Martin, E., 443
Martin, F. L., 127
Martin, J., 478
Martin, L. T., 136
Martin, M., 183
Martin, N. G., 311
Martin, P. D., 131
Martin, R. W., 545
Martin, T., 111
Martin-Diener, E., 266
Martinengo, G., 55
Martinez, A. M., 425
Martinez, G. M., 294, 356, 358, 359, 360
Martinez, M., 65
Martinez-Torteya, C., 74, 75
Martinovich, Z., 178
Martire, L. M., 505, 544, 547, 596
Martone, D. J., 424
Maruti, S. S., 260, 261
Marvan, M. L., 316
Marx, B. P., 291
Marxer, F., 584
Mason, G. A., 424
Mason, K. M., 133
Massie, M. J., 493, 494
Massler, A., 233, 235
Mastroianni, L., Jr., 330, 361
Masuhara, M., 268
Matheson, I., 426
Mathew, N. T., 562
Mathiason, M. A., 163
Matsubayashi, H., 344
Matsuda, D. J., 39
Matsumoto, T., 316
Matt, K. S., 543, 545

Matteson, A. V., 285
Matthews, K. A., 231, 232, 448, 502, 583, 584, 588
Matthews, T. J., 372
Matthey, S., 400
Matthiesen, A. S., 420
Mattila, H., 400
Mattis, J. S., 542
Maunder, R. G., 519
Maurer, T. J., 55
Mauri, M., 225, 226, 397
Maurin, E., 454
Maxwell, L., 496
May, E., 10
May, J. W., 207
Mayer, E. A., 514, 516, 517, 525
Mayer-Davis, E. J., 259
Mayers, L. B., 212
Mayeux, R., 583, 584
Mays, V. M., 31, 33, 34, 37
Mazas, C. A., 128
Mazinani, R., 318
Mazure, C. M., 130, 134
Mazzeo, S., 180
Mazzuca, S. A., 544
McArthur, S., 556
McAuley, E., 264, 269, 574
McAuslan, P., 106
McCabe, M., 181
McCabe, M. P., 430
McCabe, R. E., 519
McCabe, S. E., 105
McCall, L., 28
McCarthy, E. P., 154
McCaul, K. A., 94, 100
McCaul, K. D., 491
McCauley, J., 290, 522, 542
McChargue, D. E., 129, 130, 135
McClelland, G., 482
McCloskey, K., 64–87
McCloskey, L. A., 294
McClung, M. W., 294
McCole, S. D., 164
McCollum, E., 81
McCorkle, R., 496
McCormick, L., 174, 176, 178
McCoy, A., 127
McCullough, D., 107
McDade, T., 230
McDaniel, M., 430
McDermott, B. E., 211
McDermott, M., 235
McDonald, B. C., 495
McDonald, M., 103
McDonell, M. B., 164
McElmurray, C. T., 268
McEnany, G., 228
McEwen, B. S., 53, 584, 585, 588, 589
McFall, B. A., 422
McGarvey, S. T., 155
McGill, B., 183
McGlade, M. S., 82
McGlone, K., 545

McGonagle, K. A., 394, 586
McGovern, P., 55, 419
McGovern, S., 526
McGowen, K. R., 405
McGrath, B. J., 49
McGrath, C., 101
McGreal, D., 374
McGregor, B. A., 505
McGurl, J., 571
McHugh, M., 49, 297
McIntosh, V. V., 187, 215
McIntyre, R. S., 264
McJunkin, C., 414
McKay, K., 365
McKee, M. D., 405
McKee, S., 130, 134, 135
McKenna, J. J., 230
McKeown, L., 67
McKeown, R. E., 72
McKinlay, J., 450
McKinlay, S., 445, 450, 452
McKinley, N. M., 185, 285
McLatchie, E., 493
McLaughlin, S. A., 496
Mclean, L. M., 390, 397, 398, 399
McLean, P. D., 478
McMahon, B. T., 482
McMahon, P. M., 65, 66
McManus, A. J., 362
McMillan, C., 130
McNair, L. D., 104
McNair, R., 295
Mcnamara, P. M., 260
McNeely, M. L., 505
McNeilly, A. S., 415
McPhee, S. J., 492
McPherson, K. M., 469
McQueen, K., 421, 423
McQuillan, J., 359
McTiernan, A., 260, 491
Mead, G. E., 264
Mead, P. B., 131
Meade, M. A., 483
Meaden, P. M., 309
Meads, C., 187
Mearin, F., 514, 515
Mechanic, D., 405
Meckel, R. A., 4
Mehringer, A. M., 130
Mehta, F. S., 124
Meier, P., 107
Meier, U. C., 568
Meijer, G. A., 161
Meinlschmidt, G., 422
Meireles, S. I., 125
Meirow, D., 341
Meis, L., 82
Mekos, D., 129
Melancon, C. H., 496
Melby, M., 453
Melbye, M., 372
Meleis, A., 375
Melin, A., 236

Mellor, D., 181
Meltzer, L. J., 240
Meltzer-Brody, S., 400
Melville, J., 391, 402
Melvin, P., 67
Menacker, F., 372
Menard, W., 214
Mendelson, B., 391
Mendelson, W. B., 225
Menees, S. B., 525, 528
Menezes, A. M., 127
Menzel, J., 183
Mercer, R. T., 419
Merikangas, K. R., 315, 586
Merline, A. C., 105
Mermelstein, R., 129
Merriman, G., 287
Mesmer, C., 527
Messeri, P. A., 137
Messman, T. L., 291
Messman-Moore, T. L., 291
Meston, C., 287, 288
Metcalfe, C., 129
Meyer, E., 208
Meyer, M. H., 361
Meyer-Bahlburg, H., 296
Meyers, A. W., 131, 135
Mezick, E. J., 244
Mezzacappa, E. S., 419, 420, 422
Miaskowski, C., 493, 498
Michael, Y. L., 495, 498, 504
Michels, K. B., 262, 417
Michels, T. C., 371
Midanik, L. T., 104
Mignone, T., 82
Miilunpalo, S., 260
Milgrom, J., 181, 229
Milkie, M. A., 51, 53
Millar, K., 493
Miller, B. A., 105
Miller, B. C., 379
Miller, G. E., 547
Miller, J. H., 108
Miller, J. P., 164
Miller, L., 394, 399, 450
Miller, M. N., 405
Miller, S., 453
Miller, V., 520, 527
Miller, W. C., 35, 296
Miller, W. R., 111, 112
Miller, Y. D., 266
Milletich, R., 82
Millman, R. P., 155
Mills, E. J., 133
Minarik, P. A., 232
Mindell, J. A., 228, 229, 230, 240
Miner, M. H., 291
Minh, T. D., 312
Miniño, A. M., 372
Minnis, A. M., 296
Mircea, C. N., 332
Mirocha, J., 526

Mirowsky, J., 48, 51
Mishell, D., 416
Mishra, G. D., 126
Missmer, S. A., 337, 496
Mitchell, A. J., 493
Mitchell, D., 225, 227
Mitchell, E. M., 369
Mitchell, E. S., 232, 233
Mitchell, J. E., 176, 188, 190
Mitchell, K. S., 527
Mitchell, P., 187
Mitra, M., 71
Mitsonis, C. I., 574
Mittica, P., 557
Miyachi, M., 257
Mizes, J., 131, 135
Moayyedi, P., 526
Moe, K. E., 232, 237
Moen, P., 54, 55
Mohanty, M., 482
Mohapatra, S., 482
Mohler, B., 427, 428
Mohler, J. L., 213
Mohler-Kuo, M., 102
Mojtabai, R., 405
Mojzisch, A., 48
Mokdad, A. H., 269
Moline, M., 229
Molix, L. A., 506
Mols, F., 502
Monagle, L., 315
Monane, M., 239
Monninkhof, E. M., 261
Monteiro, M. G., 108
Montgomery, G. H., 505
Montgomery, P., 264
Montgomery-Downs, H. E., 229, 230
Monti, P. M., 112
Montori, V. M., 319
Montplaisir, J., 238
Mood, D. W., 505
Moolchan, E. T., 124
Moon-Howard, J., 131, 137
Moore, A. M., 370
Moore, G. E., 164
Moore, K., 398, 572
Moos, B. S., 112
Moos, R. H., 112, 421
Mora, S., 258
Moradi, B., 185, 202, 285
Morales-Aleman, M. M., 35
Moran, J., 7
Morantz, R. M., 46
Morbeck, D. E., 360
Moreira, P., 163
Moreno, A. Y., 138
Morgan, K., 238
Morgenstern, J., 112
Morgenstern, L. B., 592
Morgenthaler, T., 236, 242
Moriarty, B. W., 212
Morin, A. K., 317

Morin, C. M., 242
Morin, M. C., 238
Moritani, T., 316
Morland-Schultz, K., 425
Morley, S., 527
Morokoff, P. J., 281–304
Morokoff, P. M., 283
Morris, A. M., 358
Morris, J., 517
Morris, K. S., 574
Morris, M., 549
Morris, R. K., 368
Morris, S. N., 332
Morrison, D. M., 34
Morrison, J. A., 155, 331
Morrison, J. H., 584
Morris-Yates, A., 521
Morrow-Howell, N., 56
Morry, M., 184, 284
Mors, O., 229
Morse, C. A., 319
Morse, G., 316, 317
Morse, J., 430, 449
Mortensen, P. B., 229
Mortola, J. F., 311
Mosca, L., 592, 593, 594, 597
Moschiano, F., 559, 562
Moser, R., 498
Moses-Kolko, E. L., 394, 401
Mosher, W. D., 294, 360, 371
Moskowitz, J. T., 504
Moss, N. E., 35
Moss, T. P., 205
Mostyn, B. J., 376
Mostyn, T., 429
Motl, R. W., 573, 574
Mott, S. L., 365
Moum, T., 359
Mouradian, V. E., 71
Mourão-Carvalhal, I., 163
Mousa, K., 125
Moy, I., 335
Moyer, A., 111, 491
Moyers, T. B., 111
Mu, P.-F., 340, 347, 349
Muehlenkamp, J. J., 177
Mueller, D., 137, 138
Muellerleile, P. A., 29
Mugisha, E., 375
Mukamal, K. J., 100
Mulder, A., 363
Mullan, B., 505
Mullen, P. D., 131, 479
Muller, R., 482
Mullings, L., 28
Mullington, J. M., 224
Mulrow, C. D., 542
Mumenthaler, M. S., 99
Munafo, M. R., 129
Muncy, R., 4
Mundy, L., 361
Munk-Olsen, T., 229
Munné, M., 102

Munro Prescott, H., 6, 7, 12
Munster, P. N., 500
Muntaner, C., 48
Murnen, S., 183
Murphy, C., 82
Murphy, D. K., 206
Murphy, F., 213
Murphy, P. J., 233, 237
Murphy, S. L., 372
Murray, B. J., 227, 228, 229, 230, 241, 242
Murray, C., 360, 377, 378
Murray, C. D., 515, 517
Murray, C. J. L., 313
Murray, G., 493
Murray, L., 399, 401
Murray, M., 207, 474
Murrie, D., 255
Murtagh, D. R., 242
Murtagh, M. J., 443
Musante, G. J., 156
Muse, K. N., 320
Mustard, C., 48
Muthusami, K. R., 336, 337
Mwenifumbo, J. C., 132
Myers, J. K., 478
Myhr, K. M., 572
Myhre, E. B., 212
Myran, D., 527

Naccarato, R., 526
Nachtigall, R. D., 350
Naci, H., 573
Naessen, T., 314
Nagata, C., 234
Nagle, C. M., 418
Nagy, G., 416
Nair, S., 376
Nair, U. S., 123–148
Naismith, R. T., 573
Najman, J. M., 373
Nakamura, J., 284
Nakamura, K., 340
Naliboff, B., 516, 517
Namenek, R. J., 130
Nanda, R., 526
Nandurkar, S., 521
Napolitano, M., 135, 160
Nappi, R. E., 558, 560, 561
Narayan, K. M. V., 259
Näring, G., 546
Nash, B. R., 424
Nash, C. O., 223–254
Nash, K. R., 72, 73
Nast, I., 422
Nathanson, A., 81
National Cancer Institute, 25
National Center for Health Statistics, 266, 269
National Center for Victims of Crime, 287
National Committee for Quality Assurance (NCQA), 456

National Heart, Lung, and Blood Institute (NHLBI), 157
National Institute for Clinical Excellence (NICE), 186, 188, 189
National Institute of Justice, 288
National Institute on Alcohol Abuse and Alcoholism (NIAAA), 93, 94, 99, 108
National Institutes of Health (NIH), 139, 157, 161, 231, 444, 450, 457
National Research Council (NRC), 56, 95, 114, 163, 390, 391, 394, 399, 400, 401, 402, 404, 407
National Sleep Foundation (NSF), 223, 240
Nauta, H., 189
Navarrete-Navarrete, N., 544
Naylor, H., 319
Nazoo, J. Y., 429
Nduati, R., 426
Ndukwe, G., 363
Neale, M. C., 103, 311, 527
Nechas, E., 21
Nedstrand, E., 236
Nedungadi, T. P., 257
Nee, J., 309, 443
Neese, R. E., 478
Neff, R. A., 266
Negishi, H., 416
Neiderhiser, J. M., 379
Neighbors, C. J., 265
Neighbors, H. W., 37
Neilands, T. B., 38
Nelson, A. R., 355–388
Nelson, C. B., 394, 586
Nelson, D. B., 233
Nelson, D. E., 107
Nelson, H. D., 236
Nelson, J., 14, 20
Nelson, J. P., 81
Nelson, J. W., 151
Nelson, S., 548
Nemecek, D. A., 206
Nemecek, J. R., 206
Nemessury, J., 177
Nery, F. G., 544
Neugebauer, R., 371, 373
Neumann, C. A., 129
Neumann, I. D., 419, 420
Newcomer, R., 595
Newland, P. K., 573
Newman, D. L., 400
Newman, J. P., 210
Newman, K., 35, 37
Newport, D. J., 393
Newton, C. R., 342, 362
Newton, K. M., 236
Nezu, A. M., 565
Nezu, C. M., 565
Ng, J., 155
Niaura, R., 129, 134, 135, 137, 138
Nicassio, P. M., 546

Nichols, T. R., 129
Nichter, M., 124
Nicolaidis, C., 64
Nicole-Smith, L., 450
Nielsen, K., 136
Nieman, L. K., 314
Niemasik, E. E., 506
Niesel, M., 48
Nieuwenhuyse, H., 330
Nigam, M. P., 562
NIOSH, 47
Nishioka, E., 422, 424
Nissen, E., 420
Nitz, J. C., 265
Nixon, E., 453
Noakes, M., 331
Noar, S. M., 28, 29
Nobakht, M., 177
Noceda, G., 425
Noh, S., 478
Nolen-Hoeksema, S., 98, 477
Noll, J. G., 287
Noll, S., 184
Nollet, F., 476
Nolst Trenité, G. J., 203
Noonan, R., 68
Noorbala, A. A., 348, 349
NORA, 47
Norman, C., 481
Norman, J. E., Jr., 568
Norman, P., 173
Norman, R. J., 331
Norris, A., 369
Norris, A. E., 29
Norris, D. L., 174
Norris, S. M., 64
Northouse, L. L., 505
Norton, C., 525
Norton, D., 233
Nosek, M., 479, 480, 482
Nossent, J. C., 543
Notelovitz, M., 160
Nouer, S. S., 81
Novick, D. M., 389–413
Novielli, K. D., 596
Novotny, J. A., 161
Novotny, T. E., 124
Nowosielski, K., 312
Noyes, B. B., 596
Nussbaum, R. L., 590
Nyberg, S., 314
Nygren, K. G., 328
Nyren, O., 207

Oates, G., 55
Oates, M., 363
Oberman, M., 396
Oberrecht, L., 268
Obi, B., 137
Obot, I. S., 103
O'Brien, A. R., 575
O'Brien, P. E., 155
O'Brien, P. M., 306, 320

O'Connell, J., 444
O'Conner, T. G., 392
O'Connor, M., 173
O'Connor, P. J., 264, 557
Oddens, B. J., 330
O'Dea, J., 181
O'Dell, A., 66
O'Donnell, J. M., 206
O'Dougherty, M., 268
Office of Applied Statistics, SAMHSA, 114
Office of Juvenile Justice and Delinquency Prevention, 114
Office of the U.S. Surgeon General, 101, 114
Office on Women's Health, 21
Ogburn, E., 102
Ogden, C. L., 32, 149
Ogden, J., 156
Oguma, Y., 260
O'Hara, M. W., 365, 390, 391, 393, 394, 399, 421
O'Hara, R., 99
Ohayon, M. M., 231, 232, 234
Ohkawara, K., 257
Ohlin, A., 163
Ohlsen, L., 206
Ohlson, L. O., 152
Ojajärvi, A., 499
Okamoto, T., 268
Oke, S., 391
Okereke, O. I., 586
Okun, B., 339
Okun, M., 228
Oldenberg, H. S. A., 505
Olds, D., 287
O'Leary, K. D., 68
O'Leary-Kelly, A. M., 50
Olesen, V., 38
Olfson, M., 405
Olivardia, R., 184
Olkin, R., 467–490
Olsen, J., 372
Olsen, J. R., 126
Olsen, S., 101
Olsen, S. A., 575
Olsen, S. F., 335
Olson, A. K., 264
Olson, C. L., 154
Olson, C. M., 163
Olsson, M., 573
O'Mahen, H. A., 405, 406
O'Malley, P. M., 105
O'Malley, S., 110, 134
Oman, D., 470
Omodei, U., 334
Omu, A. E., 311
Omu, F. E., 311
O'Neal, H. A., 264
O'Neill, C., 362
Ong, J., 244
Opwis, K., 575
Oranye, N. O., 311

Oreland, L., 315
Orlando, R. C., 526
Orleans, T., 107
Ormrod, R., 67
Ornitz, A. W., 316
O'Rourke, P., 400
Orr, M., 296
Orr, S. T., 375
Orr, W. C., 518
Ory, M. G., 596
Ose, L., 210
Öst, L., 545
Ostbye, T., 152
Oster, G., 156
Osterlund, M. K., 589
Ostir, G. V., 494
Ostrove, J. M., 35
O'Sullivan, L. F., 292
Otero-Sabogal, R., 492
Ott, P., 584
Otten, R., 128
Ottens, A. J., 570
Otto, M. W., 214
Ovbiagele, B., 588
Owen, N., 256, 265
Owens, J. A., 230
Owens, J. F., 231, 232
Owens, R. G., 498
Ownby, R. L., 586, 587
Oyebode, F., 392

Pacheco, A., 397
Pack, A., 228
Paddison, P. L., 311, 316
Padez, C., 163
Padian, N. S., 296
Paeratakul, S., 162
Pagano, M. E., 112
Paget, S., 545
Pahel, L., 430
Paik, A., 282
Paiker, J., 225
Paikoff, R. L., 181
Palarea, R. E., 64
Palesh, O. G., 291
Palfai, T. G., 311, 316
Paliwal, P., 130
Palladino, C. L., 375
Palm, B., 205
Palmer, G., 484
Palmer, J. T., 311
Palmer, M. G., 361
Palmer J. L., 492
Palsson, O., 519, 525, 527
Palta, M., 238, 243
Paluska, S. A., 265
Pan, A., 586
Panconesi, A., 560, 565
Pandi-Perumal, S. R., 241
Panhuysen, G. E. M., 174
Panwar, V. S., 519
Paolucci, E. O., 287
Papandreou, K., 478

Paradiso, S., 594
Parag, V., 594
Paranjape, A., 64
Paras, M. L., 523
Pare, P., 515
Parisi, R. A., 153
Park, A. J., 206
Park, C. L., 491, 499
Park, E. R., 136, 137
Park, H. J., 517, 523
Park, L. E., 201
Park, S., 526
Parker, B., 71
Parkin, L., 320
Parks, S. M., 596
Parlow, J. L., 260
Parpal, H., 567
Parra-Medina, D., 31, 37, 38, 40
Parry, B., 225, 226, 227, 233, 393
Partinen, M., 240
Partridge, A. H., 496
Pasick, R. J., 491
Paskett, E. D., 503
Pataky, Z., 156
Pate, R. R., 259
Patnaik, J. L., 294
Patrick, D. L., 515
Patrick, K., 265
Patterson, J. T., 13
Patterson, R. E., 262
Patterson, S. K., 528
Pattichis, K., 565
Patton, G. C., 130
Paul, D. R., 161
Pauli, E. M., 331
Paull, K., 427
Paulozzi, L. J., 66
Paulsen, V., 231, 233
Paulus, W. E., 334
Pavelka, M., 444
Pawlak, C. R., 543
Paxton, S., 181, 229
Payne, J. L., 311, 314
Pazol, K., 367, 368
Pearce, L., 358
Pearlin, L. I., 52
Pearlstein, T., 309, 312, 313, 319
Pearson, H., 376
Pearson, J. L., 391
Pearson, T. A., 163
Peat, C. M., 177, 180, 182
Pechacek, T. F., 123
Pecorari, G., 205
Pecori, L., 211
Peden, A., 544
Pedersen, C. A., 424
Pederson, C. B., 229
Peer, M., 307
Peeters, A., 153
Peeters, P. H., 207
Peindl, K., 390, 398
Pekmezi, D., 255–277
Pelligrino, D. A., 588

Pendell, G., 358
Penner, I. K., 575
Penninx, B. W., 263
Peppone, L. J., 127
Peralta-Ramírez, M. I., 543
Perdrizet-Chevallier, C., 494
Pereda, N., 287
Perez, A., 416
Perez, S., 82
Pérez-Escamilla, R., 429
Pérez-García, M., 543
Perez-Stable, E. J., 128, 256, 492
Perfetti, T. A., 125
Pericak-Vance, M. A., 590
Perkins, K. A., 131, 132, 135, 136
Perkins, L. L., 206
Perlen, S., 401
Perlis, M., 236, 242
Perna, F. M., 264
Pero, C. D., 203
Perone, J., 178
Perovic, S., 213
Perraton, L. G., 264
Perreault, L., 157
Perri, L. M., 544
Perri, M. G., 158, 160
Perry, A. W., 204
Pers, M., 206
Persing, J. A., 202
Pertschuk, M. J., 202, 204, 209
Peter, R., 585
Peterlin, B. L., 561
Petersen, D. M., 502
Petersen, L., 497
Petersilia, J. R., 482
Peterson, A. E., 416
Peterson, B. D., 342
Peterson, B. L., 152
Peterson, C. B., 188
Peterson, G., 424
Peterson, R., 76
Petrea, R. E., 582
Petry, N. M., 268
Pettinati, H. M., 110
Peyerl, N. L., 177
Pfeiffer, C., 548
Phalen, L., 484
Phelan, J., 38, 40
Phelan, S., 155, 161, 162
Philips, M. T., 31
Phillips, A., 401
Phillips, D. H., 127
Phillips, K., 175, 177, 178, 184, 189, 214
Phillips, L. J., 573
Phillips, R. S., 154
Phillips, S. F., 527
Physical Activity Guidelines Advisory Committee, 255, 256, 257, 260, 261, 268
Piasecki, T. M., 134
Piazza, M., 129
Pico-Alfonso, M. A., 73, 74, 75

Pien, G. W., 228, 230, 231, 233, 234, 243
Pierce, J. P., 128, 262
Pierpaoli, W., 236
Pierson, R. A., 332
Piesse, C., 520
Pike, C. J., 583, 588
Pike, K., 187
Pike, M. C., 418
Pilling, S., 189
Pilpel, H. F., 11
Pilver, C. E., 311, 312, 315
Pimentel, M., 526
Pinchasov, B. B., 264
Pincus, H. A., 405
Pindborg, J. J., 124
Pinel, J. P., 264
Pinelli, G., 331
Pinelli, J., 427
Pinksy, J. L., 470
Pinneau, S. R., 47
Pinto, A., 260
Pinto, B. M., 130, 265
Pinto, C., 519
Piontek, C. M., 393
Piotrkowski, C. S., 51
Pisacane, A., 427
Pi-Sunyer, F. X., 152, 154
Pitt, B., 421
Pittion-Vouyovitch, S., 567
Pittler, M. H., 545
Pittman, J. F., 52
Piza-Katzer, H., 211
Plant, K., 545
Platz, C., 396
Plaud, J. J., 106
Pleck, J., 48
Plichta, S., 72, 73, 74
Plinta, R., 312
Plotnick, R. D., 359
Plu-Bureau,G., 416
Plummer, S., 71
Poehlman, E. T., 160
Pohjasvaara, T., 227
Polen, M. R., 107
Polis, C. B., 370
Polito, S., 574
Pollard, C., 477
Pollmacher, T., 228
Polman, C. H., 570
Polo-Kantola, P., 240
Polonsky, K. S., 154
Polosa, R., 138
Polusny, M. A., 287, 290
Pomerleau, C. S., 130, 131, 134, 135
Pomerleau, O. F., 130, 134
Pompeii, L. A., 49
Ponder, P. K., 124
Pons-Estel, G. J., 541
Ponten, B., 206
Pope, C., 177
Pope, H., 178, 184
Popper, S., 398

Porcelli, P., 526
Porter, L. S., 503, 505
Posmontier, B., 137, 229
Posner, J. A., 358, 450
Post, R. M., 309
Postma, D., 126
Potagas, C., 574
Poulos, R., 76
Poulose, B. K., 162
Powe, B. D., 502
Powell, L. H., 152
Powell, S. H., 108
Powell-Kennedy, H., 230
Power, J., 295
Poynter, B., 594
Pozo, C., 504
Pradhan, E. K., 545
Prather, C. M., 527
Pratt, B., 173
Prentice, A., 416
Prentice, P., 152
Prescott, C. A., 103
Prescott, E., 126
Prescott, H. M., 3–24
Presnell, K., 181
Pressman, S. D., 548
Preston, P., 476
Preveza, E., 478
Preveza, N., 478
Price, M., 505
Price, T. R., 594
Prince, C. B., 375
Prince, L. B., 328–354
Prinz, P. N., 239
Prior, A., 527
Prior, J., 441, 442, 455
Pritchard, G., 468
Prochaska, J. O., 29, 30
Project MATCH Research Group,
     110, 113
Protopopescu, X., 316
Prunty, M. C., 572
Pruzinsky, P., 183, 186
Pruzinsky, T., 202
Pryor, J. B., 50
Psaros, C., 375
Ptacek, R., 315
Puder, K. L., 515
Pugin, E., 416
Pugliesi, K. L., 56
Pukkala, E., 207, 359
Pulerwitz, J., 34, 295
Pulzi, P., 211
Purcell, K., 269
Purewal, S., 376, 377
Purushotham A. D., 493
Putilov, A. A., 264
Putnam, F. W., 287, 299, 482

Qaqish, B., 442
Quadflieg, N., 178
Quandt, S. A., 545
Queensbury, C. P., 164

Qui, C., 228
Quigley, B. M., 521
Quigley, E. M., 526
Quina, K., 285
Quinn, A., 445
Quinn, D., 184

Rabago, D., 231
Rabin, R. F., 77
Radat, F., 562
Radel, L., 363, 379
Radojevic, V., 546
Radojicic, Z. I., 213
Radu, E. W., 575
Rafaelli, M., 283
Raghaven, R., 68
Rahemtul, C. K., 201
Rahmanian, S. D., 126
Raikes, A., 521
Raine, T., 296
Rainville, J., 484
Raitasalo, R., 400
Raj, A., 31, 34, 35
Rajan, M., 64, 65
Rajewska, J., 233
Ram, K. T., 417
Ramagopalan, S. V., 568
Ramchandani, P., 229
Ramchandani, V. A., 99
Ramirez, A. G., 503
Ramisetty-Mikler, S., 99, 101
Ramos, M. G., 319
Ramussen, K. M., 416
Rand, M. R., 67, 71
Randall, C. L., 106, 110
Randall, P. K., 110
Ranjbaran, Z., 518
Rankin, M., 204, 209
Rao, S. S., 525, 526
Raphael, D., 67
Rapport, F., 348
Rasgon, N., 315
Rash, C. J., 131
Rasker, J. J., 545, 547
Raskind, M. A., 239
Rasmussen, B. K., 557, 558, 560, 561,
     562, 564
Ratcliffe, S. J., 35
Ratner, P. A., 136
Rattray, A., 330
Rauchfuss, M., 374
Rauprich, O., 363
Rausch, M., 575
Ravussin, E., 151
Ray, L. A., 112
Raymond, N., 190
Raynor, H. A., 159
Raynor, L. C., 400
Rea, D. W., 262
Rea, M. F., 416, 426
Reagan, L. J., 18
Reay, R., 400, 404, 405
Redding, C. A., 29

Rediehs, M. H., 237
Redline, S., 238
Redon, J., 153
Reed, D., 470
Reed, E., 31, 35
Reed, J., 10, 67
Reed, M. L., 563
Rees, T. D., 204
Reeves, M. J., 582, 591
Regan, S., 136
Regestein, Q. R., 232, 233
Rego, S. A., 243
Rehan, S., 453
Rehkopf, D. H., 31
Rehm, J., 99, 100
Reich, M., 494
Reichborn-Kjennerud, T., 179
Reichmann, S. K., 156
Reid, R. L., 226
Reig Ferrer, A., 132
Reigle, B. S., 260
Reinlib, L., 541
Reis, J. S., 237
Reiss, D., 379
Relia, S., 243
Rellini, A., 286, 288
Relyea, G., 130
Remes, A., 568
Remes-Troche, J., 514
Remington, G., 264
Rempel, J. K., 430
Rempel, L. A., 430
Ren, L., 35
Rende, R., 129
Renn, H., 362
Rennard, S. I., 151
Renner, L., 81
Rennison, C. M., 67, 68
Resick, P. A., 290
Resnick, H. S., 106, 290
Resnick, S. M., 589
Reunanen, M., 568
Revak, J., 185
Revenson, T. A., 540, 541, 542, 546,
     548, 549
Rexrode, K. M., 258, 586
Reyes, H. L., 82
Reylea, G., 131
Reynolds, F., 452, 454
Reynolds, K. A., 499, 549
Reynoso, J. T., 132
Rhatigan, D., 81
Rhomberg, M., 211
Ricciardelli, L., 173–198
Richards, J. G., 365
Richards, P., 549
Richardson, C. R., 269
Richardson, H. B., 366
Rich-Edwards, J. W., 330, 331, 416,
     417, 428
Richelsen, B., 161
Richter, D. L., 266
Rickels, K., 311, 320, 330, 361

Rickert, V. I., 269, 285
Rickman, L. S., 212
Riedel, B. W., 240
Riedl, A., 516, 517, 518
Rief, W., 177, 214
Riemann, D., 263
Riemsma, R. P., 545, 547
Rietman, J. S., 496
Riffenburgh, R. H., 212
Rigero, B. A., 424
Righetti-Veltema, M., 399, 400
Rigotti, N. A., 136
Riksen-Walraven, J. M., 423
Riley, E. P., 101
Rimington, M. R., 376
Rimm, A. A., 131, 152
Rimm, E. B., 100
Ringel, Y., 516, 523
Ringwalt, C. L., 107
Rinker, B., 427
Rintala, D. H., 480
Riordan, J., 415, 422, 425, 426
Ripley, B. D., 574
Ristock, J., 70
Ritchie, H. L., 392
Ritchie, K., 587
Ritsher, J., 373
Ritter, P., 545
Ritter, P. L., 545
Ritterband, L. M., 244
Rivera-Tovar, A. D., 311
Roark, S., 76, 77
Robbins, L., 545, 547
Roberts, J., 228, 400
Roberts, L., 515
Roberts, M. R., 135
Roberts, R. E., 56
Roberts, T., 181, 184, 185, 212, 284
Robertson, D., 442
Robertson, E., 394
Robertson, N. P., 568
Robinson, B. E., 291
Robinson, E., 331
Robinson, I. C., 415
Robinson, J., 130
Robinson, J. C., 520
Robinson, J. P., 51, 53
Robinson, K., 398
Robinson, R. G., 594
Robinson, R. L., 312
Robison, J., 54
Roca, C., 441
Rocha, F. L., 319
Rodgman, A., 125
Rodin, J., 130
Rodriguez, M. B., 283
Roe, L. S., 159
Roederer, T., 567
Roehling, P. V., 55
Roehrs, T. A., 232
Roger, V. L., 582, 583, 584, 588, 591
Rogers, B. A., 478
Rogers, G. G., 225

Rogers, M. E., 268
Rogers, N. L., 223, 268
Rogers, R., 373
Rogers, T., 130
Rohan, T. E., 126
Rohrich, R. J., 210
Rojnic Kuzman, M., 311
Roles, P., 379
Rollnick, S., 111
Rolls, B., 159
Rom, W. N., 125
Romanchik, B., 379
Romanoff, N. R., 548
Romans-Clarkson, S. E., 370, 371
Romesberg, T. L., 373
Rondo, P. H., 400
Rondon, M. B., 82
Room, R., 107
Rooney, B. L., 163
Roos, S. S., 340
Rosado, V., 163
Rosales M., 492
Rosamond, W., 592
Rosario, E. R., 583
Rosario, M., 296
Rose, J. S., 285
Rose, R., 82
Rosen, D., 82
Rosen, K., 81, 342
Rosen, R. C., 282
Rosenbaum, P., 484
Rosenberg, K. R., 181
Rosenberg, M. J., 127
Rosenstock, I. M., 29
Rosenthal, D., 369
Rosenzweig, S., 545
Rosner, B., 260, 498
Rosner, B. A., 262
Ross, C. E., 48, 51
Ross, H., 123
Ross, L., 19
Ross, L. E., 229, 365, 390, 392, 397, 398, 399
Ross, R., 258
Ross, S., 398
Rossi, A. S., 589
Rossi, B. V., 337
Rossi, J. S., 29, 285
Rossi, N., 204
Rossner, S., 163
Rossouw, J. E., 589
Rostosky, S., 448
Rotenberg, B. W., 205
Roth, E. K., 394, 401
Roth, S., 543
Rothblum, E., 156, 287, 447
Rothermel, J., 241
Rothfield, P., 446
Rothman, D., 14
Rothschild, A. K., 393
Rotkin, I. D., 8
Rotnitzky, A., 152
Roubenoff, R., 164

Rouleau, I., 238
Roush, S. F., 231
Rousseau, V., 53
Rowe, H., 369
Rowe, J. W., 585
Rowe-Jones, J., 204
Rowland, J. H., 502
Rowley, D. L., 31, 375
Royak-Shaler, R., 72
Royal-Lawson, M., 399
Roy-Byrne, P., 309
Rozario, P. A., 56
Ruan, W. J., 105
Rubinow, D., 309, 314, 441
Ruble, D. N., 420
Rudd, R., 34, 295
Ruddell, J. L., 479
Rudolph, K. D., 399
Rudy, T. E., 544
Ruggero, C. J., 396, 397, 398
Ruggiero, K. J., 290
Ruiz, M. E., 82
Ruland, C. M., 498
Rumpler, W. V., 161
Rundell, K. W., 212
Runmarker, B., 570
Runtz, M. G., 291
Rupley, D. C., 152
Rushton, D., 375
Russell, A., 517
Russell, G., 186
Russell, M., 52, 53
Ruzek, S., 14, 15, 38
Ryan, D. H., 162
Ryan, J., 587
Rybakowski, J. K., 233
Rychnovsky, J. D., 229
Rzepski, B., 515

Sable, K., 524
Sabogal, F., 492
Sachchithanantham, K., 152
Sack, D. A., 225
Sack, R. L., 239
Sacks, F. M., 159
Sadeghi, H., 205
Safer, D. L., 210
Saghafi, E. M., 505
Sahin, F. K., 228
Sahota, P. K., 227
Saia, T. L., 544
Saigal, S., 484
Sainsbury, A., 164
Saito, Y. A., 514, 521, 526, 527
Saitz, R., 107, 111
Sajatovic, M., 399
Sakita, M., 549
Saladin, M. E., 134
Salamoun, M. M., 75
Salans, L. B., 155
Salewski, L., 233
Sallis, J., 256, 263, 265
Salomon, A., 69

Salt, E., 544
Salthouse, T. A., 55
Saltzman, L. E., 65, 66, 69, 76
Salvi, E., 557
Sambira, A., 81
Samdal, F., 210
Samet, J. M., 123, 124, 125
Sammel, M. D., 231, 233, 320
Sanchez, D. T., 283, 285
Sanchez-Johnsen, L., 178
Sanchez-Lorente, S., 65
Sanday, P. R., 290, 291
Sanderman, R., 498
Sanders, R., 399
Sanderson, T., 549
Sandfort, T. G. M., 296
Sandler, M., 391, 422
Sandler, R. S., 515
Sangalli, M. R., 228
Sanghvi, R., 285
Sanjuan, P. M., 106
Sansone, L., 176
Sansone, R., 176
Santana, M. C., 35
Santelli, J., 296
Santonastaso, P., 177
Santoro, N., 443, 453
Santos, R. A., 205
Santy, E. E., 229
Sapolsky, R. M., 520, 585
Saraiya, M., 373
Sargent, L., 269
Sarkisian, C. A., 267
Sarsour, K., 241
Sartor, C. E., 105
Sartorio, A., 158
Sarwer, D. B., 189, 199–222
Satcher, S., 405
Sato, M., 549
Sattler, G., 210
Sattler, J. I., 206
Saunders, B., 106
Saunders, J. B., 108
Saunders, L., 469
Sauro, K. M., 564
Sauter, S. L., 47, 51
Savas, L. S., 523
Saver, J. L., 588
Savi, L., 562
Sawaya, G., 443, 589
Sawyer, J., 559
Saxena, R., 269
Sayegh, R., 318
Sayer, A., 48
Sayer, L. C., 53
Saykin, A. J., 495
Sbaragli, C., 339
Scali, J., 587
Scanlan, J. M., 582
Scaramella, L. V., 379
Scarinci, I., 295
Schacter, L. M., 155
Schafer, J., 102

Schaffler, N., 570
Schapira, D. V., 153
Scharf, D., 132
Scharlach, A. E., 56
Scharrer, E., 183
Schauberger, C. S., 163
Schauberger, C. W., 163
Schauffler, G., 7, 9
Scheid, V., 454
Scheier, M. F., 503, 504
Schenker, E., 341
Schenker, J. G., 341
Scherag, S., 179, 180
Schernhammer, E. S., 238
Schetter, C. D., 414–439
Schiaffino, K. M., 546
Schieroni, F., 559
Schiff, I., 126
Schiffman, S., 132
Schiller, C. E., 365
Schlebusch, L., 205, 206
Schlegel, R. J., 506
Schloredt, K. A., 288
Schlossman, S., 4
Schlundt, D. G., 159
Schmidt, L., 342, 343
Schmidt, P., 309, 314, 441
Schmidt, U., 189
Schmitz, K. H., 261, 505
Schmulson, M., 516, 525, 526
Schnall, P. L., 47
Schnebly, S., 373
Schneider, J. A., 587
Schneider, S., 542
Schneiderman, I., 424
Schnittker, J., 54
Schnohr, P., 126
Schoendorf, K. C., 375
Schoenfeld, P., 514, 518, 526
Schofield, M. J., 126
Scholle, S. H., 405
Schonberger, L. B., 471
Schooler, C., 47, 55
Schoones, J. W., 265
Schover, L. R., 496, 497
Schreiber, G. B., 130
Schrijvers, C. T. M., 131
Schubert, C. R., 236
Schulenberg, J. E., 105
Schulkin, J., 402
Schulman, K. A., 39
Schultz, K. S., 56
Schulz, A. J., 28
Schulz, R., 505, 547, 596
Schulz-Hardt, S., 48
Schumaker, H. D., 154
Schumann, B. C., 130
Schuster, D. P., 268
Schuster, M. A., 68
Schuster, M. M., 520
Schwab, R. J., 230
Schwartz, J., 107
Schwartz, S. A., 398

Schwartz, S. M., 242
Schwarz, E. B., 416, 417
Schwarz, J. C., 289
Schweizer, E., 312
Schwenk, T. L., 265
Schwochaum, S., 50
Scipio, C. D., 544
Scofield, L., 541
Scott, J., 132, 429
Scott, M., 400
Scroggie, J., 574
Sears, J., 374
Sears, M., 374
Sears, R., 374
Sears, S. F., 160
Sears, S. R., 499
Sears, W., 374
Seawell, A. H., 540, 544
Secher, N., 101, 335
Secker-Walker, R. H., 131
Sedlak, M. W., 4
Seeman, T., 53, 585
Seetha, P., 49
Seewaldt, V. L., 505
Sefl, T., 35
Segal, Z. V., 527
Segerstrom, A. B., 259
Segerstrom, S. C., 503
Segesten, K., 545
Segre, L., 399
Segui, J., 544
Seidel, D., 585
Seidell, J. C., 153
Seideman, R. Y., 317
Seifer D. B., 347
Seimyr, L., 422
Seitz, H. K., 99
Sejbaek, C. S., 342
Sejourne, N., 373
Sejvar, J. J., 471
Selfe, T., 454
Seligman, M. E., 548
Sellers, E. M., 132
Seltman, H., 502
Selye, H., 50
Sempos, C. T., 99
Senn, T. E., 287
Serdula, M. K., 107
Serletti, J. M., 215
Serra, J., 517
Seshadri, S., 582
Severino, S. K., 226
Sezgin, E., 177
Sfagos, K., 574
Shaath, N., 526
Shafey, O., 123
Shai, I., 159
Shang, S.-P., 330
Shanks, N., 420
Shapiro, B. L., 289
Shapiro, C. L., 496
Sharkey, K., 232, 233, 235, 241
Sharma, B. R., 377

Sharma, M., 269
Sharma, V., 390, 392, 395, 396
Sharp, T., 164
Sharpe, L., 572
Sharpe, M., 330
Sharples, K., 320
Shaughn O'Brien, P. M., 318
Shaver, J., 232, 241
Shaver, J. F., 225
Shaver, J. L. F., 231, 233, 240
Shaver, S., 319
Shaw, D., 391, 399
Sheard, C., 363
Shearer, S. L., 288
Shechter, A., 223, 225, 226, 239, 240, 318
Sheeran, L., 455
Sheeshka, J., 429
Shehab, D., 360, 363
Sheldon, T. A., 526
Shelley, G. A., 65, 66
Shepard, J. W., 242
Shepertycky, M. R., 243
Shepherd, J. E., 588
Shepherd, S. J., 526
Sheps, S., 340
Sherbourne, C., 401
Sheridan, D. J., 72, 73
Sherins, R. J., 337
Sherman, B., 443
Sherrard, W., 362
Sherwood, A., 232
Sherwood, H. S., 268
Sherwood, N. E., 160
Shi, Y., 124
Shibui, K., 226
Shields, P., 126
Shields, S. A., 28
Shiffman, S., 131, 132, 133
Shih, Y. C., 515
Shimizu, H., 234
Shinew, K. J., 479
Shiovitz, T. M., 318
Shipley, R. H., 206
Shisslak, C. M., 215
Shlay, J. C., 294
Shockley, K. M., 52
Shoham, A., 418
Sholtes, D., 244
Shoo, R., 521
Shorey, R., 81
Short, P. F., 498, 504
Shreffler, K. M., 359
Shumaker, S. A., 589
Shurgaja, A. M., 264
Shwarz, M., 137
Shyti, R., 561
Sibonga, J. D., 99
Sickmund, M., 67
Siddall, P. J., 481
Siddiqui, O., 129
Sidora, K. J., 287
Sieber, S. D., 46, 52

Siegel, D. M., 540
Siegel, J. A., 291
Siegel, R., 491, 492
Siegrist, J., 584
Signal, T. L., 228
Sihm, F., 206
Sillilman, J., 19
Silver, A. G., 204
Silverman, D. G., 355
Silverman, J. G., 35
Silverstein, M. J., 207
Simmons, K. W., 287
Simon, A. E., 502
Simon, J., 189
Simoni, J. M., 281, 294
Simons, E. G., 376
Simonsick, E. M., 469
Simopoulos, A. P., 431
Simpson, A. J., 362
Simpson, H. W., 359
Simpson, S., 238
Sin, D., 126
Sinclair, V. G., 548, 574
Sinforiani, E., 556, 591, 592
Singer, B. H., 585
Singh, S., 295, 370
Siniscalchi, J., 214
Siskind, V., 418
Sison, G. F., 549
Sit, D. K., 393, 396, 397
Sitaker, M., 69
Sitnyakowsky, L., 151
Siu, C., 493
Siu, L. L., 498
Sjögren, B., 422
Sjöström, L., 161, 162
Skelly, J. M., 131
Skene, D. J., 233, 236, 237, 241
Skinner, L., 106
Skinner, L. J., 289
Skokan, L. A., 549
Skoog Svanberg, A., 339
Skouteris, H., 181, 229
Skrundz, M., 422
Skrzypulec-Plinta, V., 312
Skulkans, V., 453
Skumanich, S., 374
Slade, P., 362, 370, 373
Slagsvold, B., 359
Slater, P., 51
Slaughter, R., 208
Slavin, J. L., 526
Slawta, J. N., 568
Slep, A. M., 81
Slof Op't, L., 180
Slupchynskyj, O., 203
Small, B. J., 505
Smedley, M., 361
Smeenk, J. M. J., 342
Smeets, M. A. M., 174
Smeltzer, S. C., 572
Smirnov, A. V., 568
Smith, B., 548

Smith, B. W., 543, 548
Smith, C. A., 544
Smith, D. W., 130
Smith, H., 526
Smith, J. A. Z., 366
Smith, J. F., 333
Smith, J. L., 427, 430
Smith, J. V., 129
Smith, K., 350
Smith, K. E., 46
Smith, L. A., 108
Smith, M. A., 592
Smith, M. D., 517
Smith, M. J., 309
Smith, M. T., 242
Smith, P. H., 72
Smith, S., 392, 395, 404
Smith, S. S., 134
Smithson, E., 477
Smolak, L., 173
Snider, P. R., 504
Snively, T. A., 134
Snyder, P., 502
Soares, C. N., 223, 227, 228, 230, 240, 241, 242, 307
Soares, J. M., 236
Sobel, E. L., 56
Sobel, J., 156
Sobsey, D., 482
Social Issues Research Centre, 103
Sockol, L. E., 392
Soderberg, S., 573
Soderfeldt, B., 48
Soderstrom-Anttila, V., 376, 377
Soeken, K., 544
Soerjomataram, I., 359
Sogaard, A. J., 256
Sokka, T., 539
Solomon, C. G., 259
Solomon, L. J., 131
Sommer, B., 210, 453
Sondheimer, S. J., 320
Song, I. H., 311
Song, L., 505
Sonne, S. C., 106
Sonntag, H., 130
Sorlie, T., 211, 215
Soules, M., 440, 441, 448
Southern, S., 526
Sowers, J. R., 583
Sowers, M., 164
Spangaro, J., 76, 78, 79
Spathonis, K. M., 265
Spear, S. L., 210
Speck, R. M., 268
Specker, S., 190
Spector, I. P., 361
Spelten, E. R., 504
Sperber, A. D., 514, 517
Sperry, S., 201
Spiers, M. V., 556–580, 581–603
Spiers, P., 318

Spiller, R., 517
Spinnato, J. A., 524
Spitz, A. M., 76
Spitze, G., 48, 56
Spitzer, J., 199–222
Spitzer, R., 175
Spoor, S., 155
Spring, B., 129, 135
Sridhara, S. K., 370
Srinivasan, V., 226
Stacy, R., 269
Stafford, R., 456
Stahlhut, R. W., 151
Staines, G., 52
Stallones, L., 391
Stanton, A. L., 491–513, 548
Staples, F. R., 208
Starkey, P., 318
Starkstein, S. E., 594
Starr, P., 14
Staska, S., 184, 284
Staten, D., 469
Staum, R., 48
Stearns, V., 235
Steel, P., 50
Stefanick, M., 456
Stein, M. B., 130
Stein, M. D., 107
Stein, M. T., 374
Steinbrook, R., 162
Steiner, M., 229, 233, 305–327
Steiner, T. J., 565
Steinhausen, H., 178
Stenager, E., 569
Stenberg, U., 498
Stepanski, E. J., 518
Stephen, E. H., 360
Stephens, M. A., 56
Stephenson, M., 371
Stepleman, L., 82
Sterba, K. R., 546
Sterk, C. E., 294
Stern, L., 159
Sternfeld, B., 164, 305
Sterns, A. A., 56
Sterns, H. L., 56
Sterzik, K., 334, 338
Stevens, C. M., 127
Stevens, J., 258
Stevens, R. G., 240
Stevens, S. L., 130
Stewart, A. J., 131
Stewart, D. E., 331, 421, 496
Stewart, S. H., 106
Stewart, W. F., 20, 557, 558, 559, 560, 563, 564
Stibal, J., 50
Stice, E., 155, 181, 182
Stieglitz, J., 444
Stiles, T. C., 520
Stine, K., 295
Stinson, F. S., 102, 110
Stith, S. M., 81, 82

Stockwell, T., 100
Stokes, D. A., 566
Stoller, E. P., 56
Stoller, L. M., 50
Stolz, H. E., 56
Stores, G., 229
Stoskopf, B., 484
Stotland, N. E., 163
Stotts, A. L., 131
Stout, A. L., 318
Stout, J. E., 376
Stout, R. L., 112
Stovall, E., 506
Stovner, L. J., 557
Strachan, M., 185, 190
Strand, E. B., 548
Straub, R. H., 543
Strawderman, M. S., 163
Strecher, V. J., 29
Strehler, E., 334
Streiner, D. L., 484
Streissguth, A. P., 101
Stremler, R., 229
Stridsberg, M., 314
Striegel-Moore, R. H., 175, 181, 527
Strobel, R. J., 153
Strober, M., 179
Strobino, D. M., 375
Stroebe, W., 150
Strohl, K. P., 153, 155
Strohle, A., 265
Stromer, S., 183
Strosberg, J. M., 548
Stroud, L. R., 126
Stuart, S., 365, 391, 399
Stubita, E., 562
Stucky, N. L., 560
Studd, J. W., 321
Stuebe, A., 400, 416, 417, 428
Stuenkel, C., 443, 444, 456
Stuifbergen, A., 570, 573
Stunkard, A. J., 156
Stuppy, D. J., 212
Sturdee, D., 234
Sturgis, S. H., 7
Stussman, B., 265
Su, T. P., 562
Suarez, L., 503
Suarez, M., 283
Subramanian, S. V., 31
Suchday, S., 131
Sue, D. W., 475, 484
Sugarman, M., 429
Sugiyama, Y., 344
Sularz, A., 74
Sullivan, C. E., 229
Sullivan, C. M., 35
Sullivan, G., 451
Sullivan, L. M., 156
Sullivan, P., 179, 482
Sumartojo, E., 38
Sumowski, J. F., 569

Sun, Q., 586
Sundermann, E. E., 587, 590
Sundstrom, I., 314, 315
Sundström-Poromaa, I., 315, 339
Susheela, S., 369
Susman, E. J., 154
Sutcliffe, N., 546
Sutton, M. Y., 36
Sutton-Tyrrell, K., 583
Svanberg, A., 339
Svedlund, J., 527
Sveindottir, H., 311
Swaab, D. F., 237, 239
Swaak, A. J., 543
Swain, A. M., 390, 394, 421
Swami, V., 183, 200, 201
Swan, G. E., 131
Swanson, H. H., 424
Swanson, L. M., 394, 400
Swartz, H., 391
Swartz, M., 394, 586
Swedmark, J., 525
Sweet, S. N., 257
Swider, S. M., 521
Swindle, R., 241, 305, 312
Swinson, R. P., 519
Sykes, M. A., 519
Symanski, E., 49
Syme, S. L., 35
Synder, H. N., 67
Szilagyi, P. G., 402
Szmukler, G., 186

Taal, E., 545, 547
Tabata, I., 257
Tabb, K. M., 391
Tack, J., 515
Taddio, A., 391
Tagliabue, A., 331
Takasuta, N., 234
Talcott, G. W., 135
Talley, A. E., 506
Talley, N. J., 518, 519, 521, 522, 525, 526
Tambs, K., 179
Tamminen, T., 422
Tamres, L. K., 499
Tan, C. C., 49
Tanaka, S., 257
Tang, S. T., 496
Tang, T., 331
Tang, T. N., 517
Tangen, C., 590
Tanko, L. B., 126
Tanner, J. M., 5
Tansey, M. A., 566
Tantleff-Dunn, S., 182, 183, 184
Targett, P., 469
Taris, T. W., 47
Tarpley, M., 542
Tarrant, M., 156
Tarrier, T., 400
Tashkin, D. P., 133

Task Force of the National Advisory Council on Alcohol Abuse and Alcoholism, 114
Taskila, T., 499
Taskin, O., 225
Tate, D., 478
Tate, D. F., 159, 160
Tate, D. G., 479
Tate, R., 445
Tatrow, K., 505
Tauras, J., 129
Tausig, M., 54
Taveras, E. M., 422
Taylor, A., 262, 263, 391
Taylor, C., 190
Taylor, D. J., 240, 317
Taylor, J., 99, 206
Taylor, L. A., 483
Taylor, R. S., 258
Taylor, S. E., 549, 586
Tedeschi, R. G., 499
Teede, H. J., 163
Teitelman, A. M., 35
Teixeira, C., 397
Tejada-Vera, B, 372
Telch, C., 189
Telofski, L. S., 229
Templeton, A. A., 337
Tennant, C. C., 520
Tennen, H., 548
Tennstedt, S., 596
Teplin, L. A., 482
Tepper, S. J., 557, 558, 565
Teran-Santos, J., 238
Teri, L., 595
Terry, P. D., 126
Terry-Humen, E., 296
Tervo, R. C., 484
Tesluk, P. E., 55
Testa, M., 105, 286
Teti, D. M., 400
Teti, M., 31, 36
Texiera, M. E., 156
Thabane, M., 520
Thalabard, J. C., 416
Thaw, J., 176
Thearle, M. J., 373
Theisen, S., 447
Theobald, H., 101
Theofrastous, J. P., 390
Theorell, T., 47, 48, 584
Thies, W., 582, 596
Thilaganathan, B., 357
Thio, I. M., 404
Thoennes, N., 66, 69, 70, 289
Thoits, P. A., 52
Thomas, L. T., 53
Thomas, R., 258
Thombs, B. D., 594
Thompson, A. B., 137
Thompson, B., 14
Thompson, D., 156
Thompson, E. H., 503

Thompson, J. K., 173–198, 201, 211, 285
Thompson, K., 183
Thompson, M. P., 66
Thompson, P. D., 518
Thompson, R., 69
Thompson E. H., 503
Thoresen, M., 548
Thorley, A., 181
Thornton, A., 356, 358
Thorp, J., 430
Thorpy, M. J., 239
Thoyre, S., 368
Thune, I., 260
Thurston, R. C., 232, 584
Thys-Jacobs, S., 318
Tian, J., 318
Tichenor, V., 359
Ticoll, M., 482
Tiefenthaler, J., 81
Tiggemann, M., 156, 177, 183, 185
Tillisch, K., 520
Tilmann, A., 233
Timbang, N., 70
Timko, C. A., 178
Ting, T., 312
Tinney, L., 363
Tipton, N. G., 81
Tirone, V., 292
Tishler, P. V., 238
Tiu, A. Y., 371
Tiwari, A., 82
Tjaden, P., 66, 69, 70, 289
Tobias, A., 568
Tobin, T., 69
Todd, M., 233
Toedter, L., 374, 375
Tokar, D., 185
Tokmakidis, S. P., 260
Tolgyes, T., 177
Toll, B., 128, 134
Tolman, R. M., 82
Tolonen, U., 227
Tolstrupp, J. S., 336
Tomenson, B., 524, 527
Tomeo, C. A., 129
Tomich, P. L., 499, 549
Tone, A., 10
Toner, B. B., 514, 517, 524, 527
Tong, X., 588
Tonigan, J. S., 111, 112
Toossi, M., 46
Torelli, P., 558, 559
Toriumi, D. M., 203
Torner, L., 420
Toth, E., 305
Toubro, S., 159
Toussaint, L., 479
Touvra, A. M., 260
Towfighi, A., 588
Townsend, T. G., 477
Tozzi, F., 526
Tracy, A. J., 55

Tracy, J. K., 233
Tranah, G., 235
Traustadóttir, T., 545
Travarthan, W. R., 233
Travis, C., 448
Treas, J., 56
Treloar, A., 448
Treloar, S. A., 311, 314
Tremblay, A., 455
Tremblay, G. M., 239
Trenkwalder, C., 228
Trentham-Dietz, A., 495
Trethewey, A., 447
Tretter, S., 545
Trevisan, M., 99
Trexler, K., 526
Trickett, P. K., 287
Trijsburg, R. W., 493
Trimble, M., 181
Trinder, J., 226
Tristano, A. G., 540
Trivedi, M. H., 264
Trocki, K., 104
Trogdon, J. G., 156
Trombini, G., 204
Trombley, M., 429
Trost, S., 163
Trupin, L., 542
Tsa, L., 234
Tsagareli, V., 331
Tsai, C.-F., 330
Tsai, V. W., 102
Tsatsoulis, A., 589
Tschann, J. M., 33
Tschudin, S., 312
Tsutsumi, A., 584, 585
Tucco, L., 592
Tucker, K. L., 99
Tufik, S., 236, 238
Tugade, M. M., 548
Tuinstra, J., 498
Tunceli, K., 498
Tuomilehto, J., 157, 259
Tureck, R., 330, 361
Turner, C., 400
Turner, E. C., 588
Turner, H., 67
Turner, J., 52
Turner, L. R., 135
Turner, M. G., 68
Turner, M. J., 527
Turner, R. J., 478
Turner, R. T., 99
Turok, X. P., 256
Turton, P., 373, 374
Tutty, L., 76
Tuunainen, A., 237
Tverdal, A., 126, 256
Tweedy, K., 232
Tweeten, S. S., 212
Twenge, J., 184
Tworoger, S. S., 238
Tylka, T., 185, 285

Tyndale, R. F., 132
Tyszka, A. C., 573
Tzortzis, V., 571

Udden, J., 257
Uhles, M., 243
Uhl-Hochgraber, K., 312
Ullione, M., 573
Umansky, L., 431
UNAIDS, 36
Unal, A., 177
Unver, S., 177
Upadhyaya, H. P., 134
Upchurch, R., 545
Upton, R. L., 181
Urban, M. A., 287
Urponen, H., 240
Urquiza, A. J., 291
Usai, S., 565
U.S. Bureau of Labor Statistics, 470
U.S. Census Data, 469, 470
U.S. Department of Health and
   Human Services, 26, 40, 126, 127,
   129, 405
U.S. Department of Health and
   Human Services, Office on
   Women's Health, 427
U.S. Department of Justice, 67
U.S. Department of Labor, 54
U.S. National Library of Medicine,
   426
U.S. Preventive Task Force, 390, 403
Ushiroyama, T., 316
Ussher, M. H., 262, 263
Utian, W., 442
Uttal, L., 39
Uvnäs-Moberg, K., 420, 425

Vaca, F. E., 102
Vaddiparti, K., 81
Vainio, H., 126
Valdes, V., 416
Valente, T., 129
Valoski, A., 160
Van, P., 375
Vanable, P. A., 287
van Balen, F., 359, 377
van Berlo, W., 289
van Beurden, M., 505
Van Bruggen, L. K., 291
Vance, J. C., 373
van Dam, A. P., 543
Van de Goor, L. A. M., 105
Vandelanotte, C., 265
van den Akker, O. B., 376, 377
Van den Berg, M. H., 265
van den Berg, P., 183
van den Hoogen, F., 546
van den Hout, M. A., 373
van den Maagdenberg, A., 561
van de Poll-Franse, L. V., 502
van der Knapp, H. C., 160
van der Merwe, A. B., 340

van de Ven, M., 128
van Dijk, F. J., 499
Vandivere, S., 363, 364, 365, 366, 379
Van Dongen, H. P. A., 224
Van Driel, M., 314
Vandvik, P. O., 518
van Dyck, R., 263
van Furth, E., 180
Van Harrison, R. V., 47
van Helmond, T., 546
Van Hook, M. P., 401
van Lankveld, W., 546
van Leengoed, E., 424
van Middendorp, H., 544
van Mierlo, C., 160
VanMill, J. G., 263
van Minnen, A., 342
van Niekerk, A., 377
Van Oers, J. A. M., 105
Van Oss Marón, B., 283, 295
Van Riper, M., 368
Van Ryn, M., 39
van Schaik, D. J., 405
Van Thiel, D., 337
van Tilburg, M. A., 522
van 't Spijker, A., 493
Van Wagner, V., 420
VanZile-Tamsen, C., 286
van Zyl, L., 377
Vardy, J., 495
Vardy, T. C., 574
Vargo, M. M., 498
Varin, F., 226
Varma, D., 81
Varnado-Sullivan, P., 176
Varnavides, K., 319
Vasey, J. J., 498
Vashisht, A., 321
Vasilaki, E. I., 111
Vásquez, E., 542
Vaughan, R. A., 373
Vaz, N., 420
Veale, D., 205, 214
Velicer, W. F., 29, 30
Vena, J., 261
Veneracion, M., 427
Ventura, S. J., 371
Verbeek, J. H., 499
Verbrugge, L., 469
Verduyn, C., 400, 401
Verhaak, C. M., 342
Vermeulen, M., 48
Vesga-Lopez, O., 390, 391
Vesselinova-Jenkins, C. K., 518
Vestal, K. D., 68
Vestbo, J., 126
Viana, A. G., 366
Victoria, C. G., 127
Vida Estacio, E., 474
Vieten, C., 230
Vigod, S., 305–327, 392
Viguera, A. C., 391, 392, 393, 394
Villeneuve, P. J., 207

Viner, R., 152
Vingerhoets, A. J., 362, 502, 543
Violato, C., 287
Vishnu, A., 454
Vitaliano, P. P., 582, 596
Vitek, M. P., 590
Vitiello, M. V., 239
Vitousek, K., 186, 187
Vliet Vlieland, T. P., 265
Voas, R. B., 102
Voda, A., 443, 445, 446, 449, 451, 452
Vodermaier, A., 493
Voelbel, G. T., 569
Vogel, J. S., 129
Vogel, L., 469, 470
Vogeltanz, N. D., 98, 99, 103, 105
Vogeltanz-Holm, N., 91–122
Vogelzangs, N., 263
Volaklis, K. A., 260
Volgsten, H., 339, 350
Vollmann, J., 363
Vongruenigen, V., 491
Von Korff, M. R., 522, 564
Voorhees, C. C., 128, 130
Voydanoff, P., 52, 53
Vu, M. B., 255
Vukadinovic, V. V., 213
Vulink, N. C., 214
Vuori, I., 240

Waalen, J., 76
Wack, J. T., 130
Wadden, T. A., 158, 159, 160, 161,
   162, 202, 204, 209
Wade, T., 177, 179
Wadkins, H. I., 402
Wagman, J. S., 8
Wagner, G., 154
Wahlgren D. R., 139
Waidmann, T., 469
Waisman, E., 207
Wake, M., 229
Wald, A., 524
Waldron, I., 48, 129
Walker, A. M., 424
Walker, C. H., 424
Wall, G. C., 519
Wallberg, M., 571
Wallston, K., 541, 544, 548
Walsh, B., 174, 187, 188
Walsh, C. P., 427
Walsh, J. K., 241
Walster, E., 474
Walster, G. W., 474
Walters, E. E., 494
Walters, J. F., 233
Waltman, N. L., 268
Wang, H., 164
Wang, J. H., 528
Wang, P., 331
Wang, S. J., 562
Wang, S. S., 162
Wang, W., 334

Wang, Y., 474
Wanner, M., 266, 268
Warburton, A. L., 72, 73, 78
Ward, E., 491, 492
Ward, T., 454
Wardle, J., 502
Warnecke, R., 131
Warner, P., 311, 316
Warnock, J. K., 519
Warren, A. M., 477
Warren, K. G., 572
Warren, M. P., 181
Wasik, S. L., 356, 358
Watanabe, K., 454
Waterman, P. D., 31
Waters, W. E., 557
Wathen, C. N., 76
Watkins, E., 12
Watkins, S., 400
Watson, A. C. H., 206
Watson, T., 174
Watt, R. G., 429
Watts, C., 64, 287
Waugh, M. S., 127
Waxman, B. F., 482
Weaver, A. L., 526
Weaver, T. L., 289
Webb, J. R., 479
Webb, M. S., 131
Webb, P. M., 418
Webb, V., 229
Webb, W., 208, 238
Weber, L., 31, 37, 38, 40
Webster, T. F., 151
Wechsler, H., 102
Wechsler, N. F., 11
Wee, C. C., 154
Weekley, C. K., III, 131
Weeks, J. C., 496
Weerth, C., 423
Wegener, S., 477
Wehman, P., 469
Wehr, T., 225, 227
Wehrer, J., 414
Wehrie, R., 228
Weiderpass, E., 126
Weiland, N. G., 588
Weinberg, J., 101
Weiner, D. A., 482
Weinstein, A. R., 258
Weinstock, J., 268
Weisberg, R., 214
Weisman, C. S., 15
Weisman, M. H., 546
Weisman, O., 424
Weismann, R. E., 155
Weisner, C., 107, 112
Weiss, S. J., 230
Weiss, T., 549
Weissman, M. M., 478, 586
Weitz, T. A., 371
Weitzmann, M., 52
Wekking, E. M., 543

Weller, A., 424
Weller, W. E., 494
Welles, S. L., 35
Wellisch, D., 207
Wells, J. A., 47, 48
Wells, K. B., 401
Wells, K. E., 206
Wells, S., 96
Welsh, J. A., 366
Welte, J. W., 99
Weng, H. H., 454
Wenger, N. K., 593
Wenzel, A., 397
Wenzel, L., 497
Wenzel, L. B., 499
Werner, C., 362
Werner, S., 420
Werth, E., 225
Wertheim, E. H., 181, 229
Wessel, T. R., 258
Wessinger, S., 519
West, A. E., 400
West, B., 105
West, C. M., 291
West, J., 443
West, J. D., 495
West, J. R., 101
West, M., 469
Westergaard, L. G., 333
Westerstahl, A., 362
Westerterp, K. R., 161, 255
Westhoff, C., 127
Westman, M., 51
Westrom, L., 296
Wetter, D. W., 128
Wewers, M. E., 126, 134
Wey, P. D., 204
Wezeman, F., 101
Whelan, A. M., 319
Whitaker, L. A., 202, 204, 209
Whitaker, R. C., 131
White, A., 454
White, A. R., 592
White, B., 477
White, D. L., 523
White, P., 137
Whiteford, L. M., 362
Whitehead, R., 416
Whitehead, W. E., 514, 515, 517,
  518, 519, 520, 521, 522, 524,
  525, 527
Whiteman, D. C., 418
White-Traut, R., 415
Whitlock, E. P., 107, 111
Whitson, H. E., 591
Whorwell, P. J., 515, 517, 518, 520,
  524, 525, 526, 527
Widstrom, A. M., 420, 422
Wiebe, S., 225
Wiegand, B., 229
Wiemann, C. M., 285
Wigger, A., 420
Wiggins, M., 49

Wiggs, L., 229
Wijma, K., 236
Wilburn, K., 394
Wilcox, S., 266, 268
Wildes, J., 175, 179, 189
Wilfley, D., 173, 175, 186, 188,
  189
Wilhelm, S., 177, 214
Wilhelmsen, I., 518
Wilkerson, B., 104
Willard, S. G., 211, 215
Willett, W. C., 152, 260, 262, 318,
  417
Willey J. S., 492
Williams, D. M., 265
Williams, D. R., 35, 37
Williams, I. C., 595
Williams, J., 175
Williams, K. C. D., 201
Williams, L. M., 291
Williams, L. S., 594
Williams, M., 228
Williams, M. A., 259
Williams, P., 285, 294
Williamson, D., 176
Williamson, D. A., 162
Williamson, D. F., 259
Williamson, K., 570
Willinger, M., 230
Willness, C. R., 50
Wilsnack, R. W., 93, 97, 103,
  104
Wilsnack, S. C., 91–122, 289
Wilson, C., 160
Wilson, G., 186, 187, 188
Wilson, K., 133
Wilson, P. M., 132
Wilson, R., 443, 587
Wilson, T., 173, 175, 187, 188
Winberg, J., 420
Windle, R. J., 420
Wing, R. R., 155, 157, 159, 160,
  162, 547
Wing, Y. K., 223, 240
Wingate, D. L., 518
Wingood, G. M., 31, 33, 34, 285,
  287, 294
Wingrove, J., 308
Winickoff, J., 137
Winking, J., 444
Winnick, J. J., 268
Winter, A. C., 563
Winter, L., 596
Winter, M. A., 400
Winterich, J., 445, 453
Winters, C., 160
Winzelberg, A., 190
Wirz, M., 482
Wisborg, K., 101, 335
Wisner, K., 390, 391, 393, 394, 398,
  401
Wittchen, H. U., 130
Wittmann, L., 549

Wohlfahrt, J., 372
Wohlgemuth, W., 232
Wolf, A. W., 230
Wolf, J., 16
Wolf, P. A., 156
Wolfe, D., 180
Wolfson, A. R., 223, 228, 229
Wolfson, C., 582
Wolitzky-Taylor, K. B., 290
Wollan, P., 402
Wollenhaupt, J., 469
Wolman, W., 215
Womble, L. G., 162
Women's Health, 21
Women's Health Initiative Steering
   Committee, 456, 457
Wonderlich, S. A., 176, 478
Wonders, K., 260
Wong, D., 474
Wong, F., 496
Wong, J., 82, 226
Wood, C. L., 158
Woodhouse, L. M., 211
Woodland, M. B., 373
Woods, A. B., 71
Woods, N., 225, 232, 233
Woodward, S., 232, 233
Woolfenden, S., 173
Woolhouse, H., 401, 404
Worden, J. W., 373, 374
World Health Organization (WHO),
   72, 73, 75, 163, 414, 443–444, 454,
   467, 468
Worthman, J., 429
Wortman, C. B., 477
Wragg, R., 594, 595
Wright, B., 479
Wright, C., 82, 331
Wright, J., 212
Wright, K., 226, 227
Wright, M. O., 523
Writing Group for the Women's
   Health Initiative Investigators, 235,
   443, 456, 457
Wu, A. H., 261
Wu, A. W., 494
Wu, L., 107
Wu, P., 133
Wu, R., 134
Wyatt, G. E., 287
Wyatt, K., 318, 319
Wycokk, S. C., 82
Wyman, J. F., 589

Wynder, E. L., 125
Wynter, K. H., 363

Xu, J., 154, 372, 373, 492
Xu, Q., 590
Xue, F., 126, 262

Yaffe, K., 443, 587, 589,
   590, 595
Yaggi, H. K., 238
Yalom, I. D., 421
Yamaguchi, K., 105
Yamanaka, H., 125
Yamazaki, Y., 549
Yan, Y., 37
Yanez, B., 491–513
Yang, C. K., 230
Yang, D., 261
Yang, H.-C., 496
Yang, L., 424
Yang, M., 305
Yang, P. C., 230
Yanovski, J. A., 210
Yao, J. F., 518
Yapa, C., 594
Yasuda, S., 469
Yates, A., 215
Yates, H. A., 574
Yawn, B. P., 154, 402
Ybarra, O., 283
Ye, Y. J., 56
Yeasavage, J. A., 99
Yee, J. L., 596
Yee, S., 376, 377
Yen, S. C., 320
Yen, S. S., 226
Yi, H., 95
Ylikorkala, O., 400
Yoder, J., 185
Yonkers, K. A., 390, 392, 393, 394,
   395, 396, 397, 398, 399, 401
Yoon, S. Y., 123, 124, 125
York, J. L., 99
York-Crowe, E. E., 162
Yoshida, K., 396
Young, A. S., 401
Young, M. E., 480
Young, T., 231, 232, 238, 243
Young, V. L., 206
Young-DeMarco, L., 356, 358
Youngstedt, S. D., 264
Yount, S. M., 229
Yu, F., 589

Yuker, H., 484
Yurchesen, M. E., 235

Zaadstra, B. M., 154
Zador, P. L., 102
Zaffke, M. E., 228
Zagoory-Sharon, O., 424
Zak, R., 229
Zakocs, R. C., 102
Zald, D. H., 155
Zambaldi, C. F., 398
Zang, E. A., 125
Zarcadoolas, C., 369
Zaslavsky, A. M., 589
Zatzick, D., 402
Zautra, A. J., 543, 545, 548
Zavos, P. M., 338
Zawacki, T., 106
Zawitz, M. W., 66, 67
Zayas, L. H., 405
Zea, M. C., 477
Zebracki, K., 469
Zelman, D. C., 481
Zeman, M. V., 132
Zemp, E., 312
Zerbe, K. J., 177
Zervas, I., 574
Zerwic, J., 592
Zgierska, A., 231
Zhang, B., 223, 240
Zhang, C. L., 259
Zhang, J., 582
Zhang, L., 505
Zhang, M., 334
Zhang, Q., 474
Zierler, S., 31, 36
Zillmer, E., 583, 592
Zimmer, B., 182
Zimmerman, B., 526
Zimmerman, C., 64, 287
Zinc, A., 469
Zinsmeister, A. R., 521, 526, 527
Zinzow, H. M., 290
Znoj, H., 346
Zois, C. E., 260
Zojaji, R., 205
Zolnoun, D., 400
Zschoche, S., 46
Zucker, A. N., 128, 131
Zuniga, C. D., 106
Zuttermeister, P. C., 236
Zwi, A., 76
Zwickl, S., 287

Subject Index

AAP (American Academy of Pediatrics), 230
AARP (American Association of Retired Persons), 56
Abdominal pain, 515. *See also* Irritable bowel syndrome (IBS)
Abdominoplasty, 199, 211
Abortion
  contextual factors, 368–369
  decision-making about, 369–370
  elective, 367, 368–369
  history of, 17–19
  induced, 367
  psychosocial consequences of, 370–371
  and race, 368
  reasons for choosing, 370
  social support after, 371
  spontaneous, 101, 337
  therapeutic, 367–368
Abuse
  childhood (*see* Childhood sexual abuse (CSA))
  and disability, 482–483
  emotional, 64
  and irritable bowel syndrome, 522–523
  by relatives, 69
  sexual (*see* Sexual abuse)
Accidents, automobile, 102
Acculturation. *See also* Culture
  and PMDD, 312
  and rheumatic disease, 542
  and risky sexual behavior, 295
Acetylcholinesterase inhibitors, 575
ACOG (American College of Obstetricians and Gynecologists), 21
ACTH, 419, 574
Actigraphy, 224
Active sex, 282–286
Activities of daily living, 150, 468
Acupuncture, 319, 329
  and hot flashes, 454
  and infertility, 333–335
Addiction, 98. *See also* Alcohol use; Substance abuse
Adipose tissue, 318
Adjustment, 467, 472, 476
  and benefit finding, 499–500
  and cancer, 494–495, 500–501, 504

to rheumatic disease, 545
Adjustment disorder, 339
Adjuvant therapy, 492–493
Adolescents
  and abdominal pain, 515
  and abortion, 368
  and anorexia nervosa, 178
  and body dysmorphic disorder (BDD), 178
  and body piercing, 212
  and cosmetic medical procedures, 203–204
  and dating violence, 68
  and early sexual debut, 296
  and eating disorders, 177
  engagement in disliked sexual activities, 293
  growth and development, 4–6
  healthy sexuality, 296–297
  history of health, 3–4
  and migraine headaches, 563
  and peer pressure, 182
  and physical activity, 255–256, 261, 269–270
  and pregnancy, 7–8, 372
  and regular gynecological exams, 7, 8–9
  and rheumatic disease, 540–541
  and rhinoplasty, 204
  and smoking, 128
  and tattoos, 212
  and venereal disease, 19
Adoption, 363–366, 375–376, 378–379
Adrenaline, 341
Advanced sleep phase disorder (ASPD), 239
Aerobic exercise, 260, 268, 318. *See also* Physical activity
African American women. *See also* Minority women; Women of color
  and abortion, 368
  and alcohol use, 99, 104
  and Alzheimer's disease, 583
  awareness about heart disease, 591–592
  and breastfeeding, 429
  and cancer mortality, 492, 502–503
  and cardiovascular disease, 128
  as caregivers, 595

and childlessness, 357
and colorectal cancer, 525
and condom use, 294
and cosmetic medical procedures, 203
and disability, 469
and effects of childhood sexual abuse, 287
employment with disabilities, 470
and fertility treatments, 360
and fetal loss, 372, 375
and heart disease, 583, 587
and HIV/AIDS, 32
and infertility, 346, 347, 349
and IPV victimization, 69, 82
leading causes of death in, 26
and menopause, 453–454
and mental health treatment, 405
and migraine headaches, 558
and obesity, 32
and physical activity, 267, 270
and PMDD, 312, 315
and rheumatic disease, 541, 542
and sexual assertiveness, 285
and sexual dysfunction, 282
and sexual revictimization, 291
and sleep, 234
and smoking, 128, 131, 137
and sterilization, 18
and STIs, 35
and stroke, 583
Age
  and adjustment to cancer, 503
  and alcohol use, 103–105
  and cosmetic medical procedures, 203–204
  and disability, 469
  and infertility, 336
  and IPV homicides, 67
  and nonlethal IPV assaults, 68
Agency, 476
  in childbearing, 355–388
  and disability, 479
  and sexuality, 298
Aging. *See also* Older women
  and cosmetic medical procedures, 208–211
  and disability, 593
  and eating disorders, 181
  and gender, 443
  importance of studying, 590–591

medicalization of, 203
most common disorders in women, 581
and physical activity, 256
and reproductive health, 440
and sleep, 236–239
Agoraphobia, 75
AIDS. *See* HIV/AIDS
Alaska Native women, 26, 289, 375, 468–469
Alcoholics Anonymous, 112
Alcoholism, 95
Alcohol use, 91–122
  among girls, 95
  assessment, intervention and prevention of problems, 106–114
  and cancer morbidity and mortality, 99–100
  and cardiovascular disease, 99, 100
  and disability, 483
  and education level, 104
  and employment, 103–105
  and ethnicity, 103–105
  gender differences, 98, 99, 102–103, 106–114
  and genetics, 103
  health and social consequences of drinking, 99–102
  and infertility, 101, 329, 335–337
  intervention programs, 92
  overview of use by women, 92–99
  during pregnancy, 101–102, 115, 335, 337
  prevention of risky drinking, 114
  and race, 103–106
  and rape, 290
  and reproductive health, 101
  risk factors for women's problem drinking, 102–106
  and risky behaviors, 95
  screening for problems, 106–108
  and smoking, 129–130
  treatment programs, 92, 110–114
  use across the lifespan, 94
Alcohol use disorders (AUD), 93, 96–98
  across lifespan by race/ethnicity, 99
  and genetics, 103
  and insomnia, 241
Alcohol Use Disorders Identification Test (AUDIT), 108
Aleut. *See* Alaska Native women
Allen, Edward, 8–9
Allopregnanolone, 314
ALS (amyotrophic lateral sclerosis), 471
Alternative birthing practices, 17
Alzheimer's disease, 556, 581–603
  and caregivers, 595–596
  commonalities in epidemiology with heart disease and heart disease, 581–591

and cortisol, 585
costs of, 582
course of, 591–596
and depression, 586–587, 594–595
diagnosis, 583–584
and disability, 591–596
and ethnicity, 583
gender differences, 582–583
and genetics, 589–591
psychosocial risk factors, 584–587
statistics, 582
and stress, 584–586
symptoms of, 592–593
Amantadine hydrochloride, 575
Amenorrhea, 174
  and infertility, 331
  lactational, 416
American Academy of Pediatrics (AAP), 230
American Association of Retired Persons (AARP), 56
American Changing Lives Study (Rozario), 56
American College of Obstetricians and Gynecologists (ACOG), 21, 360
American College of Sports Medicine, 261
American Indian women
  and alcohol use, 99, 103–104
  and cancer, 26
  cultural considerations following fetal mortality, 375
  and disability, 468–469
  and rape, 289
American Migraine Prevalence and Prevention Study, 557
American Psychological Association Task Force on the Sexualization of Girls, 284
American Society for Prophylaxis in Obstetrics (ASPO), 16
American Society for Reproductive Medicine (ASRM), 328, 360
American Society of Plastic Surgeons (ASPS), 199
Americans with Disabilities Act, 328, 467
AMH hormone, 346–347
Amniocentesis, 356–357
Amyotrophic lateral sclerosis (ALS), 471
Anal sex, 293
Androgenization, 320
Androgens, 333, 442, 557
Anemia, 307
Anger, 587
Anomalies, congenital, 372
Anorexia nervosa (AN), 173–174. *See also* Eating disorders
  and cosmetic medical procedures, 214–215
  course and prognosis, 178

and heritability, 179
and infertility, 331
and irritable bowel syndrome, 526–527
key diagnostic features, 173–174
and liposuction, 210–211
and migraine headaches, 563
mortality, 178
treatment options, 186–187
Antenatal period
  anxiety symptoms, 397–400
  burden of psychiatric symptoms, 390–391
  consequences of mood symptoms during, 399–400
  depressive symptoms, 391–392
  hypomania and manic symptoms, 392–393
  identifying women in need of help during, 401–404
  obsessive-compulsive disorder, 397
  and psychiatric symptoms, 389
Anterior cingulate cortex (ACC), 515–516
Anti-aging cosmetic surgical procedures, 208–211
Antibiotics, 518, 526
Anticonvulsants, 565
Antidepressants
  and breastfeeding mothers, 422
  and eating disorders, 186, 187, 188
  and irritable bowel syndrome, 526
  and migraine headaches, 565
  and physical activity, 264
  and PMDD, 319–320
  for puerperal psychiatric disorders, 405
  and sleep, 227, 235, 241
  and smoking cessation, 132
Antidiarrheal loperamide, 525
Antirape movement, 19–20
Antispasmodics, 525
Anxiety
  after perinatal loss, 374
  and alcohol use, 102, 106
  during antenatal period, 399–400
  and breast cancer, 501
  and cancer, 494
  and disability, 478
  and eating disorders, 173, 176, 181
  and heart disease, 587
  and infertility, 329, 330, 340
  and insomnia, 241
  and intimate partner violence, 75
  and migraine headaches, 562–563
  and physical activity, 263–264
  during postpartum period, 400
  sexual, 282
  and sexual assault, 290
  and smoking, 129–130
  and vascular disease, 586
  and work-family conflict, 53

Anxiety disorders
   associated with pregnancy, 397–399
   and fetal loss, 373
   and infertility, 339
   and irritable bowel syndrome, 519
   premenstrual exacerbation of
      symptoms, 308
   screening for, 403–404
Apnea, 238. *See also* Obstructive sleep
   apnea (OSA)
Appearance, physical, 284–285. *See
   also* Cosmetic medical procedures
Appearance anxiety, 182, 185, 201,
   284
Appearance comparison, 183
Aricept, 575
Arms, Suzanne, 17
Arthritis, 469, 470, 539, 542. *See also*
   Rheumatic diseases
Arthritis Self-Management Program
   (ASMP), 545
Artificial insemination, 329
Asian American women. *See also*
   Minority women; Women of
   color
   and alcohol use, 104
   and Alzheimer's disease, 583
   and cancer, 26
   and cosmetic medical procedures,
      203
   and disability, 469
   and infertility, 346, 347
   and menopause, 453
   and migraine headaches, 558
   and PMDD, 312; 315
   and rheumatic disease, 541
ASPO (American Society for
   Prophylaxis in Obstetrics), 16
ASPS (American Society of Plastic
   Surgeons), 199
Assault, 64. *See also* Abuse; Intimate
   partner violence (IPV); Rape;
   Sexual assault
Assertiveness, sexual, 285–286, 288,
   293, 296
Assessment, psychological
   of cosmetic medical procedures
      patients, 215–216
Assisted reproductive technology
   (ART), 329–330, 359–361, 363.
   See also Infertility
Asthma, 127
Atherosclerotic disease, 126, 584
AUDIT screening tool, 108, 109
Aura, 558–559, 560
Autoimmune disorders, 307, 539,
   567
Autonomic nervous system, 341, 515
Autonomy, sexual, 283
Avonex, 575

Baby blues, 393–394, 421
Baby boomers, 446

Back pain, 517
Baclofen, 575
Bacterial vaginosis, 295
Baird, Bill, 11–12
Bariatric surgery, 156, 162, 211
Battering. *See* Assault
Bed-sharing, 230
Behavioral interventions
   for depression after stroke, 594
   and eating disorders, 186
   and infertility, 344
   for migraine headaches, 565–566
   and smoking cessation, 133
   and weight loss, 157–159
Behavioral shaping, 133–134
Behavior disorders, 129–130
Behavior problems, 127
Behavior theories, psychosocial health,
   29–31
Benefit finding, 499–500, 548–549
Benzodiazepines, 241
Beta-blockers, 565
Bias, 472
Bidis, 124
Binge drinking, 290. *See also* Alcohol
   use
Binge eating, 174, 339
Binge-eating disorder (BED), 173,
   175
   and cognitive behavioral therapy
      (CBT), 191
   course and prognosis, 178
   demographics, 175
   treatment options, 188–189
Biofeedback, 319, 525, 544, 565–566
Bipolar disorder, 586
   and intimate partner violence, 75
   and physical activity, 264
   postpartum, 396, 397
   during pregnancy, 392–393
   premenstrual exacerbation of
      symptoms, 308
   and premenstrual mood
      disturbance, 309
Birth control. *See* Contraception
Birth defects, 373
Birth rates, 10
Bisexual women. *See also* Lesbian
   women; Same-sex relationships
   and adoption, 366
   and alcohol use, 104
   and childhood sexual abuse, 287
   and rape, 289
   and sexual revictimization, 291
Black cohosh, 236, 242
Black women. *See* African American
   women
Bladder control, 573
Blepharoplasty, 203, 208–209
Bloating, 317, 516–517
Blood alcohol levels (BALs), 99
Blood pressure, 157, 260. *See also*
   Hypertension

Blood sugar, 259
Blunt force trauma, 72
BMI (body mass index), 149
   and infertility, 330–333, 346
   and liposuction, 210
   and menarche, 152
   and obesity, 152–154
   and physical activity, 258
   and PMDD, 318
Body adornment, 199–222
Body appearance dissatisfaction, 182
Body contouring procedures, 211
Body dysmorphic disorder (BDD),
   175–176
   and cognitive behavioral therapy
      (CBT), 191
   and cosmetic medical procedures,
      202, 213–214, 216
   course and prognosis, 178
   prevalence, 177
   and rhinoplasty, 205
   treatment options, 189
Body esteem, 185
Body fat, 257, 318
Body image
   and abdominoplasty, 211
   and binge-eating disorder, 175
   and body piercing/tattoos, 212
   and breast augmentation, 206–207,
      208
   and bulimia nervosa, 188
   and cosmetic medical procedures,
      201–202, 214–215, 216
   and eating disorders, 173, 181
   and irritable bowel syndrome, 517
   and media, 183–184
   in middle age and beyond, 182
   and multiple sclerosis, 573
   and obesity, 156
   and sexual maturity, 181
   and smoking cessation, 135
   and toys, 184
Body mass index. *See* BMI (body mass
   index)
Body monitoring, 285
Body piercing, 212–213
Body shame, 182, 184–185, 201, 285
Body surveillance, 185, 285
Bodywork, 333
Bonding, maternal, 423–425
Bone density, 99, 256, 451
Bone disease, 456
Bone loss, 444
Botox (*Botulinum* toxin) injections,
   199, 200, 209, 210
Bowels. *See* Irritable bowel syndrome
   (IBS)
Brain
   variations in men and women,
      556–557
Breast augmentation, cosmetic, 199,
   205–208, 215
Breast cancer, 5, 125, 491

and alcohol use, 100, 115
and anxiety, 501
and breastfeeding, 418–419
and childlessness, 359
and depression, 493–494, 501–502
and employment, 499
and fatigue, 495
and hormone therapy, 457
mortality, 262
and overweight, 153
and pain, 496
and physical activity, 255, 260–262, 268
and shift work, 239–240
side effects of treatment, 495–496
and sleep problems, 495
and smoking, 127, 262
surgery, 492
treatment, 492
Breastfeeding, 127, 152, 414–439
biology of, 415–416
and breast cancer, 418–419
and ethnicity, 429
factors that discourage, 414, 426–427
fathers' response to, 430
as form of contraception, 416
labor and economic costs, 427–428
and maternal bonding, 423–425
mental health benefits of, 419–425
and metabolic syndrome, 416–418
and multiple sclerosis, 572
negative effects of, 430
nutritional demands of, 426
and ovarian cancer, 418–419
physical costs of, 425–427
physical health benefits of, 416–419
and postpartum depression, 421–423
potential maternal costs of, 425–431
reasons for deciding to, 414
and sex, 430
and sleep, 229–230
social costs, 428–431
time commitment, 427
and type 2 diabetes, 417–418, 428
and weight gain, 153
and weight loss, 416–418
Breasts
and breastfeeding, 426–427
tenderness, 441, 450
Breathing, sleep-disordered, 231
Bright light therapy, 227, 239, 240, 264, 319
Bulimia nervosa (BN), 174–175. *See also* Eating disorders
and cognitive behavioral therapy (CBT), 191
and cosmetic medical procedures, 214–215
course and prognosis, 178
demographics, 175
and heritability, 179

and irritable bowel syndrome, 526–527
and liposuction, 210–211
and migraine headaches, 563
treatment options, 187–188
Bupropion, 132–133, 134
Burden, 472
Buspirone, 315
Buxton, D. Lee, 11

Cachexia, 174
Caffeine, 240, 331, 372
Calcitonin gene-related peptide (CGRP), 560
Calcium, 318
Caloric intake, 150, 160
and anorexia nervosa, 174
and eating disorders, 189
CAM. *See* Complementary and alternative medicine (CAM)
Cancer, 26, 491–513. *See also specific type*
and alcohol use, 99–100
and anxiety, 494
and childbearing, 496–497
cognitive-behavioral interventions, 505
coping processes, 503–504
and depression, 493–494, 504
directions for application and research, 505–506
effect on employment, 498–499, 504
epidemiology, 491–492
and ethnicity, 502–503
and fatigue, 495
finding benefit in experience of, 499–500
and gender, 493
and hormone therapy, 457
importance of social support, 504
incidence rates, 491
and infertility, 329, 496–497
interventions, 504–505
medical factors, 500–502
mortality, 491–492, 502–503
and overweight, 153
and pain, 495–496
and physical activity, 255, 505
physical effects, 495–496
and psychological health, 493–494, 501–502
and quality of life, 493–500, 500–504
and reproductive health, 496–497
screening, 491
sexual and reproductive consequences, 496–497
side effects of treatment, 495–496
and sleep problems, 495
social domain, 497–498
and sociodemographic factors, 502–503

staging, 492–493
and stress, 502
surgical intervention, 492–493
survival rate, 492
and tobacco use, 125–126, 128
treatment, 492–493
Candidiasis, 425
Carbohydrates, 318
Cardiac abnormalities
and obesity, 153
and obstructive sleep apnea, 242
Cardiomyopathy, 99
Cardiovascular disease (CVD), 581
and African Americans, 128
and alcohol use, 99, 100
costs of, 582
and hypertension, 260
and job strain, 47
and physical activity, 258
and smoking, 125, 126, 127, 262
and weight loss, 157
Caregiving, 56, 57, 498, 595–596
Caucasian women. *See* White women
Cell phones, 269–270
Centers for Disease Control and Prevention, 93, 294
and infertility, 328
and intimate partner violence, 65
unintended pregnancy, 295
Central nervous system, 442, 515, 567
Cervarix, 295
Cervical cancer, 8, 9, 125–126, 295, 296
Cesarean section, 17. *See also* Childbirth
CGRP (calcitonin gene-related peptide), 560
Chamomile, 242
Change of life. *See* Menopause
Chasteberry, 319
Chemical exposure, 329
Chemical peels, 199, 209, 210
Chemotherapy, 329, 492–493, 495, 500
Chewing tobacco, 124
Child abuse. *See* Childhood sexual abuse (CSA)
Child Abuse Prevention and Treatment Act, 286
Childbearing. *See also* Pregnancy
and cancer, 496–497
decision-making about, 355–357
delaying, 356, 358
and multiple sclerosis, 572
and psychiatric symptoms, 389
psychology of agency in, 355–388
and rheumatic diseases, 539–540
societal changes, 356
that assists others to have children, 375–379
Childbirth, 15–17
Childbirth Without Fear (Dick-Read), 16

Child health
  history of, 3–4
  and physical activity, 255
  and smoking, 127
Childhood sexual abuse (CSA), 19,
    286–288. *See also* Sexual abuse
  and alcohol use, 105
  definition and prevalence, 286–287
  and healthy sexuality, 298
  and irritable bowel syndrome,
    522–523
  and lesbian women, 287
  and risky sexual behaviors, 287
  sexual health consequences of,
    287–288
  and sexual revictimization, 291–292
Childhood victimization, 105
Child labor, 4
Childlessness, 10, 357–359
Child mortality, 3
Chiropractic treatment, 319
Choices. *See* Agency
Cholesterol, high
  and cardiovascular risk, 588
  and lifestyle risk factors, 584
  and weight loss, 157
Chorionic villus sampling (CVS), 356
Chromosomal abnormality, 372
Chronic disease, 539. *See also*
    Rheumatic diseases
  and cognitive-behavioral
    interventions, 544–545
  and family coping strategies, 546
  and physical activity, 258–262
  and quality of life, 544
Chronic obstructive pulmonary
    disease (COPD), 126, 243
Chronic pelvic pain, 289, 518
Chutta, 124
Circadian rhythm, 224, 226, 236, 237,
    239, 319
  during menopause, 233
  and PMDD, 318
Cirrhosis, 99
Citalopram, 319
Civil rights, 14
Classism, 27
Climacteric. *See* Menopause
Clomipramine, 319
Clonidine, 236
Cluster headaches, 559. *See also*
    Migraine headaches
Cognition, 556
  and age-related dysfunction, 585
  and estrogen, 588–589
  and hormone therapy, 589
  and multiple sclerosis, 569
  and obesity, 156
  and sleep, 232–233
  and well-being, 479
Cognitive behavioral therapy (CBT)
  and alcohol use, 112, 113–114
  and body image, 216

and cancer, 505
and depression, 405
and eating disorders, 185–186,
    187–189, 190, 191
and infertility, 343–344
and insomnia, 242
and irritable bowel syndrome, 527
and menopause, 236
and multiple sclerosis, 574
and perimenopausal distress, 455
and PMDD, 319
and rheumatic disease, 544–545,
    546–547
and smoking cessation, 135–136
Cognitive functioning
  and alcohol use, 99
  and physical activity, 256
Cognitive impairment, 468, 587. *See
    also* Alzheimer's disease
Cognitive rehabilitation, 575
Coitus, early, 8
Colitis, ulcerative, 523
Collagen, 209
College women. *See also* Young
    women
  and body piercing, 212
  and cosmetic medical procedures,
    200, 201
  and rape, 68, 290–291
  and risky drinking, 114
  and sexual compliance, 292–293
Colon cancer, 255
Colonoscopy, 525
Colorectal cancer, 525
Combahee River Collective, 28
COMBINE study, 92, 113–114
Co-mothering, 362
Complementary and alternative
    medicine (CAM), 319
  and infertility, 333–335
  and menopause, 455
  and multiple sclerosis, 575
  and rheumatoid disease, 545
Compliance, 476
  sexual, 292–293
Comstock Law, 9, 10
Concentration problems, 330
Conception, delayed, 126
Condoms, 34, 36–37, 285, 294–295.
    See also Contraception
Congressional Caucus for Womens's
    Issues, 21
Connective tissue. *See* Rheumatic
    diseases
Consciousness raising, 14–15
Consensual sex, 286–292
Constipation, 525, 526
Consumer Attitudes Survey, 200
Contraception, 12, 14. *See also*
    Pregnancy
  breastfeeding as form of, 416
  and childbearing options, 356, 358
  complications from, 320

emergency, 20, 290
history of, 9–13
hormonal, 12–13
and intimate partner violence, 294
and multiple sclerosis, 571
physician-controlled, 10–11
and PMDD, 320
and rheumatic diseases, 540
and sleep, 227
and smoking, 126–127
and stroke risk, 588
Controlling tactics, 65
Co-parenting, 430
COPD. *See* Chronic obstructive
    pulmonary disease (COPD)
Coping behaviors, 316
  and cancer, 503–504
  and child relinquishment, 379
  and chronic illness, 546
  and disability, 475–476
  following perinatal loss, 374–375
  and infertility, 343
  and irritable bowel syndrome,
    520–521
  and menopause, 454–455
  and multiple sclerosis, 574
  and rheumatic disease, 542
Cordocentesis, 357
Core body temperature (cBT), 226,
    233, 236, 237
Coronary artery disease, 584
Coronary heart disease (CHD)
  and alcohol use, 99, 100
  and hormone therapy, 456–457,
    589
  and obesity, 152, 153
  and physical activity, 255, 258
Corticotropic-releasing hormone
    (CRH), 516
Cortisol, 419, 420–421, 585
Co-sleeping, 230
Cosmetic medical procedures, 185,
    189, 199–222
  increased acceptance of, 200–201
  minimally invasive, 209–210
  motivations for, 200–204
  and psychiatric disorders, 213–215
  psychological assessment of patients,
    215–216
  restorative, 208–211
  type-changing, 204–208
Cotinine, 337
Couples. *See also* Relationships,
    intimate
  and cancer, 498
  therapy, 329
CPAP (continuous positive airway
    pressure) therapy, 231, 243
Cramps, leg, 228
CRH (corticotropic-releasing
    hormone), 516
Criminal justice system, 19, 64
Crohn's disease, 523

Cryopreservation, 360
Culture. *See also* Acculturation
    and breastfeeding, 429
    and cancer, 503
    expectations, 281
    and fetal mortality, 375
    and infertility, 347–348
    and menopause, 452–454
    and migraine headaches, 558
    and mind-body relationship,
        474–475
    and older women, 445–446
CVD. *See* Cardiovascular disease
    (CVD)

Daily Record of Severity of Problems
    (DRSP), 309–311
DALY (disability-adjusted life years),
    312–313
Danazol, 320
Date rape, 289
Dating violence, 68
Davis, Katherine Bement, 6, 10
DDT, 151
Death
    after myocardial infarction, 591
    from cancer, 491
    from cardiovascular disease, 258
    early, 255
    from heart disease, 592
    infant, 372, 373–374
    leading causes for women, 26, 581
    neonatal, 372, 373–374
    and obesity, 32
    from stroke, 591
Decision-making. *See* Agency
Deep vein thrombosis, 320
Demand-control model, 47–48
Dementia, 569, 583, 589, 596. *See also*
    Alzheimer's disease
Depo-Provera, 12–13
Depression, 47. *See also* Major
    depressive disorder
    and adoption, 365–366
    after perinatal loss, 374
    and alcohol use, 106
    and Alzheimer's disease, 586–587,
        594–595
    among caregivers, 595–596
    antenatal, 391–392, 399–400
    and breast cancer, 493–494,
        501–502
    and cancer, 493–494, 504
    childhood, 400
    and disability, 477–478, 482
    and eating disorders, 173, 176, 181,
        182
    emotional psychosocial issues,
        594–595
    and heart disease, 586–587, 594–595
    and infertility, 329, 330, 340,
        343–344, 349, 363
    and insomnia, 241

and intimate partner violence, 74, 75
    and irritable bowel syndrome, 520
    and menopause, 233, 455, 587
    during midlife, 450
    and migraine headaches, 562–563
    and miscarriage, 373
    and multiple sclerosis, 569–570, 573
    and obstructive sleep apnea, 243
    and physical activity, 255, 263–264
    and PMDD, 311
    postpartum, 229, 311, 393–395,
        421–423
    during pregnancy, 391
    and rheumatic disease, 544
    and sexual assault, 290
    and sleep, 226
    and smoking, 129, 130, 134–135
    sociodemographic and
        environmental risk factors, 399
    and stroke, 586–587, 594–595
Depressive disorder not otherwise
    specified, 306
DES (diethylstilbestrol), 5
Diabetes
    and fetal loss, 372
    gender differences, 583
    gestational, 259
    and lifestyle risk factors, 584
    and obesity, 152
    and physical activity, 258–260
    premenstrual exacerbation of
        symptoms, 307
    and smoking, 262
    and weight loss, 157
Diabetes mellitus. *See* Type 2 diabetes
Diabetes Prevention Program, 157,
    158
Diagnostic and Statistical Manual. See
    DSM (Diagnostic and Statistical
    Manual)
Diagnostic testing, prenatal, 356–357
Dick-Read, Grantley, 16
Dietary interventions
    and hot flashes, 454–455
    for irritable bowel syndrome,
        526–527
    and PMDD, 317–318
    for weight loss, 159–160
Dieting, 162–163
    and eating disorders, 177–178, 181
Digestive system, 515
Dilation and curettage (D&C), 367
Dilation and evacuation (D&E), 367
Dilation and extraction (D&X), 367
Disability
    age at onset, 593
    and agency, 476
    and anxiety, 478
    categories, 467–468
    conceptualizing, 472–476
    conclusions and recommendations,
        485–486

in context, 468–470
    coping behaviors, 475–476
    and depression, 477–478, 482
    differentiating from illness,
        468
    dimensions of, 470–471
    and education level, 591–593
    and employment, 469, 470
    factors of clinical importance,
        480–485
    and falls, 481–482
    and fatigue, 480
    language of, 471–472
    and medical trauma, 483–484
    and mental health, 479
    migraine-related, 559–560
    models of, 472–474
    and multiple sclerosis, 573
    and pain, 481
    physical cocomitants of, 480–482
    and positive outcomes, 478–479
    and psychiatric disorders, 468
    psychosocial dimensions of, 471
    and realigning of values, 479
    response to, 476–480
    as result of lack of awareness and
        education, 591–593
    and socioeconmic status, 469
    and stigma, 484–485
    and substance abuse, 483
    and vascular diseases, 582, 593
    and violence, 482–483
    what it is, 467–468
    women's responses to, 467–490
Disabled women
    and nonlethal IPV assaults, 71
Discrimination, 156, 469
Diseases of adaptation, 50
Disenfranchised grief, 379
Disordered eating. *See* Eating disorders
Dispositional optimism, 503
Dissociative disorders
    and intimate partner violence, 75
Distress
    and cancer, 493, 498
    and infertility, 345
    and irritable bowel syndrome, 517
    during perimenopause and
        menopause, 454–455
    psychological, 587
Divorce, 8
Domestic abuse, 68. *See also* Intimate
    partner violence (IPV)
Dominance, sexual, 282–284
Donepezil, 575
Donor eggs/sperm, 360, 362–363,
    375, 376–377
Down syndrome, 372
Drinking. *See* Alcohol use
Drospirenone, 320
Drug abuse
    and fetal loss, 372
    and smoking, 129–130

Drug therapy. *See* Pharmacotherapy
DSM (*Diagnostic and Statistical Manual*),
    467, 468
  and mood disorders, 306–307
Duloxetine, 319
Dyslipidemia, 157
Dysmenorrhea, 226, 307, 518
Dyspareunia, 289
Dysthymic disorder, 520
  and infertility, 330, 339
  premenstrual exacerbation of
    symptoms, 308

Eastern medicine, 454
Eating disorders, 173–198. *See also*
    Anorexia nervosa (AN); Bulimia
    nervosa (BN)
  among older women, 177, 181–182
  and breast augmentation, 206
  challenges to treatment,
    189–190
  comorbidity, 176
  and cosmetic medical procedures,
    202, 214–215
  course and prognosis, 178–179
  developmental stages, 180–182
  diagnostic features, 173–179
  future research, 190–191
  gender differences, 177, 180
  and genetics, 179–180, 190–191
  and infertility, 331, 339–340
  and irritable bowel syndrome, 517,
    527
  and liposuction, 211
  main classifications of, 173
  and migraine headaches, 563
  mortality, 173, 178
  and obesity, 173
  prevalence rates, 176–178
  psychological/sociocultural factors,
    182–183
  risk factors for, 179–185
  and serotonin, 180
  and sexual assault, 290
  and sociocultural values, 190
  treatment options, 185–190
Eating disorders not otherwise
    specified (EDNOS), 175, 179,
    189, 191
Ecological systems theory, 51
Edinburgh Postnatal Depression Scale
    (EPDS), 403, 404
Education level
  and alcohol use, 104
  and cancer mortality, 492
  and childlessness, 357–358
  and disability, 591–593
  and PMMD, 312
Egg donation, 360, 362–363, 375,
    376–377
Eisenstadt v. Baird, 12
Elderly women. *See* Aging; Older
    women

Emaciation, 174
Embolism, pulmonary, 320
Emotion, 556
Emotional exhaustion, 47, 48
Emotional injury, 65
Employment. *See also* Working
    women
  and alcohol use, 103–105
  and cancer, 498–499, 504
  and caregiving, 56, 57
  and disability, 469, 470
  flexible work schedules, 52
  full-time *vs.* part-time, 48
  and life stage variations, 53–54
  and migraine headaches, 564
  and multiple sclerosis, 573
  productivity, 312–313
  in service industries, 47–48
  and sexual harassment, 49–50, 57
  and sleep, 234
  and stressful working conditions, 57
  structure, 53
  and well-being, 53
  of women over 50, 55–56
  and women's health, 46–63
  of women with young children,
    54–55
Endocrine-disrupting chemicals, 151
Endocrine system, 154
Endocrinology, reproductive, 356
Endometriosis, 289, 307, 328, 332,
    336
Endorphins, 264–265, 341
Energy balance, 150
  and reproductive health, 331, 333
Energy density, 159
Epilepsy, 99, 307, 474–475
Epinephrine, 341
Episodic drinking, 95
Epstein-Barr virus, 568
Equality, gender
  and medical research, 20–22
Erectile dysfunction, 337
Estradiol, 237, 320, 442, 588–589
Estrogen, 237, 314, 333, 334, 416,
    418, 430, 457, 556, 586, 588
  and cognition, 588–589
  and menopause, 451
  and migraine headaches, 557,
    560–561
  and multiple sclerosis, 571
  and obesity, 153
  and perimenopause, 441, 442, 443,
    450
  and postmenopause, 442, 456
  role in diseases of aging, 593
  and sleep, 235
  and vascular disease, 588
Estrone, 442
Eszoplicone, 235
Ethnicity. *See also* Race
  and alcohol use, 103–105
  and breastfeeding, 429

  and cancer, 502–503
  and cosmetic medical procedures,
    203
  and disability, 468–469
  and employment with disabilities,
    470
  and heart disease, 583
  and infertility, 346–348, 349
  and IPV assaults, 67, 69
  and irritable bowel syndrome, 528
  and menopause, 234
  and rheumatic disease, 541–542
  and smoking initiation, 129
  and vascular diseases, 583–584
Evidence-based interventions
  and smoking cessation, 133
  for women's problem drinking, 110
Exchange theory, 52
Excitement seeking behavior, 212
Exercise. *See also* Physical activity
  and cancer, 505
  and infertility, 330–333
  and irritable bowel syndrome, 526
  and PMDD, 317, 318
  and smoking cessation, 135
Exer-games, 265, 269
Exhaustion, emotional, 47, 48
Exner, Max J., 6
Expanded Disability Status Scale, 573
Exploitation, sexual, 297, 298
Eyelid surgery, 199

Facelift surgery, 208–209
Facial skeletal procedures, 199, 204,
    205
Falls, risk of, 256, 476, 481–482
Familial hemiplegic migraine (FHM),
    561. *See also* Migraine headaches
Family
  and chronic illness, 546
  and disability, 484
  influence on having cosmetic
    medical procedures, 201
  and irritable bowel syndrome, 522,
    524–525
  and rheumatic disease, 541, 546
Family and Medical Leave Act, 54,
    359, 427
Family planning. *See* Contraception
Family therapy, 186
Fatigue, 594
  cancer-related, 495
  and disability, 480
  and multiple sclerosis, 568–569,
    573
  and perimenopause, 449
  and physical activity, 261, 262
Fellatio, 293
Femininity, 281, 440
Feminism, 14–15, 202
Fenfluramine, 315
Fertility. *See also* Infertility;
    Menopause

and growth hormones, 5
and menopause, 446
preservation options, 360
psychiatric disorders, 338–340
treatments, 356, 360–363
Fetal alcohol syndrome (FAS), 101
Fetal growth restriction (FGR), 372
Fetal health
    and alcohol use, 101, 115
    and IPV, 71
Fetal loss, 331, 371–375
Fetal reduction, 356, 367, 368
Fibromyalgia, 240–241, 517
Fight-or-flight response, 341, 564
Final menstrual period (FMP), 440,
    448
Flow, 284, 285
Fluoxetine, 186, 188, 319, 426
Fluvoxamine, 319
Folic acid, 231
Follicles, 442
Follicle-stimulating hormone. See
    FSH (follicle-stimulating
    hormone)
Food, 150
    intolerances, 526
    and migraine headaches, 562
Forcible rape, 290. See also Rape
Fractures, 256, 457
Framework Convention on Tobacco
    Control, 125
FSH (follicle-stimulating hormone),
    329, 346, 441, 442
Functional disabilities, 468

GABA-A, 314, 315
Gabapentin, 236
Gametes, 360, 362–363, 375
Gardasil, 295
Gas, intestinal, 517
Gastrointestinal problems. See Irritable
    bowel syndrome (IBS)
Gateway hypothesis, 129–130
Gay liberation, 13–14
Gender
    and aging, 443
    and alcohol use, 98, 99, 102–103,
        106–114
    and Alzheimer's disease, 582–583
    and cancer, 493
    and cosmetic medical procedures,
        199, 200, 202
    and depression after heart attack,
        594
    and depression following cancer,
        493
    differences in sexual dysfunction,
        282
    and disability, 469, 470
    and eating disorders, 177, 180
    expectations for sex, 282, 284, 296
    and heart attack, 582–583
    and IPV homicides, 66–67

and irritable bowel syndrome, 514
and multiple sclerosis, 567
neurological differences between
    men and women, 561
and neurological disorders, 556
and nonlethal IPV assaults, 67–68
role expectations, 281, 293
and sleep, 223, 236, 240
socialization, 281
and tobacco use, 123–124
and vascular diseases, 582–583
Gender, Race, Class and Health (Schulz
    & Mullings), 28
Genetics, 356
    and alcohol use, 103
    and Alzheimer's disease, 589–591
    and eating disorders, 179–180,
        190–191
    and heart disease, 589–591
    and irritable bowel syndrome,
        521–522
    and migraine headaches, 561–562
    and multiple sclerosis, 567–568
    and obesity/weight gain, 149–150
    premenstrual dysphoric disorder
        (PMDD), 311, 313–314
    and vascular disease, 589–591
Genital enhancement, 213
Genital warts, 295
Geography, 568
Gestational diabetes, 259
Gestations, multiple, 356, 372
Girls
    and cosmetic medical procedures,
        203–204
    eating and weight-related disorders,
        173
    focus on physical appearance, 284
    reproductive health and alcohol
        use, 101
    and risky drinking, 95, 114
    and tobacco use, 124
Global Burden of Disease, 312–313
Globalization, 124
Glucocorticoid (GC) response, 585
Glucose tolerance, 154
GnRH (gonadotropin-releasing
    hormone), 320, 329, 334, 341
Gonadotropins, 237, 329, 334, 341
Graph theory analysis, 561
Grief, 374
    and child relinquishment, 379
    and fetal loss, 373
Griswold v. Connecticut, 11
Group therapy, 329, 574
Guided imagery, 319
Guilt
    and breastfeeding, 431
    and child relinquishment, 379
Gynecological cancer, 492
    and cognitive-behavioral
        interventions, 505
    and employment, 499

sexual and reproductive quality of
    life, 496–497
Gynecological problems, 307,
    517–518
routine annual checkups, 7, 8–9

Harassment, sexual, 49–50, 284–285,
    447
Hardiness, 477
Harm reduction therapy, 133–134
Harvard Study of Moods and Cycles,
    312
Haseltine, Florence, 21
Hate crimes, 482
Headache, 449, 556, 559. See also
    Migraine headaches
Health. See also Women's health
    maternal (see Maternal health)
    and micro-aggressions, 475–476
    psychological (see Psychological
        health)
    reproductive (see Reproductive
        health)
    sexual (see Sexual health)
Health and Safety Needs of Older
    Workers (NRC), 56
Health behavior
    psychological theories of, 29–31
    psychosocial theories of, 26–27
    and structural interventions, 38
    technology-based interventions,
        265–266
Health Belief Model (HBM), 26, 29,
    33–34
Health centers, neighborhood, 14
Health Information National Trends
    Survey (HINTS), 25
Health promotion, 26, 573
Health psychology, 474, 475, 479,
    484–485
Health-seeking behavior
    and irritable bowel syndrome, 514
    and obesity, 153–154
Healy, Bernadine, 22
Heart attack
    aftermath, 591–596
    and caregivers, 595–596
    gender differences, 582–583
    and obstructive sleep apnea, 242
    symptoms of, 592
Heart disease, 26, 491, 581–603
    commonalities in epidemiology
        with stroke and Alzheimer's,
        581–591
    costs of, 582
    and death, 592
    and depression, 586–587, 594–595
    and disability, 591–596
    and ethnicity, 583
    and genetics, 589–591
    and hormone therapy, 457
    and physical activity, 255
    and poverty, 474

Heart disease (*Continued*)
  psychosocial risk factors, 584–587
  and sex steroid hormones, 588–589
  and smoking, 126
  statistics, 582
  and stress, 584–586
Heart palpitations, 449
Height, 5, 6
Hemoencephalography (HEG), 566
Herbal therapy, 236, 242
  and hot flashes, 454–455
  and infertility, 333
  and PMDD, 319
Heritability. *See* Genetics
Heterosexual women, 27
  and childhood sexual abuse, 287
  and rape, 289
  and self-objectification, 284–285
  and sexual compliance, 292–293
  and sexual dominance and passivity, 283
HGH (human growth hormone), 5
High blood pressure. *See* Hypertension
Highs Scale, 403
HINTS (Health Information National Trends Survey), 25
Hip fractures, 256
Hirsutism, 320
Hispanic women. *See also* Latinas
  and adoption, 364
  and Alzheimer's disease, 583
  awareness about heart disease, 591–592
  as caregivers, 595
  and childlessness, 357
  and condom use, 295
  cultural considerations following fetal mortality, 375
  and disability, 469
  and fertility treatments, 360
  and infertility, 346, 347, 349
  and menopause, 453
  and rheumatic disease, 541, 542
  and sexual dominance and passivity, 283
  and sexual dysfunction, 282
  and sleep, 234
HIV/AIDS, 283
  and childhood sexual abuse, 287
  and condom use, 34, 36–37
  contextualizing among women, 33–35
  and infertility, 329
  and intersectionality, 27
  limitations of individualistic approaches to women's health, 31
  and media, 32
  and sexism, 38
  and sexual and relationship power, 34–35

and social inequality, 37–38
  and socioeconomic status, 35–37
Holland-Rantos, 10
Home Oriented Maternity Experience (HOME), 17
Homeostatic drive, 224
Homicides, 66–67
Hormones, 237, 557
  and Alzheimer's disease, 588–589
  and breastfeeding, 416
  changes caused by obesity, 154
  and heart disease, 588–589
  and irritable bowel syndrome, 524
  and menopause, 441
  and migraine headaches, 557, 558, 560–561
  and pregnancy, 390
  and premenstrual dysphoric disorder, 314, 320–321
  and reproduction, 331
  and sleep, 226, 231–232
  and smoking cessation, 134
  and stress, 586
  and stroke, 588–589
Hormone therapy, 235, 450, 454, 492–493
  and cancer, 457
  and coronary heart disease, 456–457
  and obstructive sleep apnea, 243
  and perimenopause, 455
  postmenopausal, 455–458
  and vascular disease, 589
Hostility, 587
Hot flashes, 231, 234, 236, 441, 447–448, 450, 451–452. *See also* Menopause
  among cultures, 452–453
  coping with, 454–455
  and perimenopause, 449
  pharmacotherapy, 235
  and sleep disturbances, 232–233, 495
HPV (human papilloma virus), 9, 126, 295, 296
Human growth hormone (hGH), 5
Human papillomavirus (HPV), 9, 126, 295, 296
Hyoscine, 525
Hyperandrogenism, 333
Hyperfemininity, 285–286
Hyperhydrosis, 209
Hyperinsulinemia, 333
Hyperlipidemia, 583
Hypersensitivity, visceral, 515, 517, 519
Hypertension, 583, 584
  and cardiovascular disease, 260
  and fetal loss, 372
  and lifestyle risk factors, 584
  and obesity, 152, 153, 157
  and obstructive sleep apnea, 242

and physical activity, 255, 260
  and smoking, 262
  and weight loss, 157
  and work-family conflict, 53
Hypnotherapy, 527
Hypnotics, 240, 241
Hypoglycemia, 154
Hypomania, 390–391, 392–393, 395–396
Hypopnea, 243
Hypothalamic hormones, 441
Hypothalamic-pituitary adrenal (HPA) axis, 316, 516, 564, 585–586
Hypothyroidism, 307
Hysterectomy, 451, 454, 492, 497, 518

IBS. *See* Irritable bowel syndrome (IBS)
Illness
  adjusting to, 545
  differentiating from disability, 468
  modeling, 522
  stress-related, 47
Immaculate Deception (Arms), 17
Immigrant women, 82, 312, 429
Immune system, 575
IMPACT study, 256
Incapacitated rape, 290. *See also* Rape
Income. *See* Socioeconomic status
Incontinence, 525
Industrialization, 4
Inequality, social, 37–38
Infant mortality, 3
Infections, 373, 425–426
Infertility, 328–354. *See also* Assisted reproductive technology (ART)
  and age, 336
  and alcohol use, 101, 329, 335–337
  and cancer, 329, 496–497
  causes, 328–329
  cultural factors, 347–348
  differences in access to and use of care, 347
  and ethnicity, 346–348, 349
  future research directions, 348–350
  impact of psychological interventions for, 343–346
  lifestyle factors that impact, 330–339
  medicalization of, 348
  and obesity, 329, 330–331, 333
  physician-patient relationship, 350
  prevalence, 328
  psychological effects of, 330, 340–342
  and race, 346–348
  and smoking, 126, 329, 335, 337–338
  social support and relationship quality, 342–343

and stress, 329, 340–342
treatment, 329–330, 333–335
and underweight, 332
Inflammatory diseases, 539
Insomnia, 223, 229, 231, 232, 236,
238. See also Sleep; Sleep
disorders
and cancer, 495
chronic, 240–242
and cognitive behavioral therapy
(CBT), 242
and irritable bowel syndrome,
518
and perimenopause, 449, 450
pharmacologic treatments for,
241–242
and physical activity, 264
Insulin
and infertility, 333
resistance, 152, 154, 164
Intercourse, 6. See also Sex
Interferons, 574, 575
Internal focus, 284
Internalization, 182
International Classification of
Functioning, Disability and
Health (ICF), 467
International Classification of Headache
Disorders, 2nd ed., 558
International Society for Premenstrual
Disorders Consensus Statement,
306
Internet
and health information
dissemination, 26
and physical activity intervention,
265–266, 268–269
Interpersonal relationships
and infertility, 345
and irritable bowel syndrome,
524–525
and PMDD, 312–313
Interpersonal therapy, 186, 188, 189,
527
Intersectionality, 25–45
defined, 27
history of, 27–28
and psychology, 39
and women's health, 38–39
Interventions
for cancer, 504–505
for migraine headaches, 565–566
for multiple sclerosis, 574–575
for puerperal psychiatric symptoms,
400–401
for rheumatic disease, 544–545,
545–548
for weight loss, 157–163
for women's problem drinking,
110–111
Interviewing, motivational, 111
Intimacy
and cancer, 498

Intimate partner violence (IPV),
64–87. See also Rape
and alcohol use, 102
and condom use, 294
definition of, 64–66
factors that influence leaving
relationship, 81
future directions, 81–82
and homicides, 66–67
and lesbian or transgender women,
70–71
and minority women, 82
negative health effects, 72–76
nonlethal assaults against pregnant
women, 71–72
overcoming attitudinal barriers to
screening, 79–81
and people with disabilities, 71
physical effects, 72–73
and poverty, 69–70
psychological effects of, 73–75
risk factors for, 66–72
Intoxication, 96. See also Alcohol use
Intra-cytoplasmic sperm injection
(ICSI), 334
Intrauterine cranial decompression,
367
Intrauterine insemination (IUI), 329,
360, 361
Intraventricular hemorrhage, 373
In vitro fertilization (IVF), 329–330,
334, 360
and alcohol consumption, 336
costs, 361
demographics of, 347
and exercise, 332
and psychosocial intervention,
345–346
and stress, 350
Iron supplements, 231
Irritability, 309, 317
Irritable bowel syndrome (IBS),
514–538
across the female lifespan, 521–525
among women veterans, 523
and anxiety, 519–520
and back pain, 517
biological factors, 515–519
and bloating, 516–517
comorbid psychiatric disorders,
519–521
coping behaviors, 520–521
and depression, 520
diagnosis, 514
dietary management, 526–527
and fibromyalgia, 517
future directions, 527–529
and genetics, 521–522
hormones, menstrual cycle and
menopause, 524
impact of ethnicity and race, 528
and interpersonal relationships,
524–525

management of, 525–527
medical comorbidity, 516–519
and pain, 515–516
prevalence, 514
psychological factors, 519–521
psychological management, 527
and race, 528
risk factors for, 522
and sleep problems, 518–519
social factors, 521
treatment, 515
urogenital and gynecological
symptoms, 517–518
and violence against women,
522–523
Ischemic stroke, 100, 126. See also
Stroke
Isolation, social, 504, 519
IVF. See In vitro fertilization (IVF)

Job strain model, 47
Joints, 449. See also Rheumatic
diseases

Karmel, Marjorie, 16
Kava kava, 242
Kidney disease, 372
Kinsey, Alfred, 7

Labor force. See Employment
Lactation, 415–416, 419, 425–431.
See also Breastfeeding
Lactational amenorrhea, 416
LactMed, 426
Lamaze, Ferdinand, 16
Laser skin resurfacing, 199, 209, 210
Late adulthood. See Older women
Latinas. See also Hispanic women
and alcohol use, 99
and arthritis, 541
and cancer, 503
and condom use, 295
and cosmetic medical procedures,
203
leading causes of death in, 26
and physical activity promotion,
266–267, 269
and PMDD, 312, 315
and rheumatic disease, 542, 547,
548–549
and sexual dominance and passivity,
283
and sexual dysfunction, 282
Lavender, 242
Laxatives, 526
Learning disabilities, 468
Leptin, 331, 333
Lesbian women. See also Same-sex
relationships
and adoptions, 366
and alcohol use, 104, 105–106
and childhood sexual abuse, 287
and childlessness, 359

Lesbian women (*Continued*)
   and fertility treatment, 360, 362
   and intimate partner violence,
      70–71
   and menopause, 446–447, 453
   and pregnancy, 359
   and rape, 289
   and self-objectification, 284–285
   sexual satisfaction, 294
Life expectancy
   and disability, 469
   gender differences, 583
   and multiple sclerosis, 569
   and obesity, 153
Lifestyle
   and hot flashes, 454–455
   and infertility, 329, 330–339
   and menopause, 453
   modification, 157, 161
   and PMDD, 317–318
   sedentary, 255, 269
   and vascular diseases, 584
Light therapy, 227, 239, 240, 264, 319
Likert rating scale, 309
Limbic system, 515
Lipid profile, 255, 588. *See also*
      Hyperlipidemia
Liposuction, 199, 209, 210–211, 215
Liver diseases, 99, 100
Loneliness, 570
Look AHEAD study, 158
Loss, 182, 373, 379
perinatal, 371–375
Low birth weight, 127, 400
Lower urinary tract, 517–518
Low-income women. *See also*
      Poverty; Socioeconomic status
      (SES)
   and cancer, 502
   and health, 27
   and HIV/AIDS, 33–34
   and physical activity promotion,
      266–268
   and pregnancy weight gain, 163
L-tryptophan, 315
LUMINA (Lupus in Minorities:
      Nature versus Nurture) study,
      541
Lumpectomy, 492. *See also* Breast
      cancer
Lung cancer, 125, 127, 128, 255
Lupron, 6
Lupus, 372. *See also* Systemic lupus
      erythematosus
Lupus in Minorities: Nature versus
      Nurture (LUMINA) study, 541
Luteinizing hormone (LH), 237, 334,
      341, 441
Lymphedema, 496

Major depressive disorder. *See also*
      Depression
   and cancer, 493–494

etiology of, 315
   and infertility, 330, 339
   and miscarriage, 373
   physiology of, 316
   and PMDD, 312
   premenstrual exacerbation of
      symptoms, 308–309
Major depressive episode with
      postpartum onset (MDE-PP),
      394–395
Male-factor infertility, 329, 337
Mammography, 154. *See also* Breast
      cancer
Mandatory reporting, 76
Mania, 392–393. *See also* Bipolar
      disorder
Manley, Helen, 7–8
Marital satisfaction, 182, 342–343
Marital status
   and alcohol use, 103–105
   and childlessness, 357
   and disability, 470
   early, 7, 8
Marriage. *See* Marital status
Mason, James O., 21
Massage therapy, 319
Mastectomy, 492, 496. *See also* Breast
      cancer
Mastitis, 425
Masturbation, 6
Maternal bonding, 423–425
Maternal health, 14, 414–439
Maternity leave, 55, 427–428
Media
   and body image, 183–184
   and cosmetic medical procedures,
      200–201
   and eating disorders, 182
   and health information
      dissemination, 25–26
   and medicalized childbirth, 16–17
   and smoking initiation, 128
Medicaid, 14
Medical model of disability, 472–474
Medicare, 14
Medications. *See also* Pharmacotherapy
   and breastfeeding, 426
   for multiple sclerosis, 574–575
   and nicotine withdrawal, 132–133
   and sleep, 239
   for weight loss, 161–162
Medicine
   gender-based, 22
   socialized, 4
Meditation, 333
Melatonin, 226, 233, 236, 237, 239,
      240, 241, 341
Memory problems, 330, 449, 569. *See
      also* Alzheimer's disease
Men. *See also* Gender
   and infertility, 336–337, 338
Menarche
   declining age of, 5

   and eating disorders, 181
   and weight gain, 152
Menopause, 440–463. *See also* Hot
      flashes; Midlife women; Older
      women; Perimenopause;
      Postmenopausal women
   average age of, 448
   biology of, 441–445
   and bone loss, 444
   coping with distress, 454–455
   cross-cultural and social class
      variations, 452–454
   cultural and ethnic factors of, 234
   cultural attitudes toward, 445–446
   defined, 440
   and depression, 233, 455, 587
   and irritable bowel syndrome, 524
   and lesbian women, 446–447, 453
   and life stage, 445–447
   medicalization of, 453
   and multiple sclerosis, 571
   normal course of, 447–449
   and physical activity, 261, 264
   and race, 453–454
   signs and symptoms, 449–454
   and sleep, 231–236
   and smoking, 126
   and stroke, 588
   surgical, 450–451
   and weight gain, 152, 164, 257
Menstrual cycle
   and alcohol use, 101
   and anorexia nervosa, 174
   biology of, 441
   end of (*see* Menopause)
   final, 440, 448
   irregularities, 289
   and irritable bowel syndrome, 524
   manipulation of, 320–321
   and menopause, 442
   and migraine headaches, 560
   and mood, 305
   and perimenopause, 448–449
   and shift work, 239–240
   and sleep, 224–227
   and smoking, 126–127
   and smoking cessation, 134
Menstrual socialization, 315–316
Mental health, 7
   and abortion, 370
   adoptive parents', 365–366
   and breastfeeding, 419–425
   and disabilities, 479
   and intimate partner violence, 75
   and IPV screening, 80–81
   maternal, 414–439
   and migraine headaches, 562–563
   and multiple sclerosis, 569–570
   and physical activity, 263–265,
      268
   and rheumatic disease, 544
Mental retardation, 101
Meritocracy, 36

Metabolic syndrome, 416–418
Metabolism, 150–151
Metformin, 331
Micro-aggressions, 475–476, 484–485
Microdermabrasion, 199, 209
Micropigmentation, 212–213
Midlife women. *See also* Menopause
  and body image, 182
  and colorectal cancer, 525
  and fetal loss, 372
  and menopause, 445
  and migraine headaches, 557
  and neurological disorders, 556
  and rheumatic disease, 539
  and sleep, 233
  and stroke, 588
Midwifery, 15, 17
Mifepristone, 367
Migraine Disability Assessment
    (MIDAS), 559–560
Migraine headaches, 556, 557–567
  and anxiety, 562–563
  and auras, 558–559, 560
  biological factors, 560–561
  and depression, 562–563
  diagnosis, 558–560
  disability caused by, 559–560
  and eating disorders, 563
  epidemiology, 557–558
  and food triggers, 562
  frequency of, 559
  genetic factors, 561–562
  interventions and treatment
    methods, 565–566
  menstrual, 450
  mental health issues, 562–563
  pharmacological treatments, 559
  and pregnancy, 560
  premenstrual exacerbation of
    symptoms, 307
  prevalence, 557, 558
  prodrome, 559
  role of estrogen in, 557, 560–561
  and sleep disturbances, 562
  and socioeconomic status, 563–564
  and stress, 564–565
  and work, 564
Mind-body relationship, 454,
    474–475, 545, 565
Mind-body techniques, 329
Mindfulness-based interventions, 545
Mini International Psychiatric
    Interview (MINI), 339
Minority women. *See also* African
    American women; Asian
    American women; Women of
    color
  and infertility, 349
  and IPV victimization, 82
  and physical activity promotion,
    266–268
Miscarriage, 126, 335, 336, 346,
    371–372, 373

Mobile Mums, 266
Modafinil, 240
Modeling, illness, 522
Molecular genetics, 131–132
"Mommy Makeovers," 211
Monoamines, 264
Mood
  and cancer, 493
  and irritable bowel syndrome, 520
  and menopause, 455
  and menstrual cycle, 305
  and perimenopause, 449
  pharmacotherapy, 235
  and sleep, 233–234
Mood disorders
  and alcohol use, 102, 106
  during antenatal period, 399–400
  and *DSM*-5, 306–307
  and intimate partner violence, 75
  and multiple sclerosis, 569–570
  during postpartum period, 229, 400
  related to pregnancy, 391–396
  screening for, 403–404
  and vascular disease, 586–587
  and work-family conflict, 53
Mood disturbances, premenstrual, 308
Moral model of disability, 472–474
Morbidity and mortality
  and alcohol use, 99–100
  and breast augmentation, 207
  breast cancer, 262
  and cancer, 491–492, 502–503
  and depression after heart attack,
    594
  and eating disorders, 173, 178
  fetal, 371–375
  infant and child, 3
  leading causes for women, 26
  and obesity, 152, 153
  tobacco use, 125–128
Morning-after pill, 20
Morris, John McLean, 20
Mosher, Clelia Duel, 6
Motherhood
  early, 7, 8
  and women's employment, 51
Mother-infant attachments, 401
Multiple gestation, 356, 372
Multiple sclerosis (MS), 469, 471, 556,
    567–575
  cognitive symptoms, 569
  coping strategies, 574
  and depression, 569–570, 573
  diagnosis, 568, 570–571
  disease course, 570–571
  and environmental factors, 568
  epidemiology and theories of
    etiology, 567–568
  and fatigue, 568–569, 573
  and genetics, 567–568
  intervention and treatment
    methods for, 574–575
  mental health issues, 569–570

  and pain, 573
  and physical activity, 573, 574
  and pregnancy, 571, 572
  prevalence, 567
  psychosocial factors, 573–574
  and quality of life, 573
  reproductive issues, 571
  sexual functioning, 571–572
  and social support, 573
  and stress, 573–574
  symptoms, 568–569
Murder, 66–67
Myelin, 567, 574
Myocardial infarction (MI), 126, 591

Naltrexone, 113
Naps, 227, 237, 238, 240
NAPSAC (National Association of
    Parents and Professionals for Safe
    Alternatives in Childbirth), 17
NARAL (National Abortion Rights
    Action League), 18
Nardil, 426
National Abortion Rights Action
    League (NARAL), 18
National Alliance for Caregiving, 56
National Association of Parents and
    Professionals for Safe Alternatives
    in Childbirth (NAPSAC), 17
National Coalition of Anti-Violence
    Programs (NCAVP), 70
National Committee for Quality
    Assurance, 456
National Crime Victimization Survey,
    67, 68
National Epidemiologic Survey of
    Alcohol and Related Conditions
    (NESARC), 91, 93, 101, 102, 105
National Health Interview Survey
    (NHIS), 93, 94, 95
National Heart, Lung, and Blood
    Institute (NHLBI), 157
National Institute on Alcohol Abuse
    and Alcoholism (NIAAA), 92
National Institutes of Health (NIH),
    21, 92
National Institutes of Mental Health,
    308
National Intimate Partner and Sexual
    Violence Survey, 288
National Latino and Asian American
    Survey, 312
National Longitudinal Alcohol
    Epidemiologic Survey (NLAES),
    93
National Longitudinal Study of
    Adolescent Health, 293
National Organization for Women
    (NOW), 18, 20
National Prevention Strategy (U.S. Dept.
    of Health and Human Services),
    26, 40
National Sexual Health Survey, 296

National Study of Health and Life Experiences of Women (NSHLEW), 93–94
National Survey of American Life, 312
National Violence Against Women Survey (NVAWS), 70, 288–289
Native American women. *See* American Indian women
Natural childbirth, 16
Nausea, 495
NCAVP (National Coalition of Anti-Violence Programs), 70
Necrotizing enterocolitis, 373
Negative affect
  and cancer, 493
  and infertility, 345
  and smoking, 130, 134–135
Neoadjuvant therapy, 492
Neonatal death, 372, 373–374
Nerve damage, 99
NESARC (National Epidemiologic Survey of Alcohol and Related Conditions), 91, 93, 101, 102, 105
Neurofeedback, 566
Neurological disorders, 556–580
  factors related to variations in men and women, 556–557
  gender differences, 556
Neuropathy, peripheral, 318
Neuroticism, 342, 587
Neurotransmitters
  and migraine headaches, 561
  and premenstrual dysphoric disorder, 314–315
New Left Activism, 13
NHIS (National Health Interview Survey), 93, 94
NHLBI (National Heart, Lung, and Blood Institute), 157
NIAAA (National Institute on Alcohol Abuse and Alcoholism), 92
Nicotine, 125, 128, 337–338
  factors associated with dependence on, 130–132
  replacement therapy, 132, 151, 263
  withdrawal medications, 132–133, 137–138
Nightmares, 243
Night sweats, 232, 234
NIH (National Institutes of Health), 21, 92
Nitrates, 562
NK-cells, 344
NLAES (National Longitudinal Alcohol Epidemiologic Survey), 93
Nonconsensual sex, 286, 288, 293, 298
Nonsteroidal anti-inflammatory drugs (NSAIDs), 227

NOW (National Organization for Women), 18, 20
NREM (non-rapid eye movement) sleep, 224
NSAIDs (nonsteroidal anti-inflammatory drugs), 227
NSHLEW (National Study of Health and Life Experiences of Women), 93–94
Nurses' Health Study, 152–153, 155, 156, 258, 259, 262
  and breastfeeding, 418
  and cancer, 495, 497
  and PMDD, 318
Nursing. *See* Breastfeeding
Nutrition. *See also* Food
  and infertility, 330–333
NVAWS (National Violence Against Women Survey), 70, 288–289

Obesity, 32, 149–172. *See also* Overweight; Weight gain
  and biological processes, 154
  causes of, 149–152
  consequences of, 152–157
  and discrimination, 156
  and eating disorders, 173
  and energy balance, 150
  and fetal loss, 372
  future directions, 164
  and infertility, 329, 330–331, 333
  and lifestyle risk factors, 584
  maternal, 152
  medical consequences of, 152–155
  and metabolism, 150–151
  and mortality, 152, 153
  and physical activity, 257
  and poverty, 474
  prevention, 163
  psychosocial consequences of, 155–156
  public health costs, 156–157
  and reproductive health, 154–155
  and sleep problems, 155
  treatments for, 157–164
Objectification, sexual, 184–185, 202, 284–285, 297, 447
Objectification theory, 184–185, 202
Obsessive-compulsive disorder (OCD), 264, 397, 398
  and eating disorders, 176
  and fetal loss, 373
  and infertility, 339
Obstructive sleep apnea (OSA), 223, 231, 235, 239, 242–243
  and obesity, 153
  and pregnancy, 228
Occupational therapy, 575
Office of Research on Women's Health, 22
Office on Women's Health (OWH), 22

Older women. *See also* Aging; Menopause; Postmenopausal women
  and caregiving, 56
  and cosmetic medical procedures, 201
  cultural attitudes toward, 445–446
  and diabetes, 583
  and disability, 469
  and eating disorders, 177, 181–182
  and fecal incontinence, 525
  and hormone therapy, 589
  and hyperlipidemia, 583
  and hypertension, 583
  and migraine headaches, 561
  and physical activity, 256
  and premenstrual syndrome, 312
  and sleep, 236–239, 241
Oophorectomy, 492, 497. *See also* Ovaries
Oppression, 27
Optimism, dispositional, 503
Oral cancer, 124
Oral contraception. *See* Contraception
Orlistat, 161
Osteoporosis, 126, 320, 451, 568
Otitis, 127
Otoplasty, 204
Our Bodies, Ourselves (Boston Women's Health Collective), 15
Ovarian cancer, 418–419, 494, 496
Ovaries, 320–321, 328. *See also* Oophorectomy
Overfeeding, 150
Overweight, 149, 150, 153, 257. *See also* Obesity
Ovulation
  disrupted, 328
  inducing, 329
  medically induced, 360
  suppression of, 320
Oxytocin, 415, 416, 420–421, 422, 423–424, 425, 586

PADS (post-adoption depression syndrome), 365–366
Pain, 64
  back, 517
  and cancer surgery, 495–496
  chronic, 548
  coping behavior, 543
  and disability, 481
  and irritable bowel syndrome, 515–516
  and multiple sclerosis, 573
  pelvic, 288, 289, 518
Pancreatic cancer, 100
Panic disorder, 75, 339, 398, 519
Pap smears, 7, 8, 154
Parental leave, 57

Parents/parenthood. *See also* Childbearing
  decisions related to initiation of, 357–366
  influence on smoking initiation, 128–129
  role in eating disorders, 182
  societal changes in, 356
Parkinson's disease, 556
Paroxetine, 319, 426
Partners, sexual, 296, 498. *See also* Relationships, intimate
PasosHacia La Salud study, 269
Passivity, sexual, 283–284, 297
Patient Protection and Affordable Care Act, 428
Patients' rights, 14
Paxil, 426
PCBs, 151
PCOS (polycystic ovarian syndrome), 328, 331, 372
Peers
  influence on having cosmetic medical procedures, 201
  and physical activity, 269–270
  role in eating disorders, 182
  and smoking initiation, 128–129
Pelvic examinations, 7
Pelvic inflammatory disease, 296, 328
Pelvic pain, 288, 289
Penn Ovarian Aging Study, 346
Peppermint oil, 525
Perimenopause, 441
  biology of, 441–445
  coping with distress, 454–455
  defined, 440
  and life stage, 445–447
  and menstrual cycle, 448–449
  normal course of, 447–449
  signs and symptoms, 449–454
  and sleep, 231, 233
  why it's important, 448
Perinatal loss, 371–375
Periodic limb movements during sleep (PLMS), 238. *See also* Restless legs syndrome (RLS)
Periods. *See* Menstrual cycle
Peripheral vascular atherosclerosis, 126
Perphenazine, 426
Personality disorders
  and alcohol use, 102
  and intimate partner violence, 75
  premenstrual exacerbation of symptoms, 308
  premenstrual exacerbations of symptoms, 309
Pharmacotherapy. *See also* Medications
  and cancer, 505
  and eating disorders, 186, 189
  and infertility, 329–330
  and insomnia, 241–242
  for migraine headaches, 559, 565

for multiple sclerosis, 574–575
and PMDD, 319–320
for problem drinking, 113–114
for puerperal psychiatric disorders, 405
and sleep, 235–236
for smoking cessation, 138
Phenelzine, 426
Phototherapy, 240
Physical activity, 255–277
  and adolescents, 261, 269–270
  and BMI, 258
  and breast cancer, 260–262, 268
  and cancer, 255, 505
  and cardiovascular disease, 258
  and chronic disease prevention and management, 258–262
  and diabetes, 258–260
  and hypertension, 260
  internet and technology interventions, 265–266
  and irritable bowel syndrome, 526
  for mental health, 263–265, 268
  and multiple sclerosis, 573, 574
  and obesity/weight gain, 150, 257
  optimal dose, 255, 268
  promotion, 266–268
  and sleep, 238
  and smoking cessation, 262–263, 268
  for weight loss, 160–161
Physical disabilities, 467
Physical injury, 65, 67–72
Physical therapy, 575
Physician-patient relationship, 350, 360, 544–545
Physician Readiness to Manage Intimate Partner Violence Survey (PREMIS), 81
Physostigmine, 575
Phytoestrogens, 236
Planned Parenthood League, 11, 12
Plastic surgery. *See* Cosmetic medical procedures
PMDD. *See* Premenstrual dysphoric disorder (PMDD)
PMS. *See* Premenstrual syndrome (PMS)
Polio, 476, 482
Polycystic ovarian syndrome (PCOS), 328, 331, 372
Polypharmacy, 239
Polysomnography, 224
Port Huron Statement, 13
Positive affect, 548
Post-abortion syndrome, 370–371
Post-adoption depression syndrome (PADS), 365–366
Postmenopausal women, 440, 441, 442, 449. *See also* Aging; Older women
  and hormone therapy, 455–458, 589

and migraine headaches, 561
and physical activity, 261
and sleep, 236–237
Postnatal period
  anxiety symptoms during, 397–399, 400
  depressive symptoms during, 393–395
  hypomanic symptoms during, 395–396
  identifying women in need of help during, 401–404
  obsessive-compulsive disorder, 397
  and physical activity, 266
  psychiatric symptoms during, 389, 390–391
  psychotic symptoms during, 396–397
Postpartum Depression Screening Scale (PDSS), 403, 404
Postpartum health, 54–55
  and abdominoplasty, 211
  bipolar disorder, 397
  and depression, 363, 421–423
  major depressive episode with postpartum onset (MDE-PP), 394–395
  and multiple sclerosis, 572
  and physical activity, 256, 264
  and PMDD, 311
  psychosis, 396, 421
  and sleep, 228–229
  and smoking cessation, 136–137
  and weight gain, 163
Posttraumatic growth, 499–500, 549
Posttraumatic stress disorder (PTSD), 243
  and alcohol use, 106
  and disability, 477, 478
  and fetal loss, 373
  and intimate partner violence, 74, 75
  and irritable bowel syndrome, 523
  and sexual assault, 289–290
Poverty. *See also* Low-income women; Socioeconomic status (SES)
  and disability, 469, 480
  and heart disease, 474
  and nonlethal IPV assaults, 69–70
  and obesity, 474
  and rheumatic disease, 541–542
Power, sexual, 34, 285, 295
Prednisone, 574
Preeclampsia, 372, 400
Pregnancy. *See also* Abortion; Childbearing; Contraception; Infertility
  after perinatal loss, 374
  and alcohol use, 101–102, 115, 335, 337
  and assisted reproductive technology, 359–361
  decisions related to ending, 367–375

Pregnancy (*Continued*)
  decisions related to initiation of,
    357–366
  and eating disorders, 181
  high risk, 356
  history of, 15–17
  and hypomania, 390–391
  loss, 371–375
  and migraine headaches, 560
  and mood symptoms, 391–396
  and multiple sclerosis, 571, 572
  and nonlethal IPV assaults, 71–72
  and obesity, 154
  perinatal loss, 371–375
  and physical activity, 256, 259
  and psychiatric symptoms, 389–413
  and rheumatic diseases, 539–540
  risk factors and etiology for loss,
    372–373
  and sleep, 227–228
  and smoking, 124–125, 127, 136,
    337
  and stroke, 588
  and suicide, 391
  teenage, 7–8, 372
  and underweight, 331
  unintended, 294, 295, 368
  and weight gain, 152, 163
Premarital sex, 7
Premature birth, 8, 372–373
Premenopausal women, 261, 440
Premenstrual dysphoric disorder
    (PMDD), 305–327
  and acculturation, 312
  biological factors, 313–315
  diagnosis of, 305–311
  difference from PMS, 306
  and disability-adjusted life years,
    312–313
  and education level, 312
  future directions, 321–322
  heritability, 311
  and hormonal treatments, 320
  and hormones, 314
  impact of, 312–313
  and life stress, 316
  management of, 316–321
  and neurotransmitters, 314–315
  pharmacotherapy, 319–320
  physical disorders as differential
    diagnoses, 307
  potential etiologic factors, 313–316
  prevalence and demographic
    correlates, 311–312
  and psychiatric disorders, 307–309
  and psychoeducation, 317
  psychosocial factors, 315–316
  and psychosocial function, 312–313
  relaxation skills and structured
    psychotherapies, 318–319
  and sexual abuse, 316
  and sleep, 225–226
  treatment, 306, 314–315

Premenstrual Symptoms Screening
    Tool (PSST), 309
Premenstrual syndrome (PMS)
  and BMI, 318
  difference from PMDD, 306
  and older women, 312
  and sleep, 225–226
  treatment, 306
PREMIS (Physician Readiness to
    Manage Intimate Partner
    Violence Survey), 81
Prenatal screening, 356–357
Preterm births, 296, 400
Prevention, disease, 26
Primary infertility, 328. *See also*
    Infertility
Primary ovarian insufficiency, 328
Primary-progressive multiple sclerosis,
    570. *See also* Multiple sclerosis
    (MS)
Problematic social support, 546. *See*
    also Social support
Prodrome, 559
Productivity, lost, 156, 312–313
Progesterone, 226, 314, 416, 441, 556
Progestin, 456
Project MATCH, 111, 112, 113
Prolactin, 415–416, 420, 423–424
Promiscuity, sexual, 287
Prostitution, 8
Prozac, 426
Psychiatric disorders
  and cosmetic surgery patients,
    213–215
  and disability, 468
  effects on women and their families,
    399–400
  and fertility, 339–340
  and infertility, 330
  and irritable bowel syndrome,
    519–521
  and pregnancy, 389–413
  and premenstrual dysphoric
    disorder, 307–309
  during puerperal period, 390
  screening for, 403–404
  sociodemographic and
    environmental risk factors, 399
Psychodynamic therapy, 527
Psychoeducation, 317
  for antenatal depressive symptoms,
    392
  during childbearing years, 389
  for hypomanic and manic
    symptoms, 393
  and multiple sclerosis, 574
  for postnatal baby blues, 394
  for postnatal bipolar symptoms, 396
  for postpartum psychosis, 397
Psychological health
  and alcohol use, 102
  and cancer, 493–494, 501–502
  and eating disorders, 173, 182

  and fetal loss, 373–374
  and infertility, 329, 330, 343–346
  and rheumatic disease, 543
  and social support, 48
Psychopathology
  and cosmetic surgery patients, 213
  and facelift surgery, 208
Psychoprophylactics, 16
Psychosis, postpartum, 396, 421
Psychosocial function
  and disability, 471
  and eating disorders, 173
  and obesity, 155–156
  and PMDD, 312–313, 315–316
  and pregnancy, 390
  and vascular diseases, 584–587
Psychosocial intervention
  and infertility, 344–345, 347–348
  and rheumatic disease, 546,
    547–548
Psychosocial stressors, 361–363
Psychotherapy, 405
  and irritable bowel syndrome, 527
  and multiple sclerosis, 574
  and PMDD, 318–319
  supportive-expressive group, 544
Psychotic disorders
  associated with pregnancy, 396–397
  and intimate partner violence, 75
PTSD. *See* Posttraumatic stress
    disorder (PTSD)
Puberty, 5–6, 154
Public health
  and alcohol use, 103
  and birth control, 10
  and disease prevention, 26
  and obesity, 156–157
  and rape, 290–291
  and smoking, 137–139
Puerperal period
  and anxiety disorders, 397–399
  identifying women in need of help
    during, 401–404
  and obsessive-compulsive disorder,
    398
  and psychiatric disorders, 389, 390,
    406–407
Pulmonary embolism, 320
Purgatives, 174, 175

Qi therapy, 319, 333
Quad marker screening test, 356
Quality of life
  and benefit finding, 499–500
  and cancer, 493–500, 500–504
  and chronic illness, 544
  and disability, 479
  and incontinence, 525
  and irritable bowel syndrome, 515,
    519, 523
  and multiple sclerosis, 573
  and obesity, 155–156
  and physical activity, 261

and pregnancy, 390
and religion, 542

Race. *See also* Ethnicity
  and abortion, 368
  and alcohol use, 103–106
  and cancer, 503
  and HIV-related risks, 287
  and infertility, 346–348
  and IPV homicides, 67
  and irritable bowel syndrome,
    528
  and menopause, 453–454
  and multiple sclerosis, 568
  and nonlethal IPV assaults, 69
  and reproductive rights, 18
  and smoking, 124, 131
Racism, 18, 27
Radiotherapy, 492–493, 495
Ramelton, 235, 241
Rape, 19–20, 288–291. *See also*
    Intimate partner violence (IPV);
    Sexual assault
  and American Indian women, 289
  barriers to reporting, 290
  definition and prevalence, 288–289
  and disability, 482
  and lesbian women, 289
  and sexual health, 289–291
  of young adult women on college
    campuses, 68
Rebif, 575
Recreation. *See* Physical activity
Rectal cancer, 100
Red clover isoflavone, 236
Rehabilitation Act, 467–468
Relapsing-remitting multiple sclerosis,
    570. *See also* Multiple sclerosis
    (MS)
Relationships, intimate
  and cancer, 498
  healthy, 297
  and infertility, 342–343
  integrating with sexual goals,
    296–299
  and irritable bowel syndrome, 520,
    524–525
  and PMDD, 312–313
  and power, 34, 295
  and rheumatic disease, 545–546
  and sexual assault, 290
  violence within, 64–87
Relationships, parental, 366
Relaxation therapy, 236, 318–319,
    344
Religion
  and childlessness, 359
  and rheumatic disease, 542–543
Relinquishment, child, 375–376,
    378–379
REM (rapid eye movement) sleep,
    224, 237
Reproductive aging. *See* Menopause

Reproductive health. *See also* Sexual
    health; Women's health
  advances in medicine, 356–357
  and aging (*see* Menopause)
  and alcohol use, 101–102
  and cancer, 496–497
  and childhood sexual abuse,
    287–288
  difficulties related to shift work,
    239–240
  infertility, 328–354
  and multiple sclerosis, 571
  and obesity, 154–155
  psychiatric symptoms and
    pregnancy, 389–413
  and smoking, 126–127
Reproductive rights, 17–19
Research, medical
  and gender equality, 20–22
Resilience, 477, 484, 543, 548–549
Respect, 297–298
Respiratory diseases, 126, 127, 153.
    See also Smoking
Respiratory distress syndrome, 373
Restless legs syndrome (RLS), 223,
    228, 231
Restorative procedures, 208–211
Revictimization, sexual, 291–292
Rheumatic diseases, 539–555
  adapting to, 541
  and benefit finding, 548–549
  coping behavior, 542
  differences across demographics and
    culture, 541–543
  and ethnicity, 541–542
  future directions, 549
  and poverty, 541–542
  and pregnancy, 539–540
  psychosocial interventions for,
    547–548
  and resilience, 548–549
  and sexuality, 540–541
  social roles, 541
  stressors and challenges, 543
Rheumatoid arthritis (RA), 539–555.
    See also Rheumatic diseases
  interpersonal-level stress and
    interventions, 545–548
  premenstrual exacerbation of
    symptoms, 307
  and reproductive choices, 539–540
Rhinoplasty, 199, 203, 204–205
Rhytidectomy, 208–209
Rifaximin, 526
Risk perception, 33–34
Risk-taking behaviors, 212
Risky behaviors
  drinking, 95, 96, 114
  sexual, 35, 285, 287, 288, 289, 294,
    296
  and socioeconomic status, 36
Roe v. Wade, 17–19
Role enhancement theory, 51–52

Ross, Loretta, 20
Rotkin, Isadore D., 8

Safe sex, 294–296
Saffron, 319
Same-sex relationships. See also
    Bisexual women; Lesbian women
  and adoption, 366
  and childbearing, 356, 359–360
  engagement in disliked sexual
    activities, 293–294
  and sexual compliance, 293
  and STIs, 295
Sanger, Margaret, 9, 10
SART (Society for Assisted
    Reproductive Technology), 347
Satisfaction
  and childlessness, 359
  and disability, 469–470
  sexual, 282, 284, 430, 540
SAWR (Society for the Advancement
    of Women's Health Research), 21
Scarcity hypothesis, 46, 51
Schizoaffective disorder, 396
Schizophrenia, 264, 396
Schroeder, Patricia, 21
Screening
  for abuse, 483
  for alcohol problems, 106–108
  for cancer, 491
  for colorectal cancer, 525
  for depression and anxiety, 478
  for IPV, 76–81
  premenstrual symptoms, 309
  prenatal, 356–357
  preventative, 154
  for puerperal psychiatric disorders,
    390, 402–404
SeamosActivas, 266–267
Secondary infertility, 328. *See also*
    Infertility
Secondary progressive multiple
    sclerosis, 570. *See also* Multiple
    sclerosis (MS)
Secondhand smoke, 124–125, 127
Sedentary lifestyle, 255, 269
Segregation, occupational, 48–49
Selective estrogen receptormodulator
    (SERM), 589
Self-confidence, 264
Self-efficacy, 30
  and disability, 479
  and irritable bowel syndrome, 521
  and multiple sclerosis, 574
Self-esteem
  and cosmetic medical procedures,
    201
  and eating disorders, 181
  and infertility, 330
  and irritable bowel syndrome, 521
  and multiple sclerosis, 573
  and obesity, 156
  and sexual assault, 290

Self-guided dieting, 162–163
Self-harm, 173
Self-image, 207
Self-objectification, 184, 284–285
Sensory disabilities, 467–468
Sequenced Treatment Alternatives to Depression (STAR-D), 308–309
SERM (selective estrogen receptormodulator), 589
Serotonin, 180, 314, 320, 321, 519
  and migraine headaches, 560, 565
Sertraline, 264, 319
Service industries, 47–48
Sex
  active, 282–286
  and breastfeeding, 430
  casual, 286
  consensual, 286–292
  education, 6–9
  engaging in disliked activities, 293–294
  goals for, 296
  nonconsensual, 286, 288, 293, 298
  premarital, 7
  safe, 294–296
  that is wanted and liked, 292–294
  unprotected, 288, 299
Sexism, 14–15, 27, 38
Sex Roles journal, 28
Sex steroid hormones, 560–561
Sexual abuse, 19, 297. *See also* Childhood sexual abuse (CSA)
  and disability, 482
  and irritable bowel syndrome, 522–523
  and PMDD, 316
  and premenstrual dysphoric disorder, 311
  and sexual assertiveness, 286
Sexual assault, 19–20, 64. *See also* Rape
  and alcohol use, 102
  and intimate partner violence, 67–72
  and risky behavior, 289
  and sexual functioning, 289
  and teens, 68
Sexual assertiveness, 285–286, 288, 293, 296
Sexual autonomy, 283
Sexual Behavior in the Human Female (Kinsey), 7
Sexual compliance, 292–293
Sexual debut, early, 296
Sexual desire, 430
Sexual development, early, 154
Sexual dysfunction, 282, 289, 518
Sexual dysfunction disorders, 75, 106, 154
Sexual harassment, 49–50, 57, 447
Sexual health, 281–304. *See also* Reproductive health; Women's health

adolescent, 296–297
  and cancer, 496–497
  and obesity, 154–155
  and rape, 289–291
Sexual insistence, 297
Sexuality
  and disability, 480
  healthy, 281–282, 297, 298
  and irritable bowel syndrome, 524–525
  and menopause, 447
  and multiple sclerosis, 571–572
  and rheumatic disease, 540–541
  and sex education, 6–9
Sexualization, 284–285
Sexually transmitted diseases. *See* STDs (sexually transmitted diseases)
Sexual maturity, 5–6, 181
Sexual minority women. *See* Bisexual women; Lesbian women
Sexual objectification, 184–185, 202, 284–285, 297, 447
Sexual promiscuity, 287
Sexual revictimization, 291–292
Sexual satisfaction, 282, 284, 294, 296
Sexual victimization, 288
Sheppard-Towner Maternity and Infancy Act, 4
Shift work, 53, 239–240
Sibutramine, 161–162
Sick leave, 57
SIDS (sudden infant death syndrome), 127, 230
Single women
  and abortion, 368
  and childbearing, 356
  and childlessness, 359
  and fertility treatment, 360, 362
  and fetal loss, 372
Slee, Noah, 10
Sleep, 223–254. *See also* Insomnia
  and aging, 236–239
  average hours needed, 224
  and bed-sharing, 230
  and breastfeeding, 229–230
  challenges, 239–243
  and circadian rhythm, 233
  and depression, 226
  deprivation, 223, 229
  and dysmenorrhea, 226
  efficiency, 225, 229
  future directions, 243–244
  and hormones, 226, 231–232
  and hot flashes, 231, 232–233
  measuring, 224
  and menopause, 231–236
  and menstrual cycle, 224–227
  and mood, 233–234
  and oral contraceptives, 227
  pharmacological management of, 235–236
  and physical activity, 255

and PMDD, 225–226, 317
  and PMS, 225–226
  during postpartum period, 228–229
  and pregnancy, 227–228
  role of cognitions, 232–233
  treatments for premenstrual disturbances, 226–227
Sleep apnea. *See* Obstructive sleep apnea (OSA)
Sleep disorders. *See also* Insomnia
  among aging women, 237–239
  and cancer, 495
  and intimate partner violence, 75
  and irritable bowel syndrome, 518–519
  and migraine headaches, 562
  and obesity, 155
  and physical activity, 264
  and smoking cessation, 137
Sleep in America Poll, 223, 224
Sleepiness, daytime, 223
Sleep-onset latency (SOL), 225
SLESH (Systemic Lupus Erythematosus Self-Help Course), 545, 547
SMART (Self-Management and Recovery Training) program, 113
Smoking. *See also* Tobacco use
  and alcohol use, 100
  and breast cancer, 262
  and cardiovascular disease, 125, 126, 127, 262
  cessation and relapse, 132–137
  current trends, 123–125
  and delayed conception, 126
  factors associated with dependence on, 130–132
  gateway hypothesis, 129–130
  health disparities and high-risk groups, 127–128
  and infertility, 329, 335, 337–338
  initiation and ethnicity, 129
  maternal, 124–125, 127, 136, 337
  and miscarriage, 126
  and molecular genetics, 131–132
  psychiatric comorbidity, 129–130
  psychological factors, 129
  psychosocial correlates of initiation, 128–130
  public health priorities, 137–139
  and race, 124, 131
  rise in prevalence among females, 124
  sociocultural factors, 137
  and socioeconomic factors, 131
  and stroke, 126
  and weight concerns, 129, 130–131, 135–136
  and women, 123–148
Smoking cessation
  counseling, 133, 268
  and physical activity, 262–263, 268

and pregnancy, 136
   unique challenges for women, 134
   and weight gain, 151
Snoring, 228, 231, 238
Snowe, Olympia, 21
SNRIs (serotonin-norepinephrine
   reuptake inhibitors), 236, 319
Snuff, 124
Social abuse, 483
Social appearance comparison, 183
Social cognitive processes, 34
Social cognitive theory (SCT), 26, 30,
   267
Social hygiene, 6–7
Social isolation, 504, 519
Socialization
   gender, 281, 294
   menstrual, 315–316
Socialized medicine, 4
Social model of disability, 472–474
Social networking
   and health behaviors, 266
   support groups, 375
Social phobias, 130, 176
Social power, 202
Social stressors, 105. See also Stressors
Social support, 48
   and adjustment to cancer, 504
   after stroke or heart attack, 594
   for fertility treatments, 362
   and fetal loss, 373
   and infertility, 342–343
   and irritable bowel syndrome, 527
   and multiple sclerosis, 573
   post-abortion, 371
   and rheumatic disease, 546
Society for Assisted Reproductive
   Technology (SART), 347
Society for the Advancement of
   Women's Health Research
   (SAWR), 21
Socioeconomic status (SES). See also
   Low-income women; Poverty
   and alcohol use, 103–105
   and cancer, 502–503
   and cancer mortality, 492
   and childlessness, 359
   and disability, 469
   and health messages, 36–37
   and HIV risk, 35–37
   and infertility, 346–348
   and menopause, 453–454
   and migraine headaches, 563–564
   and rheumatic disease, 541–542
   and smoking, 124, 131
Soft tissue fillers, 199, 209
Somatization, 290, 517, 520
Somatoform disorders, 75
Soy, 236
Sperm, 329, 336–337
Spinal cord injury (SCI), 469–470,
   478, 481, 482
Spirituality. See Religion

Spontaneous abortion, 101, 337
SSRIs (selective serotonin reuptake
   inhibitors), 189, 235, 236, 264,
   519
   and irritable bowel syndrome, 526
   and PMDD, 314–315, 319, 321
Stages of Change model, 26, 30
Stages of Reproductive Aging
   Workshop (STRAW), 441, 448
Stalking, 64, 65
STAR-D (Sequenced Treatment
   Alternatives to Depression),
   308–309
STDs (sexually transmitted diseases), 6,
   7, 287, 290, 294, 295, 299
Step Into Motion, 265
Stepped care approach, 133–134
Stereotypes, 483
Sterilization, 11, 17–19, 321, 482
Steroids, 556, 574–575, 589
Stigma
   and abortion, 369, 370
   and breastfeeding, 429–430
   and disability, 484–485
   and fertility treatments, 362
   and irritable bowel syndrome, 521,
      527
   and mental health, 405
   and obesity, 156
Stillbirth, 371, 372, 373
Stimulants, 240
STIs (sexually transmitted infections),
   6, 32, 35
Strangulation, 72
STRAW (Stages of Reproductive
   Aging Workshop), 441, 448
Strength training, 260, 268. See also
   Physical activity
Stress
   and Alzheimer's disease, 584–586
   among caregivers, 595–596
   and breastfeeding, 419
   and cancer, 502
   and child relinquishment, 379
   and coronary heart disease, 584
   dysfunctional response to, 316
   and fetal loss, 372
   and hormones, 586
   and illness, 47
   and infertility, 329, 340–342
   interpersonal, 545–548
   and irritable bowel syndrome, 515
   and IVF, 350
   management, 344
   and migraine headaches, 564–565
   and multiple sclerosis, 573–574
   and PMDD, 316, 318–319
   psychological, 520
   and rheumatic disease, 543
   and smoking cessation, 136–137
   and stroke, 584–586
Stressors
   and disability, 475–476

and irritable bowel syndrome, 520
   perception of, 479
   psychosocial for fertility treatments,
      361–363
   related to adoption, 364–365
   work-family conflict, 51
Stress theory, 52–53
Stroke, 26, 556, 581–603
   aftermath, 591–596
   and alcohol use, 100
   and anxiety, 478
   and caregivers, 595–596
   commonalities in epidemiology
      with heart disease and
      Alzheimer's, 581–591
   and depression, 586–587, 594–595
   and disability, 591–596
   and ethnicity, 583
   gender differences, 582–583
   and genetics, 589–591
   and hormone therapy, 589
   and menopause, 588
   and obstructive sleep apnea, 242
   and physical activity, 255
   and pregnancy, 588
   psychosocial risk factors, 584–587
   recognizing symptoms of, 592
   and sex steroid hormones, 588–589
   and smoking, 126
   statistics, 582
   and stress, 584–586
Students for a Democratic Society
   (SDS), 13
Study of Women's Health Across the
   Nation (SWAN), 346
Subarachnoid hemorrhage, 126
Subfertility, 335, 336–337
Submission, sexual, 282–284
Substance abuse. See also Alcohol use
   and disability, 483
   and intimate partner violence, 75
   and physical activity, 264, 268
   and sexual assault, 290
   and work-family conflict, 53
Sudden infant death syndrome (SIDS),
   127, 230
Suicide, 74, 173, 207–208, 391, 397,
   520
Support groups
   for infertility, 344
   and irritable bowel syndrome, 521
   online, 375
   for women's problem drinking,
      112–113
Surgery
   abdominal, 518
   bariatric, 156, 162, 211
   for cancer, 492–493
   cosmetic (see Cosmetic medical
      procedures)
   pain following, 495–496
   for weight loss, 162
Surrogacy, 360–361, 377–378

SWAN (Study of Women's Health Across the Nation), 231, 346
Swedish Obese Subjects Study, 162
Symmetrel, 575
Systemic disabilities, 468
Systemic lupus erythematosus, 307, 539–540, 543–544. *See also* Rheumatic diseases
Systemic Lupus Erythematosus Self-Help Course (SLESH), 545, 547
Systems theory, 51

T'ai chi, 545
Tallness, 5
Tamoxifen, 589
Tattoos, 212–213
Technology
  and health behavior interventions, 266
  and physical activity intervention, 265–266, 268–269
Teens. *See also* Adolescents
  and cosmetic medical procedures, 203–204
  and dating violence, 68
  and pregnancy, 7–8, 372
  and smoking initiation, 128–129
Tension-type headaches, 559. *See also* Migraine headaches
Terman, Lewis, 4
Testosterone, 333, 337, 557
Text messaging, 266
Thank You, Dr. Lamaze (Karmel), 16
Theory of Planned Behavior (TPB), 26, 29–30
Theory of Reasoned Action (TRA), 26, 29–30
Therapy
  family, 186
  group, 329, 574
  guided imagery, 319
  individual, 329
  interpersonal, 186, 188, 189, 527
  psychodynamic, 527
Thermoregulation, 233, 451
Third-party reproduction, 375–379
Thromboembolic complications, 320
Thrush, 425
Timing hypothesis, 457–458
Tobacco use. *See also* Smoking
  adult use, 123
  and behavioral science, 138–139
  and cancer, 125–126
  and fetal loss, 372
  gender gap, 123–124
  morbidity and mortality, 125–128
  and oral cancer, 124
  stemming use of, 124
  types of products, 124
Toxins, exposure to, 151, 329, 372
Toys, 184
Trans-fatty acids, 331

Transgender women, 70–71
Transtheoretical model (TTM), 26, 30, 267
Trauma, medical, 483–484
Traumatic brain injury (TBI), 478, 483, 556
Treir Social Stress Task, 419
Triglycerides, 157
Trilafon, 426
Tripartite influence model, 182
Triptan, 565
Truth, Sojourner, 27–28
Tryptophan, 315, 318
Tubal factor infertility, 346
Tumors, cancerous, 492, 493
Turner syndrome, 372
TWEAK screening tool, 108, 110
Twilight sleep, 16
2008 Guidelines for gamete and embryo donation, 376
Type 2 diabetes. *See also* Diabetes
  and alcohol use, 99
  and breastfeeding, 417–418, 428
  and obesity, 152–153
  and physical activity, 255, 258–260
  and weight loss, 158
Tyramine, 562

Ulcerative colitis, 523
Ultrasound, 356, 357
Underweight, 173, 331, 332–333. *See also* Eating disorders
Unequal Treatment (Nechas), 21
Unmarried women. *See* Single women
Urogenital problems, 517–518
U.S. Preventative Services Task Force, 76, 107
U.S. v. One Package of Japanese Pessaries, 11
Uterus, 328. *See also* Reproductive health

Vaccinations, 4, 9, 138, 295
Vacuum aspiration, 367. *See also* Abortion
Vaginosis, bacterial, 295, 299
Valerian, 242
Values, realignment of, 479
Varenicline, 132, 133
Varicocele, 329
Vascular diseases, 583–584
  and genetics, 589–591
Vascular system, 581
Vasodilation, 560
Vasomotor symptoms, 233
Venaflaxine, 319
Venereal diseases, 6, 8, 19
Venous thromboembolic disorders, 320
Veterans, women, 523
Victimization, 297. *See also* Childhood sexual abuse (CSA); Sexual abuse
  and alcohol use, 106
  sexual, 286, 288

Violence
  and alcohol use, 102, 106
  and disability, 482–483
  and irritable bowel syndrome, 522–523
  within relationships (*see* Intimate partner violence (IPV))
Violence Against Women journal, 65
Virginia Adult Twin Study, 103
Viruses, 151, 568
Visceral hypersensitivity, 515, 517, 519
Vision problems, 569
Vitamin B_6, 318
Vitamin D, 568
VitexAgnusCastus, 319
Vulnerable women
  and IPV victimization, 69, 82

Wagenen, Gertrude van, 20
Walking, 258, 260, 262, 264. *See also* Physical activity
Weaning, 429–430
Weight, 31–32
  and infertility, 329
  influences on, 151–152
  and smoking, 129, 130–131
  and smoking cessation, 135–136
Weight gain. *See also* Obesity
  and breastfeeding, 153
  causes of, 149–152
  influences on women's, 151–152
  and menopause, 152, 164, 257
  and perimenopause, 449
  and physical activity, 255
  and pregnancy, 152, 163
  prevention, 163
  and smoking cessation, 151
  and toxins, 151
  and viruses, 151
Weight loss, 155. *See also* Eating disorders
  and abdominoplasty, 211
  and anorexia nervosa, 174
  behavioral interventions, 157–159
  benefits of, 157
  and breastfeeding, 416–418
  and cardiovascular disease, 157
  dietary interventions, 159–160
  and eating disorders, 189
  medications for, 161–162
  and physical activity, 257
  physical activity interventions, 160–161
  and PMDD, 318
  and pregnancy outcomes, 154
  self-guided dieting, 162–163
  surgery for, 162
  treatment options, 157–163
Weight-related disorders, 173–198. *See also* Eating disorders
Well-being
  adoptive parents', 365–366

and disability, 479
following perinatal loss, 374
and infertility, 339
and menopause, 450
psychological, 339
and rheumatic disease, 541
sexual, 496
and sexual harassment, 50
and sexuality, 281
spiritual, 542
and work-family balance, 53
Wet-nursing, 414
What to Expect When You're Expecting
    (Murkoff), 15
White women
  age of sexual maturity, 5
  and alcohol use, 99, 103–104
  birthrate, 10
  and childlessness, 357
  and cosmetic medical procedures,
    203
  and disability, 469
  employment with disabilities, 470
  and fertility treatments, 360
  and heart disease, 26, 583
  and infertility, 346, 347
  and intimate partner violence, 67,
    69
  and menopause, 453, 454
  and migraine headaches, 558
  and obesity, 32
  and rheumatic disease, 541
  and sexual dominance and passivity,
    283
  and sexual dysfunction, 282
  and sleep, 234
  and smoking, 131
  and smoking cessation, 137
  and STIs, 35
  and surrogacy, 378
Wii Fit, 265, 269
Wisconsin Sleep Cohort Study, 231
Women. *See also* African American
    women; Asian American
    women; White women
  and aging, 581 (*see also* Aging)
  and alcohol use, 91–122
  and Alzheimer's disease, 581–603
  and breastfeeding, 414–439
  and cancer, 491–513
  as caregivers, 56
  and chronic insomnia, 240
  and clinical research, 21–22
  cosmetic medical procedures and
    body adornment, 199–222
  and depression, 47, 586–587
  and disability, 467–490, 593
  eating and weight-related disorders,
    173–198
  and employment, 54–55, 55–56
    (*see also* Working women)
  feelings about menopause, 446
  and heart disease, 581–603

height of, 6
and HIV/AIDS, 27
and infertility, 328–354
influences on weight, 151–152
and irritable bowel syndrome,
    514–538
leading causes of death in, 26, 581,
    592
life expectancy, 583
low-income (*see* Low-income
    women)
and menopause, 440–463
and neurological disorders,
    556–580
and obesity, 149–172
and obstructive sleep apnea,
    242–243
and premenstrual dysphoric
    disorder, 305–327
and psychiatric disorders, 399–400,
    404–406
psychiatric symptoms and
    pregnancy, 389–413
and rheumatic disease, 539–555
with school-age children, 55
and sexual harassment, 57
sexual health, 281–304
and sleep through the lifespan,
    223–254
and smoking, 123–148
social inequality and HIV risk,
    37–38
and stress, 584–586
and stroke, 581–603
and tattoos, 212
and weight, 31–32
Women for Sobriety (WFS), 112–113
Women of color. *See also* African
    American women; American
    Indian women; Asian American
    women; Hispanic women;
    Latinas; Minority women
  and HIV/AIDS, 32, 33–34
  and IPV homicides, 67
  leading causes of death in, 26
  and nonlethal IPV assaults, 69
  and obesity, 32
  and reproductive rights, 19
Women's health. *See also* Maternal
    health; Reproductive health;
    Sexual health
  and employment, 46–63
  history of, 3–24, 13–15
  and intersectionality, 25–45
  and occupational segregation, 48–49
  and physical activity, 255–277
  postpartum, 54–55
  providers and IPV, 81–82
  and sexism, 38
  and sexual harassment, 49–50
  and smoking, 125–128
  and work-family balance, 51–56
  and working conditions, 47–50

Women's Health Equity Act, 22
Women's Health Initiative, 235,
    456–457, 589
Women's Interagency IVF Study,
    346–347
Women's liberation, 14
Work. *See* Employment; Working
    women
Work-family balance, 51–56, 57, 585
Working women. *See also*
    Employment
  and breastfeeding, 427–428
  and cancer, 498–499, 504
  and disability, 469
  and health, 46–63
  and healthy working conditions,
    47–50
  and migraine headaches, 564
  and multiple sclerosis, 573
  and vascular disease risk, 585
World Health Organization (WHO)
  and breastfeeding, 414
  and disability, 468
  disability-adjusted life years,
    312–313
  and effects of IPV on women, 74
  and menopause, 443–444
  and migraine headache, 557
  and smoking, 123, 125

Yoga, 230, 264, 319, 329, 333, 505,
    545
Young women. *See also* College
    women
  and abortion, 368
  and cancer, 503
  and cosmetic medical procedures,
    201
  and eating disorders, 177
  engagement in disliked sexual
    activities, 293
  and infertility following cancer,
    496–497
  and irritable bowel syndrome, 515,
    521–522
  and migraine headaches, 557,
    563
  and multiple sclerosis, 567, 571
  and neurological disorders, 556
  and premenstrual dysphoric
    disorder, 311–312
  and rheumatic disease, 539, 540–541
  and risky drinking, 114
  and sexual assertiveness, 285
Youth
  and drinking, 95, 114
  and physical activity, 255
  and tobacco use, 124
Youth Risk Behavior Surveillance
    (YRBSS), 255, 256

Zaleplon, 241
Zolpidem, 230, 235, 241